Collins easy learning
German
Dictionary

HarperCollins Publishers
Westerhill Road
Bishopbriggs
Glasgow
G64 2QT

Ninth Edition 2019

10 9 8 7 6 5 4 3 2

ISBN 978-0-00-830026-5

www.collins.co.uk
www.collinsdictionary.com

A catalogue record for this book is
available from the British Library

Typeset by Sharon McTeir Creative Publishing
Services and Davidson Publishing Solutions,
Glasgow

Printed in Italy by Grafica Veneta S.p.A.

Acknowledgements
We would like to thank those authors and
publishers who kindly gave permission for
copyright material to be used in the Collins
Corpus. We would also like to thank Times
Newspapers Ltd for providing valuable data.

Collins gratefully acknowledge the help of the
examining boards, whom we have consulted
throughout this project, and whose word lists
and exam papers we carefully studied when
compiling this dictionary in order to ensure
appropriate coverage and support for GCSE
and other exams of a similar level.

EDITOR
Susie Beattie

CONTRIBUTORS
Persephone Lock, Maggie Seaton,
Anna Stevenson, Silke Zimmermann

FOR THE PUBLISHER
Maree Airlie, Gerry Breslin, Helen Newstead,
Sheena Shanks

TECHNICAL SUPPORT
Agnieszka Urbanowicz

MIX
Paper from
responsible sources
FSC™ C007454

Abbreviations used in this dictionary

fem	=	feminine
gen	=	genitive
masc	=	masculine
neut	=	neuter
pl	=	plural
sing	=	singular

Contents

Glossary of grammar terms

Accusative case
the form of nouns, adjectives, pronouns and articles used in German to show the direct object of a verb and after certain prepositions.

> Ich sehe **den Hund**. I see the dog.
> ('the dog' is the direct object)
> Das ist **für ihn** sehr wichtig. That is very important to him.
> (the preposition 'für' is always followed by the accusative case)

Adjective
a 'describing' word that tells you more about a person or thing, such as their appearance, colour, size or other qualities, for example, *pretty*, *blue*, *big*, and, in German, groß, billig, interessant.

> ein **großes** Haus a big house
> die **französiche** Mannschaft the French team

Adverb
a word usually used with verbs, adjectives or other adverbs that gives more information about when, where, how or in what circumstances something happens or to what degree something is true, for example, *quickly*, *happily*, *now*, *extremely*, *very*. In contrast to English, most German adverbs are simply adjectives used as adverbs. Unlike adjectives, however, they don't change and add different endings. For example, schlecht.

> Ich habe sehr **schlecht** geschlafen. I slept really **badly**.

Some adverbs which are **not** also adjectives in German are: normalerweise, meistens, wieder.

> Freitags bin ich **meistens** zu Hause. I'm usually at home on Fridays.
> Gestern war er **wieder** krank. He was ill again yesterday.

Article
a word like *the*, *a* and *an*, which is used in front of a noun. In German, the form of the article depends on whether the noun it is used with is masculine,

feminine or neuter and whether it is singular or plural. It also depends on the case of the noun. Some German articles are der, die, ein or eine.

> **die** Frauen the women
> **ein** Hund a dog

Case

the grammatical function of a noun in a sentence. See **accusative case**, **dative case**, **genitive case**.

Conjunction

a word such as *and*, *because*, or *but* that links two words or phrases of a similar type or two parts of a sentence, for example, *Diane and I have been friends for years*; *I left because I was bored*. Common German conjunctions are oder, aber, und.

> Wir wollten ins Kino, **aber** wir hatten kein Geld.
> We wanted to go to the cinema, but we had no money.
> Susi **und** Marcel Susi and Marcel

Dative case

the form of nouns, adjectives, pronouns and articles used in German to show the indirect object of a verb and after certain verbs and prepositions.

> Sie gab **der Frau** das Buch. She gave the book to the woman.
> ('the woman' is the indirect object of the verb)
> Nach **dem Essen** gingen wir aus. After our meal we went out.
> (the preposition 'nach' is always followed by the dative case)

Gender

whether a noun, article, pronoun or adjective is feminine, masculine or neuter. Some German examples are der (= masculine), die (= feminine) and das (=neuter).

> **Der Hund** hatte laut gebellt. The dog had barked loudly.
> **Die Hauptstadt** ist Wien. The capital city is Vienna.

Genitive case

the form of nouns, adjectives, pronouns and articles used in German to show that something belongs to someone and after certain verbs and prepositions.

> Das Auto **der Frau** ist schwarz. The woman's car is black.
> ('the car' belongs to 'the woman')
> trotz **des schlechten Wetters** despite the bad weather
> (the preposition 'trotz' is followed by the genitive case)

Nominative case

the basic form of nouns, pronouns, adjectives and articles used in German and the one you find in the dictionary. It is used for the subject of the sentence and after the verbs sein (*to be*) and werden (*to be, to become*).

> **Die Katze** schläft. The cat is sleeping.
> ('the cat' is the subject of the sentence)
> Sie ist **eine gute Lehrerin**. She is a good teacher.
> (after the verb 'sein')

Noun

a 'naming' word for a living being, thing or idea, for example, *woman, desk, happiness, Andrew* and, in German, Haus, Hund, Stadt.

> die **Schule** school
> das **Buch** book

Preposition

a word such as *at, for, with, into* or *from*, which is usually followed by a noun, pronoun or, in English, a word ending in *-ing*. Prepositions show how people and things relate to the rest of the sentence, for example, *She's <u>at</u> home*; *a tool <u>for</u> cutting grass*; *It's <u>from</u> David*. Some German prepositions are auf, bei, zu. The noun after a preposition must be followed by the accusative, dative or genitive case.

> Er wohnt immer noch **bei** seinen Eltern. He still lives with his parents.
> Wir sind **zum** Essen eingeladen. We're invited for dinner.

Pronoun

a word which you use instead of a noun, when you do not need or want to name someone or something directly, for example, *it*, *you*, *none* and, in German, ich, mich, es.

> **Ich** wohne in Berlin. I live in Berlin.
> **Es** ist nicht schwierig. It's not difficult.

Verb

a 'doing' word which describes what someone or something does, is, or what happens to them, for example, *be*, *sing*, *live*. Some common verbs in German are gehen, machen, sein.

> Carla **geht** montags ins Kino. Carla goes to the cinema on Mondays.
> Ruby **ist** sehr klug. Ruby is very clever.

Guide to entries

Star symbol indicates core vocabulary	★**fahren** VERB [21]
Number refers to where verb is conjugated in full	**PRESENT TENSE** ich fahre wir fahren du fährst ihr fahrt er/sie/es fährt sie/Sie fahren **PERFECT TENSE** ist/hat gefahren
Verb tables for common irregular verbs	For the perfect tense use **haben** when the verb has an object and **sein** when there is no object.
Language tips give key grammar points	1 to drive □ Er hat mich nach Hause gefahren. **He drove me home.** □ Er ist sehr schnell gefahren. **He drove very fast.**
Translations underlined to find them quickly	■ **ein Rennen fahren** to drive in a race
Examples show how the translation is used	2 to go □ Der Intercity fährt stündlich. **The Intercity train goes every hour.**
	3 to leave □ Wann seid ihr gefahren? **When did you leave?**
Numbers clearly point out different senses	4 to sail □ Das Schiff fährt nach Amerika. **The ship's sailing to America.** □ Wir sind mit dem Schiff nach Amerika gefahren. **We sailed to America.**
Important phrases set out separately	■ **Rad fahren** to cycle □ Früher bin ich viel Rad gefahren. **I used to cycle a lot.** ■ **mit dem Auto fahren** to go by car ■ **mit dem Zug fahren** to go by train □ Seid ihr mit dem Zug gefahren? **Did you go by train?**
Article to show gender of German noun	★der **Fahrer** (PL die **Fahrer**) MASC NOUN
Gender of German nouns clearly labelled	★der **Fan** (PL die **Fans**) MASC NOUN fan □ Sie ist ein Fan von Ariana Grande. **She's an Ariana Grande fan.**
All plural forms given for German nouns	**fand** VERB ▷ see **finden**
Look at the main verb for information about common irregular verb forms	★**fangen** (PRESENT TENSE **fängt**, IMPERFECT **fing**, PERFECT TENSE **hat gefangen**) VERB [23] to catch
Cultural notes offer additional information	★der **Fasching** (PL die **Faschinge**) MASC NOUN carnival **DID YOU KNOW...?** The German carnival season lasts from 11 November to Shrove Tuesday but most events, fancy-dress processions and parties take place in the week leading up to Ash Wednesday.

Guide to entries

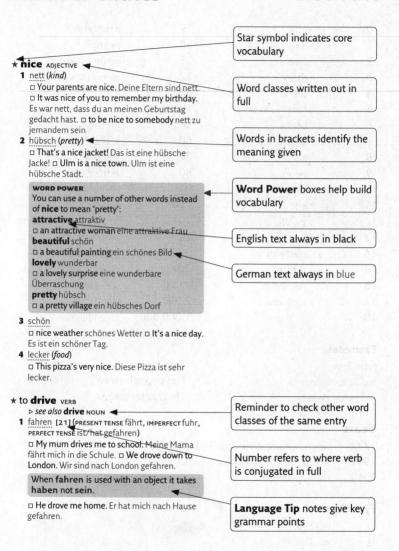

Star symbol indicates core vocabulary

★ **nice** ADJECTIVE
1 nett (*kind*)
  □ Your parents are nice. Deine Eltern sind nett.
  □ It was nice of you to remember my birthday.
  Es war nett, dass du an meinen Geburtstag
  gedacht hast. □ **to be nice to somebody** nett zu
  jemandem sein

Word classes written out in full

2 hübsch (*pretty*)
  □ That's a nice jacket! Das ist eine hübsche
  Jacke! □ Ulm is a nice town. Ulm ist eine
  hübsche Stadt.

Words in brackets identify the meaning given

> **WORD POWER**
> You can use a number of other words instead
> of **nice** to mean 'pretty':
> **attractive** attraktiv
> □ an attractive woman eine attraktive Frau
> **beautiful** schön
> □ a beautiful painting ein schönes Bild
> **lovely** wunderbar
> □ a lovely surprise eine wunderbare
> Überraschung
> **pretty** hübsch
> □ a pretty village ein hübsches Dorf

Word Power boxes help build vocabulary

English text always in black

German text always in blue

3 schön
  □ nice weather schönes Wetter □ It's a nice day.
  Es ist ein schöner Tag.
4 lecker (*food*)
  □ This pizza's very nice. Diese Pizza ist sehr
  lecker.

★ to **drive** VERB
  ▷ *see also* **drive** NOUN
1 fahren [21] (PRESENT TENSE fährt, IMPERFECT fuhr,
  PERFECT TENSE ist/hat gefahren)
  □ My mum drives me to school. Meine Mama
  fährt mich in die Schule. □ We drove down to
  London. Wir sind nach London gefahren.

Reminder to check other word classes of the same entry

Number refers to where verb is conjugated in full

> When **fahren** is used with an object it takes
> **haben** not **sein**.

  □ He drove me home. Er hat mich nach Hause
  gefahren.

Language Tip notes give key grammar points

In order to provide additional practice with dictionary skills, free downloadable
resources are now available for teachers and learners of German at
www.collins.co.uk/easylearningresources.

Numbers

0	null	19	neunzehn
1	eins	20	zwanzig
2	zwei	21	einundzwanzig
3	drei	22	zweiundzwanzig
4	vier	30	dreißig
5	fünf	40	vierzig
6	sechs	50	fünfzig
7	sieben	60	sechzig
8	acht	70	siebzig
9	neun	80	achtzig
10	zehn	90	neunzig
11	elf	100	(ein)hundert
12	zwölf	101	(ein)hundert(und)eins
13	dreizehn	200	zweihundert
14	vierzehn	300	dreihundert
15	fünfzehn	301	dreihundert(und)eins
16	sechzehn	1,000	(ein)tausend
17	siebzehn	2,000	zweitausend
18	achtzehn	1,000,000	eine Million

Examples

zehn Euro	ten euros
auf Seite neunzehn	on page nineteen
in Kapitel sieben	in chapter seven

Years

1722	siebzehnhundertzweiundzwanzig
1995	neunzehnhundertfünfundneunzig
2010	zweitausendzehn

Fractions

½	ein halb
⅓	ein Drittel
⅔	zwei Drittel
¼	ein Viertel
¾	drei Viertel
⅕	ein Fünftel

0.5	null komma fünf (0,5)
3.4	drei komma vier (3,4)
10%	zehn Prozent
100%	hundert Prozent

1st	erste(r, s)
2nd	zweite(r, s)
3rd	dritte(r, s)
4th	vierte(r, s)
5th	fünfte(r, s)
6th	sechste(r, s)
7th	siebte(r, s)
8th	achte(r, s)
9th	neunte(r, s)
10th	zehnte(r, s)
11th	elfte(r, s)
12th	zwölfte(r, s)
13th	dreizehnte(r, s)
14th	vierzehnte(r, s)
15th	fünfzehnte(r, s)
16th	sechzehnte(r, s)
17th	siebzehnte(r, s)
18th	achtzehnte(r, s)
19th	neunzehnte(r, s)
20th	zwanzigste(r, s)
21st	einundzwanzigste(r, s)
22nd	zweiundzwanzigste(r, s)
30th	dreißigste(r, s)
100th	hundertste(r, s)
101st	hunderterste(r, s)
1000th	tausendste(r, s)

Examples

Er wohnt im fünften Stock	He lives on the fifth floor.
Es war das achte Mal	It was the eighth time.
Jeder zehnte Mann/jede zehnte Frau	one in ten men/women

Time

Wie spät ist es? Es ist...   **What time is it? It's ...**

ein Uhr

zehn nach eins

Viertel nach eins

halb zwei

zwanzig vor zwei

Viertel vor zwei

Um wie viel Uhr?   **At what time?**

um Mitternacht

um zwölf Uhr mittags

um ein Uhr (nachmittags)

um acht Uhr (abends)

um 11:15 Uhr or
elf Uhr fünfzehn

um 20:45 Uhr or
zwanzig Uhr fünfundvierzig

In German times are often given in the twenty-four hour clock.

Aa

der **Aal** (PL die **Aale**) MASC NOUN
eel

★ **ab** PREPOSITION, ADVERB

The preposition **ab** takes the dative.

1 from
◻ Kinder ab zwölf Jahren **children from the age
of twelve** ◻ ab morgen **from tomorrow**

2 off
◻ Die Straße geht nach links ab. **The road goes
off to the left.** ◻ Der Knopf ist ab. **The button
has come off.** ◻ Ab nach Hause! **Off you go
home!**
■ **ab sofort** as of now
■ **ab und zu** now and then

★ **abbiegen** (IMPERFECT **bog ab**, PERFECT TENSE **ist
abgebogen**) VERB

1 to turn off
◻ Sie bog an der Kreuzung nach links ab. **At the
crossroads she turned off to the left.**

2 to bend
◻ Die Hauptstraße biegt nach rechts ab. **The
main road bends to the right.**

die **Abbildung** FEM NOUN
illustration

abbrechen (PRESENT TENSE **bricht ab**,
IMPERFECT **brach ab**, PERFECT TENSE **hat
abgebrochen**) VERB [11]

1 to break off
◻ Sie brach einen blühenden Zweig ab. **She
broke off a flowering branch.**

2 to pull down
◻ Das alte Gebäude muss abgebrochen
werden. **The old building will have to be pulled
down.**

3 to stop
◻ Es ist schon spät, wir sollten abbrechen. **It's
late now; we ought to stop.**

4 to cut off
◻ Unser Telefongespräch wurde abgebrochen.
Our phone call was cut off.

5 to abort
◻ Das dauert zu lang, du solltest das Programm
abbrechen. **It's taking too long; you should
abort the program.**

abbuchen (PERFECT TENSE **hat abgebucht**)
VERB [4]

to debit
◻ Der Betrag wird von Ihrem Konto abgebucht.
The amount will be debited from your account.

★ der **Abend** (PL die **Abende**) MASC NOUN
evening
◻ Sie macht jeden Abend einen Spaziergang.
She goes for a walk every evening. ◻ guten
Abend **good evening**
■ **zu Abend essen** to have dinner
■ **heute Abend** this evening

★ das **Abendbrot** NEUT NOUN
supper

★ das **Abendessen** (PL die **Abendessen**) NEUT
NOUN
dinner
◻ Zum Abendessen gibt es Spaghetti. **There's
spaghetti for dinner.**

★ **abends** ADVERB
in the evening

★ das **Abenteuer** (PL die **Abenteuer**) NEUT
NOUN
adventure

★ **aber** CONJUNCTION, ADVERB

1 but
◻ Er wollte mit uns mitkommen, aber seine
Eltern haben es nicht erlaubt. **He wanted to
come with us, but his parents wouldn't let him.**

2 however
◻ Ich möchte nach Ägypten reisen. Ich habe
aber kein Geld. **I'd like to go to Egypt. However, I
haven't got any money.**
■ **Das ist aber schön!** That's really nice.
■ **Nun ist aber Schluss!** Now that's enough!

★ **abfahren** (PRESENT TENSE **fährt ab**, IMPERFECT
fuhr ab, PERFECT TENSE **ist abgefahren**) VERB
[21]
to leave
◻ Wir fahren morgen sehr früh ab. **We're
leaving very early tomorrow.** ◻ Wann fährt dein
Zug ab? **When does your train leave?**

★ die **Abfahrt** FEM NOUN
departure

★ der **Abfall** (PL die **Abfälle**) MASC NOUN
rubbish no pl

★ der **Abfalleimer** (PL die **Abfalleimer**) MASC
NOUN
rubbish bin

Numbers in brackets refer to verb tables on pages 697 to 706.

abfällig – abholen

abfällig ADJECTIVE
disparaging

★**abfliegen** (IMPERFECT **flog ab**, PERFECT TENSE **ist abgeflogen**) VERB [25]
to take off
□ Die Maschine ist mit Verspätung abgeflogen. **The plane was late taking off.**
■ Um wie viel Uhr fliegt ihr ab? **What time does your plane leave?**

★**der Abflug** (PL die **Abflüge**) MASC NOUN
1 departure
□ Wir müssen zwei Stunden vor Abflug am Flughafen sein. **We have to be at the airport two hours before departure.**

2 takeoff
□ Die Maschine stürzte kurz nach dem Abflug ab. **The plane crashed shortly after takeoff.**

abfragen (PERFECT TENSE **hat abgefragt**) VERB [4]
1 to test orally
□ die Vokabeln abfragen **to give an oral vocabulary test**

2 to call up
□ Sie können die Abfahrtszeiten am Computer abfragen. **You can call up departure times on the computer.**

das Abführmittel (PL die **Abführmittel**) NEUT NOUN
laxative

★**das Abgas** (GEN des **Abgases**, PL die **Abgase**) NEUT NOUN
exhaust fumes *pl*

abgeben (PRESENT TENSE **gibt ab**, IMPERFECT **gab ab**, PERFECT TENSE **hat abgegeben**) VERB [28]
1 to hand in
□ Die Klassenarbeiten müssen am Ende der Stunde abgegeben werden. **Tests must be handed in at the end of the lesson.**

2 to pass
□ Sie gab den Ball an den Mittelstürmer ab. **She passed the ball to the centre-forward.**
■ sich mit jemandem abgeben **to associate with somebody**
■ sich mit etwas abgeben **to bother with something** □ Mit solch dummen Fragen will ich mich nicht abgeben. **I don't want to bother with such stupid questions.**
■ jemandem etwas abgeben **to let somebody have something**

abgelegen ADJECTIVE
remote

★**abgemacht** ADJECTIVE
agreed
□ Wir trafen uns zur abgemachten Zeit. **We met at the agreed time.**
■ Abgemacht! **OK!**

abgesehen ADJECTIVE
■ es auf jemanden abgesehen haben **to be out to get somebody**

■ es auf etwas abgesehen haben **to be after something**
■ abgesehen von ... **apart from ...**
□ Abgesehen von ein paar Fehlern war der Aufsatz sehr gut. **The essay was very good, apart from a few mistakes.**

abgewöhnen (PERFECT TENSE **hat abgewöhnt**) VERB [38]
■ sich etwas abgewöhnen **to give something up** □ Ich will mir das Rauchen abgewöhnen. **I want to give up smoking.**

der Abhang (PL die **Abhänge**) MASC NOUN
slope

abhängen (1) (PERFECT TENSE **hat abgehängt**) VERB [4]
1 to take down
□ Weil ihr das Bild nicht mehr gefiel, hängte sie es ab. **She took the picture down because she didn't like it any more.**

2 to unhitch
□ Er hängte den Wohnwagen ab, bevor er in die Stadt fuhr. **He unhitched the caravan before he drove into town.**

3 to shake off
□ Den Räubern gelang es, die Polizei abzuhängen. **The robbers managed to shake off the police.**

abhängen (2) (IMPERFECT **hing ab**, PERFECT TENSE **hat abgehangen**) VERB [35]
■ von jemandem abhängen **to depend on somebody**
■ von etwas abhängen **to depend on something** □ Es hängt vom Wetter ab. **It depends on the weather.**

★**abhängig** ADJECTIVE
■ abhängig von **dependent on**

abheben (IMPERFECT **hob ab**, PERFECT TENSE **hat abgehoben**) VERB
1 to answer
□ Meine Großeltern scheinen nicht zu Hause zu sein, es hebt nämlich keiner ab. **My grandparents don't seem to be at home as nobody's answering the phone.**

2 to withdraw
□ Ich muss Geld vom Sparbuch abheben. **I'll have to withdraw some money from my savings account.**

3 to take off
□ Wir sahen zu, wie das Flugzeug abhob. **We watched the plane take off.**

4 to lift off
□ Die Rakete hob senkrecht ab. **The rocket lifted off vertically.**
■ sich von etwas abheben **to stand out against something** □ Das Muster hebt sich gut vom Hintergrund ab. **The pattern stands out well against this background.**

★**abholen** (PERFECT TENSE **hat abgeholt**) VERB [4]

★ = core vocabulary

1 to collect

□ Der Restmüll wird einmal in der Woche abgeholt. Rubbish is collected once a week.

2 to pick up

□ Ich hole dich um sieben ab. I'll pick you up at seven.

★das **Abi** NEUT NOUN (*Umgangssprache*)
A levels

★das **Abitur** NEUT NOUN
A levels

der **Abiturient** (GEN des Abiturienten, PL die Abiturienten) MASC NOUN
A level student

die **Abiturientin** FEM NOUN
A level student

abkürzen (PERFECT TENSE hat abgekürzt)
VERB [36]
to abbreviate

□ Man kann 'bitte wenden' mit b. w. abkürzen. You can abbreviate 'please turn over' to PTO.
■ den Weg abkürzen to take a short cut

die **Abkürzung** FEM NOUN

1 abbreviation

□ Die Abkürzung für Künstliche Intelligenz ist KI. The abbreviation for artificial intelligence is AI.

2 shortcut

□ Wir haben eine Abkürzung genommen. We took a shortcut.

abladen (PRESENT TENSE lädt ab, IMPERFECT lud ab, PERFECT TENSE hat abgeladen) VERB
to unload

ablaufen (PRESENT TENSE läuft ab, IMPERFECT lief ab, PERFECT TENSE ist abgelaufen) VERB
[43]

1 to expire

□ Ihr Pass ist leider abgelaufen. Unfortunately, your passport has expired.

2 to drain away

□ Der Abfluss ist verstopft, und deshalb läuft das Wasser nicht ab. The waste pipe is blocked, and that's why the water won't drain away.

★**ablehnen** (PERFECT TENSE hat abgelehnt)
VERB [4]

1 to turn down

□ Sie hat das Amt der Klassensprecherin abgelehnt. She turned down being class representative. □ Mein Antrag auf ein Stipendium wurde abgelehnt. My application for a grant was turned down.

2 to disapprove of

□ Ich lehne eine solche Arbeitseinstellung ab. I disapprove of such an attitude to work.

ablenken (PERFECT TENSE hat abgelenkt) VERB
[4]
to distract

□ Lenk ihn nicht von seiner Arbeit ab. Don't distract him from his work.

■ vom Thema ablenken to change the subject

abliefern (PERFECT TENSE hat abgeliefert)
VERB [88]

1 to drop off

□ Wir haben die Kinder wieder wohlbehalten zu Hause abgeliefert. We dropped the children off at home safe and sound.

2 to hand in

□ Bis wann musst du das Referat abliefern? When do you have to hand your assignment in by?

■ etwas bei jemandem abliefern to take something to somebody □ Wir haben das gefundene Handy beim Fundbüro abgeliefert. We took the mobile phone we found to the lost property office.

abmachen (PERFECT TENSE hat abgemacht)
VERB [4]

1 to take off

□ Weißt du, wie man den Deckel abmacht? Do you know how to take the lid off?

2 to agree

□ Wir haben abgemacht, dass wir uns um sieben Uhr treffen. We agreed to meet at seven.

3 to sort out

□ Ihr solltet das untereinander abmachen, wer heute aufräumt. Sort out amongst yourselves who's going to clear up today.

die **Abmachung** FEM NOUN
agreement

die **Abnahme** FEM NOUN
decrease

□ eine weitere Abnahme der Teilnehmerzahlen a further decrease in attendance

★**abnehmen** (PRESENT TENSE nimmt ab, IMPERFECT nahm ab, PERFECT TENSE hat abgenommen) VERB [52]

1 to remove

□ Bei diesem Auto kann man das Verdeck abnehmen. You can remove the hood on this car.

■ Als das Telefon klingelte, nahm sie ab. When the telephone rang, she answered it.
■ jemandem etwas abnehmen to take something away from somebody □ Ihr wurde der Führerschein abgenommen. They took away her driving licence.

2 to decrease

□ Die Zahl der Teilnehmer hat stark abgenommen. The number of participants has decreased dramatically.

3 to lose weight

□ Warum willst du denn abnehmen? Why do you want to lose weight? □ Ich habe schon zwei Kilo abgenommen. I've already lost two kilos.

4 to buy

□ Wenn Sie mehr als zehn Stück abnehmen, bekommen Sie einen Rabatt. If you buy more than ten you get a discount. □ Hat sie dir diese

Numbers in brackets refer to verb tables on pages 697 to 706.

3

Geschichte wirklich abgenommen? Did she really buy that story? (*Umgangssprache*)

das **Abonnement** (PL die **Abonnements**) NEUT NOUN
subscription

abonnieren (PERFECT TENSE hat abonniert) VERB [76]
to subscribe to

★ **abräumen** (PERFECT TENSE hat abgeräumt) VERB [4]
to clear away
□ Sie räumte die Teller ab. She cleared away the plates.
■ **den Tisch abräumen** to clear the table

abreagieren (PERFECT TENSE hat abreagiert) VERB [4]
■ **etwas an jemandem abreagieren** to take something out on somebody
■ **sich abreagieren** to calm down

★ die **Abreise** FEM NOUN
departure

★ **abreisen** (PERFECT TENSE ist abgereist) VERB [4]
to leave

Abs. ABBREVIATION (= *Absender*)
sender

die **Absage** FEM NOUN
refusal

absagen (PERFECT TENSE hat abgesagt) VERB [4]
1 to call off
□ Die Vorstellung wurde abgesagt, weil ein Schauspieler krank war. The performance was called off because one of the actors was ill.
2 to turn down
□ eine Einladung absagen to turn down an invitation

der **Absatz** (GEN des **Absatzes**, PL die **Absätze**) MASC NOUN
1 heel
□ Die Absätze von deinen Schuhen sind ganz schief. The heels of your shoes are worn down.
2 paragraph
□ Hier solltest du einen Absatz machen. You need to start a new paragraph here.
3 sales *pl*
□ Der Absatz an mobilen Lautsprechern ist gestiegen. Sales of portable speakers have risen.

abschaffen (PERFECT TENSE hat abgeschafft) VERB [4]
1 to abolish
□ Wann wurde in Deutschland die Todesstrafe abgeschafft? When was the death sentence abolished in Germany?
2 to get rid of
□ Ich werde mein Auto abschaffen. I'm going to get rid of my car.

abscheulich ADJECTIVE
abominable

★ **abschicken** (PERFECT TENSE hat abgeschickt) VERB [4]
to send off

der **Abschied** (PL die **Abschiede**) MASC NOUN
parting
■ **von jemandem Abschied nehmen** to say goodbye to somebody

★ der **Abschleppdienst** (PL die **Abschleppdienste**) MASC NOUN
breakdown service

★ **abschleppen** (PERFECT TENSE hat abgeschleppt) VERB [4]
to tow
□ ein Auto abschleppen to tow a car

★ **abschließen** (IMPERFECT schloss ab, PERFECT TENSE hat abgeschlossen) VERB
1 to lock
□ Ich schließe meinen Schreibtisch immer ab. I always lock my desk.
2 to conclude
□ einen Vertrag abschließen to conclude a contract

abschließend ADJECTIVE, ADVERB
in conclusion
□ Abschließend möchte ich noch Folgendes sagen: ... In conclusion I would like to say this: ...

★ die **Abschlussprüfung** FEM NOUN
final exam

abschneiden (IMPERFECT schnitt ab, PERFECT TENSE hat abgeschnitten) VERB [60]
1 to cut
□ Kannst du mir bitte eine Scheibe Brot abschneiden? Can you cut me a slice of bread, please?
2 to do
□ Sie hat in der Prüfung sehr gut abgeschnitten She did very well in the exam.

abschrecken (PERFECT TENSE hat abgeschreckt) VERB [4]
to deter
□ Diese Maßnahmen sollen Jugendliche davon abschrecken, Drogen zu nehmen. These measures are intended to deter young people from taking drugs.

★ **abschreiben** (IMPERFECT schrieb ab, PERFECT TENSE hat abgeschrieben) VERB [61]
to copy
□ Er wurde dabei erwischt, wie er von seinem Nachbarn abgeschrieben hat. He was caught copying from his neighbour. □ Schreibt diesen Satz bitte in eure Hefte ab. Please copy this sentence into your exercise books.

absehbar ADJECTIVE
foreseeable
□ in absehbarer Zeit in the foreseeable future
■ **Das Ende ist absehbar.** The end is in sight.

abseits ADVERB
apart
□ Sie stand etwas abseits von den anderen. She was standing somewhat apart from the others.

das **Abseits** NEUT NOUN
offside (*in football*)
■ im Abseits stehen to be offside

★ der **Absender** (PL die **Absender**) MASC NOUN
sender

absetzen (PERFECT TENSE **hat abgesetzt**) VERB [36]

1 to drop off
□ Ich setze dich am Bahnhof ab. I'll drop you off at the station.

2 to take off
□ Willst du nicht deinen Motorradhelm absetzen? Don't you want to take your helmet off?

3 to drop
□ Dieser Sprachkurs musste vom Programm abgesetzt werden. This language course had to be dropped from the syllabus.
■ die Pille absetzen to stop taking the pill

die **Absicht** FEM NOUN
intention
□ Das war nicht meine Absicht. That was not my intention.
■ mit Absicht on purpose

absichtlich ADJECTIVE, ADVERB
deliberate
□ eine absichtliche Beleidigung a deliberate insult
■ etwas absichtlich tun to do something deliberately

absolut ADJECTIVE, ADVERB
absolute
■ Das ist absolut unmöglich. That's absolutely impossible.
■ Ich habe absolut keine Lust. I really don't feel like it.

★ **abspülen** (PERFECT TENSE **hat abgespült**) VERB [4]
to rinse
□ Er spülte die Teller ab. He rinsed the plates.
■ Geschirr abspülen to wash up

der **Abstand** (PL die **Abstände**) MASC NOUN
distance
□ Abstand halten to keep one's distance

abstellen (PERFECT TENSE **hat abgestellt**) VERB [4]

1 to put down
□ Der Koffer ist so schwer, ich muss ihn kurz abstellen. The case is so heavy that I'll have to put it down for a moment.

2 to park
□ Wir haben das Auto am Stadtrand abgestellt. We parked the car on the outskirts of town.

3 to switch off
□ Kannst du bitte das Radio abstellen? Can you switch the radio off, please?

die **Abstimmung** FEM NOUN
vote

abstreiten (IMPERFECT **stritt ab**, PERFECT TENSE **hat abgestritten**) VERB
to deny

abstürzen (PERFECT TENSE **ist abgestürzt**) VERB [36]

1 to fall
□ Mathis ist beim Klettern abgestürzt. Mathis fell while climbing.

2 to crash
□ Die Maschine ist kurz nach dem Start abgestürzt. The plane crashed shortly after takeoff.

★ das **Abteil** (PL die **Abteile**) NEUT NOUN
compartment

★ die **Abteilung** FEM NOUN

1 department
□ Sie wurde in eine andere Abteilung versetzt. She was transferred to another department.

2 ward
□ In welcher Abteilung liegt Mathis? Which ward is Mathis in?

die **Abtreibung** FEM NOUN
abortion

★ **abtrocknen** (PERFECT TENSE **hat abgetrocknet**) VERB [53]
to dry

abwärts ADVERB
down

der **Abwasch** MASC NOUN
washing-up
□ den Abwasch machen to do the washing-up

★ **abwaschen** (PRESENT TENSE **wäscht ab**, IMPERFECT **wusch ab**, PERFECT TENSE **hat abgewaschen**) VERB [89]

1 to wash
□ Wer muss heute das Geschirr abwaschen? Whose turn is it to wash the dishes today?

2 to wash off
□ Wasch dir mal die Soße vom Gesicht ab! Wash that gravy off your face.

das **Abwasser** (PL die **Abwässer**) NEUT NOUN
sewage *no pl*

die **Abwechslung** FEM NOUN
change
□ zur Abwechslung for a change

abwerten (PERFECT TENSE **hat abgewertet**) VERB [2]
to devalue

abwertend ADJECTIVE, ADVERB
derogatory
□ sich abwertend über etwas äußern to talk in a derogatory way about something

Numbers in brackets refer to verb tables on pages 697 to 706.

5

abwesend ADJECTIVE
absent

die **Abwesenheit** FEM NOUN
absence

abwischen (PERFECT TENSE **hat abgewischt**) VERB [4]
to wipe
□ Er wischte die Tafel ab. He wiped the board.

abzählen (PERFECT TENSE **hat abgezählt**) VERB [4]
to count

das **Abzeichen** (PL die **Abzeichen**) NEUT NOUN
badge

abziehen (IMPERFECT **zog ab**, PERFECT TENSE **hat/ist abgezogen**) VERB [96]

> For the perfect tense use **haben** when the verb has an object and **sein** when there is no object.

1 to take out
□ Er zog den Zündschlüssel ab. He took out the ignition key.
2 to withdraw
□ Sie haben ihre Truppen aus der Stadt abgezogen. They have withdrawn their troops from the town.
3 to deduct
□ Die Steuer wird vom Gehalt abgezogen. Tax is deducted from earnings.
■ Er ist beleidigt abgezogen. He went away in a huff. (*Umgangssprache*)

abzüglich PREPOSITION

> The preposition **abzüglich** takes the genitive.

less
□ das Gehalt abzüglich der Steuern earnings less tax

die **Achsel** FEM NOUN
1 shoulder
□ mit den Achseln zucken to shrug one's shoulders
2 armpit

★**acht** NUMBER
▷ see also die **Acht** (1) NOUN
eight
■ acht Tage a week

die **Acht** (1) FEM NOUN
▷ see also **acht** NUMBER
eight
□ Schreibe eine Acht. Write the figure eight.

die **Acht** (2) FEM NOUN
attention
■ sich in Acht nehmen to beware □ Du solltest dich vor ihr in Acht nehmen! You should beware of her.
■ etwas außer Acht lassen to disregard something
■ Acht geben ▷ see **achtgeben**

achte ADJECTIVE
eighth
□ Sie wiederholte den Satz ein achtes Mal. She repeated the sentence for an eighth time. □ Er kam als Achter. He was the eighth to arrive.

achten VERB [2]
to respect
□ Ich achte deine Meinung. I respect your opinion. □ Sie ist sehr geachtet. She's highly respected.
■ auf etwas achten to pay attention to something □ Du solltest auf die Verkehrsschilder achten. You should pay attention to the road signs.
■ auf jemanden achten to take notice of somebody □ Achte nicht auf ihn! Don't take any notice of him!

die **Achterbahn** FEM NOUN
roller coaster

achtgeben (PRESENT TENSE **gibt acht**, IMPERFECT **gab acht**, PERFECT TENSE **hat achtgegeben**) VERB [28]
to pay attention
□ Du solltest etwas mehr auf die Rechtschreibung achtgeben! You should pay a bit more attention to spelling.
■ auf jemanden achtgeben to keep an eye on somebody □ Würden Sie mal bitte kurz auf meinen Sohn achtgeben? Would you keep an eye on my son for a minute, please?
■ Gib acht! Look out!

achtmal ADVERB
eight times

★die **Achtung** FEM NOUN
respect
□ Ich habe große Achtung vor ihr. I've great respect for her.
■ Achtung! Look out!
■ Achtung Stufe! Mind the step.
■ Achtung, Achtung, hier eine Durchsage! Your attention, please. Here is an announcement.
■ Alle Achtung! Well done!

★**achtzehn** NUMBER
eighteen

★**achtzig** NUMBER
eighty

der **Acker** (PL die **Äcker**) MASC NOUN
field

addieren (PERFECT TENSE **hat addiert**) VERB [76]
to add

der **Adel** MASC NOUN
nobility

die **Ader** FEM NOUN
vein

ADHS ABBREVIATION (= *Aufmerksamkeitsdefizit/ Hyperaktivitätsstörung*)
ADHD

★ = core vocabulary

das **Adjektiv** (PL die **Adjektive**) NEUT NOUN
adjective

der **Adler** (PL die **Adler**) MASC NOUN
eagle

adlig ADJECTIVE
noble

adoptieren (PERFECT TENSE **hat adoptiert**)
VERB [76]
to adopt

die **Adoption** FEM NOUN
adoption

die **Adoptiveltern** PL NOUN
adoptive parents *pl*

das **Adoptivkind** (PL die **Adoptivkinder**)
NEUT NOUN
adopted child

★ die **Adresse** FEM NOUN
address

adressieren (PERFECT TENSE **hat adressiert**)
VERB [76]
to address
□ An wen soll ich den Brief adressieren? To
whom should I address the letter?

der **Advent** MASC NOUN
Advent

★ der **Adventskalender** (PL die
Adventskalender) MASC NOUN
Advent calendar

★ der **Adventskranz** (PL die **Adventskränze**)
MASC NOUN
Advent wreath

das **Adverb** (PL die **Adverbien**) NEUT NOUN
adverb

★ der **Affe** (GEN des **Affen**, PL die **Affen**) MASC
NOUN
monkey

★ **Afrika** NEUT NOUN
Africa
■ aus Afrika from Africa
■ nach Afrika to Africa

★ der **Afrikaner** (PL die **Afrikaner**) MASC NOUN
African

★ die **Afrikanerin** FEM NOUN
African

afrikanisch ADJECTIVE
African

Ägypten NEUT NOUN
Egypt
■ nach Ägypten to Egypt

der **Ägypter** (PL die **Ägypter**) MASC NOUN
Egyptian

die **Ägypterin** FEM NOUN
Egyptian

ägyptisch ADJECTIVE
Egyptian

ähneln VERB [34]
■ jemandem ähneln to resemble somebody
□ Sie ähnelt ihrer Mutter. She resembles her
mother.
■ Sie ähneln sich. They are alike.

ahnen VERB [38]
1 to know
□ Ich habe geahnt, dass er nicht kommen
würde. I knew he wouldn't come. □ Das konnte
ich doch nicht ahnen! How was I supposed to
know that?
2 to sense
□ Das Tier hat die Gefahr geahnt und ist schnell
verschwunden. The animal sensed the danger
and quickly disappeared.

★ **ähnlich** ADJECTIVE
similar
□ Unsere Kleider sind sehr ähnlich. Our dresses
are very similar.
■ Sein Auto sieht ähnlich aus wie meines.
His car looks like mine.
■ Er ist seinem Vater sehr ähnlich. He's
very like his father.
■ Das sieht ihr ähnlich! That's typical of her.

die **Ähnlichkeit** FEM NOUN
similarity

★ die **Ahnung** FEM NOUN
1 idea
□ Ich habe keine Ahnung, ob er kommt. I've no
idea whether he's coming.
■ Er hat von Computerspielen keine
Ahnung. He doesn't know the first thing about
computer games.
2 hunch
□ Er hatte eine Ahnung, dass etwas Schlimmes
geschehen würde. He had a hunch that
something terrible would happen.

ahnungslos ADJECTIVE
unsuspecting

★ das **Aids** (GEN des **Aids**) NEUT NOUN
AIDS *sing* (= *Acquired Immune Deficiency
Syndrome*)
□ Jonas ist an Aids gestorben. Jonas died of
AIDS.

der **Akademiker** (PL die **Akademiker**) MASC
NOUN
university graduate

die **Akademikerin** FEM NOUN
university graduate

akademisch ADJECTIVE
academic

der **Akkusativ** (PL die **Akkusative**) MASC
NOUN
accusative

die **Akne** FEM NOUN
acne
□ Sie hat Akne. She's got acne.

die **Akte** FEM NOUN
file
■ **etwas zu den Akten legen** to file
something away

★ die **Aktentasche** FEM NOUN
briefcase

die **Aktie** FEM NOUN
share
□ in Aktien investieren to invest in shares

die **Aktion** FEM NOUN
1 campaign
□ eine Aktion für den Frieden a campaign for
peace
2 operation
□ Wir alle nahmen an der Aktion teil. We all
took part in the operation.
■ **in Aktion treten** to go into action □ In
solchen Fällen tritt die Feuerwehr in Aktion. In
cases like these, the fire brigade goes into
action.

★ **aktiv** ADJECTIVE
active

★ die **Aktivität** FEM NOUN
activity

★ **aktuell** ADJECTIVE
1 topical
□ ein aktuelles Thema a topical issue
2 up-to-date
□ ein aktueller Fahrplan an up-to-date
timetable

> **BE CAREFUL!**
> aktuell does not mean **actual**.

der **Akzent** (PL die **Akzente**) MASC NOUN
1 accent
□ Sie spricht mit einem amerikanischen Akzent.
She speaks with an American accent.
2 emphasis
□ Der Akzent liegt auf Benutzerfreundlichkeit.
The emphasis is on user-friendliness.

albern ADJECTIVE
silly
■ **sich albern benehmen** to act silly

der **Albtraum** (PL die **Albträume**) MASC NOUN
nightmare

★ das **Album** (PL die **Alben**) NEUT NOUN
album

die **Algebra** FEM NOUN
algebra

★ der **Alkohol** MASC NOUN
alcohol

★ **alkoholfrei** ADJECTIVE
nonalcoholic

der **Alkoholiker** (PL die **Alkoholiker**) MASC
NOUN
alcoholic

die **Alkoholikerin** FEM NOUN
alcoholic

★ **alkoholisch** ADJECTIVE
alcoholic

das **All** NEUT NOUN
space
■ **Sind wir allein im All?** Are we alone in the
universe?

★ **alle** ADJECTIVE, PRONOUN
▷ see also **alles** PRONOUN
1 all the
□ Alle Schüler sollten kommen. All the pupils
should come.
2 all
□ Nicht alle Kinder mögen Schokolade. Not all
children like chocolate.
3 all of them
□ Wir haben alle gesehen. We saw all of them.
■ **Sie kamen alle.** They all came.
■ **wir alle** all of us
■ **Ich habe alle beide eingeladen.** I've
invited both of them.
4 every
□ alle vier Jahre every four years □ alle fünf
Meter every five metres
■ **Die Milch ist alle.** The milk's all gone.
■ **etwas alle machen** to finish something up

★ die **Allee** (PL die **Alleen**) FEM NOUN
avenue

★ **allein** ADJECTIVE, ADVERB, CONJUNCTION
1 alone
□ Sie lebt allein. She lives alone. □ Du allein
kannst das entscheiden. You alone can decide.
2 on one's own
□ Sie hat das ganz allein geschrieben. She wrote
that all on her own. □ Seit ich allein bin, habe
ich mehr Zeit. Since I've been on my own, I've
had more time.
■ **Er fühlt sich allein.** He feels lonely.
■ **nicht allein** not only

★ der/die **Alleinerziehende** (GEN des/der
Alleinerziehenden, PL die
Alleinerziehenden) MASC/FEM NOUN
single parent
□ Er ist Alleinerziehender. He's a single parent.

★ **alleinstehend** ADJECTIVE
single

allerbeste ADJECTIVE
very best
□ Felix ist mein allerbester Schüler. Felix is my
very best pupil.

allerdings ADVERB
1 though
□ Der Urlaub war schön, allerdings etwas kurz.
The holiday was nice, though it was rather
short.
2 certainly
□ Das ist allerdings schwierig. That's certainly
difficult.

★ die **Allergie** FEM NOUN
allergy

★ **allergisch** ADJECTIVE
allergic
□ Sie ist allergisch gegen Katzen. **She's allergic to cats.**

das **Allerheiligen** NEUT NOUN
All Saints' Day

DID YOU KNOW...?
Allerheiligen (November 1st) is a public holiday in those parts of Germany where most of the population are Roman Catholics.

allerlei ADJECTIVE
all sorts of
□ allerlei Sachen **all sorts of things**

allerletzte ADJECTIVE
very last
□ zum allerletzten Mal **for the very last time**

★ **alles** PRONOUN
▷ see also **alle** ADJECTIVE, PRONOUN
everything
□ Wir haben alles Mögliche versucht. **We've tried everything.** □ Sie haben alles aufgegessen. **They've eaten everything up.** □ alles, was er sagt **everything he says**
■ **alles in Allem** all in all
■ **Alles Gute!** All the best!

★ **allgemein** ADJECTIVE
general
■ **im Allgemeinen** in general

allmählich ADJECTIVE, ADVERB
1 gradual
□ eine allmähliche Besserung **a gradual improvement**
2 gradually
□ Es wird allmählich wärmer. **It's gradually getting warmer.**
■ **Allmählich solltest du das wissen.** You should know that by now.

★ der **Alltag** MASC NOUN
everyday life

allzu ADVERB
all too
□ allzu oft **all too often**
■ **allzu viel** far too much

die **Alm** FEM NOUN
alpine pasture

★ die **Alpen** FEM PL NOUN
Alps pl

das **Alphabet** (PL die Alphabete) NEUT NOUN
alphabet

alphabetisch ADJECTIVE
alphabetical
□ alphabetisch geordnet **arranged in alphabetical order**

★ der **Alptraum** (PL die Alpträume) MASC NOUN
nightmare

★ **als** CONJUNCTION
1 when
□ Als ich ein Kind war ... **When I was a child ...**
2 as
□ Sie kam, als ich gerade gehen wollte. **She arrived as I was about to leave.** □ Ich als Lehrerin weiß, ... **As a teacher, I know ...**
■ **gerade, als ...** just as ...
■ **als ob** as if □ Er tat, als ob er nichts bemerkt hätte. **He acted as if he hadn't noticed anything.**
3 than
□ Sie ist älter als ich. **She's older than me.** □ Ich kam später als er. **I came later than he did.**
■ **lieber als ...** rather than ... □ Ich mag Süßes lieber als Salziges. **I like sweet things rather than savoury things.**
■ **nichts als Ärger** nothing but trouble

★ **also** ADVERB, CONJUNCTION, EXCLAMATION
1 then
□ Was sollen wir also tun? **What shall we do, then?** □ Du willst also nicht mit. **You don't want to come along, then.** □ Du hast es also gewusst. **You did know then.**
2 so
□ Es war schon spät, also bin ich nach Hause gegangen. **It had got late, so I went home.**
3 well
□ Also ich gehe jetzt! **Well, I'm off now.** □ Also, Sie fahren immer geradeaus ... **Well, keep going straight on ...**
■ **Also gut!** Okay then.
■ **Also, so was!** Well really!
■ **Na also!** There you are then!

BE CAREFUL!
The German word also does not mean **also**.

★ **alt** ADJECTIVE
old
□ Wie alt bist du? **How old are you?** □ Felix ist zehn Jahre alt. **Felix is ten years old.** □ Sein Auto ist älter als unseres. **His car is older than ours.**
■ **meine ältere Schwester** my elder sister
■ **alles beim Alten lassen** to leave everything as it was

der **Altar** (PL die Altäre) MASC NOUN
altar

★ das **Alter** (PL die Alter) NEUT NOUN
1 age
□ In deinem Alter sollte man das wissen. **You ought to know that at your age.**
2 old age
□ Im Alter sind die Menschen oft einsam. **People are often lonely in old age.**
■ **im Alter von** at the age of

das **Altglas** (GEN des Altglases) NEUT NOUN
used glass

Numbers in brackets refer to verb tables on pages 697 to 706.

9

der **Altglascontainer** (PL die
Altglascontainer) MASC NOUN
bottle bank

★ **altmodisch** ADJECTIVE
old-fashioned

★ das **Altpapier** NEUT NOUN
waste paper

★ die **Altstadt** (PL die **Altstädte**) FEM NOUN
old town

die **Alufolie** FEM NOUN
tinfoil

das **Aluminium** NEUT NOUN
aluminium

★ **am** = an dem
  ■ am fünften März on the fifth of March
  ■ am höchsten the highest
  ■ am schönsten the most beautiful

die **Ameise** FEM NOUN
ant

★ **Amerika** NEUT NOUN
America
  ■ aus Amerika from America
  ■ in Amerika in America
  ■ nach Amerika to America

★ der **Amerikaner** (PL die **Amerikaner**) MASC
NOUN
American

★ die **Amerikanerin** FEM NOUN
American

★ **amerikanisch** ADJECTIVE
American

★ die **Ampel** FEM NOUN
traffic lights pl
  □ Die Ampel ist grün. The traffic lights are at
  green.

die **Amsel** FEM NOUN
blackbird

das **Amt** (PL die **Ämter**) NEUT NOUN
office
  □ Welches Amt ist für Kindergeld zuständig?
  Which office deals with child benefit?

amtlich ADJECTIVE
official

★ **amüsant** ADJECTIVE
amusing

★ **amüsieren** (PERFECT TENSE hat amüsiert)
VERB [76]
to amuse
  □ Diese Geschichte hat uns sehr amüsiert. The
  story amused us very much.
  ■ sich amüsieren to enjoy oneself □ Wir
  haben uns blendend amüsiert. We enjoyed
  ourselves immensely.

★ **an** PREPOSITION, ADVERB
  ▷ see also **am**

Use the accusative to express movement or a
change of place. Use the dative when there is
no change of place.

1 on
  □ Das Wort stand an der Tafel. The word was
  written on the blackboard. □ Der Lehrer schrieb
  das Wort an die Tafel. The teacher wrote the
  word on the blackboard. □ Köln liegt am Rhein.
  Cologne is on the Rhine. □ Christoph hat am
  neunten November Geburtstag. Christoph's
  birthday is on the ninth of November. □ an
  diesem Tag on this day

2 to
  □ Er ging ans Fenster. He went to the window.
  □ Wir waren gestern am Meer. We went to the
  seaside yesterday. □ Wir wollen morgen ans
  Meer fahren. We want to go to the seaside
  tomorrow. □ Ich habe einen Brief an meine
  Mutter geschrieben. I've written a letter to my
  mother.

3 by
  □ Ihr Haus liegt an der Autobahn. Their house is
  by the motorway.
  ■ an Ostern at Easter
  ■ an etwas denken to think of something
  ■ reich an Nährstoffen rich in nutrients
  ■ an etwas sterben to die of something
  ■ an und für sich actually □ Das ist an und für
  sich ganz einfach. Actually, it's quite simple.
  ■ an die hundert about a hundred
  ■ von heute an from today onwards
  ■ Das Licht ist an. The light's on.
  ■ ohne etwas an with nothing on
  ■ eine Frage an dich a question for you
  ■ an diesem Ort in this place
  ■ unten am Fluss down by the river

★ die **Ananas** (PL die **Ananas**) FEM NOUN
pineapple

★ **anbauen** (PERFECT TENSE hat angebaut) VERB
[4]
1 to build on(to)
  □ eine Garage ans Haus anbauen to build a
  garage onto the house
2 to cultivate
  □ Reis anbauen to cultivate rice

anbei ADVERB
enclosed

★ **anbieten** (IMPERFECT bot an, PERFECT TENSE hat
angeboten) VERB [8]
to offer
  □ Ich bot ihr eine Tasse Kaffee an. I offered her a
  cup of coffee.
  ■ anbieten, etwas zu tun to volunteer to do
  something □ Er hat angeboten, mir beim
  Umzug zu helfen. He volunteered to help me
  move house.

der **Anblick** (PL die **Anblicke**) MASC NOUN
sight

★ = core vocabulary

anbrechen (PRESENT TENSE **bricht an**, IMPERFECT **brach an**, PERFECT TENSE **ist/hat angebrochen**) VERB [11]

> For the perfect tense use **haben** when the verb has an object and **sein** when there is no object.

1 to break into
□ Für diese Reise müsste ich meine Ersparnisse anbrechen. **To buy it, I'd have to break into my savings.**

2 to break
□ wenn der Tag anbricht **when day breaks**

3 to dawn
□ Ein neues Zeitalter ist angebrochen. **A new age has dawned.**

anbrennen (IMPERFECT **brannte an**, PERFECT TENSE **ist angebrannt**) VERB [12]
to burn
□ Der Kuchen ist angebrannt. **The cake's burnt.**

andauernd ADJECTIVE, ADVERB

1 continual
□ diese andauernden Unterbrechungen **these continual interruptions**

2 constantly
□ Er stört andauernd. **He's constantly interrupting.**

★ **das Andenken** (PL **die Andenken**) NEUT NOUN

1 memory
□ zum Andenken an eine schöne Zeit **in memory of a wonderful time**

2 souvenir
□ Ich habe mir aus dem Urlaub einige Andenken mitgebracht. **I brought a few souvenirs back from my holiday.**

andere ADJECTIVE, PRONOUN

1 other
□ Nein, nicht dieses Buch, gib mir bitte das andere. **No, not that book, please give me the other one.**

2 different
□ Er hat jetzt eine andere Freundin. **He's got a different girlfriend now.**

3 another
□ ein anderes Mal **another time** □ Wir werden das an einem anderen Tag machen. **We'll do that another day.**
▪ **kein anderer** nobody else
▪ **die anderen** the others □ Martin ist noch da, die anderen sind schon gegangen. **Martin's still here, the others have already left.**
▪ **etwas anderes** something else □ von etwas anderem sprechen **to talk about something else**

andererseits ADVERB
on the other hand
□ Einerseits ..., andererseits ... **On the one hand ..., on the other hand ...**

andermal ADVERB
▪ **ein andermal** some other time

★ **ändern** VERB [88]
to alter
□ Ich habe das Kleid ändern lassen. **I've had the dress altered.**
▪ **sich ändern** to change □ Sie hat sich in letzter Zeit sehr geändert. **She's changed a lot recently.** □ Wenn sich die Lage nicht ändert ... **If the situation doesn't change ...**

★ **anders** ADVERB
differently
□ So geht das nicht, du musst das anders machen. **Not like that – you have to do it differently.**
▪ **anders als** different from □ Sie ist ganz anders als ihr Bruder. **She's quite different from her brother.** □ Sie hat das anders als ich übersetzt. **She translated it differently from me.**
▪ **Wer anders?** Who else?
▪ **jemand anders** somebody else
▪ **irgendwo anders** somewhere else
▪ **anders aussehen** to look different

★ **anderthalb** ADJECTIVE
one and a half

die Änderung FEM NOUN
alteration

andeuten (PERFECT TENSE **hat angedeutet**) VERB [2]
to hint
□ Sie hat angedeutet, dass sie weiß, wer es war. **She's hinted that she knows who it was.**

die Andeutung FEM NOUN
hint
▪ **Sie hat eine Andeutung gemacht, dass sie es weiß.** She hinted that she knew.

anerkennend ADJECTIVE, ADVERB
appreciative

die Anerkennung FEM NOUN

1 appreciation
□ Ihr Album fand nicht die entsprechende Anerkennung. **Her album didn't get the appreciation it deserved.**

2 recognition
□ Dieser neue Staat hofft auf Anerkennung durch die Bundesrepublik. **This new country is hoping for recognition by the Federal Republic.**

anfahren (PRESENT TENSE **fährt an**, IMPERFECT **fuhr an**, PERFECT TENSE **hat/ist angefahren**) VERB [21]

1 to hit
□ Er hat einen Fußgänger angefahren. **He hit a pedestrian.**

2 to start up
□ beim Anfahren **when starting up**

der Anfall (PL **die Anfälle**) MASC NOUN
fit
□ Sie hatte einen epileptischen Anfall. **She had an epileptic fit.** □ Wenn er das erfährt, bekommt er einen Anfall. **If he finds out, he'll have a fit.** (*Umgangssprache*)

Anfang – angehen

★ der **Anfang** (PL die **Anfänge**) MASC NOUN
beginning
□ von Anfang an right from the beginning □ am Anfang at the beginning □ Anfang Mai at the beginning of May
■ zu Anfang first

★ **anfangen** (PRESENT TENSE **fängt an**, IMPERFECT **fing an**, PERFECT TENSE **hat angefangen**) VERB [23]
1 to begin
□ Es fängt an zu regnen. It's beginning to rain.
2 to start
□ Der Film hat schon angefangen. The film's already started. □ Hast du den Aufsatz schon angefangen? Have you already started your essay?
■ Damit kann ich nichts anfangen. It doesn't mean anything to me.
■ Das fängt ja gut an! That's a good start!

★ der **Anfänger** (PL die **Anfänger**) MASC NOUN
beginner

★ die **Anfängerin** FEM NOUN
beginner

★ **anfassen** (PERFECT TENSE **hat angefasst**) VERB [31]
1 to touch
□ Fass den Hund besser nicht an! You'd better not touch the dog.
2 to treat
□ Du solltest die Kinder nicht immer so rau anfassen! You shouldn't treat the children so roughly.
■ mit anfassen to lend a hand □ Kannst du mal mit anfassen, den Schrank wegzuschieben? Can you lend a hand shifting this cupboard to one side?
■ sich anfassen to feel □ Samt fasst sich weich an. Velvet feels soft.

sich **anfreunden** (PERFECT TENSE **hat sich angefreundet**) VERB [4]
1 to make friends
□ Ich habe mich in den Ferien mit einer Engländerin angefreundet. I made friends with an English girl during the holidays.
2 to become friends
□ Die beiden haben sich angefreundet. The two of them have become friends.

anfühlen (PERFECT TENSE **hat angefühlt**) VERB [4]
to feel
□ Fühl mal meine Stirn an, ich glaube, ich habe Fieber. Feel my forehead, I think I've got a temperature. □ Der Stoff fühlt sich weich an. The material feels soft.

die **Angabe** FEM NOUN
1 information no pl
□ Die Angaben waren falsch. The information was wrong.

2 serve (tennis)
□ Wer hat Angabe? Whose serve is it?
■ Das ist doch alles nur Angabe! That's nothing but show.

angeben (PRESENT TENSE **gibt an**, IMPERFECT **gab an**, PERFECT TENSE **hat angegeben**) VERB [28]
1 to give
□ Geben Sie bitte Ihre Personalien an. Please give your personal details.
2 to state
□ Sie hat angegeben, dass sie zu dem Zeitpunkt zu Hause war. She stated that she was at home at the time.
3 to indicate
□ Alle Raststätten sind auf der Karte angegeben. All service areas are indicated on the map.
4 to show off
□ Glaub ihm kein Wort, er gibt nur an. Don't believe a word he says – he's just showing off.

★ der **Angeber** (PL die **Angeber**) MASC NOUN
show-off (Umgangssprache)

angeblich ADJECTIVE, ADVERB
1 alleged
□ Sie ist die angebliche Täterin. She's the alleged culprit.
2 allegedly
□ Angeblich hat sie es getan. Allegedly, she did it.

★ das **Angebot** (PL die **Angebote**) NEUT NOUN
offer
□ Ich nehme dein Angebot an. I accept your offer.
■ ein Angebot an etwas a selection of something □ Das Kaufhaus hat ein großes Angebot an Tablets. The department store has a large selection of tablets.
■ Angebot und Nachfrage supply and demand

angehen (IMPERFECT **ging an**, PERFECT TENSE **hat/ist angegangen**) VERB [29]

For the perfect tense use haben when the verb has an object and sein when there is no object.

1 to concern
□ Diese Angelegenheit geht mich nichts an. This matter doesn't concern me.
■ Was geht dich das an? What business is it of yours?
■ was ... angeht as regards ... □ Was die Ferien angeht, haben wir noch nichts entschieden. As regards the holidays, we still haven't decided anything.
2 to tackle
□ Ich weiß noch nicht so richtig, wie ich das Thema angehen soll. I'm not really sure how to tackle the subject.

★ = core vocabulary

3 to go on
□ Das Licht ging an. The light went on.

der/die **Angehörige** (GEN des/der **Angehörigen**, PL die **Angehörigen**) MASC/FEM NOUN
close relative
□ Er ist ein Angehöriger von mir. He's a close relative of mine.

die **Angel** FEM NOUN
1 fishing rod
2 hinge (of door)

> **BE CAREFUL!**
> The German word **Angel** does not mean **angel**.

die **Angelegenheit** FEM NOUN
1 matter
□ Ich werde diese Angelegenheit prüfen. I'll look into the matter.
2 affair
□ Das ist meine Angelegenheit. That's my affair.

★**angeln** VERB [34]
1 to catch
□ Sie hat eine große Forelle geangelt. She caught a large trout.
2 to fish
□ Sonntags geht Alex immer angeln. Alex always goes fishing on Sundays.

★**angenehm** ADJECTIVE, ADVERB
pleasant
■ Angenehm! Pleased to meet you.

angesehen ADJECTIVE
respected

★der/die **Angestellte** (GEN des/der **Angestellten**, PL die **Angestellten**) MASC/FEM NOUN
employee
□ Er ist nur ein kleiner Angestellter. He's just a lowly employee.

angewiesen ADJECTIVE
■ auf jemanden angewiesen sein to be dependent on somebody
■ auf etwas angewiesen sein to be dependent on something

angewöhnen (PERFECT TENSE hat angewöhnt) VERB [38]
■ jemandem etwas angewöhnen to teach somebody something □ Sie sollten Ihrem Sohn bessere Manieren angewöhnen. You ought to teach your son better manners.
■ sich etwas angewöhnen to get into the habit of doing something □ Ich habe es mir angewöhnt, jeden Morgen um sieben Uhr aufzustehen. I've got into the habit of getting up at seven every morning.

die **Angewohnheit** FEM NOUN
habit
□ Das ist so eine Angewohnheit von ihr. That's a habit of hers.

★**angreifen** (IMPERFECT griff an, PERFECT TENSE hat angegriffen) VERB
1 to attack
□ Ich wurde von einem Hund angegriffen. I was attacked by a dog.
2 to criticize
□ Sie wurde wegen dieser Aussage von ihren Freunden angegriffen. She was criticized by her friends for what she said.

der **Angriff** (PL die **Angriffe**) MASC NOUN
attack
■ etwas in Angriff nehmen to make a start on something

★die **Angst** (PL die **Ängste**) FEM NOUN
fear
■ vor jemandem Angst haben to be afraid of somebody
■ vor etwas Angst haben to be afraid of something
■ Ich habe Angst vor der Prüfung. I'm worried about the exam.
■ Angst um jemanden haben to be worried about somebody
■ jemandem Angst machen to scare somebody

★**ängstlich** ADJECTIVE, ADVERB
1 scared
□ Nun sei doch nicht so ängstlich, der Hund tut dir nichts! There's no need to be scared, the dog won't harm you.
2 anxious
□ 'Wird er wieder gesund?', fragte sie ängstlich. 'Will he get well again?', she asked anxiously.

★**anhaben** (PRESENT TENSE hat an, IMPERFECT hatte an, PERFECT TENSE hat angehabt) VERB [32]
to have on
□ Sie hatte heute die rote Jacke an. She had her red jacket on today.
■ jemandem nichts anhaben können to have nothing on somebody □ Ich bin unschuldig, die Polizei kann mir nichts anhaben. I'm innocent, the police have got nothing on me.

★**anhalten** (PRESENT TENSE hält an, IMPERFECT hielt an, PERFECT TENSE hat angehalten) VERB [33]
1 to stop
□ Können wir bitte anhalten, mir ist schlecht. Can we stop please? I feel sick. □ Kannst du bitte das Auto anhalten? Can you stop the car please?
2 to last
□ Das wird nicht lange anhalten. It won't last long.
■ die Luft anhalten to hold one's breath

der **Anhalter** (PL die **Anhalter**) MASC NOUN
hitchhiker
■ per Anhalter fahren to hitchhike

anhand – anmachen

anhand PREPOSITION

The preposition **anhand** takes the genitive.

with the help of
□ Wir werden das anhand der Unterlagen prüfen. We'll check that with the help of the documents.

der **Anhang** (PL die **Anhänge**) MASC NOUN
appendix

der **Anhänger** (PL die **Anhänger**) MASC NOUN
1 supporter
□ Er ist Anhänger von Schalke. He's a Schalke supporter.
2 trailer (on car)
3 label
□ Mach einen Anhänger mit deinem Namen und deiner Adresse an deinen Koffer. Put a label with your name and address on your case.
4 pendant
□ Sie trug eine Kette mit Anhänger. She was wearing a chain with a pendant.

die **Anhängerin** FEM NOUN
supporter
□ Sie ist Anhängerin von Schalke. She's a Schalke supporter.

anhören (PERFECT TENSE hat angehört) VERB [4]
to listen to
□ Wir haben CDs angehört. We listened to CDs.
■ **jemandem etwas anhören** to hear something in somebody's voice □ Man hat ihr ihre Aufregung angehört. You could hear the excitement in her voice.
■ **sich anhören** to sound □ Der Vorschlag hört sich gut an. That sounds a good suggestion.

der **Anker** (PL die **Anker**) MASC NOUN
anchor

die **Ankleidekabine** FEM NOUN
changing cubicle

anklicken (PERFECT TENSE hat angeklickt) VERB [4]
to click on (computer)
□ ein Icon anklicken to click on an icon

★ ankommen (IMPERFECT kam an, PERFECT TENSE ist angekommen) VERB [40]
to arrive
□ Wir kommen morgen Nachmittag an. We'll arrive tomorrow afternoon. □ Ist der Brief schon angekommen? Has the letter arrived yet?
■ **bei jemandem gut ankommen** to go down well with somebody □ Das Stück ist bei den Zuschauern gut angekommen. The play went down well with the audience.
■ **bei jemandem schlecht ankommen** to go down badly with somebody □ Der Witz ist offensichtlich schlecht angekommen. The joke clearly went down badly.
■ **es kommt darauf an** it depends □ Es kommt darauf an, wie das Wetter ist. It depends what the weather's like.

■ **wenn es darauf ankommt** ...when it really matters ...
■ **es darauf ankommen lassen** to wait and see

★ ankreuzen (PERFECT TENSE hat angekreuzt) VERB [36]
to mark with a cross

ankündigen (PERFECT TENSE hat angekündigt) VERB [4]
to announce

★ die **Ankunft** (PL die **Ankünfte**) FEM NOUN
arrival

★ die **Anlage** FEM NOUN
1 gardens pl
□ Wir sind in der Anlage spazieren gegangen. We went for a walk in the gardens.
2 plant
□ Das ist eine neuartige Anlage zum Recycling von Kunststoff. That's a new plastics recycling plant.
3 investment
□ Wir raten zu einer Anlage in Immobilien. We would advise investment in real estate.

der **Anlass** (GEN des **Anlasses**, PL die **Anlässe**) MASC NOUN
occasion
□ ein festlicher Anlass a festive occasion
■ **ein Anlass zu etwas** cause for something □ Das ist ein Anlass zum Feiern. That's cause for celebration.
■ **aus Anlass** on the occasion of □ Aus Anlass ihres fünfzigsten Geburtstags ... On the occasion of her fiftieth birthday ...
■ **Anlass zu etwas geben** to give cause for something □ Ihr Sohn gibt keinen Anlass zu Klagen. Your son doesn't give cause for complaint.

der **Anlasser** (PL die **Anlasser**) MASC NOUN
starter (of car)

die **Anleitung** FEM NOUN
instructions pl

der **Anlieger** (PL die **Anlieger**) MASC NOUN
resident
□ 'Anlieger frei' 'residents only'

★ anmachen (PERFECT TENSE hat angemacht) VERB [4]
1 to put on
□ Mach bitte das Licht an. Please put the light on.
2 to light
□ Wir haben ein Feuer angemacht. We lit a fire.
3 to dress
□ Er macht den Salat immer mit Zitrone an. He always dresses his salads with lemon.
4 to chat up (Umgangssprache)
□ Ich glaube, der Typ versucht, dich anzumachen. I think that bloke is trying to chat you up.

★ = core vocabulary

★ **anmelden**(PERFECT TENSE **hat angemeldet**)
VERB [54]

1 to announce

▢ Sie hat für morgen ihren Besuch angemeldet.
She's announced that she'll visit us tomorrow.

▪ **jemanden anmelden 1** to make an
appointment for somebody ▢ Er hat seinen
Sohn für morgen beim Zahnarzt angemeldet.
He's made a dental appointment for his son for
tomorrow. **2** to put somebody's name down
▢ Habt ihr Max schon im Gymnasium
angemeldet? Have you already put Max's name
down for grammar school?

▪ **sich anmelden 1** to make an appointment
▢ Ich muss mich beim Zahnarzt anmelden. I
must make an appointment with the dentist.
2 to put one's name down ▢ Sie hat sich für
einen Judokurs angemeldet. She's put her
name down for a judo course.

2 to report

▢ Alle Besucher müssen sich beim Pförtner
anmelden. All visitors must report to the
gatehouse.

3 to sign in (*on website*)

▢ Bevor Sie einkaufen können, müssen Sie sich
anmelden. You need to sign in before you can
start shopping.

4 to register

▢ Haben Sie sich schon beim
Einwohnermeldeamt angemeldet? Have you
already registered with the residents'
registration office?

DID YOU KNOW...?
Anyone moving to a new address in
Germany is required by law to register (**sich
anmelden**) at the residents' registration
office (**Einwohnermeldeamt**).

★ die **Anmeldung** FEM NOUN
registration

▢ Schluss für Anmeldungen ist der erste Mai.
The deadline for registrations is the first of May.

★ **annehmen**(PRESENT TENSE **nimmt an**,
IMPERFECT **nahm an**, PERFECT TENSE **hat
angenommen**) VERB [1]

1 to accept

▢ Sie wollte das Geschenk nicht annehmen.
She didn't want to accept the present. ▢ Danke
für die Einladung, ich nehme gerne an. Thank
you for the invitation, which I'm happy to
accept.

2 to take

▢ Er hat den Namen seiner Frau angenommen.
He took his wife's name.

▪ **ein Kind annehmen** to adopt a child

3 to believe

▢ Die Polizei nimmt an, dass er der Täter war.
The police believe he did it.

4 to suppose

▢ Nehmen wir einmal an, es wäre so. Let's
suppose that was the case.

▪ **angenommen** ...supposing ...
▢ Angenommen, er kommt nicht. Supposing he
doesn't come.

▪ **angenommen dass** ...assuming that ...
▢ Angenommen, dass sie kommt, sollten wir
auch vegetarisch kochen. Assuming that she's
coming, we should make something vegetarian
as well.

anordnen(PERFECT TENSE **hat angeordnet**)
VERB [53]

1 to arrange

▢ Er ordnete die Blumen zu einem hübschen
Gesteck an. He arranged the flowers into a
pretty bouquet.

2 to order

▢ Wer hat das angeordnet? Who ordered that?

★ **anprobieren**(PERFECT TENSE **hat anprobiert**)
VERB [76]
to try on

die **Anrede** FEM NOUN
form of address

▢ Für verheiratete und unverheiratete Frauen
benutzt man die Anrede 'Frau'. 'Frau' is the
form of address used for married and unmarried
women.

★ der **Anruf**(PL die **Anrufe**) MASC NOUN
phone call

★ der **Anrufbeantworter**(PL die
Anrufbeantworter) MASC NOUN
answering machine

★ **anrufen**(IMPERFECT **rief an**, PERFECT TENSE **hat
angerufen**) VERB [56]
to phone

▢ Hat jemand angerufen? Did anyone phone?
▢ Ich muss mal eben meine Eltern anrufen. I
must just phone my parents.

ans= an das

anschalten(PERFECT TENSE **hat
angeschaltet**) VERB [2]
to switch on

★ **anschauen**(PERFECT TENSE **hat angeschaut**)
VERB [4]

1 to look at

▢ Schau mich an! Look at me. ▢ Willst du dir
mal die Fotos anschauen? Do you want to look
at the photos?

2 to see

▢ Den Film will ich mir unbedingt anschauen. I
must go and see that film.

anscheinend ADVERB
apparently

der **Anschlag**(PL die **Anschläge**) MASC NOUN

1 notice

▢ Sie machte einen Anschlag am Schwarzen
Brett. She put a notice on the notice board.

2 attack

▢ Es gab einen Anschlag auf den Präsidenten.
There's been an attack on the President.

Numbers in brackets refer to verb tables on pages 697 to 706.

15

anschließen – Anspruch

anschließen (IMPERFECT TENSE **schloss an**, PERFECT TENSE **hat angeschlossen**) VERB

to connect

□ Der Computer ist noch nicht angeschlossen. The computer hasn't been connected yet.

■ **sich jemandem anschließen** to join somebody □ Wir gehen ins Kino, willst du dich uns nicht anschließen? We're going to the cinema. Do you want to join us?

■ **Ich schließe mich dieser Meinung an.** I endorse this view.

anschließend ADJECTIVE, ADVERB

1 subsequent

□ die daran anschließende Diskussion the subsequent discussion

2 adjacent

□ das anschließende Grundstück the adjacent plot of land

3 afterwards

□ Wir waren essen, und anschließend sind wir ins Kino gegangen. We had a meal and afterwards went to the cinema.

★**der Anschluss** (GEN **des Anschlusses**, PL **die Anschlüsse**) MASC NOUN

connection

□ Sie haben Anschluss an einen Zug nach Paris. You have a connection with a train to Paris. □ Ich habe endlich meinen Anschluss ans Internet. I finally have an internet connection.

■ **im Anschluss an** following □ Im Anschluss an die Ansprache findet ein Empfang statt. Following the speech there will be a reception.

■ **Anschluss finden** to make friends □ Sie hat in der neuen Klasse schnell Anschluss gefunden. She quickly made friends in her new class.

★**sich anschnallen** (PERFECT TENSE **hat sich angeschnallt**) VERB [4]

to fasten one's seat belt

★**die Anschrift** FEM NOUN

address

★**ansehen** (PRESENT TENSE **sieht an**, IMPERFECT **sah an**, PERFECT TENSE **hat angesehen**) VERB [64]

▷ *see also* das **Ansehen** NOUN

1 to look at

□ Sieh mich an! Look at me. □ Willst du dir mal die Fotos ansehen? Do you want to look at the photos?

2 to see

□ Den Film will ich mir unbedingt ansehen. I must go and see that film. □ Man hat ihr ihre Enttäuschung angesehen. You could see the disappointment in her face.

3 to regard

□ Sie wird als eine Expertin auf diesem Gebiet angesehen. She's regarded as an expert in this field.

■ **Sieh mal einer an!** Well, fancy that!

das Ansehen NEUT NOUN

▷ *see also* ansehen VERB

1 respect

□ Sie genießt großes Ansehen bei ihren Kollegen. She enjoys great respect among her colleagues.

2 reputation

□ Ein solches Benehmen könnte unserem Ansehen schaden. Behaviour like that could damage our reputation.

die Ansicht FEM NOUN

view

□ eine Postkarte mit der Ansicht des Matterhorns a postcard with a view of the Matterhorn □ Wenn Sie meine Ansicht in dieser Sache hören wollen ... If you want to hear my view on this business ... □ meiner Ansicht nach in my view

■ **zur Ansicht** on approval

★**die Ansichtskarte** FEM NOUN

picture postcard

ansprechen (PRESENT TENSE **spricht an**, IMPERFECT **sprach an**, PERFECT TENSE **hat angesprochen**) VERB [70]

1 to approach

□ Mich hat ein wildfremder Mann angesprochen. I was approached by a complete stranger.

2 to appeal to

□ Diese Art von Malerei spricht mich nicht an. This style of painting doesn't appeal to me.

3 to ask

□ Ich werde Herrn Arnold ansprechen, ob er uns vielleicht hilft. I'll ask Mr Arnold if he'll maybe help us.

4 to mention

□ Sie hat dieses Problem bis jetzt noch nicht angesprochen. She hasn't mentioned this problem yet.

■ **auf etwas ansprechen** to respond to something □ Der Patient spricht auf die Medikamente nicht an. The patient isn't responding to the drugs.

der Anspruch (PL **die Ansprüche**) MASC NOUN

demand

□ Sie war den Ansprüchen ihres Berufs nicht gewachsen. She wasn't up to the demands of her job.

■ **hohe Ansprüche haben** to demand a lot

■ **hohe Ansprüche an jemanden stellen** to demand a lot of somebody

■ **Anspruch auf etwas haben** to be entitled to something □ Ich habe Anspruch auf eine Erklärung. I'm entitled to an explanation.

■ **etwas in Anspruch nehmen** to take advantage of something □ Wir sollten dieses Angebot in Anspruch nehmen. We should take advantage of this offer.

■ **Ihr Beruf nimmt sie sehr in Anspruch.** Her job's very demanding.

★ = core vocabulary

anständig ADJECTIVE

decent

▫ ein anständiges Essen a decent meal

▪ sich anständig benehmen to behave oneself

anstatt PREPOSITION, CONJUNCTION

The preposition anstatt takes the genitive.

instead of

▫ Sie kam anstatt ihres Bruders. She came instead of her brother.

anstecken (PERFECT TENSE hat angesteckt) VERB [4]

▪ Er hat die halbe Klasse mit seiner Grippe angesteckt. He gave half the class his flu.

▪ Lachen steckt an. Laughter is infectious.

▪ sich anstecken to catch something▫ Pass auf, dass du dich nicht ansteckst. Be careful you don't catch anything.▫ Ich habe mich bei ihm angesteckt. I caught it from him.

ansteckend ADJECTIVE

infectious

▫ eine ansteckende Krankheit an infectious disease

anstelle PREPOSITION

The preposition anstelle takes the genitive.

instead of

▫ Anstelle der Mutter hat seine Tante unterschrieben. His aunt has signed instead of his mother.▫ Pralinen anstelle von Blumen chocolates instead of flowers

★**anstellen** (PERFECT TENSE hat angestellt) VERB [4]

1 to turn on

▫ Kannst du mal bitte den Fernseher anstellen? Can you turn the television on, please?

2 to employ

▫ Damals war sie an der Universität angestellt. She was employed by the university back then.

3 to do

▫ Wie soll ich es bloß anstellen, dass er es erlaubt? What can I do to get him to allow it?

▫ Was stellen wir denn heute Nachmittag an? What shall we do this afternoon?

4 to be up to (Umgangssprache)

▫ Was hat er denn schon wieder angestellt? What has he been up to this time?

▪ sich anstellen 1 to queue▫ Musstet ihr euch für die Karten lange anstellen? Did you have to queue for long for the tickets? 2 to act▫ Sie hat sich wirklich dumm angestellt. She acted really stupidly.

▪ Stell dich nicht so an. Don't make such a fuss.

anstrengen (PERFECT TENSE hat angestrengt) VERB [4]

▪ Die Reise hat mich sehr angestrengt. The journey took a lot out of me.

▪ Streng deinen Kopf an! Use your head!

▪ sich anstrengen to make an effort

★**anstrengend** ADJECTIVE

tiring

die **Anstrengung** FEM NOUN

effort

die **Antarktis** FEM NOUN

the Antarctic

▫ in der Antarktis in the Antarctic▫ in die Antarktis to the Antarctic

der **Anteil** (PL die Anteile) MASC NOUN

share

▫ Ich möchte meinen Anteil am Gewinn haben. I would like to have my share of the profit.

▪ Anteil nehmen an 1 to sympathize with▫ Ich nehme Anteil an deinem Pech. I sympathize with you in your bad luck. 2 to take part in▫ Sie nahm Anteil an der Debatte. She took part in the debate.

die **Antenne** FEM NOUN

aerial

antiautoritär ADJECTIVE

anti-authoritarian

das **Antibiotikum** (PL die Antibiotika) NEUT NOUN

antibiotic

antik ADJECTIVE

antique

die **Antiquitäten** FEM PL NOUN

antiques pl

der **Antrag** (PL die Anträge) MASC NOUN

1 application

▫ Sie stellte einen Antrag auf Arbeitslosenunterstützung. She put in an application for unemployment benefit.

2 motion

▫ der Antrag der Opposition the motion put by the opposition

antun (IMPERFECT tat an, PERFECT TENSE hat angetan) VERB [81]

▪ jemandem etwas antun to do something to somebody▫ Das kannst du deinen Eltern nicht antun! You can't do that to your parents.

▪ jemandem ein Unrecht antun to wrong somebody▫ Uns ist ein großes Unrecht angetan worden. We've been cruelly wronged.

▪ sich Zwang antun to force oneself▫ Tu dir keinen Zwang an! Don't force yourself!

▪ sich etwas antun to kill oneself▫ Wenn ich durchfalle, dann tue ich mir was an. If I fail, I'll kill myself.

★die **Antwort** FEM NOUN

answer

▫ jemandem eine Antwort geben to give somebody an answer

★**antworten** VERB [2]

to answer

▫ Antworte bitte! Please answer.

Numbers in brackets refer to verb tables on pages 697 to 706.

17

Anwalt – App

- **auf etwas antworten**to answer something
  □ Sie konnte auf diese Frage nicht antworten.
  She couldn't answer the question.
- **jemandem antworten**to answer
  somebody □ Wo warst du? Antworte mir
  gefälligst!Where have you been? Answer me,
  will you!

der **Anwalt**(PL die **Anwälte**) MASC NOUN
  lawyer

die **Anwältin** FEM NOUN
  lawyer

die **Anweisung** FEM NOUN
  instruction
  □ Folgen Sie bitte den Anweisungen Ihres
  Führers.Please follow your guide's instructions.
  □ Anweisung haben, etwas zu tunto have
  instructions to do something

anwenden(IMPERFECT **wendete**or **wandte
  an** PERFECT TENSE **hat angewendet**or
  angewandt) VERB
  1 to use
  □ Welche Software wenden Sie an?What
  software do you use? □ Gewalt anwendento
  use violence
  2 to apply (law, rule)

★ die **Anwendung** FEM NOUN
  application

anwesend ADJECTIVE
  present

die **Anwesenheit** FEM NOUN
  presence

die **Anzahl** FEM NOUN
  number
  □ je nach Anzahl der Teilnehmeraccording to
  the number of participants □ eine große Anzahl
  an Fehlerna large number of mistakes

anzahlen(PERFECT TENSE **hat angezahlt**) VERB
  [4]
  ■ **fünfzig Euro anzahlen**to pay fifty euros
  deposit
  ■ **ein Auto anzahlen**to put down a deposit
  on a car

die **Anzahlung** FEM NOUN
  deposit
  □ eine Anzahlung leistento pay a deposit

das **Anzeichen**(PL die **Anzeichen**) NEUT
  NOUN
  sign

★ die **Anzeige** FEM NOUN
  advertisement
  □ Ich habe ihn über eine Anzeige
  kennengelernt.I met him through an
  advertisement.
  ■ **Anzeige gegen jemanden erstatten**to
  report somebody to the police
  ■ **Ich möchte Anzeige wegen Diebstahls
  erstatten.**I wish to report a theft.

anzeigen(PERFECT TENSE **hat angezeigt**) VERB
  [4]
  1 to show
  □ Der Tachometer zeigt die Geschwindigkeit
  an.The speedometer shows the speed.
  2 to report
  □ Ich werde Sie wegen Ruhestörung anzeigen!
  I'll report you for breach of the peace! □ Ich
  habe einen Diebstahl anzuzeigen.I wish to
  report a theft.

★ **anziehen**(IMPERFECT **zog an** PERFECT TENSE **hat
  angezogen**) VERB [96]
  1 to put on
  □ Ich muss mir nur noch die Schuhe anziehen.I
  just have to put my shoes on.
  2 to dress
  □ Kannst du bitte die Kinder anziehen?Can you
  dress the children, please? □ Er war sehr schick
  angezogen.He was dressed very elegantly.
  3 to attract
  □ Der Zoo zieht viele Besucher an.The zoo
  attracts a lot of visitors.
  ■ **sich von jemandem angezogen fühlen**
  to feel attracted to somebody
  4 to tighten (screw)
  ■ **sich anziehen**to get dressed

★ der **Anzug**(PL die **Anzüge**) MASC NOUN
  suit

★ **anzünden**(PERFECT TENSE **hat angezündet**)
  VERB [54]
  to light
  □ Ich habe eine Kerze angezündet.I lit a candle.

★ der **Apfel**(PL die **Äpfel**) MASC NOUN
  apple

das **Apfelmus**(GEN des **Apfelmuses**) NEUT
  NOUN
  apple purée

★ der **Apfelsaft**(PL die **Apfelsäfte**) MASC NOUN
  apple juice

★ die **Apfelsine** FEM NOUN
  orange

die **Apfeltasche** FEM NOUN
  apple turnover

★ die **Apotheke** FEM NOUN
  chemist's
  □ in der Apothekeat the chemist's □ zur
  Apotheketo the chemist's

★ der **Apotheker**(PL die **Apotheker**) MASC
  NOUN
  pharmacist
  □ Er ist Apotheker.He's a pharmacist.

★ die **Apothekerin**(PL die **Apothekerinnen**)
  FEM NOUN
  pharmacist
  □ Sie ist Apothekerin.She's a pharmacist.

die **App**(PL die **Apps**) FEM NOUN
  app (for mobile)
  □ eine Handy-Appa mobile app

★ = core vocabulary

★ der **Apparat** (PL die **Apparate**) MASC NOUN
  1 gadget
    □ Mit diesem Apparat kann man Dosen zerkleinern. You can crush tins with this gadget.
  2 camera
  3 telephone
    □ Wer war am Apparat? Who was on the telephone?
    ■ **Am Apparat!** Speaking!
  4 set (TV)

★ das **Appartement** (PL die **Appartements**) NEUT NOUN
  flat

★ der **Appetit** MASC NOUN
  appetite
    ■ **Ich habe keinen Appetit.** I'm not hungry.
    ■ **Guten Appetit!** Enjoy your meal!

★ die **Aprikose** FEM NOUN
  apricot

★ der **April** (GEN des April or Aprils, PL die **Aprile**) MASC NOUN
  April
    □ im April in April □ am dritten April on the third of April □ Ulm, den 3. April 2019 Ulm, 3 April 2019 □ Heute ist der dritte April. Today is the third of April.
    ■ **April, April!** April Fool!

  der **Araber** (PL die **Araber**) MASC NOUN
  Arab

  die **Araberin** FEM NOUN
  Arab

  arabisch ADJECTIVE
    ■ **arabische Länder** Arab countries
    ■ **die arabische Sprache** Arabic

★ die **Arbeit** FEM NOUN
  1 job
    □ Das ist eine sehr anstrengende Arbeit. That's a very tiring job. □ Er sucht eine Arbeit auf dem Bau. He's looking for a job on a building site.
  2 work no pl
    □ Ich habe im Moment viel Arbeit. I've got a lot of work at the moment. □ Sie hat keine Arbeit. She's out of work. □ Das war eine Arbeit! That was hard work.
  3 dissertation
    □ Sie schreibt eine Arbeit über englische Ortsnamen. She's writing a dissertation on English place names.
  4 test
    □ Ich habe in der Arbeit eine Fünf geschrieben. I got an 'E' in the test. □ Morgen schreiben wir in Mathe eine Arbeit. We've got a maths test tomorrow.
    ■ **in Arbeit sein** to be in hand □ Ihre Reparatur ist in Arbeit. Your repair work is in hand.

★ **arbeiten** VERB [2]
  to work
    □ Sie arbeitet hart. She works hard. □ Sie

arbeitet als Elektrikerin bei der Firma Müller. She works as an electrician for Müller's. □ Seine Nieren arbeiten nicht richtig. His kidneys don't work properly.
    ■ **sich durch etwas arbeiten** to work one's way through something

★ der **Arbeiter** (PL die **Arbeiter**) MASC NOUN
  worker

★ die **Arbeiterin** FEM NOUN
  worker

★ der **Arbeitgeber** (PL die **Arbeitgeber**) MASC NOUN
  employer

★ die **Arbeitgeberin** (PL die **Arbeitgeberinnen**) FEM NOUN
  employer

★ der **Arbeitnehmer** (PL die **Arbeitnehmer**) MASC NOUN
  employee
    □ Als Arbeitnehmer hat man gewisse Rechte. As an employee you have certain rights.

★ die **Arbeitnehmerin** (PL die **Arbeitnehmerinnen**) FEM NOUN
  employee
    □ Als Arbeitnehmerin hat man gewisse Rechte. As an employee you have certain rights.

★ das **Arbeitsamt** (PL die **Arbeitsämter**) NEUT NOUN
  job centre

  die **Arbeitsbedingungen** PL NOUN
  working conditions pl

  die **Arbeitserlaubnis** (PL die **Arbeitserlaubnisse**) FEM NOUN
  work permit

★ **arbeitslos** ADJECTIVE
  unemployed

★ der/die **Arbeitslose** (GEN des/der **Arbeitslosen**, PL die **Arbeitslosen**) MASC/FEM NOUN
  unemployed person
    □ Ein Arbeitsloser hat die Stelle bekommen. An unemployed person got the job.
    ■ **die Arbeitslosen** the unemployed

★ die **Arbeitslosigkeit** FEM NOUN
  unemployment

★ der **Arbeitsort** (PL die **Arbeitsorte**) MASC NOUN
  place of work

★ der **Arbeitsplatz** (GEN des **Arbeitsplatzes**, PL die **Arbeitsplätze**) MASC NOUN
  1 job
    □ Suchen Sie einen neuen Arbeitsplatz? Are you looking for a new job?
  2 desk
    □ Frau Marr ist im Moment nicht an ihrem Arbeitsplatz. Ms Marr isn't at her desk at the moment.

die **Arbeitszeit** FEM NOUN
working hours *pl*
■ gleitende Arbeitszeit flexitime

★das **Arbeitszimmer** (PL die
Arbeitszimmer) NEUT NOUN
study

der **Architekt** (GEN des **Architekten**, PL die
Architekten) MASC NOUN
architect
□ Er ist Architekt. He's an architect.

die **Architektin** (PL die **Architektinnen**)
FEM NOUN
architect
□ Sie ist Architektin. She's an architect.

die **Architektur** FEM NOUN
architecture

Argentinien NEUT NOUN
Argentina
■ nach Argentinien to Argentina

der **Ärger** MASC NOUN
1 anger
□ Er hat seinen Ärger über die Verspätung an
mir ausgelassen. He took out his anger at the
delay on me.
2 trouble
□ Wenn du das machst, bekommst du Ärger. If
you do that, you'll get into trouble.
■ Ärger mit etwas haben to have trouble
with something □ Hast du wieder Ärger mit
deinem Computer? Are you having trouble with
your computer again?

★**ärgerlich** ADJECTIVE
1 annoying
□ Diese dauernden Störungen sind sehr
ärgerlich. These constant interruptions are very
annoying.
2 angry
□ Ich bin auf ihn ärgerlich. I'm angry with him.
□ Er ist über die Verzögerung ärgerlich. He's
angry at the delay.
■ jemanden ärgerlich machen to annoy
somebody

★**ärgern** VERB [88]
to annoy
□ Du sollst deine Schwester nicht immer
ärgern! Don't keep annoying your sister.
■ sich ärgern to be annoyed □ Ich habe mich
über diesen Fehler sehr geärgert. I was very
annoyed about that mistake.

die **Arktis** FEM NOUN
the Arctic
□ in der Arktis in the Arctic

★**arm** ADJECTIVE
▷ see also der **Arm** NOUN
poor
□ Er ist ärmer als ich. He's poorer than me.

★der **Arm** (PL die **Arme**) MASC NOUN
▷ see also **arm** ADJECTIVE
arm

■ jemanden auf den Arm nehmen to pull
somebody's leg (*Umgangssprache*) □ Du willst
mich wohl auf den Arm nehmen? You're pulling
my leg.

★das **Armband** (PL die **Armbänder**) NEUT
NOUN
bracelet

★die **Armbanduhr** FEM NOUN
wristwatch

die **Armee** FEM NOUN
army

der **Ärmel** (PL die **Ärmel**) MASC NOUN
sleeve

der **Ärmelkanal** MASC NOUN
the English Channel

die **Armut** FEM NOUN
poverty

arrangieren (PERFECT TENSE **hat arrangiert**)
VERB [76]
to arrange
□ Sie hat ein Treffen der beiden arrangiert. She
arranged for them both to meet.

★die **Art** (PL die **Arten**) FEM NOUN
1 way
□ Ich mache das auf meine Art. I do that my
way.
2 kind
□ Ich mag diese Art Obst nicht. I don't like this
kind of fruit. □ Häuser aller Art all kinds of
houses
3 species
□ Diese Art ist vom Aussterben bedroht. This
species is in danger of extinction.
■ Es ist nicht seine Art, das zu tun. It's not
like him to do that.

★der **Artikel** (PL die **Artikel**) MASC NOUN
article

die **Arznei** FEM NOUN
medicine

das **Arzneimittel** (PL die **Arzneimittel**)
NEUT NOUN
drug (*medicine*)

★der **Arzt** (PL die **Ärzte**) MASC NOUN
doctor
□ Karim ist Arzt. Karim's a doctor.

★die **Ärztin** FEM NOUN
doctor
□ Jutta ist Ärztin. Jutta's a doctor.

ärztlich ADJECTIVE
medical
■ Die Wunde muss ärztlich behandelt
werden. The wound will have to be treated by
a doctor.

das **As** NEUT NOUN ▷ see das **Ass**

die **Asche** (PL die **Aschen**) FEM NOUN
ash

★ = core vocabulary

★ der **Aschenbecher** (PL die **Aschenbecher**)
MASC NOUN
ashtray

der **Aschermittwoch** MASC NOUN
Ash Wednesday
□ am Aschermittwoch on Ash Wednesday

der **Asiat** (GEN des **Asiaten**, PL die **Asiaten**)
MASC NOUN
Asian

die **Asiatin** FEM NOUN
Asian

asiatisch ADJECTIVE
Asian

★ **Asien** NEUT NOUN
Asia
▪ aus Asien from Asia
▪ nach Asien to Asia

aß VERB ▷ see essen

das **Ass** (GEN des **Asses**, PL die **Asse**) NEUT
NOUN
ace
□ das Herzass the ace of hearts

★ der **Assistent** (GEN des **Assistenten**, PL die
Assistenten) MASC NOUN
assistant

★ die **Assistentin** FEM NOUN
assistant

der **Ast** (PL die **Äste**) MASC NOUN
branch

das **Asthma** NEUT NOUN
asthma
□ Sie hat Asthma. She's got asthma.

die **Astrologie** FEM NOUN
astrology

der **Astronaut** (GEN des **Astronauten**, PL die
Astronauten) MASC NOUN
astronaut
□ Er ist Astronaut. He's an astronaut.

die **Astronautin** (PL die **Astronautinnen**)
FEM NOUN
astronaut
□ Sie ist Astronaut. She's an astronaut.

die **Astronomie** FEM NOUN
astronomy

das **Asyl** (PL die **Asyle**) NEUT NOUN
asylum
□ um Asyl bitten to ask for asylum
▪ ein Obdachlosenasyl a hostel for the
homeless

der **Asylbewerber** (PL die **Asylbewerber**)
MASC NOUN
asylum-seeker

die **Asylbewerberin** FEM NOUN
asylum-seeker

★ der **Atem** MASC NOUN
breath
□ außer Atem out of breath

★ **atemlos** ADJECTIVE
breathless

★ der **Atlantik** MASC NOUN
the Atlantic
□ eine Insel im Atlantik an island in the Atlantic

der **Atlas** (GEN des **Atlasses**, PL die **Atlasse** or
Atlanten) MASC NOUN
atlas

★ **atmen** VERB [3]
to breathe

die **Atmosphäre** FEM NOUN
atmosphere

das **Atom** (PL die **Atome**) NEUT NOUN
atom

atomar ADJECTIVE
atomic

die **Atombombe** FEM NOUN
atom bomb

die **Atomwaffen** FEM PL NOUN
atomic weapons pl

atomwaffenfrei ADJECTIVE
nuclear-free

★ **attraktiv** ADJECTIVE
attractive
□ attraktiv aussehen to look attractive

ätzend ADJECTIVE
1 rubbish (Umgangssprache)
□ Die Musik ist ätzend. The music's rubbish.
2 corrosive
3 caustic

★ **auch** ADVERB
1 also
□ Yogazubehör verkaufen wir auch. We also sell
yoga equipment.
2 too
□ Das ist auch schön. That's nice, too. □ Ich
auch. Me too.
▪ Ich auch nicht. Me neither.
▪ auch nicht not ... either □ Nein, das Kleid
gefällt mir auch nicht. No, I don't like that dress
either.
▪ Auch das noch! That's all we needed!
3 even
□ Auch wenn das Wetter schlecht ist. Even if
the weather's bad. □ ohne auch nur zu fragen
without even asking
▪ wer auch whoever □ Wer das auch gesagt
hat, ich glaube es nicht. I don't believe it,
whoever said it.
▪ was auch whatever □ Was du auch sagst, ich
finde es schön. Whatever you say, I think it's
nice.
▪ wie dem auch sei be that as it may □ Wie
dem auch sei, ich gehe jetzt trotzdem. Be that
as it may, I'm still going.
▪ wie sehr er sich auch bemühte however
much he tried

Numbers in brackets refer to verb tables on pages 697 to 706.

21

auf – auffangen

★ **auf** PREPOSITION, ADVERB

1 on

> Use the accusative to express movement or a change of place. Use the dative when there is no change of place.

□ Stell die Suppe bitte auf den Tisch. **Please put the soup on the table.** □ Die Suppe steht auf dem Tisch. **The soup's on the table.**
- **auf dem Land** in the country
- **auf der ganzen Welt** in the whole world
- **auf Deutsch** in German
- **bis auf ihn** except for him
- **auf einmal** at once
- **auf seinen Vorschlag hin** at his suggestion

2 open

> □ Das Fenster ist auf. **The window's open.** □ Die Geschäfte sind am Sonntag nicht auf. **The shops aren't open on Sunday.**

3 up

> □ Ist er schon auf? **Is he up yet?** □ Ich bin schon seit sieben Uhr auf. **I've been up since seven.**
- **auf und ab** up and down
- **auf und davon** up and away

aufatmen (PERFECT TENSE **hat aufgeatmet**) VERB [4]
to heave a sigh of relief

★ **aufbauen** (PERFECT TENSE **hat aufgebaut**) VERB [4]
to build up

aufbekommen (IMPERFECT **bekam auf**, PERFECT TENSE **hat aufbekommen**) VERB [40]

1 to get open
> □ Ich bekomme das Fenster nicht auf. **I can't get the window open.**

2 to be given homework
> □ Wir haben heute nichts aufbekommen. **We weren't given any homework today.**

aufbewahren (PERFECT TENSE **hat aufbewahrt**) VERB [38]
to keep
> □ Sie bewahrt ihre Ersparnisse in einer Blechdose auf. **She keeps her savings in a tin.**

aufblasen (PRESENT TENSE **bläst auf**, IMPERFECT **blies auf**, PERFECT TENSE **hat aufgeblasen**) VERB
to inflate

aufbleiben (IMPERFECT **blieb auf**, PERFECT TENSE **ist aufgeblieben**) VERB [10]

1 to stay open
> □ Heute bleiben die Geschäfte länger auf. **The shops stay open longer today.**

2 to stay up
> □ Heute dürft ihr ausnahmsweise länger aufbleiben. **Today you can stay up late for once.**

aufbrechen (PRESENT TENSE **bricht auf**, IMPERFECT **brach auf**, PERFECT TENSE **hat/ist aufgebrochen**) VERB [11]

> For the perfect tense use **haben** when the verb has an object and **sein** when there is no object.

1 to break open
> □ Die Diebe haben den Safe aufgebrochen. **The thieves broke the safe open.**

2 to open up
> □ Die Wunde ist wieder aufgebrochen. **The wound has opened up again.**

3 to set off
> □ Wann seid ihr aufgebrochen? **When did you set off?**

aufbringen (IMPERFECT **brachte auf**, PERFECT TENSE **hat aufgebracht**) VERB [13]

1 to open
> □ Ich bringe das Konservenglas nicht auf. **I can't open the jar.**

2 to raise
> □ Wie soll ich nur das Geld für die Reparatur aufbringen? **However am I going raise the money for the repairs?**
- **Verständnis für etwas aufbringen** to be able to understand something

aufeinander ADVERB
on top of each other
> □ Leg die Handtücher aufeinander. **Put the towels on top of each other.**
- **aufeinander schießen** to shoot at one another
- **aufeinander vertrauen** to trust each other

★ **der Aufenthalt** (PL die **Aufenthalte**) MASC NOUN

1 stay
> □ Während unseres Aufenthalts in London ... **During our stay in London ...**

2 stop
> □ Der Zug hat fünf Minuten Aufenthalt in Ulm. **The train has a five-minute stop in Ulm.**

aufessen (PRESENT TENSE **isst auf**, IMPERFECT **aß auf**, PERFECT TENSE **hat aufgegessen**) VERB [20]
to eat up

auffallen (PRESENT TENSE **fällt auf**, IMPERFECT **fiel auf**, PERFECT TENSE **ist aufgefallen**) VERB [22]
to be conspicuous
- **jemandem auffallen** to strike somebody
> □ Es fiel mir auf, dass sie sich recht seltsam benahm. **It struck me that she was behaving rather strangely.**

auffällig ADJECTIVE
conspicuous
- **auffällig gekleidet sein** to be dressed strikingly

auffangen (PRESENT TENSE **fängt auf**, IMPERFECT **fing auf**, PERFECT TENSE **hat aufgefangen**) VERB [23]
to catch

★ = core vocabulary

★ **aufführen** (PERFECT TENSE **hat aufgeführt**)
VERB [4]
1 to perform
  □ ein Stück aufführen to perform a play
2 to list
  □ Alle Fachausdrücke sind im Anhang
  aufgeführt. All technical terms are listed in the
  appendix.
  ■ **sich aufführen** to behave

★ die **Aufführung** FEM NOUN
performance

★ die **Aufgabe** FEM NOUN
1 task
  □ Vier Kinder zu erziehen ist eine schwierige
  Aufgabe. Bringing up four children is a difficult
  task.
2 question
  □ Ich konnte die zweite Aufgabe in der
  Mathearbeit nicht lösen. I couldn't solve the
  second question in the maths test.
3 homework no pl
  □ Hast du deine Aufgaben schon gemacht?
  Have you done your homework yet?

★ **aufgeben** (PRESENT TENSE **gibt auf**, IMPERFECT
gab auf, PERFECT TENSE **hat aufgegeben**) VERB
[28]
1 to give up
  □ Du solltest das Rauchen aufgeben. You
  should give up smoking.
2 to post
  □ Ich habe das Paket an dich vor drei Tagen
  aufgegeben. I posted the parcel to you three
  days ago.
3 to check in
  □ Du kannst den Koffer ja vor der Reise
  aufgeben. You can check in your suitcase before
  you travel.
  ■ **eine Anzeige aufgeben** to place an
  advertisement
  ■ **Ich gebe auf!** I give up.

aufgehen (IMPERFECT **ging auf**, PERFECT TENSE
ist aufgegangen) VERB [29]
1 to rise
  □ Der Mond ist aufgegangen. The moon has
  risen.
2 to open
  □ Die Tür ging auf, und Christoph kam herein.
  The door opened and Christoph came in.
  ■ **Zwanzig durch sechs geht nicht auf.** Six
  into twenty doesn't go.

aufgeregt ADJECTIVE
excited

aufgrund PREPOSITION

The preposition **aufgrund** takes the genitive.

1 because of
  □ Das Spiel ist aufgrund des schlechten Wetters
  ausgefallen. The game was cancelled because
  of the bad weather.

2 on the basis of
  □ Sie wurde aufgrund von Indizien überführt.
  She was convicted on the basis of
  circumstantial evidence.

aufhaben (PRESENT TENSE **hat auf**, IMPERFECT
hatte auf, PERFECT TENSE **hat aufgehabt**) VERB
[32]
1 to have on
  □ Sie hatte einen roten Hut auf. She had a red
  hat on.
2 to have homework to do
  □ Wir haben heute in Englisch nichts auf. We
  haven't got any English homework to do today.
3 to be open
  □ Der Supermarkt hat bis um zehn Uhr abends
  auf. The supermarket is open until 10 in the
  evening.

★ **aufhalten** (PRESENT TENSE **hält auf**, IMPERFECT
hielt auf, PERFECT TENSE **hat aufgehalten**)
VERB [33]
1 to detain
  □ Ich möchte dich nicht aufhalten. I don't want
  to detain you.
2 to halt
  □ Anscheinend ist die Vergrößerung des
  Ozonlochs aufgehalten worden. Apparently the
  growth in the ozone hole has been halted.
3 to hold open
  □ Kannst du mir bitte die Tür aufhalten? Can
  you hold the door open for me, please?
  ■ **Sie hielt die Hand auf.** She held out her
  hand.
  ■ **sich aufhalten 1** to live □ Sie hat sich lange
  im Ausland aufgehalten. She lived abroad for a
  long time. **2** to stay □ Ich möchte mich nicht
  lange aufhalten. I don't want to stay long.
  ■ **sich mit etwas aufhalten** to waste time
  over something □ Mit solchen Kinderspielen
  halte ich mich doch nicht auf. I'm not wasting
  my time over such childish games.

aufhängen (PERFECT TENSE **hat aufgehängt**)
VERB [35]
to hang up (washing, picture)
  ■ **sich aufhängen** to hang oneself □ Er hat
  gedroht, sich aufzuhängen. He's threatened to
  hang himself.

aufheben (IMPERFECT **hob auf**, PERFECT TENSE
hat aufgehoben) VERB
1 to pick up
  □ Sie hob das Heft, das auf den Boden gefallen
  war, auf. She picked up the exercise book which
  had fallen on the floor.
2 to keep
  □ Sie hat alle seine Briefe aufgehoben. She's
  kept all his letters.
  ■ **gut aufgehoben sein** to be well looked
  after □ Unsere Tochter ist bei ihrer Oma gut
  aufgehoben. Our daughter's being well looked
  after at her granny's.

aufhören – aufpumpen

★ **aufhören** (PERFECT TENSE **hat aufgehört**) VERB [4]
to stop
□ Der Regen hat aufgehört. The rain's stopped.
▪ **aufhören, etwas zu tun** to stop doing something □ Hör endlich auf, dich dauernd zu beklagen. Will you stop complaining all the time!

★ der **Aufkleber** (PL die **Aufkleber**) MASC NOUN
sticker

auflassen (PRESENT TENSE **lässt auf**, IMPERFECT **ließ auf**, PERFECT TENSE **hat aufgelassen**) VERB [42]
1 to leave open
□ Lass bitte das Fenster auf. Please leave the window open.
2 to keep on
□ Kann ich meine Mütze auflassen? Can I keep my hat on?

★ **auflegen** (PERFECT TENSE **hat aufgelegt**) VERB [4]
to hang up
□ Sie hat einfach aufgelegt. She simply hung up.

auflesen (PRESENT TENSE **liest auf**, IMPERFECT **las auf**, PERFECT TENSE **hat aufgelesen**) VERB [45]
to pick up
□ etwas von der Straße auflesen to pick something up off the street

auflösen (PERFECT TENSE **hat aufgelöst**) VERB [4]
1 to dissolve
□ Du solltest die Tablette in Wasser auflösen. You should dissolve the tablet in water.
2 to break up
□ Die Polizei hat die Demonstration aufgelöst. The police broke up the demonstration.
▪ **sich auflösen** to dissolve □ Der Zucker hatte sich schnell im Tee aufgelöst. The sugar had quickly dissolved in the tea.
▪ **wenn sich der Nebel aufgelöst hat** when the fog has lifted
▪ **in Tränen aufgelöst sein** to be in tears

★ **aufmachen** (PERFECT TENSE **hat aufgemacht**) VERB [4]
1 to open
□ Kannst du bitte die Tür aufmachen? Can you open the door, please? □ Wann machen die Geschäfte auf? When do the shops open?
2 to undo
□ Ich schaffe es nicht, den Reißverschluss aufzumachen. I can't undo the zip.
▪ **sich aufmachen** to set out □ Wir machten uns nach London auf. We set out for London.

aufmerksam ADJECTIVE
attentive
▪ **jemanden auf etwas aufmerksam machen** to point something out to somebody
□ Ich habe ihn auf das Schloss aufmerksam gemacht. I pointed the castle out to him.

die **Aufmerksamkeit** FEM NOUN
attention
□ Darf ich um Ihre Aufmerksamkeit bitten! May I have your attention?
▪ **Wir sollten ihnen eine kleine Aufmerksamkeit mitbringen.** We ought to take them a little something.

★ die **Aufnahme** FEM NOUN
1 welcome
□ Wir fanden eine sehr freundliche Aufnahme in unserer Partnerstadt. We were given a very friendly welcome in our twin town.
2 recording
□ Wir haben uns die Aufnahme des Konzerts angehört. We listened to a recording of the concert.
3 photograph
□ Möchtest du die Aufnahmen sehen, die ich in den Ferien gemacht habe? Would you like to see the photographs I took on holiday?

die **Aufnahmeprüfung** FEM NOUN
entrance test

★ **aufnehmen** (PRESENT TENSE **nimmt auf**, IMPERFECT **nahm auf**, PERFECT TENSE **hat aufgenommen**) VERB [52]
1 to take
□ Wie hat sie die Nachricht aufgenommen? How did she take the news?
2 to record
□ eine Sendung aufnehmen to record a programme
3 to photograph
□ Diesen tollen Sonnenuntergang muss ich aufnehmen. I must photograph this wonderful sunset.
4 to admit
□ Was muss man tun, um in den Tennisklub aufgenommen zu werden? What do you have to do to be admitted to the tennis club?
▪ **es mit jemandem aufnehmen können** to be able to compete with somebody

★ **aufpassen** (PERFECT TENSE **hat aufgepasst**) VERB [31]
to pay attention
□ Ich habe heute im Unterricht nicht aufgepasst. I didn't pay attention in class today.
▪ **auf jemanden aufpassen** to look after somebody □ Ich muss auf meinen kleinen Bruder aufpassen. I have to look after my little brother.
▪ **auf etwas aufpassen** to look after something □ Kannst du mal eben auf meinen Koffer aufpassen? Can you look after my suitcase for a moment?
▪ **Aufgepasst!** Look out!

aufpumpen (PERFECT TENSE **hat aufgepumpt**) VERB [4]
to pump up

★ aufräumen (PERFECT TENSE **hat aufgeräumt**)
VERB [4]
to tidy up
□ Ich darf erst raus, wenn ich mein Zimmer aufgeräumt habe. **I can't go out until I've tidied up my room.**

aufrecht ADJECTIVE
upright

aufrechterhalten (PRESENT TENSE **erhält aufrecht**, IMPERFECT **erhielt aufrecht**, PERFECT TENSE **hat aufrechterhalten**) VERB [33]
to maintain

aufregen (PERFECT TENSE **hat aufgeregt**) VERB [4]
to excite
■ **sich aufregen** to get excited

aufregend ADJECTIVE
exciting

aufs = auf das

★ der Aufsatz (GEN **des Aufsatzes**, PL die **Aufsätze**) MASC NOUN
essay
□ Wir haben heute in Deutsch einen Aufsatz geschrieben. **We wrote an essay in today's German lesson.**

aufschieben (IMPERFECT **schob auf**, PERFECT TENSE **hat aufgeschoben**) VERB
1 to push open
□ Man kann diese Tür aufschieben. **You can push this door open.**
2 to put off
□ Wir haben unsere Abreise noch einmal aufgeschoben. **We put off our departure once again.**

★ aufschlagen (PRESENT TENSE **schlägt auf**, IMPERFECT **schlug auf**, PERFECT TENSE **hat aufgeschlagen**) VERB [59]
1 to open
□ ein Buch aufschlagen **to open a book**
□ Schlagt Seite 111 auf. **Open your books at page 111.**
2 to pitch
□ Sie schlugen ihre Zelte auf. **They pitched their tents.**
3 to go up (prices)
□ Butter hat wieder aufgeschlagen. **The price of butter has gone up again.**
4 to serve (tennis)
□ Du schlägst auf. **It's your turn to serve.**

★ aufschließen (IMPERFECT **schloss auf**, PERFECT TENSE **hat aufgeschlossen**) VERB
to unlock
□ Schließ bitte die Tür auf! **Please unlock the door.** □ Sie schloss auf und ging hinein. **She unlocked the door and went in.**

aufschlussreich ADJECTIVE
informative

★ der Aufschnitt (PL die **Aufschnitte**) MASC NOUN
cold meat

★ aufschreiben (IMPERFECT **schrieb auf**, PERFECT TENSE **hat aufgeschrieben**) VERB [61]
to write down

das Aufsehen NEUT NOUN
stir
□ Ihre Talkshow hat Aufsehen erregt. **Her chat show caused a stir.**

aufsehenerregend ADJECTIVE
sensational

auf sein VERB [65] ▷ see auf

aufsetzen (PERFECT TENSE **hat aufgesetzt**) VERB [36]
to put on
□ Setz dir eine Mütze auf! **Put a hat on.**
■ Ich setze das Teewasser auf. **I'll put the kettle on.**
■ **sich aufsetzen** to sit up □ Der Patient setzte sich auf. **The patient sat up.**

★ die Aufsicht FEM NOUN
supervision
■ **die Aufsicht haben** to be in charge

★ aufstehen (IMPERFECT **stand auf**, PERFECT TENSE **ist/hat aufgestanden**) VERB [72]

Use **sein** for 'to get up' and **haben** for 'to be open'.

1 to get up
□ Wann bist du heute Morgen aufgestanden? **When did you get up this morning?** □ Sie stand auf und ging. **She got up and left.**
2 to be open
□ Die Tür hat aufgestanden, also ging ich hinein. **The door was open, so I went in.**

aufstellen (PERFECT TENSE **hat aufgestellt**) VERB [4]
1 to pitch
□ Wir haben unser Zelt am Waldrand aufgestellt. **We pitched our tent at the edge of the woods.**
2 to stand up
□ Der Sonnenschirm ist umgefallen, kannst du ihn wieder aufstellen? **The sunshade has fallen over, could you stand it back up?**
3 to set up
□ Sie stellte die Schachfiguren auf. **She set up the chess pieces.**
■ eine Liste aufstellen **to draw up a list**
■ einen Rekord aufstellen **to set a record**
■ jemanden für ein Spiel aufstellen **to pick somebody for a game**
■ **sich aufstellen** to line up □ Stellt euch bitte in Zweierreihen auf! **Please line up in twos.**

auftauchen (PERFECT TENSE **ist aufgetaucht**) VERB [4]
to appear

auftauen (PERFECT TENSE **hat/ist aufgetaut**) VERB [4]

> For the perfect tense use **haben** when the verb has an object and **sein** when there is no object.

1 to thaw
□ Der Schnee taute auf. The snow thawed.
2 to defrost
□ Ich habe die Pizza im Mikrowellenherd aufgetaut. I've defrosted the pizza in the microwave.

aufteilen (PERFECT TENSE **hat aufgeteilt**) VERB [4]
to divide up
□ Wir wurden in drei Gruppen aufgeteilt. We were divided up into three groups.

der **Auftrag** (PL die **Aufträge**) MASC NOUN
orders *pl*
□ Ich habe den Auftrag, Sie davon zu unterrichten, dass ... I have orders to inform you that ...
■ **im Auftrag von** on behalf of □ Ich komme im Auftrag der Firma Haehnle & Co. I'm here on behalf of Haehnle and Co.

auftreten (PRESENT TENSE **tritt auf**, IMPERFECT **trat auf**, PERFECT TENSE **ist aufgetreten**) VERB [79]

1 to appear
□ Dieser Schauspieler tritt erst im dritten Akt auf. This actor doesn't appear until the third act.
2 to occur
□ Sollten Probleme auftreten, wende dich an uns. If any problems occur, get in touch with us.
3 to behave
□ Er ist ziemlich unbeliebt, weil er immer so überheblich auftritt. He's quite unpopular because he always behaves so arrogantly.

★ **aufwachen** (PERFECT TENSE **ist aufgewacht**) VERB [4]
to wake up

aufwachsen (PRESENT TENSE **wächst auf**, IMPERFECT **wuchs auf**, PERFECT TENSE **ist aufgewachsen**) VERB [87]
to grow up

aufwecken (PERFECT TENSE **hat aufgeweckt**) VERB [4]
to wake up

aufzählen (PERFECT TENSE **hat aufgezählt**) VERB [4]
to list

★ der **Aufzug** (PL die **Aufzüge**) MASC NOUN
lift
□ Wir sind mit dem Aufzug nach oben gefahren. We went up in the lift.

★ das **Auge** (PL die **Augen**) NEUT NOUN
eye
□ Sie hat dunkle Augen. She's got dark eyes.
■ **unter vier Augen** in private

★ der **Augenblick** (PL die **Augenblicke**) MASC NOUN
moment
■ **im Augenblick** at the moment

die **Augenbraue** FEM NOUN
eyebrow

★ der **August** (GEN des **Augustes** or **August**, PL die **Auguste**) MASC NOUN
August
□ im August in August □ am fünften August on 5 August □ Ulm, den 5. August 2019 Ulm, 5 August 2019 □ Heute ist der fünfte August. Today is the fifth of August.

★ die **Aula** (PL die **Aulen**) FEM NOUN
assembly hall

★ **aus** PREPOSITION, ADVERB

> The preposition **aus** takes the dative.

1 out of
□ Sie nahm ein Bonbon aus der Tüte. She took a sweet out of the bag. □ aus dem Fenster out of the window
2 from
□ Wenn er aus der Schule kommt, ist er immer sehr müde. When he comes home from school he's always very tired. □ Ich komme aus Deutschland. I come from Germany. □ Er ist aus Berlin. He's from Berlin.
3 made of
□ Die Vase ist aus Porzellan. The vase is made of china.
■ **aus Erfahrung** from experience
■ **aus Spaß** for fun
■ **aus Freundschaft** out of a sense of friendship
4 finished
□ wenn das Kino aus ist when the film's finished □ Komm sofort nach Hause, wenn die Schule aus ist. Come straight home when school has finished.
■ **Wann ist die Schule aus?** When does school finish?
5 off
□ Der Fernseher ist aus. The television's off.
■ **Licht aus!** Lights out!
■ **Sie können meinen Mann nicht sprechen, er ist aus.** You can't speak to my husband. He's out.
■ **von sich aus** of one's own accord
■ **von mir aus** as far as I'm concerned □ Von mir aus kann er zu Hause bleiben. He can stay at home as far as I'm concerned.

ausatmen (PERFECT TENSE **hat ausgeatmet**) VERB [2]
to breathe out

ausbeuten (PERFECT TENSE **hat ausgebeutet**) VERB [2]
to exploit

★ = core vocabulary

ausbilden (PERFECT TENSE hat ausgebildet)
VERB [54]
to train
□ Sie bildet Lehrlinge aus. **She trains apprentices.** □ Er ist ausgebildeter Krankenpfleger. **He's a qualified nurse.**

★**die Ausbildung** FEM NOUN
training
□ eine solide Ausbildung **a decent training**

★**der Ausbildungsplatz** (GEN des Ausbildungsplatzes, PL die Ausbildungsplätze) MASC NOUN
training job

die Ausdauer FEM NOUN
stamina

ausdenken (IMPERFECT dachte aus, PERFECT TENSE hat ausgedacht) VERB [14]
■ **sich etwas ausdenken** to think something up □ Da hast du dir aber was Witziges ausgedacht. **You've certainly thought up something imaginative.**

★**der Ausdruck (1)** (PL die Ausdrücke) MASC NOUN
expression
□ Sie hat im Ferienlager ein paar schlimme Ausdrücke gelernt. **She's learned a few nasty expressions at summer camp.** □ Als Ausdruck meiner Dankbarkeit habe ich ihm Blumen geschenkt. **I gave him flowers as an expression of my gratitude.** □ Ich kann am Ausdruck in deinem Gesicht sehen, dass dir das nicht passt. **I can see by your expression that it doesn't suit you.**

★**der Ausdruck (2)** (PL die Ausdrucke) MASC NOUN
printout
□ Kannst du mir von der Datei einen Ausdruck machen? **Can you do me a printout of the file?**

★**ausdrucken** (PERFECT TENSE hat ausgedruckt) VERB [4]
to print out
□ Soll ich dir die Namen ausdrucken? **Shall I print out the names for you?**

★**ausdrücken** (PERFECT TENSE hat ausgedrückt) VERB [4]
to express
□ Ich weiß nicht, wie man das auf Englisch ausdrückt. **I don't know how to express it in English.**

ausdrücklich ADJECTIVE, ADVERB
explicit
□ Sie hat dir das ausdrücklich verboten. **She explicitly forbade you to do it.**

auseinander ADVERB
apart
□ weit auseinander **far apart**

auseinanderhalten (PRESENT TENSE hält auseinander, IMPERFECT hielt auseinander,
PERFECT TENSE hat auseinandergehalten)
VERB [33]
to distinguish

auseinandernehmen (PRESENT TENSE nimmt auseinander, IMPERFECT nahm auseinander, PERFECT TENSE hat auseinandergenommen) VERB [52]
to take to pieces

★**die Ausfahrt** FEM NOUN
exit
□ Wir müssen an der nächsten Ausfahrt raus. **We have to take the next exit.**

★**ausfallen** (PRESENT TENSE fällt aus, IMPERFECT fiel aus, PERFECT TENSE ist ausgefallen) VERB [22]
1 to be cancelled
□ Der Sportunterricht fällt heute aus. **PE has been cancelled today.**
2 to break down
□ Die Heizung ist mal wieder ausgefallen. **The heating has broken down again.**
■ **Wenn der Strom ausfällt, ...** If there's a power cut ...
3 to fall out
□ Ihm sind die Haare ausgefallen, als er noch ziemlich jung war. **His hair fell out when he was still quite young.**
■ **Die Arbeit ist sehr schlecht ausgefallen.** The results of the test were awful.

★**der Ausflug** (PL die Ausflüge) MASC NOUN
outing
□ einen Ausflug machen **to go on an outing**

ausfragen (PERFECT TENSE hat ausgefragt) VERB [4]
to question

die Ausfuhr FEM NOUN
export

ausführen (PERFECT TENSE hat ausgeführt) VERB [4]
1 to carry out
□ Sie hat ihren Plan ausgeführt. **She carried out her plan.**
2 to export
□ Waren ausführen **to export goods**
■ **jemanden ausführen** to take somebody out □ Er hat mich zum Essen ausgeführt. **He took me out for a meal.**
■ **einen Hund ausführen** to take a dog for a walk

ausführlich ADJECTIVE, ADVERB
1 detailed
□ ein ausführlicher Bericht **a detailed report**
2 in detail
□ Sie hat mir ausführlich erzählt, wie es in den Ferien war. **She told me in detail what her holidays were like.**

★**ausfüllen** (PERFECT TENSE hat ausgefüllt) VERB [4]

Numbers in brackets refer to verb tables on pages 697 to 706.

27

to fill in

□ Füllt bitte die Lücken im Text aus. Please fill in the gaps in the text. □ Hast du den Antrag schon ausgefüllt? Have you filled in the application form yet?

die **Ausgabe** FEM NOUN

1 expenditure *no pl*

□ Wir hatten in der letzten Zeit viele Ausgaben. We've had a lot of expenditure recently.

2 edition

□ Sie hat eine sehr alte Ausgabe von Goethes Werken. She's got a very old edition of Goethe's works.

3 issue

□ Ich habe das in der letzten Ausgabe meines Computermagazins gelesen. I read it in the last issue of my computer magazine.

★ der **Ausgang** (PL die **Ausgänge**) MASC NOUN

1 exit

□ Ich warte dann am Ausgang auf euch. I'll wait for you at the exit, then.

■ 'Kein Ausgang' 'No exit'

2 ending

□ Der Film hat einen sehr traurigen Ausgang. The film has a very sad ending.

3 result

□ Welchen Ausgang hatte das Spiel? What was the result of the match?

★ **ausgeben** (PRESENT TENSE **gibt aus**, IMPERFECT **gab aus**, PERFECT TENSE **hat ausgegeben**) VERB [28]

1 to spend

□ Wir haben auf dem Volksfest hundert Euro ausgegeben. We spent a hundred euros at the fair.

2 to distribute

□ Du musst dich da vorn anstellen, da werden die Karten ausgegeben. You have to queue at the front there. That's where the tickets are being distributed.

■ **einen ausgeben** to stand a round (*Umgangssprache*) □ Ich habe heute Geburtstag, darum gebe ich einen aus. It's my birthday today, so I'm standing a round.

■ **sich für jemanden ausgeben** to pass oneself off as somebody □ Sie hat sich für meine Schwester ausgegeben. She passed herself off as my sister.

■ **sich als etwas ausgeben** to pretend to be something □ Er hat sich als Computerfachmann ausgegeben. He pretended to be a computer expert.

★ **ausgehen** (IMPERFECT **ging aus**, PERFECT TENSE **ist ausgegangen**) VERB [29]

1 to go out

□ Sollen wir heute Abend ausgehen? Shall we go out this evening? □ Anna will mit dir ausgehen. Anna wants to go out with you. □ Plötzlich ging das Licht aus. Suddenly the light went out.

2 to run out

□ Mir geht langsam das Geld aus. I'm running out of money. □ Ihnen ging das Benzin aus. They ran out of petrol.

■ **Wie ist das Spiel ausgegangen?** How did the game end?

■ **schlecht ausgehen** to turn out badly

■ **Wir können davon ausgehen, dass ...** We can assume that ...

ausgelassen ADJECTIVE
exuberant

★ **ausgenommen** CONJUNCTION
except

□ Alle kamen, ausgenommen Rana. Everyone came except Rana.

■ **Anwesende sind ausgenommen.** Present company excepted.

ausgerechnet ADVERB

■ **ausgerechnet heute** today of all days

■ **ausgerechnet du** you of all people

ausgeschlossen ADJECTIVE
impossible

□ Ich halte das für ausgeschlossen. I think that's impossible.

★ **ausgezeichnet** ADJECTIVE, ADVERB

1 excellent

□ Max ist ein ausgezeichneter Koch. Max is an excellent cook.

2 excellently

□ Sie hat es ausgezeichnet gemacht. She did it excellently.

ausgiebig ADJECTIVE
substantial

□ Das Frühstück war sehr ausgiebig. Breakfast was very substantial.

■ **ausgiebig schlafen** to have a good sleep

■ **sich ausgiebig erholen** to have a good long rest

aushalten (PRESENT TENSE **hält aus**, IMPERFECT **hielt aus**, PERFECT TENSE **hat ausgehalten**) VERB [33]

■ **Ich halte diese Hitze nicht aus!** I can't stand this heat.

■ **Das ist nicht zum Aushalten.** It's unbearable.

★ sich **auskennen** (IMPERFECT **kannte sich aus**, PERFECT TENSE **hat sich ausgekannt**) VERB [39]

1 to know about

□ Sie kennt sich mit Kindern gut aus. She knows a lot about children.

2 to know one's way around

□ Er kennt sich in Stuttgart aus. He knows his way around Stuttgart.

★ **auskommen** (IMPERFECT **kam aus**, PERFECT TENSE **ist ausgekommen**) VERB [40]

■ **mit jemandem auskommen** to get on with somebody □ Ich komme mit meinen Eltern gut aus. I get on well with my parents.

★ = core vocabulary

■ **mit etwas auskommen** to manage on something □ Die ganze Familie muss mit hundert Euro in der Woche auskommen. The whole family has to manage on a hundred euros a week.

★ die **Auskunft** (PL die **Auskünfte**) FEM NOUN
1 information *no pl*
□ Nähere Auskunft erhalten Sie unter der folgenden Nummer. For further information ring the following number.
2 information office
□ Fragen Sie bei der Auskunft, wann der nächste Zug nach Bremen geht. Ask at the information office when the next train leaves for Bremen.
■ **Telefonauskunft** directory inquiries *pl*
□ Ruf doch die Auskunft an! Ring directory inquiries.

auslachen (PERFECT TENSE **hat ausgelacht**) VERB [4]
to laugh at
□ Sie hat mich nur ausgelacht. She just laughed at me.

★ das **Ausland** NEUT NOUN
■ **im Ausland** abroad □ Er lebt im Ausland. He lives abroad.
■ **ins Ausland** abroad □ Nach dem Examen möchte sie ins Ausland gehen. After the exams she wants to go abroad.

★ der **Ausländer** (PL die **Ausländer**) MASC NOUN
foreigner
□ Ihr Mann ist Ausländer. Her husband's a foreigner.

★ die **Ausländerin** FEM NOUN
foreigner
□ Seine Frau ist Ausländerin. His wife's a foreigner.

ausländisch ADJECTIVE
foreign

das **Auslandsgespräch** (PL die **Auslandsgespräche**) NEUT NOUN
international call

auslassen (PRESENT TENSE **lässt aus**, IMPERFECT **ließ aus**, PERFECT TENSE **hat ausgelassen**) VERB [42]
1 to leave out
□ Die nächste Übung können wir auslassen. We can leave out the next exercise.
■ **Ich lasse heute das Mittagessen aus.** I'm skipping lunch today.
2 to leave off
□ Heute lass ich den Fernseher aus. I'm leaving the television off today. □ Bei der Hitze kannst du die Jacke auslassen. You can leave your jacket off in this heat.
■ **seine Wut an jemandem auslassen** to take one's anger out on somebody

ausleeren (PERFECT TENSE **hat ausgeleert**)

VERB [4]
to empty

★ **ausleihen** (IMPERFECT **lieh aus**, PERFECT TENSE **hat ausgeliehen**) VERB
to lend
□ Kannst du mir deinen Roller ausleihen? Can you lend me your scooter?
■ **sich etwas ausleihen** to borrow something
□ Ich habe mir das Tablet meiner Schwester ausgeliehen. I've borrowed my sister's tablet.

ausloggen (PERFECT TENSE **hat ausgeloggt**)
VERB [4]
to log off (*computer*)

★ **ausmachen** (PERFECT TENSE **hat ausgemacht**) VERB [48]
1 to turn off
□ Mach bitte das Radio aus, die Musik stört mich. Please turn the radio off. The music's disturbing me.
■ **das Licht ausmachen** to switch off the light
2 to put out
□ Bitte mach das Feuer aus, bevor du ins Bett gehst. Please put the fire out before you go to bed.
3 to arrange
□ Habt ihr schon einen Termin für das Fest ausgemacht? Have you arranged a date for the party yet? □ Ich habe mit ihr ausgemacht, dass wir uns um fünf Uhr treffen. I've arranged to meet her at five.
4 to settle
□ Macht das unter euch aus. Settle the matter between you.
5 to mind
□ Es macht mir nichts aus, wenn ich allein gehen muss. I don't mind having to go alone. □ Macht es Ihnen etwas aus, wenn ...? Would you mind if ...?

die **Ausnahme** FEM NOUN
exception

ausnahmsweise ADVERB
for once

ausnützen (PERFECT TENSE **hat ausgenützt**)
VERB [4]
to use

★ **auspacken** (PERFECT TENSE **hat ausgepackt**)
VERB [4]
to unpack

ausprobieren (PERFECT TENSE **hat ausprobiert**) VERB [4]
to try out

der **Auspuff** (PL die **Auspuffe**) MASC NOUN
exhaust

ausrechnen (PERFECT TENSE **hat ausgerechnet**) VERB [4]
to calculate

die **Ausrede** FEM NOUN

Numbers in brackets refer to verb tables on pages 697 to 706.

29

ausreichen - außergewöhnlich

excuse

ausreichen VERB [4]
to be enough

★**ausreichend** ADJECTIVE
1 sufficient
□ ausreichend Geld sufficient money
2 adequate

> **DID YOU KNOW...?**
> German grades range from one (**sehr gut**) to six (**ungenügend**).

die **Ausreise** FEM NOUN
departure
■ bei der Ausreise when leaving the country

★**ausrichten** (PERFECT TENSE hat ausgerichtet) VERB [4]
1 to tell
□ Ich werde es ihm ausrichten. I'll tell him.
■ Richte bitte an deine Eltern schöne Grüße aus. Please give my regards to your parents.
2 to gear to
□ Wir müssen unser Veranstaltungsangebot mehr auf Jugendliche ausrichten. We must gear our events more to young people.

★**ausrufen** (IMPERFECT rief aus, PERFECT TENSE hat ausgerufen) VERB [56]
to cry out
■ jemanden ausrufen lassen to page somebody

das **Ausrufezeichen** (PL die Ausrufezeichen) NEUT NOUN
exclamation mark

★sich **ausruhen** (PERFECT TENSE hat sich ausgeruht) VERB [4]
to rest

ausrüsten (PERFECT TENSE hat ausgerüstet) VERB [4]
to equip

die **Ausrüstung** FEM NOUN
equipment no pl

★**ausschalten** (PERFECT TENSE hat ausgeschaltet) VERB [2]
to switch off

ausschlafen (PRESENT TENSE schläft aus, IMPERFECT schlief aus, PERFECT TENSE hat ausgeschlafen) VERB [58]
to have a good sleep
■ Morgen kann ich ausschlafen. I can have a lie-in tomorrow.
■ Ich bin nicht ausgeschlafen. I didn't get enough sleep.

ausschließlich ADVERB, PREPOSITION
1 exclusively
□ Der Schulhof ist ausschließlich für Schüler dieser Schule. The school yard is exclusively for pupils of this school.
2 except

□ Wir haben jeden Tag geöffnet ausschließlich Sonntag. We're open every day except Sunday.

ausschneiden (IMPERFECT schnitt aus, PERFECT TENSE hat ausgeschnitten) VERB [60]
to cut out

★**aussehen** (PRESENT TENSE sieht aus, IMPERFECT sah aus, PERFECT TENSE hat ausgesehen) VERB [64]
▷ see also das **Aussehen** NOUN
to look
□ Sie sieht wirklich gut aus. She looks really good. □ Wie siehst du denn aus? What do you look like! □ Es sieht nach Regen aus. It looks like rain. □ Es sieht schlecht aus. Things look bad.

das **Aussehen** NEUT NOUN
▷ see also **aussehen** VERB
appearance

aus sein VERB [65] ▷ see **aus**

★**außen** ADVERB
on the outside
□ Außen ist es rot. It's red on the outside.

die **Außenpolitik** FEM NOUN
foreign policy

der **Außenseiter** (PL die Außenseiter) MASC NOUN
outsider

★**außer** PREPOSITION, CONJUNCTION

> The preposition **außer** takes the dative.

1 apart from
□ Außer dir haben das alle verstanden. Everyone has understood apart from you. □ Wer war noch da außer Emma? Apart from Emma, who was there?
■ außer Haus out □ Er ist heute den ganzen Tag außer Haus. He's out all day today.
■ außer Landes abroad
■ außer Gefahr out of danger
■ außer Betrieb out of order
■ außer sich sein to be beside oneself □ Sie war außer sich vor Wut. She was beside herself with rage.
2 if ... not
□ Wir machen morgen ein Picknick, außer es regnet. We're having a picnic tomorrow if it doesn't rain.

★**außerdem** CONJUNCTION
in addition

äußere ADJECTIVE
1 outer
□ Sie bildeten einen äußeren und einen inneren Kreis. They formed an outer and an inner circle.
2 external
□ Nur zur äußeren Anwendung. For external use only.

außergewöhnlich ADJECTIVE
unusual

★ = core vocabulary

★ außerhalb PREPOSITION, ADVERB

> The preposition **außerhalb** takes the genitive.

1 outside
□ Es liegt außerhalb der Stadt. It's outside the town.

2 out of town
□ Sie wohnt nicht in Ulm, sondern ziemlich weit außerhalb. She doesn't live in Ulm, but quite a way out of town.
■ **außerhalb der Saison** out of season

äußern VERB [88]
to express
□ Sie hat den Wunsch geäußert, allein in die Ferien fahren zu dürfen. She's expressed the wish to be allowed to go on holiday alone.
■ **eine Meinung äußern** to give an opinion
□ Willst du nicht auch deine Meinung äußern? Don't you want to give your opinion, too?
■ **sich äußern** to comment □ Sie wollte sich zu dem Vorwurf nicht äußern. She didn't wish to comment on the accusation.

außerordentlich ADJECTIVE, ADVERB
exceptional
□ Sie hat eine außerordentliche Begabung. She's exceptionally gifted. □ Sie ist außerordentlich intelligent. She's exceptionally intelligent.

★ äußerst ADVERB
▷ see also **äußerste** ADJECTIVE
extremely

äußerste ADJECTIVE
▷ see also **äußerst** ADVERB
utmost
□ Diese Sache ist von äußerster Wichtigkeit. This matter is of the utmost importance.

die Äußerung FEM NOUN
remark

★ die Aussicht FEM NOUN
1 view
□ Vom Hotel aus hat man eine schöne Aussicht aufs Meer. You have a wonderful view of the sea from the hotel.

2 prospect
□ Die Aussicht auf diese Stelle hat ihr neuen Mut gegeben. The prospect of this job gave her new hope. □ Das sind ja schöne Aussichten! What a prospect!
■ **etwas in Aussicht haben** to have the prospect of something □ Sie hat eine Stelle bei Collins in Aussicht. She has the prospect of a job with Collins.

ausspannen (PERFECT TENSE **hat ausgespannt**) VERB [4]
to relax

★ die Aussprache FEM NOUN
1 pronunciation
□ Die Aussprache der Wörter ist mit phonetischen Zeichen angegeben. The pronunciation of the words is shown by phonetic symbols.

2 frank discussion
□ Ich hatte gestern eine lange Aussprache mit ihm. I had a long, frank discussion with him yesterday.

★ aussprechen (PRESENT TENSE **spricht aus**, IMPERFECT **sprach aus**, PERFECT TENSE **hat ausgesprochen**) VERB [70]
to pronounce
□ Wie spricht man dieses Wort aus? How do you pronounce this word?
■ **sich mit jemandem aussprechen** to talk things out with somebody □ Meinst du nicht, wir sollten uns einmal aussprechen? Don't you think we ought to talk things out?
■ **sich gegen etwas aussprechen** to speak out against something □ Die Mehrheit hat sich gegen eine Klassenfahrt nach Helgoland ausgesprochen. The majority spoke out against a school trip to Heligoland.
■ **sich für etwas aussprechen** to speak out in favour of something □ Die Lehrer haben sich für eine Verlängerung der Pausenzeiten ausgesprochen. The teachers spoke out in favour of longer breaks.
■ **Lass ihn doch aussprechen!** Let him finish.

★ aussteigen (IMPERFECT **stieg aus**, PERFECT TENSE **ist ausgestiegen**) VERB [74]
to get off
□ Ich sah, wie sie aus der Straßenbahn ausstieg. I saw her get off the tram.

ausstellen (PERFECT TENSE **hat ausgestellt**) VERB [4]
1 to exhibit
□ Im Museum werden zurzeit Bilder von Chagall ausgestellt. Pictures by Chagall are currently being exhibited in the museum.

2 to be on display
□ Im Schaufenster war exotisches Obst ausgestellt. Exotic fruit was on display in the window.

3 to switch off
□ Die Heizung wird im Mai ausgestellt. The heating's switched off in May.

4 to write
□ Die Lehrerin hat ihm ein gutes Zeugnis ausgestellt. The teacher wrote him a good report.

5 to issue
□ Auf welchem Amt werden Pässe ausgestellt? Which office issues passports?

★ die Ausstellung FEM NOUN
exhibition

aussterben (PRESENT TENSE **stirbt aus**, IMPERFECT **starb aus**, PERFECT TENSE **ist**

ausgestorben) VERB [75]
to die out

★ der **Ausstieg** MASC NOUN
1 exit
□ Der Ausstieg ist hinten. The exit is at the back.
2 abandonment
□ der Ausstieg aus der Atomenergie abandonment of nuclear energy

aussuchen (PERFECT TENSE **hat ausgesucht**)
VERB [4]
to choose
□ Such dir ein Eis aus. Choose yourself an ice cream.

★ der **Austausch** (GEN des **Austausches**) MASC
NOUN
exchange
□ ein Schüleraustausch a school exchange

★ **austauschen** (PERFECT TENSE **hat ausgetauscht**) VERB [4]
1 to replace
□ Ich habe die Festplatte ausgetauscht. I've replaced the hard disk.
2 to substitute
□ Der Mittelstürmer wurde ausgetauscht. The centre-forward was substituted.

austeilen (PERFECT TENSE **hat ausgeteilt**) VERB
[4]
to give out

★ **austragen** (PRESENT TENSE **trägt aus**, IMPERFECT **trug aus**, PERFECT TENSE **hat ausgetragen**)
VERB [77]
1 to deliver
□ Morgens trägt er immer die Post aus. In the morning he always delivers the post.
2 to hold
□ Der Wettkampf wird im Olympiastadion ausgetragen. The competition will be held in the Olympic ® stadium.

★ **Australien** NEUT NOUN
Australia
■ aus Australien from Australia
■ in Australien in Australia
■ nach Australien to Australia

der **Australier** (PL die **Australier**) MASC NOUN
Australian

die **Australierin** FEM NOUN
Australian

australisch ADJECTIVE
Australian

austreten (PRESENT TENSE **tritt aus**, IMPERFECT **trat aus**, PERFECT TENSE **ist ausgetreten**) VERB
[79]
■ aus etwas austreten to leave something
□ Sie ist aus dem Verein ausgetreten. She's left the club.
■ Ich muss mal austreten. I need to go to the loo. (*Umgangssprache*)

austrinken (IMPERFECT **trank aus**, PERFECT
TENSE **hat ausgetrunken**) VERB [80]
1 to drink up
□ Sie tranken aus und gingen. They drank up and left.
2 to finish
□ Lass mich noch schnell meinen Saft austrinken. Let me just quickly finish my juice.

★ der **Ausverkauf** (PL die **Ausverkäufe**) MASC
NOUN
clearance sale

★ **ausverkauft** ADJECTIVE
1 sold out
□ Die Vorstellung ist leider ausverkauft. The performance is sold out, I'm afraid.
2 full
□ Das Kino war ausverkauft. The cinema was full.

★ die **Auswahl** FEM NOUN
selection
□ Sie haben eine große Auswahl an Schuhen. They have a large selection of shoes.

auswählen (PERFECT TENSE **hat ausgewählt**)
VERB [4]
to select

auswandern (PERFECT TENSE **ist ausgewandert**) VERB [88]
to emigrate
□ Sie sind nach Neuseeland ausgewandert. They emigrated to New Zealand.

auswärts ADVERB
1 in another town
□ Sie wohnt in Calw, arbeitet aber auswärts. She lives in Calw but works in another town.
2 away
□ Unsere Mannschaft spielt nächste Woche auswärts. Our team's playing away next week.
■ auswärts essen to eat out

das **Auswärtsspiel** (PL die **Auswärtsspiele**) NEUT NOUN
away game

der **Ausweg** (PL die **Auswege**) MASC NOUN
way out

★ der **Ausweis** (PL die **Ausweise**) MASC NOUN
1 identity card
□ Der Polizist wollte meinen Ausweis sehen. The police officer wanted to see my identity card.
2 card
□ Wenn du Schüler bist und deinen Ausweis zeigst, bekommst du Ermäßigung. If you're a student and show them your card, you get a reduction.

auswendig ADVERB
by heart
□ etwas auswendig lernen to learn something by heart

auswerten (PERFECT TENSE **hat ausgewertet**) VERB [4]
to evaluate

★ **ausziehen** (IMPERFECT **zog aus**, PERFECT TENSE **hat/ist ausgezogen**) VERB [96]

> For the perfect tense use **haben** when the verb has an object and **sein** when there is no object.

1 to take off
□ Sie hat ihren Mantel nicht ausgezogen. She didn't take off her coat.

2 to undress
□ Kannst du bitte die Kinder ausziehen und ins Bett bringen? Can you undress the children and put them to bed, please?
■ **sich ausziehen** to undress □ Haben die Kinder sich schon ausgezogen? Have the children undressed yet?

3 to move out
□ Meine Nachbarn sind letzte Woche ausgezogen. My neighbours moved out last week.

der/die **Auszubildende** (GEN des/der **Auszubildenden**, PL die **Auszubildenden**) MASC/FEM NOUN
trainee

★ das **Auto** (PL die **Autos**) NEUT NOUN
car
■ **Auto fahren** to drive

★ die **Autobahn** FEM NOUN
motorway

★ das **Autobahnkreuz** (GEN des **Autobahnkreuzes**, PL die **Autobahnkreuze**) NEUT NOUN
motorway intersection

★ der **Autobus** (GEN des **Autobusses**, PL die **Autobusse**) MASC NOUN
bus

der **Autofahrer** (PL die **Autofahrer**) MASC NOUN
motorist

die **Autofahrerin** FEM NOUN
motorist

das **Autogramm** (PL die **Autogramme**) NEUT NOUN
autograph

das **Autokennzeichen** (PL die **Autokennzeichen**) NEUT NOUN
registration number

★ der **Automat** (GEN des **Automaten**, PL die **Automaten**) MASC NOUN
machine

automatisch ADJECTIVE
automatic
□ Die Türen schließen automatisch. The doors close automatically.

★ der **Autor** (PL die **Autoren**) MASC NOUN
author

das **Autoradio** (PL die **Autoradios**) NEUT NOUN
car radio

das **Autorennen** (PL die **Autorennen**) NEUT NOUN
motor racing

★ die **Autorin** FEM NOUN
author

autoritär ADJECTIVE
authoritarian

die **Autorität** FEM NOUN
authority

der **Autounfall** (PL die **Autounfälle**) MASC NOUN
car accident

die **Axt** (PL die **Äxte**) FEM NOUN
axe

der/die **Azubi** (PL die **Azubis**) MASC/FEM NOUN
apprentice
□ Sie ist Azubi bei einem Goldschmied. She's an apprentice goldsmith.
■ **Damals war er noch Azubi.** He was still a trainee then.

Numbers in brackets refer to verb tables on pages 697 to 706.

33

Bb

★das **Baby** (PL die **Babys**) NEUT NOUN
baby

★**babysitten** (PERFECT TENSE **hat babygesittet**)
VERB [2]
to babysit

★der **Babysitter** (PL die **Babysitter**) MASC
NOUN
babysitter

★die **Babysitterin** FEM NOUN
babysitter

der **Bach** (PL die **Bäche**) MASC NOUN
stream

die **Backe** FEM NOUN
cheek

★**backen** (PRESENT TENSE **bäckt**, IMPERFECT
backte or **buk**, PERFECT TENSE **hat gebacken**)
VERB [48]
to bake

★der **Bäcker** (PL die **Bäcker**) MASC NOUN
baker
□ beim Bäcker at the baker's □ zum Bäcker to
the baker's

★die **Bäckerei** FEM NOUN
baker's

★die **Bäckerin** (PL die **Bäckerinnen**) FEM NOUN
baker

★der **Backofen** (PL die **Backöfen**) MASC NOUN
oven

★das **Bad** (PL die **Bäder**) NEUT NOUN
▷ see also das **Badezimmer**
1 bath
■ ein Bad im Meer a swim in the sea
2 bathroom
□ Du bist schon seit einer halben Stunde im
Bad! You've been in the bathroom for an hour!

★der **Badeanzug** (PL die **Badeanzüge**) MASC
NOUN
bathing suit

★die **Badehose** FEM NOUN
swimming trunks *pl*

die **Bademütze** FEM NOUN
bathing cap

★**baden** VERB [54]
to have a bath
■ jemanden baden to bath somebody □ Das

Baby muss noch gebadet werden. The baby still
has to be bathed.
■ sich baden to have a bath

Baden-Württemberg NEUT NOUN
Baden-Württemberg

DID YOU KNOW...?
Baden-Württemberg is one of the 16
Länder. Its capital is Stuttgart. Baden-
Württemberg is home to the cuckoo clock and
to Mercedes-Benz and Porsche.

★der **Badeort** MASC NOUN
spa

★das **Badetuch** (PL die **Badetücher**) NEUT
NOUN
bath towel

★die **Badewanne** FEM NOUN
bath (*tub*)

★das **Badezimmer** (PL die **Badezimmer**)
NEUT NOUN
bathroom

das **Badminton** (GEN des **Badminton**) NEUT
NOUN
badminton

★die **Bahn** (PL die **Bahnen**) FEM NOUN
1 railway
□ Er arbeitet bei der Bahn. He works for the
railway.
■ mit der Bahn fahren to go by train
2 tram
3 lane
□ Die Schwimmerin auf Bahn drei liegt in
Führung. The swimmer in lane three is in the
lead.
■ auf die schiefe Bahn geraten to go off the
rails

die **Bahnfahrt** FEM NOUN
railway journey

★der **Bahnhof** (PL die **Bahnhöfe**) MASC NOUN
station
□ auf dem Bahnhof at the station □ zum
Bahnhof to the station

★die **Bahnhofshalle** FEM NOUN
station concourse

★der **Bahnsteig** (PL die **Bahnsteige**) MASC
NOUN
platform

★ = core vocabulary

★ der **Bahnübergang** (PL die **Bahnübergänge**) MASC NOUN
level crossing

★ **bald** ADVERB
1 soon
□ Es wird bald Frühling. It'll soon be spring.
■ **Bis bald!** See you later.
2 almost
□ Ich hätte bald was gesagt. I almost said something.
■ **Wird's bald!** Get a move on!

BE CAREFUL!
The German word bald does not mean **bald**.

der **Balkan** MASC NOUN
Balkans pl
■ **auf dem Balkan** in the Balkans

der **Balken** (PL die **Balken**) MASC NOUN
beam

★ der **Balkon** (PL die **Balkons** or **Balkone**) MASC NOUN
balcony

★ der **Ball** (PL die **Bälle**) MASC NOUN
ball
□ Die Kinder spielen mit dem Ball. The children are playing with the ball. □ Mit wem kommst du zum Ball? Who are you going to the ball with?

das **Ballett** (PL die **Ballette**) NEUT NOUN
ballet

der **Ballon** (PL die **Ballons** or **Ballone**) MASC NOUN
balloon

der **Bambus** (GEN des **Bambusses**, PL die **Bambusse**) MASC NOUN
bamboo

★ die **Banane** FEM NOUN
banana

★ **band** VERB ▷ see binden

★ der **Band (1)** (PL die **Bände**) MASC NOUN
▷ see also die **Band** NOUN, das **Band** NOUN
volume
□ ein Lexikon in fünf Bänden an encyclopedia in five volumes

★ die **Band (2)** (PL die **Bands**) FEM NOUN
▷ see also der **Band** NOUN, das **Band** NOUN
band
□ Sie spielt Gitarre in einer Band. She plays the guitar in a band.

★ das **Band (3)** (PL die **Bänder**) NEUT NOUN
▷ see also der **Band** NOUN, die **Band** NOUN
1 ribbon
□ Das Kind hatte ein rotes Band im Haar. The child had a red ribbon in her hair.
2 production line
□ Meine Mutter arbeitet am Band. My mother works on the production line.
■ **am laufenden Band** nonstop

★ die **Bank (1)** (PL die **Bänke**) FEM NOUN
bench
□ Sie saß auf einer Bank im Park. She was sitting on a park bench.

★ die **Bank (2)** (PL die **Banken**) FEM NOUN
bank
□ Ich muss Geld von der Bank holen. I'll have to get money from the bank.

das **Bankkonto** (PL die **Bankkonten**) NEUT NOUN
bank account

die **Bankleitzahl** FEM NOUN
bank sort code

★ die **Banknote** FEM NOUN
banknote

bankrott ADJECTIVE
bankrupt
□ Die Firma ist bankrott. The firm is bankrupt.
■ **Bankrott machen** to go bankrupt

bar ADJECTIVE
▷ see also die **Bar** NOUN
■ **bares Geld** cash
■ **etwas bar bezahlen** to pay cash for something

★ die **Bar** (PL die **Bars**) FEM NOUN
▷ see also **bar** ADJECTIVE
bar

der **Bär** (GEN des **Bären**, PL die **Bären**) MASC NOUN
bear

barfuß ADJECTIVE
barefoot

★ das **Bargeld** NEUT NOUN
cash

der **Barren** (PL die **Barren**) MASC NOUN
parallel bars pl

★ der **Bart** (PL die **Bärte**) MASC NOUN
beard

bärtig ADJECTIVE
bearded

★ **Basel** NEUT NOUN
Basle
■ **nach Basel** to Basle

die **Basis** (PL die **Basen**) FEM NOUN
basis

der **Bass** (GEN des **Basses**, PL die **Bässe**) MASC NOUN
bass

★ **basteln** VERB [34]
to make things
□ Ich bastle gern. I like making things.
■ **etwas basteln** to make something □ Ich habe einen Untersetzer gebastelt. I've made a coaster.

bat VERB ▷ see bitten

Numbers in brackets refer to verb tables on pages 697 to 706.

35

Batterie - beantworten

★ die **Batterie** FEM NOUN
battery

der **Bau** (PL die **Bauten**) MASC NOUN

1 construction
□ Das Haus ist noch im Bau. The house is still under construction.

2 building
□ In New York gibt es viele beeindruckende Bauten. There are many impressive buildings in New York.

3 building site
□ In den Ferien arbeitet er auf dem Bau. He works on a building site in the holidays.

★ der **Bauarbeiter** (PL die **Bauarbeiter**) MASC NOUN
building worker

★ die **Bauarbeiterin** FEM NOUN
building worker

★ der **Bauch** (PL die **Bäuche**) MASC NOUN
stomach
□ Mir tut der Bauch weh. My stomach's sore.

der **Bauchnabel** (PL die **Bauchnabel**) MASC NOUN
belly button

die **Bauchschmerzen** MASC PL NOUN
stomachache *sing*

★ **bauen** VERB [38]
to build
□ Meine Eltern haben das Haus gebaut, in dem wir wohnen. My parents built the house we live in.

★ der **Bauer** (GEN des **Bauern**, PL die **Bauern**) MASC NOUN

1 farmer
□ Friedas Vater ist Bauer. Frieda's father is a farmer.

2 pawn
□ Sie zog mit dem Bauer. She moved the pawn.

★ die **Bäuerin** FEM NOUN

1 farmer
□ Sie möchte Bäuerin werden. She would like to be a farmer.

2 farmer's wife

★ der **Bauernhof** (PL die **Bauernhöfe**) MASC NOUN
farm

baufällig ADJECTIVE
dilapidated

★ der **Baum** (PL die **Bäume**) MASC NOUN
tree

★ die **Baumwolle** FEM NOUN
cotton
□ eine Tischdecke aus Baumwolle a cotton tablecloth

★ die **Baustelle** FEM NOUN
building site

der **Bayer** (GEN des **Bayern**, PL die **Bayern**) MASC NOUN
Bavarian

die **Bayerin** FEM NOUN
Bavarian

★ **Bayern** NEUT NOUN
Bavaria

> **DID YOU KNOW...?**
> **Bayern** is one of the 16 **Länder**. Its capital is München (Munich). Bavaria has the longest political tradition of any of the Länder, and since 1945 has developed into an important industrial region.

bayrisch ADJECTIVE
Bavarian

beabsichtigen (PERFECT TENSE hat **beabsichtigt**) VERB [7]
to intend
□ Ich beabsichtige, ins Ausland zu fahren. I intend to go abroad.

beachten (PERFECT TENSE hat beachtet) VERB [2]

1 to pay attention to
□ Beachte ihn nicht! Don't pay any attention to him. □ Du solltest den Hinweis auf der Packung beachten. You should pay attention to the instructions on the packet.

2 to obey
□ Man muss die Verkehrsregeln beachten. You have to obey the traffic regulations.

3 to observe
□ Sie hat die Vorfahrt nicht beachtet. She didn't observe the right of way.

beachtlich ADJECTIVE
considerable

★ der **Beamte** (GEN des **Beamten**, PL die **Beamten**) MASC NOUN

1 official
□ Der Beamte stempelte meinen Pass ab. The official stamped my passport.

2 civil servant

> **DID YOU KNOW...?**
> In Germany all public employees are classed as civil servants. They enjoy a certain social status and have many privileges.

□ Deutsche Lehrer sind Beamte. German teachers are civil servants.

★ die **Beamtin** FEM NOUN
civil servant
□ Meine Mutter ist Beamtin. My mother's a civil servant.

beantragen (PERFECT TENSE hat beantragt) VERB [7]
to apply for

★ **beantworten** (PERFECT TENSE hat beantwortet) VERB [2]
to answer

★**bearbeiten** (PERFECT TENSE hat bearbeitet)
VERB [2]

1 to deal with
□ Welches Thema hat sie in ihrer Diplomarbeit bearbeitet? **What subject did she deal with in her dissertation?**

2 to process
□ Wir haben Ihren Antrag noch nicht bearbeitet. **We haven't processed your application yet.**

3 to treat
□ Er hat den Fleck mit Fleckenmittel bearbeitet. **He treated the stain with stain remover.**
■ **jemanden bearbeiten** to work on somebody (*Umgangssprache*)□ Ich werde meine Mutter bearbeiten, dass sie mich gehen lässt. **I'll work on my mother and get her to let me go.**

★**der Becher** (PL die Becher) MASC NOUN

1 mug
□ Auf ihrem Schreibtisch stand ein Becher mit Kaffee. **There was a mug of coffee on her desk.**

2 carton

3 tub

das Becken (PL die Becken) NEUT NOUN

1 sink
□ Er ließ Wasser ins Becken laufen. **He ran water into the sink.**

2 pool

3 pelvis
■ **ein breites Becken** broad hips

4 cymbals

★**sich bedanken** (PERFECT TENSE hat sich bedankt) VERB [7]
to say thank you
□ Hast du dich auch bedankt? **Did you say thank you?**
■ **sich bei jemandem bedanken** to say thank you to somebody

der Bedarf MASC NOUN
demand
□ je nach Bedarf **according to demand**
■ **bei Bedarf** if necessary
■ **Bedarf an etwas haben** to be in need of something□ Wir haben Bedarf an Aushilfskräften. **We're in need of temporary workers.**

bedauerlich ADJECTIVE
regrettable

★**bedauern** (PERFECT TENSE hat bedauert) VERB [88]

1 to be sorry for
□ Wir bedauern es sehr, dass wir nicht kommen können. **We're very sorry that we can't come.**
■ **Ich bedauere!** I'm sorry!
■ **Ich bedauere kein Wort.** I don't regret a single word!

2 to pity
□ Ich bedaure dich wirklich! **I really pity you!**

die Bedenken PL NOUN
doubts *pl*
□ Ich habe Bedenken, ob das klappt. **I have my doubts as to whether it'll work.**
■ **Hast du keine Bedenken, wenn du deine Eltern so anlügst?** Don't you feel bad about lying to your parents like that?

bedenklich ADJECTIVE

1 dubious
□ Das sind sehr bedenkliche Methoden. **These are very dubious methods.**

2 dangerous
□ Die Lage ist bedenklich. **The situation is dangerous.**
■ **Ihr Gesundheitszustand ist bedenklich.** Her state of health is giving cause for concern.

★**bedeuten** (PERFECT TENSE hat bedeutet) VERB [2]
to mean
□ Was bedeutet dieser Ausdruck? **What does this expression mean?**□ Was hat das zu bedeuten? **What's that supposed to mean?**□ Er bedeutet mir sehr viel. **He means a lot to me.**

bedeutend ADJECTIVE

1 important
□ Er ist ein bedeutender Wissenschaftler. **He's an important scientist.**

2 considerable
□ Sie haben eine bedeutende Summe dafür bezahlt. **They paid a considerable sum for it.**
■ **bedeutend besser** considerably better
■ **bedeutend schlechter** considerably worse

die Bedeutung FEM NOUN

1 meaning
□ die Bedeutung eines Worts **the meaning of a word**

2 importance
□ eine Erfindung von großer Bedeutung **an invention of great importance**

★**bedienen** (PERFECT TENSE hat bedient) VERB [7]

1 to serve
□ Wir wurden sehr schnell bedient. **We were served very quickly.**

2 to operate
□ Er bedient die Druckmaschine. **He operates the printing press.**
■ **sich bedienen** to help oneself□ Bitte bedien dich! **Please help yourself.**

★**die Bedienung** FEM NOUN

1 service
□ In diesem Geschäft ist die Bedienung schlecht. **The service is very poor in this shop.**

2 waiter
waitress
□ Wir haben bei der Bedienung ein Bier bestellt. **We ordered a beer from the waitress.**

3 shop assistant
□ Die Bedienung im Kaufhaus war äußerst

b

Numbers in brackets refer to verb tables on pages 697 to 706.

37

unfreundlich. The shop assistant in the department store was extremely unfriendly.

4 service charge

□ Die Bedienung ist im Preis enthalten. The service charge is included in the price.

★ die **Bedingung** FEM NOUN
condition

□ unter der Bedingung, dass ... on condition that ...

bedrohen (PERFECT TENSE **hat bedroht**) VERB [7]
to threaten

das **Bedürfnis** (GEN des **Bedürfnisses** PL die **Bedürfnisse**) NEUT NOUN
need

★ das **Beefsteak** (PL die **Beefsteaks**) NEUT NOUN
steak

■ deutsches Beefsteak hamburger

★ sich **beeilen** (PERFECT TENSE **hat sich beeilt**) VERB [7]
to hurry

beeindrucken (PERFECT TENSE **hat beeindruckt**) VERB [7]
to impress

beeindruckend ADJECTIVE
impressive

beeinflussen (PRESENT TENSE **beeinflusst** IMPERFECT **beeinflusste** PERFECT TENSE **hat beeinflusst**) VERB [7]
to influence

★ **beenden** (PERFECT TENSE **hat beendet**) VERB [54]
to end

die **Beerdigung** FEM NOUN
funeral

die **Beere** FEM NOUN
1 berry
2 grape

★ der **Befehl** (PL die **Befehle**) MASC NOUN
command

befehlen (PRESENT TENSE **befiehlt**, IMPERFECT **befahl** PERFECT TENSE **hat befohlen**) VERB
1 to order

□ Der General hat den Rückzug befohlen. The general ordered his men to retreat.

2 to give orders

□ Du hast hier nicht zu befehlen! You're not the one who gives the orders here!

■ jemandem etwas befehlen to order somebody to do something

befestigen (PERFECT TENSE **hat befestigt**) VERB [7]
to fix

□ Die Regalbretter sind mit Schrauben an der Wand befestigt. The shelves are fixed to the wall with screws.

★ sich **befinden** (IMPERFECT **befand sich** PERFECT TENSE **hat sich befunden**) VERB [24]
to be

□ Er befindet sich zurzeit im Ausland. He's abroad at the moment.

befolgen (PERFECT TENSE **hat befolgt**) VERB [7]
to obey

befördern (PERFECT TENSE **hat befördert**) VERB [88]
1 to carry

□ Die städtischen Busse befördern täglich viele Menschen. The municipal buses carry many people every day.

2 to promote

□ Sie ist zur Abteilungsleiterin befördert worden. She's been promoted to head of department.

die **Beförderung** FEM NOUN
1 transport

□ Das Rote Kreuz übernimmt die Beförderung der Hilfsgüter. The Red Cross undertakes the transport of emergency supplies.

2 promotion

□ Bei einer Beförderung bekommt man auch mehr Geld. Promotion also means more money.

befragen (PERFECT TENSE **hat befragt**) VERB [7]
to question

befreien (PERFECT TENSE **hat befreit**) VERB [7]
1 to set free

□ Die Geiseln sind noch nicht befreit. The hostages haven't been set free yet.

2 to exempt

□ Sie ist vom Sportunterricht befreit. She's exempt from PE lessons.

befreundet ADJECTIVE
■ mit jemandem befreundet sein to be friends with somebody □ Ich bin mit Petra seit Jahren befreundet. I've been friends with Petra for years.

befriedigen (PERFECT TENSE **hat befriedigt**) VERB [7]
to satisfy

★ **befriedigend** ADJECTIVE
satisfactory

DID YOU KNOW...?
German grades range from one (sehr gut) to six (ungenügend).

befristet ADJECTIVE
limited

befürchten (PERFECT TENSE **hat befürchtet**) VERB [2]
to fear

befürworten (PERFECT TENSE **hat befürwortet**) VERB [2]
to support

begabt ADJECTIVE
talented

die **Begabung** FEM NOUN
talent

begann VERB ▷ see **beginnen**

★ **begegnen** (PERFECT TENSE **ist begegnet**) VERB
[53]

■ **jemandem begegnen** to meet somebody
□ Ich bin ihr heute schon einmal begegnet. I've met her once today already. □ Wir sind uns das erste Mal in London begegnet. The first time we met was in London. □ Eine solche Frechheit ist mir noch nie begegnet. I've never met such cheek.

die **Begegnung** FEM NOUN
meeting

begehen (IMPERFECT **beging**, PERFECT TENSE **hat begangen**) VERB [29]
to commit
□ Er hat einen Mord begangen. He committed a murder.

begehren (PERFECT TENSE **hat begehrt**) VERB
[7]
to desire

begehrt ADJECTIVE
1 in demand
2 eligible

begeistern (PERFECT TENSE **hat begeistert**)
VERB [88]
to thrill
□ Der Film hat mich begeistert. I was thrilled with the film.

■ **sich für etwas begeistern** to get enthusiastic about something

★ **begeistert** ADJECTIVE
enthusiastic

★ **begießen** (IMPERFECT **begoss**, PERFECT TENSE **hat begossen**) VERB
to water
□ Sie begoss ihre Rosen. She watered her roses.
■ **Das muss begossen werden!** That calls for a drink!

★ der **Beginn** MASC NOUN
beginning
□ zu Beginn at the beginning

★ **beginnen** (IMPERFECT **begann**, PERFECT TENSE **hat begonnen**) VERB [5]
to start

der **Begleitbrief** (PL die **Begleitbriefe**) MASC
NOUN
covering letter

★ **begleiten** (PERFECT TENSE **hat begleitet**) VERB
[2]
to accompany
□ Er hat mich zum Konzert begleitet. He accompanied me to the concert.

beglückwünschen (PERFECT TENSE **hat beglückwünscht**) VERB [7]
to congratulate

□ Alle meine Freunde haben mich zur bestandenen Prüfung beglückwünscht. All my friends congratulated me on passing the exam.

begonnen VERB ▷ see **beginnen**

begraben (PRESENT TENSE **begräbt**, IMPERFECT **begrub**, PERFECT TENSE **hat begraben**) VERB
to bury

begreifen (IMPERFECT **begriff**, PERFECT TENSE **hat begriffen**) VERB
to understand

der **Begriff** (PL die **Begriffe**) MASC NOUN
term
□ Das ist ein Begriff aus der Architektur. That is an architectural term.
■ **im Begriff sein, etwas zu tun** to be about to do something □ Ich war im Begriff zu gehen. I was about to go.
■ **schwer von Begriff** slow on the uptake
■ **sich einen Begriff von etwas machen** to imagine something □ Du machst dir keinen Begriff, wie schwierig das war. You can't imagine how difficult it was.

begründen (PERFECT TENSE **hat begründet**)
VERB [54]
to justify

die **Begründung** FEM NOUN
justification

★ **begrüßen** (PERFECT TENSE **hat begrüßt**) VERB
[31]
to welcome
□ Ich begrüße diese Änderung sehr. I very much welcome this change.
■ **herzlich begrüßt werden** to receive a warm welcome

die **Begrüßung** FEM NOUN
welcome

behaglich ADJECTIVE
cosy

behalten (PRESENT TENSE **behält**, IMPERFECT **behielt**, PERFECT TENSE **hat behalten**) VERB
[33]
1 to keep
□ Kann ich das Buch noch ein paar Tage behalten? Can I keep the book for another couple of days?
2 to remember
□ Ich kann ihren Namen nie behalten. I can never remember her name.

der **Behälter** (PL die **Behälter**) MASC NOUN
container

★ **behandeln** (PERFECT TENSE **hat behandelt**)
VERB [34]
1 to treat
□ Wir wurden sehr freundlich behandelt. We were treated in a very friendly manner. □ Die Wunde muss behandelt werden. The wound will have to be treated. □ Welcher Arzt behandelt Sie? Which doctor is treating you?

Behandlung – beilegen

2 to deal with
□ Der Film behandelt das Thema Jugendkriminalität. The film deals with the subject of juvenile delinquency.

★ **die Behandlung** FEM NOUN
treatment

behaupten (PERFECT TENSE **hat behauptet**) VERB [2]
to claim

beherrschen (PERFECT TENSE **hat beherrscht**) VERB [7]

1 to master
□ Ich beherrsche diese Technik noch nicht. I haven't mastered this technique yet.

2 to control
□ Er konnte seine Wut nicht mehr beherrschen. He couldn't control his anger any longer.
■ **sich beherrschen** to control oneself

★ **behilflich** ADJECTIVE
helpful
■ **jemandem bei etwas behilflich sein** to help somebody with something

behindern (PERFECT TENSE **hat behindert**) VERB [88]
to hinder

behindert ADJECTIVE
disabled

der/die Behinderte (GEN **des/der Behinderten**, PL **die Behinderten**) MASC/FEM NOUN
disabled person
■ **die Behinderten** people with disabilities

die Behinderung FEM NOUN

1 obstruction
□ Das Fahrzeug stellt eine Behinderung des Verkehrs dar. The vehicle is an obstruction to traffic.

2 handicap
□ Sie hat gelernt, mit ihrer Behinderung zu leben. She's learned to live with her handicap.

die Behörde FEM NOUN
authorities pl

★ **bei** PREPOSITION

> The preposition **bei** takes the dative.

1 near
□ Unser Haus ist beim Bahnhof. Our house is near the station. □ bei München near Munich

2 at
□ Felix ist zurzeit bei seiner Großmutter. Felix is at his grandmother's at the moment □ Wenn man bei fremden Leuten zu Besuch ist ... When you're at other people's houses ... □ beim Friseur at the hairdresser's □ bei Nacht at night □ bei uns at our place

3 with
□ bei seinen Eltern wohnen to live with one's parents □ Wenn du bei mir bist, habe ich keine Angst. When you're with me, I'm not afraid.

■ **Ich habe kein Geld bei mir.** I don't have any money on me.
■ **bei einer Firma arbeiten** to work for a firm
□ Sie arbeitet bei der Post. She works for the post office.
■ **beim Militär** in the army

4 on
□ bei meiner Ankunft on my arrival □ bei der Abreise on departure

5 during
□ beim Abendessen during dinner
■ **beim Fahren** while driving
■ **bei solcher Hitze** in such heat
■ **bei Nebel** in fog
■ **bei Regen** if it rains

beibringen (IMPERFECT **brachte bei**, PERFECT TENSE **hat beigebracht**) VERB [13]
■ **jemandem etwas beibringen** to teach somebody something □ Sie hat mir Schwimmen beigebracht. She taught me to swim.

★ **beide** ADJECTIVE, PRONOUN
> see also **beides** PRONOUN
both
□ Ich habe beide Bücher gelesen. I've read both books. □ Ich will beide. I want both of them.
□ jeder der beiden both of them □ Meine Eltern haben das beide verboten. Both my parents have forbidden it.
■ **meine beiden Brüder** both my brothers
■ **die ersten beiden** the first two
■ **wir beide** we two
■ **einer von beiden** one of the two

★ **beides** PRONOUN
> see also **beide** ADJECTIVE, PRONOUN
both
□ Ich möchte beides. I want both of them.
□ Beides ist schön. Both of them are lovely.
■ **alles beides** both of them

beieinander ADVERB
together

der Beifall MASC NOUN
applause
■ **Beifall spenden** to applaud

beige ADJECTIVE
beige

das Beil (PL **die Beile**) NEUT NOUN
axe

die Beilage FEM NOUN

1 supplement
□ eine Beilage zur Samstagszeitung a supplement in Saturday's paper

2 side dish

★ **beilegen** (PERFECT TENSE **hat beigelegt**) VERB [4]

1 to enclose
□ Ich lege einen Scheck bei. I enclose a cheque.

2 to settle
□ Der Streit war schnell beigelegt. The argument was quickly settled.

★ = core vocabulary

das **Beileid** NEUT NOUN
sympathy
□ Wir haben ihr unser Beileid ausgesprochen. We offered her our sympathy.
■ herzliches Beileid deepest sympathy

beiliegend ADVERB
enclosed

beim = bei dem

★das **Bein** (PL die Beine) NEUT NOUN
leg

beinahe ADVERB
almost

beisammen ADVERB
together

beiseite ADVERB
to one side
□ Sie schob ihren Teller beiseite. She pushed her plate to one side.

beiseitelassen (PRESENT TENSE lässt beiseite, IMPERFECT ließ beiseite, PERFECT TENSE hat beiseitegelassen) VERB [42]
to leave
□ Diese Frage sollten wir im Moment beiseitelassen. We should leave this question for the moment.

beiseitelegen VERB [4]
to put by
□ Ich habe ein paar Hundert Euro beiseitegelegt. I've got a few hundred euros put by.

beiseiteschaffen VERB [4]
to put by
□ Er hat sehr viel Geld beiseitegeschafft. He's put a lot of money by.

★das **Beispiel** (PL die Beispiele) NEUT NOUN
example
■ sich an jemandem ein Beispiel nehmen to take a leaf out of somebody's book □ Du solltest dir an deinem Bruder ein Beispiel nehmen. You should take a leaf out of your brother's book.
■ zum Beispiel for example

beispielsweise ADVERB
for example

★**beißen** (IMPERFECT biss, PERFECT TENSE hat gebissen) VERB [6]
1 to bite
□ Mein Hund beißt nicht. My dog doesn't bite.
□ Sie biss in den Apfel. She bit into the apple.
2 to burn
□ Der Rauch beißt mich in den Augen. The smoke's burning my eyes.
■ sich beißen to clash □ Rosa beißt sich mit Orange. Pink clashes with orange.

der **Beitrag** (PL die Beiträge) MASC NOUN
1 contribution
□ einen Beitrag zu etwas leisten to make a contribution to something

■ Beiträge für die Zeitung articles for the newspaper
2 membership fee
□ Der Beitrag für den Klub wird am Monatsanfang fällig. Membership fees for the club are due at the beginning of the month.
3 premium
□ die Beiträge zur Krankenversicherung the health insurance premiums

beitragen (PRESENT TENSE trägt bei, IMPERFECT trug bei, PERFECT TENSE hat beigetragen) VERB [77]
■ zu etwas beitragen to contribute to something □ Er trägt selten etwas zum Unterricht bei. He seldom contributes anything to the lesson.

bekämpfen (PERFECT TENSE hat bekämpft) VERB [7]
to fight
□ ein Feuer bekämpfen to fight a fire
■ sich bekämpfen to fight □ Diese beiden Parteien bekämpfen sich seit Jahren. These two parties have been fighting for years.

★**bekannt** ADJECTIVE
1 well-known
□ Sie ist eine bekannte Schauspielerin. She's a well-known actress.
2 familiar
□ Bekannte Wörter brauche ich nicht nachzuschlagen. I don't have to look up familiar words. □ Sie kommt mir bekannt vor. She seems familiar. □ Das kommt mir bekannt vor. That sounds familiar.
■ mit jemandem bekannt sein to know somebody □ Wir sind seit Jahren mit den Bauers bekannt. We've known the Bauers for years.
■ für etwas bekannt sein to be known for something □ Sie ist für ihren Witz bekannt. She's known for her humour.
■ Das ist mir bekannt. I know that.
■ etwas bekannt geben to announce something publicly
■ etwas bekannt machen to announce something

★der/die **Bekannte** (GEN des/der Bekannten, PL die Bekannten) MASC/FEM NOUN
acquaintance
□ Sie hat viele Bekannte, aber wenig Freunde. She has a lot of acquaintances but few friends.

bekanntgeben VERB [28] ▷ see bekannt

bekanntlich ADVERB
as you know
□ Rauchen macht bekanntlich süchtig. As you know, smoking is addictive.

bekanntmachen VERB [48] ▷ see bekannt

★sich **beklagen** (PERFECT TENSE hat sich beklagt) VERB [7]

Bekleidung – Bemerkung

to complain

□ Die Schüler haben sich darüber beklagt, dass sie Hausaufgaben aufbekommen haben. The pupils complained about being given homework.

die **Bekleidung** FEM NOUN
clothing

★ **bekommen** (IMPERFECT **bekam**, PERFECT TENSE **hat bekommen**) VERB [40]

1 to get

□ Was hast du zum Geburtstag bekommen? What did you get for your birthday? □ Sie hat in Englisch eine schlechte Note bekommen. She got bad marks in English. □ Wir haben nichts zu essen bekommen. We didn't get anything to eat.

■ **Hunger bekommen** to feel hungry
■ **Durst bekommen** to feel thirsty
■ **Angst bekommen** to become afraid
■ **ein Kind bekommen** to have a baby
□ Unsere Deutschlehrerin bekommt ein Kind. Our German teacher's having a baby.

2 to catch

□ Ich habe den letzten Bus gerade noch bekommen. I just caught the last bus.

■ **Das fette Essen ist ihm nicht bekommen**. The fatty food didn't agree with him.

■ **Was bekommen Sie?** What would you like?
■ **Bekommen Sie schon?** Are you being served?

■ **Was bekommen Sie dafür?** How much do I owe you?

BE CAREFUL!
bekommen does not mean **to become**.

belasten (PERFECT TENSE **hat belastet**) VERB [2]

1 to burden

□ Ich möchte dich nicht mit meinen Problemen belasten. I don't want to burden you with my problems.

2 to load

□ Der Aufzug darf mit maximal zehn Personen belastet werden. The lift's maximum load is ten people.

3 to pollute

□ Unsere Umwelt ist mit zu vielen Schadstoffen belastet. The environment is polluted by too many harmful substances.

4 to debit

□ Wir werden Ihr Konto mit diesem Betrag belasten. We will debit this amount from your account.

5 to incriminate

□ Die Zeugin hat den Angeklagten belastet. The witness incriminated the accused.

belästigen (PERFECT TENSE **hat belästigt**) VERB [7]

to pester

■ **jemanden sexuell belästigen** to sexually harass somebody

★ **belegt** ADJECTIVE

■ **ein belegtes Brot** an open sandwich
■ **belegt sein** to be engaged □ Die Nummer ist belegt. The number's engaged.

beleidigen (PERFECT TENSE **hat beleidigt**) VERB [7]

to insult

die **Beleidigung** FEM NOUN
insult

★ **Belgien** NEUT NOUN
Belgium

■ **aus Belgien** from Belgium
■ **in Belgien** in Belgium
■ **nach Belgien** to Belgium

★ der **Belgier** (PL die **Belgier**) MASC NOUN
Belgian

★ die **Belgierin** FEM NOUN
Belgian

★ **belgisch** ADJECTIVE
Belgian

beliebig ADJECTIVE, ADVERB

1 any you like

□ in beliebiger Reihenfolge in any order you like □ eine beliebige Anzahl any number you like

2 as you like

□ beliebig oft as often as you like □ beliebig viel as much as you like □ beliebig viele as many as you like

★ **beliebt** ADJECTIVE
popular

□ sich bei jemandem beliebt machen to make oneself popular with somebody

die **Beliebtheit** FEM NOUN
popularity

bellen VERB [38]
to bark

belohnen (PERFECT TENSE **hat belohnt**) VERB [7]
to reward

die **Belohnung** FEM NOUN
reward

□ zur Belohnung as a reward

belügen (IMPERFECT **belog**, PERFECT TENSE **hat belogen**) VERB [47]
to lie to

belustigen (PERFECT TENSE **hat belustigt**) VERB [7]
to amuse

★ **bemerken** (PERFECT TENSE **hat bemerkt**) VERB [7]
to notice

□ Ich habe keine Änderung bemerkt. I haven't noticed any change.

die **Bemerkung** FEM NOUN
remark

bemitleiden (PERFECT TENSE **hat bemitleidet**) VERB [7]
to pity

sich **bemühen** (PERFECT TENSE **hat sich bemüht**) VERB [7]
to make an effort
□ Er hat sich bemüht, höflich zu bleiben. He made an effort to remain polite.
■ **Bemühen Sie sich nicht.** Don't trouble yourself.
■ **sich um eine neue Arbeit bemühen** to try and find a new job
■ **Ich werde mich bemühen!** I'll do my best!

benachrichtigen (PERFECT TENSE **hat benachrichtigt**) VERB [7]
to inform

die **Benachrichtigung** FEM NOUN
notification

benachteiligt ADJECTIVE
disadvantaged

★ sich **benehmen** (PRESENT TENSE **benimmt sich**, IMPERFECT **benahm sich**, PERFECT TENSE **hat sich benommen**) VERB [52]
▷ see also das **Benehmen** NOUN
to behave
□ sich anständig benehmen to behave properly
□ Sie haben sich furchtbar benommen. They behaved terribly. □ Benimm dich! Behave yourself!

das **Benehmen** NEUT NOUN
▷ see also **benehmen** VERB
behaviour

beneiden (PERFECT TENSE **hat beneidet**) VERB [54]
to envy
□ Er ist nicht zu beneiden. I don't envy him.
■ **jemanden um etwas beneiden** to envy somebody something □ Ich beneide dich um deine schöne Wohnung. I envy you your lovely flat.

beneidenswert ADJECTIVE, ADVERB
enviable
■ **Sie ist beneidenswert reich.** She's enviably rich.

benoten (PERFECT TENSE **hat benotet**) VERB [2]
to mark

★ **benutzen** (PERFECT TENSE **hat benutzt**) VERB [36]
to use

der **Benutzer** (PL die **Benutzer**) MASC NOUN
user

benutzerfreundlich ADJECTIVE
user-friendly

die **Benutzerin** FEM NOUN
user

der **Benutzername** (GEN des **Benutzernamens**, PL die **Benutzernamen**) MASC NOUN
username
□ Was ist dein Benutzername? What's your username?

die **Benutzung** FEM NOUN
use

★ das **Benzin** NEUT NOUN
petrol

★ **beobachten** (PERFECT TENSE **hat beobachtet**) VERB [2]
to observe

★ **bequem** ADJECTIVE
1 comfortable
□ ein bequemer Stuhl a comfortable chair
■ **eine bequeme Ausrede** a convenient excuse
2 lazy
□ Er ist zu bequem, sich selbst etwas zu kochen. He's too lazy to cook himself something.

beraten (PRESENT TENSE **berät**, IMPERFECT **beriet**, PERFECT TENSE **hat beraten**) VERB
1 to give advice
□ Der Mann vom Arbeitsamt hat mich gut beraten. The man at the job centre gave me good advice.
■ **Lassen Sie sich von Ihrem Arzt beraten.** Consult your doctor.
2 to discuss
□ Wir müssen das weitere Vorgehen beraten. We have to discuss further action.
■ **gut beraten sein** to be well advised
■ **schlecht beraten sein** to be ill advised

berauben (PERFECT TENSE **hat beraubt**) VERB [7]
to rob

berechnen (PERFECT TENSE **hat berechnet**) VERB [53]
to charge
□ Was berechnen Sie für eine Beratung? What do you charge for a consultation?

bereit ADJECTIVE
ready
□ Wir sind bereit abzufahren. We're ready to leave. □ Das Essen ist bereit. Dinner's ready.
■ **bereit sein, etwas zu tun** to be prepared to do something □ Ich bin nicht bereit, noch länger zu warten. I'm not prepared to wait any longer.
■ **etwas bereit haben** to have something ready □ Sie hat immer eine Ausrede bereit. She always has an excuse ready.

★ **bereiten** (PERFECT TENSE **hat bereitet**) VERB [2]
to cause
□ Das hat mir einige Schwierigkeiten bereitet. That caused me some problems.
■ **Die Kinder bereiten mir sehr viel Freude.** The children give me a great deal of pleasure.

bereits ADVERB
already

Numbers in brackets refer to verb tables on pages 697 to 706.

43

bereuen – beschäftigen

bereuen (PERFECT TENSE **hat bereut**) VERB [7]
to regret

★ **der Berg** (PL die **Berge**) MASC NOUN
1 mountain
□ Im Winter fahren wir in die Berge zum Skifahren. **In winter we go skiing in the mountains.**
2 hill
□ Hinter unserem Haus ist ein kleiner Berg. **There's a small hill behind our house.**

der Bergbau MASC NOUN
mining

das Bergsteigen NEUT NOUN
mountaineering
□ Bergsteigen ist ihr Hobby. **Her hobby's mountaineering.** □ Sie ist beim Bergsteigen verunglückt. **She had a mountaineering accident.**

der Bergsteiger (PL die **Bergsteiger**) MASC NOUN
mountaineer

die Bergwacht FEM NOUN
mountain rescue service

das Bergwerk (PL die **Bergwerke**) NEUT NOUN
mine

der Bericht (PL die **Berichte**) MASC NOUN
report

berichten (PERFECT TENSE **hat berichtet**) VERB [2]
to report
□ Die Zeitungen haben nichts über diesen Zwischenfall berichtet. **The newspapers didn't report anything about this incident.**

Berlin NEUT NOUN
Berlin

DID YOU KNOW...?
Berlin is one of the 16 **Länder**. It is a 'city-state' like Bremen and Hamburg. From 1963 to 1989 it was divided by the Berlin Wall. After Germany was reunified, it became the capital city again.

berücksichtigen (PERFECT TENSE **hat berücksichtigt**) VERB [7]
to bear in mind

★ **der Beruf** (PL die **Berufe**) MASC NOUN
occupation
□ Welchen Beruf hat dein Vater? **What's your father's occupation?**
■ **Sie ist Lehrerin von Beruf. She's a teacher by profession.**

★ **beruflich** ADJECTIVE
professional
■ **beruflich unterwegs sein to be away on business**

★ **der Berufsberater** (PL die **Berufsberater**) MASC NOUN
careers adviser

★ **die Berufsberaterin** FEM NOUN
careers adviser

★ **die Berufsschule** FEM NOUN
technical college

★ **berufstätig** ADJECTIVE
working
□ Seit wann ist deine Mutter wieder berufstätig? **When did your mother start working again?**

der Berufsverkehr MASC NOUN
rush-hour traffic

beruhigen (PERFECT TENSE **hat beruhigt**) VERB [18]
to calm down
□ Dem Lehrer gelang es nicht, die Klasse zu beruhigen. **The teacher didn't manage to calm the class down.** □ Beruhige dich doch! **Calm down!**
■ **sich beruhigen to calm down** □ Die Lage hat sich beruhigt. **Things have calmed down.**

das Beruhigungsmittel (PL die **Beruhigungsmittel**) NEUT NOUN
tranquillizer

★ **berühmt** ADJECTIVE
famous

★ **berühren** (PERFECT TENSE **hat berührt**) VERB [18]
1 to touch
□ Er berührte meinen Arm. **He touched my arm.**
2 to affect
□ Die Armut der Menschen hat mich sehr berührt. **The poverty of the people affected me deeply.**
3 to touch on
□ Ich kann diese Frage heute nur berühren. **I can only touch on this question today.**
■ **sich berühren to touch** □ Die beiden Drähte berührten sich. **The two wires touched.**

die Berührung FEM NOUN
contact
□ mit etwas in Berührung kommen **to come into contact with something**

★ **beschädigen** (PERFECT TENSE **hat beschädigt**) VERB [7]
to damage

beschaffen (PERFECT TENSE **hat beschafft**) VERB [7]
to get
□ Ich muss mir ein Visum beschaffen. **I have to get a visa.** □ Können Sie mir nicht einen Job beschaffen? **Can't you get me a job?**

beschäftigen (PERFECT TENSE **hat beschäftigt**) VERB [18]
1 to occupy
□ Kannst du nicht irgendwie die Kinder beschäftigen? **Can't you occupy the children somehow?** □ Diese Frage beschäftigt mich seit Langem. **This question has been occupying me for a long time.**

b

2 to employ
□ Unsere Firma beschäftigt zweihundert Leute. Our company employs two hundred people.
■ **sich beschäftigen** to occupy oneself □ Sebastian hat Mühe, sich allein zu beschäftigen. **Sebastian has difficulty occupying himself.**
■ **sich beschäftigen mit** to deal with □ Der Artikel beschäftigt sich mit Jugendarbeitslosigkeit. **The article deals with youth unemployment.**

★ **beschäftigt** ADJECTIVE
busy

die **Beschäftigung** FEM NOUN
work
□ Er sucht eine Beschäftigung. **He's looking for work.**
■ **Sie ist zurzeit ohne Beschäftigung.** She is unemployed at the moment.

★ der **Bescheid** (PL die **Bescheide**) MASC NOUN
information no pl
□ Ich warte auf den Bescheid des Konsulats. **I'm waiting for information from the consulate.**
■ **Bescheid wissen** to know □ Weiß deine Mutter Bescheid, dass du hier bist? **Does your mother know that you're here?** □ Ich weiß Bescheid. **I know.**
■ **über etwas Bescheid wissen** to know a lot about something □ Sie weiß über Grammatik gut Bescheid. **She knows a lot about grammar.**
■ **jemandem Bescheid sagen** to let somebody know

bescheiden ADJECTIVE
modest

die **Bescheinigung** FEM NOUN
certificate
□ Du brauchst eine Bescheinigung über die Teilnahme am Kurs. **You need a certificate showing that you attended the course.** □ eine Bescheinigung des Arztes **a doctor's certificate**

★ die **Bescherung** FEM NOUN
giving out of Christmas presents
■ **Da haben wir die Bescherung!** What did I tell you!

beschimpfen (PERFECT TENSE hat **beschimpft**) VERB [18]
to swear at

beschleunigen (PERFECT TENSE hat **beschleunigt**) VERB [7]
1 to increase
□ Wir müssen das Arbeitstempo beschleunigen. **We have to increase our work rate.**
2 to accelerate
□ Das Auto vor mir beschleunigte. **The car in front of me accelerated.**

★ **beschließen** (IMPERFECT **beschloss**, PERFECT TENSE hat **beschlossen**) VERB
to decide

□ Wir haben beschlossen, nach Spanien zu fahren. **We decided to go to Spain.**

der **Beschluss** (GEN des **Beschlusses**, PL die **Beschlüsse**) MASC NOUN
decision

beschränken (PERFECT TENSE hat **beschränkt**) VERB [18]
to limit
□ Wir müssen unsere Ausgaben beschränken. **We have to limit our spending.**
■ **sich auf etwas beschränken** to restrict oneself to something □ Ich werde mich auf ein paar Worte beschränken. **I'll restrict myself to a few words.**

beschränkt ADJECTIVE
1 limited
□ Diese Regel hat nur beschränkte Gültigkeit. **This regulation only has limited validity.**
2 stupid
□ Wie kann man nur so beschränkt sein? **How can anyone be so stupid?**

★ **beschreiben** (IMPERFECT **beschrieb**, PERFECT TENSE hat **beschrieben**) VERB [61]
to describe
□ Können Sie den Täter beschreiben? **Can you describe the culprit?**

★ die **Beschreibung** FEM NOUN
description

beschützen (PERFECT TENSE hat **beschützt**) VERB [7]
to protect
□ Ich möchte euch vor diesen Gefahren beschützen. **I want to protect you from these dangers.**

die **Beschwerde** FEM NOUN
complaint
□ Wenn Sie eine Beschwerde haben, dann wenden Sie sich an den Geschäftsführer. **If you have a complaint, then please contact the manager.**
■ **Beschwerden** trouble □ Mein Knie macht mir immer noch Beschwerden. **My knee's still giving me trouble.**

★ sich **beschweren** (PERFECT TENSE hat sich **beschwert**) VERB [18]
to complain
□ Deine Lehrerin hat sich über dich beschwert. **Your teacher has complained about you.**

beseitigen (PERFECT TENSE hat **beseitigt**) VERB [7]
to remove

der **Besen** (PL die **Besen**) MASC NOUN
broom

besetzen (PERFECT TENSE hat **besetzt**) VERB [7]
1 to occupy
□ Napoleons Truppen haben weite Teile Deutschlands besetzt. **Napoleon's troops occupied large areas of Germany.**

b

2 to fill

□ Der Posten soll mit einer Frau besetzt werden. **The position is to be filled by a woman.** □ Die Stelle ist noch nicht besetzt. **The position hasn't been filled yet.**

★ **besetzt** ADJECTIVE

1 full

□ Der Zug war voll besetzt. **The train was full.**

2 engaged

□ Es ist besetzt. **It's engaged.**

3 taken

□ Ist der Platz hier besetzt? **Is this seat taken?**

★ **besichtigen** (PERFECT TENSE **hat besichtigt**) VERB [18]

to visit

★ die **Besichtigung** FEM NOUN

visit

besitzen (IMPERFECT **besaß**, PERFECT TENSE **hat besessen**) VERB [68]

1 to own

□ Sie besitzen ein Haus am Meer. **They own a house by the seaside.**

2 to have

□ Sie besitzt das Talent, sich mit allen zu zerstreiten. **She has the talent of quarrelling with everyone.**

★ der **Besitzer** (PL die **Besitzer**) MASC NOUN

owner

besondere ADJECTIVE

special

□ Das sind besondere Umstände. **Those are special circumstances.**

■ keine besonderen Kennzeichen no distinguishing features

die **Besonderheit** FEM NOUN

peculiarity

★ **besonders** ADVERB

particularly

□ Es hat mir nicht besonders gefallen. **I didn't particularly like it.**

★ **besorgen** (PERFECT TENSE **hat besorgt**) VERB [18]

to get

□ Kannst du mir nicht einen Ferienjob besorgen? **Can't you get me a holiday job?** □ Soll ich dir ein Taxi besorgen? **Shall I get you a taxi?** □ Ich muss Milch und Eier besorgen. **I'll have to get milk and eggs.**

besorgt ADJECTIVE

worried

□ Sie ist sehr besorgt um dich. **She's very worried about you.**

★ **besprechen** (PRESENT TENSE **bespricht**, IMPERFECT **besprach**, PERFECT TENSE **hat besprochen**) VERB [70]

to discuss

□ Das muss ich mit deiner Mutter besprechen. **I'll have to discuss it with your mother.**

die **Besprechung** FEM NOUN

1 meeting

□ Frau Airlie ist in einer Besprechung. **Ms Airlie is in a meeting.**

2 review

□ Hast du die Besprechung dieses Films gelesen? **Have you read the review of this film?**

★ **besser** ADJECTIVE, ADVERB

better

□ eine bessere Note a better mark □ Du gehst jetzt besser nach Hause. **You'd better go home now.**

■ Es geht ihm besser. **He's feeling better.**

■ je schneller, desto besser the quicker the better

★ sich **bessern** VERB [88]

to improve

□ Das Wetter hat sich gebessert. **The weather's improved.**

★ die **Besserung** FEM NOUN

improvement

■ Gute Besserung! Get well soon!

der **Bestandteil** (PL die **Bestandteile**) MASC NOUN

1 component

□ Hier werden die einzelnen Bestandteile der Maschine zusammengesetzt. **The individual components of the machine are assembled here.**

2 ingredient

□ Die Bestandteile sind in Gramm angegeben. **The ingredients are given in grams.**

■ sich in seine Bestandteile auflösen to fall to pieces

★ **bestätigen** (PERFECT TENSE **hat bestätigt**) VERB [18]

1 to confirm

□ Ich kann bestätigen, dass sie die Wahrheit gesagt hat. **I can confirm that she told the truth.**

2 to acknowledge

□ Hiermit bestätigen wir den Erhalt Ihres Briefes. **We hereby acknowledge receipt of your letter.**

■ sich bestätigen to prove to be true □ Mein Verdacht hat sich bestätigt. **My suspicion proved to be true.**

beste ADJECTIVE

best

□ Sie ist die beste Schülerin der Klasse. **She's the best pupil in the class.** □ So ist es am besten. **It's best that way.**

■ Am besten gehst du gleich. **You'd better go at once.**

■ jemanden zum Besten haben to pull somebody's leg

■ einen Witz zum Besten geben to tell a joke

■ Es ist nur zu deinem Besten. **It's for your own good.**

■ **Ich habe mein Bestes getan.** I did my best.

bestechen (PRESENT TENSE **besticht**, IMPERFECT **bestach**, PERFECT TENSE **hat bestochen**) VERB
to bribe

die **Bestechung** FEM NOUN
bribery *no pl*

★ das **Besteck** (PL die **Bestecke**) NEUT NOUN
cutlery *no pl*

★ **bestehen** (IMPERFECT **bestand**, PERFECT TENSE **hat bestanden**) VERB [72]
1 to be
 □ Es besteht die Möglichkeit, einen Sprachkurs zu belegen. There's the chance of registering for a language course. □ Es besteht keine Hoffnung mehr, sie jemals wiederzusehen. There's no more hope of ever seeing her again.
2 to exist
 □ Die Firma besteht seit hundert Jahren. The firm has existed for a hundred years.
 ■ **etwas bestehen** to pass something □ Ich hoffe, dass ich die Prüfung bestehe. I hope I pass the exam.
 ■ **auf etwas bestehen** to insist on something □ Wir bestehen auf sofortiger Bezahlung. We insist on immediate payment.
 ■ **bestehen aus** to consist of □ Eine Fußballmannschaft besteht aus elf Spielern. A football team consists of eleven players.

bestehlen (PRESENT TENSE **bestiehlt**, IMPERFECT **bestahl**, PERFECT TENSE **hat bestohlen**) VERB [73]
 ■ **jemanden bestehlen** to rob somebody

★ **bestellen** (PERFECT TENSE **hat bestellt**) VERB [7]
1 to order
 □ Ich habe über das Internet ein Kleid bestellt. I've ordered a dress online. □ Haben Sie schon bestellt? Have you ordered yet? □ Wir sollten ein Taxi bestellen. We should order a taxi.
2 to reserve
 □ Ich habe einen Tisch beim Chinesen bestellt. I've reserved a table at the Chinese restaurant.
3 to send for
 □ Der Direktor hat mich zu sich bestellt. The headmaster sent for me.
 ■ **Bestell deiner Mutter schöne Grüße.** Give my regards to your mother.
 ■ **Soll ich ihr etwas von dir bestellen?** Shall I give her a message from you?

die **Bestellung** FEM NOUN
order
 ■ **auf Bestellung** to order

bestenfalls ADVERB
at best

bestens ADVERB
very well
 □ Die Geschäfte gehen bestens. Business is going very well.

bestimmen (PERFECT TENSE **hat bestimmt**) VERB [7]
to decide
 □ Du kannst bestimmen, wer mitkommen soll. You can decide who's coming. □ Wer bestimmt hier, was gemacht werden muss? Who decides what has to be done?
 ■ **Du hast hier nichts zu bestimmen!** You're not the one who decides here!
 ■ **für jemanden bestimmt sein** to be meant for somebody □ Diese Bemerkung war für mich bestimmt. This comment was meant for me.
 ■ **für etwas bestimmt sein** to be intended for something □ Dieses Geld ist für die Anschaffung von Computern bestimmt. This money's intended for the purchase of computers.

★ **bestimmt** ADJECTIVE, ADVERB
1 certain
 □ Wir treffen uns immer zu einer bestimmten Zeit. We always meet at a certain time. □ Die Teilnehmer sollten eine bestimmte Anzahl nicht überschreiten. The participants shouldn't exceed a certain number.
2 particular
 □ Ich suche ein ganz bestimmtes Buch. I'm looking for a particular book.
 ■ **Suchen Sie etwas Bestimmtes?** Are you looking for something in particular?
 ■ **der bestimmte Artikel** the definite article
 ■ **Ich habe ihn bestimmt gesehen.** I'm sure I've seen him.
 ■ **Das hat er bestimmt nicht so gemeint.** I'm sure that's not how he meant it.
 ■ **Das hat sie bestimmt vergessen.** She's bound to have forgotten.

★ **bestrafen** (PERFECT TENSE **hat bestraft**) VERB [7]
to punish

★ der **Besuch** (PL die **Besuche**) MASC NOUN
1 visit
 □ Deutschland bereitet sich auf den Besuch der Königin vor. Germany's preparing for the Queen's visit. □ bei unserem Besuch in London during our visit to London
 ■ **Der Schulbesuch ist Pflicht.** School attendance is compulsory.
2 visitor
 □ Ist euer Besuch noch da? Is your visitor still there? □ Besuch haben to have visitors
 ■ **bei jemandem einen Besuch machen** to pay somebody a visit
 ■ **bei jemandem zu Besuch sein** to be visiting somebody
 ■ **zu Besuch kommen** to be visiting
 □ Nächste Woche kommt Onja zu Besuch. Onja's visiting us next week.

Numbers in brackets refer to verb tables on pages 697 to 706.

47

b

besuchen – betrunken

★ **besuchen** (PERFECT TENSE **hat besucht**) VERB [7]

1 to visit
  □ Hast du schon das Planetarium besucht? Have you visited the planetarium yet?
  ■ **Besuch uns mal wieder!** Come again!

2 to attend
  □ Sie besucht das Gymnasium. She attends grammar school. □ Der Vortrag war sehr gut besucht. The lecture was very well attended.
  ■ **Wir haben ein Konzert besucht.** We went to a concert.

der **Besucher** (PL die **Besucher**) MASC NOUN
  visitor

die **Besucherin** FEM NOUN
  visitor

betätigen (PERFECT TENSE **hat betätigt**) VERB [7]
  ■ **die Hupe betätigen** to sound the horn
  ■ **einen Schalter betätigen** to press a switch
  ■ **die Bremse betätigen** to apply the brakes
  ■ **Du solltest dich sportlich betätigen.** You should do some sport.

die **Bete** FEM NOUN
  ■ **Rote Bete** beetroot

beteiligen (PERFECT TENSE **hat beteiligt**) VERB [7]
  ■ **sich an etwas beteiligen** to take part in something □ Ines beteiligte sich nicht an der Diskussion. Ines didn't take part in the discussion.
  ■ **Alle werden am Gewinn beteiligt.** Everyone will share in the winnings.

beten VERB [2]
  to pray

der **Beton** (PL die **Betons**) MASC NOUN
  concrete

betonen (PERFECT TENSE **hat betont**) VERB [7]
  to stress

die **Betonung** FEM NOUN
  stress
  □ Wo liegt die Betonung bei diesem Wort? Where's the stress in this word?

beträchtlich ADJECTIVE, ADVERB

1 considerable
  □ eine beträchtliche Summe a considerable amount

2 considerably
  □ Es hat beträchtlich länger gedauert. It took considerably longer.

der **Betrag** (PL die **Beträge**) MASC NOUN
  amount

betragen (PRESENT TENSE **beträgt**, IMPERFECT **betrug**, PERFECT TENSE **hat betragen**) VERB [77]
  ▷ *see also* das **Betragen** NOUN
  to come to
  □ Die Reparatur betrug dreihundert Euro. The repair came to three hundred euros.
  ■ **sich betragen** to behave □ Ich hoffe, die

Kinder haben sich ordentlich betragen. I hope the children behaved well.

★ das **Betragen** NEUT NOUN
  ▷ *see also* **betragen** VERB
  behaviour
  □ Ich werde mich über dein schlechtes Betragen beschweren. I'm going to complain about your bad behaviour.

betreffen (PRESENT TENSE **betrifft**, IMPERFECT **betraf**, PERFECT TENSE **hat betroffen**) VERB [78]
  to concern
  ■ **was mich betrifft** as far as I'm concerned

★ **betreten** (PRESENT TENSE **betritt**, IMPERFECT **betrat**, PERFECT TENSE **hat betreten**) VERB [79]
  to enter
  □ Sie klopfte, bevor sie das Zimmer betrat. She knocked before entering the room.
  ■ **'Betreten verboten'** 'Keep out'

★ der **Betrieb** (PL die **Betriebe**) MASC NOUN

1 firm
  □ Unser Betrieb beschäftigt dreihundert Menschen. Our firm employs three hundred people.

2 operation
  □ Die Maschine ist jetzt in Betrieb. The machine is now in operation.
  ■ **In der Stadt war heute viel Betrieb.** It was really busy in town today.
  ■ **außer Betrieb sein** to be out of order □ Der Fahrstuhl ist außer Betrieb. The lift's out of order.

das **Betriebssystem** (PL die **Betriebssysteme**) NEUT NOUN
  operating system

sich **betrinken** (IMPERFECT **betrank sich**, PERFECT TENSE **hat sich betrunken**) VERB [80]
  to get drunk

betroffen ADJECTIVE

1 full of concern
  □ Sie machte ein betroffenes Gesicht. Her face was full of concern.

2 affected
  ■ **von etwas betroffen sein** to be affected by something □ Wir sind über diese Nachricht zutiefst betroffen. We are deeply affected by the news.

betrügen (IMPERFECT **betrog**, PERFECT TENSE **hat betrogen**) VERB

1 to cheat
  □ Der Händler hat dich betrogen. The dealer's cheated you.

2 to defraud
  □ Er hat die Firma um Millionen betrogen. He defrauded the company of millions.

3 to be unfaithful to
  □ Hast du deine Freundin schon mal betrogen? Have you ever been unfaithful to your girlfriend?

★ **betrunken** ADJECTIVE
  drunk

★ = core vocabulary

★das **Bett** (PL die **Betten**) NEUT NOUN
bed
□ ins Bett gehen **to go to bed** □ das Bett machen **to make the bed**

★die **Bettdecke** FEM NOUN
blanket

betteln VERB [34]
to beg

das **Bettlaken** (PL die **Bettlaken**) NEUT NOUN
sheet

der **Bettler** (PL die **Bettler**) MASC NOUN
beggar

die **Bettlerin** FEM NOUN
beggar

★das **Betttuch** (PL die **Betttücher**) NEUT NOUN
sheet

★die **Bettwäsche** FEM NOUN
bed linen

★das **Bettzeug** NEUT NOUN
bedding

beugen VERB [38]
to bend
□ Ich kann den Arm nicht beugen. **I can't bend my arm.**
■ **sich beugen** to bow □ Ich beuge mich der Mehrheit. **I bow to the majority.**

die **Beule** FEM NOUN
1 bump
□ eine Beule am Kopf **a bump on the head**
2 dent
□ Das Auto hat eine Beule. **The car has a dent in it.**

beunruhigen (PERFECT TENSE **hat beunruhigt**) VERB [7]
to alarm

beurteilen (PERFECT TENSE **hat beurteilt**) VERB [7]
to judge
□ Ich beurteile die Leute nicht nach ihrem Aussehen. **I don't judge people on their appearance.**

der **Beutel** (PL die **Beutel**) MASC NOUN
1 bag
□ Mehrere Länder haben Plastikbeutel verboten. **Several countries have banned plastic bags.**
2 purse
□ Er nahm zehn Euro aus dem Beutel. **He took ten euros from the purse.**

die **Bevölkerung** FEM NOUN
population

★**bevor** CONJUNCTION
before
□ Sie war gegangen, bevor ich es ihr sagen konnte. **She left before I could tell her.**

bevorstehen (IMPERFECT TENSE **stand bevor**, PERFECT TENSE **hat bevorgestanden**) VERB [72]

to be imminent
□ Die Prüfung steht bevor. **The exam's imminent.**
■ **jemandem bevorstehen** to be in store for somebody □ Da steht uns ja einiger Ärger bevor. **There's trouble in store for us.**

★**bevorzugen** (PERFECT TENSE **hat bevorzugt**) VERB [7]
to prefer

sich **bewähren** (PERFECT TENSE **hat sich bewährt**) VERB [7]
to prove oneself
□ Er hat sich als mein Freund bewährt. **He proved himself to be my friend.** □ Diese Methode hat sich bewährt. **This method has proved itself.**

bewährt ADJECTIVE
tried and tested
□ Das ist eine bewährte Methode. **That's a tried and tested method.**
■ **Sie ist eine bewährte Mitarbeiterin. She's a reliable colleague.**

★**bewegen** (PERFECT TENSE **hat bewegt**) VERB [7]
to move
■ **sich bewegen** to move
■ **jemanden zu etwas bewegen** to persuade somebody to do something

beweglich ADJECTIVE
1 movable
□ Die Puppe hat bewegliche Beine. **The doll has movable legs.**
2 agile
□ Sie ist trotz ihres Alters noch sehr beweglich. **She's still very agile despite her age.**

bewegt ADJECTIVE
1 eventful
□ Sie hatte ein bewegtes Leben. **She had an eventful life.**
2 touched
□ Wir waren von seinen Worten sehr bewegt. **We were very touched by his words.**

die **Bewegung** FEM NOUN
1 movement
□ Mir fällt jede Bewegung schwer. **Every movement is difficult for me.**
2 motion
□ Sie setzte das Fahrzeug in Bewegung. **She set the vehicle in motion.**
3 exercise
□ Du brauchst mehr Bewegung. **You need more exercise.**

der **Beweis** (PL die **Beweise**) MASC NOUN
1 proof
□ Die Polizei hat keine Beweise. **The police don't have any proof.**

b

2 sign
□ als Beweis meiner Freundschaft as a sign of my friendship

beweisen (IMPERFECT **bewies**, PERFECT TENSE **hat bewiesen**) VERB

1 to prove
□ Ich kann nicht beweisen, dass sie das gesagt hat. I can't prove that she said it. □ Die Polizei kann nichts beweisen. The police can't prove anything.

2 to show
□ Er hat sehr viel Mut bewiesen. He showed great courage.

★ sich **bewerben** (PRESENT TENSE **bewirbt sich**, IMPERFECT **bewarb sich**, PERFECT TENSE **hat sich beworben**) VERB [90]
to apply
□ Es haben sich dreißig Kandidaten beworben. Thirty candidates have applied. □ Sie hat sich bei Siemens um einen Ausbildungsplatz beworben. She applied to Siemens for an apprenticeship.

der **Bewerber** (PL die **Bewerber**) MASC NOUN
applicant

die **Bewerberin** (PL die **Bewerber**) FEM NOUN
applicant

★ die **Bewerbung** FEM NOUN
application

bewerten (PERFECT TENSE **hat bewertet**) VERB [2]
to assess
□ Der Lehrer hat unsere Aufsätze zu bewerten. The teacher has to assess our essays.

bewirken (PERFECT TENSE **hat bewirkt**) VERB [7]

1 to bring about
□ Dieses natürliche Heilmittel kann auch eine schnelle Besserung bewirken. This natural remedy can also bring about a rapid improvement.

2 to achieve
□ Meine Bitte hat nichts bewirkt. My request didn't achieve anything.
■ Ich konnte bei ihm nichts bewirken. I couldn't get anywhere with him.

bewohnen (PERFECT TENSE **hat bewohnt**) VERB [7]
to live in
□ Das Haus wird von drei Familien bewohnt. Three families live in the house.

der **Bewohner** (PL die **Bewohner**) MASC NOUN

1 inhabitant
□ die Bewohner des Landes the inhabitants of the country

2 resident
□ die Bewohner des Hauses the residents of the house

die **Bewohnerin** (PL die **Bewohnerinnen**) FEM NOUN

1 inhabitant
□ die Bewohnerinnen des Landes the inhabitants of the country

2 resident
□ die Bewohnerin des Hauses the resident of the house

★ **bewölkt** ADJECTIVE
cloudy

★ die **Bewölkung** FEM NOUN
clouds pl

bewundern (PERFECT TENSE **hat bewundert**) VERB [88]
to admire

die **Bewunderung** FEM NOUN
admiration

bewusst ADJECTIVE

1 conscious
□ umweltbewusst environmentally conscious

2 deliberate
□ Er hat ganz bewusst gelogen. He lied quite deliberately.
■ sich einer Sache bewusst sein to be aware of something □ Ich bin mir der Konsequenzen bewusst. I'm aware of the consequences.
■ Ihr wurde plötzlich bewusst, dass ... She suddenly realized that ...

bewusstlos ADJECTIVE
unconscious
■ bewusstlos werden to lose consciousness

die **Bewusstlosigkeit** FEM NOUN
unconsciousness

das **Bewusstsein** NEUT NOUN
consciousness
■ bei Bewusstsein conscious

★ **bezahlen** (PERFECT TENSE **hat bezahlt**) VERB [7]
to pay
□ Er bezahlte die Rechnung. He paid the bill.

die **Bezahlung** FEM NOUN
payment

bezeichnen (PERFECT TENSE **hat bezeichnet**) VERB [53]

1 to mark
□ Bezeichnen Sie die Stelle mit einem Kreuz. Mark the spot with a cross.

2 to call
□ Sie hat mich als Lügnerin bezeichnet. She called me a liar.

bezeichnend ADJECTIVE
typical
□ Das ist bezeichnend für sie! That's typical of her!

beziehen (IMPERFECT **bezog**, PERFECT TENSE **hat bezogen**) VERB [96]

1 to cover
□ Sie beschloss, alle Kissen zu beziehen. She

★ = core vocabulary

decided to cover all the cushions.
■ **das Bett beziehen** to change the bed

2 to move into
□ Wann könnt ihr euer neues Haus beziehen? When can you move into your new house?

3 to get
□ Wir beziehen unsere Kartoffeln direkt vom Bauern. We get our potatoes straight from the farm. □ Sie beziehen Arbeitslosenhilfe. They get unemployment benefit.

4 to subscribe to
□ Ich beziehe eine Tageszeitung. I subscribe to a daily newspaper.
■ **sich beziehen** to cloud over □ Der Himmel bezieht sich. It's clouding over.
■ **sich auf etwas beziehen** to refer to something □ Sein Beispiel bezog sich auf das Tierreich. His example referred to the animal kingdom.

★ die **Beziehung** FEM NOUN

1 relationship
□ Er hat eine Beziehung mit einer verheirateten Frau. He has a relationship with a married woman.

2 relations *pl*
□ unsere Beziehungen zu dieser Firma our relations with this company □ diplomatische Beziehungen diplomatic relations

3 connection
□ Es besteht eine Beziehung zwischen den beiden Straftaten. There's a connection between the two crimes.
■ **in dieser Beziehung** in this respect
■ **Beziehungen haben** to have contacts □ Er kann bestimmt etwas für dich tun, er hat schließlich Beziehungen. I'm sure he can do something for you, he has contacts.
■ **eine Beziehung zu etwas haben** to be able to relate to something □ Ich habe keine Beziehung zu moderner Kunst. I can't relate to modern art.

★ der **Bezirk** (PL die **Bezirke**) MASC NOUN
district

der **Bezug** (PL die **Bezüge**) MASC NOUN
cover
□ Das Sofa hatte einen bunten Bezug. The sofa had a brightly-coloured cover.
■ **in Bezug auf** regarding □ in Bezug auf Kinder regarding children
■ **Bezug nehmen auf** to refer to

bezüglich PREPOSITION

> The preposition **bezüglich** takes the genitive.

with reference to
□ Bezüglich Ihrer Anfrage können wir Ihnen mitteilen ... With reference to your inquiry we can inform you that ...

bezweifeln (PERFECT TENSE **hat bezweifelt**)
VERB [34]
to doubt
□ Ich bezweifle das. I doubt it.

★ der **BH** (PL die **BHs**) MASC NOUN (= *Büstenhalter*)
bra

die **Bibel** FEM NOUN
Bible

★ die **Bibliothek** (PL die **Bibliotheken**) FEM NOUN
library

der **Bibliothekar** (PL die **Bibliothekare**)
MASC NOUN
librarian

die **Bibliothekarin** FEM NOUN
librarian

biegen (IMPERFECT **bog**, PERFECT TENSE **hat gebogen**) VERB

1 to bend
□ Sie bog den Draht zur Seite. She bent the wire to one side.

2 to turn
□ Du musst an der Ampel rechts in die Seitenstraße biegen. You have to turn right at the lights, into the side street.
■ **sich biegen** to bend □ Die Bäume bogen sich im Wind. The trees were bending in the wind.

★ die **Biene** FEM NOUN
bee

★ das **Bier** (PL die **Biere** or **Bier**) NEUT NOUN
beer
□ Zwei Bier, bitte! Two beers, please!

★ der **Bierkeller** (PL die **Bierkeller**) MASC NOUN
beer cellar

★ **bieten** (IMPERFECT **bot**, PERFECT TENSE **hat geboten**) VERB [8]

1 to offer
□ Dieser Job bietet mir die Möglichkeit, meine Englischkenntnisse anzuwenden. This job offers me the chance to use my knowledge of English.

2 to bid
□ Sie hat zweihundert Euro für den Stuhl geboten. She bid two hundred euros for the chair. □ Wer bietet mehr? Any more bids?
■ **sobald sich die Gelegenheit bietet** as soon as the opportunity arises
■ **sich etwas bieten lassen** to put up with something □ Eine solche Frechheit lasse ich mir nicht bieten. I won't put up with such cheek.

★ das **Bild** (PL die **Bilder**) NEUT NOUN

1 picture
□ ein Bild von Picasso a picture by Picasso
■ **ein Bild der Verwüstung** a scene of destruction

2 photo
□ Hast du ein Bild von deinem Freund? Have you got a photo of your boyfriend?

bilden – bis

bilden VERB [54]

1 to form
□ Bildet einen Kreis. **Form a circle.** □ Wie wird der Plural dieses Worts gebildet? **How do you form the plural of this word?**

2 to set up
□ Sie haben einen Ausschuss gebildet. **They set up a committee.**
■ **sich eine Meinung bilden** to form an opinion□ In dieser Frage habe ich mir noch keine Meinung gebildet. **I haven't formed an opinion on this question yet.**
■ **sich bilden 1** to form□ Am Himmel bildeten sich dunkle Wolken. **Dark clouds formed in the sky. 2** to educate oneself□ Sie macht Kurse, um sich zu bilden. **She attends courses in order to educate herself.**

★**der Bildschirm** (PL die **Bildschirme**) MASC NOUN
screen

der Bildschirmschoner (PL die **Bildschirmschoner**) MASC NOUN
screen saver

★**die Bildung** FEM NOUN

1 education
□ Sie hat eine gute Bildung. **She has a good education.**

2 formation
□ Die Bildung des Plurals im Englischen ist ziemlich regelmäßig. **The formation of the plural in English is quite regular.** □ die Bildung der Regierung **the formation of the government**

★**billig** ADJECTIVE
cheap

der Billigflieger (PL die **Billigflieger**) MASC NOUN
low-cost airline

der Billigjob (PL die **Billigjobs**) MASC NOUN
low-paid job

die Binde FEM NOUN

1 bandage
□ eine elastische Binde **an elastic bandage**

2 sanitary towel
□ Sie benützt lieber Binden als Tampons. **She prefers sanitary towels to tampons.**

binden (IMPERFECT **band**, PERFECT TENSE **hat gebunden**) VERB
to tie
□ Die Tomaten werden an einen Stock gebunden. **The tomatoes are tied to a cane.** □ Sie band die Haare zu einem Pferdeschwanz. **She tied her hair back into a ponytail.**
■ **ein Buch binden** to bind a book
■ **sich binden** to get involved□ Sie möchte sich in ihrem Alter noch nicht binden. **She doesn't want to get involved at her age.**

der Bindestrich (PL die **Bindestriche**) MASC NOUN
hyphen

der Bindfaden (PL die **Bindfäden**) MASC NOUN
string

die Bindung FEM NOUN

1 tie
□ meine emotionale Bindung an meine Eltern **my emotional ties to my parents**

2 bindings *pl*
□ Bei einem Sturz müsste die Bindung aufgehen. **When you fall the bindings should come open.**

Bio- PREFIX
organic

die Biokost FEM NOUN
organic food

der Biokraftstoff (PL die **Biokraftstoffe**) MASC NOUN
biofuel

der Bioladen (PL die **Bioläden**) MASC NOUN
health food shop

die Bio-Lebensmittel NEUT PL NOUN
organic food

★**die Biologie** FEM NOUN
biology

biologisch ADJECTIVE, ADVERB

1 biological

2 organic
■ **biologisch abbaubar** biodegradable

der Biomüll MASC NOUN
organic waste

die Birke FEM NOUN
birch

★**die Birne** FEM NOUN

1 pear
□ Zum Nachtisch gab es Birnen mit Schokoladensoße. **There were pears with chocolate sauce for dessert.**

2 bulb
□ Benutzt du auch energieeffiziente Birnen? **Do you also use energy-saving bulbs?**

★**bis** PREPOSITION, CONJUNCTION

The preposition **bis** takes the accusative.

1 until
□ Sie bleibt bis Ende August in England. **She's staying in England until the end of August.** □ Du hast bis Montag Zeit. **You have until Monday.** □ bis es dunkel wird **until it gets dark**
■ **bis auf weiteres** until further notice

2 by
□ Das Referat muss bis nächsten Montag fertig sein. **The assignment must be finished by next Monday.**
■ **bis in die Nacht** into the night
■ **bis bald** see you later
■ **bis gleich** see you soon

3 as far as
□ Ich fahre bis Köln. **I'm going as far as Cologne.**
■ **bis hierher** this far

★ = core vocabulary

■ **von ... bis ...** from ... to ...□ von Köln bis Bonn from Cologne to Bonn□ von Anfang Mai bis Ende Juni from the beginning of May to the end of June

4 up to

□ Kinder bis drei fahren umsonst. Children up to three travel free.□ bis zu dreißig Grad up to thirty degrees

■ **zehn bis zwanzig** ten to twenty

■ **bis zu** up to□ Ich kann bis zu drei Personen mitnehmen. I can take up to three people.

■ **bis auf** apart from□ Bis auf Jan sind alle mitgekommen. Everybody came along apart from Jan.

bisher ADVERB
up to now

bisherig ADJECTIVE
previous

biss VERB ▷ see beißen

der **Biss** (GEN des Bisses, PL die Bisse) MASC NOUN
bite

★**bisschen** ADJECTIVE, ADVERB
bit
□ ein bisschen a bit

bissig ADJECTIVE

1 vicious
■ **Vorsicht, bissiger Hund!** Beware of the dog!

2 cutting
□ Er machte eine bissige Bemerkung. He made a cutting remark.

bist VERB ▷ see sein

das **Bit** (PL die Bits) NEUT NOUN
bit
□ Bits und Bytes bits and bytes

★**bitte** EXCLAMATION
▷ see also die **Bitte** NOUN

1 please
□ Kann ich bitte noch etwas Saft haben? Can I have some more juice, please?□ Darf ich? — Aber bitte! May I? — Please do.
■ **Wie bitte?** Pardon?
■ **Hier bitte!** Here you are.
■ **Bitte warten.** Please hold the line. (phone)

2 don't mention it
□ Vielen Dank für die Hilfe! — Bitte! Many thanks for your help! — Don't mention it!
■ **Bitte schön!** It was a pleasure.
■ **Bitte sehr!** You're welcome.

die **Bitte** FEM NOUN
▷ see also **bitte** EXCLAMATION
request
□ Ich habe eine Bitte. I have a request.□ auf seine Bitte hin at his request

★**bitten** (IMPERFECT **bat**, PERFECT TENSE **hat gebeten**) VERB [9]
■ **jemanden um etwas bitten** to ask somebody for something

★**bitter** ADJECTIVE
bitter

blamieren (PERFECT TENSE **hat blamiert**) VERB [76]
■ **sich blamieren** to make a fool of oneself
■ **jemanden blamieren** to let somebody down

die **Blase** FEM NOUN

1 bubble
□ Die Blase platzte. The bubble burst.

2 blister
□ Ich habe Blasen an den Füßen. I've got blisters on my feet.

3 bladder
□ Sie hat eine schwache Blase. She has a weak bladder.

blasen (PRESENT TENSE **bläst**, IMPERFECT **blies**, PERFECT TENSE **hat geblasen**) VERB
to blow

das **Blasinstrument** (PL die Blasinstrumente) NEUT NOUN
wind instrument

★die **Blaskapelle** FEM NOUN
brass band

die **Blasmusik** FEM NOUN
brass band music

★**blass** ADJECTIVE
pale
□ Als sie das hörte, wurde sie blass. When she heard that, she turned pale.

★das **Blatt** (PL die Blätter) NEUT NOUN

1 leaf
□ Im Herbst fallen die Blätter von den Bäumen. In autumn, the leaves fall from the trees.

2 sheet
□ ein Blatt Papier a sheet of paper

3 newspaper
□ In welchem Blatt hast du die Anzeige aufgegeben? Which newspaper did you place the advertisement in?

★**blau** ADJECTIVE

1 blue
□ Er hat blaue Augen. He has blue eyes.

2 sloshed (Umgangssprache)
□ Gestern Abend warst du ganz schön blau. You were absolutely sloshed yesterday evening.
■ **ein blaues Auge** a black eye
■ **ein blauer Fleck** a bruise
■ **eine Fahrt ins Blaue** a mystery tour

das **Blech** (PL die Bleche) NEUT NOUN

1 sheet metal

2 baking tray

das **Blei** NEUT NOUN
lead

bleiben – bloß

★ **bleiben** (IMPERFECT **blieb**, PERFECT TENSE **ist geblieben**) VERB [10]

1 to stay
□ Wie lange bleiben Sie hier? How long are you staying here? □ Hoffentlich bleibt das Wetter schön. I hope the weather will stay fine.
■ **bei etwas bleiben** to stick to something
□ Ich bleibe bei meiner Meinung. I'm sticking to my opinion.

2 to be left
□ Vom Kuchen war nur noch ein Stück für mich geblieben. There was only one piece of cake left for me.
■ **Bleibt es bei morgen zehn Uhr?** Is ten o'clock tomorrow morning still on?
■ **Wo bleibt sie denn?** Where's she got to?

bleich ADJECTIVE
pale
□ Als er das hörte, wurde er bleich. When he heard that, he turned pale.

★ **bleifrei** ADJECTIVE
unleaded

★ der **Bleistift** (PL die **Bleistifte**) MASC NOUN
pencil

blendend ADJECTIVE
marvellous
□ Du siehst blendend aus. You look marvellous.
■ **sich blendend amüsieren** to have a wonderful time
■ **Mir geht's blendend.** I'm feeling great.

★ der **Blick** (PL die **Blicke**) MASC NOUN

1 glance
□ Ich habe mit einem Blick gesehen, dass das nicht gut gehen kann. I saw at a glance that it couldn't work.
■ **Er warf einen Blick auf die Uhr.** He glanced at the clock.

2 look
□ Sie warf mir einen verzweifelten Blick zu. She gave me a desperate look.

3 view
□ Das Zimmer hat einen herrlichen Blick auf die Berge. The room has a wonderful view of the mountains.
■ **auf den ersten Blick** at first glance

★ **blicken** VERB [48]
to look
□ Sie blickte zur Seite. She looked to one side.
■ **sich blicken lassen** to show one's face □ Er hat sich hier nie wieder blicken lassen. He's never shown his face here again.
■ **Das lässt tief blicken!** That's very revealing!

blieb VERB ▷ see **bleiben**

★ **blind** ADJECTIVE

1 blind
□ Er ist auf einem Auge blind. He's blind in one eye.

2 tarnished
□ Der Spiegel war blind geworden. The mirror had become tarnished.

der **Blinddarm** (PL die **Blinddärme**) MASC NOUN
appendix
□ Er wurde am Blinddarm operiert. He had his appendix out.

blinzeln VERB [88]
to blink

★ der **Blitz** (PL die **Blitze**) MASC NOUN
lightning no pl
□ Der Blitz schlug in den Baum ein. The tree was struck by lightning.

★ **blitzen** VERB [36]
■ **Es blitzt.** There's a flash of lightning.

das **Blitzlicht** (PL die **Blitzlichter**) NEUT NOUN
flashlight

★ der **Block** (PL die **Blöcke**) MASC NOUN

1 block
□ Meine Freundin wohnt im nächsten Block. My friend lives in the next block.

2 pad
□ Er riss ein Blatt vom Block. He tore a sheet from the pad.

★ die **Blockflöte** FEM NOUN
recorder

★ **blöd** ADJECTIVE
stupid
□ Du bist blöd! You're stupid!
■ **blöd fragen** to ask stupid questions □ Wer blöd fragt, bekommt auch eine blöde Antwort. I you ask a stupid question, then you get a stupid answer.

★ der **Blödsinn** MASC NOUN
nonsense

das **Blog** (PL die **Blogs**) NEUT NOUN

> You can also say **der Blog**.

blog
□ Du solltest ein Blog darüber schreiben. You should write a blog about it.

bloggen VERB [4]
to blog
□ Ich habe schon lange nicht mehr gebloggt. I haven't blogged for a long time.

★ **blond** ADJECTIVE

1 blond
□ Er hat blonde Haare. He has blond hair.

2 blonde
□ Meine Schwester ist blond. My sister's blonde. □ Sie hat ihre Haare blond gefärbt. She dyed her hair blonde.

★ **bloß** ADVERB, ADJECTIVE
only
□ Er hat bloß einen Fehler gemacht. He only made one mistake. □ Wenn das bloß schon fertig wäre! If only it was finished.
■ **Lass das bloß!** Don't do that!
■ **Wie ist das bloß passiert?** How on earth did that happen?
■ **Wo ist er bloß?** Where's he got to?

★ = core vocabulary

- **mit bloßem Auge** with the naked eye
- **der bloße Gedanke** the very thought
- **bloßer Neid** sheer envy

blühen VERB [38]
to be in bloom
□ Zurzeit blüht der Flieder. The lilac's in bloom at the moment.

★ die **Blume** FEM NOUN
flower
□ Sie hat mir einen Strauß Blumen mitgebracht. She brought me a bunch of flowers.

★ das **Blumenbeet** (PL die **Blumenbeete**) NEUT NOUN
flowerbed

★ der **Blumenkohl** (PL die **Blumenkohle**) MASC NOUN
cauliflower

★ die **Bluse** FEM NOUN
blouse

★ das **Blut** NEUT NOUN
blood

★ der **Blutdruck** MASC NOUN
blood pressure

die **Blüte** FEM NOUN
blossom

★ **bluten** VERB [2]
to bleed
□ Meine Nase blutet. My nose is bleeding.

★ die **Blutprobe** FEM NOUN
blood test

die **Blutvergiftung** FEM NOUN
blood poisoning

der **Bock** MASC NOUN
1 billy goat
2 ram (*male sheep*)
■ **Bock haben, etwas zu tun** to fancy doing something (*Umgangssprache*) □ Ich habe heute überhaupt keinen Bock auf die Schule. I don't fancy school today at all.

★ die **Bockwurst** (PL die **Bockwürste**) FEM NOUN
frankfurter

★ der **Boden** (PL die **Böden**) MASC NOUN
1 soil
□ Der Boden ist in dieser Gegend sehr fruchtbar. The soil in this area is very fertile. □ auf deutschem Boden on German soil
2 floor
□ Wir haben auf dem Boden gesessen. We sat on the floor.
3 bottom
□ Das Schiff sank auf den Boden des Meers. The ship sank to the bottom of the sea. □ Das Fass hat einen hölzernen Boden. The barrel has a wooden bottom.
4 attic
□ Wir haben die alten Möbel auf den Boden gebracht. We put the old furniture into the attic.

die **Bodenschätze** MASC PL NOUN
mineral resources *pl*

★ der **Bodensee** MASC NOUN
Lake Constance
□ eine Stadt am Bodensee a town on Lake Constance

★ die **Bohne** FEM NOUN
bean

bohren VERB [38]
1 to bore
□ Sie bohrte ein Loch in das Brett. She bored a hole in the shelf.
2 to drill
□ Der Zahnarzt musste nicht bohren. The dentist didn't have to drill. □ In der Nordsee wird nach Erdöl gebohrt. They're drilling for oil in the North Sea.
■ **in der Nase bohren** to pick one's nose

der **Bohrer** (PL die **Bohrer**) MASC NOUN
drill

die **Bohrmaschine** FEM NOUN
drill

die **Bombe** FEM NOUN
bomb

★ der **Bonbon** (PL die **Bonbons**) MASC NOUN

You can also say **das Bonbon**.

sweet

★ das **Boot** (PL die **Boote**) NEUT NOUN
boat

★ der **Bord** MASC NOUN
▷ *see also* das **Bord** NOUN
■ **an Bord** on board

★ das **Bord** (PL die **Borde**) NEUT NOUN
▷ *see also* der **Bord** NOUN
shelf
□ Er brachte über dem Schreibtisch ein Bord für seine Bücher an. He put up a shelf over his desk for his books.

borgen VERB [38]
to borrow
□ Das gehört nicht mir, das habe ich mir geborgt. That doesn't belong to me, I borrowed it.
■ **jemandem etwas borgen** to lend somebody something □ Meine Schwester hat mir ihr Rennrad geborgt. My sister lent me her racing bike.

die **Börse** FEM NOUN
1 purse
□ Sie nahm zehn Euro aus ihrer Börse. She took ten euros out of her purse.
2 stock exchange
□ Diese Aktien werden an der Börse gehandelt. These shares are traded on the stock exchange.

★ **böse** ADJECTIVE
1 bad
□ Er ist ein böser Mensch. He's a bad man. □ Die Kinder waren böse. The children were bad. □ Sie hat eine böse Erkältung. She has a bad cold.

b

Bosnien - bravo

2 angry
□ Ich habe ihm einen bösen Brief geschrieben. I wrote him an angry letter.
■ **böse werden** to get angry□ Wenn du das noch einmal tust, werde ich böse. If you do that again, I'll get angry.□ Bist du mir noch böse? Are you still angry with me?
■ **auf jemanden böse sein** to be angry with somebody□ Ich bin böse auf Martin, weil er nicht gekommen ist. I'm angry with Martin because he didn't come.
■ **eine böse Überraschung** a nasty shock
■ **Mit ihm sieht es böse aus.** It doesn't look too good for him.

Bosnien NEUT NOUN
Bosnia

bot VERB ▷ seebieten

die **Botschaft** FEM NOUN
1 message
□ Kannst du ihm eine Botschaft übermitteln? Can you give him a message?
2 embassy
□ Sie müssen das Visum auf der Botschaft beantragen. You have to apply to the embassy for a visa.

boxen VERB [48]
to box

der **Boxer** (PLdie **Boxer**) MASC NOUN
boxer

die **Boxerin** FEM NOUN
boxer

brach VERB ▷ seebrechen

brachte VERB ▷ seebringen

★der **Brand** (PLdie **Brände**) MASC NOUN
fire

Brandenburg NEUT NOUN
Brandenburg

DID YOU KNOW...?
Brandenburg is one of the 16Länder. Its capital is Potsdam, which is famous as the residence of Frederick the Great, the 18th-century king of Prussia. Agriculture and forestry are still important parts of the economy.

Brasilien NEUT NOUN
Brazil
■ **aus Brasilien** from Brazil
■ **nach Brasilien** to Brazil

★**braten** (PRESENT TENSE **brät**, IMPERFECT **briet**, PERFECT TENSE **hat gebraten**) VERB
▷ see alsoder **Braten** NOUN
1 to roast
□ Wir haben das Hähnchen im Backofen gebraten. We roasted the chicken in the oven.
2 to fry
□ Sie briet die Kartoffeln in der Pfanne. She fried the potatoes in the frying pan.

★der **Braten** (PLdie **Braten**) MASC NOUN
▷ see alsobraten VERB
roast

★das **Brathähnchen** (PLdie **Brathähnchen**)
NEUT NOUN
roast chicken

★die **Bratkartoffeln** FEM PL NOUN
fried potatoes pl

die **Bratpfanne** FEM NOUN
frying pan

★die **Bratwurst** (PLdie **Bratwürste**) FEM NOUN
fried sausage

der **Brauch** (PLdie **Bräuche**) MASC NOUN
custom

brauchbar ADJECTIVE
1 usable
□ Hast du einen brauchbaren Föhn? Do you have a usable hairdryer?
2 capable
□ Sie ist eine sehr brauchbare Mitarbeiterin. She's a very capable colleague.

★**brauchen** VERB [48]
1 to need
□ Wir brauchen noch Brot und Butter. We still need bread and butter.□ Dazu brauche ich mindestens zwei Tage. I'll need at least two days for that.
2 to have to
□ Du brauchst heute nicht zu kommen. You don't have to come today.□ Du brauchst nur Bescheid zu sagen, dann helfe ich dir. You only have to let me know and I'll help you.
■ **Das kann ich gut brauchen.** I could really do with that.

die **Brauerei** FEM NOUN
brewery

★**braun** ADJECTIVE
1 brown
□ Sie hat braune Haare und braune Augen. She has brown hair and brown eyes.
2 tanned
□ Wir kamen ganz braun aus den Ferien zurück. We came back all tanned from our holidays.

★die **Braut** (PLdie **Bräute**) FEM NOUN
bride

★der **Bräutigam** (PLdie **Bräutigame**) MASC
NOUN
bridegroom

das **Brautpaar** (PLdie **Brautpaare**) NEUT
NOUN
bride and groom pl

★**brav** ADJECTIVE
good
□ Die Kinder waren brav. The children were good.
■ **Er ist ganz brav ins Bett gegangen.** He went to bed as good as gold.

BE CAREFUL!
brav does not mean **brave**.

bravo! EXCLAMATION
well done!

★ die **BRD** FEM NOUN (= *Bundesrepublik Deutschland*)
Federal Republic of Germany

★ **brechen** (PRESENT TENSE **bricht**, IMPERFECT **brach**, PERFECT TENSE **hat/ist gebrochen**) VERB [11]

> For the perfect tense use **haben** when the verb has an object and **sein** when there is no object. Use **haben** for 'to vomit'.

1 to break
□ Der Zweig ist gebrochen. The branch broke. □ Ich habe den Stock in zwei Teile gebrochen. I broke the stick in two. □ Ich habe mir den rechten Arm gebrochen. I've broken my right arm. □ Sie hat ihr Versprechen gebrochen. She broke her promise. □ einen Rekord brechen to break a record

2 to vomit
□ Ihm wurde schlecht, und er musste brechen. He felt ill and had to vomit.

★ **breit** ADJECTIVE
wide
□ Das ist ein breiter Fluss. That's a wide river. □ Das Brett ist fünfzehn Zentimeter breit. The plank is fifteen centimetres wide.

das **Breitband** NEUT NOUN
broadband

der **Breitbandanschluss** (PL die **Breitbandanschlüsse**) MASC NOUN
broadband connection

die **Breite** FEM NOUN
width
□ die Breite des Tisches the width of the table

Bremen NEUT NOUN
Bremen

> **DID YOU KNOW...?**
> The 'Free Hanseatic City of Bremen' is one of the 16 **Länder**. It is a 'city-state' like Berlin and Hamburg, and is made up of the cities Bremen and Bremerhaven. It is the smallest **Land**, but the second-oldest city-republic in the world.

★ die **Bremse** FEM NOUN
1 brake
□ Sie trat auf die Bremse. She stepped on the brakes.
2 horsefly
□ Wir sind von Bremsen gestochen worden. We were bitten by horseflies.

★ **bremsen** VERB [36]
to brake
□ Als er das Kind sah, bremste er. When he saw the child, he braked.
■ Sie versuchte, das Auto zu bremsen. She tried to stop the car.
■ Sie ist nicht zu bremsen. There's no stopping her.

★ **brennen** (IMPERFECT **brannte**, PERFECT TENSE **hat gebrannt**) VERB [12]

1 to burn
□ Das Holz ist zu nass, es brennt nicht. The wood's too wet, it won't burn. □ Im Wohnzimmer brennt Licht. There's a light burning in the living room. □ Der Schnaps brennt auf der Zunge. The schnapps burns your tongue. □ ein Loch in etwas brennen to burn a hole in something

2 to be on fire
□ Das Haus brannte. The house was on fire.
■ sich brennen to burn oneself □ Ich habe mich an der heißen Platte gebrannt. I've burned myself on the hot plate.
■ darauf brennen, etwas zu tun to be dying to do something □ Ich brenne darauf, deinen Freund kennenzulernen. I'm dying to meet your boyfriend.
■ eine CD/DVD brennen to burn a CD/DVD

die **Brennnessel** FEM NOUN
stinging nettle

der **Brennstoff** (PL die **Brennstoffe**) MASC NOUN
fuel

das **Brett** (PL die **Bretter**) NEUT NOUN
1 board
□ Die Hütte bestand aus ein paar zusammengenagelten Brettern. The hut consisted of a few boards nailed together. □ Sie stellte die Schachfiguren aufs Brett. She set up the chessmen on the board.
2 shelf
□ Die Gewürze stehen auf einem Brett über dem Herd. The spices are on a shelf above the cooker.
■ das Schwarze Brett the notice board
■ Ich hatte ein Brett vor dem Kopf. My mind went blank.

die **Brezel** FEM NOUN
pretzel

bricht VERB ▷ *see* **brechen**

★ der **Brief** (PL die **Briefe**) MASC NOUN
letter

★ der **Brieffreund** (PL die **Brieffreunde**) MASC NOUN
pen friend

★ die **Brieffreundin** FEM NOUN
pen friend

★ der **Briefkasten** (PL die **Briefkästen**) MASC NOUN
1 letterbox
2 postbox

★ die **Briefmarke** FEM NOUN
stamp

★ die **Brieftasche** FEM NOUN
wallet

★ der **Briefträger** (PL die **Briefträger**) MASC NOUN
postman
□ Günter ist Briefträger. Günter's a postman.

Numbers in brackets refer to verb tables on pages 697 to 706.

57

★ **die Briefträgerin** FEM NOUN
postwoman
□ Meine Tante ist Briefträgerin. My aunt's a
postwoman.

★ **der Briefumschlag** (PL die
Briefumschläge) MASC NOUN
envelope

der Briefwechsel (PL die Briefwechsel)
MASC NOUN
correspondence

brief VERB ▷ see **braten**

★ **die Brille** FEM NOUN
1 glasses pl
□ Lesley trägt eine Brille. Lesley wears glasses.
□ eine Brille a pair of glasses
2 goggles pl
□ Beim Schweißen sollte man eine Brille
tragen. You should wear goggles when welding.
3 toilet seat
□ Ich hasse es, wenn Männer die Brille oben
lassen. I hate it when men leave the toilet seat
up.

★ **bringen** (IMPERFECT **brachte**, PERFECT TENSE **hat
gebracht**) VERB [13]
1 to bring
□ Unsere Gäste haben uns einen schönen
Blumenstrauß gebracht. Our guests have
brought us a lovely bunch of flowers. □ Kann
ich meine Schwester mit zur Party bringen? Can
I bring my sister to the party?
2 to take
□ Meine Freunde haben mich zum Flughafen
gebracht. My friends took me to the airport.
□ jemanden nach Hause bringen to take
somebody home
3 to bring in
□ Diese Anlage bringt fünf Prozent Zinsen. This
investment brings in five per cent interest.
4 to publish
□ Alle Zeitungen brachten diese Geschichte auf
der ersten Seite. All the newspapers published
this story on the first page.
5 to be on
□ Sieh mal in der Zeitung nach, was das Theater
bringt. Look in the paper to see what's on at the
theatre.
▪ **jemanden zu etwas bringen** to make
somebody do something □ Sie hat mich zum
Lachen gebracht. She made me laugh. □ Du
bringst mich noch zur Verzweiflung. You make
me despair.
▪ **jemanden dazu bringen, etwas zu tun** to
get somebody to do something □ Wie hast du
deine Eltern dazu gebracht, dass sie das erlaubt
haben? How did you get your parents to let you
do that?
▪ **es über sich bringen, etwas zu tun** to
bring oneself to do something □ Ich habe es
nicht über mich gebracht, ihr das zu sagen. I
couldn't bring myself to tell her.

▪ **jemanden um etwas bringen** to cheat
somebody out of something □ Der Betrüger hat
die alte Frau um ihre ganzen Ersparnisse
gebracht. The swindler cheated the old lady out
of all her savings.
▪ **jemanden in Gefahr bringen** to put
somebody in danger
▪ **Unser Computer bringt's nicht.** Our
computer's rubbish. (Umgangssprache)
▪ **Das bringt nichts!** That's no use!

★ **der Brite** (GEN des **Briten**, PL die **Briten**) MASC
NOUN
Briton
▪ **die Briten** the British

★ **die Britin** FEM NOUN
Briton

★ **britisch** ADJECTIVE
British

die Brombeere FEM NOUN
blackberry

★ **die Broschüre** FEM NOUN
brochure

★ **das Brot** (PL die **Brote**) NEUT NOUN
1 bread no pl
□ Haben wir noch Brot im Haus? Do we still
have some bread in the house?
2 loaf
□ Kannst du für die Party drei Brote holen? Can
you get three loaves for the party?

★ **das Brötchen** (PL die **Brötchen**) NEUT NOUN
roll

browsen (PERFECT TENSE **hat gebrowst**) VERB
[38]
to browse

der Browser (PL die **Browser**) MASC NOUN
web browser

der Bruch (PL die **Brüche**) MASC NOUN
1 fracture
□ Sie wurde mit einem Bruch ins Krankenhaus
eingeliefert. She was taken to hospital with a
fracture.
▪ **zu Bruch gehen** to get broken □ Die ganzen
Teller sind zu Bruch gegangen. All the plates got
broken.
2 hernia
□ Trag das nicht allein, du hebst dir sonst einen
Bruch! Don't carry that on your own, you'll give
yourself a hernia!
3 fraction
□ Das Rechnen mit Brüchen haben wir noch
nicht gelernt. We haven't learned fractions yet.

★ **die Brücke** FEM NOUN
bridge

★ **der Bruder** (PL die **Brüder**) MASC NOUN
brother

brüllen VERB [38]
to roar
□ Der Löwe brüllte. The lion roared.

■ Er brüllte vor Schmerz. He screamed with pain.

brummen VERB [38]

1 to growl
□ Der Bär brummte. The bear growled.

2 to buzz
□ Eine dicke Fliege brummte durchs Zimmer. A huge fly buzzed around the room.
■ etwas brummen to mumble something
□ Er hat irgendetwas Unfreundliches gebrummt. He mumbled something unfriendly.

★der **Brunnen** (PL die Brunnen) MASC NOUN

1 fountain
□ Am Marktplatz steht ein Brunnen. There's a fountain in the market square.

2 well
□ Wasser aus dem Brunnen water from the well

★die **Brust** (PL die Brüste) FEM NOUN
breast

das **Brustschwimmen** NEUT NOUN
breaststroke

★**brutal** ADJECTIVE
brutal

★die **Brutalität** FEM NOUN
brutality

brutto ADVERB
gross

★das **Buch** (PL die Bücher) NEUT NOUN
book

die **Buche** FEM NOUN
beech tree

★**buchen** VERB [48]
to book
□ Wir haben eine Reise nach Kreta gebucht. We've booked a trip to Crete.

★die **Bücherei** FEM NOUN
library

★das **Bücherregal** (PL die Bücherregale) NEUT NOUN
bookcase

★der **Buchhalter** (PL die Buchhalter) MASC NOUN
accountant

★die **Buchhalterin** FEM NOUN
accountant

★die **Buchhandlung** FEM NOUN
bookshop

★der **Buchladen** (PL die Buchläden) MASC NOUN
bookshop

★die **Büchse** FEM NOUN
tin
□ Sie bewahrt den Tee in einer Büchse auf. She keeps her tea in a tin.

der **Büchsenöffner** (PL die Büchsenöffner) MASC NOUN
tin opener

★der **Buchstabe** (GEN des Buchstabens, PL die Buchstaben) MASC NOUN
letter of the alphabet

★**buchstabieren** (PERFECT TENSE hat buchstabiert) VERB [76]
to spell

buchstäblich ADVERB
literally
□ Sie kam buchstäblich in der letzten Minute. She arrived at literally the last minute.

sich **bücken** VERB [48]
to bend down

★die **Bude** FEM NOUN
stall
□ die Buden auf dem Jahrmarkt the stalls at the fair
■ Kommt ihr noch mit auf meine Bude? Do you want to come back to my place?

★das **Büfett** (PL die Büfetts) NEUT NOUN
sideboard
■ kaltes Büfett cold buffet

der **Bügel** (PL die Bügel) MASC NOUN
hanger

das **Bügeleisen** (PL die Bügeleisen) NEUT NOUN
iron
□ Ich habe mir die Hand am Bügeleisen verbrannt. I burnt my hand on the iron.

★**bügeln** VERB [34]
to iron

★die **Bühne** FEM NOUN
stage
□ auf der Bühne stehen to be on stage

buk VERB ▷ see backen

Bulgarien NEUT NOUN
Bulgaria
■ aus Bulgarien from Bulgaria
■ nach Bulgarien to Bulgaria

★der **Bummel** (PL die Bummel) MASC NOUN
stroll
□ Wir machten einen Bummel an der Donau entlang. We went for a stroll along the Danube.

★**bummeln** VERB [88]

Use sein to form the perfect tense for 'to stroll' and haben for 'to dawdle'.

1 to stroll
□ Wir sind durch die Stadt gebummelt. We strolled through the town.

2 to dawdle
□ Heute hast du auf dem Heimweg aber gebummelt. You've really been dawdling on your way home today.

der **Bund** (PL die Bünde) MASC NOUN

1 association
□ Die Bauern schlossen sich zu einem Bund zusammen. The farmers formed an association.
■ Bund und Länder the Federal Government and the Länder

Bundes- – bzw.

2 waistband

□ Die Hose ist am Bund zu eng. The trousers are too tight at the waistband.

Bundes- PREFIX

Federal

★ der **Bundeskanzler** (PL die **Bundeskanzler**) MASC NOUN

Federal Chancellor

★ die **Bundeskanzlerin** FEM NOUN

Federal Chancellor

das **Bundesland** (PL die **Bundesländer**) NEUT NOUN

state

die **Bundesliga** FEM NOUN

Premier League

der **Bundesrat** MASC NOUN

upper chamber of the German Parliament

> **DID YOU KNOW...?**
> The **Bundesrat** is not directly elected, but is made up of representatives of the 16 **Länder**. In many cases, **Bundesrat** approval is required before laws (particularly amendments to the constitution) can be passed.

die **Bundesregierung** FEM NOUN

Federal government

★ die **Bundesrepublik** FEM NOUN

Federal Republic

□ die Bundesrepublik Deutschland the Federal Republic of Germany

★ die **Bundesstraße** FEM NOUN

federal road

der **Bundestag** MASC NOUN

German Parliament

> **DID YOU KNOW...?**
> The **Bundestag** is the German parliamentary assembly, elected every four years.

die **Bundeswehr** FEM NOUN

German Armed Forces *pl*

> **DID YOU KNOW...?**
> The **Bundeswehr** has consisted of career servicemen and -women since conscription (for men only) was abolished in 2011/12.

★ **bunt** ADJECTIVE

1 brightly-coloured

□ Sie hatte einen bunten Pulli an. She was wearing a brightly-coloured jumper.

2 mixed

□ Unsere Klasse ist ein buntes Häufchen. Our class is a mixed bunch.

■ Mir wird es zu bunt. It's getting too much for me.

der **Buntstift** (PL die **Buntstifte**) MASC NOUN

coloured pencil

★ die **Burg** (PL die **Burgen**) FEM NOUN

castle

der **Bürger** (PL die **Bürger**) MASC NOUN

citizen

die **Bürgerin** FEM NOUN

citizen

★ **bürgerlich** ADJECTIVE

1 civil

□ bürgerliche Rechte civil rights

2 middle-class

□ eine gute bürgerliche Familie a good middle-class family

der **Bürgermeister** (PL die **Bürgermeister**) MASC NOUN

mayor

die **Bürgermeisterin** FEM NOUN

mayor

★ der **Bürgersteig** (PL die **Bürgersteige**) MASC NOUN

pavement

★ das **Büro** (PL die **Büros**) NEUT NOUN

office

die **Büroklammer** FEM NOUN

paper clip

★ die **Bürste** FEM NOUN

brush

★ **bürsten** (PERFECT TENSE **hat gebürstet**) VERB [2]

to brush

★ der **Bus** (GEN des **Busses**, PL die **Busse**) MASC NOUN

bus

□ mit dem Bus fahren to go by bus

★ der **Busbahnhof** (PL die **Busbahnhöfe**) MASC NOUN

bus station

der **Busch** (PL die **Büsche**) MASC NOUN

bush

der **Busen** (PL die **Busen**) MASC NOUN

bosom

★ der **Busfahrer** (PL die **Busfahrer**) MASC NOUN

bus driver

★ die **Busfahrerin** FEM NOUN

bus driver

★ die **Bushaltestelle** FEM NOUN

bus stop

★ die **Buslinie** FEM NOUN

bus route

das **Bußgeld** (PL die **Bußgelder**) NEUT NOUN

fine

★ der **Büstenhalter** (PL die **Büstenhalter**) MASC NOUN

bra

★ die **Butter** FEM NOUN

butter

★ das **Butterbrot** (PL die **Butterbrote**) NEUT NOUN

(piece of) bread and butter

bzw. ABBREVIATION (= *beziehungsweise*)

or

★ = core vocabulary

Cc

ca. ABBREVIATION (= *circa*)
approx.

★ das **Café** (PL die **Cafés**) NEUT NOUN
café
□ Sonntags gehen wir immer ins Café. On Sundays we always go to a café.

die **Cafeteria** (PL die **Cafeterias**) FEM NOUN
cafeteria

das **Callcenter** (PL die **Callcenter**) NEUT NOUN
call centre

campen VERB [38]
to camp

★ der **Campingplatz** (GEN des **Campingplatzes**, PL die **Campingplätze**) MASC NOUN
campsite

★ die **CD** (PL die **CDs**) FEM NOUN
CD

★ die **CD-ROM** (PL die **CD-ROMs**) FEM NOUN
CD-ROM

★ der **CD-Spieler** (PL die **CD-Spieler**) MASC NOUN
CD player

das **Cello** (PL die **Cellos** *or* **Celli**) NEUT NOUN
cello
□ Ich spiele Cello. I play the cello.

★ der **Cent** (PL die **Cents**) MASC NOUN
cent

★ der **Champignon** (PL die **Champignons**) MASC NOUN
button mushroom

★ die **Chance** FEM NOUN
chance

das **Chaos** (GEN des **Chaos**) NEUT NOUN
chaos

chaotisch ADJECTIVE
chaotic

★ der **Charakter** (PL die **Charakter**) MASC NOUN
character

charmant ADJECTIVE
charming

der **Charterflug** (PL die **Charterflüge**) MASC NOUN
charter flight

der **Chat** (PL die **Chats**) MASC NOUN
chat (*internet*)

der **Chatroom** (PL die **Chatrooms**) MASC NOUN
chat room

chatten VERB [2]
to chat
□ Wir haben den ganzen Abend über gechattet. We chatted all evening.

★ der **Chef** (PL die **Chefs**) MASC NOUN
1 head
□ Er ist Chef einer großen Firma. He's the head of a large company.
2 boss
□ Da muss ich den Chef fragen. I'll have to ask my boss.

★ die **Chefin** FEM NOUN
boss

★ die **Chemie** FEM NOUN
chemistry

der **Chemiker** (PL die **Chemiker**) MASC NOUN
industrial chemist

chemisch ADJECTIVE
chemical
■ chemische Reinigung dry cleaning

der **Chicorée** MASC NOUN
chicory

Chile NEUT NOUN
Chile
■ aus Chile from Chile
■ nach Chile to Chile

★ **China** NEUT NOUN
China
■ aus China from China
■ nach China to China

der **Chinese** (GEN des **Chinesen**, PL die **Chinesen**) MASC NOUN
Chinese
■ die Chinesen the Chinese

die **Chinesin** FEM NOUN
Chinese

chinesisch ADJECTIVE
Chinese

★ die **Chips** MASC PL NOUN
crisps *pl*

Chirurg – Cyberkriminalität

BE CAREFUL!
The German word **Chips** does not mean **chips**.

★der **Chirurg** (GEN des **Chirurgen**, PL die **Chirurgen**) MASC NOUN
surgeon

die **Chirurgie** FEM NOUN
surgery

★die **Chirurgin** FEM NOUN
surgeon

das **Chlor** NEUT NOUN
chlorine

★der **Chor** (PL die **Chöre**) MASC NOUN
choir
□ Sie singt im Chor. She sings in a choir.

der **Christ** (GEN des **Christen**, PL die **Christen**) MASC NOUN
Christian
□ Er ist Christ. He's a Christian.

die **Christin** FEM NOUN
Christian
□ Sie ist Christin. She's a Christian.

christlich ADJECTIVE
Christian

circa ADVERB
approximately

cm ABBREVIATION (= *Zentimeter*)
cm

★die **Cola** (PL die **Colas**) FEM NOUN
Coke®

★der **Computer** (PL die **Computer**) MASC NOUN
computer

★die **Computeranlage** FEM NOUN
computer system

das **Computerspiel** (PL die **Computerspiele**) NEUT NOUN
computer game

★**cool** ADJECTIVE
cool

★der **Cousin** (PL die **Cousins**) MASC NOUN
cousin

★die **Cousine** FEM NOUN
cousin

★die **Creme** (PL die **Cremes**) FEM NOUN
1 cream
□ eine Handcreme a hand cream
2 polish
□ Hast du schwarze Schuhcreme? Do you have any black shoe polish?
3 cream dessert
□ eine Schokoladencreme a chocolate cream dessert

das **Crowdfunding** NEUT NOUN
crowdfunding

der **Curry** MASC NOUN
curry powder

★die **Currywurst** (PL die **Currywürste**) FEM NOUN
curried sausage

die **Cyberkriminalität** FEM NOUN
cybercrime

★ = core vocabulary

Dd

★da ADVERB, CONJUNCTION

1 there
□ Da ist es schön. It's beautiful there.□ da draußen out there□ Da haben wir Glück gehabt. We were lucky there.
■ **da sein** to be there

2 here
□ Da liegt ja meine Brille. Here are my glasses. □ Da bin ich. Here I am.
■ **Ist noch Milch da?** Is there any milk left?

3 since
□ Da du gerade hier bist ... Since you're here ...

4 because
□ Ich komme nicht, da ich mir den Fuß verstaucht habe. I'm not coming because I've sprained my foot.

★dabei ADVERB

■ **nahe dabei** close by□ Er stand nahe dabei. He was standing close by.
■ **Sie hatten ihren Hund dabei.** They had their dog with them.
■ **Was ist schon dabei?** What of it?
■ **Es ist doch nichts dabei, wenn ...** It doesn't matter if ...
■ **Bleiben wir dabei.** Let's leave it at that.
■ **Es bleibt dabei.** That's settled.
■ **dabei sein** to be there□ Ich bin dabei gewesen. I was there.
■ **Er war gerade dabei, zu gehen.** He was just about to leave.

★das Dach (PL die **Dächer**) NEUT NOUN
roof

★der Dachboden (PL die **Dachböden**) MASC NOUN
attic

dachte VERB ▷ see **denken**

der Dackel (PL die **Dackel**) MASC NOUN
dachshund

dadurch ADVERB, CONJUNCTION

1 through it
□ Er muss dadurch gekrochen sein. He must have crawled through it.

2 that's why
□ Dadurch habe ich mich verspätet. That's why I was late.

3 as a result
□ Der Zug hatte Verspätung, dadurch haben wir unseren Anschluss verpasst. The train was late,

and as a result we missed our connection.
■ **dadurch, dass** because□ Dadurch, dass sie kein Englisch kann ... Because she doesn't speak any English ...

dafür ADVERB

1 for it
□ Was hast du dafür bezahlt? How much did you pay for it?□ Was bekomme ich dafür? What will I get for it?
■ **Er ist bekannt dafür.** He's well-known for that.

2 instead
□ Wenn du nicht mit ins Schwimmbad kannst, dann komm dafür doch mit ins Kino. If you can't come with us to the swimming pool, then come along to the cinema instead.
■ **Sie kann nichts dafür.** She can't help it.

★dagegen ADVERB, CONJUNCTION

1 against it
□ Was hast du dagegen? What have you got against it?□ Ich war dagegen. I was against it.
■ **Ich habe nichts dagegen.** I don't mind.
■ **Dagegen kann man nichts tun.** You can't do anything about it.

2 into it
□ Er sah den Baum nicht und rannte dagegen. He didn't see the tree and ran into it.

3 for it
□ Das ist jetzt mein Ball, ich habe meine Murmeln dagegen getauscht. This is my ball now — I swapped my marbles for it.

4 by comparison
□ Dagegen ist unser Haus klein. Our house is small by comparison.

5 however
□ Sie wollte gehen, er dagegen wollte bleiben. She wanted to leave; however he wanted to stay.

★daheim ADVERB
at home

★daher ADVERB, CONJUNCTION

1 from there
□ Daher komme ich gerade. I've just come from there.

2 that's where
□ Das war ein schwerer Unfall; daher hat er sein kaputtes Bein. It was a serious accident; that's where he got his bad leg.

d

3 that's why
□ Sie war krank und konnte daher nicht mitkommen. She was ill, and that's why she couldn't come.

★ **dahin** ADVERB
there
□ Dahin gehe ich jetzt. I'm going there now.

dahinten ADVERB
over there

dahinter ADVERB
behind it
□ Er versteckte sich dahinter. He hid behind it.

dahinterkommen (IMPERFECT **kam dahinter**, PERFECT TENSE **ist dahintergekommen**) VERB [40]
to find out
□ Meine Mutter ist dahintergekommen, dass ich gestern nicht bei dir war. My mother has found out that I wasn't at your place yesterday.

★ **damals** ADVERB
in those days

★ die **Dame** FEM NOUN
1 lady
2 queen (chess, cards)
3 draughts sing
□ Dame ist mein Lieblingsspiel. Draughts is my favourite game.

★ **damit** ADVERB, CONJUNCTION
1 with it
□ Wisch damit den Tisch ab. Wipe the table with it.
2 by that
□ Was meint er damit? What does he mean by that?
■ **Was willst du damit sagen?** What are you getting at?
■ **Genug damit!** That's enough of that!
■ **Damit eilt es nicht.** There's no hurry.
3 so that
□ Ich sage dir das, damit du das weißt. I'm telling you so that you know.

der **Dampf** (PL die **Dämpfe**) MASC NOUN
steam
■ **giftige Dämpfe** toxic fumes

dampfen VERB [48]
1 to vape
2 to puff

★ der **Dampfer** (PL die **Dampfer**) MASC NOUN
steamer
□ mit dem Dampfer fahren to go by steamer
■ **Du bist auf dem falschen Dampfer.** (Umgangssprache) You've got the wrong idea.

★ **danach** ADVERB
1 afterwards
□ Ich habe etwas getrunken, und danach fühlte ich mich besser. I had something to drink and afterwards felt much better.

2 accordingly
□ Verhalte dich bitte danach. Please behave accordingly.

★ der **Däne** (GEN des **Dänen**, PL die **Dänen**) MASC NOUN
Dane

daneben ADVERB
1 beside it
□ Sein Stuhl stand daneben. His chair was beside it.
2 by comparison
□ Er ist sehr klug, daneben wirkt sie ziemlich dumm. He's very clever, and she seems rather stupid by comparison.

★ **Dänemark** NEUT NOUN
Denmark
■ **aus Dänemark** from Denmark
■ **nach Dänemark** to Denmark

★ die **Dänin** FEM NOUN
Dane

dänisch ADJECTIVE
Danish

★ **dank** PREPOSITION
▷ see also der **Dank** NOUN

dank takes the genitive or dative.

thanks to
□ Dank meiner Schwester habe ich noch rechtzeitig davon erfahren. Thanks to my sister I found out about it in time.

★ der **Dank** MASC NOUN
▷ see also **dank** PREPOSITION
thanks pl
□ Unser Dank gilt vor allem Herrn Morris. Our thanks to Mr Morris in particular.
■ **Vielen Dank!** Many thanks.

★ **dankbar** ADJECTIVE
grateful
□ Ich bin dir sehr dankbar. I'm very grateful to you.
■ **eine dankbare Aufgabe** a rewarding task

★ **danke** EXCLAMATION
thank you
■ **Danke sehr!** Thank you.
■ **Danke schön!** Thank you very much.
■ **Nein, danke!** No, thanks.

★ **danken** VERB [38]
to thank
□ Ich möchte dir dafür danken. I'd like to thank you for that.
■ **Nichts zu danken!** Don't mention it!

★ **dann** ADVERB
then
■ **dann und wann** now and then

daran ADVERB
1 on it
□ ein Päckchen mit einem Zettel daran a parcel with a label on it

★ = core vocabulary

2 of it
   □ Er ist daran gestorben. He died of it. □ Ich habe nicht daran gedacht. I didn't think of it.
   ■ **Es liegt daran, dass ...** This is because ...
   ■ **das Beste daran** the best thing about it
   ■ **Ich war nahe daran, zu gehen.** I was on the point of going.

darauf ADVERB

1 on it
   □ Nimm einen Untersetzer und stelle den Topf darauf. Take a mat and put the pan on it.

2 afterwards
   □ kurz darauf shortly afterwards
   ■ **die Tage darauf** the following days
   ■ **am Tag darauf** the next day
   ■ **Er ging darauf zu.** He walked towards it.
   ■ **Es kommt ganz darauf an, ob ...** It all depends whether ...

daraus ADVERB

1 out of it
   □ Sie nahm einen Keks daraus. She took a biscuit out of it.

2 of it
   □ Was ist daraus geworden? What became of it?
   ■ **Daraus geht hervor, dass ...** This means that ...

darf VERB ▷ see **dürfen**

darin ADVERB

in it
   □ eine Dose mit Keksen darin a tin with biscuits in it
   ■ **Darin sehe ich kein Problem.** I don't see any problem there.

der **Darm** (PL die **Därme**) MASC NOUN
intestine

darstellen (PERFECT TENSE **hat dargestellt**) VERB [4]
to portray
   □ etwas in einem günstigen Licht darstellen to portray something in a good light

darüber ADVERB

1 over it
   □ ein Tisch mit einer Lampe darüber a table with a light over it □ Da war eine Brücke, wir sind aber nicht darüber gefahren. There was a bridge, but we didn't drive over it.

2 about it
   □ Wir haben darüber gesprochen. We talked about it. □ Denk mal darüber nach. Think about it.

3 more
   □ Sie verdient fünftausend oder vielleicht sogar darüber. She earns five thousand or maybe even more.

darum ADVERB, CONJUNCTION

1 round it
   □ Sie machte ein rotes Band darum. She put a red ribbon round it.
   ■ **Es geht darum, dass ...** The important thing is to ...

   ■ **Er würde viel darum geben, wenn ...** He would give a lot to ...

2 that's why
   □ Darum bin ich nicht gekommen. That's why I didn't come.
   ■ **Ich tue es darum, weil ...** I'm doing it because ...

darunter ADVERB

1 under it
   □ Der Topf ist heiß, leg einen Untersetzer darunter. The pot's hot, put a mat under it.
   ■ **ein Stockwerk darunter** one floor below

2 less
   □ Sie verdient nur zweitausend Euro oder vielleicht sogar darunter. She only earns two thousand euros or maybe even less.
   ■ **Was verstehst du darunter?** What do you understand by that?

★ **das** ARTICLE, PRONOUN

   das is the definite neuter article.

1 the
   □ das Auto the car
   ■ **das Leben** life
   ■ **Er hat sich das Knie verletzt.** He's hurt his knee.

2 who
   □ das Kind, das dir das gesagt hat the child who told you
   ■ **das Kind, das du gesehen hast** the child you saw

3 which
   □ das Fahrrad, das du da siehst the bike which you can see over there
   ■ **das mit dem roten Sattel** the one with the red saddle

4 that
   □ Das habe ich nicht gehört. I didn't hear that.
   ■ **das da** that one

dasein VERB ▷ see **da**

★ **dass** CONJUNCTION

that
   □ Ich bin böse, dass er nicht gekommen ist. I'm annoyed that he didn't come. □ Ich weiß, dass du besser in Mathe bist als ich. I know you're better at maths than me.

dasselbe PRONOUN
the same
   □ dasselbe Kind the same child

dastehen (IMPERFECT **stand da**, PERFECT TENSE **hat dagestanden**) VERB [72]
to stand there

die **Datei** FEM NOUN
file

die **Daten** NEUT PL NOUN
data *pl*

die **Datenbank** (PL die **Datenbanken**) FEM NOUN
data base

die **Datenverarbeitung** FEM NOUN
data processing

der **Dativ** (PL die **Dative**) MASC NOUN
dative

★das **Datum** (PL die **Daten**) NEUT NOUN
date

die **Dauer** FEM NOUN
1 duration
  □ für die Dauer meines Aufenthalts for the duration of my stay
2 length
  □ die Dauer einer Reise the length of a journey
  □ die Dauer eines Anrufs the length of a call
  ▪ von Dauer sein to be permanent
  ▪ Ihr Glück war nur von kurzer Dauer. Their happiness was only short-lived.
  ▪ auf die Dauer 1 in the long run□ Auf die Dauer wird ihm das langweilig werden. He'll get bored with it in the long run. 2 indefinitely □ Auf die Dauer geht das aber nicht. That can't go on indefinitely.

★**dauern** VERB [88]
to last
  □ Der Krieg hat zehn Jahre gedauert. The war lasted ten years.
  ▪ Der Film hat fast drei Stunden gedauert. The film was nearly three hours long.
  ▪ lange dauern to take a long time□ Das hat lange gedauert. That took a long time.□ Es hat sehr lang gedauert, bis er ... It took him a long time to ...
  ▪ Wie lange dauert das denn noch? How much longer is this going to take?

dauernd ADJECTIVE, ADVERB
constant
  □ Ich konnte sein dauerndes Stöhnen nicht ertragen. I couldn't stand his constant moaning.
  ▪ Musst du mich dauernd stören? Do you have to constantly interrupt me?

die **Dauerwelle** FEM NOUN
perm

★der **Daumen** (PL die **Daumen**) MASC NOUN
thumb
  ▪ Ich drücke dir die Daumen. I'll keep my fingers crossed for you.

davon ADVERB
1 of them
  □ Sie nahm zwei davon. She took two of them.
  ▪ Sie nahm hundert Gramm davon. She took a hundred grams.
2 away
  □ Er lief davon. He ran away.
3 from it
  □ Sie hat den Knopf davon abgetrennt. She removed the button from it.
  ▪ Sie bekommt Kopfschmerzen davon. It gives her a headache.

  ▪ davon abgesehen apart from that
4 about it
  □ davon sprechen to talk about it□ Sie weiß nichts davon. She doesn't know anything about it.
  ▪ Was habe ich davon? What's the point?
  ▪ Das kommt davon! That's what you get.

davonkommen (IMPERFECT kam davon , PERFECT TENSE ist davongekommen) VERB [40]
to escape
  □ Wir sind noch einmal davongekommen. We've had a lucky escape.

davor ADVERB
1 in front of it
  □ Ich stellte mich davor. I stood in front of it.
2 first
  □ Du solltest davor aber noch zum Friseur. You ought to go to the hairdresser's first.
  ▪ Ich habe dich davor gewarnt. I warned you about it.

dazu ADVERB
with it
  □ Was sollen wir dazu trinken? What shall we drink with it?
  ▪ ein Beispiel dazu an example of this
  ▪ seine Gedanken dazu his thoughts on this
  ▪ dazu fähig sein to be capable of it
  ▪ und dazu noch and in addition

dazwischen ADVERB
1 in between
  □ Wir können dazwischen ja eine Pause machen. We can have a break in between.
2 between them
  □ Siehst du die beiden Pfosten, stell dich dazwischen. You see the two posts? Go and stand between them.□ der Unterschied dazwischen the difference between them

dazwischenkommen (IMPERFECT kam dazwischen , PERFECT TENSE ist dazwischengekommen) VERB [40]
  ▪ Es ist etwas dazwischengekommen. Something's cropped up.

★die **DDR** (GENDER DDR) FEM NOUN (=*Deutsche Demokratische Republik*)
GDR
  □ die ehemalige DDR the former GDR

★die **Decke** FEM NOUN
1 ceiling
  □ Wir haben die Decke des Kinderzimmers gestrichen. We've painted the ceiling of the children's room.
2 blanket
  □ eine Wolldecke a woollen blanket
  ▪ eine Tischdecke a tablecloth

der **Deckel** (PL die **Deckel**) MASC NOUN
lid

★**decken** VERB [38]
to cover

□ Er deckte die Hand über seine Augen. **He covered his eyes with his hand.**
■ **den Tisch decken** to lay the table

dehnen VERB [38]
to stretch
□ Er dehnte sich und gähnte. **He stretched and yawned.**

★ **dein** ADJECTIVE
1 your
□ Dein Englischlehrer ist nett. **Your English teacher's nice.** □ Hat deine Mutter das erlaubt? **Did your mother let you?** □ Ist das dein Buch? **Is that your book?** □ Wo sind deine Eltern? **Where are your parents?**
2 yours
□ Der Bleistift hier, ist das deiner? **Is this pencil yours?** □ Meine Mutter heißt Ulla, wie heißt deine? **My mother's called Ulla; what's yours called?** □ Mein Fahrrad ist kaputt, kann ich deins benutzen? **My bike's broken; can I use yours?**

deinetwegen ADVERB
1 for your sake
□ Ich habe deinetwegen darauf verzichtet. **I did without for your sake.**
2 on your account
□ Er hat sich deinetwegen aufgeregt. **He got upset on your account.**

deklinieren (PERFECT TENSE **hat dekliniert**) VERB [76]
to decline

der **Delphin** (PL die **Delphine**) MASC NOUN
dolphin

dem ARTICLE, PRONOUN

dem is the dative of **der** and **das**.

the
□ auf dem Tisch **on the table**
■ **Gib es dem Mann.** Give it to the man.
■ **der Mann, dem ich es gegeben habe** the man I gave it to

demnächst ADVERB
shortly

die **Demokratie** FEM NOUN
democracy

demokratisch ADJECTIVE
democratic

die **Demonstration** FEM NOUN
demonstration

demonstrieren (PERFECT TENSE **hat demonstriert**) VERB [76]
to demonstrate

den ARTICLE, PRONOUN

den is the accusative of **der**.

the
□ Ich sehe den Mann. **I can see the man.**
□ durch den Wald **through the wood**

■ **Er hat sich den Fuß verletzt.** He's hurt his foot.
■ **der Mann, den ich gesehen habe** the man I saw

denen PRONOUN

denen is the dative of **die** (plural).

1 whom
■ **die Leute, denen ich die Bücher gegeben habe** the people I gave the books to
■ **die Leute, denen ich helfen wollte** the people I wanted to help
2 which
□ Probleme, denen wir nicht gewachsen sind **problems which we can't cope with**

denkbar ADJECTIVE
conceivable

★ **denken** (IMPERFECT **dachte**, PERFECT TENSE **hat gedacht**) VERB [14]
to think

★ das **Denkmal** (PL die **Denkmäler**) NEUT NOUN
monument

★ **denn** CONJUNCTION, ADVERB
1 because
□ Ich habe sie nicht gesehen, denn sie war schon weg. **I didn't see her because she had already left.**
2 than
□ besser denn je **better than ever**
■ **es sei denn ...** unless ...
■ **Warum denn?** But why?

dennoch CONJUNCTION
nevertheless

★ **deprimiert** ADJECTIVE
depressed

der ARTICLE, PRONOUN

der is the definite masculine article and genitive and dative of **die**.

1 the
□ der Mann **the man**
■ **der Tod** death
■ **das Auto der Frau** the woman's car
■ **Gib es der Frau.** Give it to the woman.
2 who
□ der, der dir das gesagt hat **the person who told you that**
■ **die Frau, der ich es gegeben habe** the woman I gave it to
3 which
□ der Computer, der mir gehört **the computer which belongs to me**
■ **der mit der Brille** the one with glasses
■ **der da** that one

derselbe PRONOUN
the same
□ derselbe Mann **the same man**

deshalb ADVERB
that's why

der **Desktop** (PL die **Desktops**) MASC NOUN
desktop (*computer*)

der **Desktop-PC** (PL die **Desktop-PCs**) MASC
NOUN
desktop PC

dessen PRONOUN

dessen is the genitive of **der** and **das**.

whose
□ mein Freund, dessen Schwester krank ist my
friend whose sister is ill

desto ADVERB
all the
□ desto besser all the better
■ **je ... desto ...** the ... the ... □ Je mehr er sagte,
desto wütender wurde sie. The more he said,
the angrier she became. □ je eher, desto besser
the earlier the better

deswegen CONJUNCTION
that's why
□ Hat er deswegen so geschimpft? Is that why
he was so mad?
■ **Es ist spät, deswegen gehen wir jetzt.**
It's late, so we're leaving.
■ **Ich sage das deswegen, weil ...** The
reason I'm saying this is that ...

deutlich ADJECTIVE, ADVERB
1 clear
□ mit deutlicher Stimme in a clear voice
2 clearly
□ Drück dich bitte deutlicher aus. Please speak
more clearly. □ Es war deutlich zu sehen. It was
clearly visible.
■ **ein deutlicher Unterschied** a distinct
difference

★ **deutsch** ADJECTIVE
▷ *see also* das **Deutsch** NOUN
German

★ das **Deutsch** (GEN des **Deutschen**) NEUT
NOUN
▷ *see also* **deutsch** ADJECTIVE
German
□ Er lernt Deutsch in der Schule. He's learning
German at school.
■ **auf Deutsch** in German

★ der/die **Deutsche** (GEN des/der **Deutschen**,
PL die **Deutschen**) MASC/FEM NOUN
German
■ **Ich bin Deutscher.** I'm German.

★ **Deutschland** NEUT NOUN
Germany
■ **aus Deutschland** from Germany
■ **in Deutschland** in Germany
■ **nach Deutschland** to Germany

★ der **Dezember** (GEN des **Dezember** *or*
Dezembers, PL die **Dezember**) MASC NOUN
December
□ im Dezember in December □ am vierten
Dezember on the fourth of December

□ Erlangen, den 5. Dezember 2019 Erlangen, 5
December 2019 □ Heute ist der sechste
Dezember. Today is the sixth of December.

der **DGB** MASC NOUN (= *Deutscher
Gewerkschaftsbund*)
German trade union federation

d. h. ABBREVIATION (= *das heißt*)
i.e.

das **Dia** (PL die **Dias**) NEUT NOUN
slide

diagonal ADJECTIVE
diagonal

der **Dialekt** (PL die **Dialekte**) MASC NOUN
dialect

der **Diamant** (GEN des **Diamanten**, PL die
Diamanten) MASC NOUN
diamond

★ die **Diät** FEM NOUN
diet
□ Er muss Diät halten. He has to stick to a strict
diet.

dich PRONOUN

dich is the accusative of **du**.

1 you
□ Ich habe dich gesehen. I saw you.
2 yourself
□ Sieh dich mal im Spiegel an. Look at yourself
in the mirror.

★ **dicht** ADJECTIVE, ADVERB
1 dense
□ dichte Wälder dense woods
2 thick
□ dichter Nebel thick fog
3 watertight
□ Ist der Behälter dicht? Is the container
watertight?
■ **Die Gasleitung war nicht dicht.** There
was a leak in the gas pipe.
■ **dichter Verkehr** heavy traffic
■ **dicht an** close to □ Geh nicht zu dicht ans
Feuer. Don't go too close to the fire.

der **Dichter** (PL die **Dichter**) MASC NOUN
poet

die **Dichterin** FEM NOUN
poet

★ **dick** ADJECTIVE
1 thick
□ Das Brett ist drei Zentimeter dick. The plank's
three centimetres thick.
2 fat
□ Hör auf, du bist nicht zu dick. Stop it, you're
not too fat.

der **Dickkopf** (PL die **Dickköpfe**) MASC NOUN
■ **einen Dickkopf haben** to be stubborn

die **Dickmilch** FEM NOUN
soured milk

★ = core vocabulary

die ARTICLE, PRONOUN

> die is the definite feminine article and the definite article plural.

1 the
  □ die Frau the woman □ die Kinder the children
  ■ **die Liebe** love
  ■ **Er hat sich die Hand verletzt.** He's hurt his hand.

2 who
  □ die, die dir das gesagt hat the person who told you that
  ■ **die Frau, die du gesehen hast** the woman you saw

3 which
  □ die Uhr, die mir gehört the watch which belongs to me
  ■ **die mit der Brille** the one with glasses
  ■ **die da** that one

★der **Dieb** (PL die Diebe) MASC NOUN
  thief

★die **Diebin** FEM NOUN
  thief

★der **Diebstahl** (PL die Diebstähle) MASC NOUN
  theft

★die **Diele** FEM NOUN
  hall
  □ Sie stand vor dem Spiegel in der Diele. She stood in front of the mirror in the hall.

★**dienen** (PERFECT TENSE hat gedient) VERB [38]
  to serve
  □ Es dient einem guten Zweck. It serves a useful purpose.
  ■ **Womit kann ich Ihnen dienen?** What can I do for you?

★der **Dienst** (PL die Dienste) MASC NOUN
  service
  ■ **Dienst haben** to be on duty

der **Dienstag** (PL die Dienstage) MASC NOUN
  Tuesday
  □ am Dienstag on Tuesday

dienstags ADVERB
  on Tuesdays

dies PRONOUN
1 this
  □ Dies ist unser Haus. This is our house.
2 these
  □ Dies sind meine Bücher. These are my books.

diese PRONOUN
1 this
  □ Die Ferien fangen Ende dieser Woche an. The holidays start at the end of this week.
2 these
  □ diese Bücher these books
3 this one
  □ Ich möchte diesen hier. I'd like this one.
4 these ones
  □ Ich suche ein Paar Sandalen, kann ich diese

anprobieren? I'm looking for a pair of sandals; can I try these ones on?

★der **Diesel** MASC NOUN
  diesel

dieselbe PRONOUN
  the same
  □ dieselbe Frau the same woman

★**diesmal** ADVERB
  this time

★**digital** ADJECTIVE
  digital
  □ die digitale Revolution the digital revolution

das **Digitalfernsehen** NEUT NOUN
  digital television

das **Diktat** (PL die Diktate) NEUT NOUN
  dictation

diktieren (PERFECT TENSE hat diktiert) VERB [76]
  to dictate

★das **Ding** (PL die Dinge) NEUT NOUN
  thing

★das **Diplom** (PL die Diplome) NEUT NOUN
  diploma

die **Diplomatie** FEM NOUN
  diplomacy

diplomatisch ADJECTIVE
  diplomatic

dir PRONOUN

> dir is the dative of du.

1 you
  □ Ich habe es dir doch gesagt. I told you so.
2 to you
  □ Ich habe es dir gestern gegeben. I gave it to you yesterday.

★**direkt** ADJECTIVE, ADVERB
  direct
  □ Ich stehe in direkter Verbindung mit ihr. I'm in direct contact with her. □ Der Flug geht direkt. It's a direct flight.

★der **Direktor** (PL die Direktoren) MASC NOUN
1 director
  □ der Direktor der Firma the director of the company
2 headmaster
  □ Mein Bruder musste gestern zum Direktor. My brother was sent to the headmaster yesterday.

★die **Disco** (PL die Discos) FEM NOUN
  disco

★die **Diskothek** FEM NOUN
  disco

★die **Diskussion** FEM NOUN
  discussion
  ■ **zur Diskussion stehen** to be under discussion

d

d

das **Diskuswerfen** NEUT NOUN
throwing the discus

diskutieren (PERFECT TENSE **hat diskutiert**)
VERB [76]
to discuss
□ Wir haben über Politik diskutiert. **We
discussed politics.**

★ **doch** ADVERB, CONJUNCTION
1 after all
□ Sie ist doch noch gekommen. **She came after
all.**
2 anyway
□ Du machst ja doch, was du willst. **You do
what you want anyway.**
3 but
□ Ich habe ihn eingeladen, doch er hatte keine
Lust. **I invited him, but he didn't feel like it.** □ Sie
ist doch noch so jung. **But she's still so young.**
4 yes

> **doch** is used to contradict a negative
> statement.

□ Ich dachte, du magst keine Süßigkeiten. —
Doch! **I thought you didn't like sweets. — Yes I
do.** □ Das ist nicht wahr. — Doch! **That's not
true. — Yes it is!**
■ **Komm doch.** Do come.
■ **Lass ihn doch.** Just leave him.

★ der **Doktor** (PL die **Doktoren**) MASC NOUN
doctor
□ Er ist Doktor der Philosophie. **He's a doctor of
philosophy.**

das **Dokument** NEUT NOUN
document

★ der **Dokumentarfilm** (PL die
Dokumentarfilme) MASC NOUN
documentary

dolmetschen VERB [48]
to interpret

der **Dolmetscher** (PL die **Dolmetscher**)
MASC NOUN
interpreter

die **Dolmetscherin** FEM NOUN
interpreter

★ der **Dom** (PL die **Dome**) MASC NOUN
cathedral

★ die **Donau** FEM NOUN
Danube

★ der **Donner** (PL die **Donner**) MASC NOUN
thunder *no pl*

★ **donnern** VERB [88]
to thunder
□ Es donnerte. **It was thundering.**

★ der **Donnerstag** (PL die **Donnerstage**) MASC
NOUN
Thursday
□ am Donnerstag **on Thursday**

★ **donnerstags** ADVERB
on Thursdays

★ **doof** ADJECTIVE
thick (*Umgangssprache*)

★ das **Doppelbett** (PL die **Doppelbetten**)
NEUT NOUN
double bed

die **Doppelfenster** NEUT PL NOUN
double glazing *sing*

das **Doppelhaus** (GEN des **Doppelhauses**,
PL die **Doppelhäuser**) NEUT NOUN
semidetached house

der **Doppelpunkt** (PL die **Doppelpunkte**)
MASC NOUN
colon

★ die **Doppelstunde** FEM NOUN
double period

doppelt ADJECTIVE
1 double
□ die doppelte Menge **double the amount**
2 twice the
□ der doppelte Preis **twice the price** □ die
doppelte Geschwindigkeit **twice the speed**
■ **doppelt so viel** twice as much
■ **in doppelter Ausführung** in duplicate

★ das **Doppelzimmer** (PL die
Doppelzimmer) NEUT NOUN
double room

★ das **Dorf** (PL die **Dörfer**) NEUT NOUN
village

★ **dort** ADVERB
there
■ **dort drüben** over there

dorther ADVERB
from there

★ **dorthin** ADVERB
there
□ Wir gehen jetzt dorthin. **We're going there
now.**

★ die **Dose** FEM NOUN
tin

★ der **Dosenöffner** (PL die **Dosenöffner**) MASC
NOUN
tin opener

der **Dotter** (PL die **Dotter**) MASC NOUN
yolk

downloaden VERB [36]
to download

das **Drachenfliegen** NEUT NOUN
hang-gliding
□ Sie ist beim Drachenfliegen verunglückt. **She
had a hang-gliding accident.**

der **Draht** (PL die **Drähte**) MASC NOUN
wire
■ **auf Draht sein** to be on the ball

★ = core vocabulary

drahtlos ADJECTIVE
wireless
□ drahtlose Kommunikation wireless communication

★ das **Drama** (PL die **Dramen**) NEUT NOUN
drama

★ **dran** ADVERB
■ Jetzt bin ich dran! It's my turn now.
■ Wer ist dran? Whose turn is it?
■ gut dran sein to be well-off
■ schlecht dran sein to be in a bad way

drauf ADVERB ▷ see darauf

★ **draußen** ADVERB
outside

der **Dreck** MASC NOUN
dirt

★ **dreckig** ADJECTIVE
dirty
□ Mach deine Kleider nicht dreckig. Don't get your clothes dirty.

. **drehen** VERB [38]
to turn
□ Dreh mal deinen Kopf zur Seite. Turn your head to one side. □ Du musst an dem Rad drehen. You have to turn the wheel.
■ eine Zigarette drehen to roll a cigarette
■ einen Film drehen to shoot a film
■ sich drehen to turn □ Das Rad drehte sich schnell. The wheel was turning fast.
■ Es dreht sich um … It's about …

drei NUMBER
▷ see also die **Drei** NOUN
three

die **Drei** FEM NOUN
▷ see also **drei** NUMBER
1 three
2 satisfactory

DID YOU KNOW…?
German grades range from one (sehr gut) to six (ungenügend).

das **Dreieck** (PL die **Dreiecke**) NEUT NOUN
triangle

dreieckig ADJECTIVE
triangular

dreihundert NUMBER
three hundred

das **Dreikönigsfest** NEUT NOUN
Epiphany

DID YOU KNOW…?
In Germany Epiphany is celebrated every year on January 6, and in some Länder it is a public holiday. It marks the visit of the Three Wise Men to Jesus and is often commemorated by special church services.

dreimal ADVERB
three times

★ **dreißig** NUMBER
thirty

dreiviertel NUMBER
three-quarters

die **Dreiviertelstunde** FEM NOUN
three-quarters of an hour
□ Eine Dreiviertelstunde war vergangen. Three-quarters of an hour had passed.

★ **dreizehn** NUMBER
thirteen

drin ADVERB ▷ see darin

★ **dringend** ADJECTIVE
urgent

★ **drinnen** ADVERB
inside

★ **dritte** ADJECTIVE
third
□ Sie nahm beim dritten Klingeln ab. She answered on the third ring. □ Er kam als Dritter. He was the third to arrive.
■ die Dritte Welt the Third World
■ das Dritte Reich the Third Reich

★ das **Drittel** (PL die **Drittel**) NEUT NOUN
third

drittens ADVERB
thirdly

★ die **Droge** FEM NOUN
drug

★ **drogenabhängig** ADJECTIVE
addicted to drugs

★ die **Drogerie** FEM NOUN
chemist's shop

★ der **Drogist** (GEN des **Drogisten**, PL die **Drogisten**) MASC NOUN
pharmacist

die **Drogistin** FEM NOUN
pharmacist

drohen VERB [38]
to threaten
□ jemandem drohen to threaten somebody

die **Drohne** FEM NOUN
drone

★ **drüben** ADVERB
over there

der **Druck** (PL die **Drucke**) MASC NOUN
1 pressure
□ Der Behälter muss viel Druck aushalten. The container has to withstand a lot of pressure.
■ jemanden unter Druck setzen to put pressure on somebody
2 printing
□ der Druck eines Buches the printing of a book
3 print
□ An der Wand hingen Drucke. There were prints on the wall.

drücken – durchblicken

★**drücken** VERB [38]

1 to press

□ Er drückte auf den Knopf. **He pressed the button.**

■ **Sie drückte ihm die Hand.** She squeezed his hand.

2 to pinch

□ Meine Schuhe drücken. **My shoes pinch.**

■ **sich vor etwas drücken** to get out of something□ Du willst dich bloß wieder vor dem Abwasch drücken. **You just want to get out of washing up again.**

★**der Drucker** (PL die **Drucker**) MASC NOUN
printer

die Drucksache FEM NOUN
printed matter *no pl*

die Drüse FEM NOUN
gland

der Dschungel (PL die **Dschungel**) MASC NOUN
jungle

du PRONOUN
you

□ Hast du das gesehen? **Did you see that?**

■ **du sagen** to use the 'du' form of address

> **DID YOU KNOW...?**
> Only use **du** when speaking to one person, and when the person is your own age or younger. Use **ihr** for several people of your own age or younger. If in doubt use the polite form **Sie**.

sich ducken VERB [48]
to duck

der Dudelsack (PL die **Dudelsäcke**) MASC NOUN
bagpipes *pl*

□ Er spielt Dudelsack. **He plays the bagpipes.**

★**der Duft** (PL die **Düfte**) MASC NOUN
scent

★**duften** VERB [2]
to smell

□ Hier duftet es nach Kaffee. **It smells of coffee here.**

★**dumm** ADJECTIVE

1 stupid

□ Das ist die dümmste Ausrede, die ich je gehört habe. **That's the stupidest excuse I've ever heard.**

2 bad

□ Es ist wirklich zu dumm, dass du nicht gekommen bist. **It's really too bad that you didn't come.**

■ **der Dumme sein** to draw the short straw

dummerweise ADVERB
stupidly

die Dummheit FEM NOUN

1 stupidity

□ Deine Dummheit ist wirklich grenzenlos. **Your stupidity really knows no bounds.**

2 stupid mistake

□ Es war eine Dummheit, ihr das zu erzählen. **It was a stupid mistake telling her that.**

■ **Dummheiten machen** to do something stupid□ Mach bloß keine Dummheiten! **Don't do anything stupid.**

der Dummkopf (PL die **Dummköpfe**) MASC NOUN
idiot

★**dunkel** ADJECTIVE
dark

□ Im Zimmer war es dunkel. **It was dark in the room.**

■ **eine dunkle Stimme** a deep voice

■ **eine dunkle Ahnung** a vague idea

■ **dunkle Gestalten** sinister figures

■ **dunkle Geschäfte** shady dealings

■ **im Dunkeln tappen** to grope about in the dark

■ **ein Dunkles** a dark beer

die Dunkelheit FEM NOUN
dark

□ Er hat Angst vor der Dunkelheit. **He's afraid of the dark.**

★**dünn** ADJECTIVE
thin

der Dunst (PL die **Dünste**) MASC NOUN
haze

★**durch** PREPOSITION, ADVERB

> The preposition **durch** takes the accusative.

1 through

□ durch den Wald **through the wood**□ Ich habe die Stelle durch meinen Onkel bekommen. **I got the job through my uncle.**□ durch seine Bemühungen **through his efforts**

2 throughout

□ die ganze Nacht durch **throughout the night**□ den Sommer durch **throughout the summer**

3 owing to

□ Durch die Verspätung haben wir den Anschluss verpasst. **Owing to the delay we missed our connection.**

■ **Tod durch Herzschlag** death from a heart attack

■ **durch die Post** by post

■ **durch und durch** completely□ Wir waren durch und durch nass. **We were completely soaked.**

durcharbeiten (PERFECT TENSE **hat durchgearbeitet**) VERB [15]
to work without a break

durchblicken (PERFECT TENSE **hat durchgeblickt**) VERB [15]
to understand

■ **Bei Computern blickt Tobias durch.** Tobias knows his stuff with computers. (*Umgangssprache*)

★ = core vocabulary

■ **etwas durchblicken lassen** to hint at something

durchdrehen (PERFECT TENSE **ist durchgedreht**) VERB [15]
to crack up (*Umgangssprache*)

durcheinander ADVERB
▷ *see also* das **Durcheinander** NOUN

1 in a mess
□ Warum ist dein Zimmer so durcheinander? Why is your room in such a mess?

2 confused
□ Ich war völlig durcheinander. I was completely confused.
■ **Du bringst mich ganz durcheinander.** You completely confuse me.

das **Durcheinander** NEUT NOUN
▷ *see also* durcheinander ADVERB
mess
□ In ihrem Zimmer war ein völliges Durcheinander. Her room was in a complete mess.

durchfahren (PRESENT TENSE **fährt durch**, IMPERFECT **fuhr durch**, PERFECT TENSE **ist durchgefahren**) VERB [21]

1 to drive through
□ Wir sind durch einen Tunnel durchgefahren. We drove through a tunnel.

2 to drive without a break
□ Wir sind die ganze Nacht durchgefahren. We drove all night without a break.
■ **Der Zug fährt bis Hamburg durch.** The train runs direct to Hamburg.

die **Durchfahrt** (PL die **Durchfahrten**) FEM NOUN
way through
□ auf unserer Durchfahrt durch Frankreich on our way through France
■ **'Durchfahrt verboten'** 'no through road'

der **Durchfall** MASC NOUN
diarrhoea

durchfallen (PRESENT TENSE **fällt durch**, IMPERFECT **fiel durch**, PERFECT TENSE **ist durchgefallen**) VERB [22]

1 to fall through
□ Die Münze ist durch dieses Gitter durchgefallen. The coin fell through this grating.

2 to fail
□ Sie ist in der Prüfung durchgefallen. She failed the exam.

durchführen (PERFECT TENSE **hat durchgeführt**) VERB [4]
to carry out

der **Durchgang** (PL die **Durchgänge**) MASC NOUN
passageway
□ Zwischen den Häusern ist ein schmaler Durchgang. There's a narrow passageway between the houses.

durchgehen (IMPERFECT **ging durch**, PERFECT TENSE **ist durchgegangen**) VERB [29]

1 to go through
□ durch einen Tunnel durchgehen to go through a tunnel

2 to break loose
□ Das Pferd ist durchgegangen. The horse has broken loose.
■ **jemandem etwas durchgehen lassen** to let somebody get away with something
■ **ein durchgehender Zug** a through train

durchkommen (IMPERFECT **kam durch**, PERFECT TENSE **ist durchgekommen**) VERB [40]

1 to get through
□ Obwohl die Öffnung sehr schmal war, sind wir durchgekommen. Although the opening was very narrow, we got through.

2 to pass
□ Es war knapp, aber ich bin durchgekommen. It was a close shave, but I passed.

3 to pull through
□ Er war schwer verletzt, ist aber durchgekommen. He was seriously injured, but he pulled through.

durchlassen (PRESENT TENSE **lässt durch**, IMPERFECT **ließ durch**, PERFECT TENSE **hat durchgelassen**) VERB [42]
to let through
□ Der Ordner wollte uns nicht durchlassen. The steward didn't want to let us through.
■ **Der Behälter lässt Wasser durch.** The container isn't watertight.

durchlesen (PRESENT TENSE **liest durch**, IMPERFECT **las durch**, PERFECT TENSE **hat durchgelesen**) VERB [45]
to read through

durchmachen (PERFECT TENSE **hat durchgemacht**) VERB [15]
to go through
□ Sie hat viel durchgemacht in ihrem Leben. She's been through a lot in her life.
■ **die Nacht durchmachen** to make a night of it

der **Durchmesser** (PL die **Durchmesser**) MASC NOUN
diameter

durchnehmen (PRESENT TENSE **nimmt durch**, IMPERFECT **nahm durch**, PERFECT TENSE **hat durchgenommen**) VERB [52]
to do
□ Wir nehmen gerade Shakespeare durch. We're doing Shakespeare just now.

die **Durchreise** FEM NOUN
journey through
□ die Durchreise durch die Schweiz the journey through Switzerland
■ **Ich bin nur auf der Durchreise.** I'm just passing through.

durchs = durch das

Numbers in brackets refer to verb tables on pages 697 to 706.

73

der **Durchschnitt** MASC NOUN
average
□ über dem Durchschnitt above average
□ unter dem Durchschnitt below average
■ im Durchschnitt on average

durchschnittlich ADJECTIVE, ADVERB
1 average
□ Ich habe durchschnittliche Noten. My marks
are average.
2 on average
□ Durchschnittlich brauche ich eine Stunde für
die Hausaufgaben. On average, my homework
takes me an hour.

durchsetzen (PERFECT TENSE **hat
durchgesetzt**) VERB [15]
■ sich durchsetzen to assert oneself □ Er
kann sich nicht durchsetzen. He doesn't know
how to assert himself.
■ Du solltest dich mehr durchsetzen. You
should be more assertive.
■ seinen Kopf durchsetzen to get one's way

durchsichtig ADJECTIVE
transparent

durchsuchen (PERFECT TENSE **hat
durchsucht**) VERB [18]
to search

★ **dürfen** (PRESENT TENSE **darf**, IMPERFECT **durfte**,
PERFECT TENSE **hat gedurft** or **dürfen**) VERB [16]
to be allowed to
□ Ich darf das. I'm allowed to do that. □ Er darf
das nicht. He's not allowed to do that. □ Ich
habe leider nicht gedurft. Unfortunately, I
wasn't allowed.
■ Darf ich? May I?
■ Darf ich ins Kino? Can I go to the cinema?

> The past participle **dürfen** is used when
> **dürfen** is a modal auxiliary.

■ etwas tun dürfen to be allowed to do
something □ Ich habe das nicht tun dürfen. I
wasn't allowed to do that. □ Die Kinder haben
gestern länger aufbleiben dürfen. The children
were allowed to stay up late yesterday.
■ darf nicht must not □ Das darf nicht
geschehen. That must not happen.

■ Da darf sie sich nicht wundern. That
shouldn't surprise her.
■ Das darf nicht wahr sein! I don't believe it!
■ Darf ich Sie bitten, das zu tun? Could I ask
you to do that?
■ Was darf es sein? What can I do for you?
■ Das dürfen Sie mir glauben. You can take
my word for it.
■ Das dürfte genug sein. That should be
enough.
■ Es dürfte Ihnen bekannt sein, dass ... As
you will probably know ...

★ der **Durst** MASC NOUN
thirst
■ Durst haben to be thirsty

★ **durstig** ADJECTIVE
thirsty

★ die **Dusche** FEM NOUN
shower

★ **duschen** VERB [48]
to have a shower
■ sich duschen to have a shower

düster ADJECTIVE
1 dark
□ Hier drin ist es so düster. It's so dark in here.
2 gloomy

★ das **Dutzend** (PL die **Dutzende** or **Dutzend**)
NEUT NOUN
dozen
□ zwei Dutzend Bücher two dozen books

★ **duzen** VERB [36]
to address someone as 'du'

> **DID YOU KNOW...?**
> The familiar form of address **du** (plural **ihr**)
> is used when addressing family members,
> friends, children under 16 and pets.

der **DVD-Player** (PL die **DVD-Player**) MASC
NOUN
DVD player

dynamisch ADJECTIVE
dynamic

★ der **D-Zug** (PL die **D-Züge**) MASC NOUN
through train

Ee

die **Ebbe** FEM NOUN
low tide
□ bei Ebbe at low tide

★ **eben** ADJECTIVE, ADVERB
1 flat
□ eine ebene Fläche a flat surface
2 just
□ Er ist eben erst gegangen. He's just gone.
3 exactly
□ Eben, das sage ich ja. That's exactly what I'm saying.
■ **eben deswegen** that's precisely why

die **Ebene** FEM NOUN
1 plain
□ Wir sahen auf die Ebene hinunter. We looked down onto the plain.
2 level
□ Das muss auf höherer Ebene entschieden werden. That has to be decided at a higher level.

ebenfalls ADVERB
likewise

★ **ebenso** ADVERB
just as
□ Sie ist ebenso groß wie ihr Bruder. She's just as tall as her brother.

die **E-Card** (PL die **E-Cards**) FEM NOUN
e-card

das **Echo** (PL die **Echos**) NEUT NOUN
echo

echt ADJECTIVE, ADVERB
1 real
□ echtes Gold real gold
■ **Der Geldschein ist nicht echt.** That banknote's a fake.
2 really
□ Die Party war echt gut. The party was really good.
■ **Echt?** Really?

die **Ecke** FEM NOUN
corner
□ um die Ecke round the corner

der **Edelstein** (PL die **Edelsteine**) MASC NOUN
precious stone

die **EDV** FEM NOUN (= *elektronische Datenverarbeitung*)
electronic data processing

★ **egal** ADJECTIVE
all the same
□ Das ist mir egal. It's all the same to me.
■ **Das ist egal.** That makes no difference.
■ **Egal, ob ...** It doesn't matter whether ...

egoistisch ADJECTIVE
selfish

★ **ehe** CONJUNCTION
▷ *see also* die **Ehe** NOUN
before
□ Ehe ich es vergesse, ... Before I forget, ...

★ die **Ehe** FEM NOUN
▷ *see also* **ehe** CONJUNCTION
marriage

★ die **Ehefrau** FEM NOUN
wife

★ **ehemalig** ADJECTIVE
former

★ der **Ehemann** (PL die **Ehemänner**) MASC NOUN
husband

★ das **Ehepaar** (PL die **Ehepaare**) NEUT NOUN
married couple *pl*

eher ADVERB
sooner
□ Das hättest du eher sagen müssen. You should have said that sooner.
■ **Das kommt schon eher der Wahrheit nahe.** That's more like the truth.

die **Ehre** FEM NOUN
honour

ehrgeizig ADJECTIVE
ambitious

★ **ehrlich** ADJECTIVE
honest

die **Ehrlichkeit** FEM NOUN
honesty

★ das **Ei** (PL die **Eier**) NEUT NOUN
egg

die **Eiche** FEM NOUN
oak

das **Eichhörnchen** (PL die **Eichhörnchen**) NEUT NOUN
squirrel

Eid - eindeutig

der Eid (PL die **Eide**) MASC NOUN
oath
□ einen Eid schwören to swear an oath

der Eierbecher (PL die **Eierbecher**) MASC
NOUN
egg cup

der Eifer MASC NOUN
enthusiasm

die Eifersucht FEM NOUN
jealousy

★**eifersüchtig** ADJECTIVE
jealous
□ Er ist eifersüchtig auf seine kleine Schwester.
He's jealous of his little sister.

eifrig ADJECTIVE
eager

das Eigelb (PL die **Eigelb**) NEUT NOUN
egg yolk

★**eigen** ADJECTIVE
own
□ meine eigene Meinung my own opinion

die Eigenart FEM NOUN
peculiarity
□ Wir haben alle unsere Eigenarten. We all have
our own peculiarities.

eigenartig ADJECTIVE
peculiar

★**die Eigenschaft** FEM NOUN
quality

eigensinnig ADJECTIVE
obstinate

★**eigentlich** ADJECTIVE, ADVERB
1 actual
□ Er ist der eigentliche Besitzer. He's the actual
owner.
2 actually
□ Eigentlich wollte ich heute nicht weggehen.
Actually I didn't want to go out today.
■ **Eigentlich nicht.** Not really.

das Eigentum NEUT NOUN
property

der Eigentümer (PL die **Eigentümer**) MASC
NOUN
owner

die Eigentümerin FEM NOUN
owner

sich **eignen** VERB [53]
to be suited
□ Er eignet sich nicht für diese Stelle. He's not
suited to this position.

★**eilen** VERB [38]
to be urgent
□ Das eilt nicht. It's not urgent.

eilig ADJECTIVE
urgent

□ Ich muss zuerst die eiligen Dinge erledigen.
I'll have to do the urgent things first.
■ **es eilig haben** to be in a hurry

★**der Eilzug** (PL die **Eilzüge**) MASC NOUN
fast stopping train

der Eimer (PL die **Eimer**) MASC NOUN
bucket

★**ein** ARTICLE, NUMBER
1 a
□ ein Mann a man □ eine Frau a woman □ ein
Kind a child
an
□ ein Ei an egg □ eine Stunde an hour
2 one
□ Es war nur ein Kind da. There was only one
child there. □ Ich möchte nur einen. I only want
one.
3 somebody
□ Wenn einer dir das sagt, glaube es nicht. If
somebody tells you that, don't believe it.
4 you
□ Da kann einem die Lust vergehen. It's enough
to put you off.

★**einander** PRONOUN
each other

einatmen (PERFECT TENSE hat **eingeatmet**)
VERB [3]
to breathe in

★**die Einbahnstraße** FEM NOUN
one-way street

einbilden (PERFECT TENSE hat **eingebildet**)
VERB [54]
■ **sich etwas einbilden** to imagine
something □ Das bildest du dir nur ein. You're
imagining it.

★**einbrechen** (PRESENT TENSE **bricht ein**,
IMPERFECT **brach ein**, PERFECT TENSE **ist
eingebrochen**) VERB [11]
to break in
□ Bei ihnen wurde eingebrochen. Their house
has been broken into. □ Er ist in das Haus
eingebrochen. He broke into the house.

★**der Einbrecher** (PL die **Einbrecher**) MASC
NOUN
burglar

★**die Einbrecherin** FEM NOUN
burglar

der Einbruch (PL die **Einbrüche**) MASC NOUN
break-in
□ In dieser Gegend gibt es häufiger Einbrüche.
There are a lot of break-ins in this area.
■ **bei Einbruch der Nacht** at nightfall
■ **vor Einbruch der Nacht** before nightfall

eindeutig ADJECTIVE
clear
□ eine eindeutige Antwort geben to give a clear
answer

★ = core vocabulary

★der **Eindruck** (pl die Eindrücke) MASC NOUN
impression

eindrucksvoll ADJECTIVE
impressive

★**eine** ▷ see ein

eineinhalb NUMBER
one and a half

einer ▷ see ein

einerseits ADVERB
on the one hand
□ Einerseits ..., andererseits ... On the one
hand ..., on the other hand ...

eines ▷ see ein

★**einfach** ADJECTIVE, ADVERB
1 easy
□ Das war eine einfache Frage. That was an
easy question. □ Das ist nicht einfach. That isn't
easy.
2 simple
□ aus dem einfachen Grund ... for the simple
reason ... □ Sie leben in sehr einfachen
Verhältnissen. They live very simple lives.
3 single
□ eine einfache Fahrkarte a single ticket
4 simply
□ Ich will das einfach nicht. I simply don't want
it. □ Er wollte einfach nicht begreifen. He simply
didn't want to understand.

die **Einfachheit** FEM NOUN
simplicity

★die **Einfahrt** FEM NOUN
entrance

der **Einfall** (pl die Einfälle) MASC NOUN
idea
□ Das war so ein Einfall von mir. It was just an
idea. □ Du hast manchmal Einfälle! You do
come up with strange ideas sometimes!

einfallen (PRESENT TENSE fällt ein , IMPERFECT
fiel ein , PERFECT TENSE ist eingefallen) VERB
[22]
■ **jemandem einfallen** to occur to somebody
□ Mir ist das Wort nicht eingefallen. The word
didn't occur to me.
■ **Das fällt mir gar nicht ein.** I wouldn't
dream of it.
■ **sich etwas einfallen lassen** to come up
with a good idea □ Meine Freunde haben sich
zu meinem Geburtstag etwas Tolles einfallen
lassen. My friends came up with a really great
idea for my birthday.

★das **Einfamilienhaus** (GEN des
Einfamilienhauses , pl die
Einfamilienhäuser) NEUT NOUN
detached (family) house

einfarbig ADJECTIVE
plain

der **Einfluss** (GEN des Einflusses , pl die
Einflüsse) MASC NOUN
influence
□ Er hat einen schlechten Einfluss auf dich. He
has a bad influence on you.

einfrieren (IMPERFECT fror ein , PERFECT TENSE
hat/ist eingefroren) VERB

> For the perfect tense use haben when the
> verb has an object and sein when there is
> no object.

to freeze
□ Wir haben die Reste eingefroren. We've
frozen the left-overs. □ Die Leitung ist
eingefroren. The pipe has frozen.

die **Einfuhr** FEM NOUN
import

die **Eingabe** FEM NOUN
input
□ die Eingabe von Daten data input

★der **Eingang** (pl die Eingänge) MASC NOUN
entrance

eingeben (PRESENT TENSE gibt ein , IMPERFECT
gab ein , PERFECT TENSE hat eingegeben) VERB
[28]
to enter
□ Bilal hat den Text in den Computer
eingegeben. Bilal entered the text into the
computer.

eingebildet ADJECTIVE
conceited
□ Sie ist furchtbar eingebildet. She's terribly
conceited.
■ **Ihre Krankheit ist nur eingebildet.** Her
illness is all in the imagination.

eingehen (IMPERFECT ging ein , PERFECT TENSE
ist eingegangen) VERB [29]
1 to die
□ Mir ist schon wieder eine Pflanze
eingegangen. Another of my plants has died.
2 to shrink
□ Der Pulli ist in der Wäsche eingegangen. The
pullover shrank in the wash.
■ **auf etwas eingehen** to comment on
something □ Er ist auf meinen Vorschlag nicht
eingegangen. He didn't comment on my
suggestion.

eingenommen ADJECTIVE
■ **eingenommen von** taken with □ Ich war
sofort von dem Plan eingenommen. I was
immediately taken with the plan.

eingeschrieben ADJECTIVE
registered
□ ein eingeschriebener Brief a registered letter

eingestellt ADJECTIVE
■ **auf etwas eingestellt sein** to be prepared
for something □ Ich war nicht auf Ihren Besuch
eingestellt. I wasn't prepared for your visit.

Numbers in brackets refer to verb tables on pages 697 to 706.

77

e

eingewöhnen – einlaufen

sich **eingewöhnen** (PERFECT TENSE **hat sich eingewöhnt**) VERB [7]
■ sich eingewöhnen into settle down in
□ Sie hat sich gut in der neuen Schule eingewöhnt. She's settled down very well in her new school.

★ **eingießen** (IMPERFECT **goss ein**, PERFECT TENSE **hat eingegossen**) VERB
to pour
□ Darf ich Ihnen noch Kaffee eingießen? Can I pour you some more coffee?

eingreifen (IMPERFECT **griff ein**, PERFECT TENSE **hat eingegriffen**) VERB
to intervene

der/die **Einheimische** (GEN des/der **Einheimischen**, PL die **Einheimischen**) MASC/FEM NOUN
local
□ Wir sollten einen Einheimischen fragen. We should ask a local.

die **Einheit** FEM NOUN
unity

DID YOU KNOW...?
Der Tag der Deutschen Einheit (the Day of German Unity) is a national holiday celebrated on 3 October. It marks the reunification of Germany in 1990 and is a public holiday throughout Germany

einholen (PERFECT TENSE **hat eingeholt**) VERB [4]
1 to catch up with
□ Wir werden euch sicher bald einholen. We'll soon catch up with you.
2 to make up
□ Wir haben die Verspätung nicht mehr eingeholt. We didn't make up the delay.

einhundert NUMBER
a hundred

einig ADJECTIVE
■ sich einig sein to be in agreement
■ einig werden to reach an agreement

★ **einige** ADJECTIVE, PRONOUN
1 some
□ einige Bücher some books □ einige von uns some of us
■ einiges quite a lot of things □ Wir haben einiges gesehen. We saw quite a lot of things.
2 several
□ Wir sind dort einige Tage geblieben. We stayed there several days. □ Bei dem Konzert sind einige früher gegangen. Several people left the concert early.

sich **einigen** VERB [38]
to agree
□ Wir haben uns auf diesen Termin geeinigt. We agreed on this date.

einigermaßen ADVERB
1 somewhat
□ Ich war einigermaßen erstaunt. I was somewhat surprised.
2 reasonably
□ Diesmal hast du dich wenigstens einigermaßen angestrengt. At least this time you've tried reasonably hard. □ Das Wetter war einigermaßen trocken. The weather was reasonably dry.

die **Einigung** FEM NOUN
agreement

★ der **Einkauf** (PL die **Einkäufe**) MASC NOUN
purchase
■ Einkäufe machen to go shopping

★ **einkaufen** (PERFECT TENSE **hat eingekauft**) VERB [4]
1 to buy
□ Wir müssen Brot einkaufen. We'll have to buy bread.
2 to shop
□ Wir kaufen meist samstags ein. We usually shop on Saturdays.
■ einkaufen gehen to go shopping

★ der **Einkaufsbummel** (PL die **Einkaufsbummel**) MASC NOUN
shopping spree

★ die **Einkaufsliste** FEM NOUN
shopping list

★ der **Einkaufswagen** (PL die **Einkaufswagen**) MASC NOUN
1 shopping trolley
2 basket (online)

★ das **Einkaufszentrum** (PL die **Einkaufszentren**) NEUT NOUN
shopping centre

★ der **Einkaufszettel** (PL die **Einkaufszettel**) MASC NOUN
shopping list

einklammern (PERFECT TENSE **hat eingeklammert**) VERB [4]
to put in brackets

das **Einkommen** (PL die **Einkommen**) NEUT NOUN
income

★ **einladen** (PRESENT TENSE **lädt ein**, IMPERFECT **lud ein**, PERFECT TENSE **hat eingeladen**) VERB
1 to invite
□ Sie hat mich zu ihrer Party eingeladen. She's invited me to her party.
■ jemanden ins Kino einladen to take somebody to the cinema
■ Ich lade dich ein. I'll treat you.
2 to load
□ Kannst du bitte die Koffer ins Auto einladen? Can you load the cases into the car, please?

★ die **Einladung** FEM NOUN
invitation

einlaufen (PRESENT TENSE **läuft ein**, IMPERFECT **lief ein**, PERFECT TENSE **ist eingelaufen**) VERB [43]

1 to come in
□ Das Schiff läuft in den Hafen ein. The ship is coming into the harbour.

2 to shrink
□ Mein Pullover ist eingelaufen. My jumper has shrunk.

sich **einleben** (PERFECT TENSE **hat sich eingelebt**) VERB [4]
to settle down
□ Wir haben uns in unserer neuen Schule gut eingelebt. We've settled down well in our new school.

die **Einleitung** FEM NOUN
introduction

einleuchten (PERFECT TENSE **hat eingeleuchtet**) VERB [4]
■ **jemandem einleuchten** to make sense to somebody □ Das leuchtet mir nicht ein. That doesn't make sense to me.

einleuchtend ADJECTIVE
clear

einloggen (PERFECT TENSE **hat eingeloggt**) VERB [4]
to log on (computer)

★ **einlösen** VERB [4]
to cash
□ Kann ich diesen Scheck einlösen? Can I cash this cheque?
■ **ein Versprechen einlösen** to keep a promise

★ **einmal** ADVERB
1 once
□ Wenn du das erst einmal begriffen hast ... Once you've understood it ...
■ **Es war einmal ...** Once upon a time there was ...
■ **noch einmal** once more
■ **auf einmal** all at once □ Auf einmal waren alle weg. All at once they were all gone.

2 one day
□ Das wirst du schon einmal begreifen. You'll understand it one day.
■ **Nehmen wir einmal an: ...** Let's just suppose: ...
■ **nicht einmal** not even

einmalig ADJECTIVE
1 unique
□ Das ist eine einmalige Gelegenheit. This is a unique opportunity.

2 single
□ Das erfordert nur eine einmalige Überprüfung. That requires only a single check.

3 fantastic
□ Das war eine einmalige Party. That was a fantastic party.

sich **einmischen** (PERFECT TENSE **hat sich eingemischt**) VERB [4]
to interfere

□ Ich will mich nicht in deine Angelegenheiten einmischen. I don't want to interfere in your affairs.

★ **einpacken** (PERFECT TENSE **hat eingepackt**) VERB [4]
to pack
□ Hast du deine Zahnbürste eingepackt? Have you packed your toothbrush?

einplanen (PERFECT TENSE **hat eingeplant**) VERB [4]
to plan for

★ **einreichen** (PERFECT TENSE **hat eingereicht**) VERB [4]
to hand in

die **Einreise** FEM NOUN
entry
■ **bei der Einreise** when entering the country

einreisen (PERFECT TENSE **ist eingereist**) VERB [4]
■ **in ein Land einreisen** to enter a country

einrichten (PERFECT TENSE **hat eingerichtet**) VERB [2]
1 to furnish
□ Sie haben ihr Haus antik eingerichtet. They've furnished their house with antiques.

2 to set up
□ Die Stadt hat eine Beratungsstelle eingerichtet. The town has set up an advice bureau.
■ **sich auf etwas einrichten** to prepare for something □ Wir hatten uns auf mehr Besucher eingerichtet. We had prepared for more visitors.

die **Einrichtung** FEM NOUN
1 furnishings pl
□ Die farbenfrohe Einrichtung gefiel mir gut. I liked the colourful furnishings.

2 facility
□ städtische Einrichtungen municipal facilities

einrosten (PERFECT TENSE **ist eingerostet**) VERB [4]
to get rusty

★ **eins** NUMBER
▷ see also die **Eins** NOUN
one
□ Ich habe nur eins bekommen. I only got one.
■ **Es ist mir alles eins.** It's all the same to me.

★ die **Eins** (PL die **Einsen**) FEM NOUN
▷ see also **eins** NUMBER
1 one
2 very good

DID YOU KNOW...?
German grades range from one (**sehr gut**) to six (**ungenügend**).

★ **einsam** ADJECTIVE
1 lonely
□ Ich fühle mich einsam. I'm feeling lonely.

Numbers in brackets refer to verb tables on pages 697 to 706.

79

einsammeln – einsteigen

2 remote
□ eine einsame Gegend a remote area

einsammeln (PERFECT TENSE **hat eingesammelt**) VERB [4]
to collect

★**einschalten** (PERFECT TENSE **hat eingeschaltet**) VERB [2]
to switch on
□ Schalt mal das Radio ein. Switch the radio on.

einschl. ABBREVIATION (= *einschließlich*)
incl.

★**einschlafen** (PRESENT TENSE **schläft ein**, IMPERFECT **schlief ein**, PERFECT TENSE **ist eingeschlafen**) VERB [58]
to fall asleep

einschließen (IMPERFECT **schloss ein**, PERFECT TENSE **hat eingeschlossen**) VERB
1 to lock in
□ Er hat mich im Badezimmer eingeschlossen. He locked me in the bathroom.
2 to lock away
□ Du solltest die Wertsachen einschließen. You should lock away the valuables.
3 to include
□ Der Preis schließt die Verpflegung ein. The price includes all meals.
■ **sich einschließen** to lock oneself in □ Sie hat sich in ihrem Zimmer eingeschlossen. She locked herself in her room.

★**einschließlich** ADVERB, PREPOSITION

> The preposition **einschließlich** takes the genitive.

1 inclusive
□ Wir sind vom zehnten bis einschließlich fünfzehnten Juni weg. We're away from the tenth to the fifteenth of June inclusive.
2 including
□ Das macht zwanzig Euro einschließlich Bedienung. That's twenty euros including service.

einschränken (PERFECT TENSE **hat eingeschränkt**) VERB [4]
1 to restrict
□ Dadurch wurde unsere Freiheit eingeschränkt. This restricted our freedom.
2 to reduce
□ Wir müssen die Kosten einschränken. We'll have to reduce costs.
■ **sich einschränken** to cut down

★sich **einschreiben** (IMPERFECT **schrieb sich ein**, PERFECT TENSE **hat sich eingeschrieben**) VERB [61]
> *see also* das **Einschreiben** NOUN
1 to register
□ Hast du dich für den Kurs eingeschrieben? Have you registered for the course?
2 to enrol
□ sich an der Universität einschreiben to enrol at university

★das **Einschreiben** (PL die **Einschreiben**)
NEUT NOUN
> *see also* einschreiben VERB
recorded delivery

einschüchtern (PERFECT TENSE **hat eingeschüchtert**) VERB [88]
to intimidate

einsehen (PRESENT TENSE **sieht ein**, IMPERFECT **sah ein**, PERFECT TENSE **hat eingesehen**) VERB [64]
to see
□ Siehst du das nicht ein? Don't you see that?

einseitig ADJECTIVE
one-sided

einsenden (IMPERFECT **sendete ein** *or* **sandte ein**, PERFECT TENSE **hat eingesendet** *or* **hat eingesandt**) VERB
to send in

einsetzen (PERFECT TENSE **hat eingesetzt**) VERB [36]
1 to put in
□ Setzt das richtige Wort ein. Put in the correct word.
2 to bet
□ Wie viel Geld hast du eingesetzt? How much money did you bet?
3 to use
□ An den Schulen werden immer mehr Computer eingesetzt. More and more computers are being used in schools.
4 to set in
□ Wenn der Winter einsetzt ... When winter sets in ...
■ **sich einsetzen** to work hard □ Du solltest dich in der Schule etwas mehr einsetzen. You should work harder at school.
■ **sich für jemanden einsetzen** to support somebody

die **Einsicht** FEM NOUN
■ **zu der Einsicht kommen, dass ...** to come to the conclusion that ...

einsilbig ADJECTIVE
1 monosyllabic
□ ein einsilbiges Wort a monosyllabic word
2 uncommunicative
□ Er war sehr einsilbig. He was very uncommunicative.

einsperren (PERFECT TENSE **hat eingesperrt**) VERB [4]
to lock up

einsprachig ADJECTIVE
monolingual

der **Einspruch** (PL die **Einsprüche**) MASC NOUN
objection

★**einsteigen** (IMPERFECT **stieg ein**, PERFECT TENSE **ist eingestiegen**) VERB [74]

★ = core vocabulary

1 to get on
□ Wir sind in den Bus eingestiegen. We got on the bus.
■ **Bitte einsteigen!** All aboard!

2 to climb in
□ Wir sind durchs Kellerfenster ins Haus eingestiegen. We climbed into the house through the cellar window.

★**einstellen** (PERFECT TENSE **hat eingestellt**) VERB [4]

1 to adjust
□ den Spiegel einstellen to adjust the mirror
■ **eine Kamera einstellen** to focus a camera

2 to tune in to
□ Welchen Sender hast du da eingestellt? Which station have you tuned in to?

3 to stop
□ Sie haben die Produktion eingestellt. They've stopped production.

4 to employ
□ Sie wurde als Sekretärin eingestellt. She was employed as a secretary.
■ **sich auf etwas einstellen** to prepare oneself for something □ Stell dich besser auf eine lange Warterei ein. You'd better prepare yourself for a long wait.

die **Einstellung** FEM NOUN

1 attitude
□ Ich mag deine Einstellung nicht. I don't like your attitude.

2 setting
□ Bitte überprüfen Sie Ihre Einstellungen. Please check your settings. (on computer)

★der **Einstieg** MASC NOUN
entrance
□ Der Einstieg ist vorn. The entrance is at the front.

einstimmen (PERFECT TENSE **hat eingestimmt**) VERB [4]
to join in
□ Alle stimmten in das Lied ein. Everyone joined in the singing.
■ **sich auf etwas einstimmen** to get oneself in the right mood for something

eintägig ADJECTIVE
one-day

eintausend NUMBER
a thousand

eintönig ADJECTIVE
monotonous

★der **Eintopf** (PL die **Eintöpfe**) MASC NOUN
stew

der **Eintrag** (PL die **Einträge**) MASC NOUN
entry
□ ein Eintrag im Wörterbuch a dictionary entry

eintragen (PRESENT TENSE **trägt ein**, IMPERFECT **trug ein**, PERFECT TENSE **hat eingetragen**) VERB [77]

to write
□ Tragt die Vokabeln in euer Heft ein. Write the vocabulary in your exercise book.
■ **sich eintragen** to put one's name down
□ Hast du dich schon in die Liste eingetragen? Have you put your name down on the list yet?

einträglich ADJECTIVE
profitable

eintreffen (PRESENT TENSE **trifft ein**, IMPERFECT **traf ein**, PERFECT TENSE **ist eingetroffen**) VERB [78]

1 to arrive
□ Sobald die Gäste eintreffen ... As soon as the guests arrive ...

2 to come true
□ Die Prophezeiung ist tatsächlich eingetroffen. The prophecy actually came true.

★**eintreten** (PRESENT TENSE **tritt ein**, IMPERFECT **trat ein**, PERFECT TENSE **ist eingetreten**) VERB [79]
■ **eintreten in 1** to enter □ Er ist ins Zimmer eingetreten. He entered the room. **2** to join □ Wann bist du in den Tennisklub eingetreten? When did you join the tennis club?
■ **Es ist eine Verzögerung eingetreten.** There has been a delay.

★der **Eintritt** (PL die **Eintritte**) MASC NOUN
admission
□ Wie viel kostet der Eintritt? How much does the admission cost?
■ **'Eintritt frei'** 'Admission free'

★das **Eintrittsgeld** (PL die **Eintrittsgelder**) NEUT NOUN
admission charge

★die **Eintrittskarte** FEM NOUN
admission ticket

★**einverstanden** ADJECTIVE
■ **einverstanden sein** to agree □ Bist du mit dem Vorschlag einverstanden? Do you agree to the suggestion?
■ **Einverstanden!** Okay!

der **Einwanderer** (PL die **Einwanderer**) MASC NOUN
immigrant

die **Einwanderin** FEM NOUN
immigrant

einwandern (PERFECT TENSE **ist eingewandert**) VERB [88]
to immigrate

die **Einwegflasche** FEM NOUN
nonreturnable bottle

einweihen (PERFECT TENSE **hat eingeweiht**) VERB [4]
to open
□ Morgen wird die neue Brücke eingeweiht. The new bridge is being opened tomorrow.
■ **jemanden in etwas einweihen** to initiate somebody into something □ Wir haben die

e

Numbers in brackets refer to verb tables on pages 697 to 706.

81

Neue in unseren Klub eingeweiht. We've initiated the newcomer into our club.
- **jemanden in ein Geheimnis einweihen** to let somebody in on a secret

★ **einwerfen** (PRESENT TENSE **wirft ein**, IMPERFECT **warf ein**, PERFECT TENSE **hat eingeworfen**) VERB [92]
to smash
□ Ich habe eine Scheibe eingeworfen. I've smashed a pane.
- **einen Brief einwerfen** to post a letter
- **Geld einwerfen** to insert money

★ der **Einwohner** (PL die **Einwohner**) MASC NOUN
inhabitant

★ die **Einwohnerin** FEM NOUN
inhabitant

das **Einwohnermeldeamt** (PL die **Einwohnermeldeämter**) NEUT NOUN
registration office

DID YOU KNOW…?
Anyone moving to a new address in Germany is required by law to register (**sich anmelden**) at the residents' registration office (**Einwohnermeldeamt**).

★ der **Einwurf** (PL die **Einwürfe**) MASC NOUN
1 slot
□ Sie steckte den Brief in den Einwurf. She put the letter through the slot.
2 throw-in (sport)
□ Der Schiedsrichter gab einen Einwurf. The referee gave a throw-in.

die **Einzahl** FEM NOUN
singular

einzahlen (PERFECT TENSE **hat eingezahlt**) VERB [4]
to pay

★ das **Einzelbett** (PL die **Einzelbetten**) NEUT NOUN
single bed

der **Einzelfahrschein** (PL die **Einzelfahrscheine**) MASC NOUN
single ticket

die **Einzelheit** FEM NOUN
detail

★ das **Einzelkind** (PL die **Einzelkinder**) NEUT NOUN
only child

★ **einzeln** ADJECTIVE, ADVERB
1 single
□ Jeder einzelne Schüler wurde befragt. Every single pupil was asked.
2 odd
□ Ich habe ein paar einzelne Socken. I've got a couple of odd socks.
3 one at a time
□ Bitte einzeln eintreten. Please come in one at a time.

- **einzeln angeben** to specify
- **der Einzelne** the individual
- **ins Einzelne gehen** to go into details

das **Einzelteil** (PL die **Einzelteile**) NEUT NOUN
component

★ das **Einzelzimmer** (PL die **Einzelzimmer**) NEUT NOUN
single room

einziehen (IMPERFECT **zog ein**, PERFECT TENSE **ist/hat eingezogen**) VERB [96]

For the perfect tense use **haben** when the verb has an object and **sein** when there is no object.

1 to retract
- **den Kopf einziehen** to duck one's head
2 to collect
3 to move in
□ Wann sind die neuen Nachbarn eingezogen? When did the new neighbours move in?

★ **einzig** ADJECTIVE
only
□ Er ist unser einziges Kind. He's our only child.
- **das Einzige** the only thing
- **der/die Einzige** the only one

einzigartig ADJECTIVE
unique

★ das **Eis** (PL die **Eis**) NEUT NOUN
1 ice
□ Es war Eis auf dem See. There was ice on the lake.
2 ice cream
□ Möchtest du ein Eis? Would you like an ice cream?

der **Eisbär** (GEN des **Eisbären**, PL die **Eisbären**) MASC NOUN
polar bear

der **Eisberg** (PL die **Eisberge**) MASC NOUN
iceberg

★ das **Eisen** (PL die **Eisen**) NEUT NOUN
iron
□ Die Brücke ist aus Eisen. The bridge is made of iron.

★ die **Eisenbahn** FEM NOUN
railway

eisern ADJECTIVE
iron
□ eine eiserne Stange an iron rod
- **die eiserne Reserve** emergency reserves

das **Eishockey** NEUT NOUN
ice hockey

eisig ADJECTIVE
icy

eiskalt ADJECTIVE
1 ice-cold
□ ein eiskaltes Getränk an ice-cold drink

★ = core vocabulary

2 icy cold
□ In diesem Zimmer ist es eiskalt. This room's icy cold.

der **Eiswürfel** (PL die Eiswürfel) MASC NOUN
ice cube

eitel ADJECTIVE
vain

der **Eiter** MASC NOUN
pus

das **Eiweiß** (PL die Eiweiße) NEUT NOUN
1 egg white
□ Das Eiweiß zu Schnee schlagen. Whisk the egg whites until stiff.
2 protein
□ eine eiweißreiche Diät a diet rich in protein

der **Ekel** MASC NOUN
disgust

ekelhaft ADJECTIVE
disgusting

sich **ekeln** VERB [34]
to disgust
■ sich vor etwas ekeln to find something disgusting □ Ich ekle mich vor Nacktschnecken. I find slugs disgusting.

der **Elch** (PL die Elche) MASC NOUN
elk

★ der **Elefant** (GEN des Elefanten, PL die Elefanten) MASC NOUN
elephant

elegant ADJECTIVE
elegant

★ der **Elektriker** (PL die Elektriker) MASC NOUN
electrician

★ die **Elektrikerin** FEM NOUN
electrician

★ **elektrisch** ADJECTIVE
electric

★ die **Elektrizität** FEM NOUN
electricity

★ das **Elektrogerät** NEUT NOUN
electrical appliance

★ der **Elektroherd** (PL die Elektroherde) MASC NOUN
electric cooker

die **Elektronik** FEM NOUN
electronics *sing*
□ Sie studiert Elektronik. She is studying electronics. □ Die Elektronik am Auto ist kaputt. There's something wrong with the electronics in the car.

elektronisch ADJECTIVE
electronic
□ elektronische Post electronic mail
□ elektronischer Briefkasten electronic mailbox

das **Element** (PL die Elemente) NEUT NOUN
element

elend ADJECTIVE
▷ *see also* das **Elend** NOUN
miserable
□ Ich fühle mich so elend. I feel so miserable.

das **Elend** NEUT NOUN
▷ *see also* **elend** ADJECTIVE
misery

elf NUMBER
eleven
□ Sie ist elf. She's eleven.

der **Elfmeter** (PL die Elfmeter) MASC NOUN
penalty

der **Ellbogen** (PL die Ellbogen) MASC NOUN
elbow

★ die **Eltern** PL NOUN
parents *pl*

das **Elterngeld** (PL die Elterngelder) NEUT NOUN
child benefit

die **Elternschaft** FEM NOUN
parenthood

★ der **Elternteil** (PL die Elternteile) MASC NOUN
parent
□ beide Elternteile both parents

die **E-Mail** (PL die E-Mails) FEM NOUN
email
□ Meine E-Mail-Adresse ist ... My email address is ...

das **Emoticon** (PL die Emoticons) NEUT NOUN
emoticon

★ der **Empfang** (PL die Empfänge) MASC NOUN
1 reception
□ Wart ihr auch bei dem Empfang? Were you at the reception too?
2 receipt
□ Bitte bestätigen Sie den Empfang der Ware. Please acknowledge receipt of the goods.
■ in Empfang nehmen to receive

★ **empfangen** (PRESENT TENSE **empfängt**, IMPERFECT **empfing**, PERFECT TENSE **hat empfangen**) VERB [23]
to receive

der **Empfänger** (PL die Empfänger) MASC NOUN
receiver

empfänglich ADJECTIVE
susceptible
□ Sie ist für Schmeicheleien sehr empfänglich. She's very susceptible to flattery.

die **Empfängnisverhütung** FEM NOUN
contraception

★ **empfehlen** (PRESENT TENSE **empfiehlt**, IMPERFECT **empfahl**, PERFECT TENSE **hat empfohlen**) VERB [17]
to recommend
□ Dieses Restaurant ist zu empfehlen. This restaurant is to be recommended.

e

empfinden – Entfernung

empfinden (IMPERFECT **empfand**, PERFECT TENSE **hat empfunden**) VERB [24]
to feel
□ Ich empfinde nichts für sie. I don't feel anything for her.

★empfindlich ADJECTIVE
1 sensitive
□ Er ist ein sehr empfindlicher Mensch. He's very sensitive.
2 touchy
□ Sie ist schrecklich empfindlich. She's terribly touchy.

empfohlen VERB ▷ see empfehlen

★das Ende (PL die **Enden**) NEUT NOUN
end
■ **am Ende 1** at the end □ am Ende des Zuges at the end of the train **2** in the end □ Am Ende ist er dann doch mitgekommen. He came in the end.
■ **zu Ende gehen** to come to an end
■ **zu Ende sein** to be finished
■ **Ende Dezember** at the end of December

★enden VERB [54]
to end

endgültig ADJECTIVE
definite

★endlich ADVERB
finally
□ Ich bin endlich fertig. I've finally finished.
□ Hast du das endlich begriffen? Have you finally understood it?
■ **Endlich!** At last!
■ **Komm endlich!** Come on!

endlos ADJECTIVE
endless

★das Endspiel (PL die **Endspiele**) NEUT NOUN
final

★die Endstation FEM NOUN
terminus

die Endung FEM NOUN
ending

★die Energie FEM NOUN
energy
□ seine ganze Energie für etwas einsetzen to devote all one's energies to something

energisch ADJECTIVE
energetic

★eng ADJECTIVE
1 narrow
□ ein enger Durchgang a narrow passageway
2 tight
□ Die Hose ist mir zu eng. The trousers are too tight for me.
3 close
□ Wir sind eng befreundet. We are close friends.

die Enge FEM NOUN
narrowness

■ **jemanden in die Enge treiben** to drive somebody into a corner

der Engel (PL die **Engel**) MASC NOUN
angel

★England NEUT NOUN
England
■ **aus England** from England
■ **in England** in England
■ **nach England** to England

★der Engländer (PL die **Engländer**) MASC NOUN
Englishman
■ **Er ist Engländer.** He's English.
■ **die Engländer** the English

★die Engländerin FEM NOUN
Englishwoman
■ **Sie ist Engländerin.** She's English.

★englisch ADJECTIVE
▷ see also das **Englisch** NOUN
English

★das Englisch (GEN des **Englischen**) NEUT NOUN
▷ see also **englisch** ADJECTIVE
English
□ Er lernt Englisch in der Schule. He's learning English at school.

der Engpass (GEN des **Engpasses**, PL die **Engpässe**) MASC NOUN
bottleneck

★der Enkel (PL die **Enkel**) MASC NOUN
grandson
■ **alle ihre Enkel** all her grandchildren

★die Enkelin FEM NOUN
granddaughter

★das Enkelkind (PL die **Enkelkinder**) NEUT NOUN
grandchild

★enorm ADJECTIVE
enormous
□ Er verdient enorm viel Geld. He earns an enormous amount of money.

entdecken (PERFECT TENSE **hat entdeckt**) VERB [18]
to discover

die Ente FEM NOUN
duck

entfernen (PERFECT TENSE **hat entfernt**) VERB [18]
to remove

★entfernt ADJECTIVE
distant
□ ein entfernter Verwandter a distant relative
■ **weit entfernt** far away
■ **weit davon entfernt sein, etwas zu tun** to be far from doing something
■ **nicht im Entferntesten** not in the slightest

die Entfernung FEM NOUN
distance

★ = core vocabulary

entfreunden VERB [54]
to unfriend

entführen (PERFECT TENSE **hat entführt**) VERB [18]
to kidnap

entgegen PREPOSITION

entgegen takes the dative.

contrary to
□ entgegen meinen Anweisungen contrary to my instructions

entgegenkommen (IMPERFECT **kam entgegen**, PERFECT TENSE **ist entgegengekommen**) VERB [40]
1 to come towards
□ Uns kam ein Lastwagen entgegen. A lorry came towards us.
2 to meet half way
□ Ich werde Ihnen entgegenkommen, sagen wir zwanzig Euro. I'll meet you half way, let's say twenty euros.

entgegenkommend ADJECTIVE
obliging

entgehen (IMPERFECT **entging**, PERFECT TENSE **ist entgangen**) VERB [29]
■ jemandem entgehen to escape somebody's attention □ Dieser Fehler ist mir entgangen. That mistake escaped my attention.
■ sich etwas entgehen lassen to miss something □ Das Konzert will ich mir nicht entgehen lassen. I'm not going to miss the concert.

enthalten (PRESENT TENSE **enthält**, IMPERFECT **enthielt**, PERFECT TENSE **hat enthalten**) VERB [33]
to contain
□ Dieses Fass enthält radioaktiven Müll. This drum contains radioactive waste.
■ sich enthalten to abstain □ Sie hat sich bei der Abstimmung enthalten. She abstained from voting.

★**entkommen** (IMPERFECT **entkam**, PERFECT TENSE **ist entkommen**) VERB [40]
to escape

★**entlang** PREPOSITION

entlang takes the accusative or the dative.

along
□ Entlang der Mauer wuchs Efeu. Ivy was growing along the wall. □ Wir gingen den Fluss entlang. We walked along the river.

entlassen (PRESENT TENSE **entlässt**, IMPERFECT **entließ**, PERFECT TENSE **hat entlassen**) VERB [42]
1 to release
□ Er wurde aus dem Gefängnis entlassen. He was released from prison.
2 to make redundant
□ 500 Arbeiter mussten entlassen werden. 500 workers had to be made redundant.

entrüstet ADJECTIVE
outraged

entschädigen (PERFECT TENSE **hat entschädigt**) VERB [18]
to compensate
□ jemanden für etwas entschädigen to compensate somebody for something

★**entscheiden** (IMPERFECT **entschied**, PERFECT TENSE **hat entschieden**) VERB
to decide
■ sich entscheiden to make up one's mind

entscheidend ADJECTIVE
decisive

die **Entscheidung** FEM NOUN
decision

entschieden ADJECTIVE
1 decided
□ Es ist entschieden, wir fahren nach Rom. It's been decided that we're going to Rome.
2 resolute
□ ein sehr entschiedener Mensch a very resolute person

sich **entschließen** (IMPERFECT **entschloss sich**, PERFECT TENSE **hat sich entschlossen**) VERB
to decide

entschlossen ADJECTIVE
determined

der **Entschluss** (GEN des **Entschlusses**, PL die **Entschlüsse**) MASC NOUN
decision

★**entschuldigen** (PERFECT TENSE **hat entschuldigt**) VERB [18]
1 to excuse
□ Entschuldige bitte die Verspätung. Please excuse the delay.
2 to apologize
□ Du solltest dich besser bei ihm entschuldigen. You'd better apologize to him.

★die **Entschuldigung** FEM NOUN
1 apology
□ Hat sie deine Entschuldigung angenommen? Did she accept your apology?
■ jemanden um Entschuldigung bitten to apologize to somebody
2 excuse
□ Krankheit ist keine Entschuldigung. Illness is no excuse.
■ Entschuldigung! Sorry.
■ Entschuldigung ... Excuse me ...
□ Entschuldigung, können Sie mir sagen, wie spät es ist? Excuse me, could you tell me what time it is?

★**entsetzlich** ADJECTIVE
dreadful

entsetzt ADJECTIVE, ADVERB
horrified

Numbers in brackets refer to verb tables on pages 697 to 706.

85

Entsorgung – Erdkunde

die **Entsorgung** FEM NOUN
waste disposal

★ sich **entspannen** (PERFECT TENSE **hat sich
entspannt**) VERB [18]

1 to relax
□ Entspann dich! Relax!

2 to ease
□ Die Lage hat sich entspannt. The situation
has eased.

entsprechen (PRESENT TENSE **entspricht**,
IMPERFECT **entsprach**, PERFECT TENSE **hat
entsprochen**) VERB [70]

1 to meet
□ Sie hat den Anforderungen nicht
entsprochen. She didn't meet the
requirements.

2 to comply with
□ Dieses Gerät entspricht nicht den Normen.
This appliance doesn't comply with the
standards.

entsprechend ADJECTIVE, ADVERB

1 appropriate
□ Die entsprechende Antwort ankreuzen. Tick
the appropriate answer.

2 accordingly
□ Benimm dich entsprechend. Behave
accordingly.

★ **enttäuschen** (PERFECT TENSE **hat enttäuscht**)
VERB [18]
to disappoint

★ **enttäuschend** ADJECTIVE
disappointing

★ die **Enttäuschung** FEM NOUN
disappointment

★ **entweder** CONJUNCTION
either
■ **entweder ... oder ...** either ... or ...

★ **entwerten** VERB [18]
to cancel
□ Du musst die Fahrkarte erst entwerten. You
have to cancel your ticket first.

★ der **Entwerter** (PL die **Entwerter**) MASC NOUN
ticket stamping machine

> **DID YOU KNOW...?**
> When you travel by train or tram (and
> sometimes by bus) you have to stamp your
> ticket in an **Entwerter**. The machines are
> either on the platforms or inside the vehicles.

entwickeln (PERFECT TENSE **hat entwickelt**)
VERB [34]

1 to develop
□ Fähigkeiten entwickeln to develop skills
□ einen Film entwickeln to develop a film

2 to show
□ Sie hat eine enorme Energie entwickelt. She
showed terrific energy.

■ **sich entwickeln** to develop □ Das Geschäft
entwickelt sich gut. The business is developing
well.

die **Entwicklung** FEM NOUN
development

die **Entwicklungshilfe** FEM NOUN
development aid

das **Entwicklungsland** (PL die
Entwicklungsländer) NEUT NOUN
developing country

sich **entzünden** (PERFECT TENSE **hat sich
entzündet**) VERB [18]
to become inflamed
□ Die Wunde hat sich entzündet. The wound
has become inflamed.

die **Entzündung** FEM NOUN
inflammation

entzwei ADVERB
broken
□ Die Vase ist entzwei. The vase is broken.

der **Enzian** (PL die **Enziane**) MASC NOUN
gentian

er PRONOUN

1 he
□ Er ist größer als ich. He's taller than me.

2 it
□ Schöner Ring, ist er neu? Lovely ring, is it
new?

3 him
□ Er ist es. It's him. □ Er war es nicht, ich war's.
It wasn't him, it was me.

erben VERB [38]
to inherit

★ **erbrechen** (PRESENT TENSE **erbricht**, IMPERFECT
erbrach, PERFECT TENSE **hat erbrochen**) VERB
[11]
to vomit

die **Erbschaft** FEM NOUN
inheritance

★ die **Erbse** FEM NOUN
pea

das **Erdbeben** (PL die **Erdbeben**) NEUT NOUN
earthquake

★ die **Erdbeere** FEM NOUN
strawberry

★ die **Erde** FEM NOUN
earth
■ **zu ebener Erde** at ground level
■ **auf der ganzen Erde** all over the world

das **Erdgas** (GEN des **Erdgases**) NEUT NOUN
natural gas

★ das **Erdgeschoss** (GEN des **Erdgeschosses**,
PL die **Erdgeschosse**) NEUT NOUN
ground floor
□ im Erdgeschoss on the ground floor

★ die **Erdkunde** FEM NOUN
geography

★ = core vocabulary

die **Erdnuss** (PLdie **Erdnüsse**) FEM NOUN
peanut

das **Erdöl** NEUT NOUN
mineral oil

sich **ereignen** (PERFECT TENSEhat sich
ereignet) VERB [53]
to happen

das **Ereignis** (GENdes **Ereignisses** , PLdie
Ereignisse) NEUT NOUN
event

★**erfahren** (PRESENT TENSEerfährt , IMPERFECT
erfuhr , PERFECT TENSEhat erfahren) VERB [21]
▷ see alsoerfahren ADJECTIVE

1 to hear
□ Ich habe erfahren, dass du heiraten willst. I've
heard that you want to get married.

2 to experience
□ Sie hat im Leben viel Gutes erfahren. She's
experienced a lot of good things in her life.

★**erfahren** ADJECTIVE
▷ see alsoerfahren VERB
experienced
□ Er ist ein erfahrener Lehrer. He's an
experienced teacher.

★die **Erfahrung** FEM NOUN
experience

erfassen (PERFECT TENSEhat erfasst) VERB [31]

1 to understand
□ Ich habe den Text noch nicht erfasst. I haven't
understood the text yet.

2 to register
□ Alle Aidsfälle werden erfasst. All AIDS cases
are registered.

erfinden (IMPERFECTerfand , PERFECT TENSEhat
erfunden) VERB [24]
to invent

der **Erfinder** (PLdie **Erfinder**) MASC NOUN
inventor

die **Erfinderin** FEM NOUN
inventor

erfinderisch ADJECTIVE
inventive

die **Erfindung** FEM NOUN
invention

★der **Erfolg** (PLdie **Erfolge**) MASC NOUN
success
■ **Erfolg versprechend** promising
■ **Viel Erfolg!** Good luck!

erfolglos ADJECTIVE
unsuccessful

★**erfolgreich** ADJECTIVE
successful

erfolgversprechend ADJECTIVE ▷ seeder
Erfolg

erforderlich ADJECTIVE
necessary

erfreulicherweise ADVERB
happily

erfreut ADJECTIVE
pleased
□ Über mein gutes Zeugnis war ich sehr erfreut.
I was very pleased with my good report.

erfrieren (IMPERFECTerfror , PERFECT TENSEist
erfroren) VERB
to freeze to death
□ Er ist erfroren. He froze to death.
■ **Die Pflanze ist erfroren.** The plant was
killed by frost.

die **Erfrischung** FEM NOUN
refreshment

erfüllen (PERFECT TENSEhat erfüllt) VERB [7]
to fulfil
□ Er hat ihr den Wunsch erfüllt. He fulfilled her
wish.
■ **sich erfüllen** to come true□ Die
Prophezeiung hat sich erfüllt. The prophecy
came true.

ergänzen (PERFECT TENSEhat ergänzt) VERB
[36]
to complete
□ Ergänzt den Satz. Complete the sentence.
■ **sich ergänzen** to complement one another

★das **Ergebnis** (GENdes **Ergebnisses** , PLdie
Ergebnisse) NEUT NOUN
result

ergreifen (IMPERFECTergriff , PERFECT TENSEhat
ergriffen) VERB

1 to seize
□ Er ergriff meine Hand. He seized my hand.
□ die Gelegenheit ergreifen to seize the
opportunity
■ **einen Beruf ergreifen** to take up a
profession
■ **Maßnahmen gegen etwas ergreifen** to
take measures against something

2 to move
□ Ihr Schicksal hat uns sehr ergriffen. Her fate
moved us deeply.

ergreifend ADJECTIVE
moving

ergriffen ADJECTIVE
deeply moved

★**erhalten** (PRESENT TENSEerhält , IMPERFECT
erhielt , PERFECT TENSEhat erhalten) VERB [33]

1 to receive
□ Sie hat den ersten Preis erhalten. She
received first prize.

2 to preserve
□ Das Gebäude sollte erhalten werden. The
building should be preserved.
■ **gut erhalten** in good condition

★**erhältlich** ADJECTIVE
obtainable

e

erheitern(PERFECT TENSE **hat erheitert**) VERB [88]
to amuse

erhitzen(PERFECT TENSE **hat erhitzt**) VERB [7]
to heat

★ sich **erholen**(PERFECT TENSE **hat sich erholt**) VERB [19]
1 to recover
□ Der Patient muss sich nach der Operation erholen. The patient needs to recover after the operation.
2 to have a rest
□ Wir haben uns in den Ferien gut erholt. We had a good rest when we were on holiday.

erholsam ADJECTIVE
restful

die **Erholung** FEM NOUN
rest
□ Wir fahren zur Erholung ans Meer. We're going to the sea for a rest.

★ **erinnern**(PERFECT TENSE **hat erinnert**) VERB [88]
■ **erinnern an** to remind of □ Du erinnerst mich an meine Schwester. You remind me of my sister. □ Erinnere mich bitte daran, dass wir noch Butter kaufen müssen. Remind me that we still have to buy butter.
■ **sich erinnern** to remember □ Ich kann mich nicht erinnern. I can't remember. □ Erinnerst du dich noch an unser Abenteuer in Erlangen? Can you still remember our adventure in Erlangen?

★ die **Erinnerung** FEM NOUN
1 memory
□ Wir haben Erinnerungen ausgetauscht. We swapped memories.
2 souvenir
□ eine Erinnerung an meinen Russlandaufenthalt a souvenir of my stay in Russia

★ **erkältet** ADJECTIVE
■ **erkältet sein** to have a cold

★ die **Erkältung** FEM NOUN
cold

erkennbar ADJECTIVE
recognizable

★ **erkennen**(IMPERFECT **erkannte**, PERFECT TENSE **hat erkannt**) VERB [39]
1 to recognize
□ Ich hätte dich fast nicht erkannt. I would hardly have recognized you.
2 to see
□ Jetzt erkenne ich, dass das ein Fehler war. I see now that it was a mistake.

★ **erklären**(PERFECT TENSE **hat erklärt**) VERB [19]
to explain

die **Erklärung** FEM NOUN
explanation
■ **eine Liebeserklärung** a declaration of love

★ sich **erkundigen**(PERFECT TENSE **hat sich erkundigt**) VERB [19]
■ **sich erkundigen nach** to inquire about □ Wir sollten uns nach den Abfahrtszeiten erkundigen. We should inquire about departure times.
■ **Er hat sich nach dir erkundigt.** He was asking about you.

★ **erlauben**(PERFECT TENSE **hat erlaubt**) VERB [19]
■ **jemandem etwas erlauben** to allow somebody to do something □ Mein Vater hat mir erlaubt auszugehen. My father allowed me to go out.
■ **sich etwas erlauben** to allow oneself something □ Ich erlaube mir jetzt ein Bier. Now I'm going to allow myself a beer.
■ **Was erlaubst du dir denn eigentlich?** How dare you!

★ die **Erlaubnis**(PL die **Erlaubnisse**) FEM NOUN
permission

erleben(PERFECT TENSE **hat erlebt**) VERB [19]
1 to experience
□ Eine solche Frechheit habe ich selten erlebt. I've seldom experienced such cheek.
■ **Wir haben in den Ferien viel Schönes erlebt.** We had a lovely time on holiday.
■ **Sie hat viel Schlimmes erlebt.** She's had a lot of bad experiences.
2 to live through
□ Mein Opa hat den Zweiten Weltkrieg erlebt. My grandpa lived through the Second World War.
3 to live to see
□ Ich möchte die Geburt deines Kindes noch erleben. I would like to live to see the birth of your child.

das **Erlebnis**(GEN des **Erlebnisses**, PL die **Erlebnisse**) NEUT NOUN
experience

erledigen(PERFECT TENSE **hat erledigt**) VERB [19]
1 to see to
□ Ich habe heute noch viel zu erledigen. I've a lot to see to today.
2 to do
□ Hast du deine Hausaufgaben schon erledigt? Have you done your homework already?
3 to wear out (Umgangssprache)
□ Die Wanderung hat mich ziemlich erledigt. The hike's really worn me out.

die **Erleichterung** FEM NOUN
relief
□ Das war eine Erleichterung! That was a relief!

der **Erlös**(GEN des **Erlöses**, PL die **Erlöse**) MASC NOUN
proceeds pl
□ Der Erlös geht an soziale Projekte. The proceeds will go to social projects.

★ = core vocabulary

erlösen (PERFECT TENSE **hat erlöst**) VERB [7]
to save
□ Sie erlöste ihn aus einer gefährlichen Lage.
She saved him from a dangerous situation.

die **Ermahnung** FEM NOUN
admonition

★ die **Ermäßigung** FEM NOUN
reduction

ermöglichen (PERFECT TENSE **hat ermöglicht**)
VERB [7]
■ **jemandem etwas ermöglichen** to make
something possible for somebody

ermorden (PERFECT TENSE **hat ermordet**) VERB
[53]
to murder

★ **ermüdend** ADJECTIVE
tiring

ermutigen (PERFECT TENSE **hat ermutigt**)
VERB [7]
to encourage

ernähren (PERFECT TENSE **hat ernährt**) VERB
[19]
to support
□ Sie hat eine Familie zu ernähren. She has a
family to support.
■ **sich von etwas ernähren** to live on
something □ Sie ernähren sich hauptsächlich
von Reis. They live mainly on rice.

ernennen (IMPERFECT **ernannte**, PERFECT TENSE
hat ernannt) VERB [39]
to appoint

erneuern (PERFECT TENSE **hat erneuert**) VERB
[88]
to renew

★ **ernst** ADJECTIVE
▷ see also der **Ernst** NOUN
serious

der **Ernst** MASC NOUN
▷ see also **ernst** ADJECTIVE
seriousness
■ **Das ist mein Ernst.** I'm quite serious.
■ **im Ernst** in earnest

ernsthaft ADJECTIVE, ADVERB
1 serious
□ ein ernsthaftes Gespräch a serious talk
2 seriously
□ Glaubst du das ernsthaft? Do you seriously
believe that?

ernstlich ADJECTIVE, ADVERB
serious
■ **ernstlich besorgt** seriously concerned

die **Ernte** FEM NOUN
harvest

ernten VERB [2]
to harvest
□ Es ist Zeit, die Kirschen zu ernten. It's time to
harvest the cherries.
■ **Lob ernten** to earn praise

erobern (PERFECT TENSE **hat erobert**) VERB [88]
to conquer

erotisch ADJECTIVE
erotic

erpressen (PERFECT TENSE **hat erpresst**) VERB
[7]
1 to blackmail
□ Du willst mich wohl erpressen? Are you trying
to blackmail me?
2 to extort
□ Er hat von ihm Geld erpresst. He extorted
money from him.

erraten (PRESENT TENSE **errät**, IMPERFECT **erriet**,
PERFECT TENSE **hat erraten**) VERB
to guess

die **Erregung** FEM NOUN
excitement

★ **erreichen** (PERFECT TENSE **hat erreicht**) VERB
[19]
1 to reach
□ Wir haben Hamburg am späten Nachmittag
erreicht. We reached Hamburg in the late
afternoon.
2 to catch
□ Wir haben den Zug nicht mehr erreicht. We
didn't manage to catch the train.
3 to achieve
□ seinen Zweck erreichen to achieve one's
purpose □ Was willst du damit erreichen? What
do you aim to achieve by this?
■ **So erreichst du bei mir gar nichts.** You
won't get anywhere with me by doing that.

★ das **Ersatzteil** (PL die **Ersatzteile**) NEUT NOUN
spare part

erschaffen (IMPERFECT **erschuf**, PERFECT TENSE
hat erschaffen) VERB
to create

★ **erscheinen** (IMPERFECT **erschien**, PERFECT
TENSE **ist erschienen**) VERB [57]
to appear

erschießen (IMPERFECT **erschoss**, PERFECT
TENSE **hat erschossen**) VERB
to shoot dead

★ **erschöpft** ADJECTIVE
exhausted

die **Erschöpfung** FEM NOUN
exhaustion

★ **erschrecken** (1) (PERFECT TENSE **hat
erschreckt**) VERB [19]
to frighten
□ Hast du mich erschreckt! You really
frightened me!

★ **erschrecken** (2) (PRESENT TENSE **erschrickt**,
IMPERFECT **erschrak**, PERFECT TENSE **ist
erschrocken**) VERB [19]
to be frightened
□ Ich bin furchtbar erschrocken, als plötzlich

German – English

e

Numbers in brackets refer to verb tables on pages 697 to 706.

89

erschreckend – erzeugen

das Licht ausging. I was terribly frightened
when the light suddenly went out.

erschreckend ADJECTIVE
alarming

★**erschrocken** ADJECTIVE
frightened

ersetzen (PERFECT TENSE **hat ersetzt**) VERB
[36]
to replace
□ Du musst die Vase ersetzen. You'll have to
replace that vase.
■ jemandem die Unkosten ersetzen to pay
somebody's expenses

die **Ersparnisse** FEM PL NOUN
savings *pl*

★**erst** ADVERB
1 first
□ Erst will ich wissen, was das kostet. First I
want to know what it costs. □ Mach erst mal die
Arbeit fertig. Finish your work first.
■ Wenn du das erst mal hinter dir hast, ...
Once you've got that behind you, ...
2 only
□ Das ist erst gestern passiert. That happened
only yesterday. □ Er ist gerade erst
angekommen. He's only just arrived.
3 not until
□ Er hat es erst gemacht, als ich es ihm
befohlen habe. He didn't do it until I told him.
□ erst morgen not until tomorrow □ erst um 5
Uhr not until 5 o'clock

erstaunlich ADJECTIVE
astonishing

erstaunt ADJECTIVE
astonished

★**erste** ADJECTIVE
first
□ Ich habe gerade mein erstes Auto gekauft.
I've just bought my first car. □ Er kam als Erster.
He was the first to arrive.
■ Erste Hilfe first aid

erstechen (PRESENT TENSE **ersticht**, IMPERFECT
erstach, PERFECT TENSE **hat erstochen**) VERB
to stab to death

★**erstens** ADVERB
firstly

ersticken (PERFECT TENSE **ist erstickt**) VERB
[19]
1 to suffocate
□ Ich bin fast erstickt. I almost suffocated.
2 to smother
□ Er versuchte, die Flammen zu ersticken. He
tried to smother the flames.
■ in Arbeit ersticken to be snowed under
with work (*Umgangssprache*)

erstklassig ADJECTIVE
first-class

erstmals ADVERB
for the first time

ertragen (PRESENT TENSE **erträgt**, IMPERFECT
ertrug, PERFECT TENSE **hat ertragen**) VERB [77]
to stand
□ Ich kann die Schmerzen kaum ertragen. I can
hardly stand the pain. □ Sie erträgt es nicht,
wenn man ihr widerspricht. She can't stand
being contradicted.

erträglich ADJECTIVE
bearable

ertrinken (IMPERFECT **ertrank**, PERFECT TENSE
ist ertrunken) VERB [80]
to drown

★**erwachsen** ADJECTIVE
grown-up

★der/die **Erwachsene** (GEN des/der
Erwachsenen, PL die **Erwachsenen**) MASC/
FEM NOUN
adult
□ Erwachsene können das nicht verstehen.
Adults can't understand that.

erwähnen (PERFECT TENSE **hat erwähnt**) VERB
[19]
to mention

die **Erwärmung** FEM NOUN
warming
□ globale Erwärmung global warming
□ Erwärmung der Erdatmosphäre warming of
the earth's atmosphere

★**erwarten** (PERFECT TENSE **hat erwartet**) VERB
[2]
to expect
□ Er erwartet zu viel von uns. He's expecting too
much of us.
■ Wir können es kaum erwarten, dass die
Ferien beginnen. We can hardly wait for the
holidays to begin.

erweisen (IMPERFECT **erwies**, PERFECT TENSE **hat
erwiesen**) VERB
■ sich erweisen als to prove to be □ Er erwies
sich als guter Schüler. He proved to be a good
pupil.

erwerben (PRESENT TENSE **erwirbt**, IMPERFECT
erwarb, PERFECT TENSE **hat erworben**) VERB
[90]
to acquire

das **Erz** (GEN des **Erzes**, PL die **Erze**) NEUT NOUN
ore

★**erzählen** (PERFECT TENSE **hat erzählt**) VERB
[19]
to tell

★die **Erzählung** FEM NOUN
story

erzeugen (PERFECT TENSE **hat erzeugt**) VERB
[19]

1 to produce
□ In dieser Gegend wird Wein erzeugt. **Wine is produced in this region.**

2 to generate
□ Strom erzeugen **to generate electricity**

das **Erzeugnis** (GEN des **Erzeugnisses**, PL die **Erzeugnisse**) NEUT NOUN
produce *no pl*
□ ausländische Erzeugnisse **foreign produce**

erziehen (IMPERFECT **erzog**, PERFECT TENSE **hat erzogen**) VERB [96]
to bring up
□ Sie hat fünf Kinder erzogen. **She brought up five children.** □ Sie sollten ihre Kinder zu etwas mehr Höflichkeit erziehen. **They should bring their children up to be more polite.**

die **Erziehung** FEM NOUN
education

es PRONOUN
it
□ Es ist rot. **It's red.** □ Ich habe es nicht gesehen. **I didn't see it.** □ Es schneit. **It's snowing.**

der **Esel** (PL die **Esel**) MASC NOUN
donkey

essbar ADJECTIVE
edible

★**essen** VERB [20]

PRESENT TENSE	
ich esse	wir essen
du isst	ihr esst
er/sie/es isst	sie/Sie essen
PERFECT TENSE	
hat gegessen	

▷ *see also* das **Essen** NOUN
to eat

★das **Essen** (PL die **Essen**) NEUT NOUN
▷ *see also* **essen** VERB

1 meal
□ Komm doch am Freitag zum Essen. **Why don't you come for a meal on Friday?.**

2 food
□ Das Essen war lecker. **The food was delicious.**

★der **Essig** (PL die **Essige**) MASC NOUN
vinegar

★das **Esszimmer** (PL die **Esszimmer**) NEUT NOUN
dining room

★die **Etage** FEM NOUN
floor
□ Wir wohnen in der dritten Etage. **We live on the third floor.**

die **Etagenbetten** NEUT PL NOUN
bunk beds *pl*

das **E-Ticket** (PL die **E-Tickets**) NEUT NOUN
e-ticket

das **Etikett** (PL die **Etikette** *or* **Etiketten**) NEUT NOUN
label
□ Lies mal, was auf dem Etikett steht. **Read what's on the label.**

etliche PL PRONOUN
quite a few
□ etliche Leute **quite a few people**

das **Etui** (PL die **Etuis**) NEUT NOUN
case
□ ein Brillenetui **a glasses case**

★**etwa** ADVERB
1 about
□ Es waren etwa zwanzig. **There were about twenty.**
2 for instance
□ Leute wie etwa Jochen wissen das eben nicht. **People like Jochen, for instance, just don't know that.**
■ Soll das etwa heißen, dass ...? **Is that supposed to mean that ...?**
■ Du willst doch nicht etwa schon gehen! **You're not going already, are you?**

etwaig ADJECTIVE
possible

★**etwas** PRONOUN, ADVERB
1 something
□ Wir sollten ihr etwas schenken. **We should give her something.**
2 anything
□ Hast du nicht etwas gehört? **Haven't you heard anything?**
3 a little
□ Wir sollten uns etwas ausruhen. **We should have a little rest.** □ Nur etwas Milch bitte. **Just a little milk, please.** □ Sie ist etwas kleiner als ihre Schwester. **She is a little smaller than her sister.**

★die **EU** FEM NOUN (= *Europäische Union*)
EU (= *European Union*)

euch PRONOUN

euch is the accusative and dative of **ihr**.

1 you
□ Ich habe euch gesehen. **I saw you.** □ Ich komme mit euch. **I'll come with you.**
2 yourselves
□ Seht euch mal im Spiegel an. **Look at yourselves in the mirror.**
3 to you
□ Sie hat es euch gegeben. **She gave it to you.**

★**euer** PRONOUN, ADJECTIVE
1 your
□ Euer Deutschlehrer ist nett. **Your German teacher is nice.** □ Wenn das eure Mutter erlaubt. **If your mother lets you.** □ Ist das euer Haus? **Is that your house?**
2 yours
□ Das ist nicht unser Computer, das ist eurer.

That's not our computer, that's yours. □ Unsere Mutter heißt Samira, wie heißt eure? Our mother's called Samira, what's yours called? □ Wenn es in unserem Haus nicht geht, feiern wir in eurem. If it's not OK in our house, then we'll celebrate in yours.

die **Eule** FEM NOUN
owl

eure ▷ see **euer**

eures ▷ see **euer**

euretwegen ADVERB
1 for your sakes
□ Wir sind euretwegen nicht in Urlaub gefahren. We didn't go on holiday for your sakes.
2 on your account
□ Er hat sich euretwegen aufgeregt. He got upset on your account.

★ der **Euro** (PL die **Euros** or **Euro**) MASC NOUN
euro
□ Das kostet zehn Euro. It costs ten euros.

★ **Europa** NEUT NOUN
Europe
■ aus Europa from Europe
■ in Europa in Europe
■ nach Europa to Europe

★ der **Europäer** (PL die **Europäer**) MASC NOUN
European

★ die **Europäerin** FEM NOUN
European

★ **europäisch** ADJECTIVE
European

e. V. ABBREVIATION (= *eingetragener Verein*)
registered society

evangelisch ADJECTIVE
Protestant

eventuell ADVERB, ADJECTIVE
perhaps

□ Eventuell komme ich später nach. Perhaps I'll come on later.
■ **Eventuelle Fragen wird mein Kollege gerne beantworten.** My colleague will be pleased to answer any questions you may have.

BE CAREFUL!
eventuell does not mean **eventual**.

ewig ADJECTIVE
eternal

die **Ewigkeit** FEM NOUN
eternity

★ das **Examen** (PL die **Examen**) NEUT NOUN
exam

explodieren (PERFECT TENSE **ist explodiert**)
VERB [76]
to explode

die **Explosion** FEM NOUN
explosion

exportieren (PERFECT TENSE **hat exportiert**)
VERB [76]
to export

★ **extra** ADVERB, ADJECTIVE
1 separately
□ Schicke den USB-Stick lieber extra. It'd be better to send the USB stick separately.
2 specially
□ Das wurde extra für sie angefertigt. That was made specially for her. □ Ich bin extra wegen dir gekommen. I came specially because of you.
3 on purpose
□ Das hat er extra gemacht. He did that on purpose.
4 extra
□ Ich habe das extra schnell gemacht. I did it extra quickly. □ Das sind extra starke Pfefferminzbonbons. These are extra strong peppermints.

extrem ADJECTIVE
extreme

Ff

★ die **Fabrik** FEM NOUN
factory

> **BE CAREFUL!**
> Fabrik does not mean **fabric**.

der **Fabrikarbeiter** (PL die **Fabrikarbeiter**)
MASC NOUN
factory worker

die **Fabrikarbeiterin** FEM NOUN
factory worker

★ das **Fach** (PL die **Fächer**) NEUT NOUN
1 shelf
□ Das ist mein Fach im Schrank. This is my shelf
in the cupboard.
2 pigeonhole
□ Jeder Lehrer hat im Lehrerzimmer ein Fach.
Every teacher has a pigeonhole in the staff
room.
3 subject
□ In welchem Fach bist du am besten? What
subject are you best at?

der **Facharzt** (GEN des **Facharztes**, PL die
Fachärzte) MASC NOUN
specialist (*doctor*)

die **Fachärztin** FEM NOUN
specialist (*doctor*)

der **Fachausdruck** (PL die **Fachausdrücke**)
MASC NOUN
technical term

die **Fachfrau** FEM NOUN
expert

★ die **Fachhochschule** FEM NOUN
college

der **Fachmann** (PL die **Fachleute**) MASC NOUN
expert

★ die **Fachschule** FEM NOUN
technical college

die **Fackel** FEM NOUN
torch

der **Faden** (PL die **Fäden**) MASC NOUN
thread

fähig ADJECTIVE
capable
□ Sie ist eine sehr fähige Lehrerin. She's a very
capable teacher.
■ **fähig sein, etwas zu tun** to be capable of

doing something □ Bist du fähig, diesen Text zu
übersetzen? Are you capable of translating this
text?

die **Fähigkeit** FEM NOUN
ability

die **Fahne** FEM NOUN
flag

★ der **Fahrausweis** (GEN des **Fahrausweises**,
PL die **Fahrausweise**) MASC NOUN
ticket
□ Die Fahrausweise, bitte. Tickets, please.

die **Fahrbahn** FEM NOUN
carriageway

★ die **Fähre** FEM NOUN
ferry

★ **fahren** VERB [21]

> **PRESENT TENSE**
> ich fahre   wir fahren
> du fährst   ihr fahrt
> er/sie/es fährt   sie/Sie fahren
> **PERFECT TENSE**
> ist/hat gefahren

> For the perfect tense use **haben** when the
> verb has an object and **sein** when there is
> no object.

1 to drive
□ Er hat mich nach Hause gefahren. He drove
me home. □ Er ist sehr schnell gefahren. He
drove very fast.
■ **ein Rennen fahren** to drive in a race
2 to go
□ Der Intercity fährt stündlich. The Intercity
train goes every hour.
3 to leave
□ Wann seid ihr gefahren? When did you leave?
4 to sail
□ Das Schiff fährt nach Amerika. The ship's
sailing to America. □ Wir sind mit dem Schiff
nach Amerika gefahren. We sailed to America.
■ **Rad fahren** to cycle □ Früher bin ich viel Rad
gefahren. I used to cycle a lot.
■ **mit dem Auto fahren** to go by car
■ **mit dem Zug fahren** to go by train □ Seid
ihr mit dem Zug gefahren? Did you go by train?

★ der **Fahrer** (PL die **Fahrer**) MASC NOUN
driver

★die Fahrerin FEM NOUN
driver

★der Fahrgast (PL die **Fahrgäste**) MASC NOUN
passenger

★das Fahrgeld (PL die **Fahrgelder**) NEUT NOUN
fare
□ Bitte das Fahrgeld abgezählt bereithalten.
Please have exact fare ready.

★die Fahrkarte FEM NOUN
ticket
□ Die Fahrkarten, bitte. Tickets, please.

der Fahrkartenautomat (GEN des
Fahrkartenautomaten, PL die
Fahrkartenautomaten) MASC NOUN
ticket machine

★der Fahrkartenschalter (PL die
Fahrkartenschalter) MASC NOUN
ticket office

fahrlässig ADJECTIVE
negligent

der Fahrlehrer (PL die **Fahrlehrer**) MASC
NOUN
driving instructor

die Fahrlehrerin FEM NOUN
driving instructor

★der Fahrplan (PL die **Fahrpläne**) MASC NOUN
timetable

fahrplanmäßig ADJECTIVE
scheduled

★der Fahrpreis (GEN des **Fahrpreises**, PL die
Fahrpreise) MASC NOUN
fare

die Fahrprüfung FEM NOUN
driving test

★das Fahrrad (PL die **Fahrräder**) NEUT NOUN
bicycle

der Fahrradweg (PL die **Fahrradwege**)
MASC NOUN
cycle lane

★der Fahrschein (PL die **Fahrscheine**) MASC
NOUN
ticket
□ Die Fahrscheine, bitte. Tickets, please.

der Fahrscheinentwerter (PL die
Fahrscheinentwerter) MASC NOUN
ticket stamping machine

DID YOU KNOW...?
When you travel by train or tram (and
sometimes by bus) you have to stamp your
ticket in a **Fahrscheinentwerter**. The
machines are either on the platforms or inside
the vehicles.

★die Fahrschule FEM NOUN
driving school

★der Fahrstuhl (PL die **Fahrstühle**) MASC NOUN
lift

★die Fahrt FEM NOUN
1 journey
□ Die Fahrt nach Hamburg war lang. It was a
long journey to Hamburg.
2 trip
□ Am Wochenende haben wir eine Fahrt in den
Schwarzwald gemacht. We went on a trip to the
Black Forest at the weekend.
■ **Gute Fahrt!** Have a good journey.

die Fahrtkosten PL NOUN
travelling expenses *pl*

★das Fahrzeug (PL die **Fahrzeuge**) NEUT NOUN
vehicle

fair ADJECTIVE
fair
□ Das ist nicht fair! That's not fair!

der Faktor (PL die **Faktoren**) MASC NOUN
factor

die Fakultät FEM NOUN
faculty

der Falke (GEN des **Falken**, PL die **Falken**)
MASC NOUN
falcon

★der Fall (PL die **Fälle**) MASC NOUN
case
□ Die Polizei untersucht den Fall. The police are
investigating the case. □ In diesem Fall mache
ich eine Ausnahme. I'll make an exception in
this case. □ Welcher Fall steht nach 'außer'?
Which case does 'außer' take?
■ **auf jeden Fall** definitely □ Ich komme auf
jeden Fall. I'll definitely come.
■ **für alle Fälle** just in case □ Nimm für alle
Fälle einen Schirm mit. Take an umbrella, just in
case.
■ **Auf keinen Fall!** No way!

die Falle FEM NOUN
trap

★fallen (PRESENT TENSE **fällt**, IMPERFECT **fiel**,
PERFECT TENSE **ist gefallen**) VERB [22]
to fall
■ **etwas fallen lassen 1** to drop something
□ Lass es nicht fallen! Don't drop it! **2** to
abandon something □ Wir haben die Idee, in
Frankreich Ferien zu machen, wieder fallen
lassen. We've abandoned the idea of spending
our holidays in France.
■ **eine Bemerkung fallen lassen** to make a
remark

fällen VERB [38]
■ **einen Baum fällen** to fell a tree
■ **ein Urteil fällen** to pronounce judgement

fallenlassen VERB [42] ▷ *see* fallen

fällig ADJECTIVE
due

★falls ADVERB
if

★ = core vocabulary

der **Fallschirm** (PL die **Fallschirme**) MASC
NOUN
parachute

★**falsch** ADJECTIVE
1 wrong
□ Die Antwort war falsch. The answer was wrong.
■ **jemanden falsch verstehen** to get somebody wrong
2 false
□ falsche Zähne false teeth

fälschen VERB [38]
to forge

die **Fälschung** FEM NOUN
forgery

die **Falte** FEM NOUN
1 fold
□ eine Falte im Papier a fold in the paper
2 crease
■ **Die Hose ist voller Falten.** The trousers are all creased.
3 wrinkle
■ **Ihr Gesicht ist voller Falten.** Her face is all wrinkled.
4 pleat
□ eine Rockfalte a pleat in a skirt

falten VERB [2]
to fold

faltig ADJECTIVE
1 wrinkled
□ Er hat ein faltiges Gesicht. He's got a wrinkled face.
2 creased
□ Deine Hose ist ganz faltig. Your trousers are all creased.

★die **Familie** FEM NOUN
family

★der **Familienname** (GEN des **Familiennamens**, PL die **Familiennamen**) MASC NOUN
surname

★der **Familienstand** (PL die **Familienstände**) MASC NOUN
marital status

★der **Fan** (PL die **Fans**) MASC NOUN
fan
□ Sie ist ein Fan von Ariana Grande. She's an Ariana Grande fan.

fand VERB ▷ see finden

★**fangen** (PRESENT TENSE **fängt**, IMPERFECT **fing**, PERFECT TENSE **hat gefangen**) VERB [23]
to catch

die **Fantasie** FEM NOUN
imagination no pl

fantasielos ADJECTIVE
unimaginative

fantasieren (PERFECT TENSE **hat fantasiert**) VERB [76]
to fantasize

□ Er fantasierte von einem Lottogewinn. He fantasized about a win on the lottery.

fantasievoll ADJECTIVE
imaginative

★**fantastisch** ADJECTIVE
fantastic

★die **Farbe** FEM NOUN
1 colour
□ Rosa ist Olis Lieblingsfarbe. Pink is Oli's favourite colour.
2 paint
□ Hast du Farben, ich möchte was malen? I'd like to do some painting, have you got any paints?

farbecht ADJECTIVE
colourfast

färben VERB [38]
to dye
□ Sie hat ihre Haare gefärbt. She's dyed her hair.

farbenblind ADJECTIVE
colour-blind

★der **Farbfilm** (PL die **Farbfilme**) MASC NOUN
colour film

das **Farbfoto** (PL die **Farbfotos**) NEUT NOUN
colour photograph

farbig ADJECTIVE
coloured

farblos ADJECTIVE
colourless

★der **Farbstift** (PL die **Farbstifte**) MASC NOUN
coloured pencil

der **Farbstoff** (PL die **Farbstoffe**) MASC NOUN
dye

der **Farbton** (PL die **Farbtöne**) MASC NOUN
shade

der **Fasan** (PL die **Fasane** or **Fasanen**) MASC NOUN
pheasant

★der **Fasching** (PL die **Faschinge**) MASC NOUN
carnival

> **DID YOU KNOW...?**
> The German carnival season lasts from 11 November to Shrove Tuesday but most events, fancy-dress processions and parties take place in the week leading up to Ash Wednesday.

★der **Faschingsdienstag** MASC NOUN
Shrove Tuesday

die **Faser** FEM NOUN
fibre

das **Fass** (GEN des **Fasses**, PL die **Fässer**) NEUT NOUN
barrel
□ ein Weinfass a wine barrel
■ **ein Ölfass** an oil drum
■ **Bier vom Fass** draught beer

fassen – Feierabend

fassen (PERFECT TENSE **hat gefasst**) VERB [31]
1 to grasp
□ Er fasste mich am Arm. He grasped my arm.
2 to hold
□ Der Behälter fasst zwanzig Liter. The container holds twenty litres.
3 to understand
□ Ich kann es nicht fassen, dass du das noch immer nicht gemacht hast. I can't understand why you still haven't done it.
■ **nicht zu fassen** unbelievable
■ **sich fassen** to calm down

die **Fassung** FEM NOUN
1 composure
□ Er hat die Fassung verloren. He lost his composure.
■ **jemanden aus der Fassung bringen** to upset somebody
2 version
□ der Text in einer neuen Fassung the text in a new version

fassungslos ADJECTIVE
speechless

★ **fast** ADVERB
almost

> **BE CAREFUL!**
> The German word **fast** does not mean **fast**.

fasten VERB [2]
to fast

> **BE CAREFUL!**
> The German word **fasten** does not mean **to fasten**.

★ die **Fastenzeit** FEM NOUN
Lent

die **Fastnacht** FEM NOUN
carnival

> **DID YOU KNOW...?**
> The German carnival season lasts from 11 November to Shrove Tuesday but most events, fancy-dress processions and parties take place in the week leading up to Ash Wednesday.

★ **faul** ADJECTIVE
1 rotten
□ Der Apfel ist faul. The apple's rotten.
2 lazy
□ Er ist der faulste Schüler. He's our laziest pupil.
■ **eine faule Ausrede** a lame excuse
■ **Daran ist etwas faul.** There's something fishy about it. (*Umgangssprache*)

faulen VERB [38]
to rot

★ **faulenzen** VERB [36]
to laze about

die **Faust** (PL die **Fäuste**) FEM NOUN
fist
■ **auf eigene Faust** off one's own bat

★ der **FCKW** MASC NOUN
(= *Fluorchlorkohlenwasserstoff*)
CFC (= *chlorofluorocarbon*)

★ der **Februar** (GEN des **Februar** or **Februars**, PL die **Februare**) MASC NOUN
February
□ im Februar in February □ am dritten Februar on the third of February □ Bonn, den 3. Februar 2019 Bonn, 3 February 2019 □ Heute ist der zweite Februar. Today is the second of February.

fechten (PRESENT TENSE **ficht**, IMPERFECT **focht**, PERFECT TENSE **hat gefochten**) VERB
to fence

die **Feder** FEM NOUN
1 feather
□ Er hatte eine Feder am Hut. He had a feather in his hat.
2 spring
□ Die Federn des Betts sind ausgeleiert. The bed springs have worn out.

der **Federball** (PL die **Federbälle**) MASC NOUN
1 shuttlecock
2 badminton

das **Federbett** (PL die **Federbetten**) NEUT NOUN
continental quilt

die **Fee** FEM NOUN
fairy

fegen VERB [38]
to sweep

fehl ADJECTIVE
■ **fehl am Platz** out of place

★ **fehlen** VERB [38]
1 to be absent
□ Er hat gestern in der Schule gefehlt. He was absent from school yesterday.
2 to be missing
□ Da fehlt ein Knopf. There's a button missing.
□ Wer fehlt? Is anyone missing?
■ **Mir fehlt das nötige Geld.** I haven't got the money.
■ **Du fehlst mir.** I miss you.
■ **Was fehlt ihm?** What's wrong with him?

★ der **Fehler** (PL die **Fehler**) MASC NOUN
1 mistake
□ Wie viele Fehler hast du gemacht? How many mistakes did you make?
2 fault
□ Sein einziger Fehler ist, dass er den Mund nicht halten kann. His only fault is that he can't keep his mouth shut.

★ die **Feier** FEM NOUN
celebration

★ der **Feierabend** (PL die **Feierabende**) MASC NOUN
clocking-off time
■ **Feierabend machen** to clock off
■ **Wann hat dein Vater Feierabend?** When does your father finish work?

feierlich ADJECTIVE
solemn

die **Feierlichkeit** FEM NOUN
festivity

★**feiern** VERB [88]
to celebrate

★der **Feiertag** (PLdie **Feiertage**) MASC NOUN
holiday
□ ein öffentlicher Feiertag a public holiday

feige ADJECTIVE
▷ see alsodie **Feige** NOUN
cowardly

die **Feige** FEM NOUN
▷ see alsofeige ADJECTIVE
fig

★der **Feigling** (PLdie **Feiglinge**) MASC NOUN
coward

die **Feile** FEM NOUN
file
□ eine Nagelfeile a nailfile

feilschen VERB [38]
to haggle

★**fein** ADJECTIVE
1 fine
□ feiner Sand fine sand
2 refined
□ feine Leute refined people
■ Fein! Great!

der **Feind** (PLdie **Feinde**) MASC NOUN
enemy

feindlich ADJECTIVE
hostile

die **Feindschaft** FEM NOUN
hostility

★das **Feld** (PLdie **Felder**) NEUT NOUN
1 field
□ Auf diesem Feld wächst Hafer. There are oats
growing in this field.
2 pitch
□ ein Fußballfeld a football pitch
3 square
□ Sie rückte mit ihrem Bauern ein Feld vor. She
moved her pawn forward one square.

der **Fels** (GENdes **Felsen**, PLdie **Felsen**) MASC
NOUN
rock
■ die weißen Felsen von Dover the white
cliffs of Dover

feminin ADJECTIVE
feminine

★das **Fenster** (PLdie **Fenster**) NEUT NOUN
window

★der **Fensterladen** (PLdie **Fensterläden**)
MASC NOUN
shutter

die **Fensterscheibe** FEM NOUN
windowpane

★die **Ferien** PL NOUN
holidays pl
■ Ferien haben to be on holiday

★der **Ferienjob** (PLdie **Ferienjobs**) MASC NOUN
holiday job

der **Ferienkurs** (GENdes **Ferienkurses**, PL
die **Ferienkurse**) MASC NOUN
vacation course

das **Ferienlager** (PLdie **Ferienlager**) NEUT
NOUN
holiday camp

fern ADJECTIVE, ADVERB
distant
□ in ferner Zukunft in the distant future
■ fern von hier a long way from here
■ der Ferne Osten the Far East

die **Fernbedienung** FEM NOUN
remote control

das **Ferngespräch** (PLdie **Ferngespräche**)
NEUT NOUN
long-distance call

das **Fernglas** (GENdes **Fernglases**, PLdie
Ferngläser) NEUT NOUN
binoculars pl
□ ein Fernglas a pair of binoculars

der **Fernsehapparat** (PLdie
Fernsehapparate) MASC NOUN
television set

★**fernsehen** (PRESENT TENSEsieht fern,
IMPERFECTsah fern, PERFECT TENSEhat
ferngesehen) VERB [64]
▷ see alsodas **Fernsehen** NOUN
to watch television

★das **Fernsehen** NEUT NOUN
▷ see alsofernsehen VERB
television
□ im Fernsehen on television

★der **Fernseher** (PLdie **Fernseher**) MASC NOUN
television set

★der **Fernsehfilm** (PLdie **Fernsehfilme**)
MASC NOUN
TV film

★die **Fernsehsendung** FEM NOUN
TV programme

★die **Fernsehserie** FEM NOUN
TV series

der **Fernsprecher** (PLdie **Fernsprecher**)
MASC NOUN
telephone

die **Fernsteuerung** FEM NOUN
remote control

die **Ferse** FEM NOUN
heel
□ Ich habe eine Blase an der Ferse. I've got a
blister on my heel.

★**fertig** ADJECTIVE
1 ready
□ Das Essen ist fertig. Dinner's ready.

Numbers in brackets refer to verb tables on pages 697 to 706.

97

2 finished

□ Der Aufsatz ist fertig. The essay's finished.
□ Bist du mit deinen Hausaufgaben fertig?
Have you finished your homework?
■ **etwas fertig machen** to finish something
□ Ich muss noch die Matheaufgaben fertig
machen. I've just got to finish my maths
homework.
■ **sich fertig machen** to get ready

fertigbringen (IMPERFECT **brachte fertig**
PERFECT TENSE **hat fertiggebracht**) VERB [13]
■ **es fertigbringen, etwas zu tun** to bring
oneself to do something □ Ich bringe es nicht
fertig, ihr das zu sagen. I can't bring myself to
tell her.

das **Fertiggericht** (PL die **Fertiggerichte**)
NEUT NOUN
ready meal

fertigmachen VERB [48]
■ **jemanden fertigmachen 1** to wear
somebody out □ Die Radtour hat mich
fertiggemacht. The cycling trip wore me out.
2 to tear somebody off a strip (*Umgangssprache*)
□ Meine Englischlehrerin hat mich heute
fertiggemacht. My English teacher tore me off a
strip today.

fesselnd ADJECTIVE
captivating

★ **fest** ADJECTIVE, ADVERB
▷ *see also* das **Fest** NOUN
firm
□ Er hielt sie mit festem Griff. He had a firm grip
of her. □ Er hat einen festen Händedruck. He
has a firm handshake.
■ **ein festes Einkommen** a regular income
■ **fest schlafen** to sleep soundly
■ **feste Nahrung** solids *pl*

★ das **Fest** (PL die **Feste**) NEUT NOUN
▷ *see also* **fest** ADJECTIVE, ADVERB
1 party
□ Ben macht am Samstag ein Fest. Ben is
having a party on Saturday.
2 festival
□ das Backnanger Straßenfest the Backnang
Street Festival
■ **Frohes Fest!** Happy Christmas!

★ **festhalten** (PRESENT TENSE **hält fest,** IMPERFECT
hielt fest, PERFECT TENSE **hat festgehalten**)
VERB [33]
to keep hold of
□ Du musst das Steuer festhalten. You must
keep hold of the wheel.
■ **sich festhalten an** to hold on to □ Sie hielt
sich am Geländer fest. She held on to the
banister.

die **Festigkeit** FEM NOUN
strength

festlegen (PERFECT TENSE **hat festgelegt**) VERB
[4]
to fix

□ einen Termin festlegen to fix a date
■ **sich festlegen** to commit oneself

festlich ADJECTIVE
festive

festmachen (PERFECT TENSE **hat
festgemacht**) VERB [48]
1 to fix
□ Habt ihr den Termin schon festgemacht?
Have you fixed the date yet?
2 to moor
□ Wir haben das Boot im Hafen festgemacht.
We moored the boat in the harbour.

die **Festnahme** FEM NOUN
arrest

festnehmen (PRESENT TENSE **nimmt fest,**
IMPERFECT **nahm fest,** PERFECT TENSE **hat
festgenommen**) VERB [52]
to arrest

das **Festnetz** (PL die **Festnetze**) NEUT NOUN
landline
■ **aus dem Festnetz anrufen** to call from a
landline

die **Festplatte** FEM NOUN
hard disk

die **Festspiele** NEUT PL NOUN
festival *sing*

feststehen (IMPERFECT **stand fest,** PERFECT
TENSE **hat festgestanden**) VERB [72]
to be certain
□ So viel steht fest: ... This much is certain: ...

feststellen (PERFECT TENSE **hat festgestellt**)
VERB [4]
1 to establish
□ Wir konnten nicht feststellen, wer das
geschrieben hatte. We couldn't establish who'd
written it.
2 to see
□ Ich stelle fest, dass du schon wieder nicht
aufgepasst hast. I see that you haven't been
paying attention again.
3 to detect
□ Wir haben da einen Fehler festgestellt. We've
detected an error.

★ der **Festtag** MASC NOUN
1 holiday
□ Frohe Festtage! Happy Holidays! (*Christmas
and New Year*)
2 special day

★ **fett** ADJECTIVE
▷ *see also* das **Fett** NOUN
fat
□ Er ist zu fett. He's too fat.
■ **fettes Essen** greasy food
■ **fette Schrift** bold type

★ das **Fett** (PL die **Fette**) NEUT NOUN
▷ *see also* **fett** ADJECTIVE
fat

★ = core vocabulary

fettarm ADJECTIVE
low-fat
□ Der fettarme Joghurt schmeckt nicht gut. The low-fat yoghurt doesn't taste good.
■ fettarme Milch semi-skimmed milk

★ **fettig** ADJECTIVE
greasy

der **Fetzen** (PL die **Fetzen**) MASC NOUN
scrap
□ ein Fetzen Papier a scrap of paper

★ **feucht** ADJECTIVE
1 damp
□ etwas mit einem feuchten Tuch abwischen to wipe something with a damp cloth
2 humid
□ Das Klima ist sehr feucht. The climate's very humid.

die **Feuchtigkeit** FEM NOUN
1 moisture
□ Salz zieht Feuchtigkeit an. Salt attracts moisture.
2 humidity
□ hohe Luftfeuchtigkeit high humidity

★ das **Feuer** (PL die **Feuer**) NEUT NOUN
fire

★ der **Feuerlöscher** (PL die **Feuerlöscher**) MASC NOUN
fire extinguisher

★ die **Feuerwehr** (PL die **Feuerwehren**) FEM NOUN
fire brigade

das **Feuerwehrauto** (PL die **Feuerwehrautos**) NEUT NOUN
fire engine

★ die **Feuerwehrfrau** FEM NOUN
firefighter

★ der **Feuerwehrmann** (PL die **Feuerwehrleute** or **Feuerwehrmänner**) MASC NOUN
firefighter

★ das **Feuerwerk** (PL die **Feuerwerke**) NEUT NOUN
fireworks pl
□ Wir waren beim Feuerwerk. We went to the fireworks.

★ das **Feuerzeug** (PL die **Feuerzeuge**) NEUT NOUN
lighter

★ das **Fieber** (PL die **Fieber**) NEUT NOUN
1 fever
□ Das Fieber wird sich in ein paar Tagen senken. The fever will pass in a couple of days.
2 temperature
□ Hast du Fieber? Have you got a temperature?

fiel VERB ▷ see fallen

fies ADJECTIVE
nasty

die **Figur** FEM NOUN
1 figure (body)
2 character (in book)

die **Filiale** FEM NOUN
branch

★ der **Film** (PL die **Filme**) MASC NOUN
film

filmen VERB [38]
to film

der **Filter** (PL die **Filter**) MASC NOUN
filter

filtern VERB [88]
to filter

★ der **Filzstift** (PL die **Filzstifte**) MASC NOUN
felt-tip pen

das **Finanzamt** (PL die **Finanzämter**) NEUT NOUN
Inland Revenue Office

finanziell ADJECTIVE
financial

finanzieren (PERFECT TENSE hat finanziert) VERB [76]
to finance

★ **finden** (IMPERFECT fand, PERFECT TENSE hat gefunden) VERB [24]
1 to find
□ Hast du deinen Radiergummi gefunden? Have you found your rubber?
2 to think
□ Ich finde, er sieht gut aus. I think he's good-looking. □ Ich finde sie nicht attraktiv. I don't think she's attractive.
■ Ich finde nichts dabei, wenn ... I don't see what's wrong with ... □ Ich finde nichts dabei, wenn man mal einen Tag faulenzt. I don't see what's wrong with lazing about for one day.
■ Das wird sich finden. Things will work out.

fing VERB ▷ see fangen

★ der **Finger** (PL die **Finger**) MASC NOUN
finger

der **Fingerabdruck** (PL die **Fingerabdrücke**) MASC NOUN
fingerprint
■ genetische Fingerabdrücke genetic fingerprinting

der **Fingernagel** (PL die **Fingernägel**) MASC NOUN
fingernail

★ der **Finne** (GEN des **Finnen**, PL die **Finnen**) MASC NOUN
Finn

★ die **Finnin** FEM NOUN
Finn

★ **finnisch** ADJECTIVE
Finnish

★ **Finnland** NEUT NOUN
Finland

finster – fleißig

- **aus Finnland** from Finland
- **nach Finnland** to Finland

finster ADJECTIVE

1 dark
□ Hier ist es aber finster. **It's dark in here.**

2 sinister
□ finstere Gestalten **sinister figures**
- **ein finsteres Gesicht** a grim face

die **Finsternis** FEM NOUN
darkness

★die **Firma** (PL die **Firmen**) FEM NOUN
firm

★der **Fisch** (PL die **Fische**) MASC NOUN
fish
□ Ich habe fünf Fische. **I've got five fish.**
- **Fische** Pisces *sing* □ Adelheid ist Fisch.
Adelheid's Pisces.

★**fischen** VERB [48]
to fish
□ Sonntags geht Alex immer fischen. **Alex always goes fishing on Sundays.**

der **Fischer** (PL die **Fischer**) MASC NOUN
fisherman

die **Fischerei** FEM NOUN
fishing

die **Fischerin** FEM NOUN
fisherman

★**fit** ADJECTIVE
fit
□ Ich halte mich mit Schwimmen fit. **I keep fit by swimming.**

das **Fitnesscenter** (PL die **Fitnesscenter**)
NEUT NOUN
fitness centre

das **Fitnessstudio** (PL die **Fitnessstudios**)
NEUT NOUN
gym

fix ADJECTIVE
- **fix und fertig 1** finished □ Alles war fix und fertig. **Everything was finished. 2** all in
(*Umgangssprache*)□ Ich bin fix und fertig. **I'm all in.**

★**flach** ADJECTIVE

1 flat
□ Norddeutschland ist flach. **North Germany's flat.**

2 shallow
□ Ich brauche eine flache Schale. **I need a shallow bowl.**

der **Flachbildschirm** (PL die
Flachbildschirme) MASC NOUN
flat screen
□ ein Fernseher mit Flachbildschirm a flatscreen TV

die **Fläche** FEM NOUN
area
□ eine Fläche von hundert Quadratkilometern an area of a hundred square kilometres

das **Flachland** NEUT NOUN
lowland

flackern VERB [88]
to flicker

die **Flagge** FEM NOUN
flag

★die **Flamme** FEM NOUN
flame

★die **Flasche** FEM NOUN
bottle
□ eine Flasche Mineralwasser a bottle of mineral water

der **Flaschenöffner** (PL die
Flaschenöffner) MASC NOUN
bottle-opener

flauschig ADJECTIVE
fluffy

der **Fleck** (PL die **Flecke**) MASC NOUN

1 stain
□ Der Wein hat einen Fleck auf dem Teppich gemacht. **The wine left a stain on the carpet.**

2 spot
□ Das ist ein hübscher Fleck. **This is a beautiful spot.**

das **Fleckenmittel** (PL die **Fleckenmittel**)
NEUT NOUN
stain remover

fleckig ADJECTIVE

1 spotted
□ Ein Dalmatiner hat ein fleckiges Fell. **A Dalmatian has a spotted coat.**

2 stained
□ Die Tischdecke ist ganz fleckig. **The tablecloth's all stained.**

die **Fledermaus** (PL die **Fledermäuse**) FEM
NOUN
bat

★das **Fleisch** NEUT NOUN
meat
□ Ich esse kein Fleisch. **I don't eat meat.**

★der **Fleischer** (PL die **Fleischer**) MASC NOUN
butcher

★die **Fleischerei** FEM NOUN
butcher's

★die **Fleischerin** FEM NOUN
butcher

der **Fleiß** (GEN des **Fleißes**) MASC NOUN
hard work
□ Mit etwas Fleiß könntest du deine Noten verbessern. **With a bit of hard work you could improve your marks.**

★**fleißig** ADJECTIVE
hard-working
□ Silke ist eine fleißige Schülerin. **Silke's a hard-working pupil.**
- **Ich war heute schon fleißig.** **I've already done quite a bit of work today.**

German-English

flexibel ADJECTIVE
flexible

flicken VERB [48]
to mend

★ **die Fliege** FEM NOUN
1 fly
□ Er tut keiner Fliege etwas zuleide. He wouldn't hurt a fly.
2 bow tie
□ Er trug eine Fliege. He was wearing a bow tie.

★ **fliegen** (IMPERFECT **flog**, PERFECT TENSE **ist geflogen**) VERB [25]
to fly

fliehen (IMPERFECT **floh**, PERFECT TENSE **ist geflohen**) VERB [26]
to flee

die Fliese FEM NOUN
tile

das Fließband (PL die **Fließbänder**) NEUT NOUN
assembly line

★ **fließen** (IMPERFECT **floss**, PERFECT TENSE **ist geflossen**) VERB [27]
to flow

★ **fließend** ADJECTIVE, ADVERB
1 running
□ fließendes Wasser running water
2 fluent
□ Sie spricht fließend Englisch. She is fluent in English.

flink ADJECTIVE
nimble

die Flitterwochen FEM PL NOUN
honeymoon *sing*

flitzen (PERFECT TENSE **ist geflitzt**) VERB [48]
to dash

die Flocke FEM NOUN
flake
□ eine Schneeflocke a snowflake

flog VERB ▷ *see* **fliegen**

der Floh (PL die **Flöhe**) MASC NOUN
flea

der Flohmarkt (PL die **Flohmärkte**) MASC NOUN
flea market

floss VERB ▷ *see* **fließen**

die Flosse FEM NOUN
1 fin
□ die Flosse eines Hais a shark's fin
2 flipper
□ Er hat seine Flossen mit ins Schwimmbad genommen. He took his flippers with him to the swimming baths.

★ **die Flöte** FEM NOUN
1 flute
□ Alia spielt Flöte. Alia plays the flute.
2 recorder
□ Phil spielt Flöte. Phil plays the recorder.

fluchen VERB [38]
to curse

flüchtig ADJECTIVE
at large
□ Der Einbrecher ist noch flüchtig. The burglar's still at large.
■ **jemanden nur flüchtig kennen** to know somebody only superficially

der Flüchtling (PL die **Flüchtlinge**) MASC NOUN
refugee

★ **der Flug** (PL die **Flüge**) MASC NOUN
flight
□ Der Flug nach Atlanta ist verspätet. The flight to Atlanta's been delayed.

das Flugblatt (PL die **Flugblätter**) NEUT NOUN
leaflet

der Flügel (PL die **Flügel**) MASC NOUN
1 wing
□ die Flügel des Adlers the eagle's wings
2 grand piano
□ Im Musikzimmer steht ein Flügel. There's a grand piano in the music room.

★ **der Fluggast** (PL die **Fluggäste**) MASC NOUN
airline passenger

die Fluggesellschaft FEM NOUN
airline

★ **der Flughafen** (PL die **Flughäfen**) MASC NOUN
airport

der Fluglotse (GEN des **Fluglotsen**, PL die **Fluglotsen**) MASC NOUN
air traffic controller

der Flugplan (PL die **Flugpläne**) MASC NOUN
flight schedule

★ **der Flugplatz** (GEN des **Flugplatzes**, PL die **Flugplätze**) MASC NOUN
1 airport
□ Wir bringen dich zum Flugplatz. We'll take you to the airport.
2 airfield
□ Dieser Flugplatz ist nur für Privatflugzeuge. This airfield is only for private planes.

★ **der Flugschein** (PL die **Flugscheine**) MASC NOUN
plane ticket

★ **das Flugticket** (PL die **Flugtickets**) NEUT NOUN
plane ticket

★ **das Flugzeug** (PL die **Flugzeuge**) NEUT NOUN
aeroplane

die Flugzeugentführung FEM NOUN
hijacking

das Fluor NEUT NOUN
fluorine

★ **der Flur** (PL die **Flure**) MASC NOUN
corridor

f

Fluss – Forschung

BE CAREFUL!
Flur does not mean **floor**.

★ der **Fluss** (GEN des **Flusses**, PL die **Flüsse**)
MASC NOUN
river

★ das **Flüsschen** (PL die **Flüsschen**) NEUT NOUN
little river

flüssig ADJECTIVE
liquid

die **Flüssigkeit** FEM NOUN
liquid

★ **flüstern** VERB [88]
to whisper

★ die **Flut** (PL die **Fluten**) FEM NOUN
1 flood
□ Wir haben eine Flut von Briefen bekommen.
We received a flood of letters.
2 high tide
□ Das Schiff läuft bei Flut aus. The ship sails at high tide.

das **Flutlicht** (PL die **Flutlichter**) NEUT NOUN
floodlight

★ der **Föhn** (PL die **Föhne**) MASC NOUN
1 foehn (warm dry alpine wind)
2 hair dryer

föhnen VERB [38]
to blow-dry

★ die **Folge** FEM NOUN
1 result
□ Er starb an den Folgen des Unfalls. He died as a result of the accident.
■ **etwas zur Folge haben** to result in something □ Deine Faulheit wird schlechte Noten zur Folge haben. Your laziness will result in bad marks.
■ **Folgen haben** to have consequences □ Das wird schlimme Folgen haben. That'll have serious consequences.
2 episode
□ Hast du die letzte Folge der 'Lindenstraße' gesehen? Did you see the latest episode of 'Lindenstraße'?
■ **ein Roman in Folgen** a serialized novel

★ **folgen** (PERFECT TENSE **ist gefolgt**) VERB [38]
to follow
□ Uns ist ein grünes Auto gefolgt. We were followed by a green car. □ Folgen Sie dem Wagen da. Follow that car. □ Ich konnte ihm nicht folgen. I couldn't follow what he was saying.
■ **Meine Kinder folgen nicht immer.** My children don't always do what they're told.

★ **folgend** ADJECTIVE
following

die **Folgerung** FEM NOUN
conclusion

folglich ADVERB
consequently

folgsam ADJECTIVE
obedient

die **Folie** FEM NOUN
foil

★ **followen** VERB [38]
to follow (on social media)

foltern VERB [88]
to torture

der **Fön**® (PL die **Föne**) MASC NOUN
hair dryer

fordern VERB [88]
to demand

die **Forderung** FEM NOUN
demand

★ die **Forelle** FEM NOUN
trout
□ drei Forellen three trout

★ die **Form** FEM NOUN
1 shape
□ Das Auto hat eine elegante Form. The car has an elegant shape.
2 mould
□ Das Metall wird in eine Form gegossen. The metal is poured into a mould.
3 baking tin

das **Format** (PL die **Formate**) NEUT NOUN
format

formatieren (PERFECT TENSE **hat formatiert**)
VERB [76]
to format

die **Formel** FEM NOUN
formula

formen VERB [38]
to form

förmlich ADJECTIVE
formal

★ das **Formular** (PL die **Formulare**) NEUT NOUN
form
□ ein Formular ausfüllen to fill in a form

formulieren (PERFECT TENSE **hat formuliert**)
VERB [76]
to formulate

der **Forscher** (PL die **Forscher**) MASC NOUN
1 research scientist
□ Die Forscher haben noch keinen Impfstoff gegen Aids entwickelt. Research scientists have still not developed an AIDS vaccine.
2 explorer
□ Ein Gruppe von Forschern ist im Amazonasgebiet verschollen. A group of explorers is missing in the Amazon region.

die **Forscherin** FEM NOUN
1 research scientist
2 explorer

die **Forschung** FEM NOUN
research no pl

★ = core vocabulary

fort ADVERB
gone
□ Mein Geldbeutel ist fort. My purse is gone.
■ **und so fort** and so on
■ **in einem fort** on and on
■ **Fort mit dir!** Away with you!

sich **fortbewegen** (PERFECT TENSE **hat sich fortbewegt**) VERB [4]
to move

fortbleiben (IMPERFECT **blieb fort**, PERFECT TENSE **ist fortgeblieben**) VERB [10]
to stay away

fortfahren (PRESENT TENSE **fährt fort**, IMPERFECT **fuhr fort**, PERFECT TENSE **ist fortgefahren**) VERB [21]
1 to leave
□ Sie sind gestern fortgefahren. They left yesterday.
2 to continue
□ Er fuhr in seiner Rede fort. He continued with his speech.

fortgeschritten ADJECTIVE
advanced

★ der **Fortschritt** (PL die **Fortschritte**) MASC NOUN
progress *no pl*
□ Fortschritte machen to make progress

fortschrittlich ADJECTIVE
progressive

fortsetzen (PERFECT TENSE **hat fortgesetzt**) VERB [15]
to continue

die **Fortsetzung** FEM NOUN
1 continuation *no pl*
□ die Fortsetzung des Krieges the continuation of the war
2 sequel
□ Hast du die Fortsetzung gelesen? Have you read the sequel?
■ **Fortsetzung folgt** to be continued

★ das **Foto** (PL die **Fotos**) NEUT NOUN
photo

★ der **Fotoapparat** (PL die **Fotoapparate**) MASC NOUN
camera

★ der **Fotograf** (GEN des **Fotografen**, PL die **Fotografen**) MASC NOUN
photographer

BE CAREFUL!
Fotograf does not mean **photograph**.

★ die **Fotografie** FEM NOUN
1 photography
□ Die Fotografie ist sein Hobby. His hobby is photography.
2 photograph
□ Ich habe eine Fotografie davon gesehen. I've seen a photograph of it.

★ **fotografieren** (PERFECT TENSE **hat fotografiert**) VERB [76]
1 to take a photo of
□ Kannst du uns mal fotografieren? Can you take a photo of us?
2 to take photographs
□ Ich fotografiere in den Ferien nie. I never take photographs on holiday.

★ die **Fotografin** FEM NOUN
photographer

das **Fotohandy** (PL die **Fotohandys**) NEUT NOUN
camera phone

die **Fotokopie** FEM NOUN
photocopy

Fr. ABBREVIATION (= *Frau*)
1 Mrs
2 Ms

die **Fracht** FEM NOUN
freight
□ Frachtkosten freight charges

★ die **Frage** FEM NOUN
question
□ Könntest du bitte meine Frage beantworten? Could you please answer my question?
□ jemandem eine Frage stellen to ask somebody a question
■ **in Frage kommen/stellen** ▷ *see* **infrage**

der **Fragebogen** (PL die **Fragebogen**) MASC NOUN
questionnaire

★ **fragen** VERB [38]
to ask
□ Kann ich dich was fragen? Can I ask you something?

das **Fragezeichen** (PL die **Fragezeichen**) NEUT NOUN
question mark

fraglich ADJECTIVE
doubtful
□ Es ist sehr fraglich, ob wir kommen können. It's very doubtful whether we can come.

★ der **Franken** (PL die **Franken**) MASC NOUN
franc
□ Er bezahlte 50 Franken. He paid 50 francs.
■ **der Schweizer Franken** the Swiss franc

frankieren (PERFECT TENSE **hat frankiert**) VERB [76]
■ **einen Brief frankieren** to put a stamp on a letter
■ **ein frankierter Rückumschlag** a stamped self-addressed envelope

★ **Frankreich** NEUT NOUN
France
■ **aus Frankreich** from France
■ **in Frankreich** in France
■ **nach Frankreich** to France

Numbers in brackets refer to verb tables on pages 697 to 706.

103

Franzose – Freude

★ der **Franzose** (GEN des **Franzosen**, PL die **Franzosen**) MASC NOUN
Frenchman
■ **Er ist Franzose.** He's French.
■ **die Franzosen** the French

★ die **Französin** FEM NOUN
Frenchwoman
■ **Sie ist Französin.** She's French.

★ **französisch** ADJECTIVE
▷ see also das **Französisch** NOUN
French

das **Französisch** (GEN des **Französischen**) NEUT NOUN
▷ see also **französisch** ADJECTIVE
French
□ **Er lernt Französisch in der Schule.** He's learning French at school.

fraß VERB ▷ see **fressen**

★ die **Frau** FEM NOUN
1 woman
□ **Sie ist eine nette Frau.** She's a nice woman.
2 wife
□ **Herr Arnold ist mit seiner Frau gekommen.** Mr Arnold came with his wife.
■ **Sehr geehrte Frau Braun 1** Dear Mrs Braun **2** Dear Ms Braun

DID YOU KNOW...?
Generally **Frau** is used to address all women whether married or not.

■ **Frau Doktor** Doctor

der **Frauenarzt** (GEN des **Frauenarztes**, PL die **Frauenärzte**) MASC NOUN
gynaecologist

die **Frauenärztin** FEM NOUN
gynaecologist

★ das **Fräulein** (PL die **Fräulein**) NEUT NOUN
Miss
□ **Liebes Fräulein Dümmler** Dear Miss Dümmler

DID YOU KNOW...?
Fräulein is hardly ever used nowadays and **Frau** is used instead to address all women whether married or not.

★ **frech** ADJECTIVE
cheeky

die **Frechheit** FEM NOUN
cheek

★ **frei** ADJECTIVE
free
■ **Ist der Platz hier frei?** Is this seat taken?
■ **Soll ich einen Platz für dich frei halten?** Shall I keep a seat for you?
■ **'Einfahrt frei halten'** 'Keep clear'
■ **Wir haben im Moment keine freien Stellen.** We haven't got any vacancies at the moment.
■ **ein freier Mitarbeiter** a freelancer
■ **im Freien** in the open air

★ das **Freibad** (PL die **Freibäder**) NEUT NOUN
open-air swimming pool

□ **Im Sommer gehe ich gern ins Freibad.** I like going to the open-air swimming pool in the summer.

freigebig ADJECTIVE
generous

★ **freihalten** VERB [33] ▷ see **frei**

die **Freiheit** FEM NOUN
1 freedom
2 liberty
□ **sich Freiheiten herausnehmen** to take liberties

freilassen (PRESENT TENSE **lässt frei**, IMPERFECT **ließ frei**, PERFECT TENSE **hat freigelassen**) VERB [42]
to free

die **Freiminuten** PL NOUN (mobile phone)
free minutes pl

★ der **Freitag** (PL die **Freitage**) MASC NOUN
Friday
□ **am Freitag** on Friday

★ **freitags** ADVERB
on Fridays

★ **freiwillig** ADJECTIVE
voluntary

★ die **Freizeit** FEM NOUN
spare time
□ **Was machst du in deiner Freizeit?** What do you do in your spare time?

★ die **Freizeitbeschäftigung** FEM NOUN
leisure activity

das **Freizeitzentrum** (PL die **Freizeitzentren**) NEUT NOUN
leisure centre

★ **fremd** ADJECTIVE
1 strange
□ **eine fremde Umgebung** strange surroundings
2 foreign
□ **fremde Länder und Sprachen** foreign countries and languages
■ **Ich bin in London fremd.** I'm a stranger to London.

der **Fremdenverkehr** MASC NOUN
tourism

★ das **Fremdenzimmer** (PL die **Fremdenzimmer**) NEUT NOUN
guest room

★ die **Fremdsprache** FEM NOUN
foreign language

das **Fremdwort** (PL die **Fremdwörter**) NEUT NOUN
foreign word

fressen (PRESENT TENSE **frisst**, IMPERFECT **fraß**, PERFECT TENSE **hat gefressen**) VERB
to eat
□ **Er frisst wie ein Schwein.** He eats like a pig.

★ die **Freude** FEM NOUN
1 joy
□ **Welche Freude!** What joy!

2 delight

□ Zu meiner Freude hatten wir gestern keine Schule. **To my delight we didn't have any school yesterday.**

■ **Er hat viel Freude an seinem Mountainbike.** He's delighted with his mountain bike.

■ **Das wird den Kindern Freude machen.** That'll please the children.

■ **Ich wollte dir eine Freude machen.** I wanted to make you happy.

★**freuen** VERB [38]

■ **sich freuen** to be glad □ Ich freue mich, dass du gekommen bist. **I'm glad you've come.**

■ **sich auf etwas freuen** to look forward to something □ Wir freuen uns darauf, euch zu sehen. **We're looking forward to seeing you.**

■ **sich über etwas freuen** to be pleased with something □ Sie hat sich sehr über das Geschenk gefreut. **She was very pleased with the present.**

■ **Dein Brief hat mich sehr gefreut.** Your letter made me very happy.

■ **Freut mich!** Pleased to meet you.

★der **Freund** (PL die **Freunde**) MASC NOUN

1 friend

□ Alle meine Freunde waren da. **All my friends were there.**

2 boyfriend

□ Hast du einen Freund? **Have you got a boyfriend?**

★die **Freundin** FEM NOUN

1 friend

□ Maja kommt mit ihrer Freundin. **Maja's coming with her friend.**

2 girlfriend

□ Tobias hat keine Freundin. **Tobias hasn't got a girlfriend.**

★**freundlich** ADJECTIVE

1 friendly

□ Die Leute waren sehr freundlich. **The people were very friendly.** □ ein freundliches Lächeln a friendly smile

2 kind

□ Das ist sehr freundlich von Ihnen. **That's very kind of you.**

freundlicherweise ADVERB

kindly

□ Er hat uns freundlicherweise geholfen. **He kindly helped us.**

die **Freundlichkeit** FEM NOUN

friendliness

die **Freundschaft** FEM NOUN

friendship

der **Frieden** (PL die **Frieden**) MASC NOUN

peace

■ **im Frieden** in peacetime

der **Friedhof** (PL die **Friedhöfe**) MASC NOUN

cemetery

friedlich ADJECTIVE

peaceful

★**frieren** (IMPERFECT **fror**, PERFECT TENSE **hat gefroren**) VERB

to freeze

□ Ich friere. **I'm freezing.**

■ **Es friert mich.** I'm freezing.

■ **Letzte Nacht hat es gefroren.** It was frosty last night.

★die **Frikadelle** FEM NOUN

rissole

★**frisch** ADJECTIVE

fresh

□ frische Milch fresh milk □ ein frischer Wind a fresh wind □ Nimm ein frisches Blatt. Take a fresh sheet of paper.

■ **Frisch gestrichen!** Wet paint!

■ **sich frisch machen** to freshen oneself up

★der **Friseur** (PL die **Friseure**) MASC NOUN

hairdresser

★die **Friseurin** FEM NOUN

hairdresser

★die **Friseuse** FEM NOUN

hairdresser

frisieren (PERFECT TENSE **hat frisiert**) VERB [76]

■ **jemanden frisieren** to do somebody's hair

■ **sich frisieren** to do one's hair □ Er frisierte sich vor dem Spiegel. **He did his hair in front of the mirror.**

frisst VERB ▷ see **fressen**

die **Frist** FEM NOUN

deadline

□ eine Frist einhalten to meet a deadline

die **Frisur** FEM NOUN

hairdo

Frl. ABBREVIATION (= *Fräulein*)

Miss

★**froh** ADJECTIVE

happy

□ frohe Gesichter happy faces

■ **Ich bin froh, dass ...** I'm glad that ...

★**fröhlich** ADJECTIVE

cheerful

die **Fröhlichkeit** FEM NOUN

cheerfulness

fromm ADJECTIVE

devout

fror VERB ▷ see **frieren**

der **Frosch** (PL die **Frösche**) MASC NOUN

frog

★der **Frost** (PL die **Fröste**) MASC NOUN

frost

□ ein strenger Frost a hard frost

frösteln VERB [88]

to shiver

★die **Frucht** (PL die **Früchte**) FEM NOUN

fruit

fruchtbar ADJECTIVE
1 fruitful
□ ein fruchtbares Gespräch a fruitful conversation
2 fertile
□ fruchtbarer Boden fertile soil

★ der **Fruchtsaft** (PL die **Fruchtsäfte**) MASC NOUN
fruit juice

★ **früh** ADJECTIVE, ADVERB
early
□ Komm lieber etwas früher. It's better if you come a bit earlier.
■ heute früh this morning

★ **früher** ADJECTIVE, ADVERB
1 former
□ eine frühere Schülerin unserer Schule a former pupil of our school
2 once
□ Hier stand früher ein Haus. A house once stood here.
■ Früher war das anders. That used to be different.

frühestens ADVERB
at the earliest

das **Frühjahr** (PL die **Frühjahre**) NEUT NOUN
spring
□ im Frühjahr in spring

★ der **Frühling** (PL die **Frühlinge**) MASC NOUN
spring
□ im Frühling in spring

★ das **Frühstück** NEUT NOUN
breakfast

★ **frühstücken** VERB [38]
to have breakfast

frustrieren (PERFECT TENSE **hat frustriert**) VERB [76]
to frustrate

der **Fuchs** (GEN des **Fuchses**, PL die **Füchse**) MASC NOUN
fox

fügen VERB [38]
to join
□ Er fügte ein Teil an ein anderes. He joined one piece to another.
■ sich fügen to be obedient

★ **fühlen** VERB [38]
to feel
□ Fühl mal, wie weich das ist. Feel how soft it is.
□ Ich fühle mich wohl. I feel fine.

fuhr VERB ▷ see fahren

★ **führen** VERB [38]
1 to lead
□ Sie führte uns nach draußen. She led us outside.
■ ein Geschäft führen to run a business
2 to be winning
□ Welche Mannschaft führt? Which team's winning?

★ der **Führer** (PL die **Führer**) MASC NOUN
1 leader
□ der Parteiführer the party leader
2 guide
□ Unser Führer zeigte uns alle Sehenswürdigkeiten. Our guide showed us all the sights.
3 guidebook
□ Hast du einen Führer von Rom? Have you got a guidebook of Rome?

★ der **Führerschein** (PL die **Führerscheine**) MASC NOUN
driving licence
■ den Führerschein machen to take one's driving test

★ die **Führung** FEM NOUN
1 lead
□ Unsere Mannschaft liegt in Führung. Our team is in the lead.
2 leadership
□ Er übernahm die Führung der Partei. He took over the leadership of the party.
3 management
□ Das Geschäft hat unter neuer Führung wiedereröffnet. The business has reopened under new management.
4 guided tour
□ Führungen durchs Museum finden stündlich statt. There are guided tours of the museum every hour.

★ **füllen** VERB [38]
1 to fill
□ Sie füllte das Glas bis zum Rand. She filled the glass to the brim.
2 to stuff
□ Heute gibt es gefüllte Paprika. We're having stuffed peppers today.

★ der **Füller** (PL die **Füller**) MASC NOUN
fountain pen

die **Füllung** FEM NOUN
filling

das **Fundament** (PL die **Fundamente**) NEUT NOUN
foundations pl

★ das **Fundbüro** (PL die **Fundbüros**) NEUT NOUN
lost property office

fundiert ADJECTIVE
sound
□ fundierte Englischkenntnisse a sound knowledge of English

★ **fünf** NUMBER
▷ see also die **Fünf** NOUN
five

die **Fünf** FEM NOUN
▷ see also **fünf** NUMBER
1 five
2 poor

★ = core vocabulary

fünfte ADJECTIVE
fifth
□ Ich erkläre dir das jetzt zum fünften Mal. This is the fifth time I've explained this to you. □ Er kam als Fünfter. He was the fifth to arrive.

★ **fünfzehn** NUMBER
fifteen

★ **fünfzig** NUMBER
fifty

der **Funke** (GEN des **Funkens**, PL die **Funken**) MASC NOUN
spark

funkeln VERB [88]
to sparkle

das **Funkgerät** (PL die **Funkgeräte**) NEUT NOUN
radio set

das **Funkloch** (PL die **Funklöcher**) NEUT NOUN
dead spot (*mobile phone*)

die **Funktion** FEM NOUN
function

★ **funktionieren** (PERFECT TENSE **hat funktioniert**) VERB [76]
to work

die **Funktionstaste** FEM NOUN
function key

★ **für** PREPOSITION

The preposition **für** takes the accusative.

for
□ Das ist für dich. This is for you.
■ **was für** what kind of □ Was für ein Fahrrad hast du? What kind of bike have you got?
■ **das Für und Wider** the pros and cons

★ die **Furcht** FEM NOUN
fear

★ **furchtbar** ADJECTIVE
terrible

fürchten VERB [2]
to be afraid
□ Ich fürchte mich vor diesem Mann. I'm afraid of that man.

fürchterlich ADJECTIVE
awful

füreinander ADVERB
for each other

fürs = **für das**

★ der **Fuß** (GEN des **Fußes**, PL die **Füße**) MASC NOUN
1 foot
□ Mir tun die Füße weh. My feet hurt.
2 leg
□ Der Tisch hat vier Füße. The table's got four legs.
■ **zu Fuß** on foot

★ der **Fußball** (PL die **Fußbälle**) MASC NOUN
football

der **Fußballplatz** (GEN des **Fußballplatzes**, PL die **Fußballplätze**) MASC NOUN
football pitch

das **Fußballspiel** (PL die **Fußballspiele**) NEUT NOUN
football match

der **Fußballspieler** (PL die **Fußballspieler**) MASC NOUN
footballer

die **Fußballspielerin** FEM NOUN
footballer

★ der **Fußboden** (PL die **Fußböden**) MASC NOUN
floor

★ der **Fußgänger** (PL die **Fußgänger**) MASC NOUN
pedestrian

★ die **Fußgängerin** FEM NOUN
pedestrian

★ die **Fußgängerzone** FEM NOUN
pedestrian precinct

der **Fußweg** (PL die **Fußwege**) MASC NOUN
footpath

das **Futter** (PL die **Futter**) NEUT NOUN
1 feed
□ Die Krankheit entstand durch verseuchtes Futter. The disease was the result of contaminated feed.
2 food
□ Hast du Futter für die Katze gekauft? Have you bought cat food?
3 lining
□ Der Mantel hat ein Futter aus Pelz. The coat has a fur lining.

★ **füttern** VERB [88]
1 to feed
□ Kannst du bitte das Baby füttern? Can you feed the baby, please?
2 to line
□ Der Mantel ist gefüttert. The coat's lined.

das **Futur** (PL die **Future**) NEUT NOUN
future

f

Gg

g ABBREVIATION (= *Gramm*)
g

gab VERB ▷ *see* geben

★ die **Gabel** FEM NOUN
fork

gähnen VERB [38]
to yawn

★ die **Galerie** FEM NOUN
gallery

der **Gamer** (PL die **Gamer**) MASC NOUN
gamer (*on computer*)

die **Gamerin** FEM NOUN
gamer (*on computer*)

gammeln VERB [88]
to bum around (*Umgangssprache*)

★ der **Gang** (PL die **Gänge**) MASC NOUN
1 corridor
□ Häng deinen Mantel im Gang auf. Hang your coat up in the corridor.
2 aisle
□ Ich hätte gern einen Platz am Gang. I'd like an aisle seat.
3 gear
□ Mein Fahrrad hat zehn Gänge. My bike has ten gears.
4 course
□ Das war erst der zweite Gang, und ich bin schon satt. That was only the second course and I'm full already. □ der Gang der Dinge the course of events
■ **etwas in Gang bringen** to get something off the ground □ Sie hat das Projekt in Gang gebracht. She got the project off the ground.

die **Gans** (PL die **Gänse**) FEM NOUN
goose

das **Gänseblümchen** (PL die **Gänseblümchen**) NEUT NOUN
daisy

die **Gänsehaut** FEM NOUN
goose pimples *pl*

★ **ganz** ADJECTIVE, ADVERB
1 whole
□ die ganze Welt the whole world □ ganz Europa the whole of Europe
■ **sein ganzes Geld** all his money
2 quite
□ ganz gut quite good
■ **ganz und gar nicht** not at all
■ **Es sieht ganz so aus.** It really looks like it.

★ **ganztags** ADVERB
full time
□ ganztags arbeiten to work full time

★ die **Ganztagsschule** FEM NOUN
all-day school

★ die **Ganztagsstelle** FEM NOUN
full-time job

gar ADJECTIVE, ADVERB
done
□ Die Kartoffeln sind gar. The potatoes are done.
■ **gar nicht** not at all □ Sie hat sich gar nicht gefreut. She was not at all pleased. □ gar nicht schlecht not bad at all
■ **gar nichts** nothing at all □ Ich habe gar nichts zu tun. I have nothing at all to do. □ Ich habe gar nichts verstanden. I didn't understand anything at all.
■ **gar niemand** nobody at all □ Es war gar niemand da. There was nobody there at all.

★ die **Garage** FEM NOUN
garage (*for parking*)

garantieren (PERFECT TENSE **hat garantiert**) VERB [76]
to guarantee
■ **Er kommt garantiert.** He's sure to come.

★ die **Garderobe** FEM NOUN
cloakroom
□ Ich habe meinen Mantel an der Garderobe abgegeben. I left my coat in the cloakroom.

★ die **Gardine** FEM NOUN
curtain
□ die Gardinen zuziehen to shut the curtains

★ der **Garten** (PL die **Gärten**) MASC NOUN
garden

★ das **Gas** (GEN des **Gases**, PL die **Gase**) NEUT NOUN
gas
□ Wir kochen mit Gas. We cook with gas.
■ **Gas geben** to accelerate

der **Gasherd** (PL die **Gasherde**) MASC NOUN
gas cooker

das **Gaspedal** (PL die **Gaspedale**) NEUT NOUN
accelerator

★ die **Gasse** FEM NOUN
lane
□ die schmalen Gassen der Altstadt the narrow lanes of the old town

★ = core vocabulary

★ der **Gast** (PL die **Gäste**) MASC NOUN
guest
□ Wir haben Gäste aus England. **We've got guests from England.**
■ **bei jemandem zu Gast sein** to be somebody's guest

★ das **Gästehaus** (GEN des **Gästehauses**, PL die **Gästehäuser**) NEUT NOUN
guest house

gastfreundlich ADJECTIVE
hospitable

★ die **Gastfreundschaft** FEM NOUN
hospitality

★ der **Gastgeber** (PL die **Gastgeber**) MASC NOUN
host

★ die **Gastgeberin** FEM NOUN
hostess

★ das **Gasthaus** (GEN des **Gasthauses**, PL die **Gasthäuser**) NEUT NOUN
inn

★ der **Gasthof** (PL die **Gasthöfe**) MASC NOUN
inn

★ die **Gaststätte** FEM NOUN
pub

> **DID YOU KNOW...?**
> In Germany there's practically no difference between pubs and restaurants. You can eat or drink in a **Gaststätte**, families are welcome and the opening hours are flexible.

★ das **Gebäck** (PL die **Gebäcke**) NEUT NOUN
pastry
□ Kuchen und Gebäck **cakes and pastries**

gebären (PRESENT TENSE **gebiert**, IMPERFECT **gebar**, PERFECT TENSE **hat geboren**) VERB
to give birth to

★ das **Gebäude** (PL die **Gebäude**) NEUT NOUN
building

★ **geben** (PRESENT TENSE **gibt**, IMPERFECT **gab**, PERFECT TENSE **hat gegeben**) VERB [28]
to give
□ Gib ihm bitte das Geld. **Please give him the money.** □ Kannst du dieses Buch bitte deiner Mutter geben. **Could you give this book to your mother, please.**
■ **Karten geben** to deal
■ **es gibt** there is □ Hier gibt es ein schönes Freibad. **There's a lovely open-air pool here.** □ In Stuttgart gibt es viele Parks. **There are many parks in Stuttgart.**
■ **Wenn wir zu spät kommen, gibt es Ärger.** There will be trouble if we arrive late.
■ **Was gibt's?** What's up?
■ **Was gibt es im Kino?** What's on at the cinema?
■ **sich geschlagen geben** to admit defeat
■ **Das wird sich schon geben.** That'll sort itself out.

das **Gebet** (PL die **Gebete**) NEUT NOUN
prayer

gebeten VERB ▷ *see* **bitten**

★ das **Gebiet** (PL die **Gebiete**) NEUT NOUN
1 area
□ ein bewaldetes Gebiet **a wooded area**
2 field
□ Er ist Experte auf diesem Gebiet. **He's an expert in this field.**

gebildet ADJECTIVE
cultured

★ das **Gebirge** (PL die **Gebirge**) NEUT NOUN
mountain chain
□ Die Alpen sind ein großes Gebirge. **The Alps are a large mountain chain.**
■ **ins Gebirge fahren** to go to the mountains

das **Gebiss** (GEN des **Gebisses**, PL die **Gebisse**) NEUT NOUN
1 teeth *pl*
□ Sie hat ein gesundes Gebiss. **She's got healthy teeth.**
2 dentures *pl*
□ Opas Gebiss lag auf dem Tisch. **Grandpa's dentures were lying on the table.**

gebissen VERB ▷ *see* **beißen**

geblieben VERB ▷ *see* **bleiben**

★ **geboren** VERB ▷ *see* **gebären**

★ **geboren** ADJECTIVE
1 born
□ Wann bist du geboren? **When were you born?**
2 née
□ Frau Dümmler, geborene Schnorr **Mrs Dümmler, née Schnorr**

geboten VERB ▷ *see* **bieten**

gebracht VERB ▷ *see* **bringen**

gebraten ADJECTIVE
fried

★ **gebrauchen** (PERFECT TENSE **hat gebraucht**) VERB [48]
to use
■ **Das kann ich gut gebrauchen.** I could really do with that.

★ die **Gebrauchsanweisung** FEM NOUN
directions for use *pl*
□ Wo ist die Gebrauchsanweisung? **Where are the directions for use?**

gebraucht ADJECTIVE
used

der **Gebrauchtwagen** (PL die **Gebrauchtwagen**) MASC NOUN
second-hand car

★ **gebrochen** VERB ▷ *see* **brechen**

★ die **Gebühr** FEM NOUN
fee

die **Gebühreneinheit** FEM NOUN
unit (*telephone*)

★ **gebührenpflichtig** ADJECTIVE
subject to a charge
■ **eine gebührenpflichtige Verwarnung** a fine

gebunden – gefasst

gebunden VERB ▷ *see* **binden**

★ **die Geburt** FEM NOUN
birth
□ bei der Geburt at the birth

gebürtig ADJECTIVE
native of
□ ein gebürtiger Schweizer a native of
Switzerland

★ **das Geburtsdatum** (PL die **Geburtsdaten**)
NEUT NOUN
date of birth

★ **der Geburtsort** (PL die **Geburtsorte**) MASC
NOUN
birthplace

★ **der Geburtstag** (PL die **Geburtstage**) MASC
NOUN
birthday
□ Herzlichen Glückwunsch zum Geburtstag!
Happy Birthday!

das Gebüsch (PL die **Gebüsche**) NEUT NOUN
bushes *pl*

gedacht VERB ▷ *see* **denken**

das Gedächtnis (GEN des **Gedächtnisses**, PL
die **Gedächtnisse**) NEUT NOUN
memory
□ Ich habe ein schlechtes Gedächtnis. I've got a
bad memory.

der Gedanke (GEN des **Gedankens**, PL die
Gedanken) MASC NOUN
thought
■ sich über etwas Gedanken machen to
think about something □ Ich habe mir
Gedanken über das gemacht, was du gesagt
hast. I've thought about what you said.

der Gedankenstrich (PL die
Gedankenstriche) MASC NOUN
dash

gedeihen (IMPERFECT **gedieh**, PERFECT TENSE **ist
gediehen**) VERB
to thrive

das Gedenken NEUT NOUN
■ zum Gedenken an jemanden in memory
of somebody

das Gedicht (PL die **Gedichte**) NEUT NOUN
poem

das Gedränge NEUT NOUN
crush
□ Vor der Kinokasse herrschte großes
Gedränge. There was a huge crush at the
cinema box office.

die Geduld FEM NOUN
patience

sich **gedulden** (PERFECT TENSE **hat sich
geduldet**) VERB [7]
to be patient

★ **geduldig** ADJECTIVE
patient

gedurft VERB ▷ *see* **dürfen**

★ **geehrt** ADJECTIVE
■ Sehr geehrter Herr Butterfeld Dear Mr
Butterfeld

geeignet ADJECTIVE
suitable

★ **die Gefahr** FEM NOUN
1 danger
□ in Gefahr schweben to be in danger
2 risk
□ Gefahr laufen, etwas zu tun to run the risk of
doing something □ auf eigene Gefahr at one's
own risk

gefährden (PERFECT TENSE **hat gefährdet**)
VERB [7]
to endanger

★ **gefährlich** ADJECTIVE
dangerous

das Gefälle (PL die **Gefälle**) NEUT NOUN
gradient

★ **gefallen (1)** VERB [22] ▷ *see* **fallen**

★ **gefallen (2)** (PRESENT TENSE **gefällt**, IMPERFECT
gefiel, PERFECT TENSE **hat gefallen**) VERB [22]
▷ *see also* der **Gefallen** NOUN
to like
□ Es gefällt mir. I like it. □ Das Geschenk hat ihr
gefallen. She liked the present. □ Er gefällt mir.
I like him. □ Das gefällt mir an ihm. That's one
thing I like about him.
■ sich etwas gefallen lassen to put up with
something □ Eine solche Frechheit lasse ich mir
nicht gefallen. I'm not putting up with cheek
like that.

der Gefallen (PL die **Gefallen**) MASC NOUN
▷ *see also* **gefallen** VERB
favour
□ Könntest du mir einen Gefallen tun? Could
you do me a favour?

gefangen VERB ▷ *see* **fangen**
■ jemanden gefangen nehmen to take
somebody prisoner

der/die Gefangene (GEN des/der
Gefangenen, PL die **Gefangenen**) MASC/FEM
NOUN
prisoner
□ Ein Gefangener ist geflohen. A prisoner has
escaped.

gefangennehmen VERB [52] ▷ *see*
gefangen

die Gefangenschaft FEM NOUN
captivity

das Gefängnis (GEN des **Gefängnisses**, PL
die **Gefängnisse**) NEUT NOUN
prison

die Gefängnisstrafe FEM NOUN
prison sentence

das Gefäß (GEN des **Gefäßes**, PL die **Gefäße**)
NEUT NOUN
container

gefasst ADJECTIVE
composed

□ Sie war sehr gefasst. **She was very composed.**
■ **auf etwas gefasst sein to be prepared for something** □ Ich war schon aufs Schlimmste gefasst. **I was prepared for the worst.**

geflogen VERB ▷ *see* **fliegen**

geflossen VERB ▷ *see* **fließen**

★ das **Geflügel** NEUT NOUN
poultry

gefragt ADJECTIVE
in demand
□ Er ist ein sehr gefragter Künstler. **He's an artist very much in demand.** □ Handwerker sind sehr gefragt. **Tradesmen are in great demand.**

gefräßig ADJECTIVE
greedy

das **Gefrierfach** (PL die **Gefrierfächer**) NEUT NOUN
icebox

die **Gefriertruhe** FEM NOUN
deep-freeze

gefroren ADJECTIVE
frozen

★ das **Gefühl** (PL die **Gefühle**) NEUT NOUN
feeling
□ Sie hat ein Gefühl für Kunst. **She's got a feeling for art.**
■ **etwas im Gefühl haben to have a feel for something**

gefüllt ADJECTIVE
stuffed
□ gefüllte Auberginen **stuffed aubergines**

★ **gefunden** VERB ▷ *see* **finden**

gegangen VERB ▷ *see* **gehen**

gegeben VERB ▷ *see* **geben**

★ **gegen** PREPOSITION

The preposition **gegen** takes the accusative.

1 against
□ Ich bin gegen diese Idee. **I'm against this idea.** □ nichts gegen jemanden haben **to have nothing against somebody**
■ **ein Mittel gegen Schnupfen something for colds**
■ **Williams gegen Wozniacki Williams versus Wozniacki**

2 towards
□ gegen Osten **towards the east** □ gegen Abend **towards evening**
■ **gegen einen Baum fahren to drive into a tree**

3 round about
□ gegen drei Uhr **round about three o'clock**

★ die **Gegend** FEM NOUN
area
□ die Gegend um Ulm **the area around Ulm**

das **Gegenmittel** (PL die **Gegenmittel**) NEUT NOUN
antidote

der **Gegensatz** (GEN des **Gegensatzes**, PL die **Gegensätze**) MASC NOUN
contrast
■ **Im Gegensatz zu mir ist er gut in Mathe. Unlike me, he's good at maths.**

gegenseitig ADJECTIVE
mutual
□ gegenseitiges Vertrauen **mutual trust**
■ **sich gegenseitig helfen to help each other**

★ der **Gegenstand** (PL die **Gegenstände**) MASC NOUN
object

★ das **Gegenteil** NEUT NOUN
opposite
□ Das ist das Gegenteil von schön. **That's the opposite of lovely.**
■ **im Gegenteil on the contrary**

★ **gegenüber** PREPOSITION, ADVERB

The preposition **gegenüber** takes the dative.

1 opposite
□ Die Apotheke ist gegenüber. **The chemist's is opposite.** □ Er saß mir gegenüber. **He sat opposite me.**

2 towards
□ Sie waren mir gegenüber sehr freundlich. **They were very friendly towards me.**

der **Gegenverkehr** MASC NOUN
oncoming traffic

die **Gegenwart** FEM NOUN
present
□ in der Gegenwart leben **to live in the present**

gegessen VERB ▷ *see* **essen**

der **Gegner** (PL die **Gegner**) MASC NOUN
opponent

gegrillt ADJECTIVE
grilled

das **Gehackte** (GEN des **Gehackten**) NEUT NOUN
mince
□ Ein Kilo Gehacktes, bitte. **A kilo of mince, please.**

★ das **Gehalt** (PL die **Gehälter**) NEUT NOUN
salary
□ Er verdient ein gutes Gehalt. **He earns a good salary.**

gehässig ADJECTIVE
spiteful

geheim ADJECTIVE
secret
□ geheim halten **to keep secret**

das **Geheimnis** (GEN des **Geheimnisses**, PL die **Geheimnisse**) NEUT NOUN
1 secret
□ Kannst du ein Geheimnis behalten? **Can you keep a secret?**
2 mystery
□ die Geheimnisse der Erde **the Earth's mysteries**

g

geheimnisvoll ADJECTIVE
mysterious

die **Geheimnummer** FEM NOUN
ex-directory number
■ **Wir haben eine Geheimnummer.** We're ex-directory.

★ **gehen** VERB [29]

IMPERFECT	
ich ging	wir gingen
du gingst	ihr gingt
er/sie/es ging	sie/Sie gingen
PERFECT TENSE	
ist gegangen	

1 to go
□ Wir gehen jetzt. We're going now.
□ schwimmen gehen to go swimming

2 to walk
□ Sollen wir gehen oder den Bus nehmen? Shall we walk or go by bus?
■ **Wie geht es dir?** How are you?
■ **Wie geht's?** How are things?
■ **Mir geht's gut.** I'm fine.
■ **Ihm geht's gut.** He's fine.
■ **Es geht.** Not bad.
■ **Geht das?** Is that possible?
■ **Geht's noch?** Can you manage?
■ **Das geht nicht.** That's not on.
■ **um etwas gehen** to be about something
□ In dem Film geht es um einen Bankraub. The film's about a bank robbery.
■ **Hier geht es um sehr viel Geld.** There's a lot of money at stake here.

der **Gehilfe** (GEN des **Gehilfen**, PL die **Gehilfen**) MASC NOUN
assistant

die **Gehilfin** FEM NOUN
assistant

das **Gehirn** (PL die **Gehirne**) NEUT NOUN
brain

die **Gehirnerschütterung** FEM NOUN
concussion

gehoben VERB ▷ see heben

geholfen VERB ▷ see helfen

gehorchen (PERFECT TENSE hat gehorcht) VERB [48]
to obey
□ Du solltest deinem Vater gehorchen. You should obey your father. □ Ein Hund sollte lernen zu gehorchen. A dog should learn to obey.

★ **gehören** (PERFECT TENSE hat gehört) VERB [38]
■ **jemandem gehören** to belong to somebody
□ Dieses Buch gehört mir. This book belongs to me.
■ **Das gehört sich einfach nicht.** That just isn't done.

gehörlos ADJECTIVE
profoundly deaf

gehorsam ADJECTIVE
▷ see also der **Gehorsam** NOUN
obedient

der **Gehorsam** MASC NOUN
▷ see also **gehorsam** ADJECTIVE
obedience

der **Gehweg** (PL die **Gehwege**) MASC NOUN
pavement

der **Geier** (PL die **Geier**) MASC NOUN
vulture

★ die **Geige** FEM NOUN
violin
□ Kaila spielt Geige. Kaila plays the violin.

geil ADJECTIVE
cool (Umgangssprache)
□ Das war eine geile Party. That was a cool party. □ ein geiler Song a cool song

die **Geisel** FEM NOUN
hostage

der **Geist** (PL die **Geister**) MASC NOUN
1 ghost
2 mind
□ Er hat einen regen Geist. He has a lively mind
■ **Seine Rede sprühte vor Geist.** His speech was very witty.

geisteskrank ADJECTIVE
mentally ill

die **Geisteskrankheit** FEM NOUN
mental illness

geistig ADJECTIVE
intellectual
□ ihre geistigen Fähigkeiten her intellectual capabilities
■ **geistige Getränke** alcoholic drinks
■ **geistig behindert** mentally handicapped

der **Geiz** (GEN des **Geizes**) MASC NOUN
meanness

der **Geizhals** (GEN des **Geizhalses**, PL die **Geizhälse**) MASC NOUN
miser

★ **geizig** ADJECTIVE
mean

gekannt VERB ▷ see kennen

gekonnt VERB ▷ see können

gekonnt ADJECTIVE
skilful

das **Gel** (PL die **Gele**) NEUT NOUN
gel

das **Gelächter** NEUT NOUN
laughter

geladen VERB ▷ see laden

geladen ADJECTIVE
1 loaded
□ eine geladene Waffe a loaded weapon
2 invited
□ geladene Gäste invited guests
■ **geladen sein** to be furious □ Meine Mutter war geladen. My mother was furious.

★ = core vocabulary

gelähmt ADJECTIVE
paralysed

das Gelände (PL die **Gelände**) NEUT NOUN
1 grounds *pl*
□ auf dem Gelände der Schule on the school grounds
2 terrain
□ unwegsames Gelände difficult terrain
■ **durchs Gelände fahren** to go cross-country
■ **ein Baugelände** a building site

★ **gelangweilt** ADJECTIVE
bored

gelassen VERB ▷ *see* **lassen**

gelassen ADJECTIVE
calm
□ Sie blieb gelassen. She remained calm.

geläufig ADJECTIVE
common
□ ein geläufiger Begriff a common term
■ **Das ist mir nicht geläufig.** I'm not familiar with that.

★ **gelaunt** ADJECTIVE
■ **gut gelaunt** in a good mood
■ **schlecht gelaunt** in a bad mood
■ **Wie ist er gelaunt?** What sort of mood's he in?

★ **gelb** ADJECTIVE
1 yellow
2 amber
□ Die Ampel war gelb. The traffic lights were at amber.

★ **das Geld** (PL die **Gelder**) NEUT NOUN
money
■ **Geld verdienen** to earn money
■ **etwas zu Geld machen** to sell something off

der Geldautomat (GEN des **Geldautomaten**, PL die **Geldautomaten**) MASC NOUN
cash machine

★ **der Geldbeutel** (PL die **Geldbeutel**) MASC NOUN
purse

der Geldschein (PL die **Geldscheine**) MASC NOUN
banknote

★ **die Geldstrafe** FEM NOUN
fine

das Geldstück (PL die **Geldstücke**) NEUT NOUN
coin

★ **die Geldtasche** FEM NOUN
wallet

★ **der Geldwechsel** MASC NOUN
changing of money
□ Beim Geldwechsel muss man eine Gebühr bezahlen. There is a charge for changing money.
■ **'Geldwechsel'** 'bureau de change'

gelegen VERB ▷ *see* **liegen**

★ **die Gelegenheit** FEM NOUN
1 opportunity
□ Sobald ich eine Gelegenheit bekomme ... As soon as I get an opportunity ... □ bei jeder Gelegenheit at every opportunity
2 occasion
□ Bei dieser Gelegenheit trug sie das blaue Kostüm. On this occasion she wore her blue suit.

gelegentlich ADVERB
1 occasionally
□ Gelegentlich gehe ich ganz gern ins Kino. I occasionally like going to the cinema.
2 some time or other
□ Ich werde mich gelegentlich darum kümmern. I'll do it some time or other.

das Gelenk (PL die **Gelenke**) NEUT NOUN
joint (*in body*)

gelenkig ADJECTIVE
supple

gelernt ADJECTIVE
skilled

geliehen VERB ▷ *see* **leihen**

★ **gelingen** (IMPERFECT **gelang**, PERFECT TENSE **ist gelungen**) VERB
to succeed
□ Sein Plan ist ihm nicht gelungen. His plan didn't succeed.
■ **Es ist mir gelungen, ihn zu überzeugen.** I succeeded in convincing him.
■ **Der Kuchen ist gelungen.** The cake turned out well.

gelten (PRESENT TENSE **gilt**, IMPERFECT **galt**, PERFECT TENSE **hat gegolten**) VERB
to be valid
□ Dein Ausweis gilt nicht mehr. Your passport is no longer valid.
■ **es gilt, etwas zu tun** it's necessary to do something □ Es gilt, sich zu entscheiden. It's necessary to make a decision.
■ **jemandem gelten** to be aimed at somebody □ Diese Bemerkung hat dir gegolten. This comment was aimed at you.
■ **etwas gelten lassen** to accept something
■ **Was gilt die Wette?** What do you bet?

gelungen VERB ▷ *see* **gelingen**

gelungen ADJECTIVE
successful

das Gemälde (PL die **Gemälde**) NEUT NOUN
painting
□ ein Gemälde von Rembrandt a painting by Rembrandt

★ **gemein** ADJECTIVE
mean
□ Das war gemein! That was mean!
■ **etwas gemein haben mit** to have something in common with □ Mit solchen

g

Leuten habe ich nichts gemein. I don't have anything in common with people like that.

gemeinsam ADJECTIVE, ADVERB

1 joint
□ gemeinsame Anstrengungen joint efforts

2 together
□ Wir sind gemeinsam zum Lehrer gegangen. We went together to the teacher. □ ein gemeinsames Abendessen dinner together
■ **etwas gemeinsam haben** to have something in common □ Wir haben viel gemeinsam. We've a lot in common.

★ **gemischt** ADJECTIVE
mixed

gemocht VERB ▷ see **mögen**

★ das **Gemüse** (PL die **Gemüse**) NEUT NOUN
vegetables pl
□ Gemüse ist gesund. Vegetables are healthy.

gemusst VERB ▷ see **müssen**

★ **gemütlich** ADJECTIVE

1 cosy
□ eine gemütliche Wohnung a cosy flat
■ **ein gemütlicher Abend** a pleasant evening

2 good-natured
□ Sie ist ein gemütlicher Mensch. She's good-natured.

das **Gen** (PL die **Gene**) NEUT NOUN
gene

genannt VERB ▷ see **nennen**

★ **genau** ADJECTIVE, ADVERB

1 exact
□ Ich brauche genaue Zahlen. I need exact figures.

2 accurate
□ Diese Übersetzung ist nicht sehr genau. This translation isn't very accurate.

3 exactly
□ Genau das habe ich auch gesagt. That's exactly what I said. □ Sie hatte genau dasselbe Kleid an. She was wearing exactly the same dress. □ Das ist genau anders herum. That's exactly the opposite.
■ **etwas genau nehmen** to take something seriously
■ **genau genommen** strictly speaking

die **Genauigkeit** FEM NOUN
accuracy

★ **genauso** ADVERB
■ **genauso gut** just as good

genehmigen (PERFECT TENSE **hat genehmigt**) VERB [7]
to approve
■ **sich etwas genehmigen** to treat oneself to something □ Ich werde mir jetzt ein Eis genehmigen. I'm going to treat myself to an ice cream.

die **Genehmigung** FEM NOUN

1 permission
□ Für den Umbau brauchen wir eine Genehmigung. We need permission for the conversion.

2 permit
□ Hier ist meine Genehmigung. Here's my permit.

die **Generation** FEM NOUN
generation

★ **Genf** NEUT NOUN
Geneva
■ **der Genfer See** Lake Geneva

genial ADJECTIVE
brilliant

das **Genick** (PL die **Genicke**) NEUT NOUN
back of the neck
■ **sich das Genick brechen** to break one's neck

das **Genie** (PL die **Genies**) NEUT NOUN
genius

genießbar ADJECTIVE

1 edible
□ Das Essen war nicht genießbar. The meal wasn't edible.

2 drinkable
□ Probier mal, ob der Tee genießbar ist. Try the tea and see if it's drinkable.

genießen (IMPERFECT **genoss**, PERFECT TENSE **hat genossen**) VERB
to enjoy
□ Wir haben die Ferien genossen. We enjoyed our holidays.

genmanipuliert ADJECTIVE
genetically modified
□ genmanipulierte Lebensmittel genetically modified food

genommen VERB ▷ see **nehmen**

die **Gentechnologie** FEM NOUN
genetic engineering

★ **genug** ADJECTIVE
enough
□ Wir haben genug Geld. We've got enough money. □ gut genug good enough

★ **genügen** (PERFECT TENSE **hat genügt**) VERB [38]
to be enough
□ Das genügt noch nicht. That isn't enough.
■ **jemandem genügen** to be enough for somebody □ Genügt dir das eine Stück? Is one piece enough for you?

genügend ADJECTIVE
sufficient

der **Genuss** (GEN des **Genusses**, PL die **Genüsse**) MASC NOUN

1 pleasure
□ Es war ein Genuss! That was sheer pleasure!

2 consumption
□ der Genuss von Alkohol the consumption of alcohol
■ **in den Genuss von etwas kommen** to receive the benefit of something

★ = core vocabulary

genüsslich ADVERB
with relish

★ **geöffnet** ADJECTIVE
open

die **Geografie** FEM NOUN
geography

die **Geometrie** FEM NOUN
geometry

★ das **Gepäck** NEUT NOUN
luggage

★ die **Gepäckannahme** FEM NOUN
luggage office

★ die **Gepäckausgabe** FEM NOUN
baggage reclaim

gepflegt ADJECTIVE
1 well-groomed
□ gepflegte Hände well-groomed hands
2 well-kept
□ ein gepflegter Park a well-kept park

★ **gerade** ADJECTIVE, ADVERB
1 straight
□ eine gerade Strecke a straight stretch
2 upright
□ eine gerade Haltung an upright posture
■ **eine gerade Zahl** an even number
3 just
□ Du kommst gerade richtig. You've come just at the right time. □ Das ist es ja gerade! That's just it! □ Er wollte gerade aufstehen. He was just about to get up.
■ **gerade erst** only just □ Ich bin gerade erst gekommen. I've only just arrived.
■ **gerade noch** only just □ Das geht gerade noch. That's only just OK.
■ **gerade deshalb** that's exactly why
■ **gerade du** you of all people □ Warum gerade ich? Why me of all people?
■ **nicht gerade** not exactly □ Das war nicht gerade nett. That wasn't exactly nice.

★ **geradeaus** ADVERB
straight ahead

gerannt VERB ▷ see rennen

★ das **Gerät** (PL die **Geräte**) NEUT NOUN
1 gadget
□ ein Gerät zum Papierschneiden a gadget for cutting paper
2 appliance
□ ein Haushaltsgerät a household appliance
3 tool
□ ein Gartengerät a garden tool
4 apparatus no pl
□ Wir haben heute an den Geräten geturnt. We did gymnastics on the apparatus today.
5 equipment no pl
□ Geräte zum Angeln fishing equipment

geraten (PRESENT TENSE **gerät**, IMPERFECT **geriet**, PERFECT TENSE **ist geraten**) VERB
1 to thrive
□ Hier geraten die Pflanzen. Plants thrive here.

2 to turn out
□ Ihre Kinder sind alle gut geraten. All their children have turned out well. □ Der Kuchen ist mir nicht geraten. The cake hasn't turned out well.
■ **in etwas geraten** to get into something □ Wir sind in den Stau geraten. We got into a traffic jam.
■ **in Angst geraten** to get frightened
■ **nach jemandem geraten** to take after somebody

geräuchert ADJECTIVE
smoked

★ das **Geräusch** (PL die **Geräusche**) NEUT NOUN
sound

★ **gerecht** ADJECTIVE
fair
□ Das ist nicht gerecht! That's not fair!

die **Gerechtigkeit** FEM NOUN
justice

das **Gerede** NEUT NOUN
gossip
□ Das ist alles nur Gerede. That's all just gossip.

gereizt ADJECTIVE
irritable

★ das **Gericht** (PL die **Gerichte**) NEUT NOUN
1 court
□ Wir sehen uns vor Gericht. I'll see you in court.
2 dish
□ ein leckeres Gericht a tasty dish
■ **das Jüngste Gericht** the Last Judgement

gerieben VERB ▷ see reiben

gering ADJECTIVE
1 small
□ eine geringe Menge a small amount
2 low
□ geringe Beteiligung low participation
■ **eine geringe Zeit** a short time

geringschätzig ADJECTIVE
disparaging

geringste ADJECTIVE
least
□ Das ist meine geringste Sorge. That's the least of my worries.

geritten VERB ▷ see reiten

★ **gern** ADVERB
gladly
□ Das habe ich gern getan. I did it gladly.
■ **gern mögen** to like □ Ich mag diese Art von Musik gern. I like this kind of music.
■ **etwas gern tun** to like doing something □ Ich schwimme gern. I like swimming.
■ **Ich hätte gern ...** I'd like ... □ Ich hätte gern ein Zitroneneis. I'd like a lemon ice cream.
■ **Ja, gern!** Yes, please.
■ **Gern geschehen!** It's a pleasure.

gernhaben (PRESENT TENSE **hat gern**, IMPERFECT **hatte gern**, PERFECT TENSE **hat gerngehabt**) VERB [32]

gerochen – geschnitten

to like
□ Ich habe sie sehr gern. I like her a lot.

gerochen VERB ▷ *see* riechen

★ der **Geruch** (PL die Gerüche) MASC NOUN
smell

das **Gerücht** (PL die Gerüchte) NEUT NOUN
rumour

das **Gerümpel** NEUT NOUN
junk

★ **gesalzen** VERB ▷ *see* salzen

★ **gesalzen** ADJECTIVE
■ gesalzene Preise (*Umgangssprache*) hefty
prices

gesamt ADJECTIVE
whole
□ die gesamte Klasse the whole class
■ die gesamten Kosten the total cost
■ gesamte Werke complete works
■ im Gesamten all in all

★ die **Gesamtschule** FEM NOUN
comprehensive school

DID YOU KNOW…?
Gesamtschulen are the exception rather
than the rule in Germany.

gesandt VERB ▷ *see* senden

★ das **Geschäft** (PL die Geschäfte) NEUT NOUN
1 shop
□ In welchem Geschäft hast du das gekauft?
Which shop did you buy that in?
2 business *no pl*
□ Die Geschäfte gehen gut. Business is good.
3 deal
□ Ich schlage dir ein Geschäft vor. I'll make a
deal with you. □ Das war ein gutes Geschäft.
That was a good deal.

★ die **Geschäftsfrau** FEM NOUN
businesswoman

★ der **Geschäftsmann** (PL die
Geschäftsmänner) MASC NOUN
businessman

die **Geschäftszeiten** FEM PL NOUN
business hours *pl*

★ **geschehen** (PRESENT TENSE geschieht,
IMPERFECT geschah, PERFECT TENSE ist
geschehen) VERB
to happen
□ Was ist geschehen? What's happened? □ Was
ist mit ihm geschehen? What's happened to
him?

gescheit ADJECTIVE
clever

★ das **Geschenk** (PL die Geschenke) NEUT
NOUN
present

★ die **Geschichte** FEM NOUN
1 story
□ eine lustige Geschichte a funny story

2 history
□ die deutsche Geschichte German history
3 business
□ die Geschichte mit dem verschwundenen
Pass the business of the missing passport

geschichtlich ADJECTIVE
historical

geschickt ADJECTIVE
skilful

★ **geschieden** VERB ▷ *see* scheiden

★ **geschieden** ADJECTIVE
divorced

geschienen VERB ▷ *see* scheinen

★ das **Geschirr** NEUT NOUN
crockery
□ In welchem Schrank steht das Geschirr? What
cupboard is the crockery kept in?
■ das Geschirr spülen to do the dishes

★ die **Geschirrspülmaschine** FEM NOUN
dishwasher

das **Geschirrtuch** (PL die Geschirrtücher)
NEUT NOUN
dish cloth

★ das **Geschlecht** (PL die Geschlechter) NEUT
NOUN
1 sex
□ ein Kind weiblichen Geschlechts a child of the
female sex
2 gender
□ Welches Geschlecht hat dieses Substantiv?
What gender is this noun?

die **Geschlechtskrankheit** FEM NOUN
sexually transmitted disease

der **Geschlechtsverkehr** MASC NOUN
sexual intercourse

★ **geschlossen** VERB ▷ *see* schließen

★ **geschlossen** ADJECTIVE
shut
■ 'Geschlossen' 'Closed'

★ der **Geschmack** (PL die Geschmäcke) MASC
NOUN
taste
□ Das ist nicht nach meinem Geschmack. This
is not to my taste.
■ Geschmack an etwas finden to come to
like something □ Sie hat inzwischen
Geschmack an Handball gefunden. In the
meantime she's come to like handball.

geschmacklos ADJECTIVE
1 tasteless
□ Die Suppe war ziemlich geschmacklos. The
soup was pretty tasteless.
2 in bad taste
□ Das war ein geschmackloser Witz. That joke
was in bad taste.

geschmackvoll ADJECTIVE
tasteful

geschnitten VERB ▷ *see* schneiden

★ = core vocabulary

geschossen VERB ▷ *see* **schießen**

geschrieben VERB ▷ *see* **schreiben**

geschrien VERB ▷ *see* **schreien**

geschützt ADJECTIVE
protected

das **Geschwätz** NEUT NOUN
chatter

★ **geschwätzig** ADJECTIVE
talkative

★ die **Geschwindigkeit** FEM NOUN
speed

die **Geschwindigkeitsbeschränkung**
FEM NOUN
speed limit

★ die **Geschwindigkeitskontrolle** FEM
NOUN
speed check

★ die **Geschwister** PL NOUN
brothers and sisters *pl*

geschwommen VERB ▷ *see* **schwimmen**

das **Geschwür** (PL die **Geschwüre**) NEUT
NOUN
ulcer

gesellig ADJECTIVE
sociable

die **Gesellschaft** FEM NOUN
1 society
□ die Gesellschaft verändern to change society
2 company
□ jemandem Gesellschaft leisten to keep
somebody company

gesessen VERB ▷ *see* **sitzen**

das **Gesetz** (GEN des **Gesetzes**, PL die
Gesetze) NEUT NOUN
law

gesetzlich ADJECTIVE
legal
▪ gesetzlicher Feiertag public holiday

★ das **Gesicht** (PL die **Gesichter**) NEUT NOUN
face

der **Gesichtsausdruck** MASC NOUN
expression

★ **gespannt** ADJECTIVE
1 strained
□ Die Lage im Nahen Osten bleibt gespannt.
The situation in the Middle East remains
strained.
2 eager
□ gespannte Zuhörer eager listeners
▪ Ich bin gespannt, ob ... I wonder
whether ...
▪ auf etwas gespannt sein to look forward
to something □ Ich bin auf das Fest gespannt.
I'm looking forward to the party.

das **Gespenst** (PL die **Gespenster**) NEUT
NOUN
ghost

★ **gesperrt** ADJECTIVE
closed off

★ das **Gespräch** (PL die **Gespräche**) NEUT NOUN
1 conversation
□ ein langes Gespräch a long conversation
2 call
□ Frau Morris, ein Gespräch für Sie. Mrs Morris,
there's a call for you.

gesprächig ADJECTIVE
talkative

gesprochen VERB ▷ *see* **sprechen**

gesprungen VERB ▷ *see* **springen**

die **Gestalt** FEM NOUN
1 shape
□ die Gestalt der Skulptur the shape of the
sculpture
▪ Gestalt annehmen to take shape □ Mein
Referat nimmt langsam Gestalt an. My
assignment is slowly taking shape.
2 figure
□ Ich konnte eine dunkle Gestalt im Garten
erkennen. I could see a dark figure in the
garden.
▪ in Gestalt von in the form of

gestalten (PERFECT TENSE **hat gestaltet**) VERB
[2]
to lay out
□ Wer hat euren Garten gestaltet? Who laid out
your garden?
▪ Wie gestaltest du deine Freizeit? How do
you spend your spare time?

gestanden VERB ▷ *see* **stehen**

das **Geständnis** (GEN des **Geständnisses**, PL
die **Geständnisse**) NEUT NOUN
confession

der **Gestank** MASC NOUN
stench

★ **gestatten** (PERFECT TENSE **hat/ist gestattet**)
VERB [2]
to allow
▪ Gestatten Sie? May I?

★ **gestattet** ADJECTIVE
permitted
□ Das ist nicht gestattet. That is not permitted.

die **Geste** FEM NOUN
gesture

gestehen (IMPERFECT **gestand**, PERFECT TENSE
hat gestanden) VERB [72]
to confess

das **Gestein** (PL die **Gesteine**) NEUT NOUN
rock
□ vulkanisches Gestein volcanic rock

das **Gestell** (PL die **Gestelle**) NEUT NOUN
1 frame
□ ein Brillengestell spectacle frames
2 rack
□ ein Gestell für Weinflaschen a wine rack

★ **gestern** ADVERB
yesterday

g

German - English

gestohlen – gewiss

- **gestern Abend** yesterday evening
- **gestern Morgen** yesterday morning

gestohlen VERB ▷ *see* **stehlen**

★ **gestorben** VERB ▷ *see* **sterben**

gestört ADJECTIVE
disturbed

★ **gestreift** ADJECTIVE
striped

★ **gesund** ADJECTIVE
healthy
- **wieder gesund werden** to get better

★ die **Gesundheit** FEM NOUN
health
- **Gesundheit!** Bless you!

gesungen VERB ▷ *see* **singen**

getan VERB ▷ *see* **tun**

★ das **Getränk** (PL die **Getränke**) NEUT NOUN
drink

★ die **Getränkekarte** FEM NOUN
wine list

sich **getrauen** (PERFECT TENSE **hat sich getraut**) VERB [7]
to dare
□ Sie hat sich nicht getraut hineinzugehen. She didn't dare go in.

das **Getreide** (PL die **Getreide**) NEUT NOUN
cereals *pl*

★ **getrennt** ADJECTIVE
separate

das **Getriebe** (PL die **Getriebe**) NEUT NOUN
gearbox

getrieben VERB ▷ *see* **treiben**

getroffen VERB ▷ *see* **treffen**

getrunken VERB ▷ *see* **trinken**

geübt ADJECTIVE
experienced

gewachsen VERB ▷ *see* **wachsen**

gewachsen ADJECTIVE
- **jemandem gewachsen sein** to be a match for somebody □ Sie war ihrem Gegner gewachsen. She was a match for her opponent.
- **Er ist den Kindern nicht gewachsen.** He can't cope with the children.
- **einer Sache gewachsen sein** to be up to something □ Meinst du, du bist dieser Aufgabe gewachsen? Do you think you're up to this job?

gewagt ADJECTIVE
risky

★ die **Gewalt** FEM NOUN
1 force
□ die Gewalt des Aufpralls the force of the impact
2 power
□ die staatliche Gewalt the power of the state
3 violence
□ Gewalt gegen Kinder violence against children
- **mit aller Gewalt** with all one's might

★ **gewaltig** ADJECTIVE
tremendous
□ eine gewaltige Menge a tremendous amount
- **Sie hat sich gewaltig angestrengt.** She tried tremendously hard.
- **ein gewaltiger Irrtum** a huge mistake

★ **gewalttätig** ADJECTIVE
violent

gewann VERB ▷ *see* **gewinnen**

das **Gewässer** (PL die **Gewässer**) NEUT NOUN
waters *pl*

das **Gewebe** (PL die **Gewebe**) NEUT NOUN
1 fabric
□ ein feines Gewebe a fine fabric
2 tissue
□ Die Gewebeprobe hat ergeben, dass alles in Ordnung ist. The tissue samples showed that there's nothing wrong.

das **Gewehr** (PL die **Gewehre**) NEUT NOUN
gun

die **Gewerkschaft** FEM NOUN
trade union

> **DID YOU KNOW...?**
> Unions in Germany are mainly organized within the **Deutscher Gewerkschaftsbund (DGB)**.

der **Gewerkschaftsbund** MASC NOUN
trade union confederation

gewesen VERB ▷ *see* **sein**

das **Gewicht** (PL die **Gewichte**) NEUT NOUN
weight
□ das Gewicht meines Koffers the weight of my case

der **Gewinn** (PL die **Gewinne**) MASC NOUN
profit
□ Wir haben dieses Jahr einen Gewinn gemacht. We've made a profit this year.
□ etwas mit Gewinn verkaufen to sell something at a profit

★ **gewinnen** (IMPERFECT **gewann**, PERFECT TENSE **hat gewonnen**) VERB [30]
to win
□ Sie hat den ersten Preis gewonnen. She won first prize.
- **im Lotto gewinnen** to have a win on the lottery
- **an etwas gewinnen** to gain in something
□ Die Stadt hat an Beliebtheit gewonnen. The town has gained in popularity.

der **Gewinner** (PL die **Gewinner**) MASC NOUN
winner

die **Gewinnerin** (PL die **Gewinnerin**) FEM NOUN
winner

gewiss ADJECTIVE, ADVERB
certain
□ Zwischen den beiden besteht eine gewisse Ähnlichkeit. There's a certain similarity between them.

■ **Das weiß ich ganz gewiss.** I'm certain about that.

■ **Das hat sie gewiss vergessen.** She must have forgotten.

das **Gewissen** (PL die Gewissen) NEUT NOUN
conscience

gewissenhaft ADJECTIVE
conscientious

gewissermaßen ADVERB
more or less

die **Gewissheit** FEM NOUN
certainty

★ das **Gewitter** (PL die Gewitter) NEUT NOUN
thunderstorm

gewöhnen (PERFECT TENSE hat gewöhnt)
VERB [75]

■ **sich an etwas gewöhnen** to get used to something □ Ich muss mich erst an die neue Rechtschreibung gewöhnen. **I have to get used to the new spelling rules.**

■ **jemanden an etwas gewöhnen** to teach somebody something □ Der Klassenlehrer hat versucht, seine Klasse an Disziplin zu gewöhnen. **The form teacher tried to teach his class discipline.**

die **Gewohnheit** FEM NOUN
habit
□ Es ist so eine Gewohnheit von mir, morgens Kaffee zu trinken. **It's a habit of mine to drink coffee in the morning.** □ zur Gewohnheit werden **to become a habit**

■ **aus Gewohnheit** from habit

★ **gewöhnlich** ADJECTIVE

1 usual
□ Ich bin heute früh zu der gewöhnlichen Zeit aufgestanden. **I got up at my usual time this morning.**

■ **Ich stehe gewöhnlich um sieben Uhr auf.** I usually get up at seven o'clock.

2 ordinary
□ Das sind ganz gewöhnliche Leute. **They're quite ordinary people.**

■ **wie gewöhnlich** as usual

gewohnt ADJECTIVE
usual
□ Mir fehlt die gewohnte Umgebung. **I miss my usual surroundings.**

■ **etwas gewohnt sein** to be used to something □ Ich bin es nicht gewohnt, dass man mir widerspricht. **I'm not used to being contradicted.**

gewonnen VERB ▷ see **gewinnen**

geworden VERB ▷ see **werden**

geworfen VERB ▷ see **werfen**

das **Gewürz** (GEN des Gewürzes, PL die Gewürze) NEUT NOUN
spice

gewusst VERB ▷ see **wissen**

die **Gezeiten** PL NOUN
tides pl

gezogen VERB ▷ see **ziehen**

gezwungen VERB ▷ see **zwingen**

★ **gibt** VERB ▷ see **geben**

die **Gier** FEM NOUN
greed

gierig ADJECTIVE
greedy
□ gierig nach Geld **greedy for money**

★ **gießen** (IMPERFECT goss, PERFECT TENSE hat gegossen) VERB
to pour
□ Sie goss mir Wein ins Glas. **She poured wine into my glass.**

■ **die Blumen gießen** to water the flowers
■ **Es gießt in Strömen.** It's pouring.

die **Gießkanne** FEM NOUN
watering can

das **Gift** (PL die Gifte) NEUT NOUN
poison

BE CAREFUL!
The German word **Gift** does not mean **gift**.

giftig ADJECTIVE
poisonous
□ eine giftige Pflanze **a poisonous plant**

ging VERB ▷ see **gehen**

★ der **Gipfel** (PL die Gipfel) MASC NOUN

1 peak
□ die schneebedeckten Gipfel **the snow-covered peaks**

2 height
□ Das ist der Gipfel der Unverschämtheit. **That's the height of impudence.**

die **Giraffe** FEM NOUN
giraffe

das **Girokonto** (PL die Girokonten) NEUT NOUN
current account

★ die **Gitarre** FEM NOUN
guitar
□ Ich spiele Gitarre. **I play the guitar.**

glänzen VERB [36]
to shine
□ Ihr Gesicht glänzte vor Freude. **Her face shone with joy.**

glänzend ADJECTIVE

1 shining
□ ein glänzendes Metall **shining metal**

2 brilliant
□ Das war eine glänzende Leistung. **That was a brilliant achievement.**

★ das **Glas** (GEN des Glases, PL die Gläser) NEUT NOUN
glass

die **Glasscheibe** FEM NOUN
pane

★ **glatt** ADJECTIVE

1 smooth

g

Glatteis – gliedern

□ Der Tisch hat eine glatte Oberfläche. The table has a smooth surface.

2 slippery

□ Pass auf, die Straßen sind glatt. Be careful, the streets are slippery.
■ **eine glatte Absage** a flat refusal
■ **eine glatte Lüge** a downright lie
■ **Das habe ich glatt vergessen.** It completely slipped my mind.

★ das **Glatteis** (GEN des **Glatteises**) NEUT NOUN
black ice

□ Bei Glatteis sollte man vorsichtig fahren. When there's black ice, you have to drive carefully.

das **Glätteisen** (PL die **Glätteisen**) NEUT NOUN
hair straighteners pl

★ die **Glatze** FEM NOUN
■ **Er hat eine Glatze.** He's bald.
■ **eine Glatze bekommen** to go bald

★ **glauben** VERB [38]

1 to believe

□ Ich habe kein Wort geglaubt. I didn't believe a word.

2 to think

□ Ich glaube, wir sind hier nicht willkommen. I don't think we're welcome here.
■ **jemandem glauben** to believe somebody
□ Ich glaube dir. I believe you.
■ **an etwas glauben** to believe in something
□ Glaubst du an ein Leben nach dem Tod? Do you believe in life after death?

glaubwürdig ADJECTIVE

1 credible

□ Das ist keine besonders glaubwürdige Geschichte. That story's not particularly credible.

2 trustworthy

□ Er ist ein glaubwürdiger Mensch. He's a trustworthy person.

★ **gleich** ADJECTIVE, ADVERB

1 same

□ Wir haben das gleiche Problem. We have the same problem.

2 identical

□ Bei einem Würfel sind alle Seiten gleich. All the sides of a cube are identical.

3 the same

□ Ich behandle alle meine Kinder gleich. I treat all my children the same. □ Sie waren genau gleich angezogen. They were dressed exactly the same.
■ **gleich groß** the same size

4 equal

□ Wir wollen für die gleiche Arbeit auch die gleiche Bezahlung. We want equal pay for equal work.

5 straight away

□ Ich werde ihn gleich anrufen. I'll call him straight away.
■ **Ich bin gleich fertig.** I'll be ready in a minute.

■ **Es ist mir gleich.** It's all the same to me.
■ **Zwei mal zwei gleich vier.** Two times two equals four.
■ **gleich nach** right after □ Wir sind gleich nach dem Mittagessen abgefahren. We left right after lunch.
■ **gleich neben** right next to □ Wir wohnen gleich neben der Schule. We live right next to the school.

gleichaltrig ADJECTIVE
of the same age

□ gleichaltrige Schüler pupils of the same age
□ Sie sind gleichaltrig. They're the same age.

gleichartig ADJECTIVE
similar

die **Gleichberechtigung** FEM NOUN
equal rights pl

□ die Gleichberechtigung der Frau equal rights for women

gleichen (IMPERFECT **glich**, PERFECT TENSE **hat geglichen**) VERB
■ **jemandem gleichen** to be like somebody
□ Du gleichst deinem Vater. You're like your father.
■ **einer Sache gleichen** to be like something
□ Unser Haus gleicht eurem. Our house is like yours.
■ **sich gleichen** to be alike

★ **gleichfalls** ADVERB
■ **Danke gleichfalls!** The same to you.

gleichgeschlechtlich ADJECTIVE
same-sex
■ **gleichgeschlechtliche Ehe** same-sex marriage

das **Gleichgewicht** NEUT NOUN
balance

gleichgültig ADJECTIVE

1 indifferent

□ Er zeigte sich ihr gegenüber ziemlich gleichgültig. He seemed to be quite indifferent to her.

2 not important

□ Es ist doch gleichgültig, wie wir das machen. It's not important how we do it.

gleichzeitig ADVERB
at the same time

□ Ich kann doch nicht drei Dinge gleichzeitig tun. I can't do three things at the same time.

★ das **Gleis** (GEN des **Gleises**, PL die **Gleise**) NEUT NOUN

1 line

□ die Straßenbahngleise the tram lines

2 platform

□ Achtung auf Gleis drei. Attention on platform three.

der **Gletscher** (PL die **Gletscher**) MASC NOUN
glacier

gliedern VERB [88]
to structure

★ = core vocabulary

□ Du musst deinen Aufsatz besser gliedern. You must structure your essay better.

glitzern VERB [88]

1 to glitter
□ Das Wasser glitzerte in der Sonne. The water glittered in the sun.

2 to twinkle
□ Die Sterne glitzerten. The stars twinkled.

die **Globalisierung** FEM NOUN
globalization

die **Glocke** FEM NOUN
bell
■ etwas an die große Glocke hängen to shout something from the rooftops

★ das **Glück** NEUT NOUN

1 luck
□ Ein vierblättriges Kleeblatt bringt Glück. A four-leaf clover brings good luck.
■ Glück haben to be lucky □ Ich habe in der Prüfung viel Glück gehabt. I was very lucky in the exam.
■ Viel Glück! Good luck!
■ zum Glück fortunately

2 happiness
□ Sie strahlte vor Glück. She was beaming with happiness.

★ **glücklich** ADJECTIVE

1 happy
□ Ich bin sehr glücklich mit ihm. I'm very happy with him. □ Das waren glückliche Tage. Those were happy days.

2 lucky
□ Das war ein glücklicher Zufall. That was a lucky coincidence.

glücklicherweise ADVERB
fortunately

★ der **Glückwunsch** (PL die Glückwünsche) MASC NOUN
congratulations pl
□ Herzlichen Glückwunsch zur bestandenen Prüfung. Congratulations on passing your exam.
■ Herzlichen Glückwunsch zum Geburtstag. Happy Birthday.

die **Glühbirne** FEM NOUN
light bulb

GmbH ABBREVIATION (= Gesellschaft mit beschränkter Haftung)
limited company

★ das **Gold** NEUT NOUN
gold

★ **golden** ADJECTIVE
golden

★ der **Goldfisch** (PL die Goldfische) MASC NOUN
goldfish
□ Ich habe zwei Goldfische. I've got two goldfish.

der **Golf** (PL die Golfe) MASC NOUN
▷ see also das Golf NOUN
gulf
□ der Persische Golf the Persian Gulf

das **Golf** NEUT NOUN
▷ see also der Golf NOUN
golf
□ Mein Vater spielt Golf. My father plays golf.

der **Golfplatz** (GEN des Golfplatzes, PL die Golfplätze) MASC NOUN
golf course

der **Golfstrom** MASC NOUN
the Gulf Stream

gönnen VERB [38]
■ sich etwas gönnen to treat oneself to something □ Ich werde mir ein Stück Kuchen gönnen. I'm going to treat myself to a piece of cake.
■ Sie gönnt mir meinen Erfolg nicht. She begrudges me my success.

googeln VERB [88]
to google

★ der **Gott** (PL die Götter) MASC NOUN
god
■ Mein Gott! For heaven's sake! □ Mein Gott, wie kann man nur so dumm sein! For heaven's sake, how can you be so stupid!
■ Um Gottes willen! For heaven's sake! □ Um Gottes willen, tu das bloß nicht! For heaven's sake don't do that!
■ Grüß Gott! Hello!
■ Gott sei Dank! Thank God!

die **Göttin** FEM NOUN
goddess

göttlich ADJECTIVE
divine

das **Grab** (PL die Gräber) NEUT NOUN
grave

graben (PRESENT TENSE gräbt, IMPERFECT grub, PERFECT TENSE hat gegraben) VERB
▷ see also der Graben NOUN
to dig

der **Graben** (PL die Gräben) MASC NOUN
▷ see also graben VERB
ditch

★ der **Grad** (PL die Grad) MASC NOUN
degree
□ dreißig Grad im Schatten thirty degrees in the shade

die **Grafikkarte** FEM NOUN
graphics card
□ Welche Grafikkarte hast du in deinem PC? What graphics card do you have in your PC?

grafisch ADJECTIVE
graphic

★ das **Gramm** (PL die Gramme or Gramm) NEUT NOUN
gram
□ hundert Gramm Käse a hundred grams of cheese

Numbers in brackets refer to verb tables on pages 697 to 706.

121

Grammatik - grob

die **Grammatik** FEM NOUN
grammar

graphisch ADJECTIVE ▷ *see* **grafisch**

★ das **Gras** (GEN des **Grases**, PL die **Gräser**) NEUT
NOUN
grass

grässlich ADJECTIVE
horrible

die **Gräte** FEM NOUN
bone
□ Dieser Fisch hat zu viele Gräten. This fish has too many bones in it.

★ **gratis** ADVERB
free of charge

★ **gratulieren** (PERFECT TENSE **hat gratuliert**)
VERB [76]
■ **jemandem gratulieren** to congratulate somebody □ Wir gratulierten ihr zum bestandenen Examen. We congratulated her on passing her exam.
■ **Gratuliere!** Congratulations!

★ **grau** ADJECTIVE
grey

★ das **Graubrot** (PL die **Graubrote**) NEUT NOUN
brown bread

der **Gräuel** (PL die **Gräuel**) MASC NOUN
horror
□ die Gräuel des Bürgerkriegs the horrors of civil war
■ **Das ist mir ein Gräuel.** I loathe it.

grauenhaft ADJECTIVE
horrible

grauhaarig ADJECTIVE
grey-haired

grausam ADJECTIVE
cruel

die **Grausamkeit** FEM NOUN
cruelty

greifen (IMPERFECT **griff**, PERFECT TENSE **hat gegriffen**) VERB
■ **nach etwas greifen** to reach for something □ Er griff nach meiner Hand. He reached for my hand.
■ **um sich greifen** to spread □ Das Feuer griff schnell um sich. The fire spread quickly.

grell ADJECTIVE
harsh
□ eine grelle Farbe a harsh colour
■ **ein greller Schrei** a piercing scream

★ die **Grenze** FEM NOUN
1 border
□ Wir sind an der Grenze kontrolliert worden. Our papers were checked at the border.
2 boundary
□ Der Zaun ist die Grenze zum Grundstück des Nachbarn. The fence marks the boundary with our neighbour's property.

3 limit
□ die Grenzen des guten Geschmacks the limits of good taste

grenzen VERB [36]
■ **an etwas grenzen** to border on something □ Unser Grundstück grenzt an das von Schmidts. Our property borders on the Schmidt's.
■ **Das grenzt an Wahnsinn.** It verges on madness.

grenzenlos ADJECTIVE
boundless

der **Greuel** MASC NOUN ▷ *see* der **Gräuel**

★ der **Grieche** (GEN des **Griechen**, PL die **Griechen**) MASC NOUN
Greek

★ **Griechenland** NEUT NOUN
Greece
■ **aus Griechenland** from Greece
■ **nach Griechenland** to Greece

★ die **Griechin** FEM NOUN
Greek

★ **griechisch** ADJECTIVE
▷ *see also* das **Griechisch** NOUN
Greek

das **Griechisch** (GEN des **Griechischen**)
NEUT NOUN
▷ *see also* **griechisch** ADJECTIVE
Greek

der **Grieß** (GEN des **Grießes**) MASC NOUN
semolina

der **Griff** (PL die **Griffe**) MASC NOUN
1 handle
□ Halte dich da an dem Griff fest. Hold on to the handle.
2 hold
□ Ich habe Judogriffe geübt. I've been practising judo holds.

griffbereit ADJECTIVE
handy
□ etwas griffbereit halten to keep something handy

★ der **Grill** (PL die **Grills**) MASC NOUN
grill

★ **grillen** VERB [48]
1 to grill
□ gegrillter Fisch grilled fish
2 to have a barbecue
□ Wir wollen am Sonntag grillen. We'd like to have a barbecue on Sunday.

grinsen VERB [38]
to grin

★ die **Grippe** FEM NOUN
flu

grob ADJECTIVE
1 coarse
□ grober Sand coarse sand
2 rough

★ = core vocabulary

□ Sei nicht so grob zu deiner Schwester. Don't be so rough with your sister.

3 serious
□ ein grober Fehler a serious mistake

★ **groß** ADJECTIVE, ADVERB

1 big
□ Das war mein größter Fehler. That was my biggest mistake. □ Sie haben ein großes Haus. They have a big house.

2 tall
□ Mein Bruder ist viel größer als ich. My brother is much taller than me. □ Wie groß bist du? How tall are you?

3 great
□ Das war eine große Leistung. That was a great achievement. □ Sie war eine große Politikerin. She was a great politician.
■ **großen Hunger haben** to be very hungry
■ **die großen Ferien** the summer holidays
■ **Er hat sich nicht groß angestrengt.** He didn't try very hard.
■ **im Großen und Ganzen** on the whole

★ **großartig** ADJECTIVE
splendid

★ **Großbritannien** NEUT NOUN
Great Britain
■ **aus Großbritannien** from Great Britain
■ **in Großbritannien** in Great Britain
■ **nach Großbritannien** to Great Britain

★ die **Größe** FEM NOUN

1 size
□ Welche Schuhgröße hast du? What size shoes do you take?

2 height
□ Im Pass steht bei den Angaben zur Person auch die Größe. Your height's also included in your passport under personal details.

★ die **Großeltern** PL NOUN
grandparents pl

★ die **Großmutter** (PL die **Großmütter**) FEM NOUN
grandmother

großschreiben (IMPERFECT **schrieb groß**, PERFECT TENSE **hat großgeschrieben**) VERB [61]
to write in capitals

★ die **Großstadt** (PL die **Großstädte**) FEM NOUN
city

größtenteils ADVERB
for the most part

★ der **Großvater** (PL die **Großväter**) MASC NOUN
grandfather

★ **großzügig** ADJECTIVE, ADVERB
generous
□ Meine Eltern sind sehr großzügig. My parents are very generous. □ Sie hat großzügig darauf verzichtet. She generously did without.

★ **grün** ADJECTIVE
green
□ Die Ampel ist grün. The traffic lights are at green.

★ der **Grund** (PL die **Gründe**) MASC NOUN

1 reason
□ Nenn mir einen Grund, warum wir das nicht so machen können. Give me one reason why we can't do it like this.
■ **Aus welchem Grund ist er so böse?** Why is he so angry?

2 ground
□ Das Haus ist auf felsigem Grund gebaut. The house is built on rocky ground.

3 bottom
□ Das Schiff sank auf den Grund des Meeres. The ship sank to the bottom of the sea.
■ **im Grunde genommen** basically
■ **auf Grund** ▷ see **aufgrund**
■ **zu Grunde** ▷ see **zugrunde**

gründen VERB [54]
to found
□ Wir haben einen Fanklub gegründet. We've founded a fan club.

gründlich ADJECTIVE, ADVERB
thorough
□ eine gründliche Vorbereitung zur Prüfung thorough preparation for the exam □ Wir haben das Haus gründlich geputzt. We cleaned the house thoroughly.
■ **Ich habe mich gründlich geirrt.** I was completely wrong.

der **Grundsatz** (GEN des **Grundsatzes**, PL die **Grundsätze**) MASC NOUN
principle

grundsätzlich ADJECTIVE, ADVERB

1 fundamental
□ Es bleibt die grundsätzliche Frage, ob das erlaubt werden soll. The fundamental question remains: should it be allowed?

2 basically
□ Grundsätzlich bin ich ja dafür, aber ... Basically I'm in favour, but ...

3 on principle
□ Ich bin grundsätzlich gegen die Prügelstrafe. I'm against corporal punishment on principle.

★ die **Grundschule** FEM NOUN
primary school

die **Grünen** MASC PL NOUN
the Greens pl

grunzen VERB [36]
to grunt

★ die **Gruppe** FEM NOUN
group

★ der **Gruselfilm** (PL die **Gruselfilme**) MASC NOUN
horror film

gruselig ADJECTIVE
creepy (Umgangssprache)

Numbers in brackets refer to verb tables on pages 697 to 706.

123

Gruß – Gymnastik

★ **der Gruß** (GEN des **Grußes**, PL die **Grüße**)
MASC NOUN
greeting
- **viele Grüße** best wishes
- **mit freundlichen Grüßen** yours sincerely
- **Grüße an** regards to □ **Grüße an deine Eltern.** Regards to your parents.

★ **grüßen** VERB [31]
to say hello
□ Sie hat mich nicht gegrüßt. She didn't say hello to me.
- **Grüß Lorna von mir.** Give Lorna my regards.
- **Lorna läßt dich grüßen.** Lorna sends her regards.

★ **gucken** VERB [38]
to look

★ **der Gulasch** (PL die **Gulaschs**) MASC NOUN
goulash

★ **die Gulaschsuppe** FEM NOUN
goulash soup

★ **gültig** ADJECTIVE
valid

★ **das Gummi** (PL die **Gummis**) NEUT NOUN

You can also say **der Gummi**.

rubber
□ Die Reifen sind aus Gummi. The tyres are made of rubber.

das Gummiband (PL die **Gummibänder**)
NEUT NOUN
elastic band
□ Sie machte ein Gummiband um das Geschenk. She put an elastic band round the present.

das Gummibärchen (PL die **Gummibärchen**) NEUT NOUN
jelly bear

★ **günstig** ADJECTIVE
convenient
□ Morgen wäre günstig. Tomorrow would be convenient.
- **eine günstige Gelegenheit** a favourable opportunity
- **Das habe ich günstig bekommen.** It was a bargain.

★ **die Gurke** FEM NOUN
cucumber
□ Sie mag Gurkensalat nicht. She doesn't like cucumber salad.
- **saure Gurke** gherkin

der Gurt (PL die **Gurte**) MASC NOUN
belt

★ **der Gürtel** (PL die **Gürtel**) MASC NOUN
belt

★ **gut** ADJECTIVE, ADVERB
1 good
□ Ich habe gute Noten bekommen. I got good marks. □ Sie ist ein guter Mensch. She's a good

person. □ Das ist ein guter Witz. That's a good joke.
- **In Englisch habe ich 'gut'.** I got a B in English.

DID YOU KNOW...?
German grades range from one (**sehr gut**) to six (**ungenügend**).

- **Alles Gute!** All the best.
- **also gut** all right then □ Also gut, ich komme. All right then, I'll come.
2 well
□ Sie hat das gut gemacht. She did it well. □ Ich kenne ihn gut. I know him well.
- **gut schmecken** to taste good
- **gut drei Stunden** a good three hours
- **Das kann gut sein.** That may well be.
- **Gut, aber ...** OK, but ...
- **Lass es gut sein.** That'll do.
- **Es ist zum Glück gut gegangen.** Fortunately it came off.
- **Mir geht's gut.** I'm fine.
- **gut gemeint** well-meant □ ein gut gemeinter Rat a well-meant piece of advice
- **gut tun** ▷ see guttun

die Güter NEUT PL NOUN
goods pl

gutgehen VERB [29] ▷ see gut

gutgemeint ADJECTIVE ▷ see gut

das Guthaben (PL die **Guthaben**) NEUT NOUN
credit

gütig ADJECTIVE
kind

gutmütig ADJECTIVE
good-natured

der Gutschein (PL die **Gutscheine**) MASC
NOUN
voucher

guttun (IMPERFECT **tat gut**, PERFECT TENSE **hat gutgetan**) VERB [81]
- **jemandem guttun** to do somebody good
□ Die Pause hat mir gutgetan. The break did me good.

★ **das Gymnasium** (PL die **Gymnasien**) NEUT
NOUN
grammar school

BE CAREFUL!
The German word **Gymnasium** does not mean **gymnasium**.

★ **die Gymnastik** FEM NOUN
keep-fit
□ Ich mache einmal in der Woche Gymnastik. I do keep-fit once a week.

Hh

★ das **Haar** (PL die **Haare**) NEUT NOUN
hair
□ Sie hat dunkle Haare. She's got dark hair.
■ um ein Haar nearly

die **Haarbürste** FEM NOUN
hairbrush

der **Haarglätter** (PL die **Haarglätter**) MASC NOUN
hair straighteners *pl*

★ **haben** VERB [32]

PRESENT TENSE	
ich habe	wir haben
du hast	ihr habt
er/sie/es hat	sie/Sie haben
PERFECT TENSE	
hat gehabt	

to have
□ Ich habe einen neuen Pulli. I've got a new pullover. □ Sie hat ihn nicht gesehen. She hasn't seen him.
■ Welches Datum haben wir heute? What's the date today?
■ Hunger haben to be hungry
■ Angst haben to be afraid
■ Woher hast du das? Where did you get that from?
■ Was hast du denn? What's the matter with you?
■ Ich hätte gern ... I would like ...

das **Hackfleisch** NEUT NOUN
mince

★ der **Hafen** (PL die **Häfen**) MASC NOUN
harbour

★ die **Hafenstadt** (PL die **Hafenstädte**) FEM NOUN
port

der **Hafer** MASC NOUN
oats *pl*

die **Haferflocken** FEM PL NOUN
porridge oats *pl*

haftbar ADJECTIVE
responsible
□ Eltern sind für ihre Kinder haftbar. Parents are responsible for their children.

haften VERB [2]
to stick

□ Der Klebstreifen haftet nicht. The adhesive tape isn't sticking.
■ haften für to be responsible for

die **Haftpflichtversicherung** FEM NOUN
third party insurance

★ der **Hagel** MASC NOUN
hail

★ **hageln** VERB [88]
■ Es hagelt. It's hailing.

★ der **Hahn** (PL die **Hähne**) MASC NOUN
1 cock
□ Der Hahn krähte. The cock crowed.
2 tap
□ Der Hahn tropft. The tap's dripping.

★ das **Hähnchen** (PL die **Hähnchen**) NEUT NOUN
chicken
□ Heute gibt es Hähnchen. We're having chicken today.

der **Hai** (PL die **Haie**) MASC NOUN
shark

der **Haken** (PL die **Haken**) MASC NOUN
1 hook
□ Häng deinen Anorak an den Haken. Hang your anorak up on the hook.
2 catch
□ Die Sache hat einen Haken. There's a catch.

★ **halb** ADJECTIVE
half
□ ein halber Kuchen half a cake □ eine halbe Stunde half an hour
■ halb eins half past twelve

halbieren (PERFECT TENSE **hat halbiert**) VERB [76]
to halve

das **Halbjahr** (PL die **Halbjahre**) NEUT NOUN
six months *pl*

halbjährlich ADJECTIVE
half-yearly

★ die **Halbpension** FEM NOUN
half board

★ **halbtags** ADVERB
■ halbtags arbeiten to work part-time

★ die **Halbtagsarbeit** FEM NOUN
part-time job

half – Handel

half VERB ▷ *see* **helfen**

★ die **Hälfte** FEM NOUN
half

★ die **Halle** FEM NOUN
hall
□ eine Messehalle an exhibition hall

★ das **Hallenbad** (PL die **Hallenbäder**) NEUT NOUN
indoor swimming pool

hallo EXCLAMATION
hello!

★ der **Hals** (GEN des **Halses**, PL die **Hälse**) MASC NOUN
1 neck
□ Ich habe einen steifen Hals. I've got a stiff neck.
2 throat
□ Mir tut der Hals weh. My throat's sore.
■ **Hals über Kopf** in a rush

★ die **Halskette** FEM NOUN
necklace

★ die **Halsschmerzen** MASC PL NOUN
sore throat *sing*
□ Ich habe Halsschmerzen. I've got a sore throat.

das **Halstuch** (PL die **Halstücher**) NEUT NOUN
scarf

halt EXCLAMATION
stop!

haltbar ADJECTIVE
durable
□ Das ist ein sehr haltbares Material. That's a very durable material.
■ **Butter ist nur begrenzt haltbar.** Butter only keeps for a limited time.
■ **'Mindestens haltbar bis …'** 'Best before …'

★ **halten** (PRESENT TENSE **hält**, IMPERFECT **hielt**, PERFECT TENSE **hat gehalten**) VERB [33]
1 to hold
□ Er hielt sie an der Hand. He held her by the hand. □ Kannst du das mal halten? Can you hold that for a moment?
2 to keep
□ Obst hält nicht lange. Fruit doesn't keep long.
3 to last
□ Ihre Freundschaft hat lange gehalten. Their friendship has lasted a long time.
4 to stop
□ Der Bus hielt vor dem Rathaus. The bus stopped in front of the town hall.
■ **halten für** to regard as □ Man hält ihn für den besten Chirurgen in Deutschland. He's regarded as being the best surgeon in Germany.
■ **Ich habe sie für deine Mutter gehalten.** I took her for your mother.
■ **halten von** to think of □ Sie hält viel von dir. She thinks a lot of you. □ Ich halte nichts von

dieser Methode. I don't think much of this method.
■ **sich rechts halten** to keep to the right

★ die **Haltestelle** FEM NOUN
stop
□ Wo ist die Straßenbahnhaltestelle? Where's the tram stop?

haltmachen VERB [48]
to stop

die **Haltung** FEM NOUN
1 posture
□ Er hat eine aufrechte Haltung. He has an upright posture.
2 attitude
□ Ich bewundere deine Haltung in dieser Frage. I admire your attitude in this issue.

Hamburg NEUT NOUN
Hamburg

DID YOU KNOW…?
The 'Free Hanseatic City of Hamburg' is one of the 16 **Länder**. It is a 'city-state' like Bremen and Berlin, and is Germany's principal seaport.

der **Hammer** (PL die **Hämmer**) MASC NOUN
hammer

der **Hamster** (PL die **Hamster**) MASC NOUN
hamster

hamstern VERB [88]
to hoard

★ die **Hand** (PL die **Hände**) FEM NOUN
hand

die **Handarbeit** FEM NOUN
1 manual work
□ Handarbeit macht ihm mehr Spaß als geistige Arbeit. He enjoys manual work more than intellectual work.
2 needlework
□ Sie verbringt manche Abende mit Handarbeiten. She spends some evenings in with her needlework.

★ der **Handball** MASC NOUN
handball

die **Handbremse** FEM NOUN
handbrake

das **Handbuch** (PL die **Handbücher**) NEUT NOUN
manual

der **Händedruck** MASC NOUN
handshake

der **Handel** MASC NOUN
1 trade
□ der Handel mit Osteuropa trade with Eastern Europe □ fairer Handel fair trade
■ **Dieses Gerät ist überall im Handel erhältlich.** This appliance is available in all shops and retail outlets.

★ = core vocabulary

German-English

2 deal

□ Wir haben einen Handel abgeschlossen. **We have concluded a deal.**

handeln VERB [34]

1 to act

□ Wir müssen schnell handeln. **We'll have to act quickly.**

2 to trade

□ Er handelt mit Gebrauchtwaren. **He trades in second-hand goods.**

■ **mit jemandem handeln** to bargain with somebody □ Ich habe versucht, mit ihm zu handeln, aber er wollte es mir nicht billiger geben. **I tried to bargain with him but he didn't want to give it to me any cheaper.**

■ **Es handelt sich um ...** It's about ... □ Sie wollte mir nicht sagen, worum es sich handelt. **She didn't want to tell me what it was about.**

■ **handeln von** to be about □ Die Geschichte handelt von einer kranken Frau. **The story's about a sick woman.**

die **Handelsschule** FEM NOUN
business school

das **Handgepäck** NEUT NOUN
hand luggage

★ der **Händler** (PL die **Händler**) MASC NOUN
dealer

□ Ich habe meinen Computerhändler danach gefragt. **I asked my computer dealer about it.**

★ die **Händlerin** FEM NOUN
dealer

handlich ADJECTIVE
handy

★ die **Handlung** FEM NOUN

1 act

□ Das war eine unüberlegte Handlung. **That was a rash act.**

2 plot

□ Ich habe die Handlung des Buches nicht genau verstanden. **I didn't really understand the plot of the book.**

3 shop

□ eine Eisenwarenhandlung an ironmonger's shop

die **Handschrift** FEM NOUN
handwriting

★ der **Handschuh** (PL die **Handschuhe**) MASC NOUN
glove

★ die **Handtasche** FEM NOUN
handbag

★ das **Handtuch** (PL die **Handtücher**) NEUT NOUN
towel

★ das **Handy** (PL die **Handys**) NEUT NOUN
mobile phone

BE CAREFUL!
The German word **Handy** does not mean **handy**.

der **Hang** (PL die **Hänge**) MASC NOUN
slope

★ **hängen (1)** (IMPERFECT **hängte**, PERFECT TENSE **hat gehängt**) VERB [48]
to hang

□ Sie hat die Wäsche auf die Leine gehängt. **She hung her washing on the line.** □ Sie hängten den Verbrecher. **They hanged the criminal.**

★ **hängen (2)** (IMPERFECT **hing**, PERFECT TENSE **hat gehangen**) VERB [35]
to hang

□ An der Wand hing ein Bild von Picasso. **A painting by Picasso was hanging on the wall.**
■ **hängen an** to be attached to □ Sie hat sehr an ihrem Vater gehangen. **She was very attached to her father.**

hänseln VERB [88]
to tease

die **Hansestadt** (PL die **Hansestädte**) FEM NOUN
Hanseatic town

DID YOU KNOW...?
The **Hanse** (Hanseatic League) was a powerful association of cities which dominated Baltic trade in the Middle Ages. Even today, Bremen, Hamburg, Lübeck, Rostock and Wismar still call themselves **Hansestädte**.

harmlos ADJECTIVE
harmless

harmonisch ADJECTIVE
harmonious

★ **hart** ADJECTIVE
hard

□ hart wie Stein as hard as stone □ Wir haben hart gearbeitet. **We worked hard.**
■ **harte Worte** harsh words
■ **Das ist hart.** That's tough.
■ **ein hart gekochtes Ei** a hard-boiled egg

★ **hartnäckig** ADJECTIVE
stubborn

das **Haschisch** (GEN des **Haschisch**) NEUT NOUN
hashish

der **Hase** (GEN des **Hasen**, PL die **Hasen**) MASC NOUN
hare

die **Haselnuss** (PL die **Haselnüsse**) FEM NOUN
hazelnut

der **Hass** (GEN des **Hasses**) MASC NOUN
hatred

★ **hassen** (PERFECT TENSE **hat gehasst**) VERB [31]
to hate

h

hässlich – Haustier

★ **hässlich** ADJECTIVE
1 ugly
□ Das ist aber ein hässlicher Hund! That's a really ugly dog!
2 nasty
□ Es ist hässlich, so etwas zu sagen. It's nasty to say things like that.

hast VERB ▷ *see* **haben**

hastig ADJECTIVE
hasty

hat, hatte VERB ▷ *see* **haben**

der **Haufen** (PL die **Haufen**) MASC NOUN
heap
□ In ihrem Schlafzimmer lag ein Haufen schmutziger Wäsche. There was a heap of dirty washing lying in her bedroom.
■ **ein Haufen ...** heaps of ... (*Umgangssprache*)
□ Ich habe einen Haufen Fehler gemacht. I've made heaps of mistakes. □ Er hat einen Haufen Geld dafür bezahlt. He paid heaps of money for it. □ ein Haufen Leute heaps of people

häufen VERB [38]
■ **sich häufen** 1 to accumulate □ Der Müll häufte sich in den Straßen. The rubbish accumulated in the streets. 2 to be on the increase □ Die Fälle von Asthma häufen sich. Cases of asthma are on the increase.

★ **häufig** ADJECTIVE, ADVERB
1 frequent
□ sein häufiges Fehlen his frequent absences
2 frequently
□ Er fehlt häufig. He is frequently absent.

★ der **Hauptbahnhof** (PL die **Hauptbahnhöfe**) MASC NOUN
main station

hauptberuflich ADVERB
full-time
□ Er ist hauptberuflich als Gärtner tätig. He's employed full-time as a gardener.

das **Hauptfach** (PL die **Hauptfächer**) NEUT NOUN
main subject

★ das **Hauptgericht** (PL die **Hauptgerichte**) NEUT NOUN
main course

die **Hauptsache** FEM NOUN
main thing
□ Hauptsache, du bist gesund. The main thing is that you're healthy.

die **Hauptsaison** (PL die **Hauptsaisons**) FEM NOUN
high season

★ die **Hauptschule** FEM NOUN
secondary school

★ die **Hauptstadt** (PL die **Hauptstädte**) FEM NOUN
capital
□ Berlin ist die Hauptstadt von Deutschland. Berlin's the capital of Germany.

★ die **Hauptstraße** FEM NOUN
main street

★ die **Hauptverkehrszeit** FEM NOUN
rush hour

das **Hauptwort** (PL die **Hauptwörter**) NEUT NOUN
noun

★ das **Haus** (GEN des **Hauses**, PL die **Häuser**) NEUT NOUN
house
■ **nach Hause** home □ Ich muss jetzt nach Hause. I'll have to go home now.
■ **zu Hause** at home

die **Hausarbeit** FEM NOUN
1 housework no pl
□ Meine Mutter erledigt immer noch die Mehrheit der Hausarbeit. My mother still does the majority of the housework.
2 homework no pl
□ Wir haben eine Hausarbeit zum Thema Umweltverschmutzung auf. We've got homework on the subject of pollution.

der **Hausarzt** (GEN des **Hausarztes**, PL die **Hausärzte**) MASC NOUN
family doctor

die **Hausärztin** FEM NOUN
family doctor

die **Hausaufgaben** FEM PL NOUN
homework no pl
□ Heute waren die Hausaufgaben nicht schwierig. Our homework wasn't difficult today

★ die **Hausfrau** FEM NOUN
housewife

★ der **Haushalt** (PL die **Haushalte**) MASC NOUN
1 household
□ den Haushalt führen to run the household
2 budget
□ der Haushalt für 2019 the 2019 budget

★ der **Hausmeister** (PL die **Hausmeister**) MASC NOUN
caretaker

★ die **Hausmeisterin** FEM NOUN
caretaker

★ die **Hausnummer** FEM NOUN
house number

der **Hausschlüssel** (PL die **Hausschlüssel**) MASC NOUN
front-door key

der **Hausschuh** (PL die **Hausschuhe**) MASC NOUN
slipper

★ das **Haustier** (PL die **Haustiere**) NEUT NOUN
pet

★ = core vocabulary

★ die **Haustür** FEM NOUN
front door

★ die **Hauswirtschaft** FEM NOUN
home economics *sing*

die **Haut** (PL die **Häute**) FEM NOUN
skin

Hbf. ABBREVIATION (= *Hauptbahnhof*)
central station

der **Hebel** (PL die **Hebel**) MASC NOUN
lever

★ **heben** (IMPERFECT **hob**, PERFECT TENSE **hat
gehoben**) VERB
to lift

die **Hecke** FEM NOUN
hedge

die **Hefe** FEM NOUN
yeast

★ das **Heft** (PL die **Hefte**) NEUT NOUN
1 exercise book
□ Schreibt die Verbesserung in euer Heft. Write
the correction in your exercise books.
2 issue
□ Hast du noch das letzte Heft von 'Geo'? Have
you got the latest issue of 'Geo'?

die **Heftklammer** FEM NOUN
paper clip

★ das **Heftpflaster** (PL die **Heftpflaster**) NEUT
NOUN
sticking plaster

die **Heide** FEM NOUN
moor
□ Wir haben einen Spaziergang durch die Heide
gemacht. We went for a walk over the moor.
■ **die Lüneburger Heide** Lüneburg Heath

das **Heidekraut** NEUT NOUN
heather

die **Heidelbeere** FEM NOUN
blueberry

heilbar ADJECTIVE
curable

heilen (PERFECT TENSE **hat/ist geheilt**) VERB
[38]

For the perfect tense use **haben** when the
verb has an object and **sein** when there is
no object.

1 to cure
□ Viele Arten von Krebs kann man heilen. Many
kinds of cancer can be cured.
2 to heal
□ Die Wunde ist schnell geheilt. The wound
healed quickly.

heilig ADJECTIVE
holy

der **Heiligabend** (PL die **Heiligabende**)
MASC NOUN
Christmas Eve

der/die **Heilige** (GEN des/der **Heiligen**, PL die
Heiligen) MASC/FEM NOUN
saint
□ Er ist auch kein Heiliger. He's no saint.

das **Heilmittel** (PL die **Heilmittel**) NEUT
NOUN
remedy

★ **heim** ADVERB
▷ *see also* das **Heim** NOUN
home
□ Ich muss jetzt heim. I'll have to go home now.

das **Heim** (PL die **Heime**) NEUT NOUN
▷ *see also* **heim** ADVERB
home
□ ein Heim für Kinder mit Lernschwierigkeiten
a home for children with learning difficulties

★ die **Heimat** FEM NOUN
homeland
□ Deutschland ist meine Heimat. Germany's
my homeland.

★ **heimatlos** ADJECTIVE
homeless

★ die **Heimfahrt** FEM NOUN
journey home

heimgehen (IMPERFECT **ging heim**, PERFECT
TENSE **ist heimgegangen**) VERB [29]
to go home

heimlich ADJECTIVE
secret
□ Sie haben ein heimliches Treffen vereinbart.
They arranged a secret meeting.

die **Heimreise** FEM NOUN
journey home

das **Heimspiel** (PL die **Heimspiele**) NEUT
NOUN
home game

★ der **Heimweg** (PL die **Heimwege**) MASC NOUN
way home

★ das **Heimweh** NEUT NOUN
homesickness

die **Heirat** FEM NOUN
marriage

★ **heiraten** VERB [2]
to get married
□ Sie heiraten morgen. They're getting married
tomorrow.
■ **jemanden heiraten** to marry somebody

heiser ADJECTIVE
hoarse

die **Heiserkeit** FEM NOUN
hoarseness

★ **heiß** ADJECTIVE
hot
□ Mir ist heiß. I'm hot. □ heiße Schokolade hot
chocolate

h

heißen – herausnehmen

★ **heißen** (IMPERFECT **hieß**, PERFECT TENSE **hat geheißen**) VERB

1 to be called
□ Er heißt Marek. He's called Marek.

2 to mean
□ Das heißt, dass wir morgen früh aufstehen müssen. That means that we'll have to get up early tomorrow.
■ **Es heißt ...** It is said ...
■ **das heißt** that is (to say)

★ **heiter** ADJECTIVE

1 cheerful
□ Ich war in heiterer Laune. I was in a cheerful mood.

2 bright
□ Das Wetter wird heiter bis bewölkt. The weather will be cloudy with bright spells.

★ **heizen** VERB [36]
to heat

der **Heizkörper** (PL die **Heizkörper**) MASC NOUN
radiator

★ die **Heizung** FEM NOUN
heating

hektisch ADJECTIVE
hectic

der **Held** (GEN des **Helden**, PL die **Helden**) MASC NOUN
hero

die **Heldin** FEM NOUN
heroine

★ **helfen** (PRESENT TENSE **hilft**, IMPERFECT **half**, PERFECT TENSE **hat geholfen**) VERB [37]
to help
□ Kann ich dir helfen? Can I help you? □ Die Tablette hat geholfen. The pill helped.
□ jemandem bei etwas helfen to help somebody with something
■ **sich zu helfen wissen** to be resourceful
□ Er weiß sich zu helfen. He's very resourceful.
■ **Es hilft nichts, du musst ...** It's no use, you'll have to ...

★ **hell** ADJECTIVE
bright
□ Hier ist es schön hell. It's nice and bright here.
■ **Sie hat einen hellen Teint.** She has a clear complexion.
■ **eine helle Farbe** a light colour
■ **ein Helles** a light beer

hellblau ADJECTIVE
light blue

hellblond ADJECTIVE
light-blond

der **Helm** (PL die **Helme**) MASC NOUN
helmet

★ das **Hemd** (PL die **Hemden**) NEUT NOUN
shirt
■ **ein Unterhemd** a vest

die **Hemmung** FEM NOUN
inhibition
□ Er hat furchtbare Hemmungen. He has terrible inhibitions.

die **Henne** FEM NOUN
hen

★ **her** ADVERB
ago
□ Das ist fünf Jahre her. That was five years ago.
■ **von ... her** from ... □ von England her from England □ von weit her from a long way away
■ **Wo bist du her?** Where do you come from?
■ **Komm her zu mir.** Come here.
■ **Her damit!** Hand it over!

herab ADVERB
down

herabhängen (IMPERFECT **hing herab**, PERFECT TENSE **hat herabgehangen**) VERB [35]
to hang down

herablassend ADJECTIVE
condescending

heran ADVERB
■ **Näher heran!** Come closer!

herauf ADVERB
up
□ Komm hier herauf. Come up here.

heraus ADVERB
out

herausbekommen (IMPERFECT **bekam heraus**, PERFECT TENSE **hat herausbekommen**) VERB [40]

1 to get out
□ Ich habe den Fleck nicht herausbekommen. didn't get the stain out.

2 to find out
□ Ich muss herausbekommen, warum er das gemacht hat. I'll have to find out why he did it.

herausfordern (PERFECT TENSE **hat herausgefordert**) VERB [15]
to challenge

herauskommen (IMPERFECT **kam heraus**, PERFECT TENSE **ist herausgekommen**) VERB [40]
to come out
□ Die Maus ist aus ihrem Loch herausgekommen. The mouse came out of its hole.
■ **Dabei kommt nichts heraus.** Nothing wi come of it.

herausnehmen (PRESENT TENSE **nimmt heraus**, IMPERFECT **nahm heraus**, PERFECT TENSE **hat herausgenommen**) VERB [52]
to take out
□ Sie hat das Lesezeichen aus dem Buch herausgenommen. She took the bookmark ou of the book.
■ **sich etwas herausnehmen** to take liberties □ Du nimmst dir wirklich etwas zu vie heraus. You really do take far too many libertie

★ = core vocabulary

sich **herausstellen** (PERFECT TENSE **hat sich herausgestellt**) VERB [15]
to turn out
□ Es stellte sich heraus, dass ... It turned out that ...

herausziehen (IMPERFECT **zog heraus**, PERFECT TENSE **hat herausgezogen**) VERB [96]
to pull out

herb ADJECTIVE
bitter
□ eine herbe Enttäuschung a bitter disappointment □ ein herber Geschmack a bitter taste

★ **herbei** ADVERB
over
□ Alle eilten herbei. Everyone hurried over.

★ die **Herbergseltern** PL NOUN
wardens pl (in youth hostel)

herbringen (IMPERFECT **brachte her**, PERFECT TENSE **hat hergebracht**) VERB [13]
to bring here

★ der **Herbst** (PL die **Herbste**) MASC NOUN
autumn
□ im Herbst in autumn

★ die **Herbstferien** PL NOUN
autumn holidays pl

herbstlich ADJECTIVE
autumnal

★ der **Herd** (PL die **Herde**) MASC NOUN
cooker
□ ein Herd mit vier Platten a cooker with four rings

die **Herde** FEM NOUN
herd
□ eine Herde Kühe a herd of cows
■ eine Schafherde a flock of sheep

★ **herein** ADVERB
in
□ Noch mehr Menschen drängten herein. Even more people pushed their way in. □ Das Wasser strömte herein. The water poured in.
■ Herein! Come in!

hereinbitten (IMPERFECT **bat herein**, PERFECT TENSE **hat hereingebeten**) VERB [9]
to ask in

hereinfallen (PRESENT TENSE **fällt herein**, IMPERFECT **fiel herein**, PERFECT TENSE **ist hereingefallen**) VERB [22]
■ auf etwas hereinfallen to fall for something □ Auf einen solch plumpen Trick falle ich nicht herein. I'm not falling for an obvious trick like that. □ Sie ist auf einen Betrüger hereingefallen. She fell for a swindler.

hereinkommen (IMPERFECT **kam herein**, PERFECT TENSE **ist hereingekommen**) VERB [40]
to come in

hereinlassen (PRESENT TENSE **lässt herein**, IMPERFECT **ließ herein**, PERFECT TENSE **hat hereingelassen**) VERB [42]
to let in

hereinlegen (PERFECT TENSE **hat hereingelegt**) VERB [4]
■ jemanden hereinlegen to take somebody for a ride (Umgangssprache) □ Er will dich bloß hereinlegen. He's just trying to take you for a ride.

hergeben (PRESENT TENSE **gibt her**, IMPERFECT **gab her**, PERFECT TENSE **hat hergegeben**) VERB [28]
to hand over
□ Gib das Buch her! Hand over the book!
■ sich zu etwas hergeben to lend one's name to something

hergehen (IMPERFECT **ging her**, PERFECT TENSE **ist hergegangen**) VERB [29]
■ hinter jemandem hergehen to follow somebody
■ Es geht hoch her. There are a lot of goings-on. (Umgangssprache)

herhören (PERFECT TENSE **hat hergehört**) VERB [4]
to listen
□ Alle mal herhören! Listen everybody!

der **Hering** (PL die **Heringe**) MASC NOUN
herring

herkommen (IMPERFECT **kam her**, PERFECT TENSE **ist hergekommen**) VERB [40]
to come
□ Komm mal her! Come here!

die **Herkunft** (PL die **Herkünfte**) FEM NOUN
origin

das **Heroin** NEUT NOUN
heroin

★ der **Herr** (GEN des **Herrn**, PL die **Herren**) MASC NOUN
1 gentleman
□ Meine Herren! Gentlemen!
■ Er muss immer den großen Herrn spielen! He always has to play the big man!
2 Lord
□ Herr, gib uns Frieden! Lord, give us peace.
3 Mr
□ Herr Mosbacher Mr Mosbacher
■ Mein Herr! Sir!

★ **herrlich** ADJECTIVE
marvellous

herrschen VERB [48]
1 to reign
□ Wann hat Karl der Große geherrscht? When did Charlemagne reign?
2 to be
□ Hier herrschen ja schöne Zustände. This is a fine state of affairs. □ Es herrscht noch Ungewissheit, wann das gemacht werden soll. It's still uncertain when it's to be done.

herstellen – Heuschnupfen

herstellen (PERFECT TENSE **hat hergestellt**) VERB [4]
to manufacture

der **Hersteller** (PL die **Hersteller**) MASC NOUN
manufacturer

die **Herstellerin** FEM NOUN
manufacturer

die **Herstellung** FEM NOUN
manufacture

herüber ADVERB
1 over here
□ Er kam langsam zu uns herüber. **He came slowly over to us.**
2 across
□ Sie versuchte, zu uns herüberzuschwimmen. **She tried to swim across to us.**

★ **herum** ADVERB
round
□ Mach ein rotes Band herum. **Tie a red band round it.**
■ **um etwas herum** round something □ Sie gingen ums Haus herum. **They went round the house.**

herumführen (PERFECT TENSE **hat herumgeführt**) VERB [4]
to show around

herumgehen (IMPERFECT **ging herum**, PERFECT TENSE **ist herumgegangen**) VERB [29]
to walk about
□ Wir sind ein paar Stunden in der Stadt herumgegangen. **We walked about the town for a couple of hours.**
■ **um etwas herumgehen** to walk round something □ Sie ging um den Tisch herum. **She walked round the table.**

sich **herumsprechen** (PRESENT TENSE **spricht sich herum**, IMPERFECT **sprach sich herum**, PERFECT TENSE **hat sich herumgesprochen**) VERB [70]
to get around

herunter ADVERB
down

heruntergekommen ADJECTIVE
run-down

herunterkommen (IMPERFECT **kam herunter**, PERFECT TENSE **ist heruntergekommen**) VERB [40]
1 to come down
□ Sie ist zu uns heruntergekommen. **She came down to us.**
2 to become run-down
□ Das Haus ist in den letzten Jahren ziemlich heruntergekommen. **The house has become rather run-down in the past few years.**

herunterladen (PRESENT TENSE **lädt herunter**, IMPERFECT **lud herunter**, PERFECT TENSE **hat heruntergeladen**) VERB
to download (computer)
□ eine Datei herunterladen to download a file

hervorbringen (IMPERFECT **brachte hervor**, PERFECT TENSE **hat hervorgebracht**) VERB [13]
to produce

★ **hervorragend** ADJECTIVE
excellent

hervorrufen (IMPERFECT **rief hervor**, PERFECT TENSE **hat hervorgerufen**) VERB [56]
to cause

★ das **Herz** (GEN des **Herzens**, PL die **Herzen**) NEUT NOUN
1 heart
□ Es bricht mir fast das Herz. **It almost breaks my heart.**
2 hearts sing
□ Herz ist Trumpf. **Hearts is trumps.**

der **Herzinfarkt** (PL die **Herzinfarkte**) MASC NOUN
heart attack

★ **herzlich** ADJECTIVE
warm
□ ein herzlicher Empfang a warm welcome
■ **Wir wurden herzlich begrüßt. We were warmly welcomed.**
■ **Herzlich willkommen in Bamberg.** Welcome to Bamberg.
■ **Herzlichen Glückwunsch!** Congratulations.
■ **Herzliche Grüße. Best wishes.**

herzlos ADJECTIVE
heartless

der **Herzschlag** (PL die **Herzschläge**) MASC NOUN
1 heartbeat
□ bei jedem Herzschlag with every heartbeat
2 heart attack
□ Er hat einen Herzschlag bekommen. **He had a heart attack.**

Hessen NEUT NOUN
Hesse

DID YOU KNOW...?
Hessen is one of the 16 Länder. Its capital i Wiesbaden, yet its biggest city is Frankfurt am Main, which is Germany's principal financial centre and home to the Bundesbank.

das **Heu** NEUT NOUN
hay
■ **Geld wie Heu** stacks of money

heulen VERB [38]
1 to howl
□ Die Wölfe heulten. **The wolves were howling.**
2 to cry
□ Jetzt fang nicht gleich an zu heulen. **Now don't start crying.**

★ der **Heuschnupfen** MASC NOUN
hay fever
□ Sie leidet an Heuschnupfen. **She suffers from hay fever.**

★ = core vocabulary

★ heute ADVERB

today
- **heute Abend** this evening
- **heute Morgen** this morning
- **heute früh** this morning

heutig ADJECTIVE

today's
□ die heutige Jugend today's youth

★ heutzutage ADVERB

nowadays

die **Hexe** FEM NOUN

witch

der **Hexenschuss** (GEN des **Hexenschusses**) MASC NOUN

lumbago

hielt VERB ▷ see **halten**

★ hier ADVERB

here
□ hier drinnen in here
- **Hier spricht Lisa.** This is Lisa.
- **hier bleiben** to stay here

★ hierher ADVERB

here

hiesig ADJECTIVE

local
□ die hiesige Bevölkerung the local population

hieß VERB ▷ see **heißen**

★ die **Hilfe** FEM NOUN

help no pl
- **Erste Hilfe** first aid
- **Hilfe!** Help!

hilflos ADJECTIVE

helpless

hilfreich ADJECTIVE

helpful

★ hilfsbereit ADJECTIVE

ready to help

hilft VERB ▷ see **helfen**

★ die **Himbeere** FEM NOUN

raspberry

★ der **Himmel** (PL die **Himmel**) MASC NOUN

1 sky
□ ein wolkenloser Himmel a cloudless sky

2 heaven
□ in den Himmel kommen to go to heaven

himmelblau ADJECTIVE

sky-blue

die **Himmelsrichtung** FEM NOUN

- **die vier Himmelsrichtungen** the four points of the compass

himmlisch ADJECTIVE

heavenly

★ hin ADVERB

- **hin und zurück** there and back
- **hin und her** to and fro
- **Wo ist er hin?** Where has he gone?
- **auf meine Bitte hin** at my request

★ hinab ADVERB

down

★ hinauf ADVERB

up

hinaufsteigen (IMPERFECT **stieg hinauf**, PERFECT TENSE **ist hinaufgestiegen**) VERB [74]

to climb
□ Wir sind auf den Berg hinaufgestiegen. We climbed up the mountain.

★ hinaus ADVERB

out

★ hinausgehen (IMPERFECT **ging hinaus**, PERFECT TENSE **ist hinausgegangen**) VERB [29]

to go out
□ Sie ist kurz hinausgegangen. She's gone out for a minute.
- **über etwas hinausgehen** to exceed something □ Das geht weit über meine Erwartungen hinaus. That far exceeds my expectations.

hinausschieben (IMPERFECT **schob hinaus**, PERFECT TENSE **hat hinausgeschoben**) VERB

to put off
□ Sie haben die Entscheidung hinausgeschoben. They put the decision off.

hinauswerfen (PRESENT TENSE **wirft hinaus**, IMPERFECT **warf hinaus**, PERFECT TENSE **hat hinausgeworfen**) VERB [92]

to throw out

hindern VERB [88]

- **jemanden an etwas hindern** to prevent somebody from doing something □ Ich konnte ihn nicht am Weggehen hindern. I couldn't prevent him from going.

das **Hindernis** (GEN des **Hindernisses**, PL die **Hindernisse**) NEUT NOUN

obstacle

★ hinein ADVERB

in
□ Hinein mit dir! In you go!

★ hineingehen (IMPERFECT **ging hinein**, PERFECT TENSE **ist hineingegangen**) VERB [29]

to go in
□ Geh doch hinein. Go in.
- **hineingehen in** to go into □ Sie traute sich nicht, ins Zimmer hineinzugehen. She didn't dare go into the room.

die **Hinfahrt** FEM NOUN

outward journey

★ hinfallen (PRESENT TENSE **fällt hin**, IMPERFECT **fiel hin**, PERFECT TENSE **ist hingefallen**) VERB [22]

to fall
□ Sie stolperte und fiel hin. She stumbled and fell.

h

der **Hinflug** (PL die **Hinflüge**) MASC NOUN
outward flight

hinhalten (PRESENT TENSE **hält hin**, IMPERFECT
hielt hin, PERFECT TENSE **hat hingehalten**)
VERB [33]
to hold out
□ Sie hielt ihren Teller hin. She held out her
plate.
■ **jemanden hinhalten** to put somebody off

hinken VERB [38]
to limp

★ **hinlegen** (PERFECT TENSE **hat hingelegt**) VERB
[4]
to put down
□ Leg das Buch dort drüben hin. Put the book
down over there.
■ **sich hinlegen** to lie down

hinnehmen (PRESENT TENSE **nimmt hin**,
IMPERFECT **nahm hin**, PERFECT TENSE **hat
hingenommen**) VERB [52]
to put up with
□ Das kann ich nicht länger hinnehmen. I can't
put up with this any longer.

die **Hinreise** FEM NOUN
outward journey

★ sich **hinsetzen** (PERFECT TENSE **hat sich
hingesetzt**) VERB [15]
to sit down

hinstellen (PERFECT TENSE **hat hingestellt**)
VERB [4]
to put
□ Wo soll ich die Vase hinstellen? Where shall I
put the vase?
■ **Er stellte sich vor den Lehrer hin.** He
went and stood in front of the teacher.

★ **hinten** ADVERB
at the back
□ Er sitzt ganz hinten. He sits at the very back.

★ **hinter** PREPOSITION

Use the accusative to express movement or a
change of place. Use the dative when there is
no change of place.

1 behind
□ Stell dich hinter deine Schwester. Stand
behind your sister. □ Ich saß hinter ihr. I was
sitting behind her.
2 after
□ Wir hatten kurz hinter Köln eine Panne. We
broke down just after Cologne.

hintere ADJECTIVE
back
□ die hinteren Reihen the back rows
■ **der hintere Reifen** the rear tyre

hintereinander ADVERB
one after the other
■ **dreimal hintereinander** three times in a
row

der **Hintergrund** (PL die **Hintergründe**)
MASC NOUN
background

hinterher ADVERB
afterwards

der **Hintern** (GEN des **Hintern**, PL die
Hintern) MASC NOUN
bottom

das **Hinterrad** (PL die **Hinterräder**) NEUT
NOUN
back wheel

hinüber ADVERB
over

hinübergehen (IMPERFECT **ging hinüber**,
PERFECT TENSE **ist hinübergegangen**) VERB [29
to go over

★ **hinunter** ADVERB
down

hinunterschlucken (PERFECT TENSE **hat
hinuntergeschluckt**) VERB [4]
to swallow

der **Hinweg** (PL die **Hinwege**) MASC NOUN
way there
□ auf dem Hinweg on the way there

der **Hinweis** (GEN des **Hinweises**, PL die
Hinweise) MASC NOUN
1 hint
□ Er hat mir nicht den kleinsten Hinweis
gegeben, wie ich das machen soll. He didn't
give me the slightest hint as to how I was
supposed to do it.
2 instruction
□ Hinweise zur Bedienung operating
instructions

hinweisen (IMPERFECT **wies hin**, PERFECT TENSE
hat hingewiesen) VERB
■ **jemanden auf etwas hinweisen** to point
something out to somebody □ Er wies mich
darauf hin, dass ... He pointed out to me that ...

★ **hinzufügen** (PERFECT TENSE **hat hinzugefügt**
VERB [15]
to add

das **Hirn** (PL die **Hirne**) NEUT NOUN
brain

der **Hirsch** (PL die **Hirsche**) MASC NOUN
stag

★ **historisch** ADJECTIVE
historic

★ die **Hitparade** FEM NOUN
charts pl

★ die **Hitze** FEM NOUN
heat

★ **hitzefrei** ADJECTIVE
■ **hitzefrei haben** to have time off school
because of excessively hot weather

die **Hitzewelle** FEM NOUN
heat wave

der **Hitzschlag** (PL die Hitzschläge) MASC NOUN
heatstroke

★ **hoch** ADJECTIVE
▷ see also das **Hoch** NOUN
high
□ zehn Meter hoch ten metres high

Before a noun or after an article, use **hohe**.

□ ein hoher Zaun a high fence
■ **Das ist mir zu hoch.** That's beyond me.

das **Hoch** (PL die Hochs) NEUT NOUN
▷ see also **hoch** ADJECTIVE
1 cheer
□ Ein Hoch auf die Gastgeber! Three cheers for the hosts!
2 area of high pressure
□ ein Hoch über dem Atlantik an area of high pressure over the Atlantic

hochachtungsvoll ADVERB
yours faithfully

hochbegabt ADJECTIVE
extremely talented

das **Hochdeutsch** (GEN des Hochdeutschen) NEUT NOUN
High German

der **Hochdruck** MASC NOUN
high pressure

das **Hochhaus** (GEN des Hochhauses, PL die Hochhäuser) NEUT NOUN
multistorey building

hochheben (IMPERFECT hob hoch, PERFECT TENSE hat hochgehoben) VERB
to lift up

hochladen (PRESENT TENSE lädt hoch, IMPERFECT lud hoch, PERFECT TENSE hat hochgeladen) VERB
to upload (computer)
□ eine Datei hochladen to upload a file

hochnäsig ADJECTIVE
stuck-up

die **Hochsaison** (PL die Hochsaisons) FEM NOUN
high season

die **Hochschule** FEM NOUN
1 college
2 university

der **Hochsommer** (PL die Hochsommer) MASC NOUN
high summer

der **Hochsprung** (PL die Hochsprünge) MASC NOUN
high jump

★ **höchst** ADVERB
extremely

höchste ADJECTIVE
highest
□ Die Zugspitze ist der höchste Berg Deutschlands. The Zugspitze is the highest mountain in Germany.

höchstens ADVERB
at most

die **Höchstgeschwindigkeit** FEM NOUN
maximum speed

höchstwahrscheinlich ADVERB
most probably

★ die **Hochzeit** FEM NOUN
wedding

der **Hochzeitstag** (PL die Hochzeitstage) MASC NOUN
1 wedding day
□ An ihrem Hochzeitstag trug sie einen Hosenanzug in Weiss. She wore a white trouser suit on her wedding day.
2 wedding anniversary
□ Morgen ist ihr zehnter Hochzeitstag. It's their tenth wedding anniversary tomorrow.

★ der **Hocker** (PL die Hocker) MASC NOUN
stool

★ der **Hof** (PL die Höfe) MASC NOUN
1 yard
□ Die Kinder spielen im Hof. The children are playing in the yard.
2 farm
□ Dieser Bauer hat den größten Hof im Dorf. This farmer has the largest farm in the village.

★ **hoffen** VERB [38]
to hope
□ Ich hoffe, er kommt noch. I hope he's coming.
■ **auf etwas hoffen** to hope for something
□ Wir hoffen auf besseres Wetter. We're hoping for better weather.

★ **hoffentlich** ADVERB
hopefully
□ Hoffentlich kommt er bald. Hopefully he'll come soon. □ Das passiert hoffentlich nie wieder. Hopefully that won't happen again.
■ **Hoffentlich nicht.** I hope not.

★ die **Hoffnung** FEM NOUN
hope

hoffnungslos ADJECTIVE
hopeless

★ **hoffnungsvoll** ADJECTIVE
hopeful

★ **höflich** ADJECTIVE
polite

h

Höflichkeit – Hotel

die Höflichkeit FEM NOUN
politeness

hohe ADJECTIVE

> hohe is the form of hoch used before a noun.

high
□ ein hoher Zaun a high fence

die Höhe FEM NOUN
height

der Höhepunkt (PL die Höhepunkte) MASC. NOUN
climax
□ der Höhepunkt des Abends the climax of the evening

★ **höher** ADJECTIVE, ADVERB
higher
□ Die Eiche ist höher als die Birke. The oak tree is taller than the birch tree.

hohl ADJECTIVE
hollow

die Höhle FEM NOUN
cave

★ **holen** VERB [38]
to get
□ Ich hole ihn. I'll get him.
■ jemanden holen lassen to send for somebody

★ **Holland** NEUT NOUN
Holland
■ aus Holland from Holland
■ in Holland in Holland
■ nach Holland to Holland

★ **der Holländer** (PL die Holländer) MASC NOUN
Dutchman
■ Er ist Holländer. He's Dutch.
■ die Holländer the Dutch

★ **die Holländerin** FEM NOUN
Dutchwoman
■ Sie ist Holländerin. She's Dutch.

★ **holländisch** ADJECTIVE
Dutch

die Hölle FEM NOUN
hell

★ **das Holz** (GEN des Holzes, PL die Hölzer) NEUT NOUN
wood

die Holzkohle FEM NOUN
charcoal

die Homepage FEM NOUN
home page

homosexuell ADJECTIVE
homosexual

★ **der Honig** (PL die Honige) MASC NOUN
honey

die Honigmelone FEM NOUN
honeydew melon

der Hopfen (PL die Hopfen) MASC NOUN
hops pl

hörbar ADJECTIVE
audible

das Hörbuch (PL die Hörbücher) NEUT NOUN
audio book

horchen VERB [48]
1 to listen
□ Er horchte auf das kleinste Geräusch. He listened for the slightest noise.
2 to eavesdrop
□ Du hast an der Tür gehorcht! You've been eavesdropping at the door!

★ **hören** VERB [38]
to hear
□ Ich höre dich nicht. I can't hear you.
■ Musik hören to listen to music
■ Radio hören to listen to the radio

★ **der Hörer** (PL die Hörer) MASC NOUN
receiver
□ Sie hat einfach den Hörer aufgelegt. She simply put down the receiver.

der Horizont (PL die Horizonte) MASC NOUN
horizon
□ am Horizont on the horizon

horizontal ADJECTIVE
horizontal

das Horn (PL die Hörner) NEUT NOUN
horn

★ **der Horror** MASC NOUN
horror

★ **der Horrorfilm** (PL die Horrorfilme) MASC NOUN
horror film

der Horrorroman (PL die Horrorromane) MASC NOUN
horror novel

★ **die Hose** FEM NOUN
trousers pl
□ eine Hose a pair of trousers

> **BE CAREFUL!**
> The German word Hose does not mean hose.

★ **der Hosenanzug** (PL die Hosenanzüge) MASC NOUN
trouser suit

die Hosentasche FEM NOUN
trouser pocket

der Hosenträger (PL die Hosenträger) MASC NOUN
braces pl

★ **das Hotel** (PL die Hotels) NEUT NOUN
hotel

Hr. ABBREVIATION (= *Herr*)
Mr

★ **hübsch** ADJECTIVE
pretty

★ der **Hubschrauber** (PL die Hubschrauber)
MASC NOUN
helicopter

der **Huf** (PL die Hufe) MASC NOUN
hoof

das **Hufeisen** (PL die Hufeisen) NEUT NOUN
horseshoe

die **Hüfte** FEM NOUN
hip

★ der **Hügel** (PL die Hügel) MASC NOUN
hill

hügelig ADJECTIVE
hilly

★ das **Huhn** (PL die Hühner) NEUT NOUN
chicken
□ Huhn mit Reis chicken with rice

die **Hummel** FEM NOUN
bumblebee

★ der **Humor** MASC NOUN
humour
■ Humor haben to have a sense of humour

★ **humorvoll** ADJECTIVE
humorous

★ der **Hund** (PL die Hunde) MASC NOUN
dog

hundemüde ADJECTIVE
dog-tired (*Umgangssprache*)

hundert NUMBER
a hundred

★ der **Hunger** MASC NOUN
hunger
■ Hunger haben to be hungry

★ **hungrig** ADJECTIVE
hungry

die **Hupe** FEM NOUN
horn
□ auf die Hupe drücken to sound the horn

hupen VERB [38]
to sound the horn

hüpfen (PERFECT TENSE **ist gehüpft**) VERB [38]
to hop

der **Hürdenlauf** (PL die Hürdenläufe) MASC
NOUN
hurdles *pl*

★ **husten** VERB [2]
▷ *see also* der **Husten** NOUN
to cough

★ der **Husten** MASC NOUN
▷ *see also* **husten** VERB
cough
□ Sie hat Husten. She has a cough.

das **Hustenbonbon** (PL die
Hustenbonbons) NEUT NOUN
cough drop

der **Hustensaft** (PL die Hustensäfte) MASC
NOUN
cough mixture

★ der **Hut** (PL die Hüte) MASC NOUN
▷ *see also* die **Hut** NOUN
hat

★ die **Hut** FEM NOUN
▷ *see also* der **Hut** NOUN
■ auf der Hut sein to be on one's guard

hüten VERB [2]
to look after
□ Silke hütet heute Abend unsere Kinder.
Silke's looking after our children this evening.
■ ein Geheimnis hüten to keep a secret
■ sich hüten, etwas zu tun to take care not
to do something □ Ich werde mich hüten, ihr
das zu sagen. I'll take care not to say that to her.
■ sich hüten vor to be on one's guard against
□ Hüte dich vor ihm, er lügt. Be on your guard
against him, he's a liar.

★ die **Hütte** FEM NOUN
hut

das **Hybridauto** (PL die Hybridautos) NEUT
NOUN
hybrid car

hygienisch ADJECTIVE
hygienic

hysterisch ADJECTIVE
hysterical
□ Sie wurde hysterisch. She became hysterical.

h

Ii

★ ICE ABBREVIATION (= *Intercityexpress*)
Intercity Express train

ich PRONOUN

I
□ Ich weiß nicht. **I don't know.**
■ Ich bin's! **It's me!**

das Icon (PL die Icons) NEUT NOUN
icon (*computer*)
□ ein Icon anklicken **to click on an icon**

ideal ADJECTIVE
▷ *see also* das **Ideal** NOUN
ideal

das Ideal (PL die Ideale) NEUT NOUN
▷ *see also* **ideal** ADJECTIVE
ideal

★ die Idee FEM NOUN
idea

identifizieren (PERFECT TENSE hat
identifiziert) VERB [76]
to identify

identisch ADJECTIVE
identical

die Identität FEM NOUN
identity

der Identitätsdiebstahl MASC NOUN
identity theft
□ Identitätsdiebstahl im Internet ist ein
wachsendes Problem. **Identity theft online is a**
growing problem.

die Ideologie FEM NOUN
ideology

ideologisch ADJECTIVE
ideological

der Idiot (GEN des Idioten, PL die Idioten)
MASC NOUN
idiot

die Idiotin FEM NOUN
idiot

idiotisch ADJECTIVE
idiotic

der Igel (PL die Igel) MASC NOUN
hedgehog

ihm PRONOUN

ihm is the dative of er and es.

1 him
□ Kannst du ihm sagen, wie spät es ist? **Can you**
tell him what the time is?
2 to him
□ Gib es ihm! **Give it to him.**
3 it
□ Das Meerschweinchen hat Hunger, gib ihm
was zu essen. **The guinea pig's hungry, give it**
something to eat.

ihn PRONOUN

ihn is the accusative of er.

him
□ Ich habe ihn gesehen. **I saw him.**

ihnen PRONOUN
▷ *see also* **Ihnen** PRONOUN

ihnen is the dative of sie (plural).

1 them
□ Ich sage es ihnen. **I'll tell them.**
2 to them
□ Gib es ihnen. **Give it to them.**

Ihnen PRONOUN
▷ *see also* **ihnen** PRONOUN

Ihnen is the dative of Sie.

1 you
□ Darf ich Ihnen etwas zu trinken anbieten?
May I offer you something to drink?
2 to you
□ Darf ich Ihnen das geben? **May I give this to**
you?

★ ihr PRONOUN
▷ *see also* **Ihr** ADJECTIVE, **ihr** ADJECTIVE
1 you
□ Habt ihr das gesehen? **Did you see that?**

DID YOU KNOW...?
Use **ihr** when you are talking to several people
of your own age or younger. If in doubt use
the polite form **Sie**.

□ Ihr seid es. **It's you.**

ihr is also the dative of sie (singular).

2 her
□ Kannst du ihr das bitte ausrichten? **Can you**
please tell her? □ Er steht neben ihr. **He's**
standing beside her.
3 to her
□ Gib es ihr. **Give it to her.**

★ = core vocabulary

★ **ihr** ADJECTIVE
▷ *see also* **Ihr** ADJECTIVE, **ihr** PRONOUN

1 her
□ Ihr Vater ist nett. **Her father's nice.** □ Ihre Mutter hat mir das gesagt. **Her mother told me.** □ Das ist ihr Fahrrad. **That's her bike.**

2 hers
□ Das ist nicht ihr Füller, ihrer ist schwarz. **That's not her pen, hers is black.** □ Meine Mutter heißt Ulla, ihre auch. **My mother's called Ulla, so is hers.** □ Mein Fahrrad war kaputt, also habe ich ihres genommen. **My bike was broken, so I took hers.**

3 their
□ Das ist ihr Lehrer. **That's their teacher.** □ Ihre Englischlehrerin ist netter als unsere. **Their English teacher's nicer than ours.** □ Ihr Haus liegt gleich neben unserem. **Their house is right next door to ours.**

4 theirs
□ Das ist nicht ihr Lehrer, ihrer heißt Herr Schulz. **That's not their teacher, theirs is called Mr Schulz.** □ Unsere Schule macht einen Wandertag, ihre nicht. **Our school is going rambling, theirs isn't.**

★ **Ihr** ADJECTIVE
▷ *see also* **ihr** ADJECTIVE, PRONOUN

1 your
□ Ihr Vater ist nett. **Your father's nice.** □ Ihre Mutter hat mir das gesagt. **Your mother told me.** □ Ist das Ihr Fahrrad? **Is that your bike?** □ Leben Ihre Eltern noch? **Are your parents still alive?**

2 yours
□ Das ist nicht Ihr Füller, Ihrer ist hier. **That's not your pen, yours is here.** □ Meine Mutter heißt Ulla, wie heißt Ihre? **My mother's called Ulla, what's yours called?** □ Mein Fahrrad ist kaputt, kann ich Ihres nehmen? **My bike's broken, can I take yours?**

ihretwegen ADVERB
▷ *see also* **Ihretwegen**

ihretwegen refers to **sie** (singular or plural).

1 for her sake
□ Ich habe ihretwegen auf den Urlaub verzichtet. **I went without a holiday for her sake.**

2 on her account
□ Er hat sich ihretwegen furchtbar aufgeregt. **He got terribly upset on her account.**

3 as far as she's concerned
□ Sie sagt, dass du ihretwegen ruhig gehen kannst. **She says that as far as she's concerned you can go.**

4 for their sake
□ Wir haben ihretwegen auf den Urlaub verzichtet. **We went without a holiday for their sake.**

5 on their account
□ Er hat sich ihretwegen furchtbar aufgeregt. **He got terribly upset on their account.**

6 as far as they're concerned
□ Sie sagen, dass du ihretwegen ruhig gehen kannst. **They say that as far as they're concerned you can go.**

Ihretwegen ADVERB
▷ *see also* **ihretwegen**

Ihretwegen refers to **Sie**.

1 for your sake
□ Ich habe Ihretwegen auf den Urlaub verzichtet. **I went without a holiday for your sake.**

2 on your account
□ Er hat sich Ihretwegen furchtbar aufgeregt. **He got terribly upset on your account.**

★ die **Illustrierte** (GEN der **Illustrierten**) FEM NOUN
magazine

im = in dem

★ der **Imbiss** (GEN des **Imbisses**, PL die **Imbisse**) MASC NOUN
snack

★ der **Imbissstand** (PL die **Imbissstände**) MASC NOUN
hot-dog stand

★ die **Imbissstube** FEM NOUN
snack bar

immatrikulieren (PERFECT TENSE hat **immatrikuliert**) VERB [76]
to register (*at university*)

★ **immer** ADVERB
always
□ Du kommst immer zu spät. **You're always late.**
■ **immer wieder** again and again
■ **immer noch** still
■ **immer noch nicht** still not
■ **für immer** forever
■ **immer wenn ich ...** every time I ...
■ **immer schöner** more and more beautiful
■ **immer trauriger** sadder and sadder
■ **wer auch immer** whoever
■ **was auch immer** whatever

immerhin ADVERB
at least

das **Imperfekt** (PL die **Imperfekte**) NEUT NOUN
imperfect

impfen VERB [38]
to vaccinate
□ jemanden gegen etwas impfen **to vaccinate somebody against something**

der **Impfstoff** (PL die **Impfstoffe**) MASC NOUN
vaccine

die **Impfung** FEM NOUN
vaccination

der **Import** (PL die **Importe**) MASC NOUN
import

importieren – Inhaber

importieren (PERFECT TENSE **hat importiert**)
VERB [76]
to import

improvisieren (PERFECT TENSE **hat
improvisiert**) VERB [76]
to improvise

imstande ADJECTIVE
▪ **imstande sein, etwas zu tun** to be able to
do something

★ **in** PREPOSITION

> Use the accusative to express movement or a
> change of place. Use the dative when there is
> no change of place.

1 in
□ Es ist im Schrank. It's in the cupboard. □ Sie
ist in der Stadt. She's in town. □ Sie wurde rot
im Gesicht. She went red in the face.

2 into
□ Lege es in diese Schublade. Put it into this
drawer. □ Sie geht in die Stadt. She's going into
town.
▪ **in der Schule sein** to be at school
▪ **in die Schule gehen** to go to school
▪ **in diesem Jahr** this year
▪ **heute in zwei Wochen** two weeks today
▪ **in sein** to be in □ E-bikes sind jetzt in. E-bikes
are in at the moment.

inbegriffen ADVERB
included

der **Inder** (PL die **Inder**) MASC NOUN
Indian

die **Inderin** FEM NOUN
Indian

der **Indianer** (PL die **Indianer**) MASC NOUN
Native American

die **Indianerin** FEM NOUN
Native American

indianisch ADJECTIVE
Native American

★ das **Indien** NEUT NOUN
India
▪ **aus Indien** from India
▪ **nach Indien** to India

indisch ADJECTIVE
Indian

★ die **Industrie** FEM NOUN
industry

★ das **Industriegebiet** (PL die
Industriegebiete) NEUT NOUN
industrial area

der **Infarkt** (PL die **Infarkte**) MASC NOUN
coronary

die **Infektion** FEM NOUN
infection

der **Infinitiv** (PL die **Infinitive**) MASC NOUN
infinitive

infizieren (PERFECT TENSE **hat infiziert**) VERB
[76]
to infect
□ Sie hat ihren Bruder infiziert. She infected her
brother.
▪ **sich bei jemandem infizieren** to catch
something from somebody

die **Inflation** FEM NOUN
inflation

infolge PREPOSITION

> The preposition **infolge** takes the genitive.

as a result of

infolgedessen ADVERB
consequently

★ die **Informatik** FEM NOUN
computer science

★ der **Informatiker** (PL die **Informatiker**)
MASC NOUN
computer scientist

★ die **Informatikerin** FEM NOUN
computer scientist

★ die **Information** FEM NOUN
information no pl
□ Weitere Informationen lassen wir Ihnen
zukommen. We will send you further
information.

informieren (PERFECT TENSE **hat informiert**)
VERB [76]
to inform
▪ **sich über etwas informieren** to find out
about something □ Ich werde mich über die
Bedingungen informieren. I'll find out about the
terms.
▪ **sich über jemanden informieren** to make
enquiries about somebody □ Ich habe mich
über ihn informiert. I've made enquiries about
him.

infrage ADVERB
▪ **etwas infrage stellen** to question
something
▪ **nicht infrage kommen** to be out of the
question

★ der **Ingenieur** (PL die **Ingenieure**) MASC NOUN
engineer

★ die **Ingenieurin** FEM NOUN
engineer

die **Ingenieurschule** FEM NOUN
school of engineering

der **Ingwer** MASC NOUN
ginger

der **Inhaber** (PL die **Inhaber**) MASC NOUN
owner
□ Wir müssen den Inhaber des Hauses fragen,
ob das geht. We'll have to ask the owner of the
house if it's all right.
▪ **der Inhaber einer Lizenz** the licence
holder

★ = core vocabulary

die **Inhaberin** FEM NOUN
owner

der **Inhalt** (PL die **Inhalte**) MASC NOUN
1 contents *pl*
□ Der Inhalt der Flasche war grün. **The contents of the bottle were green.**
2 content
□ Fasse den Inhalt dieser Geschichte zusammen. **Summarize the content of this story.**
3 volume
□ Berechne den Inhalt des Würfels. **Calculate the volume of the cube.**

die **Inhaltsangabe** FEM NOUN
summary

das **Inhaltsverzeichnis** (GEN des **Inhaltsverzeichnisses**, PL die **Inhaltsverzeichnisse**) NEUT NOUN
table of contents

inkl. ABBREVIATION (= *inklusive*)
incl.

★ **inklusive** PREPOSITION, ADVERB

The preposition **inklusive** takes the genitive.

1 inclusive of
□ ein Computer inklusive Bildschirm **a computer inclusive of monitor**
2 included
□ Die Bedienung ist inklusive. **Service is included.**

★ das **Inland** NEUT NOUN
■ im In- und Ausland **at home and abroad**

das **Inlineskate** (PL die **Inlineskates**) NEUT NOUN
Rollerblade®

das **Inlineskaten** NEUT NOUN
rollerblading

★ **innen** ADVERB
inside

die **Innenpolitik** FEM NOUN
domestic policy

innenpolitisch ADJECTIVE
internal

★ die **Innenstadt** (PL die **Innenstädte**) FEM NOUN
town centre

innere ADJECTIVE
internal
□ innere Blutungen **internal bleeding** □ die inneren Angelegenheiten des Landes **the internal matters of the country**

★ **innerhalb (1)** PREPOSITION
▷ *see also* **innerhalb** ADVERB

The preposition **innerhalb** takes the genitive.

1 within
2 during
□ Der Bus fährt nur innerhalb der Woche, nicht an Wochenenden. **The bus only runs during the week, not at the weekend.**

★ **innerhalb (2)** ADVERB
▷ *see also* **innerhalb** PREPOSITION
■ **innerhalb von** within
□ Das muss innerhalb von zwei Tagen gemacht werden. **That must be done within two days.**

inoffiziell ADJECTIVE
unofficial

ins = in das

★ **insbesondere** ADVERB
particularly

die **Inschrift** FEM NOUN
inscription

★ das **Insekt** (PL die **Insekten**) NEUT NOUN
insect

★ die **Insel** FEM NOUN
island

★ **insgesamt** ADVERB
in all
□ Er hat insgesamt drei Fahrräder. **He has three bikes in all.** □ Insgesamt waren dreihundert Leute gekommen. **In all, three hundred people came.**

der **Instinkt** (PL die **Instinkte**) MASC NOUN
instinct

★ das **Instrument** (PL die **Instrumente**) NEUT NOUN
instrument

intellektuell ADJECTIVE
intellectual

★ **intelligent** ADJECTIVE
intelligent

die **Intelligenz** FEM NOUN
intelligence

intensiv ADJECTIVE
intensive

★ der **Intercityexpress** (GEN des **Intercityexpresses**, PL die **Intercityexpresse**) MASC NOUN
Intercity Express train

★ der **Intercityzug** (PL die **Intercityzüge**) MASC NOUN
Intercity train

★ **interessant** ADJECTIVE
interesting

★ das **Interesse** (PL die **Interessen**) NEUT NOUN
interest
■ **Interesse haben an** to be interested in
□ Hast du Interesse an einem gebrauchten Notebook? **Are you interested in a used notebook?** □ Jonathan scheint Interesse an dir zu haben. **Jonathan seems to be interested in you.**

★ **interessieren** (PERFECT TENSE hat **interessiert**) VERB [76]

i

to interest
□ Es interessiert mich, was du in den Ferien erlebt hast. I'm interested to know what you did in your holidays.
■ **sich interessieren für** to be interested in
□ Ich interessiere mich für Kunst. I'm interested in art.

★ das **Internat** (PL die **Internate**) NEUT NOUN
boarding school

international ADJECTIVE
international

★ das **Internet** NEUT NOUN
internet

der **Internet-Anbieter** (PL die **Internet-Anbieter**) MASC NOUN
Internet Service Provider

der **Internetbenutzer** (PL die **Internetbenutzer**) MASC NOUN
internet user

die **Internetbenutzerin** FEM NOUN
internet user

das **Internet-Café** (PL die **Internet-Cafés**) NEUT NOUN
internet café

das **Internet-Mobbing** NEUT NOUN
online bullying

die **Internetseite** (PL die **Internetseiten**) FEM NOUN
web page

interpretieren (PERFECT TENSE **hat interpretiert**) VERB [76]
to interpret

intransitiv ADJECTIVE
intransitive

inwiefern ADVERB
how far
□ Ich weiß nicht, inwiefern das stimmt. I don't know how far that's right.

★ **inzwischen** ADVERB
meanwhile

der **Irak** MASC NOUN
Iraq
■ **aus dem Irak** from Iraq
■ **im Irak** in Iraq
■ **in den Irak** to Iraq

irakisch ADJECTIVE
Iraqi

der **Iran** MASC NOUN
Iran
■ **aus dem Iran** from Iran
■ **im Iran** in Iran
■ **in den Iran** to Iran

iranisch ADJECTIVE
Iranian

★ der **Ire** (GEN des **Iren**, PL die **Iren**) MASC NOUN
Irishman
■ **die Iren** the Irish

★ **irgend** ADVERB
at all
□ Komm, wenn es irgend geht. Come if it's at all possible.

★ **irgendein** ADJECTIVE
1 some
□ Irgendein Mann hat mir das gesagt. Some man told me. □ Irgendeine Ausrede wird dir schon einfallen. You'll think of some excuse.
2 any
□ Ich will nicht irgendeinen Computer. I don't just want any computer. □ Gibt es nicht irgendeine Möglichkeit? Isn't there any chance? □ Welchen Kuli willst du? — Irgendeinen. Which pen do you want? — Any one.

irgendetwas PRONOUN
1 something
□ irgendetwas Schönes something nice
2 anything
□ Hast du irgendetwas gehört? Did you hear anything?

irgendjemand PRONOUN
1 somebody
□ Das hat mir irgendjemand gesagt. Somebody told me.
2 anybody
□ Hast du irgendjemanden gesehen? Did you see anybody?

★ **irgendwann** ADVERB
sometime

★ **irgendwas** PRONOUN
1 something
□ Er murmelte irgendwas. He murmured something.
2 anything
□ Was soll ich anziehen? — Irgendwas. What shall I wear? — Anything.

★ **irgendwie** ADVERB
somehow

★ **irgendwo** ADVERB
somewhere

★ die **Irin** FEM NOUN
Irishwoman

★ **irisch** ADJECTIVE
Irish

★ **Irland** NEUT NOUN
Ireland
■ **aus Irland** from Ireland
■ **in Irland** in Ireland
■ **nach Irland** to Ireland

die **Ironie** FEM NOUN
irony

ironisch ADJECTIVE
ironic
□ Das war ironisch gemeint. That was meant to be ironic.

irre ADJECTIVE, ADVERB

1 mad
□ Wer ist denn auf diese irre Idee gekommen?
Who thought up this mad idea?

2 fantastic
□ Das war ein irres Konzert. **That was a fantastic concert.**

3 incredibly
□ Er ist irre schnell gefahren. **He drove incredibly fast.** □ Die Party war irre gut. **The party was incredibly good.**

irreführen (PERFECT TENSE **hat irregeführt**)
VERB [4]
to mislead

irren VERB [38]

> Use **haben** to form the perfect tense for 'to be mistaken' but **sein** for 'to wander about'.

to wander about
□ Sie ist durch die Straßen geirrt. **She wandered about the streets.**
■ **sich irren** to be mistaken □ Du hast dich geirrt. **You were mistaken.**

der **Irrtum** (PL die **Irrtümer**) MASC NOUN
mistake

der **Islam** MASC NOUN
Islam

Island NEUT NOUN
Iceland
■ **nach Island** to Iceland

Israel NEUT NOUN
Israel
■ **aus Israel** from Israel
■ **nach Israel** to Israel

der/die **Israeli** (PL die **Israelis**) MASC/FEM NOUN
Israeli
□ Sie ist mit einem Israeli verheiratet. **She is married to an Israeli.**

israelisch ADJECTIVE
Israeli

isst VERB ▷ see **essen**

ist VERB ▷ see **sein**

★ **Italien** NEUT NOUN
Italy
■ **aus Italien** from Italy
■ **in Italien** in Italy
■ **nach Italien** to Italy

★ der **Italiener** (PL die **Italiener**) MASC NOUN
Italian

★ die **Italienerin** FEM NOUN
Italian

★ **italienisch** ADJECTIVE
Italian

i

Jj

★ **ja** ADVERB
  1 yes
  □ Hast du das gesehen? — Ja. Did you see that?
  — Yes, I did.
  ▪ **Ich glaube ja.** I think so.
  2 really?
  □ Ich habe mir ein neues Auto gekauft. — Ach
  ja? I've bought a new car. — Really?
  ▪ **Du kommst, ja?** You're coming, aren't you?
  ▪ **Sei ja vorsichtig!** Do be careful.
  ▪ **Sie wissen ja, dass ...** As you know, ...
  ▪ **Tu das ja nicht!** Don't you dare do that!
  ▪ **Ich habe es ja gewusst.** I just knew it.
  ▪ **ja, also ...** well ... □ Ja, also wenn ihr alle geht,
  dann gehe ich mit. Well, if you're all going, then
  I'm going too.

die **Jacht** FEM NOUN
  yacht

★ die **Jacke** FEM NOUN
  1 jacket
  □ Sie trug einen blauen Rock und eine schwarze
  Jacke. She was wearing a blue skirt and a black
  jacket.
  2 cardigan
  □ Wenn es dir kalt ist, solltest du eine Jacke
  anziehen. If you're cold, you should put on a
  cardigan.

das **Jackett** (PL die **Jacketts**) NEUT NOUN
  jacket

die **Jagd** (PL die **Jagden**) FEM NOUN
  1 hunt
  □ Er fiel während der Jagd vom Pferd. He fell off
  his horse during the hunt.
  2 hunting
  □ Alan geht oft zur Jagd. Alan often goes
  hunting.

jagen VERB [38]

  Use **haben** to form the perfect tense for 'to
  hunt' or 'to chase' but **sein** for 'to race'.

  1 to hunt
  □ Sonntags gehen sie jagen. They go hunting
  on Sundays. □ Meine Katze jagt Mäuse. My cat
  hunts mice.
  2 to chase
  □ Die Polizei hat die Bankräuber gejagt, aber
  nicht eingeholt. The police chased the bank
  robbers but didn't catch them.

  3 to race
  □ Wir sind mit ihr ins Krankenhaus gejagt. We
  raced with her to the hospital.
  ▪ **Damit kann man mich jagen.** I can't stand
  that.

★ das **Jahr** (PL die **Jahre**) NEUT NOUN
  year
  □ Ich bin vierzehn Jahre alt. I'm fourteen years
  old.
  ▪ **die Neunzigerjahre** the nineties

★ die **Jahreszeit** FEM NOUN
  season
  ▪ **zu jeder Jahreszeit** throughout the year
  □ Man bekommt inzwischen zu jeder Jahreszeit
  Erdbeeren. You can now get strawberries
  throughout the year.

  der **Jahrgang** (PL die **Jahrgänge**) MASC NOUN
  year
  □ Sie ist mein Jahrgang. She was born in the
  same year as me. □ Welcher Jahrgang bist du?
  In which year were you born?

★ das **Jahrhundert** (PL die **Jahrhunderte**)
  NEUT NOUN
  century

★ **jährlich** ADJECTIVE, ADVERB
  yearly

★ der **Jahrmarkt** (PL die **Jahrmärkte**) MASC
  NOUN
  funfair

★ das **Jahrtausend** (PL die **Jahrtausende**)
  NEUT NOUN
  millennium

  jähzornig ADJECTIVE
  hot-tempered

  die **Jalousie** FEM NOUN
  Venetian blind

  der **Jammer** MASC NOUN
  misery
  ▪ **Es ist ein Jammer, dass ...** It's a crying
  shame that ...

  jammern VERB [88]
  to whine
  □ Hör auf zu jammern! Stop whining.

★ der **Januar** (GEN des **Januar** or **Januars**, PL die
  Januare) MASC NOUN
  January

★ = core vocabulary

Japan – joggen

□ im Januar **in January** □ am dritten Januar **on the third of January** □ Ulm, den 3. Januar 2019 **Ulm, 3 January 2019** □ Heute ist der dritte Januar. **Today is the third of January.**

★ **Japan** NEUT NOUN
Japan
■ aus Japan **from Japan**
■ nach Japan **to Japan**

der **Japaner** (PL die **Japaner**) MASC NOUN
Japanese

die **Japanerin** FEM NOUN
Japanese

japanisch ADJECTIVE
▷ see also das **Japanisch** NOUN
Japanese

das **Japanisch** (GEN des **Japanischen**) NEUT NOUN
▷ see also **japanisch** ADJECTIVE
Japanese

jaulen VERB [38]
to howl

★ **jawohl** ADVERB
yes

★ **je** ADVERB, CONJUNCTION
1 ever
□ Warst du je in Italien? **Have you ever been to Italy?** □ Hast du so was je gesehen? **Did you ever see anything like it?** □ besser denn je **better than ever**
2 each
□ Wir haben je zwei Stück bekommen. **We got two pieces each.** □ Sie zahlten je zehn Euro. **They paid ten euros each.**
■ je nach **depending on** □ Je nach Größe sind sie verschieden teuer. **Prices vary depending on size.**
■ je nachdem **it depends** □ Wir kommen vielleicht etwas später, je nachdem, wie lange wir unterwegs sind. **We'll perhaps be a little late, it depends how long we take to get there.**
■ je nachdem, ob ... **depending on whether ...** □ Wir kommen vielleicht mit den Kindern, je nachdem ob sie Lust haben. **We'll come with the children depending on whether they feel like it or not.**
■ je ... umso ... **the ... the ...** □ Je schneller er fuhr, umso mehr Angst hatte sie. **The faster he drove, the more frightened she was.**
■ je eher, desto besser **the sooner the better**

★ die **Jeans** (PL die **Jeans**) FEM NOUN
jeans pl
■ eine Jeans **a pair of jeans** □ Ich habe mir eine neue Jeans gekauft. **I've bought myself a new pair of jeans.**

jede PRONOUN
1 every
□ Jeder Schüler bekommt ein Zeugnis. **Every pupil receives a report.** □ Ich besuche sie jede Woche. **I visit her every week.** □ Er gab jedem

Mädchen ein Bonbon. **He gave every girl a sweet.**
■ jeder **everybody** □ Jeder weiß, dass das nicht erlaubt ist. **Everybody knows that that's not allowed.**
2 each
□ Jeder von euch bekommt ein Stück. **Each of you will get a piece.** □ Jede seiner Freundinnen war anders. **Each of his girlfriends was different.** □ Jedes der Kinder hat mir etwas geschenkt. **Each child gave me something.**
■ jedes Mal **every time**

jedenfalls ADVERB
in any case

jederzeit ADVERB
at any time

jedoch ADVERB
however

jemals ADVERB
ever

★ **jemand** PRONOUN
1 somebody
□ Jemand hat mir gesagt, dass du krank bist. **Somebody told me that you were ill.**
2 anybody
□ War jemand zu Hause? **Was anybody at home?**

jene PRONOUN
1 that
□ in jener Zeit **at that time**
2 those
□ in jenen Tagen **in those days**
3 that one
□ Ich möchte jenen hier. **I'd like that one.**
4 those ones
□ Kann ich jene anprobieren? **Can I try those ones on?**

★ **jetzt** ADVERB
now
□ Sie ist jetzt in der Schweiz. **She's in Switzerland now.**

jeweils ADVERB
■ jeweils zwei zusammen **two at a time**
■ zu jeweils fünf Euro **at five euros each**

★ der **Job** (PL die **Jobs**) MASC NOUN
(Umgangssprache)
job

das **Jod** NEUT NOUN
iodine

jodeln VERB [88]
to yodel

★ **joggen** VERB [48]

Use haben for the perfect tense when you describe the activity and sein when you describe the motion.

to jog
□ Früher habe ich oft gejoggt. **I used to jog a lot.**

German-English

j

Numbers in brackets refer to verb tables on pages 697 to 706. **145**

☐ Wir sind durch den Wald gejoggt. We jogged through the woods.

★ das **Jogging** NEUT NOUN
jogging

der **Jogginganzug** (PL die **Jogginganzüge**) MASC NOUN
tracksuit

★ der **Joghurt** (PL die **Joghurts**) MASC NOUN
yoghurt

★ der **Jogurt** (PL die **Jogurts**) MASC NOUN
yogurt

die **Johannisbeere** FEM NOUN
redcurrant
☐ Johannisbeeren sind mir zu sauer. Redcurrants are too sour for me.
■ **Schwarze Johannisbeere** blackcurrant

★ der **Journalist** (GEN des **Journalisten**, PL die **Journalisten**) MASC NOUN
journalist

★ die **Journalistin** FEM NOUN
journalist

jubeln VERB [34]
to rejoice

das **Jubiläum** (PL die **Jubiläen**) NEUT NOUN
anniversary
☐ Nächstes Jahr feiert unsere Schule ihr zwanzigjähriges Jubiläum. Our school's celebrating its twentieth anniversary next year.

jucken VERB [38]
to be itchy
☐ Meine Nase juckt. My nose is itchy. ☐ Es juckt mich am Arm. My arm's itchy.

der **Jude** (GEN des **Juden**, PL die **Juden**) MASC NOUN
Jew

die **Jüdin** FEM NOUN
Jew

jüdisch ADJECTIVE
Jewish

★ die **Jugend** FEM NOUN
youth
☐ In meiner Jugend habe ich Fußball gespielt. I used to play football in my youth. ☐ die Jugend von heute the youth of today

★ die **Jugendherberge** FEM NOUN
youth hostel

★ der **Jugendklub** (PL die **Jugendklubs**) MASC NOUN
youth club

jugendlich ADJECTIVE
youthful
☐ Er hat ein jugendliches Gesicht. He has a youthful face. ☐ Sie sieht sehr jugendlich aus. She looks very youthful.

★ der/die **Jugendliche** (GEN des/der **Jugendlichen**, PL die **Jugendlichen**) MASC/FEM NOUN
teenager
☐ Ich habe einen Jugendlichen dabei beobachtet, wie er die Wand besprüht hat. I watched a teenager spray the wall.

★ das **Jugendzentrum** (PL die **Jugendzentren**) NEUT NOUN
youth centre

★ der **Juli** (GEN des **Juli** or **Julis**, PL die **Julis**) MASC NOUN
July
☐ im Juli in July ☐ am dritten Juli on the third of July ☐ Ulm, den 3. Juli 2019 Ulm, 3 July 2019 ☐ Heute ist der dritte Juli. Today is the third of July.

★ **jung** ADJECTIVE
young
☐ Er ist drei Jahre jünger als ich. He's three years younger than me.

★ der **Junge** (GEN des **Jungen**, PL die **Jungen**) MASC NOUN
▷ see also das **Junge** NOUN
boy
☐ In unserer Klasse gibt es zehn Jungen und fünfzehn Mädchen. There are ten boys and fifteen girls in our class. ☐ Ich sehe den Jungen nicht. I can't see the boy.

★ das **Junge** (GEN des **Jungen**, PL die **Jungen**) NEUT NOUN
▷ see also der **Junge** NOUN
young animal
■ **eine Löwin mit ihren Jungen** a lioness with her young

die **Jungfrau** FEM NOUN
1 virgin
2 Virgo
☐ Veronika ist Jungfrau. Veronika's Virgo.

jüngste ADJECTIVE
1 youngest
☐ Er ist der jüngste Schüler der Klasse. He's the youngest pupil in the class.
2 latest
☐ die jüngsten Entwicklungen the latest developments

★ der **Juni** (GEN des **Juni** or **Junis**, PL die **Junis**) MASC NOUN
June
☐ im Juni in June ☐ am fünfzehnten Juni on the fifteenth of June ☐ Ulm, den 3. Juni 2019 Ulm, 3 June 2019 ☐ Heute ist der dritte Juni. Today is the third of June.

★ der **Juwelier** (PL die **Juweliere**) MASC NOUN
jeweller

Kk

das **Kabel** (PL die **Kabel**) NEUT NOUN
1 wire
□ Das Kabel des Telefons ist zu kurz. The telephone wire is too short.
2 cable
□ Das Kabel der Seilbahn muss regelmäßig überprüft werden. The cable on the cable car has to be checked regularly.

das **Kabelfernsehen** NEUT NOUN
cable television

kabellos ADJECTIVE
wireless
□ kabellose Lautsprecher wireless speakers

★ die **Kabine** FEM NOUN
1 cabin
□ Wir hatten zu zweit eine Kabine auf dem Schiff. The two of us shared a cabin on the ship.
2 cubicle
□ Sie können das Kleid dort hinten in der Kabine anprobieren. You can try the dress on in the cubicle over there.

der **Käfer** (PL die **Käfer**) MASC NOUN
beetle

★ der **Kaffee** (PL die **Kaffees** or **Kaffee**) MASC NOUN
coffee
□ Herr Ober, zwei Kaffee bitte. Two coffees please, waiter.

★ die **Kaffeekanne** FEM NOUN
coffeepot

★ die **Kaffeepause** FEM NOUN
coffee break
□ Wir machten Kaffeepause. We had a coffee break.

★ der **Käfig** (PL die **Käfige**) MASC NOUN
cage

kahl ADJECTIVE
bald
□ sein kahler Kopf his bald head
■ die kahlen Bäume im Winter the bare trees in winter
■ kahl geschoren shaven

★ der **Kakao** (PL die **Kakaos** or **Kakao**) MASC NOUN
cocoa
□ Herr Ober, zwei Kakao bitte. Two cups of cocoa please, waiter.

das **Kalb** (PL die **Kälber**) NEUT NOUN
calf (*animal*)

★ das **Kalbfleisch** NEUT NOUN
veal

★ der **Kalender** (PL die **Kalender**) MASC NOUN
1 calendar
□ An der Wand hing ein Kalender mit Bildern von Picasso. A calendar with pictures by Picasso was hanging on the wall.
2 diary
□ Sie holte ihren Kalender aus der Tasche. She got her diary out of her bag.

der **Kalk** MASC NOUN
1 lime (*stone*)
2 calcium
□ Ein Mangel an Kalk kann zu schlechten Zähnen führen. A lack of calcium can lead to bad teeth.

die **Kalorie** FEM NOUN
calorie

kalorienarm ADJECTIVE
low in calories

★ **kalt** ADJECTIVE
cold
□ Heute ist es kälter als gestern. It's colder today than yesterday. □ Mir ist kalt. I'm cold.
■ etwas kalt stellen to chill something □ Du solltest den Weißwein kalt stellen. You should chill the white wine.

★ die **Kälte** FEM NOUN
1 cold
□ Bei dieser Kälte gehe ich nicht raus. I'm not going out in this cold.
2 coldness
□ Die Kälte des Wassers hat uns vom Baden abgehalten. The coldness of the water stopped us from bathing.

kam VERB ▷ see **kommen**

das **Kamel** (PL die **Kamele**) NEUT NOUN
camel

★ die **Kamera** (PL die **Kameras**) FEM NOUN
camera

der **Kamerad** (GEN des **Kameraden**, PL die **Kameraden**) MASC NOUN
friend

die **Kameradin** FEM NOUN
friend

k

Numbers in brackets refer to verb tables on pages 697 to 706.

Kamin – kaputt

der Kamin (PL die Kamine) MASC NOUN
open fire
- **Wir saßen am Kamin.** We sat by the fire.

★ **der Kamm** (PL die Kämme) MASC NOUN
comb

★ **kämmen** VERB [38]
to comb
□ Sie kann es nicht leiden, wenn man sie kämmt. She can't stand having her hair combed. □ Ich muss meiner kleinen Schwester die Haare kämmen. I have to comb my little sister's hair.
- **sich kämmen** to comb one's hair

der Kampf (PL die Kämpfe) MASC NOUN
1 fight
□ der Kampf zwischen Tyson und Bruno the fight between Tyson and Bruno
2 contest
□ Dieses Jahr findet der Kampf um den Pokal in Großbritannien statt. The contest for the cup is taking place in Great Britain this year.
3 struggle
□ Ich habe die Prüfung geschafft, aber es war ein Kampf. I passed the exam but it was a struggle.

kämpfen VERB [38]
to fight

Kanada NEUT NOUN
Canada
- **aus Kanada** from Canada
- **in Kanada** in Canada
- **nach Kanada** to Canada

der Kanadier (PL die Kanadier) MASC NOUN
Canadian

die Kanadierin FEM NOUN
Canadian

kanadisch ADJECTIVE
Canadian

★ **der Kanal** (PL die Kanäle) MASC NOUN
1 canal
□ Diese beiden Flüsse sind durch einen Kanal verbunden. These two rivers are connected by a canal.
2 drain

die Kanalinseln FEM PL NOUN
the Channel Islands pl

★ **der Kanaltunnel** (PL die Kanaltunnel) MASC NOUN
the Channel Tunnel

★ **der Kanarienvogel** (PL die Kanarienvögel) MASC NOUN
canary

der Kandidat (GEN des Kandidaten, PL die Kandidaten) MASC NOUN
candidate

die Kandidatin FEM NOUN
candidate

das Känguru (PL die Kängurus) NEUT NOUN
kangaroo

★ **das Kaninchen** (PL die Kaninchen) NEUT NOUN
rabbit

der Kanister (PL die Kanister) MASC NOUN
can
□ ein Benzinkanister a petrol can

kann VERB ▷ see **können**

★ **das Kännchen** (PL die Kännchen) NEUT NOUN
pot
□ ein Kännchen Kaffee a pot of coffee
- **ein Kännchen mit Milch** a jug of milk

★ **die Kanne** FEM NOUN
1 pot (for coffee)
2 churn (for milk)
3 watering can

die Kante FEM NOUN
edge

★ **die Kantine** FEM NOUN
canteen
□ Mittags isst sie in der Kantine. She eats in the canteen at lunchtime.

★ **das Kanu** (PL die Kanus) NEUT NOUN
canoe
- **Kanu fahren** to go canoeing

der Kanzler (PL die Kanzler) MASC NOUN
chancellor

die Kanzlerin FEM NOUN
chancellor

★ **kapieren** (PERFECT TENSE hat kapiert) VERB [76]
to understand
□ Ich habe heute in Mathe nichts kapiert. I didn't understand anything in maths today. □ Hast du das endlich kapiert? Have you finally understood?

das Kapital NEUT NOUN
capital (money)

der Kapitän (PL die Kapitäne) MASC NOUN
captain

die Kapitänin FEM NOUN
captain

das Kapitel (PL die Kapitel) NEUT NOUN
chapter

die Kappe FEM NOUN
cap

★ **kaputt** ADJECTIVE
1 broken
□ Mein Computer ist kaputt. My computer's broken.
- **Am Auto ist etwas kaputt.** There's something wrong with the car.
- **kaputt machen** to break □ Mach mir bloß mein Fahrrad nicht kaputt! Don't you dare break

★ = core vocabulary

my bike! □ Sie hat den Teller kaputt gemacht.
She's broken the plate.

2 knackered (*Umgangssprache*)
□ Ich bin von der Wanderung total kaputt. I'm
completely knackered after the walk.

kaputtgehen (IMPERFECT **ging kaputt**,
PERFECT TENSE **ist kaputtgegangen**) VERB [29]

1 to break
□ Mein Computer ist gestern kaputtgegangen.
My computer broke yesterday.

2 to wear out (*material*)

3 to die (*plant*)

4 to break up (*relationship*)

★ **kaputtmachen** (PERFECT TENSE **hat
kaputtgemacht**) VERB [48]
to wear out
□ Die viele Arbeit macht mich noch kaputt. All
this work is wearing me out.
■ **sich kaputtmachen** to wear oneself out
□ Du solltest mal Ferien machen, du machst
dich ja kaputt. You should take a holiday, you're
wearing yourself out.

die **Kapuze** FEM NOUN
hood
□ ein Anorak mit Kapuze an anorak with a hood

★ der **Karfreitag** MASC NOUN
Good Friday

die **Karibik** FEM NOUN
the Caribbean
□ Wir fahren in die Karibik. We're going to the
Caribbean. □ Wir machen in der Karibik Ferien.
We're spending our holidays in the Caribbean.

★ **kariert** ADJECTIVE

1 checked
□ Sie hatte ein kariertes Kleid an. She was
wearing a checked dress.

2 squared
□ Für Mathe brauchst du ein Heft mit kariertem
Papier. You need an exercise book with squared
paper for maths.

die **Karies** FEM NOUN
tooth decay
□ Sie hat Karies. She has tooth decay.

★ der **Karneval** (PL die **Karnevale** or
Karnevals) MASC NOUN
carnival

DID YOU KNOW...?
The German carnival season lasts from 11
November to Shrove Tuesday but most
events, fancy-dress processions and parties
take place in the week leading up to Ash
Wednesday.

das **Karo** (PL die **Karos**) NEUT NOUN

1 square
□ Das Muster bestand aus kleinen Karos. The
pattern was made up of little squares.

2 diamonds *sing*
□ Karo ist Trumpf. Diamonds is trumps.

★ die **Karotte** FEM NOUN
carrot

die **Karriere** FEM NOUN
career
■ **Karriere machen** to get on □ Für Frauen ist
es schwerer, in der Politik Karriere zu machen.
It's harder for women to get on in politics.

★ die **Karte** FEM NOUN

1 card
□ Sie hat uns aus dem Urlaub eine Karte
geschickt. She sent us a card from her holiday.
□ Ich weiß nicht, welche Karte ich ausspielen
soll. I don't know which card I should play.
■ **die Gelbe Karte** the yellow card
■ **die Rote Karte** the red card

2 map
□ Sieh mal auf der Karte nach, wie weit wir
noch fahren müssen. Look on the map to see
how far we still have to go.

3 menu
□ Der Ober brachte uns die Karte. The waiter
brought us the menu.

4 ticket
□ Kannst du Karten fürs Konzert besorgen? Can
you get us tickets for the concert? □ Ich fahre
morgen nach Bonn, die Karte habe ich schon
gekauft. I'm going to Bonn tomorrow, I've
already bought my ticket.
■ **alles auf eine Karte setzen** to put all one's
eggs in one basket

das **Kartenspiel** (PL die **Kartenspiele**) NEUT
NOUN

1 card game
□ Ich habe ein neues Kartenspiel gelernt. I've
learned a new card game.

2 pack of cards
□ Hast du ein Kartenspiel da? Have you got a
pack of cards?

★ die **Kartoffel** FEM NOUN
potato

★ der **Kartoffelbrei** MASC NOUN
mashed potatoes *pl*

★ der **Kartoffelsalat** (PL die **Kartoffelsalate**)
MASC NOUN
potato salad

★ der **Karton** (PL die **Kartons**) MASC NOUN

1 cardboard
□ Wir haben das Bild auf Karton aufgezogen.
We mounted the picture on cardboard.

2 cardboard box
□ Sie packte die Bücher in einen Karton. She
packed the books in a cardboard box.

das **Karussell** (PL die **Karussells**) NEUT NOUN
roundabout
□ Ich möchte Karussell fahren. I'd like to go on
the roundabout.

★ der **Käse** (PL die **Käse**) MASC NOUN
cheese

k

der **Käsekuchen** (PL die Käsekuchen) MASC NOUN
cheesecake

die **Kaserne** FEM NOUN
barracks pl
□ In unserer Nähe gibt es eine Kaserne. There's a barracks near us.

★ die **Kasse** FEM NOUN
1 till
□ Die meisten Geschäfte haben elektronische Kassen. Most shops have electronic tills.
2 checkout
□ an der Kasse at the checkout □ Es war nur eine von fünf Kassen besetzt. Only one of the five checkouts was open.
3 box office
□ Sie können Ihre Karten telefonisch vorbestellen und an der Kasse abholen. You may order your tickets in advance and collect them from the box office.
4 ticket office
□ Karten fürs Fußballspiel bekommen Sie auch an der Kasse des Stadions. You can also get tickets for the football match at the ticket office in the stadium.
5 cash box
□ Alle Barbeträge bewahren wir in dieser Kasse auf. We keep all the cash in this cash box.
6 health insurance
□ Bei welcher Kasse sind Sie versichert? What health insurance have you got?

DID YOU KNOW...?
In Germany one can choose between different health insurance schemes. There is no 'National Health Service'.

■ gut bei Kasse sein to be in the money (Umgangssprache)

★ der **Kassenzettel** (PL die Kassenzettel) MASC NOUN
receipt

kassieren (PERFECT TENSE hat kassiert) VERB [76]
to take
□ Die Polizei hat seinen Führerschein kassiert. The police took his driving licence.
■ Der Parkwächter hat zehn Euro Parkgebühren kassiert. The parking attendant charged us ten euros to park the car.
■ Darf ich kassieren? Would you like to pay now?

★ der **Kassierer** (PL die Kassierer) MASC NOUN
cashier

★ die **Kassiererin** FEM NOUN
cashier

die **Kastanie** FEM NOUN
1 chestnut
2 chestnut tree

der **Kasten** (PL die Kästen) MASC NOUN
1 box
□ Er warf den Brief in den Kasten. He put the letter in the box.
2 case
□ Sie legte die Geige zurück in den Kasten. She put the violin back in its case.
■ ein Kasten Bier a crate of beer

der **Katalog** (PL die Kataloge) MASC NOUN
catalogue

der **Katalysator** (PL die Katalysatoren) MASC NOUN
catalytic converter
□ ein Auto mit Katalysator a car with catalytic converter

katastrophal ADJECTIVE, ADVERB
catastrophic
■ katastrophal schlecht appallingly bad

die **Katastrophe** FEM NOUN
disaster

die **Kategorie** FEM NOUN
category

der **Kater** (PL die Kater) MASC NOUN
1 tomcat
□ Wir haben einen Kater und eine Katze. We have a tomcat and a female cat.
2 hangover
□ Nach der Party hatte ich einen furchtbaren Kater. I had a terrible hangover after the party.

★ die **Kathedrale** FEM NOUN
cathedral

katholisch ADJECTIVE
Catholic

★ die **Katze** FEM NOUN
cat
■ für die Katz for nothing

kauen VERB [38]
to chew

der **Kauf** (PL die Käufe) MASC NOUN
purchase
□ der Kauf eines Autos the purchase of a car
■ ein guter Kauf a bargain

★ **kaufen** VERB [38]
to buy

der **Käufer** (PL die Käufer) MASC NOUN
buyer

die **Käuferin** FEM NOUN
buyer

★ die **Kauffrau** FEM NOUN
businesswoman

★ das **Kaufhaus** (GEN des Kaufhauses, PL die Kaufhäuser) NEUT NOUN
department store

★ der **Kaufmann** (PL die Kaufleute) MASC NOUN
1 businessman
□ ein erfolgreicher Kaufmann a successful businessman

2 grocer
□ zum Kaufmann gehen to go to the grocer's

★ der **Kaugummi** (PL die **Kaugummis**) MASC NOUN
chewing gum *no pl*

★ **kaum** ADVERB
hardly
□ Ich habe kaum geschlafen. I hardly slept.

★ die **Kegelbahn** FEM NOUN
skittle alley

★ **kegeln** VERB [88]
to play skittles

die **Kehle** FEM NOUN
throat

der **Keil** (PL die **Keile**) MASC NOUN
wedge

der **Keim** (PL die **Keime**) MASC NOUN
1 shoot
□ Eine Woche nach der Aussaat zeigen sich die ersten Keime. The first shoots appear a week after sowing.
2 germ
□ Das Mittel tötete die Keime ab. The medicine killed the germs.
■ **etwas im Keim ersticken** to nip something in the bud

★ **kein** ADJECTIVE, PRONOUN

When combined with a noun, kein is used for masculine and neuter nouns, keine for feminine and plural nouns. On its own keiner is used for masculine, keine for feminine and plural, and keines or keins for neuter.

1 not … any
□ Ich habe keine Geschwister. I don't have any brothers or sisters. □ Ich will keinen Streit. I don't want any quarrelling. □ Er zeigt kein Interesse an Computern. He doesn't show any interest in computers. □ Von den Autos hat mir keines gefallen. I didn't like any of the cars.
2 no
□ Kein Tier könnte in diesem Klima überleben. No animal could survive in this climate.
■ **'Kein Zutritt'** 'No entry'
■ **Ich habe keine Lust.** I don't feel like it.
■ **Ich habe keinen Hunger.** I'm not hungry.
3 nobody
□ Alle waren eingeladen, es ist aber keiner gekommen. Everybody was invited but nobody came.
■ **Ich kenne hier keinen.** I don't know anybody here.

keinerlei ADJECTIVE
no … whatsoever
□ Ich habe damit keinerlei Probleme. I don't have any problems with it whatsoever.

keinesfalls ADVERB
on no account

keineswegs ADVERB
by no means

★ der **Keks** (PL die **Kekse**) MASC NOUN
biscuit

★ der **Keller** (PL die **Keller**) MASC NOUN
cellar

★ der **Kellner** (PL die **Kellner**) MASC NOUN
waiter

★ die **Kellnerin** FEM NOUN
waitress

★ **kennen** (IMPERFECT **kannte**, PERFECT TENSE **hat gekannt**) VERB [39]
to know
□ Ich kenne ihn nicht. I don't know him. □ Ich kenne London gut. I know London well.

★ **kennenlernen** VERB [4]
1 to meet
□ Sie hat ihre Freundin bei einem Fußballspiel kennengelernt. She met her girlfriend at a football match.
2 to get to know
□ Ich würde ihn gern besser kennenlernen. I'd like to get to know him better.
■ **sich kennenlernen 1** to meet □ Wir haben uns auf einer Party kennengelernt. We met at a party. **2** to get to know each other □ Wir haben uns im Laufe der Zeit immer besser kennengelernt. We got to know each other better and better as time went on.

die **Kenntnis** (PL die **Kenntnisse**) FEM NOUN
knowledge *no pl*
□ Deutschkenntnisse wären von Vorteil. Knowledge of German would be an advantage.
■ **etwas zur Kenntnis nehmen** to note something
■ **jemanden in Kenntnis setzen** to inform somebody

das **Kennzeichen** (PL die **Kennzeichen**) NEUT NOUN
1 mark
□ unveränderliche Kennzeichen distinguishing marks
2 registration
□ das Auto mit dem Kennzeichen S-MJ 2714 the car with the registration S-MJ 2714

der **Kerl** (PL die **Kerle**) MASC NOUN
bloke
■ **Sie ist ein netter Kerl.** She's a good sort.

der **Kern** (PL die **Kerne**) MASC NOUN
1 pip
□ Viele Sorten von Klementinen haben keine Kerne. Many types of clementines don't have any pips.
2 stone
□ der Kern der Kirsche the cherry stone
3 kernel (*of nut*)
4 nucleus
5 core

k

Kernenergie – Kirmes

□ der Reaktorkern the reactor core
■ **Wir sollten zum Kern des Problems kommen.** We should get to the heart of the problem.

die **Kernenergie** FEM NOUN
nuclear energy

das **Kernkraftwerk** (PL die **Kernkraftwerke**) NEUT NOUN
nuclear power station

die **Kerze** FEM NOUN
1 candle
□ Sie zündete eine Kerze an. She lit a candle.
2 plug
□ Bei der Inspektion werden die Kerzen erneuert. The plugs are changed while the car is being serviced.

★ die **Kette** FEM NOUN
chain

keuchen VERB [48]
to pant

der **Keuchhusten** MASC NOUN
whooping cough
□ Meine Schwester hat Keuchhusten. My sister has whooping cough.

die **Keule** FEM NOUN
1 club
□ Er schlug ihm mit einer Keule über den Kopf. He hit him over the head with a club.
2 leg
□ Beim Hähnchen mag ich am liebsten die Keule. My favourite part of a chicken is the leg.

das **Kfz** (GEN des **Kfz** or **Kfzs**, PL die **Kfzs**) NEUT NOUN (= *Kraftfahrzeug*)
motor vehicle

kg ABBREVIATION (= *Kilogramm*)
kg

kichern VERB [88]
to giggle

der **Kiefer** (PL die **Kiefer**) MASC NOUN
▷ *see also* die **Kiefer** NOUN
jaw

die **Kiefer** FEM NOUN
▷ *see also* der **Kiefer** NOUN
pine tree

der **Kies** MASC NOUN
gravel

★ das **Kilo** (PL die **Kilos** or **Kilo**) NEUT NOUN
kilo
□ Ich muss ein paar Kilos loswerden. I need to lose a couple of kilos. □ Ich hätte gern zwei Kilo Tomaten. Can I have two kilos of tomatoes.
■ **Ich wiege fünfundfünfzig Kilo.** I weigh eight and a half stone.

★ das **Kilogramm** (PL die **Kilogramme** or **Kilogramm**) NEUT NOUN
kilogram
□ zwei Kilogramm Äpfel two kilograms of apples

★ der **Kilometer** (PL die **Kilometer**) MASC NOUN
kilometre
■ **mit achtzig Kilometern pro Stunde** at fifty miles per hour

★ das **Kind** (PL die **Kinder**) NEUT NOUN
child
■ **von Kind auf** from childhood
■ **ein Kind bekommen** to have a baby

★ der **Kindergarten** (PL die **Kindergärten**) MASC NOUN
kindergarten

der **Kindergärtner** (PL die **Kindergärtner**) MASC NOUN
kindergarten teacher

die **Kindergärtnerin** FEM NOUN
kindergarten teacher

das **Kindergeld** NEUT NOUN
child benefit

★ die **Kinderkrippe** FEM NOUN
crèche

die **Kinderlähmung** FEM NOUN
polio
□ Sie hatte als Kind Kinderlähmung. She had polio as a child.

kinderleicht ADJECTIVE
child's play
□ Es war kinderleicht. It was child's play.

★ das **Kindermädchen** (PL die **Kindermädchen**) NEUT NOUN
nanny

★ der **Kinderpfleger** (PL die **Kinderpfleger**) MASC NOUN
paediatric nurse

die **Kinderpflegerin** FEM NOUN
paediatric nurse

die **Kindertagesstätte** FEM NOUN
day nursery

der **Kinderwagen** (PL die **Kinderwagen**) MASC NOUN
pram

die **Kindheit** FEM NOUN
childhood

kindisch ADJECTIVE
childish
■ **sich kindisch benehmen** to behave childishly

das **Kinn** (PL die **Kinne**) NEUT NOUN
chin

★ das **Kino** (PL die **Kinos**) NEUT NOUN
cinema
□ ins Kino gehen to go to the cinema

★ der **Kiosk** (PL die **Kioske**) MASC NOUN
kiosk

★ die **Kirche** FEM NOUN
church

★ die **Kirmes** (PL die **Kirmessen**) FEM NOUN
funfair

German - English

★ die **Kirsche** FEM NOUN
cherry

★ das **Kissen** (PL die **Kissen**) NEUT NOUN
1 cushion
□ Auf dem Sofa lagen bunte Kissen. There were brightly-coloured cushions on the sofa.
2 pillow
□ Er schläft ohne Kissen. He sleeps without a pillow.

kitschig ADJECTIVE
kitschy

kitzeln VERB [34]
to tickle

kitzlig ADJECTIVE
ticklish
□ Ich bin kitzlig an den Füßen. My feet are ticklish. □ Das ist eine ganz kitzlige Angelegenheit. That's a very ticklish matter.

★ **klagen** VERB [38]
1 to wail
□ 'Hätte ich doch nur auf dich gehört', klagte er. 'If only I had listened to you', he wailed.
2 to complain
□ Sie klagt dauernd über ihre Kinder. She's constantly complaining about her children.
□ Sie klagt in letzter Zeit oft über Kopfschmerzen. She's been complaining of headaches a lot recently.
3 to sue
□ Wir werden gegen ihn klagen. We're going to sue him.
■ **Sie hat mir ihr Leid geklagt.** She poured out her sorrows to me.

die **Klammer** (PL die **Klammern**) FEM NOUN
1 bracket
□ Sie schrieb in Klammern eine Erklärung dazu. She wrote an explanation in brackets.
2 peg (clothes peg)
3 brace (for teeth)
□ Viele Kinder müssen eine Klammer tragen. Many children have to wear a brace.

der **Klang** (PL die **Klänge**) MASC NOUN
sound

die **Klappe** FEM NOUN
1 flap
□ Über dem Briefkasten ist eine Klappe. There's a flap over the letterbox.
2 valve
□ Die Klappe an seinem Herzen hat ein Loch. His heart valve has a hole in it.
3 trap (Umgangssprache)
□ Er soll die Klappe halten. He should keep his trap shut.
■ **Sie hat eine große Klappe.** She's got a big mouth.

★ **klappen** VERB [48]
1 to work
□ Das kann ja nicht klappen. That won't work.

□ Das Experiment hat geklappt. The experiment worked.
2 to tip
□ Sie klappte den Sitz nach oben. She tipped up the seat. □ Er klappte den Deckel der Kiste nach hinten. He tipped the lid of the chest back.

klappern VERB [88]
to rattle

★ **klar** ADJECTIVE
clear
□ Das Wasser ist sehr klar. The water is very clear. □ Ich brauche einen klaren Kopf. I need a clear head. □ eine klare Antwort a clear answer □ Mir ist nicht klar, was er eigentlich will. I'm not clear about what he really wants.
■ **sich über etwas im Klaren sein** to be clear about something □ Bist du dir über die Konsequenzen im Klaren? Are you clear about the consequences?
■ **Na klar!** Of course!

klären VERB [38]
1 to clarify
□ Wir sollten diese Frage klären. We should clarify this matter.
2 to purify
□ In dieser Anlage wird das Abwasser geklärt. The sewage is purified in this plant.
■ **sich klären** to clear itself up □ Dieses Problem hat sich inzwischen geklärt. The problem has cleared itself up in the meantime.

die **Klarheit** FEM NOUN
1 clarity
■ **Wir brauchen in dieser Sache Klarheit.** This matter must be clarified.
2 clearness
□ die Klarheit des Wassers the clearness of the water

die **Klarinette** FEM NOUN
clarinet
□ Oliver spielt Klarinette. Oliver plays the clarinet.

klarstellen (PERFECT TENSE **hat klargestellt**) VERB [4]
to make clear
□ Ich möchte doch mal klarstellen, dass ich das nie gesagt habe. I would like to make it quite clear that I never said that.

★ **klasse** ADJECTIVE
▷ see also die **Klasse** NOUN
smashing (Umgangssprache)
□ Er ist ein klasse Lehrer. He's a smashing teacher.

die **Klasse** FEM NOUN
▷ see also **klasse** ADJECTIVE
class
□ Wir sind in der ersten Klasse gefahren. We travelled first class. □ Unsere Klasse fährt nach England. Our class is going to England.
■ **große Klasse sein** to be great □ Unser

k

Sportlehrer ist große Klasse. Our sports teacher's really great.

★ die **Klassenarbeit** FEM NOUN
test

DID YOU KNOW...?
The **Klassenarbeit** is the main form of assessment in German schools. Over the school year, German pupils write between 6 and 8 **Klassenarbeiten**, usually 45 minutes long, in their core subjects (generally maths, German and English).

□ Wir schreiben morgen in Englisch eine Klassenarbeit. We've got a written English test tomorrow.

das **Klassenbuch** (PL die **Klassenbücher**) NEUT NOUN
class register

★ die **Klassenfahrt** (PL die **Klassenfahrten**) FEM NOUN
class trip

★ der **Klassenkamerad** (GEN des **Klassenkameraden**, PL die **Klassenkameraden**) MASC NOUN
classmate

★ die **Klassenkameradin** FEM NOUN
classmate

der **Klassenlehrer** (PL die **Klassenlehrer**) MASC NOUN
class teacher

die **Klassenlehrerin** FEM NOUN
class teacher

★ der **Klassensprecher** (PL die **Klassensprecher**) MASC NOUN
class representative

★ die **Klassensprecherin** FEM NOUN
class representative

★ das **Klassenzimmer** (PL die **Klassenzimmer**) NEUT NOUN
classroom

★ **klassisch** ADJECTIVE
classical

der **Klatsch** (GEN des **Klatsches**) MASC NOUN
gossip
□ Hast du schon den neuesten Klatsch gehört? Have you heard the latest gossip?

klatschen VERB [48]
1 to clap
□ Die Zuschauer klatschten. The audience clapped.
2 to gossip
□ Über das Königshaus wird viel geklatscht. There's a lot of gossip about the royal family.
3 to batter
□ Der Regen klatschte gegen die Scheiben. The rain battered against the panes.
■ **jemandem Beifall klatschen** to applaud somebody

klauen (PERFECT TENSE **hat geklaut**) VERB [38] (*Umgangssprache*)
to pinch

★ das **Klavier** (PL die **Klaviere**) NEUT NOUN
piano
□ Emma spielt Klavier. Emma plays the piano.

kleben VERB [38]
to stick
□ Ich habe die zerbrochene Vase wieder geklebt. I've stuck the broken vase together again. □ Das klebt nicht. It doesn't stick.
■ **etwas an etwas kleben** to stick something on something □ Sie hat das Bild der Gruppe an ihre Wand geklebt. She stuck the picture of the band on her wall.
■ **an etwas kleben** to stick to something □ An der Windschutzscheibe klebten lauter tote Insekten. There were lots of dead insects stuck to the windscreen.
■ **jemandem eine kleben** to thump somebody (*Umgangssprache*)

klebrig ADJECTIVE
sticky

der **Klebstoff** (PL die **Klebstoffe**) MASC NOUN
glue

der **Klebstreifen** (PL die **Klebstreifen**) MASC NOUN
adhesive tape

der **Klee** MASC NOUN
clover

★ das **Kleid** (PL die **Kleider**) NEUT NOUN
dress
□ Sie trug ein rotes Kleid. She was wearing a red dress.
■ **Kleider** clothes *pl* □ Wir haben viele Kleider weggegeben. We have given away lots of clothes.

der **Kleiderbügel** (PL die **Kleiderbügel**) MASC NOUN
coat hanger

★ der **Kleiderschrank** (PL die **Kleiderschränke**) MASC NOUN
wardrobe

★ die **Kleidung** FEM NOUN
clothing

das **Kleidungsstück** (PL die **Kleidungsstücke**) NEUT NOUN
garment

★ **klein** ADJECTIVE
small
□ ein kleines Kind a small child □ ein kleiner Betrag a small amount
■ **als ich klein war** when I was little

★ das **Kleingeld** NEUT NOUN
small change

★ der **Klempner** (PL die **Klempner**) MASC NOUN
plumber

★ = core vocabulary

★ die **Klempnerin** FEM NOUN
plumber

★ **klettern** (PERFECT TENSE ist geklettert) VERB [88]
to climb

★ **klicken** VERB [48]
to click (computer)
□ mit der Maus klicken to click on the mouse

★ das **Klima** (PL die Klimas) NEUT NOUN
climate

die **Klimaanlage** FEM NOUN
air conditioning

der **Klimawandel** MASC NOUN
climate change
□ Wir müssen den Kampf gegen den Klimawandel gewinnen. We must win the battle against climate change.

★ die **Klingel** FEM NOUN
bell

★ **klingeln** VERB [34]
to ring
■ Es klingelte. The doorbell rang.

der **Klingelton** (PL die Klingeltöne) MASC NOUN
ringtone (of mobile phone)

klingen (IMPERFECT klang, PERFECT TENSE hat geklungen) VERB
to sound
□ Das Klavier klingt verstimmt. The piano sounds out of tune. □ Der Vorschlag klingt gut. The suggestion sounds good. □ Du klingst deprimiert. You sound depressed.

★ die **Klinik** FEM NOUN
clinic

die **Klinke** FEM NOUN
handle (of door)

die **Klippe** FEM NOUN
cliff

★ das **Klo** (PL die Klos) NEUT NOUN
loo (Umgangssprache)

der **Klon** (PL die Klone) MASC NOUN
clone

klonen VERB [38]
to clone
□ ein geklontes Schaf a cloned sheep

★ **klopfen** VERB [38]
1 to knock
□ Sie klopfte an die Tür. She knocked on the door.
■ Es klopft. There's somebody knocking on the door.
2 to pound
□ Mein Herz klopfte vor Aufregung. My heart was pounding with excitement.
■ jemandem auf die Schulter klopfen to tap somebody on the shoulder

das **Kloster** (PL die Klöster) NEUT NOUN
1 monastery
2 convent

★ der **Klub** (PL die Klubs) MASC NOUN
club (association)

★ **klug** ADJECTIVE
intelligent

die **Klugheit** FEM NOUN
intelligence

km ABBREVIATION (= Kilometer)
km

knabbern VERB [88]
to nibble
□ Er knabberte an einem Keks. He nibbled a biscuit.

das **Knäckebrot** NEUT NOUN
crispbread

knacken VERB [48]
to crack
□ Nüsse knacken to crack nuts □ einen Code knacken to crack a code
■ ein Auto knacken to break into a car

der **Knall** (PL die Knalle) MASC NOUN
bang
□ Die Tür schlug mit einem lauten Knall zu. The door closed with a loud bang.

knapp ADJECTIVE
1 tight
□ Meine Schuhe tun mir weh, sie sind zu knapp. My shoes are hurting me, they're too tight.
2 scarce
□ Wasser ist knapp. Water is scarce.
■ knapp bei Kasse short of money
3 just
□ Sie ist knapp fünfzehn Jahre alt. She is not quite fifteen. □ Wir haben knapp verloren. We only just lost.
■ eine knappe Stunde just under an hour
■ knapp unter just under □ Das kostet knapp unter tausend Euro. That costs just under a thousand euros.

kneifen (IMPERFECT kniff, PERFECT TENSE hat gekniffen) VERB
1 to pinch
□ Er hat mich in den Arm gekniffen. He pinched my arm.
2 to back out
□ Als er springen sollte, hat er gekniffen. When it was his turn to jump, he backed out.

★ die **Kneipe** FEM NOUN
pub

★ das **Knie** (PL die Knie) NEUT NOUN
knee

der **Kniestrumpf** (PL die Kniestrümpfe) MASC NOUN
knee-length sock

der **Knoblauch** MASC NOUN
garlic

k

der **Knöchel** (PL die **Knöchel**) MASC NOUN
1 knuckle
□ Ich habe mir die Knöchel an der rechten Hand geschürft. I've scraped the knuckles of my right hand.
2 ankle
□ Bei dem Sprung habe ich mir den Knöchel verstaucht. I sprained my ankle when I jumped.

der **Knochen** (PL die **Knochen**) MASC NOUN
bone

★ der **Knödel** (PL die **Knödel**) MASC NOUN
dumpling

★ der **Knopf** (PL die **Knöpfe**) MASC NOUN
button

der **Knoten** (PL die **Knoten**) MASC NOUN
1 knot
□ Sie machte einen Knoten in die Schnur. She tied a knot in the string.
2 bun
□ Sie trug das Haar in einem Knoten. She wore her hair in a bun.
3 lump
□ Sie hat einen Knoten in der Brust entdeckt. She noticed a lump in her breast.

der **Knüppel** (PL die **Knüppel**) MASC NOUN
1 cudgel
□ Die Robbenbabys werden mit Knüppeln erschlagen. The baby seals are beaten to death with cudgels.
2 truncheon
□ Die Polizisten gingen mit Knüppeln gegen die Demonstranten vor. The police used truncheons against the demonstrators.
3 joystick

★ der **Koch** (PL die **Köche**) MASC NOUN
cook

★ **kochen** VERB [48]
1 to cook
□ Was kochst du heute? What are you cooking today? □ Ich koche gern. I like cooking.
■ Sie kann gut kochen. She's a good cook.
2 to boil
□ Das Wasser kocht. The water's boiling.

★ der **Kocher** (PL die **Kocher**) MASC NOUN
cooker

★ die **Köchin** FEM NOUN
cook

der **Kochtopf** (PL die **Kochtöpfe**) MASC NOUN
saucepan

★ der **Koffer** (PL die **Koffer**) MASC NOUN
suitcase

★ der **Kofferraum** (PL die **Kofferräume**) MASC NOUN
boot (of car)

★ der **Kohl** MASC NOUN
cabbage

die **Kohle** FEM NOUN
1 coal
□ Wir heizen mit Kohle. We use coal for heating.

2 charcoal
□ Wir brauchen noch Kohle zum Grillen. We need charcoal for the barbecue.
3 dough (money)
■ Ich habe keine Kohle. I'm broke. (Umgangssprache)

das **Kohlenhydrat** (PL die **Kohlenhydrate**) NEUT NOUN
carbohydrate

die **Kohlensäure** FEM NOUN
carbon dioxide
■ Mineralwasser mit Kohlensäure sparkling mineral water

die **Kokosnuss** (PL die **Kokosnüsse**) FEM NOUN
coconut

★ der **Kollege** (GEN des **Kollegen**, PL die **Kollegen**) MASC NOUN
colleague

★ die **Kollegin** FEM NOUN
colleague

★ **Köln** NEUT NOUN
Cologne
■ nach Köln to Cologne

★ der **Komfort** MASC NOUN
luxury
□ ein Auto mit allem Komfort a luxury car

die **Komfortzone** FEM NOUN
comfort zone

der **Komiker** (PL die **Komiker**) MASC NOUN
comedian

die **Komikerin** FEM NOUN
comedian

★ **komisch** ADJECTIVE
funny
□ ein komischer Film a funny film □ ein komisches Gefühl a funny feeling

das **Komma** (PL die **Kommas**) NEUT NOUN
comma
■ zwei Komma drei (2,3) two point three (2.3)

★ **kommen** VERB [40]

IMPERFECT	
ich kam	wir kamen
du kamst	ihr kamt
er/sie/es kam	sie/Sie kamen
PERFECT TENSE	
ist gekommen	

1 to come
□ Wann ist der Brief gekommen? When did the letter come? □ Kommst du auch zur Party? Are you coming to the party too?
■ Komm gut nach Hause! Safe journey home.
2 to get
□ Wie komme ich zum Bahnhof? How do I get to the station?

★ = core vocabulary

■ unter ein Auto kommen to be run over by a car

3 to appear
  □ Es wird Frühling, die Schneeglöckchen kommen schon. Spring is coming, the snowdrops are appearing.

4 to go
  □ Er ist gestern ins Krankenhaus gekommen. He went into hospital yesterday. □ Das kommt in den Schrank. That goes in the cupboard.
  ■ Mit sechs kommt man in die Schule. You start school at six.
  ■ Wer kommt zuerst? Who's first?
  ■ Jetzt kommst du an die Reihe. It's your turn now.
  ■ kommenden Sonntag next Sunday
  ■ kommen lassen to send for □ Ich habe mir die neueste GPS-Uhr kommen lassen. I've sent for a new GPS watch. □ Der Direktor hat ihn kommen lassen. The headmaster sent for him.
  ■ auf etwas kommen to think of something □ Darauf bin ich nicht gekommen. I didn't think of that.
  ■ Wie kommst du auf die Idee? What gave you that idea?
  ■ Ich komme nicht auf seinen Namen. His name escapes me.
  ■ Er kommt aus Bayern. He comes from Bavaria.
  ■ Sie ist durchs Abitur gekommen. She got through her Abitur.
  ■ ums Leben kommen to lose one's life □ Sie ist bei einem Unfall ums Leben gekommen. She lost her life in an accident.
  ■ Das kommt davon! That's what you get!
  ■ zu sich kommen to come round □ Die Patientin ist noch nicht wieder zu sich gekommen. The patient hasn't come round again yet.
  ■ zu etwas kommen 1 to get something □ Wie bist du zu dem Computer gekommen? How did you get the computer? 2 to get round to something □ Ich mache das, sobald ich dazu komme. I'll do it as soon as I get round to it.

★ die **Kommode** FEM NOUN
  chest of drawers

der **Kommunismus** (GEN des Kommunismus) MASC NOUN
  communism

★ die **Komödie** FEM NOUN
  comedy

kompatibel ADJECTIVE
  compatible

das **Kompliment** (PL die Komplimente) NEUT NOUN
  compliment
  □ Er hat ihr zu ihrer Übersetzung ein Kompliment gemacht. He complimented her on her translation.

★ **kompliziert** ADJECTIVE
  complicated

der **Komponist** (GEN des Komponisten, PL die Komponisten) MASC NOUN
  composer

die **Komponistin** FEM NOUN
  composer

★ das **Kompott** (PL die Kompotte) NEUT NOUN
  compote

★ der **Konditor** (PL die Konditoren) MASC NOUN
  pastry cook

★ die **Konditorei** FEM NOUN
  cake shop

★ die **Konditorin** FEM NOUN
  pastry cook

das **Kondom** (PL die Kondome) NEUT NOUN
  condom

der **Konflikt** (PL die Konflikte) MASC NOUN
  conflict

★ der **König** (PL die Könige) MASC NOUN
  king

★ die **Königin** FEM NOUN
  queen

königlich ADJECTIVE
  royal

das **Königreich** (PL die Königreiche) NEUT NOUN
  kingdom
  ■ das Vereinigte Königreich the United Kingdom

die **Konjugation** FEM NOUN
  conjugation

konjugieren (PERFECT TENSE hat konjugiert) VERB [76]
  to conjugate

die **Konjunktion** FEM NOUN
  conjunction

der **Konjunktiv** (PL die Konjunktive) MASC NOUN
  subjunctive

die **Konkurrenz** FEM NOUN
1 competition
  □ Auf diesem Sektor ist die Konkurrenz groß. Competition is keen in this sector.
2 competitors pl
  □ Sie ist zur Konkurrenz gegangen. She's gone over to our competitors.

★ **können** VERB [41]

PRESENT TENSE	
ich kann	wir können
du kannst	ihr könnt
er/sie/es kann	sie/Sie können
PERFECT TENSE	
hat gekonnt/können	

▷ see also das **Können** NOUN

The past participle **können** is used when **können** is a modal auxiliary.

Numbers in brackets refer to verb tables on pages 697 to 706.

157

Können – Korkenzieher

1 can

□ Kannst du schwimmen? **Can you swim?** □ Sie kann keine Mathematik. **She can't do mathematics.** □ Sie hat nicht früher kommen können. **She couldn't come earlier.** □ Kann ich mit? **Can I come with you?** □ Ich kann nicht ... **I can't ...**

2 to be able to

□ Morgen werde ich nicht kommen können. **I won't be able to come tomorrow.**

■ **Ich kann nicht mehr. 1** I can't go on. □ Ich mache jetzt Schluss, ich kann nicht mehr. **I'll have to stop now, I can't go on. 2** I'm full up. □ Willst du noch ein Stück Kuchen? — Nein danke, ich kann nicht mehr. **Would you like another piece of cake? — No thanks, I'm full up.**

3 may

□ Kann ich gehen? **May I go?** □ Sie könnten recht haben. **You may be right.**

■ **Es kann sein, dass ...** It may be that ... □ Es kann sein, dass ich etwas später komme. **It may be that I'll come a little later.**

■ **Ich kann nichts dafür.** It's not my fault.

■ **Das kann sein.** That's possible.

4 to know

□ Er kann viele Geschichtszahlen. **He knows a lot of historical dates.**

■ **Können Sie Deutsch?** Can you speak German?

das **Können** NEUT NOUN
▷ see also **können** VERB
ability

□ Sie hat ihr Können bewiesen. **She has proved her ability.**

konnte VERB ▷ see **können**

konservativ ADJECTIVE
conservative

die **Konserve** FEM NOUN
tinned food

die **Konservenbüchse** FEM NOUN
tin

der **Konsonant** (GEN des **Konsonanten**, PL die **Konsonanten**) MASC NOUN
consonant

der **Kontakt** (PL die **Kontakte**) MASC NOUN
contact

die **Kontaktlinsen** FEM PL NOUN
contact lenses pl

der **Kontinent** (PL die **Kontinente**) MASC NOUN
continent

★ das **Konto** (PL die **Konten**) NEUT NOUN
account

□ Geld auf ein Konto einzahlen **to pay money into an account**

★ die **Kontrolle** FEM NOUN
control

□ die Passkontrolle **passport control** □ Sie hat die Kontrolle über das Fahrzeug verloren. **She lost control of the vehicle.** □ etwas unter Kontrolle haben **to have something under control**

★ der **Kontrolleur** (PL die **Kontrolleure**) MASC NOUN
inspector

★ die **Kontrolleurin** FEM NOUN
inspector

★ **kontrollieren** (PERFECT TENSE hat kontrolliert) VERB [76]
to check

□ Kann ich bitte Ihre Fahrkarten kontrollieren? **May I check your tickets please?**

sich **konzentrieren** (PERFECT TENSE hat sich konzentriert) VERB [76]
to concentrate

□ Ich kann mich nicht konzentrieren. **I can't concentrate.**

★ das **Konzert** (PL die **Konzerte**) NEUT NOUN
1 concert

□ Wir waren gestern Abend im Konzert. **We were at a concert yesterday evening.**

2 concerto

□ ein Konzert für Klavier und Violine **a concerto for piano and violin**

★ der **Kopf** (PL die **Köpfe**) MASC NOUN
head

der **Kopfhörer** (PL die **Kopfhörer**) MASC NOUN
headphones pl

★ das **Kopfkissen** (PL die **Kopfkissen**) NEUT NOUN
pillow

★ der **Kopfsalat** (PL die **Kopfsalate**) MASC NOUN
lettuce

die **Kopfschmerzen** MASC PL NOUN
headache sing

□ Ich habe Kopfschmerzen. **I've got a headache.**

die **Kopie** FEM NOUN
copy

★ **kopieren** (PERFECT TENSE hat kopiert) VERB [76]
to copy

□ kopieren und einfügen **to copy and paste**

das **Kopiergerät** (PL die **Kopiergeräte**) NEUT NOUN
photocopier

★ der **Korb** (PL die **Körbe**) MASC NOUN
basket

■ **jemandem einen Korb geben** to turn somebody down

der **Korken** (PL die **Korken**) MASC NOUN
cork

der **Korkenzieher** (PL die **Korkenzieher**) MASC NOUN
corkscrew

das **Korn** (PL die **Körner**) NEUT NOUN
corn

der **Körper** (PL die **Körper**) MASC NOUN
body

der **Körperteil** (PL die **Körperteile**) MASC
NOUN
part of the body

★ **korrigieren** (PERFECT TENSE **hat korrigiert**)
VERB [76]
to correct

die **Kosmetik** FEM NOUN
cosmetics pl

kosmetisch ADJECTIVE
cosmetic

die **Kost** FEM NOUN
1 food
□ Sie ernährt sich von gesunder Kost. She eats
healthy food.
2 board
□ Für Kost und Unterkunft ist gesorgt. Board
and lodging will be provided.

★ **kostbar** ADJECTIVE
precious
□ Du vergeudest meine kostbare Zeit. You're
wasting my precious time.

★ **kosten** VERB [2]
▷ see also die **Kosten** NOUN
1 to cost
□ Mein Fahrrad hat zweitausend Euro gekostet.
My bike cost two thousand euros.
■ **Was kostet …?** How much is …?
2 to taste
□ Willst du die Soße mal kosten? Would you like
to taste the sauce? □ Koste mal, ob das
schmeckt. Taste it and see if it's good.

★ die **Kosten** PL NOUN
▷ see also **kosten** VERB
1 costs pl
□ die Kosten tragen to bear the costs
2 expense
□ Bei vielen Kindern hat man auch viele Kosten.
Lots of children mean a lot of expense.
■ **auf jemandes Kosten** at somebody's
expense □ Sie ist auf Kosten der Firma zu der
Konferenz gefahren. She went to the
conference at the company's expense.

★ **kostenlos** ADJECTIVE
free of charge

★ **köstlich** ADJECTIVE
1 hilarious
□ Das war ein köstlicher Film. That was a
hilarious film. □ ein köstlicher Witz a hilarious
joke
2 delicious (food)
■ **sich köstlich amüsieren** to have a
marvellous time

★ das **Kostüm** (PL die **Kostüme**) NEUT NOUN
costume
■ **ein Damenkostüm** a ladies' suit

★ das **Kotelett** (PL die **Koteletts**) NEUT NOUN
chop

krabbeln (PERFECT TENSE **ist gekrabbelt**) VERB
[88]
to crawl

der **Krach** MASC NOUN
1 crash
□ Die Vase fiel mit einem lauten Krach zu
Boden. The vase fell on the ground with a loud
crash.
2 noise
□ Unsere Nachbarn machen viel Krach. Our
neighbours make a lot of noise.
3 row
□ Sie hat Krach mit ihrem Freund. She had a
row with her boyfriend.

★ die **Kraft** (PL die **Kräfte**) FEM NOUN
strength
□ Samson hat seine Kraft verloren. Samson lost
his strength.
■ **Er hat viel Kraft.** He's very strong.
■ **mit aller Kraft** with all one's might
■ **Kinder kosten viel Kraft.** Children require
a lot of energy.
■ **Sie scheint magische Kräfte zu haben.**
She seems to have magic powers.
■ **Das Gesetz tritt am ersten August in
Kraft.** The law comes into effect on the first of
August.

das **Kraftfahrzeug** (PL die **Kraftfahrzeuge**)
NEUT NOUN
motor vehicle

★ **kräftig** ADJECTIVE, ADVERB
1 strong
□ Er ist ein kräftiger Junge. He is a strong boy.
2 hard
□ ein kräftiger Schlag a hard blow □ kräftig
schütteln to shake hard
■ **kräftig üben** to practise a lot □ Wenn du
kräftig übst, dann schaffst du es. If you practise
a lot, you'll do it.

das **Krafttraining** NEUT NOUN
weight training

das **Kraftwerk** (PL die **Kraftwerke**) NEUT
NOUN
power station

der **Kragen** (PL die **Kragen**) MASC NOUN
collar

die **Kralle** FEM NOUN
1 claw
□ die Krallen der Katze the cat's claws
2 talon
□ die Krallen des Vogels the bird's talons

der **Kram** MASC NOUN
stuff (Umgangssprache)
□ Ich habe den ganzen Kram weggeworfen. I
threw all the stuff away.
■ **Mach doch deinen Kram allein!** Do it
yourself!

k

krank – kriechen

■ **Das passt mir nicht in den Kram.** It doesn't suit me.

★ **krank** ADJECTIVE
ill
□ Ich bin krank. I'm ill. □ Ich habe eine kranke Mutter. My mother's ill.

★ das **Krankenhaus** (GEN des Krankenhauses, PL die Krankenhäuser) NEUT NOUN
hospital

★ die **Krankenkasse** FEM NOUN
health insurance

> **DID YOU KNOW...?**
> In Germany one can choose between different health insurance schemes. There is no 'National Health Service'.

★ der **Krankenpfleger** (PL die Krankenpfleger) MASC NOUN
male nurse

★ der **Krankenschein** (PL die Krankenscheine) MASC NOUN
health insurance card

★ die **Krankenschwester** FEM NOUN
nurse

die **Krankenversicherung** FEM NOUN
health insurance

★ der **Krankenwagen** (PL die Krankenwagen) MASC NOUN
ambulance

★ die **Krankheit** FEM NOUN
illness

krankschreiben (IMPERFECT schrieb krank, PERFECT TENSE hat krankgeschrieben) VERB [61]
■ **jemanden krankschreiben** to give somebody a sick note □ Der Arzt hat ihn für eine Woche krankgeschrieben. The doctor gave him a sick note for a week.

kratzen VERB [36]
to scratch
■ **sich kratzen** to scratch oneself

das **Kraut** (PL die Kräuter) NEUT NOUN
1 herb
□ eine Salatsoße mit frischen Kräutern a salad dressing with fresh herbs
2 sauerkraut
□ Heute gibt es Würstchen mit Kraut. We're having sausages and sauerkraut today.

★ die **Krawatte** FEM NOUN
tie

kreativ ADJECTIVE
creative

★ der **Krebs** (GEN des Krebses, PL die Krebse) MASC NOUN
1 crab
□ Krebse bewegen sich seitlich voran. Crabs move sideways.

2 cancer
□ Sie ist an Krebs gestorben. She died of cancer.
3 Cancer
□ Beate ist Krebs. Beate's Cancer.

der **Kredit** (PL die Kredite) MASC NOUN
credit
□ auf Kredit on credit

★ die **Kreditkarte** FEM NOUN
credit card

★ die **Kreide** FEM NOUN
chalk

★ der **Kreis** (GEN des Kreises, PL die Kreise) MASC NOUN
1 circle
□ Stellt euch im Kreis auf. Form a circle. □ mein Freundeskreis my circle of friends □ im Kreis gehen to go round in circles
2 district
□ Blaubeuren liegt im Kreis Ulm. Blaubeuren is in the district of Ulm.

kreischen VERB [38]
to shriek
□ Sie kreischte laut. She shrieked loudly.

der **Kreislauf** MASC NOUN
circulation
□ Sie hat einen labilen Kreislauf. She has bad circulation.

★ der **Kreisverkehr** (PL die Kreisverkehre) MASC NOUN
roundabout

das **Kreuz** (GEN des Kreuzes, PL die Kreuze) NEUT NOUN
1 cross
□ Sie markierte die Stelle mit einem Kreuz. She marked the place with a cross.
2 back
□ Mir tut das Kreuz weh. My back's sore.
3 clubs *sing*
□ Kreuz ist Trumpf. Clubs is trumps.

★ die **Kreuzung** FEM NOUN
1 crossroads *sing*
□ An der Kreuzung fährst du links. You go left at the crossroads.
2 cross
□ Das ist eine Kreuzung zwischen Pferd und Esel. It's a cross between a horse and a donkey.

das **Kreuzworträtsel** (PL die Kreuzworträtsel) NEUT NOUN
crossword puzzle

kriechen (IMPERFECT kroch, PERFECT TENSE ist gekrochen) VERB
1 to crawl
□ Das Baby kroch zur Tür. The baby crawled towards the door. □ Der Verkehr kriecht. The traffic is crawling.
2 to grovel
□ Er kriecht vor seinem Chef. He's grovelling to his boss.

k

der **Krieg** (PL die **Kriege**) MASC NOUN
war

★ **kriegen** VERB [38]
to get
□ Ich kriege einen Schnupfen. I'm getting a cold.
■ Sie kriegt ein Kind. She's going to have a baby.

★ der **Krimi** (PL die **Krimis**) MASC NOUN
thriller
■ Ich lese gern Krimis. I like reading crime novels.

★ der **Kriminalfilm** (PL die **Kriminalfilme**) MASC NOUN
crime thriller

★ der **Kriminalroman** (PL die **Kriminalromane**) MASC NOUN
detective story

kriminell ADJECTIVE
criminal

die **Krise** FEM NOUN
crisis

kritisch ADJECTIVE
critical

★ **kritisieren** (PERFECT TENSE hat kritisiert) VERB [76]
to criticize

Kroatien NEUT NOUN
Croatia
■ aus Kroatien from Croatia
■ nach Kroatien to Croatia

die **Krone** FEM NOUN
crown

die **Kröte** FEM NOUN
toad

★ der **Krug** (PL die **Krüge**) MASC NOUN
1 jug
□ Sie stellte einen Krug Saft auf den Tisch. She put a jug of juice on the table.
2 beer mug
□ Sie trinkt ihr Bier immer aus einem Krug. She always drinks her beer out of a beer mug.

krumm ADJECTIVE
■ ein krummer Rücken a hunched back
■ Mach nicht so einen krummen Rücken. Don't slouch.
■ Sitz nicht so krumm. Sit up straight.

★ die **Küche** FEM NOUN
1 kitchen
2 cooking
□ die französische Küche French cooking

★ der **Kuchen** (PL die **Kuchen**) MASC NOUN
1 cake
□ ein Marmorkuchen a marble cake
2 flan
□ ein Obstkuchen a fruit flan

der **Kuckuck** (PL die **Kuckucke**) MASC NOUN
cuckoo

★ die **Kuckucksuhr** FEM NOUN
cuckoo clock

die **Kugel** FEM NOUN
1 bullet
□ Er wurde von einer Kugel getroffen. He was hit by a bullet.
2 ball
□ Die Wahrsagerin hat eine Kugel aus Glas. The fortune teller has a crystal ball.

★ der **Kugelschreiber** (PL die **Kugelschreiber**) MASC NOUN
Biro®

★ die **Kuh** (PL die **Kühe**) FEM NOUN
cow

★ **kühl** ADJECTIVE
cool
□ Abends wurde es kühl. In the evenings it got cool.

der **Kühler** (PL die **Kühler**) MASC NOUN
radiator (in car)

★ der **Kühlschrank** (PL die **Kühlschränke**) MASC NOUN
fridge

die **Kühltruhe** FEM NOUN
freezer

kühn ADJECTIVE
bold

★ der **Kuli** (PL die **Kulis**) MASC NOUN
Biro®

die **Kultur** FEM NOUN
1 culture
■ Kultur haben to be cultured
2 civilization
□ die abendländische Kultur Western civilization

der **Kulturbeutel** (PL die **Kulturbeutel**) MASC NOUN
toilet bag

kulturell ADJECTIVE
cultural

der **Kümmel** (PL die **Kümmel**) MASC NOUN
caraway seed

der **Kummer** MASC NOUN
sorrow
■ Hast du Kummer? Have you got problems?

kümmern VERB [38]
to concern
□ Was kümmert mich seine Kritik? Why should his criticism concern me?
■ Das kümmert mich nicht. That doesn't worry me.
■ sich um jemanden kümmern to look after somebody
■ sich um etwas kümmern to see to something □ Kannst du dich um meine Pflanzen kümmern? Can you see to my plants?
□ Ich kümmere mich darum, dass das gemacht wird. I'll see to it that it's done.

German - English

k

Kunde - Küste

★ der **Kunde** (GEN des **Kunden**, PL die **Kunden**) MASC NOUN
customer

kündigen VERB [38]
1 to hand in one's notice
□ Die Arbeit gefällt mir nicht, ich werde kündigen. I don't like the job, I'm going to hand in my notice.
■ **Der Chef hat ihr gekündigt.** The boss gave her her notice.
■ **die Wohnung kündigen** to give notice on one's flat
2 to cancel
□ Ich habe mein Abonnement gekündigt. I've cancelled my subscription.

die **Kündigung** FEM NOUN
notice
□ Er reichte seine Kündigung ein. He handed in his notice.

★ die **Kundin** FEM NOUN
customer

die **Kundschaft** FEM NOUN
customers pl

★ die **Kunst** (PL die **Künste**) FEM NOUN
1 art
□ Er interessiert sich für Kunst. He's interested in art.
2 knack
□ Sie beherrscht die Kunst, andere zu überzeugen. She's got the knack of persuading others.
■ **Das ist doch keine Kunst.** It's easy.

der **Künstler** (PL die **Künstler**) MASC NOUN
artist

die **Künstlerin** FEM NOUN
artist

künstlerisch ADJECTIVE
artistic
□ künstlerisch begabt sein to have artistic talents

★ **künstlich** ADJECTIVE
artificial

★ der **Kunststoff** (PL die **Kunststoffe**) MASC NOUN
synthetic material

das **Kunststück** (PL die **Kunststücke**) NEUT NOUN
trick

das **Kunstwerk** (PL die **Kunstwerke**) NEUT NOUN
work of art

★ das **Kupfer** NEUT NOUN
copper (metal)

die **Kupplung** FEM NOUN
clutch
□ Bei Automatikwagen gibt es keine Kupplung.

Automatic cars don't have a clutch.

★ die **Kur** FEM NOUN
health cure
□ eine Kur machen to take a health cure

der **Kurort** (PL die **Kurorte**) MASC NOUN
health resort

★ der **Kurs** (GEN des **Kurses**, PL die **Kurse**) MASC NOUN
1 course
□ Ich mache einen Kurs, um Spanisch zu lernen. I'm doing a course to learn Spanish.
2 rate
□ Wie ist der Kurs des Pfunds? What's the rate for the pound?

★ die **Kurve** FEM NOUN
1 bend
□ Ein Auto bog um die Kurve. A car came round the bend.
2 curve
□ die Kurve eines Schaubilds the curve on a graph

★ **kurz** ADJECTIVE
short
□ Sie hat kurze Haare. She has short hair. □ Sie hat eine kurze Rede gehalten. She made a short speech.
■ **kurz gesagt** in short
■ **zu kurz kommen** to come off badly
■ **den Kürzeren ziehen** to get the worst of it

die **Kürze** FEM NOUN
shortness

kürzen VERB [36]
1 to shorten
□ Du solltest den Aufsatz etwas kürzen. You should shorten your essay a little.
2 to cut
□ Mein Vater hat mir das Taschengeld gekürzt. My father has cut my pocket money.

die **Kurzgeschichte** FEM NOUN
short story

★ **kürzlich** ADVERB
recently

kurzsichtig ADJECTIVE
short-sighted

★ die **Kusine** FEM NOUN
cousin

★ der **Kuss** (GEN des **Kusses**, PL die **Küsse**) MASC NOUN
kiss

★ **küssen** VERB [48]
to kiss
□ Sie hat mich geküsst. She kissed me.
■ **sich küssen** to kiss □ Sie küssten sich. They kissed.

★ die **Küste** FEM NOUN
coast

★ = core vocabulary

LI

l ABBREVIATION (= *Liter*)
l

★ das **Labor** (PL die **Labore** *or* **Labors**) NEUT
NOUN
lab

★ **lächeln** VERB [34]
▷ *see also* das **Lächeln** NOUN
to smile

★ das **Lächeln** NEUT NOUN
▷ *see also* **lächeln** VERB
smile

★ **lachen** VERB [48]
to laugh

★ **lächerlich** ADJECTIVE
ridiculous

★ der **Lachs** (GEN des **Lachses**, PL die **Lachse**)
MASC NOUN
salmon
□ drei Lachse three salmon

der **Lack** (PL die **Lacke**) MASC NOUN
1 varnish
□ Er hat das Holz mit Lack behandelt. He
treated the wood with varnish.
2 paint
□ Der Lack an meinem Auto ist stumpf
geworden. The paint on my car has become
dull.

laden (PRESENT TENSE **lädt**, IMPERFECT **lud**,
PERFECT TENSE **hat geladen**) VERB
▷ *see also* der **Laden** NOUN
1 to load
□ Wir haben das Gepäck ins Auto geladen. We
loaded the luggage into the car. □ Das
Programm wird geladen. The program is being
loaded. □ eine Waffe laden to load a weapon
2 to charge
□ Ich muss meinen Akku laden. I need to
charge my phone.
3 to summon
□ Ich wurde als Zeugin geladen. I was
summoned as a witness.

★ der **Laden** (PL die **Läden**) MASC NOUN
▷ *see also* **laden** VERB
1 shop
□ In welchem Laden hast du das gekauft?
Which shop did you buy it in?

2 shutter
□ Im Sommer machen wir tagsüber die Läden
zu. In summer we close the shutters during the
day.

die **Ladung** FEM NOUN
1 cargo
□ Das Flugzeug hatte zu viel Ladung an Bord.
The plane had too much cargo on board.
2 loading
□ Ein Arbeiter ist bei der Ladung des Schiffes
verunglückt. A worker was injured while loading
the ship.
3 summons *sing*
□ Wenn Sie eine Ladung als Zeuge bekommen,
müssen Sie erscheinen. If you receive a
summons to appear as a witness, you have to
attend.
4 charge
□ eine Ladung Dynamit a charge of dynamite

★ die **Lage** FEM NOUN
1 situation
□ Die politische Lage in Syrien ist brisant. The
political situation in Syria is explosive.
2 layer
□ Die Torte bestand aus mehreren Lagen. The
gateau was made up of several layers.
■ **in der Lage sein, etwas zu tun** to be in a
position to do something

das **Lager** (PL die **Lager**) NEUT NOUN
1 camp
□ Er fährt im Sommer in ein Lager der
Pfadfinder. He's going to a scout camp in the
summer.
2 warehouse
□ Die Fabrik hat ein eigenes Lager. The factory
has its own warehouse.
3 stockroom
□ Die Verkäuferin hat im Lager nachgesehen.
The sales assistant looked in the stockroom.

lagern VERB [88]
1 to store
□ kühl lagern to store in a cool place □ trocken
lagern to store in a dry place
2 to lay down
□ Der Verletzte sollte auf der Seite gelagert
werden. The injured person should be laid down
on his side.

lahm – langfristig

3 to camp
□ Die Wandergruppe lagerte am Fluss. The group of hikers camped by the river.

lahm ADJECTIVE
1 lame
□ Das Pferd ist lahm. The horse is lame.
2 slow
□ Er ist furchtbar lahm. He is terribly slow.

lähmen VERB [38]
to paralyse

die **Lähmung** FEM NOUN
paralysis

der **Laib** (PL die **Laibe**) MASC NOUN
loaf

der **Laie** (GEN des **Laien**, PL die **Laien**) MASC NOUN
layman

das **Laken** (PL die **Laken**) NEUT NOUN
sheet (*on bed*)

die **Lakritze** FEM NOUN
liquorice

das **Lamm** (PL die **Lämmer**) NEUT NOUN
lamb

★ das **Lammfleisch** NEUT NOUN
lamb (*meat*)

★ die **Lampe** FEM NOUN
lamp

★ das **Land** (PL die **Länder**) NEUT NOUN
1 country
□ Italien ist ein schönes Land. Italy is a beautiful country. □ Am Wochenende fahren wir aufs Land. We're going to the country at the weekend.
■ **auf dem Land** in the country
■ **an Land** on land □ Wenn wir wieder an Land sind … When we're on land again …
2 state
□ Die Bundesrepublik besteht aus sechzehn Ländern. The Federal Republic consists of sixteen states.

die **Landebahn** FEM NOUN
runway

★ **landen** (PERFECT TENSE **ist gelandet**) VERB [54]
to land

die **Landeskunde** FEM NOUN
regional and cultural studies *pl*

★ die **Landkarte** FEM NOUN
map

★ der **Landkreis** (GEN des **Landkreises**, PL die **Landkreise**) MASC NOUN
administrative district

> **DID YOU KNOW…?**
> The German administrative hierarchy starts with the **Stadt/Gemeinde** (town/community), and continues via the **Landkreis** (administrative district) and **Land** (federal state) to the **Bund** (federation).

die **ländlich** ADJECTIVE
rural

★ die **Landschaft** FEM NOUN
1 countryside
□ Die toskanische Landschaft ist sehr schön. The Tuscan countryside is very beautiful.
2 landscape
□ Turner hat viele Landschaften gemalt. Turner painted many landscapes.

★ die **Landstraße** FEM NOUN
country road

die **Landung** FEM NOUN
landing
□ Das Flugzeug verunglückte bei der Landung. The plane crashed on landing.

der **Landwirt** (PL die **Landwirte**) MASC NOUN
farmer

die **Landwirtschaft** FEM NOUN
agriculture

★ **lang** ADJECTIVE
1 long
□ Sie hat lange Haare. She has long hair. □ Das war eine lange Rede. That was a long speech. □ Sie war länger als erwartet weg. She was away longer than expected. □ Es wird nicht lang dauern. It won't take long.
2 tall
□ Mathis ist der Längste in unserer Klasse. Mathis is the tallest in our class.

langatmig ADJECTIVE
long-winded

★ **lange** ADVERB
for a long time
□ Sie war lange krank. She was ill for a long time.
■ **lange dauern** to last a long time
■ **lange brauchen** to take a long time

die **Länge** FEM NOUN
length
□ Sie hat die Länge und Breite des Zimmers ausgemessen. She measured the length and breadth of the room. □ die Länge eines Films the length of a film

langen VERB [38]
to be enough
□ Das Fleisch hat nicht für alle gelangt. There wasn't enough meat to go round. □ Das Geld hat für ein Geschenk nicht gelangt. There wasn't enough money to get a present.
■ **Es langt mir.** I've had enough.
■ **nach etwas langen** to reach for something
□ Er langte nach dem Apfel. He reached for the apple.

die **Langeweile** FEM NOUN
boredom

langfristig ADJECTIVE, ADVERB
long-term
□ eine langfristige Besserung a long-term

★ = core vocabulary

improvement □ Wir müssen langfristig planen. We have to plan long-term.

der **Langlauf** MASC NOUN
cross-country skiing
□ Sie macht gern Langlauf. She likes to go cross-country skiing.

länglich ADJECTIVE
longish

★ **langsam** ADJECTIVE, ADVERB
1 slow
2 slowly
□ langsam fahren to drive slowly
■ Das wird langsam langweilig. This is getting boring.

die **Langsamkeit** FEM NOUN
slowness

der **Langschläfer** (PL die Langschläfer) MASC NOUN
late riser

die **Langspielplatte** FEM NOUN
LP

längst ADVERB
■ Das ist längst fertig. That was finished a long time ago.
■ Das weiß ich längst. I've known that for a long time.
■ Er ist längst nicht so gescheit wie seine Schwester. He's far from being as bright as his sister.

längste ADJECTIVE
longest
□ der längste Tag des Jahres the longest day of the year

★ **langweilen** VERB [38]
to bore
□ Langweile ich dich? Am I boring you?
■ sich langweilen to be bored

★ **langweilig** ADJECTIVE
boring

langwierig ADJECTIVE
lengthy

★ der **Lappen** (PL die Lappen) MASC NOUN
rag
□ mit einem feuchten Lappen with a damp rag

der **Laptop** (PL die Laptops) MASC NOUN
laptop

★ der **Lärm** MASC NOUN
noise

der **Laser** (PL die Laser) MASC NOUN
laser

★ **lassen** (PRESENT TENSE lässt, IMPERFECT ließ, PERFECT TENSE gelassen or lassen) VERB [42]

The past participle lassen is used when lassen is a modal auxiliary.

1 to stop
□ Du solltest das Rauchen lassen. You should

stop smoking. □ Er kann das Trinken nicht lassen. He can't stop drinking. □ Sie kann's nicht lassen. She won't stop doing it.
■ Lass das! Stop that!
2 to leave
□ Kann ich die Kinder hier lassen? Can I leave the children here? □ jemanden allein lassen to leave somebody alone □ Wir haben das Auto zu Hause gelassen. We left the car at home.
□ etwas lassen, wie es ist to leave something as it is □ Lass mal, ich mache das schon. Leave it, I'll do it.
■ Lassen wir das! Let's leave it.
■ Lass mich! Leave me alone.
■ jemanden irgendwohin lassen to let somebody go somewhere □ Sie lässt die Katze nicht ins Schlafzimmer. She doesn't let the cat into the bedroom. □ jemanden ins Haus lassen to let somebody into the house
■ etwas machen lassen to have something done □ Ich habe mir den Katalog schicken lassen. I had the catalogue sent to me. □ Sie hat sich die Haare schneiden lassen. She had her hair cut.
■ jemanden etwas tun lassen to let somebody do something □ Sie hat uns nicht ins Kino gehen lassen. She didn't let us go to the cinema.
■ jemanden warten lassen to keep somebody waiting
■ Das lässt sich machen. That can be done.
■ Lass uns gehen. Let's go.

lässig ADJECTIVE
casual

die **Last** FEM NOUN
load
□ Er stöhnte unter der schweren Last. He groaned under the heavy load.
■ jemandem zur Last fallen to be a burden to somebody

lästern VERB [88]
to make nasty remarks
□ Lästert ihr schon wieder über eure Lehrerin? Are you making nasty remarks about your teacher again?

lästig ADJECTIVE
tiresome

★ der **Lastwagen** (PL die Lastwagen) MASC NOUN
lorry

★ das **Latein** NEUT NOUN
Latin

Lateinamerika NEUT NOUN
Latin America

die **Laterne** FEM NOUN
1 lantern
□ Die Kinder trugen Laternen. The children carried lanterns.

2 streetlamp
□ Vor unserem Haus steht eine Laterne. There's a streetlamp in front of our house.

der **Lauch** (PL die **Lauche**) MASC NOUN
leek

★ der **Lauf** (PL die **Läufe**) MASC NOUN
1 run
□ Er machte einen Lauf durch den Wald. He went for a run through the forest.
2 race
□ Sie hat den Lauf über vierhundert Meter gewonnen. She won the four-hundred-metre race.
3 course
□ der Lauf des Flusses the course of the river
□ im Laufe der Woche in the course of the week
□ einer Sache ihren Lauf lassen to let something take its course

die **Laufbahn** FEM NOUN
career

★ **laufen** (PRESENT TENSE **läuft**, IMPERFECT **lief**, PERFECT TENSE **ist gelaufen**) VERB [43]
1 to run
□ Sie liefen so schnell sie konnten. They ran as fast as they could. □ Sie läuft Marathon. She runs marathons.
2 to walk
□ Wir mussten nach Hause laufen. We had to walk home.

laufend ADJECTIVE, ADVERB
1 running
□ bei laufendem Motor with the engine running
2 current
□ die laufenden Ausgaben current expenses
■ auf dem Laufenden sein to be up to date
■ auf dem Laufenden halten to keep up to date
3 always
□ Musst du mich laufend stören? Do you always have to interrupt me?

★ der **Läufer** (PL die **Läufer**) MASC NOUN
1 runner
□ Die Läufer standen am Start. The runners were at the start. □ Im Flur liegt ein roter Läufer. There's a red runner in the hall.
2 bishop
□ Sie zog mit dem Läufer. She moved her bishop.

★ die **Läuferin** FEM NOUN
runner

die **Laufmasche** FEM NOUN
ladder (in tights)

das **Laufwerk** (PL die **Laufwerke**) NEUT NOUN
drive (of computer)
□ Mein alter Laptop hat ein DVD-Laufwerk. My old laptop has a DVD drive.

die **Laune** FEM NOUN
mood

□ Was hat sie für eine Laune? What kind of mood is she in? □ Ich habe gute Laune. I'm in a good mood. □ Ich bin deine Launen leid. I'm fed up with your bad moods.

★ **launisch** ADJECTIVE
1 temperamental
□ Sie ist ein sehr launischer Mensch. She's very temperamental.
2 bad-tempered
□ Er war heute schrecklich launisch. He was terribly bad-tempered today.

die **Laus** (PL die **Läuse**) FEM NOUN
louse

★ **laut** ADJECTIVE, ADVERB, PREPOSITION
▷ see also der **Laut** NOUN
1 loud
□ Ich mag laute Musik nicht. I don't like loud music.
2 noisy
□ Hier ist es schrecklich laut. It's terribly noisy here.
3 loudly
□ Sie schrie so laut sie konnte. She screamed as loudly as she could.
■ laut lesen to read aloud
4 according to
□ Laut unserem Vertrag ... According to our contract ...

der **Laut** (PL die **Laute**) MASC NOUN
▷ see also **laut** ADJECTIVE, ADVERB, PREPOSITION
sound

lauten VERB [2]
1 to go
□ Wie lautet die zweite Strophe des Lieds? How does the second verse of the song go?
2 to be
□ Das Urteil lautete auf zehn Jahre Gefängnis. The sentence was ten years' imprisonment.

läuten VERB [2]
to ring
□ Die Glocken läuten. The bells are ringing.
□ Ich habe geläutet, es hat aber niemand aufgemacht. I rang but nobody answered.

lauter ADVERB
nothing but
□ Sie hat lauter Lügen erzählt. She told nothing but lies.

die **Lautschrift** FEM NOUN
phonetics pl

der **Lautsprecher** (PL die **Lautsprecher**) MASC NOUN
loudspeaker

die **Lautstärke** FEM NOUN
volume

lauwarm ADJECTIVE
lukewarm

★ = core vocabulary

die **Lawine** FEM NOUN
avalanche

★ **leben** VERB [38]
▷ see also das **Leben** NOUN
to live

★ das **Leben** (PL die **Leben**) NEUT NOUN
▷ see also **leben** VERB
life
■ **ums Leben kommen** to lose one's life □ Er
ist bei einem Unfall ums Leben gekommen. He
lost his life in an accident.

lebend ADJECTIVE
living

★ **lebendig** ADJECTIVE
1 alive
□ Er konnte lebendig aus den Trümmern
geborgen werden. He was rescued from the
ruins alive.
2 lively
□ Sie ist ein sehr lebendiges Kind. She's a very
lively child.

★ die **Lebensgefahr** FEM NOUN
mortal danger
□ Die Geiseln waren in Lebensgefahr. The
hostages were in mortal danger.
■ 'Lebensgefahr!' 'danger!'

lebensgefährlich ADJECTIVE
1 dangerous
□ eine lebensgefährliche Kurve a dangerous
corner
2 critical
□ eine lebensgefährliche Krankheit a critical
illness □ lebensgefährlich verletzt critically
injured

die **Lebenshaltungskosten** PL NOUN
cost of living sing

lebenslänglich ADJECTIVE
for life
■ **Er hat eine lebenslängliche
Gefängnisstrafe bekommen.** He received a
life sentence.

★ der **Lebenslauf** (PL die **Lebensläufe**) MASC
NOUN
CV (= curriculum vitae)

★ die **Lebensmittel** NEUT PL NOUN
food sing

★ das **Lebensmittelgeschäft** (PL die
Lebensmittelgeschäfte) NEUT NOUN
grocer's shop

der **Lebensstandard** MASC NOUN
standard of living

die **Lebensversicherung** FEM NOUN
life insurance

★ die **Leber** FEM NOUN
liver

★ die **Leberwurst** (PL die **Leberwürste**) FEM
NOUN
liver sausage

das **Lebewesen** (PL die **Lebewesen**) NEUT
NOUN
creature

★ **lebhaft** ADJECTIVE
lively

der **Lebkuchen** (PL die **Lebkuchen**) MASC
NOUN
gingerbread

lecken VERB [48]
1 to leak
□ Der Behälter leckt. The container's leaking.
2 to lick
□ Die Katze leckte sich das Fell. The cat licked
its fur. □ Sie leckte am Eis. She licked her ice
cream.

★ **lecker** ADJECTIVE
delicious
□ lecker schmecken to taste delicious

★ das **Leder** (PL die **Leder**) NEUT NOUN
leather

die **Lederhose** FEM NOUN
leather trousers pl

> **DID YOU KNOW...?**
> **Lederhosen** are the traditional dress in
> South Germany and Austria.

★ **ledig** ADJECTIVE
single
□ 'Familienstand: ledig' 'Marital status: single'

★ **leer** ADJECTIVE
empty
□ eine leere Flasche an empty bottle □ leere
Drohungen empty threats
■ **ein leeres Blatt Papier** a blank sheet of
paper
■ **ein leerer Blick** a vacant expression
■ **leer machen** to empty

die **Leere** FEM NOUN
emptiness

leeren VERB [38]
to empty

legal ADJECTIVE
legal

★ **legen** VERB [38]
1 to put
□ Sie legte das Kind ins Bett. She put the child
to bed. □ Leg das Besteck in die Schublade. Put
the cutlery in the drawer. □ Er legte das Buch
aus der Hand. He put the book down.
2 to lay
□ Sie legten den Verletzten auf eine Decke.
They laid the injured man on a blanket. □ Sie
legte ihren Mantel über den Stuhl. She laid her
coat over the chair. □ ein Ei legen to lay an egg
■ **sich legen** 1 to lie down □ Sie legte sich auf
das Sofa. She lay down on the sofa. □ Ich lege
mich ins Bett. I'm going to lie down. 2 to drop
□ Der Wind hat sich gelegt. The wind has
dropped.

Lehne – leise

- **Das wird sich legen.** That will sort itself out.

die **Lehne** FEM NOUN
1 arm
□ Sie saß auf der Lehne des Sofas. She sat on the arm of the sofa.
2 back
□ Der Sessel hat eine hohe Lehne. The chair has a high back.

lehnen VERB [38]
to lean

★ der **Lehnstuhl** (PL die Lehnstühle) MASC NOUN
armchair

★ die **Lehre** FEM NOUN
1 apprenticeship
□ bei jemandem in die Lehre gehen to serve one's apprenticeship with somebody
2 lesson
□ Lass dir das eine Lehre sein! Let that be a lesson to you!

★ **lehren** (PERFECT TENSE hat gelehrt) VERB [38]
to teach

★ der **Lehrer** (PL die Lehrer) MASC NOUN
teacher

★ die **Lehrerin** FEM NOUN
teacher

★ das **Lehrerzimmer** (PL die Lehrerzimmer) NEUT NOUN
staff room

★ der **Lehrling** (PL die Lehrlinge) MASC NOUN
apprentice

der **Lehrplan** (PL die Lehrpläne) MASC NOUN
syllabus

★ die **Lehrstelle** FEM NOUN
apprenticeship

die **Leiche** FEM NOUN
corpse

★ **leicht** ADJECTIVE
1 light
□ leichtes Gepäck light luggage
2 easy
□ Die Klassenarbeit war leicht. The class test was easy.
- **es sich leicht machen** to make things easy for oneself □ Du machst es dir wirklich zu leicht. You really make things too easy for yourself.

★ die **Leichtathletik** FEM NOUN
athletics *sing*

leichtfallen VERB [22]
- **jemandem leichtfallen** to be easy for somebody

leichtmachen VERB [48] ▷ *see* leicht

der **Leichtsinn** MASC NOUN
carelessness

leichtsinnig ADJECTIVE
careless

★ **leid** ADJECTIVE
▷ *see also* das **Leid** NOUN
- **etwas leid sein** to be tired of something
□ Ich bin deine ewigen Klagen leid. I'm tired of your constant complaining.

das **Leid** NEUT NOUN
▷ *see also* **leid** ADJECTIVE
sorrow
- **zu Leide** ▷ *see* zuleide

★ **leiden** (IMPERFECT **litt**, PERFECT TENSE **hat gelitten**) VERB [44]
to suffer
□ Sie leidet an Asthma. She suffers from asthma. □ Wir leiden unter der Hitze. We're suffering from the heat.
- **jemanden gut leiden können** to like somebody
- **Ich kann ihn nicht leiden.** I can't stand him.

★ **leider** ADVERB
unfortunately
□ Ich kann leider nicht kommen. Unfortunately I can't come.
- **Ja, leider.** Yes, I'm afraid so.
- **Leider nicht.** I'm afraid not. □ Er hat mir leider nicht geholfen. I'm afraid he didn't help me.

leidtun (IMPERFECT **tat leid**, PERFECT TENSE **hat leidgetan**) VERB [81]
- **Es tut mir leid.** I'm sorry.
- **Er tut mir leid.** I'm sorry for him.

★ **leihen** (IMPERFECT **lieh**, PERFECT TENSE **hat geliehen**) VERB
to lend
□ Kannst du mir fünfzig Euro leihen? Can you lend me fifty euros?
- **sich etwas leihen** to borrow something
□ Das ist nicht mein Fahrrad, ich habe es mir von meiner Schwester geliehen. That's not my bike, I've borrowed it from my sister.

der **Leim** (PL die Leime) MASC NOUN
glue

die **Leine** FEM NOUN
1 line
□ Sie hängte die Wäsche auf die Leine. She hung the washing on the line.
2 lead
□ Hunde müssen an der Leine geführt werden. Dogs must be kept on a lead.

das **Leinen** (PL die Leinen) NEUT NOUN
linen

★ **leise** ADJECTIVE, ADVERB
1 quiet
□ Seid bitte leise. Please be quiet.
2 quietly
□ Sie sprach mit leiser Stimme. She spoke quietly. □ Sie kam ganz leise ins Zimmer. She came into the room very quietly.

★ **leisten** VERB [2]
  1 to do
    □ Du hast gute Arbeit geleistet. **You've done a good job.**
  2 to achieve
    □ Sie hat viel geleistet im Leben. **She's achieved a lot in her life.**
    ■ **jemandem Gesellschaft leisten** to keep somebody company
    ■ **sich etwas leisten** to treat oneself to something □ Ich leiste mir heute einen freien Tag. **I'm going to treat myself to a day off today.**
    ■ **sich etwas leisten können** to be able to afford something □ Ich kann mir keinen neuen Computer leisten. **I can't afford a new computer.** □ Ich kann es mir nicht leisten, schon wieder zu spät zu kommen. **I can't afford to be late again.**

★ die **Leistung** FEM NOUN
  1 performance
    □ Sie haben die Leistung des Motors verbessert. **They've improved the performance of the engine.**
    ■ **schulische Leistungen** school results
  2 achievement
    □ eine sportliche Leistung **a sporting achievement** □ Das war wirklich eine Leistung! **That really was an achievement.**

leiten VERB [2]
  1 to direct
    □ Das Wasser wird durch Rohre geleitet. **The water is directed through pipes.**
  2 to lead
    □ eine Partei leiten **to lead a party**
  3 to run
    □ Wer leitet diese Firma? **Who runs this company?**
  4 to chair
    □ Wer hat die Versammlung geleitet? **Who chaired the meeting?**
    ■ **Metall leitet Strom besonders gut.** Metal is a good conductor of electricity.

★ der **Leiter** (PL die **Leiter**) MASC NOUN
  ▷ *see also* die **Leiter** NOUN
  head
    □ der Leiter des Museums **the head of the museum**

★ die **Leiter** FEM NOUN
  ▷ *see also* der **Leiter** NOUN
  ladder
    □ eine Leiter hinaufklettern **to climb a ladder**

★ die **Leiterin** FEM NOUN
  head
    □ die Leiterin einer Buchhandlung **the manager of a bookshop**

die **Leitung** FEM NOUN
  1 management
    □ Ihr wurde die Leitung der Abteilung übertragen. **She was entrusted with the management of the department.**

  2 direction
    □ der Jugendchor unter Leitung von ... **the youth choir under the direction of ...**
  3 pipe
    □ In unserer Straße werden neue Leitungen für Wasser und Gas verlegt. **They're laying new water and gas pipes in our road.**
  4 cable
    □ Die Leitung steht unter Strom. **The cable is live.**
  5 line
    □ Alle Leitungen waren besetzt. **All the lines were busy.**
    ■ **eine lange Leitung haben** to be slow on the uptake

die **Lektion** FEM NOUN
  lesson

★ die **Lektüre** FEM NOUN
  1 reading
    □ Stör sie nicht bei der Lektüre. **Don't disturb her while she's reading.**
  2 reading matter
    □ Das ist die richtige Lektüre für die Ferien. **That's the right reading matter for the holidays.**
  3 set text
    □ Welche Lektüre habt ihr dieses Jahr in Englisch? **What are your set texts in English this year?**

    BE CAREFUL!
    Lektüre does not mean **lecture.**

lenken VERB [38]
  to steer
    □ ein Fahrzeug lenken **to steer a car**

das **Lenkrad** (PL die **Lenkräder**) NEUT NOUN
  steering wheel

★ **lernen** VERB [38]
  to learn

die **Lernplattform** FEM NOUN
  VLE (*virtual learning environment*)

das **Lesebuch** (PL die **Lesebücher**) NEUT NOUN
  reading book

★ **lesen** (PRESENT TENSE **liest**, IMPERFECT **las**, PERFECT TENSE **hat gelesen**) VERB [45]
  to read

leserlich ADJECTIVE
  legible
    □ eine leserliche Handschrift **legible handwriting** □ leserlich schreiben **to write legibly**

das **Lesezeichen** (PL die **Lesezeichen**) NEUT NOUN
  bookmark

★ **letzte** ADJECTIVE
  1 last
    □ In der letzten Arbeit habe ich eine Zwei geschrieben. **I got a 'B' in the last test.** □ Ich

habe noch einen letzten Wunsch. I have one last wish. □ letzte Woche last week □ zum letzten Mal for the last time
■ **als Letzter** last □ Frank kam als Letzter. Frank arrived last.
2 latest
□ Laut letzten Informationen kam es zu schweren Unruhen. According to latest reports there were serious riots.

★ **letztens** ADVERB
lately

leuchten VERB [2]
to shine
□ jemandem ins Gesicht leuchten to shine a light in somebody's face

der **Leuchter** (PL die Leuchter) MASC NOUN
candlestick

der **Leuchtstift** (PL die Leuchtstifte) MASC NOUN
highlighter

der **Leuchtturm** (PL die Leuchttürme) MASC NOUN
lighthouse

★ die **Leute** PL NOUN
people pl

das **Lexikon** (PL die Lexika) NEUT NOUN
encyclopedia

★ das **Licht** (PL die Lichter) NEUT NOUN
light

das **Lichtjahr** (PL die Lichtjahre) NEUT NOUN
light year

das **Lid** (PL die Lider) NEUT NOUN
eyelid

der **Lidschatten** (PL die Lidschatten) MASC NOUN
eyeshadow

★ **lieb** ADJECTIVE
dear
□ Liebe Bettina Dear Bettina □ Lieber Herr Schlüter Dear Mr Schlüter
■ **Das ist lieb von dir.** That's nice of you.
■ **jemanden lieb haben** to be fond of somebody

★ die **Liebe** FEM NOUN
love

★ **lieben** VERB [38]
to love

liebenswürdig ADJECTIVE
kind

die **Liebenswürdigkeit** FEM NOUN
kindness

★ **lieber** ADVERB
rather
□ Ich hätte jetzt lieber einen Kaffee. I'd rather have a coffee just now. □ Ich gehe lieber nicht. I'd rather not go.
■ **Lass das lieber!** I'd leave that if I were you.

■ **etwas lieber haben** to prefer something
□ Was hast du lieber, Mathe oder Chemie? What do you prefer, maths or chemistry?

der **Liebesbrief** (PL die Liebesbriefe) MASC NOUN
love letter

die **Liebesgeschichte** FEM NOUN
love story

der **Liebeskummer** MASC NOUN
■ **Liebeskummer haben** to be lovesick

★ der **Liebesroman** (PL die Liebesromane) MASC NOUN
romantic novel

liebevoll ADJECTIVE
loving

liebhaben VERB [32] ▷ see lieb

der **Liebling** (PL die Lieblinge) MASC NOUN
darling

Lieblings- PREFIX
favourite
□ Was ist dein Lieblingsfach? What's your favourite subject?

liebste ADJECTIVE
favourite
□ Der Winter ist meine liebste Jahreszeit. Winter is my favourite season.
■ **am liebsten** best □ Am liebsten lese ich Kriminalromane. I like detective stories best.

★ das **Lied** (PL die Lieder) NEUT NOUN
song

lief VERB ▷ see laufen

★ **liefern** VERB [88]
1 to deliver
□ Wir liefern die Möbel ins Haus. We deliver the furniture to your door.
2 to supply
□ Die Windkraftanlage liefert den Strom für die ganze Stadt. The wind turbine supplies electricity to the whole city.
■ **den Beweis liefern** to produce proof

★ der **Lieferwagen** (PL die Lieferwagen) MASC NOUN
van

★ **liegen** (IMPERFECT lag, PERFECT TENSE hat gelegen) VERB [46]
1 to lie
□ Sie lag auf dem Bett. She lay on the bed. □ Wir haben den ganzen Tag am Strand gelegen. We lay on the beach all day. □ Auf meinem Schreibtisch liegt eine Menge Papier. There's a lot of paper lying on my desk.
■ **Es lag viel Schnee.** There was a lot of snow.
2 to be
□ Unser Haus liegt sehr zentral. Our house is very central. □ Ulm liegt an der Donau. Ulm is on the Danube.
■ **nach Süden liegen** to face south

★ = core vocabulary

■ **Mir liegt viel daran.** It matters a lot to me.
■ **Mir liegt nichts daran.** It doesn't matter to me.
■ **Es liegt bei dir, ob …** It's up to you whether …
■ **Sprachen liegen mir nicht.** Languages are not my thing.
■ **Woran liegt es?** How come?
■ **Das liegt am Wetter.** It's because of the weather.
■ **liegen bleiben 1** to lie in □ Morgen ist Sonntag, da kann ich liegen bleiben. It's Sunday tomorrow, so I can lie in. **2** not to get up □ Der verletzte Spieler blieb liegen. The injured player didn't get up. **3** to be left behind □ Der Schirm ist liegen geblieben. The umbrella's been left behind.
■ **etwas liegen lassen** to leave something □ Ich muss diese Arbeit liegen lassen. I'll have to leave this job. □ Ich habe meinen Schirm liegen lassen. I've left my umbrella.

der **Liegestuhl** (PL die **Liegestühle**) MASC NOUN
deck chair

der **Liegewagen** (PL die **Liegewagen**) MASC NOUN
couchette

★ der **Lift** (PL die **Lifte** or **Lifts**) MASC NOUN
lift (elevator)

★ die **Liga** (PL die **Ligen**) FEM NOUN
league

★ **lila** ADJECTIVE
purple
□ Sie hatte einen lila Hut auf. She was wearing a purple hat.

★ die **Limo** (PL die **Limos**) FEM NOUN
lemonade

★ die **Limonade** FEM NOUN
lemonade

★ das **Lineal** (PL die **Lineale**) NEUT NOUN
ruler
□ einen Strich mit dem Lineal ziehen to draw a line with a ruler

★ die **Linie** FEM NOUN
line

linke ADJECTIVE
▷ see also die **Linke** NOUN
left
□ In Großbritannien fährt man auf der linken Seite. In Great Britain they drive on the left. □ Mein linkes Auge tut weh. My left eye's hurting. □ Er hat sich den linken Arm gebrochen. He broke his left arm.

die **Linke** (GEN der **Linken**) FEM NOUN
▷ see also **linke** ADJECTIVE
1 left
□ Zu Ihrer Linken sehen Sie das Rathaus. On your left you'll see the town hall.

2 left hand
□ Er schlug mit der Linken zu. He hit out with his left hand.

★ **links** ADVERB
left
□ links abbiegen to turn left
■ **links überholen** to overtake on the left
■ **Er schreibt mit links.** He writes with his left hand.
■ **Links sehen Sie das Rathaus.** On the left you'll see the town hall.
■ **links von der Kirche** to the left of the church
■ **links von mir** on my left
■ **links wählen** to vote for a left-wing party
■ **etwas mit links machen** to do something easily

der **Linkshänder** (PL die **Linkshänder**) MASC NOUN
■ **Er ist Linkshänder.** He's left-handed.

die **Linkshänderin** FEM NOUN
■ **Sie ist Linkshänderin.** She's left-handed.

die **Linkskurve** FEM NOUN
left-hand bend

der **Linksverkehr** MASC NOUN
driving on the left
■ **In Großbritannien ist Linksverkehr.** They drive on the left in Britain.

die **Linse** FEM NOUN
1 lentil
□ Linsensuppe lentil soup
2 lens
□ die Linse der Kamera the camera lens

★ die **Lippe** FEM NOUN
lip

★ der **Lippenstift** (PL die **Lippenstifte**) MASC NOUN
lipstick

★ der **Liter** (PL die **Liter**) MASC NOUN

You can also say das **Liter**.

litre

★ die **Literatur** FEM NOUN
literature

die **Lizenz** FEM NOUN
licence

★ der **Lkw** (GEN des **Lkw** or **Lkws**, PL die **Lkws**) MASC NOUN (= Lastkraftwagen)
lorry

der **Lkw-Fahrer** (PL die **Lkw-Fahrer**) MASC NOUN
lorry driver

die **Lkw-Fahrerin** FEM NOUN
lorry driver

das **Lob** NEUT NOUN
praise

loben – loslaufen

★ **loben** VERB [38]
to praise

★ **das Loch** (PL die **Löcher**) NEUT NOUN
hole

locker ADJECTIVE
1 loose
　□ ein lockerer Zahn a loose tooth
2 relaxed
　□ eine lockere Atmosphäre a relaxed atmosphere

lockerlassen (PRESENT TENSE **lässt locker**, IMPERFECT **ließ locker**, PERFECT TENSE **hat lockergelassen**) VERB [42]
　■ nicht lockerlassen not to let up □ Er ließ nicht locker mit seinen Fragen. He didn't let up with his questions.

★ **lockig** ADJECTIVE
curly

★ **der Löffel** (PL die **Löffel**) MASC NOUN
spoon
　■ ein Löffel Zucker a spoonful of sugar

die Logik FEM NOUN
logic

logisch ADJECTIVE
logical

★ **der Lohn** (PL die **Löhne**) MASC NOUN
1 wages pl
　□ Freitags wird der Lohn ausbezahlt. The wages are paid on Fridays.
2 reward
　□ Das ist jetzt der Lohn für meine Mühe! That's the reward for my efforts.

★ **lohnen** VERB [38]
　■ Das lohnt sich. It's worth it.

lohnend ADJECTIVE
worthwhile

die Lohnsteuer FEM NOUN
income tax

das Lokal (PL die **Lokale**) NEUT NOUN
pub

die Lokomotive FEM NOUN
locomotive

das Lorbeerblatt (PL die **Lorbeerblätter**) NEUT NOUN
bay leaf

★ **los** ADJECTIVE
　▷ see also das **Los** NOUN
loose
　□ Die Schraube ist los. The screw's loose.
　■ Dort ist viel los. There's a lot going on there.
　■ Dort ist nichts los. There's nothing going on there.
　■ Was ist los? What's the matter?
　■ Los! Go on!

das Los (GEN des **Loses**, PL die **Lose**) NEUT NOUN
　▷ see also **los** ADJECTIVE
lottery ticket

□ Mein Los hat gewonnen. My lottery ticket has won.

losbinden (IMPERFECT **band los**, PERFECT TENSE **hat losgebunden**) VERB
to untie

★ **löschen** VERB [48]
to put out
　□ ein Feuer löschen to put out a fire □ das Licht löschen to put out the light
　■ den Durst löschen to quench one's thirst
　■ eine Datei löschen to delete a file

die Löschtaste FEM NOUN
delete key

lose ADJECTIVE
loose
　□ lose Blätter loose sheets □ etwas lose verkaufen to sell something loose
　■ ein loses Mundwerk a big mouth

★ **lösen** VERB [38]
1 to solve
　□ ein Rätsel lösen to solve a puzzle □ ein Problem lösen to solve a problem
2 to loosen
　□ Kannst du diesen Knoten lösen? Can you loosen the knot?
　■ etwas von etwas lösen to remove something from something □ Sie löste das Etikett vom Glas. She removed the label from the jar.
　■ sich lösen 1 to come loose □ Eine Schraube hatte sich gelöst. A screw had come loose. 2 to dissolve □ Die Tablette löst sich in Wasser. The pill dissolves in water. 3 to resolve itself □ Das Problem hat sich inzwischen gelöst. The problem has resolved itself in the meantime.
　■ eine Fahrkarte lösen to buy a ticket

losfahren (PRESENT TENSE **fährt los**, IMPERFECT **fuhr los**, PERFECT TENSE **ist losgefahren**) VERB [21]
to leave

losgehen (IMPERFECT **ging los**, PERFECT TENSE **ist losgegangen**) VERB [29]
1 to set out
　□ Wir sollten so langsam losgehen. It's time we were setting out.
2 to start
　□ Wann geht der Film los? When does the film start?
　■ auf jemanden losgehen to go for somebody □ Er ging mit einem Messer auf sie los. He went for her with a knife.

loslassen (PRESENT TENSE **lässt los**, IMPERFECT **ließ los**, PERFECT TENSE **hat losgelassen**) VERB [42]
to let go of

loslaufen (PRESENT TENSE **läuft los**, IMPERFECT **lief los**, PERFECT TENSE **ist losgelaufen**) VERB [43]
to run off

löslich ADJECTIVE
soluble

die Lösung FEM NOUN
solution
□ Weißt du die Lösung des Rätsels? Do you
know the solution to the puzzle?

das Lotto (PL die **Lottos**) NEUT NOUN
National Lottery

die Lottozahlen FEM PL NOUN
winning lottery numbers *pl*

★ **der Löwe** (GEN des **Löwen**, PL die **Löwen**)
MASC NOUN
1 lion
2 Leo
□ Manfred ist Löwe. Manfred's Leo.

die Lücke FEM NOUN
gap

★ **die Luft** (PL die **Lüfte**) FEM NOUN
air
□ Ich brauche frische Luft. I need some fresh
air.
■ **in der Luft liegen** to be in the air
■ **jemanden wie Luft behandeln** to ignore
somebody

der Luftballon (PL die **Luftballons** or
Luftballone) MASC NOUN
balloon

★ **der Luftdruck** MASC NOUN
atmospheric pressure

das Luftkissenboot (PL die
Luftkissenboote) NEUT NOUN
hovercraft

die Luftmatratze FEM NOUN
air bed

★ **die Luftpost** FEM NOUN
airmail
□ per Luftpost by airmail

die Luftverschmutzung FEM NOUN
air pollution

★ **die Lüge** FEM NOUN
lie

★ **lügen** (IMPERFECT **log**, PERFECT TENSE **hat
gelogen**) VERB [47]
to lie
□ Ich müsste lügen, wenn ... I would be lying
if ...
■ **Er lügt ständig.** He's always telling lies.

der Lügner (PL die **Lügner**) MASC NOUN
liar

die Lunge FEM NOUN
lung

die Lungenentzündung FEM NOUN
pneumonia

die Lupe FEM NOUN
magnifying glass
■ **unter die Lupe nehmen** to scrutinize

★ **die Lust** FEM NOUN
■ **Lust haben, etwas zu tun** to feel like doing
something □ Hast du Lust, ins Kino zu gehen?
Do you feel like going to the cinema?
■ **keine Lust haben, etwas zu tun** not to
feel like doing something □ Sie hatte keine Lust,
mit auf die Party zu kommen. She didn't feel
like coming to the party.
■ **Lust auf etwas haben** to feel like
something □ Ich habe Lust auf eine kalte
Limonade. I feel like some cold lemonade.

★ **lustig** ADJECTIVE
funny
□ eine lustige Geschichte a funny story

lutschen VERB [48]
to suck
□ am Daumen lutschen to suck one's thumb

der Lutscher (PL die **Lutscher**) MASC NOUN
lollipop

★ **Luxemburg** NEUT NOUN
Luxembourg
■ **aus Luxemburg** from Luxembourg
■ **nach Luxemburg** to Luxembourg

★ **der Luxus** (GEN des **Luxus**) MASC NOUN
luxury

Mm

m ABBREVIATION (= *Meter*)
m

★ **machen** VERB [48]

PRESENT TENSE	
ich mache	wir machen
du machst	ihr macht
er/sie/es macht	sie/Sie machen
PERFECT TENSE	
hat gemacht	

1 to do
  □ Hausaufgaben machen to do one's homework □ etwas sorgfältig machen to do something carefully □ Was machst du heute Nachmittag? What are you doing this afternoon?
  ■ **eine Prüfung machen** to sit an exam
  ■ **den Führerschein machen** to take driving lessons
2 to make
  □ aus Holz gemacht made of wood □ Kaffee machen to make coffee □ einen Fehler machen to make a mistake □ Krach machen to make a noise □ jemanden traurig machen to make somebody sad □ Das macht müde. It makes you tired.
  ■ **Schluss machen** to finish
  ■ **ein Foto machen** to take a photo
3 to cause
  □ Das hat mir viel Mühe gemacht. This caused me a lot of trouble. □ viel Arbeit machen to cause a lot of work
  ■ **Das macht die Kälte.** It's the cold that does that.
4 to be
  □ Drei und fünf macht acht. Three and five is eight. □ Was macht das? How much is that? □ Das macht acht Euro. That's eight euros.
  ■ **Was macht die Arbeit?** How's the work going?
  ■ **Was macht dein Bruder?** How's your brother doing?
  ■ **Das macht nichts.** That doesn't matter.
  ■ **Die Kälte macht mir nichts.** I don't mind the cold.
  ■ **sich machen** to come on □ Eine Zwei in Physik, du machst dich! A 'B' in physics, you're coming on!
  ■ **sich nichts aus etwas machen** not to be very keen on something □ Ich mache mir nichts aus Süßigkeiten. I'm not very keen on sweets.

  ■ **Mach's gut!** Take care!
  ■ **Mach schon!** Come on!

die **Macht** (PL die **Mächte**) FEM NOUN
power

★ das **Mädchen** (PL die **Mädchen**) NEUT NOUN
girl

★ der **Mädchenname** (GEN des **Mädchennamens**, PL die **Mädchennamen**) MASC NOUN
maiden name

mag VERB ▷ *see* **mögen**

★ das **Magazin** NEUT NOUN
magazine
  □ Ich habe das in einem Magazin gelesen. I read it in a magazine.

★ der **Magen** (PL die **Magen** or **Mägen**) MASC NOUN
stomach

★ die **Magenschmerzen** MASC PL NOUN
stomachache *sing*
  □ Ich habe Magenschmerzen. I've got stomachache.

★ die **Magenverstimmung** FEM NOUN
stomach upset

★ **mager** ADJECTIVE
1 lean
  □ mageres Fleisch lean meat
2 thin
  □ Er ist furchtbar mager. He's terribly thin.

der **Magnet** (GEN des **Magnets** or **Magneten**, PL die **Magneten**) MASC NOUN
magnet

magnetisch ADJECTIVE
magnetic

★ die **Mahlzeit** FEM NOUN
meal
  □ Wir essen drei Mahlzeiten am Tag. We eat three meals a day.

★ der **Mai** (GEN des **Mai** or **Mais**, PL die **Maie**) MASC NOUN
May
  □ im Mai in May □ am sechsten Mai on 6 May □ Ulm, den 6. Mai 2019 Ulm, 6 May 2019 □ Heute ist der sechste Mai. Today is the sixth of May.
  ■ **der Erste Mai** May Day

★ = core vocabulary

★ der **Maifeiertag** MASC NOUN
May Day

mailen (PERFECT TENSE **hat gemailt**) VERB [38]
to email
□ Hast du es gemailt? Did you email it?

die **Mailingliste** (PL die **Mailinglisten**) FEM NOUN
mailing list

der **Mais** (GEN des **Maises**) MASC NOUN
maize

die **Majonäse** FEM NOUN
mayonnaise

★ **mal** ADVERB
▷ see also das **Mal** NOUN
times
□ zwei mal fünf two times five □ Wir haben sechsmal geklingelt. We rang six times.
■ Warst du schon mal in Paris? Have you ever been to Paris?

★ das **Mal** (PL die **Male**) NEUT NOUN
▷ see also **mal** ADVERB
1 time
□ das fünfte Mal the fifth time □ zum ersten Mal for the first time □ Wie viele Male hast du es versucht? How many times have you tried?
2 mark
□ Sie hat ein rotes Mal im Gesicht. She has a red mark on her face.

★ **malen** VERB [38]
to paint

der **Maler** (PL die **Maler**) MASC NOUN
painter

★ **malerisch** ADJECTIVE
picturesque

das **Mallorca** NEUT NOUN
Majorca
■ nach Mallorca to Majorca

malnehmen (PRESENT TENSE **nimmt mal**, IMPERFECT **nahm mal**, PERFECT TENSE **hat malgenommen**) VERB [52]
to multiply

das **Malz** (GEN des **Malzes**) NEUT NOUN
malt

die **Mama** (PL die **Mamas**) FEM NOUN
mum (Umgangssprache)

★ **man** PRONOUN
you
□ Man kann nie wissen. You never know. □ Wie schreibt man das? How do you spell that?
■ Man sagt, ... They say ...
■ Man hat mir gesagt ... I was told that ...

★ der **Manager** (PL die **Manager**) MASC NOUN
manager

manche PRONOUN
some
□ Manche Bücher sind langweilig. Some books are boring.

★ **manchmal** ADVERB
sometimes

die **Mandarine** FEM NOUN
mandarin orange

die **Mandel** FEM NOUN
1 almond
□ ein Kuchen mit Nüssen und Mandeln a cake with nuts and almonds
2 tonsil
□ Sie hat entzündete Mandeln. Her tonsils are inflamed.

der **Mangel** (PL die **Mängel**) MASC NOUN
1 lack
□ Schlafmangel lack of sleep
2 shortage
□ Der Mangel an Lehrern führt zu immer größeren Klassen. The shortage of teachers is leading to bigger classes.
3 fault
□ Das Gerät weist mehrere Mängel auf. The appliance has several faults.

★ **mangelhaft** ADJECTIVE
1 poor
□ Er hat mangelhaft bekommen. He got a poor mark.

DID YOU KNOW...?
German grades range from one (**sehr gut**) to six (**ungenügend**).

2 faulty
□ Mangelhafte Waren kann man zurückgehen lassen. You can return faulty goods.

mangels PREPOSITION

The preposition **mangels** takes the genitive.

for lack of
□ Er wurde mangels Beweisen freigesprochen. He was acquitted for lack of evidence.

die **Manieren** PL NOUN
manners pl
□ Sie hat keine Manieren. She doesn't have any manners.

★ der **Mann** (PL die **Männer**) MASC NOUN
1 man
□ Es war ein Mann am Telefon. There was a man on the phone.
2 husband
□ Frau Maier kam mit ihrem Mann. Mrs Maier came with her husband.
■ seinen Mann stehen to hold one's own
■ Alle Mann an Deck! All hands on deck!

★ **männlich** ADJECTIVE
1 male
□ meine männlichen Kollegen my male colleagues
■ eine männliche Person a man
2 masculine
□ ein männliches Substantiv a masculine noun

m

Mannschaft – Maß

★ die **Mannschaft** FEM NOUN
1 team
  □ die deutsche Mannschaft the German team
2 crew
  □ der Kapitän und seine Mannschaft the captain and his crew

★ der **Mantel** (PL die **Mäntel**) MASC NOUN
  coat
  □ Er hatte einen Mantel an. He was wearing a coat.

★ die **Mappe** FEM NOUN
1 briefcase
2 folder

BE CAREFUL!
Mappe does not mean **map**.

das **Märchen** (PL die **Märchen**) NEUT NOUN
  fairy tale

★ die **Margarine** FEM NOUN
  margarine

die **Marine** FEM NOUN
  navy
  □ Er ist bei der Marine. He's in the navy.

die **Marionette** FEM NOUN
  puppet

die **Marke** FEM NOUN
1 brand
  □ Für diese Marke sieht man in letzter Zeit viel Werbung. There's been a lot of advertising for this brand recently.
2 make
  □ Welche Marke fährt dein Vater? What make of car does your father drive?
3 voucher
  ■ eine Briefmarke a postage stamp

★ die **Markenware** FEM NOUN
  branded goods pl

markieren (PERFECT TENSE **hat markiert**) VERB [76]
  to mark
  □ Sie hat die Stelle mit Leuchtstift markiert. She marked the place with a highlighter.

★ der **Markt** (PL die **Märkte**) MASC NOUN
  market

★ der **Marktplatz** (GEN des **Marktplatzes**, PL die **Marktplätze**) MASC NOUN
  market place

★ die **Marmelade** FEM NOUN
  jam
  □ Erdbeermarmelade strawberry jam
  ■ Orangenmarmelade marmalade

der **Marmor** (PL die **Marmore**) MASC NOUN
  marble

★ der **März** (GEN des **März** or **Märzes**, PL die **Märze**) MASC NOUN
  March
  □ im März in March □ am dritten März on the third of March □ Bern, den 3. März 2019 Bern, 3 March 2019 □ Heute ist der dritte März. Today is the third of March.

die **Masche** FEM NOUN
1 mesh no pl
  □ Das Netz hatte feine Maschen. The net had a very fine mesh.
2 stitch
  ■ Das ist die neueste Masche. That's the latest thing.

★ die **Maschine** FEM NOUN
1 machine
  □ Werkzeug wird heutzutage von Maschinen hergestellt. Nowadays tools are manufactured by machines. □ Kannst du die schmutzige Wäsche bitte in die Maschine tun? Can you put the dirty washing in the machine?
2 engine
  □ Dieses Motorrad hat eine starke Maschine. This motorbike has a powerful engine.
3 typewriter
  □ Bevor es Computer gab, hat man mit der Maschine geschrieben. Before computers, one used to write with a typewriter.
4 plane

das **Maschinengewehr** (PL die **Maschinengewehre**) NEUT NOUN
  machine gun

die **Masern** PL NOUN
  measles sing
  □ Masern sind bei Erwachsenen ziemlich gefährlich. Measles is quite dangerous for adults.

die **Maske** FEM NOUN
  mask

sich **maskieren** (PERFECT TENSE **hat sich maskiert**) VERB [76]
1 to disguise oneself
  □ Die Täter hatten sich maskiert. The culprits had disguised themselves.
2 to dress up
  □ Als was wirst du dich maskieren? What are you dressing up as?
  ■ Die Bankräuber waren maskiert. The bank robbers were masked.

das **Maß (1)** (GEN des **Maßes**, PL die **Maße**) NEUT NOUN
1 measure
  □ In Deutschland werden metrische Maße verwendet. Metric measures are used in Germany.
  ■ Wie sind die Maße des Zimmers? What are the measurements of the room?
2 extent
  □ Sie war zu einem hohen Maß selbst schuld. To a large extent she had only herself to blame.

die **Maß (2)** (GEN der **Maß**, PL die **Maß** or die **Maßen**) FEM NOUN
  litre of beer

die **Massage** FEM NOUN
massage

die **Masse** FEM NOUN
mass

massenhaft ADVERB
masses of (*Umgangssprache*)
□ Du hast massenhaft Fehler gemacht. You've made masses of mistakes.

die **Massenmedien** NEUT PL NOUN
mass media *pl*

massieren (PERFECT TENSE **hat massiert**) VERB
[76]
to massage
□ Kannst du mir bitte den Rücken massieren? Can you massage my back, please?

★ **mäßig** ADJECTIVE
moderate

die **Maßnahme** FEM NOUN
step
□ Maßnahmen ergreifen to take steps

der **Maßstab** (PL die **Maßstäbe**) MASC NOUN
1 standard
□ Dieses Gerät setzt neue Maßstäbe. This appliance sets new standards.
2 scale
□ In welchem Maßstab ist diese Karte? What's the scale of this map?

der **Mast** (PL die **Maste** or **Masten**) MASC NOUN
1 mast
□ Am Mast hing die britische Fahne. The Union Jack was hanging from the mast.
2 pylon
□ Neben unserem Garten steht ein Hochspannungsmast. There's a high-tension pylon beside our garden.

das **Material** (PL die **Materialien**) NEUT NOUN
material
□ Aus welchem Material ist das gemacht? What material is it made of? □ Ich sammle Material für mein Referat. I'm collecting material for my assignment.

materialistisch ADJECTIVE
materialistic
□ materialistisch eingestellt sein to be materialistic

★ die **Mathe** FEM NOUN
maths *sing* (*Umgangssprache*)

★ die **Mathematik** FEM NOUN
mathematics *sing*
□ Mathematik ist mein Lieblingsfach. Mathematics is my favourite subject.

mathematisch ADJECTIVE
mathematical

die **Matratze** FEM NOUN
mattress

★ der **Matrose** (GEN des **Matrosen**, PL die **Matrosen**) MASC NOUN
sailor

der **Matsch** MASC NOUN
1 mud
□ Deine Schuhe sind voller Matsch. Your shoes are covered in mud.
2 slush

matschig ADJECTIVE
1 muddy
□ Nach dem Regen war der Weg sehr matschig. The path was very muddy after the rain.
2 slushy
□ Bei matschigem Schnee macht das Skifahren keinen Spaß. Skiing isn't fun when the snow is slushy.

matt ADJECTIVE
1 weak
□ Bei der Hitze fühle ich mich so matt. I feel so weak in this heat.
2 dull
□ Ihre Augen waren ganz matt. Her eyes were really dull.
3 matt
□ Möchten Sie die Abzüge Hochglanz oder matt? Would you like the prints glossy or matt?
4 mate
□ Schach und matt checkmate

die **Matte** FEM NOUN
mat

★ die **Mauer** FEM NOUN
wall

das **Maul** (PL die **Mäuler**) NEUT NOUN
mouth
□ Die Katze hatte einen Vogel im Maul. The cat had a bird in its mouth.
■ Halt's Maul! Shut your face! (*Umgangssprache*)

der **Maulkorb** (PL die **Maulkörbe**) MASC NOUN
muzzle

der **Maulwurf** (PL die **Maulwürfe**) MASC NOUN
mole

der **Maurer** (PL die **Maurer**) MASC NOUN
bricklayer

★ die **Maus** (PL die **Mäuse**) FEM NOUN
mouse
□ Sie hat Angst vor Mäusen. She's afraid of mice. □ Du musst zweimal mit der Maus klicken. You have to click the mouse twice.

die **Mausefalle** FEM NOUN
mousetrap

★ der **Mausklick** (PL die **Mausklicks**) MASC NOUN
mouse click
■ per Mausklick by clicking the mouse

die **Maut** FEM NOUN
toll
□ Auf einigen Autobahnen wird eine Maut erhoben. You have to pay a toll on some motorways.

m

maximal – mein

maximal ADJECTIVE, ADVERB

1 maximum
- □ der maximale Betrag the maximum amount

2 at most
- □ Wir können maximal eine Woche wegfahren. We can go away for a week at most.

die **Mayonnaise** FEM NOUN
mayonnaise

★ der **Mechaniker** (PL die **Mechaniker**) MASC NOUN
mechanic

mechanisch ADJECTIVE, ADVERB

1 mechanical
- □ Das Gerät hat einen mechanischen Schaden. The appliance has a mechanical fault.

2 mechanically
- □ etwas mechanisch tun to do something mechanically

meckern VERB [88]
to moan
- □ Müsst ihr über alles meckern? Do you have to moan about everything?

das **Mecklenburg-Vorpommern** NEUT NOUN
Mecklenburg-Western Pomerania

DID YOU KNOW...?
Mecklenburg-Vorpommern is one of the 16 Länder. Its capital is Schwerin. It is Germany's most rural and thinly populated Land, and is becoming increasingly popular with tourists.

die **Medaille** FEM NOUN
medal

die **Medien** NEUT PL NOUN
media *pl*

die **Medienwissenschaft** FEM NOUN
media studies *pl*

★ das **Medikament** (PL die **Medikamente**) NEUT NOUN
drug
- □ verschreibungspflichtige Medikamente prescribed drugs

★ die **Medizin** FEM NOUN
medicine

medizinisch ADJECTIVE
medical

★ das **Meer** (PL die **Meere**) NEUT NOUN
sea
- □ Wir wohnen am Meer. We live by the sea.

die **Meeresfrüchte** FEM PL NOUN
seafood

der **Meeresspiegel** MASC NOUN
sea level

der **Meerrettich** MASC NOUN
horseradish

★ das **Meerschweinchen** (PL die **Meerschweinchen**) NEUT NOUN
guinea pig

★ das **Mehl** (PL die **Mehle**) NEUT NOUN
flour

★ **mehr** ADJECTIVE, ADVERB
more
- □ Seit sie selbständig ist, muss sie mehr arbeiten. Since she became self-employed, she's had to work more.
- ■ Diese Internetseite ist nicht mehr aktuell. This website is no longer up to date.

mehrdeutig ADJECTIVE
ambiguous

★ **mehrere** ADJECTIVE
several

mehreres PRONOUN
several things

mehrfach ADJECTIVE, ADVERB

1 many
- □ Dieses Gerät hat mehrfache Verwendungsmöglichkeiten. This gadget has many uses.

2 repeated
- □ Es ist mir erst nach mehrfachen Versuchen gelungen. I only managed after repeated attempts. □ Ich habe mehrfach versucht, dich zu erreichen. I've tried repeatedly to get hold of you.

★ das **Mehrfamilienhaus** (GEN des **Mehrfamilienhauses**, PL die **Mehrfamilienhäuser**) NEUT NOUN
block of flats

die **Mehrheit** FEM NOUN
majority

mehrmalig ADJECTIVE
repeated

mehrmals ADVERB
repeatedly

die **Mehrwertsteuer** FEM NOUN
value added tax

die **Mehrzahl** FEM NOUN

1 majority
- □ Die Mehrzahl der Schüler besitzt einen Computer. The majority of pupils have a computer.

2 plural
- □ Wie heißt die Mehrzahl von 'woman'? What's the plural of 'woman'?

meiden (IMPERFECT **mied**, PERFECT TENSE **hat gemieden**) VERB
to avoid

★ **mein** ADJECTIVE, PRONOUN

1 my
- □ Mein Englischlehrer ist nett. My English teacher's nice. □ Meine Mutter erlaubt es nicht. My mother won't allow it. □ Ich finde mein Buch nicht. I can't find my book.

2 mine

□ Das ist nicht mein Füller, meiner ist blau. That's not my pen, mine's blue. □ Seine Mutter heißt Anne, meine auch. His mother's called Anne, so's mine. □ Wenn dein Fahrrad kaputt ist, kannst du meins nehmen. If your bike's broken you can use mine.

★ **meinen** VERB [38]

1 to think

□ Ich meine, wir sollten jetzt gehen. I think we should go now. □ Was meint deine Mutter zu deinem Freund? What does your mother think about your boyfriend? □ Sollen wir sie zur Party einladen, was meinst du? Should we invite her to the party? What do you think?

2 to say

□ Unser Lehrer meint, wir sollten am Wochenende keine Aufgaben machen. Our teacher says that we shouldn't do any homework at the weekend.

3 to mean

□ Was meint er mit diesem Wort? What does he mean by this word? □ Ich verstehe nicht, was du meinst. I don't understand what you mean. □ So habe ich das nicht gemeint. I didn't mean it like that.

■ **Das will ich meinen!** I should think so.

meinetwegen ADVERB

1 for my sake

□ Ihr müsst meinetwegen nicht auf euren Urlaub verzichten. You don't have to do without your holiday for my sake.

2 on my account

□ Hat er sich meinetwegen so aufgeregt? Did he get so upset on my account?

3 as far as I'm concerned

□ Meinetwegen kannst du gehen. As far as I'm concerned you can go.

4 go ahead

□ Kann ich das machen? — Meinetwegen. Can I do that? — Go ahead.

★ die **Meinung** FEM NOUN

opinion

□ Er hat mich nach meiner Meinung zu diesem Punkt gefragt. He asked for my opinion on this subject.

■ **meiner Meinung nach** in my opinion □ Meiner Meinung nach sollten Kinder nicht so viel fernsehen. In my opinion children shouldn't watch so much television.

■ **Ganz meine Meinung!** I quite agree.

■ **jemandem die Meinung sagen** to give somebody a piece of one's mind

BE CAREFUL!
Meinung does not mean **meaning**.

die **Meinungsumfrage** FEM NOUN

opinion poll

meist ADVERB

usually

□ Samstags bin ich meist zu Hause. I'm usually at home on Saturdays.

★ **meiste** ADJECTIVE

most

□ Die meisten Bücher habe ich schon gelesen. I've already read most of the books. □ Hast du die Bücher alle gelesen? — Ja, die meisten. Have you read all the books? — Yes, most of them. □ Die meisten von euch kennen dieses Wort sicher. Most of you must know this word.

■ **am meisten** **1** most □ Darüber hat sie sich am meisten aufgeregt. This upset her most.
2 the most □ Er hat am meisten gewonnen. He won the most.

★ **meistens** ADVERB

usually

□ Samstags bin ich meistens zu Hause. I'm usually at home on Saturdays.

der **Meister** (PL die **Meister**) MASC NOUN

1 champion

□ Er ist deutscher Meister im Ringen. He's the German wrestling champion.

2 master craftsman

□ Der Meister bildet Lehrlinge aus. The master craftsman trains apprentices.

★ die **Meisterschaft** FEM NOUN

championship

□ Wer hat die Meisterschaft gewonnen? Who won the championship?

★ **melden** (PERFECT TENSE **hat gemeldet**) VERB [54]

to report

□ Er meldete den Diebstahl bei der Polizei. He reported the theft to the police.

■ **sich melden** **1** to answer (phone) □ Es meldet sich niemand. There's no answer. **2** to put one's hand up (in school)

■ **sich polizeilich melden** to register with the police

die **Melodie** FEM NOUN

tune

die **Melone** FEM NOUN

melon

das **Meme** (PL die **Memes**) NEUT NOUN

meme

★ die **Menge** FEM NOUN

1 quantity

□ etwas in großen Mengen bestellen to order a large quantity of something

2 crowd

□ Ich habe ihn in der Menge verloren. I lost him in the crowd.

■ **eine Menge** a lot of □ Du hast eine Menge Fehler gemacht. You've made a lot of mistakes. □ Hast du CDs? — Ja, eine Menge. Have you got any CDs? — Yes, lots.

★ der **Mensch** (GEN des **Menschen**, PL die **Menschen**) MASC NOUN

human being

□ Es heißt, dass sich der Mensch durch die Sprache vom Tier unterscheidet. It's said that what distinguishes human beings from animals is language. □ Es schadet dem Menschen auch. It damages human beings too.
■ **Wie viele Menschen?** How many people?
■ **kein Mensch** nobody

der **Menschenverstand** MASC NOUN
■ **gesunder Menschenverstand** common sense

die **Menschheit** FEM NOUN
mankind

menschlich ADJECTIVE
human

★ das **Menü** (PL die **Menüs**) NEUT NOUN
set meal

merken VERB [38]
to notice
□ Hat sie gemerkt, dass ich gefehlt habe? Did she notice that I wasn't there? □ Ich habe den Fehler nicht gemerkt. I didn't notice the mistake.
■ **sich etwas merken** to remember something □ Dieses Wort kann ich mir nie merken. I can never remember that word.
■ **Das werd' ich mir merken!** I won't forget that in a hurry!

merkwürdig ADJECTIVE
odd
■ **sich merkwürdig benehmen** to behave strangely

★ die **Messe** FEM NOUN
1 fair
□ Auf der Messe wurden die neuesten Modelle gezeigt. The latest models were shown at the fair.
2 mass
□ Sie geht jeden Sonntag zur Messe. She goes to mass every Sunday.

★ **messen** (PRESENT TENSE **misst**, IMPERFECT **maß**, PERFECT TENSE **hat gemessen**) VERB
to measure
□ Hast du die Länge gemessen? Have you measured the length?
■ **bei jemandem Fieber messen** to take somebody's temperature
■ **Mit ihm kannst du dich nicht messen.** You're no match for him.

★ das **Messer** (PL die **Messer**) NEUT NOUN
knife

das **Messgerät** (PL die **Messgeräte**) NEUT NOUN
gauge

das **Messing** NEUT NOUN
brass

★ das **Metall** (PL die **Metalle**) NEUT NOUN
metal

★ der **Meter** (PL die **Meter**) MASC NOUN
metre

die **Methode** FEM NOUN
method

★ der **Metzger** (PL die **Metzger**) MASC NOUN
butcher
□ Er ist Metzger. He's a butcher. □ beim Metzger at the butcher's □ zum Metzger to the butcher's

★ die **Metzgerei** FEM NOUN
butcher's

miauen VERB [7]
to miaow

mich PRONOUN

mich is the accusative of ich.

1 me
□ Er hat mich zu seiner Party eingeladen. He's invited me to his party.
2 myself
□ Ich sehe mich im Spiegel. I can see myself in the mirror.

die **Miene** FEM NOUN
look
■ **eine finstere Miene machen** to look grim

★ **mies** ADJECTIVE
lousy (*Umgangssprache*)
□ Mir geht's mies. I feel lousy.

★ die **Miete** FEM NOUN
rent
■ **zur Miete wohnen** to live in rented accommodation

★ **mieten** VERB [2]
1 to rent

DID YOU KNOW...?
It is far more usual to live in rented accommodation in Germany than it is in Britain. Flats are mainly rented unfurnished.

□ Wir haben eine Ferienwohnung gemietet. We've rented a holiday flat.
2 to hire
□ Man kann am Flughafen ein Auto mieten. You can hire a car at the airport.

das **Mietshaus** (GEN des **Mietshauses**, PL die **Mietshäuser**) NEUT NOUN
block of rented flats

der **Mietvertrag** (PL die **Mietverträge**) MASC NOUN
lease

★ der **Mietwagen** (PL die **Mietwagen**) MASC NOUN
rental car

das **Mikroblog** (PL die **Mikroblogs**) NEUT NOUN
microblog

das **Mikrofon** (PL die **Mikrofone**) NEUT NOUN
microphone

das **Mikroskop** (PL die **Mikroskope**) NEUT NOUN
microscope

★ = core vocabulary

★ die **Mikrowelle** FEM NOUN
microwave

★ die **Milch** FEM NOUN
milk

mild ADJECTIVE
1 mild
□ eine milde Seife a mild soap □ mildes Wetter
mild weather
2 lenient
□ ein mildes Urteil a lenient sentence □ ein
milder Richter a lenient judge

das **Militär** NEUT NOUN
army
□ zum Militär gehen to join the army

militärisch ADJECTIVE
military

die **Milliarde** FEM NOUN
billion

der **Millimeter** (PL die **Millimeter**) MASC
NOUN
millimetre

die **Million** FEM NOUN
million

der **Millionär** (PL die **Millionäre**) MASC NOUN
millionaire
□ Er ist Millionär. He's a millionaire.

die **Minderheit** FEM NOUN
minority
□ in der Minderheit sein to be in the minority

minderjährig ADJECTIVE
underage
□ Sie ist noch minderjährig. She's still
underage.

der/die **Minderjährige** (GEN des/der
Minderjährigen, PL die **Minderjährigen**)
MASC/FEM NOUN
minor
□ Minderjährige dürfen keinen Alkohol kaufen.
Minors are not allowed to buy alcohol.

minderwertig ADJECTIVE
inferior

das **Mindestalter** NEUT NOUN
minimum age

mindeste ADJECTIVE
■ das Mindeste the least □ Das ist das
Mindeste, was du tun kannst. That's the least
you can do.
■ nicht im Mindesten not in the least □ Sie
war nicht im Mindesten überrascht. She wasn't
in the least surprised.
■ zum Mindesten at least □ Zum Mindesten
hättest du ja anrufen können. You could at least
have phoned.

mindestens ADVERB
at least

das **Mineral** (PL die **Minerale** or **Mineralien**)
NEUT NOUN
mineral

★ das **Mineralwasser** (PL die
Mineralwasser) NEUT NOUN
mineral water

der **Minirock** (PL die **Miniröcke**) MASC NOUN
miniskirt

★ der **Minister** (PL die **Minister**) MASC NOUN
minister (in government)

das **Ministerium** (PL die **Ministerien**) NEUT
NOUN
ministry

★ **minus** ADVERB
minus

★ die **Minute** FEM NOUN
minute

mir PRONOUN

mir is the dative of ich.

1 me
□ Kannst du mir sagen, wie spät es ist? Can you
tell me the time?
2 to me
□ Gib es mir! Give it to me.
■ mir nichts, dir nichts just like that □ Sie
war mir nichts, dir nichts verschwunden. She
disappeared just like that.

★ **mischen** VERB [48]
to mix

die **Mischung** FEM NOUN
mixture

miserabel ADJECTIVE
dreadful
□ Mir geht's miserabel. I feel dreadful.

missbilligen (PERFECT TENSE **hat missbilligt**)
VERB [49]
to disapprove of

der **Missbrauch** MASC NOUN
abuse

der **Misserfolg** (PL die **Misserfolge**) MASC
NOUN
failure

misshandeln (PERFECT TENSE **hat
misshandelt**) VERB [88]
to ill-treat

missmutig ADJECTIVE
sullen

misstrauen (PERFECT TENSE **hat misstraut**)
VERB [49]
▷ see also das **Misstrauen** NOUN
■ jemandem misstrauen to mistrust
somebody

das **Misstrauen** NEUT NOUN
▷ see also **misstrauen** VERB
suspicion

misstrauisch ADJECTIVE
suspicious

★ das **Missverständnis** (GEN des
Missverständnisses, PL die

m

missverstehen – Mitschülerin

Missverständnisse) NEUT NOUN
misunderstanding

missverstehen (IMPERFECT **missverstand,**
PERFECT TENSE **hat missverstanden**) VERB [72]
to misunderstand

der **Mist** MASC NOUN

1 manure
□ Im Frühling werden die Felder mit Mist
gedüngt. **The fields are fertilized with manure in
the spring.**

2 rubbish (*Umgangssprache*)
□ Warum isst du so einen Mist? **Why do you eat
such rubbish?** □ Heute kommt wieder nur Mist
im Fernsehen. **There's nothing but rubbish on
TV again today.** □ Du redest Mist. **You're talking
rubbish.**
■ Mist! Blast!

BE CAREFUL!
The German word Mist does not mean **mist**.

die **Mistel** FEM NOUN
mistletoe

★ **mit** PREPOSITION, ADVERB

The preposition **mit** takes the dative.

1 with
□ Er ist mit seiner Freundin gekommen. **He
came with his girlfriend.** □ mit Filzstift
geschrieben **written with a felt-tip pen**

2 by
□ mit dem Auto **by car** □ mit der Bahn **by train**
□ mit dem Bus **by bus**
■ **mit zehn Jahren** at the age of ten
■ **Sie ist mit die Beste in ihrer Klasse. She
is one of the best in her class.**
■ **Wollen Sie mit? Do you want to come
along?**

der **Mitarbeiter** (PL die **Mitarbeiter**) MASC
NOUN

1 colleague
□ meine Mitarbeiter und ich **my colleagues
and I**

2 collaborator
□ die Mitarbeiter an diesem Projekt **the
collaborators on this project**

3 employee
□ Die Firma hat 500 Mitarbeiter. **The company
has 500 employees.**

★ **mitbringen** (IMPERFECT **brachte mit,** PERFECT
TENSE **hat mitgebracht**) VERB [13]
to bring along
□ Kann ich meine Freundin mitbringen? **Can I
bring my girlfriend along?**

miteinander ADVERB
with each another

der **Mitesser** (PL die **Mitesser**) MASC NOUN
blackhead

★ **mitfahren** (PRESENT TENSE **fährt mit,** IMPERFECT
fuhr mit, PERFECT TENSE **ist mitgefahren**) VERB
[21]

to come too
□ Wir fahren nach Berlin. Willst du mitfahren?
**We're going to Berlin. Do you want to come
too?**
■ Ich fahre nicht mit. I'm not going.
■ Willst du mit uns im Auto mitfahren? D
you want a lift in our car?

mitgeben (PRESENT TENSE **gibt mit,** IMPERFECT
gab mit, PERFECT TENSE **hat mitgegeben**) VER
[28]
to give

★ das **Mitglied** (PL die **Mitglieder**) NEUT NOUN
member

die **Mitgliedschaft** FEM NOUN
membership

mithelfen (PRESENT TENSE **hilft mit,** IMPERFECT
half mit, PERFECT TENSE **hat mitgeholfen**)
VERB [37]
to help

★ **mitkommen** (IMPERFECT **kam mit,** PERFECT
TENSE **ist mitgekommen**) VERB [40]

1 to come along
□ Willst du nicht mitkommen? **Wouldn't you
like to come along?**

2 to keep up
□ In Mathe komme ich nicht mit. **I can't keep
up in maths.**

★ das **Mitleid** NEUT NOUN

1 sympathy
■ Ich habe wirklich Mitleid mit dir. I really
sympathize with you.

2 pity
□ Er kennt kein Mitleid. **He knows no pity.**

★ **mitmachen** (PERFECT TENSE **hat mitgemach**
VERB [48]
to join in

★ **mitnehmen** (PRESENT TENSE **nimmt mit,**
IMPERFECT **nahm mit,** PERFECT TENSE **hat
mitgenommen**) VERB [52]

1 to take
□ Kannst du den Brief zur Post mitnehmen?
Can you take the letter to the post office? □ Ich
habe meine Freundin zur Party mitgenommen
I took my girlfriend to the party.

2 to take away
□ Die Polizei ist gekommen und hat sie
mitgenommen. **The police came and took her
away.**

3 to affect
□ Die Scheidung ihrer Eltern hat sie sehr
mitgenommen. **Her parents' divorce really
affected her.**
■ zum Mitnehmen to take away

der **Mitschüler** (PL die **Mitschüler**) MASC
NOUN
schoolmate

die **Mitschülerin** FEM NOUN
schoolmate

mitspielen VERB [4]
to join in
□ Willst du nicht mitspielen? Don't you want to join in?
■ Wer hat bei dem Match mitgespielt? Who played in the match?

der Mittag (PL die Mittage) MASC NOUN
midday
□ gegen Mittag around midday
■ zu Mittag essen to have lunch
■ heute Mittag at lunchtime
■ morgen Mittag tomorrow lunchtime
■ gestern Mittag yesterday lunchtime

das Mittagessen (PL die Mittagessen) NEUT NOUN
lunch

mittags ADVERB
at lunchtime

die Mittagspause FEM NOUN
lunch break

die Mitte FEM NOUN
middle

mitteilen VERB [4]
■ jemandem etwas mitteilen to inform somebody of something

die Mitteilung FEM NOUN
communication

das Mittel (PL die Mittel) NEUT NOUN
means sing
□ Wir werden jedes Mittel einsetzen, um die Genehmigung zu bekommen. We will use every means to gain approval. □ ein Mittel zum Zweck a means to an end
■ ein Mittel gegen Husten something for a cough
■ ein Mittel gegen Flecken a stain remover
■ öffentliche Mittel public funds

Mitteleuropa NEUT NOUN
Central Europe

mittelgroß ADJECTIVE
1 medium-sized
□ Bremen ist eine mittelgroße Stadt. Bremen is a medium-sized city.
2 of medium height
□ Christine ist mittelgroß. Christine is of medium height.

mittelmäßig ADJECTIVE
mediocre

das Mittelmeer NEUT NOUN
the Mediterranean

der Mittelpunkt (PL die Mittelpunkte) MASC NOUN
centre

der Mittelstürmer (PL die Mittelstürmer) MASC NOUN
centre-forward

mitten ADVERB
in the middle
□ mitten auf der Straße in the middle of the street □ mitten am Tag in the middle of the day □ mitten in der Nacht in the middle of the night

die Mitternacht FEM NOUN
midnight
□ um Mitternacht at midnight

mittlere ADJECTIVE
1 middle
□ Das mittlere von den Fahrrädern ist meins. The bike in the middle is mine. □ Der mittlere Teil des Buches ist langweilig. The middle section of the book is boring.
2 average
□ Die mittleren Temperaturen liegen bei zwanzig Grad. The average temperature is twenty degrees.
■ mittleren Alters middle-aged □ eine Frau mittleren Alters a middle-aged woman
■ mittlere Reife O-levels pl

mittlerweile ADVERB
meanwhile

der Mittwoch (PL die Mittwoche) MASC NOUN
Wednesday
□ am Mittwoch on Wednesday

mittwochs ADVERB
on Wednesdays

mobben VERB [48] (Umgangssprache)
to bully
■ in der Schule/am Arbeitsplatz gemobbt werden to be bullied at school/at work

das Mobbing NEUT NOUN (Umgangssprache)
bullying
■ das Internet-Mobbing online bullying

die Möbel NEUT PL NOUN
furniture sing

der Möbelwagen (PL die Möbelwagen) MASC NOUN
removal van

das Mobiltelefon (PL die Mobiltelefone) NEUT NOUN
mobile phone

möblieren (PERFECT TENSE hat möbliert) VERB [76]
to furnish
□ Sie hat ihre Wohnung sehr geschmackvoll möbliert. She has furnished her flat very tastefully.
■ möbliert wohnen to live in furnished accommodation

möchte VERB ▷ see mögen

die Mode FEM NOUN
fashion

das Modell (PL die Modelle) NEUT NOUN
model

m

Numbers in brackets refer to verb tables on pages 697 to 706.

183

★ **modern** ADJECTIVE
modern

modernisieren (PERFECT TENSE **hat modernisiert**) VERB [76]
to modernize

★ **modisch** ADJECTIVE
fashionable
□ Jane trägt sehr modische Kleidung. Jane wears very fashionable clothes.

mogeln VERB [88]
to cheat

★ **mögen** VERB [50]

PRESENT TENSE	
ich mag	wir mögen
du magst	ihr mögt
er/sie/es mag	sie/Sie mögen
PERFECT TENSE	
hat gemocht/mögen	

The past participle **mögen** is used when **mögen** is a modal auxiliary.

to like
□ Ich mag Süßes. I like sweet things. □ Ich habe sie noch nie gemocht. I've never liked her.
■ **Ich möchte ...** I'd like ... □ Ich möchte ein Erdbeereis. I'd like a strawberry ice cream. □ Er möchte in die Stadt. He'd like to go into town. □ Möchtest du ...? Would you like ...?
■ **Ich möchte nicht, dass du ...** I wouldn't like you to ... □ Ich möchte nicht, dass du dich übergangen fühlst. I wouldn't like you to feel you were being ignored.
■ **Ich mag nicht mehr.** I've had enough.
■ **etwas tun mögen** to like to do something □ Magst du noch mit zu mir kommen? Would you like to come back to my place? □ Möchtest du etwas essen? Would you like something to eat?
■ **etwas nicht tun mögen** not to want to do something □ Sie mag nicht bleiben. She doesn't want to stay. □ Ich möchte nicht, dass du so spät nach Hause kommst. I don't want you coming home so late.

★ **möglich** ADJECTIVE
possible
□ Das ist gar nicht möglich! That's not possible. □ so viel wie möglich as much as possible □ so viele wie möglich as many as possible □ so bald wie möglich as soon as possible

möglicherweise ADVERB
possibly

★ **die Möglichkeit** FEM NOUN
possibility
■ **nach Möglichkeit** if possible

möglichst ADVERB
as ... as possible
□ Komm möglichst bald. Come as soon as possible.

die Möhre FEM NOUN
carrot

★ **der Moment** (PL die **Momente**) MASC NOUN
moment
□ Wir müssen den richtigen Moment abwarten We have to wait for the right moment.
■ **im Moment** at the moment
■ **Moment mal!** Just a moment.

momentan ADJECTIVE, ADVERB
1 momentary
□ Das ist nur eine momentane Schwäche. It's only a momentary weakness.
2 at the moment
□ Ich bin momentan sehr beschäftigt. I'm very busy at the moment.

die Monarchie FEM NOUN
monarchy

★ **der Monat** (PL die **Monate**) MASC NOUN
month

monatelang ADVERB
for months

★ **monatlich** ADJECTIVE, ADVERB
monthly

die Monatskarte FEM NOUN
monthly ticket

★ **der Mond** (PL die **Monde**) MASC NOUN
moon

monetarisieren VERB [76]
to monetize

★ **der Montag** (PL die **Montage**) MASC NOUN
Monday
□ am Montag on Monday

★ **montags** ADVERB
on Mondays

das Moor (PL die **Moore**) NEUT NOUN
moor

die Moral FEM NOUN
1 morals pl
□ Er hat keine Moral. He hasn't got any morals.
2 moral
□ Und die Moral der Geschichte ist: ... And the moral of the story is: ...

moralisch ADJECTIVE
moral

★ **der Mord** (PL die **Morde**) MASC NOUN
murder

der Mörder (PL die **Mörder**) MASC NOUN
murderer

BE CAREFUL!
Mörder does not mean **murder**.

die Mörderin FEM NOUN
murderer

★ **morgen** ADVERB
▷ see also der **Morgen** NOUN
tomorrow

★ = core vocabulary

- **morgen früh** tomorrow morning
- **Bis morgen!** See you tomorrow!

★ der **Morgen** (PL die **Morgen**) MASC NOUN
▷ *see also* **morgen** ADVERB
morning
□ Wir haben den ganzen Morgen Unterricht. We've got lessons all morning.
- **Guten Morgen!** Good morning.

★ **morgens** ADVERB
in the morning
□ Morgens bin ich immer müde. I'm always tired in the morning.
- **von morgens bis abends** from morning to night

morgig ADJECTIVE
tomorrow's
□ das morgige Fest tomorrow's party
- **der morgige Tag** tomorrow

★ die **Mosel** FEM NOUN
Moselle

das **Motiv** (PL die **Motive**) NEUT NOUN
motive
□ Was war sein Motiv? What was his motive?

motivieren (PERFECT TENSE **hat motiviert**) VERB [76]
to motivate

★ der **Motor** (PL die **Motoren**) MASC NOUN
1 engine
□ Das Auto hat einen starken Motor. The car has a powerful engine.
2 motor
□ ein Außenbordmotor an outboard motor

das **Motorboot** (PL die **Motorboote**) NEUT NOUN
motorboat

★ das **Motorrad** (PL die **Motorräder**) NEUT NOUN
motorcycle

die **Möwe** FEM NOUN
seagull

der **MP3-Spieler** (PL die **MP3-Spieler**) MASC NOUN
MP3 player

MRT ABBREVIATION
(= *Magnetresonanztomographie*)
MRI

die **Mücke** FEM NOUN
midge

der **Mückenstich** (PL die **Mückenstiche**) MASC NOUN
midge bite

müde ADJECTIVE
tired
□ Ich bin sehr müde. I'm very tired.

die **Müdigkeit** FEM NOUN
tiredness

die **Mühe** FEM NOUN
trouble
□ Das macht gar keine Mühe. That's no trouble.
- **mit Müh und Not** with great difficulty
- **sich Mühe geben** to go to a lot of trouble
□ Die Gastgeberin hat sich viel Mühe gegeben. The hostess went to a lot of trouble.
- **sich mehr Mühe geben** to try harder

die **Mühle** FEM NOUN
1 mill
□ In dieser Mühle wird Korn gemahlen. Corn is ground in this mill.
2 grinder
□ Hast du eine Mühle, um den Kaffee zu mahlen? Do you have a grinder for the coffee?

mühsam ADJECTIVE, ADVERB
1 arduous
- **ein mühsames Geschäft** a painstaking business
2 with difficulty
- **Ich habe es mühsam gefunden.** I struggled to find it.

★ der **Müll** MASC NOUN
refuse

die **Müllabfuhr** FEM NOUN
1 disposal of rubbish
□ Die Gebühren für die Müllabfuhr sollen erhöht werden. The charges for the disposal of rubbish are to be increased.
2 dustmen pl
□ Morgen kommt die Müllabfuhr. The dustmen come tomorrow.

der **Mülleimer** (PL die **Mülleimer**) MASC NOUN
rubbish bin

★ die **Mülltonne** FEM NOUN
dustbin

multiplizieren (PERFECT TENSE **hat multipliziert**) VERB [76]
to multiply

der **Mumps** (GEN des **Mumps**) MASC NOUN
mumps sing
□ Mumps ist sehr unangenehm. Mumps is very unpleasant.

★ **München** NEUT NOUN
Munich
- **nach München** to Munich

★ der **Mund** (PL die **Münder**) MASC NOUN
mouth
- **Halt den Mund!** Shut up! (*Umgangssprache*)

die **Mundharmonika** FEM NOUN
mouth organ

★ **mündlich** ADJECTIVE
oral
□ eine mündliche Prüfung an oral exam

die **Munition** FEM NOUN
ammunition

Münster – MwSt

★ das **Münster** (PL die **Münster**) NEUT NOUN
   cathedral

munter ADJECTIVE
   lively

★ die **Münze** FEM NOUN
   coin

murmeln VERB [34]
   to mumble
   □ Er murmelte irgendwas vor sich hin. **He mumbled something.**

mürrisch ADJECTIVE
   sullen

die **Muschel** FEM NOUN
1 mussel
   □ Ich esse gern Muscheln. **I like mussels.**
2 shell
   □ Wir haben am Strand Muscheln gesammelt. **We collected shells on the beach.**
3 receiver
   □ Du musst in die Muschel sprechen. **You have to speak into the receiver.**

★ das **Museum** (PL die **Museen**) NEUT NOUN
   museum

★ die **Musik** FEM NOUN
   music

musikalisch ADJECTIVE
   musical
   □ musikalisch begabt sein **to be musically gifted**

★ der **Musiker** (PL die **Musiker**) MASC NOUN
   musician

das **Musikinstrument** (PL die **Musikinstrumente**) NEUT NOUN
   musical instrument

★ **musizieren** (PERFECT TENSE hat musiziert) VERB [76]
   to make music

der **Muskel** (PL die **Muskeln**) MASC NOUN
   muscle

das **Müsli** (PL die **Müsli**) NEUT NOUN
   muesli

★ **müssen** VERB [51]

PRESENT TENSE	
ich muss	wir müssen
du musst	ihr müsst
er/sie/es muss	sie/Sie müssen
PERFECT TENSE	
hat gemusst/müssen	

   The past participle müssen is used when müssen is a modal auxiliary.

1 must
   □ Ich muss es tun. **I must do it.**
2 to have to
   □ Er hat gehen müssen. **He had to go.** □ Ich musste es tun. **I had to do it.** □ Er muss es nicht tun. **He doesn't have to do it.** □ Muss ich? **Do I have to?**
   ■ Muss das sein? **Is that really necessary?**
   ■ Es muss nicht wahr sein. **It needn't be true.**
   ■ Sie hätten ihn fragen müssen. **You should have asked him.**
   ■ Es muss geregnet haben. **It must have rained.**
   ■ Ich muss mal. **I need the loo.** (*Umgangssprache*)

das **Muster** (PL die **Muster**) NEUT NOUN
1 pattern
   □ ein Kleid mit einem geometrischen Muster **a dress with a geometric pattern**
2 sample
   □ Lass dir von dem Stoff doch ein Muster geben. **Ask them to give you a sample of the material.**

der **Mut** MASC NOUN
   courage
   ■ Nur Mut! **Cheer up!**
   ■ jemandem Mut machen **to encourage somebody**
   ■ zu Mute ▷ see zumute

mutig ADJECTIVE
   courageous

★ die **Mutter (1)** (PL die **Mütter**) FEM NOUN
   mother
   □ Meine Mutter erlaubt das nicht. **My mother doesn't allow that.**

★ die **Mutter (2)** (PL die **Muttern**) FEM NOUN
   nut
   □ Hast du die Mutter zu dieser Schraube gesehen? **Have you seen the nut for this bolt?**

die **Muttersprache** FEM NOUN
   mother tongue

der **Muttertag** (PL die **Muttertage**) MASC NOUN
   Mother's Day

★ die **Mutti** (PL die **Muttis**) FEM NOUN
   mummy (*Umgangssprache*)

★ die **Mütze** FEM NOUN
   cap

MwSt ABBREVIATION (= *Mehrwertsteuer*)
   VAT (= *value added tax*)

★ = core vocabulary

Nn

★ na EXCLAMATION

well
□ Na, kommst du mit? Well, are you coming?
- **Na gut.** Okay then.
- **Na ja, ...** Well, ...

der **Nabel** (PL die **Nabel**) MASC NOUN
navel

★ nach PREPOSITION, ADVERB

> The preposition **nach** takes the dative.

1 to
□ nach Berlin to Berlin □ nach Italien to Italy
- **nach Süden** south
- **nach links** left
- **nach rechts** right
- **nach oben** up
- **nach hinten** back

2 after
□ Ich fange nach Weihnachten damit an. I'll
start on it after Christmas. □ die nächste Straße
nach der Kreuzung the first street after the
crossroads □ einer nach dem anderen one after
the other □ Nach Ihnen! After you! □ Ihm nach!
After him!

3 past
□ zehn nach drei ten past three

4 according to
□ Nach unserer Englischlehrerin wird das so
geschrieben. According to our English teacher,
that's how it's spelt.
- **nach und nach** little by little
- **nach wie vor** still

★ der Nachbar (GEN des **Nachbarn**, PL die
Nachbarn) MASC NOUN
neighbour

★ die Nachbarin FEM NOUN
neighbour

die **Nachbarschaft** FEM NOUN
neighbourhood

★ nachdem CONJUNCTION

1 after
□ Nachdem er gegangen war, haben wir Witze
erzählt. After he left we told jokes.

2 since
□ Nachdem du sowieso zur Post gehst,
könntest du mein Päckchen aufgeben? Since
you're going to the post office anyway, could
you post my parcel?

- **je nachdem** it depends □ Du kommst doch
auch mit? — Je nachdem. You're coming along
too, aren't you? — It depends.
- **je nachdem, ob** depending on whether
□ Wir kommen mit dem Rad oder dem Auto, je
nachdem, ob es regnet oder nicht. We'll be
coming by bike or by car, depending on whether
it rains or not.

★ nachdenken (IMPERFECT **dachte nach**,
PERFECT TENSE **hat nachgedacht**) VERB [14]
- **nachdenken über** to think about □ Ich
habe über deine Frage nachgedacht. I've been
thinking about your question.

nachdenklich ADJECTIVE
pensive

nacheinander ADVERB
one after the other

nachgeben (PRESENT TENSE **gibt nach**,
IMPERFECT **gab nach**, PERFECT TENSE **hat
nachgegeben**) VERB [28]

1 to give way
□ Das Brett hat nachgegeben. The plank gave
way.

2 to give in
□ Ich werde nicht nachgeben. I won't give in.

★ nachgehen (IMPERFECT **ging nach**, PERFECT
TENSE **ist nachgegangen**) VERB [29]
- **jemandem nachgehen** to follow somebody
- **einer Sache nachgehen** to look into
something □ Wir werden Ihrer Beschwerde
nachgehen. We will look into your complaint.
- **Die Uhr geht nach.** The clock is slow.

nachgiebig ADJECTIVE
indulgent

★ nachher ADVERB
afterwards

die **Nachhilfestunde** FEM NOUN
private lesson

der **Nachhilfeunterricht** MASC NOUN
extra tuition

★ nachholen (PERFECT TENSE **hat nachgeholt**)
VERB [4]

1 to catch up on
□ Weil er gefehlt hat, muss er jetzt viel
nachholen. As he was absent, he's got a lot to
catch up on.

2 to make up for

nachkommen – nachsitzen

□ Wir konnten meinen Geburtstag nicht feiern, werden das aber nachholen. We weren't able to celebrate my birthday, but we'll make up for it.

■ eine Prüfung nachholen to do an exam at a later date

nachkommen (IMPERFECT **kam nach**, PERFECT TENSE **ist nachgekommen**) VERB [40]
to come later

□ Wir gehen schon mal, du kannst ja später nachkommen. We'll go on and you can come later.

■ einer Verpflichtung nachkommen to fulfil an obligation

nachlassen (PRESENT TENSE **lässt nach**, IMPERFECT **ließ nach**, PERFECT TENSE **hat nachgelassen**) VERB [42]

1 to deteriorate

□ Seine Leistungen haben merklich nachgelassen. His marks have deteriorated considerably.

■ Ihr Gedächtnis lässt nach. Her memory is going.

■ Er hat nachgelassen. He's got worse.

2 to ease off

□ Die Schmerzen haben nachgelassen. The pain has eased off.

3 to die down

□ sobald der Sturm nachlässt as soon as the storm dies down

nachlässig ADJECTIVE
careless

■ etwas nachlässig machen to do something carelessly □ Sie macht ihre Hausaufgaben ziemlich nachlässig. She does her homework pretty carelessly.

nachlaufen (PRESENT TENSE **läuft nach**, IMPERFECT **lief nach**, PERFECT TENSE **ist nachgelaufen**) VERB [43]

■ jemandem nachlaufen to run after somebody □ Sie hat ihren Schirm vergessen, lauf ihr schnell nach. She's forgotten her umbrella. Quick, run after her.
to chase

□ Er läuft allen Mädchen nach. He chases all the girls.

nachmachen (PERFECT TENSE **hat nachgemacht**) VERB [4]

1 to copy

□ Macht alle meine Bewegungen nach. Copy all my movements.

2 to imitate

□ Sie kann unsere Mathelehrerin gut nachmachen. She's good at imitating our maths teacher.

3 to forge

□ ein Gemälde nachmachen to forge a painting

■ Das ist nicht echt, sondern nachgemacht. This isn't genuine, it's a fake.

★ der **Nachmittag** (PL die **Nachmittage**) MASC NOUN
afternoon

□ am Nachmittag in the afternoon

■ heute Nachmittag this afternoon

★ **nachmittags** ADVERB
in the afternoon

★ der **Nachname** (GEN des **Nachnamens**, PL die **Nachnamen**) MASC NOUN
surname

□ Wie heißt du mit Nachnamen? What's your surname?

nachprüfen (PERFECT TENSE **hat nachgeprüft**) VERB [4]
to check

■ Sie prüfte nach, ob ihr Handy noch funktionierte. She checked if her mobile was still working.

★ die **Nachricht** FEM NOUN

1 news *sing*

□ Wir haben noch keine Nachricht von ihr. We still haven't had any news of her.

■ die Nachrichten the news □ Was kommt in den Nachrichten? What's on the news?

2 message

□ Kannst du ihm eine Nachricht von mir übermitteln? Can you give him a message from me?

nachschlagen (PRESENT TENSE **schlägt nach**, IMPERFECT **schlug nach**, PERFECT TENSE **hat nachgeschlagen**) VERB [59]
to look up (*in dictionary*)

★ **nachsehen** (PRESENT TENSE **sieht nach**, IMPERFECT **sah nach**, PERFECT TENSE **hat nachgesehen**) VERB [64]
to check

□ Sieh mal nach, ob noch genügend Brot da ist. Check whether we've still got enough bread. □ Ich habe im Wörterbuch nachgesehen. I've checked in the dictionary. □ Mein Vater sieht immer meine Englischaufgaben nach. My father always checks my English homework.

■ jemandem etwas nachsehen to forgive somebody something □ Den kleinen Fehler sollten wir ihm nachsehen. We ought to forgive him this little mistake.

■ das Nachsehen haben to come off worst

nachsenden (IMPERFECT **sendete** or **sandte nach**, PERFECT TENSE **hat nachgesendet** or **nachgesandt**) VERB
to send on

□ Ich habe ihr den Brief nachgesendet. I've sent the letter on to her.

nachsichtig ADJECTIVE
lenient

★ **nachsitzen** (IMPERFECT **saß nach**, PERFECT TENSE **hat nachgesessen**) VERB [68]

■ nachsitzen müssen to be kept in □ Er musste nachsitzen, weil er seine Hausaufgaben vergessen hatte. He was kept in because he had forgotten to do his homework.

★ = core vocabulary

German-English

★ die Nachspeise FEM NOUN
pudding
□ Was gibt's als Nachspeise? **What's for pudding?**

★ nächste ADJECTIVE
▷ *see also* **nahe, näher**
1 next
□ Wir nehmen den nächsten Zug. **We'll take the next train.** □ Beim nächsten Mal passt du besser auf. **Be more careful next time.**
□ nächstes Jahr **next year**
■ **als Nächstes** next □ Was machen wir als Nächstes? **What'll we do next?**
■ **Der Nächste bitte!** Next, please!
2 nearest
□ Wo ist hier die nächste Post? **Where's the nearest post office?**

★ die Nacht (PL die **Nächte**) FEM NOUN
night
■ **Gute Nacht!** Good night.

★ der Nachteil (PL die **Nachteile**) MASC NOUN
disadvantage

das Nachthemd (PL die **Nachthemden**)
NEUT NOUN
nightshirt

★ der Nachtisch MASC NOUN
pudding
□ Was gibt's zum Nachtisch? **What's for pudding?**

★ der Nachtklub (PL die **Nachtklubs**) MASC
NOUN
night club

das Nachtleben NEUT NOUN
nightlife

nachträglich ADJECTIVE, ADVERB
1 subsequent
□ eine nachträgliche Korrektur **a subsequent correction**
■ **nachträgliche Glückwünsche** belated best wishes
2 later
□ Nachträglich habe ich eingesehen, dass das ein Fehler war. **I later realized that it was a mistake.**

★ die Nachtruhe FEM NOUN
sleep
□ Ich brauche meine Nachtruhe. **I need my sleep.**

★ nachts ADVERB
at night

der Nacken (PL die **Nacken**) MASC NOUN
nape of the neck

nackt ADJECTIVE
naked
□ Er war nackt. **He was naked.**
■ **nackte Arme** bare arms
■ **nackte Tatsachen** plain facts

die Nadel FEM NOUN
1 needle
□ Ich brauche Nadel und Faden. **I need a needle and thread.**
2 pin
□ Ich habe mich an der Nadel des Ansteckers gestochen. **I've pricked myself on the pin of my badge.**

der Nagel (PL die **Nägel**) MASC NOUN
nail

die Nagelfeile FEM NOUN
nailfile

der Nagellack (PL die **Nagellacke**) MASC
NOUN
nail varnish

nagelneu ADJECTIVE
brand-new

nagen VERB [38]
to gnaw
□ an etwas nagen **to gnaw on something**

★ nahe ADJECTIVE, ADVERB, PREPOSITION
▷ *see also* **näher, nächste**
1 near
□ in der nahen Zukunft **in the near future**
■ **nahe bei** near □ nahe bei der Kirche **near the church**
2 close
□ Der Bahnhof ist ganz nah. **The station's quite close.** □ nahe Verwandte **close relatives** □ nahe Freunde **close friends** □ Unser Haus ist nahe der Universität. **Our house is close to the university.** □ den Tränen nahe **close to tears**
■ **mit jemandem nah verwandt sein** to be closely related to somebody
■ **der Nahe Osten** the Middle East
■ **Die Prüfungen rücken näher.** The exams are getting closer.
■ **nahe daran sein, etwas zu tun** to be close to doing something □ Ich war nahe daran aufzugeben. **I was close to giving up.**
■ **nahe liegend** ▷ *see* naheliegend

★ die Nähe FEM NOUN
■ **in der Nähe** near □ Unsere Schule liegt in der Nähe des Bahnhofs. **Our school is near the station.** □ Ich wohne in der Nähe von Rostock. **I live near Rostock.**
■ **aus der Nähe** close up □ wenn man das aus der Nähe betrachtet **if you look at it close up**

nahelegen VERB [4]
■ **jemandem etwas nahelegen** to suggest something to somebody

naheliegend ADJECTIVE
obvious

★ nähen VERB [38]
to sew

näher ADJECTIVE, ADVERB
▷ *see also* **nahe, nächste**
nearer

□ Die Straßenbahnhaltestelle ist näher als die Bushaltestelle. The tram stop is nearer than the bus stop.
■ **Näheres** details *pl* □ Ich wüsste gern Näheres. I'd like to have more details.
■ **näher kommen** to get closer

sich **nähern** VERB [88]
to get closer
□ Wir näherten uns dem Bahnhof. We were approaching the station.

nahezu ADVERB
nearly

nahm VERB ▷ *see* nehmen

die **Nähmaschine** FEM NOUN
sewing machine

die **Nähnadel** FEM NOUN
needle

nahrhaft ADJECTIVE
nourishing

★ die **Nahrung** FEM NOUN
food
□ feste Nahrung solid food

das **Nahrungsmittel** (PL die **Nahrungsmittel**) NEUT NOUN
foodstuffs *pl*

die **Naht** (PL die **Nähte**) FEM NOUN
seam
□ Die Hose ist an der Naht geplatzt. The trousers have split along the seam.

der **Nahverkehr** MASC NOUN
local traffic

★ der **Nahverkehrszug** (PL die **Nahverkehrszüge**) MASC NOUN
local train

★ der **Name** (GEN des **Namens**, PL die **Namen**) MASC NOUN
name
□ Mein Name ist ... My name is ...
■ **im Namen von** on behalf of

nämlich ADVERB
1 you see
□ Sie ist nämlich meine beste Freundin. You see, she's my best friend.
2 that is (to say)
□ Nächstes Jahr, nämlich im März ... Next year, that is to say in March ...

nannte VERB ▷ *see* nennen

nanu EXCLAMATION
well, well!

die **Narbe** FEM NOUN
scar

die **Narkose** FEM NOUN
anaesthetic

naschen VERB [48]
■ Sie nascht gern. She's got a sweet tooth.
■ Wer hat von der Torte genascht? Who's been at the cake?

★ die **Nase** FEM NOUN
nose
□ Meine Nase blutet. My nose is bleeding.
■ **die Nase vollhaben** to be fed up

das **Nasenbluten** NEUT NOUN
nosebleed
□ Ich hatte Nasenbluten. I had a nosebleed.

★ **nass** ADJECTIVE
wet
□ Nach dem Regen war die Wäsche noch nässer. After the rain, the washing was even wetter.

die **Nässe** FEM NOUN
wetness

die **Nation** FEM NOUN
nation

die **Nationalhymne** FEM NOUN
national anthem

★ die **Nationalität** FEM NOUN
nationality

★ die **Natur** FEM NOUN
1 country
□ Wir gehen gern in der Natur spazieren. We like to go for a walk in the country.
2 constitution
□ Sie hat eine robuste Natur. She's got a strong constitution.

★ **natürlich** ADJECTIVE, ADVERB
1 natural
□ Das ist ihre natürliche Haarfarbe. That's her natural hair colour.
2 of course
□ Wir kommen natürlich. Of course we'll come.
□ Sie hat das natürlich wieder vergessen. She's forgotten it again, of course. □ Ja, natürlich! Yes of course.

das **Naturschutzgebiet** (PL die **Naturschutzgebiete**) NEUT NOUN
nature reserve

der **Naturschutzpark** (PL die **Naturschutzparks**) MASC NOUN
national park

die **Naturwissenschaft** FEM NOUN
natural science

der **Naturwissenschaftler** (PL die **Naturwissenschaftler**) MASC NOUN
scientist

der **Navi** MASC NOUN
1 GPS
2 sat nav

★ der **Nebel** (PL die **Nebel**) MASC NOUN
1 mist
2 fog

nebelig ADJECTIVE
1 misty
2 foggy

★ = core vocabulary

neben PREPOSITION

> Use the accusative to express movement or a change of place. Use the dative when there is no change of place.

1 next to
□ Dein Rad steht neben meinem. **Your bike's next to mine.** □ Stell dein Rad neben meines. **Put your bike next to mine.**

2 apart from
> **neben** takes the dative in this sense.

□ Neben den Sehenswürdigkeiten haben wir uns auch ein Theaterstück angesehen. **Apart from the sights, we also saw a play.**

nebenan ADVERB
next door

nebenbei ADVERB

1 at the same time
□ Ich kann nicht Hausaufgaben machen und nebenbei fernsehen. **I can't do my homework and watch TV at the same time.**

2 on the side
□ Sie hat nebenbei noch einen anderen Job. **She has another job on the side.**
■ Sie sagte ganz nebenbei, dass sie nicht mitkommen wollte. **She mentioned quite casually that she didn't want to come along.**
■ Nebenbei bemerkt, ... **Incidentally, ...**

nebeneinander ADVERB
side by side

das **Nebenfach** (PL die **Nebenfächer**) NEUT NOUN
subsidiary subject

der **Nebenfluss** (GEN des **Nebenflusses**, PL die **Nebenflüsse**) MASC NOUN
tributary

nebenher ADVERB

1 on the side
□ Sie verdient nebenher noch Geld durch Zeitungaustragen. **She also earns money on the side doing a paper round.**

2 at the same time
□ Sie bügelt und sieht nebenher fern. **She does the ironing and watches TV at the same time.**

3 alongside
□ Wir sind mit dem Rad gefahren, der Hund lief nebenher. **We rode our bikes and the dog ran alongside.**

die **Nebenstraße** FEM NOUN
side street

neblig ADJECTIVE

1 misty

2 foggy

nee ADVERB (*Umgangssprache*)
no
□ Nee, das mache ich lieber später. **No, I'd rather do that later.**

★ der **Neffe** (GEN des **Neffen**, PL die **Neffen**)
MASC NOUN
nephew

negativ ADJECTIVE
▷ *see also* das **Negativ** NOUN
negative
□ HIV-negativ **HIV-negative**

das **Negativ** (PL die **Negative**) NEUT NOUN
▷ *see also* **negativ** ADJECTIVE
negative
□ Kann ich von den Bildern das Negativ haben? **Can I have the negatives of these pictures?**

★ **nehmen** (PRESENT TENSE **nimmt**, IMPERFECT **nahm**, PERFECT TENSE **hat genommen**) VERB
[52]
to take
□ Sie nahm fünf Euro aus dem Geldbeutel. **She took five euros out of her purse.** □ Wir nehmen besser den Bus in die Stadt. **We'd better take the bus into town.** □ Hast du deine Medizin genommen? **Have you taken your medicine?** □ Nimm ihn nicht ernst! **Don't take him seriously.**
■ Ich nehme ein Erdbeereis. **I'll have a strawberry ice cream.**
■ Nimm dir doch bitte! **Please help yourself.**

der **Neid** MASC NOUN
envy

★ **neidisch** ADJECTIVE
envious
□ Sie ist neidisch auf ihren Bruder. **She's envious of her brother.**

★ **nein** ADVERB
no
□ Hast du das gesehen? — Nein. **Did you see that? — No, I didn't.**
■ Ich glaube nein. **I don't think so.**

die **Nelke** FEM NOUN

1 carnation
□ Er brachte mir einen Strauß Nelken. **He brought me a bunch of carnations.**

2 clove
□ Zum Glühwein braucht man Nelken. **You need cloves to make mulled wine.**

★ **nennen** (IMPERFECT **nannte**, PERFECT TENSE **hat genannt**) VERB [39]

1 to call
□ Sie haben ihren Sohn Rafael genannt. **They called their son Rafael.** □ Die Band nennt sich 'Die Zerstörer'. **The band call themselves 'The Destroyers'.** □ Wie nennt man ...? **What do you call ...?**

2 to name
□ Kannst du mir einen Fluss in England nennen? **Can you name a river in England?**

das **Neonlicht** NEUT NOUN
neon light

die **Neonröhre** FEM NOUN
strip light

der **Nerv** (PL die **Nerven**) MASC NOUN
nerve
■ **jemandem auf die Nerven gehen** to get on somebody's nerves

der **Nervenzusammenbruch** (PL die **Nervenzusammenbrüche**) MASC NOUN
nervous breakdown

★ **nervös** ADJECTIVE
nervous

die **Nervosität** FEM NOUN
nervousness

das **Nest** (PL die **Nester**) NEUT NOUN
1 nest
□ Der Vogel hat ein Nest gebaut. The bird has built a nest.
2 dump (*Umgangssprache*)
□ Wiblingen ist ein Nest. Wiblingen is a dump.

der **Netball** MASC NOUN
netball

★ **nett** ADJECTIVE
1 lovely
□ Vielen Dank für den netten Abend. Thanks for a lovely evening.
2 nice
□ Wir haben uns nett unterhalten. We had a nice talk.
3 kind
□ Wären Sie vielleicht so nett, mir zu helfen? Would you be so kind as to help me? □ Das war sehr nett von dir. That was very kind of you.

netto ADVERB
net
□ Sie verdient dreitausend Euro netto. She earns three thousand euros net.

★ das **Netz** (GEN des **Netzes**, PL die **Netze**) NEUT NOUN
1 net
□ Die Fischer werfen ihre Netze aus. The fishermen cast their nets. □ Der Ball ging ins Netz. The ball went into the net.
2 network
□ ein weitverzweigtes Netz an Rohren an extensive network of pipes □ einen Computer ans Netz anschließen to connect a computer to the network

das **Netzwerk** (PL die **Netzwerke**) NEUT NOUN
network
■ **ein soziales Netzwerk** a social networking site

netzwerken (PERFECT TENSE **hat genetzwerkt**) VERB [38]
to network (*computer*)

★ **neu** ADJECTIVE
new
□ Ist der Pulli neu? Is that pullover new? □ Sie hat einen neuen Freund. She's got a new boyfriend. □ Ich bin neu hier. I'm new here.
■ **neue Sprachen** modern languages
■ **neueste** latest □ die neuesten Nachrichten the latest news
■ **seit Neuestem** recently
■ **neu schreiben** to rewrite
■ **Das ist mir neu!** That's news to me.

neuartig ADJECTIVE
new kind of
□ ein neuartiges Wörterbuch a new kind of dictionary

die **Neugier** FEM NOUN
curiosity

★ **neugierig** ADJECTIVE
curious

die **Neuheit** FEM NOUN
new product
□ Auf der Messe werden alle Neuheiten vorgestellt. All new products are presented at the trade fair.

die **Neuigkeit** FEM NOUN
news *sing*
□ Gibt es irgendwelche Neuigkeiten? Is there any news?

★ das **Neujahr** NEUT NOUN
New Year
■ **An Neujahr habe ich meine Schwester besucht.** I visited my sister on New Year's Day.

★ **neulich** ADVERB
the other day

★ **neun** NUMBER
nine

neunte ADJECTIVE
ninth
□ Heute ist der neunte Juni. Today is the ninth of June.

★ **neunzehn** NUMBER
nineteen

★ **neunzig** NUMBER
ninety

Neuseeland NEUT NOUN
New Zealand
■ **aus Neuseeland** from New Zealand
■ **nach Neuseeland** to New Zealand

der **Neuseeländer** (PL die **Neuseeländer**) MASC NOUN
New Zealander

die **Neuseeländerin** FEM NOUN
New Zealander

neutral ADJECTIVE
neutral

das **Neutrum** (PL die **Neutra** or **Neutren**) NEUT NOUN
neuter

★ **nicht** ADVERB
not

★ = core vocabulary

□ Ich bin nicht müde. **I'm not tired.** □ Er ist es nicht. **It's not him.**
■ **Er raucht nicht. 1** He isn't smoking. **2** He doesn't smoke.
■ **Ich kann das nicht. — Ich auch nicht.** I can't do it. — Neither can I.
■ **Nicht! Don't!**
■ **Nicht berühren!** Do not touch!
■ **Du bist müde, nicht wahr?** You're tired, aren't you?
■ **Das ist schön, nicht wahr?** It's nice, isn't it?
■ **Was du nicht sagst!** You don't say!

★ die **Nichte** FEM NOUN
niece

★ der **Nichtraucher** (PL die **Nichtraucher**)
MASC NOUN
nonsmoker

★ **nichts** PRONOUN
nothing
□ nichts zu verzollen nothing to declare
□ nichts Neues nothing new
■ **Ich habe nichts gesagt.** I didn't say anything.
■ **Nichts ist so wie früher.** Things aren't what they used to be.
■ **Das macht nichts.** It doesn't matter.
■ **für nichts und wieder nichts** for nothing

der **Nick** (PL die **Nicks**) MASC NOUN
username
□ Was ist dein Nick? What's your username?

nicken VERB [48]
to nod

der **Nickname** (GEN des **Nicknamens**, PL die **Nicknamen**) MASC NOUN
username
□ Was ist dein Nickname? What's your username?

★ **nie** ADVERB
never
□ Das habe ich nie gesagt. I never said that.
□ Das werde ich nie vergessen. I'll never forget that. □ Das habe ich noch nie gehört. I've never heard that. □ Ich war noch nie in Indien. I've never been to India.
■ **nie wieder** never again □ Tu das nie wieder. Don't ever do that again.
■ **nie mehr** never again □ Sie hat nie mehr geschrieben. She never wrote to me again.
■ **nie und nimmer** no way □ Das kann nie und nimmer stimmen. There's no way that can be right.

nieder ADJECTIVE, ADVERB
1 low
□ ein niederer Rang a low rank
■ **ein niederer Beamter** a low-ranking government officer
2 base
□ niedere Instinkte base instincts

■ **Nieder mit ...!** Down with ...! □ Nieder mit dem Diktator! Down with the dictator!

niedergeschlagen ADJECTIVE
dejected

die **Niederlage** FEM NOUN
defeat

★ die **Niederlande** NEUT PL NOUN
the Netherlands *pl*
■ **aus den Niederlanden** from the Netherlands
■ **in den Niederlanden** in the Netherlands
■ **in die Niederlande** to the Netherlands

der **Niederländer** (PL die **Niederländer**)
MASC NOUN
Dutchman
■ **Er ist Niederländer.** He's Dutch.

die **Niederländerin** FEM NOUN
Dutchwoman
■ **Sie ist Niederländerin.** She's Dutch.

★ **niederländisch** ADJECTIVE
Dutch

Niedersachsen NEUT NOUN
Lower Saxony

DID YOU KNOW...?
Niedersachsen is one of the 16 Länder. Its capital is Hannover. Its most important industries are mining and car manufacturing (Volkswagen). The Hannover Industrial Fair is the largest in the world.

★ der **Niederschlag** (PL die **Niederschläge**)
MASC NOUN
precipitation
■ **heftige Niederschläge** heavy rain
■ **radioaktiver Niederschlag** radioactive fallout

niedlich ADJECTIVE
sweet
□ niedlich aussehen to look sweet

★ **niedrig** ADJECTIVE
1 low
□ Die Decke ist sehr niedrig. The ceiling is very low. □ niedrige Temperaturen low temperatures
2 shallow
□ Hier ist der Fluss niedriger. The river is shallower here.
3 base
□ niedrige Motive base motives

niemals ADVERB
never

★ **niemand** PRONOUN
1 nobody
□ Niemand hat mir Bescheid gesagt. Nobody told me.
2 not ... anybody
□ Ich habe niemanden gesehen. I haven't seen anybody. □ Sie hat mit niemandem darüber

gesprochen. She hasn't mentioned it to anybody.

die Niere FEM NOUN
kidney

nieseln VERB [88]
to drizzle

niesen VERB [38]
to sneeze

die Niete FEM NOUN

1 stud
□ Jeans mit Nieten jeans with studs

2 blank
□ Ich habe eine Niete gezogen. I've drawn a blank.
■ In Mathe ist er eine Niete. He's useless at maths.

nimmt VERB ▷ see **nehmen**

nirgends ADVERB

1 nowhere
□ Nirgends sonst gibt es so schöne Blumen. Nowhere else will you find such beautiful flowers.

2 not ... anywhere
□ Hier gibt es nirgends ein Schwimmbad. There isn't a swimming pool anywhere here. □ Ich habe ihn nirgends gesehen. I haven't seen him anywhere.

nirgendwo ADVERB ▷ see **nirgends**

nirgendwohin ADVERB ▷ see **nirgends**

das Niveau (PL die **Niveaus**) NEUT NOUN
level

★ **noch** ADVERB, CONJUNCTION
still
□ Ich habe noch Hunger. I'm still hungry. □ Das kann noch passieren. That might still happen. □ Das ist noch besser. That's better still.
■ Bleib doch noch ein bisschen! Stay a bit longer.
■ Das wirst du noch lernen. You'll learn.
■ Er wird noch kommen. He'll come.
■ heute noch today
■ noch am selben Tag the very same day
■ noch vor einer Woche only a week ago
■ Wer noch? Who else? □ Wer war noch da? Who else was there?
■ Was noch? What else? □ Was will er noch? What else does he want?
■ noch nicht not yet □ Ich bin noch nicht fertig. I haven't finished yet.
■ noch nie never □ Ich war noch nie in Leeds. I've never been to Leeds.
■ immer noch still □ Du bist ja immer noch da! How come you're still here? □ Das Haus ist immer noch nicht fertig. The house still isn't finished.
■ noch einmal again
■ noch dreimal three more times
■ noch einer another one
■ noch größer even bigger

■ Geld noch und noch loads of money (Umgangssprache)
■ weder ... noch ... neither ... nor ...

nochmals ADVERB
again

der Nominativ (PL die **Nominative**) MASC NOUN
nominative

★ **Nordamerika** NEUT NOUN
North America

★ **der Norden** MASC NOUN
north

Nordirland NEUT NOUN
Northern Ireland
■ aus Nordirland from Northern Ireland
■ in Nordirland in Northern Ireland
■ nach Nordirland to Northern Ireland

★ **nördlich** ADJECTIVE, PREPOSITION, ADVERB
northerly
□ Wir fuhren in nördlicher Richtung. We drove in a northerly direction.
■ nördlich einer Sache to the north of something □ Das Kraftwerk liegt nördlich der Stadt. The power station is to the north of the city.
■ nördlich von north of □ Düsseldorf liegt nördlich von Köln. Düsseldorf is north of Cologne.

der Nordosten MASC NOUN
northeast

der Nordpol MASC NOUN
North Pole
□ am Nordpol at the North Pole □ zum Nordpol to the North Pole

Nordrhein-Westfalen NEUT NOUN
North Rhine-Westphalia

DID YOU KNOW...?
Nordrhein-Westfalen is one of the 16 Länder. Its capital is Düsseldorf. It is Germany's most densely populated state, and includes the Ruhr district.

★ **die Nordsee** FEM NOUN
North Sea
□ Wir fahren an die Nordsee. We're going to the North Sea. □ Wir waren an der Nordsee. We've been to the North Sea.

der Nordwesten MASC NOUN
northwest

die Norm FEM NOUN
standard
□ Für die meisten technischen Geräte gibt es Normen. There are set standards for most technical equipment.

★ **normal** ADJECTIVE
normal

★ **das Normalbenzin** NEUT NOUN
regular petrol

★ **normalerweise** ADVERB
normally

★ **Norwegen** NEUT NOUN
Norway
- **aus Norwegen** from Norway
- **nach Norwegen** to Norway

★ der **Norweger** (PL die **Norweger**) MASC NOUN
Norwegian

★ die **Norwegerin** FEM NOUN
Norwegian

★ **norwegisch** ADJECTIVE
Norwegian

die **Not** FEM NOUN
- **zur Not** if necessary □ Zur Not kannst du ja später nachkommen. You can join us later if necessary.

★ der **Notausgang** (PL die **Notausgänge**)
MASC NOUN
emergency exit

★ die **Notbremse** FEM NOUN
emergency brake

★ der **Notdienst** (PL die **Notdienste**) MASC NOUN
emergency service

★ die **Note** FEM NOUN
1 mark
□ Max hat gute Noten. Max has got good marks.
2 note
□ Welche Note hast du eben gespielt? What note did you just play?

★ der **Notfall** (PL die **Notfälle**) MASC NOUN
emergency

notfalls ADVERB
if need be

notieren (PERFECT TENSE **hat notiert**) VERB [76]
to note down

★ **nötig** ADJECTIVE
necessary
□ wenn nötig if necessary
- **etwas nötig haben** to need something

die **Notiz** FEM NOUN
1 note
□ Sein Kalender ist voller Notizen. His diary is full of notes.
2 item
□ Das stand heute in einer kleinen Notiz in der Zeitung. There was a short item on it in the newspaper today.
- **Notiz nehmen von** to take notice of □ Er hat von mir überhaupt keine Notiz genommen. He didn't take any notice of me at all.

das **Notizbuch** (PL die **Notizbücher**) NEUT NOUN
notebook

notlanden (PERFECT TENSE **ist notgelandet**)
VERB [54]
to make an emergency landing

★ der **Notruf** (PL die **Notrufe**) MASC NOUN
emergency call

★ **notwendig** ADJECTIVE
necessary

★ der **November** (GEN des **November** or **Novembers**, PL die **November**) MASC NOUN
November
□ im November in November □ am neunten November on the ninth of November
□ Freiburg, den 9. November 2019 Freiburg, 9 November 2019 □ Heute ist der neunte November. Today is the ninth of November.

Nr. ABBREVIATION (= *Nummer*)
No.

nüchtern ADJECTIVE
1 sober
□ Nach drei Gläsern Wein bist du nicht mehr nüchtern. After three glasses of wine you aren't sober any more. □ nüchterne Tatsachen sober facts
2 with an empty stomach
□ Kommen Sie nüchtern ins Krankenhaus. Come to the hospital with an empty stomach.
- **auf nüchternen Magen** on an empty stomach
- **eine Lage nüchtern betrachten** to look at a situation rationally

★ die **Nudel** FEM NOUN
noodle
□ Es waren Nudeln in der Suppe. There were noodles in the soup.
- **Nudeln** pasta *sing* □ Nudeln sind meine Lieblingsspeise. Pasta is my favourite food.

★ **null** NUMBER
▷ see also die **Null** NOUN
1 nil
□ Sie haben eins zu null gespielt. They won one nil.
2 no
□ Ich hatte null Fehler. I had no mistakes.
- **null Uhr** midnight
- **null und nichtig** null and void

★ die **Null** FEM NOUN
▷ see also **null** NUMBER
1 zero
□ Du musst zuerst eine Null wählen. You have to dial zero first.
2 nonentity
□ Er ist doch eine völlige Null. He's a complete nonentity.

★ die **Nullerjahre** PL NOUN
noughties (*the 2000s*)

★ die **Nummer** FEM NOUN
1 number
□ Ich kann seine Nummer auswendig. I know his number by heart.
2 size
□ Die Schuhe sind eine Nummer zu groß. These shoes are a size too big.

n

nummerieren - nutzlos

nummerieren (PERFECT TENSE **hat nummeriert**) VERB [76]
to number

das **Nummernschild** (PL die **Nummernschilder**) NEUT NOUN
number plate

★ **nun** ADVERB, EXCLAMATION
1 now
   □ von nun an from now on
2 well
   □ Nun, was gibt's Neues? Well, what's new?
   ■ Das ist nun mal so. That's the way it is.

★ **nur** ADVERB
only
   □ Das hat nur zwanzig Euro gekostet. It only cost twenty euros. □ Es sind nur fünf Leute da gewesen. There were only five people there.
   ■ Wo bleibt er nur? Where on earth can he be?
   ■ Was hat sie nur? What on earth's wrong with her?

★ die **Nuss** (PL die **Nüsse**) FEM NOUN
nut

★ **nutzen** VERB [36]
   ▷ see also der **Nutzen** NOUN
to help

□ Sprachkenntnisse können dir im Ausland viel nutzen. Knowing a language can help you a lot abroad.
   ■ etwas nutzen to make use of something
   □ Du solltest die Zeit nutzen. You ought to make use of the time.
   ■ Das nutzt ja doch nichts. That's pointless.
   ■ Es nutzt alles nichts, wir müssen ... There's no getting around it, we'll have to ...

★ der **Nutzen** MASC NOUN
   ▷ see also **nutzen** VERB
   ■ von Nutzen useful □ Sprachkenntnisse sind immer von Nutzen. It's always useful to know a foreign language.
   ■ Das ist zu deinem Nutzen. It's for your own good.

★ **nützen** VERB [36] ▷ see **nutzen**

nützlich ADJECTIVE
useful
   □ sich nützlich machen to make oneself useful

★ **nutzlos** ADJECTIVE
useless

★ = core vocabulary

Oo

die **Oase** FEM NOUN
oasis

★ **ob** CONJUNCTION
1 whether
□ Ich weiß nicht, ob ich kommen kann. I don't know whether I can come.
2 if
□ Sie fragt, ob du auch kommst. She wants to know if you're coming too.
■ **Ob das wohl wahr ist?** Can that be true?
■ **Und ob!** You bet!

★ **obdachlos** ADJECTIVE
homeless

★ **oben** ADVERB
on top
□ oben auf dem Schrank on top of the cupboard
■ **oben auf dem Berg** up on the mountain
■ **Die Schlafzimmer sind oben.** The bedrooms are upstairs.
■ **nach oben** up □ Der Fahrstuhl fährt nach oben. The lift is going up. □ Ich gehe nach oben in mein Zimmer. I'm going up to my room.
■ **von oben** down □ Der Fahrstuhl kommt von oben. The lift is coming down. □ Bringst du mir von oben die Bettwäsche mit? Bring the bed clothes down with you.
■ **oben ohne** topless
■ **Befehl von oben** orders from above

der **Ober** (PL die Ober) MASC NOUN
waiter
■ **Herr Ober!** Waiter!

obere ADJECTIVE
▷ see also **oberste** ADJECTIVE
upper
□ die oberen Stockwerke the upper floors
■ **die oberen Klassen** the senior classes

die **Oberfläche** FEM NOUN
surface

oberflächlich ADJECTIVE
superficial
□ Er ist sehr oberflächlich in seiner Arbeit. His work is very superficial.
■ **jemanden nur oberflächlich kennen** to know somebody only slightly

★ das **Obergeschoss** (GEN des Obergeschosses, PL die Obergeschosse) NEUT NOUN
upper storey

der **Oberschenkel** (PL die Oberschenkel) MASC NOUN
thigh

die **Oberschule** FEM NOUN
grammar school

oberste ADJECTIVE
▷ see also **obere** ADJECTIVE
topmost
□ Das Buch steht auf dem obersten Regalbrett. The book is on the topmost shelf.
■ **Sie ist in der obersten Klasse.** She's in the top class.

★ die **Oberstufe** FEM NOUN
upper school

das **Oberteil** (PL die Oberteile) NEUT NOUN
upper part

die **Oberweite** FEM NOUN
bust measurement

★ **obgleich** CONJUNCTION
although
□ Obgleich sie müde war, blieb sie lange auf. Although she was tired, she stayed up late.

das **Objekt** (PL die Objekte) NEUT NOUN
object

objektiv ADJECTIVE
▷ see also das **Objektiv** NOUN
objective

das **Objektiv** (PL die Objektive) NEUT NOUN
▷ see also **objektiv** ADJECTIVE
lens (of camera)

★ das **Obst** NEUT NOUN
fruit

der **Obstkuchen** (PL die Obstkuchen) MASC NOUN
fruit tart

★ **obwohl** CONJUNCTION
although
□ Obwohl sie müde war, blieb sie lange auf. Although she was tired, she stayed up late.

der **Ochse** (GEN des Ochsen, PL die Ochsen) MASC NOUN
ox

öde ADJECTIVE
dull
□ eine öde Landschaft a dull landscape

oder - Ökostrom

■ **Diese Arbeit ist echt öde.** This job's really the pits. (*Umgangssprache*)

★ **oder** CONJUNCTION
or
□ entweder ich oder du either me or you
■ **Das stimmt, oder?** That's right, isn't it?

★ der **Ofen** (PL die Öfen) MASC NOUN
1 oven
□ Der Kuchen ist im Ofen. The cake's in the oven.
2 heater
■ **Mach bitte den Ofen an, mir ist kalt.** Put the fire on, I'm cold.

★ **offen** ADJECTIVE
open
□ Das Fenster ist offen. The window's open.
□ Die Banken sind bis sechzehn Uhr offen. The banks are open until four o'clock. □ Sie ist ein sehr offener Mensch. She's a very open person.
■ **offen gesagt** to be honest
■ **Ich gebe dir eine offene Antwort.** I'll be frank with you.
■ **eine offene Stelle** a vacancy

offenbleiben (IMPERFECT **blieb offen**, PERFECT TENSE **ist offengeblieben**) VERB [10]
to remain open
□ Diese Möglichkeit bleibt uns noch offen. This option remains open to us.

offensichtlich ADJECTIVE, ADVERB
1 obvious
□ ein offensichtlicher Fehler an obvious mistake
2 obviously
□ Er ist offensichtlich nicht zufrieden. He's obviously dissatisfied.

★ **öffentlich** ADJECTIVE
public
□ öffentliche Verkehrsmittel public transport

die **Öffentlichkeit** FEM NOUN
public
□ Die Öffentlichkeit wurde nicht informiert. The public were not informed. □ in aller Öffentlichkeit in public

offiziell ADJECTIVE
official

der **Offizier** (PL die Offiziere) MASC NOUN
officer

die **Offizierin** FEM NOUN
officer

★ **öffnen** VERB [53]
to open
□ jemandem die Tür öffnen to open the door for somebody

★ der **Öffner** (PL die Öffner) MASC NOUN
opener

die **Öffnung** FEM NOUN
opening

★ die **Öffnungszeiten** FEM PL NOUN
opening times *pl*

★ **oft** ADVERB
▷ *see also* **öfter** ADVERB
often
□ Wie oft warst du schon in London? How often have you been to London?

öfter ADVERB
▷ *see also* **oft** ADVERB
more often
□ Ich würde dich gern öfter besuchen. I would like to visit you more often.
■ **Sie war in letzter Zeit öfter krank.** She's been ill a lot recently.

öfters ADVERB
often

★ **ohne** PREPOSITION, CONJUNCTION

The preposition **ohne** takes the accusative.

without
□ Ich fahre ohne meine Eltern in Ferien. I'm going on holiday without my parents. □ Ich habe das ohne Wörterbuch übersetzt. I translated it without a dictionary. □ Sie ist gegangen, ohne Bescheid zu sagen. She left without telling anyone. □ ohne zu fragen without asking
■ **Das ist nicht ohne.** It's not half bad. (*Umgangssprache*)
■ **ohne weiteres** easily □ Das ist ohne weiteres in einer Woche zu schaffen. That can easily be done in a week.
■ **Du kannst doch nicht so ohne weiteres gehen.** You can't just leave.

ohnmächtig ADJECTIVE
■ **ohnmächtig werden** to faint
■ **Sie ist ohnmächtig.** She's fainted.

★ das **Ohr** (PL die Ohren) NEUT NOUN
ear
■ **Er hat sehr gute Ohren.** His hearing is very good.

die **Ohrenschmerzen** MASC PL NOUN
earache *sing*
□ Sie hat Ohrenschmerzen. She's got earache.

die **Ohrfeige** FEM NOUN
slap across the face

ohrfeigen VERB [38]
■ **jemanden ohrfeigen** to slap somebody across the face

der **Ohrring** (PL die Ohrringe) MASC NOUN
earring

ökologisch ADJECTIVE
ecological

der **Ökostrom** MASC NOUN
green electricity
□ Wir produzieren mit Ökostrom. We use green electricity.

der **Ökotourismus** (GEN des **Ökotourismus**) MASC NOUN
ecotourism

★ der **Oktober** (GEN des **Oktober** or **Oktobers**, PL die **Oktober**) MASC NOUN
October
□ im Oktober in October □ am dritten Oktober on the third of October □ Kiel, den 3. Oktober 2019 Kiel, 3 October 2019. □ Heute ist der dritte Oktober. Today is the third of October.

★ das **Oktoberfest** (PL die **Oktoberfeste**) NEUT NOUN
Munich beer festival

★ das **Öl** (PL die **Öle**) NEUT NOUN
oil

die **Ölheizung** FEM NOUN
oil-fired central heating

ölig ADJECTIVE
oily

oliv ADJECTIVE
olive-green

die **Olive** FEM NOUN
olive

die **Ölsardine** FEM NOUN
sardine

der **Ölwechsel** (PL die **Ölwechsel**) MASC NOUN
oil change

die **Olympiade** FEM NOUN
Olympic Games ® pl

der **Olympiasieger** (PL die **Olympiasieger**) MASC NOUN
Olympic ® champion

die **Olympiasiegerin** FEM NOUN
Olympic ® champion

olympisch ADJECTIVE
Olympic ®

★ die **Oma** (PL die **Omas**) FEM NOUN
granny (Umgangssprache)

★ das **Omelett** (PL die **Omeletts**) NEUT NOUN
omelette

★ der **Onkel** (PL die **Onkel**) MASC NOUN
uncle

online ADVERB
online

★ der **Opa** (PL die **Opas**) MASC NOUN
grandpa (Umgangssprache)

die **Oper** FEM NOUN
1 opera
□ eine Oper von Verdi an opera by Verdi
2 opera house
□ Die Mailänder Oper ist berühmt. The Milan opera house is famous.

★ die **Operation** FEM NOUN
operation

der **Operationssaal** (PL die **Operationssäle**) MASC NOUN
operating theatre

die **Operette** FEM NOUN
operetta

★ **operieren** (PERFECT TENSE **hat operiert**) VERB [76]
to operate on
□ jemanden operieren to operate on somebody
■ **Sie muss operiert werden.** She has to have an operation.
■ **Sie wurde am Auge operiert.** She had an eye operation.

das **Opfer** (PL die **Opfer**) NEUT NOUN
1 sacrifice
□ Das war ein großes Opfer für ihn. It was a great sacrifice for him.
2 victim
□ Der Unfall hat viele Opfer gefordert. The accident claimed a lot of victims.

die **Opposition** FEM NOUN
opposition

die **Optik** FEM NOUN
optics sing

der **Optiker** (PL die **Optiker**) MASC NOUN
optician

optimal ADJECTIVE, ADVERB
optimum
□ Das ist die optimale Lösung. That's the optimum solution.
■ **Sie hat das optimal gelöst.** She solved it in the best possible way.
■ **Wir haben den Platz optimal genutzt.** We made the best possible use of the space available.

der **Optimismus** (GEN des **Optimismus**) MASC NOUN
optimism

der **Optimist** (GEN des **Optimisten**, PL die **Optimisten**) MASC NOUN
optimist

★ **optimistisch** ADJECTIVE
optimistic

★ **orange** ADJECTIVE
▷ see also die **Orange** NOUN
orange

★ die **Orange** FEM NOUN
▷ see also **orange** ADJECTIVE
orange

★ der **Orangensaft** (PL die **Orangensäfte**) MASC NOUN
orange juice

★ das **Orchester** (PL die **Orchester**) NEUT NOUN
orchestra

★ **ordentlich** ADJECTIVE, ADVERB
1 tidy
□ Seine Wohnung ist sehr ordentlich. His flat's

ordinär – Österreich

very tidy. □ Ich bin ein ordentlicher Mensch. I'm a tidy person.

2 decent
□ Das sind ordentliche Leute. They're decent people. □ Das ist doch kein ordentliches Gehalt. That's not a decent wage. □ eine ordentliche Portion a decent portion
▪ **Ich brauche jetzt etwas Ordentliches zu essen.** Now I need a decent meal.

3 respectable
□ Das ist eine ordentliche Leistung. That's a respectable achievement. □ Du solltest dir einen ordentlichen Beruf aussuchen. You ought to look for a respectable job.

4 neatly
□ Du solltest ordentlicher schreiben. You should write more neatly.

5 properly
□ Kannst du dich nicht ordentlich benehmen? Can't you behave properly?
▪ **Es hat ordentlich geschneit.** There's been a fair bit of snow.
▪ **Sie haben ihn ordentlich verprügelt.** They beat him up good and proper. (*Umgangssprache*)

ordinär ADJECTIVE
vulgar
▪ **sich ordinär ausdrücken** to use vulgar expressions

ordnen VERB [53]
to put in order

★ der **Ordner** (PL die **Ordner**) MASC NOUN
file

★ die **Ordnung** FEM NOUN
order
□ Ruhe und Ordnung law and order
▪ **Sie liebt Ordnung.** She likes everything to be in its place.
▪ **Das hat schon alles seine Ordnung.** Everything is as it should be.
▪ **Ordnung machen** to tidy up □ Du solltest in deinem Zimmer Ordnung machen. You should tidy up your room.
▪ **Mit meinem Auto ist etwas nicht in Ordnung.** Something's wrong with my car.
▪ **etwas wieder in Ordnung bringen** to repair something □ Er hat das defekte Gerät wieder in Ordnung gebracht. He repaired the faulty appliance.
▪ **Ist alles in Ordnung?** Is everything okay?
▪ **In Ordnung!** Okay!

das **Organ** (PL die **Organe**) NEUT NOUN
organ
□ die inneren Organe internal organs
▪ **Er hat ein lautes Organ.** He's got a loud voice.

die **Organisation** FEM NOUN
organization

organisch ADJECTIVE
organic

★ **organisieren** (PERFECT TENSE **hat organisiert**) VERB [76]
to organize
□ Wer hat das Fest organisiert? Who organized the party?

die **Orgel** FEM NOUN
organ
□ Sie spielt Orgel. She plays the organ.

der **Orient** MASC NOUN
Orient

orientalisch ADJECTIVE
oriental

sich **orientieren** (PERFECT TENSE **hat sich orientiert**) VERB [76]

1 to find one's way around
□ Ich brauche einen Stadtplan, um mich besser orientieren zu können. I need a city map to be able to find my way around better.

2 to find out
□ Ich muss mich orientieren, wie das gehandhabt wird. I'll have to find out what the procedure is.

originell ADJECTIVE
original
□ ein origineller Einfall an original idea

der **Orkan** (PL die **Orkane**) MASC NOUN
hurricane

★ der **Ort** (PL die **Orte**) MASC NOUN
place
▪ **an Ort und Stelle** on the spot

die **Orthografie** FEM NOUN
spelling

örtlich ADJECTIVE
local

das **Ortsgespräch** (PL die **Ortsgespräche**) NEUT NOUN
local phone call

★ der **Osten** MASC NOUN
east

das **Osterei** (PL die **Ostereier**) NEUT NOUN
Easter egg

die **Osterferien** PL NOUN
Easter holidays *pl*

★ das **Ostern** (PL die **Ostern**) NEUT NOUN
Easter
□ an Ostern at Easter

★ **Österreich** NEUT NOUN
Austria

DID YOU KNOW...?
Austria borders Germany, the Czech Republic, Slovakia, Hungary, Slovenia, Italy and Switzerland. Its capital is Vienna.

- **aus Österreich** from Austria
- **in Österreich** in Austria
- **nach Österreich** to Austria

★ der **Österreicher** (PL die **Österreicher**)
MASC NOUN
Austrian

★ die **Österreicherin** FEM NOUN
Austrian

★ **österreichisch** ADJECTIVE
Austrian

DID YOU KNOW…?
People in Austria speak a dialect of German.

★ **östlich** ADJECTIVE, PREPOSITION, ADVERB
easterly
  □ Wir fuhren in östlicher Richtung. We drove in an easterly direction.
  ■ **östlich einer Sache** to the east of something □ Das Kraftwerk liegt östlich der Stadt. The power station is to the east of the city.
  ■ **östlich von** east of □ Jena liegt östlich von Erfurt. Jena is east of Erfurt.

★ die **Ostsee** FEM NOUN
Baltic
  □ Wir fahren an die Ostsee. We're going to the Baltic. □ Wir waren an der Ostsee. We've been to the Baltic.

★ **oval** ADJECTIVE
oval

der **Ozean** (PL die **Ozeane**) MASC NOUN
ocean

das **Ozon** NEUT NOUN
ozone

das **Ozonloch** (PL die **Ozonlöcher**) NEUT NOUN
ozone hole

die **Ozonschicht** FEM NOUN
ozone layer

o

Pp

★ das **Paar** (PL die **Paare**) NEUT NOUN
1 pair
□ Ich habe ein Paar Schuhe gekauft. I've bought a pair of shoes.
2 couple
□ Sie sind ein sehr glückliches Paar. They're a very happy couple.
■ **ein paar** a few

paarmal ADVERB
■ **ein paarmal** a few times

★ das **Päckchen** (PL die **Päckchen**) NEUT NOUN
1 small parcel
□ Wie viel kostet ein Päckchen ins Ausland? How much does it cost to post a small parcel abroad?
2 packet
□ Sie raucht ein Päckchen pro Tag. She smokes a packet a day.

★ **packen** VERB [38]
1 to pack
□ Hast du deinen Koffer schon gepackt? Have you already packed your suitcase?
2 to grasp
□ Sie packte mich am Arm. She grasped my arm.
■ **Er hat die Prüfung nicht gepackt.** He didn't manage to get through the exam.

das **Packpapier** NEUT NOUN
brown paper

★ die **Packung** FEM NOUN
1 packet
□ eine Packung Tee a packet of tea □ eine Packung Zigaretten a packet of cigarettes
2 box
□ eine Packung Pralinen a box of chocolates

★ das **Paket** (PL die **Pakete**) NEUT NOUN
1 packet
□ Ich habe ein Paket Waschpulver gekauft. I bought a packet of washing powder.
2 parcel
□ Die Gebühren für Pakete stehen in dieser Liste. Parcel rates are in this list.

die **Paketannahme** FEM NOUN
parcels office

der **Palast** (PL die **Paläste**) MASC NOUN
palace

die **Palme** FEM NOUN
palm tree

★ die **Pampelmuse** FEM NOUN
grapefruit

die **Pandemie** FEM NOUN
pandemic
□ eine Grippepandemie a flu pandemic

die **Panik** FEM NOUN
panic

panisch ADJECTIVE
■ **panische Angst vor etwas haben** to be terrified of something
■ **panisch reagieren** to panic

★ die **Panne** FEM NOUN
1 breakdown
□ Wir hatten eine Panne auf der Autobahn. We had a breakdown on the motorway.
2 slip
□ Mir ist da eine kleine Panne passiert. I made a slight slip.

der **Panzer** (PL die **Panzer**) MASC NOUN
1 tank
□ Die Armee setzte Panzer ein. The army used tanks.
2 shell
□ der Panzer einer Schildkröte a tortoise's shell

der **Papa** (PL die **Papas**) MASC NOUN
daddy (*Umgangssprache*)

★ der **Papagei** (PL die **Papageien**) MASC NOUN
parrot

★ das **Papier** (PL die **Papiere**) NEUT NOUN
paper

der **Papierkorb** (PL die **Papierkörbe**) MASC NOUN
wastepaper basket

die **Papiertüte** FEM NOUN
paper bag

die **Pappe** FEM NOUN
cardboard

der **Paprika** (PL die **Paprikas**) MASC NOUN
1 paprika
□ Ich habe das Hähnchen mit Paprika gewürzt. I've seasoned the chicken with paprika.
2 pepper
□ Heute gibt es gefüllte Paprikas. We're having stuffed peppers today.

der **Papst** (PL die **Päpste**) MASC NOUN
pope

★ = core vocabulary

das **Paradies** (GEN des **Paradieses**, PL die **Paradiese**) NEUT NOUN
paradise

parallel ADJECTIVE
parallel

die **Parallele** FEM NOUN
parallel

paralympisch ADJECTIVE
Paralympic

das **Pärchen** (PL die **Pärchen**) NEUT NOUN
couple
□ Auf der Parkbank saß ein Pärchen. There was a couple sitting on the bench in the park.

das **Parfüm** (PL die **Parfüms** or **Parfüme**) NEUT NOUN
perfume

der **Pariser** (PL die **Pariser**) MASC NOUN
Parisian

die **Pariserin** FEM NOUN
Parisian

★ der **Park** (PL die **Parks**) MASC NOUN
park

★ die **Parkanlage** FEM NOUN
park

★ **parken** VERB [38]
to park

★ das **Parkett** (PL die **Parkette** or **Parketts**) NEUT NOUN
stalls pl (theatre)

★ das **Parkhaus** (GEN des **Parkhauses**, PL die **Parkhäuser**) NEUT NOUN
multistorey car park

die **Parklücke** FEM NOUN
parking space

★ der **Parkplatz** (GEN des **Parkplatzes**, PL die **Parkplätze**) MASC NOUN
car park

die **Parkscheibe** FEM NOUN
parking disc

★ der **Parkschein** MASC NOUN
car-park ticket

die **Parkuhr** FEM NOUN
parking meter

★ das **Parkverbot** (PL die **Parkverbote**) NEUT NOUN
■ Hier ist Parkverbot. You're not allowed to park here.

das **Parlament** (PL die **Parlamente**) NEUT NOUN
parliament

die **Partei** FEM NOUN
party (political)
■ Partei für jemanden ergreifen to take somebody's side

parteiisch ADJECTIVE
biased

das **Parterre** (PL die **Parterres**) NEUT NOUN
1 ground floor
□ Wir wohnen im Parterre. We live on the ground floor.
2 stalls pl (theatre)

★ der **Partner** (PL die **Partner**) MASC NOUN
partner

★ die **Partnerin** FEM NOUN
partner

★ die **Partnerstadt** (PL die **Partnerstädte**) FEM NOUN
twin town

★ die **Party** (PL die **Partys**) FEM NOUN
party
□ eine Party veranstalten to have a party

★ der **Pass** (GEN des **Passes**, PL die **Pässe**) MASC NOUN
1 passport
□ Ist dein Pass noch gültig? Is your passport still valid?
2 pass
□ Im Winter ist der Pass gesperrt. The pass is closed in winter.

★ die **Passage** FEM NOUN
passage
■ eine Einkaufspassage a shopping arcade

★ der **Passagier** (PL die **Passagiere**) MASC NOUN
passenger

★ **passen** VERB [31]
1 to fit
□ Die Hose passt nicht. The trousers don't fit.
□ Es ist zu groß und passt nicht in meinen Koffer. It's too big and doesn't fit in my suitcase.
2 to suit
□ Passt dir Dienstag? Does Tuesday suit you?
□ Dieser Termin passt mir nicht. That date doesn't suit me.
■ Es passt mir nicht, dass du so frech bist. I don't like you being so cheeky.
■ zu etwas passen to go with something
□ Der Rock passt nicht zu deiner Bluse. The skirt doesn't go with your blouse.
■ zu jemandem passen to be right for somebody □ Er passt nicht zu dir. He's not right for you.
3 to pass
□ Auf die Frage muss ich passen. I'll have to pass on that question.

passend ADJECTIVE
1 matching
□ Ich muss jetzt dazu passende Schuhe kaufen. I now must buy some matching shoes.
2 appropriate
□ Sie hat ein paar passende Worte gesprochen. She said a few appropriate words.
3 convenient
□ Das ist nicht die passende Gelegenheit. This isn't a convenient time.

P

★ **passieren** (PERFECT TENSE **ist passiert**) VERB
[76]
to happen
□ Was ist passiert? **What happened?** □ Mir ist
etwas Lustiges passiert. **Something funny
happened to me.**

passiv ADJECTIVE, ADVERB
▷ see also das **Passiv** NOUN
passive
□ passives Rauchen **passive smoking** □ passiv
zusehen **to watch passively**

das **Passiv** (PL die **Passive**) NEUT NOUN
▷ see also **passiv** ADJECTIVE, ADVERB
passive

das **Passivrauchen** NEUT NOUN
passive smoking

die **Passkontrolle** FEM NOUN
passport control

das **Passwort** (PL die **Passwörter**) NEUT
NOUN
password

die **Pastete** FEM NOUN
pie (savoury)

der **Pate** (GEN des **Paten**, PL die **Paten**) MASC
NOUN
godfather

das **Patenkind** (PL die **Patenkinder**) NEUT
NOUN
godchild

das **Patent** (PL die **Patente**) NEUT NOUN
patent

★ der **Patient** (GEN des **Patienten**, PL die
Patienten) MASC NOUN
patient

★ die **Patientin** FEM NOUN
patient

die **Patin** FEM NOUN
godmother

die **Patrone** FEM NOUN
cartridge

pauken VERB [38]
1 to swot (Umgangssprache)
□ Vor der Prüfung habe ich ziemlich gepaukt. **I
swotted quite a lot before the test.**
2 to swot up (Umgangssprache)
□ Ich muss Vokabeln pauken. **I have to swot up
my vocabulary.**

die **Pauschalreise** FEM NOUN
package tour

★ die **Pause** FEM NOUN
1 break
□ eine Pause machen **to have a break** □ die
große Pause **the long break**
2 interval
□ In der Pause haben wir über das Stück
gesprochen. **We talked about the play during
the interval.**

der **Pazifik** MASC NOUN
Pacific

★ das **Pech** NEUT NOUN
bad luck
□ Das war Pech! **That was bad luck.**
■ **Pech haben** to be unlucky
■ **Pech!** Hard luck!

das **Pedal** (PL die **Pedale**) NEUT NOUN
pedal

★ **peinlich** ADJECTIVE
1 embarrassing
□ eine peinliche Frage **an embarrassing
question**
2 awkward
□ eine peinliche Angelegenheit **an awkward
situation**
■ **Das ist mir aber peinlich.** I'm dreadfully
sorry.
■ **peinlich genau** painstakingly □ Sie hat das
peinlich genau überprüft. **She checked it
painstakingly.**

die **Peitsche** FEM NOUN
whip

die **Pelle** FEM NOUN
skin

der **Pelz** (GEN des **Pelzes**, PL die **Pelze**) MASC
NOUN
fur

das **Pendel** (PL die **Pendel**) NEUT NOUN
pendulum

pendeln (PERFECT TENSE **ist gependelt**) VERB
[34]
to commute
□ Er pendelt zwischen Tübingen und Stuttgart.
He commutes between Tübingen and Stuttgart

der **Pendelverkehr** MASC NOUN
1 shuttle service
□ Die Fluggesellschaft hat einen Pendelverkehr
zwischen Köln und Berlin eingerichtet. **The
airline set up a shuttle service between Cologne
and Berlin.**
2 commuter traffic
□ Zwischen Tübingen und Stuttgart besteht ein
reger Pendelverkehr. **There is heavy commuter
traffic between Tübingen and Stuttgart.**

der **Pendler** (PL die **Pendler**) MASC NOUN
commuter

penetrant ADJECTIVE
1 overpowering
□ ein penetranter Geruch **an overpowering
smell**
2 pushy
□ ein penetranter Vertreter **a pushy salesman**
■ **penetrant werden** to get aggressive

der **Penis** (GEN des **Penis**, PL die **Penisse**)
MASC NOUN
penis

★ = core vocabulary

pennen VERB [48]
to kip (Umgangssprache)
□ Ich habe auf dem Fußboden gepennt. I kipped on the floor.
■ Er pennt. He's having a kip.

der **Penner** (PL die Penner) MASC NOUN
dosser (Umgangssprache)

die **Pension** FEM NOUN
1 pension
□ Er bezieht eine ordentliche Pension. He gets a decent pension.
■ in Pension gehen to retire
2 guesthouse
□ Wir haben in einer Pension übernachtet. We stayed overnight in a guesthouse.

pensioniert ADJECTIVE
retired

perfekt ADJECTIVE
▷ see also das Perfekt NOUN
perfect
□ ein perfektes Alibi a perfect alibi □ perfekt passen to fit perfectly

das **Perfekt** (PL die Perfekte) NEUT NOUN
▷ see also perfekt ADJECTIVE
perfect

die **Periode** FEM NOUN
period

die **Perle** FEM NOUN
pearl

perplex ADJECTIVE
dumbfounded

die **Person** FEM NOUN
person
■ Ich für meine Person ... Personally I ...

das **Personal** NEUT NOUN
staff
□ das Personal der Firma the staff of the company □ das Hotelpersonal the hotel staff

der **Personalausweis** (GEN des Personalausweises, PL die Personalausweise) MASC NOUN
identity card

der **Personalchef** (PL die Personalchefs) MASC NOUN
personnel manager

die **Personalien** FEM PL NOUN
particulars pl

das **Personalpronomen** (PL die Personalpronomen) NEUT NOUN
personal pronoun

der **Personenzug** (PL die Personenzüge) MASC NOUN
passenger train

persönlich ADJECTIVE, ADVERB
1 personal
□ das persönliche Fürwort the personal pronoun □ persönlich werden to get personal

2 in person
□ persönlich erscheinen to appear in person
3 personally
□ jemanden persönlich kennen to know somebody personally □ Das war nicht persönlich gemeint. It wasn't meant personally.

★ die **Persönlichkeit** FEM NOUN
personality

die **Perücke** FEM NOUN
wig

der **Pessimist** (GEN des Pessimisten, PL die Pessimisten) MASC NOUN
pessimist

★ **pessimistisch** ADJECTIVE
pessimistic

die **Pest** FEM NOUN
plague
■ jemanden wie die Pest hassen to loathe somebody

die **Petersilie** FEM NOUN
parsley

das **Petroleum** NEUT NOUN
paraffin

der **Pfad** (PL die Pfade) MASC NOUN
path

★ der **Pfadfinder** (PL die Pfadfinder) MASC NOUN
boy scout

★ die **Pfadfinderin** FEM NOUN
girl guide

★ das **Pfand** (PL die Pfänder) NEUT NOUN
1 deposit
□ Auf der Flasche ist ein Pfand von siebzig Cent. There's a deposit of seventy cents on the bottle.
2 forfeit
□ Wer die Frage nicht beantworten kann, muss ein Pfand geben. Anyone who cannot answer the question must pay a forfeit.

die **Pfandflasche** FEM NOUN
returnable bottle

die **Pfanne** FEM NOUN
frying pan

der **Pfannkuchen** (PL die Pfannkuchen) MASC NOUN
pancake

der **Pfarrer** (PL die Pfarrer) MASC NOUN
parish priest

Pfd. ABBREVIATION (= Pfund)
pound (weight)

★ der **Pfeffer** (PL die Pfeffer) MASC NOUN
pepper

das **Pfefferkorn** (PL die Pfefferkörner) NEUT NOUN
peppercorn

das **Pfefferminzbonbon** (PL die Pfefferminzbonbons) NEUT NOUN
peppermint

P

Pfefferminze – pfuschen

die **Pfefferminze** FEM NOUN
mint

die **Pfeffermühle** FEM NOUN
pepper mill

★ die **Pfeife** FEM NOUN
1 whistle
□ die Pfeife des Schiedsrichters the referee's whistle
2 pipe
□ Mein Bruder raucht Pfeife. My brother smokes a pipe.

pfeifen (IMPERFECT **pfiff**, PERFECT TENSE **hat gepfiffen**) VERB
to whistle

der **Pfeil** (PL die **Pfeile**) MASC NOUN
arrow

★ das **Pferd** (PL die **Pferde**) NEUT NOUN
horse

das **Pferderennen** (PL die **Pferderennen**) NEUT NOUN
1 race meeting
□ Er geht regelmäßig zu Pferderennen. He regularly goes to race meetings.
2 horse-racing
□ Ich interessiere mich nicht für Pferderennen. I'm not interested in horse-racing.

der **Pferdeschwanz** (GEN des **Pferdeschwanzes**, PL die **Pferdeschwänze**) MASC NOUN
ponytail

der **Pferdestall** (PL die **Pferdeställe**) MASC NOUN
stable

★ das **Pfingsten** (GEN des **Pfingsten**, PL die **Pfingsten**) NEUT NOUN
Whitsun
□ an Pfingsten at Whitsun

der **Pfirsich** (PL die **Pfirsiche**) MASC NOUN
peach

★ die **Pflanze** FEM NOUN
plant

★ **pflanzen** VERB [36]
to plant

★ das **Pflaster** (PL die **Pflaster**) NEUT NOUN
1 plaster
□ Sie klebte ein Pflaster auf die Wunde. She put a plaster on the cut.
2 paving stones pl
□ Jemand hatte das Pflaster in der Fußgängerzone bemalt. Somebody had been painting on the paving stones in the pedestrian precinct.

★ die **Pflaume** FEM NOUN
plum

die **Pflege** FEM NOUN
1 care
□ Diese Pflanze braucht nicht viel Pflege. This plant doesn't need much care. □ ein Mittel zur Pflege von Leder a leather-care product
2 nursing
□ Ein krankes Baby braucht viel Pflege. A sick baby needs a lot of nursing.
■ ein Kind in Pflege geben to have a child fostered

die **Pflegeeltern** PL NOUN
foster parents pl

pflegeleicht ADJECTIVE
easy-care
□ ein pflegeleichter Stoff an easy-care fabric

pflegen VERB [38]
1 to nurse
□ Sie pflegt ihre kranke Mutter. She's nursing her sick mother.
2 to look after
□ Unsere Nachbarn pflegen ihren Rasen. Our neighbours look after their lawns.
■ gepflegte Hände well-cared-for hands
■ gepflegt aussehen to look well-groomed

der **Pfleger** (PL die **Pfleger**) MASC NOUN
male nurse

★ die **Pflicht** FEM NOUN
duty
□ Es ist deine Pflicht, dich darum zu kümmern. It's your duty to take care of it.

pflichtbewusst ADJECTIVE
conscientious

★ das **Pflichtfach** (PL die **Pflichtfächer**) NEUT NOUN
compulsory subject

★ **pflücken** VERB [48]
to pick
□ Wir haben Himbeeren gepflückt. We picked raspberries. □ einen Strauß pflücken to pick a bunch of flowers

der **Pförtner** (PL die **Pförtner**) MASC NOUN
doorman

der **Pfosten** (PL die **Pfosten**) MASC NOUN
post
□ Der Ball traf den Pfosten. The ball hit the post

die **Pfote** FEM NOUN
paw
□ Der Hund hat schmutzige Pfoten. The dog's paws are dirty.

pfui EXCLAMATION
ugh!

★ das **Pfund** (PL die **Pfunde** or **Pfund**) NEUT NOUN
pound
□ drei Pfund Äpfel three pounds of apples
□ dreißig britische Pfund thirty pounds sterling

pfuschen VERB [38]
to be sloppy (Umgangssprache)
■ Die Handwerker haben gepfuscht. The craftsmen produced sloppy work.

★ = core vocabulary

■ jemandem ins Handwerk pfuschen to stick one's nose into somebody's business

die **Pfütze** FEM NOUN
puddle

die **Phantasie** FEM NOUN ▷ see die **Fantasie**

phantasieren VERB ▷ see **fantasieren**

phantastisch ADJECTIVE ▷ see **fantastisch**

die **Philosophie** FEM NOUN
philosophy

philosophisch ADJECTIVE
philosophical

phlegmatisch ADJECTIVE
lethargic

die **Phonetik** FEM NOUN
phonetics pl
□ Die Phonetik steht in eckigen Klammern. Phonetics are given in square brackets.

phonetisch ADJECTIVE
phonetic

das **Photo** NEUT NOUN ▷ see das **Foto**

★ die **Physik** FEM NOUN
physics sing
□ Physik ist mein Lieblingsfach. Physics is my favourite subject.

der **Physiker** (PL die **Physiker**) MASC NOUN
physicist

die **Physikerin** FEM NOUN
physicist

physisch ADJECTIVE
physical

der **Pickel** (PL die **Pickel**) MASC NOUN
1 pimple
□ Du hast einen Pickel auf der Nase. You've got a pimple on your nose.
2 pickaxe
□ Die Arbeiter haben den Straßenbelag mit Pickeln aufgeschlagen. The workers broke up the road surface with pickaxes.
3 ice axe
□ Die Bergsteiger hatten Seile und Pickel dabei. The mountaineers had ropes and ice axes with them.

★ das **Picknick** (PL die **Picknicks**) NEUT NOUN
picnic
□ Picknick machen to have a picnic

der **Piepser** (PL die **Piepser**) MASC NOUN
bleeper (Umgangssprache)

das **Pik** (PL die **Pik**) NEUT NOUN
spades sing
□ Pik ist Trumpf. Spades is trumps.

★ **pikant** ADJECTIVE
spicy

★ die **Pille** FEM NOUN
pill
□ Sie nimmt die Pille. She's on the pill.

★ der **Pilot** (GEN des **Piloten**, PL die **Piloten**) MASC NOUN
pilot

das **Pils** (GEN des **Pils**, PL die **Pils**) NEUT NOUN
Pilsner lager

★ der **Pilz** (GEN des **Pilzes**, PL die **Pilze**) MASC NOUN
1 mushroom
□ eine Soße mit Pilzen a mushroom sauce
2 toadstool
□ Diese Pilze sind giftig. These toadstools are poisonous.

pinkeln VERB [88]
to pee (Umgangssprache)

der **Pinsel** (PL die **Pinsel**) MASC NOUN
paintbrush

die **Pinzette** FEM NOUN
tweezers pl
□ eine Pinzette a pair of tweezers

der **Pirat** (GEN des **Piraten**, PL die **Piraten**) MASC NOUN
pirate

die **Piste** FEM NOUN
1 run
□ Wir sind die blaue Piste runtergefahren. We skied down the blue run.
2 runway
□ Das Flugzeug stand auf der Piste und wartete auf die Starterlaubnis. The plane stood on the runway waiting for clearance for takeoff.

die **Pistole** FEM NOUN
pistol

★ der **Pkw** (GEN des **Pkw** or **Pkws**, PL die **Pkws**) MASC NOUN (= Personenkraftwagen)
car

plagen VERB [38]
to bother
□ Was plagt dich denn? What's bothering you?
■ Sie muss sich in der Schule ziemlich plagen. She finds school hard going.

★ das **Plakat** (PL die **Plakate**) NEUT NOUN
poster

★ der **Plan** (PL die **Pläne**) MASC NOUN
1 plan
□ Unser Plan war, vor ihm da zu sein. Our plan was to arrive before him.
2 map
□ Hast du einen Plan von München? Have you got a map of Munich?

★ **planen** VERB [38]
to plan
□ Wir planen unseren nächsten Urlaub. We're planning our next holiday.
■ einen Mord planen to plot a murder

der **Planet** (GEN des **Planeten**, PL die **Planeten**) MASC NOUN
planet

P

planmäßig – plump

★ planmäßig ADJECTIVE

1 according to plan
□ Alles verlief planmäßig. **Everything went according to plan.**

2 scheduled
□ planmäßige Ankunft **scheduled arrival**

3 on time
□ Die Maschine ist planmäßig gelandet. **The plane landed on time.**

★ das Plastik NEUT NOUN
▷ *see also* die **Plastik** NOUN
plastic
□ Plastik ist eine enorme Belastung für die Umwelt. **Plastic is an enormous burden on the environment.**

★ die Plastik FEM NOUN
▷ *see also* das **Plastik** NOUN
sculpture

der Plastikbeutel (PL die **Plastikbeutel**) MASC NOUN
plastic bag

die Plastiktüte FEM NOUN
plastic bag

platt ADJECTIVE
flat
□ ein platter Reifen **a flat tyre** □ plattes Land **flat country**
■ etwas platt drücken **to flatten something**
■ Ich bin platt! **I'm flabbergasted!**
(*Umgangssprache*)

plattdeutsch ADJECTIVE
low German

★ die Platte FEM NOUN

1 plate
□ Sie stellte den Topf auf die Platte. **She put the saucepan on the plate.**
■ eine Platte mit Käseaufschnitt **a platter of assorted cheeses**

2 record
□ Sie hat alle Platten der Beatles. **She's got all the Beatles' records.**

der Plattenspieler (PL die **Plattenspieler**) MASC NOUN
record player

★ der Platz (GEN des **Platzes**, PL die **Plätze**) MASC NOUN

1 place
□ Das ist ein schöner Platz zum Zelten. **That's a good place to pitch a tent.** □ Das Buch steht nicht an seinem Platz. **The book isn't in its place.** □ der erste Platz **the first place**

2 seat
□ Wir hatten Plätze in der ersten Reihe. **We had seats in the front row.** □ Ist hier noch ein Platz frei? **Are all these seats taken?**
■ Platz nehmen **to take a seat**

3 room
□ Das Sofa braucht zu viel Platz. **The sofa takes up too much room.** □ jemandem Platz machen **to make room for somebody**

4 square
□ Auf dem Platz vor der Kirche ist zweimal die Woche Markt. **There's a market twice a week on the square in front of the church.**

5 playing field
■ Der Schiedsrichter schickte ihn vom Platz. **The referee sent him off.**

das Plätzchen (PL die **Plätzchen**) NEUT NOUN

1 spot
□ ein hübsches Plätzchen **a beautiful spot**

2 biscuit
□ Zum Kaffee gab es Plätzchen. **There were biscuits with the coffee.**

platzen (PERFECT TENSE **ist geplatzt**) VERB [36]

1 to burst
□ Der Luftballon ist geplatzt. **The balloon has burst.**

2 to explode
□ In der Innenstadt ist gestern eine Bombe geplatzt. **A bomb exploded in the town centre yesterday.**
■ vor Wut platzen **to be livid**
(*Umgangssprache*)

★ die Platzkarte FEM NOUN
seat reservation

★ plaudern VERB [88]
to chat

pleite ADJECTIVE
▷ *see also* die **Pleite** NOUN
broke (*Umgangssprache*)
□ Ich bin total pleite. **I'm stony-broke.**

die Pleite FEM NOUN
▷ *see also* **pleite** ADJECTIVE

1 bankruptcy
□ die Pleite einer Firma **the bankruptcy of a company**
■ Pleite machen **to go bust** (*Umgangssprache*)

2 flop (*Umgangssprache*)
□ Die Veranstaltung war eine Pleite. **The event was a flop.**

die Plombe FEM NOUN
filling
□ Ich habe noch keine einzige Plombe. **I still haven't got a single filling.**

★ plötzlich ADJECTIVE, ADVERB

1 sudden
□ ihr plötzliches Erscheinen **her sudden appearance**

2 suddenly
□ Sie war plötzlich weg. **Suddenly she was gone.**

plump ADJECTIVE
clumsy
□ plumpe Bewegungen **clumsy movements**
■ ein plumper Körper **a shapeless body**
■ eine plumpe Lüge **a blatant lie**

★ = core vocabulary

der **Plural** (PL die **Plurale**) MASC NOUN
plural

★ **plus** ADVERB
▷ see also das **Plus** NOUN
plus

das **Plus** (GEN des **Plus**) NEUT NOUN
▷ see also **plus** ADVERB
1 plus
□ Steht vor der Zahl ein Plus oder ein Minus? Is there a plus or a minus in front of the figure?
2 profit
□ Die Firma hat dieses Jahr ein Plus gemacht. The company has made a profit this year.
3 advantage
□ Sprachkenntnisse sind immer ein Plus. Language skills are always an advantage.

das **Plutonium** NEUT NOUN
plutonium

★ **PLZ** ABBREVIATION (= Postleitzahl)
postcode

der **Po** (PL die **Pos**) MASC NOUN
bum (Umgangssprache)

★ der **Pokal** (PL die **Pokale**) MASC NOUN
1 cup
□ Welche Mannschaft hat den Pokal gewonnen? Which team won the cup?
2 goblet
□ Sie tranken Wein aus Pokalen. They drank wine out of goblets.

das **Pokalspiel** (PL die **Pokalspiele**) NEUT NOUN
cup tie

der **Pol** (PL die **Pole**) MASC NOUN
pole
□ am Pol at the Pole

★ der **Pole** (GEN des **Polen**, PL die **Polen**) MASC NOUN
Pole
■ **Er ist Pole.** He's Polish.

★ **Polen** NEUT NOUN
Poland
■ **aus Polen** from Poland
■ **nach Polen** to Poland

die **Police** FEM NOUN
insurance policy

polieren (PERFECT TENSE **hat poliert**) VERB [76]
to polish

die **Polin** FEM NOUN
Pole
■ **Sie ist Polin.** She's Polish.

★ die **Politik** FEM NOUN
1 politics sing
□ Politik interessiert mich nicht. Politics doesn't interest me.
2 policy
□ die Politik Großbritanniens in Bezug auf Immigration Great Britain's policy on immigration

★ der **Politiker** (PL die **Politiker**) MASC NOUN
politician

politisch ADJECTIVE
political

★ die **Polizei** FEM NOUN
police

> Note that **Polizei** is used with a singular verb and 'police' with a plural verb.

□ Die Polizei ist noch nicht da. The police haven't arrived yet.

der **Polizeibeamte** (GEN des **Polizeibeamten**, PL die **Polizeibeamten**) MASC NOUN
police officer
□ Wir wurden von einem Polizeibeamten angehalten. We were stopped by a police officer.

die **Polizeibeamtin** FEM NOUN
police officer
□ Sie ist Polizeibeamtin. She's a police officer.

polizeilich ADJECTIVE
■ **Er wird polizeilich gesucht.** The police are looking for him.

★ das **Polizeirevier** (PL die **Polizeireviere**) NEUT NOUN
police station

die **Polizeistunde** FEM NOUN
closing time (of bars)

★ die **Polizeiwache** FEM NOUN
police station

★ der **Polizist** (GEN des **Polizisten**, PL die **Polizisten**) MASC NOUN
police officer
□ Oliver ist Polizist. Oliver's a police officer.
□ Wir brauchen einen Polizisten. We need a police officer.

★ die **Polizistin** FEM NOUN
police officer
□ Susi ist Polizistin. Susi's a police officer.

★ **polnisch** ADJECTIVE
Polish

★ die **Pommes** FEM PL NOUN
chips pl
□ Pommes mit Mayonnaise chips with mayonnaise

die **Pommes frites** FEM PL NOUN
chips pl
□ Würstchen mit Pommes frites sausages and chips

pompös ADJECTIVE
ostentatious

das **Pony** (PL die **Ponys**) NEUT NOUN
▷ see also der **Pony** NOUN
pony
□ Wir sind auf Ponys geritten. We rode ponies.

P

der Pony (PL die **Ponys**) MASC NOUN
▷ *see also* das **Pony** NOUN
fringe
□ Sie trägt einen Pony. **She's got a fringe.**

★ **der Pop** MASC NOUN
pop

★ **die Popmusik** FEM NOUN
pop music

poppig ADJECTIVE
bright
□ poppige Farben **bright colours**

★ **der Popstar** (PL die **Popstars**) MASC NOUN
pop star

die Pore FEM NOUN
pore

die Pornografie FEM NOUN
pornography

porös ADJECTIVE
porous

der Porree (PL die **Porrees**) MASC NOUN
leek

★ **das Portemonnaie** (PL die
Portemonnaies) NEUT NOUN
purse

★ **der Portier** (PL die **Portiers**) MASC NOUN
porter

★ **die Portion** FEM NOUN
portion
□ eine große Portion **a big portion** □ Zwei
Portionen Pommes frites, bitte. **Two portions of
chips, please.**
■ Dazu gehört eine ordentliche Portion
Mut. **You need quite a bit of courage for that.**

★ **das Portmonee** (PL die **Portmonees**) NEUT
NOUN
purse

das Porto (PL die **Portos**) NEUT NOUN
postage

★ **Portugal** NEUT NOUN
Portugal
■ **aus Portugal** from Portugal
■ **nach Portugal** to Portugal

★ **der Portugiese** (GEN des **Portugiesen**, PL die
Portugiesen) MASC NOUN
Portuguese

★ **die Portugiesin** FEM NOUN
Portuguese

★ **portugiesisch** ADJECTIVE
Portuguese

★ **das Porzellan** NEUT NOUN
1 porcelain
□ eine Figur aus Porzellan **a porcelain figurine**
2 china
□ Das Porzellan habe ich von meiner Oma
geerbt. **I inherited the china from my grandma.**

die Posaune FEM NOUN
trombone
□ Fatima spielt Posaune. **Fatima plays the
trombone.**

positiv ADJECTIVE
positive
□ HIV-positiv **HIV-positive**

das Possessivpronomen (PL die
Possessivpronomen) NEUT NOUN
possessive pronoun

★ **die Post** FEM NOUN
1 post office
□ Bring bitte das Päckchen zur Post. **Please take
the parcel to the post office.**
2 mail
□ Ist Post für mich gekommen? **Was there any
mail for me?**

★ **das Postamt** (PL die **Postämter**) NEUT NOUN
post office

der Postausgang (PL die **Postausgänge**)
MASC NOUN
outbox

der Postbote (GEN des **Postboten**, PL die
Postboten) MASC NOUN
postman

die Postbotin FEM NOUN
postwoman

der Posteingang (PL die **Posteingänge**)
MASC NOUN
inbox

posten VERB [2]
to post (*on forum*, *blog*)
□ Wann hast du das gepostet? **When did you
post that?**

der Posten (PL die **Posten**) MASC NOUN
1 post
□ Sie hat einen guten Posten als Psychologin.
She's got a good post as a psychologist.
2 item
□ Dieser Posten ist nicht auf der Preisliste
aufgeführt. **This item doesn't appear on the
price list.**

★ **das Poster** (PL die **Poster**) NEUT NOUN
poster

das Postfach (PL die **Postfächer**) NEUT NOUN
post office box

★ **die Postkarte** FEM NOUN
postcard

postlagernd ADVERB
poste restante

★ **die Postleitzahl** FEM NOUN
postcode

postwendend ADVERB
by return of post

das Postwertzeichen (PL die
Postwertzeichen) NEUT NOUN
postage stamp

die **Pracht** FEM NOUN
splendour

prächtig ADJECTIVE, ADVERB
1 magnificent
□ ein prächtiges Haus a magnificent house
2 marvellous
□ Wir haben uns prächtig amüsiert. We had a marvellous time.

prachtvoll ADJECTIVE
splendid

das **Prädikat** (PL die Prädikate) NEUT NOUN
predicate
□ Subjekt und Prädikat eines Satzes subject and predicate of a sentence

prahlen VERB [38]
to brag

der **Praktikant** (GEN des Praktikanten, PL die Praktikanten) MASC NOUN
trainee

die **Praktikantin** FEM NOUN
trainee

das **Praktikum** (GEN des Praktikums, PL die Praktika) NEUT NOUN
practical training
□ Sie absolviert ihr Praktikum. She's doing her practical training.

★ **praktisch** ADJECTIVE
1 practical
□ ein praktischer Mensch a practical person
□ eine praktische Lösung a practical solution
□ praktische Erfahrung practical experience
2 handy
□ ein praktisches Gerät a handy gadget
■ praktischer Arzt general practitioner
■ praktisch begabt sein to be good with one's hands

★ die **Praline** FEM NOUN
chocolate

die **Präposition** FEM NOUN
preposition

das **Präsens** (GEN des Präsens) NEUT NOUN
present tense

das **Präservativ** (PL die Präservative) NEUT NOUN
condom

★ der **Präsident** (GEN des Präsidenten, PL die Präsidenten) MASC NOUN
president

die **Praxis** (PL die Praxen) FEM NOUN
1 practical experience
□ Ihr fehlt die Praxis. She lacks practical experience.
■ etwas in die Praxis umsetzen to put something into practice
2 surgery
□ Kommen Sie zur Behandlung in die Praxis. Come to the surgery for treatment.

3 practice
□ Mein Anwalt hat seine eigene Praxis aufgemacht. My solicitor has opened his own practice.

★ der **Preis** (GEN des Preises, PL die Preise) MASC NOUN
1 price
□ Die Preise für Computer sind gefallen. Computer prices have fallen.
2 prize
□ Ihr Hund hat einen Preis gewonnen. Her dog's won a prize.
■ um keinen Preis not at any price □ Das mache ich um keinen Preis. I won't do it at any price.

preisgünstig ADJECTIVE
inexpensive

die **Preislage** FEM NOUN
price range

das **Preisschild** (PL die Preisschilder) NEUT NOUN
price tag

der **Preisträger** (PL die Preisträger) MASC NOUN
prizewinner

★ **preiswert** ADJECTIVE
inexpensive

die **Prellung** FEM NOUN
bruise

der **Premierminister** (PL die Premierminister) MASC NOUN
prime minister

die **Presse** FEM NOUN
press

pressen VERB [31]
to press

der **Priester** (PL die Priester) MASC NOUN
priest

die **Priesterin** FEM NOUN
priest

★ **prima** ADJECTIVE
super
□ Es ist ein prima Hotel. It's a super hotel.

der **Prinz** (GEN des Prinzen, PL die Prinzen) MASC NOUN
prince

die **Prinzessin** FEM NOUN
princess

das **Prinzip** (PL die Prinzipien) NEUT NOUN
principle
■ aus Prinzip as a matter of principle

privat ADJECTIVE
private

der **Privatpatient** (GEN des Privatpatienten, PL die Privatpatienten) MASC NOUN
private patient

P

Privatschule – protestieren

die **Privatschule** FEM NOUN
fee-paying school

★ **pro** PREPOSITION

> The preposition **pro** takes the accusative.

per
□ zehn Euro pro Person ten euros per person
■ einmal pro Woche once a week

die **Probe** FEM NOUN
1 test
□ Wir müssen eine Probe machen, ob er geeignet ist. We need to do a test to see if he's suitable. □ Wir haben morgen in Englisch noch eine Probe! We've got another English test tomorrow!
2 sample
□ Die Probe wird im Labor untersucht. The sample's being examined in the laboratory.
3 rehearsal
□ die letzte Probe vor der Aufführung the final rehearsal before the performance
■ jemanden auf die Probe stellen to test somebody

★ **probieren** (PERFECT TENSE **hat probiert**) VERB [76]
to try
□ Probier mal eine andere Methode. Try a different method. □ Willst du mal von dem Käse probieren? Would you like to try some of the cheese?
■ Ich werde probieren, ob ich das kann. I'll give it a try.

★ das **Problem** (PL die **Probleme**) NEUT NOUN
problem
□ Kein Problem! No problem.

das **Produkt** (PL die **Produkte**) NEUT NOUN
product

die **Produktion** FEM NOUN
1 production
□ die Produktion von Luxusautos the production of luxury cars
2 output
□ Wir müssen unsere Produktion erhöhen. We must increase our output.

produzieren (PERFECT TENSE **hat produziert**) VERB [76]
to produce

der **Professor** (PL die **Professoren**) MASC NOUN
professor

die **Professorin** FEM NOUN
professor

★ der **Profi** (PL die **Profis**) MASC NOUN
pro (Umgangssprache)
□ Er spielt wie ein Profi. He plays like a pro.

der **Profit** (PL die **Profite**) MASC NOUN
profit

profitieren (PERFECT TENSE **hat profitiert**) VERB [76]
to profit
□ von etwas profitieren to profit from something

★ das **Programm** (PL die **Programme**) NEUT NOUN
1 programme
□ das Programm des heutigen Abends this evening's programme
2 program
□ Für die Kalkulation arbeite ich mit einem anderen Programm. I've got a different program for spreadsheets.

★ **programmieren** (PERFECT TENSE **hat programmiert**) VERB [76]
to program

★ der **Programmierer** (PL die **Programmierer**) MASC NOUN
programmer

★ das **Projekt** (PL die **Projekte**) NEUT NOUN
project

der/die **Promi** MASC/FEM NOUN
celebrity

das **Promille** (PL die **Promille**) NEUT NOUN
alcohol level
□ Er hatte drei Promille. He had an alcohol level of three hundred milligrams in a hundred millilitres of blood.

das **Pronomen** (PL die **Pronomen**) NEUT NOUN
pronoun

die **Proportion** FEM NOUN
proportion

★ der **Prospekt** (PL die **Prospekte**) MASC NOUN
brochure

> **BE CAREFUL!**
> Prospekt does not mean **prospect**.

prost EXCLAMATION
cheers!

die **Prostituierte** (GEN der **Prostituierten**) FEM NOUN
prostitute

die **Prostitution** FEM NOUN
prostitution

das **Protein** (PL die **Proteine**) NEUT NOUN
protein

der **Protest** (PL die **Proteste**) MASC NOUN
protest

★ **protestantisch** ADJECTIVE
Protestant

protestieren (PERFECT TENSE **hat protestiert**) VERB [76]
to protest
□ Wir protestieren gegen diese Maßnahmen. We're protesting against these measures.

★ = core vocabulary

das **Protokoll** (PL die **Protokolle**) NEUT NOUN

1 minutes pl
□ Wer schreibt das Protokoll der heutigen Besprechung? Who is taking the minutes of today's meeting?

2 statement
□ Bitte unterschreiben Sie hier. Please sign here.

protzen VERB [48]
to show off
□ Sie protzt mit ihrem neuen Mountainbike. She's showing off with her new mountain bike.

protzig ADJECTIVE
showy
□ ein protziges Auto a showy car

der **Proviant** (PL die **Proviante**) MASC NOUN
provisions pl

provisorisch ADJECTIVE
provisional

provozieren (PERFECT TENSE **hat provoziert**) VERB [76]
to provoke

★ das **Prozent** (PL die **Prozente**) NEUT NOUN
per cent
□ zehn Prozent ten per cent

der **Prozess** (GEN des **Prozesses**, PL die **Prozesse**) MASC NOUN
trial
□ Der Prozess fängt nächste Woche an. The trial starts next week.
■ **einen Prozess gewinnen** to win a case

★ **prüfen** VERB [38]

1 to test
□ Sie wollte meine Deutschkenntnisse prüfen. She wanted to test my knowledge of German.
□ Wir werden morgen in Chemie geprüft. We're having a chemistry test tomorrow.

2 to check
□ Vor der Reise sollte man den Ölstand prüfen. You should check the oil before your journey.

der **Prüfer** (PL die **Prüfer**) MASC NOUN
examiner

★ die **Prüfung** FEM NOUN

1 examination
□ Sie hat die Prüfung bestanden. She's passed the examination.

2 check
□ Bei der Prüfung der Bremsen haben wir einen Defekt festgestellt. During a check on the brakes we found a fault.

der **Prügel** (PL die **Prügel**) MASC NOUN
stick
□ Er schlug ihn mit einem Prügel. He hit him with a stick.
■ **Prügel bekommen** to get a beating (Umgangssprache) □ Ich habe als Kind nie Prügel bekommen. I never got a beating as a child.

■ Er hat von der Gang Prügel bekommen. The gang beat him up.

die **Prügelei** FEM NOUN
fight

prügeln VERB [34]
to beat
□ Eltern sollten ihre Kinder nicht prügeln. Parents shouldn't beat their children.
■ **sich prügeln** to fight □ Ich will mich nicht mit dir prügeln. I don't want to fight you.
■ **Die beiden haben sich in der Pause geprügelt.** The two of them had a fight in the break.

die **Prügelstrafe** FEM NOUN
corporal punishment

psychisch ADJECTIVE
psychological

der **Psychologe** (GEN des **Psychologen**, PL die **Psychologen**) MASC NOUN
psychologist
□ Ihr Vater ist Psychologe. Her father is a psychologist.

die **Psychologie** FEM NOUN
psychology

psychologisch ADJECTIVE
psychological

die **Pubertät** FEM NOUN
puberty
□ während der Pubertät during puberty

★ das **Publikum** NEUT NOUN
audience
□ Am Ende des Stückes klatschte das Publikum. The audience clapped at the end of the play.

★ der **Pudding** (PL die **Puddinge** or **Puddings**) MASC NOUN
blancmange

der **Puder** (PL die **Puder**) MASC NOUN
powder

der **Pulli** (PL die **Pullis**) MASC NOUN
(Umgangssprache)
pullover

★ der **Pullover** (PL die **Pullover**) MASC NOUN
pullover

★ der **Puls** (GEN des **Pulses**, PL die **Pulse**) MASC NOUN
pulse
■ **jemandem den Puls fühlen** to take somebody's pulse

das **Pult** (PL die **Pulte**) NEUT NOUN
desk

das **Pulver** (PL die **Pulver**) NEUT NOUN
powder

die **Pumpe** FEM NOUN
pump

pumpen VERB [38]

1 to pump

P

Numbers in brackets refer to verb tables on pages 697 to 706.

213

Punkt - Pyramide

□ Das Öl wird durch die Pipeline gepumpt. The oil's pumped along the pipeline.

2 to lend

□ Kannst du mir mal dein iPad® pumpen? Can you lend me your iPad®?

3 to borrow

□ Ich habe mir das Rad meiner Schwester gepumpt. I've borrowed my sister's bike.

★ der **Punkt** (PL die **Punkte**) MASC NOUN

1 full stop

□ Am Satzende steht ein Punkt. A full stop goes at the end of a sentence.

2 point

□ In diesem Punkt gebe ich dir recht. On this point I agree with you.

3 dot

□ Das Schiff war nur noch ein kleiner Punkt am Horizont. The ship was only a small dot on the horizon. □ Sie trug ein rotes T-Shirt mit weißen Punkten. She was wearing a red T-Shirt with white dots.

★ **pünktlich** ADJECTIVE, ADVERB

1 punctual

□ Sie ist nicht sehr pünktlich. She's not very punctual.

2 on time

□ Der Zug kam pünktlich an. The train arrived on time.

die **Pünktlichkeit** FEM NOUN
punctuality

★ die **Puppe** FEM NOUN
doll

pur ADJECTIVE

pure

□ Das ist pures Gold. That's pure gold. □ Das ist doch der pure Wahnsinn. But that's pure madness.

■ **etwas pur trinken** to drink something neat
■ **Whisky pur** neat whisky

die **Pute** FEM NOUN
turkey

der **Puter** (PL die **Puter**) MASC NOUN
turkey

★ **putzen** VERB [36]

1 to clean

□ Er putzt jeden Samstag das Haus. He cleans the house every Saturday.

2 to wipe

□ Putz dir die Schuhe, bevor du reinkommst. Wipe your shoes before you come in.

■ **sich die Nase putzen** to blow one's nose
□ Putz dir mal die Nase! Blow your nose.
■ **sich die Zähne putzen** to brush one's teeth

★ die **Putzfrau** FEM NOUN
cleaner

★ der **Putzmann** (PL die **Putzmänner**) MASC NOUN
cleaner

das **Puzzle** (PL die **Puzzles**) NEUT NOUN
jigsaw

★ der **Pyjama** (PL die **Pyjamas**) MASC NOUN
pyjamas pl
□ ein Pyjama a pair of pyjamas

die **Pyramide** FEM NOUN
pyramid

P

★ = core vocabulary

Qq

qm ABBREVIATION (= *Quadratmeter*)
m²

das **Quadrat** (PL die Quadrate) NEUT NOUN
square

quadratisch ADJECTIVE
square

der **Quadratmeter** (PL die Quadratmeter)
MASC NOUN
square metre
□ eine Wohung von achtzig Quadratmetern a
flat of eighty square metres

die **Qual** FEM NOUN
1 agony
□ Treppensteigen ist für sie eine Qual. Climbing
the stairs is agony for her.
2 anguish *no pl*
□ Die Qualen, die ich vor dieser Operation
ausgestanden habe ... The anguish I went
through before that operation ...

quälen VERB [38]
to treat cruelly
□ Tiere quälen to treat animals cruelly
■ **sich quälen 1** to struggle □ Sie quälte sich
die Treppe hinauf. She struggled up the steps.
2 to torment oneself □ Quäl dich nicht so!
Don't torment yourself like that.
■ **Er muss sich in der Schule ziemlich
quälen.** School's quite a trial for him.

die **Qualifikation** (PL die Qualifikationen)
FEM NOUN
qualification

qualifiziert ADJECTIVE
qualified

die **Qualität** FEM NOUN
quality

die **Qualle** FEM NOUN
jellyfish
□ zwei Quallen two jellyfish

der **Qualm** MASC NOUN
thick smoke

qualmen VERB [38]
to smoke
□ Der Schornstein qualmt. The chimney is
smoking.

die **Quantität** FEM NOUN
quantity

der **Quark** MASC NOUN
quark

der **Quarz** (GEN des Quarzes) MASC NOUN
quartz

quasseln VERB [88]
to natter (*Umgangssprache*)

der **Quatsch** MASC NOUN
rubbish (*Umgangssprache*)
□ Erzähl keinen Quatsch! Don't talk rubbish!
■ **Quatsch machen** to fool around
■ **Mach keinen Quatsch!** Don't be foolish!

quatschen VERB [48]
to natter (*Umgangssprache*)

die **Quelle** FEM NOUN
1 spring
□ heiße Quellen hot springs
2 source
□ aus zuverlässiger Quelle from a reliable
source

quer ADVERB
1 diagonally
□ Die Streifen auf dem Stoff verlaufen quer. The
stripes run diagonally across the material.
■ **quer auf dem Bett** across the bed
2 at right angles
□ Die Mannstraße verläuft quer zur
Müllerstraße. Mann Street runs at right angles
to Müller Street.

die **Querflöte** FEM NOUN
flute
□ Cordula spielt Querflöte. Cordula plays the
flute.

querschnittsgelähmt ADJECTIVE
paraplegic

die **Querstraße** FEM NOUN
■ **eine Straße mit vielen Querstraßen** a
road with a lot of side streets off it
■ **Biegen Sie an der zweiten Querstraße
links ab.** Take the second street on the left.

quetschen VERB [48]
1 to squash
□ Pass auf, dass die Tomaten nicht gequetscht
werden. Mind the tomatoes don't get squashed.

q

Quetschung – Quittung

2 <u>to cram</u>
□ Sie quetschte das Kleid noch in ihren Koffer. She crammed the dress into her case.
■ **Ich habe mir den Finger in der Tür gequetscht.** I trapped my finger in the door.

die **Quetschung** FEM NOUN
<u>bruise</u>

quitt ADJECTIVE
<u>quits</u>
□ Jetzt sind wir quitt. We're quits now.

★ die **Quittung** FEM NOUN
<u>receipt</u>
□ Brauchen Sie eine Quittung? Do you need a receipt?

q

★ = core vocabulary

Rr

★ der **Rabatt** (PL die **Rabatte**) MASC NOUN
discount

die **Rache** FEM NOUN
revenge

der **Rachen** (PL die **Rachen**) MASC NOUN
throat

rächen VERB [48]
- **etwas rächen** to avenge something
- **sich rächen** to take revenge
- **Das wird sich rächen.** You'll pay for that.

★ das **Rad** (PL die **Räder**) NEUT NOUN
1 wheel
2 bike
□ Wir sind mit dem Rad gekommen. **We came by bike.**
- **Rad fahren** to cycle

der **Radar** (PL die **Radare**) MASC NOUN

You can also say das **Radar**.

radar

die **Radarkontrolle** FEM NOUN
radar-controlled speed check

radeln (PERFECT TENSE **ist geradelt**) VERB [88]
to cycle
□ Wir sind an den Bodensee geradelt. **We cycled to Lake Constance.**

★ **radfahren** VERB [21] ▷ see das **Rad**

★ der **Radfahrer** (PL die **Radfahrer**) MASC NOUN
cyclist

der **Radfahrweg** (PL die **Radfahrwege**) MASC NOUN
cycle track

★ der **Radiergummi** (PL die **Radiergummis**) MASC NOUN
rubber

das **Radieschen** (PL die **Radieschen**) NEUT NOUN
radish

★ das **Radio** (PL die **Radios**) NEUT NOUN
radio

radioaktiv ADJECTIVE
radioactive

die **Radioaktivität** FEM NOUN
radioactivity

das **Radrennen** (PL die **Radrennen**) NEUT NOUN

1 cycle race
□ Er hat an dem Radrennen teilgenommen. **He took part in the cycle race.**
2 cycle racing
□ Sie begeistert sich für Radrennen. **She's a cycle racing fan.**

der **Radsport** MASC NOUN
cycling

der **Rahm** MASC NOUN
cream

der **Rahmen** (PL die **Rahmen**) MASC NOUN
frame
□ der Rahmen eines Bildes **the frame of a picture**
- **im Rahmen des Möglichen** within the bounds of possibility

die **Rakete** FEM NOUN
rocket

★ der **Rand** (PL die **Ränder**) MASC NOUN
1 edge
□ Er stand am Rand des Schwimmbeckens. **He stood on the edge of the swimming pool.**
2 rim
□ der Rand der Tasse **the rim of the cup**
- **eine Brille mit Goldrand** a pair of gold-rimmed glasses
3 margin
□ Lass an der Seite des Blattes einen Rand. **Leave a margin at the edge of the page.**
4 ring
□ In der Badewanne waren dunkle Ränder. **There were dark rings in the bath tub.**
5 verge
□ Die Firma steht am Rand des Bankrotts. **The company's on the verge of bankruptcy.**
- **außer Rand und Band** out of control

randalieren (PERFECT TENSE **hat randaliert**) VERB [76]
to go on the rampage

★ der **Rang** (PL die **Ränge**) MASC NOUN
1 rank (*military*)
□ Sie steht im Rang eines Hauptmanns. **She has the rank of captain.**
2 circle (*theatre*)
□ erster Rang **dress circle** □ zweiter Rang **upper circle**

Numbers in brackets refer to verb tables on pages 697 to 706.

r

★ der **Rappen** (PL die **Rappen**) MASC NOUN
rappen
□ Der Schweizer Franken hat hundert Rappen.
There are one hundred rappen in a Swiss franc.

DID YOU KNOW...?
In the French-speaking part of Switzerland
you talk about **centime** rather than **Rappen**.

rasch ADJECTIVE, ADVERB
quick
□ Das war rasch gemacht. That was quickly
done.
■ Ich gehe noch rasch beim Bäcker
vorbei. I'll just pop round to the baker's.

rasen (PERFECT TENSE **ist gerast**) VERB [88]
▷ see also der **Rasen** NOUN
to race
□ Wir sind durch die engen Straßen gerast. We
raced along the narrow streets.

★ der **Rasen** (PL die **Rasen**) MASC NOUN
▷ see also **rasen** VERB
lawn

der **Rasenmäher** (PL die **Rasenmäher**)
MASC NOUN
lawnmower

★ der **Rasierapparat** (PL die **Rasierapparate**)
MASC NOUN
shaver

die **Rasiercreme** (PL die **Rasiercremes**)
FEM NOUN
shaving cream

★ **rasieren** (PERFECT TENSE **hat rasiert**) VERB [76]
to shave
■ sich rasieren to shave

die **Rasierklinge** FEM NOUN
razor blade

das **Rasiermesser** (PL die **Rasiermesser**)
NEUT NOUN
razor

die **Rasse** FEM NOUN
1 race
□ Rassenunruhen race riots
2 breed
□ Welche Rasse ist Ihr Hund? What breed is
your dog?

der **Rassismus** (GEN des **Rassismus**) MASC
NOUN
racism

der **Rassist** (PL die **Rassisten**) MASC NOUN
racist

die **Rassistin** FEM NOUN
racist

rassistisch ADJECTIVE
racist

die **Rast** FEM NOUN
rest
■ Rast machen to stop for a break

rasten VERB [2]
to rest

★ das **Rasthaus** (PL die **Rasthäuser**) NEUT
NOUN
services pl (motorway)

★ der **Rasthof** (PL die **Rasthöfe**) MASC NOUN
services pl (motorway)

★ der **Rastplatz** (GEN des **Rastplatzes**, PL die
Rastplätze) MASC NOUN
lay-by

★ die **Raststätte** FEM NOUN
service area

die **Rasur** FEM NOUN
shaving

★ der **Rat** MASC NOUN
advice no pl
□ Frag doch deine Partnerin um Rat. Ask your
partner for advice.
■ ein Rat a piece of advice
■ Ich weiß keinen Rat. I don't know what to
do.
■ jemanden zu Rate ziehen to consult
somebody

die **Rate** FEM NOUN
instalment

★ **raten** (PRESENT TENSE **rät**, IMPERFECT **riet**, PERFECT
TENSE **hat geraten**) VERB
to guess
□ Rat mal, wie alt ich bin. Guess how old I am.
■ jemandem raten to advise somebody □ Sie
hat mir geraten, einen Arzt aufzusuchen. She
advised me to see a doctor.

★ das **Rathaus** (GEN des **Rathauses**, PL die
Rathäuser) NEUT NOUN
town hall

die **Ration** FEM NOUN
ration

rationalisieren (PERFECT TENSE **hat
rationalisiert**) VERB [76]
to rationalize

rationell ADJECTIVE
efficient

ratlos ADJECTIVE
at a loss
□ Ich bin ratlos, was ich tun soll. I'm at a loss as
to what to do.
■ Sie sah mich ratlos an. She gave me a
helpless look.

der **Ratschlag** (PL die **Ratschläge**) MASC
NOUN
(piece of) advice
□ Ich habe viele Ratschläge bekommen. I've
been given a lot of advice.

das **Rätsel** (PL die **Rätsel**) NEUT NOUN
1 puzzle
□ Sie löst gern Rätsel. She likes solving puzzles.
2 mystery
□ Das ist mir ein Rätsel. It's a mystery to me.

r

rätselhaft ADJECTIVE
mysterious
■ **Es ist mir rätselhaft.** It's a mystery to me.

★ die **Ratte** FEM NOUN
rat

rau ADJECTIVE
1 rough
□ raue Haut rough skin
2 husky
□ eine raue Stimme a husky voice
3 sore
□ ein rauer Hals a sore throat
4 harsh
□ raues Wetter harsh weather □ ein rauer Wind a harsh wind
■ **Hier herrschen raue Sitten.** People here have rough-and-ready ways.

der **Raub** MASC NOUN
robbery

das **Raubtier** (PL die **Raubtiere**) NEUT NOUN
predator

★ der **Rauch** MASC NOUN
smoke

★ **rauchen** VERB [48]
to smoke
■ '**Rauchen verboten**' 'No smoking'

★ der **Raucher** (PL die **Raucher**) MASC NOUN
smoker

räuchern VERB [88]
to smoke
□ Fisch räuchern to smoke fish

rauh ADJECTIVE ▷ see **rau**

★ der **Raum** (PL die **Räume**) MASC NOUN
1 space
□ Sie haben eine Rakete in den Raum geschossen. They launched a rocket into space. □ Raum und Zeit space and time
2 room
□ Eine Wohnung mit vier Räumen ist nicht groß genug für uns. A four-roomed flat isn't big enough for us. □ Dieses Gerät braucht wenig Raum. This appliance doesn't take up much room.
3 area
□ Im Raum Stuttgart kommt es morgen zu Gewittern. There will be thunderstorms in the Stuttgart area tomorrow.

räumen VERB [38]
1 to clear
□ Die Polizei hat das besetzte Haus geräumt. The police cleared the squat.
2 to vacate
□ Bitte räumen Sie Ihr Zimmer bis spätestens zehn Uhr. Please vacate your room by ten o'clock at the latest.
3 to clear away
□ Könnt ihr bitte das Geschirr vom Tisch räumen? Could you clear away the dishes, please?

4 to put away
□ Räum bitte deine Spielsachen in den Schrank. Please put your toys away in the cupboard.

die **Raumfähre** FEM NOUN
space shuttle

die **Raumfahrt** FEM NOUN
space travel

der **Rauminhalt** (PL die **Rauminhalte**) MASC NOUN
volume

räumlich ADJECTIVE
spatial

die **Räumlichkeiten** FEM PL NOUN
premises pl

das **Raumschiff** (PL die **Raumschiffe**) NEUT NOUN
spaceship

der **Rausch** (PL die **Räusche**) MASC NOUN
■ **einen Rausch haben** to be drunk
■ **seinen Rausch ausschlafen** to sleep it off

das **Rauschgift** (PL die **Rauschgifte**) NEUT NOUN
drug

der/die **Rauschgiftsüchtige** (GEN des/der **Rauschgiftsüchtigen**, PL die **Rauschgiftsüchtigen**) MASC/FEM NOUN
drug addict

sich **räuspern** VERB [88]
to clear one's throat

reagieren (PERFECT TENSE **hat reagiert**) VERB [76]
1 to react
□ Wie hat sie auf diesen Vorwurf reagiert? How did she react to the allegation?
2 to respond
□ Die Bremsen haben nicht reagiert. The brakes didn't respond.

die **Reaktion** FEM NOUN
reaction

reaktionär ADJECTIVE
reactionary

der **Reaktor** (PL die **Reaktoren**) MASC NOUN
reactor

realisieren (PERFECT TENSE **hat realisiert**) VERB [76]
1 to fulfil
□ Er hat seine Träume realisiert. He's fulfilled his dreams.
2 to carry out
□ Wir sollten diese Pläne realisieren. We ought to carry out these plans.
3 to realize
□ Sie hat nicht realisiert, dass er schon weg war. She didn't realize that he had already left.

realistisch ADJECTIVE
realistic

r

Reality-Fernsehen – Rechte

das Reality-Fernsehen NEUT NOUN
reality TV

die Realityshow (PL die Realityshows) FEM NOUN
reality show

das Reality-TV NEUT NOUN
reality TV

★ **die Realschule** FEM NOUN
secondary school

> **DID YOU KNOW...?**
> Pupils enter **Realschule** at the age of about ten, and leave after six years. It is not as academically oriented as the **Gymnasium**.

★ **rechnen** VERB [53]
▷ *see also* das **Rechnen** NOUN
to work out
□ Lass mich rechnen, wie viel das wird. Let me work out how much that's going to be.
■ **gut rechnen können** to be good at arithmetic
■ **Özil wird zu den besten Fußballspielern gerechnet.** Özil is regarded as one of the best footballers.
■ **rechnen zu** to class as □ Man rechnet Mexico City zu den Megastädten. Mexico City is classed as one of the megacities.
■ **rechnen mit 1** to reckon with □ Mit wie vielen Besuchern können wir rechnen? How many visitors can we reckon with? **2** to reckon on □ Mit dieser Reaktion hatte ich nicht gerechnet. I hadn't reckoned on this reaction.
■ **rechnen auf** to count on □ Wir rechnen auf deine Unterstützung. We're counting on your support.

★ **das Rechnen** NEUT NOUN
▷ *see also* **rechnen** VERB
arithmetic
□ Maria ist gut im Rechnen. Maria's good at arithmetic.

★ **der Rechner** (PL die **Rechner**) MASC NOUN
1 calculator
□ Ich habe das mit meinem Rechner nachgerechnet. I've checked it with my calculator.
2 computer
□ Er hat sich für seinen Rechner einen neuen Prozessor gekauft. He's bought a new CPU for his computer.

★ **die Rechnung** FEM NOUN
1 calculations *pl*
□ Meine Rechnung ergibt, dass wir noch zweihundert Euro haben. According to my calculations, we still have two hundred euros left.
2 invoice
□ Die Rechnung liegt der Sendung bei. The invoice is enclosed.

★ **recht** ADJECTIVE, ADVERB
▷ *see also* das **Recht** NOUN

1 right
□ Es war nicht recht, dass du sie belogen hast. It wasn't right of you to lie to her. □ Dies ist nicht der rechte Moment, um darüber zu sprechen. This isn't the right moment to talk about it.
■ **Wenn ich dich recht verstehe ...** If I understand you correctly ...
■ **Das geschieht dir recht!** Serves you right!
2 quite
□ Das scheint recht einfach. It seems quite simple.
■ **jemandem recht sein** to be all right with somebody □ Wenn es deiner Mutter recht ist, übernachte ich gern bei euch. If it's all right with your mother, I'd like to stay the night at your place.
■ **Das ist mir recht.** That suits me.
■ **es jemandem recht machen** to please somebody □ Dir kann man es auch nie recht machen! There's no pleasing you.
■ **recht haben** to be right □ Wer hat nun recht? Who's right? □ Er will immer recht haben. He always has to be right.
■ **jemandem recht geben** to agree with somebody □ Ich muss dir recht geben, das war nicht nett. I have to agree with you – that wasn't nice.
■ **Jetzt erst recht!** Now more than ever.

★ **das Recht** (PL die **Rechte**) NEUT NOUN
▷ *see also* **recht** ADJECTIVE, ADVERB

1 right
□ Es ist mein Recht, das zu erfahren. It's my right to know that. □ Ich habe ein Recht auf eine Erklärung. I've got a right to an explanation.
■ **im Recht sein** to be in the right □ Obwohl er im Recht war, hat er nachgegeben. Although he was in the right, he gave in.
■ **etwas mit Recht tun** to be right to do something □ Sie hat sich mit Recht beschwert. She was right to complain.
2 law
□ Sie wurde nach deutschem Recht zu zehn Jahren Gefängnis verurteilt. She was sentenced under German law to ten years' imprisonment.
■ **Recht sprechen** to administer justice

★ **rechte** ADJECTIVE
▷ *see also* die **Rechte** NOUN, das **Rechte** NOUN
right
□ In Deutschland fährt man auf der rechten Seite. They drive on the right in Germany. □ Mein rechtes Auge tut weh. My right eye's hurting. □ Er hat sich den rechten Arm gebrochen. He broke his right arm.

die Rechte (GEN der **Rechten**) FEM NOUN
▷ *see also* **rechte** ADJECTIVE, das **Rechte** NOUN
1 right
□ Zu Ihrer Rechten sehen Sie das Rathaus. On your right you'll see the town hall.

2 right hand
□ Er schlug mit der Rechten zu. **He hit out with his right hand.**

3 right-wing
□ eine Partei der Rechten **a right-wing party**

das **Rechte** (GEN des **Rechten**) NEUT NOUN
▷ *see also* die **Rechte** NOUN, **rechte** ADJECTIVE
right thing
□ Pass auf, dass du das Rechte sagst. **Make sure you say the right thing.**

rechteckig ADJECTIVE
rectangular

rechtfertigen VERB [38]
to justify
□ Wie kannst du dein Verhalten rechtfertigen? **How can you justify your behaviour?**
■ **sich rechtfertigen** to justify oneself

rechtmäßig ADJECTIVE
lawful

★ **rechts** ADVERB
right
□ rechts abbiegen **to turn right**
■ **rechts überholen** to overtake on the right
■ **Er schreibt mit rechts.** He writes with his right hand.
■ **Rechts sehen Sie das Rathaus.** On the right you'll see the town hall.
■ **rechts von der Kirche** to the right of the church
■ **rechts von mir** on my right
■ **rechts wählen** to vote for a right-wing party

★ der **Rechtsanwalt** (PL die **Rechtsanwälte**)
MASC NOUN
lawyer

★ die **Rechtsanwältin** FEM NOUN
lawyer

die **Rechtschreibung** FEM NOUN
spelling

der **Rechtshänder** (PL die **Rechtshänder**)
MASC NOUN
■ **Er ist Rechtshänder.** He's right-handed.

die **Rechtshänderin** FEM NOUN
■ **Sie ist Rechtshänderin.** She's right-handed.

die **Rechtskurve** FEM NOUN
right-hand bend

der **Rechtsverkehr** MASC NOUN
driving on the right
■ **In Deutschland ist Rechtsverkehr.** They drive on the right in Germany.

★ **rechtzeitig** ADJECTIVE, ADVERB
in time
□ Ich bitte um rechtzeitige Benachrichtigung. **Please let me know in time.** □ Wir sind rechtzeitig angekommen. **We arrived in time.**

★ **recyceln** (PERFECT TENSE **hat recycelt**) VERB [7]
to recycle

der **Redakteur** (PL die **Redakteure**) MASC
NOUN
editor

die **Redaktion** FEM NOUN
1 editorial staff
□ Die Redaktion hat das Manuskript abgelehnt. **The editorial staff rejected the manuscript.**
2 editorial office
□ Er arbeitet in unserer Redaktion. **He works in our editorial office.**

die **Rede** FEM NOUN
speech
□ Er hat eine witzige Rede gehalten. **He made an amusing speech.**
■ **jemanden zur Rede stellen** to take somebody to task

★ **reden** VERB [54]
1 to talk
□ Wir haben über das Wetter geredet. **We talked about the weather.** □ Du redest Unsinn. **You're talking nonsense.**
2 to speak
□ Ich werde mit deiner Mutter reden. **I'll speak to your mother.** □ Ich rede nicht gern vor so vielen Menschen. **I don't like speaking in front of so many people.**
3 to say
□ Was reden die Leute über uns? **What are people saying about us?**

die **Redewendung** FEM NOUN
expression

der **Redner** (PL die **Redner**) MASC NOUN
speaker

reduzieren (PERFECT TENSE **hat reduziert**)
VERB [76]
to reduce

das **Referat** (PL die **Referate**) NEUT NOUN
1 assignment
□ Ich muss in Geografie ein Referat schreiben. **I have to write an assignment in geography.**
2 paper
□ Sie hat ein Referat über Shakespeare gehalten. **She gave a paper on Shakespeare.**
3 section
□ Er ist Leiter des Referats Umweltschutz. **He's head of the environmental protection section.**

reflexiv ADJECTIVE
reflexive

die **Reform** FEM NOUN
reform

★ das **Regal** (PL die **Regale**) NEUT NOUN
1 bookcase
□ In ihrem Regal stehen viele Krimis. **There are a lot of detective stories in her bookcase.**
2 rack
□ ein Regal für Weinflaschen **a wine rack**
3 shelf
□ Auf dem Regal standen Kräuter. **There were herbs on the shelf.**

Regel – Reihenfolge

die **Regel** FEM NOUN

1 rule

□ Keine Regel ohne Ausnahme. The exception proves the rule.

2 period

□ Meine Regel ist ausgeblieben. I've missed a period.

★ **regelmäßig** ADJECTIVE, ADVERB

regular

□ in regelmäßigen Abständen at regular intervals □ Die Busse verkehren regelmäßig. The buses run regularly.

die **Regelmäßigkeit** FEM NOUN

regularity

regeln VERB [34]

1 to direct

□ Ein Polizist regelte den Verkehr. A police officer was directing the traffic.

2 to control

□ die Lautstärke regeln to control the volume

3 to settle

□ Ich habe da noch eine Sache mit ihm zu regeln. I've still got something to settle with him.

4 to arrange

□ Wir haben das so geregelt, dass sie abwäscht und ich putze. We've arranged things so that she washes the dishes and I do the cleaning.

■ **sich von selbst regeln** to take care of itself

★ der **Regen** (PL die **Regen**) MASC NOUN

rain

der **Regenbogen** (PL die **Regenbogen**) MASC NOUN

rainbow

★ der **Regenmantel** (PL die **Regenmäntel**) MASC NOUN

raincoat

★ der **Regenschauer** (PL die **Regenschauer**) MASC NOUN

shower

★ der **Regenschirm** (PL die **Regenschirme**) MASC NOUN

umbrella

regieren (PERFECT TENSE **hat regiert**) VERB [76]

1 to govern

□ Wer regiert zurzeit Ungarn? Who governs Hungary nowadays?

2 to reign

□ Wann hat Elisabeth die Erste regiert? When did Elizabeth the First reign?

die **Regierung** FEM NOUN

1 government

□ die deutsche Regierung the German government

2 reign

□ England unter der Regierung von Elisabeth der Zweiten England during the reign of Elizabeth the Second

★ **regnen** VERB [53]

to rain

□ Es regnet. It's raining.

★ **regnerisch** ADJECTIVE

rainy

das **Reh** (PL die **Rehe**) NEUT NOUN

deer

reiben (IMPERFECT **rieb**, PERFECT TENSE **hat gerieben**) VERB [61]

1 to rub

□ Warum reibst du dir die Augen? Why are you rubbing your eyes?

2 to grate

□ Er rieb Käse über die Kartoffeln. He grated cheese over the potatoes.

die **Reibung** FEM NOUN

friction

★ **reich** ADJECTIVE

rich

★ **reichen** VERB [48]

1 to be enough

□ Der Kuchen wird nicht für alle reichen. There won't be enough cake for everybody.

2 to give

□ Sie reichte mir die Hand. She gave me her hand.

■ **jemandem etwas reichen** to pass somebody something □ Kannst du mir bitte die Butter reichen? Can you pass me the butter, please?

■ **Nur ein Salat reicht ihm nicht.** A salad won't be enough for him.

■ **Mir reicht's!** I've had enough.

★ **reif** ADJECTIVE

1 ripe

□ Die Äpfel sind noch nicht reif. The apples aren't ripe yet.

2 mature

□ Für sein Alter ist er schon sehr reif. He's very mature for his age.

★ der **Reifen** (PL die **Reifen**) MASC NOUN

tyre

□ Mir ist ein Reifen geplatzt. I've got a burst tyre.

★ der **Reifendruck** MASC NOUN

tyre pressure

★ die **Reifenpanne** FEM NOUN

puncture

★ die **Reihe** FEM NOUN

row

□ Stellt euch in einer Reihe auf. Stand in a row. □ Wir saßen in der zweiten Reihe. We sat in the second row.

■ **der Reihe nach** in turn

■ **Er ist an der Reihe.** It's his turn.

■ **an die Reihe kommen** to have one's turn

die **Reihenfolge** FEM NOUN

order

★ = core vocabulary

□ alphabetische Reihenfolge alphabetical order

★ das **Reihenhaus** (GEN des **Reihenhauses**, PL die **Reihenhäuser**) NEUT NOUN
terraced house

★ **rein** ADJECTIVE, ADVERB

1 pure
□ Das ist reines Gold. That's pure gold. □ reine Seide pure silk

2 clean
□ Damit wird die Wäsche rein. This will get the washing clean. □ reine Luft clean air
■ reine Haut clear skin

3 sheer
□ Das ist der reine Wahnsinn. That's sheer madness. □ Das ist das reinste Vergnügen. It's sheer pleasure.

4 purely
□ Rein technisch ist das machbar. From a purely technical point of view it's feasible.
■ rein gar nichts absolutely nothing
■ etwas ins Reine schreiben to make a fair copy of something
■ etwas ins Reine bringen to clear something up

5 in
□ Deckel auf und rein mit dem Müll. Off with the lid and in with the rubbish. □ Los rein mit dir, Zeit fürs Bett! Come on, in you come, it's time for bed.

der **Reinfall** (PL die **Reinfälle**) MASC NOUN
let-down

die **Reinheit** FEM NOUN
purity
□ die Reinheit des Biers the purity of beer
■ Für die Reinheit Ihrer Wäsche ... To get your washing really clean ...

★ **reinigen** VERB [38]
to clean

★ die **Reinigung** FEM NOUN

1 cleaning
□ ein Mittel zur Reinigung der Polster a cleaning agent for upholstery

2 cleaner's sing
□ Bring bitte meine Hose in die Reinigung. Please take my trousers to the cleaner's.
■ chemische Reinigung 1 dry cleaning □ Bei diesem Stoff empfehlen wir eine chemische Reinigung. We recommend dry cleaning for this material. 2 dry cleaner's □ Im Einkaufszentrum gibt es auch eine chemische Reinigung. There's also a dry cleaner's in the shopping centre.

★ der **Reis** (GEN des **Reises**) MASC NOUN
rice

★ die **Reise** FEM NOUN
journey
□ Auf meiner letzten Reise durch Ägypten habe ich viel gesehen. I saw a lot on my last journey through Egypt.

■ **Reisen** travels □ Auf ihren Reisen hat sie viel erlebt. She has experienced a lot on her travels.
■ **Gute Reise!** Have a good journey.

das **Reiseandenken** (PL die **Reiseandenken**) NEUT NOUN
souvenir

★ das **Reisebüro** (PL die **Reisebüros**) NEUT NOUN
travel agency

★ der **Reiseführer** (PL die **Reiseführer**) MASC NOUN

1 guidebook
□ Ich habe einen Reiseführer für Griechenland gekauft. I've bought a guidebook to Greece.

2 travel guide
□ Unser Reiseführer hat uns alles erklärt. Our travel guide explained everything to us.

★ der **Reiseleiter** (PL die **Reiseleiter**) MASC NOUN
courier

★ **reisen** (PERFECT TENSE **ist gereist**) VERB [36]
to travel
□ Ich reise gern. I like travelling.
■ **reisen nach** to go to □ In den Sommerferien wollen wir nach Griechenland reisen. We want to go to Greece in the summer holidays.

★ der/die **Reisende** (GEN des/der **Reisenden**, PL die **Reisenden**) MASC/FEM NOUN

1 traveller

2 passenger
□ Sie war die einzige Reisende im letzten Zug nach Basel. She was the only passenger on the last train to Basel.

★ der **Reisepass** (GEN des **Reisepasses**, PL die **Reisepässe**) MASC NOUN
passport

★ der **Reisescheck** (PL die **Reiseschecks**) MASC NOUN
traveller's cheque

★ das **Reiseziel** (PL die **Reiseziele**) NEUT NOUN
destination

reißen (IMPERFECT **riss**, PERFECT TENSE **hat/ist gerissen**) VERB

Use **haben** to form the perfect tense. Use **sein** to form the perfect tense for 'to break'.

1 to tear
□ Sie riss ihren Brief in tausend Stücke. She tore her letter into a thousand pieces. □ Er riss sich die Kleider vom Leib. He tore his clothes off.

2 to break
□ Das Seil ist gerissen. The rope has broken.

3 to snatch
□ Er hat mir den Geldbeutel aus der Hand gerissen. He snatched my purse from my hand.

4 to drag
□ Sie hat ihn zu Boden gerissen. She dragged him to the floor.

5 to wrench

□ Er riss das Steuer nach links. He wrenched the steering wheel to the left.

6 to tug

□ Er riss an der Leine. He tugged at the rope.

■ **Witze reißen** to crack jokes

■ **etwas an sich reißen** to seize something

□ Er hat versucht, die Macht an sich zu reißen. He tried to seize power.

■ **sich um etwas reißen** to scramble for something □ Die Kinder haben sich um die Luftballons gerissen. The children scrambled for the balloons.

der **Reißverschluss** (GEN des **Reißverschlusses**, PL die **Reißverschlüsse**) MASC NOUN

zip

★ **reiten** (IMPERFECT **ritt**, PERFECT TENSE **ist geritten**) VERB

to ride

der **Reiter** (PL die **Reiter**) MASC NOUN

rider

★ die **Reitschule** FEM NOUN

riding school

der **Reiz** (GEN des **Reizes**, PL die **Reize**) MASC NOUN

1 charm

□ der Reiz dieser Stadt the charm of this town

2 appeal

□ der Reiz der Großstadt the appeal of the big city

reizbar ADJECTIVE

irritable

reizen VERB [36]

1 to appeal to

□ Diese Arbeit reizt mich sehr. The work greatly appeals to me. □ Es würde mich reizen, mal nach Kreta zu fahren. The idea of going to Crete appeals to me.

2 to annoy

□ Du musst den Hund nicht reizen. Don't annoy the dog.

3 to irritate

□ Der Rauch reizt die Augen. Smoke irritates the eyes.

reizend ADJECTIVE

charming

reizvoll ADJECTIVE

attractive

★ die **Reklame** FEM NOUN

1 advertising

□ Im Fernsehen gibt es viel zu viel Reklame. There's far too much advertising on television.

2 advertisement

□ zehn Seiten Reklame ten pages of advertisements

der **Rekord** (PL die **Rekorde**) MASC NOUN

record

□ Der Rekord liegt bei zehn Metern. The record is ten metres. □ einen neuen Rekord aufstellen to set a new record

der **Rektor** (PL die **Rektoren**) MASC NOUN

1 headteacher

□ Der Rektor ist bei uns für die Stundenpläne zuständig. At our school, the headteacher's in charge of timetables.

2 vice-chancellor

□ Zu Semesterbeginn hält der Rektor eine Rede. At the beginning of term the vice-chancellor gives a speech.

das **Rektorat** (PL die **Rektorate**) NEUT NOUN

headteacher's office

□ Hannah, du sollst aufs Rektorat gehen. Hannah, you're to go to the headteacher's office.

relativ ADVERB

relatively

□ Das ist relativ einfach. That's relatively easy.

★ **relaxt** ADJECTIVE

relaxed

★ die **Religion** FEM NOUN

religion

religiös ADJECTIVE

religious

das **Rendezvous** (GEN des **Rendezvous**, PL die **Rendezvous**) NEUT NOUN

date

□ Sie hatte gestern Abend ein Rendezvous. She had a date last night.

★ **rennen** (IMPERFECT **rannte**, PERFECT TENSE **ist gerannt**) VERB [55]

▷ see also das **Rennen** NOUN

to run

das **Rennen** (PL die **Rennen**) NEUT NOUN

▷ see also **rennen** VERB

race

□ ein Pferderennen a horse race □ ein Autorennen a motor race

der **Rennfahrer** (PL die **Rennfahrer**) MASC NOUN

racing driver

das **Rennpferd** (PL die **Rennpferde**) NEUT NOUN

racehorse

der **Rennwagen** (PL die **Rennwagen**) MASC NOUN

racing car

renovieren (PERFECT TENSE **hat renoviert**) VERB [76]

to renovate

rentabel ADJECTIVE

1 lucrative

□ eine rentable Arbeit a lucrative job

2 profitable

□ Das wäre nicht rentabel. That wouldn't be profitable.

★ = core vocabulary

die **Rente** FEM NOUN
pension
■ in Rente gehen to retire

BE CAREFUL!
Rente does not mean **rent**.

sich **rentieren** (PERFECT TENSE hat sich
rentiert) VERB [76]
to be profitable
□ Das Geschäft rentiert sich nicht mehr. The
business is no longer profitable.
■ Das hat sich rentiert. That was worthwhile.

★ der **Rentner** (PL die **Rentner**) MASC NOUN
pensioner

★ die **Reparatur** FEM NOUN
repair

★ die **Reparaturwerkstatt** (PL die
Reparaturwerkstätten) FEM NOUN
garage (*repair shop*)

★ **reparieren** (PERFECT TENSE hat repariert)
VERB [76]
to repair

die **Reportage** FEM NOUN
1 report
□ Ich habe eine Reportage über die globale
Erwärmung gelesen. I read a report about global
warming.
2 live commentary
□ Hast du im Radio die Reportage des
Europapokalspiels gehört? Did you hear the live
commentary on the European cup game on the
radio?

★ der **Reporter** (PL die **Reporter**) MASC NOUN
reporter

die **Republik** FEM NOUN
republic

republikanisch ADJECTIVE
republican

das **Reservat** (PL die **Reservate**) NEUT NOUN
reservation

die **Reserve** FEM NOUN
reserve

das **Reserverad** (PL die **Reserveräder**) NEUT
NOUN
spare wheel

★ **reservieren** (PERFECT TENSE hat reserviert)
VERB [76]
to reserve
□ Ich habe einen Tisch für heute Abend
reservieren lassen. I've reserved a table for this
evening.

★ die **Reservierung** FEM NOUN
reservation

der **Respekt** MASC NOUN
respect

respektieren (PERFECT TENSE hat
respektiert) VERB [76]
to respect

respektlos ADJECTIVE
disrespectful

respektvoll ADJECTIVE
respectful

der **Rest** (PL die **Reste**) MASC NOUN
1 rest
□ Den Rest bezahle ich später. I'll pay the rest
later. □ Die meisten sind früher gegangen, der
Rest hat noch lange gefeiert. Most left early, but
the rest carried on celebrating for a long time.
2 left-over
□ Heute gab's die Reste von gestern. Today we
had yesterday's left-overs.
■ die Reste the remains □ Das sind die Reste
der alten Stadtmauer. These are the remains of
the old town walls.

★ das **Restaurant** (PL die **Restaurants**) NEUT
NOUN
restaurant

restaurieren (PERFECT TENSE hat restauriert)
VERB [76]
to restore

restlich ADJECTIVE
remaining

der **Restmüll** MASC NOUN
non-recyclable waste

★ das **Resultat** (PL die **Resultate**) NEUT NOUN
result

★ **retten** VERB [2]
to rescue

der **Rettich** (PL die **Rettiche**) MASC NOUN
radish

★ die **Rettung** FEM NOUN
1 rescue
□ Alle zeigten bei der Rettung großen Mut. They
all showed great courage during the rescue.
2 salvation
□ Das war meine Rettung. That was my
salvation.
3 hope
□ seine letzte Rettung his last hope

das **Rettungsboot** (PL die **Rettungsboote**)
NEUT NOUN
lifeboat

★ der **Rettungsdienst** (PL die
Rettungsdienste) MASC NOUN
rescue service

der **Rettungsring** (PL die **Rettungsringe**)
MASC NOUN
lifebelt

★ der **Rettungswagen** (PL die
Rettungswagen) MASC NOUN
ambulance

die **Reue** FEM NOUN
remorse
□ Der Täter zeigt keine Reue. The culprit
doesn't show any remorse.

German-English

★ das Revier (PL die **Reviere**) NEUT NOUN

1 police station
□ Die Polizistin nahm ihn mit aufs Revier. The police officer took him to the police station.

2 territory
□ Der Hund verteidigte sein Revier. The dog was defending his territory.

die Revolution FEM NOUN
revolution

★ der Revolver (PL die **Revolver**) MASC NOUN
revolver

★ das Rezept (PL die **Rezepte**) NEUT NOUN

1 recipe
□ Kannst du mir mal das Rezept von deinem Käsekuchen geben? Can you give me your cheesecake recipe?

2 prescription
□ Dieses Medikament bekommt man nur auf Rezept. You can only get this medicine on prescription.

★ die Rezeption FEM NOUN
reception

rezeptpflichtig ADJECTIVE
available only on prescription
■ rezeptpflichtige Medikamente prescribed drugs

der Rhabarber MASC NOUN
rhubarb

★ der Rhein MASC NOUN
Rhine

DID YOU KNOW...?
The Rhine is 1320 km long and the entire 865 km which flows through Germany is navigable, making it an important inland waterway. It flows past such important cities as Karlsruhe, Mannheim, Ludwigshafen, Mainz, Cologne, Düsseldorf and Duisburg.

Rheinland-Pfalz NEUT NOUN
Rhineland-Palatinate

DID YOU KNOW...?
Rheinland-Pfalz is one of the 16 Länder. Its capital is Mainz. It is home to the BASF chemicals giant and to Germany's biggest television network, ZDF (Channel 2).

das Rheuma NEUT NOUN
rheumatism
□ Meine Oma hat Rheuma. My granny's got rheumatism.

der Rhythmus (GEN des **Rhythmus**, PL die **Rhythmen**) MASC NOUN
rhythm

richten VERB [2]
to point
□ Er richtete das Fernrohr zum Himmel. He pointed the telescope at the sky.
■ eine Waffe auf jemanden richten to aim a weapon at somebody

■ etwas an jemanden richten to address something to somebody □ Der Brief war an meine Eltern gerichtet. The letter was addressed to my parents.
■ Ich richte mich ganz nach dir. I'll do whatever you want.
■ sich nach etwas richten **1** to conform to something □ Auch du solltest dich danach richten, wie wir das hier machen. You should conform to our way of doing things. **2** to be determined by something □ Das Angebot richtet sich nach der Nachfrage. Supply is determined by demand.

der Richter (PL die **Richter**) MASC NOUN
judge

★ richtig ADJECTIVE, ADVERB

1 right
□ Es war nicht richtig von dir, ihn zu belügen. It wasn't right of you to lie to him. □ Das war nicht die richtige Antwort. That wasn't the right answer.
■ Bin ich hier richtig? Have I come to the right place?
■ der Richtige the right person
■ das Richtige the right thing

2 correctly
□ Du hast das nicht richtig geschrieben. You haven't written that correctly.

3 proper
□ Ich will ein richtiges Motorrad und keinen Roller. I want a proper motorbike, not a scooter.

4 really
□ Wir waren richtig froh, als es vorbei war. We were really glad when it was over.

★ die Richtung FEM NOUN
direction
□ Wir gehen in die falsche Richtung. We are going in the wrong direction. □ in östlicher Richtung in an easterly direction

rieb VERB ▷ see **reiben**

★ riechen (IMPERFECT **roch**, PERFECT TENSE **hat gerochen**) VERB
to smell
□ Ich rieche Gas. I can smell gas. □ Das riecht gut. That smells good. □ Ich kann nichts riechen. I can't smell anything.
■ an etwas riechen to smell something □ Sie roch an der Rose. She smelled the rose.
■ nach etwas riechen to smell of something □ Hier riecht es nach Benzin. It smells of petrol here.
■ Ich kann ihn nicht riechen. I can't stand him.

rief VERB ▷ see **rufen**

der Riegel (PL die **Riegel**) MASC NOUN

1 bolt
□ Sie schob den Riegel vor die Tür. She bolted the door.

2 bar

★ = core vocabulary

□ Für unterwegs haben wir einen Schokoriegel mitgenommen. We've brought a bar of chocolate to eat on the way.

der Riese(GEN des **Riesen**, PL die **Riesen**) MASC NOUN
giant

riesengroß ADJECTIVE
gigantic

riesig ADJECTIVE
huge

riet VERB ▷ *see* **raten**

das Rind(PL die **Rinder**) NEUT NOUN
1 ox (*male*)
2 cow (*female*)
 ▪ **Rinder**cattle
3 beef
 □ Wir essen kaum noch Rind. We hardly eat beef any more.

die Rinde FEM NOUN
1 rind
 □ Er schnitt die Rinde vom Käse ab. He cut the rind off the cheese.
2 crust
 □ frisches Brot mit knuspriger Rinde fresh crusty bread
3 bark
 □ Er ritzte ihren Namen in die Rinde einer Eiche. He carved her name into the bark of an oak tree.

★ **das Rindfleisch** NEUT NOUN
beef

★ **der Ring**(PL die **Ringe**) MASC NOUN
ring

das Ringbuch(PL die **Ringbücher**) NEUT NOUN
ring binder

das Ringen NEUT NOUN
wrestling
 □ Ringen ist sein Hobby. His hobby is wrestling.

der Ringkampf(PL die **Ringkämpfe**) MASC NOUN
wrestling bout

ringsum ADVERB
all around
 □ Wir sahen ringsum Menschen. We saw people all around. □ Er blickte ringsum. He looked all around.

die Rippe FEM NOUN
rib

das Risiko(PL die **Risiken**) NEUT NOUN
risk

riskant ADJECTIVE
risky

riskieren(PERFECT TENSE **hat riskiert**) VERB
[76]
to risk

der Riss(GEN des **Risses**, PL die **Risse**) MASC NOUN
1 crack
 □ Die Maus verschwand durch einen Riss in der Mauer. The mouse disappeared into a crack in the wall. □ Der trockene Boden war voller Risse. The dry soil was full of cracks.
2 tear
 □ Er hatte einen Riss in der Hose. There was a tear in his trousers.

rissig ADJECTIVE
1 cracked
 □ Von der Trockenheit ist die Erde rissig geworden. The soil is cracked as a result of the drought.
2 chapped
 □ Vom vielen Waschen hat sie ganz rissige Hände. Her hands are all chapped from doing so much washing.

ritt VERB ▷ *see* **reiten**

der Rivale(GEN des **Rivalen**, PL die **Rivalen**) MASC NOUN
rival

die Robbe FEM NOUN
seal
 □ ein Robbenbaby a seal pup

der Roboter(PL die **Roboter**) MASC NOUN
robot

roch VERB ▷ *see* **riechen**

★ **der Rock** (PL die **Röcke**) MASC NOUN
skirt

der Roggen MASC NOUN
rye

roh ADJECTIVE
1 raw
 □ rohes Fleisch raw meat □ Karotten esse ich am liebsten roh. I like carrots best raw.
2 callous
 □ Sei nicht so roh. Don't be so callous.
3 rough
 □ Er hat ihn ziemlich roh mit sich gezogen. He dragged him off pretty roughly.

das Rohr(PL die **Rohre**) NEUT NOUN
1 pipe
 □ Das Abwasser wird durch Rohre in die Kanalisation geleitet. Sewage is fed into the sewer via pipes.
2 cane
 □ ein Stuhl aus Rohr a cane chair
3 reeds *pl*
 □ In dem Teich wuchs Rohr. Reeds were growing in the pond.

der Rohstoff(PL die **Rohstoffe**) MASC NOUN
raw material

der Rolladen MASC NOUN ▷ *see* der **Rollladen**

★ **das Rollbrett**(PL die **Rollbretter**) NEUT NOUN
skateboard

Rolle – Routenplaner

die Rolle FEM NOUN

1 role
□ Der Schauspieler hat die Rolle des Königs gut gespielt. The actor was good in the role of the king. □ Die Rolle der Frau hat sich geändert. The role of women has changed.

2 castor
□ ein Stuhl mit Rollen a chair with castors

3 roll
□ eine Rolle Toilettenpapier a roll of toilet paper

4 reel
□ Sie hat den Faden von der Rolle abgewickelt. She unwound the thread from the reel.
■ **keine Rolle spielen** not to matter □ Das Wetter spielt keine Rolle. The weather doesn't matter.
■ **eine wichtige Rolle spielen bei** to play a major role in □ Er hat bei der Planung des Abschlussfestes eine wichtige Rolle gespielt. He played a major role in organizing the end-of-term party.

rollen (PERFECT TENSE **hat/ist gerollt**) VERB [38]

For the perfect tense use **haben** when the verb has an object and **sein** when there is no object.

to roll
□ Sie haben den Stein den Berg hinuntergerollt. They rolled the stone down the hill. □ Der Ball ist direkt vor ein Auto gerollt. The ball rolled right in front of a car.

★ **der Roller** (PL die **Roller**) MASC NOUN
scooter

der Rollladen (PL die **Rollläden**) MASC NOUN
shutter

★ **der Rollschuh** (PL die **Rollschuhe**) MASC NOUN
roller skate

★ **der Rollstuhl** (PL die **Rollstühle**) MASC NOUN
wheelchair

★ **die Rolltreppe** FEM NOUN
escalator

★ **Rom** NEUT NOUN
Rome
■ **nach Rom** to Rome

★ **der Roman** (PL die **Romane**) MASC NOUN
novel

romantisch ADJECTIVE
romantic

römisch ADJECTIVE
Roman

röntgen VERB [54]
to X-ray

★ **rosa** ADJECTIVE
pink
□ Er hatte ein rosa Hemd an. He was wearing a pink shirt.

★ **die Rose** FEM NOUN
rose

★ **der Rosenkohl** MASC NOUN
Brussels sprouts pl
□ Rosenkohl ist mein Lieblingsgemüse. Brussels sprouts are my favourite vegetable.

★ **der Rosenmontag** (PL die **Rosenmontage**) MASC NOUN
Monday before Shrove Tuesday

DID YOU KNOW...?
Rosenmontag is an important day in the carnival festivities. Cities such as Cologne, Düsseldorf and Mainz traditionally have long processions with carnival floats on **Rosenmontag**.

die Rosine FEM NOUN
raisin

der Rost (PL die **Roste**) MASC NOUN
rust
□ An diesem Auto ist viel Rost. This car has a lot of rust on it.
■ **ein Bratrost** a grill

rosten (PERFECT TENSE **ist gerostet**) VERB [2]
to rust

rösten VERB [2]

1 to roast
□ geröstete Erdnüsse roasted peanuts

2 to toast
□ Brot rösten to toast bread

3 to grill
□ Würstchen auf dem Grill rösten to grill sausages

rostig ADJECTIVE
rusty

★ **rot** ADJECTIVE
red
□ Sein Gesicht wurde immer röter. His face got redder and redder.
■ **in den roten Zahlen** in the red
■ **das Rote Meer** the Red Sea

die Röteln PL NOUN
German measles sing
□ Röteln sind für schwangere Frauen gefährlich. German measles is dangerous for pregnant women.

rothaarig ADJECTIVE
red-haired

★ **der Rotkohl** MASC NOUN
red cabbage

★ **der Rotwein** (PL die **Rotweine**) MASC NOUN
red wine

die Roulade FEM NOUN
beef olive

die Route FEM NOUN
route

der Routenplaner (PL die **Routenplaner**) MASC NOUN
route planner

★ = core vocabulary

★ der **Router** MASC NOUN
router

★ der **Rowdy** (PL die Rowdys) MASC NOUN
hooligan

das **RSI-Syndrom** NEUT NOUN (= *Repetitive-Strain-Injury-Syndrom*)
RSI

die **Rübe** FEM NOUN
beet
□ Der Bauer füttert die Kühe mit Rüben. **The farmer feeds his cows on beet.**
■ **Gelbe Rübe** carrot
■ **Rote Rübe** beetroot

rüber ADVERB
over
□ Komm hier rüber, da siehst du besser. **Come over here, you'll get a better view.** □ Ich geh mal zu den Nachbarn rüber. **I'm just going over to our neighbours.**

rücken (PERFECT TENSE ist/hat gerückt) VERB [38]
▷ *see also* der **Rücken** NOUN

For the perfect tense use **haben** when the verb has an object and **sein** when there is no object.

1 to move over
□ Rück mal ein bisschen. **Move over a bit.**
2 to shift
□ Sie rückten den Schrank zur Seite. **They shifted the cupboard to one side.**

★ der **Rücken** (PL die Rücken) MASC NOUN
▷ *see also* **rücken** VERB
back
□ Sie schläft auf dem Rücken. **She sleeps on her back.**

das **Rückenmark** NEUT NOUN
spinal cord

die **Rückenschmerzen** MASC PL NOUN
backache *sing*

das **Rückenschwimmen** NEUT NOUN
backstroke

★ die **Rückfahrkarte** FEM NOUN
return ticket

★ die **Rückfahrt** FEM NOUN
return journey

der **Rückflug** (PL die Rückflüge) MASC NOUN
return flight

★ die **Rückgabe** FEM NOUN
return

rückgängig ADJECTIVE
■ **etwas rückgängig machen** to cancel something

das **Rückgrat** (PL die Rückgrate) NEUT NOUN
spine

die **Rückkehr** FEM NOUN
return
□ bei unserer Rückkehr **on our return**

das **Rücklicht** (PL die Rücklichter) NEUT NOUN
rear light

★ die **Rückreise** FEM NOUN
return journey

die **Rücksicht** FEM NOUN
consideration
■ **auf jemanden Rücksicht nehmen** to show consideration for somebody □ Du solltest mehr Rücksicht auf deine Mitschüler nehmen. **You should show more consideration for your fellow pupils.**

rücksichtslos ADJECTIVE
inconsiderate
■ **ein rücksichtsloser Fahrer** a reckless driver

rücksichtsvoll ADJECTIVE
considerate

der **Rücksitz** (PL die Rücksitze) MASC NOUN
back seat
□ Dieser Sportwagen hat keine Rücksitze. **This sports car has no back seats.**
■ **auf dem Rücksitz** in the back

★ der **Rückspiegel** (PL die Rückspiegel) MASC NOUN
rear-view mirror

das **Rückspiel** (PL die Rückspiele) NEUT NOUN
return match

der **Rücktritt** (PL die Rücktritte) MASC NOUN
resignation

★ **rückwärts** ADVERB
backwards
□ rückwärts zählen to count backwards

der **Rückwärtsgang** (PL die Rückwärtsgänge) MASC NOUN
reverse gear

der **Rückweg** (PL die Rückwege) MASC NOUN
way back

das **Ruder** (PL die Ruder) NEUT NOUN
1 oar
□ ein Boot mit zwei Rudern a boat with two oars
2 rudder
□ Der Steuermann steht am Ruder. **The helmsman stands at the rudder.**

das **Ruderboot** (PL die Ruderboote) NEUT NOUN
rowing boat

★ **rudern** (PERFECT TENSE hat/ist gerudert) VERB [88]

Use **haben** for the perfect tense when you describe the activity and **sein** when you describe the motion.

to row
□ Zuerst hat er gerudert, dann sie. **First he**

r

Numbers in brackets refer to verb tables on pages 697 to 706.

229

rowed, then she did. □ Wir sind über den See gerudert. We rowed across the lake.

der **Ruf**(PL die **Rufe**) MASC NOUN

1 shout

□ Wir hörten seine Rufe. We heard his shouts.

2 reputation

□ Das schadet seinem Ruf. This will damage his reputation.

★ **rufen**(IMPERFECT **rief**, PERFECT TENSE **hat gerufen**) VERB [56]

1 to call out

□ Ich habe gerufen, es hat mich aber niemand gehört. I called out, but nobody heard me.

■ **Der Patient rief nach der Schwester.** The patient called for the nurse.

2 to call

□ Wir sollten den Arzt rufen. We ought to call the doctor. □ Sie hat mir ein Taxi gerufen. She called me a taxi.

3 to shout

□ Sie rief um Hilfe. She shouted for help.

die **Rufnummer** FEM NOUN

telephone number

★ die **Ruhe** FEM NOUN

1 rest

□ Nach den anstrengenden Tagen brauche ich etwas Ruhe. After the strain of the last few days I need a rest.

2 peace

□ Jetzt kann ich in Ruhe arbeiten. Now I can work in peace.

3 peace and quiet

□ Die Kinder sind weg, ich genieße die Ruhe. The children are out and I'm enjoying the peace and quiet.

■ **in aller Ruhe**calmly

■ **jemanden aus der Ruhe bringen**to unsettle somebody □ Dieser Anruf hat mich aus der Ruhe gebracht. The phone call unsettled me.

4 silence

□ Ich bitte um etwas mehr Ruhe. I would ask you for a bit more silence.

■ **Ruhe!**Silence!

■ **jemanden in Ruhe lassen**to leave somebody alone □ Lass endlich deine Schwester in Ruhe. Will you leave your sister alone!

■ **sich zur Ruhe setzen**to retire

der **Ruhestand** MASC NOUN

retirement

■ **Mein Vater ist im Ruhestand.** My father is retired.

die **Ruhestörung** FEM NOUN

breach of the peace

★ der **Ruhetag** MASC NOUN

day off

□ einen Ruhetag einlegen to have a day off

■ 'Mittwochs Ruhetag' 'closed on Wednesdays'

★ **ruhig** ADJECTIVE, ADVERB

1 quiet

□ Im Haus war alles ruhig. The house was completely quiet. □ Die Kinder haben ruhig gespielt. The children played quietly. □ Seid endlich ruhig! Will you be quiet!

2 still

□ Bleib ruhig stehen, dann tut dir der Hund nichts. If you keep still the dog won't hurt you.

■ **eine ruhige Hand**a steady hand

3 calm

□ Wie kannst du so ruhig bleiben? How can you stay so calm? □ Ich bin ganz ruhig in die Prüfung gegangen. I went quite calmly into the exam.

■ **ein ruhiges Gewissen**a clear conscience

■ **Kommen Sie ruhig herein!**Come on in.

der **Ruhm** MASC NOUN

fame

★ das **Rührei**(PL die **Rühreier**) NEUT NOUN

scrambled eggs pl

rühren VERB [38]

1 to stir

□ Sie rührte mit dem Löffel in der Soße. She stirred the sauce with the spoon.

2 to move

□ Ich kann meine Beine nicht rühren. I can't move my legs.

■ **sich rühren**to move □ Sie hatte so Angst, dass sie sich nicht rührte. She was so afraid that she didn't move.

■ **jemanden rühren**to move somebody □ Die Armut der Kinder hat uns gerührt. The children's poverty moved us.

rührend ADJECTIVE

touching

□ eine rührende Geschichte a touching story

□ Er ist rührend naiv. He's touchingly naive.

die **Ruine** FEM NOUN

ruin

ruinieren (PERFECT TENSE **hat ruiniert**) VERB [76]

to ruin

der **Rumäne**(GEN des **Rumänen**, PL die **Rumänen**) MASC NOUN

Romanian

Rumänien NEUT NOUN

Romania

■ **aus Rumänien**from Romania

■ **nach Rumänien**to Romania

die **Rumänin** FEM NOUN

Romanian

rumänisch ADJECTIVE

Romanian

der **Rummelplatz**(GEN des **Rummelplatzes**, PL die **Rummelplätze**) MASC NOUN

fairground

★ = core vocabulary

rund ADJECTIVE, ADVERB

1 round

□ Sie hat ein rundes Gesicht. She's got a round face.

2 about

□ Das kostet rund hundert Euro. It costs about a hundred euros.

■ **rund um etwas** around something □ Die Stadtmauer geht rund um die Stadt. The town walls go around the town.

die **Runde** FEM NOUN

1 lap

□ Das Auto fuhr ein paar Runden. The car drove a few laps. □ Sie liegt in der letzten Runde in Führung. She's in the lead on the last lap.

2 round

□ Diese Runde zahle ich. I'll get this round.

DID YOU KNOW...?
It isn't usual to buy rounds in Germany. Normally people just order what they want from the waiter, and pay when they leave. You can, however, buy a round (**eine Runde schmeißen**) if you're feeling generous.

3 group

□ Wir waren eine gesellige Runde. We were a sociable group.

■ **über die Runden kommen** (*Umgangssprache*) to get by

die **Rundfahrt** FEM NOUN

round trip

der **Rundfunk** MASC NOUN

broadcasting

■ **im Rundfunk** on the radio

runter ADVERB

1 off

□ Runter vom Tisch! Get off the table!

2 down

□ Dann ging's den Berg runter. Then off we went down the mountain.

runterladen (PRESENT TENSE **lädt runter**, IMPERFECT **lud runter**, PERFECT TENSE **hat runtergeladen**) VERB

to download (*computer*)

□ eine Datei runterladen to download a file

der **Ruß** (GEN des **Rußes**) MASC NOUN

soot

★ der **Russe** (GEN des **Russen**, PL die **Russen**) MASC NOUN

Russian

der **Rüssel** (PL die **Rüssel**) MASC NOUN

1 snout

□ der Rüssel eines Schweins a pig's snout

2 trunk

□ der Rüssel eines Elefanten an elephant's trunk

rußig ADJECTIVE

sooty

★ die **Russin** FEM NOUN

Russian

★ **russisch** ADJECTIVE

Russian

★ **Russland** NEUT NOUN

Russia

■ **aus Russland** from Russia

■ **nach Russland** to Russia

die **Rüstung** FEM NOUN

1 suit of armour

□ In der Burg standen ein paar rostige Rüstungen. There were a couple of rusty suits of armour in the castle.

2 armaments *pl*

□ Es wird viel Geld für Rüstung ausgegeben. A lot of money is spent on armaments.

die **Rutschbahn** FEM NOUN

slide

rutschen (PERFECT TENSE **ist gerutscht**) VERB [48]

1 to slip

□ Sie ist auf dem Eis gerutscht und hingefallen. She slipped and fell on the ice. □ Der Teller ist mir aus der Hand gerutscht. The plate slipped out of my hand.

2 to move over

□ Rutsch mal ein bisschen! Move over a bit.

r

Ss

★ der **Saal** (PL die **Säle**) MASC NOUN
hall

das **Saarland** NEUT NOUN
Saarland

> **DID YOU KNOW...?**
> The **Saarland** is one of the 16 **Länder**. Its capital is Saarbrücken. While its coal and steel industries have been in crisis, it still has flourishing ceramics and glass industries.

★ die **Sache** FEM NOUN
1 thing
□ Räum bitte deine Sachen weg. **Please put your things away.** □ Pack warme Sachen ein. **Pack warm things.** □ Was machst du denn für Sachen? **The things you do!**
2 matter
□ Wir sollten diese Sache ausdiskutieren. **We should discuss this matter fully.** □ Die Polizei wird dieser Sache nachgehen. **The police will investigate this matter.**
3 job
□ Es ist deine Sache, dich darum zu kümmern. **It's your job to see to it.**
■ **Mach keine Sachen!** Don't be silly!
■ **zur Sache** to the point □ Komm endlich zur Sache! **Get to the point!**

sachlich ADJECTIVE
1 objective
□ ein sehr sachlicher Bericht **a very objective report** □ Du solltest sachlich bleiben. **You should remain objective.**
2 factual
□ Was er sagt, ist sachlich falsch. **What he says is factually inaccurate.**

sächlich ADJECTIVE
neuter

Sachsen NEUT NOUN
Saxony

> **DID YOU KNOW...?**
> **Sachsen** is one of the 16 **Länder**. Its capital is Dresden. Its largest city, Leipzig, is famous for its industrial fair and was one of the main centres of the peaceful revolt against the DDR regime.

Sachsen-Anhalt NEUT NOUN
Saxony-Anhalt

> **DID YOU KNOW...?**
> **Sachsen-Anhalt** is one of the 16 **Länder**. Its capital is Magdeburg. It has a rich cultural past: Martin Luther and Georg Friedrich Händel were born here, and the Bauhaus school of architecture was situated in Dessau.

sächsisch ADJECTIVE
Saxon

sachte ADVERB
softly

der **Sack** (PL die **Säcke**) MASC NOUN
sack

die **Sackgasse** FEM NOUN
cul-de-sac

★ der **Saft** (PL die **Säfte**) MASC NOUN
juice

saftig ADJECTIVE
juicy

die **Säge** FEM NOUN
saw

★ **sagen** VERB [38]
1 to say
□ Ich kann noch nicht sagen, ob ich komme. **I can't say yet if I'll come.** □ Habe ich etwas Falsches gesagt? **Have I said something wrong?** □ Wie sagt man 'danke' auf Japanisch? **How do you say 'thank you' in Japanese?** □ Was sagst du zu meinem Vorschlag? **What do you say to my suggestion?**
■ **Man sagt, dass ...** It's said that ...
2 to tell
□ Kannst du ihm bitte sagen, er soll seine Eltern anrufen. **Can you tell him to call his parents.** □ Ich werde es ihr sagen. **I'll tell her.** □ Sag ihm er solle das nicht tun. **Tell him he shouldn't do it.**
■ **etwas zu jemandem sagen** to call somebody something □ Die Kinder sagen Onja zu mir. **The children call me Onja.**
■ **zu sagen haben** to have a say □ Du hast hier nichts zu sagen. **You don't have a say in this matter.**
■ **Das hat nichts zu sagen.** It doesn't mean anything.

sägen VERB [38]
to saw

sagenhaft ADJECTIVE

1 legendary
□ der sagenhafte König Artus the legendary King Arthur

2 terrific (*Umgangssprache*)
□ Das war ein sagenhaftes Glück. That was terrific luck.

sah VERB ▷ *see* **sehen**

die **Sahne** FEM NOUN
cream

die **Saison** (PL die **Saisons**) FEM NOUN
season

die **Saite** FEM NOUN
string

das **Saiteninstrument** (PL die **Saiteninstrumente**) NEUT NOUN
stringed instrument

der **Salat** (PL die **Salate**) MASC NOUN

1 salad
□ Es gab verschiedene Salate. There were various salads.

2 lettuce
□ Am liebsten mag ich grünen Salat. I like lettuce best.

die **Salbe** FEM NOUN
ointment

das **Salz** (GEN des **Salzes**) NEUT NOUN
salt

salzen (PERFECT TENSE **hat gesalzen**) VERB
to salt

salzig ADJECTIVE
salty

die **Salzkartoffeln** FEM PL NOUN
boiled potatoes *pl*

die **Salzstange** FEM NOUN
pretzel stick

das **Salzwasser** NEUT NOUN
salt water

der **Samen** (PL die **Samen**) MASC NOUN
seed
□ Hast du die Blumensamen schon ausgesät? Have you sown the flower seeds yet?

sammeln VERB [34]

1 to collect
□ Sie sammelt Kunst. She collects art. □ Sie sammeln für ein Waisenhaus. They're collecting for an orphanage. □ Altpapier wird gesammelt und wiederverwertet. Waste paper is collected and recycled.

2 to gather
□ Wir haben Pilze gesammelt. We gathered mushrooms.

die **Sammlung** FEM NOUN
collection

der **Samstag** (PL die **Samstage**) MASC NOUN
Saturday
□ am Samstag on Saturday

★ **samstags** ADVERB
on Saturdays

samt PREPOSITION
▷ *see also* der **Samt** NOUN

The preposition **samt** takes the dative.

with
□ Sie kamen samt Kindern und Hund. They came with their children and dog.

der **Samt** (PL die **Samte**) MASC NOUN
▷ *see also* **samt** PREPOSITION
velvet

★ der **Sand** MASC NOUN
sand

★ die **Sandale** FEM NOUN
sandal

sandig ADJECTIVE
sandy

der **Sandkasten** (PL die **Sandkästen**) MASC NOUN
sandpit

der **Sandstrand** (PL die **Sandstrände**) MASC NOUN
sandy beach

sandte VERB ▷ *see* **senden**

sanft ADJECTIVE
gentle
□ etwas sanft berühren to touch something gently

sang VERB ▷ *see* **singen**

der **Sänger** (PL die **Sänger**) MASC NOUN
singer

die **Sängerin** FEM NOUN
singer

der **Sankt Nikolaus** MASC NOUN
St Nicholas

DID YOU KNOW...?
Sankt Nikolaus (Tag) (St Nicholas' Day) is on December 6 and marks the start of the festive season in Roman Catholic parts of Germany. Traditionally, children leave their shoes outside the door when they go to bed on December 5, and awake the next day to find them full of small gifts.

die **Sardine** FEM NOUN
sardine

der **Sarg** (PL die **Särge**) MASC NOUN
coffin

der **Sarkasmus** (GEN des **Sarkasmus**, PL die **Sarkasmen**) MASC NOUN
sarcasm

saß VERB ▷ *see* **sitzen**

der **Satellit** (GEN des **Satelliten**, PL die **Satelliten**) MASC NOUN
satellite

S

Satellitenfernsehen – schade

★ **das Satellitenfernsehen** NEUT NOUN
satellite television

★ **satt** ADJECTIVE
1 full
□ Ich bin satt. I'm full.
■ **Wir sind nicht satt geworden.** We didn't get enough to eat.
■ **sich satt essen** to eat one's fill
■ **satt machen** to be filling
■ **jemanden satt sein** to be fed up with somebody
2 rich
□ satte Farben rich colours □ ein sattes Rot a rich red

der Sattel (PL die **Sättel**) MASC NOUN
saddle

der Satz (GEN des **Satzes**, PL die **Sätze**) MASC NOUN
1 sentence
□ Bitte antworte mit einem ganzen Satz. Please answer in a complete sentence.
■ **ein Nebensatz** a subordinate clause
■ **ein Adverbialsatz** an adverbial clause
2 theorem
□ der Satz des Pythagoras Pythagoras' theorem
3 set
□ Nadal hat den ersten Satz verloren. Nadal lost the first set. □ ein Satz Schraubenschlüssel a set of screwdrivers
4 rate
□ Die Krankenversicherung hat ihre Sätze erhöht. The health insurance has increased its rates.

das Satzzeichen (PL die **Satzzeichen**) NEUT NOUN
punctuation mark

★ **sauber** ADJECTIVE
1 clean
□ Die Wäsche ist nicht sauber geworden. The washing hasn't come up clean.
2 fine
□ Du bist mir ein sauberer Freund! You're a fine friend!
■ **sauber machen** to clean

die Sauberkeit FEM NOUN
cleanness

saubermachen VERB [48] ▷ see **sauber**

die Sauce FEM NOUN
sauce

★ **sauer** ADJECTIVE
1 sour
□ Der Apfel ist sauer. The apple is sour. □ Die Milch ist sauer geworden. The milk has turned sour.
2 acid
□ saurer Regen acid rain
3 cross
□ Ich bin sauer auf meine Freundin. I'm cross with my girlfriend.

die Sauerei FEM NOUN
1 scandal
□ Es ist eine Sauerei, dass wir länger arbeiten müssen. It's a scandal that we have to work longer hours.
2 mess
□ Wer hat denn die Sauerei im Bad gemacht? Who made the mess in the bathroom?
3 obscenity
□ Über solche Sauereien kann ich nicht lachen. I can't laugh at such obscenities.

★ **das Sauerkraut** NEUT NOUN
sauerkraut (pickled cabbage)

der Sauerstoff MASC NOUN
oxygen

saufen (PRESENT TENSE **säuft**, IMPERFECT **soff**, PERFECT TENSE **hat gesoffen**) VERB
to booze (Umgangssprache)

saugen (IMPERFECT **saugte** or **sog**, PERFECT TENSE **hat gesaugt** or **gesogen**) VERB
to suck

das Säugetier (PL die **Säugetiere**) NEUT NOUN
mammal

der Säugling (PL die **Säuglinge**) MASC NOUN
infant

die Säule FEM NOUN
column

die Sauna (PL die **Saunas**) FEM NOUN
sauna

die Säure FEM NOUN
acid
□ Die Säure hat den Stein zerfressen. The acid has eaten away at the stone.

das Saxofon (PL die **Saxofone**) NEUT NOUN
saxophone
□ Er spielt Saxofon. He plays the saxophone.

★ **die S-Bahn** FEM NOUN
suburban railway

die SB-Tankstelle FEM NOUN
self-service petrol station

★ **das Schach** NEUT NOUN
chess
□ Ich kann nicht Schach spielen. I can't play chess.

das Schachbrett (PL die **Schachbretter**) NEUT NOUN
chessboard

die Schachfigur FEM NOUN
chessman

★ **die Schachtel** FEM NOUN
box

★ **schade** ADJECTIVE, EXCLAMATION
a pity
□ Es ist schade um das gute Essen. It's a pity to waste good food. □ Das ist aber schade. That's a pity.

★ = core vocabulary

■ **Wie schade!** What a pity! □ Wie schade, dass du nicht mitkommen kannst. What a pity you can't come.

■ **für etwas zu schade sein** to be too good for something □ Diese Decke ist doch zu schade für ein Picknick. This blanket is too good for a picnic.

■ **sich für etwas zu schade sein** to consider oneself too good for something □ Du bist dir für so eine Arbeit wohl zu schade? So you consider yourself too good for a job like that?

der **Schädel**(PL die Schäde) MASC NOUN
skull

★ **schaden** VERB [54]
▷ *see also* der **Schaden**NOUN

■ **jemandem schaden** to harm somebody □ Ich habe den Eindruck, dass sie mir schaden will. I've got the feeling that she wants to harm me.

■ **einer Sache schaden** to damage something □ Das hat unserem Ruf geschadet. That's damaged our reputation.

■ **es kann nicht schaden ...** it can't do any harm ... □ Es kann nicht schaden, wenn du die Vokabeln noch einmal wiederholst. It can't do any harm for you to go over the vocabulary once more.

★ der **Schaden**(PL die Schäden) MASC NOUN
▷ *see also* schaden VERB

1 damage
□ Der Schaden an seinem Auto war nicht so groß. The damage to his car wasn't too bad.

2 injury
□ Sie hat den Unfall ohne Schaden überstanden. She came out of the accident without injury.

3 disadvantage
□ Es soll dein Schaden nicht sein. It won't be to your disadvantage.

der **Schadenersatz**(GEN des Schadenersatzes) MASC NOUN
compensation

schädigen(PERFECT TENSE hat geschädigt) VERB [38]
to damage

schädlich ADJECTIVE
harmful
□ Rauchen ist schädlich. Smoking is harmful.

der **Schadstoff**(PL die Schadstoffe) MASC NOUN
harmful substance

★ das **Schaf**(PL die Schafe) NEUT NOUN
sheep
□ zehn Schafe ten sheep

der **Schäferhund**(PL die Schäferhunde) MASC NOUN
Alsatian

★ **schaffen (1)**(IMPERFECT schuf PERFECT TENSE hat geschaffen) VERB
to create
□ Die Regierung will neue Arbeitsplätze schaffen. The government wants to create new jobs.

★ **schaffen (2)**(IMPERFECT schaffte PERFECT TENSE hat geschafft) VERB [48]
to manage
□ Die Übersetzung schaffe ich heute noch. I'll manage that translation today. □ Er schafft das nicht allein. He won't manage to do that on his own. □ Wir haben den Zug gerade noch geschafft. We just managed to catch the train.

■ **eine Prüfung schaffen** to pass an exam
■ **Ich bin geschafft!** I'm shattered!

★ der **Schal**(PL die Schale or Schals) MASC NOUN
scarf

★ die **Schale** FEM NOUN

1 skin
□ eine Bananenschale a banana skin

2 peel *no pl*
□ die Kartoffelschale the potato peel □ eine Zitronenschale lemon peel

3 shell
□ Die Nussschalen nicht in den Kompost werfen. Don't throw the nutshells onto the compost heap. □ Diese Eier haben sehr dünne Schalen. These eggs have very thin shells.

4 bowl
□ Auf dem Tisch stand eine Schale mit Obst. There was a bowl of fruit on the table.

schälen VERB [38]

1 to peel
□ einen Apfel schälen to peel an apple

2 to shell
□ Nüsse schälen to shell nuts

■ **sich schälen** to peel □ Meine Nase schält sich. My nose is peeling.

der **Schall** MASC NOUN
sound

die **Schallmauer** FEM NOUN
sound barrier

★ die **Schallplatte** FEM NOUN
record

schalten VERB [2]

1 to switch
□ den Herd auf 'aus' schalten to switch the oven to 'off'

2 to change gear
□ Du solltest schalten. You should change gear.
■ **in den vierten Gang schalten** to change into fourth

3 to catch on *(Umgangssprache)*
□ Ich habe zu spät geschaltet. I caught on too late.

★ der **Schalter**(PL die Schalter) MASC NOUN

1 counter
□ Zahlen Sie bitte am Schalter dort drüben. Please pay at the counter over there.

Numbers in brackets refer to verb tables on pages 697 to 706.

235

S

2 switch
□ Wo ist der Lichtschalter? Where is the light switch?

das **Schaltjahr** (PL die **Schaltjahre**) NEUT NOUN
leap year

sich **schämen** VERB [38]
to be ashamed
□ sich einer Sache schämen to be ashamed of something

die **Schande** FEM NOUN
disgrace

★ **scharf** ADJECTIVE
1 sharp
□ ein scharfes Messer a sharp knife □ eine scharfe Kurve a sharp corner
■ ein scharfer Wind a biting wind
2 hot
□ Indisches Essen ist schärfer als deutsches. Indian food is hotter than German food.
■ scharfe Munition live ammunition
■ scharf schießen to shoot with live ammunition
■ scharf nachdenken to think hard
■ auf etwas scharf sein to be mad about something (*Umgangssprache*) □ Er ist ganz scharf auf Gummibärchen. He is mad about jelly bears.
■ auf jemanden scharf sein to fancy somebody □ Ich glaube, Sonja ist scharf auf dich. I think Sonja fancies you.

der **Schatten** (PL die **Schatten**) MASC NOUN
1 shadow
2 shade
□ Wir saßen im Schatten. We sat in the shade.

schattig ADJECTIVE
shady

der **Schatz** (GEN des **Schatzes**, PL die **Schätze**) MASC NOUN
1 treasure
□ der Schatz der Piraten the pirates' treasure
2 darling
□ Du bist ein Schatz! You're a darling! □ Mein Schatz. My darling.

das **Schätzchen** (PL die **Schätzchen**) NEUT NOUN
darling

schätzen VERB [36]
1 to guess
□ Schätz mal, wie viel das gekostet hat. Guess how much that cost.
■ Man kann sein Alter schlecht schätzen. It's difficult to tell how old he is.
2 to value
□ Ich werde die alte Uhr schätzen lassen. I'm going to have the old clock valued.
3 to appreciate
□ Ich schätze deine Hilfe sehr. I really appreciate your help.

das **Schaubild** (PL die **Schaubilder**) NEUT NOUN
diagram

★ **schauen** VERB [38]
to look
□ Schau mal an die Tafel. Look at the board.

★ der **Schauer** (PL die **Schauer**) MASC NOUN
1 shower
□ Für morgen sind Schauer angesagt. Showers are forecast for tomorrow.
2 shudder
□ Ein Schauer überlief sie. A shudder ran through her body.

die **Schaufel** FEM NOUN
shovel

★ das **Schaufenster** (PL die **Schaufenster**) NEUT NOUN
shop window

★ der **Schaufensterbummel** (PL die **Schaufensterbummel**) MASC NOUN
window shopping

die **Schaukel** FEM NOUN
swing

schaukeln VERB [34]
to swing

der **Schaumgummi** MASC NOUN
foam rubber

★ das **Schauspiel** NEUT NOUN
play (*theatre*)

★ der **Schauspieler** (PL die **Schauspieler**) MASC NOUN
actor

★ die **Schauspielerin** FEM NOUN
actress

★ der **Scheck** (PL die **Schecks**) MASC NOUN
cheque

das **Scheckheft** (PL die **Scheckhefte**) NEUT NOUN
cheque book

★ die **Scheckkarte** FEM NOUN
cheque card

★ die **Scheibe** FEM NOUN
slice
□ Sie belegte das Brot mit mehreren Scheiben Wurst. She put several slices of cold meat on the bread.

der **Scheibenwischer** (PL die **Scheibenwischer**) MASC NOUN
windscreen wiper

scheiden (IMPERFECT schied, PERFECT TENSE hat geschieden) VERB
■ sich scheiden lassen to get a divorce
■ geschieden sein to be divorced

die **Scheidung** FEM NOUN
divorce

★ = core vocabulary

★ der **Schein** (PL die **Scheine**) MASC NOUN

1 light
  □ beim Schein einer Kerze by the light of a candle

2 appearance
  □ Der Schein trügt. Appearances are deceptive.

3 note
  □ Er hat in großen Scheinen bezahlt. He paid in large notes.

4 certificate
  □ Am Ende des Semesters bekommt man einen Schein. You get a certificate at the end of the semester.

  ■ **etwas zum Schein tun** to pretend to do something □ Er ging zum Schein auf den Vorschlag ein. He pretended to go along with the suggestion.

scheinbar ADVERB
  apparently

★ **scheinen** (IMPERFECT **schien**, PERFECT TENSE **hat geschienen**) VERB [57]

1 to shine
  □ Die Sonne scheint. The sun is shining.

2 to seem
  □ Sie scheint glücklich zu sein. She seems to be happy.

★ der **Scheinwerfer** (PL die **Scheinwerfer**) MASC NOUN

1 headlamp
  □ Die Scheinwerfer des entgegenkommenden Autos haben mich geblendet. The headlamps of the approaching car blinded me.

2 floodlight
  □ Die Scheinwerfer beleuchteten das Stadion. The floodlights lit the stadium.

3 spotlight
  □ Das Gemälde wird von einem Scheinwerfer angestrahlt. The painting is lit up by a spotlight.

scheitern (PERFECT TENSE **ist gescheitert**) VERB [88]
  to fail

der **Schenkel** (PL die **Schenkel**) MASC NOUN
  thigh

★ **schenken** VERB [38]

1 to give
  □ Was haben dir deine Eltern zum Geburtstag geschenkt? What did your parents give you for your birthday? □ Das habe ich geschenkt bekommen. I was given it as a present.

2 to pour
  □ Sie schenkte ihm noch etwas Rotwein ins Glas. She poured some more red wine into his glass.

  ■ **sich etwas schenken** to skip something □ Die Geigenstunde werde ich mir heute schenken. I'm going to skip my violin lesson today.

  ■ **Das ist geschenkt!** **1** That's a giveaway! **2** That's worthless!

★ die **Schere** FEM NOUN

1 scissors pl
  □ eine Schere a pair of scissors

2 shears pl
  □ Wo ist die Schere, um die Hecke zu schneiden? Where are the shears for cutting the hedge?

der **Scherz** (GEN des **Scherzes**, PL die **Scherze**) MASC NOUN
  joke
  □ Das war doch nur ein Scherz! It was only a joke.

  ■ **zum Scherz** for fun

scheußlich ADJECTIVE
  dreadful
  □ Das Wetter war scheußlich. The weather was dreadful.

  ■ **Das tut scheußlich weh.** It hurts dreadfully.

★ der **Schi** (PL die **Schi** or **Schier**) MASC NOUN ▷ see der **Ski**

die **Schicht** FEM NOUN

1 layer
  □ Auf dem Weg lag eine Schicht Sand. There was a layer of sand on the path.

2 class
  □ soziale Schichten social classes

3 shift
  □ Mein Vater arbeitet Schicht. My father works shifts.

schick ADJECTIVE
  stylish
  □ ein schicker Hosenanzug a stylish trouser suit
  ■ **schick angezogen** stylishly dressed

★ **schicken** VERB [48]
  to send
  □ Ich habe ihr ein Päckchen geschickt. I've sent her a parcel. □ Sie hat ihren Sohn zum Bäcker geschickt. She sent her son to the baker's.

das **Schicksal** NEUT NOUN
  fate

★ **schieben** (IMPERFECT **schob**, PERFECT TENSE **hat geschoben**) VERB
  to push
  □ Wir mussten das Auto schieben. We had to push the car. □ Könnt ihr mal schieben? Could you lot push?
  ■ **die Schuld auf jemanden schieben** to put the blame on somebody

★ der **Schiedsrichter** (PL die **Schiedsrichter**) MASC NOUN

1 referee
  □ Der Schiedsrichter pfiff das Spiel an. The referee blew the whistle to start the game.

2 umpire
  □ Bei einem Tennisspiel sagt der Schiedsrichter den Spielstand an. In a tennis match the umpire gives the score.

S

schief ADJECTIVE, ADVERB
crooked
□ Die Wände des Hauses sind schief. The walls of the house are crooked.
■ **Das Bild hängt schief.** The picture isn't hanging straight.
■ **der Schiefe Turm von Pisa** the Leaning Tower of Pisa
■ **ein schiefer Blick** a funny look
■ **Er hatte seinen Hut schief aufgesetzt.** He was wearing his hat at an angle.

schiefgehen (IMPERFECT **ging schief**, PERFECT TENSE **ist schiefgegangen**) VERB [29]
to go wrong

schielen VERB [38]
to squint

schien VERB ▷ *see* scheinen

die **Schiene** FEM NOUN
1 rail
□ Die Schienen sind verrostet. The rails have rusted.
2 splint
□ Sie hatte den Arm in einer Schiene. She had her arm in a splint.

schießen (IMPERFECT **schoss**, PERFECT TENSE **hat geschossen**) VERB
1 to shoot
□ Nicht schießen! Don't shoot! □ Sie hat ein Kaninchen geschossen. She shot a rabbit. □ Er hat auf einen Polizisten geschossen. He shot at a police officer.
2 to kick
□ Sie schoss den Ball ins Tor. She kicked the ball into the goal.

★ das **Schiff** (PL die **Schiffe**) NEUT NOUN
ship

die **Schifffahrt** FEM NOUN
shipping

der **Schikoree** MASC NOUN
chicory

★ das **Schild** (PL die **Schilder**) NEUT NOUN
sign
□ Das ist eine Einbahnstraße, hast du das Schild nicht gesehen? This is a one-way street, didn't you see the sign?
■ **ein Namensschild** a nameplate

die **Schildkröte** FEM NOUN
1 tortoise
2 turtle

der **Schimmel** (PL die **Schimmel**) MASC NOUN
1 mould
□ Auf dem Käse ist Schimmel. There's mould on the cheese.
2 white horse
□ Sie ritt auf einem Schimmel. She rode a white horse.

schimmelig ADJECTIVE
mouldy

der **Schimpanse** (GEN des **Schimpansen**, PL die **Schimpansen**) MASC NOUN
chimpanzee

schimpfen VERB [38]
to scold
□ Hat deine Mutter geschimpft? Did your mother scold you?
■ **auf jemanden schimpfen** to curse somebody □ Schüler schimpfen gern auf ihre Lehrer. Pupils like cursing their teachers.
■ **über etwas schimpfen** to complain about something □ Meine Kinder schimpfen über zu viel Hausaufgaben. My children complain about having too much homework.

das **Schimpfwort** (PL die **Schimpfwörter**) NEUT NOUN
term of abuse

★ der **Schinken** (PL die **Schinken**) MASC NOUN
ham

der **Schirm** (PL die **Schirme**) MASC NOUN
umbrella
□ Nimm einen Schirm mit! Take an umbrella!
■ **der Sonnenschirm** the sunshade
■ **eine Mütze mit Schirm** a peaked cap

die **Schlacht** FEM NOUN
battle

schlachten VERB [2]
to slaughter

das **Schlachtfeld** (PL die **Schlachtfelder**) NEUT NOUN
battlefield

der **Schlachthof** (PL die **Schlachthöfe**) MASC NOUN
slaughterhouse

★ der **Schlaf** MASC NOUN
sleep

★ der **Schlafanzug** (PL die **Schlafanzüge**) MASC NOUN
pyjamas *pl*
□ ein Schlafanzug a pair of pyjamas

★ **schlafen** (PRESENT TENSE **schläft**, IMPERFECT **schlief**, PERFECT TENSE **hat geschlafen**) VERB [58]
to sleep
□ Hast du gut geschlafen? Did you sleep well? □ Schlaf gut! Sleep well.
■ **schlafen gehen** to go to bed

schlaff ADJECTIVE
1 exhausted
□ Nach der Gartenarbeit war ich total schlaff. I was completely exhausted after working in the garden.
2 slack
□ Das Seil ist zu schlaff. The rope is too slack.

★ **schlaflos** ADJECTIVE
sleepless

der **Schlafsaal** (PL die **Schlafsäle**) MASC NOUN
dormitory

★ = core vocabulary

★ der **Schlafsack** (PL die **Schlafsäcke**) MASC NOUN
sleeping bag

die **Schlaftablette** FEM NOUN
sleeping pill

★ das **Schlafzimmer** (PL die **Schlafzimmer**) NEUT NOUN
bedroom

der **Schlag** (PL die **Schläge**) MASC NOUN
1 blow
□ ein Schlag auf den Kopf a blow to the head
□ Ich bin durchgefallen, das ist ein Schlag. I've failed, that's a blow.

2 stroke
□ Mein Opa hat einen Schlag gehabt und ist gelähmt. My granddad's had a stroke and he's now paralysed.

3 shock
□ Fass nicht an den Draht, sonst bekommst du einen Schlag. Don't touch that wire, otherwise you'll get a shock.
■ **Er hat von seinem Vater Schläge bekommen.** His father gave him a hiding. (*Umgangssprache*)
■ **mit einem Schlag** all at once

★ **schlagen** (PRESENT TENSE **schlägt**, IMPERFECT **schlug**, PERFECT TENSE **hat geschlagen**) VERB [59]
1 to beat
□ Meine Eltern haben mich noch nie geschlagen. My parents have never beaten me.
□ Schottland hat Holland vier zu eins geschlagen. Scotland beat Holland four one.
□ Ihr Herz schlug schneller. Her heart beat faster.
■ **Sahne schlagen** to whip cream

2 to hit
□ Sie schlug mit dem Hammer auf den Nagel. She hit the nail with the hammer. □ Sie schlug mit der Faust auf den Tisch. She hit the table with her fist.
■ **Er schlägt den Nagel in die Wand.** He hammers the nail into the wall.

3 to strike
□ Die Uhr schlägt zehn. The clock strikes ten.
□ Es hat eben zehn geschlagen. It's just struck ten.
■ **nach jemandem schlagen** to take after somebody □ Sie schlägt nach ihrer Mutter. She takes after her mother.
■ **sich gut schlagen** to do well □ Er hat sich in der Prüfung gut geschlagen. He did well in the exam.

★ der **Schlager** (PL die **Schlager**) MASC NOUN
hit

der **Schläger** (PL die **Schläger**) MASC NOUN
1 thug
□ Franz ist ein Schläger. Franz is a thug.

2 bat
□ Baseball und Tischtennis spielt man mit einem Schläger. You play baseball and table tennis with a bat.

3 racket
□ Für Tennis, Federball und Squash braucht man einen Schläger. You need a racket for tennis, badminton and squash.
■ **ein Golfschläger** a golf club
■ **ein Hockeyschläger** a hockey stick

die **Schlägerei** FEM NOUN
fight

schlagfertig ADJECTIVE
quick-witted

★ die **Schlagsahne** FEM NOUN
whipped cream

die **Schlagzeile** FEM NOUN
headline

★ das **Schlagzeug** (PL die **Schlagzeuge**) NEUT NOUN
drums pl
□ Sie spielt Schlagzeug. She plays the drums.
□ Am Schlagzeug: Yasmin Braun. On drums: Yasmin Braun.

der **Schlamm** MASC NOUN
mud

schlampen VERB [38]
to be sloppy (*Umgangssprache*)
□ Bei den Hausaufgaben hast du geschlampt. Your homework's sloppy.

schlampig ADJECTIVE
sloppy (*Umgangssprache*)

★ die **Schlange** FEM NOUN
1 snake
□ eine giftige Schlange a poisonous snake

2 queue
□ Vor dem Kino stand eine lange Schlange. There was a long queue outside the cinema.
■ **Schlange stehen** to queue □ Wir mussten für die Karten Schlange stehen. We had to queue for the tickets.

★ **schlank** ADJECTIVE
slim
□ Sie ist sehr schlank. She's very slim.

die **Schlankheitskur** FEM NOUN
diet
□ eine Schlankheitskur machen to be on a diet

schlapp ADJECTIVE
worn out
□ Ich fühle mich schlapp. I feel worn out.

★ **schlau** ADJECTIVE
cunning

der **Schlauch** (PL die **Schläuche**) MASC NOUN
1 hose
□ Er hat den Garten mit dem Schlauch gespritzt. He watered the garden with the hose.

S

2 inner tube

□ Ich brauche einen neuen Schlauch für mein Fahrrad. I need a new inner tube for my bike.

das **Schlauchboot** (PL die **Schlauchboote**) NEUT NOUN

rubber dinghy

★ **schlecht** ADJECTIVE, ADVERB

1 bad

□ Er ist in Mathe schlecht. He is bad at maths. □ Meine Augen werden immer schlechter. My eyes are getting worse.

■ **ein schlechtes Gewissen** a guilty conscience

2 badly

□ Ich habe schlecht geschlafen. I slept badly.

■ **schlecht gelaunt** in a bad mood

■ **Mir ist schlecht.** I feel sick.

■ **ein schlecht bezahlter Job** a poorly paid job

■ **Ihm geht es schlecht.** He's in a bad way.

schlechtmachen VERB [48]

■ **jemanden schlechtmachen** to run somebody down □ Du solltest ihn nicht dauernd schlechtmachen. You shouldn't constantly run him down.

schleichen (IMPERFECT **schlich**, PERFECT TENSE **ist geschlichen**) VERB

to creep

die **Schleife** FEM NOUN

1 loop

□ Der Fluss macht eine Schleife. The river makes a loop.

2 bow

□ Sie hatte eine Schleife im Haar. She had a bow in her hair.

Schleswig-Holstein NEUT NOUN

Schleswig-Holstein

DID YOU KNOW...?

Schleswig-Holstein is one of the 16 **Länder**. Its capital is Kiel. It is Germany's northernmost state, bordered by Denmark, the North Sea and the Baltic.

schleudern (PERFECT TENSE **hat/ist geschleudert**) VERB [88]

For the perfect tense use **haben** when the verb has an object and **sein** when there is no object.

1 to hurl

□ Sie hat das Buch in die Ecke geschleudert. She hurled the book into the corner.

2 to spin

□ Du solltest die nasse Wäsche schleudern. You should spin the wet washing.

3 to skid

□ Das Auto ist geschleudert. The car skidded.

schlief VERB ▷ see **schlafen**

schließen (IMPERFECT **schloss**, PERFECT TENSE **hat geschlossen**) VERB

to shut

□ Schließ bitte das Fenster. Please shut the window. □ Wann schließen die Geschäfte? When do the shops shut? □ Sie hatte die Augen geschlossen. She had her eyes shut. □ Der Betrieb wurde geschlossen. The company was shut down.

■ **mit jemandem Freundschaft schließen** to make friends with somebody

■ **etwas aus etwas schließen** to gather something from something □ Aus dem, was er sagte, schließe ich, dass er nicht mitkommen will. I gather from what he said that he doesn't want to come.

schließlich ADVERB

1 finally

2 eventually

□ Der Motor hat gestottert, aber schließlich hat er versagt. The engine spluttered but eventually failed.

■ **schließlich doch** after all

★ **schlimm** ADJECTIVE

bad

schlimmer ADJECTIVE

worse

schlimmste ADJECTIVE

worst

□ mein schlimmster Feind my worst enemy

schlimmstenfalls ADVERB

at the worst

★ der **Schlips** MASC NOUN

tie (*necktie*)

der **Schlitten** (PL die **Schlitten**) MASC NOUN

sledge

□ Im Winter sind wir viel Schlitten gefahren. We went sledging a lot in the winter.

★ der **Schlittschuh** (PL die **Schlittschuhe**) MASC NOUN

skate

■ **Schlittschuh laufen** to skate

der **Schlitz** (GEN des **Schlitzes**, PL die **Schlitze**) MASC NOUN

1 slit

□ Der Rock hat hinten einen Schlitz. The skirt has a slit at the back.

2 slot

□ Du musst das Zwei-Euro-Stück in den Schlitz werfen. You have to put the two-euro coin in the slot.

3 flies *pl*

□ Der Schlitz an deiner Hose ist auf. Your flies are open.

schloss VERB ▷ see **schließen**

★ das **Schloss** (GEN des **Schlosses**, PL die **Schlösser**) NEUT NOUN

★ = core vocabulary

1 lock

□ Sie steckte den Schlüssel ins Schloss. She put the key in the lock.

2 clasp

□ Kannst du mir bitte das Schloss an meiner Kette aufmachen? Can you please open the clasp of my necklace?

3 chateau

□ das Schloss Versailles the chateau of Versailles

der **Schluckauf** MASC NOUN

hiccups pl

□ Er hatte einen Schluckauf. He had hiccups.

schlucken VERB [48]

to swallow

schlug VERB ▷ see **schlagen**

der **Schluss** (GEN des **Schlusses**, PL die **Schlüsse**) MASC NOUN

1 end

□ am Schluss des Jahres at the end of the year

2 ending

□ Das Buch hat einen traurigen Schluss. The book has a sad ending.

3 conclusion

□ Ich habe meine Schlüsse gezogen. I've drawn my conclusions.

■ **zum Schluss** finally □ Zum Schluss haben wir noch ein Lied gesungen. Finally we sang a song.

■ **Schluss machen** to finish □ Wir sollten langsam Schluss machen. We should be finishing now.

■ **mit jemandem Schluss machen** to finish with somebody □ Warum hast du mit Florian Schluss gemacht? Why did you finish with Florian?

der **Schlüssel** (PL die **Schlüssel**) MASC NOUN

key

□ Wo ist mein Fahrradschlüssel? Where's the key for my bike? □ der Schlüssel zum Erfolg the key to success

das **Schlüsselbein** (PL die **Schlüsselbeine**) NEUT NOUN

collar bone

der **Schlüsselbund** (PL die **Schlüsselbunde**) MASC NOUN

bunch of keys

der **Schlüsselring** (PL die **Schlüsselringe**) MASC NOUN

keyring

der **Schlussverkauf** MASC NOUN

sales pl

□ Dieses Kleid habe ich im Schlussverkauf bekommen. I got this dress in the sales.

schmackhaft ADJECTIVE

tasty

schmal ADJECTIVE

1 narrow

□ ein schmaler Durchgang a narrow passageway

2 thin

□ Er hat ein schmales Gesicht. He has a thin face.

BE CAREFUL!

schmal does not mean **small**.

★ **schmecken** VERB [48]

to taste

□ Wie schmeckt eine Mango? What does a mango taste like? □ Das schmeckt gut. That tastes good.

■ **Es schmeckt ihm.** He likes it.

schmeicheln VERB [38]

■ **jemandem schmeicheln** to flatter somebody

schmeißen (IMPERFECT **schmiss**, PERFECT TENSE **hat geschmissen**) VERB

to throw

schmelzen (PRESENT TENSE **schmilzt**, IMPERFECT **schmolz**, PERFECT TENSE **ist geschmolzen**) VERB

to melt

□ Das Eis ist geschmolzen. The ice has melted.

der **Schmerz** (GEN des **Schmerzes**, PL die **Schmerzen**) MASC NOUN

1 pain

□ ein stechender Schmerz in der Seite a stabbing pain in the side

2 grief

□ Sie verbarg ihren Schmerz über diesen Verlust. She hid her grief over her loss.

★ **schmerzen** (PERFECT TENSE **hat geschmerzt**) VERB [36]

to hurt

das **Schmerzmittel** (PL die **Schmerzmittel**) NEUT NOUN

painkiller

die **Schmerztablette** FEM NOUN

painkiller

der **Schmetterling** (PL die **Schmetterlinge**) MASC NOUN

butterfly

★ die **Schminke** FEM NOUN

make-up

★ **schminken** VERB [38]

to make up

□ Hast du dir die Augen geschminkt? Have you made up your eyes?

■ **Ich schminke mich selten.** I seldom use make-up.

★ der **Schmuck** MASC NOUN

1 jewellery

□ Sie trägt selten Schmuck. She seldom wears jewellery.

2 decoration

□ bunte Kugeln als Schmuck für den Weihnachtsbaum bright baubles as Christmas tree decorations

S

schmücken VERB [48]
to decorate

schmuggeln VERB [34]
to smuggle

schmusen VERB [38]
to cuddle
□ Sie hat mit Felix geschmust. She cuddled Felix.

der **Schmutz** (GEN des **Schmutzes**) MASC NOUN
dirt

★ **schmutzig** ADJECTIVE
dirty

der **Schnabel** (PL die **Schnäbel**) MASC NOUN
beak
□ Der Schnabel der Amsel ist gelb. The blackbird's beak is yellow.

die **Schnalle** FEM NOUN
buckle

★ der **Schnaps** (GEN des **Schnapses**, PL die **Schnäpse**) MASC NOUN
schnapps

schnarchen VERB [48]
to snore

schnaufen VERB [38]
to puff

die **Schnauze** FEM NOUN
1 nose
□ Der Hund hat eine kalte Schnauze. The dog has a cold nose.
2 gob (Umgangssprache)
□ Halt die Schnauze! Shut your gob!
■ die Schnauze von etwas voll haben to be fed up with the back teeth of something

sich **schnäuzen** VERB [36]
to blow one's nose

die **Schnecke** FEM NOUN
snail
■ eine Nacktschnecke a slug

★ der **Schnee** MASC NOUN
snow
□ Heute Nacht ist viel Schnee gefallen. A lot of snow fell last night.

der **Schneeball** (PL die **Schneebälle**) MASC NOUN
snowball

der **Schneemann** (PL die **Schneemänner**) MASC NOUN
snowman

★ **schneiden** (IMPERFECT **schnitt**, PERFECT TENSE **hat geschnitten**) VERB [60]
to cut
□ Kannst du bitte Brot schneiden? Can you cut some bread, please? □ jemandem die Haare schneiden to cut somebody's hair □ Du solltest dir die Haare schneiden lassen. You should have your hair cut.

■ sich schneiden 1 to cut oneself □ Ich habe mich geschnitten. I've cut myself. □ Ich habe mir in den Finger geschnitten. I've cut my finger. 2 to intersect □ Die beiden Geraden schneiden sich. The two straight lines intersect.

★ **schneien** VERB [38]
■ Es schneit. It's snowing.

★ **schnell** ADJECTIVE, ADVERB
1 fast
□ Sie hat ein schnelles Auto. She has a fast car.
□ Sie ist schnell gefahren. She drove fast.
2 quickly
□ Ich rief schnell einen Krankenwagen. I quickly phoned for an ambulance.

die **Schnelligkeit** FEM NOUN
speed

★ der **Schnellimbiss** (GEN des **Schnellimbisses**, PL die **Schnellimbisse**) MASC NOUN
snack bar

schnellstens ADVERB
as quickly as possible

★ der **Schnellzug** (PL die **Schnellzüge**) MASC NOUN
express train

sich **schneuzen** VERB [36] ▷ see **schnäuzen**

schnitt VERB ▷ see **schneiden**

der **Schnitt** (PL die **Schnitte**) MASC NOUN
1 cut
□ Der Schnitt blutet. The cut's bleeding. □ Das Kleid hat einen eleganten Schnitt. The dress has an elegant cut.
2 average
□ Ich habe im Zeugnis einen Schnitt von drei. I've got an average of C in my report.
3 pattern
□ Hast du zu dem Rock einen Schnitt? Have you got a pattern for this skirt?

der **Schnittlauch** MASC NOUN
chive

die **Schnittstelle** FEM NOUN
interface

die **Schnittwunde** FEM NOUN
cut

★ das **Schnitzel** (PL die **Schnitzel**) NEUT NOUN
escalope
□ Ich bestelle mir ein Schnitzel. I'm going to order an escalope.

schnitzen VERB [48]
to carve

der **Schnorchel** (PL die **Schnorchel**) MASC NOUN
snorkel

der **Schnuller** (PL die **Schnuller**) MASC NOUN
dummy
□ Das Baby saugte am Schnuller. The baby sucked the dummy.

★ = core vocabulary

der **Schnupfen** (PL die **Schnupfen**) MASC
NOUN
cold
□ Meine Schwester hat Schnupfen. My sister
has a cold.

die **Schnur** (PL die **Schnüre**) FEM NOUN
1 string
□ Du solltest eine Schnur um das Päckchen
machen. You should put string round the
parcel.
2 flex
□ Die Schnur von der Lampe ist zu kurz. The flex
of the lamp is too short.

der **Schnurrbart** (PL die **Schnurrbärte**)
MASC NOUN
moustache

der **Schnürsenkel** (PL die **Schnürsenkel**)
MASC NOUN
shoelace

der **Schock** (PL die **Schocks**) MASC NOUN
shock

schockieren (PERFECT TENSE hat schockiert)
VERB [76]
to shock

die **Schokolade** FEM NOUN
chocolate
□ eine heiße Schokolade a hot chocolate

schon ADVERB
1 already
□ Ich bin schon fertig. I've already finished.
2 yet
□ Ist er schon da? Is he there yet?
■ Warst du schon einmal da? Have you ever
been there?
■ Ich war schon einmal da. I've been there
before.
■ Das war schon immer so. That's always
been the case.
■ Hast du schon gehört? Have you heard?
■ schon oft often
■ schon der Gedanke the very thought
■ Du wirst schon noch sehen. You'll see.
■ Das wird schon noch gut. That'll be OK.
■ ja schon, aber ... yes, but ...
■ schon möglich possible
■ Schon gut! OK!
■ Du weißt schon. You know.
■ Komm schon! Come on!

schön ADJECTIVE
1 beautiful
□ Sie haben ein schönes Haus. They have a
beautiful house.
2 nice
□ Es waren schöne Ferien. The holidays were
nice. □ Schönes Wochenende! Have a nice
weekend.
■ sich schön machen to make oneself look
nice
■ Schöne Grüße an deine Eltern! Regards
to your parents.

■ ganz schön frech pretty damn cheeky
(Umgangssprache)
■ na schön very well □ Na schön, dann geht
halt spielen. Very well then, go and play.

schonend ADJECTIVE, ADVERB
gentle
□ jemandem etwas schonend beibringen to
break something gently to somebody

die **Schönheit** FEM NOUN
beauty

sich **schönmachen** VERB [48] ▷ see schön

schöpfen VERB [38]
to ladle
□ Sie schöpfte Suppe in die Teller. She ladled
soup into the plates.
■ Luft schöpfen to get some air

die **Schöpfung** FEM NOUN
creation

der **Schornstein** (PL die **Schornsteine**)
MASC NOUN
chimney

schoss VERB ▷ see schießen

★ der **Schotte** (GEN des **Schotten**, PL die
Schotten) MASC NOUN
Scot
■ Er ist Schotte. He's Scottish.

★ die **Schottin** FEM NOUN
Scot
■ Sie ist Schottin. She's Scottish.

★ **schottisch** ADJECTIVE
Scottish

★ **Schottland** NEUT NOUN
Scotland
■ aus Schottland from Scotland
■ in Schottland in Scotland
■ nach Schottland to Scotland

schräg ADJECTIVE
sloping
□ Das Haus hat ein schräges Dach. The house
has a sloping roof.
■ schräg gegenüber diagonally opposite

der **Schrägstrich** (PL die **Schrägstriche**)
MASC NOUN
slash

★ der **Schrank** (PL die **Schränke**) MASC NOUN
1 cupboard
□ Der Besen ist im Schrank in der Küche. The
broom's in the cupboard in the kitchen.
2 wardrobe
□ Ich räume meine Kleider in den Schrank. I'll
put my clothes away in the wardrobe.

die **Schranke** FEM NOUN
barrier

die **Schraube** FEM NOUN
1 screw
2 bolt

der Schraubenschlüssel(PL die Schraubenschlüssel) MASC NOUN
spanner

der Schraubenzieher(PL die Schraubenzieher) MASC NOUN
screwdriver

★ **der Schreck** MASC NOUN
fright
□ Ich habe einen furchtbaren Schreck bekommen. I got a terrible fright.

schreckhaft ADJECTIVE
jumpy

schrecklich ADJECTIVE, ADVERB
1 terrible
□ Wir hatten schreckliches Wetter. The weather was terrible.
2 terribly
□ Das tut schrecklich weh. It hurts terribly. □ Es tut mir schrecklich leid. I'm terribly sorry.

der Schrei(PL die Schreie) MASC NOUN
1 scream
□ Als er die Spinne sah, stieß er einen Schrei aus. When he saw the spider he let out a scream.
2 shout
□ Wir hörten einen Schrei um Hilfe. We heard a shout for help.

★ **schreiben**(IMPERFECT schrieb, PERFECT TENSE hat geschrieben) VERB [61]
1 to write
□ Ich habe ihr einen E-mail geschrieben. I've written her an email. □ Wir sollten uns schreiben. We should write to each other.
2 to spell
□ Wie schreibt man seinen Namen? How do you spell his name?

die Schreibmaschine FEM NOUN
typewriter

★ **der Schreibtisch**(PL die Schreibtische) MASC NOUN
desk

★ **die Schreibwaren** FEM PL NOUN
stationery *sing*

das Schreibzeug NEUT NOUN
writing materials *pl*

★ **schreien**(IMPERFECT schrie, PERFECT TENSE hat geschrien) VERB [62]
1 to scream
□ Sie schrie vor Schmerzen. She screamed with pain.
2 to shout
□ Wir haben geschrien, du hast uns aber nicht gehört. We shouted but you didn't hear us.

der Schreiner(PL die Schreiner) MASC NOUN
joiner

schrieb VERB ▷ *see* schreiben

die Schrift FEM NOUN
1 writing
□ Sie hat eine schöne Schrift. She has lovely writing.
2 font
□ Welche Schrift soll ich für das Dokument nehmen? Which font should I use for the document?

★ **schriftlich** ADJECTIVE, ADVERB
written
□ eine schriftliche Entschuldigung a written apology
■ **etwas schriftlich festhalten** to put something in writing

der Schriftsteller(PL die Schriftsteller) MASC NOUN
writer

schrill ADJECTIVE
shrill

der Schritt(PL die Schritte) MASC NOUN
1 step
□ Er machte einen vorsichtigen Schritt nach vorn. He took a careful step forward.
2 walk
□ Ich habe dich an deinem Schritt erkannt. I recognized you by your walk.
3 pace
□ Sie ging mit schnellen Schritten nach Hause. She walked home at a brisk pace.
■ **Schritt fahren** to drive at walking pace

der Schrott MASC NOUN
scrap metal

schrumpfen(PERFECT TENSE ist geschrumpft) VERB [38]
1 to shrink
□ Der Pulli ist in der Wäsche geschrumpft. The pullover shrank in the wash.
2 to shrivel
□ Die Äpfel sind geschrumpft. The apples have shrivelled.

die Schublade FEM NOUN
drawer

schüchtern ADJECTIVE
shy

★ **der Schuh**(PL die Schuhe) MASC NOUN
shoe

die Schuhcreme(PL die Schuhcremes) FEM NOUN
shoe polish

die Schuhgröße FEM NOUN
shoe size
□ Welche Schuhgröße hast du? What shoe size are you?

★ **die Schularbeiten** FEM PL NOUN
homework *sing*
□ Hast du deine Schularbeiten schon gemacht? Have you done your homework?

★ = core vocabulary

die **Schulaufgaben** FEM PL NOUN
homework *sing*
□ Heute haben wir keine Schulaufgaben bekommen.We didn't get any homework today.

★ das **Schulbuch**(PL die Schulbücher) NEUT NOUN
school book

schuld ADJECTIVE
▷ *see also* die Schuld NOUN
■ an etwas schuld sein to be to blame for something □ Du bist an der Verspätung schuld. You are to blame for the delay.
■ Er ist schuld.It's his fault.

★ die **Schuld** FEM NOUN
▷ *see also* schuld ADJECTIVE
1 guilt
□ Seine Schuld konnte nicht bewiesen werden. His guilt couldn't be proved.
2 fault
□ Es war deine Schuld, dass wir zu spät kamen. It was your fault that we arrived late.
■ jemandem Schuld geben to blame somebody

schulden VERB [54]
▷ *see also* die Schulden NOUN
to owe
□ Was schulde ich dir?How much do I owe you?

die **Schulden** FEM PL NOUN
▷ *see also* schulden VERB
debt *sing*
□ Ich muss noch meine Schulden bei dir bezahlen.I still have to pay off my debts to you.
□ Staatsschulden national debt

★ **schuldig** ADJECTIVE
guilty
□ Meinst du, dass die Angeklagte schuldig ist? Do you think that the accused is guilty?
■ jemandem etwas schuldig sein to owe somebody something □ Was bin ich dir schuldig?How much do I owe you?

★ der **Schuldirektor**(PL die Schuldirektoren) MASC NOUN
headmaster

★ die **Schuldirektorin** FEM NOUN
headmistress

★ die **Schule** FEM NOUN
school
□ in der Schule at school

der **Schüler**(PL die Schüler) MASC NOUN
pupil

die **Schülerin** FEM NOUN
pupil

die **Schulferien** PL NOUN
school holidays *pl*

★ **schulfrei** ADJECTIVE
■ ein schulfreier Tag a holiday

■ Sonntag ist schulfrei.Sunday isn't a school day.

★ der **Schulhof**(PL die Schulhöfe) MASC NOUN
playground

das **Schuljahr**(PL die Schuljahre) NEUT NOUN
school year

der **Schulleiter**(PL die Schulleiter) MASC NOUN
head teacher

die **Schulleiterin** FEM NOUN
head teacher

schulpflichtig ADJECTIVE
of school age

die **Schulstunde** FEM NOUN
period

der **Schultag**(PL die Schultage) MASC NOUN
■ mein erster Schultag my first day at school

die **Schultasche** FEM NOUN
school bag

★ die **Schulter** FEM NOUN
shoulder

das **Schulzeugnis**(GEN des Schulzeugnisses, PL die Schulzeugnisse) NEUT NOUN
school report

die **Schürze** FEM NOUN
apron

der **Schuss**(GEN des Schusses, PL die Schüsse) MASC NOUN
shot
□ Wir hörten einen Schuss.We heard a shot.

die **Schüssel** FEM NOUN
bowl

die **Schusswaffe** FEM NOUN
firearm

der **Schuster**(PL die Schuster) MASC NOUN
cobbler

der **Schutt** MASC NOUN
rubble
□ Der Schutt von der Baustelle wird morgen weggebracht.The rubble from the building site will be removed tomorrow.
■ Schutt abladen verboten!No dumping!

schütteln VERB [34]
to shake
■ sich schütteln to shake oneself
■ sich vor Ekel schütteln to shudder with disgust □ Als ich die Schlange sah, hat es mich vor Ekel geschüttelt.I shuddered with disgust when I saw the snake.

schütten VERB [2]
1 to pour
□ Soll ich dir Saft ins Glas schütten?Shall I pour you some juice?

2 to spill
□ Pass auf, dass du den Kaffee nicht auf die Tischdecke schüttest. **Be careful that you don't spill coffee on the tablecloth.**
■ **Es schüttet. It's pouring down.**

★ der **Schutz** (GEN des **Schutzes**) MASC NOUN
1 protection
□ Zum Schutz gegen die Sonne solltest du dich eincremen. **You should put some cream on to protect against the sun.**
2 shelter
□ Sie suchten Schutz in der Berghütte. **They took shelter in a mountain hut.**
■ **jemanden in Schutz nehmen** to stand up for somebody

der **Schütze** (GEN des **Schützen**, PL die **Schützen**) MASC NOUN
1 marksman
□ Er ist ein guter Schütze. **He's a good marksman.**
2 Sagittarius
□ Martin ist Schütze. **Martin's Sagittarius.**

schützen VERB [36]
to protect
□ Die Pflanzen sollten vor zu großer Hitze geschützt werden. **The plants should be protected from too much heat.** □ Diese Creme schützt die Haut gegen Sonnenbrand. **This cream protects the skin from sunburn.**
■ **sich gegen etwas schützen** to protect oneself from something □ Schützen Sie sich gegen Sonnenbrand. **Protect yourself from sunburn.**

★ **schwach** ADJECTIVE
weak
□ Ihre Stimme wurde immer schwächer. **Her voice became weaker and weaker.**
■ **Das war eine schwache Leistung! That wasn't very good.**

die **Schwäche** FEM NOUN
weakness

der **Schwächling** (PL die **Schwächlinge**) MASC NOUN
weakling

der **Schwachsinn** MASC NOUN
balderdash

schwachsinnig ADJECTIVE
idiotic
□ So eine schwachsinnige Idee! **What an idiotic idea!**

★ der **Schwager** (PL die **Schwäger**) MASC NOUN
brother-in-law

★ die **Schwägerin** FEM NOUN
sister-in-law

★ **schwamm** VERB ▷ see **schwimmen**

der **Schwamm** (PL die **Schwämme**) MASC NOUN
sponge

schwanger ADJECTIVE
pregnant
□ Sie ist im dritten Monat schwanger. **She's three months pregnant.**

schwanken VERB [38]
1 to sway
□ Das Schiff schwankte. **The ship swayed.**
2 to stagger
□ Er schwankte und fiel dann um. **He staggered and fell down.**
3 to fluctuate
□ Die Temperaturen schwanken. **Temperatures are fluctuating.** □ Der Kurs des Pfunds schwankt. **The exchange rate of the pound is fluctuating.**

der **Schwanz** (GEN des **Schwanzes**, PL die **Schwänze**) MASC NOUN
tail

schwänzen VERB [36]
to skive off (*Umgangssprache*)
□ Ich habe heute die Turnstunde geschwänzt. **I skived off PE today.**

der **Schwarm** (PL die **Schwärme**) MASC NOUN
swarm
□ ein Schwarm Fliegen **a swarm of flies**
■ **Er ist mein Schwarm. I have a crush on him.** (*Umgangssprache*)

schwärmen (PERFECT TENSE **hat/ist geschwärmt**) VERB [38]

Use **sein** to form the perfect tense for 'to swarm'.

to swarm
□ Die Bienen sind aus dem Bienenstock geschwärmt. **The bees swarmed out of the hive.**
■ **schwärmen für** to have a crush on (*Umgangssprache*) □ Er schwärmt für seinen Mathelehrer. **He has a crush on his maths teacher.**
■ **schwärmen von** to rave about □ Er hat von dem Konzert geschwärmt. **He raved about the concert.**

★ **schwarz** ADJECTIVE
black
□ Der Himmel wurde immer schwärzer. **The sky turned blacker and blacker.**
■ **Schwarzes Brett** notice board
■ **ins Schwarze treffen** to hit the bull's eye

★ das **Schwarzbrot** (PL die **Schwarzbrote**) NEUT NOUN
brown rye bread

der/die **Schwarze** (GEN des/der **Schwarzen**, PL die **Schwarzen**) MASC/FEM NOUN
black person

schwarzfahren (PRESENT TENSE **fährt schwarz**, IMPERFECT **fuhr schwarz**, PERFECT TENSE **ist schwarzgefahren**) VERB [21]

- **Sie fährt in der Straßenbahn immer schwarz.** She never pays her tram fare.

schwarzsehen (PRESENT TENSE **sieht schwarz**, IMPERFECT **sah schwarz**, PERFECT TENSE **hat schwarzgesehen**) VERB [64]
to look on the black side of things
□ Sieh doch nicht immer so schwarz. Don't always look on the black side of things.

★ der **Schwarzwald** MASC NOUN
Black Forest

schwarz-weiß ADJECTIVE
black and white

schwätzen VERB [48]
to chatter

der **Schwätzer** (PL die **Schwätzer**) MASC NOUN
windbag (*Umgangssprache*)

★ der **Schwede** (GEN des **Schweden**, PL die **Schweden**) MASC NOUN
Swede
- **Er ist Schwede.** He's Swedish.

★ **Schweden** NEUT NOUN
Sweden
- **aus Schweden** from Sweden
- **nach Schweden** to Sweden

★ die **Schwedin** FEM NOUN
Swede

★ **schwedisch** ADJECTIVE
Swedish

★ **schweigen** (IMPERFECT **schwieg**, PERFECT TENSE **hat geschwiegen**) VERB
1 to be silent
□ Die Kinder finden es schwierig, mehr als fünf Minuten lang zu schweigen. The children find it difficult to be silent for more than five minutes.
2 to stop talking
□ Sag ihm, er soll schweigen. Tell him to stop talking.

★ das **Schwein** (PL die **Schweine**) NEUT NOUN
pig
- **Schwein haben** to be really lucky □ Da hatten wir ja noch mal Schwein. We were really lucky there.

der **Schweinebraten** (PL die **Schweinebraten**) MASC NOUN
roast pork

★ das **Schweinefleisch** NEUT NOUN
pork

die **Schweinegrippe** FEM NOUN
swine flu

der **Schweiß** (GEN des **Schweißes**) MASC NOUN
sweat

★ die **Schweiz** FEM NOUN
Switzerland

schwarzsehen – Schwiegervater

DID YOU KNOW...?
Switzerland is bordered by Germany, Austria, Liechstenstein, Italy and France. Its capital is Berne and its currency the Swiss franc. Roughly 60% of the population (mainly in the North and East) speak a German dialect. French, Italian and Rhaeto-Romanic are also spoken.

- **aus der Schweiz** from Switzerland
- **in der Schweiz** in Switzerland
- **in die Schweiz** to Switzerland

★ der **Schweizer** (PL die **Schweizer**) MASC NOUN
Swiss
- **die Schweizer** the Swiss

★ die **Schweizerin** FEM NOUN
Swiss

★ **schweizerisch** ADJECTIVE
Swiss

★ **schwer** ADJECTIVE, ADVERB
1 heavy
□ Ich habe einen schweren Koffer. I have a heavy suitcase. □ Er hat eine schwere Erkältung. He has a heavy cold.
- **Ich habe einen schweren Kopf.** I've got a headache.
2 difficult
□ Die Mathearbeit war schwer. The maths test was difficult.
- **Er ist schwer verletzt.** He's badly injured.

schwerfallen (PRESENT TENSE **fällt schwer**, IMPERFECT **fiel schwer**, PERFECT TENSE **ist schwergefallen**) VERB [22]
- **jemandem schwerfallen** to be difficult for somebody □ Das dürfte dir nicht schwerfallen. That shouldn't be too difficult for you.

das **Schwert** (PL die **Schwerter**) NEUT NOUN
sword

★ die **Schwester** FEM NOUN
1 sister
□ Meine Schwester ist jünger als ich. My sister's younger than me.
2 nurse
□ Die Schwester hat mir eine Schmerztablette gegeben. The nurse gave me a painkiller.

die **Schwiegereltern** PL NOUN
parents-in-law *pl*

★ die **Schwiegermutter** (PL die **Schwiegermütter**) FEM NOUN
mother-in-law

★ der **Schwiegersohn** (PL die **Schwiegersöhne**) MASC NOUN
son-in-law

★ die **Schwiegertochter** (PL die **Schwiegertöchter**) FEM NOUN
daughter-in-law

★ der **Schwiegervater** (PL die **Schwiegerväter**) MASC NOUN
father-in-law

★ **schwierig** ADJECTIVE
difficult

★ **die Schwierigkeit** FEM NOUN
difficulty

★ **das Schwimmbad** (PL die
Schwimmbäder) NEUT NOUN
swimming pool

★ **das Schwimmbecken** (PL die
Schwimmbecken) NEUT NOUN
swimming pool

★ **schwimmen** (IMPERFECT **schwamm**, PERFECT
TENSE **ist geschwommen**) VERB [63]
1 to swim
□ Er kann nicht schwimmen. He can't swim.
2 to float
□ Auf dem Fluss schwammen Äste. Branches
were floating on the river.

der **Schwindel** MASC NOUN
1 dizzy spell
□ Bei hohem Fieber muss man auch mit
Schwindel rechnen. If you have a high
temperature, you can also expect to have dizzy
spells.
2 fraud
□ Der Schwindel wurde entdeckt. The fraud was
discovered.

schwindelfrei ADJECTIVE
■ schwindelfrei sein to have a good head for
heights □ Ich bin nicht schwindelfrei. I don't
have a good head for heights.

schwindeln VERB [34]
to fib (Umgangssprache)

★ **schwindlig** ADJECTIVE
dizzy
■ Mir ist schwindlig. I feel dizzy.

★ **schwitzen** VERB [36]
to sweat

schwören (IMPERFECT **schwor**, PERFECT TENSE
hat geschworen) VERB
to swear

schwul ADJECTIVE
gay

schwül ADJECTIVE
close

der/die **Schwule** (GEN des/der **Schwulen**, PL
die **Schwulen**) MASC/FEM NOUN
gay person

der **Schwung** (PL die **Schwünge**) MASC NOUN
swing
□ Sie setzte das Pendel in Schwung. She started
the pendulum swinging.
■ jemanden in Schwung bringen to get
somebody going

★ **sechs** NUMBER
▷ see also die **Sechs** NOUN
six

die **Sechs** FEM NOUN
▷ see also **sechs** NUMBER

1 six
2 unsatisfactory

DID YOU KNOW...?
German grades range from one (**sehr gut**) to
six (**ungenügend**).

sechste ADJECTIVE
sixth
□ Er kam als Sechster. He was the sixth to
arrive.

das **Sechstel** (PL die **Sechstel**) NEUT NOUN
sixth

★ **sechzehn** NUMBER
sixteen

★ **sechzig** NUMBER
sixty

★ **die See** FEM NOUN
▷ see also der **See** NOUN
sea
□ auf See at sea
■ an die See fahren to go to the seaside

★ **der See** (PL die **Seen**) MASC NOUN
▷ see also die **See** NOUN
lake
□ der Genfer See Lake Geneva

der **Seehund** (PL die **Seehunde**) MASC NOUN
seal

★ **seekrank** ADJECTIVE
seasick

die **Seele** FEM NOUN
soul

seelenruhig ADVERB
calmly

das **Segel** (PL die **Segel**) NEUT NOUN
sail

★ **das Segelboot** (PL die **Segelboote**) NEUT
NOUN
yacht

das **Segelfliegen** NEUT NOUN
gliding

das **Segelflugzeug** (PL die **Segelflugzeuge**
NEUT NOUN
glider

★ **segeln** (PERFECT TENSE **ist gesegelt**) VERB [34]
to sail

das **Segelschiff** (PL die **Segelschiffe**) NEUT
NOUN
sailing ship

der **Segen** (PL die **Segen**) MASC NOUN
blessing

★ **sehen** (PRESENT TENSE **sieht**, IMPERFECT **sah**,
PERFECT TENSE **hat gesehen**) VERB [64]
1 to see
□ Hast du den Film schon gesehen? Have you
seen the film yet?
■ siehe Seite fünf see page five

2 to look
□ Sieh mal an die Tafel. **Look at the board.**
■ **schlecht sehen** to have bad eyesight □ Sie sieht schlecht. **She has bad eyesight.**
■ **mal sehen, ob ...** let's see if ... □ Mal sehen, ob Post für mich gekommen ist. **Let's see if there's any post for me.**
■ **Kommst du mit? — Mal sehen.** Are you coming? — I'll see.

× sehenswert ADJECTIVE
worth seeing

die **Sehenswürdigkeiten** FEM PL NOUN
sights pl

sich **sehnen** VERB [38]
■ **sich sehnen nach** to long for

die **Sehnsucht** (PL die **Sehnsüchte**) FEM NOUN
longing

sehnsüchtig ADJECTIVE
longing

× sehr ADVERB

1 very
□ Das ist sehr schön. **That's very nice.**
■ **sehr gut** very good

> **DID YOU KNOW...?**
> German grades range from one (**sehr gut**) to six (**ungenügend**).

2 a lot
□ Er hat sehr geweint. **He cried a lot.**
■ **zu sehr** too much
■ **Sehr geehrter Herr Ahlers** Dear Mr Ahlers

× die Seide FEM NOUN
silk

× die Seife FEM NOUN
soap

× die Seifenoper FEM NOUN
soap opera

das **Seil** (PL die **Seile**) NEUT NOUN

1 rope
□ Sie hatten ihn mit einem Seil gefesselt. **They had tied him up with a rope.**

2 cable
□ das Seil des Skilifts **the cable of the ski lift**

× die Seilbahn FEM NOUN
cable car

× sein VERB [65]

PRESENT TENSE	
ich bin	wir sind
du bist	ihr seid
er/sie/es ist	sie/Sie sind

PERFECT TENSE	
ist gewesen	

> *see also* **sein** ADJECTIVE

to be
□ Ich bin müde. **I'm tired.** □ Du bist doof. **You're stupid.** □ Er ist reich. **He's rich.** □ Sie ist Lehrerin. **She's a teacher.** □ Es ist kalt. **It's cold.**

□ Wir sind Schüler am Gymnasium. **We're pupils at the grammar school.** □ Wir waren dort. **We were there.** □ Wir sind im Schwimmbad gewesen. **We've been to the swimming pool.** □ Seien Sie nicht böse. **Don't be angry.**
□ Morgen bin ich in Rom. **Tomorrow I'll be in Rome.**
■ **Das wäre gut.** That would be a good thing.
■ **Wenn ich Sie wäre ...** If I were you ...
■ **Das wär's.** That's it.
■ **Mir ist kalt.** I'm cold.
■ **Was ist?** What's the matter?
■ **Ist was?** Is something the matter?
■ **es sei denn, dass ...** unless ...
■ **wie dem auch sei** be that as it may
■ **Wie wäre es mit ...?** How about ...?
■ **Lass das sein!** Stop that!

★ sein ADJECTIVE

> *see also* **sein** VERB

1 his
□ Sein Deutschlehrer ist nett. **His German teacher's nice.** □ Seine Mutter erlaubt das nicht. **His mother doesn't allow it.** □ Das ist sein Buch. **That's his book.** □ Seine Eltern sind klasse. **His parents are great.** □ Das ist nicht mein Kuli, das ist seiner. **That's not my pen, it's his.** □ Meine Mutter heißt Anne, seine auch. **My mother's called Anne, so is his.**

2 its
□ Der Fuchs kam aus seiner Höhle. **The fox came out of its lair.** □ Jedes Buch hat seinen Platz. **Each book has its place.**

seiner PRONOUN

> **seiner** is the genitive of **er**.

of him
□ Wir gedenken seiner. **We're thinking of him.**

seinetwegen ADVERB

1 for his sake
□ Ihr müsst seinetwegen nicht auf euren Urlaub verzichten. **You don't have to do without your holiday for his sake.**

2 on his account
□ Hat sie sich seinetwegen so aufgeregt? **Did she get so upset on his account?**

3 as far as he's concerned
□ Er sagt, dass du seinetwegen gehen kannst. **He says that as far as he's concerned you can go.**

★ seit PREPOSITION, CONJUNCTION

> The preposition **seit** takes the dative.

1 since
□ Seit er verheiratet ist, spielt er nicht mehr Fußball. **He's stopped playing football since he got married.** □ Seit letztem Jahr habe ich nichts mehr von ihm gehört. **I haven't heard anything from him since last year.**

2 for
□ Er ist seit einer Woche hier. **He's been here for a week.** □ seit Langem for a long time

Numbers in brackets refer to verb tables on pages 697 to 706.

249

★ **seitdem** ADVERB, CONJUNCTION
<u>since</u>
□ Seitdem sie im Gymnasium ist, hat sie kaum mehr Zeit. Since she's been going to grammar school, she's hardly had any time.
■ **Ich habe seitdem nichts mehr von ihr gehört.** I haven't heard from her since then.

★ **die Seite** FEM NOUN
1 <u>side</u>
□ Die rechte Seite des Autos war beschädigt. The right side of the car was damaged.
2 <u>page</u>
□ Das steht auf Seite fünfzig. It's on page fifty.

der Sekretär MASC NOUN
<u>secretary</u>

das Sekretariat (PL die **Sekretariate**) NEUT NOUN
<u>secretary's office</u>

die Sekretärin FEM NOUN
<u>secretary</u>

★ **der Sekt** (PL die **Sekte**) MASC NOUN
<u>sparkling wine</u>

★ **die Sekunde** FEM NOUN
<u>second</u>
□ zehn Sekunden ten seconds

★ **selber** PRONOUN = **selbst**

★ **selbst** PRONOUN, ADVERB
1 <u>on one's own</u>
□ Das Kind kann sich selbst anziehen. The child can get dressed on her own. □ Ich werde schon selbst eine Lösung finden. I'll find a solution on my own.
■ **ich selbst** I myself
■ **er selbst** he himself
■ **wir selbst** we ourselves
■ **Sie ist die Liebenswürdigkeit selbst.** She's kindness itself.
■ **Sie braut ihr Bier selbst.** She brews her own beer.
■ **von selbst** by itself □ Die Bombe ist von selbst losgegangen. The bomb went off by itself.
2 <u>even</u>
□ Selbst meine Großmutter findet Adele gut. Even my grandmother likes Adele.
■ **selbst wenn** even if □ Du musst das machen, selbst wenn du keine Lust hast. You have to do it even if you don't feel like it.

selbständig ADJECTIVE ▷ see **selbstständig**

★ **die Selbstbedienung** FEM NOUN
<u>self-service</u>

selbstbewusst ADJECTIVE
<u>self-confident</u>

der Selbstmord (PL die **Selbstmorde**) MASC NOUN
<u>suicide</u>
□ Selbstmord begehen to commit suicide

der Selbstmordanschlag (PL die **Selbstmordanschläge**) MASC NOUN
<u>suicide attack</u>

selbstsicher ADJECTIVE
<u>self-assured</u>

selbstständig ADJECTIVE
1 <u>independent</u>
□ Du solltest langsam selbstständiger werden. It's about time you started to become more independent. □ ein selbstständiger Staat an independent country
2 <u>on one's own</u>
□ Kannst du das nicht selbstständig entscheiden? Can't you decide on your own?
■ **sich selbstständig machen** to become self-employed □ Sie hat sich als Übersetzerin selbstständig gemacht. She set herself up as a self-employed translator.

die Selbstverpflegung FEM NOUN
<u>self-catering</u>

selbstverständlich ADJECTIVE, ADVERB
1 <u>obvious</u>
□ Das ist für mich durchaus nicht selbstverständlich. It's not at all obvious to me.
■ **Es ist doch selbstverständlich, dass man da hilft.** It goes without saying that you should help.
■ **Ich halte das für selbstverständlich.** I take that for granted.
2 <u>of course</u>
□ Ich habe mich selbstverständlich sofort bedankt. Of course I said thank you immediately. □ Kommt er mit? — Selbstverständlich. Is he coming? — Of course. □ Ich habe selbstverständlich nicht unterschrieben. Of course I didn't sign.

das Selbstvertrauen NEUT NOUN
<u>self-confidence</u>

★ **das Selfie** (PL die **Selfies**) NEUT NOUN
<u>selfie</u>

★ **der Selfie-Stick** (PL die **Selfie-Sticks**) MASC NOUN
<u>selfie stick</u>

selig ADJECTIVE
1 <u>blissful</u>
□ Er hatte ein seliges Lächeln auf dem Gesicht. He had a blissful smile on his face.
2 <u>overjoyed</u>
□ Sie war selig, als sie ihn sah. She was overjoyed to see him.

der Sellerie MASC NOUN
<u>celeriac</u>

★ **selten** ADJECTIVE, ADVERB
1 <u>rare</u>
□ eine seltene Pflanze a rare plant
2 <u>rarely</u>
□ Wir gehen selten ins Kino. We rarely go to the cinema.

★ = core vocabulary

seltsam ADJECTIVE
curious

das Semester(PL die Semester) NEUT NOUN
semester

das Seminar(PL die Seminare) NEUT NOUN
seminar
□ Ich mache dieses Semester ein Seminar über Steinbeck. I'm doing a seminar on Steinbeck this semester.

die Sendefolge FEM NOUN
series

senden(IMPERFECT sendete or sandte, PERFECT TENSE hat gesendet or gesandt) VERB
1 to send
□ Bitte senden Sie mir Ihren neuesten Katalog. Please send me your latest catalogue.
2 to broadcast
□ Der Spielfilm wird im dritten Programm gesendet. The film will be broadcast on Channel three. □ Wir senden bis Mitternacht. We broadcast until midnight.

die Sendereihe FEM NOUN
series

die Sendung FEM NOUN
1 transmission
□ Während der Sendung darf das Studio nicht betreten werden. Nobody's allowed to enter the studio during transmission.
2 programme
□ Kennst du die Sendung 'Tiere im Zoo'? Do you know the programme 'Animals in the Zoo'?
3 consignment
□ Für Sie ist eine Sendung mit Mustern angekommen. A consignment of samples has arrived for you.

der Senf(PL die Senfe) MASC NOUN
mustard

die Sensation FEM NOUN
sensation

sensibel ADJECTIVE
sensitive
□ Sie ist ein sehr sensibler Mensch. She's a very sensitive person.

> **BE CAREFUL!**
> sensibel does not mean **sensible**.

sentimental ADJECTIVE
sentimental
□ Nun werd nicht sentimental! Now don't get sentimental.

der September MASC NOUN
September
□ im September in September □ am elften September on the eleventh of September □ Ulm, den 10. September 2007 Ulm, 10 September 2007 □ Heute ist der elfte September. Today is the eleventh of September.

★ **die Serie** FEM NOUN
series *sing*

seriös ADJECTIVE
respectable

> **BE CAREFUL!**
> seriös does not mean **serious**.

der Server(PL die Server) MASC NOUN
server

das Service(GEN des Service or Services, PL die Service) NEUT NOUN
▷ *see also* der Service NOUN
set
□ Sie hat ein hübsches Teeservice aus Porzellan. She has a lovely china tea set.

der Service(GEN des Service, PL die Services) MASC NOUN
▷ *see also* das Service NOUN
service
□ In dem Hotel ist der Service ausgezeichnet. The service in the hotel is excellent.

★ **die Serviette** FEM NOUN
serviette

servus EXCLAMATION
1 hello!
2 goodbye!

★ **der Sessel**(PL die Sessel) MASC NOUN
armchair

der Sessellift(PL die Sessellifte) MASC NOUN
chairlift

★ **setzen** VERB [36]
to put
□ Er setzte das Kind auf den Stuhl. He put the child on the chair. □ Sie setzte das Glas an den Mund. She put the glass to her lips. □ Hast du meinen Namen auf die Liste gesetzt? Have you put my name on the list? □ ein Komma setzen to put a comma
■ **jemandem eine Frist setzen** to set somebody a deadline
■ **sich setzen 1** to settle □ Der Kaffeesatz hat sich gesetzt. The coffee grounds have settled.
2 to sit down □ Setz dich doch! Do sit down!
□ Sie setzte sich aufs Sofa. She sat down on the sofa.
■ **auf etwas setzen** to bet on something □ Er hat hundert Euro auf die Nummer zwei gesetzt. He bet a hundred euros on number two.

die Seuche FEM NOUN
epidemic

seufzen VERB [36]
to sigh

sexuell ADJECTIVE
sexual

das Shampoo(PL die Shampoos) NEUT NOUN
shampoo

Sibirien NEUT NOUN
Siberia

sich – sie

★ **sich** PRONOUN

1 himself
  □ Er redet mit sich selbst. **He's talking to himself.**
  herself
  □ Sie spricht nicht gern über sich selbst. **She doesn't like to talk about herself.** □ Sie wäscht sich. **She's washing herself.** □ Sie hat sich einen Pullover gekauft. **She bought herself a jumper.**
  itself
  □ Das Boot hat sich wieder aufgerichtet. **The boat righted itself.**

2 themselves
  □ Meine Eltern haben sich ein neues Auto gekauft. **My parents have bought themselves a new car.** □ Sie bleiben gern unter sich. **They keep themselves to themselves.**

3 each other
  □ Sie lieben sich. **They love each other.**
  ■ **Sie wäscht sich die Haare.** She's washing her hair.
  ■ **Er schneidet sich die Nägel.** He's cutting his nails.
  ■ **Man fragt sich, ob …** One wonders whether …
  ■ **Sie wiederholen sich.** You're repeating yourself.
  ■ **Haben Sie Ihren Ausweis bei sich?** Do you have your pass on you?
  ■ **Dieser Artikel verkauft sich gut.** This article sells well.

★ **sicher** ADJECTIVE, ADVERB

1 safe
  □ Das ist ein sehr sicheres Auto. **It's a very safe car.**

2 certain
  □ Der Termin ist noch nicht sicher. **The date isn't certain yet.**
  ■ **Ich bin nicht sicher.** I'm not sure.

3 reliable
  ■ eine sichere Methode a reliable method
  ■ **vor jemandem sicher sein** to be safe from somebody □ In einer Großstadt ist man vor Taschendieben nicht sicher. **You're never safe from pickpockets in a city.**
  ■ **vor etwas sicher sein** to be safe from something □ Bei ihr ist man vor Überraschungen nie sicher. **With her you're never safe from surprises.**

4 definitely
  □ Sie kommt sicher nicht mehr. **She's definitely not coming anymore.**
  ■ **Er weiß das sicher schon.** I'm sure he knows that already.
  ■ **sicher nicht** surely not
  ■ **Aber sicher!** Of course!

★ die **Sicherheit** FEM NOUN
  safety no pl
  □ Tragen Sie einen Helm zu Ihrer eigenen Sicherheit. **Wear a helmet for your own safety.**

□ Diese Maßnahmen dienen der Sicherheit de Fluggäste. **These measures are for passenger safety.**
  ■ **Hier sind wir in Sicherheit.** We're safe here.
  ■ **Ich kann nicht mit Sicherheit sagen, ob ich komme.** I can't say for sure if I'll come.

★ der **Sicherheitsgurt** (PL die **Sicherheitsgurte**) MASC NOUN
  seat belt

★ **sicherlich** ADVERB
  certainly

sichern VERB [88]
  to secure
  □ Maßnahmen, die Arbeitsplätze sichern measures to secure jobs
  ■ **Daten sichern** to back up data □ Die Daten werden stündlich in der Cloud gesichert. **The data is backed up onto the cloud every hour.**
  ■ **jemandem etwas sichern** to secure something for somebody □ Ich habe dir einen guten Platz gesichert. **I've secured a good plac for you.**

die **Sicherung** FEM NOUN

1 securing
  □ Maßnahmen zur Sicherung der Arbeitsplätz measures for securing jobs

2 fuse
  □ Die Sicherung ist durchgebrannt. **The fuse has blown.**

die **Sicherungskopie** FEM NOUN
  backup copy

die **Sicht** FEM NOUN
  view
  □ Wir hatten eine gute Sicht auf die Berge. **We had a good view of the mountains.** □ Du versperrst mir die Sicht. **You're blocking my view.**
  ■ **auf lange Sicht** on a long-term basis
  ■ **aus jemandes Sicht** as somebody sees it □ Aus meiner Sicht ist das zu schaffen. **As I see it, it can be done.**

sichtbar ADJECTIVE
  visible

★ **sie** PRONOUN
  ▷ see also **Sie** PRONOUN

1 she
  □ Sie ist sehr klug. **She's very clever.**

2 it
  □ Schöne Tasche, ist sie neu? **Lovely bag, is it new?** □ Kann ich deine Tasche haben, oder brauchst du sie noch? **Can I have your bag or d you need it?**

3 her
  □ Ich kenne sie nicht. **I don't know her.**

4 they
  □ Sie sind alle gekommen. **They all came.**

5 them
  □ Ich habe sie alle eingeladen. **I've invited all c them.**

Sie PRONOUN

▷ *see also* **sie** PRONOUN

you

□ Möchten Sie mitkommen? Would you like to come? □ Ich kenne Sie. I know you.

DID YOU KNOW...?

The formal form of address **Sie** (singular and plural) is used when addressing people you don't know or your superiors. Teachers say **Sie** to children over the age of 16.

das **Sieb** (PL die **Siebe**) NEUT NOUN

1 sieve

□ Wir sollten das Mehl durch ein Sieb schütten. We should rub the flour through a sieve.

2 strainer

□ Hast du ein Teesieb? Have you got a tea strainer?

sieben NUMBER

seven

siebte ADJECTIVE

seventh

□ Er kam als Siebter. He was the seventh to arrive.

siebzehn NUMBER

seventeen

siebzig NUMBER

seventy

die **Siedlung** FEM NOUN

1 settlement

□ eine indianische Siedlung an Indian settlement

2 estate

□ Sie wohnt in unserer Siedlung. She lives on our estate.

der **Sieg** (PL die **Siege**) MASC NOUN

victory

siegen VERB [38]

to win

□ Welche Mannschaft hat gesiegt? Which team won?

der **Sieger** (PL die **Sieger**) MASC NOUN

winner

□ Deutschland war 2014 Sieger der Fußballweltmeisterschaft. Germany was the winner of the 2014 World Cup.

siehe VERB ▷ *see* **sehen**

siezen VERB [36]

to address as 'Sie'

DID YOU KNOW...?

The formal form of address **Sie** (singular and plural) is used when addressing people you don't know or your superiors. Teachers say **Sie** to children over the age of 16.

die **Silbe** FEM NOUN

syllable

★ das **Silber** NEUT NOUN

silver

★ das **Silvester** (PL die **Silvester**) NEUT NOUN

New Year's Eve

simsen VERB [36] (*Umgangssprache*)

to text

★ **singen** (IMPERFECT **sang**, PERFECT TENSE **hat gesungen**) VERB [66]

to sing

der **Singular** (PL die **Singulare**) MASC NOUN

singular

sinken (IMPERFECT **sank**, PERFECT TENSE **ist gesunken**) VERB [67]

1 to sink

□ Das Schiff ist gesunken. The ship has sunk.

2 to fall

□ Die Preise für Computer sind gesunken. The prices of computers have fallen.

★ der **Sinn** (PL die **Sinne**) MASC NOUN

1 sense

□ die fünf Sinne the five senses

2 meaning

□ Ich verstehe den Sinn dieses Satzes nicht. I don't understand the meaning of this sentence. □ Was ist der Sinn des Lebens? What's the meaning of life?

■ **Sinn für etwas haben** to have a sense of something □ Sie hat viel Sinn für Humor. She has a great sense of humour.

■ **jemandem in den Sinn kommen** to come to somebody □ Die Idee kam mir plötzlich in den Sinn. The idea suddenly came to me.

■ **Es hat keinen Sinn.** There's no point.

sinnlos ADJECTIVE

1 pointless

□ Es ist sinnlos, das zu tun. It's pointless doing that.

2 meaningless

□ Er hat sinnloses Zeug geredet. He talked meaningless rubbish.

sinnvoll ADJECTIVE

sensible

□ Das wäre eine sinnvolle Änderung. That would be a sensible change.

die **Situation** FEM NOUN

situation

★ der **Sitz** (GEN des **Sitzes**, PL die **Sitze**) MASC NOUN

seat

★ **sitzen** (IMPERFECT **saß**, PERFECT TENSE **hat gesessen**) VERB [68]

1 to sit

□ Er saß auf dem Stuhl. He was sitting on the chair.

■ **sitzen bleiben 1** to remain seated □ Bitte bleiben Sie sitzen. Please remain seated. **2** to have to repeat a year

DID YOU KNOW...?
In Germany pupils do not automatically move up (**versetzt werden**) to the next class at the end of the school year. If their performance is not good enough, they have to repeat the school year. This is known as **sitzen bleiben**.

□ Ich habe Angst, dass ich dieses Jahr sitzen bleibe. I'm worried that I'll have to repeat this year.

2 to fit
□ Diese Hose sitzt. These trousers fit well.

der **Sitzplatz** (GEN des **Sitzplatzes**, PL die **Sitzplätze**) MASC NOUN
seat

die **Sitzung** FEM NOUN
meeting

der **Skandal** (PL die **Skandale**) MASC NOUN
scandal

Skandinavien NEUT NOUN
Scandinavia
■ **aus Skandinavien** from Scandinavia
■ **nach Skandinavien** to Scandinavia

skandinavisch ADJECTIVE
Scandinavian

das **Skelett** (PL die **Skelette**) NEUT NOUN
skeleton

★ der **Ski** (PL die **Ski** or **Skier**) MASC NOUN
ski
■ **Ski fahren** to ski

der **Skifahrer** (PL die **Skifahrer**) MASC NOUN
skier

das **Skilaufen** NEUT NOUN
skiing

der **Skilehrer** (PL die **Skilehrer**) MASC NOUN
ski instructor

der **Skilift** (PL die **Skilifte** or **Skilifts**) MASC NOUN
ski lift

der **Skorpion** (PL die **Skorpione**) MASC NOUN
1 scorpion
2 Scorpio
□ Sie ist Skorpion. She's Scorpio.

skypen VERB [38]
to Skype

der **Slip** (PL die **Slips**) MASC NOUN
pants *pl*
□ ein Slip a pair of pants

die **Slowakei** FEM NOUN
Slovakia
■ **aus der Slowakei** from Slovakia
■ **in die Slowakei** to Slovakia

die **SMS** (PL die **SMS**) FEM NOUN
text message
■ **Er hat mir eine SMS geschickt.** He texted me.

das **Snowboard** NEUT NOUN
snowboard
■ **Snowboard fahren** to go snowboarding

★ **so** ADVERB, CONJUNCTION, EXCLAMATION
1 so
□ Ich hatte mich so darauf gefreut. I was so looking forward to it. □ so schön so nice
□ zwanzig oder so twenty or so □ und so weiter and so on
■ **so groß wie ...** as big as ...
2 so much
□ Das hat ihn so geärgert, dass ... That annoyed him so much that ...
3 like that
□ Mach es nicht so. Don't do it like that.
■ **... oder so was** ... or something like that
■ **so einer wie ich** somebody like me
■ **Na so was!** Well, well!
■ **so dass** so that
■ **So?** Really?

★ **sobald** CONJUNCTION
as soon as

das **Söckchen** (PL die **Söckchen**) NEUT NOUN
ankle sock

★ die **Socke** FEM NOUN
sock

sodass CONJUNCTION
so that

★ das **Sofa** (PL die **Sofas**) NEUT NOUN
sofa

★ **sofort** ADVERB
immediately

sogar ADVERB
even

★ **sogleich** ADVERB
straight away

die **Sohle** FEM NOUN
sole

★ der **Sohn** (PL die **Söhne**) MASC NOUN
son

solch PRONOUN
such
□ Sie ist solch eine nette Frau. She's such a nice lady. □ eine solche Frechheit such a cheek
■ **ein solcher** a ... like that □ Ein solcher Fehler sollte nicht passieren. A mistake like that shouldn't happen. □ Eine solche Wohnung würde mir auch gefallen. I'd like a flat like that.

★ der **Soldat** (GEN des **Soldaten**, PL die **Soldaten**) MASC NOUN
soldier

★ die **Soldatin** FEM NOUN
soldier

solide ADJECTIVE
1 solid
□ Dieser Tisch ist aus solidem Holz. This table made of solid wood.

2 sound

□ Sie hat solide Grammatikkenntnisse. **She has a sound grasp of grammar.**

3 respectable

□ Wir führen ein solides Leben. **We lead a respectable life.** □ Er ist solide geworden. **He's become respectable.**

★ **sollen**(IMPERFECT sollte, PERFECT TENSE hat gesollt or sollen) VERB [69]

The past participle sollen is used when sollen is a modal auxiliary.

1 to be supposed to

□ Ich soll um fünf Uhr dort sein. **I'm supposed to be there at five o'clock.** □ Was soll das heißen? **What's that supposed to mean?** □ Morgen soll es schön werden. **It's supposed to be nice tomorrow.**

2 to have to

□ Du sollst sofort nach Hause. **You have to go home immediately.** □ Sie sagt, du sollst nach Hause kommen. **She says that you have to come home.**

■ Sag ihm, er soll warten. **Tell him he's to wait.**

3 should

□ Ich sollte meine Hausaufgaben machen. **I should do my homework.** □ Du hättest nicht gehen sollen. **You shouldn't have gone.** □ Was soll ich machen? **What should I do?** □ Ich hätte eigentlich nicht gesollt. **I really shouldn't have.** □ Das sollst du nicht. **You shouldn't do that.**

■ Sie soll wirklich intelligent sein. **She's said to be really intelligent.**

■ Man sollte glauben, dass ... **You would think that ...**

■ Soll ich dir helfen? **Shall I help you?**

■ Soll ich? **Shall I?**

■ Was soll das? **What's all this?**

■ Was soll's? **What the hell!** (*Umgangssprache*)

★ der **Sommer**(PL die Sommer) MASC NOUN

summer

□ im Sommer in summer

★ die **Sommerferien** PL NOUN

summer holidays *pl*

sommerlich ADJECTIVE

1 summery

□ ein sommerliches Kleid a summery dress

2 summer

□ sommerliche Kleidung summer clothes □ sommerliches Wetter summer weather

der **Sommerschlussverkauf**(PL die Sommerschlussverkäufe) MASC NOUN

summer sale

die **Sommersprossen** FEM PL NOUN

freckles *pl*

das **Sonderangebot**(PL die Sonderangebote) NEUT NOUN

special offer

sonderbar ADJECTIVE

strange

★ **sondern** CONJUNCTION

but

■ nicht nur ..., sondern auch not only ..., but also

★ der **Sonderpreis** MASC NOUN

special price

★ der **Sonnabend**(PL die Sonnabende) MASC NOUN

Saturday

□ am Sonnabend on Saturday

★ **sonnabends** ADVERB

on Saturdays

★ die **Sonne** FEM NOUN

sun

★ sich **sonnen** VERB [38]

to sun oneself

★ der **Sonnenbrand**(PL die Sonnenbrände) MASC NOUN

sunburn

★ die **Sonnenbrille** FEM NOUN

sunglasses *pl*

□ Sie trug eine Sonnenbrille. **She was wearing sunglasses.**

★ die **Sonnencreme**(PL die Sonnencremes) FEM NOUN

suntan lotion

die **Sonnenenergie** FEM NOUN

solar power

★ die **Sonnenmilch** FEM NOUN

suntan lotion

das **Sonnenöl**(PL die Sonnenöle) NEUT NOUN

suntan oil

★ der **Sonnenschein** MASC NOUN

sunshine

der **Sonnenschirm**(PL die Sonnenschirme) MASC NOUN

sunshade

★ der **Sonnenstich** MASC NOUN

sunstroke

★ **sonnig** ADJECTIVE

sunny

★ der **Sonntag**(PL die Sonntage) MASC NOUN

Sunday

□ am Sonntag on Sunday

sonntags ADVERB

on Sundays

★ **sonst** ADVERB, CONJUNCTION

1 normally

□ Was ist mit dir? Du bist doch sonst nicht so still. **What's wrong with you? You're not normally so quiet.** □ Die Kinder sind sonst eigentlich artiger. **The children normally behave better.**

2 else
□ Wer sonst? **Who else?** □ Was sonst? **What else?** □ Sonst war niemand da. **Nobody else was there.** □ sonst nichts **nothing else**
■ **sonst noch else** □ Was hast du sonst noch bekommen? **What else did you get?**
■ **Haben Sie sonst noch einen Wunsch?** Would you like anything else?
■ **Sonst noch etwas? Anything else?**
■ **sonst wo somewhere else**

3 otherwise
□ Ich habe etwas Kopfschmerzen, aber sonst geht's mir gut. **I've got a headache, otherwise I feel fine.**

sonstig ADJECTIVE
other

★ **die Sorge** FEM NOUN
worry
■ **Ich mache mir Sorgen. I'm worried.**

★ **sorgen** VERB [38]
■ **für jemanden sorgen to look after somebody**
■ **für etwas sorgen to see to something**
■ **sich um jemanden sorgen to worry about somebody**

sorgfältig ADJECTIVE
careful

★ **die Sorte** FEM NOUN
1 sort
□ Welche Sorte Äpfel ist das? **What sort of apple is that?**
2 brand
□ Welche Sorte Waschmittel verwenden Sie? **What brand of detergent do you use?**

sortieren (PERFECT TENSE **hat sortiert**) VERB [76]
1 to sort out
□ Ich bin endlich dazu gekommen, meine Urlaubsfotos zu sortieren. **I finally managed to sort out my holiday photos.**
2 to sort
□ Du musst hier klicken, um die Liste aufsteigend zu sortieren. **You need to click here to sort the list in ascending order.**

die Soße FEM NOUN
1 sauce
□ Eis mit Himbeersoße **ice cream with raspberry sauce**
2 gravy
□ Schweinebraten mit Soße **roast pork with gravy**
3 dressing
□ Salat mit einer Joghurtsoße **salad with a yoghurt dressing**

★ **das Souvenir** (PL **die Souvenirs**) NEUT NOUN
souvenir

soviel ADVERB ▷ see **viel**

soviel CONJUNCTION
as far as
□ soviel ich weiß **as far as I know**

soweit ADVERB ▷ see **weit**

soweit CONJUNCTION
as far as
□ Soweit ich weiß, kann er nicht kommen. **As far as I know, he can't come.**

sowenig ADVERB ▷ see **wenig**

sowie CONJUNCTION
as soon as
□ Ich rufe an, sowie ich Bescheid weiß. **I'll phone as soon as I know.**

sowieso ADVERB
anyway

sowohl CONJUNCTION
■ **sowohl ... als auch both ... and**

sozial ADJECTIVE
social
■ **ein soziales Netzwerk a social networking site**
■ **soziale Medien social media**

die Sozialhilfe FEM NOUN
social security
□ Sozialhilfe bekommen **to be on social security**

★ **die Sozialkunde** FEM NOUN
social studies *sing*

die Sozialversicherung FEM NOUN
social security

die Sozialwissenschaften PL NOUN
social sciences

sozusagen ADVERB
so to speak

die Spalte FEM NOUN
1 crack
□ Durch die Trockenheit hatten sich tiefe Spalten gebildet. **Deep cracks had formed as a result of the dry spell.**
2 column
□ Der Text ist in zwei Spalten gedruckt. **The text is printed in two columns.**

spalten VERB [2]
to split

★ **Spanien** NEUT NOUN
Spain
■ **aus Spanien from Spain**
■ **in Spanien in Spain**
■ **nach Spanien to Spain**

★ **der Spanier** (PL **die Spanier**) MASC NOUN
Spaniard
■ **Er ist Spanier. He's Spanish.**
■ **die Spanier the Spanish**

★ **die Spanierin** FEM NOUN
Spaniard
■ **Sie ist Spanierin. She's Spanish.**

spanisch ADJECTIVE
▷ *see also* das **Spanisch** NOUN
Spanish

das **Spanisch** (GEN des **Spanischen**) NEUT
NOUN
▷ *see also* spanisch ADJECTIVE
Spanish
□ Er lernt Spanisch in der Schule. He's learning Spanish at school.

spannend ADJECTIVE
exciting

die **Spannung** FEM NOUN
1 suspense
□ ein Film voller Spannung a film full of suspense
2 tension
□ Das führte zu Spannungen zwischen den beiden Ländern. That caused tension between the two countries.

das **Sparbuch** (PL die **Sparbücher**) NEUT
NOUN
savings book

sparen VERB [38]
to save
□ Wir müssen sparen. We have to save. □ Sie hat zweihundert Euro gespart. She's saved two hundred euros. □ Energie sparen to save energy □ Er spart für ein Mountainbike. He's saving for a mountain bike.
■ **sich etwas sparen** 1 not to bother with something □ Den Film kannst du dir sparen. Don't bother with that film. 2 to keep something to oneself □ Spar dir deine Bemerkungen. You can keep your remarks to yourself.
■ **mit etwas sparen** to be sparing with something
■ **an etwas sparen** to economize on something □ Sie spart in letzter Zeit am Essen. She's been economizing on food recently.

BE CAREFUL!
sparen does not mean **to spare**.

der **Spargel** MASC NOUN
asparagus

die **Sparkasse** FEM NOUN
savings bank

sparsam ADJECTIVE
1 economical
□ ein sparsames Auto an economical car □ Wir sollten mit den Rohstoffen sparsam umgehen. We should be economical with raw materials.
2 thrifty
□ Sie ist sehr sparsam. She's very thrifty.

das **Sparschwein** (PL die **Sparschweine**)
NEUT NOUN
piggy bank

der **Spaß** (GEN des **Spaßes**, PL die **Späße**)
MASC NOUN
fun

□ Wir hatten in den Ferien viel Spaß. We had great fun in the holidays.
■ **Er versteht keinen Spaß.** He has no sense of humour.
■ **Skifahren macht mir Spaß.** I like skiing.
■ **zum Spaß** for fun □ Ich mache den Kurs nur zum Spaß. I'm only doing the course for fun.
■ **Viel Spaß!** Have fun!

spät ADJECTIVE, ADVERB
late
□ Es wird spät. It's getting late. □ Wir kamen zu spät. We were late.
■ **Wie spät ist es?** What's the time?

später ADJECTIVE, ADVERB
later
□ Bis später! See you later!

spätestens ADVERB
at the latest

der **Spatz** (GEN des **Spatzen**, PL die **Spatzen**)
MASC NOUN
sparrow

★**spazieren** VERB [76]
■ **spazieren fahren** to go for a drive
■ **spazieren gehen** to go for a walk

★der **Spaziergang** (PL die **Spaziergänge**)
MASC NOUN
walk
□ einen Spaziergang machen to go for a walk

★der **Speck** MASC NOUN
bacon

das **Speerwerfen** NEUT NOUN
throwing the javelin

der **Speicher** (PL die **Speicher**) MASC NOUN
1 loft
□ Die alten Möbel sind auf dem Speicher. The old furniture's in the loft.
2 storehouse
□ Die alten Speicher am Hafen wurden zu Wohnungen umgebaut. The old storehouses at the harbour were converted into flats.
3 memory
□ Ich will den Speicher meines Computers erweitern. I want to expand the memory of my computer.

die **Speicherkarte** FEM NOUN
memory card
□ Wo kann ich eine Speicherkarte für meine Kamera kaufen? Where can I buy a memory card for my camera?

★**speichern** (PERFECT TENSE hat gespeichert)
VERB [88]
1 to store
□ Energie speichern to store energy
2 to save
□ eine Datei speichern to save a file

★das **Speiseeis** NEUT NOUN
ice cream

★ die **Speisekarte** FEM NOUN
menu
□ Könnte ich bitte die Speisekarte haben?**Could I have the menu please?**

★ der **Speisesaal** MASC NOUN
dining room

der **Speisewagen**(PL die Speisewagen)
MASC NOUN
dining car

die **Spende** FEM NOUN
donation

spenden VERB [54]
to donate
□ Ich habe zwanzig Euro gespendet.**I've donated twenty euros.**
■ Blut spenden**to give blood**

BE CAREFUL!
The German word spendendoes not mean to spend.

der **Spender**(PL die Spender) MASC NOUN
donor

spendieren(PERFECT TENSE hat spendiert)
VERB [76]
■ jemandem etwas spendieren**to stand somebody something** (*Umgangssprache*)
□ Mutti hat uns ein Eis spendiert.**Mum stood us all an ice cream.**

★ die **Sperre** FEM NOUN
1 barrier
□ Vor dem Eingang befand sich eine Sperre.
There was a barrier in front of the entrance.
2 ban
□ Er erhielt eine Sperre von drei Monaten.**He got a three-month ban.**

sperren(PERFECT TENSE hat gesperrt) VERB
[38]
1 to close
□ Die Polizei hat die Straße gesperrt.**The police closed the road.**
2 to obstruct
□ Es ist verboten, gegnerische Spieler zu sperren.**Obstructing the opposition is not allowed.**
3 to lock
□ Diese Dateien sind gesperrt.**These files are locked.**

die **Spezialität** FEM NOUN
speciality

★ der **Spiegel**(PL die Spiegel) MASC NOUN
mirror
□ Er sah in den Spiegel.**He looked in the mirror.**

das **Spiegelbild**(PL die Spiegelbilder) NEUT
NOUN
reflection

★ das **Spiegelei**(PL die Spiegeleier) NEUT NOUN
fried egg

★ das **Spiel**(PL die Spiele) NEUT NOUN
1 game
□ Sollen wir ein Spiel spielen?**Shall we play a game?** □ Hast du das Spiel England gegen Deutschland gesehen?**Did you see the England-Germany game?**
2 pack
□ Hast du ein Spiel Karten?**Do you have a pack of cards?**
■ ein Theaterspiel**a play**

★ **spielen** VERB [38]
to play
□ Die Kinder spielen im Garten.**The children are playing in the garden.** □ Wollen wir Tennis spielen?**Shall we play tennis?** □ Wer spielt der Hamlet?**Who's playing Hamlet?** □ Wir haben um Geld gespielt.**We played for money.**

spielend ADVERB
easily

der **Spieler**(PL die Spieler) MASC NOUN
1 player
□ Wir brauchen noch einen dritten Spieler.**We still need a third player.**
2 gambler
□ Er ist ein leidenschaftlicher Spieler.**He's a passionate gambler.**

das **Spielfeld**(PL die Spielfelder) NEUT NOUN
pitch

der **Spielfilm**(PL die Spielfilme) MASC NOUN
feature film

die **Spielkonsole** FEM NOUN
games console

★ der **Spielplatz**(GEN des Spielplatzes, PL die
Spielplätze) MASC NOUN
playground

die **Spielregel** FEM NOUN
rule
□ Ich erkläre euch die Spielregeln.**I'll explain the rules of the game to you.**

★ das **Spielzeug**(PL die Spielzeuge) NEUT
NOUN
toy

das **Spielzimmer**(PL die Spielzimmer)
NEUT NOUN
playroom

der **Spinat** MASC NOUN
spinach

die **Spinne** FEM NOUN
spider

spinnen(IMPERFECT spann, PERFECT TENSE hat
gesponnen) VERB
1 to spin
□ Wolle spinnen**to spin wool**
2 to be crazy
□ Du spinnst wohl!**You're crazy!**

die **Spionage** FEM NOUN
espionage

★ = core vocabulary

spionieren (PERFECT TENSE **hat spioniert**)
VERB [76]
to spy

spitz ADJECTIVE
pointed
- **ein spitzer Winkel** an acute angle
- **eine spitze Zunge** a sharp tongue
- **eine spitze Bemerkung** a caustic remark

★ **spitze** ADJECTIVE
great (*Umgangssprache*)
- **Das war spitze!** That was great!

★ die **Spitze** FEM NOUN
1 point
□ Die Spitze des Bleistifts ist abgebrochen. The point of the pencil has broken off.
2 peak
□ Die Spitzen der Berge waren schneebedeckt. The peaks of the mountains were covered with snow.
3 top
□ Welche Mannschaft liegt an der Spitze? Which team is top?
4 lace
□ An ihrem Kleid war ein Kragen aus Spitze. Her dress had a lace collar.

★ der **Spitzer** (PL die **Spitzer**) MASC NOUN
pencil sharpener

der **Spitzname** (GEN des **Spitznamens**, PL die **Spitznamen**) MASC NOUN
nickname

der **Splitter** (PL die **Splitter**) MASC NOUN
splinter

sponsern VERB [88]
to sponsor

★ der **Sport** MASC NOUN
sport

★ die **Sportart** FEM NOUN
sport
□ verschiedene Sportarten various sports

der **Sportler** (PL die **Sportler**) MASC NOUN
sportsman

die **Sportlerin** FEM NOUN
sportswoman

★ **sportlich** ADJECTIVE
sporty
□ Amina ist sehr sportlich. Amina is very sporty.

★ der **Sportplatz** (GEN des **Sportplatzes**, PL die **Sportplätze**) MASC NOUN
sports field

der **Sportschuh** (PL die **Sportschuhe**) MASC NOUN
trainer

★ der **Sportverein** (PL die **Sportvereine**) MASC NOUN
sports club

★ das **Sportzentrum** (PL die **Sportzentren**) NEUT NOUN
sports centre

sprach VERB ▷ *see* **sprechen**

★ die **Sprache** FEM NOUN
language

der **Sprachführer** (PL die **Sprachführer**) MASC NOUN
phrase book

★ das **Sprachlabor** (PL die **Sprachlabors** or **Sprachlabore**) NEUT NOUN
language laboratory

sprachlich ADJECTIVE
linguistic

sprachlos ADJECTIVE
speechless

die **Sprachsteuerung** FEM NOUN
voice control

sprang VERB ▷ *see* **springen**

★ **sprechen** (PRESENT TENSE **spricht**, IMPERFECT **sprach**, PERFECT TENSE **hat gesprochen**) VERB [70]
1 to talk
□ Seid bitte ruhig, wenn ich spreche. Please be quiet, I'm talking. □ Du sprichst so leise. You talk so quietly. □ Wir haben von dir gesprochen. We were talking about you.
2 to say
□ Sie hat kein Wort gesprochen. She didn't say a word.
3 to speak
□ Ich spreche Italienisch ziemlich schlecht. I speak Italian pretty badly.
- **jemanden sprechen** to speak to somebody
□ Der Direktor will dich sprechen. The headmaster wants to speak to you.
- **mit jemandem über etwas sprechen** to speak to somebody about something
- **Das spricht für ihn.** That's a point in his favour.

★ die **Sprechstunde** FEM NOUN
surgery (*doctor's*)

spricht VERB ▷ *see* **sprechen**

das **Sprichwort** (PL die **Sprichwörter**) NEUT NOUN
proverb

★ **springen** (IMPERFECT **sprang**, PERFECT TENSE **ist gesprungen**) VERB [71]
1 to jump
□ Er sprang über den Zaun. He jumped over the fence.
2 to crack
□ Das Glas ist gesprungen. The glass has cracked.

★ die **Spritze** FEM NOUN
1 syringe
□ Die Spritze muss steril sein. The syringe has to be sterile.
2 injection
□ Der Arzt hat mir eine Spritze gegeben. The doctor gave me an injection.

S

Numbers in brackets refer to verb tables on pages 697 to 706.

259

spritzen – Stachel

3 nozzle
□ Die Spritze am Gartenschlauch ist nicht dicht. The nozzle on the garden hose leaks.

spritzen (PERFECT TENSE **hat/ist gespritzt**) VERB [36]

> Use **haben** to form the perfect tense. Use **sein** to form the perfect tense for 'to spurt out'.

1 to spray
□ Er hat sein Fahrrad grün gespritzt. He's sprayed his bike green.
■ **den Garten spritzen** to water the garden
■ **jemanden nass spritzen** to splash somebody

2 to spurt out
□ Das Blut spritzte aus der Wunde. The blood spurted out of the wound.

★ der **Sprudel** (PL die **Sprudel**) MASC NOUN
mineral water
■ **süßer Sprudel** lemonade

die **Sprühdose** FEM NOUN
spray can

sprühen (PERFECT TENSE **hat/ist gesprüht**) VERB [38]

> For the perfect tense use **haben** when the verb has an object and **sein** when there is no object. Use **haben** to form the perfect tense for 'to sparkle'.

1 to spray
□ Sie hat einen Spruch an die Wand gesprüht. She sprayed a comment on the wall.

2 to fly
□ In alle Richtungen sind Funken gesprüht. Sparks flew in all directions.

3 to sparkle
□ Sie hat gestern Abend vor Witz gesprüht. She was sparkling with humour yesterday evening.

der **Sprung** (PL die **Sprünge**) MASC NOUN

1 jump
□ Das war ein weiter Sprung. That was a long jump.

2 crack
□ Die Tasse hat einen Sprung. There is a crack in the cup.

das **Sprungbrett** (PL die **Sprungbretter**) NEUT NOUN
springboard

spucken VERB [38]
to spit

die **Spüle** FEM NOUN
kitchen sink

spülen VERB [38]

1 to rinse
□ Wollsachen muss man gut spülen. Woollens have to be rinsed well.

2 to wash up
□ Wenn du spülst, dann trockne ich ab. If you wash up I'll dry.

die **Spülmaschine** FEM NOUN
dishwasher

das **Spülmittel** (PL die **Spülmittel**) NEUT NOUN
washing-up liquid

die **Spur** FEM NOUN

1 track
□ Wir sahen Spuren im Sand. We saw tracks in the sand.

2 lane
□ Der Fahrer vor mir hat plötzlich die Spur gewechselt. The driver in front of me suddenly changed lane.

3 trace
□ Auf ihrem Gesicht sah man die Spuren der Anstrengung. You could see the traces of strain on her face.
■ **eine Bremsspur** skidmarks *pl*

4 trail
□ Die Polizei verfolgte seine Spur. The police followed his trail.
■ **Das Essen war eine Spur zu scharf.** The meal was a touch too spicy.

spüren VERB [38]
to feel

★ der **Staat** (PL die **Staaten**) MASC NOUN
state
■ **die Vereinigten Staaten von Amerika** the United States of America

staatlich ADJECTIVE

1 state
□ staatliche Fördermittel state subsidies □ eine staatliche Schule a state school

2 state-run
□ eine staatliche Einrichtung a state-run organization

die **Staatsangehörigkeit** FEM NOUN
nationality

stabil ADJECTIVE

1 stable
□ Die Lage ist stabil. The situation is stable.
□ Sie ist psychisch stabil. She's mentally stable.

2 sturdy
□ stabile Möbel sturdy furniture

der **Stachel** (PL die **Stacheln**) MASC NOUN

1 spike
□ Ich habe mir die Hose an einem Stachel aufgerissen. I've torn my trousers on a spike.

2 spine
□ Ein Igel hat Stacheln. A hedgehog has spines.
□ Dieser Kaktus hat lange Stacheln. This cactus has long spines.

3 sting
□ Ich habe versucht, den Stachel der Biene herauszuziehen. I tried to take the bee sting out.

★ = core vocabulary

die **Stachelbeere** FEM NOUN
gooseberry

der **Stacheldraht** (PL die **Stacheldrähte**)
MASC NOUN
barbed wire

★ das **Stadion** (PL die **Stadien**) NEUT NOUN
stadium

★ die **Stadt** (PL die **Städte**) FEM NOUN
town

städtisch ADJECTIVE
municipal

★ der **Stadtkreis** (PL die **Stadtkreise**) MASC
NOUN
town borough

★ die **Stadtmitte** FEM NOUN
town centre

★ der **Stadtplan** (PL die **Stadtpläne**) MASC
NOUN
street map

★ der **Stadtrand** (PL die **Stadtränder**) MASC
NOUN
outskirts pl

★ die **Stadtrundfahrt** FEM NOUN
tour of the city

★ der **Stadtteil** (PL die **Stadtteile**) MASC NOUN
part of town

★ das **Stadtzentrum** (PL die **Stadtzentren**)
NEUT NOUN
city centre

stahl VERB ▷ see **stehlen**

★ der **Stahl** MASC NOUN
steel

der **Stall** (PL die **Ställe**) MASC NOUN
stable
□ Die Pferde sind im Stall. The horses are in the
stable.
■ **ein Hühnerstall** a henhouse

der **Stamm** (PL die **Stämme**) MASC NOUN
1 trunk
□ Der Baum hat einen dicken Stamm. The tree
has a thick trunk.
2 tribe
□ Er gehört zu einem uralten Stamm. He
belongs to an ancient tribe.
3 stem
□ Die Endung wird an den Stamm des Verbs
angehängt. The ending's added to the stem of
the verb.

★ **stammen** VERB [38]
■ **stammen aus** to come from

der **Stammgast** (PL die **Stammgäste**) MASC
NOUN
regular customer

der **Stammtisch** (PL die **Stammtische**)
MASC NOUN
table for the regulars

stand VERB ▷ see **stehen**

★ der **Stand** (PL die **Stände**) MASC NOUN
1 state
□ Was ist der Stand der Dinge? What's the state
of things?
2 score
□ Sie sind beim Stand von eins zu eins in die
Pause. The score was one all at half-time.
3 stand
□ An welchem Stand hast du den Luftballon
gekauft? Which stand did you buy the balloon
at?
4 level
□ Prüf mal den Ölstand. Check the oil level.
■ **zu Stande** ▷ see **zustande**

ständig ADJECTIVE
constant
□ Musst du ständig stören? Do you constantly
have to interrupt?

der **Standort** (PL die **Standorte**) MASC NOUN
location

der **Stapel** (PL die **Stapel**) MASC NOUN
pile

starb VERB ▷ see **sterben**

★ **stark** ADJECTIVE
1 strong
□ Mein Bruder ist stärker als du. My brother's
stronger than you.
2 heavy
□ starke Regenfälle heavy rain
■ **starke Kopfschmerzen** a splitting
headache
3 great (Umgangssprache)
□ Das war stark! That was great!

der **Start** (PL die **Starts**) MASC NOUN
1 start
□ Es waren über hundert Läufer am Start. There
were over a hundred runners at the start.
2 takeoff
□ Die Maschine war bereit zum Start. The
machine was ready for takeoff.

★ **starten** VERB [2]
1 to start
□ Wann startet das Rennen? When does the
race start?
2 to take off
□ Das Flugzeug startet gleich. The plane is
about to take off.

die **Startseite** (PL die **Startseiten**) FEM NOUN
home page

★ **statt** CONJUNCTION, PREPOSITION
The preposition statt takes the genitive or
the dative.

S

stattfinden – Steinbock

instead of
□ Statt nach Hause zu gehen, sind wir noch in die Disco. Instead of going home, we went to the disco. □ Sie kam statt ihres Bruders. She came instead of her brother.

★ **stattfinden** (IMPERFECT **TENSE fand statt**, PERFECT **TENSE hat stattgefunden**) VERB [24]
to take place

★ **der Stau** (PL die **Staus**) MASC NOUN
traffic jam
□ Wir sind im Stau stecken geblieben. We were stuck in a traffic jam.

der Staub MASC NOUN
dust
■ **Staub wischen** to dust

staubig ADJECTIVE
dusty

staubsaugen (PERFECT TENSE **hat staubgesaugt**) VERB [38]
to hoover

★ **der Staubsauger** (PL die **Staubsauger**)
MASC NOUN
vacuum cleaner

staunen VERB [38]
to be astonished

Std. ABBREVIATION (= *Stunde*)
hr.

★ **stechen** (PRESENT TENSE **sticht**, IMPERFECT **stach**, PERFECT TENSE **hat gestochen**) VERB
1 to prick
□ Ich habe mich mit der Nadel gestochen. I've pricked myself with the needle.
2 to sting
□ Mich hat eine Biene gestochen. A bee stung me.
3 to bite
□ Reibe dich ein, damit du nicht gestochen wirst. Rub something on so that you won't be bitten.

★ **die Steckdose** FEM NOUN
socket

★ **stecken** VERB [48]
1 to put
□ Sie steckte ihren Geldbeutel in die Tasche. She put her purse in her bag.
2 to insert
□ Stecken Sie die Münze in den Schlitz. Insert the coin into the slot.
3 to stick
□ Steck deinen Finger nicht in das Loch! Don't stick your finger in the hole.
4 to pin
□ Ich steckte das Abzeichen an meine Jacke. I pinned the badge onto my jacket.
5 to be stuck
□ Wir stecken im Stau. We are stuck in a traffic jam.
■ **Wo steckt sie nur?** Where on earth is she?

der Stecker (PL die **Stecker**) MASC NOUN
plug

die Stecknadel FEM NOUN
pin

★ **das Stehcafé** (PL die **Stehcafés**) NEUT NOUN
small area with tables but no seating in a bakery or supermarket café

★ **stehen** (IMPERFECT **stand**, PERFECT TENSE **hat gestanden**) VERB [72]
1 to stand
□ Es war so voll, dass wir stehen mussten. It was so full that we had to stand.
2 to be
□ Vor unserem Haus steht eine Kastanie. There's a chestnut tree in front of our house.
3 to say
□ In der Zeitung steht, dass das Wetter besser wird. It says in the newspaper that the weather will improve.
■ **zum Stehen kommen** to come to a halt
□ Der Verkehr kam zum Stehen. The traffic came to a halt.
■ **Es steht schlecht um ihn.** Things are bad for him.
■ **jemandem stehen** to suit somebody □ Blau steht dir gut. Blue suits you.
■ **Wie steht's? 1** How are things? **2** What's the score?
■ **stehen bleiben** to stop □ Meine Uhr ist stehen geblieben. My watch has stopped.

★ **die Stehlampe** FEM NOUN
standard lamp

★ **stehlen** (PRESENT TENSE **stiehlt**, IMPERFECT **stahl**, PERFECT TENSE **hat gestohlen**) VERB [73]
to steal

steif ADJECTIVE
stiff

★ **steigen** (IMPERFECT **stieg**, PERFECT TENSE **ist gestiegen**) VERB [74]
1 to rise
□ Der Ballon stieg zum Himmel. The balloon rose into the sky.
2 to climb
□ Sie ist auf die Leiter gestiegen. She climbed up the ladder.
■ **in etwas steigen** to get into something □ Er stieg ins Auto. He got into the car.
■ **Sie stieg in den Zug.** She got on the train.
■ **auf etwas steigen** to get on something
□ Sie stieg aufs Fahrrad. She got on her bike.

die Steigung FEM NOUN
incline

★ **steil** ADJECTIVE
steep

★ **der Stein** (PL die **Steine**) MASC NOUN
stone

der Steinbock (PL die **Steinböcke**) MASC NOUN
Capricorn
□ Er ist Steinbock. He's Capricorn.

steinig ADJECTIVE
stony

★ die **Stelle** FEM NOUN
1 place
□ Ich habe mir die Stelle im Buch angestrichen. I've marked the place in the book.
■ **an dieser Stelle** here
2 job
□ Ich suche eine neue Stelle. I'm looking for a new job.
3 office
□ Bei welcher Stelle kann man einen Pass bekommen? In which office can you get a passport?
■ **An deiner Stelle würde ich das nicht tun.** I wouldn't do it if I were you.

★ **stellen** VERB [38]
1 to put
□ Ich habe die Vase auf den Tisch gestellt. I put the vase on the table.
2 to set
□ Stell deine Uhr nach meiner. Set your watch by mine.
3 to supply
□ Die Lehrbücher werden gestellt. The course books will be supplied.
■ **sich irgendwohin stellen** to stand somewhere □ Stellt euch bitte an die Wand. Please stand against the wall.
■ **sich stellen** to give oneself up □ Der Dieb hat sich gestellt. The thief gave himself up.
■ **sich dumm stellen** to pretend to be stupid

★ die **Stellenanzeige** FEM NOUN
job advertisement

die **Stellung** FEM NOUN
position
□ In welcher Stellung schläfst du? Which position do you sleep in? □ Er hat eine gute Stellung. He has a good position.
■ **zu etwas Stellung nehmen** to comment on something

der **Stellvertreter** (PL die **Stellvertreter**) MASC NOUN
deputy

der **Stempel** (PL die **Stempel**) MASC NOUN
stamp

stempeln VERB [34]
to stamp
■ **jemanden zum Sündenbock stempeln** to make somebody a scapegoat

★ **sterben** (PRESENT TENSE **stirbt**, IMPERFECT **starb**, PERFECT TENSE **ist gestorben**) VERB [75]
to die

★ die **Stereoanlage** FEM NOUN
stereo

★ der **Stern** (PL die **Sterne**) MASC NOUN
star
□ die Sterne am Himmel the stars in the sky

das **Sternzeichen** (PL die **Sternzeichen**) NEUT NOUN
star sign
□ Was ist dein Sternzeichen? What star sign are you?

★ das **Steuer** (PL die **Steuer**) NEUT NOUN
▷ see also die **Steuer** NOUN
wheel
□ Wer saß am Steuer? Who was at the wheel?

die **Steuer** FEM NOUN
▷ see also das **Steuer** NOUN
tax
□ Wir müssen viel Steuern bezahlen. We have to pay a lot of tax.

★ das **Steuerrad** (PL die **Steuerräder**) NEUT NOUN
steering wheel

★ der **Stich** (PL die **Stiche**) MASC NOUN
1 bite
□ Das Mittel schützt vor Stichen. This gives protection from bites. □ ein Mückenstich a midge bite
■ **ein Bienenstich** a bee sting
2 stab
□ Er tötete sie mit zwölf Stichen. He killed her by stabbing her twelve times.
3 stitch
□ Sie hat den Aufhänger mit ein paar Stichen angenäht. She sewed on the loop with a couple of stitches. □ Die Wunde wurde mit drei Stichen genäht. Three stitches were put in the wound.
4 engraving
□ ein Kupferstich a copper engraving
■ **jemanden im Stich lassen** to leave somebody in the lurch

sticken VERB [38]
to embroider

der **Stickstoff** MASC NOUN
nitrogen

★ der **Stiefel** (PL die **Stiefel**) MASC NOUN
boot

das **Stiefkind** (PL die **Stiefkinder**) NEUT NOUN
stepchild

★ die **Stiefmutter** (PL die **Stiefmütter**) FEM NOUN
stepmother

★ der **Stiefvater** (PL die **Stiefväter**) MASC NOUN
stepfather

stiehlt VERB ▷ see **stehlen**

der **Stiel** (PL die **Stiele**) MASC NOUN
1 handle
□ der Stiel des Besens the broom handle
2 stem
□ Er hat den Stiel der Tulpe abgeknickt. He snapped the stem off the tulip.

S

Numbers in brackets refer to verb tables on pages 697 to 706.

263

Stier – Störung

der Stier (PL die Stiere) MASC NOUN
1 bull
  □ Der Stier wurde getötet. The bull was killed.
2 Taurus
  □ Brigitte ist Stier. Brigitte's Taurus.

★ **der Stift** (PL die Stifte) MASC NOUN
1 peg
  □ Das Brett wird mit Stiften an der Wand befestigt. The board is fixed to the wall with pegs.
2 crayon
  □ Sebastian hat lauter bunte Stifte bekommen. Sebastian got lots of coloured crayons.
3 pencil
  □ Schreib lieber mit Kuli als mit einem Stift. I'd rather you wrote with a Biro than a pencil.

stiften VERB [2]
  ■ Sie hat eine Runde Eis gestiftet. She bought us all an ice cream.
  ■ Unruhe stiften to cause trouble

der Stil (PL die Stile) MASC NOUN
  style

★ **still** ADJECTIVE
  quiet
  □ Seid mal still. Be quiet.
  ■ Sie stand ganz still. She stood quite still.

★ **die Stille** FEM NOUN
  quietness
  ■ in aller Stille quietly

stillhalten (PRESENT TENSE hält still, IMPERFECT hielt still, PERFECT TENSE hat stillgehalten) VERB [33]
  to keep still

stillschweigend ADVERB
  tacitly

★ **die Stimme** FEM NOUN
1 voice
  □ Er hat eine laute Stimme. He has a loud voice.
2 vote
  □ Er bekam nur zwanzig Stimmen. He only got twenty votes.
  ■ Wem hast du deine Stimme gegeben? Who did you vote for?

★ **stimmen** VERB [38]
1 to be right
  □ Die Übersetzung stimmt nicht. The translation isn't right. □ Das stimmt nicht! That's not right!
2 to tune
  □ ein Instrument stimmen to tune an instrument
3 to vote
  □ stimmen für to vote for □ stimmen gegen to vote against
  ■ Stimmt so! Keep the change.

die Stimmung FEM NOUN
  mood

★ **stinken** (IMPERFECT stank, PERFECT TENSE hat gestunken) VERB
  to stink

das Stipendium (PL die Stipendien) NEUT NOUN
  grant

stirbt VERB ▷ see sterben

★ **die Stirn** FEM NOUN
  forehead

★ **der Stock (1)** (PL die Stöcke) MASC NOUN
  stick
  □ Er hat ihn mit einem Stock geschlagen. He hit him with a stick.

★ **der Stock (2)** (PL die Stock or Stockwerke) MASC NOUN
  floor
  □ Wir wohnen im dritten Stock. We live on the third floor.

★ **der Stoff** (PL die Stoffe) MASC NOUN
1 fabric
  □ Das ist ein hübscher Stoff. That's a pretty fabric.
2 material
  □ Ich sammle Stoff für mein Referat. I'm collecting material for my assignment.

stöhnen VERB [38]
  to groan

stolpern (PERFECT TENSE ist gestolpert) VERB [88]
1 to stumble
  □ Er ist gestolpert und gefallen. He stumbled and fell.
2 to trip
  □ Er ist über einen Stein gestolpert. He tripped over a stone.

★ **stolz** ADJECTIVE
  proud
  □ Ich bin stolz auf dich. I'm proud of you.

stören VERB [38]
  to disturb
  □ Störe ich? Am I disturbing you? □ Ich will nicht länger stören. I won't disturb you any longer.
  ■ Stört es dich, wenn ich das Fenster aufmache? Do you mind if I open the window?
  ■ Die Leitung war gestört. It was a bad line.
  ■ sich an etwas stören to worry about something □ Stör dich nicht an der Schrift, der Inhalt ist wichtig. Don't worry about the writing it's the content that counts.

störend ADJECTIVE
  disturbing

die Störung FEM NOUN
1 interruption
  □ Diese dauernden Störungen regen mich auf. These constant interruptions are getting on my nerves.

★ = core vocabulary

2 interference

□ Es war eine Störung beim Bild. There was interference to the picture.

stoßen (PRESENT TENSE **stößt**, IMPERFECT **stieß**, PERFECT TENSE **hat gestoßen**) VERB

■ **den Kopf an etwas stoßen** to bump one's head on something □ Ich habe mir an der niedrigen Decke den Kopf gestoßen. I bumped my head on the low ceiling.

■ **sich stoßen** to bump oneself □ Sie hat einen blauen Fleck, wo sie sich gestoßen hat. She has a bruise where she bumped herself.

■ **sich an etwas stoßen** to take exception to something □ Sie hat sich an seinem schlechten Benehmen gestoßen. She took exception to his bad behaviour.

■ **an etwas stoßen** to bump into something □ Pass auf, dass du nicht an die Statue stößt. Watch out that you don't bump into the statue.

■ **auf etwas stoßen** to come across □ Heute bin ich auf dem Flohmarkt auf ein tolles Buch gestoßen. I came across a great book at the flea market today.

stottern VERB [88]
to stutter

Str. ABBREVIATION (= *Straße*)
St

die **Strafarbeit** FEM NOUN
lines *pl*
□ Ich habe eine Strafarbeit bekommen. I got lines.

die **Strafe** FEM NOUN

1 punishment
□ Zur Strafe müsst ihr länger bleiben. You'll be kept in after school as a punishment.
■ **eine Gefängnisstrafe** a prison sentence

2 fine
□ Er musste eine Strafe von fünfzig Euro bezahlen. He had to pay a fifty euro fine.

der **Strahl** (PL die **Strahlen**) MASC NOUN

1 ray
□ radioaktive Strahlen radioactive rays □ ein Sonnenstrahl a ray of sunlight
■ **ein Lichtstrahl** a beam of light

2 jet
□ ein Wasserstrahl a jet of water

strahlen VERB [38]

1 to shine
□ Die Sterne strahlten hell. The stars shone brightly.

2 to beam
□ Sie strahlte, als sie das hörte. She beamed when she heard that.

die **Strahlung** FEM NOUN
radiation

der **Strand** (PL die **Strände**) MASC NOUN

1 beach
□ Wir haben den ganzen Tag am Strand gelegen. We lay on the beach all day.

2 shore
□ Das wurde an den Strand gespült. That was washed up on the shore.

strapazieren (PERFECT TENSE **hat strapaziert**) VERB [76]

1 to be hard on
□ Du hast heute deinen Computer ganz schön strapaziert. You've been really hard on your computer today.

2 to wear out
□ Die Wanderung hat uns ziemlich strapaziert. The walk has really worn us out.

die **Straße** FEM NOUN

1 street
□ In welcher Straße wohnt Thomas? Which street does Thomas live in?

2 road
□ Wir sind die Straße entlang der Küste gefahren. We drove along the coast road.

die **Straßenbahn** FEM NOUN
tram

der **Strauß (1)** (GEN des **Straußes**, PL die **Sträuße**) MASC NOUN
bunch of flowers
□ Wir haben unserer Gastgeberin einen Strauß mitgebracht. We brought our hostess a bunch of flowers.

der **Strauß (2)** (GEN des **Straußes**, PL die **Strauße**) MASC NOUN
ostrich

die **Strecke** FEM NOUN

1 distance
□ Wir haben diese Strecke an einem Tag zurückgelegt. We covered this distance in one day. □ Bis zu ihm ist es noch eine ziemliche Strecke. It's still quite a distance to his place.

2 line
□ Auf der Strecke zwischen Stuttgart und Ulm gab es ein Zugunglück. There's been a train accident on the Stuttgart to Ulm line.

streicheln VERB [88]
to stroke

streichen (IMPERFECT **strich**, PERFECT TENSE **hat gestrichen**) VERB

1 to stroke
□ Sie strich über seine Haare. She stroked his hair.

2 to spread
□ Sie strich Honig aufs Brot. She spread honey on the bread.

3 to paint
□ Ich muss dringend mein Zimmer streichen. I really must paint my room.

4 to delete
□ Den zweiten Satz kannst du streichen. You can delete the second sentence.

5 to cancel
□ Der Direktor hat den Schulausflug gestrichen. The headmaster has cancelled the school trip.

S

★ das **Streichholz** (GEN des Streichholzes, PL
die **Streichhölzer**) NEUT NOUN
match

der **Streifen** (PL die Streifen) MASC NOUN
strip

der **Streik** (PL die Streiks) MASC NOUN
strike

streiken VERB [38]
to go on strike
■ Sie streiken. They're on strike.

★ der **Streit** (PL die Streite) MASC NOUN
argument

★ sich **streiten** (IMPERFECT stritt, PERFECT TENSE
hat gestritten) VERB
to argue
□ Sie streiten sich ständig. They argue
constantly.
■ Darüber lässt sich streiten. That's
debatable.

★ **streng** ADJECTIVE
1 strict
□ Meine Eltern sind furchtbar streng. My
parents are terribly strict.
2 severe
□ Es war ein strenger Winter. It was a severe
winter. □ Das wird streng bestraft. That will be
severely punished.
3 sharp
□ Wo kommt der strenge Geruch her? Where's
that sharp smell coming from?

★ der **Stress** (GEN des Stresses) MASC NOUN
stress
■ Ich bin im Stress! I'm stressed out.
(Umgangssprache)

stressen (PRESENT TENSE stresst, IMPERFECT
stresste, PERFECT TENSE hat gestresst) VERB
[48]
to put under stress

stressig ADJECTIVE
stressful

der **Strich** (PL die Striche) MASC NOUN
1 line
□ Mach einen Strich unter die Spalte. Draw a
line under the column.
2 stroke
□ Mit ein paar Strichen zeichnete er ein Haus.
He drew a house with a couple of strokes.

der **Strichkode** (PL die Strichkodes) MASC
NOUN
bar code

der **Strichpunkt** (PL die Strichpunkte)
MASC NOUN
semicolon

der **Strick** (PL die Stricke) MASC NOUN
rope

★ **stricken** VERB [48]
to knit

das **Stroh** NEUT NOUN
straw

★ der **Strohhalm** (PL die Strohhalme) MASC
NOUN
drinking straw

★ der **Strom** (PL die Ströme) MASC NOUN
1 current
□ der Wechselstrom alternating current
■ Vorsicht, auf dem Draht ist Strom. Be
careful, the wire is live.
2 electricity
□ Sie haben den Strom abgeschaltet. They've
cut off the electricity.
3 stream
□ Ein Strom von Zuschauern kam aus dem
Stadion. A stream of spectators was coming ou
of the stadium.
4 (large) river
□ Der Rhein ist ein Strom. The Rhine is a river.

die **Strömung** FEM NOUN
current

★ der **Strumpf** (PL die Strümpfe) MASC NOUN
stocking

★ die **Strumpfhose** FEM NOUN
tights pl
□ eine Strumpfhose a pair of tights

das **Stück** (PL die Stücke) NEUT NOUN
1 piece
□ Sie schnitt ein Stück Käse ab. She cut off a
piece of cheese.
2 play
□ Wir haben ein Stück von Brecht angesehen.
We saw a play by Brecht.

das **Stückchen** (PL die Stückchen) NEUT
NOUN
little piece

★ der **Student** (GEN des Studenten, PL die
Studenten) MASC NOUN
student
□ Ich vermiete die Wohnung an einen
Studenten. I rent the flat to a student.

★ die **Studentin** FEM NOUN
student

★ **studieren** (PERFECT TENSE hat studiert) VERB
[76]
to study
□ Mein Bruder studiert Physik. My brother's
studying physics.

★ das **Studium** (PL die Studien) NEUT NOUN
studies pl

die **Stufe** FEM NOUN
1 step
□ Vorsicht, Stufe! Mind the step!
2 stage
□ Er hat bereits eine fortgeschrittene Stufe
erreicht. He's already reached an advanced
stage. □ eine Entwicklungsstufe a stage of
development

★ = core vocabulary

der Stuhl (PL die **Stühle**) MASC NOUN
chair

stumm ADJECTIVE
1 silent
□ Sie blieb stumm. **She remained silent.**
2 with a speech impairment

stumpf ADJECTIVE
blunt
□ Er wurde mit einem stumpfen Gegenstand am Kopf getroffen. **He was hit on the head with a blunt object.**
■ **ein stumpfer Winkel** an obtuse angle

die Stunde FEM NOUN
1 hour
□ Ich komme in einer Stunde. **I'll come in an hour.**
2 lesson
□ Was haben wir in der letzten Stunde behandelt? **What did we do in the last lesson?**

der Stundenplan (PL die **Stundenpläne**) MASC NOUN
timetable

stündlich ADJECTIVE
hourly
□ stündlich verkehren to run hourly

stur ADJECTIVE
obstinate

der Sturm (PL die **Stürme**) MASC NOUN
storm

stürmen (PERFECT TENSE ist/hat gestürmt) VERB [38]

Use sein to form the perfect tense for 'to storm (out)'. Use haben to form the perfect tense for all other meanings.

to storm
□ Er ist aus dem Zimmer gestürmt. **He stormed out of the room.** □ Die Polizei hat das Gebäude gestürmt. **The police stormed the building.**
■ **Es stürmt.** There's a gale blowing.

stürmisch ADJECTIVE
stormy

der Sturz (GEN des **Sturzes**, PL die **Stürze**) MASC NOUN
1 fall
□ Bei dem Sturz hat sie sich das Bein gebrochen. **She broke her leg in the fall.**
2 overthrow
□ Alle freuten sich über den Sturz des Diktators. **Everybody was pleased about the overthrow of the dictator.**

stürzen (PERFECT TENSE hat/ist gestürzt) VERB [36]

Use sein to form the perfect tense. Use haben to form the perfect tense for 'to overthrow' and for sich stürzen.

1 to fall
□ Sie ist vom Pferd gestürzt. **She fell off a horse.**
2 to rush
□ Er kam ins Zimmer gestürzt. **He rushed into the room.**
3 to overthrow
□ Die Regierung wurde gestürzt. **The government has been overthrown.**
■ **sich stürzen** to plunge □ Sie stürzte sich ins Wasser. **She plunged into the water.**

der Sturzhelm (PL die **Sturzhelme**) MASC NOUN
crash helmet

die Stütze FEM NOUN
support

das Subjekt (PL die **Subjekte**) NEUT NOUN
subject

das Substantiv (PL die **Substantive**) NEUT NOUN
noun

subtrahieren (PERFECT TENSE hat subtrahiert) VERB [76]
to subtract

die Suche FEM NOUN
search

★**suchen** VERB [48]
to look for
□ Ich suche meinen Radiergummi. **I'm looking for my rubber.** □ Wir haben gesucht, es aber nicht gefunden. **We looked for it but couldn't find it.** □ Er wird von der Polizei gesucht. **The police are looking for him.**
■ **nach etwas suchen** to look for something
□ Wonach suchst du? **What are you looking for?**

die Suchmaschine FEM NOUN
search engine (internet)

süchtig ADJECTIVE
addicted
□ kaffeesüchtig addicted to coffee

der/die Süchtige (GEN des/der **Süchtigen**, PL die **Süchtigen**) MASC/FEM NOUN
addict

Südafrika NEUT NOUN
South Africa
■ **aus Südafrika** from South Africa
■ **nach Südafrika** to South Africa

Südamerika NEUT NOUN
South America
■ **aus Südamerika** from South America
■ **nach Südamerika** to South America

★**der Süden** MASC NOUN
south

★**südlich** ADJECTIVE, PREPOSITION, ADVERB
southerly
□ in südlicher Richtung in a southerly direction
■ **südlich einer Sache** to the south of something □ Das Kraftwerk liegt südlich der

S

Südosten - Szene

Stadt.The power station's to south of the city.
■ **südlich von**south of □ Das liegt südlich von
Rom.It is south of Rome.

der **Südosten** MASC NOUN
southeast

der **Südpol** MASC NOUN
South Pole
□ am Südpolat the South Pole

der **Südwesten** MASC NOUN
southwest

die **Summe** FEM NOUN
total

summen VERB [38]
1 to buzz
□ Die Bienen summten.The bees were buzzing.
2 to hum
□ Sie summte vor sich hin.She was humming.
□ Er hat ein Lied gesummt.He hummed a song.

die **Sünde** FEM NOUN
sin

★ das **Superbenzin** NEUT NOUN
four-star petrol

der **Superlativ**(PL die Superlative) MASC
NOUN
superlative

★ der **Supermarkt**(PL die Supermärkte)
MASC NOUN
supermarket

★ die **Suppe** FEM NOUN
soup

★ das **Surfbrett**(PL die Surfbretter) NEUT
NOUN
surfboard

★ **surfen**(PERFECT TENSE hat gesurft) VERB [38]
to surf
■ im Internet surfento surf the Net

süß ADJECTIVE
sweet

die **Süßigkeit** FEM NOUN
sweet

□ Sie isst gern Süßigkeiten.She likes eating
sweets.

der **Süßstoff**(PL die Süßstoffe) MASC NOUN
sweetener

die **Süßwaren** PL NOUN
confectionery *sing*

der **Süßwarenladen**(PL die
Süßwarenläden) MASC NOUN
sweetshop

das **Symbol**(PL die Symbole) NEUT NOUN
symbol

symmetrisch ADJECTIVE
symmetrical

die **Sympathie** FEM NOUN
fondness
□ Ihre Sympathie für ihn ist offensichtlich.Her
fondness for him is obvious.

★ **sympathisch** ADJECTIVE
likeable
□ Er ist ein sympathischer Mensch.He's a
likeable person.
■ Er ist mir sympathisch.I like him.

BE CAREFUL!
sympathischdoes not mean **sympathetic**.

★ **synchronisieren**(PERFECT TENSE hat
synchronisiert) VERB [76]
to dub
□ ein synchronisierter Filma dubbed film

das **Synonym**(PL die Synonyme) NEUT NOUN
synonym

synthetisch ADJECTIVE
synthetic

das **System**(PL die Systeme) NEUT NOUN
system

systematisch ADJECTIVE
systematic

die **Szene** FEM NOUN
scene

Tt

★ der **Tabak**(PL die **Tabake**) MASC NOUN
tobacco

die **Tabelle** FEM NOUN
table

das **Tablet**(PL die **Tablets**) NEUT NOUN
tablet (*computer*)

das **Tablett**(PL die **Tablette**) NEUT NOUN
tray

★ die **Tablette** FEM NOUN
tablet

der **Tachometer**(PL die **Tachometer**) MASC
NOUN
speedometer

tadellos ADJECTIVE
faultless

★ die **Tafel** FEM NOUN
1 blackboard
□ Der Lehrer schrieb das Wort an die Tafel. The teacher wrote the word on the blackboard.
2 foodbank
□ Die Tafeln in Deutschland arbeiten am Limit. Foodbanks in Germany are working at full capacity.
■ **eine Tafel Schokolade** a bar of chocolate

★ der **Tag**(PL die **Tage**) MASC NOUN
1 day
□ Ich war den ganzen Tag weg. I was away all day.
2 daylight
□ Wir möchten noch bei Tag ankommen. We want to arrive in daylight.
■ **an den Tag kommen** to come to light
■ **Guten Tag!** Hello!

das **Tageblatt**(PL die **Tageblätter**) NEUT
NOUN
daily newspaper

★ das **Tagebuch**(PL die **Tagebücher**) NEUT
NOUN
diary
□ ein Tagebuch führen to keep a diary

★ **tagelang** ADVERB
for days

der **Tagesanbruch** MASC NOUN
dawn
□ bei Tagesanbruch at dawn

das **Tagesgericht**(PL die **Tagesgerichte**)
NEUT NOUN
dish of the day

★ die **Tageskarte** FEM NOUN
1 menu of the day
2 day ticket

★ das **Tageslicht** NEUT NOUN
daylight

die **Tageszeit** FEM NOUN
time of day

die **Tageszeitung** FEM NOUN
daily paper

★ **täglich** ADJECTIVE, ADVERB
daily

tagsüber ADVERB
during the day

die **Taille** FEM NOUN
waist

der **Takt**(PL die **Takte**) MASC NOUN
tact
□ Sie behandelte die Sache mit viel Takt. She showed great tact in dealing with the matter.
■ **keinen Takt haben** to be tactless
■ **den Takt angeben** to keep time □ Der Lehrer gab den Takt an. The teacher kept time.
■ **im Stundentakt** at hourly intervals

die **Taktik** FEM NOUN
tactics pl
□ Das ist die falsche Taktik. Those are the wrong tactics.

taktisch ADJECTIVE
tactical
□ Das war taktisch unklug. That was a tactical mistake.

taktlos ADJECTIVE
tactless

taktvoll ADJECTIVE
tactful

★ das **Tal**(PL die **Täler**) NEUT NOUN
valley

das **Talent**(PL die **Talente**) NEUT NOUN
talent

talentiert ADJECTIVE
talented

Numbers in brackets refer to verb tables on pages 697 to 706.

t

der **Tampon** (PL die **Tampons**) MASC NOUN
tampon

der **Tank** (PL die **Tanks**) MASC NOUN
tank

★ **tanken** VERB [38]
to get petrol
□ Wir müssen noch tanken. We still have to get
petrol.

★ die **Tankstelle** FEM NOUN
petrol station

die **Tanne** FEM NOUN
fir

der **Tannenzapfen** (PL die **Tannenzapfen**)
MASC NOUN
fir cone

★ die **Tante** FEM NOUN
aunt

★ der **Tanz** (GEN des **Tanzes**, PL die **Tänze**) MASC
NOUN
dance

★ **tanzen** VERB [36]
to dance

die **Tanzschule** FEM NOUN
dancing school

DID YOU KNOW...?
It is very common for German boys and girls
to go to a **Tanzschule** when they are about
14.

★ die **Tapete** FEM NOUN
wallpaper

★ **tapezieren** (PERFECT TENSE **hat tapeziert**)
VERB [76]
to wallpaper

★ **tapfer** ADJECTIVE
brave

die **Tapferkeit** FEM NOUN
bravery

★ die **Tasche** FEM NOUN
1 pocket
□ Er hatte die Hände in der Hosentasche. He
had his hands in his trouser pockets.
2 bag
□ Sie kann ihre Tasche nicht finden. She can't
find her bag.

★ das **Taschenbuch** (PL die **Taschenbücher**)
NEUT NOUN
paperback

★ der **Taschendieb** MASC NOUN
pickpocket

★ das **Taschengeld** (PL die **Taschengelder**)
NEUT NOUN
pocket money

★ die **Taschenlampe** FEM NOUN
torch

das **Taschenmesser** (PL die
Taschenmesser) NEUT NOUN
penknife

★ der **Taschenrechner** (PL die
Taschenrechner) MASC NOUN
pocket calculator

★ das **Taschentuch** (PL die **Taschentücher**)
NEUT NOUN
handkerchief

★ die **Tasse** FEM NOUN
cup
□ eine Tasse Tee a cup of tea

★ die **Tastatur** FEM NOUN
keyboard

★ die **Taste** FEM NOUN
1 button
□ Welche Taste muss ich drücken, um die
Waschmaschine anzustellen? What button do I
have to press to start the washing machine?
2 key
□ Bei der Computertastatur gibt es eine
Hochstelltaste. There's a shift key on the
computer keyboard.

tat VERB ▷ see **tun**

die **Tat** (PL die **Taten**) FEM NOUN
1 deed
□ Das war eine tapfere Tat. That was a brave
deed. □ eine gute Tat a good deed
2 crime
□ Der Beschuldigte hat die Tat gestanden. The
accused confessed to the crime.
■ in der Tat indeed

der **Täter** (PL die **Täter**) MASC NOUN
culprit

tätig ADJECTIVE
■ tätig sein to work □ Sie ist als Journalistin
tätig. She works as a journalist.

die **Tätigkeit** FEM NOUN
1 activity
□ kriminelle Tätigkeiten criminal activities
2 occupation
□ Welche Tätigkeit übt dein Vater aus? What's
your father's occupation?

tätowieren (PERFECT TENSE **hat tätowiert**)
VERB [76]
to tattoo

die **Tätowierung** FEM NOUN
tattoo

die **Tatsache** FEM NOUN
fact

tatsächlich ADJECTIVE, ADVERB
1 actual
□ Der tatsächliche Grund war ein anderer als
der, den sie angegeben hatte. The actual reason
was different from the one she gave.
2 really
□ Das hat sie tatsächlich gesagt. She really did
say that. □ Er ist tatsächlich rechtzeitig
gekommen. He really has come in time.

★ = core vocabulary

t

★ **taub** ADJECTIVE
deaf
□ Sie ist auf dem rechten Ohr taub. She's deaf in her right ear.

die **Taube** FEM NOUN
1 pigeon
□ die Tauben auf dem Marktplatz the pigeons in the market square
2 dove
□ die Friedenstaube the dove of peace

taubstumm ADJECTIVE
deaf-mute

★ **tauchen** (PERFECT TENSE hat/ist getaucht) VERB [48]

> Use **haben** for the perfect tense when you describe the activity and **sein** when you describe the motion.

1 to dip
□ Sie hat ihren Zeh ins Wasser getaucht. She dipped her toe into the water.
2 to dive
□ Als Kind habe ich viel getaucht. I used to dive a lot as a child. □ Er ist nach dem versunkenen Schatz getaucht. He dived in search of the sunken treasure.

tauen VERB [38]
■ Es taut. It's thawing.

die **Taufe** FEM NOUN
christening

taufen VERB [38]
to christen

taugen VERB [38]
■ nichts taugen to be no good □ Das Programm taugt nichts. The program's no good.

tauschen VERB [48]
to exchange

täuschen VERB [48]
1 to deceive
□ Du hast mich bewusst getäuscht. You deliberately deceived me.
2 to be deceptive
□ Der äußere Anschein täuscht oft. Appearances are often deceptive.
■ sich täuschen to be wrong

die **Täuschung** FEM NOUN
deception
■ eine optische Täuschung an optical illusion

tausend NUMBER
thousand

★ das **Taxi** (GEN des **Taxis**, PL die **Taxis**) NEUT NOUN
taxi

der **Taxifahrer** (PL die **Taxifahrer**) MASC NOUN
taxi driver

die **Taxifahrerin** FEM NOUN
taxi driver

★ der **Taxistand** (PL die **Taxistände**) MASC NOUN
taxi rank

★ die **Technik** FEM NOUN
1 technology
□ hoch entwickelte Technik advanced technology
■ die Gentechnik genetic engineering
2 technique
□ Sie beherrscht diese Technik des Hochsprungs noch nicht. She hasn't mastered this high-jump technique yet.

der **Techniker** (PL die **Techniker**) MASC NOUN
technician

die **Technikerin** FEM NOUN
technician

★ **technisch** ADJECTIVE
technical

★ die **Technologie** FEM NOUN
technology

★ der **Tee** (PL die **Tees**) MASC NOUN
tea
□ Tee mit Milch und Zucker tea with milk and sugar □ Tee mit Zitrone lemon tea □ Kamillentee camomile tea

der **Teebeutel** (PL die **Teebeutel**) MASC NOUN
tea bag

die **Teekanne** FEM NOUN
teapot

der **Teelöffel** (PL die **Teelöffel**) MASC NOUN
teaspoon
■ ein Teelöffel Zucker a teaspoonful of sugar

der **Teer** MASC NOUN
tar

der **Teich** (PL die **Teiche**) MASC NOUN
pond

der **Teig** (PL die **Teige**) MASC NOUN
dough

★ der **Teil** (PL die **Teile**) MASC NOUN

> You can also say **das Teil**.

1 part
□ der erste Teil des Buches the first part of the book
■ das Ersatzteil the spare part
2 share
□ Ich möchte meinen Teil am Gewinn. I would like my share of the profit.
3 component part
□ Er hat das Fahrrad in seine Teile zerlegt. He dismantled the bike into its component parts.
■ zum Teil partly

★ **teilen** VERB [38]
to divide
■ mit jemandem teilen to share with somebody

teilnehmen – Terrasse

★ **teilnehmen** (PRESENT TENSE **nimmt teil,** IMPERFECT **nahm teil,** PERFECT TENSE **hat teilgenommen**) VERB [52]
  ▪ **an etwas teilnehmen** to take part in something □ Du solltest am Wettbewerb teilnehmen! You ought to take part in the competition.

der **Teilnehmer** (PL die **Teilnehmer**) MASC NOUN
  participant

die **Teilnehmerin** FEM NOUN
  participant

teils ADVERB
  partly

teilweise ADVERB
  in parts
  □ Das Buch war teilweise sehr spannend. The book was thrilling in parts.
  ▪ **Sie waren teilweise beschädigt.** Some of them were damaged.

die **Teilzeitarbeit** FEM NOUN
  part-time work

der **Teint** (PL die **Teints**) MASC NOUN
  complexion

★ das **Telefon** (PL die **Telefone**) NEUT NOUN
  telephone

der **Telefonanruf** (PL die **Telefonanrufe**) MASC NOUN
  telephone call

★ das **Telefonat** (PL die **Telefonate**) NEUT NOUN
  phone call

★ das **Telefonbuch** (PL die **Telefonbücher**) NEUT NOUN
  phone book

der **Telefonhörer** (PL die **Telefonhörer**) MASC NOUN
  receiver
  □ Er nahm den Telefonhörer ab. He picked up the receiver.

★ **telefonieren** (PERFECT TENSE **hat telefoniert**) VERB [76]
  to telephone
  ▪ **Ich habe gestern mit ihr telefoniert.** I talked to her on the phone yesterday.

telefonisch ADJECTIVE
  telephone
  □ eine telefonische Nachricht a telephone message
  ▪ **Sie können mich telefonisch erreichen.** You can contact me by phone.

★ die **Telefonnummer** FEM NOUN
  telephone number

★ die **Telefonzelle** FEM NOUN
  telephone box

★ das **Telegramm** (PL die **Telegramme**) NEUT NOUN
  telegram

das **Teleskop** (PL die **Teleskope**) NEUT NOUN
  telescope

★ der **Teller** (PL die **Teller**) MASC NOUN
  plate

das **Temperament** (PL die **Temperamente**) NEUT NOUN
  ▪ **Sie hat ein ziemlich lebhaftes Temperament.** She's quite a vivacious person.

temperamentvoll ADJECTIVE
  vivacious

★ die **Temperatur** FEM NOUN
  temperature

das **Tempo** (PL die **Tempos**) NEUT NOUN
  1 speed
  □ Er ist mit einem irren Tempo gefahren. He drove at breakneck speed.
  2 rate
  □ Wir müssen unser Arbeitstempo steigern. We must increase our work rate.

tendieren (PERFECT TENSE **hat tendiert**) VERB [76]
  ▪ **zu etwas tendieren** to tend towards something

★ das **Tennis** (GEN des **Tennis**) NEUT NOUN
  tennis

★ der **Tennisplatz** (GEN des **Tennisplatzes,** PL die **Tennisplätze**) MASC NOUN
  tennis court

der **Tennisschläger** (PL die **Tennisschläger**) MASC NOUN
  tennis racket

der **Tennisspieler** (PL die **Tennisspieler**) MASC NOUN
  tennis player

die **Tennisspielerin** FEM NOUN
  tennis player

★ der **Teppich** (PL die **Teppiche**) MASC NOUN
  carpet

★ der **Teppichboden** (PL die **Teppichböden**) MASC NOUN
  wall-to-wall carpet

★ der **Termin** (PL die **Termine**) MASC NOUN
  1 date
  □ Habt ihr schon einen Termin ausgemacht? Have you already arranged a date?
  2 deadline
  □ Ich muss den Aufsatz bis zu dem Termin fertig haben. I must have the essay finished by that deadline.
  3 appointment
  □ Ich habe einen Termin beim Zahnarzt. I've got an appointment with the dentist.

★ der **Terminkalender** (PL die **Terminkalender**) MASC NOUN
  appointments diary

★ die **Terrasse** FEM NOUN
  terrace

der **Terror** MASC NOUN
terror

der **Terrorismus** (GEN des **Terrorismus**)
MASC NOUN
terrorism

der **Terrorist** (GEN des **Terroristen**, PL die
Terroristen) MASC NOUN
terrorist

★ der **Tesafilm**® MASC NOUN
Sellotape®

★ der **Test** (PL die **Tests**) MASC NOUN
test

das **Testament** (PL die **Testamente**) NEUT
NOUN
will
□ sein Testament machen to make one's will

testen VERB [2]
to test

★ **teuer** ADJECTIVE
expensive

der **Teufel** (PL die **Teufel**) MASC NOUN
devil

der **Text** (PL die **Texte**) MASC NOUN
1 text
□ Lest den Text auf Seite zehn. Read the text on
page ten.
2 lyrics *pl*
□ Kannst du mir den Text von dem Song
übersetzen? Can you translate the lyrics of the
song for me?

die **Textilien** FEM PL NOUN
textiles *pl*

★ die **Textverarbeitung** FEM NOUN
word processing

★ das **Theater** (PL die **Theater**) NEUT NOUN
1 theatre
□ Wir gehen ins Theater. We're going to the
theatre.
■ **Theater spielen** to act
2 fuss (*Umgangssprache*)
□ Mach nicht so ein Theater! Don't make such a
fuss.

★ das **Theaterstück** (PL die **Theaterstücke**)
NEUT NOUN
play

★ die **Theke** FEM NOUN
1 bar
□ Er stand an der Theke und trank ein Bier. He
stood at the bar drinking a beer.
2 counter
□ Das bekommen Sie an der Käsetheke. You'll
get that at the cheese counter.

das **Thema** (PL die **Themen**) NEUT NOUN
subject

theoretisch ADJECTIVE
theoretical

□ Rein theoretisch betrachtet ist das richtig.
From a purely theoretical point of view, that's
correct.

die **Theorie** FEM NOUN
theory

die **Therapie** FEM NOUN
therapy

★ das **Thermometer** (PL die **Thermometer**)
NEUT NOUN
thermometer

die **Thermosflasche** FEM NOUN
Thermos®

die **These** FEM NOUN
thesis

der **Thron** (PL die **Throne**) MASC NOUN
throne

der **Thunfisch** (PL die **Thunfische**) MASC
NOUN
tuna

das **Thüringen** NEUT NOUN
Thuringia

DID YOU KNOW...?
Thüringen is one of the 16 **Länder**. Its
capital is Erfurt. With its extensive forests,
it is sometimes called 'Germany's green
heartland'. It is not only rural, however: the
Zeiss precision engineering company is based
in Jena.

ticken VERB [48]
to tick
□ Die Uhr tickte. The clock was ticking.
■ **Du tickst ja nicht richtig!** You must be out
of your mind! (*Umgangssprache*)

★ **tief** ADJECTIVE
▷ *see also* das **Tief** NOUN
1 deep
□ Wie tief ist das Wasser? How deep's the
water?
2 low (*neckline, price, note*)
□ ein tief ausgeschnittenes Kleid a low-cut
dress

das **Tief** (PL die **Tiefs**) NEUT NOUN
▷ *see also* **tief** ADJECTIVE
depression
□ ein Tief über Norddeutschland a depression
over North Germany

★ der **Tiefdruck** MASC NOUN
low pressure

die **Tiefe** FEM NOUN
depth

die **Tiefgarage** FEM NOUN
underground garage

tiefgekühlt ADJECTIVE
frozen

die **Tiefkühlkost** FEM NOUN
frozen food

t

Numbers in brackets refer to verb tables on pages 697 to 706.

273

★ die **Tiefkühltruhe** FEM NOUN
freezer

★ das **Tier** (PL die Tiere) NEUT NOUN
animal

★ der **Tierarzt** (GEN des Tierarztes, PL die Tierärzte) MASC NOUN
vet

★ der **Tiergarten** (PL die Tiergärten) MASC NOUN
zoo

tierisch ADJECTIVE, ADVERB
1 animal
□ tierische Fette animal fats
2 terrible
□ Du hast dich tierisch benommen. You behaved terribly.
3 awesome (*Umgangssprache*)
□ Das Konzert war tierisch gut. The concert was awesome.

der **Tierkreis** (GEN des Tierkreises) MASC NOUN
zodiac

die **Tierquälerei** FEM NOUN
cruelty to animals

★ der **Tiger** (PL die Tiger) MASC NOUN
tiger

die **Tinte** FEM NOUN
ink

der **Tintenfisch** (PL die Tintenfische) MASC NOUN
squid

der **Tipp** (PL die Tipps) MASC NOUN
tip

★ **tippen** VERB [38]
1 to tap
□ Sie tippte leicht an die Statue. She lightly tapped the statue.
2 to type
□ Tippst du dein Referat? Are you typing your assignment?
■ im Lotto tippen to play the lottery
■ Auf wen tippst du bei den Wahlen? Who're you tipping to win the elections?

★ der **Tippfehler** (PL die Tippfehler) MASC NOUN
typing error

Tirol NEUT NOUN
Tyrol

der **Tiroler** (PL die Tiroler) MASC NOUN
Tyrolean

die **Tirolerin** FEM NOUN
Tyrolean

★ der **Tisch** (PL die Tische) MASC NOUN
table
□ bei Tisch at table

★ die **Tischdecke** FEM NOUN
tablecloth

★ das **Tischtennis** NEUT NOUN
table tennis

das **Tischtuch** (PL die Tischtücher) NEUT NOUN
tablecloth

★ der **Titel** (PL die Titel) MASC NOUN
title

★ der **Toast** (PL die Toasts) MASC NOUN
toast

das **Toastbrot** (PL die Toastbrote) NEUT NOUN
bread for toasting

der **Toaster** (PL die Toaster) MASC NOUN
toaster

toben VERB [38]
1 to rage
□ Der Sturm tobte die ganze Nacht. The storm raged all night long.
2 to go mad
□ Wenn er das erfährt, wird er toben. If he finds out he'll go mad.
3 to romp about
□ Die Kinder toben im Garten. The children are romping about in the garden.

★ die **Tochter** (PL die Töchter) FEM NOUN
daughter

★ der **Tod** (PL die Tode) MASC NOUN
death

todernst ADJECTIVE, ADVERB
1 grave
□ ein todernstes Gesicht a grave face
2 in deadly earnest
□ Er hat das todernst gesagt. He said it in deadly earnest.

die **Todesstrafe** FEM NOUN
death penalty

todkrank ADJECTIVE
critically ill

★ **tödlich** ADJECTIVE
deadly
□ eine tödliche Waffe a deadly weapon
■ ein tödlicher Unfall a fatal accident

todmüde ADJECTIVE
exhausted

★ die **Toilette** FEM NOUN
toilet

★ das **Toilettenpapier** NEUT NOUN
toilet paper

tolerant ADJECTIVE
tolerant

★ **toll** ADJECTIVE
terrific (*Umgangssprache*)

die **Tollwut** FEM NOUN
rabies *sing*

★ die **Tomate** FEM NOUN
tomato

★ = core vocabulary

das **Tomatenmark** NEUT NOUN
tomato purée

★ der **Ton** (PL die **Töne**) MASC NOUN
1 sound
□ Es war kein Ton zu hören. Not a sound could be heard.
2 note
□ Mit welchen Ton fängt das Lied an? What note does the song start on?
3 tone of voice
□ Sein Ton gefiel mir nicht. I didn't like his tone of voice.
4 shade
□ Pastelltöne sind in. Pastel shades are in.
5 stress
□ Bei Substantiven liegt der Ton meist auf der ersten Silbe. Nouns are usually stressed on the first syllable.

die **Tonne** FEM NOUN
ton
□ Ein Blauwal wiegt bis zu 140 Tonnen. A blue whale weighs up to 140 tons.

★ der **Topf** (PL die **Töpfe**) MASC NOUN
pot

toppen VERB
to do better than
■ einen Rekord toppen to break a record

★ das **Tor** (PL die **Tore**) NEUT NOUN
1 gate
□ Das Tor war offen. The gate was open.
2 goal
□ Wer hat das zweite Tor geschossen? Who scored the second goal?

der **Torf** MASC NOUN
peat

★ die **Torte** FEM NOUN
1 gateau
2 flan

der **Torwart** (PL die **Torwarte**) MASC NOUN
goalkeeper

die **Torwartin** FEM NOUN
goalkeeper

★ **tot** ADJECTIVE
dead
■ Er war sofort tot. He was killed instantly.

★ **total** ADJECTIVE, ADVERB
1 complete
□ Das ist doch der totale Wahnsinn. But that's complete madness.
2 completely
□ Das ist total verrückt. That's completely mad.

totalitär ADJECTIVE
totalitarian

der **Totalschaden** (PL die **Totalschäden**) MASC NOUN
complete write-off

der/die **Tote** (GEN des/der **Toten**, PL die **Toten**) MASC/FEM NOUN
dead body
□ Auf der Straße lag ein Toter. There was a dead body lying in the road.
■ die Toten begraben to bury the dead

töten VERB [2]
to kill

sich **totlachen** (PERFECT TENSE hat sich totgelacht) VERB [4]
to laugh one's head off (*Umgangssprache*)

der **Touchscreen** (PL die **Touchscreens**) MASC NOUN
touchscreen

★ die **Tour** (PL die **Touren**) FEM NOUN
trip
□ auf Tour gehen to go on a trip
■ auf vollen Touren at full speed

★ der **Tourismus** (GEN des **Tourismus**) MASC NOUN
tourism

★ der **Tourist** (GEN des **Touristen**, PL die **Touristen**) MASC NOUN
tourist

★ die **Touristin** FEM NOUN
tourist

★ die **Tournee** FEM NOUN
tour
□ Beyoncé auf Tournee Beyoncé on tour □ auf Tournee gehen to go on tour

die **Tracht** FEM NOUN
traditional costume
□ Im Schwarzwald tragen die Frauen noch Tracht. Women still wear traditional costume in the Black Forest.
■ eine Tracht Prügel a sound beating

★ die **Tradition** FEM NOUN
tradition

traditionell ADJECTIVE
traditional

traf VERB ▷ *see* treffen

tragbar ADJECTIVE
portable
□ ein tragbarer Fernseher a portable TV

träge ADJECTIVE
sluggish

★ **tragen** (PRESENT TENSE **trägt**, IMPERFECT **trug**, PERFECT TENSE **hat getragen**) VERB [77]
1 to carry
□ Kannst du meinen Koffer tragen? Can you carry my case?
2 to bear
□ die Verantwortung tragen to bear responsibility
3 to wear (*clothes, glasses*)
□ Er trug eine weiße Jacke und eine Sonnenbrille. He was wearing a white jacket and sunglasses.

t

die **Tragetasche** FEM NOUN
carrier bag

tragisch ADJECTIVE
tragic

die **Tragödie** FEM NOUN
tragedy

der **Trainer**(PL die **Trainer**) MASC NOUN
coach

★ **trainieren**(PERFECT TENSE **hat trainiert**) VERB
[76]
1 to train
□ Sie trainiert täglich für den Wettkampf. She
trains for the competition every day.
2 to coach
□ Wer trainiert diese Tennisspielerin? Who
coaches this tennis player?
3 to practise
□ Diese Übung muss ich noch mehr trainieren.
I need to practise this exercise more.

★ das **Training**(PL die **Trainings**) NEUT NOUN
training no pl

★ der **Trainingsanzug**(PL die
Trainingsanzüge) MASC NOUN
track suit

trampen VERB [38]
to hitchhike

der **Tramper**(PL die **Tramper**) MASC NOUN
hitchhiker

die **Tramperin** FEM NOUN
hitchhiker

die **Träne** FEM NOUN
tear
□ in Tränen ausbrechen to burst into tears

trank VERB ▷ see **trinken**

der **Transport**(PL die **Transporte**) MASC
NOUN
transport

transportieren(PERFECT TENSE **hat
transportiert**) VERB [76]
to transport

das **Transportmittel**(PL die
Transportmittel) NEUT NOUN
means of transport sing

die **Traube** FEM NOUN
grape

★ **trauen** VERB [38]
■ **jemandem trauen** to trust somebody
■ **sich trauen** to dare □ Ich wette, du traust
dich nicht! I bet you don't dare.

der **Traum**(PL die **Träume**) MASC NOUN
dream

★ **träumen** VERB [38]
to dream
□ Ich habe von dir geträumt. I dreamt about
you.

traumhaft ADJECTIVE
wonderful

□ Es waren traumhafte Ferien. It was a
wonderful holiday.

★ **traurig** ADJECTIVE
sad

★ die **Traurigkeit** FEM NOUN
sadness

★ **treffen**(PRESENT TENSE **trifft**, IMPERFECT **traf**,
PERFECT TENSE **hat getroffen**) VERB [78]
▷ see also das **Treffen** NOUN
1 to hit
□ Er hat die Zielscheibe getroffen. He hit the
target. □ Sie wurde am Kopf getroffen. She was
hit on the head.
■ **Du hast nicht getroffen.** You missed.
2 to meet
□ Ich habe ihn gestern im Supermarkt
getroffen. I met him yesterday in the
supermarket. □ Wir sind in London auf ihn
getroffen. We met him in London.
■ **sich treffen** to meet □ Wir treffen uns am
Bahnhof. We'll meet at the station. □ Sie treffen
sich einmal in der Woche. They meet once a
week.
3 to affect
□ Die Bemerkung hat sie sehr getroffen. The
remark affected her deeply.
■ **eine Entscheidung treffen** to make a
decision
■ **Maßnahmen treffen** to take steps
■ **Es traf sich, dass ...** It so happened that ...
■ **Das trifft sich gut!** How very convenient!

das **Treffen**(PL die **Treffen**) NEUT NOUN
▷ see also **treffen** VERB
meeting

treffend ADJECTIVE
pertinent

der **Treffer**(PL die **Treffer**) MASC NOUN
1 hit
□ Das Schiff musste einen Volltreffer
hinnehmen. The ship took a direct hit.
2 goal
□ Özil hat einen Treffer erzielt. Özil scored a
goal. □ Ich hatte vier Treffer im Lotto. I got four
numbers in the lottery.

★ der **Treffpunkt**(PL die **Treffpunkte**) MASC
NOUN
meeting place

★ **treiben**(IMPERFECT **trieb**, PERFECT TENSE **hat/ist
getrieben**) VERB

Use **haben** to form the perfect tense. Use
sein to form the perfect tense for 'to drift'.

1 to drive
□ Sie trieben die Kühe auf das Feld. They drove
the cows into the field.
■ **Sport treiben** to do sport
■ **Unsinn treiben** to fool around
■ **jemanden zu etwas treiben** to drive
somebody to something □ Du treibst mich zur
Verzweiflung. You drive me to despair.

★ = core vocabulary

■ **Sie hat uns zur Eile getrieben.** She made us hurry up.

2 to drift
□ Das Schiff ist aufs Meer getrieben. The ship drifted out to sea.

das **Treibhaus** (GEN des **Treibhauses**, PL die **Treibhäuser**) NEUT NOUN
greenhouse

der **Treibhauseffekt** MASC NOUN
greenhouse effect

das **Treibhausgas** (PL die **Treibhausgase**) NEUT NOUN
greenhouse gas

der **Treibstoff** (PL die **Treibstoffe**) MASC NOUN
fuel

trennen VERB [38]
1 to separate
□ Sie konnten die beiden Schläger nur zu dritt trennen. It took three of them to separate the two thugs.

2 to make a distinction between
□ Diese beiden Begriffe muss man sauber trennen. You have to make a clear distinction between these two concepts.

3 to hyphenate
□ Wie wird dieses Wort getrennt? Where do you hyphenate this word?
■ **sich trennen** to separate □ Die beiden haben sich getrennt. The two of them have separated.
■ **Du solltest dich von ihm trennen.** You ought to leave him.
■ **sich von etwas trennen** to part with something □ Ich trenne mich ungern von dem Buch. I'm loath to part with this book.

die **Trennung** FEM NOUN
separation

★ die **Treppe** FEM NOUN
stairs pl

das **Treppenhaus** (GEN des **Treppenhauses**, PL die **Treppenhäuser**) NEUT NOUN
staircase

treten (PRESENT TENSE **tritt**, IMPERFECT **trat**, PERFECT TENSE **hat/ist getreten**) VERB [79]

For the perfect tense use **haben** when the verb has an object and **sein** when there is no object.

1 to step
□ Sie ist in die Pfütze getreten. She stepped in the puddle. □ Er trat auf die Bremse. He stepped on the brakes. □ Er trat ans Mikrofon. He stepped up to the microphone.
■ **mit jemandem in Verbindung treten** to get in touch with somebody
■ **in Erscheinung treten** to appear

2 to kick
□ Sie hat mich getreten. She kicked me. □ Sie trat nach dem Hund. She kicked the dog.

3 to tread
□ Er ist mir auf den Fuß getreten. He trod on my foot.

treu ADJECTIVE
faithful

die **Treue** FEM NOUN
faithfulness

die **Tribüne** FEM NOUN
1 grandstand
□ Die Fans auf der Tribüne pfiffen. The fans on the grandstand whistled.

2 platform
□ Der Redner stand auf einer Tribüne. The speaker stood on a platform.

der **Trichter** (PL die **Trichter**) MASC NOUN
1 funnel
□ Sie hat das Öl mit einem Trichter in die Flasche gefüllt. She used a funnel to fill the bottle with oil.

2 crater
□ Das Gelände war von Bombentrichtern übersät. The area was pitted with bomb craters.

der **Trick** (PL die **Tricks**) MASC NOUN
trick
□ Das war ein fauler Trick. That was a dirty trick.

★ der **Trickfilm** (PL die **Trickfilme**) MASC NOUN
cartoon

trieb VERB ▷ see **treiben**

trifft VERB ▷ see **treffen**

★ das **Trimester** (PL die **Trimester**) NEUT NOUN
term (university)

★ **trinkbar** ADJECTIVE
drinkable

★ **trinken** (IMPERFECT **trank**, PERFECT TENSE **hat getrunken**) VERB [80]
to drink
■ **Ich habe zu viel getrunken.** I've had too much to drink.

★ das **Trinkgeld** (PL die **Trinkgelder**) NEUT NOUN
tip
□ Er gab dem Taxifahrer ein großzügiges Trinkgeld. He gave the taxi driver a generous tip.

★ die **Trinkhalle** FEM NOUN
refreshment kiosk

★ das **Trinkwasser** (PL die **Trinkwässer**) NEUT NOUN
drinking water

★ **trocken** ADJECTIVE
dry

★ **trocknen** VERB [53]
to dry

der **Trödel** MASC NOUN
junk (Umgangssprache)

Trödelmarkt – tüchtig

der Trödelmarkt(PL die Trödelmärkte)
MASC NOUN
flea market

trödeln VERB [88]
to dawdle

die Trommel FEM NOUN
drum
□ Er spielt Trommel. He plays the drums.

das Trommelfell(PL die Trommelfelle)
NEUT NOUN
eardrum

trommeln VERB [34]
to drum

★ **die Trompete** FEM NOUN
trumpet
□ Sie spielt Trompete. She plays the trumpet.

die Tropen PL NOUN
tropics pl

★ **der Tropfen**(PL die Tropfen) MASC NOUN
drop

tropisch ADJECTIVE
tropical

der Trost MASC NOUN
consolation

trösten VERB [2]
to console

trostlos ADJECTIVE
bleak
□ eine trostlose Landschaft a bleak landscape

der Trostpreis(GEN des Trostpreises PL die
Trostpreise) MASC NOUN
consolation prize

der Trottel(PL die Trottel) MASC NOUN
prat (Umgangssprache)

★ **trotz** PREPOSITION
▷ see also der Trotz NOUN

The preposition trotz takes the dative or
genitive.

in spite of

der Trotz(GEN des Trotzes) MASC NOUN
▷ see also trotz PREPOSITION
defiance
□ ihm zum Trotz in defiance of him
■ etwas aus Trotz tun to do something
defiantly

★ **trotzdem** ADVERB
all the same
□ Ich gehe trotzdem. I'm going all the same.

trotzig ADJECTIVE
defiant

trüb ADJECTIVE
1 dull
□ Es war ein trüber Tag. It was a dull day.
2 cloudy
□ Das Wasser war trüb. The water was cloudy.

3 gloomy
□ Die Zukunftsaussichten sind ziemlich trüb.
Prospects for the future are pretty gloomy.

der Trubel MASC NOUN
hurly-burly

trübsinnig ADJECTIVE
gloomy

trug VERB ▷ see tragen

trügen(IMPERFECT trog PERFECT TENSE hat
getrogen) VERB
to be deceptive
□ Der Schein trügt. Appearances are deceptive.

die Trümmer PL NOUN
1 wreckage sing
□ die Trümmer des Flugzeugs the wreckage of
the aeroplane
2 ruins pl
□ Nach dem Bombenangriff lag die Stadt in
Trümmern. After the air raid the town was in
ruins.

die Trunkenheit FEM NOUN
drunkenness
■ Trunkenheit am Steuer drink-driving

die Truppen FEM PL NOUN
troops pl

der Truthahn(PL die Truthähne) MASC NOUN
turkey

der Tscheche(GEN des Tschechen PL die
Tschechen) MASC NOUN
Czech

die Tschechin FEM NOUN
Czech

tschechisch ADJECTIVE
Czech

tschüs EXCLAMATION
cheerio!

★ **das T-Shirt**(PL die T-Shirts) NEUT NOUN
T-shirt

★ **die Tube** FEM NOUN
tube
□ eine Tube Zahnpasta a tube of toothpaste

★ **das Tuch**(PL die Tücher) NEUT NOUN
1 cloth
□ Mit welchem Tuch soll ich abstauben? Which
cloth should I use for dusting?
2 towel
□ Nimm dir ein großes Tuch ins Schwimmbad
mit. Take a large towel with you to the
swimming baths.
3 scarf
□ Sie hatte ein seidenes Tuch um den Hals. She
wore a silk scarf around her neck.

tüchtig ADJECTIVE
competent
□ Er ist ein sehr tüchtiger Mensch. He's a very
competent person.

★ = core vocabulary

■ **Er nahm einen tüchtigen Schluck aus der Flasche.** He took a hefty swig from the bottle. (*Umgangssprache*)

die **Tulpe** FEM NOUN
tulip

★ **tun** (IMPERFECT **tat**, PERFECT TENSE **hat getan**) VERB [81]

1 to do
□ Was sollen wir jetzt tun? What shall we do now? □ Er hat den ganzen Tag nichts getan. He hasn't done anything all day. □ Was kann ich für Sie tun? What can I do for you?

2 to put
□ Sie tat die Teller in den Schrank. She put the plates in the cupboard.

3 to act
□ Tu nicht so unschuldig! Don't act so innocent.

4 to pretend
□ Sie tat, als ob sie schliefe. She pretended to be sleeping. □ Er ist nicht krank, er tut nur so. He isn't ill, he's only pretending.

■ **Der Hund tut dir bestimmt nichts.** The dog won't hurt you.

■ **Hoffentlich hast du dir bei dem Sturz nichts getan.** I hope you didn't hurt yourself when you fell.

■ **Es tut sich viel.** A lot's happening.

■ **mit etwas zu tun haben** to have something to do with something □ Seine Laune hat etwas mit seiner Krankheit zu tun. His mood has something to do with his illness.

■ **Das tut nichts zur Sache.** That's neither here nor there.

der **Tunfisch** (PL die **Tunfische**) MASC NOUN
tuna

der **Tunnel** (PL die **Tunnel**) MASC NOUN
tunnel

der **Tupfen** (PL die **Tupfen**) MASC NOUN
dot

★ die **Tür** FEM NOUN
door

★ der **Türke** (GEN des **Türken**, PL die **Türken**) MASC NOUN
Turk

★ die **Türkei** FEM NOUN
Turkey
■ **aus der Türkei** from Turkey
■ **in der Türkei** in Turkey
■ **in die Türkei** to Turkey

★ die **Türkin** FEM NOUN
Turk

türkis ADJECTIVE
turquoise

★ **türkisch** ADJECTIVE
Turkish

★ der **Turm** (PL die **Türme**) MASC NOUN
1 tower

□ die Türme der Burg the castle towers

2 steeple
□ Das Ulmer Münster hat den höchsten Kirchturm der Welt. Ulm Cathedral has the world's highest steeple.

3 rook
□ Er machte einen Zug mit dem Turm. He moved his rook.

★ **turnen** VERB [38]
▷ see also das **Turnen** NOUN

1 to do gymnastics
□ Sie turnt nicht gern. She doesn't like doing gymnastics.

2 to perform
□ Sie hat die Kür hervorragend geturnt. She performed the free programme brilliantly.

★ das **Turnen** NEUT NOUN
▷ see also **turnen** VERB

1 gymnastics *sing*
□ Die Russinnen sind im Turnen gut. The Russian women are good at gymnastics.

2 physical education
□ Wir haben in der vierten Stunde Turnen. We have PE in the fourth period.

★ die **Turnhalle** FEM NOUN
gym

die **Turnhose** FEM NOUN
gym shorts *pl*
□ eine Turnhose a pair of gym shorts

★ das **Turnier** (PL die **Turniere**) NEUT NOUN
tournament

der **Turnschuh** (PL die **Turnschuhe**) MASC NOUN
trainer
□ ein Paar Turnschuhe a pair of trainers

das **Turnzeug** NEUT NOUN
gym things *pl*
□ Wo ist mein Turnzeug? Where are my gym things?

★ die **Tüte** FEM NOUN
bag

der **TÜV** (PL die **TÜVs**) MASC NOUN
(= *Technischer Überwachungsverein*)
MOT
□ Mein Auto ist nicht durch den TÜV gekommen. My car failed its MOT.

twittern VERB [88]
to tweet (*on Twitter*)

der **Typ** (PL die **Typen**) MASC NOUN
1 type
□ Er ist ein athletischer Typ. He's an athletic type.

2 bloke (*Umgangssprache*)
□ der Typ da drüben the bloke over there

★ **typisch** ADJECTIVE
typical
□ typisch für typical of

Numbers in brackets refer to verb tables on pages 697 to 706.

279

Uu

★ die **U-Bahn** FEM NOUN
underground
□ mit der U-Bahn fahren to travel by
underground

die **U-Bahn-Station** FEM NOUN
underground station

★ **übel** ADJECTIVE
bad
□ ein übler Geruch a bad smell □ eine üble Lage
a bad situation □ Nicht übel! Not bad.
■ jemandem ist übel somebody feels sick
■ Sie hat dir die Bemerkung übel
genommen. She was offended by your
remark.

die **Übelkeit** FEM NOUN
nausea

übelnehmen VERB [52] ▷ see übel

★ **üben** VERB [38]
to practise

★ **über** PREPOSITION, ADVERB

> Use the accusative to express movement or a
> change of place. Use the dative when there is
> no change of place.

1 over
□ Über dem Tisch hängt eine Lampe. There's a
lamp hanging over the table. □ Sie legten ein
Brett über das Loch. They put a board over the
hole. □ Flugzeuge dürfen nicht über dieses
Gebiet fliegen. Planes are not allowed to fly over
this area. □ Über Weihnachten bin ich zu
Hause. I'm at home over Christmas. □ Kinder
über zwölf Jahren children over twelve years of
age □ Das hat über hundert Euro gekostet. It
cost over a hundred euros.

2 above
□ Das Flugzeug flog hoch über der Stadt. The
plane flew high above the town.
■ den ganzen Tag über all day long
■ zwei Grad über null two degrees above
zero
■ ein Scheck über zweihundert Euro a
cheque for two hundred euros

3 across
□ Er ging quer über das Feld. He went across
the field.

4 via
□ nach Köln über Aachen to Cologne via Aachen

□ über Satellit via satellite

5 about
□ Wir haben über das Wetter geredet. We
talked about the weather. □ ein Buch über ... a
book about ...

6 through
□ Ich habe den Job über einen Freund
bekommen. I got the job through a friend.
■ über jemanden lachen to laugh at
somebody
■ Er liebt ihn über alles. He loves him more
than anything.
■ über und über over and over
■ über kurz oder lang sooner or later
■ etwas über haben to be fed up with
something (*Umgangssprache*) □ Ich habe
Kartoffeln langsam über. I'm getting fed up with
potatoes.

★ **überall** ADVERB
everywhere

überaus ADVERB
exceedingly

überbieten (IMPERFECT **überbot**, PERFECT TENSE
hat überboten) VERB [8]
to outbid
□ Er bot zweitausend Euro, aber wir haben ihn
überboten. He bid two thousand euros but we
outbid him.
■ einen Rekord überbieten to break a
record
■ sich überbieten to excel oneself

der **Überblick** (PL die **Überblicke**) MASC
NOUN

1 view
□ Von hier aus hat man einen guten Überblick
über das Gelände. You can get a good view of
the area from here.

2 overview
□ ein Überblick über die unregelmäßigen
Verben an overview of irregular verbs

3 overall impression
□ Ich muss mir erst mal einen Überblick
verschaffen. I have to get an overall impression
first.
■ den Überblick verlieren to lose track of
things
■ Sie hat den Überblick über ihre Arbeit
verloren. She has no idea where she is with
her work.

★ = core vocabulary

überdenken (IMPERFECT **überdachte**, PERFECT TENSE **hat überdacht**) VERB [14]
to think over

übereifrig ADJECTIVE
overeager

übereinander ADVERB
one on top of the other
□ Sie legte die Bücher übereinander. She put one book on top of the other.
■ **übereinander sprechen** to talk about each other

überempfindlich ADJECTIVE
hypersensitive

★ **überfahren** (PRESENT TENSE **überfährt**, IMPERFECT **überfuhr**, PERFECT TENSE **hat überfahren**) VERB [21]
to run over
□ Die Katze wurde von einem Auto überfahren. The cat was run over by a car.

★ die **Überfahrt** FEM NOUN
crossing

der **Überfall** (PL die **Überfälle**) MASC NOUN
1 raid
□ ein Banküberfall a bank raid □ ein Überfall auf ein fremdes Land a raid on a foreign country
2 assault
□ Er wurde das Opfer eines Überfalls. He was the victim of an assault.

★ **überfallen** (PRESENT TENSE **überfällt**, IMPERFECT **überfiel**, PERFECT TENSE **hat überfallen**) VERB [22]
1 to attack
□ Sie ist im Park überfallen worden. She was attacked in the park.
■ **eine Bank überfallen** to raid a bank
2 to descend on
□ Am Wochenende hat mich meine Freundin mit ihren Eltern überfallen. My girlfriend and her parents descended on me at the weekend.

überfällig ADJECTIVE
overdue

überflüssig ADJECTIVE
superfluous

überfordern (PERFECT TENSE **hat überfordert**) VERB [88]
to ask too much of
□ Unser Mathelehrer überfordert uns. Our maths teacher asks too much of us.

überfüllt ADJECTIVE
1 overcrowded
□ Die Gefängnisse sind völlig überfüllt. The prisons are completely overcrowded.
2 oversubscribed
□ Der Computerkurs ist überfüllt. The computer course is oversubscribed.

der **Übergang** (PL die **Übergänge**) MASC NOUN
1 crossing
□ ein Fußgängerübergang a pedestrian crossing

2 transition
□ der Übergang vom Sommer zum Herbst the transition from summer to autumn

★ **übergeben** (PRESENT TENSE **übergibt**, IMPERFECT **übergab**, PERFECT TENSE **hat übergeben**) VERB [28]
to hand over
□ Sie hat uns die Schlüssel übergeben. She handed the keys over to us.
■ **sich übergeben** to be sick

★ **überhaupt** ADVERB
1 at all
□ Kannst du überhaupt Auto fahren? Can you drive a car at all? □ Hast du überhaupt zugehört? Have you been listening at all? □ Ich habe überhaupt keine Lust. I don't feel like it at all.
2 in general
□ Die Schotten sind überhaupt sehr freundlich. In general the Scots are very friendly.
■ **überhaupt nicht** not at all □ Der Film hat mir überhaupt nicht gefallen. I didn't like the film at all.
■ **überhaupt nichts** nothing at all □ Was hat er gesagt? — Überhaupt nichts. What did he say? — Nothing at all. □ Er hat überhaupt nichts gesagt. He didn't say anything at all.

überheblich ADJECTIVE
arrogant

★ **überholen** (PERFECT TENSE **hat überholt**) VERB [18]
1 to overtake
□ Er hat rechts überholt. He overtook on the right.
2 to check over
□ Ich muss mein Fahrrad überholen. I have to check my bike over.

überholt ADJECTIVE
out-of-date

das **Überholverbot** (PL die **Überholverbote**) NEUT NOUN
restriction on overtaking

überhören (PERFECT TENSE **hat überhört**) VERB [18]
1 not to hear
□ Sie hat das Klingeln überhört. She didn't hear the bell.
2 to ignore
□ Deine Frechheit überhöre ich. I shall ignore your cheek.

überlassen (PRESENT TENSE **überlässt**, IMPERFECT **überließ**, PERFECT TENSE **hat überlassen**) VERB [42]
■ **jemandem etwas überlassen** to leave something up to somebody □ Ich überlasse es dir, wann du das machst. I'll leave it up to you when you do it.

überlasten (PERFECT TENSE **hat überlastet**) VERB [2]
to overload

u

□ Der Aufzug war überlastet. The lift was overloaded.

■ **Ich fühle mich überlastet.** I feel overworked.

überleben (PERFECT TENSE **hat überlebt**) VERB [18]

to survive

★ **überlegen** (PERFECT TENSE **hat überlegt**) VERB [82]

▷ see also **überlegen** ADJECTIVE

to think about

□ Ich muss mir deinen Vorschlag überlegen. I'll have to think about your suggestion. □ Überleg doch mal. Think about it.

★ **überlegen** ADJECTIVE

▷ see also **überlegen** VERB

1 better

□ Er ist ihr in Englisch überlegen. He's better at English than she is.

2 convincingly

□ Unsere Mannschaft hat überlegen gewonnen. Our team won convincingly.

die **Überlieferung** FEM NOUN

tradition

überlisten (PERFECT TENSE **hat überlistet**) VERB [2]

to outwit

überm = über dem

übermäßig ADJECTIVE

excessive

★ **übermorgen** ADVERB

the day after tomorrow

übernächste ADJECTIVE

next but one

□ An der übernächsten Haltestelle muss ich aussteigen. I need to get off at the next stop but one.

★ **übernachten** (PERFECT TENSE **hat übernachtet**) VERB [2]

■ **bei jemandem übernachten** to spend the night at somebody's house

★ die **Übernachtung** FEM NOUN

overnight stay

■ **Übernachtung mit Frühstück** bed and breakfast

übernehmen (PRESENT TENSE **übernimmt**, IMPERFECT **übernahm**, PERFECT TENSE **hat übernommen**) VERB [52]

to take over

□ Er hat das Geschäft seines Vaters übernommen. He's taken over his father's business. □ Er hat das Amt des Klassensprechers übernommen. He took over as class representative.

■ **sich übernehmen** to take on too much

überprüfen (PERFECT TENSE **hat überprüft**) VERB [18]

to check

★ **überqueren** (PERFECT TENSE **hat überquert**) VERB [7]

to cross

★ **überraschen** (PERFECT TENSE **hat überrascht**) VERB [18]

to surprise

★ **überrascht** ADJECTIVE

surprised

★ die **Überraschung** FEM NOUN

surprise

überreden (PERFECT TENSE **hat überredet**) VERB [54]

to persuade

□ Kannst du sie nicht überreden mitzukommen? Can't you persuade her to come?

übers = über das

überschätzen (PERFECT TENSE **hat überschätzt**) VERB [36]

to overestimate

überschlagen (PRESENT TENSE **überschlägt**, IMPERFECT **überschlug**, PERFECT TENSE **hat überschlagen**) VERB [59]

to estimate

□ Wir sollten die Kosten für das Fest überschlagen. We should estimate how much the party will cost.

■ **eine Seite überschlagen** to miss a page

■ **Das Auto hat sich überschlagen.** The car rolled over.

überschnappen (PERFECT TENSE **ist übergeschnappt**) VERB [4]

to flip one's lid (*Umgangssprache*)

□ Du bist wohl übergeschnappt! You've flipped your lid!

die **Überschrift** FEM NOUN

heading

der **Überschuss** (GEN des **Überschusses**, PL die **Überschüsse**) MASC NOUN

surplus

□ ein Überschuss an a surplus of

überschütten (PERFECT TENSE **hat überschüttet**) VERB [2]

■ **jemanden mit etwas überschütten** to shower somebody with something □ Sie haben uns mit Geschenken überschüttet. They showered us with presents.

★ die **Überschwemmung** FEM NOUN

flood

übersehen (PRESENT TENSE **übersieht**, IMPERFECT **übersah**, PERFECT TENSE **hat übersehen**) VERB [64]

1 to overlook

□ Sie hat ein paar Fehler übersehen. She overlooked a couple of mistakes.

2 to see

□ Wir können die Folgen noch nicht übersehen. We can't see the consequences yet.

★ **übersetzen**(PERFECT TENSE **hat übersetzt**)
VERB [36]
to translate
□ Übersetzt den Text ins Englische. Translate the text into English.

der **Übersetzer**(PL die **Übersetzer**) MASC NOUN
translator

die **Übersetzerin** FEM NOUN
translator

die **Übersetzung** FEM NOUN
translation
□ Das war eine schwierige Übersetzung. That was a difficult translation.

die **Übersicht** FEM NOUN
1 view
□ Von hier aus hat man eine gute Übersicht. You get a good view from here.
2 overview
□ eine Übersicht über die unregelmäßigen Verben an overview of irregular verbs

übersichtlich ADJECTIVE
clear
□ Die Tabelle ist nicht besonders übersichtlich. The table isn't particularly clear. □ etwas übersichtlich gestalten to arrange something clearly
■ ein übersichtliches Gelände open country

überspringen(IMPERFECT **übersprang** PERFECT TENSE **hat übersprungen**) VERB [71]
1 to jump over
□ Er hat die Hürde übersprungen. He jumped over the hurdle.
2 to skip
□ Das nächste Kapitel können wir überspringen. We can skip the next chapter.

überstehen(IMPERFECT **überstand**, PERFECT TENSE **hat überstanden**) VERB [72]
1 to get over
□ Wir haben das Schlimmste überstanden. We've got over the worst.
2 to survive
□ Die Pflanze hat den Winter nicht überstanden. The plant didn't survive the winter.

übersteigen(IMPERFECT **überstieg** PERFECT TENSE **hat überstiegen**) VERB [74]
to exceed
□ Das übersteigt unsere Erwartungen. That exceeds our expectations.

überstimmen(PERFECT TENSE **hat überstimmt**) VERB [7]
to outvote

die **Überstunden** FEM PL NOUN
overtime sing
□ Er macht viele Überstunden. He does a lot of overtime.

überstürzen(PERFECT TENSE **hat überstürzt**) VERB [36]
to rush
□ Du solltest nichts überstürzen. You shouldn't rush into things.
■ **sich überstürzen** to follow one another in rapid succession □ Die Ereignisse überstürzten sich. One event followed another in rapid succession.

überstürzt ADJECTIVE
1 rash
□ eine überstürzte Entscheidung a rash decision
2 in a rush
□ Sie sind überstürzt abgereist. They left in a rush.

übertragen(PRESENT TENSE **überträgt**, IMPERFECT **übertrug** PERFECT TENSE **hat übertragen**) VERB [77]
▷ see also **übertragen** ADJECTIVE
1 to broadcast
□ Wir übertragen das Spiel live. We're broadcasting the game live.
2 to copy
□ Sie hat den Text in ihr Heft übertragen. She copied the text into her exercise book.
3 to transmit
□ eine Krankheit übertragen to transmit an illness
■ **Sie hat mir diese Aufgabe übertragen.** She has assigned this task to me.
■ **sich übertragen auf** to spread to □ Ihre Nervosität hat sich auf die Kinder übertragen. Her nervousness spread to the children.

übertragen ADJECTIVE
▷ see also **übertragen** VERB
figurative
□ die übertragene Bedeutung eines Wortes the figurative meaning of a word

übertreffen(PRESENT TENSE **übertrifft**, IMPERFECT **übertraf**, PERFECT TENSE **hat übertroffen**) VERB [78]
to surpass

übertreiben(IMPERFECT **übertrieb**, PERFECT TENSE **hat übertrieben**) VERB
to exaggerate

die **Übertreibung** FEM NOUN
exaggeration

übertrieben ADJECTIVE
excessive

überwachen(PERFECT TENSE **hat überwacht**) VERB [18]
1 to supervise
□ Wer soll die Kinder überwachen? Who will supervise the children?
2 to keep under surveillance
□ Die Polizei überwacht ihn. The police are keeping him under surveillance.

überweisen(IMPERFECT **überwies**, PERFECT TENSE **hat überwiesen**) VERB
to transfer

überwinden(IMPERFECT **überwand**, PERFECT TENSE **hat überwunden**) VERB

u

Numbers in brackets refer to verb tables on pages 697 to 706.

283

to overcome
□ Jetzt haben wir alle Schwierigkeiten überwunden. Now we've overcome all difficulties.
■ **sich überwinden** to force oneself □ Ich musste mich überwinden, das zu essen. I had to force myself to eat it.

überzeugen (PERFECT TENSE **hat überzeugt**) VERB [18]
to convince

überzeugend ADJECTIVE
convincing

die **Überzeugung** FEM NOUN
conviction
□ Er sagte es ohne große Überzeugung. He said it without much conviction.

üblich ADJECTIVE
usual

das **U-Boot** (PL die **U-Boote**) NEUT NOUN
submarine

übrig ADJECTIVE
remaining
□ Die übrigen Gäste sind auch bald gegangen. The remaining guests left soon afterwards.
■ **Ist noch Kuchen übrig?** Is there any cake left?
■ **die übrigen** the others
■ **das Übrige** the rest
■ **im Übrigen** besides
■ **übrig bleiben** to be left
■ **übrig lassen** to leave □ Habt ihr uns etwas Kuchen übrig gelassen? Have you left us any cake?

übrigens ADVERB
by the way
□ Übrigens, du schuldest mir noch zehn Euro. By the way, you still owe me ten euros.

übrighaben (PRESENT TENSE **hat übrig**, IMPERFECT **hatte übrig**, PERFECT TENSE **hat übriggehabt**) VERB [32]
■ **für jemanden etwas übrighaben** to be fond of somebody

übriglassen VERB [42] ▷ *see* **übrig**

★ die **Übung** FEM NOUN
1 practice
□ Mir fehlt die Übung. I need more practice.
□ Übung macht den Meister. Practice makes perfect.
2 exercise
□ Bitte macht jetzt Übung dreizehn. Please do exercise thirteen now. □ eine Turnübung a gym exercise

★ das **Ufer** (PL die **Ufer**) NEUT NOUN
1 bank
□ Wir saßen am Ufer des Rheins. We sat on the bank of the Rhine.
2 shore
□ Treibholz, das ans Ufer gespült wurde driftwood which was washed up onto the shore

★ die **Uhr** FEM NOUN
1 clock
□ Die Uhr am Bahnhof sollte richtig gehen. The station clock should be right.
2 watch
□ Er sah auf seine Uhr. He looked at his watch.
■ **Wie viel Uhr ist es?** What time is it?
■ **ein Uhr** one o'clock
■ **zwanzig Uhr** eight o'clock in the evening
■ **um fünf Uhr** at five o'clock

der **Uhrzeigersinn** MASC NOUN
■ **im Uhrzeigersinn** clockwise
■ **entgegen dem Uhrzeigersinn** anticlockwise

★ die **Uhrzeit** FEM NOUN
time

der **Ultraschall** MASC NOUN
ultrasound

★ **um** PREPOSITION, CONJUNCTION, ADVERB

The preposition um takes the accusative.

1 round
□ Sie legte sich einen Schal um den Hals. She wrapped a scarf round her neck. □ Wir sind um die Stadt herumgefahren. We drove round the town.
■ **um Weihnachten** around Christmas
2 at
□ um acht Uhr at eight o'clock
3 by
□ etwas um vier Zentimeter kürzen to shorten something by four centimetres
■ **um zehn Prozent teurer** ten per cent more expensive
■ **um vieles besser** better by far
4 for
□ der Kampf um den Titel the battle for the title
□ um Geld spielen to play for money
■ **um ... willen** for the sake of ...

um ... willen takes the genitive.

□ um deinetwillen for your sake □ um meiner Mutter willen for my mother's sake
■ **um ... zu** in order to ...

um ... zu is used with the infinitive.

□ Ich gehe in die Schule, um etwas zu lernen. I go to school in order to learn something.
■ **zu klug, um zu ...** too clever to ...
5 about
□ um die dreißig Leute about thirty people
■ **Die zwei Stunden sind um.** The two hours are up.

umarmen (PERFECT TENSE **hat umarmt**) VERB [7]
to hug
□ Sie umarmten sich. They hugged.

umblättern (PERFECT TENSE **hat umgeblättert**) VERB [4]
to turn over

German -English

umbringen (IMPERFECT brachte um, PERFECT TENSE hat umgebracht) VERB [13]
to kill

★ **umdrehen** (PERFECT TENSE hat umgedreht) VERB [4]
to turn round
□ Dreh das Bild mal um. Turn the picture round.
■ sich umdrehen to turn round

umfallen (PRESENT TENSE fällt um, IMPERFECT fiel um, PERFECT TENSE ist umgefallen) VERB [22]
to fall down

der **Umfang** MASC NOUN
1 extent
□ Der Umfang der Arbeiten war am Anfang nicht absehbar. The extent of the work couldn't be seen at the beginning.
2 circumference
□ Berechnet den Umfang des Kreises. Calculate the circumference of the circle.

★ die **Umfrage** FEM NOUN
poll

der **Umgang** MASC NOUN
■ erfahren im Umgang mit Kindern experienced in dealing with children
■ der Umgang mit dem Computer working with computers

die **Umgangssprache** FEM NOUN
colloquial language

umgeben (PRESENT TENSE umgibt, IMPERFECT umgab, PERFECT TENSE hat umgeben) VERB [28]
to surround

★ die **Umgebung** FEM NOUN
1 surroundings pl
□ ein Haus in schöner Umgebung a house in beautiful surroundings
2 environment
□ Diese Pflanze wächst am besten in sonniger Umgebung. This plant grows best in a sunny environment.

umgehen (1) (IMPERFECT ging um, PERFECT TENSE ist umgegangen) VERB [29]

Note that here the stress is on um.

■ mit jemandem grob umgehen to treat somebody roughly
■ mit Geld sparsam umgehen to be careful with one's money
■ Sie kann nicht gut mit Geld umgehen. She's not very good with money.

umgehen (2) (IMPERFECT umging, PERFECT TENSE hat umgangen) VERB [29]

Note that here the stress is on gehen.

to avoid
□ Dieses Problem sollten wir besser umgehen. It would be better if we could avoid this problem.

umgehend ADJECTIVE
immediate

die **Umgehungsstraße** FEM NOUN
bypass

umgekehrt ADJECTIVE, ADVERB
1 reverse
□ in umgekehrter Reihenfolge in reverse order
■ genau umgekehrt exactly the opposite
2 the other way around
□ Du musst das Bild umgekehrt hängen. You'll have to hang the picture the other way round.
□ Mach das doch umgekehrt, und fang hiermit an. Do it the other way round and start here.
■ ... und umgekehrt ... and vice versa

umhauen (PERFECT TENSE hat umgehauen) VERB [4]
1 to bowl over
□ Die Neuigkeit wird dich umhauen. The news will bowl you over.
2 to fell
□ Sie haben die alte Eiche umgehauen. They've felled the old oak tree.

sich **umhören** (PERFECT TENSE hat sich umgehört) VERB [4]
to ask around

umkehren (PERFECT TENSE hat/ist umgekehrt) VERB [4]

For the perfect tense use haben when the verb has an object and sein when there is no object.

1 to turn back
□ Wir sind auf halbem Weg umgekehrt. We turned back halfway.
2 to turn round
□ Warum hast du das Bild umgekehrt? Why did you turn the picture round?
3 to turn inside out
□ Sie hat ihre Tasche umgekehrt, den Schlüssel aber nicht gefunden. She turned her bag inside out but couldn't find the key.
4 to turn upside down
□ Kehr mal den Eimer um, dann kann ich mich draufstellen. Turn the bucket upside down so that I can stand on it.

umkippen (PERFECT TENSE hat/ist umgekippt) VERB [4]

For the perfect tense use haben when the verb has an object and sein when there is no object.

1 to tip over
□ Der Stuhl ist umgekippt. The chair tipped over.
2 to overturn
□ Sie haben das Boot umgekippt. They overturned the boat.
3 to keel over (Umgangssprache)
□ Wenn ich Blut sehe, kippe ich immer um. I keel over whenever I see blood.

★ die **Umkleidekabine** FEM NOUN
changing cubicle

u

★ der **Umkleideraum**(PL die
 Umkleideräume) MASC NOUN
 changing room

★ **umkommen**(IMPERFECT **kam um**, PERFECT
 TENSE **ist umgekommen**) VERB [40]
 to be killed
 □ Alle Passagiere sind umgekommen. All the
 passengers were killed.

 der **Umkreis**(GEN des **Umkreises**, PL die
 Umkreise) MASC NOUN
 neighbourhood
 ■ **im Umkreis von** within a radius of

 der **Umlaut**(PL die **Umlaute**) MASC NOUN
 umlaut

 umlegen(PERFECT TENSE **hat umgelegt**) VERB
 [4]
 1 to put on
 □ Du solltest dir eine Jacke umlegen. You
 should put on a jacket.
 ■ **die Kosten für etwas umlegen** to divide
 the cost of something
 2 to bump off (*Umgangssprache*)
 □ Er ist von der Mafia umgelegt worden. He was
 bumped off by the Mafia.

 umleiten(PERFECT TENSE **hat umgeleitet**)
 VERB [4]
 to divert

★ die **Umleitung** FEM NOUN
 diversion

 umrechnen(PERFECT TENSE **hat
 umgerechnet**) VERB [4]
 to convert

 die **Umrechnung** FEM NOUN
 conversion

 der **Umrechnungskurs**(GEN des
 Umrechnungskurses, PL die
 Umrechnungskurse) MASC NOUN
 rate of exchange

 der **Umriss**(GEN des **Umrisses**, PL die
 Umrisse) MASC NOUN
 outline

 umrühren(PERFECT TENSE **hat umgerührt**)
 VERB [4]
 to stir

 ums= um das

 der **Umsatz**(GEN des **Umsatzes**, PL die
 Umsätze) MASC NOUN
 turnover

 umschalten(PERFECT TENSE **hat
 umgeschaltet**) VERB [4]
 to switch
 □ Schalt bitte ins zweite Programm um. Please
 switch over to Channel two.
 ■ **Die Ampel hat auf Gelb umgeschaltet.**
 The traffic lights changed to amber.
 ■ **Wir schalten um ins Studio.** We'll now go
 back to the studio.

★ der **Umschlag**(PL die **Umschläge**) MASC
 NOUN

1 cover
 □ Alle meine Mathehefte haben einen
 schwarzen Umschlag. All my maths exercise
 books have a black cover.
2 jacket
 □ Ich habe den Umschlag von dem Wörterbuch
 abgemacht. I took the jacket off the dictionary.
3 envelope
 □ Sie steckte den Brief in den Umschlag. She
 put the letter in the envelope.

 sich **umsehen**(PRESENT TENSE **sieht sich um**,
 IMPERFECT **sah sich um**, PERFECT TENSE **hat sich
 umgesehen**) VERB [64]
 to look around
 □ Als sie Schritte hörte, sah sie sich um. When
 she heard steps, she looked around.
 ■ **sich nach etwas umsehen** to look for
 something □ Ich sehe mich zurzeit nach einer
 neuen Wohnung um. I'm looking for a new flat
 at the moment.

 umso CONJUNCTION
 so much
 □ umso besser so much the better □ umso
 schlimmer so much the worse
 ■ **Je mehr ich höre, umso weniger
 verstehe ich.** The more I hear the less I
 understand.

★ **umsonst** ADVERB
1 in vain
 □ Wir haben umsonst gewartet. We waited in
 vain.
2 for nothing
 □ Wir sind umsonst ins Museum gekommen.
 We got into the museum for nothing.
3 free of charge
 □ Diese Broschüre gibt es umsonst. This
 brochure is free of charge.

 der **Umstand**(PL die **Umstände**) MASC NOUN
 circumstance
 □ unter keinen Umständen under no
 circumstances
 ■ **Wenn es keine Umstände macht.** If it's
 no trouble.
 ■ **unter Umständen** possibly
 ■ **in anderen Umständen sein** to be
 pregnant

 umständlich ADJECTIVE
1 complicated
 □ Das ist aber umständlich, wie du das machst.
 The way you do it is complicated.
2 long-winded
 □ eine umständliche Erklärung a long-winded
 explanation

★ **umsteigen**(IMPERFECT **stieg um**, PERFECT TENSE
 ist umgestiegen) VERB [74]
 to change
 □ Wir müssen in München umsteigen. We have
 to change in Munich.

 umstellen (1)(PERFECT TENSE **hat
 umgestellt**) VERB [4]

 Note that here the stress is on **um**.

to move
□ Ich werde meinen Schreibtisch umstellen.
I'm going to move my desk.
■ **auf metrische Maße umstellen** to go over
to the metric system
■ **sich umstellen** to adapt □ Jetzt, wo das Baby
da ist, müssen wir uns umstellen. Now that the
baby's here we have to adapt.

umstellen (2) (PERFECT TENSE **hat umstellt**)
VERB [7]

Note that here the stress is on **stellen**.

to surround
□ Die Polizei hat das Haus umstellt. The police
have surrounded the house.

umstritten ADJECTIVE
controversial
□ ein umstrittenes Thema a controversial
subject

★ der **Umtausch** MASC NOUN
exchange

★ **umtauschen** (PERFECT TENSE **hat
umgetauscht**) VERB [4]
to exchange

der **Umweg** (PL die **Umwege**) MASC NOUN
detour
□ Wir haben einen Umweg gemacht. We made
a detour.

★ die **Umwelt** FEM NOUN
environment

umweltfeindlich ADJECTIVE
damaging to the environment

umweltfreundlich ADJECTIVE
environment-friendly

der **Umweltschützer** (PL die
Umweltschützer) MASC NOUN
environmentalist

★ die **Umweltverschmutzung** FEM NOUN
environmental pollution

★ **umziehen** (IMPERFECT **zog um**, PERFECT TENSE
hat/ist umgezogen) VERB [96]

Use **haben** to form the perfect tense. Use
sein to form the perfect tense for 'to move'.

1 to change
□ Ich habe Carolin heute schon zweimal
umgezogen. I've already changed Carolin's
clothes twice today.
■ **sich umziehen** to get changed □ Wenn ich
mich umgezogen habe, können wir gehen. We
can go when I've got changed.

2 to move
□ Mein Freund ist nach Bremen umgezogen.
My friend's moved to Bremen.

der **Umzug** (PL die **Umzüge**) MASC NOUN

1 move
□ Alle meine Freunde haben beim Umzug
geholfen. All my friends helped with the move.

2 procession
□ Zu Karneval finden überall Umzüge statt.

There are processions everywhere during the
Carnival.

unabhängig ADJECTIVE
independent

die **Unabhängigkeit** FEM NOUN
independence

unangebracht ADJECTIVE
uncalled-for

★ **unangenehm** ADJECTIVE
unpleasant

die **Unannehmlichkeiten** FEM PL NOUN
trouble *sing*
□ Das gibt Unannehmlichkeiten mit dem
Klassenlehrer. That'll cause trouble with the
class teacher.

unanständig ADJECTIVE
improper

★ **unartig** ADJECTIVE
naughty

unaufmerksam ADJECTIVE
inattentive

unausstehlich ADJECTIVE
intolerable

unbeabsichtigt ADJECTIVE
unintentional

unbedeutend ADJECTIVE
unimportant

★ **unbedingt** ADJECTIVE, ADVERB

1 unconditional
□ Ich verlange unbedingten Gehorsam. I
demand unconditional obedience.

2 really
□ Er wollte unbedingt nach Hause. He really
wanted to go home. □ Den Film musst du dir
unbedingt ansehen. You really have to see that
film.

unbefriedigend ADJECTIVE
unsatisfactory

unbefriedigt ADJECTIVE
unsatisfied

unbegreiflich ADJECTIVE
inconceivable

unbekannt ADJECTIVE
unknown

unbeliebt ADJECTIVE
unpopular

★ **unbequem** ADJECTIVE
uncomfortable
□ Das Bett ist unbequem. The bed's
uncomfortable.

★ **unbesetzt** ADJECTIVE
vacant

unbestimmt ADJECTIVE

1 indefinite
□ der unbestimmte Artikel the indefinite article

2 uncertain
□ Es ist noch unbestimmt, wann wir Ferien

Numbers in brackets refer to verb tables on pages 697 to 706.

287

machen. It's still uncertain when we're going on holiday.

unbewusst ADJECTIVE
unconscious

★ **und** CONJUNCTION
and
□ und so weiter and so on
■ Na und? So what?

undankbar ADJECTIVE
ungrateful

undeutlich ADJECTIVE
indistinct

★ **unehrlich** ADJECTIVE
dishonest

unempfindlich ADJECTIVE
practical
□ Wir brauchen für das Sofa einen unempfindlichen Bezug. We need a practical cover for the sofa.
■ Ich bin gegen Kälte unempfindlich. I don't feel the cold.

unendlich ADJECTIVE
infinite

★ **unentschieden** ADJECTIVE
undecided
■ unentschieden enden to end in a draw

unerfahren ADJECTIVE
inexperienced

unerfreulich ADJECTIVE
unpleasant

unerträglich ADJECTIVE
unbearable
□ Die Schmerzen sind unerträglich. The pain's unbearable.

unerwünscht ADJECTIVE
undesirable

unfähig ADJECTIVE
incapable
□ zu etwas unfähig sein to be incapable of something

unfair ADJECTIVE
unfair

★ der **Unfall** (PL die **Unfälle**) MASC NOUN
accident

★ **unfreundlich** ADJECTIVE
unfriendly

die **Unfreundlichkeit** FEM NOUN
unfriendliness

der **Unfug** MASC NOUN
1 mischief
□ Die Kinder machen dauernd Unfug. The children are always getting up to mischief.
2 nonsense
□ Red nicht so einen Unfug. Don't talk such nonsense.

der **Ungar** (GEN des **Ungarn**, PL die **Ungarn**) MASC NOUN
Hungarian

die **Ungarin** FEM NOUN
Hungarian

ungarisch ADJECTIVE
Hungarian

Ungarn NEUT NOUN
Hungary
■ aus Ungarn from Hungary
■ nach Ungarn to Hungary

die **Ungeduld** FEM NOUN
impatience

★ **ungeduldig** ADJECTIVE
impatient

ungeeignet ADJECTIVE
unsuitable

★ **ungefähr** ADJECTIVE, ADVERB
1 approximate
□ Kannst du mir eine ungefähre Zeit nennen? Can you give me an approximate time?
2 approximately
□ um ungefähr zwei Uhr at approximately two o'clock

ungefährlich ADJECTIVE
harmless

das **Ungeheuer** (PL die **Ungeheuer**) NEUT NOUN
monster
□ das Ungeheuer von Loch Ness the Loch Ness monster

ungehörig ADJECTIVE
impertinent

ungehorsam ADJECTIVE
disobedient

ungeklärt ADJECTIVE
unsolved
□ ein ungeklärtes Rätsel an unsolved puzzle

ungelegen ADJECTIVE
inconvenient
□ Ich hoffe, ich komme nicht ungelegen. I hope I haven't come at an inconvenient time.

ungelernt ADJECTIVE
unskilled
□ ein ungelernter Arbeiter an unskilled worker

ungemütlich ADJECTIVE
1 uncomfortable
□ ein ungemütlicher Stuhl an uncomfortable chair
2 disagreeable
□ Jetzt wird er ungemütlich. Now he's going to get disagreeable.

ungenau ADJECTIVE
inaccurate

ungenießbar ADJECTIVE
1 inedible
□ Das Essen war ungenießbar. The food was inedible.
2 undrinkable
□ Diese Limonade ist ungenießbar. This lemonade's undrinkable.

3 unbearable

□ Du bist heute aber ungenießbar. You're really unbearable today.

ungenügend ADJECTIVE

1 insufficient

□ eine ungenügende Menge an insufficient amount

2 unsatisfactory

DID YOU KNOW...?
German grades range from one (**sehr gut**) to six (**ungenügend**).

ungepflegt ADJECTIVE

■ **ein ungepflegter Garten** a neglected garden

■ **ungepflegte Hände** uncared-for hands

ungerade ADJECTIVE

■ **eine ungerade Zahl** an odd number

★ **ungerecht** ADJECTIVE
unjust

die **Ungerechtigkeit** FEM NOUN
injustice

ungern ADVERB
reluctantly

ungeschickt ADJECTIVE
clumsy

ungestört ADJECTIVE
undisturbed

★ **ungesund** ADJECTIVE
unhealthy

ungewiss ADJECTIVE
uncertain

die **Ungewissheit** FEM NOUN
uncertainty

ungewöhnlich ADJECTIVE
unusual

ungewohnt ADJECTIVE
unaccustomed

das **Ungeziefer** NEUT NOUN
vermin

ungezogen ADJECTIVE
rude

ungezwungen ADJECTIVE
natural

★ **unglaublich** ADJECTIVE
incredible

das **Unglück** (PL die **Unglücke**) NEUT NOUN

1 accident

□ Er ist bei einem Unglück ums Leben gekommen. He lost his life in an accident.

2 misfortune

□ Lass sie in ihrem Unglück nicht allein. Don't leave her alone in her misfortune.

3 bad luck

□ Eine schwarze Katze bringt Unglück. A black cat means bad luck.

★ **unglücklich** ADJECTIVE

1 unhappy

□ Sie ist furchtbar unglücklich. She's terribly unhappy.

2 unfortunate

□ ein unglücklicher Zufall an unfortunate coincidence □ eine unglückliche Formulierung an unfortunate choice of words

■ **Sie ist unglücklich gefallen.** She fell awkwardly.

ungültig ADJECTIVE
invalid

ungünstig ADJECTIVE
unfavourable

unheilbar ADJECTIVE
incurable

unheimlich ADJECTIVE, ADVERB

1 weird

□ Das war ein unheimliches Geräusch. That was a weird noise.

■ **Mir wird's etwas unheimlich.** I'm getting a bit scared.

2 incredibly

□ Das hat mich unheimlich gefreut. I was incredibly pleased about it.

★ **unhöflich** ADJECTIVE
impolite

★ die **Uni** (PL die **Unis**) FEM NOUN
uni (Umgangssprache)

★ die **Uniform** FEM NOUN
uniform

uninteressant ADJECTIVE
uninteresting

★ die **Universität** FEM NOUN
university

unklar ADJECTIVE
unclear

■ **über etwas im Unklaren sein** to be unclear about something □ Ich bin mir über mein Berufsziel noch im Unklaren. I'm still unclear about what I want to do.

■ **jemanden über etwas im Unklaren lassen** to leave somebody in the dark about something

unklug ADJECTIVE
unwise

die **Unkosten** PL NOUN
expenses pl

unlogisch ADJECTIVE
illogical

unlösbar ADJECTIVE
insoluble

□ ein unlösbares Problem an insoluble problem

unmissverständlich ADJECTIVE
unmistakeable

unmittelbar ADJECTIVE
immediate

★ **unmöglich** ADJECTIVE
impossible

u

German-English

die **Unmöglichkeit** FEM NOUN
impossibility

unmoralisch ADJECTIVE
immoral

unnötig ADJECTIVE
unnecessary

★ **unordentlich** ADJECTIVE
untidy

die **Unordnung** FEM NOUN
disorder

unparteiisch ADJECTIVE
impartial

unpassend ADJECTIVE
1 inappropriate
   □ unpassende Kleidung inappropriate clothes
2 inopportune
   □ zu einer unpassenden Zeit at an inopportune time

unpersönlich ADJECTIVE
impersonal
   □ das unpersönliche Fürwort the impersonal pronoun

unpraktisch ADJECTIVE
unpractical

unpünktlich ADJECTIVE
   ■ Sie ist immer unpünktlich. She's always late.

★ **unrecht** ADJECTIVE
   ▷ see also das **Unrecht** NOUN
   wrong
   □ Du tust ihr unrecht. You are doing her an injustice.
   ■ unrecht haben to be wrong

das **Unrecht** NEUT NOUN
   ▷ see also **unrecht** ADJECTIVE
   wrong
   □ ein großes Unrecht a great wrong
   ■ zu Unrecht wrongly

unregelmäßig ADJECTIVE
irregular
   □ ein unregelmäßiges Verb an irregular verb

★ **unreif** ADJECTIVE
1 not ripe
   □ Der Apfel ist noch unreif. The apple's not ripe yet.
2 immature
   □ Elisabeth ist noch furchtbar unreif. Elisabeth's still terribly immature.

unrichtig ADJECTIVE
incorrect

die **Unruhe** FEM NOUN
unrest

der **Unruhestifter** (PL die **Unruhestifter**)
MASC NOUN
troublemaker

unruhig ADJECTIVE
restless

uns PRONOUN

uns is the accusative and dative of wir.

1 us
   □ Sie haben uns eingeladen. They've invited us.
2 to us
   □ Sie haben es uns gegeben. They gave it to us.
3 ourselves
   □ Wir fragen uns, ob das sein muss. We're asking ourselves whether that is necessary.
4 each other
   □ Wir lieben uns. We love each other.

unschlagbar ADJECTIVE
invincible

die **Unschuld** FEM NOUN
innocence

unschuldig ADJECTIVE
innocent

unselbstständig ADJECTIVE
dependent

★ **unser** ADJECTIVE
1 our
   □ Unser Deutschlehrer ist nett. Our German teacher's nice. □ Unser Haus ist ganz in der Nähe der Schule. Our house is very near the school. □ Unsere Ferien in Irland waren toll. Our holidays in Ireland were great.
2 ours
   □ Das ist nicht euer Lehrer, das ist unserer. He's not your teacher, he's ours. □ Ihre Note war besser als unsere. Her mark was better than ours. □ Deine Eltern sind netter als unsere. Your parents are nicer than ours.

unseretwegen ADVERB
1 for our sake
   □ Ihr braucht unseretwegen nicht zu warten. You needn't wait for our sake.
2 because of us
   □ Hat er sich unseretwegen so aufgeregt? Did he get so upset because of us?
3 as far as we're concerned
   □ Unseretwegen kann man das gern anders machen. As far as we're concerned you're welcome to do it differently.

unsicher ADJECTIVE
1 uncertain
   □ Es ist unsicher, ob wir kommen können. It's uncertain whether we can come.
2 insecure
   □ Nala ist sehr unsicher. Nala's very insecure.

unsichtbar ADJECTIVE
invisible

der **Unsinn** MASC NOUN
nonsense
   □ Unsinn erzählen to talk nonsense
   ■ Unsinn machen to do silly things

unsportlich ADJECTIVE
not sporty
   □ Tobias ist ziemlich unsportlich. Tobias is not at all sporty.

★ = core vocabulary

u

■ **unsportliches Verhalten** unsportsmanlike behaviour

★ **unsympathisch** ADJECTIVE
unpleasant
□ ein unsympathischer Mensch an unpleasant person
■ **Er ist mir unsympathisch.** I don't like him.

★ **unten** ADVERB
1 at the bottom
□ Das beste Buch lag unten auf dem Stapel. The best book was at the bottom of the pile. □ Er stand unten an der Treppe. He was standing at the bottom of the stairs. □ unten am Berg at the bottom of the mountain
2 downstairs
□ Mutter ist unten in der Küche. Mother's downstairs in the kitchen.
■ **nach unten** down

★ **unter** PREPOSITION
1 under

Use the accusative to express movement or a change of place. Use the dative when there is no change of place.

□ Die Katze lag unter dem Tisch. The cat lay under the table. □ Der Ball rollte unter den Tisch. The ball rolled under the table.
□ unter achtzehn Jahren under eighteen years of age
2 below
□ Temperaturen unter null below-zero temperatures
3 among
□ Unter den Büchern war auch ein Atlas. There was also an atlas among the books.
■ **Sie waren unter sich.** They were by themselves.
■ **einer unter ihnen** one of them
■ **unter anderem** among other things

das **Unterbewusstsein** NEUT NOUN
subconscious

unterbrechen (PRESENT TENSE **unterbricht**, IMPERFECT **unterbrach**, PERFECT TENSE **hat unterbrochen**) VERB [11]
to interrupt

die **Unterbrechung** FEM NOUN
interruption

unterdrücken (PERFECT TENSE **hat unterdrückt**) VERB [7]
1 to suppress
□ Sie unterdrückte ein Lächeln. She suppressed a smile.
2 to oppress
□ Menschen unterdrücken to oppress people

untere ADJECTIVE
lower
□ die unteren Stockwerke the lower floors

untergehen (IMPERFECT **ging unter**, PERFECT TENSE **ist untergegangen**) VERB [29]
1 to sink

2 to set
□ sobald die Sonne untergegangen ist ... as soon as the sun has set ...
■ **Die Welt geht unter.** The world's coming to an end.
■ **Seine Rede ging im Lärm unter.** His speech was drowned out by the noise.

★ das **Untergeschoss** NEUT NOUN
basement

unterhalb PREPOSITION

The preposition **unterhalb** takes the genitive.

below
□ Ihr Haus befindet sich unterhalb der Kirche. Her house is below the church.

★ **unterhalten** (PRESENT TENSE **unterhält**, IMPERFECT **unterhielt**, PERFECT TENSE **hat unterhalten**) VERB [33]
1 to entertain
□ Sie hat uns den ganzen Abend mit lustigen Geschichten unterhalten. She entertained us with funny stories all evening.
2 to run
□ Das Schwimmbad wird von der Stadt unterhalten. The swimming pool is run by the town council.
■ **sich unterhalten** to talk □ Wir haben uns über dich unterhalten. We talked about you.

unterhaltsam ADJECTIVE
entertaining

★ die **Unterhaltung** FEM NOUN
1 talk
□ Es war eine sehr aufschlussreiche Unterhaltung. It was a very informative talk.
2 entertainment
□ Zur Unterhaltung der Gäste spielt die örtliche Musikkapelle. Entertainment will be provided by the local brass band.

das **Unterhemd** (PL die **Unterhemden**) NEUT NOUN
vest

★ die **Unterhose** FEM NOUN
underpants pl
□ eine Unterhose a pair of underpants

★ die **Unterkunft** (PL die **Unterkünfte**) FEM NOUN
accommodation no pl

der **Untermieter** (PL die **Untermieter**) MASC NOUN
lodger

★ **unternehmen** (PRESENT TENSE **unternimmt**, IMPERFECT **unternahm**, PERFECT TENSE **hat unternommen**) VERB [52]
▷ see also das **Unternehmen** NOUN
■ **Was sollen wir heute unternehmen?** What shall we do today?

das **Unternehmen** (PL die **Unternehmen**) NEUT NOUN
▷ see also **unternehmen** VERB
enterprise

u

Numbers in brackets refer to verb tables on pages 697 to 706.

291

Unternehmer – unübersichtlich

der Unternehmer (PL die Unternehmer)
MASC NOUN
entrepreneur

die Unternehmerin FEM NOUN
entrepreneur

unternehmungslustig ADJECTIVE
enterprising

★ **der Unterricht** MASC NOUN
lessons *pl*
□ Nachmittags haben wir selten Unterricht. We seldom have lessons in the afternoon.

★ **unterrichten** (PERFECT TENSE hat unterrichtet) VERB [2]
1 to teach
□ Sie unterrichtet Englisch und Französisch. She teaches English and French.
■ **Wer unterrichtet euch in Sport?** Who do you have for sport?
2 to inform
□ Wir müssen deine Eltern davon unterrichten. We'll have to inform your parents.

das Unterrichtsfach (PL die Unterrichtsfächer) NEUT NOUN
subject

der Unterrock (PL die Unterröcke) MASC NOUN
underskirt

untersagt ADJECTIVE
forbidden

unterschätzen (PERFECT TENSE hat unterschätzt) VERB [36]
to underestimate

unterscheiden (IMPERFECT unterschied, PERFECT TENSE hat unterschieden) VERB [60]
to distinguish
□ Man muss zwischen Sachlichkeit und Unfreundlichkeit unterscheiden. You have to distinguish between objectivity and unfriendliness.
■ **sich unterscheiden** to differ

★ **der Unterschied** (PL die Unterschiede) MASC NOUN
difference
■ **im Unterschied zu** as distinct from

unterschiedlich ADJECTIVE
different
□ Sie haben sehr unterschiedliche Begabungen. They have very different talents. □ Sie sind unterschiedlich groß. They're different sizes.
■ **Das Wetter war sehr unterschiedlich.** The weather was mixed.

★ **unterschreiben** (IMPERFECT unterschrieb, PERFECT TENSE hat unterschrieben) VERB [61]
to sign
□ Du musst das Zeugnis unterschreiben lassen. You have to have the report signed.

★ **die Unterschrift** FEM NOUN
signature

unterste ADJECTIVE
bottom

□ Es ist im untersten Fach. It's on the bottom shelf.
■ **Sie ist in der untersten Klasse.** She's in the first form.

sich **unterstellen (1)** (PERFECT TENSE hat sich untergestellt) VERB [4]

Note that here the stress is on **unter**.

to take shelter
□ Es hat so stark geregnet, dass wir uns unterstellen mussten. It was raining so heavily that we had to take shelter.

unterstellen (2) (PERFECT TENSE hat unterstellt) VERB [18]

Note that here the stress is on **stellen**.

to imply
□ Willst du mir vielleicht unterstellen, dass ich das absichtlich getan habe? Are you perhaps implying that I did it on purpose?

unterstreichen (IMPERFECT unterstrich, PERFECT TENSE hat unterstrichen) VERB
to underline

der Unterstrich (PL die Unterstriche) MASC NOUN
underscore

die Unterstufe FEM NOUN
lower school

★ **unterstützen** (PERFECT TENSE hat unterstützt) VERB [36]
to support

die Unterstützung FEM NOUN
support

★ **untersuchen** (PERFECT TENSE hat untersucht) VERB [18]
to examine

die Untersuchung FEM NOUN
examination

die Untertasse FEM NOUN
saucer
□ eine fliegende Untertasse a flying saucer

unterteilen (PERFECT TENSE hat unterteilt) VERB [7]
to divide up

★ **der Untertitel** (PL die Untertitel) MASC NOUN
subtitle

★ **die Unterwäsche** FEM NOUN
underwear

★ **unterwegs** ADVERB
on the way

untreu ADJECTIVE
unfaithful

untröstlich ADJECTIVE
inconsolable

unübersichtlich ADJECTIVE
unclear
□ eine unübersichtliche Darstellung an unclear presentation
■ **eine unübersichtliche Kurve** a blind corner

u

292   ★ = core vocabulary

ununterbrochen ADJECTIVE
uninterrupted

unveränderlich ADJECTIVE
unchangeable

unverantwortlich ADJECTIVE
irresponsible

unverbesserlich ADJECTIVE
incorrigible

unvergesslich ADJECTIVE
unforgettable

unverkrampft ADJECTIVE
relaxed

unvermeidlich ADJECTIVE
unavoidable

unvernünftig ADJECTIVE
foolish

★ **unverschämt** ADJECTIVE
impudent

★ die **Unverschämtheit** FEM NOUN
impudence

unverzeihlich ADJECTIVE
unpardonable

unvollständig ADJECTIVE
incomplete

unvoreingenommen ADJECTIVE
unbiased

unvorsichtig ADJECTIVE
careless

★ **unvorstellbar** ADJECTIVE
inconceivable

unwahr ADJECTIVE
untrue

unwahrscheinlich ADJECTIVE, ADVERB
1 unlikely
□ eine unwahrscheinliche Geschichte an
unlikely story
2 incredibly
□ Ich habe mich unwahrscheinlich gefreut. I
was incredibly pleased.

★ **unwichtig** ADJECTIVE
unimportant

unwirksam ADJECTIVE
ineffective

unzählig ADJECTIVE
countless

unzerbrechlich ADJECTIVE
unbreakable

unzertrennlich ADJECTIVE
inseparable

★ **unzufrieden** ADJECTIVE
dissatisfied

unzutreffend ADJECTIVE
incorrect

updaten VERB [38]
to update

uploaden VERB [36]
to upload

uralt ADJECTIVE
ancient

der **Ureinwohner** (PL die **Ureinwohner**)
MASC NOUN
original inhabitant

der **Urin** (PL die **Urine**) MASC NOUN
urine

die **Urkunde** FEM NOUN
certificate

★ der **Urlaub** (PL die **Urlaube**) MASC NOUN
holiday
□ Wir fahren morgen in Urlaub. We're going on
holiday tomorrow. □ Wo warst du im Urlaub?
Where did you go on holiday?

★ die **Ursache** FEM NOUN
cause
■ **Keine Ursache!** That's all right.

ursprünglich ADJECTIVE, ADVERB
1 original
□ Wir mussten unsere ursprünglichen Pläne
aufgeben. We had to abandon our original
plans.
2 originally
□ Ursprünglich wollten wir nach Griechenland
fahren. We originally wanted to go to Greece.

das **Urteil** (PL die **Urteile**) NEUT NOUN
1 opinion
□ Wie lautet dein Urteil? What's your opinion?
2 sentence
□ Die Richter haben das Urteil noch nicht
verkündet. The judges haven't passed sentence
yet.

urteilen VERB [38]
to judge

der **Urwald** (PL die **Urwälder**) MASC NOUN
jungle

★ die **USA** PL NOUN
USA *sing*
■ **aus den USA** from the USA
■ **in den USA** in the USA
■ **in die USA** to the USA

usw. ABBREVIATION (= *und so weiter*)
etc

u

Vv

vage ADJECTIVE
vague

★ die **Vanille** FEM NOUN
vanilla

die **Vase** FEM NOUN
vase

★ der **Vater** (PL die **Väter**) MASC NOUN
father

das **Vaterunser** (PL die **Vaterunser**) NEUT NOUN
Lord's prayer

★ der **Vati** (PL die **Vatis**) MASC NOUN
daddy (*Umgangssprache*)

das **veganisch** ADJECTIVE
vegan

★ der **Vegetarier** (PL die **Vegetarier**) MASC NOUN
vegetarian

★ die **Vegetarierin** FEM NOUN
vegetarian

vegetarisch ADJECTIVE
vegetarian

das **Veilchen** (PL die **Veilchen**) NEUT NOUN
violet

die **Vene** FEM NOUN
vein

das **Ventil** (PL die **Ventile**) NEUT NOUN
valve

der **Ventilator** (PL die **Ventilatoren**) MASC NOUN
fan

verabreden (PERFECT TENSE **hat verabredet**) VERB [54]
to arrange

□ Wir sollten Zeit und Ort des Treffens verabreden. We ought to arrange when and where to meet.

■ **sich mit jemandem verabreden** to arrange to meet somebody

■ **mit jemandem verabredet sein** to have arranged to meet somebody □ Ich bin mit meiner Mutter verabredet. I've arranged to meet my mother.

★ die **Verabredung** FEM NOUN
date

★ **verabschieden** (PERFECT TENSE **hat verabschiedet**) VERB [54]
to say goodbye to

□ Wir verabschiedeten unsere Gäste. We said goodbye to our guests.

■ **sich verabschieden** to take one's leave

verallgemeinern (PERFECT TENSE **hat verallgemeinert**) VERB [88]
to generalize

veralten (PERFECT TENSE **ist veraltet**) VERB [2]
to become obsolete

★ **veränderlich** ADJECTIVE
changeable

★ **verändern** (PERFECT TENSE **hat verändert**) VERB [88]
to change

■ **sich verändern** to change □ Sie hat sich in den letzten beiden Monaten verändert. She's changed in the last couple of months.

die **Veränderung** FEM NOUN
change

die **Veranlagung** FEM NOUN
disposition

□ eine nervöse Veranlagung a nervous disposition

veranlassen (PERFECT TENSE **hat veranlasst**) VERB [84]

■ **etwas veranlassen** to have something done

■ **sich veranlasst sehen, etwas zu tun** to be prompted to do something

veranschaulichen (PERFECT TENSE **hat veranschaulicht**) VERB [7]
to illustrate

veranstalten (PERFECT TENSE **hat veranstaltet**) VERB [2]
to organize

der **Veranstalter** (PL die **Veranstalter**) MASC NOUN
organizer

★ die **Veranstaltung** FEM NOUN
event

verantworten (PERFECT TENSE **hat verantwortet**) VERB [2]
to take responsibility for

□ Wenn das nicht klappt, hast du das zu verantworten. If it doesn't work, you'll have to take responsibility for it.

★ = core vocabulary

- **Das kann ich nicht verantworten.** I couldn't possibly allow that.

verantwortlich ADJECTIVE
responsible

★ die **Verantwortung** FEM NOUN
responsibility

verarbeiten (PERFECT TENSE **hat verarbeitet**) VERB [2]

1 to process
□ In diesem Werk wird Metall verarbeitet. Metal is processed in this factory.
■ **etwas zu etwas verarbeiten** to make something into something □ Der Plastikmüll wird zu Parkbänken verarbeitet. Plastic waste is made into park benches.

2 to digest
□ Ich muss die Reiseeindrücke erst noch verarbeiten. I still have to digest my impressions from the journey.

verärgern (PERFECT TENSE **hat verärgert**) VERB [88]
to annoy

das **Verb** (PL die **Verben**) NEUT NOUN
verb

★ der **Verband** (PL die **Verbände**) MASC NOUN

1 dressing
■ **Die Schwester hat ihm einen Verband angelegt.** The nurse dressed his wound.

2 association
□ Die Bauern haben sich zu einem Verband zusammengeschlossen. The farmers have formed an association.

der **Verbandskasten** (PL die **Verbandskästen**) MASC NOUN
first-aid box

verbergen (PRESENT TENSE **verbirgt**, IMPERFECT **verbarg**, PERFECT TENSE **hat verborgen**) VERB
to hide
■ **sich vor jemandem verbergen** to hide from somebody

★ **verbessern** (PERFECT TENSE **hat verbessert**) VERB [88]

1 to improve
□ Ich konnte meine Noten verbessern. I was able to improve my marks.

2 to correct
□ Meine Mutter hat meine Hausaufgaben verbessert. My mother corrected my homework.
■ **sich verbessern** to improve □ In Mathe habe ich mich verbessert. I've improved in maths.

★ die **Verbesserung** FEM NOUN

1 improvement
□ eine Verbesserung seiner Leistungen an improvement in his work

2 correction
□ Schreibt bitte die Verbesserung ins Heft.

Please write the correction in your exercise book.

verbiegen (IMPERFECT **verbog**, PERFECT TENSE **hat verbogen**) VERB
to bend

★ **verbieten** (IMPERFECT **verbot**, PERFECT TENSE **hat verboten**) VERB [8]
to forbid
□ Meine Mutter hat mir verboten, mit Frank auszugehen. My mother forbade me to go out with Frank.

★ **verbinden** (IMPERFECT **verband**, PERFECT TENSE **hat verbunden**) VERB

1 to combine
□ Ich habe das Nützliche mit dem Angenehmen verbunden. I was able to combine business with pleasure.

2 to bandage
□ Die Wunde muss verbunden werden. The wound has to be bandaged.
■ **jemandem die Augen verbinden** to blindfold somebody

3 to connect
□ Ein Kanal verbindet die beiden Flüsse. A canal connects the two rivers.

4 to put through
□ Können Sie mich bitte mit Frau Karl verbinden? Can you put me through to Mrs Karl, please? □ Ich verbinde! I'm putting you through.
■ **Sie sind falsch verbunden.** You've got the wrong number.

★ die **Verbindung** (PL die **Verbindungen**) FEM NOUN

1 connection
□ Es gibt eine direkte Verbindung nach München. There is a direct connection to Munich.

2 communication
■ **Unsere Verbindung wurde unterbrochen.** We were cut off.
■ **Die Verbindung mit Nepal war sehr schlecht.** The line to Nepal was really bad.
■ **eine chemische Verbindung** a compound

★ **verbleit** ADJECTIVE
leaded

verblüffen (PERFECT TENSE **hat verblüfft**) VERB [84]
to amaze

verbluten (PERFECT TENSE **ist verblutet**) VERB [2]
to bleed to death

verborgen ADJECTIVE
hidden

das **Verbot** (PL die **Verbote**) NEUT NOUN
ban
□ Die Regierung verhängte ein Verbot für Rindfleischimporte aus England. The government imposed a ban on beef imports from England.

Numbers in brackets refer to verb tables on pages 697 to 706.

295

V

verboten – verdienen

★ **verboten** ADJECTIVE
forbidden
- **Rauchen verboten!** No smoking

der **Verbrauch** MASC NOUN
consumption

verbrauchen (PERFECT TENSE hat verbraucht) VERB [84]
to use up
□ Das Gerät verbraucht viel Strom. The machine uses up a lot of electricity.

der **Verbraucher** (PL die Verbraucher) MASC NOUN
consumer

★ der **Verbrauchermarkt** (PL die Verbrauchermärkte) MASC NOUN
hypermarket

das **Verbrechen** (PL die Verbrechen) NEUT NOUN
crime

der **Verbrecher** (PL die Verbrecher) MASC NOUN
criminal

verbreiten (PERFECT TENSE hat verbreitet) VERB [2]
1 to spread
□ eine Krankheit verbreiten to spread a disease
2 to broadcast
□ eine Nachricht verbreiten to broadcast a message
- **sich verbreiten** to spread □ Die Seuche hat sich inzwischen im ganzen Land verbreitet. The epidemic has since spread all over the country.
□ Die Nachricht von seinem Tod hat sich schnell verbreitet. The news of his death spread quickly.

verbrennen (IMPERFECT verbrannte, PERFECT TENSE hat verbrannt) VERB [12]
1 to burn
□ In dieser Anlage wird Müll verbrannt. Waste is burnt in this plant.
2 to cremate
□ Sie möchte nach ihrem Tod verbrannt werden. She'd like to be cremated when she dies.

★ **verbringen** (IMPERFECT verbrachte, PERFECT TENSE hat verbracht) VERB [13]
to spend
□ Wir haben das Wochenende im Schwarzwald verbracht. We spent the weekend in the Black Forest.

verbrühen (PERFECT TENSE hat verbrüht) VERB [7]
to scald
□ Ich habe mir den Arm verbrüht. I've scalded my arm.
- **sich verbrühen** to scald oneself □ Pass auf, dass du dich nicht verbrühst. Careful you don't scald yourself.

der **Verdacht** (PL die Verdachte) MASC NOUN
suspicion

verdächtig ADJECTIVE
suspicious

verdächtigen (PERFECT TENSE hat verdächtigt) VERB [84]
to suspect

verdammt ADJECTIVE, ADVERB
damned (Umgangssprache)
□ Diese verdammten Fliegen! These damned flies!
- **Verdammt noch mal!** Damn it all!
- **Verdammt!** Damn!

verdampfen (PERFECT TENSE ist verdampft) VERB [7]
to evaporate

verdanken (PERFECT TENSE hat verdankt) VERB [84]
- **jemandem sein Leben verdanken** to owe one's life to somebody □ Sie verdankt ihm ihr Leben. She owes her life to him.

verdauen (PERFECT TENSE hat verdaut) VERB [84]
to digest

verdaulich ADJECTIVE
- **Das ist schwer verdaulich.** That's hard to digest.

die **Verdauung** FEM NOUN
digestion

verderben (PRESENT TENSE verdirbt, IMPERFECT verdarb, PERFECT TENSE hat/ist verdorben) VERB

> Use haben to form the perfect tense. Use sein to form the perfect tense for 'to go bad'.

1 to ruin
□ Du verdirbst dir bei dem schlechten Licht die Augen. You'll ruin your eyes in this bad light.
□ Er hat mir den Urlaub verdorben. He ruined my holiday.
2 to corrupt
□ Geld verdirbt den Menschen. Money corrupts people.
- **es mit jemandem verderben** to get into somebody's bad books □ Sie will es mit keinem verderben. She doesn't want to get into anybody's bad books.
3 to go bad
□ Die Wurst ist verdorben. The sausage has gone bad.

★ **verdienen** (PERFECT TENSE hat verdient) VERB [84]
1 to earn
□ Wie viel verdient deine Mutter? How much does your mother earn?
2 to deserve
□ Du hast die Strafe verdient. You deserved the punishment.

★ = core vocabulary

verdreifachen (PERFECT TENSE **hat verdreifacht**) VERB [7]
to treble

verdünnen (PERFECT TENSE **hat verdünnt**) VERB [7]
to dilute

verdunsten (PERFECT TENSE **ist verdunstet**) VERB [2]
to evaporate

verdursten (PERFECT TENSE **ist verdurstet**) VERB [2]
to die of thirst

verdutzt ADJECTIVE
nonplussed

► der **Verein** (PL die **Vereine**) MASC NOUN
club
□ ein Sportverein a sports club

vereinbar ADJECTIVE
compatible
□ mit etwas vereinbar compatible with something

vereinbaren (PERFECT TENSE **hat vereinbart**) VERB [84]
to agree on

die **Vereinbarung** FEM NOUN
agreement

vereinen (PERFECT TENSE **hat vereint**) VERB [84]
1 to unite
□ Das geteilte Land wurde wieder vereint. The divided country was reunited.
2 to reconcile
□ Ich kann das nicht mit meinem Gewissen vereinen. I can't reconcile that with my conscience.
■ **Mit vereinten Kräften schaffen wir das.** If we all pull together, we'll manage to do it.
■ die Vereinten Nationen the United Nations

vereinfachen (PERFECT TENSE **hat vereinfacht**) VERB [84]
to simplify

vereinigen (PERFECT TENSE **hat vereinigt**) VERB [84]
to unite

vereinzelt ADJECTIVE
isolated
□ vereinzelte Schauer isolated showers

vererben (PERFECT TENSE **hat vererbt**) VERB [18]
to leave
□ Meine Oma hat mir all ihre Bücher vererbt. My granny left me all her books.
■ **sich vererben** to be hereditary
□ Krampfadern vererben sich. Varicose veins are hereditary.

verfahren (PRESENT TENSE **verfährt**, IMPERFECT **verfuhr**, PERFECT TENSE **hat/ist verfahren**) VERB [21]
1 to proceed
□ Wie sollen wir verfahren? How shall we proceed?
2 to use up
□ Wir haben 50 Liter Benzin verfahren. We have used up 50 litres of petrol.
■ **Wir haben uns verfahren.** We have lost our way.

das **Verfahren** (PL die **Verfahren**) NEUT NOUN
1 process
□ Das ist ein neuartiges Verfahren zum Recyceln von Plastik. This is a new recycling process for plastic.
2 proceedings pl
□ ein Verfahren gegen jemanden einleiten to bring proceedings against somebody

die **Verfassung** FEM NOUN
1 constitution
□ Die Opposition hat eine Änderung der Verfassung beantragt. The opposition's called for an amendment to the constitution.
2 state
□ Ich bin nicht in der Verfassung, da mitzumachen. I'm in no state to join in.

verfolgen (PERFECT TENSE **hat verfolgt**) VERB [84]
1 to pursue
□ Die Polizei verfolgte die Täter. The police pursued the culprits.
■ **Die Hunde verfolgten ihre Fährte.** The dogs tracked them.
2 to persecute
□ In vielen Ländern werden Minderheiten verfolgt. Minorities are persecuted in many countries.

die **Verfolgung** FEM NOUN
1 hunt
□ Die Verfolgung der Täter war erfolgreich. The hunt for the culprits had a successful outcome.
2 persecution
□ die Verfolgung von Minderheiten the persecution of minorities

verfügbar ADJECTIVE
available

die **Verfügung** FEM NOUN
■ **etwas zur Verfügung haben** to have something at one's disposal □ Nicht alle Schüler haben einen Computer zur Verfügung. Not all pupils have a computer at their disposal.
■ **allen zur Verfügung stehen** to be open to all
■ **Ich stehe Ihnen zur Verfügung.** I am at your service.

verführen (PERFECT TENSE **hat verführt**) VERB [84]
1 to tempt
□ Verführ mich nicht, ich habe schon zwei

V

Numbers in brackets refer to verb tables on pages 697 to 706.

297

Stück Kuchen gegessen. Don't tempt me, I've already had two pieces of cake.
2 to seduce

★ die **Vergangenheit** FEM NOUN
past
□ in der Vergangenheit in the past

der **Vergaser** (PL die **Vergaser**) MASC NOUN
carburettor

vergaß VERB ▷ see vergessen

★ **vergeben** (PRESENT TENSE **vergibt**, IMPERFECT **vergab**, PERFECT TENSE **hat vergeben**) VERB [28]
to forgive
□ Kannst du mir noch einmal vergeben? Can you forgive me one more time? □ Diese Lüge werde ich dir nie vergeben. I'll never forgive you for that lie.
■ **vergeben sein** to be taken □ Tut mir leid, die Stelle ist schon vergeben. Sorry, the job's already taken.
■ **Er ist schon vergeben.** He's already spoken for.

vergeblich ADVERB, ADJECTIVE
in vain
□ Wir haben uns vergeblich bemüht. We tried, but in vain. □ All mein Reden war vergeblich. All my words were in vain.

vergehen (IMPERFECT **verging**, PERFECT TENSE **ist vergangen**) VERB [29]
to pass
■ **Wie schnell die Zeit doch vergeht!** How time flies!
■ **Mir ist der Appetit vergangen.** I've lost my appetite.
■ **sich an jemandem vergehen** to indecently assault somebody

★ **vergessen** (PRESENT TENSE **vergisst**, IMPERFECT **vergaß**, PERFECT TENSE **hat vergessen**) VERB [83]
to forget
□ Ich habe seinen Namen vergessen. I've forgotten his name.
■ **Vergiss nicht, die Blumen zu gießen.** Remember to water the flowers.

vergesslich ADJECTIVE
forgetful

vergeuden (PERFECT TENSE **hat vergeudet**) VERB [7]
to squander

vergewaltigen (PERFECT TENSE **hat vergewaltigt**) VERB [7]
to rape
□ Er hat eine Frau vergewaltigt. He raped a woman.

die **Vergewaltigung** FEM NOUN
rape

sich **vergewissern** (PERFECT TENSE **hat sich vergewissert**) VERB [88]
to make sure

★ **vergiften** (PERFECT TENSE **hat vergiftet**) VERB [2]
to poison

die **Vergiftung** FEM NOUN
poisoning

vergisst VERB ▷ see vergessen

der **Vergleich** (PL die **Vergleiche**) MASC NOUN
comparison
■ **im Vergleich zu** compared with

★ **vergleichen** (IMPERFECT **verglich**, PERFECT TENSE **hat verglichen**) VERB
to compare
□ Er hat mein Wörterbuch mit seinem verglichen. He compared my dictionary with his. □ Man kann doch Äpfel und Birnen nicht vergleichen. You can't compare apples and pears.

★ das **Vergnügen** (PL die **Vergnügen**) NEUT NOUN
pleasure
■ **Viel Vergnügen!** Have fun!

vergnügt ADJECTIVE
cheerful

vergraben (PRESENT TENSE **vergräbt**, IMPERFECT **vergrub**, PERFECT TENSE **hat vergraben**) VERB
to bury

vergrößern (PERFECT TENSE **hat vergrößert**) VERB [88]
1 to enlarge
□ Ich habe das Foto vergrößern lassen. I had the photo enlarged.
2 to extend
□ Wir wollen das Haus vergrößern. We want to extend the house.
■ **sich vergrößern** to grow larger □ Die Klasse hat sich stark vergrößert. The class has grown considerably larger.

verhaften (PERFECT TENSE **hat verhaftet**) VERB [2]
to arrest

sich **verhalten** (PRESENT TENSE **verhält sich**, IMPERFECT **verhielt sich**, PERFECT TENSE **hat sich verhalten**) VERB [33]
▷ see also das **Verhalten** NOUN
to behave
□ Er hat sich uns gegenüber sehr fair verhalten. He behaved very fairly towards us.

das **Verhalten** NEUT NOUN
▷ see also **verhalten** VERB
behaviour

★ das **Verhältnis** (GEN des **Verhältnisses**, PL die **Verhältnisse**) NEUT NOUN
1 affair
□ Er hat ein Verhältnis mit einer verheirateten Frau. He's having an affair with a married woman.
2 proportion
□ Unser Gehalt steht in keinem Verhältnis zu

★ = core vocabulary

unserer Leistung. Our salary is not in proportion to our efforts.

■ **Verhältnisse 1** conditions □ Wenn die Verhältnisse anders wären, könnten wir die Arbeit schneller beenden. If conditions were different we could get the work finished sooner. **2** background *sing* □ Er kommt aus bescheidenen Verhältnissen. He comes from a modest background.

■ **über seine Verhältnisse leben** to live beyond one's means

verhältnismäßig ADVERB
relatively

verhandeln (PERFECT TENSE **hat verhandelt**) VERB [34]
to negotiate
□ Sie verhandeln einen Waffenstillstand. They're negotiating a ceasefire.
■ **Mein Fall wird nächste Woche vor dem Arbeitsgericht verhandelt.** My case is being heard by the industrial tribunal next week.

die **Verhandlung** FEM NOUN
1 negotiation
□ die Friedensverhandlungen peace negotiations □ Wir sind mit der Firma noch in Verhandlung. We're still involved in negotiations with the company.
2 trial
□ Die Verhandlung gegen Klitt ist morgen. Klitt's trial is tomorrow.
3 hearing
□ die Verhandlung vor dem Arbeitsgericht the hearing before the industrial tribunal

verharmlosen (PERFECT TENSE **hat verharmlost**) VERB [7]
to play down

verhauen (PERFECT TENSE **hat verhauen**) VERB [7]
to beat up

verheerend ADJECTIVE
devastating

verheimlichen (PERFECT TENSE **hat verheimlicht**) VERB [7]
■ **jemandem etwas verheimlichen** to keep something secret from somebody

★ **verheiratet** ADJECTIVE
married

★ **verhindern** (PERFECT TENSE **hat verhindert**) VERB [88]
to prevent
■ **verhindert sein** to be unable to make it
□ Ich bin leider verhindert. I'm afraid I can't make it.

verhungern (PERFECT TENSE **ist verhungert**) VERB [88]
to starve to death

das **Verhütungsmittel** (PL die **Verhütungsmittel**) NEUT NOUN
contraceptive

★ sich **verirren** (PERFECT TENSE **hat sich verirrt**) VERB [84]
to get lost
□ Wir hatten uns im Nebel verirrt. We lost our way in the fog.

der **Verkauf** (PL die **Verkäufe**) MASC NOUN
sale

★ **verkaufen** (PERFECT TENSE **hat verkauft**) VERB [84]
to sell

★ der **Verkäufer** (PL die **Verkäufer**) MASC NOUN
shop assistant
□ Der Verkäufer hat uns sehr gut beraten. The shop assistant was extremely helpful.

★ die **Verkäuferin** FEM NOUN
shop assistant
□ Sie ist Verkäuferin in einer Modeboutique. She's a shop assistant in a fashion boutique.

★ der **Verkehr** MASC NOUN
traffic
□ Heute war viel Verkehr auf den Straßen. There was heavy traffic on the roads today.

★ die **Verkehrsampel** FEM NOUN
traffic lights *pl*

★ das **Verkehrsamt** (PL die **Verkehrsämter**) NEUT NOUN
tourist office

die **Verkehrsmeldung** FEM NOUN
traffic announcement

★ das **Verkehrsmittel** (PL die **Verkehrsmittel**) NEUT NOUN
means of transport *sing*

das **Verkehrsschild** (PL die **Verkehrsschilder**) NEUT NOUN
road sign

der **Verkehrsunfall** (PL die **Verkehrsunfälle**) MASC NOUN
traffic accident

das **Verkehrszeichen** (PL die **Verkehrszeichen**) NEUT NOUN
traffic sign

verkehrt ADJECTIVE
wrong
□ Das war die verkehrte Antwort. That was the wrong answer.
■ **verkehrt herum** back to front □ Du hast deinen Pulli verkehrt herum an. You've got your pullover on back to front.

sich **verkleiden** (PERFECT TENSE **hat sich verkleidet**) VERB [54]
to dress up
□ Sie verkleidete sich als Gespenst. She dressed up as a ghost.

verkleinern (PERFECT TENSE **hat verkleinert**) VERB [88]
to reduce
□ Wir sollten den Zeilenabstand verkleinern. We should reduce the line spacing.

V

■ **sich verkleinern** to grow smaller □ Die Klasse hat sich stark verkleinert. The class has grown considerably smaller.

der **Verlag** (PL die **Verlage**) MASC NOUN
publisher

verlangen (PERFECT TENSE **hat verlangt**) VERB [84]
to ask for
□ Ich verlange etwas mehr Verständnis. I'm asking for a bit more understanding. □ Wie viel hat er dafür verlangt? How much did he ask for it?
■ **etwas von jemandem verlangen** to expect something of somebody □ Unser Chemielehrer verlangt zu viel von uns. Our chemistry teacher expects too much of us.

verlängern (PERFECT TENSE **hat verlängert**) VERB [88]
1 to extend
□ Wir haben die Ferien um eine Woche verlängert. We've extended our holiday by a week.
2 to lengthen
□ Wir müssen das Seil verlängern. We'll have to lengthen the rope.

★ **verlassen** (PRESENT TENSE **verlässt**, IMPERFECT **verließ**, PERFECT TENSE **hat verlassen**) VERB [42]
▷ see also **verlassen** ADJECTIVE
to leave
□ Er hat seine Frau und Kinder verlassen. He's left his wife and children.
■ **Verlassen Sie sofort das Gebäude!** Get out of the building immediately.
■ **sich verlassen auf** to depend on □ Ich kann mich doch auf dich verlassen. I hope I can depend on you.

★ **verlassen** ADJECTIVE
▷ see also **verlassen** VERB
1 deserted
□ eine verlassene Gegend a deserted area □ der verlassene Ehemann the deserted husband
2 empty
□ ein verlassenes Haus an empty house

sich **verlaufen** (PRESENT TENSE **verläuft sich**, IMPERFECT **verlief sich**, PERFECT TENSE **hat sich verlaufen**) VERB [43]
1 to get lost
□ Wir haben uns im Wald verlaufen. We got lost in the forest.
2 to disperse
□ Nach Ende der Veranstaltung verlief sich die Menge. After the event the crowd dispersed.

verlegen ADJECTIVE
embarrassed
■ **nicht verlegen um** never at a loss for □ Sie ist nie um eine Ausrede verlegen. She's never at a loss for an excuse.

verleihen (IMPERFECT **verlieh**, PERFECT TENSE **hat verliehen**) VERB
1 to lend
□ Ich habe mein Wörterbuch an sie verliehen. I've lent her my dictionary.
2 to hire out
□ Ich suche jemanden, der Fahrräder verleiht. I'm looking for somebody who hires out bikes.
3 to award
□ Sie hat einen Preis verliehen bekommen. She was awarded a prize.

verleiten (PERFECT TENSE **hat verleitet**) VERB [2]
■ **jemanden dazu verleiten, etwas zu tun** to tempt somebody into doing something

verlernen (PERFECT TENSE **hat verlernt**) VERB [84]
to forget

★ **verletzen** (PERFECT TENSE **hat verletzt**) VERB [36]
1 to hurt
□ Deine Bemerkung hat mich verletzt. Your remark hurt me.
2 to injure
□ Sie ist schwer verletzt. She's seriously injured.
■ **ein Gesetz verletzen** to violate a law

der/die **Verletzte** (GEN des/der **Verletzten**, PL die **Verletzten**) MASC/FEM NOUN
injured person
□ Auf der Straße lag ein Verletzter. An injured person was lying in the street.

★ die **Verletzung** FEM NOUN
injury
■ **Er hatte schwere Verletzungen.** He was seriously injured.
■ **Das ist eine Verletzung der Spielregeln.** That's against the rules of the game.

sich **verlieben** (PERFECT TENSE **hat sich verliebt**) VERB [84]
■ **sich in jemanden verlieben** to fall in love with somebody

verliebt ADJECTIVE
in love
□ Ich bin in Anke verliebt. I'm in love with Anke.

★ **verlieren** (IMPERFECT **verlor**, PERFECT TENSE **hat verloren**) VERB [85]
to lose

der **Verlierer** (PL die **Verlierer**) MASC NOUN
loser

sich **verloben** (PERFECT TENSE **hat sich verlobt**) VERB [84]
■ **sich mit jemandem verloben** to get engaged to somebody

der **Verlobte** (GEN des **Verlobten**, PL die **Verlobten**) MASC NOUN
▷ see also die **Verlobte** NOUN
fiancé
□ Mathias ist mein Verlobter. Mathias is my fiancé.

★ = core vocabulary

die **Verlobte** (GEN der **Verlobten**, PL die **Verlobten**) FEM NOUN
▷ see also der **Verlobte** NOUN
fiancée
□ Leonie ist ihre Verlobte. Leonie is her fiancée.

★ die **Verlobung** FEM NOUN
engagement

verloren ADJECTIVE
lost
□ die verlorene Zeit wieder einholen to make up for lost time
■ verlorene Eier poached eggs
■ verloren gehen to get lost

verlor, verloren VERB ▷ see **verlieren**

die **Verlosung** FEM NOUN
raffle

der **Verlust** (PL die **Verluste**) MASC NOUN
loss

vermehren (PERFECT TENSE **hat vermehrt**) VERB [7]
increase
□ Die Firma hat ihren Umsatz vermehrt. The company has increased its turnover.
■ sich vermehren to reproduce □ Wie vermehren sich Regenwürmer? How do earthworms reproduce?

★ **vermeiden** (IMPERFECT **vermied**, PERFECT TENSE **hat vermieden**) VERB
to avoid

★ **vermieten** (PERFECT TENSE **hat vermietet**) VERB [2]
1 to let
□ 'Zimmer zu vermieten' 'Rooms to let'
2 to rent
□ Sie vermietet Zimmer. She rents rooms.
3 to hire out
□ Wir vermieten Boote und Fahrräder. We hire out boats and bikes.

der **Vermieter** (PL die **Vermieter**) MASC NOUN
landlord

die **Vermieterin** FEM NOUN
landlady

vermissen (PERFECT TENSE **hat vermisst**) VERB [7]
to miss
□ Ich habe dich vermisst. I missed you.
■ Ich vermisse eines meiner Bücher. One of my books is missing.

das **Vermögen** (PL die **Vermögen**) NEUT NOUN
wealth
■ ein Vermögen kosten to cost a fortune

vermuten (PERFECT TENSE **hat vermutet**) VERB [2]
1 to guess
□ Ich kann nur vermuten, was er damit gemeint hat. I can only guess what he meant by that.

■ Man vermutet, dass er im Ausland ist. He is thought to be abroad.
2 to suspect
□ Die Polizei vermutet, dass sie die Täter sind. The police suspect that they're the culprits.
3 to suppose
□ Ich vermute, dass er das noch nicht weiß. I don't suppose that he knows that yet.

vermutlich ADJECTIVE, ADVERB
1 probable
□ die vermutliche Ursache the probable cause
2 probably
□ Sie ist vermutlich schon gegangen. She has probably already left.

die **Vermutung** FEM NOUN
1 assumption
□ Das legt die Vermutung nahe, dass sie kündigen will. It seems a likely assumption that she's already gone.
2 suspicion
□ Die Polizei hat eine Vermutung, wer der Täter gewesen sein könnte. The police have a suspicion as to who the culprit could have been.

vernachlässigen (PERFECT TENSE **hat vernachlässigt**) VERB [84]
to neglect

vernichten (PERFECT TENSE **hat vernichtet**) VERB [2]
to destroy
■ Insekten vernichten to exterminate insects
■ Unkraut vernichten to eradicate weeds

die **Vernunft** FEM NOUN
reason

vernünftig ADJECTIVE
reasonable
□ Sei doch vernünftig! Be reasonable! □ ein vernünftiger Preis a reasonable price
■ etwas Vernünftiges essen to eat something decent

veröffentlichen (PERFECT TENSE **hat veröffentlicht**) VERB [84]
to publish

die **Verpackung** FEM NOUN
packing no pl

★ **verpassen** (PERFECT TENSE **hat verpasst**) VERB [7]
to miss
□ Wir haben den Anschluss nach Paris verpasst. We missed our connection to Paris.
■ jemandem eine Ohrfeige verpassen to give somebody a clip round the ear

verpflegen (PERFECT TENSE **hat verpflegt**) VERB [7]
to cater for
□ Die Flüchtlinge wurden vom Roten Kreuz verpflegt. The Red Cross catered for the refugees.

Numbers in brackets refer to verb tables on pages 697 to 706.

301

Verpflegung – verschieden

die Verpflegung FEM NOUN
food
□ Für Ihre Verpflegung wird gesorgt. Food will be laid on. □ Die Verpflegung im Schullandheim war gut. The food at the school camp was good.

verpflichten (PERFECT TENSE **hat verpflichtet**) VERB [2]
to sign
□ Der Klub will einen neuen Spieler verpflichten. The club wants to sign a new player.
■ **sich verpflichten, etwas zu tun** to promise to do something □ Du hast dich verpflichtet, für die Musik zu sorgen. You promised to organize the music.
■ **Sie haben sich verpflichtet, für Ersatz zu sorgen.** You undertook to find a replacement.
■ **verpflichtet sein, etwas zu tun** to be obliged to do something
■ **Er ist zum Stillschweigen verpflichtet.** He's sworn to silence.
■ **Das verpflichtet Sie zu nichts.** This doesn't commit you to anything.
■ **jemandem zu Dank verpflichtet sein** to be obliged to somebody

verprügeln (PERFECT TENSE **hat verprügelt**) VERB [7]
to beat up

verraten (PRESENT TENSE **verrät**, IMPERFECT **verriet** PERFECT TENSE **hat verraten**) VERB
1 to betray
□ Er hat seine Mittäter verraten. He betrayed his accomplices.
2 to report
□ Lucas hat uns beim Lehrer verraten. Lucas reported us to the teacher.
3 to tell
□ Verrate mir doch, wer es war. Tell me who it was. □ Ich habe dieses Geheimnis niemandem verraten. I haven't told anyone the secret.
■ **sich verraten** to give oneself away

verregnet ADJECTIVE
rainy

★ **verreisen** (PERFECT TENSE **ist verreist**) VERB [84]
to go away
□ Ich möchte diesen Sommer verreisen. I'd like to go away this summer.
■ **Wir wollen nach Israel verreisen.** We intend to go to Israel.

verrenken (PERFECT TENSE **hat verrenkt**) VERB [7]
to sprain
□ Er hat sich den Knöchel verrenkt. He sprained his ankle.

verrosten (PERFECT TENSE **ist verrostet**) VERB [2]
to rust

verrückt ADJECTIVE
crazy

der/die Verrückte (GEN **des/der Verrückten**, PL **die Verrückten**) MASC/FEM NOUN
maniac
□ Er ist gefahren wie ein Verrückter. He drove like a maniac.

die Verrücktheit FEM NOUN
madness

verrufen ADJECTIVE
disreputable

der Vers (GEN **des Verses**, PL **die Verse**) MASC NOUN
verse

der Versager (PL **die Versager**) MASC NOUN
failure

versalzen (PERFECT TENSE **hat versalzen**) VERB
to put too much salt in
□ Sie hat die Suppe versalzen. She put too much salt in the soup.
■ **Die Suppe ist versalzen.** There's too much salt in the soup.

versammeln (PERFECT TENSE **hat versammelt**) VERB [34]
to assemble

★ **die Versammlung** FEM NOUN
meeting

das Versandhaus (GEN **des Versandhauses**, PL **die Versandhäuser**) NEUT NOUN
mail-order firm

versäumen (PERFECT TENSE **hat versäumt**) VERB [84]
to miss
□ Ich habe wegen Krankheit drei Stunden versäumt. I missed three lessons due to illness. □ Sie sollten nicht versäumen, sich die Kathedrale anzusehen. Don't miss a visit to the cathedral.
■ **es versäumen, etwas zu tun** to fail to do something □ Sie hat es versäumt, sich rechtzeitig anzumelden. She failed to register in time.

verschenken (PERFECT TENSE **hat verschenkt**) VERB [7]
to give away

verschicken (PERFECT TENSE **hat verschickt**) VERB [7]
to send away

verschieben (IMPERFECT **verschob**, PERFECT TENSE **hat verschoben**) VERB
to postpone
□ Wir müssen das Fest verschieben. We'll have to postpone the party.

★ **verschieden** ADJECTIVE
different

★ = core vocabulary

□ Die zwei Brüder sind sehr verschieden. The two brothers are very different. □ Sie sind verschieden groß. They are different sizes.
■ **verschiedene** various □ Wir haben verschiedene Sehenswürdigkeiten besichtigt. We've seen various sights.

verschlafen (PRESENT TENSE **verschläft**, IMPERFECT **verschlief**, PERFECT TENSE **hat verschlafen**) VERB [58]
▷ see also **verschlafen** ADJECTIVE

1 to sleep in
□ Tut mir leid, ich habe verschlafen. Sorry, I slept in.

2 to sleep through
□ Er hat den ganzen Vormittag verschlafen. He slept through the whole morning.

3 to forget
□ Ich habe deinen Geburtstag total verschlafen. I completely forgot your birthday.

verschlafen ADJECTIVE
▷ see also **verschlafen** VERB

sleepy
□ Sie sah mich mit einem verschlafenen Blick an. She gave me a sleepy look. □ ein verschlafenes kleines Dorf a sleepy little village

verschlechtern (PERFECT TENSE **hat verschlechtert**) VERB [88]

to make worse
□ Das verschlechtert die Lage. That makes the situation worse.
■ **sich verschlechtern 1** to get worse □ Die Lage hat sich verschlechtert. The situation's got worse. □ In Englisch habe ich mich verschlechtert. My marks in English have got worse. **2** to deteriorate □ Sein Gesundheitszustand hat sich noch weiter verschlechtert. His condition has deteriorated even further.

verschlimmern (PERFECT TENSE **hat verschlimmert**) VERB [88]

to make worse
□ Du verschlimmerst alles, wenn du weiter lügst. You'll make everything worse if you go on lying.
■ **sich verschlimmern** to get worse □ Die Lage hat sich verschlimmert. The situation's got worse.

der **Verschluss** (GEN des **Verschlusses**, PL die **Verschlüsse**) MASC NOUN

1 cap
□ Die Flasche hat einen kindersicheren Verschluss. The bottle has a childproof cap.

2 fastening
□ Kannst du mir den Verschluss an meinem Kleid aufmachen? Can you undo the fastening of my dress?

3 catch
□ der Verschluss der Tasche the catch of the bag □ der Verschluss an einer Halskette the catch of a necklace

verschmutzen (PERFECT TENSE **hat verschmutzt**) VERB [7]

1 to soil
■ **stark verschmutzt** very dirty

2 to pollute
□ die Umwelt verschmutzen to pollute the environment

verschneit ADJECTIVE
snow-covered
□ eine verschneite Straße a snow-covered road

verschonen (PERFECT TENSE **hat verschont**) VERB [84]
■ **jemanden mit etwas verschonen** to spare somebody something □ Sie verschonte mich mit den ganzen Einzelheiten. She spared me all the details.

★ **verschreiben** (IMPERFECT **verschrieb**, PERFECT TENSE **hat verschrieben**) VERB [61]
to prescribe
□ Der Arzt hat mir Antibiotika verschrieben. The doctor prescribed me antibiotics.
■ **sich verschreiben** to make a spelling mistake

verschütten (PERFECT TENSE **hat verschüttet**) VERB [7]
to spill
□ Er hat den Kaffee verschüttet. He spilt the coffee.
■ **verschüttet werden** to be buried □ Bei dem Erdbeben wurden zahlreiche Menschen verschüttet. Many people were buried in the earthquake.

verschweigen (IMPERFECT **verschwieg**, PERFECT TENSE **hat verschwiegen**) VERB
■ **jemandem etwas verschweigen** to keep something from somebody

verschwenden (PERFECT TENSE **hat verschwendet**) VERB [7]
to waste
□ Zeit verschwenden to waste time

die **Verschwendung** FEM NOUN
waste

★ **verschwinden** (IMPERFECT **verschwand**, PERFECT TENSE **ist verschwunden**) VERB [86]
to disappear

verschwitzt ADJECTIVE
sweaty

verschwommen ADJECTIVE
blurred

das **Versehen** (PL die **Versehen**) NEUT NOUN
oversight
□ Das war ein Versehen. It was an oversight.
■ **aus Versehen** by mistake

versehentlich ADVERB
by mistake

versenden (IMPERFECT **versendete** or **versandte**, PERFECT TENSE **hat versendet** or **versandt**) VERB
to dispatch

V

versessen – verstärken

versessen ADJECTIVE
- **auf etwas versessen sein** to be mad about something (*Umgangssprache*) □ Sie ist ganz versessen auf ihn. **She's mad about him.**

★ **versetzen** (PERFECT TENSE **hat versetzt**) VERB [7]
to transfer
□ Mein Vater wird nach Berlin versetzt. **My father's being transferred to Berlin.**
- **jemanden in die nächste Klasse versetzen** to move somebody up into the next class

DID YOU KNOW…?
In Germany pupils do not automatically move up (**versetzt werden**) to the next class at the end of the school year. If their performance is not good enough, they have to repeat the school year. This is known as **sitzen bleiben**.

- **jemanden versetzen** to stand somebody up (*Umgangssprache*) □ Meine Freundin hat mich versetzt. **My girlfriend stood me up.**
- **sich in jemandes Lage versetzen** to put oneself in somebody's shoes □ Wenn du dich einmal in meine Lage versetzt … **If you put yourself in my shoes …**
- **jemandem einen Schlag versetzen** to hit somebody
- **jemandem einen Tritt versetzen** to kick somebody
- **jemanden in gute Laune versetzen** to put somebody in a good mood

verseuchen (PERFECT TENSE **hat verseucht**) VERB [7]
to contaminate

★ **versichern** (PERFECT TENSE **hat versichert**) VERB [88]
1 to assure
□ Er hat mir versichert, dass das stimmt. **He assured me that this is correct.**
2 to insure
□ Wir sind nicht gegen Diebstahl versichert. **We are not insured against theft.**

die Versicherung FEM NOUN
insurance

sich versöhnen (PERFECT TENSE **hat sich versöhnt**) VERB [84]
to make up
□ Na, habt ihr euch wieder versöhnt? **Well, have you two made up again?**
- **sich mit jemandem versöhnen** to make it up with somebody □ Ich habe mich wieder mit ihm versöhnt. **I made it up with him again.**

versorgen (PERFECT TENSE **hat versorgt**) VERB [7]
to supply
□ Über diese Windkraftanlage werden 20000 Haushalte mit Strom versorgt. **This wind turbine will power 20,000 households with electricity.**

- **einen Kranken versorgen** to look after a patient
- **eine Familie versorgen** to support a famil

sich verspäten (PERFECT TENSE **hat sich verspätet**) VERB [2]
to be late

★ **verspätet** ADJECTIVE
late
□ die verspätete Ankunft **the late arrival**
- **der verspätete Flug** the delayed flight
- **verspätete Glückwünsche** belated best wishes

★ **die Verspätung** FEM NOUN
delay
- **Verspätung haben** to be late

★ **versprechen** (PRESENT TENSE **verspricht**, IMPERFECT **versprach**, PERFECT TENSE **hat versprochen**) VERB [70]
▷ *see also* das **Versprechen** NOUN
to promise
□ Du hast es versprochen. **You promised.**
- **Ich habe mir von dem Kurs mehr versprochen.** I expected more from this course.

★ **das Versprechen** (PL **die Versprechen**) NEUT NOUN
▷ *see also* **versprechen** VERB
promise
□ Sie hat ihr Versprechen gehalten. **She kept her promise.**

der Verstand MASC NOUN
mind
□ den Verstand verlieren to go out of one's mind
- **über jemandes Verstand gehen** to be beyond somebody

verständigen (PERFECT TENSE **hat verständigt**) VERB [7]
to inform
□ Wir müssen ihre Eltern verständigen. **We must inform her parents.**
- **sich verständigen** to communicate □ Wir konnten uns auf Englisch verständigen. **We were able to communicate in English.**
- **sich auf etwas verständigen** to agree on something □ Wir haben uns auf folgendes Vorgehen verständigt. **We've agreed on the following plan of action.**

verständlich ADJECTIVE
understandable
- **sich verständlich ausdrücken** to express oneself clearly

verständnisvoll ADJECTIVE
understanding
□ Meine Eltern sind sehr verständnisvoll. **My parents are very understanding.**

verstärken (PERFECT TENSE **hat verstärkt**) VERB [7]

v

1 to strengthen
□ Wir müssen den Karton verstärken. We'll have to strengthen the box. □ ein Team verstärken to strengthen a team

2 to amplify
□ den Ton verstärken to amplify the sound
■ **Das verstärkt die Schmerzen.** That makes the pain worse.

der **Verstärker** (PL die **Verstärker**) MASC NOUN
amplifier

die **Verstärkung** FEM NOUN
reinforcements pl
□ Wir brauchen Verstärkung. We need reinforcements.

verstauchen (PERFECT TENSE **hat verstaucht**) VERB [7]
to sprain
□ Ich habe mir den Knöchel verstaucht. I've sprained my ankle.

das **Versteck** (PL die **Verstecke**) NEUT NOUN
hiding place

verstecken (PERFECT TENSE **hat versteckt**) VERB [7]
to hide

verstehen (IMPERFECT **verstand**, PERFECT TENSE **hat verstanden**) VERB [72]
to understand
□ Ich habe die Frage nicht verstanden. I didn't understand the question. □ Ich verstehe nicht. I don't understand.
■ **sich verstehen** to get on □ Die beiden verstehen sich blendend. The two of them get on marvellously.
■ **Das versteht sich von selbst.** That goes without saying.

verstopft ADJECTIVE

1 blocked
□ ein verstopfter Abfluss a blocked drain

2 constipated
□ Ich bin seit gestern verstopft. I've been constipated since yesterday.

verstreuen (PERFECT TENSE **hat verstreut**) VERB [7]
to scatter

der **Versuch** (PL die **Versuche**) MASC NOUN

1 attempt
□ Ich habe den Versuch gemacht, Spanisch zu lernen. I made an attempt to learn Spanish. □ Sie hat schon nach dem ersten Versuch aufgegeben. She gave up after the first attempt.

2 experiment
□ Versuche mit Tieren lehnen wir ab. We disapprove of experiments with animals.

versuchen (PERFECT TENSE **hat versucht**) VERB [84]
to try
□ Ich versuche zu kommen. I'll try to come.

□ Willst du mal die Soße versuchen? Would you like to try the sauce?
■ **sich an etwas versuchen** to try one's hand at something □ Ich habe mich am Töpfern versucht. I tried my hand at pottery.

vertagen (PERFECT TENSE **hat vertagt**) VERB [7]
to adjourn

vertauschen (PERFECT TENSE **hat vertauscht**) VERB [7]

1 to mix up
□ Die Babys wurden im Krankenhaus vertauscht. They mixed the babies up at the hospital. □ Er hat offensichtlich seinen Mantel mit meinem vertauscht. He must have got his coat and mine mixed up.

2 to exchange
□ Er hat seinen Sportwagen mit einem Familienwagen vertauscht. He exchanged his sports car for a family car.

verteidigen (PERFECT TENSE **hat verteidigt**) VERB [84]
to defend

der **Verteidiger** (PL die **Verteidiger**) MASC NOUN

1 defender
□ Der Verteidiger wurde gefoult. The defender was fouled.

2 defence counsel
□ Wer ist der Verteidiger des Angeklagten? Who's defence counsel?

die **Verteidigerin** FEM NOUN
defender

verteilen (PERFECT TENSE **hat verteilt**) VERB [84]

1 to hand out
□ Sie verteilte die Hefte an die Schüler. She handed the exercise books out to the pupils.

2 to spread
□ Die Salbe sollte gleichmäßig auf der Haut verteilt werden. The ointment should be spread evenly over the skin.

der **Vertrag** (PL die **Verträge**) MASC NOUN

1 contract
□ ein Arbeitsvertrag a contract of employment

2 treaty
□ ein Friedensvertrag a peace treaty

vertragen (PRESENT TENSE **verträgt**, IMPERFECT **vertrug**, PERFECT TENSE **hat vertragen**) VERB [77]

1 to be able to stand
□ Ich vertrage die Hitze nicht. I can't stand the heat.

2 to tolerate
□ Ich kann eine solche Behandlung nicht vertragen. I can't tolerate such treatment.
■ **sich vertragen** to get along □ Die beiden vertragen sich blendend. The two of them get along marvellously.

v

Numbers in brackets refer to verb tables on pages 697 to 706.

305

■ **sich wieder vertragen** to patch things up
□ Na, vertragt ihr euch wieder? Well, have you patched things up again?

verträglich ADJECTIVE
1 good-natured
□ ein verträglicher Mensch a good-natured person
2 easily digestible
□ Im Sommer sollte man nur leicht verträgliche Speisen zu sich nehmen. In summer, you should only eat easily digestible food.
■ **Das Medikament ist gut verträglich.** The drug has no side effects.

vertrauen (PERFECT TENSE **hat vertraut**) VERB [84]
▷ see also das **Vertrauen** NOUN
■ **jemandem vertrauen** to trust somebody
■ **vertrauen auf** to rely on □ Ich vertraue auf dich. I'm relying on you.
■ **Ich vertraue auf mein Glück.** I'm trusting my luck.

das **Vertrauen** NEUT NOUN
▷ see also **vertrauen** VERB
trust
□ Vertrauen zu jemandem haben to have trust in somebody

vertraulich ADJECTIVE
1 confidential
□ ein vertrauliches Gespräch a confidential talk
2 familiar
□ Ich verbitte mir diesen vertraulichen Ton. I'll not have you talking to me in such familiar way.

vertraut ADJECTIVE
familiar
□ vertraute Gesichter familiar faces

vertreiben (IMPERFECT **vertrieb**, PERFECT TENSE **hat vertrieben**) VERB
1 to drive
□ Er hat uns von seinem Grundstück vertrieben. He drove us off his land.
2 to sell
□ Wir vertreiben Hardware und Software. We sell hardware and software.
■ **sich die Zeit vertreiben** to pass the time
□ Ich habe mir die Zeit mit Kreuzworträtseln vertrieben. I passed the time doing crosswords.

vertreten (PRESENT TENSE **vertritt**, IMPERFECT **vertrat**, PERFECT TENSE **hat vertreten**) VERB [79]
1 to stand in for
□ Während ich in Urlaub bin, vertritt mich Frau Wengel. While I'm on holiday, Mrs Wengel's standing in for me.
2 to represent
□ Die Lobby vertritt die Interessen der Wirtschaft. The lobby represents business interests.
■ **eine Meinung vertreten** to hold an opinion

■ **sich den Fuß vertreten** to twist one's ank
□ Ich habe mir den Fuß vertreten. I've twisted my ankle.
■ **sich die Beine vertreten** to stretch one's legs □ Ich will mir nur etwas die Beine vertreten. I just want to stretch my legs a bit.

★ der **Vertreter** (PL die **Vertreter**) MASC NOUN
sales representative
□ Er ist Vertreter für Collins. He's a sales representative for Collins.

★ die **Vertreterin** FEM NOUN
sales representative

der **Vertrieb** (PL die **Vertriebe**) MASC NOUN
1 sale
□ Der Vertrieb von Raubkopien steht unter Strafe. The sale of pirate copies is punishable b law.
2 marketing department
□ Sie arbeitet im Vertrieb. She works in the marketing department.

sich **vertun** (IMPERFECT **vertat sich**, PERFECT TENSE **hat sich vertan**) VERB [81]
to make a mistake

verübeln (PERFECT TENSE **hat verübelt**) VERB [7]
■ **jemandem etwas verübeln** to be cross with somebody because of something

verüben (PERFECT TENSE **hat verübt**) VERB [7]
to commit

★ **verunglücken** (PERFECT TENSE **ist verunglückt**) VERB [84]
to have an accident
□ Sie sind mit dem Auto verunglückt. They've had a car accident.

verursachen (PERFECT TENSE **hat verursach** VERB [84]
to cause

verurteilen (PERFECT TENSE **hat verurteilt**) VERB [84]
to condemn

vervielfältigen (PERFECT TENSE **hat vervielfältigt**) VERB [84]
to copy

vervollständigen (PERFECT TENSE **hat vervollständigt**) VERB [7]
to complete

die **Verwaltung** FEM NOUN
administration
□ Er arbeitet in der Verwaltung. He works in administration.

verwandt ADJECTIVE
■ **mit jemandem verwandt sein** to be related to somebody

★ der/die **Verwandte** (GEN des/der **Verwandten**, PL die **Verwandten**) MASC/FEM NOUN
relative

★ = core vocabulary

□ Ein Verwandter von mir ist gestern gestorben. A relative of mine died yesterday.

die **Verwandtschaft** FEM NOUN
relations pl
□ Die ganze Verwandtschaft war eingeladen. All my relations were invited.

verwechseln (PERFECT TENSE **hat verwechselt**) VERB [34]

1 to confuse
□ Du darfst die beiden Begriffe nicht verwechseln. You mustn't confuse the two ideas.

2 to mix up
□ Sie haben offensichtlich die Mäntel verwechselt. They must have got their coats mixed up.
■ **verwechseln mit 1** to confuse with □ Ich verwechsle 'akut' immer mit 'aktuell'. I always confuse 'akut' with 'aktuell'. **2** to mistake for □ Ich habe dich mit deiner Schwester verwechselt. I mistook you for your sister.
■ **Sie sind zum Verwechseln ähnlich.** They're the spitting image of each other.

die **Verwechslung** FEM NOUN
mix-up

verweigern (PERFECT TENSE **hat verweigert**) VERB [88]
■ **jemandem etwas verweigern** to refuse somebody something □ Sie verweigerte ihm das Besuchsrecht für die Kinder. She refused him access to the children.
■ **den Gehorsam verweigern** to refuse to obey
■ **die Aussage verweigern** to refuse to testify

der **Verweis** (GEN des **Verweises**, PL die **Verweise**) MASC NOUN
reprimand
□ Er hat für sein Zuspätkommen einen schweren Verweis bekommen. He was given a severe reprimand for being late.

verwelken (PERFECT TENSE **ist verwelkt**) VERB [7]
to fade

verwenden (IMPERFECT **verwendete** or **verwandte**, PERFECT TENSE **hat verwendet** or **verwandt**) VERB

1 to use
□ Welche Software verwenden Sie? What software do you use?

2 to spend (effort, time, work)
□ Ich habe auf diesen Aufsatz viel Zeit verwendet. I spent a lot of time on this essay.

verwerten (PERFECT TENSE **hat verwertet**) VERB [2]
to utilize

verwirren (PERFECT TENSE **hat verwirrt**) VERB [84]

1 to confuse

□ Jetzt hast du mich total verwirrt. Now you've completely confused me.

2 to tangle up (thread)
□ Die Katze hat die Wolle verwirrt. The cat's tangled the wool up.

verwöhnen (PERFECT TENSE **hat verwöhnt**) VERB [84]
to spoil

verwunden (PERFECT TENSE **hat verwundet**) VERB [7]
to wound

der/die **Verwundete** (GEN des/der **Verwundeten**, PL die **Verwundeten**) MASC/FEM NOUN
injured person
□ Der Arzt versorgt gerade einen Verwundeten. The doctor is just attending to an injured person.

die **Verwundung** FEM NOUN
injury

das **Verzeichnis** (GEN des **Verzeichnisses**, PL die **Verzeichnisse**) NEUT NOUN
list
□ Am Ende des Buches ist ein Verzeichnis aller Fachbegriffe. At the end of the book there's a list of all the technical terms.
■ **das Inhaltsverzeichnis** the table of contents

verzeihen (IMPERFECT **verzieh**, PERFECT TENSE **hat verziehen**) VERB
to forgive
□ jemandem etwas verzeihen to forgive somebody for something

★ die **Verzeihung** FEM NOUN
forgiveness
■ **Verzeihung! 1** sorry □ Verzeihung, ich wollte Sie nicht treten. Sorry, I didn't mean to kick you. **2** excuse me □ Verzeihung, aber können Sie mir sagen, wie spät es ist? Excuse me, could you tell me what time it is?

verzichten (PERFECT TENSE **hat verzichtet**) VERB [2]
■ **auf etwas verzichten 1** to do without something □ Ich werde heute wohl auf meinen Mittagsschlaf verzichten müssen. It looks like I'll have to do without my afternoon nap today. □ Ich verzichte auf deine Hilfe. I can do without your help. **2** to forego something □ Er hat auf eine Bezahlung verzichtet. He forewent payment. □ Ich verzichte nicht auf meine Rechte. I won't forego my rights.

die **Verzierung** FEM NOUN
decoration

verzögern (PERFECT TENSE **hat verzögert**) VERB [88]
to delay

die **Verzögerung** FEM NOUN
delay

Numbers in brackets refer to verb tables on pages 697 to 706.

307

★ **verzollen** (PERFECT TENSE **hat verzollt**) VERB [84]
to pay duty on
□ Den Whisky müssen Sie verzollen. You have to pay duty on that whisky.
■ **Haben Sie etwas zu verzollen?** Have you anything to declare?

verzweifeln (PERFECT TENSE **ist verzweifelt**) VERB [7]
to despair

verzweifelt ADJECTIVE
desperate

die **Verzweiflung** FEM NOUN
despair

★ der **Vetter** (PL die **Vettern**) MASC NOUN
cousin

★ das **Videogerät** (PL die **Videogeräte**) NEUT NOUN
video recorder

★ der **Videorekorder** (PL die **Videorekorder**) MASC NOUN
video recorder

das **Vieh** NEUT NOUN
cattle *pl*
□ Das Vieh ist auf der Weide. The cattle are out in the meadow.

★ **viel** ADJECTIVE, ADVERB
1 a lot of
□ Sie haben viel Arbeit. They've got a lot of work.
2 much
□ ein viel diskutiertes Thema a much discussed topic □ Wir haben nicht viel Geld. We haven't got much money. □ Wir haben nicht viel gelernt. We didn't learn much.
■ **Vielen Dank!** Thank you very much.
3 a lot
□ Wir haben viel gesehen. We saw a lot.
■ **viel zu wenig** far too little
■ **Viel Glück!** Good luck.
■ **so viel** so much □ Sie hat so viel gelernt. She's learned so much. □ Rede nicht so viel. Don't talk so much.
■ **so viel(e) wie** as much as □ Sie hat so viel wie ich bekommen. She got as much as I did. □ so viel wie möglich as much as possible □ Ich habe so viele Bücher wie möglich mitgenommen. I took as many books as possible.
■ **wie viel?** how much?
■ **zu viel** too much

★ **viele** PL PRONOUN
1 a lot of
□ Sie hat viele Bücher. She's got a lot of books.
2 many
□ Er hat nicht viele Fehler gemacht. He didn't make many mistakes. □ Viele Schüler mögen Chemie nicht. Many pupils don't like chemistry.
■ **Viele wissen das nicht.** A lot of people don't know that.

vieles PRONOUN
many things *pl*
□ Vieles war neu für mich. Many things were new to me.

★ **vielleicht** ADVERB
perhaps

★ **vielmals** ADVERB
■ **Danke vielmals!** Many thanks!

vielseitig ADJECTIVE
many-sided

vielversprechend ADJECTIVE
promising

★ **vier** NUMBER
▷ *see also* die **Vier** NOUN
four

die **Vier** FEM NOUN
▷ *see also* **vier** NUMBER
1 four
2 adequate

DID YOU KNOW...?
German grades range from one (**sehr gut**) to six (**ungenügend**).

das **Viereck** (PL die **Vierecke**) NEUT NOUN
1 rectangle
2 square

★ **viereckig** ADJECTIVE
1 rectangular
2 square

vierte ADJECTIVE
fourth
□ Sie hat erst beim vierten Klingeln abgenommen. She didn't answer until the fourth ring. □ Er kam als Vierter. He was the fourth to arrive.

★ das **Viertel** (PL die **Viertel**) NEUT NOUN
quarter
□ Viertel vor zwei quarter to two

das **Vierteljahr** (PL die **Vierteljahre**) NEUT NOUN
quarter

vierteljährlich ADJECTIVE
quarterly

vierteln VERB [88]
1 to divide by four
□ wenn man den Betrag viertelt ... if you divide the amount by four ...
2 to cut into quarters
□ Sie hat den Kuchen geviertelt. She cut the cake into quarters.

★ die **Viertelstunde** FEM NOUN
quarter of an hour

★ **vierzehn** NUMBER
fourteen
■ **in vierzehn Tagen** in a fortnight

★ **vierzig** NUMBER
forty

★ = core vocabulary

V

die **Villa** (PL die **Villen**) FEM NOUN
villa

viral ADJECTIVE
viral
■ ein virales Video a viral video

virtuell ADJECTIVE
virtual
□ die virtuelle Realität virtual reality

die **Visa** PL NOUN ▷ see das **Visum**

die **Visitenkarte** FEM NOUN
business card

das **Visum** (PL die **Visa**) NEUT NOUN
visa

das **Vitamin** (PL die **Vitamine**) NEUT NOUN
vitamin

der **Vogel** (PL die **Vögel**) MASC NOUN
bird
■ einen Vogel haben to have a screw loose (*Umgangssprache*)
■ jemandem den Vogel zeigen to make a rude sign

DID YOU KNOW...?
In Germany you make a rude sign at somebody by tapping your forehead to show that you think they are stupid.

die **Vogelgrippe** FEM NOUN
bird flu

die **Vokabel** FEM NOUN
word

das **Vokabular** (PL die **Vokabulare**) NEUT NOUN
vocabulary

der **Vokal** (PL die **Vokale**) MASC NOUN
vowel

das **Volk** (PL die **Völker**) NEUT NOUN
1 people
□ das einfache Volk the simple people
2 nation
□ das deutsche Volk the German nation

das **Volksfest** (PL die **Volksfeste**) NEUT NOUN
fair

die **Volkshochschule** FEM NOUN
adult education classes *pl*

die **Volkswirtschaft** FEM NOUN
economics *sing*

voll ADJECTIVE
full
■ voll und ganz completely
■ jemanden für voll nehmen to take somebody seriously

völlig ADJECTIVE, ADVERB
1 complete
□ bis zur völligen Erschöpfung to the point of complete exhaustion
2 completely
□ Das ist völlig unmöglich. That's completely

impossible. □ Ich bin völlig deiner Meinung. I completely agree with you.

volljährig ADJECTIVE
of age
□ volljährig werden to come of age

vollkommen ADJECTIVE
perfect
□ vollkommen richtig perfectly right
■ vollkommen unmöglich completely impossible

das **Vollkornbrot** (PL die **Vollkornbrote**) NEUT NOUN
wholemeal bread *no pl*

vollmachen VERB [48]
to fill up

die **Vollmacht** FEM NOUN
power of attorney

der **Vollmond** MASC NOUN
full moon
□ bei Vollmond at full moon

die **Vollpension** FEM NOUN
full board

vollständig ADJECTIVE
complete

volltanken VERB [4]
to fill up (*car*)

vom = von dem

von PREPOSITION

von takes the dative.

1 from
□ von Hamburg nach Kiel from Hamburg to Kiel
■ von ... bis from ... to □ von morgens bis abends from morning to night
■ von ... an from ... □ Von Mai an wohnen wir in Regensburg. We'll be living in Regensburg from May.
■ von ... aus from ... □ Ich habe es vom Fenster aus gesehen. I saw it from my window.
■ etwas von sich aus tun to do something of one's own accord □ Du solltest das von dir aus machen. You should do it of your own accord.
■ von mir aus I don't mind □ Von mir aus können wir gehen. I don't mind if we go.
■ Von wo bist du? Where are you from?
■ Von wann ist der Brief? When's the letter from?
2 by
□ Ich bin von einem Hund gebissen worden. I was bitten by a dog. □ ein Gedicht von Schiller a poem by Schiller
■ von etwas kommen to be caused by something □ Der Husten kommt vom Rauchen. The cough is caused by smoking.
3 of
□ ein Freund von mir a friend of mine □ Wie nett von dir! How nice of you!
■ jeweils zwei von zehn two out of every ten

voneinander – Vorderseite

4 about

□ Er erzählte vom Urlaub. He talked about his holiday.

■ Von wegen! No way! (*Umgangssprache*)

voneinander ADVERB

from each other

★ **vor** PREPOSITION, ADVERB

Use the accusative to express movement or a change of place. Use the dative when there is no change of place.

1 in front of

□ Er stand vor dem Spiegel. He stood in front of the mirror. □ Stell den Stuhl vor das Fenster. Put the chair in front of the window.

2 before

□ Der Artikel steht vor dem Substantiv. The article goes before the noun. □ Vor der Kirche links abbiegen. Turn left just before you get to the church. □ Ich war vor ihm da. I was there before him.

3 ago

□ vor zwei Tagen two days ago □ vor einem Jahr a year ago

■ Es ist fünf vor vier. It's five to four.

■ vor Kurzem a little while ago

4 with

□ vor Wut with rage □ vor Liebe with love

■ vor Hunger sterben to die of hunger

■ vor lauter Arbeit because of work

■ vor allem above all

■ vor und zurück backwards and forwards

vorankommen (IMPERFECT **kam voran**, PERFECT TENSE **ist vorangekommen**) VERB [40]

to make progress

voraus ADVERB

ahead

□ Fahr du schon mal voraus. You go on ahead. □ Er war seiner Zeit voraus. He was ahead of his time.

■ im Voraus in advance

vorausgehen (IMPERFECT **ging voraus**, PERFECT TENSE **ist vorausgegangen**) VERB [29]

1 to go on ahead

□ Geht ihr voraus, ich komme nach. Go on ahead, I'll catch up with you.

2 to precede

□ Der Schlägerei ging ein Streit voraus. The fight was preceded by an argument.

voraussetzen (PERFECT TENSE **hat vorausgesetzt**) VERB [15]

to assume

□ Ich setze voraus, dass du auch kommst. I assume that you're coming too.

■ vorausgesetzt, dass ... provided that ...

die Voraussetzung FEM NOUN

prerequisite

■ unter der Voraussetzung, dass ... provided that ...

voraussichtlich ADVERB

probably

★ **vorbei** ADVERB

past

□ Fahren Sie am Rathaus vorbei. Drive past the town hall.

■ Ich sehe noch kurz bei ihr vorbei. I'll just pop round to her place.

■ vorbei sein to be over □ Damit ist es nun vorbei. That's all over now.

★ **vorbeigehen** (IMPERFECT **ging vorbei**, PERFECT TENSE **ist vorbeigegangen**) VERB [29]

to go past

□ Er ging vorbei, ohne zu grüßen. He went past without saying hello.

■ an etwas vorbeigehen to go past something □ Sie ist am Schaufenster vorbeigegangen, ohne es zu beachten. She went past the shop window without looking at it.

■ bei jemandem vorbeigehen to call in at somebody's □ Kannst du beim Bäcker vorbeigehen? Can you call in at the baker's? □ Ich gehe noch schnell bei meiner Freundin vorbei. I'm just going to call in at my girlfriend's.

★ **vorbeikommen** (IMPERFECT **kam vorbei**, PERFECT TENSE **ist vorbeigekommen**) VERB [40]

■ bei jemandem vorbeikommen to drop in on somebody

★ **vorbereiten** (PERFECT TENSE **hat vorbereitet**) VERB [2]

to prepare

die Vorbereitung FEM NOUN

preparation

vorbeugen (PERFECT TENSE **hat vorgebeugt**) VERB [4]

■ sich vorbeugen to lean forward

■ einer Sache vorbeugen to prevent something □ um einer Erkältung vorzubeugen to prevent a cold

die Vorbeugung FEM NOUN

prevention

□ zur Vorbeugung gegen for the prevention of

das Vorbild (PL **die Vorbilder**) NEUT NOUN

role model

□ Er ist mein Vorbild. He's my role model.

■ sich jemanden zum Vorbild nehmen to follow somebody's example □ Du solltest dir deinen Bruder zum Vorbild nehmen. You ought to follow your brother's example.

vordere ADJECTIVE

front

□ Das Haus hat einen vorderen und einen hinteren Eingang. The house has a front door and a back door.

die Vorderseite FEM NOUN

front

★ = core vocabulary

vorderste ADJECTIVE
front
□ die vorderste Reihe the front row

voreilig ADJECTIVE
hasty
□ Du solltest nicht voreilig urteilen. You shouldn't make hasty judgements.

voreingenommen ADJECTIVE
biased

vorenthalten (PRESENT TENSE **enthält vor**, IMPERFECT **enthielt vor**, PERFECT TENSE **hat vorenthalten**) VERB [33]
■ jemandem etwas vorenthalten to withhold something from somebody

vorerst ADVERB
for the moment

die **Vorfahrt** FEM NOUN
right of way
■ Vorfahrt achten! Give way!

der **Vorfall** (PL die **Vorfälle**) MASC NOUN
incident

vorführen (PERFECT TENSE **hat vorgeführt**) VERB [4]
to show

die **Vorgängerin** FEM NOUN
predecessor

vorgehen (IMPERFECT **ging vor**, PERFECT TENSE **ist vorgegangen**) VERB [29]
▷ see also das **Vorgehen** NOUN
1 to go on ahead
□ Geht ihr vor, ich komme nach. Go on ahead, I'll catch up.
2 to go up to
□ Sie ging ans Rednerpult vor. She went up to the lectern.
3 to proceed
□ Ich weiß nicht, wie wir vorgehen sollen. I don't know how we should proceed.
■ Die Uhr geht vor. The clock is fast.
■ Was geht hier vor? What's going on here?

das **Vorgehen** NEUT NOUN
▷ see also **vorgehen** VERB
action

vorgestern ADVERB
the day before yesterday

vorhaben (PRESENT TENSE **hat vor**, IMPERFECT **hatte vor**, PERFECT TENSE **hat vorgehabt**) VERB [32]
to intend
□ Wir haben vor, nach Italien zu fahren. We intend to go to Italy. □ Was hast du vor? What do you intend to do?
■ Ich habe heute viel vor. I've got a lot planned for today.
■ Hast du schon was vor? Have you got anything on?
■ Was hast du heute Abend vor? What are you doing this evening?

★ der **Vorhang** (PL die **Vorhänge**) MASC NOUN
curtain

★ **vorher** ADVERB
beforehand

die **Vorhersage** FEM NOUN
forecast

vorhersehbar ADJECTIVE
predictable

vorhersehen (PRESENT TENSE **sieht vorher**, IMPERFECT **sah vorher**, PERFECT TENSE **hat vorhergesehen**) VERB [64]
to foresee

vorhin ADVERB
just now

★ **vorig** ADJECTIVE
previous

vorkommen (IMPERFECT **kam vor**, PERFECT TENSE **ist vorgekommen**) VERB [40]
1 to happen
□ So ein Fehler sollte nicht vorkommen. A mistake like that shouldn't happen.
■ Es kommt vor, dass ich früh ins Bett gehe. I sometimes go to bed early.
■ jemandem vorkommen to seem to somebody □ Er kam mir traurig vor. He seemed sad to me. □ Das kommt mir komisch vor. That seems funny to me.
■ sich dumm vorkommen to feel stupid
□ Ich kam mir dumm vor. I felt stupid.
2 to come out
□ Komm endlich hinter dem Schrank vor. Come out from behind that cupboard, will you?

vorläufig ADJECTIVE
provisional

vorlaut ADJECTIVE
impertinent

vorlesen (PRESENT TENSE **liest vor**, IMPERFECT **las vor**, PERFECT TENSE **hat vorgelesen**) VERB [45]
to read out

vorletzte ADJECTIVE
last but one
□ Ich wohne im vorletzten Haus. My house is the last but one.

die **Vorliebe** FEM NOUN
partiality
■ eine Vorliebe für etwas haben to be partial to something □ Sie hat eine Vorliebe für Krimis. She's partial to detective stories.

★ der **Vormittag** (PL die **Vormittage**) MASC NOUN
morning
□ am Vormittag in the morning

★ **vormittags** ADVERB
in the morning

★ **vorn** ADVERB
in front

Numbers in brackets refer to verb tables on pages 697 to 706.

311

V

□ Der deutsche Schwimmer liegt vorn. The German swimmer is in front.
■ **Er stand ganz vorn in der Schlange.** He was right at the front of the queue.
■ **nach vorn** to the front
■ **von vorn anfangen** to start at the beginning
■ **wieder von vorn anfangen** to start again from the beginning

★ der **Vorname** (GEN des **Vornamens**, PL die **Vornamen**) MASC NOUN
first name

vornehm ADJECTIVE
1 distinguished
□ eine vornehme Familie a distinguished family
2 refined
□ sich vornehm ausdrücken to use refined language □ vornehme Manieren refined manners
3 posh
□ ein vornehmes Hotel a posh hotel
4 elegant
□ eine vornehme Dame an elegant lady
■ **Tu nicht so vornehm!** Don't put on airs and graces.

vornehmen (PRESENT TENSE **nimmt vor**, IMPERFECT **nahm vor**, PERFECT TENSE **hat vorgenommen**) VERB [52]
■ **sich etwas vornehmen** to resolve to do something □ Ich habe mir vorgenommen, das nie wieder zu tun. I've resolved never to do that again.

vornherein ADVERB
■ **von vornherein** from the start

★ der **Vorort** (PL die **Vororte**) MASC NOUN
suburb

der **Vorrat** (PL die **Vorräte**) MASC NOUN
stock
□ solange der Vorrat reicht while stocks last

vorrätig ADJECTIVE
in stock

der **Vorschlag** (PL die **Vorschläge**) MASC NOUN
suggestion

★ **vorschlagen** (PRESENT TENSE **schlägt vor**, IMPERFECT **schlug vor**, PERFECT TENSE **hat vorgeschlagen**) VERB [59]
to suggest

die **Vorschrift** FEM NOUN
rule
□ Das ist gegen die Vorschriften. It's against the rules.

★ die **Vorsicht** FEM NOUN
caution
■ **Vorsicht! 1** Look out! **2** Caution!
■ **Vorsicht, Stufe!** Mind the step!

★ **vorsichtig** ADJECTIVE
careful

★ die **Vorspeise** FEM NOUN
starter

der **Vorsprung** (PL die **Vorsprünge**) MASC NOUN
lead
□ Wir haben einen Vorsprung vor unseren Konkurrenten gewonnen. We have gained a lead over our competitors.

★ die **Vorstadt** (PL die **Vorstädte**) FEM NOUN
suburbs *pl*

vorstellbar ADJECTIVE
conceivable

★ **vorstellen** (PERFECT TENSE **hat vorgestellt**) VERB [4]
■ **sich etwas vorstellen** to imagine something □ Stell dir mal vor, wir wären jetzt in Urlaub. Imagine we were on holiday right now.
■ **jemanden jemandem vorstellen** to introduce somebody to somebody □ Darf ich Ihnen meinen Mann vorstellen? May I introduce my husband to you?

★ die **Vorstellung** FEM NOUN
1 performance
□ Die Vorstellung endet gegen zehn Uhr. The performance ends at about ten.
2 idea
□ Hast du eine Vorstellung, wie wir das machen sollen? Have you got any idea how we should do that? □ Du hast ja keine Vorstellung, wie weh das tut. You've no idea how much it hurts.

★ das **Vorstellungsgespräch** (PL die **Vorstellungsgespräche**) NEUT NOUN
interview *(for job)*

★ der **Vorteil** (PL die **Vorteile**) MASC NOUN
advantage
■ **im Vorteil sein** to have the advantage

der **Vortrag** (PL die **Vorträge**) MASC NOUN
talk
□ einen Vortrag halten to give a talk

vorüber ADVERB
over

vorübergehend ADJECTIVE
1 passing
□ eine vorübergehende Phase a passing phase
2 temporarily
□ Das Geschäft ist vorübergehend geschlossen. The shop's temporarily closed.

das **Vorurteil** (PL die **Vorurteile**) NEUT NOUN
prejudice

der **Vorverkauf** (PL die **Vorverkäufe**) MASC NOUN
advance booking

★ die **Vorwahl** FEM NOUN
dialling code
□ Was ist die Vorwahl von Liverpool? What's the dialling code for Liverpool?

der **Vorwand** (PL die **Vorwände**) MASC NOUN
pretext

★ **vorwärts** ADVERB
forward

★ = core vocabulary

vorwerfen (PRESENT TENSE **wirft vor**, IMPERFECT **warf vor**, PERFECT TENSE **hat vorgeworfen**) VERB [92]

■ **jemandem etwas vorwerfen** to accuse somebody of something □ Er hat mir mangelndes Interesse vorgeworfen. He accused me of lack of interest.

■ **sich nichts vorzuwerfen haben** to have nothing to reproach oneself for □ Ich habe mir nichts vorzuwerfen. I've nothing to reproach myself for.

vorwiegend ADVERB
predominantly

das **Vorwort** (PL die **Vorworte**) NEUT NOUN
preface

der **Vorwurf** (PL die **Vorwürfe**) MASC NOUN
reproach

■ **jemandem Vorwürfe machen** to reproach somebody

■ **sich Vorwürfe machen** to reproach oneself

★ **vorzeigen** (PERFECT TENSE **hat vorgezeigt**) VERB [4]
to show

★ **vorziehen** (IMPERFECT **zog vor**, PERFECT TENSE **hat vorgezogen**) VERB [96]

1 to prefer
   □ Was ziehst du vor: Kaffee oder Tee? Do you prefer coffee or tea?

2 to pull forward
   □ Du solltest den Stuhl etwas vorziehen. You should pull your chair forward a bit.

vulgär ADJECTIVE
vulgar
   □ sich vulgär ausdrücken to use vulgar language

der **Vulkan** (PL die **Vulkane**) MASC NOUN
volcano

V

Ww

die **Waage** FEM NOUN
1 scales pl
□ Die Waage stimmt nicht genau. The scales aren't accurate.
2 Libra
□ Ulla ist Waage. Ulla's Libra.

waagerecht ADJECTIVE
horizontal

★ **wach** ADJECTIVE
■ wach sein to be awake

die **Wache** FEM NOUN
guard
□ Wache stehen to stand guard

das **Wachs** (GEN des **Wachses**, PL die **Wachse**) NEUT NOUN
wax

★ **wachsen** (PRESENT TENSE **wächst**, IMPERFECT **wuchs**, PERFECT TENSE **ist gewachsen**) VERB [87]
to grow

das **Wachstum** NEUT NOUN
growth

wackelig ADJECTIVE
wobbly

die **Wade** FEM NOUN
calf
□ Ich habe mich an der Wade verletzt. I've hurt my calf.

★ die **Waffe** FEM NOUN
weapon

die **Waffel** FEM NOUN
1 waffle
□ Heute gab's zum Nachtisch Waffeln. We had waffles for dessert today.
2 wafer
□ Willst du eine Waffel zu deinem Eis? Would you like a wafer with your ice cream?

wagen VERB [38]
▷ see also der **Wagen** NOUN
■ es wagen, etwas zu tun to dare to do something
■ sich irgendwohin wagen to dare to go somewhere

★ der **Wagen** (PL die **Wagen**) MASC NOUN
▷ see also **wagen** VERB

1 car
□ Seid ihr mit dem Wagen da? Did you come by car?
2 carriage
□ ein Eisenbahnwagen a railway carriage
■ ein Pferdewagen a cart

der **Wagenheber** (PL die **Wagenheber**) MASC NOUN
jack (for car)

★ die **Wahl** (PL die **Wahlen**) FEM NOUN
1 choice
□ Du hast die Wahl. It's your choice.
2 election
□ Wann sind die nächsten Wahlen? When are the next elections?

★ **wählen** VERB [38]
1 to choose
□ Du kannst wählen, entweder das rote oder das grüne. You can choose, either the red one or the green one.
2 to vote
□ Wer wurde zum Klassensprecher gewählt? Who was voted class representative?
■ Wählt Kowalski! Vote for Kowalski.
■ Nächsten Sonntag wird gewählt. There are elections next Sunday.
3 to dial
□ Sie wählte die Nummer ihrer Freundin. She dialled her friend's number.

wählerisch ADJECTIVE
particular

★ das **Wahlfach** (PL die **Wahlfächer**) NEUT NOUN
optional subject

der **Wahnsinn** MASC NOUN
madness

wahnsinnig ADJECTIVE, ADVERB
1 mad
□ Wer hatte denn diese wahnsinnige Idee? Whose mad idea was it?
2 incredibly
□ Das Kleid war wahnsinnig schön. The dress was incredibly pretty. □ Das tut wahnsinnig weh. It's incredibly sore.

★ **wahr** ADJECTIVE
true
□ eine wahre Geschichte a true story
■ Sie ist verheiratet, nicht wahr? She's married, isn't she?

★ = core vocabulary

★ **während** PREPOSITION, CONJUNCTION

The preposition **während** takes the genitive.

1 during
□ Was hast du während der Ferien gemacht?
What did you do during the holidays?

2 while
□ Sie sah fern, während sie ihre Hausaufgaben
machte. She was watching TV while she was
doing her homework.

3 whereas
□ Er ist ganz nett, während seine Frau unhöflich
ist. He's quite nice, whereas his wife's impolite.

die **Wahrheit** FEM NOUN
truth

wahrnehmen (PRESENT TENSE **nimmt wahr**,
IMPERFECT **nahm wahr**, PERFECT TENSE **hat
wahrgenommen**) VERB [52]
to perceive

der **Wahrsager** (PL die **Wahrsager**) MASC
NOUN
fortune teller

die **Wahrsagerin** FEM NOUN
fortune teller

★ **wahrscheinlich** ADJECTIVE, ADVERB

1 likely
□ Das ist nicht sehr wahrscheinlich. That's not
very likely.

2 probably
□ Er kommt wahrscheinlich nicht. He's
probably not coming.

die **Währung** FEM NOUN
currency

der **Wal** (PL die **Wale**) MASC NOUN
whale

★ der **Wald** (PL die **Wälder**) MASC NOUN

1 wood
□ Hinter unserem Haus ist ein Wald. There's a
wood behind our house.

2 forest
□ die Wälder Kanadas the forests of Canada

★ **Wales** NEUT NOUN
Wales
■ **aus Wales** from Wales
■ **in Wales** in Wales
■ **nach Wales** to Wales

der **Walfisch** (PL die **Walfische**) MASC NOUN
whale

★ der **Waliser** (PL die **Waliser**) MASC NOUN
Welshman
■ **Er ist Waliser.** He's Welsh.
■ **die Waliser** the Welsh

die **Waliserin** FEM NOUN
Welshwoman
■ **Sie ist Waliserin.** She's Welsh.

★ **walisisch** ADJECTIVE
Welsh

die **Walnuss** (PL die **Walnüsse**) FEM NOUN
walnut

★ die **Wand** (PL die **Wände**) FEM NOUN
wall

★ der **Wanderer** (PL die **Wanderer**) MASC NOUN
rambler

★ die **Wanderin** FEM NOUN
rambler

★ **wandern** (PERFECT TENSE **ist gewandert**) VERB
[88]
to hike
□ Wir sind am Wochenende gewandert. We
went hiking at the weekend.

★ die **Wanderung** FEM NOUN
hike

★ der **Wandschrank** (PL die **Wandschränke**)
MASC NOUN
wall cupboard

★ **wann** ADVERB
when

war VERB ▷ see **sein**

die **Ware** FEM NOUN
goods pl

★ das **Warenhaus** (GEN des **Warenhauses**, PL
die **Warenhäuser**) NEUT NOUN
department store

der **Warenkorb** (PL die **Warenkörbe**) MASC
NOUN
basket (online)

warf VERB ▷ see **werfen**

warm ADJECTIVE
warm
□ Heute ist es wärmer als gestern. It's warmer
today than yesterday.
■ **ein warmes Essen** a hot meal
■ **Mir ist warm.** I'm warm.

die **Wärme** FEM NOUN
warmth

die **Wärmflasche** FEM NOUN
hot-water bottle

warnen VERB [38]
to warn
□ jemanden vor etwas warnen to warn
somebody of something

★ die **Warnung** FEM NOUN
warning

★ **warten** VERB [2]
to wait
□ Ich habe eine Stunde gewartet. I waited an
hour.
■ **warten auf** to wait for □ Ich warte draußen
auf dich. I'll wait outside for you.
■ **auf sich warten lassen** to take a long time

★ der **Wartesaal** (PL die **Wartesäle**) MASC
NOUN
waiting room (in station)

Numbers in brackets refer to verb tables on pages 697 to 706.

315

w

★ das **Wartezimmer** (PL die Wartezimmer)
NEUT NOUN
waiting room

★ **warum** ADVERB
why

★ **was** PRONOUN
1 what
  □ Was hast du gesagt? **What did you say?** □ Was
  für eine Enttäuschung! **What a disappointment!**
  ■ **Was für ein ...** What kind of ... □ Was für ein
  Fahrrad hast du? **What kind of bike do you have?**
2 something
  □ Heute gibt's was Leckeres zum Mittagessen.
  **We're having something delicious for lunch
  today.**

waschbar ADJECTIVE
washable

★ das **Waschbecken** (PL die Waschbecken)
NEUT NOUN
washbasin

★ die **Wäsche** FEM NOUN
washing
  □ Wäsche waschen **to do the washing**
  ■ **die Bettwäsche** bed linen
  ■ **die Unterwäsche** underwear

die **Wäscheklammer** FEM NOUN
clothes peg

die **Wäscheleine** FEM NOUN
washing line

★ **waschen** (PRESENT TENSE **wäscht**, IMPERFECT
wusch, PERFECT TENSE **hat gewaschen**) VERB
[89]
to wash
  ■ **sich waschen** to have a wash
  ■ **sich die Hände waschen** to wash one's
  hands □ Ich muss mir die Hände waschen. **I'll
  have to wash my hands.**

★ die **Waschmaschine** FEM NOUN
washing machine

das **Waschmittel** (PL die Waschmittel)
NEUT NOUN
detergent

★ das **Waschpulver** (PL die Waschpulver)
NEUT NOUN
washing powder

der **Waschsalon** (PL die Waschsalons)
MASC NOUN
launderette

★ das **Wasser** (PL die Wasser or Wässer) NEUT
NOUN
water

★ **wasserdicht** ADJECTIVE
waterproof

der **Wasserfall** (PL die Wasserfälle) MASC
NOUN
waterfall

die **Wasserfarbe** FEM NOUN
watercolour

★ der **Wasserhahn** (PL die Wasserhähne)
MASC NOUN
tap

der **Wassermann** MASC NOUN
Aquarius
  □ Gerda ist Wassermann. **Gerda's Aquarius.**

die **Wassermelone** FEM NOUN
water melon

der **Wasserstoff** MASC NOUN
hydrogen

die **Watte** FEM NOUN
cotton wool

★ das **WC** (PL die WCs) NEUT NOUN
WC

★ die **Webcam** (PL die Webcams) FEM NOUN
webcam

das **Web-Magazin** (PL die Web-Magazine)
NEUT NOUN
webzine

die **Webmail** FEM NOUN
webmail

★ die **Webseite** FEM NOUN
web page

★ der **Wechsel** (PL die Wechsel) MASC NOUN
change

★ der **Wechselkurs** (GEN des
Wechselkurses, PL die Wechselkurse) MASC
NOUN
rate of exchange

★ **wechseln** VERB [34]
1 to change
  □ Wir mussten einen Reifen wechseln. **We had
  to change a tyre.** □ Wie viel Geld wechselst du?
  How much money are you changing?
  ■ **Blicke wechseln** to exchange glances
2 to have change
  □ Können Sie wechseln? **Do you have any
  change?** □ Kannst du mir zwanzig Euro in
  Münzen wechseln? **Have you got change for
  twenty euros?**

★ die **Wechselstube** FEM NOUN
bureau de change

★ **wecken** VERB [38]
to wake up

★ der **Wecker** (PL die Wecker) MASC NOUN
alarm clock

weder CONJUNCTION
neither
  ■ **weder ... noch ...** neither ... nor ...

★ **weg** ADVERB
▷ see also der **Weg** NOUN
away
  □ Geh weg! **Go away!**
  ■ **Weg da!** Out of the way!
  ■ **Finger weg!** Hands off!
  ■ **Er war schon weg.** He'd already left.

★ der **Weg** (PL die **Wege**) MASC NOUN
▷ see also **weg** ADVERB

1 way
□ Es gibt sicher einen Weg, das zu reparieren.
There must be a way to repair it.

2 path
□ Ein Weg führte zur Kapelle hinauf. A path led up to the chapel.

3 route
□ Welchen Weg habt ihr genommen? Which route did you take?

■ **sich auf den Weg machen** to be on one's way

■ **jemandem aus dem Weg gehen** to keep out of somebody's way

★ **wegen** PREPOSITION

> The preposition **wegen** takes the dative or sometimes the genitive.

because of
□ Wegen dir bin ich zu spät gekommen. Because of you I arrived late. □ Wegen des schlechten Wetters wurde die Veranstaltung abgesagt. The event was cancelled because of the bad weather.

weggehen (IMPERFECT **ging weg**, PERFECT TENSE **ist weggegangen**) VERB [29]
to go away

weglassen (PRESENT TENSE **lässt weg**, IMPERFECT **ließ weg**, PERFECT TENSE **hat weggelassen**) VERB [42]
to leave out

weglaufen (PRESENT TENSE **läuft weg**, IMPERFECT **lief weg**, PERFECT TENSE **ist weggelaufen**) VERB [43]
to run away

weglegen (PERFECT TENSE **hat weggelegt**) VERB [4]
to put aside

wegmachen (PERFECT TENSE **hat weggemacht**) VERB [48]
to get rid of
□ einen Fleck wegmachen to get rid of a stain

wegmüssen (PRESENT TENSE **muss weg**, IMPERFECT **musste weg**, PERFECT TENSE **hat weggemusst** or **wegmüssen**) VERB [51]
to have to go

wegnehmen (PRESENT TENSE **nimmt weg**, IMPERFECT **nahm weg**, PERFECT TENSE **hat weggenommen**) VERB [52]
to take away

wegtun (IMPERFECT **tat weg**, PERFECT TENSE **hat weggetan**) VERB [81]
to put away

★ der **Wegweiser** (PL die **Wegweiser**) MASC NOUN
signpost

★ **wegwerfen** (PRESENT TENSE **wirft weg**, IMPERFECT **warf weg**, PERFECT TENSE **hat weggeworfen**) VERB [92]
to throw away

weh ADJECTIVE ▷ see **wehtun**

die **Wehrdienst** MASC NOUN
military service (until 2011)

> **DID YOU KNOW...?**
> Young men were generally conscripted into the **Wehrdienst** when they left school. The basic period of military service was 9 months.

der **Wehrdienstverweigerer** (PL die **Wehrdienstverweigerer**) MASC NOUN
conscientious objector (until 2011)

sich wehren VERB [38]
to defend oneself

die **Wehrpflicht** FEM NOUN
compulsory military service (until 2011)

★ **wehtun** (IMPERFECT **tat weh**, PERFECT TENSE **hat wehgetan**) VERB [81]

1 to hurt
□ Mein Bein tut weh. My leg hurts.

2 to be sore
□ Mein Hals tut weh. My throat's sore.

■ **sich wehtun** to hurt oneself □ Hast du dir wehgetan? Have you hurt yourself?

■ **jemandem wehtun** to hurt somebody □ Ich möchte dir nicht wehtun, aber das war nicht sehr intelligent. I don't want to hurt you, but that really wasn't very clever.

das **Weibchen** (PL die **Weibchen**) NEUT NOUN
female

★ **weiblich** ADJECTIVE
feminine
□ ein weibliches Substantiv a feminine noun

★ **weich** ADJECTIVE
soft
□ ein weiches Bett a soft bed

sich weigern VERB [88]
to refuse

★ das **Weihnachten** (GEN des **Weihnachten**) NEUT NOUN
Christmas
□ an Weihnachten at Christmas □ zu Weihnachten for Christmas

■ **Frohe Weihnachten!** Merry Christmas.

die **Weihnachtsferien** PL NOUN
Christmas holidays pl

★ das **Weihnachtslied** (PL die **Weihnachtslieder**) NEUT NOUN
Christmas carol

★ der **Weihnachtsmann** (PL die **Weihnachtsmänner**) MASC NOUN
Father Christmas

der **Weihnachtsmarkt** (PL die **Weihnachtsmärkte**) MASC NOUN
Christmas fair

★ der **Weihnachtstag** (PL die **Weihnachtstage**) MASC NOUN
- der erste Weihnachtstag Christmas Day
- der zweite Weihnachtstag Boxing Day

★ **weil** CONJUNCTION
because

★ die **Weile** FEM NOUN
while
□ Es wird eine Weile dauern. It'll take a while.

★ der **Wein** (PL die **Weine**) MASC NOUN
wine

der **Weinberg** (PL die **Weinberge**) MASC NOUN
vineyard

der **Weinbrand** (PL die **Weinbrände**) MASC NOUN
brandy

★ **weinen** VERB [38]
to cry
- Das ist zum Weinen. It's enough to make you cry.

das **Weinglas** (GEN des **Weinglases**, PL die **Weingläser**) NEUT NOUN
wine glass

★ die **Weinkarte** FEM NOUN
wine list

★ der **Weinkeller** (PL die **Weinkeller**) MASC NOUN
1 wine cellar
2 wine bar

★ die **Weinprobe** FEM NOUN
wine tasting

★ die **Weinstube** FEM NOUN
wine bar

★ die **Weintraube** FEM NOUN
grape

die **Weise** FEM NOUN
way
□ Die Art und Weise, wie er uns behandelt hat. The way he treated us.
- auf diese Weise in this way

die **Weisheit** FEM NOUN
wisdom

der **Weisheitszahn** (PL die **Weisheitszähne**) MASC NOUN
wisdom tooth

★ **weiß** VERB ▷ see **wissen**

★ **weiß** ADJECTIVE
white

das **Weißbrot** (PL die **Weißbrote**) NEUT NOUN
white bread

★ der **Weißwein** (PL die **Weißweine**) MASC NOUN
white wine

★ **weit** ADJECTIVE, ADVERB
1 long
□ Das ist eine weite Reise. That's a long journey. □ Das war sein weitester Wurf. That was his longest throw.
2 far
□ Wie weit ist es ...? How far is it ...? □ Nach Berlin ist es weiter als nach München. It's further to Berlin than to Munich. □ so weit wie möglich as far as possible □ Das geht zu weit. That's going too far.
3 baggy
□ Sie hatte einen weiten Pulli an. She was wearing a baggy pullover.
- ein weiter Begriff a broad idea
- so weit sein to be ready □ Ich bin so weit. I'm ready.
- Ich bin so weit zufrieden. By and large I'm quite satisfied.

weitaus ADVERB
by far

★ **weiter** ADJECTIVE, ADVERB
further
□ Wenn du noch weitere Fragen hast ... If you have any further questions ... □ Alles Weitere besprechen wir morgen. We can discuss any further details tomorrow.
- ohne weiteres just like that □ Ich kann doch nicht so ohne weiteres gehen. I can't go just like that.
- weiter nichts nothing else
- weiter niemand nobody else

★ sich **weiterbilden** (PERFECT TENSE **hat sich weitergebildet**) VERB [4]
to continue one's education

★ die **Weiterbildung** FEM NOUN
further education

die **Weiterfahrt** FEM NOUN
continuation of the journey

weitergehen (IMPERFECT **ging weiter**, PERFECT TENSE **ist weitergegangen**) VERB [29]
to go on

weiterhin ADVERB
- etwas weiterhin tun to go on doing something

weiterleiten (PERFECT TENSE **hat weitergeleitet**) VERB [4]
to pass on

★ **weitermachen** (PERFECT TENSE **hat weitergemacht**) VERB [48]
to continue

der **Weitsprung** MASC NOUN
long jump

der **Weizen** MASC NOUN
wheat

welche ADJECTIVE, PRONOUN

1 which

  □ Welcher Mann? **Which man?** □ Welche Frau? **Which woman?** □ Welches Mädchen? **Which girl?** □ Welcher von beiden? **Which of the two?** □ Welchen hast du genommen? **Which one did you take?**

2 what

  □ Welch eine Überraschung! **What a surprise!**
  ▪ **Welche Freude! What joy!**

3 some

  □ Ich habe Kirschen, willst du welche? **I have some cherries, would you like some?** □ Ich habe welche. **I have some.**

4 any

  □ Ich brauche Briefmarken, hast du welche? **I need stamps, have you got any?** □ Ich brauche Kleingeld, hast du welches? **I need change, have you got any?**

die **Welle** FEM NOUN
  wave

die **Wellenlänge** FEM NOUN
  wavelength

der **Wellensittich** (PL die **Wellensittiche**) MASC NOUN
  budgie

die **Welt** FEM NOUN
  world

das **Weltall** NEUT NOUN
  universe

weltberühmt ADJECTIVE
  world-famous

der **Weltkrieg** (PL die **Weltkriege**) MASC NOUN
  world war

der **Weltmeister** (PL die **Weltmeister**) MASC NOUN
  world champion

der **Weltraum** MASC NOUN
  space

weltweit ADJECTIVE, ADVERB
  worldwide

wem PRONOUN

  wem is the dative of **wer**.

  to whom
  ▪ **Mit wem bist du gekommen? Who did you come with?**

wen PRONOUN

  wen is the accusative of **wer**.

  whom
  ▪ **Wen hast du gesehen? Who did you see?**

wenig ADJECTIVE, ADVERB
  little
  □ Das ist ein wenig benutzter Weg. **That is a little-used path.**

  ▪ **so wenig wie** as little as □ Er arbeitet so wenig wie möglich. **He works as little as possible.** □ Ich habe so wenig Geld wie du. **I have as little money as you.**
  ▪ **zu wenig** too little
  ▪ **ein wenig** a little, a bit □ Kannst du ein wenig zur Seite rutschen? (*Umgangssprache*) **Can you move up a bit?**

wenige PL PRONOUN
  few *pl*
  □ Das wissen nur wenige. **Only a few people know that.**

weniger ADJECTIVE, ADVERB

1 less

  □ Ich habe weniger Geld als du. **I have less money than you.**

2 fewer

  □ Ich habe weniger Fehler gemacht. **I've made fewer mistakes.**

3 minus

  □ Zehn weniger drei ist sieben. **Ten minus three is seven.**

wenigste ADJECTIVE
  least
  □ Das ist das wenigste, was ich tun kann. **That's the least I can do.**

  ▪ **am wenigsten** the least □ Die Clowns haben mir am wenigsten gefallen. **I liked the clowns the least.**

wenigstens ADVERB
  at least

wenn CONJUNCTION

1 if

  □ Wenn er anruft, sag mir Bescheid. **If he calls, tell me.**
  ▪ **selbst wenn** ... even if ...
  ▪ **wenn ich doch** ... if only I ...

2 when

  □ Wenn ich nach Hause komme, dusche ich erst mal. **When I get home, the first thing I'm going to do is have a shower.**
  ▪ **immer wenn** whenever □ Immer wenn ich frage, lacht er nur. **Whenever I ask, he just laughs.**

wer PRONOUN
  who

  BE CAREFUL!
  wer does not mean **where**.

die **Werbeagentur** FEM NOUN
  advertising agency

das **Werbefernsehen** NEUT NOUN
  commercial television

werben (PRESENT TENSE **wirbt**, IMPERFECT **warb**, PERFECT TENSE **hat geworben**) VERB [90]
  to advertise
  □ Im Fernsehen wird zu viel geworben. **There's too much advertising on TV.**
  ▪ **Mitglieder werben** to recruit members

★ der **Werbespot** (PL die **Werbespots**) MASC NOUN
commercial

★ die **Werbung** FEM NOUN
1 advert
□ Hast du die Werbung für den neuen Schokoriegel gesehen? Have you seen the advert for the new chocolate bar? □ Wenn Werbung kommt, schalte ich um. I switch over when the adverts come on.
2 advertising
□ Er arbeitet in der Werbung. He works in advertising.
▪ **für etwas Werbung machen** to advertise something

★ **werden** VERB [91]

PRESENT TENSE	
ich werde	wir werden
du wirst	ihr werdet
er/sie/es wird	sie/Sie werden
PERFECT TENSE	
ist geworden/worden	

1 to become
□ Er ist Lehrer geworden. He became a teacher. □ Sie ist reich geworden. She became rich. □ Was ist aus ihm geworden? What became of him?
▪ **Erster werden** to come first
▪ **Was willst du einmal werden?** What do you want to be?
▪ **rot werden** to turn red
▪ **Es ist gut geworden.** It turned out well.
▪ **Die Fotos sind gut geworden.** The photos have come out well.
▪ **Es ist nichts geworden.** It came to nothing.
▪ **Es wird Tag.** It's getting light.
▪ **Es wird Nacht.** It's getting dark.
▪ **Mir wird kalt.** I'm getting cold.
▪ **Mir wird schlecht.** I feel sick.

2 will

werden is used to form the future tense.

□ Das muss anders werden. That'll have to change. □ Er wird es tun. He'll do it. □ Er wird das nicht tun. He won't do it. □ Sie wird in der Küche sein. She'll be in the kitchen.
▪ **Es wird gleich regnen.** It's going to rain.

3 to be

werden is used to form the passive.

□ gebraucht werden to be needed □ Er ist erschossen worden. He's been shot. □ Mir wurde gesagt, dass ... I was told that ...

4 would

werden is used to form the conditional tense.

▪ **Ich würde ...** I would ...
▪ **Er würde gern ...** He'd like to ...
▪ **Ich würde lieber ...** I'd rather ...

★ **werfen** (PRESENT TENSE **wirft**, IMPERFECT **warf**, PERFECT TENSE **hat geworfen**) VERB [92]
to throw

★ das **Werken** NEUT NOUN
1 handicrafts *sing*
2 design technology

★ die **Werkstatt** (PL die **Werkstätten**) FEM NOUN
1 workshop
□ eine Werkstatt für Behinderte a workshop for people with disabilities
2 garage
□ Das Auto ist in der Werkstatt. The car's in the garage.

★ der **Werktag** (PL die **Werktage**) MASC NOUN
working day

★ **werktags** ADVERB
on working days

das **Werkzeug** (PL die **Werkzeuge**) NEUT NOUN
tool

★ **wert** ADJECTIVE
▷ *see also* der **Wert** NOUN
worth
□ Wie viel ist das Bild wert? How much is that picture worth? □ Das ist nichts wert. It's not worth anything. □ Das ist viel wert. It's worth a lot.

der **Wert** (PL die **Werte**) MASC NOUN
▷ *see also* **wert** ADJECTIVE
value
▪ **Wert legen auf** to attach importance to
□ Sie legt großen Wert auf rechtzeitiges Erscheinen. She attaches great importance to punctuality.
▪ **Es hat doch keinen Wert.** There's no point.

★ **wertlos** ADJECTIVE
worthless

★ **wertvoll** ADJECTIVE
valuable

das **Wesen** (PL die **Wesen**) NEUT NOUN
manner
□ Er hat ein freundliches Wesen. He has a friendly manner.

wesentlich ADJECTIVE
significant

weshalb ADVERB
why

★ die **Wespe** FEM NOUN
wasp

wessen PRONOUN

wessen is the genitive of **wer**.

whose

die **Weste** FEM NOUN
waistcoat

★ der **Westen** MASC NOUN
west

★ = core vocabulary

★ westlich ADJECTIVE, PREPOSITION, ADVERB
westerly
□ in westlicher Richtung in a westerly direction
■ **westlich einer Sache** to the west of
something □ Das Kraftwerk liegt westlich der
Stadt. The power station's to the west of the
city.
■ **westlich von** west of □ Essen liegt westlich
von Bochum. Essen's west of Bochum.

weswegen ADVERB
why

★ der Wettbewerb (PL die **Wettbewerbe**)
MASC NOUN
competition

die Wette FEM NOUN
bet

wetten VERB [2]
to bet
□ Ich wette, du fällst durchs Examen. I bet you
fail the exam.

★ das Wetter NEUT NOUN
weather

★ der Wetterbericht (PL die
Wetterberichte) MASC NOUN
weather report

★ die Wetterlage (PL die **Wetterlagen**) FEM
NOUN
weather situation

★ die Wettervorhersage FEM NOUN
weather forecast

★ der Wettkampf (PL die **Wettkämpfe**) MASC
NOUN
contest

der Wettlauf (PL die **Wettläufe**) MASC NOUN
race

★ wichtig ADJECTIVE
important

der Widder (PL die **Widder**) MASC NOUN
1 ram
2 Aries
□ Angela ist Widder. Angela's Aries.

★ wider PREPOSITION

The preposition wider takes the accusative.

against
■ **wider Erwarten** contrary to expectations

widerlich ADJECTIVE
disgusting

widerspenstig ADJECTIVE
wilful

widersprechen (PRESENT TENSE
widerspricht, IMPERFECT **widersprach**,
PERFECT TENSE **hat widersprochen**) VERB [70]
■ **jemandem widersprechen** to contradict
somebody

der Widerspruch (PL die **Widersprüche**)
MASC NOUN
contradiction

der Widerstand (PL die **Widerstände**) MASC
NOUN
resistance

★ widerwillig ADJECTIVE
unwilling

★ wie ADVERB
1 how
□ Wie groß? How big? □ Wie schnell? How fast?
□ Wie schön! How lovely! □ Und wie! And how!
□ Wie wär's? How about it? □ Wie geht's dir?
How are you?
■ **Wie bitte? 1** Pardon? □ Wie bitte, was
haben Sie gesagt? Pardon, what did you say?
2 What? □ Wie bitte, du willst zweitausend
Euro von mir haben? What? You want me to
give you two thousand euros?
■ **so schön wie ...** as beautiful as ...
■ **wie ich schon sagte** as I said
2 like
□ wie du like you □ singen wie ein ... to sing like
a ...
■ **wie zum Beispiel** such as

★ wieder ADVERB
again
□ wieder da sein to be back again □ Gehst du
schon wieder? Are you off again?
■ **wieder ein ...** another ... □ wenn du wieder
einen Geldbeutel findest ... if you find another
purse ...

wiederaufbereiten (PERFECT TENSE hat
wiederaufbereitet) VERB [2]
to recycle

wiederbekommen (IMPERFECT bekam
wieder, PERFECT TENSE hat
wiederbekommen) VERB [40]
to get back

wiedererkennen (IMPERFECT erkannte
wieder, PERFECT TENSE hat wiedererkannt)
VERB [39]
to recognize

★ wiederholen (PERFECT TENSE hat wiederholt)
VERB [4]
to repeat

die Wiederholung FEM NOUN
1 repetition
□ Es darf keine Wiederholung dieses Vorfalls
geben. There must be no repetition of this
incident.
2 repeat
□ Im Fernsehen kommen zu viele
Wiederholungen. There are too many repeats
on TV.

das Wiederhören NEUT NOUN
■ **Auf Wiederhören!** Goodbye! (on telephone,
radio)

wiedersehen (PRESENT TENSE sieht wieder,
IMPERFECT sah wieder, PERFECT TENSE hat
wiedergesehen) VERB [64]

German -English

W

wiederverwerten – wirklich

to see again
- **Auf Wiedersehen!** Goodbye.

wiederverwerten (PERFECT TENSE **hat wiederverwertet**) VERB [7]
to recycle

die **Wiege** FEM NOUN
cradle

★ **wiegen** (IMPERFECT **wog**, PERFECT TENSE **hat gewogen**) VERB
to weigh
□ Ich habe mich heute früh gewogen. I weighed myself this morning.

★ **Wien** NEUT NOUN
Vienna

★ die **Wiese** FEM NOUN
meadow

★ **wieso** ADVERB
why

wie viel ADJECTIVE, PRONOUN
how much
□ Wie viel hat das gekostet? How much did it cost?
- **wie viel Menschen** how many people

★ **wievielte** ADJECTIVE
- **Zum wievielten Mal?** How many times?
- **Den Wievielten haben wir?** What's the date?

wieweit CONJUNCTION
to what extent

das **Wi-Fi** NEUT NOUN
Wi-Fi

wild ADJECTIVE
wild

wildfremd ADJECTIVE
- **ein wildfremder Mensch** a complete stranger

will VERB ▷ see **wollen**

der **Wille** (GEN des **Willens**, PL die **Willen**) MASC NOUN
will
□ Ich habe es aus freiem Willen getan. I did it of my own free will.

★ **willkommen** ADJECTIVE
welcome
□ Herzlich willkommen! Welcome!
- **jemanden willkommen heißen** to welcome somebody

wimmeln VERB [88]
- **Es wimmelt von ...** It's teeming with ...

die **Wimper** FEM NOUN
eyelash

die **Wimperntusche** FEM NOUN
mascara

★ der **Wind** (PL die **Winde**) MASC NOUN
wind

die **Windel** FEM NOUN
nappy
□ Kannst du dem Baby die Windeln wechseln? Can you change the baby's nappy?

die **Windenergie** FEM NOUN
wind energy

★ **windig** ADJECTIVE
windy
□ Es ist windig. It's windy.

die **Windmühle** FEM NOUN
windmill

der **Windpark** MASC NOUN
wind farm

die **Windpocken** PL NOUN
chickenpox *sing*
□ Windpocken sind ansteckend. Chickenpox is catching.

★ die **Windschutzscheibe** FEM NOUN
windscreen

★ das **Windsurfen** NEUT NOUN
windsurfing

der **Winkel** (PL die **Winkel**) MASC NOUN
1 angle
□ ein spitzer Winkel an acute angle
2 corner
□ Ich habe jeden Winkel des Zimmers durchsucht. I've searched every corner of the room.

★ **winken** VERB [38]
to wave
□ jemandem winken to wave to somebody

★ der **Winter** (PL die **Winter**) MASC NOUN
winter
□ im Winter in winter

winzig ADJECTIVE
tiny

wir PRONOUN
we
□ Wir kommen. We're coming.
- **wir alle** all of us
- **Wir sind's.** It's us.

die **Wirbelsäule** FEM NOUN
spine

wird VERB ▷ see **werden**

wirft VERB ▷ see **werfen**

wirken VERB [38]
1 to have an effect
□ Die Tablette wirkt schon. The pill's already having an effect.
2 to seem
□ Er wirkte traurig. He seemed sad.

★ **wirklich** ADJECTIVE, ADVERB
1 real
□ Er ist ein wirklicher Freund. He's a real friend.
2 really
□ Das ist wirklich passiert. That really

★ = core vocabulary

happened. □ Ich weiß es wirklich nicht. I really don't know.

die Wirklichkeit FEM NOUN
reality

wirksam ADJECTIVE
effective

die Wirkung FEM NOUN
effect
□ Wirkung auf etwas haben to have an effect on something

wirr ADJECTIVE
confused

der Wirsing MASC NOUN
savoy cabbage

wirst VERB ▷ see **werden**

der Wirt (PL die **Wirte**) MASC NOUN
landlord

die Wirtin FEM NOUN
landlady

★ **die Wirtschaft** FEM NOUN
1 pub
□ Wir sind in einer Wirtschaft eingekehrt. We stopped at a pub.
2 economy
□ Die Wirtschaft leidet unter der Rezession. The economy's suffering because of the recession.

wirtschaftlich ADJECTIVE
1 economical
□ Die große Packung ist wirtschaftlicher. The large packet's more economical.
2 economic
□ ein wirtschaftlicher Aufschwung an economic upswing

★ **die Wirtschaftslehre** FEM NOUN
economics *sing*

★ **das Wirtshaus** (GEN des **Wirtshauses**, PL die **Wirtshäuser**) NEUT NOUN
inn

wischen VERB [48]
to wipe

★ **wissen** VERB [93]

PRESENT TENSE	
ich weiß	wir wissen
du weißt	ihr wisst
er/sie/es weiß	sie/Sie wissen
PERFECT TENSE	
hat gewusst	

▷ *see also* das **Wissen** NOUN
to know
□ Sie weiß sehr viel. She knows a lot. □ Weißt du, wie die Hauptstadt von der Slowakei heißt? Do you know what the capital of Slovakia is called? □ Ich weiß es nicht. I don't know.
■ **Was weiß ich!** How should I know?

das Wissen NEUT NOUN
▷ *see also* **wissen** VERB
knowledge

die Wissenschaft FEM NOUN
science

der Wissenschaftler (PL die **Wissenschaftler**) MASC NOUN
scientist

wissenschaftlich ADJECTIVE
scientific

★ **die Witwe** FEM NOUN
widow
□ Sie ist Witwe. She's a widow.

★ **der Witwer** (PL die **Witwer**) MASC NOUN
widower
□ Er ist Witwer. He's a widower.

der Witz (GEN des **Witzes**, PL die **Witze**) MASC NOUN
joke
□ einen Witz erzählen to tell a joke

★ **witzig** ADJECTIVE
funny

das WLAN NEUT NOUN
Wi-Fi

★ **wo** ADVERB
where
□ Wo warst du? Where were you?

> **BE CAREFUL!**
> **wo** does not mean **who**.

woanders ADVERB
elsewhere

★ **die Woche** FEM NOUN
week
□ nächste Woche next week

★ **das Wochenende** (PL die **Wochenenden**) NEUT NOUN
weekend
□ am Wochenende at the weekend

wochenlang ADJECTIVE, ADVERB
for weeks

★ **der Wochentag** (PL die **Wochentage**) MASC NOUN
weekday

★ **wochentags** ADVERB
on weekdays

★ **wöchentlich** ADJECTIVE, ADVERB
weekly

wofür ADVERB
what ... for
□ Wofür brauchst du das Geld? What do you need the money for?

wog VERB ▷ see **wiegen**

★ **woher** ADVERB
where ... from
□ Woher sind Sie? Where do you come from?

★ **wohin** ADVERB
1 where ... to
□ Wohin zieht ihr um? Where are you moving to?

2 where
- □ Wohin gehst du? **Where are you going?**

★ **wohl** ADVERB
▷ *see also* das **Wohl** NOUN
probably
- □ Das hat er wohl vergessen. **He's probably forgotten.**
- ■ **Es ist wohl gestohlen worden. It must have been stolen.**
- ■ **Das ist doch wohl nicht dein Ernst!** Surely you're not being serious!
- ■ **Das mag wohl sein. That may well be.**
- ■ **Ob das wohl stimmt? I wonder if that's true.**
- ■ **Er weiß das sehr wohl. He knows that perfectly well.**
- ■ **Ich muss wohl oder übel hingehen. I have to go whether I like it or not.**

das **Wohl** NEUT NOUN
▷ *see also* wohl ADVERB
benefit
- □ zu eurem Wohl **for your benefit**
- ■ **Zum Wohl! Cheers!**

sich **wohlfühlen** VERB [4]
1 to be happy
- □ Ich fühle mich in diesem Haus sehr wohl. **I'm very happy in this house.**
2 to feel well
- □ Sie fühlte sich nicht wohl. **She didn't feel well.**

die **Wohltätigkeit** FEM NOUN
charity

das **Wohltätigkeitskonzert** (PL die **Wohltätigkeitskonzerte**) NEUT NOUN
charity concert

die **Wohltätigkeitsorganisation** FEM NOUN
charitable organization

die **Wohltätigkeitsveranstaltung** FEM NOUN
charity event

die **Wohltätigkeitsverein** (PL die **Wohltätigkeitsvereine**) MASC NOUN
charity

★ der **Wohnblock** (PL die **Wohnblocks**) MASC NOUN
block of flats

★ **wohnen** VERB [38]
to live
- □ Ich wohne in Bremen. **I live in Bremen.**

die **Wohngemeinschaft** FEM NOUN
- ■ **Ich wohne in einer Wohngemeinschaft. I share a flat.**

das **Wohnheim** (PL die **Wohnheime**) NEUT NOUN
1 home
- □ ein Wohnheim für ältere Menschen **a home for senior citizens**
- ■ **ein Studentenwohnheim a hall of residence**
2 hostel

★ der **Wohnort** (PL die **Wohnorte**) MASC NOUN
place of residence

der **Wohnsitz** (GEN des **Wohnsitzes**, PL die **Wohnsitze**) MASC NOUN
place of residence
- ■ **keinen festen Wohnsitz haben** (*formal*) to be homeless

★ die **Wohnung** FEM NOUN
flat

★ der **Wohnwagen** (PL die **Wohnwagen**) MASC NOUN
caravan

★ das **Wohnzimmer** (PL die **Wohnzimmer**) NEUT NOUN
living room

der **Wolf** (PL die **Wölfe**) MASC NOUN
wolf

★ die **Wolke** FEM NOUN
cloud

der **Wolkenkratzer** (PL die **Wolkenkratzer**) MASC NOUN
skyscraper

★ **wolkenlos** ADJECTIVE
cloudless

★ **wolkig** ADJECTIVE
cloudy

★ die **Wolle** FEM NOUN
wool

★ **wollen** (PRESENT TENSE **will**, IMPERFECT **wollte**, PERFECT TENSE **hat gewollt** *or* **wollen**) VERB [94]

The past participle **wollen** is used when **wollen** is a modal auxiliary.

to want
- □ Er hat nicht gewollt. **He didn't want to.** □ Er wollte das nicht. **He didn't want it.** □ Ich will nach Hause. **I want to go home.** □ Ich will, dass du mir zuhörst. **I want you to listen to me.**
- ■ **Wenn du willst. If you like.**
- ■ **etwas tun wollen to want to do something** □ Er hat unbedingt gehen wollen. **He really wanted to go.** □ Er will ein Haus kaufen. **He wants to buy a house.**
- ■ **etwas gerade tun wollen to be on the point of doing something** □ Ich wollte gerade gehen. **I was on the point of going.**
- ■ **Ich wollte, ich wäre ... I wish I were ...**

womit ADVERB
1 with which
- □ Das ist der Gegenstand, womit er erschlagen wurde. **This is the instrument with which he was killed.**
2 what ... with
- □ Womit hast du das repariert? **What did you repair it with?**

wonach ADVERB
1 what ... for
- □ Das war genau, wonach er gesucht hatte. **That was just what he had been looking for.**

2 what ... by
□ Wonach sollen wir die Uhr stellen? What shall we set the clock by?
■ der Tag, wonach er verunglückte the day before his accident

woran ADVERB
■ das Paket, woran dieser Zettel hing the parcel the note was attached to
■ Woran war dieser Zettel befestigt? What was this note attached to?
■ Woran ist er gestorben? What did he die of?

worauf ADVERB
what ... on
□ Worauf soll ich den Computer stellen? What shall I put the computer on?
■ der Tisch, worauf der Computer steht the table the computer is on

woraus ADVERB
■ das Material, woraus es hergestellt ist the material it is made of
■ das Leck, woraus Gas strömte the hole gas was pouring out of

worin ADVERB
what ... in
□ Worin war das versteckt? What was it hidden in?
■ die Schublade, worin der Schlüssel ist the drawer the key is in
■ Worin besteht der Unterschied? What's the difference?

★ **das Wort** (PL die **Wörter** or **Worte**) NEUT NOUN
word
□ Sie sprach ein paar bewegende Worte. She said a few moving words. □ Manche Wörter werden wie im Französischen ausgesprochen. Some words are pronounced as in French.
■ jemanden beim Wort nehmen to take somebody at his word □ Ich nahm sie beim Wort. I took her at her word.
■ mit anderen Worten in other words

★ **das Wörterbuch** (PL die **Wörterbücher**) NEUT NOUN
dictionary

wörtlich ADJECTIVE
literal

der Wortschatz (GEN des **Wortschatzes**) MASC NOUN
vocabulary

das Wortspiel (PL die **Wortspiele**) NEUT NOUN
pun

worüber ADVERB
■ das Thema, worüber wir reden the subject we're talking about
■ der Tisch, worüber eine Lampe hing the table a lamp was hanging over
■ Worüber kann ich meinen Mantel legen? Where can I put my coat?

worunter ADVERB
what ... under
□ Worunter hat sich die Katze verkrochen? What did the cat crawl under?
■ der Tisch, worunter die Katze lag the table the cat was lying under

★ **wovon** ADVERB
■ Das war es, wovon wir sprachen. That was what we were talking about.
■ das Essen, wovon ihm schlecht wurde the food which made him ill

wovor ADVERB
■ das Haus, wovor du stehst the house you're standing in front of
■ die Arbeit, wovor sie am meisten Angst hat the test which she's most afraid of

wozu ADVERB
1 why
□ Wozu willst du das wissen? Why do you want to know that?
2 what ... for
□ Wozu dient dieser Schalter? What's this switch for? □ Wozu brauchst du einen Computer? What do you need a computer for?

das Wrack (PL die **Wracks**) NEUT NOUN
wreck

der Wucher MASC NOUN
■ Das ist Wucher! That's daylight robbery! (Umgangssprache)

wund ADJECTIVE
sore
□ Ich habe mir die Füße beim Einkaufen wund gelaufen. My feet are sore from going round the shops.

★ **die Wunde** FEM NOUN
wound

das Wunder (PL die **Wunder**) NEUT NOUN
miracle
■ es ist kein Wunder it's no wonder

★ **wunderbar** ADJECTIVE
wonderful

wundern VERB [88]
to surprise
□ Diese Frage hat mich sehr gewundert. This question really surprised me.
■ sich wundern über to be surprised at □ Ich wundere mich immer wieder über ihr Wissen. I'm always surprised at how much she knows. □ Ich wundere mich, dass er noch nicht angerufen hat. I'm surprised that he hasn't phoned yet.

wunderschön – wütend

- **Ich muss mich schon über dich wundern.** I must say you surprise me.
- **Es wundert mich, dass du das fragst.** I'm surprised you ask.
- **Er wird sich noch wundern!** He's in for a surprise!

★ **wunderschön** ADJECTIVE
beautiful

wundervoll ADJECTIVE
wonderful

★ der **Wunsch** (PL die **Wünsche**) MASC NOUN
wish

★ **wünschen** VERB [48]
to wish
□ Ich wünsche dir viel Erfolg! I wish you every success.
- **sich etwas wünschen** to want something
□ Ich wünsche mir zum Geburtstag Inline-Skates. I want inline skates for my birthday.

wurde VERB ▷ see **werden**

der **Wurf** (PL die **Würfe**) MASC NOUN
throw

der **Würfel** (PL die **Würfel**) MASC NOUN
1 dice
□ zwei Würfel two dice □ Wir haben Würfel gespielt. We played dice.
2 cube
□ Ein Würfel hat sechs gleich große Flächen. A cube has six equal surfaces.

würfeln VERB [34]
1 to throw a dice
□ Ich bin dran mit Würfeln. It's my turn to throw the dice. □ Wir haben darum gewürfelt, wer abwaschen muss. We threw a dice to see who was going to wash up.
2 to dice
□ den Speck würfeln to dice the bacon

der **Würfelzucker** MASC NOUN
lump sugar

der **Wurm** (PL die **Würmer**) MASC NOUN
worm

★ die **Wurst** (PL die **Würste**) FEM NOUN
1 sausage
□ Leberwurst liver sausage
2 cold meat
- **eine Wurstplatte** a platter of cold meat
- **Das ist mir Wurst.** I don't give a toss. (*Umgangssprache*)

★ das **Würstchen** (PL die **Würstchen**) NEUT NOUN
sausage

die **Würze** FEM NOUN
seasoning

die **Wurzel** FEM NOUN
root

wusch VERB ▷ see **waschen**

wusste VERB ▷ see **wissen**

die **Wüste** FEM NOUN
desert

★ die **Wut** FEM NOUN
rage
- **eine Wut haben** to be furious

der **Wutanfall** (PL die **Wutanfälle**) MASC NOUN
fit of rage

★ **wütend** ADJECTIVE
furious
□ Ich bin wütend auf ihn. I'm furious with him.

W

x-beliebig ADJECTIVE
<u>any ... whatever</u>
□ Wähle eine x-beliebige Zahl. Choose any number whatever.

x-mal ADVERB
<u>any number of times</u>

□ Ich habe es ihm x-mal gesagt. I've told him any number of times.

das **Xylofon** (PL die **Xylofone**) NEUT NOUN
<u>xylophone</u>

Yy

das **Yoga** (GEN des **Yoga** or **Yogas**) NEUT NOUN
yoga

das **Ypsilon** (GEN des **Ypsilon** or **Ypsilons**, PL
die **Ypsilons**) NEUT NOUN
the letter Y

★ = core vocabulary

Zz

zaghaft ADJECTIVE
timid

zäh ADJECTIVE
1 tough
□ Das Steak ist zäh. The steak's tough. □ Ich bin zäh, ich halte es noch eine Weile aus. I'm tough, I can stand it for a bit yet.
2 slow-moving
□ Der Verkehr war zäh. Traffic was slow-moving.

★ die **Zahl** FEM NOUN
number

★ **zahlen** VERB [38]
to pay
□ Wie viel hast du dafür gezahlt? How much did you pay for it?
■ Zahlen bitte! The bill, please!

★ **zählen** VERB [38]
to count
□ Ich zähle bis drei. I'll count to three. □ Ich habe die Hefte gezählt. I've counted the exercise books.
■ zählen auf to count on □ Wir zählen auf dich. We're counting on you.
■ zählen zu to be one of □ Er zählt zu den besseren Schülern. He's one of the better pupils.

★ **zahlreich** ADJECTIVE
numerous

die **Zahlung** FEM NOUN
payment

das **Zahlwort** (PL die Zahlwörter) NEUT NOUN
numeral

zahm ADJECTIVE
tame

der **Zahn** (PL die Zähne) MASC NOUN
tooth

★ der **Zahnarzt** (GEN des Zahnarztes, PL die Zahnärzte) MASC NOUN
dentist

★ die **Zahnärztin** FEM NOUN
dentist

★ die **Zahnbürste** FEM NOUN
toothbrush

★ die **Zahncreme** (PL die Zahncremes) FEM NOUN
toothpaste

das **Zahnfleisch** NEUT NOUN
gums pl
□ Mein Zahnfleisch blutet. My gums are bleeding.

★ die **Zahnpasta** (PL die Zahnpasten) FEM NOUN
toothpaste

die **Zahnschmerzen** MASC PL NOUN
toothache sing
□ Zahnschmerzen sind sehr unangenehm. Toothache is very unpleasant.

der **Zahnstein** MASC NOUN
tartar

der **Zahnstocher** (PL die Zahnstocher) MASC NOUN
toothpick

die **Zange** FEM NOUN
1 pliers pl
□ Ich brauche eine isolierte Zange. I need a pair of insulated pliers.
2 pincers pl
□ die Zangen eines Hummers a lobster's pincers

zappeln VERB [34]
1 to wriggle
□ Der Fisch zappelt noch. The fish is still wriggling.
2 to fidget
□ Hör auf zu zappeln. Stop fidgeting.

zart ADJECTIVE
1 soft
□ zarte Haut soft skin
2 gentle
□ eine zarte Berührung a gentle touch
3 delicate
□ zarte Farben delicate colours □ Sie ist ein sehr zartes Kind. She's a very delicate child.
■ zartes Fleisch tender meat

★ **zärtlich** ADJECTIVE
loving
□ Mein Freund ist sehr zärtlich. My boyfriend's very loving. □ ein zärtlicher Kuss a loving kiss □ eine zärtliche Berührung a loving touch

die **Zauberei** FEM NOUN
magic

der **Zaun** (PL die Zäune) MASC NOUN
fence

Numbers in brackets refer to verb tables on pages 697 to 706.

z. B. ABBREVIATION (= *zum Beispiel*)
e.g.

der **Zebrastreifen** (PL die Zebrastreifen) MASC NOUN
zebra crossing

★ die **Zehe** FEM NOUN
toe
  □ die große Zehe the big toe
  ■ eine Knoblauchzehe a clove of garlic

★ **zehn** NUMBER
ten

zehnte ADJECTIVE
tenth

das **Zeichen** (PL die Zeichen) NEUT NOUN
sign

★ der **Zeichentrickfilm** (PL die Zeichentrickfilme) MASC NOUN
animated cartoon

★ **zeichnen** VERB [53]
to draw
  □ Marek kann gut zeichnen. Marek's good at drawing. □ Sie hat eine Maus gezeichnet. She's drawn a mouse.

die **Zeichnung** FEM NOUN
drawing

der **Zeigefinger** (PL die Zeigefinger) MASC NOUN
index finger

★ **zeigen** VERB [38]
1 to show
  □ Sie hat mir ihre Fotos gezeigt. She showed me her photos. □ Zeig mal, was du da hast. Show us what you've got there.
2 to point
  □ Sie zeigte auf die Tafel. She pointed to the blackboard.
  ■ zeigen auf to point at □ Man zeigt nicht mit dem Finger auf Menschen. Don't point at people.
  ■ es wird sich zeigen time will tell □ Es wird sich zeigen, ob er das kann. Time will tell whether he can do it.
  ■ Es zeigte sich, dass ... It turned out that ...
  □ Es zeigte sich, dass der Text zu schwierig war. It turned out that the text was too difficult.

der **Zeiger** (PL die Zeiger) MASC NOUN
1 hand
  □ der große und der kleine Zeiger der Uhr the big hand and the little hand of the clock
2 pointer
  □ der Zeiger der Waage the pointer of the scales

die **Zeile** FEM NOUN
line
  □ Ich schreibe ihr ein paar Zeilen. I'm going to write her a few lines.

★ die **Zeit** FEM NOUN
1 time
  □ Wir haben keine Zeit mehr. We haven't got any more time. □ Um welche Zeit seid ihr nach Hause gekommen? What time did you get home?
2 tense
  □ die Zeiten der Vergangenheit the past tenses
  ■ sich Zeit lassen to take one's time □ Da hast du dir aber viel Zeit gelassen. You've been taking your time.
  ■ von Zeit zu Zeit from time to time
  ■ Zeit raubend ▷ see zeitraubend

zeitlich ADJECTIVE
chronological

die **Zeitlupe** FEM NOUN
slow motion
  □ in Zeitlupe in slow motion

zeitnah ADJECTIVE, ADVERB
1 prompt
  □ eine zeitnahe Antwort a prompt reply
2 promptly
  □ Der Aufzug wurde zeitnah repariert. The lift was repaired promptly.

zeitraubend ADJECTIVE
time-consuming

der **Zeitraum** (PL die Zeiträume) MASC NOUN
period
  □ innerhalb dieses Zeitraums within this period

★ die **Zeitschrift** FEM NOUN
magazine

★ die **Zeitung** FEM NOUN
newspaper

die **Zeitverschwendung** FEM NOUN
waste of time
  □ Das ist doch Zeitverschwendung! That's just a waste of time.

die **Zelle** FEM NOUN
cell
  □ Im Alter sterben die Zellen ab. Cells die off in old age.

★ das **Zelt** (PL die Zelte) NEUT NOUN
tent

★ **zelten** VERB [2]
to camp

★ der **Zeltplatz** (GEN des Zeltplatzes, PL die Zeltplätze) MASC NOUN
camp site

der **Zement** (PL die Zemente) MASC NOUN
cement

zensieren (PERFECT TENSE hat zensiert) VERB [76]
1 to censor
  □ Der Film wurde zensiert. The film was censored.
2 to give a mark
  □ Wie hat deine Deutschlehrerin den Aufsatz zensiert? What mark did your German teacher give you for your essay?

die **Zensur** FEM NOUN
mark
  □ Ich habe durchweg gute Zensuren. I've got good marks in everything.

★ der **Zentimeter** (PL die Zentimeter) MASC NOUN
centimetre

der **Zentner** (PL die **Zentner**) MASC NOUN
hundredweight
□ drei Zentner three hundredweight

zentral ADJECTIVE
central

die **Zentrale** FEM NOUN
1 head office
□ Das Gerät müssen wir in der Zentrale anfordern. We'll have to order the appliance from the head office.
2 switchboard
□ Du musst dich über die Zentrale verbinden lassen. You have to go through the switchboard.

★ die **Zentralheizung** FEM NOUN
central heating *no pl*

★ das **Zentrum** (PL die **Zentren**) NEUT NOUN
centre

zerbrechen (PRESENT TENSE **zerbricht**, IMPERFECT **zerbrach**, PERFECT TENSE **hat/ist zerbrochen**) VERB [11]

For the perfect tense use **haben** when the verb has an object and **sein** when there is no object.

to break
□ Sie hat den Teller zerbrochen. She's broken the plate. □ Der Teller ist zerbrochen. The plate broke.

zerbrechlich ADJECTIVE
fragile

zerreißen (IMPERFECT **zerriss**, PERFECT TENSE **hat/ist zerrissen**) VERB

For the perfect tense use **haben** when the verb has an object and **sein** when there is no object.

1 to tear to pieces
□ Sie hat seinen Brief zerrissen. She tore his letter to pieces.
2 to tear
□ Der Umschlag ist unterwegs zerrissen. The envelope got torn in the post.

zerren VERB [38]
to drag
□ Ich muss meine Tochter jeden Tag aus dem Bett zerren. I have to drag my daughter out of bed in the morning.
■ **zerren an** to tug at □ Der Hund zerrte an der Leine. The dog tugged at its leash.

zerrissen VERB ▷ *see* **zerreißen**

zerschlagen (PRESENT TENSE **zerschlägt**, IMPERFECT **zerschlug**, PERFECT TENSE **hat zerschlagen**) VERB [59]
to smash
□ Sie haben alles Porzellan zerschlagen. They smashed all the china.
■ **sich zerschlagen** to fall through □ Unsere Ferienpläne haben sich zerschlagen. Our holiday plans have fallen through.

★ **zerstören** (PRESENT TENSE **hat zerstört**) VERB [95]
to destroy

die **Zerstörung** FEM NOUN
destruction

zerstreuen (PERFECT TENSE **hat zerstreut**) VERB [95]
1 to entertain
□ Er hat uns mit lustigen Geschichten zerstreut. He entertained us with amusing stories.
2 to scatter
□ Warum hast du die Blätter im ganzen Zimmer zerstreut? Why have you scattered the papers all over the room? □ Unsere Familie ist über ganz Deutschland zerstreut. Our family's scattered all over Germany.
■ **jemandes Angst zerstreuen** to allay somebody's fears

zerstreut ADJECTIVE
1 absent-minded
□ Er ist furchtbar zerstreut. He's terribly absent-minded.
2 scattered
□ Sie sammelte die zerstreuten Seiten auf. She picked up the scattered pages.

★ der **Zettel** (PL die **Zettel**) MASC NOUN
1 note
□ Auf dem Küchentisch liegt ein Zettel für dich. There's a note on the kitchen table for you.
2 piece of paper
□ Sie schrieb seine Telefonnummer auf einen Zettel. She wrote his phone number on a piece of paper.
3 form
□ Wenn du dem Klub beitreten willst, musst du diesen Zettel ausfüllen. If you want to join the club you'll have to fill in this form.

das **Zeug** NEUT NOUN
1 stuff (*Umgangssprache*)
□ Was ist das für ein Zeug? What's this stuff? □ mein Sportzeug my sports stuff
2 gear
□ mein Angelzeug my fishing gear
■ **dummes Zeug** nonsense □ Das ist doch dummes Zeug. That's just a lot of nonsense.
■ **das Zeug haben zu** to have the makings of □ Er hat das Zeug zum Lehrer. He has the makings of a teacher.

★ der **Zeuge** (GEN des **Zeugen**, PL die **Zeugen**) MASC NOUN
witness

die **Zeugin** FEM NOUN
witness

★ das **Zeugnis** (GEN des **Zeugnisses**, PL die **Zeugnisse**) NEUT NOUN
report
□ Oliver hat ein sehr gutes Zeugnis. Oliver's got a very good report.

die **Ziege** FEM NOUN
goat

der **Ziegel** (PL die **Ziegel**) MASC NOUN
1 brick
□ eine Mauer aus Ziegeln a brick wall

Z

Numbers in brackets refer to verb tables on pages 697 to 706.

331

2 tile
  □ Deutsche Dächer sind meist mit roten Ziegeln gedeckt. German roofs are usually covered with red tiles.

★ **ziehen** (IMPERFECT **zog**, PERFECT TENSE **hat/ist gezogen**) VERB [96]

> Use sein to form the perfect tense for 'to move' (house) and 'to roam'. Use haben for 'to move' (in chess), 'to draw' and 'to pull'.

1 to draw
  □ Er hat eine Niete gezogen. He drew a blank.
2 to pull
  □ Sie zog mich am Ärmel. She pulled at my sleeve.
3 to move
  □ Sie sind nach Basel gezogen. They've moved to Basel. □ Er zog mit seinem Turm. He moved his rook.
4 to roam
  □ Wildtiere ziehen frei durch den Nationalpark. Wild animals roam throughout the national park.
  ■ Es zieht. There's a draught.
  ■ sich in die Länge ziehen to be drawn out

★ das **Ziel** (PL die **Ziele**) NEUT NOUN
1 destination
  □ Unser heutiges Ziel ist Bonn. Our destination today is Bonn.
2 finishing line
  □ Er ging als Erster durchs Ziel. He was the first to cross the finishing line.
3 target
  □ Ulm war das Ziel eines Bombenangriffs. Ulm was the target of an air raid.
4 goal
  □ Es ist nicht mein Ziel im Leben, reich zu werden. Getting rich is not my goal in life.

zielen VERB [38]
  to aim
  □ Er hat auf seine Beine gezielt. He aimed at his legs.

die **Zielscheibe** FEM NOUN
  target
  □ Er traf die Zielscheibe mit seinem ersten Schuss. He hit the target with his first shot.

★ **ziemlich** ADJECTIVE, ADVERB
1 quite
  □ Das war eine ziemliche Katastrophe. That was quite a disaster.
2 fair
  □ eine ziemliche Menge Fehler a fair number of mistakes
3 rather
  □ Er war ziemlich sauer. He was rather cross.
  ■ ziemlich viel quite a bit □ Wir haben ziemlich viel erledigt. We've got through quite a bit.

sich **zieren** VERB [76]
  to act coy

zierlich ADJECTIVE
  dainty

die **Ziffer** FEM NOUN
  figure

zig ADJECTIVE
  umpteen (*Umgangssprache*)

★ die **Zigarette** FEM NOUN
  cigarette

die **Zigarettenschachtel** FEM NOUN
  cigarette packet

die **Zigarre** FEM NOUN
  cigar

★ das **Zimmer** (PL die **Zimmer**) NEUT NOUN
  room
  ■ 'Zimmer frei' 'Vacancies'

★ das **Zimmermädchen** (PL die **Zimmermädchen**) NEUT NOUN
  chambermaid

der **Zimmernachweis** (GEN des **Zimmernachweises**, PL die **Zimmernachweise**) MASC NOUN
  accommodation office

der **Zimt** MASC NOUN
  cinnamon

das **Zinn** NEUT NOUN
1 tin
  □ In Cornwall wurde früher Zinn abgebaut. They used to mine tin in Cornwall.
2 pewter
  □ Mein Bruder sammelt Zinn. My brother collects pewter.

der **Zins** (GEN des **Zinses**, PL die **Zinsen**) MASC NOUN
  interest *no pl*
  □ acht Prozent Zinsen eight per cent interest

★ **zirka** ADVERB
  approximately

★ der **Zirkus** (GEN des **Zirkus**, PL die **Zirkusse**) MASC NOUN
  circus

zischen VERB [48]
  to hiss

das **Zitat** (PL die **Zitate**) NEUT NOUN
  quotation

zitieren (PERFECT TENSE **hat zitiert**) VERB [76]
  to quote

★ die **Zitrone** FEM NOUN
  lemon

die **Zitronenlimonade** FEM NOUN
  lemonade

der **Zitronensaft** (PL die **Zitronensäfte**) MASC NOUN
  lemon juice

zittern VERB [88]
  to tremble
  □ vor Angst zittern to tremble with fear
  ■ Sie zitterte vor Kälte. She was shivering.

★ = core vocabulary

zivil ADJECTIVE
civil
■ **zivile Partnerschaft** civil partnership

der Zivildienst MASC NOUN
community service

DID YOU KNOW...?
Until the abolition of compulsory military service in 2011, those young men who opted out of this could choose to do **Zivildienst** or community service instead, for example with the Red Cross.

die Zivilisation FEM NOUN
civilization

zögern VERB [88]
to hesitate

★ **der Zoll** (PL die **Zölle**) MASC NOUN
1 customs pl
 □ Wir mussten am Zoll lange warten. We had to wait a long time at customs.
2 duty
 □ Darauf musst du Zoll bezahlen. You have to pay duty on that.

★ **der Zollbeamte** (GEN des **Zollbeamten**, PL die **Zollbeamten**) MASC NOUN
customs official
 □ Ein Zollbeamter hat unser Auto durchsucht. A customs official searched our car.

★ **zollfrei** ADJECTIVE
duty-free

★ **die Zollkontrolle** FEM NOUN
customs check

die Zone FEM NOUN
zone

★ **der Zoo** (PL die **Zoos**) MASC NOUN
zoo

zoologisch ADJECTIVE
zoological

der Zopf (PL die **Zöpfe**) MASC NOUN
1 plait
 □ zwei blonde Zöpfe two blonde plaits
2 pigtail
 □ Sie hatte ihre Haare zu einem Zopf zusammengebunden. She had put her hair into a pigtail.

★ **der Zorn** MASC NOUN
anger

★ **zornig** ADJECTIVE
angry

★ **zu** PREPOSITION, CONJUNCTION, ADVERB

The preposition **zu** takes the dative.

1 to
 □ zum Bahnhof gehen to go to the station □ zum Arzt gehen to go to the doctor □ zur Schule gehen to go to school □ zur Kirche gehen to go to church □ Sollen wir zu euch gehen? Shall we go to your place?
 ■ Sie sah zu ihm hin. She looked towards him.

■ **zum Fenster herein** through the window
■ **zu meiner Linken** on my left

zu is used with the infinitive.

 □ etwas zu essen something to eat □ um besser sehen zu können in order to see better □ ohne es zu wissen without knowing it

2 at
 □ zu Ostern at Easter
 ■ **zu Hause** at home
 ■ **bis zum ersten Mai** 1 until the first of May
 □ Das Sonderangebot gilt bis zum ersten Mai. The special offer is valid until the first of May.
 2 by the first of May □ Bis zum ersten Mai muss mein Referat fertig sein. My assignment has to be finished by the first of May.
 ■ **zu meinem Geburtstag** for my birthday
 ■ **zu meiner Zeit** in my time

3 with
 □ Wein zum Essen trinken to drink wine with one's meal
 ■ **sich zu jemandem setzen** to sit down beside somebody

4 on
 □ Anmerkungen zu etwas notes on something

5 for
 □ Wasser zum Waschen water for washing
 ■ **Papier zum Schreiben** paper to write on
 ■ **zu etwas werden** to develop into something □ Sie ist zu einer begabten Fußballspielerin geworden. She's developed into a talented football player.
 ■ **jemanden zu etwas machen** to make somebody something □ Sie haben mich zur Klassensprecherin gemacht. They made me class representative.
 ■ **drei zu zwei** three two □ Unsere Mannschaft hat drei zu zwei gewonnen. Our team won three two.
 ■ **das Stück zu drei Euro** at three euros each
 ■ **zum ersten Mal** for the first time
 ■ **zu meiner Freude** to my delight
 ■ **zum Scherz** as a joke
 ■ **zu Fuß** on foot
 ■ **Es ist zum Weinen.** It's enough to make you cry.

6 too
 □ zu schnell too fast □ zu sehr too much

7 closed
 □ Die Geschäfte haben zu. The shops are closed.
 ■ **zu sein** to be shut □ Das Fenster war zu. The window was shut.

das Zubehör (PL die **Zubehöre**) NEUT NOUN
accessories pl
 □ Das Zubehör kostet extra. You pay extra for the accessories.

zubereiten (PERFECT TENSE **hat zubereitet**) VERB [2]
to prepare

zubinden (IMPERFECT **band zu**, PERFECT TENSE **hat zugebunden**) VERB
to tie up

Numbers in brackets refer to verb tables on pages 697 to 706.

Z

333

zubringen (IMPERFECT **brachte zu**, PERFECT TENSE **hat zugebracht**) VERB [13]
to spend
□ Ich habe viel Zeit bei ihnen zugebracht. I spent a lot of time with them.

die **Zucchini** PL NOUN
courgette *sing*

züchten VERB [2]
1 to breed
□ Er züchtet Tauben. He breeds pigeons.
2 to grow
□ Mein Vater züchtet Rosen. My father grows roses.

zucken VERB [38]
1 to twitch
□ Seine Mundwinkel zuckten. The corners of his mouth twitched.
2 to flash
□ Ein Blitz zuckte durch die Nacht. Lightning flashed across the night sky.
■ **mit den Schultern zucken** to shrug one's shoulders

★ der **Zucker** MASC NOUN
1 sugar
□ Ich nehme keinen Zucker in den Tee. I don't take sugar in my tea.
2 diabetes
□ Meine Tante hat Zucker. My aunt's got diabetes.

der **Zuckerguss** (GEN des **Zuckergusses**, PL die **Zuckergüsse**) MASC NOUN
icing *no pl*

zudecken (PERFECT TENSE **hat zugedeckt**) VERB [4]
1 to cover up
□ Man sollte das Loch zudecken. They ought to cover up the hole.
2 to tuck up
□ Er deckte die Kinder zu. He tucked the children up.

zueinander ADVERB
1 to one another
□ Seid nett zueinander. Be nice to one another.
■ **Wir haben viel Vertrauen zueinander.** We trust each other.
2 together
□ Wir halten zueinander, egal, was kommt. Whatever happens, we'll stick together.

★ **zuerst** ADVERB
1 first
□ Was soll ich zuerst machen? What shall I do first? □ Er ist zuerst gekommen, dann kam seine Schwester. He arrived first, then his sister.
2 at first
□ Zuerst war sie noch etwas schüchtern. At first, she was still a bit shy.
■ **zuerst einmal** first of all □ Wir sollten zuerst einmal klären, was das kostet. First of all we ought to check how much it costs.

★ die **Zufahrt** FEM NOUN
approach road
■ '**keine Zufahrt**' 'no access'

der **Zufall** (PL die **Zufälle**) MASC NOUN
1 chance
□ Wie es der Zufall so wollte … As chance would have it …
■ **durch Zufall** by chance □ Ich habe es durch Zufall gefunden. I found it by chance.
2 coincidence
□ Es war schon ein Zufall, dass ich ihm in London begegnet bin. It was quite a coincidence that I met him in London. □ Was für ein glücklicher Zufall! What a happy coincidence! □ So ein Zufall! What a coincidence!

★ **zufällig** ADJECTIVE, ADVERB
1 chance
□ eine zufällige Begegnung a chance meeting
2 by chance
□ Ich habe das Restaurant ganz zufällig gefunden. I found the restaurant quite by chance.
■ **Ich habe zufällig Zeit.** I happen to have time.
3 by any chance
□ Hast du zufällig mein Heft gesehen? Have you seen my exercise book by any chance?

★ **zufrieden** ADJECTIVE
satisfied
□ Ich bin mit deinen Leistungen nicht zufrieden. I'm not satisfied with your work. □ Bist du jetzt zufrieden? Are you satisfied now? □ ein zufriedener Gesichtsausdruck a satisfied expression

zufrieren (IMPERFECT **fror zu**, PERFECT TENSE **ist zugefroren**) VERB
to freeze over
□ Der See ist zugefroren. The lake's frozen over.

★ der **Zug** (PL die **Züge**) MASC NOUN
1 train
□ Wir sind mit dem Zug gefahren. We went by train.
2 draught
□ Hier ist ein furchtbarer Zug. There's a terrible draught in here.
3 move
□ Du bist am Zug. It's your move.
4 gulp
□ Er trank das Glas auf einen Zug leer. He emptied the glass in one gulp.
5 trait
□ Sein Geiz ist ein unangenehmer Zug an ihm. His meanness is an unpleasant trait.
■ **etwas in vollen Zügen genießen** to enjoy something to the full

die **Zugabe** FEM NOUN
1 free gift
□ ein Handy als Zugabe a mobile as a free gift
2 encore
□ Die Zuhörer brüllten: 'Zugabe, Zugabe'. The audience roared: 'encore, encore'.

zugeben (PRESENT TENSE **gibt zu**, IMPERFECT **gab zu**, PERFECT TENSE **hat zugegeben**) VERB [28]
to admit
□ Gib doch zu, dass du dich getäuscht hast. Admit you were wrong. □ Sie wollte ihren Irrtum nicht zugeben. She didn't want to admit her mistake.

zugehen (IMPERFECT **ging zu**, PERFECT TENSE **ist zugegangen**) VERB [29]
to shut
□ Die Tür geht nicht zu. The door won't shut.
■ **auf jemanden zugehen** to walk up to somebody □ Sie ging auf den Mann zu und fragte ihn nach dem Weg. She walked up to the man and asked him the way.
■ **auf etwas zugehen** to walk towards something □ Sie ging auf den Eingang zu, kehrte dann aber wieder um. She walked towards the entrance but then turned back again.
■ **Es geht dort seltsam zu.** There are strange goings-on there.
■ **dem Ende zugehen** to be nearing the end

★ der **Zugführer** (PL die **Zugführer**) MASC NOUN
chief guard (*on train*)

★ die **Zugführerin** FEM NOUN
chief guard (*on train*)

zugig ADJECTIVE
draughty

zügig ADJECTIVE
swift
□ eine zügige Entscheidung a swift decision

zugreifen (IMPERFECT **griff zu**, PERFECT TENSE **hat zugegriffen**) VERB
1 to help oneself
□ Greift ungeniert zu, es ist genügend Kuchen da! Feel free to help yourselves, there's plenty of cake.
2 to seize
□ Er sah das Seil und griff zu. He saw the rope and seized it.
3 to lend a hand
□ Du könntest ruhig ein bisschen zugreifen und mich nicht alles allein machen lassen. You could at least lend a hand a bit instead of letting me do everything.

zugrunde ADVERB
■ **zugrunde gehen** to perish □ Viele fremde Kulturen sind an der westlichen zugrunde gegangen. Many foreign cultures have been destroyed by the West.
■ **zugrunde richten** to ruin □ Alkohol und Drogen haben sie zugrunde gerichtet. Alcohol and drugs have destroyed her.
■ **einer Sache etwas zugrunde legen** to base something on something □ Diesem Film liegt ein Roman zugrunde. This film is based on a novel.

zugunsten PREPOSITION

The preposition **zugunsten** takes the dative or the genitive.

in favour of
□ Das Gericht entschied zugunsten des Angeklagten. The court decided in favour of the accused.

das **Zuhause** (GEN des **Zuhause**) NEUT NOUN
home

★ **zuhören** (PERFECT TENSE **hat zugehört**) VERB [4]
to listen
□ Du hörst mir ja gar nicht zu. You're not listening to me at all.

der **Zuhörer** (PL die **Zuhörer**) MASC NOUN
listener

die **Zuhörerin** FEM NOUN
listener

zukommen (IMPERFECT **kam zu**, PERFECT TENSE **ist zugekommen**) VERB [40]
■ **auf jemanden zukommen** to come up to somebody □ Er kam auf uns zu und fragte uns, wie spät es ist. He came up to us and asked what time it was.
■ **jemandem etwas zukommen lassen** to give somebody something □ Mein Onkel hat mir etwas Geld zukommen lassen. My uncle gave me some money.
■ **etwas auf sich zukommen lassen** to take something as it comes □ Warum lässt du diese Sache nicht einfach auf dich zukommen? Why don't you just take things as they come?

★ die **Zukunft** FEM NOUN
future
□ in Zukunft in the future

★ die **Zukunftspläne** MASC PL NOUN
plans for the future

zulassen (PRESENT TENSE **lässt zu**, IMPERFECT **ließ zu**, PERFECT TENSE **hat zugelassen**) VERB [42]
1 to allow
□ Ich kann es nicht zulassen, dass du so spät noch fernsiehst. I can't allow you to watch TV so late.
2 to register
□ Hast du deinen Roller schon zugelassen? Have you registered your scooter yet?
3 to leave closed
□ Bitte lass das Fenster zu. Please leave the window closed.

zulässig ADJECTIVE
permissible

zuleide ADVERB
■ **jemandem etwas zuleide tun** to hurt somebody □ Bitte tu ihr nichts zuleide. Please don't hurt her.

zuletzt ADVERB
1 last
□ Er wurde zuletzt in der Nähe vom Hauptbahnhof gesehen. He was last seen near the main station. □ Wir sollten das zuletzt machen. We should do that last.
2 in the end

zuliebe – zurückkommen

□ Zuletzt hat sie es dann doch verstanden. In the end she understood.

zuliebe ADVERB
■ **jemandem zuliebe** to please somebody □ Er ist mir zuliebe zu Hause geblieben. He stayed at home to please me.

zum = **zu dem**

★ **zumachen** (PERFECT TENSE **hat zugemacht**) VERB [4]
1 to shut
□ Mach bitte die Tür zu. Please shut the door.
□ Wann machen die Geschäfte zu? When do the shops shut?
2 to fasten
□ Kannst du mal bitte mein Kleid zumachen? Can you fasten my dress, please?

zumindest ADVERB
at least

zumute ADVERB
■ **Wie ist ihm zumute?** How does he feel?

zumuten (PERFECT TENSE **hat zugemutet**) VERB [2]
■ **jemandem etwas zumuten** to ask something of somebody □ Das kann ich ihm nicht zumuten. I can't ask that of him.

die **Zumutung** FEM NOUN
■ **Das ist eine Zumutung!** That's asking too much.

★ **zunächst** ADVERB
first of all
□ Wir sollten zunächst diese Frage klären. We ought to clear this issue up first of all.
■ **zunächst einmal** to start with

★ **zunehmen** (PRESENT TENSE **nimmt zu**, IMPERFECT **nahm zu**, PERFECT TENSE **hat zugenommen**) VERB [52]
1 to increase
□ Der Lärm nahm zu. The noise increased.
2 to put on weight
□ Ich habe schon wieder zugenommen. I've put on weight yet again.
■ **Er hat fünf Kilo zugenommen.** He's put on five kilos.

die **Zuneigung** FEM NOUN
affection

★ die **Zunge** FEM NOUN
tongue

zur = **zu der**

sich **zurechtfinden** (IMPERFECT **fand sich zurecht**, PERFECT TENSE **hat sich zurechtgefunden**) VERB [24]
to find one's way

zurechtkommen (IMPERFECT **kam zurecht**, PERFECT TENSE **ist zurechtgekommen**) VERB [40]
to manage

zurechtlegen (PERFECT TENSE **hat zurechtgelegt**) VERB [4]
to sort out
□ Ich habe die Sachen für die Ferien schon

zurechtgelegt. I've already sorted out my things for my holiday.
■ **sich eine Ausrede zurechtlegen** to think up an excuse □ Na, welche Ausrede hast du dir denn diesmal zurechtgelegt? Well, what excuse have you thought up this time?

★ **zurück** ADVERB
back

zurückbekommen (IMPERFECT **bekam zurück**, PERFECT TENSE **hat zurückbekommen**) VERB [40]
to get back

zurückbringen (IMPERFECT **brachte zurück**, PERFECT TENSE **hat zurückgebracht**) VERB [13]
to bring back

★ **zurückerstatten** (PERFECT TENSE **hat zurückerstattet**) VERB [2]
to refund

★ **zurückfahren** (PRESENT TENSE **fährt zurück**, IMPERFECT **fuhr zurück**, PERFECT TENSE **ist/hat zurückgefahren**) VERB [21]

For the perfect tense use **haben** when the verb has an object and **sein** when there is no object.

to return
□ Wann fahrt ihr zurück? When do you return?
■ **jemanden zurückfahren** to drive somebody back □ Sie hat mich nach Hause zurückgefahren. She drove me back home.

zurückgeben (PRESENT TENSE **gibt zurück**, IMPERFECT **gab zurück**, PERFECT TENSE **hat zurückgegeben**) VERB [28]
to give back
□ Gib mir bitte mein Buch zurück. Please give me my book back.

★ **zurückgehen** (IMPERFECT **ging zurück**, PERFECT TENSE **ist zurückgegangen**) VERB [29]
1 to go back
□ Wir sollten zurückgehen, bevor es zu spät wird. We should go back before it gets too late.
2 to recede
□ Das Hochwasser ist zurückgegangen. The floodwater receded.
3 to fall
□ Die Nachfrage geht zurück. Demand is falling.
■ **zurückgehen auf** to date back to □ Die Gründung der Stadt Aachen geht auf Karl den Großen zurück. The founding of the city of Aachen dates back to Charlemagne.

zurückhaltend ADJECTIVE
reserved
□ Er ist sehr zurückhaltend. He is very reserved.

★ **zurückkehren** (PERFECT TENSE **ist zurückgekehrt**) VERB [15]
to return

★ **zurückkommen** (IMPERFECT **kam zurück**, PERFECT TENSE **ist zurückgekommen**) VERB [40]
to come back
□ Er kam nach dem Film zurück. He came back

after the film. □ Darf ich auf das zurückkommen, was Sie vorhin gesagt haben? May I come back to what you were saying earlier?

■ **Komm nicht zu spät zurück.** Don't be back too late.

zurücklegen (PERFECT TENSE **hat zurückgelegt**) VERB [15]
1 to put back
□ Leg das Buch bitte an seinen Platz zurück. Please put the book back in its place.
2 to put by
□ Wir haben für die Ferien etwas Geld zurückgelegt. We've put some money by for the holidays.
3 to put aside
□ Können Sie mir diesen Pulli bitte zurücklegen? Could you put this pullover aside for me, please?
4 to cover
□ Wir haben heute zweihundert Kilometer zurückgelegt. We've covered two hundred kilometres today.

zurücknehmen (PRESENT TENSE **nimmt zurück**, IMPERFECT **nahm zurück**, PERFECT TENSE **hat zurückgenommen**) VERB [52]
to take back

★ **zurückrufen** (PERFECT TENSE **hat zurückgerufen**) VERB [56]
to call back
□ Können Sie mich morgen zurückrufen? Can you call me back tomorrow?

zurücktreten (PRESENT TENSE **tritt zurück**, IMPERFECT **trat zurück**, PERFECT TENSE **ist zurückgetreten**) VERB [79]
1 to step back
□ Treten Sie etwas zurück bitte! Step back a bit, please.
2 to resign
□ Warum ist er zurückgetreten? Why did he resign?

zurückzahlen (PERFECT TENSE **hat zurückgezahlt**) VERB [15]
to repay
□ Du solltest endlich das geliehene Geld zurückzahlen. It's high time you repaid the money you borrowed.

★ **zurückziehen** (IMPERFECT **zog zurück**, PERFECT TENSE **hat zurückgezogen**) VERB [96]
1 to pull back
□ Sie zog die Hand zurück. She pulled her hand back.
2 to withdraw
□ ein Angebot zurückziehen to withdraw an offer
■ **sich zurückziehen** to retire □ Sie hat sich in ihr Zimmer zurückgezogen. She has retired to her room. □ Er hat sich aus dem öffentlichen Leben zurückgezogen. He has retired from public life.

zurzeit ADVERB
at the moment

zusagen (PERFECT TENSE **hat zugesagt**) VERB [4]
1 to promise
□ Er hat mir seine Hilfe zugesagt. He promised to help me.
2 to accept an invitation
□ Die meisten Gäste haben zugesagt. Most of the guests have accepted the invitation.
■ **jemandem zusagen** to appeal to somebody □ Das Konzert hat mir nicht zugesagt. The concert didn't appeal to me.

★ **zusammen** ADVERB
together

zusammenbleiben (IMPERFECT **blieb zusammen**, PERFECT TENSE **sind zusammengeblieben**) VERB [10]
to stay together

zusammenbrechen (PRESENT TENSE **bricht zusammen**, IMPERFECT **brach zusammen**, PERFECT TENSE **ist zusammengebrochen**) VERB [11]
1 to collapse
□ Das Gebäude ist zusammengebrochen. The building collapsed.
2 to break down
□ Als er von seinem Tod erfuhr, ist er zusammengebrochen. When he heard of his death he broke down.

zusammenfassen (PERFECT TENSE **hat zusammengefasst**) VERB [15]
to summarize
□ Sie fasste das Gesagte noch einmal kurz zusammen. She briefly summarized once again what had been said.

die **Zusammenfassung** FEM NOUN
summary

der **Zusammenhang** (PL die **Zusammenhänge**) MASC NOUN
connection
□ Gibt es einen Zusammenhang zwischen diesen Ereignissen? Is there a connection between these events?
■ **im Zusammenhang mit** in connection with □ Zwei Männer wurden im Zusammenhang mit dem Mord verhört. Two men were questioned in connection with the murder.
■ **aus dem Zusammenhang** out of context □ Du hast mich aus dem Zusammenhang zitiert. You've quoted me out of context.

zusammenhängen (IMPERFECT **hing zusammen**, PERFECT TENSE **hat zusammengehangen**) VERB [69]
to be connected
□ Die beiden Ereignisse hängen miteinander zusammen. The two events are connected.

zusammenkommen (IMPERFECT **kam zusammen**, PERFECT TENSE **ist zusammengekommen**) VERB [40]
1 to meet up
□ Früher sind wir öfter zusammengekommen. We used to meet up more often.
2 to come together
□ Es ist alles zusammengekommen. Everything came together.

z

Numbers in brackets refer to verb tables on pages 697 to 706.

337

zusammenlegen (PERFECT TENSE hat zusammengelegt) VERB [15]

1 to fold
□ Er legte die Wäsche zusammen. He folded the washing.

2 to merge
□ Die beiden Klassen sollen zusammengelegt werden. The two classes are to be merged.

3 to combine
□ Wir können unsere Geburtstagspartys doch zusammenlegen. We can combine our birthday parties.

4 to club together
□ Wir haben zusammengelegt und ihr ein iPad® gekauft. We clubbed together and bought her an iPad®.

zusammennehmen (PRESENT TENSE nimmt zusammen, IMPERFECT nahm zusammen, PERFECT TENSE hat zusammengenommen) VERB [52]

to summon up
□ Ich musste meinen ganzen Mut zusammennehmen. I had to summon up all my courage.

■ alles zusammengenommen all in all

■ sich zusammennehmen to pull oneself together

zusammenpassen (PERFECT TENSE hat zusammengepasst) VERB [4]

1 to be well suited
□ Die beiden passen gut zusammen. The two are well suited.

2 to go together
□ Der Pulli und die Hose passen nicht zusammen. The pullover and the trousers don't go together.

das Zusammensein NEUT NOUN

get-together
□ ein gemütliches Zusammensein a cosy get-together

zusammenstellen (PERFECT TENSE hat zusammengestellt) VERB [15]

1 to put together
□ Stellt alle Stühle zusammen. Put all the chairs together.

2 to compile
□ Ich habe eine Wunschliste zusammengestellt. I've compiled a list of presents I'd like.

★ **der Zusammenstoß** (GEN des Zusammenstoßes, PL die Zusammenstöße) MASC NOUN

collision

zusammenstoßen (PRESENT TENSE stößt zusammen, IMPERFECT stieß zusammen, PERFECT TENSE sind zusammengestoßen) VERB

to collide

zusammenzählen (PERFECT TENSE hat zusammengezählt) VERB [4]

to add up

zusätzlich ADJECTIVE, ADVERB

1 additional
□ Wir sollen eine zusätzliche Englischstunde bekommen. We're to get an additional English lesson.

2 in addition
□ Zusätzlich zu den Matheaufgaben muss ich noch Physik machen. I still have some physics to do in addition to my maths homework.

zuschauen (PERFECT TENSE hat zugeschaut) VERB [4]

to watch
□ Habt ihr beim Match zugeschaut? Did you watch the match?

★ **die Zuschauer** MASC PL NOUN

audience sing
□ Die Zuschauer haben geklatscht. The audience clapped.

★ **der Zuschlag** (PL die Zuschläge) MASC NOUN

supplement
□ Für den ICE musst du einen Zuschlag zahlen. You have to pay a supplement if you go by Intercity Express.

zusehen (PRESENT TENSE sieht zu, IMPERFECT sah zu, PERFECT TENSE hat zugesehen) VERB [64]

to watch
□ Wir haben beim Match zugesehen. We watched the match. □ Er stand nur dabei und sah zu. He just stood there watching.

■ jemandem zusehen to watch somebody
□ Ich habe ihr dabei zugesehen, wie sie ihr Zimmer aufräumte. I watched her tidy up her room.

■ zusehen, dass etwas gemacht wird to make sure something is done □ Sieh zu, dass die Kinder früh ins Bett kommen. Make sure that the children go to bed early.

zusenden (IMPERFECT sendete or sandte zu, PERFECT TENSE hat zugesendet or zugesandt) VERB

to send
□ Wir werden Ihnen unseren Prospekt zusenden. We'll send you our brochure.

der Zustand (PL die Zustände) MASC NOUN

1 state
□ Das Haus war in einem furchtbaren Zustand. The house was in an awful state. □ Das sind hier ja schreckliche Zustände. This is a terrible state of affairs.

2 condition
□ Das Auto ist noch in gutem Zustand. The car's still in good condition.

zustande ADVERB

■ zustande bringen to bring about

■ zustande kommen to come about

zuständig ADJECTIVE

■ Dafür bin ich nicht zuständig. That's not my responsibility.

■ der zuständige Beamte the official in charge

Z

zustimmen (PERFECT TENSE **hat zugestimmt**)
VERB [4]
to agree
□ Ich stimme dir zu. I agree with you.

die **Zustimmung** FEM NOUN
1 consent
□ Du brauchst die Zustimmung deiner Eltern.
You need your parents' consent.
2 approval
□ wenn das deine Zustimmung findet if that
meets with your approval

zustoßen (PRESENT TENSE **stößt zu**, IMPERFECT
stieß zu, PERFECT TENSE **ist zugestoßen**) VERB
to happen
□ Ihm ist doch hoffentlich nichts zugestoßen.
Let's hope nothing's happened to him.

★ die **Zutaten** FEM PL NOUN
ingredients pl

zutreffen (PRESENT TENSE **trifft zu**, IMPERFECT
traf zu, PERFECT TENSE **hat zugetroffen**) VERB
[78]
1 to be true
□ Es trifft nicht zu, dass ich das Buch
mitgenommen habe. It's not true that I took the
book with me.
2 to apply
□ Diese Beschreibung trifft nicht auf sie zu. This
description doesn't apply to her.

zutreffend ADJECTIVE
■ Zutreffendes bitte unterstreichen.
Please underline where applicable.

★ **zuverlässig** ADJECTIVE
reliable

zuversichtlich ADJECTIVE
confident

★ **zuviel** ADVERB ▷ see **viel**

zuvor ADVERB
before
□ der Tag zuvor the day before

zuwenig ADVERB ▷ see **wenig**

zuziehen (IMPERFECT **zog zu**, PERFECT TENSE **hat
zugezogen**) VERB [96]
1 to draw
□ Es wird dunkel, zieh bitte die Vorhänge zu. It's
getting dark, please draw the curtains.
2 to call in
□ Wir sollten einen Fachmann zuziehen. We
should call in an expert.
■ sich etwas zuziehen to catch something
□ Ich habe mir eine Erkältung zugezogen. I've
caught a cold.

zuzüglich PREPOSITION

The preposition **zuzüglich** takes the genitive.

plus
□ zweihundert Euro zuzüglich der Spesen two
hundred euros plus expenses

der **Zwang** (PL die **Zwänge**) MASC NOUN
compulsion

zwängen VERB [38]
to squeeze

zwanglos ADJECTIVE
informal
□ ein zwangloses Gespräch an informal
conversation

zwanzig NUMBER
twenty

★ **zwar** ADVERB
although
□ Ich habe das zwar gesagt, aber es war nicht so
gemeint. Although I said it, it wasn't meant like
that.
■ das ist zwar ..., aber ... that may be ... but ...
□ Das ist zwar viel, aber mir reicht es nicht. That
may be a lot, but it's not enough for me.
■ und zwar 1 to be precise □ und zwar am
Sonntag on Sunday to be precise 2 in fact
□ und zwar so schnell, dass ... in fact, so quickly
that ...

der **Zweck** (PL die **Zwecke**) MASC NOUN
1 purpose
□ Was ist der Zweck Ihres Besuchs? What's the
purpose of your visit?
2 point
□ Was ist der Zweck dieser Übung? What's the
point of this exercise? □ Es hat keinen Zweck.
There's no point.

zwecklos ADJECTIVE
pointless

★ **zwei** NUMBER
▷ see also die **Zwei** NOUN
two

die **Zwei** FEM NOUN
▷ see also **zwei** NUMBER
1 two
2 good

DID YOU KNOW...?
German grades range from one (**sehr gut**) to
six (**ungenügend**).

zweideutig ADJECTIVE
1 ambiguous
□ Sie hat sich zweideutig ausgedrückt. She
expressed herself very ambiguously.
2 suggestive
□ Er macht immer so zweideutige
Bemerkungen. He's always making such
suggestive comments.

zweierlei ADJECTIVE
two different
□ zweierlei Stoff two different kinds of material
□ Das sind doch zweierlei Dinge. They're two
different things.
■ zweierlei Meinung of differing opinions

zweifach ADJECTIVE, ADVERB
1 double
□ die zweifache Menge double the quantity
2 twice
□ Der Brief war zweifach gefaltet. The letter had
been folded twice.

Z

Zweifel – Zypern

der **Zweifel** (PL die **Zweifel**) MASC NOUN
doubt
□ ohne Zweifel without doubt

zweifelhaft ADJECTIVE
1 doubtful
□ Es ist noch zweifelhaft, ob wir kommen. It's still doubtful whether we're coming.
2 dubious
□ eine zweifelhafte Lösung a dubious solution
■ **ein zweifelhaftes Kompliment** a backhanded compliment

zweifellos ADVERB
doubtless
■ **Sie hat sich zweifellos bemüht.** There's no doubt that she tried.

zweifeln VERB [34]
■ **an etwas zweifeln** to doubt something
□ Ich zweifle an der Richtigkeit dieser Aussage. I doubt the truth of this statement.
■ **zweifeln, ob** to doubt whether □ Ich zweifle, ob wir das schaffen. I doubt whether we'll make it.

der **Zweig** (PL die **Zweige**) MASC NOUN
branch

die **Zweigstelle** FEM NOUN
branch
□ Die nächste Zweigstelle ist in Villach. The nearest branch is in Villach.

zweihundert NUMBER
two hundred

★ **zweimal** ADVERB
twice

zweisprachig ADJECTIVE
bilingual

zweispurig ADJECTIVE
two-lane

zweit ADVERB
■ **zu zweit 1** together □ Wir fahren zu zweit in die Ferien. We're going on holiday together.
2 in twos □ Stellt euch zu zweit auf. Line up in twos.

zweitbeste ADJECTIVE
second best

★ **zweite** ADJECTIVE
second
□ Er kam als Zweiter. He was the second to arrive.

★ **zweitens** ADVERB
secondly

zweitgrößte ADJECTIVE
second largest

zweitklassig ADJECTIVE
inferior

die **Zwetschge** FEM NOUN
damson

der **Zwieback** (PL die **Zwiebacke**) MASC NOUN
rusk

★ die **Zwiebel** FEM NOUN
onion
□ Sebastian mag keine Zwiebeln. Sebastian doesn't like onions.

★ der **Zwilling** (PL die **Zwillinge**) MASC NOUN
twin
□ Diese Zwillinge sehen sich zum Verwechseln ähnlich. The twins are the spitting image of each other.
■ **Zwillinge** Gemini □ Maya ist Zwilling. Maya's Gemini.

zwingen (IMPERFECT **zwang**, PERFECT TENSE **hat gezwungen**) VERB [97]
to force

zwinkern VERB [88]
to wink
□ Als sie das sagte, zwinkerte er wissend. When she said that he winked knowingly.

★ **zwischen** PREPOSITION

> Use the accusative to express movement or a change of place. Use the dative when there is no change of place.

between
□ Sie stand zwischen den beiden Mädchen. She was standing between the two girls. □ Stell deinen Stuhl zwischen unsere. Put your chair between ours.

das **Zwischending** NEUT NOUN
cross
□ Das ist ein Zwischending zwischen einem Hotel und einer Jugendherberge. It's a cross between a hotel and a youth hostel.

zwischendurch ADVERB
in between
□ Wir haben zwischendurch eine Pause gemacht. We had a break in between.

der **Zwischenfall** (PL die **Zwischenfälle**) MASC NOUN
incident

die **Zwischenfrage** FEM NOUN
question

★ **zwölf** NUMBER
twelve

Zypern NEUT NOUN
Cyprus
■ **aus Zypern** from Cyprus
■ **nach Zypern** to Cyprus
■ **in Zypern** in Cyprus

German in Action

At home

Wo wohnst du?	Where do you live?
Ich wohne ...	**I live ...**
in einem Dorf	in a village
in einer Kleinstadt	in a small town
im Stadtzentrum	in the town centre
am Stadtrand von London	in the suburbs of London
auf dem Land	in the countryside
am Meer	at the seaside
an einem Fluss	beside a river
100 km von Manchester entfernt	100 km from Manchester
nördlich von Birmingham	north of Birmingham
in einem Einzelhaus	in a detached house
in einer Doppelhaushälfte	in a semi-detached house
in einem zweistöckigen Haus	in a two-storey house
in einem Wohnblock	in a block of flats
in einer Siedlung	on a housing estate
Ich wohne in einer Wohnung ...	**I live in a flat ...**
im Erdgeschoss	on the ground floor
im ersten Stock	on the first floor
im zweiten Stock	on the second floor
im obersten Stock	on the top floor
Ich wohne ...	**I live ...**
in einem modernen Haus	in a modern house
in einem Neubau	in a new house
in einem Altbau	in an old house

Zu Hause	At home
Im Erdgeschoss ist ...	**On the ground floor there is ...**
die Küche	the kitchen
das Wohnzimmer	the living room
das Esszimmer	the dining room
die Diele	the lounge
Im Obergeschoss ist ...	**Upstairs there is ...**
mein Zimmer	my bedroom
das Zimmer meines Bruders	my brother's bedroom
das Zimmer meiner Eltern	my parents' room
das Gästezimmer	the spare bedroom
das Badezimmer	the bathroom
das Arbeitszimmer	the study
ein Garten	a garden
ein Tennisplatz	a tennis court
ein Nachbar	a neighbour
die Leute nebenan	the next-door neighbours

Von zu Hause zur Schule

	From home to school
Die Schule ist ziemlich weit von meinem Haus entfernt.	School is quite a long way from my house.
Ich wohne fünf Minuten zu Fuß von der Schule entfernt.	I live five minutes' walk from school.
Mein Vater fährt mich im Auto zur Schule.	My dad takes me to school in the car.
Ich fahre mit dem Bus zur Schule.	I go to school by bus.

Nützliche Ausdrücke

	Useful phrases
Unser Haus ist sehr klein.	Our house is very small.
Mein Zimmer ist aufgeräumt.	My room is tidy.
Mein Bruder und ich haben ein gemeinsames Zimmer.	I share my bedroom with my brother.
Mein bester Freund wohnt in derselben Straße wie ich.	My best friend lives in the same street as me.
Neben meinem Haus ist ein Tennisplatz.	There's a tennis court next to my house.
Unser Haus hat keinen Garten.	Our house doesn't have a garden.
Wir ziehen nächsten Monat um.	We're moving next month.
Wir wohnen hier seit 5 Jahren.	We've been living here for 5 years.
Ich mag unsere Wohngegend nicht.	I don't like the area where we live.
Es ist eine sehr ruhige Gegend.	It's a very quiet area.
Der öffentliche Nahverkehr in der Stadt ist ausgezeichnet.	The public transport in the town is excellent.
In meiner Gegend gibt es nicht viel zu tun.	There's not much to do in my area.
Meine neue Gegend ist viel besser als die alte.	My new area is much better than the old one.

Einige wichtige Adressen — Some important places

Einige wichtige Adressen	Some important places
ein Kino	a cinema
ein Theater	a theatre
ein Museum	a museum
ein Platz	a square
ein Park	a park
ein Restaurant	a restaurant
ein Café	a café
ein Internet-Café	an internet café
ein Geldautomat	a cash machine
das Fremdenverkehrsbüro	the tourist office
eine Kathedrale	a cathedral
eine Kirche	a church
eine Moschee	a mosque
eine Synagoge	a synagogue
ein Einkaufszentrum	a shopping centre
die Geschäfte	the shops
das Rathaus	the town hall
der Markt	the market
eine Bank	a bank
das Schwimmbad	the swimming pool
das Sportzentrum	the sports centre
das Fußballstadion	the football stadium
die Eisbahn	the ice rink
die Skateboardanlage	the skate park
der Vergnügungspark	the amusement park
die Stadtbücherei	the public library

Dinge zu sehen und zu tun — Things to see and do

Dinge zu sehen und zu tun	Things to see and do
ein Museum besuchen	go to a museum
einen Dom besuchen	visit the cathedral
die Altstadt besuchen	do a tour of the old quarter
den Fluss entlang gehen	walk along the river
den Turm hinaufgehen	go up the tower
ins Theater gehen	go to the theatre
auf eine Besichtigungstour gehen	go sightseeing

Die Stadt besuchen — Visiting the town

Die Stadt besuchen	Visiting the town
Die wichtigsten Sehenswürdigkeiten sind in der Stadtmitte.	The most important sights are in the centre of the town.
Es ist interessant, das Museum zu besuchen.	It is interesting to visit the museum.
Vergessen Sie nicht, die Altstadt zu besuchen.	Don't forget to go to the old quarter.

Verkehrsmittel — Means of transport

Verkehrsmittel	Means of transport
ein Bus	a bus
ein (Reise)bus	a coach
die U-Bahn	the underground
die Straßenbahn	the tram
der Zug	the train
der Bahnhof	the station
der Busbahnhof	the bus station
eine U-Bahn-Linie	an underground line
umsteigen	to change bus/train

Richtungen — Directions

Richtungen	Directions
gegenüber	opposite
neben	next to
in der Nähe von	near
zwischen ... und ...	between ... and ...
hinter	behind
vor	in front of
Wo ist der Busbahnhof?	Where's the bus station?
Ich suche das Fremdenverkehrsbüro.	I'm looking for the tourist office.
Gehen Sie bis zum Ende der Straße.	Go right to the end of the street.
Biegen Sie rechts ab.	Turn right.
Überqueren Sie die Brücke.	Cross the bridge.
Nehmen Sie die erste Straße links.	Take the first street on the left.
Es ist auf der rechten Seite.	It's on your right.
Es ist gegenüber dem Kino.	It's opposite the cinema.
Es ist neben dem Postamt.	It's next to the post office.
Die Bushaltestelle ist nahe an der Schule.	The bus stop is near the school.

Stadt oder Land? — Town or country?

Stadt oder Land?	Town or country?
Städte sind toll, weil es dort viele Läden gibt.	Cities are great because there are a lot of shops.
Auf dem Land ist es wunderbar ruhig.	The countryside is nice and quiet.
Ich lebe nicht gern in der Stadt, weil die Luft dort so schlecht ist.	I don't like living in town because there's so much pollution.
Auf dem Land gibt es nichts zu tun.	There is nothing to do in the country.

Describing someone

Persönlichkeit	Personality
Er/Sie ist ...	**He/She is ...**
lustig	funny
nett	nice
freundlich	friendly
unfreundlich	unfriendly
schüchtern	shy
still	quiet
lästig	annoying
großzügig	generous
gesprächig	talkative
intelligent	intelligent
schlau	clever
dumm	stupid, silly
geizig	stingy
seltsam	strange
sportbegeistert	sporty
vernünftig	mature
verantwortungsbewusst	responsible
ordentlich	tidy
unordentlich	untidy

Merkmale	Characteristics
Er/Sie ist ...	**He/She is ...**
groß	tall
klein	small
schlank	slim
dick	fat
gutaussehend	good-looking
jung	young
alt	old
Er ist etwa dreißig.	He's about thirty.
Sie ist groß, schlank und sieht ziemlich gut aus.	She's tall, slim and quite nice-looking.
Meine Schwester ist größer als ich.	My sister is taller than me.
Er ist weder dick noch schlank.	He is neither fat nor slim.
Er sieht aus wie seine Schwester.	He looks like his sister.

Was macht einen guten Freund aus?	What makes a good friend?
Er/sie versteht mich.	He/She understands me.
Er/sie steht mir bei.	He/She supports me.
Er/sie hilft mir.	He/She helps me.
Er/sie respektiert mich.	He/She respects me.
Er/sie setzt mich nicht unter Druck.	He/She doesn't put pressure on me.
Er/sie kritisiert mich nicht.	He/She doesn't criticise me.
Andrea ist meine beste Freundin, weil sie immer da ist, um mir zu helfen.	Andrea is my best friend because she is always there to help me.
Meine Freunde haben in schwierigen Zeiten immer zu mir gestanden.	My friends have always supported me in difficult times.
Ich verstehe mich mit meinen Eltern, weil sie meine Entscheidungen im Allgemeinen respektieren.	I get on with my parents because they generally respect my decisions.
Meine große Schwester hilft mir mit den Hausaufgaben, wenn ich etwas nicht verstehe.	My elder sister helps me with my homework if I don't understand it.
Rafa ist mein Freund, weil er mich versteht.	Rafa is my friend because he understands me.
Meine Großmutter hört mir zu, wenn ich Probleme habe.	My grandmother listens to me when I have problems.
Ein guter Freund belügt dich nicht.	A good friend never lies to you.

Describing someone

Farben	Colours
gelb	yellow
orange	orange
rot	red
rosa	pink
lila	purple
blau	blue
grün	green
braun	brown
grau	grey
schwarz	black
weiß	white
burgunderfarben	maroon
marineblau	navy (blue)
türkis	turquoise
beige	beige
cremefarben	cream
Für Augen:	**For eyes:**
haselnussbraun	hazel
Für Haare:	**For hair:**
blond	blonde
dunkelblond	light brown
braun	brown
dunkelbraun	dark brown
rot	red

Kleidung	Clothes
ein Pullover	a jumper
eine Hose	trousers
eine Bluse	a blouse
ein T-shirt	a T-shirt
ein Mantel	a coat
eine Jacke	a jacket
eine Strickjacke	a cardigan
ein Kapuzenpulli	a hoodie
Jeans	jeans
(eine) Leggings	leggings
ein Kleid	a dress
ein Rock	a skirt
eine Krawatte	a tie
ein Jackett	a (suit) jacket
ein Hemd	a shirt
Schuhe	shoes
Turnschuhe	trainers
Stiefel	boots
Sandalen	sandals
formelle Kleidung	formal clothes
Freizeitkleidung	casual clothes
schicke Kleidung	smart clothes
Sportkleidung	sports clothes
bequeme Kleidung	comfortable clothes

Als ich ... war

Als Kind war sie sehr freundlich.
Als Kind hatte er lange Haare.
Als mein Vater 20 war, hatte er einen Schnurrbart.
Mit 15 war er sehr schüchtern. Jetzt ist er mehr extrovertiert.
Früher war ich ziemlich klein, aber ich bin gewachsen.

When I was ...

When she was a child she was very friendly.
When he was a child he had long hair.
When my father was 20 he had a moustache.
He was very shy at 15. Now he is more extrovert.

I used to be quite short but I have grown now.

Nützliche Ausdrücke

Ich habe haselnussbraune Augen.
Er hat braune Haare.
Sie hat kurze graue Haare.
Sie hat rote Haare.
Er hat eine Glatze.
Sie hat lange lockige blonde Haare.
Er hat einen Schnurrbart/einen Bart.
Er trägt eine Brille.
Sie trägt ein hellblaues T-shirt.
Er trägt einen dunkelgrauen Anzug.
Normalerweise trage ich Jeans, aber wenn ich ausgehe, ziehe ich mir oft ein Kleid an.
Ich hasse formelle Kleidung.
Ich trage lieber Leggings, weil sie bequemer sind.

Sie tragen immer farbenfrohe Kleidung.
Diese Turnschuhe sind echt cool.
In der Schule müssen wir einen Blazer tragen.

Useful phrases

I've got hazel eyes.
He's got brown hair.
She's got short grey hair.
She's got red hair.
He's bald.
She's got long curly blonde hair.
He's got a moustache/a beard.
He wears glasses.
She's wearing a light blue T-shirt.
He's wearing a dark grey suit.
I usually wear jeans, but when I go out, I often wear a dress.
I hate formal clothes.
I prefer wearing leggings because they're more comfortable.

They always wear bright colours.
These trainers are really cool.
At school we have to wear a blazer.

School and my plans for the future

Fächer	Subjects
die Fremdsprachen	languages (French/English etc)
die Literatur	literature
die Physik	physics
die Chemie	chemistry
die Mathe	maths
die Biologie	biology
Theater	drama
der Tanz	dance
die Musik	music
die Kunst	art
die Technologie	design and technology
die Computerwissenschaft	computing
die Geographie	geography
die Geschichte	history
der Sport	PE

Es ist/Sie sind ... Ich finde es/sie ...	It's/They're ... I find it/them ...
schwierig	difficult
leicht	easy
langweilig	boring
interessant	interesting
praktisch	practical
nützlich	useful

Die Computerwissenschaft ist praktisch und das Deutsch ist nützlich, aber ich finde die Chemie schwierig.

Computing is practical and German is useful, but I find chemistry difficult.

Mein Lieblingsfach ist die Mathe, weil es gar nicht langweilig ist.

My favourite subject is maths because it is not boring at all.

Obwohl ich die Mathe hasse, finde ich die Statistik interessant.

Even though I hate maths, I find statistics interesting.

Ich kann die Literaturklasse nicht leiden, weil unser Lehrer sehr streng ist und mir auch schlechte Noten gibt.

I can't stand going to literature classes because the teacher is very strict and also gives me bad marks.

Meine Realschule/ Mein Gymnasium	My (secondary) school

Meine Schule hat ...	My school has ...
ein Klassenzimmer	a classroom
Toiletten	toilets
eine Kantine	a dinner hall/canteen
einen Schulhof	a playground
eine Bibliothek	a library
eine Turnhalle	a gymnasium
ein Labor	a lab
eine Aula	an assembly hall
ein Theater	a theatre
einen Musikraum	a music room
einen IT-Raum	an IT room
ein Lehrerzimmer	a staffroom
einen Empfang	a reception
ein Büro	an office

Der Schultag	The school day

Mein Lieblingstag ist ... weil ich ... habe/wir ... haben	My favourite day is ... because I have/we have ...
morgens	in the morning
nachmittags	in the afternoon
nach der Pause	after break

Dienstag habe ich Mathe, Computerwissenschaft und auch Französisch.

On Tuesdays, I have maths, computing and also French.

Montags ist meine erste Stunde Biologie.

I have biology first period on Monday morning.

Freitags habe ich zwei Stunden Sport.

On Fridays I do two hours of PE.

Was ist dein Lieblingstag?

What's your favourite day?

School and my plans for the future

Musikinstrumente — Musical instruments

Ich spiele ...	**I play ...**
Geige	the violin
Klavier	the piano
Gitarre	the guitar
Querflöte	the flute
Ich kann Klavier spielen.	I can play the piano.
Ich spiele Geige, seit ich acht bin.	I've been playing the violin since I was eight.
Ich spiele im Schulorchester.	I play in the school orchestra.
Ich möchte gern Gitarre lernen.	I'd like to learn to play the guitar.

Was man tut — Things to do

Hausaufgaben machen	do homework
eine Prüfung ablegen	do an exam
gute/schlechte Noten bekommen	get good/bad marks
eine Aktivität machen	do an activity
eine Matheaufgabe machen	do a maths problem
an einem Projekt über... arbeiten	do a project about ...
Notizen machen	take notes
die Fragen beantworten	answer the questions
Aufgaben machen	do exercises

Meine Pläne — My plans

Ich möchte ... studieren	**I'd like to study ...**
Medizin	medicine
Maschinenbau	engineering
Jura	law
Soziologie	sociology
Psychologie	psychology
Sprachen	languages
Architektur	architecture
Computerwissenschaft	computer science
Ich möchte ...	**I'd like to ...**
viel Geld verdienen	earn lots of money
in einem Geschäft arbeiten	work in a shop
in einer Bank arbeiten	work in a bank
in der Tourismusbranche arbeiten	work in tourism
eine Lehre machen	do an apprenticeship
einen Abschluss machen	get a qualification

Prüfungen — Exams

eine Prüfung	an exam
eine Probeprüfung	a mock exam
das Ergebnis	the results
Ich mache dieses Jahr mein GCSE.	I'm doing my GCSEs this year.
Meine erste Prüfung ist nächsten Montag.	I'm going to do my first exam next Monday.
Ich hoffe, ich bestehe meine Prüfungen.	I hope I'll pass my exams.
Ich glaube, ich bin durch die Matheprüfung gefallen.	I think I've failed my maths exam.
Ich bekomme das Ergebnis im August.	I'll get the results in August.
Ich habe in meinen Prüfungen gut abgeschnitten.	I've done well in my exams.
Ich muss Mathe lernen.	I need to revise my maths.
Ich muss mein Englisch-GCSE wiederholen.	I need to resit my English GCSE.

Meine Ziele — Ambitions

Ich habe vor zu studieren.	I'm planning to go to university.
Danach möchte ich ins Ausland gehen.	Afterwards I'd like to go abroad.
Ich möchte nach der Schule erstmal eine Reise machen.	I'd like to go travelling before university.
Ich weiß noch nicht, was ich machen will.	I don't know yet what I want to do.
Ich werde vielleicht Mathe studieren.	Maybe I'll study maths.

Jobs and hobbies

Berufe — Professions

Berufe	Professions
Ich möchte ... werden	I'd like to be ...
Rechtsanwalt/Rechtsanwältin	a solicitor
Lehrer/Lehrerin	a teacher
Zahnarzt/Zahnärztin	a dentist
Sänger/Sängerin	a singer
Friseur/Friseuse	a hairdresser
Journalist/Journalistin	a journalist
Schauspieler/Schauspielerin	an actor
Fußballprofi	a professional footballer
Musiker/Musikerin	a musician
Politiker/Politikerin	a politician
Ich glaube, dieser Beruf ist ...	I think this job is ...
gut bezahlt	well paid
schlecht bezahlt	badly paid

Sport — Sports

Sport	Sports
Ich spiele ...	I play ...
Fußball	football
Basketball	basketball
Rugby	rugby
Tennis	tennis
Tischtennis	table tennis
Ich ...	I ...
fahre Kanu	canoe
turne	do gymnastics
schwimme	swim
gehe Reiten	go horse riding
mache Leichtathletik	do athletics
wandere	go hiking
Ich mache diesen Sommer einen Segelkurs.	I'm going to do a sailing course this summer.
Ich bin noch nie Ski gefahren.	I've never been skiing.
Ich mache zweimal in der Woche Fußballtraining.	I do football training twice a week.
Ich habe an einem Leichtathletikwettkampf teilgenommen.	I took part in an athletics competition.

Die Arbeit — Work

Die Arbeit	Work
ein Lebenslauf	a CV
eine Bewerbung	a job application
sich um eine Stelle bewerben	to apply for a job
ein Vorstellungsgespräch	an interview
die Berufserfahrung	work experience
eine Ganztagsarbeit	a full-time job
eine Teilzeitarbeit	a part-time job
eine befristete/feste Stelle	a temporary/permanent job
die Arbeitszeit	work hours
ein Job	a job
eine Stelle	a job, a position
der Chef/die Chefin	the boss
der/die Angestellte	the employee
ein Büroangestellter/eine Büroangestellte	an office worker
ein/eine Auszubildende	an apprentice
die Ausbildung	training
die Erfahrung	experience
das Gehalt	salary
arbeiten	to work
arbeitslos sein	to be unemployed
im Ruhestand sein	to be retired
eine Lehre machen	to do an apprenticeship
ein Praktikum machen	to do work experience
bezahlt werden	to get paid
Ich arbeite ...	I work ...
samstags in dem Supermarkt	at the supermarket on Saturdays
in einem Kleidergeschäft	in a clothes shop
Ich babysitte.	I do baby-sitting.
Ich verdiene 7.5 Euro die Stunde.	I earn 7.5 euros an hour.
Der Job ist anstrengend.	It's a tiring job.
Ich hatte noch nie einen Job.	I've never had a job.
Ich suche mir in diesem Sommer einen Job.	I'm going to look for a job for this summer.
Meine Eltern geben mir kein Taschengeld.	My parents don't give me pocket money.

Meine Lieblingshobbys — My hobbies

Meine Lieblingshobbys	My hobbies
Ich lese gern Romane.	I like reading novels.
Ich höre gern in meinem Zimmer Musik.	I love listening to music in my room.
Ich gehe gern mit meinen Freunden in die Stadt.	I love going into town with my friends.
Ich mag Sport total gern.	I'm mad about sports.
Skateboardfahren ist echt cool.	Skateboarding is really cool.
Ich gehe lieber mit meinen Freunden aus.	I'd rather go out with my friends.
Ich hasse Aktivitäten im Freien.	I hate outdoor activities.
Ich verbringe viel Zeit an meiner Spielkonsole.	I spend a lot of time on my games console.
Ich kann nicht kochen.	I can't cook.
Ich backe gut.	I'm good at baking.

Food and health

Mahlzeiten	Meals
das Frühstück	breakfast
das Mittagessen	lunch
das Abendessen	dinner
Ich esse sehr gern ...	**I love ...**
Schokolade	chocolate
Salat	salad
Erdbeeren	strawberries
Ich esse gern ...	**I like ...**
Fisch	fish
Fleisch	meat
Käse	cheese
Eier	eggs
Bonbons	sweets
Gemüse	vegetables
Ich mag kein ...	**I don't like ...**
Mineralwasser	mineral water
Ich mag keine ...	**I don't like ...**
Bananen	bananas
Ich mag keinen ...	**I don't like ...**
Orangensaft	orange juice
Ich hasse ...	**I hate ...**
Spinat	spinach
Gemüse ist gut für die Gesundheit.	Vegetables are very good for you.
Ich esse kein Schweinefleisch.	I don't eat pork.
Ich esse viel Obst.	I eat a lot of fruit.
Ich vermeide kohlensäurehaltige Getränke.	I avoid fizzy drinks.
Ich bin Vegetarier/ Vegetarierin.	I'm a vegetarian.
Ich bin allergisch gegen Erdnüsse.	I'm allergic to peanuts.
Guten Appetit.	Enjoy your meal.
Das schmeckt.	It's very tasty.

Einige Ratschläge ...	Some advice ...
Falls du deine Lebensweise verbessern willst ...	If you want to improve your lifestyle ...
Du solltest ...	You should ...
Du musst ...	You have to ...
Es ist ratsam, ...	It's advisable to ...
zweimal pro Woche Sport zu machen.	exercise twice a week.
viel Obst zu essen.	eat lots of fruit
weniger Kaffee zu trinken.	drink less coffee.
Junk-Food zu vermeiden.	avoid junk food.

Wie ich mich fühle	How I'm feeling
Ich habe ...	**I've got ...**
Kopfschmerzen	a headache
Zahnschmerzen	toothache
Ohrenschmerzen	earache
einen rauen Hals	a sore throat
Mein Bauch tut weh.	My stomach is sore.
Meine Augen jucken.	My eyes are itchy.
Mir ist schlecht.	I feel sick.
Ich bin erkältet.	I've got a cold.
Ich habe (eine) Grippe.	I've got flu.
Ich habe mir das Bein gebrochen.	I broke my leg.
Er hat sich am Finger geschnitten.	He cut his finger.
Ich bin ...	**I am ...**
müde	tired
krank	ill
Mir ist ...	**I am ...**
kalt	cold
warm	hot
Ich habe ...	**I am ...**
Angst	scared
Durst	thirsty
Hunger	hungry

Fit bleiben	Staying healthy
Was machst du, um fit zu bleiben?	What do you do to keep fit?
Ich treibe viel Sport.	I do a lot of sport.
Ich gehe früh schlafen.	I go to bed early.
Ich gehe zu Fuß zur Schule.	I walk to school.
Du solltest jeden Tag Frischkost essen.	You should have fresh food every day.
Ich muss mehr Wasser trinken. Ich trinke nicht genug davon.	I have to drink more water. I don't drink enough.
Es ist gut für die Gesundheit.	It's good for your health.
Alkohol ist ungesund.	Alcohol is bad for your health.
Er hat eine gesunde Lebensweise.	He has a healthy lifestyle.
Ich trinke und rauche nicht.	I don't drink or smoke.

Relationships and feelings

Beziehungen	Relationships
Ich vertrage mich sehr/ganz gut mit meiner Schwester.	I get on very/quite well with my sister.
Ich vertrage mich überhaupt nicht mit meinem Bruder.	I don't get on at all with my brother.
Ich kann sie nicht leiden.	I can't stand her.
Mein bester Freund heißt Max.	My best friend is called Max.
Ich habe drei beste Freundinnen.	I've got three best friends.
Wir sind immer zusammen.	We're always together.
Ich habe mich mit Nadia gestritten.	I've had a quarrel with Nadia.
Mit Emma rede ich nicht mehr.	I'm not talking to Emma any more.

Gefühle	Emotions
Ich bin ...	I am ...
traurig	sad
erfreut	pleased
glücklich	happy
böse	angry
verliebt	in love
gekränkt	hurt
gelangweilt	bored
deprimiert	depressed
nervös	nervous
besorgt	worried
Ich habe gute/schlechte Laune.	I'm in a good/bad mood.
Ich bin in Lena verliebt.	I'm in love with Lena.
Bruno und ich haben uns getrennt.	Bruno and I have split up.
Ich freue mich, dass du kommst.	I'm pleased you're coming.
Ich bin traurig, dass ich weggehe.	I'm sad to be leaving.
Mir ist langweilig.	I'm bored.
Ich hoffe, du bist nicht allzu böse.	I hope you're not too angry.
Sie war gekränkt, dass sie nicht eingeladen war.	She was hurt that she wasn't invited.

Familienmitglieder	Members of the family
mein Vater	my father, my dad
meine Mutter	my mother, my mum
meine Eltern	my parents
mein Stiefvater	my stepfather
meine Stiefmutter	my stepmother
mein Bruder	my brother
meine Schwester	my sister
mein Halbbruder	my half-brother
meine Halbschwester	my half-sister
mein Stiefbruder	my stepbrother
meine Stiefschwester	my stepsister
mein Onkel	my uncle
meine Tante	my aunt
mein Cousin	my cousin (male)
meine Cousine	my cousin (female)
mein Großvater	my grandfather
meine Großmutter	my grandmother
meine Großeltern	my grandparents
mein Urgroßvater	my great-grandfather
meine Urgroßmutter	my great-grandmother
mein großer Bruder	my big brother
meine kleine Schwester	my little sister

Nützliche Ausdrücke	Useful phrases
Das ist meine Schwester Leonie.	This is my sister, Leonie.
Sie heiratet im nächsten Sommer.	She's getting married next summer.
Ich habe eine Zwillingsschwester.	I have a twin sister.
Ich habe einen Halbbruder.	I have a half-brother.
Ich bin Einzelkind.	I'm an only child.
Meine Eltern leben getrennt.	My parents are separated.
Meine Eltern sind geschieden.	My parents are divorced.
Mein Großvater ist letztes Jahr gestorben.	My grandfather died last year.
Meine Mutter hat wieder geheiratet.	My mother got married again.
Sie ist alleinerziehend.	She's a single mother.
Er ist alleinerziehend.	He's a single father.
Sie sind nicht verheiratet.	They are not married.

Greetings, meeting people and expressing opinions

Begrüßungen und Vorstellungen	Greetings and introductions
Guten Tag	Hello.
Guten Morgen	Good morning.
Guten Abend	Good evening.
Gute Nacht	Good night.
Bis später	See you later.
Bis bald	See you soon.
Bis morgen	See you tomorrow.
Bis Montag/nächste Woche	See you on Monday/next week.
Auf Wiedersehen/tschüss	Goodbye/Bye!
Schönen Tag!	Have a good day!
Ich möchte Ihnen meine Mutter vorstellen.	Let me introduce you to my mother.
Kennen Sie Samina schon?	Have you met Samina?
Das ist Oli.	This is Oli.
Freut mich, Sie kennenzulernen.	Nice to meet you.
Angenehm!	Pleased to meet you.

Meinungen	Opinions
Toll!	Great!/That's great!
Das ist furchtbar!	That's dreadful!
Das ist schrecklich!	That's terrible!
Cool!	Cool!
Wie gruselig!	How scary!
Wie langweilig!	How boring!
(Das ist aber) schade!	What a shame!
Wie peinlich!	How embarrassing!
Ich denke, dass ...	I think that ...
Ich finde/glaube, dass ...	I think/I believe that ...
Ich halte es für eine gute Idee.	I think it's a good idea .
Meiner Meinung nach ...	In my opinion/view ...
Für mich ...	For me ...

Ein Treffen vereinbaren / Arranging to meet someone

Möchtest du ...	**Would you like ...**
Willst du ...	**Do you want to ...**
ins Kino gehen?	go to the cinema?
Schlittschuh laufen?	go skating?
Fußball spielen?	play football?
zu mir kommen?	come to my house?
Es tut mir leid, ich muß ...	**I'm sorry, I have to ...**
meine Hausaufgaben machen.	do my homework.
die Hausarbeit machen.	do the housework.
mein Zimmer aufräumen.	tidy my room.
meinen Eltern helfen.	help my parents.
meinen Hund ausführen.	take the dog for a walk.
Ich kann nicht weil ...	**I can't because ...**
ich meine Großeltern besuche.	I'm visiting my grandparents.
ich am Wochenende weg bin.	I'm away this weekend.
ich Hausarrest habe.	I'm grounded.
ich kein Geld habe.	I don't have any money.
Treffen wir uns ...	**Shall we meet ...**
dem Kino gegenüber?	opposite the cinema?
an der Bushaltestelle?	at the bus stop?
OK.	OK.
Gut.	That's fine.
Alles klar.	Alright.
Hört sich gut an.	Sounds good to me.

Nützliche Ausdrücke / Useful phrases

Was machen wir am Wochenende?	What shall we do this weekend?
Ich kann Samstag nicht kommen, aber Sonntag Nachmittag geht.	I can't come on Saturday but Sunday afternoon is OK for me.
Wir gehen heute Abend ins Theater. Möchtest du mit uns kommen?	We are going to the theatre this evening. Would you like to come with us?
Ich möchte lieber heute zu Hause bleiben.	I'd rather not go out today.
Komm doch heute Nachmittag vorbei!	Why don't you drop by my house this afternoon?
Schade, ich bin beschäftigt.	What a shame! I've got things to do.
Auf keinen Fall! Ich hasse Sport.	No way! I hate sports.

Communications: letters and emails

Eine E-Mail — An email

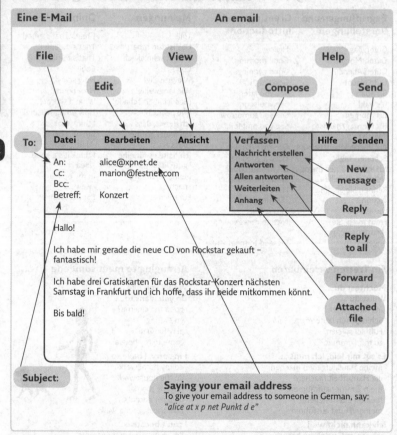

File · **Edit** · **View** · **Compose** · **Help** · **Send**

To:

Datei	Bearbeiten	Ansicht	Verfassen	Hilfe	Senden

Verfassen:
Nachricht erstellen — **New message**
Antworten — **Reply**
Allen antworten — **Reply to all**
Weiterleiten — **Forward**
Anhang — **Attached file**

An: alice@xpnet.de
Cc: marion@festnet.com
Bcc:
Betreff: Konzert

Hallo!

Ich habe mir gerade die neue CD von Rockstar gekauft – fantastisch!

Ich habe drei Gratiskarten für das Rockstar-Konzert nächsten Samstag in Frankfurt und ich hoffe, dass ihr beide mitkommen könnt.

Bis bald!

Subject:

Saying your email address
To give your email address to someone in German, say:
"alice at x p net Punkt d e"

Briefe und E-Mails — Letters and emails

Briefe und E-Mails	Letters and emails
ein Brief	a letter
eine Postkarte	a postcard
eine E-Mail	an email
Hallo	Hello
Lieber/Liebe ...	Dear ...
Sehr geehrter Herr ...	Dear Mr ...
Sehr geehrte Frau ...	Dear Mrs ...
Vielen Dank für Ihren Brief.	Thank you for your letter.
Schreib mir bald!	Write soon!
Grüß ... von mir.	Give my love to ...
Samuel lässt grüßen.	Samuel sends his best wishes.
Mit herzlichen Grüßen	Love
Gruß und Kuss	Hugs and kisses
Alles Gute	Best wishes
Mit freundlichen Grüßen	Kind regards
Ich hoffe, bald von dir zu hören.	Looking forward to hearing from you
Es tut mir leid, dass ich nicht früher geschrieben habe.	I'm sorry I didn't write earlier.
zu Händen von	for the attention of
per... verschickt	sent by

Communications: on the phone and online

Am Telefon und im Internet	On the phone and the internet
das Telefon	telephone
das Handy	mobile
das Festnetz	landline
die Vorwahl(nummer)	area code
die falsche Nummer	wrong number
eine SMS	a text
eine App	an app
ein Beitrag	a post
der Username	username
das Passwort	password
Wi-Fi	Wi-Fi
das Netz	signal
die Verbindung	connection
die Daten	data
die sozialen Medien	social media
das soziale Netzwerk	social networks
ein Blog	a blog
ein Vlog	a vlog
online	online
die Nummer wählen	to dial the number
das Telefon abnehmen	to answer the phone
auf die Taste drücken	to press the key
auflegen	to hang up
verbinden	to connect
eine Voicemail	a voice mail
eine SMS schicken	to send a text
eine Nachricht weiterleiten	to forward a message
twittern	to tweet
mit jemandem skypen	to Skype® someone
herunterladen	to download
chatten	to chat

Am Telefon und im Internet	On the phone and the internet
Abends chatte ich mit meinen Freunden.	I chat to my friends in the evenings.
Bist du auf Twitter®?	Are you on Twitter®?
Ich habe meine Urlaubsfotos auf Facebook® gestellt.	I put my holiday photos on Facebook®.
Dafür kannst du eine App herunterladen.	You can download an app for that.
Hast du Wi-Fi?	Do you have Wi-Fi?
Ich habe seinen Namen gegoogelt.	I googled his name.

Vorteile und Nachteile	Advantages and disadvantages
Das Internet ist ...	**The internet is ...**
nützlich	useful
praktisch	handy/practical
schnell	fast
aber andererseits kann es ...	**but on the other hand it can be ...**
süchtig machen	addictive
Die neue Techniken sind ...	**New technology is ...**
einfach	easy
weitverbreitet	popular
notwendig	necessary
aber sie sind auch ...	**but it is also ...**
gefährlich	dangerous

Nützliche Ausdrücke	Useful phrases
Hallo! Kann ich bitte mit ... sprechen?	Hello! Could I speak to ...?
Könnten Sie mich mit ... verbinden?	Could you put me through to ...?
Ich möchte mit ... sprechen.	I would like to speak to ...
Hallo!	Hello!
Ich werde Sie mit ihm verbinden.	I'll put you through to him.
Moment mal.	One moment, please.
Bleiben Sie am Apparat bitte.	Hold the line, please.
Ich hole ihn/sie.	I'll get him/her for you.
Tut mir leid, ich habe mich verwählt.	I'm sorry, I dialled the wrong number.
Könnten Sie ihn/sie bitten, mich zurückzurufen?	Would you ask him/her to call me back, please?
Ich rufe in einer halben Stunde wieder an.	I'll call back in half an hour.
Kannst du mich bitte zurückrufen?	Could you please call me back?
Ich habe kein Netz.	I don't have a signal.
Mein Guthaben ist alle.	I've run out of credit.
Die Verbindung ist sehr schlecht.	It's a very bad line.
Ich höre dich nicht mehr.	You're breaking up.
Schick mir eine SMS.	Send me a text.
Ich teile Videos, die ich mag, mit meinen Freunden.	I share videos that I like with my friends.
Er hat gerade ein neues Video gepostet.	He's just posted a new video.
Wir dürfen kein Handy in die Schule mitbringen.	We're not allowed mobiles in school.
Schalte dein Handy stumm.	Put your mobile on silent.
Schalten Sie Ihr Handy aus.	You have to switch your mobiles off.

My world

Das Wetter	The weather
Es ist kalt.	It's cold.
Es ist heiß.	It's hot.
Es ist ein schöner Tag.	It's a nice day.
Es ist windig.	It's windy.
Es ist sonnig.	It's sunny.
Es regnet/es schneit.	It's raining/snowing.
Es ist 30 Grad.	It's 30 degrees.
Es friert.	It's frosty.
Es ist neblig.	It's foggy.
Heute ist das Wetter schön/schlecht.	The weather is nice/bad today.

Probleme in meiner Welt	Problems in my world
Ich bin besorgt um ...	I'm worried about ...
die Umweltverschmutzung.	pollution.
die Armut.	poverty.
die Arbeitslosigkeit.	unemployment.
die Gewalttätigkeit.	violence.
die Obdachlosen.	the homeless.
den Klimawandel.	climate change.
die globale Erwärmung.	global warming.
die Wüstenbildung.	desertification.
die Entwaldung.	deforestation.
die Überschwemmungen.	floods.
die Brände.	fires.
die Kriege.	wars.
die Wanderungsbewegung.	migration.
die Kinderarbeit.	child labour.
die gefährdeten Tierarten.	endangered species.
die Pestizide.	pesticides.
die Ungleichheit.	inequality.
die mangelnde Solidarität.	lack of solidarity.
Was können wir tun?	What can we do?
Wir könnten ...	We can ...
Man sollte ...	We/one should ...
Es ist wichtig ...	It's important ...

Aktionen und gute Zwecke	Campaigns and good causes
Wir müssen ...	We have to ...
Glas/Dosen/Papier recyceln.	recycle glass/tins/paper.
Licht/Geräte nachts ausschalten.	switch off the light/devices at night.
keine Energie verschwenden.	not waste energy.
Wasser sparen.	save water.
die Umwelt schützen.	protect the environment.
öffentliche Verkehrsmittel benutzen.	use public transport.
weniger mit dem Auto fahren.	use the car less.
die CO2-Bilanz verringern.	reduce the carbon footprint.
erneuerbare Energien nutzen.	use renewable energy.
keine Plastiktüten benutzen.	avoid using plastic bags.
Produkte aus dem fairen Handel kaufen.	buy fairtrade products.
Freiwilligenarbeit leisten.	do voluntary work.
Entwicklungshelfer werden.	become an aid worker.
in einer NGO tätig sein.	collaborate with an NGO.
in einem Asyl aushelfen.	help at a refuge.
einer Wohltätigkeitsorganisation Geld spenden.	donate to a charity.
Spenden beschaffen.	fundraise.
Second-Hand-Kleidung sammeln.	collect secondhand clothes.
sich engagieren.	campaign.
gegen... protestieren.	protest against ...
gegen... demonstrieren.	demonstrate against ...

Nützliche Ausdrücke	Useful phrases
Normalerweise ist es nicht kalt im April.	It's not usually cold in April.
Im Winter gehe ich morgens laufen.	In the winter I go running in the morning.
Wenn es regnet, gehen wir in ein Museum, aber wenn es schön ist, gehen wir in den Park.	If it rains we'll go to a museum but if it's a nice day we'll go to the park.
Wenn es zu heiß ist, spielt man lieber kein Tennis.	It is better not to play tennis if it's too hot.
Wir organisieren eine Tombola, um Geld für die Krebsforschung zu sammeln.	We are going to organize a raffle to raise funds for cancer research.
Meiner Meinung nach sind Kriege und Meeresverschmutzung die zentralen Probleme der Welt.	In my view, the main world problems are wars and sea pollution.
In meiner Stadt gibt es viel Arbeitslosigkeit.	In my town there is a lot of unemployment.

Dates, festivals and holidays

Wochentage	Days of the week
Montag	Monday
Dienstag	Tuesday
Mittwoch	Wednesday
Donnerstag	Thursday
Freitag	Friday
Samstag	Saturday
Sonntag	Sunday
am Montag	on Monday
montags	on Mondays
jeden Montag	every Monday
letzten Dienstag	last Tuesday
nächsten Freitag	next Friday
Samstag in einer Woche	a week on Saturday
Samstag in zwei Wochen	two weeks on Saturday

Monate	Months of the year
Januar	January
Februar	February
März	March
April	April
Mai	May
Juni	June
Juli	July
August	August
September	September
Oktober	October
November	November
Dezember	December
Den wievielten haben wir heute?	What date is it today?
Heute ist der 16. Juni.	It's the 16th of June.
Wann ist dein Geburtstag?	What date is your birthday?
Er ist am 22. Mai.	It's the 22nd of May.

Feiertage	Festivals
Weihnachten	Christmas
Heiligabend	Christmas Eve
der erste Weihnachtsfeiertag	Christmas Day
der zweite Weihnachtsfeiertag	Boxing Day
Silvester	New Year's Eve
das Neujahr	New Year's Day
der Valentinstag	Valentine's Day
der erste April	April Fools' Day
der Karfreitag	Good Friday
Ostern	Easter
der Muttertag	Mother's Day
der Vatertag	Father's Day
Pfingsten	Whitsun
Allerheiligen	All Saints' Day
der Ramadan	Ramadan
das Eid al-Fitr	Eid
die Chanukka	Hanukkah
Frohe Weihnachten!	Happy Christmas!
April, April!	April fool!
Neujahr feiern	to celebrate New Year
Was machst du an Weihnachten?	What do you do at Christmas?

Die Ferien	Holidays
die Sommerferien	the summer holidays
die Herbstferien	the autumn half-term
die Weihnachtsferien	the Christmas holidays
die Osterferien	the Easter holidays
das Meer	the seaside
die Berge	the mountains
Was machst du in den Ferien?	What are you going to do in the holidays?
Wir fahren diesen Sommer für eine Woche nach Italien.	We're going to Italy for a week this summer.
Wir fahren dieses Jahr nicht in Urlaub.	We're not going on holiday this year.
Im Februar gehen wir immer Ski fahren.	We always go skiing in February.
Nächstes Jahr wollen wir eine Wohnung im Schwarzwald mieten.	Next year we want to rent a flat in the Black Forest.
Ich gehe gar nicht gern Campen.	I hate camping.

Building phrases

Vergleiche	Comparisons
ganz	quite
zu viel/zu viele	too much/too many
mehr (als)	more (than)
größer/kleiner (als)	bigger/smaller (than)
die Mehrheit	the majority
besser (als)	better (than)
nicht so groß/klein (wie)	not as big/small (as)
weniger (als)	less (than)
ähnlich/wie	like
genau (wie)	the same (as)
ähnlich (wie)	similar (to)
schlechter/schlimmer (als)	worse (than)
wenig/wenige	little/few
ein bißchen/ein paar	a little/a few
so ... wie ...	as ... as ...
so viel/viele ... wie ...	as much/many ... as ...

Konjunktionen	Conjunctions
trotz	despite
deshalb	so/therefore
selbst wenn	even if
obwohl	although
weil/da	as/because/since
wegen	because of
wenn	when
während	whereas
oder	or
aber	but
darum/deshalb	that's why
wenn	if
jedoch	however
vielleicht	perhaps/maybe
und	and
um ... zu	to/in order to

Präpositionen	Prepositions
an/bei/in	at
in/nach/zu	to
mit	with
ab/aus/von	from
von	of
in/an	in
auf	on
auf	towards
bis	until/up to
für	for
von/mit	by
... nach	according to ...
ohne	without

Fragen	Questions
wo?	where?
wie?	how?
welche/welcher/welches?	which?
wann?	when?
wie viel/wie viele?	how much/how many?
woher?	where ... from?
wessen?	whose?
warum?	why?
was?	what?
wer?	who?

Verneinungen	Negatives
nie	never
weder ... noch	neither ... nor ...
nichts	nothing
neimand	nobody/no one
keine/keiner/keines	none
außer	except
auch nicht	neither
nicht mehr	no longer

Bindewörter	Connectives
auch	also
außerdem	apart from
eindeutig	clearly
angenommen, (dass)	given that
das heißt	so/that is to say
einerseits ..., andererseits ...	on one hand ... on the other...
zweifellos	without doubt
wohin	where ... to
als/wenn	when
wo	where
der/die/das	that/which/who

Einige Beispiele im Kontext
Some examples in context

Meine Stadt ist klein. → Die Stadt, in der ich seit 12 Jahren wohne, ist klein und sie ist **außerdem nicht** sehr lebendig, **weil** es **keine** Aktivitäten für die Jugendlichen gibt. Das ist ärgerlich!

Ich verstehe mich sehr gut mit meiner Mutter. → Ich verstehe mich sehr gut mit meiner Mutter **weil** sie mich **immer** unterstützt, **obwohl** wir **ziemlich** verschieden sind.

Es ist wichtig, keine Energie zu verschwenden → **Um** die Umwelt **so** weit **wie** möglich **zu** schützen, ist es **meiner Meinung nach** wichtig zu recyceln und **nichts** zu verschwenden.

Aa

★ A NOUN
    die Eins *fem* (PL die Einsen) (*school mark*)
    □ I got an A for my essay. Ich habe für meinen
    Aufsatz eine Eins bekommen.

★ a ARTICLE

> In the nominative use **ein** for masculine and
> neuter nouns, **eine** for feminine nouns.

1 ein
    □ a man ein Mann □ I saw a man. Ich habe
    einen Mann gesehen. □ a child ein Kind □ an
    apple ein Apfel

2 eine
    □ a woman eine Frau □ He gave it to a woman.
    Er hat es einer Frau gegeben.

> You do not translate 'a' when you want to
> describe what somebody does for a living.

    □ He's a butcher. Er ist Metzger. □ She's a
    doctor. Sie ist Ärztin.
    ■ **once a week** einmal pro Woche
    ■ **thirty kilometres an hour** dreißig Kilometer
    in der Stunde
    ■ **thirty pence a kilo** dreißig Pence das Kilo
    ■ **a hundred pounds** einhundert Pfund

AA NOUN (= *Automobile Association*)
    der ADAC *masc*

★ to abandon VERB
1 verlassen [42] (PRESENT TENSE verlässt, IMPERFECT
    verließ, PERFECT TENSE hat verlassen) (*place*)
2 aufgeben [28] (PRESENT TENSE gibt auf, IMPERFECT
    gab auf, PERFECT TENSE hat aufgegeben) (*plan,
    idea*)

abbey NOUN
    das Kloster *neut* (PL die Klöster)

abbreviation NOUN
    die Abkürzung *fem*

★ ability NOUN
    die Fähigkeit *fem*
    ■ **to have the ability to do something** fähig
    sein [65], etwas zu tun

★ able ADJECTIVE
    ■ **to be able to do something** etwas tun
    können [41]

to abolish VERB
    abschaffen [4] (PERFECT TENSE hat abgeschafft)

★ abortion NOUN
    die Abtreibung *fem*
    ■ **She had an abortion.** Sie hat abgetrieben.

★ about PREPOSITION, ADVERB
1 wegen (*concerning*)
    □ She emailed me about the exam. Sie schickte
    mir eine E-Mail wegen der Prüfung.
2 etwa (*approximately*)
    □ It takes about ten hours. Es dauert etwa zehn
    Stunden. □ about a hundred pounds etwa
    hundert Pfund □ at about eleven o'clock um
    etwa elf Uhr
3 in ... herum (*around*)
    □ to walk about the town in der Stadt
    herumlaufen
4 über
    □ a book about London ein Buch über London
    ■ **to be about to do something** gerade etwas
    tun wollen [94] □ I was about to go out. Ich
    wollte gerade gehen.
    ■ **to talk about something** über etwas reden
    [54] □ We talked about the weather. Wir haben
    über das Wetter geredet.
    ■ **What's the film about?** Wovon handelt der
    Film?
    ■ **How about going to the cinema?** Wie
    wär's, wenn wir ins Kino gingen?

★ above PREPOSITION, ADVERB
    über
    □ above forty degrees über vierzig Grad

> Use the accusative to express movement or a
> change of place. Use the dative when there is
> no change of place.

    □ He put his hands above his head. Er hielt die
    Hände über den Kopf. □ It's in the cupboard
    above the sink. Es ist im Schrank über der Spüle.
    ■ **the flat above** die Wohnung darüber
    ■ **mentioned above** oben erwähnt
    ■ **above all** vor allem

★ abroad ADVERB
1 im Ausland
    □ She lives abroad. Sie lebt im Ausland.
2 ins Ausland
    □ to go abroad ins Ausland gehen

abrupt ADJECTIVE
    brüsk
    □ He was a bit abrupt with me. Er war etwas
    brüsk zu mir.

abruptly ADVERB
    plötzlich
    □ He got up abruptly. Er stand plötzlich auf.

absence – account

★ **absence** NOUN
die Abwesenheit *fem*

★ **absent** ADJECTIVE
abwesend

absent-minded ADJECTIVE
zerstreut
□ She's a bit absent-minded. Sie ist etwas zerstreut.

★ **absolutely** ADVERB
1 völlig (*completely*)
□ Beate's absolutely right. Beate hat völlig recht.
2 ganz sicher
□ Do you think it's a good idea? — Absolutely! Meinst du, das ist eine gute Idee? — Ganz sicher!

absurd ADJECTIVE
absurd
□ That's absurd! Das ist absurd!

★ **abuse** NOUN
▷ *see also* **abuse** VERB
der Missbrauch *masc* (*of power, drugs*)
■ **child abuse** die Kindesmisshandlung
■ **to shout abuse at somebody** jemanden beschimpfen [18]

★ to **abuse** VERB
▷ *see also* **abuse** NOUN
missbrauchen [49] (PERFECT TENSE hat missbraucht)
■ **to abuse drugs** Drogen missbrauchen [49]
■ **abused children** misshandelte Kinder

abusive ADJECTIVE
beleidigend
□ He became abusive. Er wurde beleidigend.

★ **academic** ADJECTIVE
■ **the academic year** das Studienjahr

academy NOUN
die Akademie *fem*
□ a military academy eine Militärakademie

to **accelerate** VERB
beschleunigen [7] (PERFECT TENSE hat beschleunigt)

accelerator NOUN
das Gaspedal *neut* (PL die Gaspedale)

★ **accent** NOUN
der Akzent *masc* (PL die Akzente)
□ He's got a German accent. Er hat einen deutschen Akzent.

★ to **accept** VERB
annehmen [1] (PRESENT TENSE nimmt an, IMPERFECT nahm an, PERFECT TENSE hat angenommen)
■ **to accept somebody** jemanden akzeptieren

★ **acceptable** ADJECTIVE
annehmbar

★ **access** NOUN
1 der Zugang *masc*
□ He has access to confidential information. Er hat Zugang zu vertraulichen Informationen.
2 das Besuchsrecht *neut*
□ The father has access to the children. Der Vater hat ein Besuchsrecht.

accessible ADJECTIVE
erreichbar
□ It's easily accessible. Es ist leicht erreichbar.

accessory NOUN
■ **fashion accessories** die Modeartikel *masc pl*

★ **accident** NOUN
der Unfall *masc* (PL die Unfälle)
□ to have an accident einen Unfall haben
■ **by accident 1** (*by mistake*) versehentlich
□ The burglar killed him by accident. Der Einbrecher hat ihn versehentlich getötet. **2** (*by chance*) zufällig □ She met him by accident. Sie ist ihm zufällig begegnet.

accidental ADJECTIVE
zufällig

to **accommodate** VERB
unterbringen [13] (IMPERFECT brachte unter, PERFECT TENSE hat untergebracht)
■ **The hotel can accommodate fifty people.** Das Hotel hat Platz für fünfzig Gäste.

★ **accommodation** NOUN
die Unterkunft *fem* (PL die Unterkünfte)

★ to **accompany** VERB
begleiten [2] (PERFECT TENSE hat begleitet)

accord NOUN
■ **of his own accord** aus eigenem Antrieb □ He left of his own accord. Er ist aus eigenem Antrieb gegangen.

accordingly ADVERB
entsprechend

★ **according to** PREPOSITION
laut
□ According to him, everyone had gone. Laut ihm waren alle weggegangen.

accordion NOUN
das Akkordeon *neut* (PL die Akkordeons)

★ **account** NOUN
1 das Konto *neut* (PL die Konten)
□ a bank account ein Bankkonto
■ **to do the accounts** die Buchführung machen [48]
2 der Bericht *masc* (PL die Berichte) (*report*)
■ **He gave a detailed account of what happened.** Er berichtete genau, was passiert war.
■ **to take something into account** etwas berücksichtigen [7]
■ **on account of** wegen □ We couldn't go out on account of the rain. Wir konnten wegen des Regens nicht raus.

to **account for** VERB
erklären [19]

★ = core vocabulary

□ She was ill, which accounts for her poor results. Sie war krank, was ihre schlechten Resultate erklärt.

accountable ADJECTIVE
■ **to be accountable to someone** jemandem gegenüber verantwortlich sein [65]

accountancy NOUN
die Buchführung fem

accountant NOUN
1 der Buchhalter masc (PL die Buchhalter)
die Buchhalterin fem (bookkeeper)
□ She's an accountant. Sie ist Buchhalterin.
2 der Steuerberater masc (PL die Steuerberater)
die Steuerberaterin fem (tax consultant)

accuracy NOUN
die Genauigkeit fem

★ **accurate** ADJECTIVE
genau
□ accurate information genaue Information

accurately ADVERB
genau

accusation NOUN
1 der Vorwurf masc (PL die Vorwürfe)
2 die Anklage fem (PL die Anklagen) (by police)

★ to **accuse** VERB
■ **to accuse somebody** 1 jemanden beschuldigen [84] □ She accused me of lying. Sie beschuldigte mich, ich würde lügen. 2 (police) jemanden anklagen [4] □ The police are accusing her of murder. Die Polizei klagt sie wegen Mordes an.

ace NOUN
das Ass neut (GEN des Asses, PL die Asse)
□ the ace of hearts das Herzass

★ **ache** NOUN
▷ see also **ache** VERB
der Schmerz masc (GEN des Schmerzes, PL die Schmerzen)
□ I have an ache in my side. Ich habe Schmerzen in der Seite.

to **ache** VERB
▷ see also **ache** NOUN
wehtun [81] (IMPERFECT tat weh, PERFECT TENSE hat wehgetan)
□ My leg's aching. Mein Bein tut weh.

★ to **achieve** VERB
1 erreichen [19] (PERFECT TENSE hat erreicht) (an aim)
2 erringen (IMPERFECT errang, PERFECT TENSE hat errungen) (victory)

★ **achievement** NOUN
die Leistung fem
□ That was quite an achievement. Das war eine Leistung.

★ **acid** NOUN
die Säure fem

★ **acid rain** NOUN
saurer Regen masc

acne NOUN
die Akne fem
□ She's got acne. Sie hat Akne.

to **acquit** VERB
■ **to be acquitted** freigesprochen werden [91]
□ He was acquitted of murder. Er wurde von der Mordanklage freigesprochen.

acre NOUN
der Morgen masc (PL die Morgen)

acrobat NOUN
der Akrobat masc (GEN des Akrobaten, PL die Akrobaten)
die Akrobatin fem
□ He's an acrobat. Er ist Akrobat.

★ **across** PREPOSITION, ADVERB
über

> Use the accusative to express movement or a change of place. Use the dative when there is no change of place.

□ the shop across the road der Laden über der Straße □ to walk across the road über die Straße gehen
■ **across from** (opposite) gegenüber +dat □ He sat down across from her. Er setzte sich ihr gegenüber.

★ to **act** VERB
▷ see also **act** NOUN
1 spielen [38] (in play, film)
□ He acts well. Er spielt gut. □ She's acting the part of Juliet. Sie spielt die Rolle der Julia.
2 handeln [34] (take action)
□ The police acted quickly. Die Polizei hat schnell gehandelt.
■ **She acts as his interpreter.** Sie übersetzt für ihn.

★ **act** NOUN
▷ see also **act** VERB
der Akt masc (PL die Akte) (in play)
□ in the first act im ersten Akt

★ **action** NOUN
die Handlung fem
■ **The film was full of action.** In dem Film gab es viel Action.
■ **to take firm action against somebody** hart gegen jemanden vorgehen [29]

★ **active** ADJECTIVE
aktiv
□ He's a very active person. Er ist ein sehr aktiver Mensch. □ an active volcano ein aktiver Vulkan

★ **activity** NOUN
die Tätigkeit fem
■ **outdoor activities** die Aktivitäten im Freien

★ **actor** NOUN
der Schauspieler masc (PL die Schauspieler)
□ His father is a well-known actor. Sein Vater ist ein bekannter Schauspieler.

actress – adolescent

★ **actress** NOUN

die Schauspielerin *fem*

□ Her sister is a well-known actress. Ihre Schwester ist eine bekannte Schauspielerin.

★ **actual** ADJECTIVE

wirklich

□ The film is based on actual events. Der Film basiert auf wirklichen Begebenheiten.

> **BE CAREFUL!**
> Do not translate **actual** by the German word **aktuell**.

★ **actually** ADVERB

1 wirklich (*really*)

□ Did it actually happen? Ist das wirklich passiert?

2 eigentlich (*in fact*)

□ Actually, I don't know him at all. Eigentlich kenne ich ihn überhaupt nicht.

acupuncture NOUN

die Akupunktur *fem*

AD ABBREVIATION

n. Chr. (= *nach Christus*)

□ in 800 AD im Jahre 800 n. Chr.

★ **ad** NOUN

1 die Anzeige *fem* (*in paper*)

2 die Werbung *fem* (*on TV, radio*)

to adapt VERB

bearbeiten [2] (PERFECT TENSE hat bearbeitet)

□ His novel was adapted for television. Sein Roman wurde fürs Fernsehen bearbeitet.

■ **to adapt to something** (*get used to*) sich in etwas eingewöhnen [7] □ He has adapted to his new school. Er hat sich in seiner neuen Schule eingewöhnt.

adaptor NOUN

der Adapter *masc* (PL die Adapter)

★ **to add** VERB

hinzufügen [15] (PERFECT TENSE hat hinzugefügt)

□ Add two eggs to the mixture. Fügen Sie dem Teig zwei Eier hinzu.

to add up VERB

zusammenzählen [4]

□ Add the figures up. Zähle die Zahlen zusammen.

addict NOUN

der Süchtige *masc* (GEN des Süchtigen, PL die Süchtigen)

die Süchtige *fem* (GEN der Süchtigen) (*drug addict*)

□ an addict (*man*) ein Süchtiger

■ **Martin's a football addict.** Martin ist ein Fußballnarr.

addicted ADJECTIVE

süchtig

□ She's addicted to heroin. Sie ist heroinsüchtig. □ He's addicted to YouTube. Er ist süchtig nach YouTube.

★ **addition** NOUN

■ **in addition** außerdem □ He broke his leg and, in addition, caught a cold. Er hat sich das Bein gebrochen und außerdem einen Schnupfen bekommen.

■ **in addition to** zusätzlich zu □ In addition to the price of the CD, there's a charge for postage. Zusätzlich zum Preis der CD wird eine Versandgebühr berechnet.

★ **address** NOUN

▷ see also **address** VERB

die Adresse *fem*

□ What's your address? Wie ist Ihre Adresse?

★ **to address** VERB

▷ see also **address** NOUN

1 adressieren [76] (PERFECT TENSE hat adressiert) (*envelope, letter*)

2 sprechen [70] zu (PRESENT TENSE spricht, IMPERFECT sprach, PERFECT TENSE hat gesprochen) (*speak to*)

□ She addressed the audience. Sie sprach zum Publikum.

★ **adjective** NOUN

das Adjektiv *neut* (PL die Adjektive)

★ **to adjust** VERB

einstellen [4] (PERFECT TENSE hat eingestellt)

□ He adjusted the seat to the right height. Er stellte den Stuhl auf die richtige Höhe ein.

■ **to adjust to something** (*get used to*) sich in etwas eingewöhnen [7] □ He has adjusted to his new school. Er hat sich in seiner neuen Schule eingewöhnt.

adjustable ADJECTIVE

verstellbar

★ **administration** NOUN

die Verwaltung *fem*

admiral NOUN

der Admiral *masc* (PL die Admirale)

★ **to admire** VERB

bewundern [88] (PERFECT TENSE hat bewundert)

admission NOUN

der Eintritt *masc*

□ 'admission free' 'Eintritt frei'

★ **to admit** VERB

zugeben [28] (PRESENT TENSE gibt zu, IMPERFECT gab zu, PERFECT TENSE hat zugegeben)

□ I must admit that ... Ich muss zugeben, dass ... □ He admitted that he'd done it. Er gab zu, dass er es getan hat.

adolescence NOUN

die Pubertät *fem*

adolescent NOUN

der Jugendliche *masc* (GEN des Jugendlichen, PL die Jugendlichen)

die Jugendliche *fem* (GEN der Jugendlichen)

□ an adolescent (*male*) ein Jugendlicher

★ = core vocabulary

★ to **adopt** VERB

1 adoptieren [76] (PERFECT TENSE hat adoptiert) (*child*)
□ Phil was adopted. Phil wurde adoptiert.

2 annehmen [1] (PRESENT TENSE nimmt an, IMPERFECT nahm an, PERFECT TENSE hat angenommen) (*idea*)
□ Her suggestion was adopted. Ihr Vorschlag wurde angenommen.

★ **adopted** ADJECTIVE

adoptiert

■ **an adopted son** ein Adoptivsohn

adoption NOUN

die Adoption *fem*

to **adore** VERB

bewundern [88] (PERFECT TENSE hat bewundert)

Adriatic Sea NOUN

die Adria *fem*

★ **adult** NOUN

der Erwachsene *masc* (GEN des Erwachsenen, PL die Erwachsenen)
die Erwachsene *fem* (GEN der Erwachsenen)
□ an adult (*man*) ein Erwachsener

■ **adult education** die Erwachsenenbildung

★ to **advance** VERB

▷ *see also* **advance** NOUN

1 vorrücken [4] (PERFECT TENSE ist vorgerückt) (*move forward*)
□ The troops are advancing. Die Truppen rücken vor.

2 Fortschritte machen [48] (*progress*)
□ Technology has advanced a lot. Die Technik hat große Fortschritte gemacht.

★ **advance** NOUN

▷ *see also* **advance** VERB

■ **in advance** vorher □ They bought the tickets in advance. Sie haben die Karten vorher gekauft.

advance booking NOUN

die Vorbestellung *fem*
□ Reductions are offered for advance booking. Bei Vorbestellung gibt es Rabatt.

■ **Advance booking is essential.** Es ist wichtig, vorzubestellen.

★ **advanced** ADJECTIVE

fortgeschritten

★ **advantage** NOUN

der Vorteil *masc* (PL die Vorteile)
□ Going to university has many advantages. Das Studium hat viele Vorteile.

■ **to take advantage of something** etwas ausnutzen [4] □ Let's take advantage of the good weather. Wir sollten das schöne Wetter ausnutzen.

■ **to take advantage of somebody** jemanden ausnutzen [4] □ The company was taking advantage of its employees. Die Firma nutzte ihre Angestellten aus.

★ **adventure** NOUN

das Abenteuer *neut* (PL die Abenteuer)

adverb NOUN

das Adverb *neut* (PL die Adverbien)

advert NOUN ▷ *see* **advertisement**

★ to **advertise** VERB

annoncieren [76] (PERFECT TENSE hat annonciert)
□ Jobs are advertised in the paper. Stellenangebote werden in der Zeitung annonciert.

advertisement NOUN

1 die Anzeige *fem* (*in paper*)
2 die Werbung *fem* (*on TV, radio*)

advertising NOUN

die Werbung *fem*
□ She works in advertising. Sie ist in der Werbung tätig. □ They've increased spending on advertising. Sie geben mehr Geld für Werbung aus.

★ **advice** NOUN

der Rat *masc*
□ to give somebody advice jemandem einen Rat geben

■ **a piece of advice** ein Rat □ He gave me a good piece of advice. Er gab mir einen guten Rat.

★ to **advise** VERB

raten (PRESENT TENSE rät, IMPERFECT riet, PERFECT TENSE hat geraten)
□ He advised me to wait. Er riet mir zu warten.
□ He advised me not to go. Er hat mir geraten, nicht zu gehen.

aerial NOUN

die Antenne *fem*

★ **aerobics** PL NOUN

das Aerobic *neut*
□ I'm going to aerobics tonight. Ich mache heute Abend Aerobic.

★ **aeroplane** NOUN

das Flugzeug *neut* (PL die Flugzeuge)

aerosol NOUN

der Spray *masc* (PL die Sprays)

★ **affair** NOUN

1 das Verhältnis *neut* (GEN des Verhältnisses, PL die Verhältnisse) (*romantic*)
□ to have an affair with somebody mit jemandem ein Verhältnis haben

2 die Angelegenheit *fem* (*event*)

★ to **affect** VERB

1 beeinflussen [7] (PERFECT TENSE hat beeinflusst) (*influence*)
□ Does junk food affect children's behaviour? Beeinflusst Junkfood das Verhalten von Kindern?

2 beeinträchtigen [84] (PERFECT TENSE hat beeinträchtigt) (*have effect on*)
□ The weather has affected sales. Das Wetter hat den Absatz beeinträchtigt.

affectionate – agreement

affectionate ADJECTIVE
liebevoll

★ to **afford** VERB
sich leisten [2]
□ I can't afford a new pair of jeans. Ich kann mir keine neue Jeans leisten. □ We can't afford to go on holiday. Wir können es uns nicht leisten, in Urlaub zu fahren.

★ **afraid** ADJECTIVE
■ **to be afraid of something** vor etwas Angst haben [32] □ I'm afraid of spiders. Ich habe Angst vor Spinnen.
■ **I'm afraid I can't come.** Ich kann leider nicht kommen.
■ **I'm afraid so.** Ja, leider.
■ **I'm afraid not.** Leider nicht.

★ **Africa** NOUN
Afrika neut
■ **from Africa** aus Afrika
■ **to Africa** nach Afrika

African ADJECTIVE
▷ see also **African** NOUN
afrikanisch

African NOUN
▷ see also **African** ADJECTIVE
der Afrikaner masc (PL die Afrikaner)
die Afrikanerin fem

★ **after** PREPOSITION, ADVERB, CONJUNCTION
nach +dat
□ after dinner nach dem Abendessen □ He ran after me. Er rannte mir nach.
■ **soon after** kurz danach
■ **after I'd had a rest** nachdem ich mich ausgeruht hatte
■ **After eating I left.** Nachdem ich gegessen hatte, ging ich.
■ **after all** schließlich

★ **afternoon** NOUN
der Nachmittag masc (PL die Nachmittage)
□ three o'clock in the afternoon drei Uhr nachmittags □ this afternoon heute Nachmittag □ on Saturday afternoon Samstag Nachmittag

afters PL NOUN
der Nachtisch masc sing (PL die Nachtische)

aftershave NOUN
das Aftershave neut (PL die Aftershaves)

★ **afterwards** ADVERB
danach
□ She left not long afterwards. Sie ging kurz danach.

★ **again** ADVERB
1 wieder (once more)
□ They're friends again. Sie sind wieder Freunde.
2 noch einmal (one more time)
□ Can you tell me again? Kannst du mir das noch einmal sagen?

■ **not ... again** nie mehr □ I won't go there again. Dort gehe ich nie mehr hin.
■ **Do it again!** Mach's noch mal!
■ **Not again!** Nicht schon wieder!
■ **again and again** immer wieder

★ **against** PREPOSITION
gegen
□ He leant against the wall. Er lehnte gegen die Wand. □ I'm against animal testing. Ich bin gegen Tierversuche.

★ **age** NOUN
das Alter neut (PL die Alter)
□ an age limit eine Altersgrenze
■ **at the age of sixteen** mit sechzehn
■ **I haven't seen her for ages.** Ich habe sie schon ewig nicht mehr gesehen.

★ **aged** ADJECTIVE
■ **aged ten** zehn Jahre alt

★ **agenda** NOUN
die Tagesordnung fem

★ **agent** NOUN
der Agent masc (GEN des Agenten, PL die Agenten)
die Agentin fem
■ **an estate agent** ein Immobilienmakler
■ **a travel agent** ein Reisebüro

★ **aggressive** ADJECTIVE
aggressiv

★ **ago** ADVERB
■ **two days ago** vor zwei Tagen
■ **two years ago** vor zwei Jahren
■ **not long ago** vor Kurzem
■ **How long ago did it happen?** Wie lange ist das her?

agony NOUN
■ **He was in agony.** Er hatte furchtbare Schmerzen.

★ to **agree** VERB
■ **to agree with somebody** jemandem zustimmen [4] □ I agree with your sister. Ich stimme deiner Schwester zu.
■ **to agree to do something** bereit sein [65], etwas zu tun □ He agreed to go and pick her up. Er war bereit, sie abzuholen.
■ **to agree that ...** (admit) zugeben [28], dass ... □ I agree that it's difficult. Ich gebe zu, dass das schwierig ist.
■ **Garlic doesn't agree with me.** Ich vertrage Knoblauch nicht.

agreed ADJECTIVE
ausgemacht
□ at the agreed time zur ausgemachten Zeit

★ **agreement** NOUN
die Abmachung fem
■ **to be in agreement** übereinstimmen [4]
□ Everybody was in agreement with Ray. Alle stimmten mit Ray überein.

★ **agricultural** ADJECTIVE
landwirtschaftlich

★ **agriculture** NOUN
die Landwirtschaft fem

★ **ahead** ADVERB
voraus
□ We sent him on ahead. Wir schickten ihn voraus.
■ **The Germans are five points ahead.** Die Deutschen führen mit fünf Punkten.
■ **She looked straight ahead.** Sie sah geradeaus.
■ **ahead of time** vorzeitig
■ **to plan ahead** vorausplanen [15]
■ **Go ahead!** Ja bitte!

★ **aid** NOUN
■ **in aid of charity** für wohltätige Zwecke

★ **AIDS** NOUN
das Aids neut (GEN des Aids)

★ to **aim** VERB
▷ see also **aim** NOUN
■ **to aim at** zielen [38] auf +acc □ He aimed a gun at me. Er zielte mit der Pistole auf mich.
■ **The film is aimed at children.** Der Film ist für Kinder gedacht.
■ **to aim to do something** beabsichtigen [84], etwas zu tun □ Sami aimed to leave at five o'clock. Sami beabsichtigte, um fünf Uhr zu gehen.

★ **aim** NOUN
▷ see also **aim** VERB
das Ziel neut (PL die Ziele)
□ The aim of the festival is to raise money. Ziel des Festivals ist, Geld aufzutreiben.

★ **air** NOUN
die Luft fem (PL die Lüfte)
■ **to get some fresh air** frische Luft schnappen [48]
■ **by air** mit dem Flugzeug □ I prefer to travel by air. Ich reise lieber mit dem Flugzeug.

★ **air-conditioned** ADJECTIVE
mit Klimaanlage

air conditioning NOUN
die Klimaanlage fem

Air Force NOUN
die Luftwaffe fem

air hostess NOUN
die Stewardess fem (PL die Stewardessen)
□ She's an air hostess. Sie ist Stewardess.

★ **airline** NOUN
die Fluggesellschaft fem

★ **airmail** NOUN
■ **by airmail** mit Luftpost

airplane NOUN (US)
das Flugzeug neut (PL die Flugzeuge)

★ **airport** NOUN
der Flughafen masc (PL die Flughäfen)

aisle NOUN
1 der Mittelgang masc (PL die Mittelgänge) (in church)
2 der Gang masc (PL die Gänge) (in plane)
□ an aisle seat ein Platz am Gang

★ **alarm** NOUN
der Alarm masc (PL die Alarme) (warning)
■ **a fire alarm** ein Feueralarm

alarm clock NOUN
der Wecker masc (PL die Wecker)

★ **album** NOUN
das Album neut (PL die Alben)

★ **alcohol** NOUN
der Alkohol masc

alcoholic NOUN
▷ see also **alcoholic** ADJECTIVE
der Alkoholiker masc (PL die Alkoholiker)
die Akoholikerin fem
□ He's an alcoholic. Er ist Alkoholiker.

alcoholic ADJECTIVE
▷ see also **alcoholic** NOUN
alkoholisch
□ alcoholic drinks alkoholische Getränke

alert ADJECTIVE
1 aufgeweckt (bright)
□ He's a very alert baby. Er ist ein sehr aufgewecktes Baby.
2 wachsam (paying attention)
□ We must stay alert. Wir müssen wachsam bleiben.

★ **A levels** PL NOUN
das Abitur neut sing

DID YOU KNOW...?
On average, Germans take their **Abitur** at the age of 19. The students sit examinations in a variety of subjects to attain an overall grade. If you pass, you have the right to a place at university.

alike ADVERB
■ **to look alike** sich ähnlich sehen [64] □ The two sisters look alike. Die beiden Schwestern sehen sich ähnlich.

★ **alive** ADJECTIVE
am Leben

★ **all** ADJECTIVE, PRONOUN, ADVERB
1 alle
□ all the books alle Bücher
■ **all the time** die ganze Zeit
■ **all day** den ganzen Tag
2 alles
□ He ate it all. Er hat alles gegessen. □ I ate all of it. Ich habe alles gegessen.
■ **All of us went.** Wir sind alle hingegangen.
■ **after all** schließlich □ After all, nobody can make us go. Schließlich kann uns niemand zwingen hinzugehen.

■ **all alone** ganz allein □ She's all alone. Sie ist ganz allein.

■ **not at all** überhaupt nicht □ I'm not tired at all. Ich bin überhaupt nicht müde.

■ **The score is five all.** Es steht fünf zu fünf.

★ **allergic** ADJECTIVE
allergisch
■ **to be allergic to something** allergisch gegen etwas sein [65] □ I'm allergic to cats. Ich bin allergisch gegen Katzen.

allergy NOUN
die Allergie fem (PL die Allergien)
□ Have you got any allergies? Hast du Allergien?

alley NOUN
die Gasse fem

★ to **allow** VERB
■ **to be allowed to do something** etwas tun dürfen [16] □ He's not allowed to go out at night. Er darf abends nicht ausgehen.
■ **to allow somebody to do something** jemandem erlauben [19], etwas zu tun □ His mum allowed him to go out. Seine Mama hat ihm erlaubt, auszugehen.

★ **all right** ADVERB
1 gut (okay)
□ Everything turned out all right. Alles ist gut gegangen.
■ **Are you all right?** Bist du in Ordnung?
2 okay (not bad)
□ The film was all right. Der Film war okay.
3 einverstanden (when agreeing)
□ We'll talk about it later. — All right. Wir reden später darüber. — Einverstanden.
■ **Is that all right with you?** Ist das okay?

all-round ADJECTIVE, ADVERB
■ **She's a good all-round player.** Sie ist eine gute, vielseitige Spielerin.
■ **a great all-round achievement** eine rundum gute Leistung

almond NOUN
die Mandel fem (PL die Mandeln)

★ **almost** ADVERB
fast
□ I've almost finished. Ich bin fast fertig.

★ **alone** ADJECTIVE, ADVERB
allein
□ She lives alone. Sie lebt allein.
■ **to leave somebody alone** jemanden in Ruhe lassen [42] □ Leave her alone! Lass sie in Ruhe!
■ **to leave something alone** etwas nicht anfassen [31] □ Leave my things alone! Fass meine Sachen nicht an!

★ **along** PREPOSITION, ADVERB
entlang
□ Chris was walking along the beach. Chris ging am Strand entlang.
■ **all along** die ganze Zeit □ He was lying to me all along. Er hat mich die ganze Zeit belogen.

★ **aloud** ADVERB
laut
■ **He read the poem aloud.** Er las das Gedicht vor.

★ **alphabet** NOUN
das Alphabet neut (PL die Alphabete)

★ **Alps** PL NOUN
die Alpen fem pl

★ **already** ADVERB
schon
□ Liz had already gone. Liz war schon weg.

★ **also** ADVERB
auch
BE CAREFUL!
Do not translate **also** by the German word **also**.

altar NOUN
der Altar masc (PL die Altäre)

to **alter** VERB
verändern [88] (PERFECT TENSE hat verändert)

alternate ADJECTIVE
abwechselnd
■ **on alternate days** jeden zweiten Tag

★ **alternative** NOUN
▷ see also **alternative** ADJECTIVE
die Alternative fem
□ Fruit is a healthy alternative to chocolate. Obst ist eine gesunde Alternative zu Schokolade.
■ **You have no alternative.** Du hast keine andere Wahl.
■ **There are several alternatives.** Es gibt mehrere Möglichkeiten.

★ **alternative** ADJECTIVE
▷ see also **alternative** NOUN
andere
□ an alternative solution eine andere Lösung
□ an alternative suggestion ein anderer Vorschlag
■ **alternative medicine** die alternative Medizin

alternatively ADVERB
■ **Alternatively, we could just stay at home.** Wir könnten auch zu Hause bleiben.

★ **although** CONJUNCTION
obwohl
□ Although she was tired, she stayed up late. Obwohl sie müde war, blieb sie lange auf.

★ **altogether** ADVERB
1 insgesamt (in total)
□ You owe me twenty pounds altogether. Du schuldest mir insgesamt zwanzig Pfund.
2 ganz (completely)
□ I'm not altogether happy with your work. Ich bin mit Ihrer Arbeit nicht ganz zufrieden.

aluminium (US aluminum) NOUN
das Aluminium neut

★ **always** ADVERB
immer
□ He's always moaning. Er beklagt sich immer.

am VERB ▷ *see* **be**

★ **a.m.** ABBREVIATION
morgens
□ at four a.m. um vier Uhr morgens

DID YOU KNOW...?
In Germany times are often given using the 24-hour clock.

□ at two a.m. um zwei Uhr

amateur NOUN
der Amateur *masc* (PL die Amateure)
die Amateurin *fem*
□ He's an amateur. Er ist Amateur.

to **amaze** VERB
■ **to be amazed** erstaunt sein [65] □ I was amazed that I managed to do it. Ich war erstaunt, dass ich es geschafft habe.

★ **amazing** ADJECTIVE
1 erstaunlich (*surprising*)
□ That's amazing news! Das sind erstaunliche Neuigkeiten!
2 ausgezeichnet (*excellent*)
□ Vivian's an amazing cook. Vivian ist eine ausgezeichnete Köchin.

ambassador NOUN
der Botschafter *masc* (PL die Botschafter)
die Botschafterin *fem*

amber ADJECTIVE
■ **an amber light** eine gelbe Ampel

★ **ambition** NOUN
der Ehrgeiz *masc* (GEN des Ehrgeizes)

ambitious ADJECTIVE
ehrgeizig
□ She's very ambitious. Sie ist sehr ehrgeizig.

★ **ambulance** NOUN
der Krankenwagen *masc* (PL die Krankenwagen)

amenities PL NOUN
■ **The hotel has very good amenities.** Das Hotel hat viel zu bieten.

★ **America** NOUN
Amerika *neut*
■ **from America** aus Amerika
■ **in America** in Amerika
■ **to America** nach Amerika

American ADJECTIVE
▷ *see also* **American** NOUN
amerikanisch
□ He's American. Er ist Amerikaner. □ She's American. Sie ist Amerikanerin.

American NOUN
▷ *see also* **American** ADJECTIVE
der Amerikaner *masc* (PL die Amerikaner)
die Amerikanerin *fem*
■ **the Americans** die Amerikaner

★ **among** PREPOSITION
unter +*dat*
□ I was among friends. Ich war unter Freunden.
■ **among other things** unter anderem

★ **amount** NOUN
1 der Betrag *masc* (PL die Beträge)
□ a large amount of money ein großer Geldbetrag
2 die Menge *fem*
□ a huge amount of rice eine enorme Menge Reis

amp NOUN
1 das Ampere *neut* (GEN des Ampere, PL die Ampere) (*of electricity*)
2 der Verstärker *masc* (PL die Verstärker) (*for hi-fi*)

amplifier NOUN
der Verstärker *masc* (PL die Verstärker) (*for hi-fi*)

to **amuse** VERB
belustigen [7] (PERFECT TENSE hat belustigt)
■ **He was most amused by the story.** Er fand die Geschichte sehr lustig.

amusement NOUN
das Vergnügen *neut* (PL die Vergnügen) (*enjoyment*)
■ **amusement arcade** die Spielhalle

an ARTICLE ▷ *see* **a**

to **analyse** VERB
analysieren [76] (PERFECT TENSE hat analysiert)

analysis NOUN
die Analyse *fem*

to **analyze** VERB (US)
analysieren [76] (PERFECT TENSE hat analysiert)

ancestor NOUN
der Vorfahr *masc* (GEN des Vorfahren, PL die Vorfahren)
die Vorfahrin *fem*

anchor NOUN
der Anker *masc* (PL die Anker)

ancient ADJECTIVE
alt
□ This is an ancient custom. Das ist ein alter Brauch.
■ **ancient Greece** das antike Griechenland
■ **an ancient monument** ein historisches Denkmal

★ **and** CONJUNCTION
und
□ you and me du und ich □ Two and two are four. Zwei und zwei gibt vier. □ He talked and talked. Er redete und redete.
■ **Please try and come!** Versuche bitte zu kommen!
■ **better and better** immer besser

★ **angel** NOUN
der Engel *masc* (PL die Engel)

BE CAREFUL!
Do not translate **angel** by the German word **Angel**.

Numbers in brackets refer to verb tables on pages 697 to 706.

365

anger – any

★ **anger** NOUN
die Wut *fem*

★ **angle** NOUN
der Winkel *masc* (PL die Winkel)

angler NOUN
der Angler *masc* (PL die Angler)
die Anglerin *fem*

angling NOUN
das Angeln *neut*
□ His favourite hobby is angling. Angeln ist sein Lieblingshobby.

★ **angry** ADJECTIVE
böse
□ Dad looks very angry. Papa sieht sehr böse aus.
■ **to be angry with somebody** mit jemandem böse sein [65] □ Mum's really angry with you. Mama ist sehr böse mit dir.
■ **to get angry** wütend werden [91]

★ **animal** NOUN
das Tier *neut* (PL die Tiere)

ankle NOUN
der Fußknöchel *masc* (PL die Fußknöchel)

★ **anniversary** NOUN
der Jahrestag *masc* (PL die Jahrestage)
■ **wedding anniversary** der Hochzeitstag

★ to **announce** VERB
ankündigen [4] (PERFECT TENSE hat angekündigt)

★ **announcement** NOUN
die Ankündigung *fem*

to **annoy** VERB
ärgern [88]
□ He's really annoying me. Er ärgert mich echt.
■ **to get annoyed** wütend werden [91] □ I saw that he was getting annoyed. Ich sah, dass er wütend wurde.

★ **annoying** ADJECTIVE
ärgerlich
□ It's really annoying. Es ist wirklich ärgerlich.

★ **annual** ADJECTIVE
jährlich
□ an annual meeting ein jährliches Treffen

anonymous ADJECTIVE
anonym

anorak NOUN
der Anorak *masc* (PL die Anoraks)

★ **another** ADJECTIVE

Use **noch ein** for masculine and neuter nouns, **noch eine** for feminine nouns.

1 noch ein
□ I bought another hat. Ich habe noch einen Hut gekauft. □ Would you like another piece of cake? Möchtest du noch ein Stück Kuchen?
noch eine
□ Would you like another cup of tea? Möchten Sie noch eine Tasse Tee?

Use **ein anderer** for masculine, **eine andere** for feminine and **ein anderes** for neuter nouns.

2 ein anderer (*different*)
□ Could you show me another hat? Könnten Sie mir einen anderen Hut zeigen?
eine andere
□ My girlfriend goes to another school. Meine Freundin besucht eine andere Schule.
ein anderes
□ Have you got another shirt? Haben Sie noch ein anderes Hemd?
■ **another time** ein andermal

★ to **answer** VERB
▷ *see also* **answer** NOUN
beantworten [2] (PERFECT TENSE hat beantwortet)
□ Can you answer my question? Kannst du meine Frage beantworten?
■ **Answer me!** Antworte mir!
■ **to answer the phone** ans Telefon gehen [29]
■ **to answer the door** aufmachen [4] □ Can you answer the door, please? Kannst du bitte aufmachen?

★ **answer** NOUN
▷ *see also* **answer** VERB
1 die Antwort *fem* (*to question*)
2 die Lösung *fem* (*to problem*)

answering machine NOUN
der Anrufbeantworter *masc* (PL die Anrufbeantworter)

ant NOUN
die Ameise *fem*

Antarctic NOUN
die Antarktis *fem*

anthem NOUN
■ **the national anthem** die Nationalhymne

antibiotic NOUN
das Antibiotikum *neut* (PL die Antibiotika)

antidepressant NOUN
das Antidepressivum *neut* (PL die Antidepressiva)

★ **antique** NOUN
die Antiquität *fem* (*furniture*)

antique shop NOUN
der Antiquitätenladen *masc* (PL die Antiquitätenläden)

antiseptic NOUN
das Antiseptikum *neut* (PL die Antiseptika)

★ **any** ADJECTIVE, PRONOUN, ADVERB

In most cases 'any' is not translated.

□ Would you like any bread? Möchten Sie Brot?
□ Have you got any mineral water? Haben Sie Mineralwasser?

Use **kein** for 'not any'.

★ = core vocabulary

□ We haven't got any milk left. Wir haben keine Milch mehr. □ I haven't got any money. Ich habe kein Geld. □ I haven't got any books. Ich habe keine Bücher. □ Sorry, we haven't got any. Tut mir leid, wir haben keine.

■ **any more 1** (*additional*) noch etwas
□ Would you like any more coffee? Möchten Sie noch etwas Kaffee? **2** (*no longer*) nicht mehr
□ I don't love him any more. Ich liebe ihn nicht mehr.

★ **anybody** PRONOUN
1 jemand (*in question*)
□ Has anybody got a pen? Hat jemand etwas zum Schreiben?
2 jeder (*no matter who*)
□ Anybody can learn to swim. Jeder kann schwimmen lernen.

Use **niemand** for 'not ... anybody'.

□ I can't see anybody. Ich kann niemanden sehen.

anyhow ADVERB
sowieso
□ He doesn't want to go out and anyhow he's not allowed. Er will nicht ausgehen, und er darf es sowieso nicht.

★ **anyone** PRONOUN
1 jemand (*in question*)
□ Has anyone got a pen? Hat jemand etwas zum Schreiben?
2 jeder (*no matter who*)
□ Anyone can learn to swim. Jeder kann schwimmen lernen.

Use **niemand** for 'not ... anyone'.

□ I can't see anyone. Ich kann niemanden sehen.

★ **anything** PRONOUN
1 etwas (*in question*)
□ Would you like anything to eat? Möchtest du etwas zu essen?
2 alles (*no matter what*)
□ Anything could happen. Alles könnte passieren.

Use **nichts** for 'not ... anything'.

□ I can't hear anything. Ich kann nichts hören.

★ **anyway** ADVERB
sowieso
□ He doesn't want to go out and anyway he's not allowed. Er will nicht ausgehen, und er darf es sowieso nicht.

★ **anywhere** ADVERB
1 irgendwo (*in question*)
□ Have you seen my coat anywhere? Hast du irgendwo meinen Mantel gesehen?
2 überall
□ You can buy stamps almost anywhere. Man kann fast überall Briefmarken kaufen.

Use **nirgends** for 'not ... anywhere'.

3 nirgends
□ I can't find it anywhere. Ich kann es nirgends finden.

★ **apart** ADVERB
■ **The two towns are ten kilometres apart.** Die zwei Städte liegen zehn Kilometer voneinander entfernt.
■ **apart from** abgesehen von □ Apart from that, everything's fine. Davon abgesehen ist alles in Ordnung.

★ **apartment** NOUN
die Wohnung *fem*

to **apologize** VERB
sich entschuldigen [18] (PERFECT TENSE hat sich entschuldigt)
□ He apologized for being late. Er entschuldigte sich für sein Zuspätkommen.
■ **I apologize!** Ich bitte um Entschuldigung!

apology NOUN
die Entschuldigung *fem*

★ **apostrophe** NOUN
der Apostroph *masc* (PL die Apostrophe)

app NOUN (= *application*)
die App *fem* (PL die Apps)
□ a mobile app eine Handy-App

apparatus NOUN
der Apparat *masc* (PL die Apparate)

★ **apparent** ADJECTIVE
offensichtlich

★ **apparently** ADVERB
offensichtlich

to **appeal** VERB
▷ *see also* **appeal** NOUN
bitten [9] (IMPERFECT bat, PERFECT TENSE hat gebeten)
□ They appealed for help. Sie baten um Hilfe.
■ **to appeal to somebody** (*attract*) jemanden reizen [36] □ Does that appeal to you? Reizt dich das?

appeal NOUN
▷ *see also* **appeal** VERB
der Aufruf *masc* (PL die Aufrufe)

★ to **appear** VERB
1 kommen [40] (IMPERFECT kam, PERFECT TENSE ist gekommen) (*come into view*)
□ The bus appeared around the corner. Der Bus kam um die Ecke.
■ **to appear on TV** im Fernsehen auftreten [79]
2 scheinen [57] (IMPERFECT schien, PERFECT TENSE hat geschienen) (*seem*)
□ She appeared to be asleep. Sie schien zu schlafen.

★ **appearance** NOUN
das Äußere *neut* (GEN des Äußeren) (*looks*)
□ She takes great care over her appearance. Sie achtet sehr auf ihr Äußeres.

appendicitis NOUN
die Blinddarmentzündung *fem*

appetite NOUN
der Appetit *masc*

to **applaud** VERB
klatschen [48]

applause NOUN
der Beifall *masc*

★ **apple** NOUN
der Apfel *masc* (PL die Äpfel)
■ **an apple tree** ein Apfelbaum *masc*

applicant NOUN
der Bewerber *masc* (PL die Bewerber)
die Bewerberin *fem*
□ There were a hundred applicants for the job.
Es gab hundert Bewerber für die Stelle.

★ **application** NOUN
■ **a job application** eine Bewerbung

application form NOUN
1 das Bewerbungsformular *neut* (PL die
Bewerbungsformulare) (*for job*)
2 das Anmeldeformular *neut* (PL die
Anmeldeformulare) (*for university*)

★ to **apply** VERB
■ **to apply for a job** sich für eine Stelle
bewerben [90] □ She applied for the coaching
job. Sie bewarb sich für die Stelle als Trainerin.
■ **to apply to** (*be relevant*) zutreffen [78] auf
□ This rule doesn't apply to me. Diese Regel
trifft auf mich nicht zu.

★ **appointment** NOUN
der Termin *masc* (PL die Termine)
□ I've got a dental appointment. Ich habe einen
Zahnarzttermin.

★ to **appreciate** VERB
zu schätzen wissen [93] (PRESENT TENSE weiß zu
schätzen, IMPERFECT wusste zu schätzen, PERFECT
TENSE hat zu schätzen gewusst)
□ I really appreciate your help. Ich weiß deine
Hilfe wirklich zu schätzen.

apprentice NOUN
der Lehrling *masc* (PL die Lehrlinge)

der **Lehrling** is also used for women.

□ She is an apprentice. Sie ist Lehrling.

★ to **approach** VERB
1 sich nähern [88] (*get nearer to*)
□ He approached the house. Er näherte sich
dem Haus.
2 angehen [29] (IMPERFECT ging an, PERFECT TENSE
hat angegangen) (*tackle*)
□ to approach a problem ein Problem angehen

★ **appropriate** ADJECTIVE
passend
□ That dress isn't very appropriate for an
interview. Dieses Kleid ist für ein
Vorstellungsgespräch nicht sehr passend.

★ **approval** NOUN
die Zustimmung *fem*

★ to **approve** VERB
■ **to approve of** gutheißen □ I don't approve of
his choice. Ich heiße seine Wahl nicht gut.
■ **They didn't approve of his girlfriend.** Sie
hatten etwas gegen seine Freundin.

approximate ADJECTIVE
ungefähr

apricot NOUN
die Aprikose *fem*

★ **April** NOUN
der April *masc*
□ in April im April
■ **April Fool's Day** der erste April
■ **April Fool!** April, April!

apron NOUN
die Schürze *fem*

Aquarius NOUN
der Wassermann *masc*
□ I'm Aquarius. Ich bin Wassermann.

Arab ADJECTIVE
▷ *see also* **Arab** NOUN
arabisch
□ the Arab countries die arabischen Länder

Arab NOUN
▷ *see also* **Arab** ADJECTIVE
der Araber *masc* (PL die Araber)
die Araberin *fem*

Arabic ADJECTIVE
arabisch

arch NOUN
der Bogen *masc* (PL die Bögen)

archaeologist (US **archeologist**) NOUN
der Archäologe *masc* (GEN des Archäologen, PL
die Archäologen)
die Archäologin *fem*
□ She's an archaeologist. Sie ist Archäologin.

archaeology (US **archeology**) NOUN
die Archäologie *fem*

archbishop NOUN
der Erzbischof *masc* (PL die Erzbischöfe)

archeologist NOUN (US)
der Archäologe *masc* (GEN des Archäologen, PL
die Archäologen)
die Archäologin *fem*
□ She's an archaeologist. Sie ist Archäologin.

archeology NOUN (US)
die Archäologie *fem*

architect NOUN
der Architekt *masc* (GEN des Architekten, PL die
Architekten)
die Architektin *fem*
□ She's an architect. Sie ist Architektin.

architecture NOUN
die Architektur *fem*

★ = core vocabulary

Arctic NOUN
die Arktis *fem*

are VERB ▷ *see* be

★ **area** NOUN
1 die Gegend *fem*
□ She lives in the London area. Sie lebt in der Gegend von London.
2 das Viertel *neut* (PL die Viertel)
□ my favourite area of London mein Lieblingsviertel von London
3 die Fläche *fem*
□ an area of one thousand square metres eine Fläche von eintausend Quadratmetern

Argentina NOUN
Argentinien *neut*
■ **from Argentina** aus Argentinien
■ **to Argentina** nach Argentinien

Argentinian ADJECTIVE
argentinisch

★ to **argue** VERB
streiten (IMPERFECT stritt, PERFECT TENSE hat gestritten)
□ They never stop arguing. Sie streiten dauernd.

★ **argument** NOUN
der Streit *masc* (PL die Streite)
■ **to have an argument** Streit haben [32]
□ They had an argument. Sie hatten Streit.

Aries NOUN
der Widder *masc*
□ I'm Aries. Ich bin Widder.

★ **arm** NOUN
der Arm *masc* (PL die Arme)

armchair NOUN
der Sessel *masc* (PL die Sessel)

armour (US **armor**) NOUN
die Rüstung *fem*
■ **a suit of armour** eine Rüstung

army NOUN
die Armee *fem* (PL die Armeen)

★ **around** PREPOSITION, ADVERB
1 um
□ around the corner um die Ecke
2 etwa (*approximately*)
□ around a hundred pounds etwa einhundert Pfund
3 gegen (*date, time*)
□ around eight p.m. gegen acht Uhr abends
■ **around here** 1 (*nearby*) hier in der Nähe □ Is there a chemist's around here? Gibt es hier in der Nähe eine Apotheke? 2 (*in this area*) hier in der Gegend □ He lives around here. Er wohnt hier in der Gegend.

★ to **arrange** VERB
■ **to arrange to do something** verabreden [84], etwas zu tun □ They arranged to go out together on Friday. Sie haben verabredet, am Freitag zusammen auszugehen.

■ **to arrange a meeting** ein Treffen ausmachen [48] □ Can we arrange a meeting? Können wir ein Treffen ausmachen?
■ **to arrange a party** eine Party vorbereiten [2]

arrangement NOUN
der Plan *masc* (PL die Pläne) (*plan*)
■ **They made arrangements to go out on Friday night.** Sie haben verabredet, am Freitagabend auszugehen.

★ to **arrest** VERB
▷ *see also* arrest NOUN
verhaften [2] (PERFECT TENSE hat verhaftet)
□ The police have arrested five people. Die Polizei hat fünf Leute verhaftet.

★ **arrest** NOUN
▷ *see also* arrest VERB
die Verhaftung *fem*
■ **You're under arrest!** Sie sind verhaftet!

arrival NOUN
die Ankunft *fem* (PL die Ankünfte)

★ to **arrive** VERB
ankommen [40] (IMPERFECT kam an, PERFECT TENSE ist angekommen)
□ I arrived at five o'clock. Ich bin um fünf Uhr angekommen.

arrogant ADJECTIVE
arrogant

arrow NOUN
der Pfeil *masc* (PL die Pfeile)

★ **art** NOUN
die Kunst *fem* (PL die Künste)

artery NOUN
die Arterie *fem*

art gallery NOUN
die Kunstgalerie *fem*

★ **article** NOUN
der Artikel *masc* (PL die Artikel)
□ a newspaper article ein Zeitungsartikel

artificial ADJECTIVE
künstlich

★ **artist** NOUN
der Künstler *masc* (PL die Künstler)
die Künstlerin *fem*
□ She's an artist. Sie ist Künstlerin.

artistic ADJECTIVE
künstlerisch

★ **as** CONJUNCTION, ADVERB
1 als (*while*)
□ He came in as I was leaving. Er kam herein, als ich gehen wollte.
2 da (*since*)
□ As it's Sunday, you can have a lie-in. Da es Sonntag ist, kannst du ausschlafen.
3 als (*in the role of*)
□ He works as a waiter in the holidays. In den Ferien jobbt er als Kellner.
■ **as ... as** so ... wie □ Helen's as tall as Maree.

Numbers in brackets refer to verb tables on pages 697 to 706.

369

Helen ist so groß wie Maree. □ His coat cost twice as much as mine. Sein Mantel hat doppelt so viel wie meiner gekostet.

■ **as much ... as** so viel ... wie □ I haven't got as much money as you. Ich habe nicht so viel Geld wie du.

■ **as soon as possible** sobald wie möglich □ I'll do it as soon as possible. Ich tue es sobald wie möglich.

■ **as from tomorrow** ab morgen □ As from tomorrow, the shops will stay open until ten p.m. Ab morgen haben die Geschäfte bis zehn Uhr abends auf.

■ **as if** als ob

■ **as though** als ob

Note that **als ob** is followed by the subjunctive.

□ She acted as though she hadn't seen me. Sie tat so, als ob sie mich nicht sähe.

asap ABBREVIATION (= *as soon as possible*) sobald wie möglich

ash NOUN
die Asche *fem*

ashamed ADJECTIVE
■ **to be ashamed** sich schämen [38] □ You should be ashamed of yourself! Du solltest dich schämen!

ashtray NOUN
der Aschenbecher *masc* (PL die Aschenbecher)

Asia NOUN
Asien *neut*
■ **from Asia** aus Asien
■ **to Asia** nach Asien

Asian ADJECTIVE
▷ *see also* **Asian** NOUN
asiatisch
■ **He's Asian.** Er ist Asiate.
■ **She's Asian.** Sie ist Asiatin.

Asian NOUN
▷ *see also* **Asian** ADJECTIVE
der Asiate *masc* (GEN des Asiaten, PL die Asiaten)
die Asiatin *fem*

★ to **ask** VERB
1 fragen [38] (*inquire, request*)
□ 'Have you finished?' she asked. 'Bist du fertig?' fragte sie.
■ **to ask somebody something** jemanden etwas fragen [38] □ He asked her how old she was. Er fragte sie, wie alt sie ist.
■ **to ask for something** um etwas bitten [9] □ He asked for a cup of tea. Er bat um eine Tasse Tee.
■ **to ask somebody to do something** jemanden bitten [9], etwas zu tun □ She asked him to do the shopping. Sie bat ihn einzukaufen.
■ **to ask about something** sich nach etwas erkundigen [19] □ I asked about train times to Leeds. Ich habe mich nach Zugverbindungen nach Leeds erkundigt.

■ **to ask somebody a question** jemanden etwas fragen [38]
2 einladen (PRESENT TENSE lädt ein, IMPERFECT lud ein, PERFECT TENSE hat eingeladen) (*invite*)
□ Have you asked Matthew to the party? Hast du Matthew zur Party eingeladen?
■ **He asked her out.** (*on a date*) Er hat sie um ein Rendezvous gebeten.

★ **asleep** ADJECTIVE
■ **to be asleep** schlafen [58] □ He's asleep. Er schläft.
■ **to fall asleep** einschlafen [58] □ I fell asleep in front of the TV. Ich bin beim Fernsehen eingeschlafen.

asparagus NOUN
der Spargel *masc* (PL die Spargel)

★ **aspect** NOUN
der Aspekt *masc* (PL die Aspekte)

aspirin NOUN
die Schmerztablette *fem*

assembly NOUN
die Versammlung *fem* (*in School*)

asset NOUN
der Vorteil *masc* (PL die Vorteile)
□ Her experience will be an asset. Ihre Erfahrung wird von Vorteil sein.

assignment NOUN
das Referat *neut* (PL die Referate) (*in school*)

assistance NOUN
die Hilfe *fem*

★ **assistant** NOUN
1 der Verkäufer *masc* (PL die Verkäufer)
die Verkäuferin *fem* (*in shop*)
2 der Assistent *masc* (GEN des Assistenten, PL die Assistenten)
die Assistentin *fem* (*helper*)

association NOUN
der Verband *masc* (PL die Verbände)

assortment NOUN
1 die Auswahl *fem* (*choice*)
□ a large assortment of cheeses eine große Auswahl an Käse
2 die Mischung *fem* (*mixture*)
□ an assortment of biscuits eine Keksmischung

to **assume** VERB
annehmen [1] (PRESENT TENSE nimmt an, IMPERFECT nahm an, PERFECT TENSE hat angenommen)
□ I assume she won't be coming. Ich nehme an, dass sie nicht kommt.

to **assure** VERB
versichern [88] (PERFECT TENSE hat versichert)
□ He assured me he was coming. Er versicherte mir, dass er kommt.

★ **asthma** NOUN
das Asthma *neut*
□ I've got asthma. Ich habe Asthma.

★ = core vocabulary

to astonish VERB
erstaunen [19] (PERFECT TENSE hat erstaunt)
□ She was astonished. Sie war erstaunt.

astonishing ADJECTIVE
erstaunlich

astrology NOUN
die Astrologie fem

astronaut NOUN
der Astronaut masc (GEN des Astronauten, PL die Astronauten)
die Astronautin fem

astronomy NOUN
die Astronomie fem

asylum NOUN
das Asyl neut (PL die Asyle)
□ to ask for asylum um Asyl bitten

asylum-seeker NOUN
der Asylbewerber masc (PL die Asylbewerber)
die Asylbewerberin fem

★ **at** PREPOSITION
1 um
   □ at four o'clock um vier Uhr
2 an
   □ at Christmas an Weihnachten □ What are you doing at the weekend? Was machst du am Wochenende?
   ■ at night nachts
3 mit
   □ at fifty kilometres per hour mit fünfzig Stundenkilometern
4 in
   □ at school in der Schule □ at the office im Büro
   ■ at home zu Hause
   ■ two at a time jeweils zwei
   ■ at the races beim Pferderennen

★ **at** NOUN
das At-Zeichen neut (PL die At-Zeichen) (@ symbol)

ate VERB ▷ see eat

Athens NOUN
Athen neut
   ■ from Athens aus Athen

★ **athlete** NOUN
der Athlet masc (GEN des Athleten, PL die Athleten)
die Athletin fem

athletic ADJECTIVE
athletisch

athletics NOUN
die Leichtathletik fem
   □ I like watching the athletics on TV. Ich sehe mir im Fernsehen gern Leichtathletik an.

★ **Atlantic** NOUN
der Atlantik masc

★ **atlas** NOUN
der Atlas masc (GEN des Atlasses, PL die Atlanten)

atmosphere NOUN
die Atmosphäre fem

atom NOUN
das Atom neut (PL die Atome)

★ **to attach** VERB
festbinden (IMPERFECT band fest, PERFECT TENSE hat festgebunden)
   □ They attached a rope to the car. Sie banden ein Seil am Auto fest.
   ■ Please find attached … Anbei erhalten Sie …

attached ADJECTIVE
   ■ to be attached to somebody an jemandem hängen [35] □ He's very attached to his family. Er hängt sehr an seiner Familie.

to attack VERB
   ▷ see also attack NOUN
angreifen (IMPERFECT griff an, PERFECT TENSE hat angegriffen)
   □ The dog attacked me. Der Hund hat mich angegriffen.

attack NOUN
   ▷ see also attack VERB
der Angriff masc (PL die Angriffe)

★ **attempt** NOUN
   ▷ see also attempt VERB
der Versuch masc (PL die Versuche)
   □ She gave up after several attempts. Sie gab nach mehreren Versuchen auf.

★ **to attempt** VERB
   ▷ see also attempt NOUN
versuchen [84] (PERFECT TENSE hat versucht)
   ■ to attempt to do something versuchen [84], etwas zu tun □ I attempted to write a song. Ich habe versucht, ein Lied zu schreiben.

to attend VERB
teilnehmen [52] (PRESENT TENSE nimmt teil, IMPERFECT nahm teil, PERFECT TENSE hat teilgenommen)
   □ to attend a meeting an einem Treffen teilnehmen

★ **attention** NOUN
die Aufmerksamkeit fem
   ■ to pay attention to something auf etwas achten [2] □ He didn't pay attention to what I was saying. Er hat nicht darauf geachtet, was ich sagte.

attic NOUN
der Speicher masc (PL die Speicher)

attitude NOUN
die Einstellung fem
   □ I really don't like your attitude! Mir gefällt deine Einstellung nicht!

attorney NOUN (US)
der Rechtsanwalt masc (PL die Rechtsanwälte)
die Rechtsanwältin fem
   □ My mother's an attorney. Meine Mutter ist Rechtsanwältin.

a

to **attract** VERB
anziehen [96] (IMPERFECT zog an, PERFECT TENSE
hat angezogen)
□ The Lake District attracts lots of tourists. Der
Lake District zieht viele Touristen an.

attraction NOUN
die Attraktion *fem*
□ a tourist attraction eine Touristenattraktion

★ **attractive** ADJECTIVE
attraktiv
□ She's very attractive. Sie ist sehr attraktiv.

aubergine NOUN
die Aubergine *fem*

auction NOUN
die Auktion *fem*

★ **audience** NOUN
die Zuschauer *masc pl* (*in theatre*)
□ The audience clapped. Die Zuschauer
klatschten.

audition NOUN
1 die Vorsprechprobe *fem* (*of actor*)
2 das Vorspiel *neut* (PL die Vorspiele) (*of musician*)

★ **August** NOUN
der August *masc*
□ in August im August

★ **aunt** NOUN
die Tante *fem*
□ my aunt meine Tante

aunty NOUN
die Tante *fem*
□ my aunty meine Tante

★ **au pair** NOUN
das Au-pair-Mädchen *neut* (PL die Au-pair-
Mädchen)
der Au-pair-Junge *masc* (PL die Au-pair-Jungen)
□ She's an au pair. Sie ist Au-pair-Mädchen.

Australia NOUN
Australien *neut*
■ **from Australia** aus Australien
■ **in Australia** in Australien
■ **to Australia** nach Australien

Australian ADJECTIVE
▷ *see also* **Australian** NOUN
australisch
■ **He's Australian.** Er ist Australier.
■ **She's Australian.** Sie ist Australierin.

Australian NOUN
▷ *see also* **Australian** ADJECTIVE
der Australier *masc* (PL die Australier)
die Australierin *fem*
■ **the Australians** die Australier

Austria NOUN
Österreich *neut*
■ **from Austria** aus Österreich
■ **in Austria** in Österreich
■ **to Austria** nach Österreich

Austrian ADJECTIVE
▷ *see also* **Austrian** NOUN
österreichisch
■ **He's Austrian.** Er ist Österreicher.
■ **She's Austrian.** Sie ist Österreicherin.

Austrian NOUN
▷ *see also* **Austrian** ADJECTIVE
der Österreicher *masc* (PL die Österreicher)
die Österreicherin *fem*
■ **the Austrians** die Österreicher

★ **author** NOUN
der Autor *masc* (PL die Autoren)
die Autorin *fem*
□ She's a famous author. Sie ist eine berühmte
Autorin.

autobiography NOUN
die Autobiografie *fem*

autograph NOUN
das Autogramm *neut* (PL die Autogramme)
□ May I have your autograph? Kann ich Ihr
Autogramm haben?

★ **automatic** ADJECTIVE
automatisch
□ an automatic door eine automatische Tür

automatically ADVERB
automatisch

★ **autumn** NOUN
der Herbst *masc* (PL die Herbste)
□ in autumn im Herbst

availability NOUN
die Erhältlichkeit *fem* (*of goods*)
■ **subject to availability** falls vorrätig

★ **available** ADJECTIVE
erhältlich
□ Brochures are available on request. Prospekte
sind auf Anfrage erhältlich.
■ **Is Mr Cooke available today?** Ist Herr Cooke
heute zu sprechen?

avalanche NOUN
die Lawine *fem*

avatar NOUN
der Avatar *masc* (PL die Avatare)

avenue NOUN
die Allee *fem*

★ **average** NOUN
▷ *see also* **average** ADJECTIVE
der Durchschnitt *masc* (PL die Durchschnitte)
□ on average im Durchschnitt

★ **average** ADJECTIVE
▷ *see also* **average** NOUN
durchschnittlich
□ the average price der durchschnittliche Preis

avocado NOUN
die Avocado *fem* (PL die Avocados)

★ to **avoid** VERB
1 meiden (IMPERFECT mied, PERFECT TENSE hat
gemieden)

★ = core vocabulary

□ He avoids her when she's in a bad mood. Er meidet sie, wenn sie schlechte Laune hat.

2 vermeiden

□ You should avoid going out on your own at night. Du solltest vermeiden, nachts allein auszugehen.

awake ADJECTIVE

wach

■ **to be awake** wach sein [65] □ Is she awake? Ist sie wach? □ He was still awake. Er war noch wach.

award NOUN

der Preis *masc* (PL die Preise)

□ He's won an award. Er hat einen Preis bekommen. □ the award for the best actor der Preis für den besten Schauspieler

aware ADJECTIVE

■ **to be aware that** ... sich bewusst sein [65], dass ...

■ **to be aware of something** etwas merken [38] □ We are aware of what is happening. Wir merken, was geschieht.

■ **not that I am aware of** nicht dass ich wüsste

★ **away** ADJECTIVE, ADVERB

weg (*not here*)

□ Felix is away today. Felix ist heute weg. □ He's away for a week. Er ist eine Woche lang weg.

■ **The town's two kilometres away.** Die Stadt ist zwei Kilometer entfernt.

■ **The coast is two hours away by car.** Zur Küste sind es mit dem Auto zwei Stunden.

■ **Go away!** Geh weg!

away match NOUN

das Auswärtsspiel *neut* (PL die Auswärtsspiele)

□ Our team has an away match this week. Unsere Mannschaft hat diese Woche ein Auswärtsspiel.

★ **awful** ADJECTIVE

schrecklich

□ That's awful! Das ist schrecklich!

■ **an awful lot of** ... furchtbar viel ... □ an awful lot of work furchtbar viel Arbeit □ an awful lot of mistakes furchtbar viele Fehler

awfully ADVERB

furchtbar

□ I'm awfully sorry. Es tut mir furchtbar leid.

awkward ADJECTIVE

1 schwierig (*difficult*)

□ an awkward situation eine schwierige Situation □ It's a bit awkward for me to come and see you. Es ist für mich etwas schwierig, dich zu besuchen.

2 unangenehm (*embarrassing*)

□ an awkward question eine unangenehme Frage

axe NOUN

die Axt *fem* (PL die Äxte)

Bb

BA ABBREVIATION (= *Bachelor of Arts*)
der Magister *masc* (PL die Magister)
■ **She's got a BA in History.** Sie hat einen
Magistertitel in Geschichte.

★ **baby** NOUN
das Baby *neut* (PL die Babys)

baby carriage NOUN (US)
der Buggy *masc* (PL die Buggys)

★ to **babysit** VERB
babysitten [2]
□ Veronika is babysitting for her friend.
Veronika babysittet bei ihrer Freundin.

babysitter NOUN
der Babysitter *masc* (PL die Babysitter)
die Babysitterin *fem*

babysitting NOUN
das Babysitten *neut*

★ **back** NOUN
▷ *see also* **back** ADJECTIVE, ADVERB, VERB
1 der Rücken *masc* (PL die Rücken) (*of person,
horse, book*)
2 die Rückseite *fem* (*of page, house*)
□ Write your name on the back. Schreiben Sie
Ihren Namen auf die Rückseite.
■ **in the back of the car** hinten im Auto
■ **at the back** hinten □ He's sitting at the back.
Er sitzt hinten.

★ **back** ADJECTIVE, ADVERB
▷ *see also* **back** NOUN, VERB
hintere
□ the back wheel of my bike das hintere Rad
meines Fahrrads
■ **the back seat** der Rücksitz
■ **the back door** die Hintertür
■ **to get back** zurückkommen [40] □ What
time did you get back? Wann bist du
zurückgekommen?
■ **We went there by bus and walked back.**
Wir sind mit dem Bus hingefahren und zu Fuß
zurückgegangen.
■ **He's not back yet.** Er ist noch nicht zurück.
■ **to call somebody back** jemanden
zurückrufen [56] □ I'll call back later. Ich rufe
später zurück.

★ to **back** VERB
▷ *see also* **back** NOUN, ADJECTIVE, ADVERB
■ **to back somebody** für jemanden sein [65]
□ I'm backing him. Ich bin für ihn.

to **back out** VERB
einen Rückzieher machen [48]
□ They promised to help and then backed out.
Sie haben versprochen zu helfen, haben dann
aber einen Rückzieher gemacht.

to **back up** VERB
unterstützen [36]
□ She tried to back her up. Sie hat versucht, sie
zu unterstützen

backache NOUN
die Rückenschmerzen *masc pl*
□ to have backache Rückenschmerzen haben

backbone NOUN
das Rückgrat *neut* (PL die Rückgrate)

to **backfire** VERB
schiefgehen [29] (IMPERFECT ging schief, PERFECT
TENSE ist schiefgegangen) (*go wrong*)

★ **background** NOUN
der Hintergrund *masc* (PL die Hintergründe)
□ a house in the background ein Haus im
Hintergrund □ his family background sein
familiärer Hintergrund
■ **background noise** die
Hintergrundgeräusche *neut pl*

backhand NOUN
die Rückhand *fem* (PL die Rückhände)

★ **backing** NOUN
die Unterstützung *fem* (*support*)

backpack NOUN
der Rucksack *masc* (PL die Rucksäcke)

backpacker NOUN
der Wanderer *masc* (PL die Wanderer)
die Wanderin *fem*

back pain NOUN
die Rückenschmerzen *masc pl*
□ to have back pain Rückenschmerzen haben

backside NOUN
der Hintern *masc* (GEN des Hinterns, PL die
Hintern)

backstroke NOUN
das Rückenschwimmen *neut*

backup NOUN
die Unterstützung *fem* (*support*)
■ **a backup file** eine Sicherungsdatei

★ **backwards** ADVERB
zurück

★ = core vocabulary

□ to take a step backwards einen Schritt zurück machen
■ **to fall backwards** nach hinten fallen [22]

back yard NOUN
der Hinterhof masc (PL die Hinterhöfe)

★ **bacon** NOUN
der Speck masc
□ bacon and eggs Eier mit Speck

★ **bad** ADJECTIVE
1 schlecht
□ a bad film ein schlechter Film □ the bad weather das schlechte Wetter □ to be in a bad mood schlechte Laune haben □ not bad nicht schlecht □ That's not bad at all. Das ist gar nicht schlecht.

> **WORD POWER**
> You can use a number of other words instead of **bad** to mean 'terrible':
> **awful** schrecklich
> □ an awful journey eine schreckliche Reise
> **dreadful** furchtbar
> □ a dreadful mistake ein furchtbarer Fehler
> **hopeless** hoffnungslos
> □ a hopeless team eine hoffnungslose Mannschaft
> **terrible** furchtbar
> □ a terrible book ein furchtbares Buch

■ **to be bad at something** in etwas schlecht sein [65] □ I'm really bad at maths. In Mathe bin ich wirklich schlecht.
2 schlimm (serious)
□ a bad accident ein schlimmer Unfall
3 böse (naughty)
□ You bad boy! Du böser Junge!
■ **to go bad** (food) schlecht werden [91]
■ **I feel bad about it.** Das tut mir echt leid.

badge NOUN
1 der Button masc (PL die Buttons) (metal)
2 der Aufkleber masc (PL die Aufkleber) (sticker)

★ **badly** ADVERB
schlecht
□ badly paid schlecht bezahlt
■ **badly wounded** schwer verletzt
■ **He's badly in need of some money.** Er braucht dringend Geld.

badminton NOUN
das Badminton neut
□ to play badminton Badminton spielen

bad-tempered ADJECTIVE
■ **to be bad-tempered 1** (by nature) griesgrämig sein [65] □ He's a really bad-tempered person. Er ist wirklich ein griesgrämiger Mensch. **2** (temporarily) schlechte Laune haben [32] □ He was really bad-tempered yesterday. Er hatte gestern wirklich schlechte Laune.

to **baffle** VERB
verblüffen [84] (PERFECT TENSE hat verblüfft)
□ She was baffled. Sie war verblüfft.

★ **bag** NOUN
die Tasche fem
■ **an old bag** (person) eine alte Schachtel

baggage NOUN
das Gepäck neut sing

baggage reclaim NOUN
die Gepäckausgabe fem

baggy ADJECTIVE
weit (clothes)

bagpipes PL NOUN
der Dudelsack masc (PL die Dudelsäcke)
□ Ed plays the bagpipes. Ed spielt Dudelsack.

★ to **bake** VERB
backen [48] (PRESENT TENSE bäckt, IMPERFECT backte, PERFECT TENSE hat gebacken)
□ to bake a cake einen Kuchen backen

★ **baker** NOUN
der Bäcker masc (PL die Bäcker)
die Bäckerin fem
□ He's a baker. Er ist Bäcker.

bakery NOUN
die Bäckerei fem

baking ADJECTIVE
■ **It's baking in here!** Hier ist es knallheiß!

★ **balance** NOUN
▷ see also **balance** VERB
das Gleichgewicht neut
□ to lose one's balance das Gleichgewicht verlieren

★ to **balance** VERB
▷ see also **balance** NOUN
balancieren [76] (PERFECT TENSE ist balanciert)
□ I balanced on the window ledge. Ich balancierte auf dem Fensterbrett.
■ **The boxes were carefully balanced.** Die Kartons befanden sich genau im Gleichgewicht.

balanced ADJECTIVE
ausgewogen
□ a balanced diet eine ausgewogene Ernährung

★ **balcony** NOUN
der Balkon masc (PL die Balkons)

bald ADJECTIVE
glatzköpfig
■ **to be bald** eine Glatze haben [32]

★ **ball** NOUN
der Ball masc (PL die Bälle)

ballet NOUN
das Ballett neut (PL die Ballette)

> Note that you pronounce the 'tt' in German.

□ We went to a ballet. Wir sind ins Ballett gegangen.
■ **ballet lessons** Ballettstunden

ballet dancer NOUN
der Balletttänzer masc (PL die Balletttänzer)
die Balletttänzerin fem

ballet shoes PL NOUN
die Ballettschuhe *masc pl*

★ **balloon** NOUN
der Luftballon *masc* (PL die Luftballons) (*at parties*)
■ **a hot-air balloon** ein Heißluftballon

ballpoint pen NOUN
der Kugelschreiber *masc* (PL die Kugelschreiber)

★ **ban** NOUN
▷ see also **ban** VERB
das Verbot *neut* (PL die Verbote)

★ to **ban** VERB
▷ see also **ban** NOUN
verbieten [8] (IMPERFECT verbot, PERFECT TENSE hat verboten)
□ **to ban somebody from doing something** jemandem verbieten, etwas zu tun
■ **She was banned from driving.** Sie bekam Fahrverbot.

★ **banana** NOUN
die Banane *fem*
□ **a banana skin** eine Bananenschale

★ **band** NOUN
1 die Band *fem* (PL die Bands) (*rock band*)
2 die Kapelle *fem* (*brass band*)

bandage NOUN
▷ see also **bandage** VERB
der Verband *masc* (PL die Verbände)

to **bandage** VERB
▷ see also **bandage** NOUN
verbinden (IMPERFECT verband, PERFECT TENSE hat verbunden)
□ **She bandaged his arm.** Sie verband ihm den Arm.

Band-Aid® NOUN (US)
das Heftpflaster *neut* (PL die Heftpflaster)

bandit NOUN
der Bandit *masc* (GEN des Banditen, PL die Banditen)

bang NOUN
▷ see also **bang** VERB
1 der Knall *masc* (PL die Knalle)
□ **I heard a loud bang.** Ich habe einen lauten Knall gehört.
2 der Schlag *masc* (PL die Schläge)
□ **a bang on the head** ein Schlag auf den Kopf
■ **Bang!** Peng!

to **bang** VERB
▷ see also **bang** NOUN
anschlagen [59] (PRESENT TENSE schlägt an, IMPERFECT schlug an, PERFECT TENSE hat angeschlagen) (*part of body*)
□ **I banged my head.** Ich habe mir den Kopf angeschlagen.
■ **to bang the door** die Tür zuknallen [4]
■ **to bang on the door** gegen die Tür hämmern [34]

banger NOUN
die Bratwurst *fem* (PL die Bratwürste)
□ **bangers and mash** Bratwürste mit Kartoffelbrei

★ **bank** NOUN
1 die Bank *fem* (PL die Banken) (*financial*)
2 das Ufer *neut* (PL die Ufer) (*of river, lake*)

to **bank on** VERB
sich verlassen [42] auf (PRESENT TENSE verlässt, IMPERFECT verließ, PERFECT TENSE hat verlassen)
□ **I'm banking on you coming.** Ich verlasse mich darauf, dass du kommst. □ **I wouldn't bank on it.** Ich würde mich nicht darauf verlassen.

bank account NOUN
das Bankkonto *neut* (PL die Bankkonten)

★ **banker** NOUN
der Banker *masc* (PL die Banker)
die Bankerin *fem*

bank holiday NOUN
der Feiertag *masc* (PL die Feiertage)

banknote NOUN
die Banknote *fem*

bankrupt ADJECTIVE
bankrott

banned ADJECTIVE
verboten

★ **bar** NOUN
1 die Bar *fem* (PL die Bars) (*pub*)
2 die Theke *fem* (*counter*)
■ **a bar of chocolate** eine Tafel Schokolade
■ **a bar of soap** ein Stück Seife

barbaric ADJECTIVE
barbarisch

★ **barbecue** NOUN
das Barbecue *neut* (PL die Barbecues)
■ **We could have a barbecue this evening.** Wir könnten heute Abend grillen.

barber NOUN
der Herrenfriseur *masc* (PL die Herrenfriseure)

★ **bare** ADJECTIVE
nackt

barefoot ADJECTIVE, ADVERB
barfuß
□ **They go around barefoot.** Sie laufen barfuß herum. □ **She was barefoot.** Sie war barfuß.

barely ADVERB
kaum
□ **I could barely hear her.** Ich konnte sie kaum hören.

★ **bargain** NOUN
das Schnäppchen *neut* (PL die Schnäppchen)
□ **It was a bargain!** Das war ein Schnäppchen!

barge NOUN
der Kahn *masc* (PL die Kähne)

to **bark** VERB
bellen [38]

★ = core vocabulary

barmaid NOUN
die Bardame *fem*
□ She's a barmaid. Sie ist Bardame.

barman NOUN
der Barkeeper *masc* (PL die Barkeeper)
□ He's a barman. Er ist Barkeeper.

barn NOUN
die Scheune *fem*

barrel NOUN
das Fass *neut* (GEN des Fasses, PL die Fässer)

barrier NOUN
die Schranke *fem*

bartender NOUN (US)
der Barkeeper *masc* (PL die Barkeeper)

base NOUN
1 die Basis *fem* (PL die Basen) (*basis*)
□ a good base for a successful career eine gute Basis für eine erfolgreiche Karriere
2 der Fuß *masc* (GEN des Fußes, PL die Füße) (*of lamp, mountain*)
3 der Boden *masc* (PL die Böden) (*of container*)
4 der Stützpunkt *masc* (PL die Stützpunkte) (*military*)

★ **baseball** NOUN
der Baseball *masc*
□ a baseball cap eine Baseballmütze

based ADJECTIVE
■ based on basierend auf +*dat*

★ **basement** NOUN
das Untergeschoss *neut* (GEN des Untergeschosses, PL die Untergeschosse)

to **bash** VERB
▷ *see also* **bash** NOUN
■ to bash something in etwas einschlagen [59] □ They bashed the door in. Sie schlugen die Tür ein.

bash NOUN
▷ *see also* **bash** VERB
■ I'll have a bash. Ich versuch's mal.

basic ADJECTIVE
1 elementar (*knowledge, education*)
■ basic vocabulary der Grundwortschatz
■ It's a basic model. Es ist ein Grundmodell.
2 einfach
□ The accommodation is pretty basic. Die Unterkunft ist sehr einfach.

★ **basically** ADVERB
eigentlich
□ Basically, I just don't like him. Eigentlich mag ich ihn nicht.

basics PL NOUN
die Grundlagen *fem pl*

basil NOUN
das Basilikum *neut*

basin NOUN
das Waschbecken *neut* (PL die Waschbecken) (*washbasin*)

basis NOUN
■ on a daily basis täglich
■ on a regular basis regelmäßig

★ **basket** NOUN
1 der Korb *masc* (PL die Körbe)
2 der Warenkorb *masc* (*online*)

★ **basketball** NOUN
der Basketball *masc*

bass NOUN
der Bass *masc* (GEN des Basses, PL die Bässe)
□ He plays bass. Er spielt Bass. □ He's a bass. Er singt Bass.
■ a bass drum eine Basstrommel
■ a bass guitar eine Bassgitarre

bassoon NOUN
das Fagott *neut* (PL die Fagotte)
□ I play the bassoon. Ich spiele Fagott.

★ **bat** NOUN
1 der Schläger *masc* (PL die Schläger) (*for cricket, rounders, table tennis*)
2 die Fledermaus *fem* (PL die Fledermäuse) (*animal*)

★ **bath** NOUN
1 das Bad *neut* (PL die Bäder)
□ a hot bath ein heißes Bad
■ to have a bath baden [54]
2 die Badewanne *fem* (*bathtub*)
□ There's a spider in the bath. In der Badewanne ist eine Spinne.

to **bathe** VERB
baden [54]

bathing suit NOUN (US)
der Badeanzug *masc* (PL die Badeanzüge)

★ **bathroom** NOUN
das Badezimmer *neut* (PL die Badezimmer)

baths PL NOUN
das Schwimmbad *neut* (PL die Schwimmbäder)

bath towel NOUN
das Badetuch *neut* (PL die Badetücher)

batter NOUN
der Pfannkuchenteig *masc* (*for pancakes*)

battery NOUN
die Batterie *fem*

★ **battle** NOUN
die Schlacht *fem*
□ the Battle of Hastings die Schlacht von Hastings
■ It was a battle, but we managed in the end. Es war ein Kampf, aber wir haben es schließlich geschafft.

battleship NOUN
das Schlachtschiff *neut* (PL die Schlachtschiffe)

bay NOUN
die Bucht *fem*

BC ABBREVIATION (= *before Christ*)
v. Chr. (= *vor Christus*)
□ in 200 BC im Jahre 200 v. Chr.

b

★ **to be** VERB
sein [65] (PRESENT TENSE ist, IMPERFECT war, PERFECT TENSE ist gewesen)
□ I'm tired. Ich bin müde. □ You're late. Du bist spät dran. □ She's English. Sie ist Engländerin. □ It's cold. Es ist kalt. □ It's a nice day. Es ist ein schöner Tag. □ It's four o'clock. Es ist vier Uhr. □ I'm fourteen. Ich bin vierzehn. □ We are all happy. Wir sind alle glücklich. □ I've been ill. Ich war krank. □ I've never been to Dresden. Ich war noch nie in Dresden.
■ **to be beaten** geschlagen werden [91]

> Questions like 'isn't it?' don't exist in German.

□ She's pretty, isn't she? Sie ist hübsch, nicht wahr? □ The film was good, wasn't it? Der Film war gut, nicht wahr?

> You do not translate 'a' when you want to describe somebody's occupation.

□ She's a doctor. Sie ist Ärztin. □ He's a student. Er ist Student. □ He's a bachelor. Er ist Junggeselle.
■ **I'm cold.** Mir ist kalt.
■ **I'm hungry.** Ich habe Hunger.

★ **beach** NOUN
der Strand *masc* (PL die Strände)

bead NOUN
die Perle *fem*

beak NOUN
der Schnabel *masc* (PL die Schnäbel)

beam NOUN
der Strahl *masc* (PL die Strahlen)

beans PL NOUN
die Bohnen *fem pl*
■ **baked beans** gebackene Bohnen

> **DID YOU KNOW...?**
> Few Germans eat baked beans and not many shops sell them.

■ **broad beans** dicke Bohnen
■ **green beans** grüne Bohnen
■ **kidney beans** Kidneybohnen

bean sprouts PL NOUN
die Sojasprossen *masc pl*

★ **bear** NOUN
▷ *see also* **bear** VERB
der Bär *masc* (GEN des Bären, PL die Bären)

★ **to bear** VERB
▷ *see also* **bear** NOUN
ertragen [77] (PRESENT TENSE erträgt, IMPERFECT ertrug, PERFECT TENSE hat ertragen) (*endure*)
□ I can't bear it. Ich kann es nicht ertragen.
■ **Bear up!** Kopf hoch!
■ **If you would bear with me for a moment ...** Wenn Sie sich bitte einen Moment gedulden könnten ...

beard NOUN
der Bart *masc* (PL die Bärte)

□ He's got a beard. Er hat einen Bart.
■ **a man with a beard** ein bärtiger Mann

bearded ADJECTIVE
bärtig

★ **beat** NOUN
▷ *see also* **beat** VERB
der Rhythmus *masc* (GEN des Rhythmus, PL die Rhythmen)

★ **to beat** VERB
▷ *see also* **beat** NOUN
schlagen [59] (PRESENT TENSE schlägt, IMPERFECT schlug, PERFECT TENSE hat geschlagen)
□ We beat them three nil. Wir haben sie drei zu null geschlagen.
■ **Beat it!** Hau ab! (*informal*)
■ **to beat somebody up** jemanden zusammenschlagen [59]

★ **beautiful** ADJECTIVE
schön

beautifully ADVERB
schön

★ **beauty** NOUN
die Schönheit *fem*

beauty spot NOUN
der Schönheitsfleck *masc* (PL die Schönheitsflecken)

became VERB ▷ *see* **become**

★ **because** CONJUNCTION
weil
□ I did it because ... Ich habe es getan, weil ...
■ **because of** wegen □ because of the weather wegen des Wetters

★ **to become** VERB
werden [91] (PRESENT TENSE wird, IMPERFECT wurde, PERFECT TENSE ist geworden)
□ He became famous. Er wurde berühmt.

> **BE CAREFUL!**
> Do not translate **to become** by **bekommen**.

★ **bed** NOUN
das Bett *neut* (PL die Betten)
□ in bed im Bett
■ **to go to bed** ins Bett gehen [29] □ to go to bed with somebody mit jemandem ins Bett gehen
■ **bed and breakfast** das Zimmer mit Frühstück *neut* □ How much is it for bed and breakfast? Wie viel kostet das Zimmer mit Frühstück?
■ **We stayed in a bed and breakfast.** Wir waren in einer Frühstückspension.

bedclothes PL NOUN
die Bettwäsche *fem sing*

bedding NOUN
das Bettzeug *neut*

★ **bedroom** NOUN
das Schlafzimmer *neut* (PL die Schlafzimmer)

bedsit NOUN
■ **She lives in a bedsit.** das Sie wohnt in einem möblierten Zimmer *neut.*

bedspread NOUN
die Tagesdecke *fem*

★ **bedtime** NOUN
■ **Ten o'clock is my usual bedtime.** Ich gehe normalerweise um zehn Uhr ins Bett.
■ **Bedtime!** Ab ins Bett!

bee NOUN
die Biene *fem*

★ **beef** NOUN
das Rindfleisch *neut*
■ **roast beef** das Roastbeef

★ **beefburger** NOUN
die Frikadelle *fem*

been VERB ▷ *see* **be**

★ **beer** NOUN
das Bier *neut* (PL die Biere or Bier)

When ordering more than one beer use the plural form **Bier**.

□ Two beers, please! Zwei Bier bitte!

beetle NOUN
der Käfer *masc* (PL die Käfer)

beetroot NOUN
die Rote Bete *fem*

★ **before** PREPOSITION, CONJUNCTION, ADVERB
1 vor
□ before Tuesday vor Dienstag
2 bevor
□ Wash your hands before eating. Wasch die Hände bevor du isst. □ I'll phone before I leave. Ich rufe an, bevor ich gehe.
3 schon (*already*)
□ I've seen this film before. Ich habe diesen Film schon gesehen. □ Have you been to Scotland before? Warst du schon einmal in Schottland?
■ **the day before** am Tag davor
■ **the week before** die Woche davor

beforehand ADVERB
vorher

to **beg** VERB
1 betteln [34] (*for money*)
2 anflehen [4] (PERFECT TENSE hat angefleht)
□ He begged me to stop. Er flehte mich an, aufzuhören.

began VERB ▷ *see* **begin**

beggar NOUN
der Bettler *masc* (PL die Bettler)
die Bettlerin *fem*

★ to **begin** VERB
anfangen [23] (PRESENT TENSE fängt an, IMPERFECT fing an, PERFECT TENSE hat angefangen)
■ **to begin doing something** anfangen [23] etwas zu tun

beginner NOUN
der Anfänger *masc* (PL die Anfänger)
die Anfängerin *fem*
□ I'm just a beginner. Ich bin noch Anfänger.

★ **beginning** NOUN
der Anfang *masc* (PL die Anfänge)
□ in the beginning am Anfang

begun VERB ▷ *see* **begin**

★ **behalf** NOUN
■ **on behalf of somebody** für jemanden □ on her behalf für sie

★ to **behave** VERB
sich benehmen [52] (PRESENT TENSE benimmt sich, IMPERFECT benahm sich, PERFECT TENSE hat sich benommen)
□ He behaved like an idiot. Er hat sich wie ein Idiot benommen. □ She behaved very badly. Sie hat sich sehr schlecht benommen.
■ **to behave oneself** sich anständig benehmen [52] □ Did the children behave themselves? Haben sich die Kinder anständig benommen?
■ **Behave!** Sei brav!

★ **behaviour** (US behavior) NOUN
das Benehmen *neut*

★ **behind** PREPOSITION, ADVERB
▷ *see also* **behind** NOUN
hinter

Use the accusative to express movement or a change of place. Use the dative when there is no change of place.

□ the wall behind the television die Wand hinter dem Fernseher □ The book fell behind the television. Das Buch fiel hinter den Fernseher.
■ **to be behind** (*late*) im Rückstand sein [65]
□ I'm behind with my revision. Ich bin mit dem Pauken im Rückstand.

★ **behind** NOUN
▷ *see also* **behind** PREPOSITION, ADVERB
der Hintern *masc* (GEN des Hintern, PL die Hintern)

beige ADJECTIVE
beige

Belgian ADJECTIVE
▷ *see also* **Belgian** NOUN
belgisch
■ **He's Belgian.** Er ist Belgier.
■ **She's Belgian.** Sie ist Belgierin.

Belgian NOUN
▷ *see also* **Belgian** ADJECTIVE
der Belgier *masc* (PL die Belgier)
die Belgierin *fem*
■ **the Belgians** die Belgier

★ **Belgium** NOUN
Belgien *neut*
■ **from Belgium** aus Belgien
■ **in Belgium** in Belgien
■ **to Belgium** nach Belgien

believe – beside

★ to **believe** VERB
glauben [38]
□ I don't believe you. Ich glaube dir nicht.
■ **to believe in something** an etwas glauben
[38] □ Do you believe in ghosts? Glaubst du an
Gespenster? □ to believe in God an Gott
glauben

★ **bell** NOUN
1 die Klingel *fem* (*doorbell, in school*)
■ **to ring the bell** klingeln [34]
■ **When the bell rings the children go out
into the playground.** Wenn es klingelt, gehen
die Kinder auf den Schulhof.
2 die Glocke *fem* (*in church*)
3 das Glöckchen *neut* (PL die Glöckchen)
□ Our cat has a bell on its neck. Unsere Katze
hat ein Glöckchen um den Hals.

belly NOUN
der Bauch *masc* (PL die Bäuche)

★ to **belong** VERB
gehören [38] (PERFECT TENSE hat gehört)
■ **to belong to somebody** jemandem gehören
[38] □ Who does it belong to? Wem gehört das?
□ That belongs to me. Das gehört mir.
■ **Do you belong to the club?** Bist du Mitglied
im Klub?
■ **Where does this belong?** Wo gehört das
hin?

belongings PL NOUN
die Sachen *fem pl*

★ **below** PREPOSITION, ADVERB
1 unterhalb
□ below the castle unterhalb der Burg
2 unter

Use the accusative to express movement or a
change of place. Use the dative when there is
no change of place.

□ The sun sank below the horizon. Die Sonne
sank unter den Horizont. □ We were below the
clouds. Wir waren unter den Wolken.
3 darunter
□ on the floor below im Stock darunter
■ **ten degrees below freezing** zehn Grad
unter null

★ **belt** NOUN
der Gürtel *masc* (PL die Gürtel)

beltway NOUN (US)
die Umgehungsstraße *fem*

bench NOUN
1 die Bank *fem* (PL die Bänke) (*seat*)
2 die Werkbank *fem* (PL die Werkbänke) (*for
woodwork*)

benchmark NOUN
der Maßstab *masc* (PL die Maßstäbe)

★ **bend** NOUN
▷ *see also* **bend** VERB
1 die Kurve *fem* (*in road*)
2 die Biegung *fem* (*in river*)

★ to **bend** VERB
▷ *see also* **bend** NOUN
1 beugen [38] (*leg, arm*)
□ I can't bend my arm. Ich kann den Arm nicht
beugen.
2 verbiegen (IMPERFECT verbog, PERFECT TENSE hat
verbogen) (*object*)
□ You've bent it. Du hast es verbogen.
■ **It bends easily.** Das lässt sich leicht biegen.
■ **'do not bend'** 'nicht knicken'.

to **bend down** VERB
sich bücken [48]

to **bend over** VERB
sich nach vorne beugen [38]

★ **beneath** PREPOSITION
unter

Use the accusative to express movement or a
change of place. Use the dative when there is
no change of place.

□ He placed his boots beneath the chair. Er
stellte seine Stiefel unter den Stuhl. □ She
found his jumper beneath the bed. Sie fand
seinen Pullover unter dem Bett.

★ **benefit** NOUN
▷ *see also* **benefit** VERB
der Vorteil *masc* (PL die Vorteile) (*advantage*)
■ **unemployment benefit** die
Arbeitslosenunterstützung

★ to **benefit** VERB
▷ *see also* **benefit** NOUN
profitieren [76]
□ You'll benefit from that experience. Du wirst
von dieser Erfahrung profitieren.
■ **He benefited from the change.** Die
Veränderung hat ihm gutgetan.

bent VERB ▷ *see* **bend**

bent ADJECTIVE
verbogen
□ a bent fork eine verbogene Gabel

berserk ADJECTIVE
■ **to go berserk** durchdrehen [15] □ She went
berserk. Sie hat durchgedreht.

berth NOUN
1 die Koje *fem* (*on ship*)
2 der Schlafwagenplatz *masc* (PL die
Schlafwagenplätze) (*on train*)

★ **beside** PREPOSITION
neben

Use the accusative to express movement or a
change of place. Use the dative when there is
no change of place.

□ the lamp beside the television die Lampe
neben dem Fernseher □ Put that chair beside
the television. Stell den Stuhl neben den
Fernseher.
■ **I was beside myself.** Ich war außer mir.
■ **That's beside the point.** Das tut hier nichts
zur Sache.

★ = core vocabulary

besides ADVERB

außerdem

□ Besides, it's too expensive. Und außerdem ist es zu teuer.

best ADJECTIVE, ADVERB

1 beste

□ He's the best player in the team. Er ist der beste Spieler der Mannschaft. □ Lexi's the best at maths. Lexi ist in Mathe die Beste.

2 am besten

□ Emma sings best. Emma singt am besten.

■ **to do one's best** sein Bestes tun [81] □ I did my best. Ich habe mein Bestes getan.

■ **to make the best of it** das Beste daraus machen [48] □ We'll have to make the best of it. Wir müssen das Beste daraus machen.

best man NOUN

der Trauzeuge *masc* (GEN des Trauzeugen, PL die Trauzeugen)

> **DID YOU KNOW...?**
> There is no real equivalent in Germany to 'best man'. A **Trauzeuge** is merely an official witness to the wedding ceremony.

bet NOUN

▷ *see also* **bet** VERB

die Wette *fem*

□ to make a bet eine Wette machen

to **bet** VERB

▷ *see also* **bet** NOUN

wetten [2]

□ I bet you he won't come. Wetten, dass er nicht kommt. □ I bet he forgot. Wetten, dass er es vergessen hat.

to **betray** VERB

verraten (PRESENT TENSE verrät, IMPERFECT verriet, PERFECT TENSE hat verraten)

better ADJECTIVE, ADVERB

besser

□ This one's better than that one. Dieses hier ist besser als das da. □ a better way to do it eine bessere Methode □ You'd better do it straight away. Das machst du besser sofort. □ I'd better go home. Ich gehe besser nach Hause. □ That's better! Das ist schon besser!

■ **better still** noch besser □ Go tomorrow, or better still, today. Geh morgen, oder noch besser heute.

■ **to get better 1** (*improve*) besser werden [91] □ I hope the weather gets better soon. Ich hoffe, das Wetter wird bald besser. □ My German is getting better. Mein Deutsch wird besser. **2** (*from illness*) sich erholen [19]

■ **I hope you get better soon.** Gute Besserung!

■ **to feel better** sich besser fühlen [38] □ Are you feeling better now? Fühlst du dich jetzt besser?

betting shop NOUN

das Wettbüro *neut* (PL die Wettbüros)

> **DID YOU KNOW...?**
> There are very few betting shops in Germany and betting is far less popular than in the UK.

★ **between** PREPOSITION

zwischen

> Use the accusative to express movement or a change of place. Use the dative when there is no change of place.

□ The cathedral is between the town hall and the river. Der Dom liegt zwischen dem Rathaus und dem Fluss. □ He sat down between the two girls. Er setzte sich zwischen die beiden Mädchen. □ between fifteen and twenty minutes zwischen fünfzehn und zwanzig Minuten

to **beware** VERB

■ **'Beware of the dog!'** 'Vorsicht bissiger Hund!'

to **bewilder** VERB

verwirren [84]

□ She was bewildered. Sie war verwirrt.

beyond PREPOSITION

hinter

□ There was a lake beyond the mountain. Hinter dem Berg war ein See.

■ **beyond belief** nicht zu glauben

■ **beyond repair** nicht mehr zu reparieren

biased ADJECTIVE

voreingenommen

★ **Bible** NOUN

die Bibel *fem*

★ **bicycle** NOUN

das Fahrrad *neut* (PL die Fahrräder)

★ **big** ADJECTIVE

groß

□ a big house ein großes Haus □ a bigger house ein größeres Haus □ my big brother mein großer Bruder □ her big sister ihre große Schwester

■ **He's a big guy.** Er ist kräftig gebaut.

> **WORD POWER**
> You can use a number of other words instead of **big** to mean 'large':
> **enormous** riesig
> □ an enormous cake ein riesiger Kuchen
> **gigantic** riesengroß
> □ gigantic rocks riesengroße Felsen
> **huge** riesig
> □ a huge garden ein riesiger Garten
> **massive** enorm groß
> □ a massive TV ein enorm großer Fernseher

bigheaded ADJECTIVE

eingebildet

★ **bike** NOUN

das Fahrrad *neut* (PL die Fahrräder)

□ by bike mit dem Fahrrad

Numbers in brackets refer to verb tables on pages 697 to 706.

381

bikini – black coffee

bikini NOUN
der Bikini masc (PL die Bikinis)

bilingual ADJECTIVE
zweisprachig

★ **bill** NOUN
1 die Rechnung fem
□ the gas bill die Gasrechnung
■ **Can we have the bill, please?** Können wir bitte zahlen?
2 der Geldschein masc (PL die Geldscheine) (banknote)
□ a dollar bill ein Dollarschein

★ **billion** NOUN
die Milliarde fem

bin NOUN
1 der Abfalleimer masc (PL die Abfalleimer) (indoors)
2 der Mülleimer masc (PL die Mülleimer) (outside)

bingo NOUN
das Bingo neut

binoculars PL NOUN
das Fernglas neut (PL die Ferngläser)
□ a pair of binoculars ein Fernglas

biochemistry NOUN
die Biochemie fem

★ **biodegradable** ADJECTIVE
biologisch abbaubar

biofuel NOUN
der Biokraftstoff masc (PL die Biokraftstoffe)

biography NOUN
die Biografie fem

★ **biology** NOUN
die Biologie fem

★ **bird** NOUN
der Vogel masc (PL die Vögel)

bird flu NOUN
die Vogelgrippe fem

bird-watching NOUN
■ **My hobby's bird-watching.** Mein Hobby ist das Beobachten von Vögeln.

Biro® NOUN
der Kuli masc (PL die Kulis)

★ **birth** NOUN
die Geburt fem
□ date of birth das Geburtsdatum

birth certificate NOUN
die Geburtsurkunde fem

birth control NOUN
die Empfängnisverhütung fem

★ **birthday** NOUN
der Geburtstag masc (PL die Geburtstage)
□ When's your birthday? Wann hast du Geburtstag? □ a birthday cake ein Geburtstagskuchen □ I'm going to have a birthday party. Ich gebe eine Geburtstagsparty.

★ **biscuit** NOUN
der Keks masc (PL die Kekse)

bishop NOUN
der Bischof masc (PL die Bischöfe)

★ **bit** VERB ▷ see bite

★ **bit** NOUN
das Stück neut (PL die Stücke) (piece)
□ Would you like another bit? Möchtest du noch ein Stück? □ a bit of cake ein Stück Kuche
■ **a bit 1** etwas □ He's a bit mad. Er ist etwas verrückt. □ a bit too hot etwas zu heiß **2** ein bisschen □ Wait a bit! Warte ein bisschen! □ D you play football? — A bit. Spielst du Fußball? — Ein bisschen.
■ **a bit of** (a little) etwas □ a bit of music etwas Musik □ It's a bit of a nuisance. Das ist schon etwas ärgerlich.
■ **to fall to bits** kaputtgehen [29]
■ **to take something to bits** etwas auseinandernehmen [52]
■ **bit by bit** nach und nach

bitch NOUN
1 das Miststück neut (PL die Miststücke) (rude: person)
2 die Hündin fem (female dog)

★ to **bite** VERB
▷ see also **bite** NOUN
1 beißen [6] (IMPERFECT biss, PERFECT TENSE hat gebissen) (person, dog)
2 stechen (PRESENT TENSE sticht, IMPERFECT stach, PERFECT TENSE hat gestochen) (insect)
□ I got bitten by mosquitoes. Ich bin von Mücken gestochen worden.
■ **to bite one's nails** an den Nägeln kauen [38]

★ **bite** NOUN
▷ see also **bite** VERB
1 der Stich masc (PL die Stiche) (insect bite)
2 der Biss masc (GEN des Bisses, PL die Bisse) (animal bite)
■ **to have a bite to eat** eine Kleinigkeit essen [20]

★ **bitter** ADJECTIVE
1 bitter
2 bitterkalt (weather, wind)
□ It's bitter today. Heute ist es bitterkalt.

★ **black** ADJECTIVE
schwarz
□ a black jacket eine schwarze Jacke

blackberry NOUN
die Brombeere fem

blackbird NOUN
die Amsel fem

blackboard NOUN
die Tafel fem

black coffee NOUN
der schwarze Kaffee masc (PL die schwarzen Kaffees)

★ = core vocabulary

blackcurrant NOUN
die Schwarze Johannisbeere *fem*

blackmail NOUN
▷ *see also* **blackmail** VERB
die Erpressung *fem*
□ That's blackmail! Das ist Erpressung!

to **blackmail** VERB
▷ *see also* **blackmail** NOUN
erpressen [7] (PERFECT TENSE hat erpresst)
□ He blackmailed her. Er erpresste sie.

blackout NOUN
der Stromausfall *masc* (PL die Stromausfälle) (*power cut*)
■ **to have a blackout** (*faint*) ohnmächtig werden [91]

black pudding NOUN
die Blutwurst *fem* (PL die Blutwürste)

blacksmith NOUN
der Schmied *masc*
□ He's a blacksmith. Er ist Schmied.

blade NOUN
die Klinge *fem*

to **blame** VERB
■ **Don't blame me!** Ich bin nicht schuld!
■ **I blame him.** Ich gebe ihm die Schuld.
■ **He blamed it on my sister.** Er gab meiner Schwester die Schuld.

blank ADJECTIVE
▷ *see also* **blank** NOUN
leer
■ **My mind went blank.** Ich hatte ein Brett vor dem Kopf.

blank NOUN
▷ *see also* **blank** ADJECTIVE
die Lücke *fem*
□ Fill in the blanks. Füllt die Lücken aus.

blank cheque NOUN
der Blankoscheck *masc* (PL die Blankoschecks)

★ **blanket** NOUN
die Decke *fem*

blast NOUN
■ **a bomb blast** eine Bombenexplosion

blatant ADJECTIVE
unverschämt
□ a blatant lie ein unverschämter Lügner

blaze NOUN
das Feuer *neut* (PL die Feuer)

blazer NOUN
der Blazer *masc* (PL die Blazer)

bleach NOUN
das Bleichmittel *neut* (PL die Bleichmittel)

bleached ADJECTIVE
gebleicht
□ bleached hair gebleichtes Haar

bleak ADJECTIVE
trostlos

□ The future looks bleak. Die Zukunft sieht trostlos aus.

to **bleed** VERB
bluten [2]
□ My nose is bleeding. Ich blute aus der Nase.

bleeper NOUN
der Piepser *masc* (PL die Piepser)

blender NOUN
der Mixer *masc* (PL die Mixer)

to **bless** VERB
segnen [53] (*religiously*)
■ **Bless you!** (*after sneezing*) Gesundheit!

blew VERB ▷ *see* **blow**

★ **blind** ADJECTIVE
▷ *see also* **blind** NOUN
blind

★ **blind** NOUN
▷ *see also* **blind** ADJECTIVE
das Rollo *neut* (PL die Rollos) (*fabric*)

blindfold NOUN
▷ *see also* **blindfold** VERB
die Augenbinde *fem*

to **blindfold** VERB
▷ *see also* **blindfold** NOUN
■ **to blindfold somebody** jemandem die Augen verbinden

to **blink** VERB
zwinkern [88]

bliss NOUN
■ **It was bliss!** Es war eine Wonne!

blister NOUN
die Blase *fem*

blizzard NOUN
der Schneesturm *masc* (PL die Schneestürme)

blob NOUN
der Tropfen *masc* (PL die Tropfen)
□ a blob of glue ein Tropfen Klebstoff

★ **block** NOUN
▷ *see also* **block** VERB
der Block *masc* (PL die Blöcke)
□ He lives in our block. Er lebt in unserem Block.
■ **a block of flats** ein Wohnblock *masc*

★ to **block** VERB
▷ *see also* **block** NOUN
blockieren [76] (PERFECT TENSE hat blockiert)

blockage NOUN
die Verstopfung *fem* (*in pipe or tube*)
□ The tea leaves have created a blockage in the pipe. Die Teeblätter haben eine Verstopfung im Rohr verursacht.

blog NOUN
▷ *see also* **blog** VERB
das/der Blog *neut/masc* (*internet*)

to **blog** VERB
▷ *see also* **blog** NOUN
bloggen [48]

Numbers in brackets refer to verb tables on pages 697 to 706.

383

□ He has been blogging about his school. Er hat über seine Schule gebloggt.

blogger NOUN
der Blogger *masc* (PL die Blogger)
die Bloggerin *fem*

blogpost NOUN
der Blogpost *masc* (PL die Blogposts)

bloke NOUN
der Typ *masc* (PL die Typen) (*informal*)

★ **blonde** ADJECTIVE
blond
□ She's got blonde hair. Sie hat blondes Haar.

★ **blood** NOUN
das Blut *neut*

blood pressure NOUN
der Blutdruck *masc*
□ to have high blood pressure hohen Blutdruck haben

blood sports PL NOUN
der Blutsport *masc*

blood test NOUN
die Blutuntersuchung *fem*

★ **blouse** NOUN
die Bluse *fem*

★ **blow** NOUN
▷ *see also* **blow** VERB
der Schlag *masc* (PL die Schläge)

★ to **blow** VERB
▷ *see also* **blow** NOUN
1 blasen (PRESENT TENSE bläst, IMPERFECT blies, PERFECT TENSE hat geblasen) (*person*)
2 wehen [38] (*wind*)
■ **to blow one's nose** sich die Nase putzen [36] □ Blow your nose! Putz dir die Nase!
■ **to blow a whistle** pfeifen
■ **to blow out a candle** eine Kerze ausblasen

to **blow up** VERB
1 in die Luft jagen [38]
□ The terrorists blew up a police station. Die Terroristen haben ein Polizeirevier in die Luft gejagt.
2 aufblasen
□ to blow up a balloon einen Luftballon aufblasen
■ **The house blew up.** Das Haus flog in die Luft.

blow-dry NOUN
das Föhnen *neut*
□ A cut and blow-dry, please. Schneiden und Föhnen bitte.

blown VERB ▷ *see* **blow**

★ **blue** ADJECTIVE
blau
□ a blue dress ein blaues Kleid
■ **It came out of the blue.** Das kam aus heiterem Himmel.

blues PL NOUN
der Blues *masc sing* (GEN des Blues) (*music*)

to **bluff** VERB
▷ *see also* **bluff** NOUN
bluffen [38]

bluff NOUN
▷ *see also* **bluff** VERB
der Bluff *masc* (PL die Bluffs)
□ It's just a bluff. Das ist ein Bluff.

blunder NOUN
der Schnitzer *masc* (PL die Schnitzer)

blunt ADJECTIVE
1 unverblümt (*person*)
2 stumpf (*knife*)

to **blush** VERB
rot werden [91] (PRESENT TENSE wird rot, IMPERFECT wurde rot, PERFECT TENSE ist rot geworden)

★ **board** NOUN
1 das Brett *neut* (PL die Bretter)
2 die Tafel *fem* (*blackboard*)
□ Write it on the board. Schreib es an die Tafel.
■ **It's on the board in the office.** Es hängt am schwarzen Brett im Büro. (*noticeboard*)
■ **on board** an Bord
■ **full board** die Vollpension

boarder NOUN
der Internatsschüler *masc* (PL die Internatsschüler)
die Internatsschülerin *fem*

board game NOUN
das Brettspiel *neut* (PL die Brettspiele)

boarding card NOUN
die Bordkarte *fem*

boarding school NOUN
das Internat *neut* (PL die Internate)
□ I go to boarding school. Ich gehe in ein Internat.

to **boast** VERB
prahlen [38]
□ to boast about something mit etwas prahlen

★ **boat** NOUN
das Boot *neut* (PL die Boote)

★ **body** NOUN
der Körper *masc* (PL die Körper)

bodybuilding NOUN
das Bodybuilding *neut*
□ He does bodybuilding. Er macht Bodybuilding.

bodyguard NOUN
der Leibwächter *masc* (PL die Leibwächter)

bog NOUN
das Moor *neut* (PL die Moore) (*marsh*)

★ **boil** NOUN
▷ *see also* **boil** VERB
der/das Furunkel *masc/neut* (PL die Furunkel)

to **boil** VERB
▷ see also **boil** NOUN
kochen [48]
□ to boil some water Wasser kochen □ to boil an egg ein Ei kochen □ The water's boiling. Das Wasser kocht.

to **boil over** VERB
überkochen [4]
□ The milk boiled over. Die Milch ist übergekocht.

boiled ADJECTIVE
■ a soft-boiled egg ein weich gekochtes Ei *neut*
■ boiled potatoes Salzkartoffeln *fem pl*

boiling ADJECTIVE
■ It's boiling in here! Hier ist eine Bruthitze!
■ boiling hot brütend heiß □ a boiling hot day ein brütend heißer Tag

bolt NOUN
1 der Riegel *masc* (PL die Riegel) (*on door*)
2 der Bolzen *masc* (PL die Bolzen) (*with nut*)

bomb NOUN
▷ see also **bomb** VERB
die Bombe *fem*

> Note that you pronounce the second 'b' in German.

to **bomb** VERB
▷ see also **bomb** NOUN
bombardieren [76] (PERFECT TENSE hat bombardiert)

bomber NOUN
der Bomber *masc* (PL die Bomber)

> Note that you pronounce the second 'b' in German.

bombing NOUN
der Bombenangriff *masc* (PL die Bombenangriffe)

bond NOUN
die Bindung *fem* (*between people*)
□ a strong bond eine enge Bindung

bone NOUN
1 der Knochen *masc* (PL die Knochen) (*of human, animal*)
2 die Gräte *fem* (*of fish*)

bone dry ADJECTIVE
knochentrocken

bonfire NOUN
das Feuer *neut* (PL die Feuer)

bonnet NOUN
die Motorhaube *fem* (*of car*)

bonus NOUN
1 der Bonus *masc* (PL die Bonusse) (*extra payment*)
2 der Vorteil *masc* (PL die Vorteile) (*added advantage*)

★ **book** NOUN
▷ see also **book** VERB
das Buch *neut* (PL die Bücher)

★ to **book** VERB
▷ see also **book** NOUN
buchen [48]
□ We haven't booked. Wir haben nicht gebucht.

bookcase NOUN
1 das Bücherregal *neut* (PL die Bücherregale) (*open*)
2 der Bücherschrank *masc* (PL die Bücherschränke) (*with doors*)

booklet NOUN
die Broschüre *fem*

bookmark NOUN
das Lesezeichen *neut* (PL die Lesezeichen)

bookshelf NOUN
das Bücherbrett *neut* (PL die Bücherbretter)
■ bookshelves das Bücherregal *sing*

★ **bookshop** NOUN
die Buchhandlung *fem*

to **boost** VERB
Auftrieb geben [28] (PRESENT TENSE gibt, IMPERFECT gab, PERFECT TENSE hat gegeben)
□ The win boosted our morale. Der Sieg gab uns moralischen Auftrieb.

★ **boot** NOUN
1 der Kofferraum *masc* (PL die Kofferräume) (*of car*)
2 der Stiefel *masc* (PL die Stiefel) (*footwear*)
■ football boots die Fußballschuhe *masc pl*

booze NOUN
der Alkohol *masc*

★ **border** NOUN
die Grenze *fem*

bore VERB ▷ see **bear**

★ **bored** ADJECTIVE
■ to be bored sich langweilen [38] □ I'm bored. Ich langweile mich.
■ She gets bored easily. Ihr wird schnell langweilig.

boredom NOUN
die Langeweile *fem* (GEN der Langeweile)

★ **boring** ADJECTIVE
langweilig

★ **born** ADJECTIVE
■ to be born geboren werden [91]
■ I was born in 1982. Ich bin 1982 geboren.

borne VERB ▷ see **bear**

★ to **borrow** VERB
ausleihen (IMPERFECT lieh aus, PERFECT TENSE hat ausgeliehen)
□ Can I borrow your pen? Kann ich deinen Schreiber ausleihen?
■ to borrow something from somebody sich etwas von jemandem leihen □ I borrowed some money from a friend. Ich habe mir von einem Freund Geld geliehen.

Bosnia NOUN
Bosnien *neut*

Numbers in brackets refer to verb tables on pages 697 to 706.

385

b

Bosnian - boxer

■ **from Bosnia** aus Bosnien
■ **to Bosnia** nach Bosnien

Bosnian ADJECTIVE
bosnisch

★ **boss** NOUN
der Chef masc (PL die Chefs)
die Chefin fem

to **boss around** VERB
■ **to boss somebody around** jemanden
herumkommandieren [76]

bossy ADJECTIVE
herrisch

★ **both** ADJECTIVE, PRONOUN
beide
□ We both went. Wir sind beide gegangen.
□ Emma and Jane both went. Emma und Jane
sind beide gegangen. □ Both of your answers
are wrong. Beide Antworten sind falsch. □ Both
of them have left. Beide sind gegangen. □ Both
of us went. Wir sind beide gegangen.
■ **both ... and** sowohl ... als auch □ He speaks
both French and Italian. Er spricht sowohl
Französisch als auch Italienisch.

★ **bother** NOUN
▷ see also **bother** VERB
der Ärger masc
□ We had a spot of bother with the car. Wir
hatten Ärger mit dem Auto.
■ **No bother!** Kein Problem!

★ to **bother** VERB
▷ see also **bother** NOUN
1 beunruhigen [7] (PERFECT TENSE hat beunruhigt)
(worry)
□ Is something bothering you? Beunruhigt dich
etwas?
2 stören [38] (disturb)
□ I'm sorry to bother you. Es tut mir leid, dass
ich dich störe.
■ **Don't bother!** Nicht nötig!
■ **to bother to do something** es für nötig
halten [24], etwas zu tun □ He didn't bother to
tell me about it. Er hat es nicht für nötig
gehalten, es mir zu sagen.

★ **bottle** NOUN
die Flasche fem

bottle bank NOUN
der Altglascontainer masc (PL die
Altglascontainer)

bottle-opener NOUN
der Flaschenöffner masc (PL die Flaschenöffner)

★ **bottom** NOUN
▷ see also **bottom** ADJECTIVE
1 der Boden masc (PL die Böden) (of container,
bag, sea)
2 der Hintern masc (GEN des Hinterns, PL die
Hintern) (buttocks)
3 das Ende neut (PL die Enden) (of list)
■ **at the bottom of page two** unten auf Seite
zwei

★ **bottom** ADJECTIVE
▷ see also **bottom** NOUN
unterste
□ the bottom shelf das unterste Regalbrett
■ **the bottom sheet** das Bettlaken

bought VERB ▷ see **buy**

to **bounce** VERB
hüpfen [38] (PERFECT TENSE ist gehüpft)

bouncer NOUN
der Rausschmeißer masc (PL die
Rausschmeißer)

bound ADJECTIVE
■ **He's bound to say that.** Er muss das ja
sagen.
■ **She's bound to come.** Sie kommt sicher.

boundary NOUN
die Grenze fem

bow NOUN
▷ see also **bow** VERB
1 die Schleife fem (knot)
□ to tie a bow eine Schleife machen
2 der Bogen masc (PL die Bogen)
□ a bow and arrow ein Pfeil und Bogen

to **bow** VERB
▷ see also **bow** NOUN
sich verneigen [84] (PERFECT TENSE hat sich
verneigt)

bowels PL NOUN
die Eingeweide neut pl

★ **bowl** NOUN
▷ see also **bowl** VERB
die Schale fem (for soup, cereal)

★ to **bowl** VERB
▷ see also **bowl** NOUN
werfen [92] (PRESENT TENSE wirft, IMPERFECT warf
PERFECT TENSE hat geworfen) (in cricket)

bowler NOUN
der Werfer masc (PL die Werfer)
die Werferin fem (in cricket)

bowling NOUN
das Bowling neut
■ **to go bowling** Bowling spielen [38]
■ **a bowling alley** eine Bowlingbahn

bowls SING NOUN
das Boccia neut (GEN des Boccia)

The 'cc' in **Boccia** is pronounced like 'ch'
in church.

□ to play bowls Boccia spielen

bow tie NOUN
die Fliege fem

★ **box** NOUN
die Schachtel fem
□ a box of matches eine Schachtel Streichhölze
■ **a cardboard box** ein Karton masc

boxer NOUN
der Boxer masc (PL die Boxer)

★ = core vocabulary

boxer shorts PL NOUN
die Boxershorts *pl*
□ He was wearing a pair of boxer shorts. Er trug
Boxershorts.

boxing NOUN
das Boxen *neut*

Boxing Day NOUN
■ It was Boxing Day. Es war der zweite
Weihnachtstag.

boy NOUN
der Junge *masc* (GEN des Jungen, PL die Jungen)

boyfriend NOUN
der Freund *masc* (PL die Freunde)
□ Have you got a boyfriend? Hast du einen
Freund?

bra NOUN
der BH *masc* (PL die BHs)

brace NOUN
die Zahnspange *fem* (on teeth)
□ She wears a brace. Sie hat eine Zahnspange.

bracelet NOUN
das Armband *neut* (PL die Armbänder)

brackets PL NOUN
die Klammern *fem pl*
□ in brackets in Klammern

brain NOUN
das Gehirn *neut* (PL die Gehirne)

brainy ADJECTIVE
gescheit

brake NOUN
▷ see also **brake** VERB
die Bremse *fem*

to **brake** VERB
▷ see also **brake** NOUN
bremsen [36]

branch NOUN
1 der Zweig *masc* (PL die Zweige) (of tree)
2 die Filiale *fem* (of bank)

brand NOUN
die Marke *fem*
□ a well-known brand of coffee eine bekannte
Kaffeemarke

brand name NOUN
der Markenname *masc* (GEN des
Markennamens, PL die Markennamen)

brand-new ADJECTIVE
brandneu

brandy NOUN
der Weinbrand *masc* (PL die Weinbrände)

brass NOUN
das Messing *neut* (metal)
■ the brass section die Blechbläser *masc pl*

brass band NOUN
die Blaskapelle *fem*

brat NOUN
■ He's a spoiled brat. Er ist ein verwöhnter
Balg.

★ **brave** ADJECTIVE
mutig

> **BE CAREFUL!**
> Do not translate **brave** by brav.

Brazil NOUN
Brasilien *neut*
■ from Brazil aus Brasilien
■ to Brazil nach Brasilien

★ **bread** NOUN
das Brot *neut* (PL die Brote)
□ bread and butter Brot mit Butter
■ brown bread das Graubrot
■ white bread das Weißbrot

> **DID YOU KNOW...?**
> There is a huge variety of types of bread in
> Germany which can't simply be divided into
> brown and white.

★ **break** NOUN
▷ see also **break** VERB
die Pause *fem* (rest)
□ to take a break eine Pause machen □ during
morning break während der Vormittagspause
■ the Christmas break die
Weihnachtsfeiertage *masc pl*
■ Give me a break! Mach mal halblang!

★ to **break** VERB
▷ see also **break** NOUN
1 kaputt machen [48] (PERFECT TENSE hat kaputt
gemacht)
□ Careful, you'll break something! Vorsicht, du
machst sonst was kaputt!
2 brechen [11] (PRESENT TENSE bricht, IMPERFECT
brach, PERFECT TENSE hat gebrochen) (record, law)
□ to break a promise sein Versprechen brechen
■ to break one's leg sich das Bein brechen
[11] □ I broke my leg. Ich habe mir das Bein
gebrochen.
■ He broke his arm. Er hat sich den Arm
gebrochen.
3 brechen [11] (get broken)
□ Careful, it'll break! Vorsicht, es bricht!

to **break down** VERB
eine Panne haben [32] (PRESENT TENSE hat eine
Panne, IMPERFECT hatte eine Panne, PERFECT
TENSE hat eine Panne gehabt)
□ The car broke down. Das Auto hatte eine
Panne.

to **break in** VERB
einbrechen [11] (PRESENT TENSE bricht ein,
IMPERFECT brach ein, PERFECT TENSE hat
eingebrochen)

to **break into** VERB
einbrechen [11] in (PRESENT TENSE bricht ein,
IMPERFECT brach ein, PERFECT TENSE ist
eingebrochen)
□ Thieves broke into the house. Diebe brachen
in das Haus ein.

breakdown - bright

to **break off** VERB
abbrechen [11] (PRESENT TENSE bricht ab, IMPERFECT brach ab, PERFECT TENSE hat abgebrochen)
□ I broke off a small piece. Ich habe ein kleines Stück abgebrochen.

to **break open** VERB
aufbrechen [11] (PRESENT TENSE bricht auf, IMPERFECT brach auf, PERFECT TENSE hat aufgebrochen) (door, cupboard)

to **break out** VERB
ausbrechen [11] (PRESENT TENSE bricht aus, IMPERFECT brach aus, PERFECT TENSE ist ausgebrochen)
■ **to break out in a rash** einen Ausschlag bekommen [40]

to **break up** VERB
1 sich auflösen [4] (PERFECT TENSE hat sich aufgelöst) (crowd)
2 zu Ende gehen [29] (IMPERFECT ging zu Ende, PERFECT TENSE ist zu Ende gegangen) (meeting, party)
3 sich trennen [38] (couple)
■ **to break up a fight** eine Schlägerei beenden [54]
■ **We break up next Wednesday.** Nächsten Mittwoch ist der letzte Schultag.

breakdown NOUN
1 die Panne fem (in vehicle)
□ to have a breakdown eine Panne haben
2 der Nervenzusammenbruch masc (PL die Nervenzusammenbrüche) (mental)
□ to have a breakdown einen Nervenzusammenbruch haben

breakdown van NOUN
das Pannenfahrzeug neut (PL die Pannenfahrzeuge)

★ **breakfast** NOUN
das Frühstück neut (PL die Frühstücke)
□ What would you like for breakfast? Was möchtest du zum Frühstück?
■ **to have breakfast** frühstücken [38]

break-in NOUN
der Einbruch masc (PL die Einbrüche)

break time NOUN
die Pause fem (in School)

breast NOUN
die Brust fem (PL die Brüste)
■ **chicken breast** die Hähnchenbrust

to **breast-feed** VERB
stillen [48]

breaststroke NOUN
das Brustschwimmen neut

★ **breath** NOUN
der Atem masc
□ to be out of breath außer Atem sein
■ **to have bad breath** Mundgeruch haben [32]
■ **to get one's breath back** verschnaufen [84]

★ to **breathe** VERB
atmen [3]

to **breathe in** VERB
einatmen [4]

to **breathe out** VERB
ausatmen [4]

to **breed** VERB
▷ see also **breed** NOUN
züchten [2]
□ to breed dogs Hunde züchten

breed NOUN
▷ see also **breed** VERB
die Rasse fem

breeze NOUN
die Brise fem

brewery NOUN
die Brauerei fem

bribe NOUN
▷ see also **bribe** VERB
die Bestechung fem

to **bribe** VERB
▷ see also **bribe** NOUN
bestechen (PRESENT TENSE besticht, IMPERFECT bestach, PERFECT TENSE hat bestochen)

brick NOUN
der Backstein masc (PL die Backsteine)
□ a brick wall eine Backsteinmauer

bricklayer NOUN
der Maurer masc (PL die Maurer)
die Maurerin fem

bride NOUN
die Braut fem (PL die Bräute)

bridegroom NOUN
der Bräutigam masc (PL die Bräutigame)

bridesmaid NOUN
die Brautjungfer fem

★ **bridge** NOUN
1 die Brücke fem
□ a suspension bridge eine Hängebrücke
2 das Bridge neut (GEN des Bridge)
□ to play bridge Bridge spielen

brief ADJECTIVE
kurz

briefcase NOUN
die Aktentasche fem

briefly ADVERB
kurz

briefs PL NOUN
die Unterhose fem
□ a pair of briefs eine Unterhose

★ **bright** ADJECTIVE
1 hell (light)
2 leuchtend (colour)
□ a brighter colour eine leuchtendere Farbe
■ **bright blue** hellblau

★ = core vocabulary

3 intelligent
□ He's not very bright. Er ist nicht besonders intelligent.

brilliant ADJECTIVE
1 prima (*wonderful*)
□ Brilliant! Prima!
2 glänzend (*clever*)
□ a brilliant scientist ein glänzender Wissenschaftler

to **bring** VERB
1 bringen [13] (IMPERFECT brachte, PERFECT TENSE hat gebracht)
□ Could you bring me my trainers? Könntest du mir meine Sportschuhe bringen?
2 mitbringen [13] (*bring along*)
□ Bring warm clothes. Bringt warme Kleidung mit! □ Can I bring a friend? Darf ich einen Freund mitbringen?

to **bring about** VERB
herbeiführen [4]

to **bring back** VERB
zurückbringen [13]

to **bring forward** VERB
vorverlegen [84]
□ The meeting was brought forward. Die Sitzung wurde vorverlegt.

to **bring up** VERB
aufziehen [96]
□ She brought up 5 children on her own. Sie hat fünf Kinder alleine aufgezogen.

★ **Britain** NOUN
Großbritannien *neut*
■ **from Britain** aus Großbritannien
■ **in Britain** in Großbritannien
■ **to Britain** nach Großbritannien
■ **Great Britain** Großbritannien

★ **British** ADJECTIVE
britisch
■ **He's British.** Er ist Brite.
■ **She's British.** Sie ist Britin.
■ **the British** die Briten *masc pl*
■ **the British Isles** die Britischen Inseln

Brittany NOUN
die Bretagne *fem*
■ **in Brittany** in der Bretagne

broad ADJECTIVE
breit (*wide*)
■ **in broad daylight** am helllichten Tag

broadband NOUN
das Breitband *neut*
■ **a broadband cable** ein Breitbandkabel *masc*

broadcast NOUN
▷ *see also* **broadcast** VERB
die Sendung *fem*

to **broadcast** VERB
▷ *see also* **broadcast** NOUN
senden

□ The interview was broadcast all over the world. Das Interview wurde in der ganzen Welt gesendet.

broad-minded ADJECTIVE
tolerant

★ **broccoli** SING NOUN
der Brokkoli *masc pl* (PL die Brokkoli(s))
□ Broccoli is her favourite vegetable. Ihr Lieblingsgemüse ist Brokkoli.

brochure NOUN
die Broschüre *fem*

to **broil** VERB (US)
grillen [48]

broke VERB ▷ *see* **break**

broke ADJECTIVE
■ **to be broke** (*without money*) pleite sein [65]

broken VERB ▷ *see* **break**

broken ADJECTIVE
1 kaputt
□ It's broken. Es ist kaputt.
2 gebrochen (*limb*)
□ He's got a broken arm. Er hat einen gebrochenen Arm.

bronchitis NOUN
die Bronchitis *fem*

bronze NOUN
die Bronze *fem*
□ the bronze medal die Bronzemedaille

brooch NOUN
die Brosche *fem*

broom NOUN
der Besen *masc* (PL die Besen)

★ **brother** NOUN
der Bruder *masc* (PL die Brüder)
□ my brother mein Bruder □ my big brother mein großer Bruder

brother-in-law NOUN
der Schwager *masc* (PL die Schwäger)

brought VERB ▷ *see* **bring**

★ **brown** ADJECTIVE
braun
■ **brown bread** das Graubrot

Brownie NOUN
der Wichtel *masc* (PL die Wichtel) (*Girl Guide*)

to **browse** VERB
browsen [38] (PERFECT TENSE hat gebrowst) (*computer*)
■ **to browse in a shop** sich in einem Geschäft umsehen [64]

browser NOUN
der Browser *masc* (PL die Browser) (*internet*)

bruise NOUN
der blaue Fleck *masc* (PL die blauen Flecke)

★ **brush** NOUN
▷ *see also* **brush** VERB

Numbers in brackets refer to verb tables on pages 697 to 706.

389

brush – bump

1 die Bürste *fem*

2 der Pinsel *masc* (PL die Pinsel) (*paintbrush*)

★ to **brush** VERB

▷ *see also* **brush** NOUN

bürsten [2]

■ **to brush one's hair** sich die Haare bürsten [2] □ I brushed my hair. Ich habe mir die Haare gebürstet.

■ **to brush one's teeth** die Zähne putzen [36] □ I've brushed my teeth. Ich habe die Zähne geputzt.

Brussels NOUN

Brüssel *neut*

■ **to Brussels** nach Brüssel

Brussels sprouts PL NOUN

der Rosenkohl *masc sing*

□ Do you like Brussels sprouts? Magst du Rosenkohl?

brutal ADJECTIVE

brutal

BSc ABBREVIATION (= *Bachelor of Science*)

der Magister *masc* (PL die Magister)

■ **She's got a BSc in Chemistry.** Sie hat einen Magistertitel in Chemie.

bubble NOUN

die Blase *fem*

bubble bath NOUN

das Schaumbad *neut* (PL die Schaumbäder)

bubble gum NOUN

der Bubblegum *masc* (PL die Bubblegums)

bucket NOUN

der Eimer *masc* (PL die Eimer)

buckle NOUN

die Schnalle *fem* (*on belt, watch, shoe*)

Buddhism NOUN

der Buddhismus *masc* (GEN des Buddhismus)

Buddhist ADJECTIVE

buddhistisch

buddy NOUN (US)

der Kumpel *masc* (PL die Kumpel)

★ **budget** NOUN

▷ *see also* **budget** VERB

das Budget *neut* (PL die Budgets)

★ to **budget** VERB

▷ *see also* **budget** NOUN

einplanen [4] (PERFECT TENSE hat eingeplant)

□ They budgeted $10 million for advertising. Sie planten 10 Millionen Dollar für Werbung ein.

budgie NOUN

der Wellensittich *masc* (PL die Wellensittiche)

buffet NOUN

das Büfett *neut* (PL die Büfetts)

buffet car NOUN

der Speisewagen *masc* (PL die Speisewagen)

bug NOUN

1 die Wanze *fem* (*insect*)

■ There are many bugs there. Dort gibt es viel Ungeziefer.

■ a stomach bug eine Magen-Darm-Infektion

■ There's a bug going round. Da geht etwas herum.

2 der Programmfehler *masc* (PL die Programmfehler) (*in computer*)

bugged ADJECTIVE

verwanzt

□ The room was bugged. Das Zimmer war verwanzt.

buggy NOUN

der Kinderwagen *masc* (PL die Kinderwagen)

★ to **build** VERB

bauen [38]

□ They're going to build houses here. Hier werden Häuser gebaut.

to **build up** VERB

zunehmen [52] (*increase*)

builder NOUN

1 der Bauunternehmer *masc* (PL die Bauunternehmer)

die Bauunternehmerin *fem* (*owner of firm*)

2 der Bauarbeiter *masc* (PL die Bauarbeiter)

die Bauarbeiterin *fem* (*worker*)

★ **building** NOUN

das Gebäude *neut* (PL die Gebäude)

built VERB ▷ *see* **build**

bulb NOUN

die Glühbirne *fem* (*electric*)

Bulgaria NOUN

Bulgarien *neut*

■ **from Bulgaria** aus Bulgarien

■ **to Bulgaria** nach Bulgarien

bull NOUN

der Stier *masc* (PL die Stiere)

bullet NOUN

die Kugel *fem*

bulletin board NOUN

das Schwarze Brett *neut* (PL die Schwarzen Bretter) (*computer*)

bullfighting NOUN

der Stierkampf *masc* (PL die Stierkämpfe)

bully NOUN

▷ *see also* **bully** VERB

■ **Many children are victims of online bullies.** Viele Kinder werden im Internet gemobbt.

to **bully** VERB

▷ *see also* **bully** NOUN

mobben [48] (PERFECT TENSE hat gemobbt)

bum NOUN

der Po *masc* (PL die Pos) (*informal: bottom*)

bum bag NOUN

die Gürteltasche *fem*

bump NOUN

▷ *see also* **bump into** VERB

★ = core vocabulary

b

1 die Beule *fem* (*lump*)
2 der Zusammenstoß *masc* (GEN des Zusammenstoßes, PL die Zusammenstöße) (*minor accident*)
■ **We had a bump.** Es hat gebumst.

to bump into VERB
▷ *see also* **bump** NOUN
■ **to bump into something** gegen etwas laufen [43] □ She bumped into the wall. Sie ist gegen die Wand gelaufen.
■ **We bumped into his car.** Wir sind in sein Auto gefahren.
■ **I bumped into an old friend.** Ich bin zufällig einem alten Freund begegnet.

bumper NOUN
die Stoßstange *fem*

bumpy ADJECTIVE
holperig

bun NOUN
das Brötchen *neut* (PL die Brötchen)

★ **bunch** NOUN
■ **a bunch of flowers** ein Blumenstrauß *masc*
■ **a bunch of grapes** eine Traube
■ **a bunch of keys** ein Schlüsselbund *masc*

bunches PL NOUN
die Rattenschwänze *masc pl*
□ She has her hair in bunches. Sie hat Rattenschwänze.

bungalow NOUN
der Bungalow *masc* (PL die Bungalows)

bunk NOUN
1 das Bett *neut* (PL die Betten)
2 die Koje *fem* (*on ship*)

bunk beds PL NOUN
das Etagenbett *neut sing*

★ **burger** NOUN
der Hamburger *masc* (PL die Hamburger)

★ **burglar** NOUN
der Einbrecher *masc* (PL die Einbrecher)
die Einbrecherin *fem*

to burglarize VERB (US)
einbrechen [11] in +*acc* (PRESENT TENSE bricht ein, IMPERFECT brach ein, PERFECT TENSE ist eingebrochen)
□ Her house was burglarized. Bei ihr wurde eingebrochen.

burglary NOUN
der Einbruch *masc* (PL die Einbrüche)

to burgle VERB
einbrechen [11] in +*acc* (PRESENT TENSE bricht ein, IMPERFECT brach ein, PERFECT TENSE ist eingebrochen)
□ Her house was burgled. Bei ihr wurde eingebrochen.

★ **burn** NOUN
▷ *see also* **burn** VERB
die Verbrennung *fem*

★ **to burn** VERB
▷ *see also* **burn** NOUN
1 verbrennen [12] (IMPERFECT verbrannte, PERFECT TENSE hat verbrannt) (*rubbish, documents*)
2 anbrennen lassen [42] (PRESENT TENSE lässt anbrennen, IMPERFECT ließ anbrennen, PERFECT TENSE hat anbrennen lassen) (*food*)
□ I burned the cake. Ich habe den Kuchen anbrennen lassen.
3 brennen [12] (IMPERFECT brannte, PERFECT TENSE hat gebrannt) (*CD, DVD*)
■ **to burn oneself** sich verbrennen [12] □ I burned myself on the oven door. Ich habe mich an der Ofentür verbrannt.
■ **I've burned my hand.** Ich habe mir die Hand verbrannt.
■ **to burn down** abbrennen [12] □ The factory burned down. Die Fabrik ist abgebrannt.

★ **to burst** VERB
platzen [36] (PERFECT TENSE ist geplatzt)
□ The balloon burst. Der Luftballon ist geplatzt.
■ **to burst a balloon** einen Luftballon platzen lassen [42]
■ **to burst out laughing** laut loslachen [4]
■ **to burst into flames** in Flammen aufgehen [29]
■ **to burst into tears** in Tränen ausbrechen [11]

★ **to bury** VERB
1 begraben (PRESENT TENSE begräbt, IMPERFECT begrub, PERFECT TENSE hat begraben) (*dead people, animals*)
□ We buried my guinea pig in the garden. Wir haben mein Meerschweinchen im Garten begraben.
2 vergraben (*things*)
□ My dog buries his bones. Mein Hund vergräbt seine Knochen.

★ **bus** NOUN
der Bus *masc* (GEN des Busses, PL die Busse)
□ the bus driver der Busfahrer □ the school bus der Schulbus
■ **a bus pass** (*monthly*) eine Monatskarte für den Bus

DID YOU KNOW...?
Almost all German cities operate an integrated public transport system; you can buy a weekly (**Wochenkarte**), monthly (**Monatskarte**) or yearly (**Jahreskarte**) pass which is valid for that period on all buses, trams and light railway vehicles in a particular zone.

■ **a bus station** ein Busbahnhof *masc*
■ **a bus ticket** eine Busfahrkarte

bush NOUN
der Busch *masc* (PL die Büsche)

★ **business** NOUN
1 die Firma *fem* (PL die Firmen) (*firm*)
□ He's got his own business. Er hat seine eigene Firma.

Numbers in brackets refer to verb tables on pages 697 to 706.

391

b

2 das Geschäft neut (PL die Geschäfte) (commerce)
  □ a business trip eine Geschäftsreise
  ■ He's away on business. Er ist geschäftlich unterwegs.
  ■ It's none of my business. Das geht mich nichts an.

★ **businessman** NOUN
  der Geschäftsmann masc (PL die Geschäftsleute)

★ **businesswoman** NOUN
  die Geschäftsfrau fem

busker NOUN
  der Straßenmusikant masc (GEN des Straßenmusikanten, PL die Straßenmusikanten)
  die Straßenmusikantin fem

bus stop NOUN
  die Bushaltestelle fem

bust NOUN
  der Busen masc (PL die Busen) (chest)
  ■ bust measurement die Oberweite

★ **busy** ADJECTIVE
  1 beschäftigt (person)
  2 belebt (shop, street)
  3 besetzt (phone line)
  ■ It's been a busy day. Es war viel los heute.

busy signal NOUN (US)
  das Besetztzeichen neut (PL die Besetztzeichen)

★ **but** CONJUNCTION
  aber
  □ I'd like to come, but I'm busy. Ich würde gerne kommen, aber ich habe zu tun.

butcher NOUN
  der Metzger masc (PL die Metzger)
  die Metzgerin fem
  □ He's a butcher. Er ist Metzger.

★ **butcher's** NOUN
  die Metzgerei fem

★ **butter** NOUN
  die Butter fem

butterfly NOUN
  der Schmetterling masc (PL die Schmetterlinge)

buttocks PL NOUN
  der Hintern masc sing (GEN des Hintern, PL die Hintern)

★ **button** NOUN
  der Knopf masc (PL die Knöpfe)

★ to **buy** VERB
  ▷ see also **buy** NOUN
  kaufen [38]
  □ He bought me an ice cream. Er hat mir ein Eis gekauft.
  ■ to buy something from somebody etwas von jemandem kaufen [38] □ I bought a watch from him. Ich habe von ihm eine Uhr gekauft.

★ **buy** NOUN
  ▷ see also **buy** VERB
  der Kauf masc (PL die Käufe)
  □ It was a good buy. Es war ein guter Kauf.

★ **by** PREPOSITION
  1 von
    □ They were caught by the police. Sie wurden von der Polizei erwischt. □ a painting by Picasso ein Gemälde von Picasso
  2 mit
    □ by car mit dem Auto □ by train mit dem Zug
    □ by bus mit dem Bus
  3 bei (close to)
    □ Where's the bank? — It's by the post office. Wo ist die Bank? — Sie ist bei der Post.
    ■ by day bei Tag
    ■ by night bei Nacht
  4 bis (not later than)
    □ We have to be there by four o'clock. Wir müssen bis vier Uhr dort sein.
    ■ by the time ... bis ... □ By the time I got there it was too late. Bis ich dort war, war es zu spät.
    ■ That's fine by me. Ist in Ordnung!
    ■ all by himself ganz allein
    ■ all by herself ganz allein
    ■ I did it all by myself. Ich habe es ganz allein gemacht.
    ■ by the way übrigens

★ **bye** EXCLAMATION
  tschüss!

bypass NOUN
  die Umgehungsstraße fem (road)

★ = core vocabulary

Cc

cab NOUN
das Taxi *neut* (PL die Taxis)

cabbage NOUN
der Kohl *masc*

cabin NOUN
die Kabine *fem* (*on ship*)

cabinet NOUN
■ **a bathroom cabinet** ein
Badezimmerschränkchen *neut*

cable NOUN
das Kabel *neut* (PL die Kabel)

cable car NOUN
die Drahtseilbahn *fem*

cable television NOUN
das Kabelfernsehen *neut*

cactus NOUN
der Kaktus *masc* (GEN des Kaktus, PL die
Kakteen)

cadet NOUN
■ **a police cadet** ein Polizeischüler *masc*
■ **a cadet officer** ein Offiziersanwärter *masc*

café NOUN
das Café *neut* (PL die Cafés)

cage NOUN
der Käfig *masc* (PL die Käfige)

cagoule NOUN
die Windjacke *fem*

cake NOUN
der Kuchen *masc* (PL die Kuchen)

to calculate VERB
rechnen [53]

calculation NOUN
die Rechnung *fem*

calculator NOUN
der Taschenrechner *masc* (PL die
Taschenrechner)

calendar NOUN
der Kalender *masc* (PL die Kalender)

calf NOUN
1 das Kalb *neut* (PL die Kälber) (*of cow*)
2 die Wade *fem* (*of leg*)

call NOUN
▷ *see also* **call** VERB
der Anruf *masc* (PL die Anrufe) (*by phone*)
□ Thanks for your call. Danke für Ihren Anruf.

■ **a phone call** ein Telefongespräch *neut*
■ **to be on call** (*doctor*) Bereitschaftsdienst
haben [32] □ He's on call this evening. Er hat
heute Abend Bereitschaftsdienst.

★ **to call** VERB
▷ *see also* **call** NOUN
1 anrufen [56] (IMPERFECT rief an, PERFECT TENSE hat
angerufen) (*by phone*)
□ I'll tell him you called. Ich sage ihm, dass du
angerufen hast. □ This is the number to call.
Das ist die Nummer, die du anrufen musst.
2 rufen [56] (*fetch*)
□ We called the police. Wir haben die Polizei
gerufen.
3 nennen [39] (IMPERFECT nannte, PERFECT TENSE
hat genannt) (*by name*)
□ Everyone calls him Jimmy. Alle nennen ihn
Jimmy.
■ **to be called** heißen □ He's called Fluffy. Er
heißt Fluffy. □ What's she called? Wie heißt sie?
■ **to call somebody names** jemanden
beschimpfen [18]

to call back VERB
zurückrufen [56] (*phone again*)
□ I'll call back at six o'clock. Ich rufe um sechs
Uhr zurück.

to call for VERB
abholen [4]
□ I'll call for you at half past two. Ich hole dich
um halb drei ab.

to call off VERB
absagen [4]
□ The match was called off. Das Spiel wurde
abgesagt.

call box NOUN
die Telefonzelle *fem*

call centre NOUN
das Callcenter *neut* (PL die Callcenters)

★ **calm** ADJECTIVE
ruhig

to calm down VERB
sich beruhigen [18] (PERFECT TENSE hat sich
beruhigt)
□ Calm down! Beruhige dich!

Calor gas® NOUN
das Butangas *neut*

calorie – candy

calorie NOUN
die Kalorie fem

calves PL NOUN ▷ see **calf**

camcorder NOUN
der Camcorder masc (PL die Camcorder)

came VERB ▷ see **come**

camel NOUN
das Kamel neut (PL die Kamele)

★ **camera** NOUN
1 der Fotoapparat masc (PL die Fotoapparate) (for photos)
2 die Kamera fem (PL die Kameras) (for filming, TV)

cameraman NOUN
der Kameramann masc (PL die Kameramänner)

cameraphone NOUN
das Fotohandy neut (PL die Fotohandys)

camerawoman NOUN
die Kamerafrau fem

★ to **camp** VERB
▷ see also **camp** NOUN
zelten [2]

★ **camp** NOUN
▷ see also **camp** VERB
das Lager neut (PL die Lager)
■ **a camp bed** eine Campingliege

★ **campaign** NOUN
▷ see also **campaign** VERB
die Kampagne fem

★ to **campaign** VERB
▷ see also **campaign** NOUN
sich einsetzen [36] (PERFECT TENSE hat sich eingesetzt)

□ They are campaigning for a change in the law.
Sie setzen sich für eine Gesetzesänderung ein.

camper NOUN
1 der Camper masc (PL die Camper)
die Camperin fem (person)
2 das Wohnmobil neut (PL die Wohnmobile) (van)

★ **camping** NOUN
das Camping neut
■ **to go camping** zelten [2] □ We went camping in Cornwall. Wir waren in Cornwall zelten.

camping gas NOUN
das Campinggas neut

★ **campsite** NOUN
der Zeltplatz masc (PL die Zeltplätze)

campus NOUN
das Universitätsgelände neut (PL die Universitätsgelände)

★ **can** VERB
▷ see also **can** NOUN
können [41] (PRESENT TENSE kann, IMPERFECT konnte, PERFECT TENSE hat können)

□ I can't come. Ich kann nicht kommen. □ Can I help you? Kann ich dir helfen? □ You could hire a bike. Du könntest dir ein Fahrrad mieten. □ I couldn't sleep. Ich konnte nicht schlafen. □ I can swim. Ich kann schwimmen. □ He can't drive. Er kann nicht Auto fahren. □ Can you speak German? Können Sie Deutsch?
■ **That can't be true!** Das darf nicht wahr sein
■ **You could be right.** Da könntest du recht haben.

★ **can** NOUN
▷ see also **can** VERB
1 die Dose fem (tin)
□ a can of sweetcorn eine Dose Mais □ a can of beer eine Dose Bier
2 der Kanister masc (PL die Kanister) (jerry can)
□ a can of petrol ein Benzinkanister

★ **Canada** NOUN
Kanada neut
■ **from Canada** aus Kanada
■ **in Canada** in Kanada
■ **to Canada** nach Kanada

★ **Canadian** ADJECTIVE
▷ see also **Canadian** NOUN
kanadisch
■ **He's Canadian.** Er ist Kanadier.
■ **She's Canadian.** Sie ist Kanadierin.

★ **Canadian** NOUN
▷ see also **Canadian** ADJECTIVE
der Kanadier masc (PL die Kanadier)
die Kanadierin fem

canal NOUN
der Kanal masc (PL die Kanäle)

Canaries NOUN
■ **the Canaries** die Kanarischen Inseln pl

canary NOUN
der Kanarienvogel masc (PL die Kanarienvögel)

★ to **cancel** VERB
1 absagen [4] (PERFECT TENSE hat abgesagt)
□ The match was cancelled. Das Spiel wurde abgesagt.
2 stornieren [76] (PERFECT TENSE hat storniert) (booking)
□ He cancelled his hotel booking. Er hat seine Hotelreservierung storniert.

cancellation NOUN
die Absage fem

★ **cancer** NOUN
der Krebs masc (GEN des Krebses)
□ He's got cancer. Er hat Krebs.
■ **I'm Cancer.** Ich bin Krebs.

★ **candidate** NOUN
der Kandidat masc (GEN des Kandidaten, PL die Kandidaten)
die Kandidatin fem

candle NOUN
die Kerze fem

candy NOUN (US)
1 das Bonbon neut (PL die Bonbons) (sweet)
2 die Süßigkeit fem (sweets)

★ = core vocabulary

candyfloss NOUN
die Zuckerwatte *fem*

cannabis NOUN
das Cannabis *neut* (GEN des Cannabis)

canned ADJECTIVE
in Dosen *(food)*
□ canned soup Suppe in Dosen

cannot VERB ▷ *see* **can**

canoe NOUN
das Kanu *neut* (PL die Kanus)

canoeing NOUN
■ to go canoeing Kanu fahren [21] □ We went
canoeing. Wir gingen Kanu fahren.

can-opener NOUN
der Dosenöffner *masc* (PL die Dosenöffner)

can't VERB ▷ *see* **can**

canteen NOUN
die Kantine *fem*

canvas NOUN
die Leinwand *fem* (PL die Leinwände)

★ **cap** NOUN
1 die Mütze *fem* (hat)
2 der Verschluss *masc* (GEN des Verschlusses, PL
die Verschlüsse) *(of bottle, tube)*

★ **capable** ADJECTIVE
fähig
■ to be capable of doing something etwas
tun können [41] □ She is capable of looking
after herself. Sie kann auf sich selbst aufpassen.

capacity NOUN
1 die Fähigkeit *fem*
□ She has the capacity to succeed. Sie hat die
Fähigkeit, es zu schaffen.
2 das Fassungsvermögen *neut (quantity)*
□ a capacity of fifty litres ein Fassungsvermögen
von fünfzig Litern

★ **capital** NOUN
1 die Hauptstadt *fem* (PL die Hauptstädte)
□ Cardiff is the capital of Wales. Cardiff ist die
Hauptstadt von Wales.
2 der Großbuchstabe *masc* (GEN des
Großbuchstaben, PL die Großbuchstaben)
(letter)
□ Write your address in capitals. Schreib deine
Adresse in Großbuchstaben.

capitalism NOUN
der Kapitalismus *masc* (GEN des Kapitalismus)

capital punishment NOUN
die Todesstrafe *fem*

Capricorn NOUN
der Steinbock *masc*
□ I'm Capricorn. Ich bin Steinbock.

to **capsize** VERB
kentern [88] (PERFECT TENSE ist gekentert)

★ **captain** NOUN
der Kapitän *masc* (PL die Kapitäne)

die Kapitänin *fem*
□ She's captain of the rugby team. Sie ist die
Kapitänin der Rugbymannschaft.

★ **caption** NOUN
die Bildunterschrift *fem*

to **capture** VERB
1 gefangen nehmen [52] (PRESENT TENSE nimmt
gefangen, IMPERFECT nahm gefangen, PERFECT
TENSE hat gefangen genommen) *(person)*
□ He was captured by the enemy. Er wurde vom
Feind gefangen genommen.
2 fangen [23] (PRESENT TENSE fängt, IMPERFECT fing,
PERFECT TENSE hat gefangen) *(animal)*
□ They managed to capture the lion. Sie
konnten den Löwen fangen.

★ **car** NOUN
das Auto *neut* (PL die Autos)
■ to go by car mit dem Auto fahren [21] □ We
went by car. Wir sind mit dem Auto gefahren.
■ a car crash ein Autounfall *masc*

caramel NOUN
das Karamellbonbon *neut* (PL die
Karamellbonbons) *(sweet)*

★ **caravan** NOUN
der Wohnwagen *masc* (PL die Wohnwagen)
□ a caravan site ein Campingplatz für
Wohnwagen

carbohydrate NOUN
das Kohlenhydrat *neut* (PL die Kohlenhydrate)

carbon footprint NOUN
die CO_2-Bilanz *fem*
□ We need to reduce our carbon footprint. Wir
müssen unsere CO_2-Bilanz verbessern.

car boot sale NOUN
der Flohmarkt *masc* (PL die Flohmärkte)

★ **card** NOUN
die Karte *fem*
■ a card game ein Kartenspiel *neut*

★ **cardboard** NOUN
der Karton *masc* (PL die Kartons)

cardigan NOUN
die Strickjacke *fem*

★ **care** NOUN
▷ *see also* **care** VERB
die Vorsicht *fem*
■ with care vorsichtig
■ to take care of aufpassen [4] auf +*acc* □ I
take care of the children on Saturdays. Ich passe
samstags auf die Kinder auf.
■ Take care! 1 *(Be careful!)* Sei vorsichtig!
2 *(Look after yourself!)* Pass auf dich auf!

★ to **care** VERB
▷ *see also* **care** NOUN
■ to care about achten [2] auf +*acc* □ They
care about their image. Sie achten auf ihr
Image.
■ I don't care! Das ist mir egal! □ She doesn't
care. Das ist ihr egal.

Numbers in brackets refer to verb tables on pages 697 to 706.

395

■ **to care for somebody** (*patients, old people*)
jemanden pflegen [38]

★ **career** NOUN
die Karriere *fem*

★ **careful** ADJECTIVE
vorsichtig
□ Be careful! Sei vorsichtig!

carefully ADVERB
1 sorgsam
□ She carefully avoided the subject. Sie vermied das Thema sorgsam.
2 vorsichtig (*safely*)
□ Drive carefully! Fahr vorsichtig!
■ **Think carefully!** Denk gut nach!

careless ADJECTIVE
1 schluderig (*work*)
■ **a careless mistake** ein Flüchtigkeitsfehler *masc*
2 nachlässig (*person*)
□ She's very careless. Sie ist sehr nachlässig.
3 unvorsichtig
□ a careless driver ein unvorsichtiger Fahrer

★ **caretaker** NOUN
der Hausmeister *masc* (PL die Hausmeister)
die Hausmeisterin *fem*

car ferry NOUN
die Autofähre *fem*

cargo NOUN
die Fracht *fem*

car hire NOUN
der Autoverleih *masc* (PL die Autoverleihe)

Caribbean ADJECTIVE
▷ *see also* **Caribbean** NOUN
karibisch

Caribbean NOUN
▷ *see also* **Caribbean** ADJECTIVE
1 die Karibik *fem* (*islands*)
□ We're going to the Caribbean. Wir fahren in die Karibik. □ He's from the Caribbean. Er kommt aus der Karibik.
2 das Karibische Meer *neut* (*sea*)

caring ADJECTIVE
liebevoll
■ **the caring professions** die Pflegeberufe

carnation NOUN
die Nelke *fem*

carnival NOUN
der Karneval *masc* (PL die Karnevale)

carol NOUN
■ **a Christmas carol** ein Weihnachtslied *neut*

★ **car park** NOUN
der Parkplatz *masc* (PL die Parkplätze)

carpenter NOUN
der Schreiner *masc* (PL die Schreiner)
die Schreinerin *fem*
□ He's a carpenter. Er ist Schreiner.

carpentry NOUN
die Schreinerei *fem*

★ **carpet** NOUN
der Teppich *masc* (PL die Teppiche)
□ a Persian carpet ein Perserteppich

carriage NOUN
der Eisenbahnwagen *masc* (PL die Eisenbahnwagen)

carrier bag NOUN
die Tragetasche *fem*

★ **carrot** NOUN
die Karotte *fem*

★ **to carry** VERB
tragen [77] (PRESENT TENSE trägt, IMPERFECT trug, PERFECT TENSE hat getragen)
□ He carried her bag. Er trug ihre Tasche.
■ **a plane carrying a hundred passengers**
ein Flugzeug mit hundert Passagieren an Bord

to carry on VERB
weitermachen [48]
□ Carry on! Mach weiter!
■ **She carried on talking.** Sie redete weiter.

to carry out VERB
ausführen [4] (*orders*)

carrycot NOUN
die Babytragetasche *fem*

cart NOUN
der Karren *masc* (PL die Karren)

carton NOUN
die Tüte *fem* (*of milk, juice*)

★ **cartoon** NOUN
1 der Zeichentrickfilm *masc* (PL die Zeichentrickfilme) (*film*)
2 der Cartoon *masc* (PL die Cartoons) (*in newspaper*)
■ **a strip cartoon** ein Comic *masc*

cartridge NOUN
die Patrone *fem*

to carve VERB
aufschneiden [60] (IMPERFECT schnitt auf, PERFECT TENSE hat aufgeschnitten) (*meat*)

★ **case** NOUN
1 der Koffer *masc* (PL die Koffer)
□ I've packed my case. Ich habe meinen Koffer gepackt.
2 der Fall *masc* (PL die Fälle)
□ in some cases in manchen Fällen □ Which case does 'außer' take? Welcher Fall steht nach 'außer'?
■ **in that case** in dem Fall □ I don't want it. — In that case, I'll take it. Ich will es nicht. — In dem Fall nehme ich es.
■ **in case** für den Fall □ in case it rains für den Fall, dass es regnet
■ **just in case** für alle Fälle □ Take some money, just in case. Nimm für alle Fälle Geld mit.

★ = core vocabulary

★ cash NOUN

das Bargeld *neut*

□ I desperately need some cash. Ich brauche dringend Bargeld.

- **in cash** in bar □ two thousand pounds in cash zweitausend Pfund in bar
- **to pay cash** bar bezahlen [7]
- **I'm a bit short of cash.** Ich bin etwas knapp bei Kasse.
- **a cash card** eine Geldautomatenkarte
- **the cash desk** die Kasse
- **a cash machine** ein Geldautomat *masc*
- **a cash register** eine Registrierkasse

cashew nut NOUN

die Cashewnuss *fem* (PL die Cashewnüsse)

cashier NOUN

der Kassierer *masc* (PL die Kassierer)

die Kassiererin *fem*

cashmere NOUN

der Kaschmir *masc*

□ a cashmere sweater ein Kaschmirpullover

casino NOUN

das Kasino *neut* (PL die Kasinos)

casserole NOUN

der Schmortopf *masc* (PL die Schmortöpfe)

- **a casserole dish** eine Kasserolle

cast NOUN

die Besetzung *fem*

□ After the play, we met the cast. Nach dem Stück haben wir die Besetzung kennengelernt.

casual ADJECTIVE

1 leger

□ casual clothes legere Kleidung

2 lässig

□ a casual attitude eine lässige Haltung

3 beiläufig

□ It was just a casual remark. Es war nur eine beiläufige Bemerkung.

casually ADVERB

- **to dress casually** sich leger kleiden [54]

★ casualty NOUN

die Unfallstation *fem* (hospital department)

★ cat NOUN

die Katze *fem*

□ Have you got a cat? Hast du eine Katze?

catalogue NOUN

der Katalog *masc* (PL die Kataloge)

catalytic converter NOUN

der Katalysator *masc* (PL die Katalysatoren)

catarrh NOUN

der Katarrh *masc* (PL die Katarrhe)

catastrophe NOUN

die Katastrophe *fem*

★ to catch VERB

1 fangen [23] (PRESENT TENSE fängt, IMPERFECT fing, PERFECT TENSE hat gefangen)

□ My cat catches birds. Meine Katze fängt Vögel.

- **to catch a thief** einen Dieb fassen [31]
- **to catch somebody doing something**

jemanden dabei erwischen [48] wie er etwas tut □ If they catch you smoking ... Wenn sie dich beim Rauchen erwischen ...

2 nehmen [52] (PRESENT TENSE nimmt, IMPERFECT nahm, PERFECT TENSE hat genommen) (bus, train)

□ We caught the last bus. Wir haben den letzten Bus genommen.

3 mitbekommen [40] (IMPERFECT bekam mit, PERFECT TENSE hat mitbekommen) (hear)

□ I didn't catch his name. Ich habe seinen Namen nicht mitbekommen.

- **to catch a cold** einen Schnupfen bekommen [40]

to catch up VERB

aufholen [38]

□ I'm trying to catch up: I was away last week. Ich versuche aufzuholen: ich war letzte Woche weg.

catching ADJECTIVE

ansteckend

□ It's not catching. Das ist nicht ansteckend.

catering NOUN

- **Who did the catering?** Wer hat das Essen und die Getränke geliefert?

cathedral NOUN

die Kathedrale *fem*

Catholic ADJECTIVE

▷ see also **Catholic** NOUN

katholisch

Catholic NOUN

▷ see also **Catholic** ADJECTIVE

der Katholik *masc* (GEN des Katholiken, PL die Katholiken)

die Katholikin *fem*

- **I'm a Catholic.** Ich bin katholisch.

cattle PL NOUN

das Vieh *neut sing*

caught VERB ▷ see **catch**

★ cauliflower NOUN

der Blumenkohl *masc* (PL die Blumenkohle)

★ cause NOUN

▷ see also **cause** VERB

die Ursache *fem*

□ the cause of the fire die Ursache des Feuers

★ to cause VERB

▷ see also **cause** NOUN

verursachen [84] (PERFECT TENSE hat verursacht)

□ to cause an accident einen Unfall verursachen

cautious ADJECTIVE

vorsichtig

cautiously ADVERB

vorsichtig

★ cave NOUN

die Höhle *fem*

Numbers in brackets refer to verb tables on pages 697 to 706.

397

caviar NOUN
der Kaviar *masc*

CCTV ABBREVIATION (= *closed-circuit television*)
die Videoüberwachung *fem*

CCTV camera NOUN
die Überwachungskamera *fem* (PL die Überwachungskameras)

★ **CD** NOUN (= *compact disc*)
die CD *fem* (PL die CDs)

★ **CD player** NOUN
der CD-Spieler *masc* (PL die CD-Spieler)

★ **CD-ROM** NOUN
die CD-ROM *fem* (PL die CD-ROMs)

CDT NOUN (= *Craft, Design and Technology*)
die Arbeitslehre *fem*

★ **ceasefire** NOUN
der Waffenstillstand *masc* (PL die Waffenstillstände)

★ **ceiling** NOUN
die Decke *fem*

★ to **celebrate** VERB
feiern [88] (*birthday*)

celebration NOUN
die Feier *fem*

celebrity NOUN
die Berühmtheit *fem*

celery NOUN
der Stangensellerie *masc* (GEN des Stangensellerie, PL die Stangenselleries)

★ **cell** NOUN
die Zelle *fem*

★ **cellar** NOUN
der Keller *masc* (PL die Keller)
◻ a wine cellar ein Weinkeller

cello NOUN
das Cello *neut* (PL die Celli)
◻ I play the cello. Ich spiele Cello.

cell phone NOUN (US)
das Handy *neut* (PL die Handys)

Celsius ADJECTIVE
Celsius-(*scale*)

cement NOUN
der Zement *masc*

cemetery NOUN
der Friedhof *masc* (PL die Friedhöfe)

★ **cent** NOUN
der Cent *masc* (PL die Cents *or* Cent)

> When talking about amounts of money use the plural form **Cent**.

◻ twenty cents zwanzig Cent

centenary NOUN
das hundertjährige Jubiläum *neut* (PL die hundertjährigen Jubiläen)

center NOUN (US)
das Zentrum *neut* (PL die Zentren)
◻ a sports center ein Sportzentrum

★ **centigrade** ADJECTIVE
■ **twenty degrees centigrade** zwanzig Grad Celsius

★ **centimetre** (US **centimeter**) NOUN
der Zentimeter *masc* (PL die Zentimeter)
◻ twenty centimetres zwanzig Zentimeter

★ **central** ADJECTIVE
zentral

★ **central heating** NOUN
die Zentralheizung *fem*

★ **centre** (US **center**) NOUN
das Zentrum *neut* (PL die Zentren)
◻ a sports centre ein Sportzentrum

★ **century** NOUN
das Jahrhundert *neut* (PL die Jahrhunderte)
◻ the twentieth century das zwanzigste Jahrhundert ◻ the twenty-first century das einundzwanzigste Jahrhundert

cereal NOUN
die Getreideflocken *fem pl*
◻ I have cereal for breakfast. Zum Frühstück esse ich Getreideflocken.

★ **ceremony** NOUN
die Zeremonie *fem*

★ **certain** ADJECTIVE
1 sicher
◻ I'm absolutely certain it was him. Ich bin ganz sicher, dass er es war. ◻ I don't know for certain. Ich bin mir nicht sicher.
■ **to make certain** sich vergewissern [88] ◻ I made certain the door was locked. Ich habe mich vergewissert, dass die Tür abgeschlossen war.
2 bestimmt
◻ a certain person eine bestimmte Person

★ **certainly** ADVERB
natürlich
◻ I certainly expected something better. Ich habe natürlich etwas Besseres erwartet.
■ **Certainly not!** Sicher nicht!
■ **So it was a surprise? — It certainly was!** Also war's eine Überraschung? — Und ob!

★ **certificate** NOUN
die Urkunde *fem*

CFC NOUN (= *chlorofluorocarbon*)
der FCKW *masc* (= *Fluorchlorkohlenwasserstoff*)

★ **chain** NOUN
die Kette *fem*

★ **chair** NOUN
1 der Stuhl *masc* (PL die Stühle)
◻ a table and four chairs ein Tisch und vier Stühle
2 der Sessel *masc* (PL die Sessel) (*armchair*)

★ = core vocabulary

chairlift NOUN
der Sessellift *masc* (PL die Sessellifte)

★ **chairman** NOUN
der Vorsitzende *masc* (GEN des Vorsitzenden, PL die Vorsitzenden)
□ **a chairman** ein Vorsitzender

★ **chairperson** NOUN
der Vorsitzende *masc* (GEN des Vorsitzenden, PL die Vorsitzenden)
die Vorsitzende *fem* (GEN der Vorsitzenden)

★ **chairwoman** NOUN
die Vorsitzende *fem* (GEN der Vorsitzenden)
□ **a chairwoman** eine Vorsitzende

chalet NOUN
das Ferienhaus *neut* (PL die Ferienhäuser)

chalk NOUN
die Kreide *fem*

★ **challenge** NOUN
▷ *see also* **challenge** VERB
die Herausforderung *fem*

★ to **challenge** VERB
▷ *see also* **challenge** NOUN
■ **She challenged me to a race.** Sie wollte mit mir um die Wette laufen.

challenging ADJECTIVE
anspruchsvoll
□ **a challenging job** eine anspruchsvolle Arbeit

chambermaid NOUN
das Zimmermädchen *neut* (PL die Zimmermädchen)

champagne NOUN
der Champagner *masc* (PL die Champagner)

★ **champion** NOUN
der Meister *masc* (PL die Meister)
die Meisterin *fem*

★ **championship** NOUN
die Meisterschaft *fem*

★ **chance** NOUN
1 die Chance *fem*
□ **Do you think I've got any chance?** Meinst du, ich habe eine Chance? □ **Their chances of winning are very good.** Ihre Gewinnchancen sind sehr gut.
2 die Möglichkeit *fem*
□ **a chance to travel** eine Möglichkeit, auf Reisen zu gehen
■ **I'll write when I get the chance.** Ich schreibe, sobald ich dazu komme.
■ **by chance** zufällig □ **We met by chance.** Wir haben uns zufällig kennengelernt.
■ **to take a chance** ein Risiko eingehen [29] □ **I'm taking no chances!** Ich gehe kein Risiko ein!
■ **No chance!** Auf keinen Fall!

Chancellor of the Exchequer NOUN
der Schatzkanzler *masc* (PL die Schatzkanzler)

chandelier NOUN
der Kronleuchter *masc* (PL die Kronleuchter)

★ to **change** VERB
▷ *see also* **change** NOUN
1 sich verändern [88] (PERFECT TENSE hat sich verändert)
□ **The town has changed a lot.** Die Stadt hat sich sehr verändert.
2 wechseln [34] (*money, job*)
□ **I'd like to change fifty pounds.** Ich würde gern fünfzig Pfund wechseln. □ **He wants to change his job.** Er möchte den Job wechseln.
■ **You have to change trains in Stuttgart.** Sie müssen in Stuttgart umsteigen.
■ **I'm going to change my shoes.** Ich ziehe andere Schuhe an.
■ **to change one's mind** es sich anders überlegen [82] □ **I've changed my mind.** Ich habe es mir anders überlegt.
■ **to change gear** schalten [2]
3 sich umziehen [96] (IMPERFECT zog sich um, PERFECT TENSE hat sich umgezogen)
□ **She's changing to go out.** Sie zieht sich zum Ausgehen um.
■ **to get changed** sich umziehen [96] □ **I'm going to get changed.** Ich ziehe mich um.
4 umtauschen [4] (PERFECT TENSE hat umgetauscht) (*swap*)
□ **Can I change this sweater? It's too small.** Kann ich diesen Pullover umtauschen? Er ist zu klein.

★ **change** NOUN
▷ *see also* **change** VERB
1 die Änderung *fem*
■ **There's been a change of plan.** Die Pläne haben sich geändert.
■ **a change of clothes** Kleidung zum Wechseln
■ **for a change** zur Abwechslung □ **Let's play tennis for a change.** Lass uns zur Abwechslung Tennis spielen.
2 das Kleingeld *neut* (*money*)
□ **I haven't got any change.** Ich habe kein Kleingeld.

changeable ADJECTIVE
wechselhaft

changing room NOUN
der Umkleideraum *masc* (PL die Umkleideräume)

★ **channel** NOUN
das Programm *neut* (PL die Programme) (*TV*)
□ **There's football on the other channel.** Im anderen Programm gibt es Fußball.
■ **the English Channel** der Ärmelkanal
■ **the Channel Islands** die Kanalinseln
■ **the Channel Tunnel** der Kanaltunnel

★ **chaos** NOUN
das Chaos *neut* (GEN des Chaos)

chapel NOUN
die Kapelle *fem* (*part of church*)

Numbers in brackets refer to verb tables on pages 697 to 706.

399

★ **chapter** NOUN
das Kapitel neut (PL die Kapitel)

★ **character** NOUN
1 der Charakter masc (PL die Charaktere)
□ Give me some idea of his character.
Beschreiben Sie mir seinen Charakter.
■ **She's quite a character.** Sie ist ein Unikum.
2 die Figur fem (in play, film)
□ the character played by Tom Cruise die Figur,
die Tom Cruise spielt

★ **characteristic** NOUN
das Merkmal neut (PL die Merkmale)

charcoal NOUN
die Holzkohle fem

★ **charge** NOUN
▷ see also **charge** VERB
die Gebühr fem
□ Is there a charge for delivery? Wird für die
Zustellung eine Gebühr erhoben? □ an extra
charge eine Extragebühr
■ **free of charge** kostenlos
■ **to be on a charge** angeklagt sein [65] □ He's
on a charge of murder. Er ist des Mordes
angeklagt.
■ **to be in charge** die Verantwortung haben
[32] □ Mrs Munday was in charge of the group.
Mrs Munday hatte die Verantwortung für die
Gruppe.

★ to **charge** VERB
▷ see also **charge** NOUN
1 verlangen [84] (PERFECT TENSE hat verlangt)
(money)
□ How much did he charge you? Wie viel hat er
verlangt? □ They charge ten pounds an hour.
Sie verlangen zehn Pfund die Stunde.
2 anklagen [4] (PERFECT TENSE hat angeklagt) (with
crime)
□ The police have charged him with murder.
Die Polizei hat ihn des Mordes angeklagt.

★ **charity** NOUN
die Wohltätigkeit fem
■ **She does a lot of work for charity.** Sie
arbeitet viel für die Wohltätigkeitsorganisation.
■ **He gave the money to charity.** Er hat das
Geld für wohltätige Zwecke gespendet.
■ **charity concert** das Wohltätigkeitskonzert

charm NOUN
der Charme masc

Note that the 'e' in Charme is silent.

□ He's got a lot of charm. Er hat viel Charme.

charming ADJECTIVE
bezaubernd

★ **chart** NOUN
die Grafik fem
□ The chart shows the rise of unemployment.
Die Grafik stellt den Anstieg der Arbeitslosigkeit
dar.
■ **the charts** die Hitparade sing □ This album is

number one in the charts. Dieses Album ist auf
Platz eins der Hitparade.

charter flight NOUN
der Charterflug masc (PL die Charterflüge)

★ to **chase** VERB
▷ see also **chase** NOUN
verfolgen [84] (PERFECT TENSE hat verfolgt)

★ **chase** NOUN
▷ see also **chase** VERB
die Verfolgung fem
■ **a car chase** eine Verfolgungsjagd im Auto

★ **chat** NOUN
1 das Schwätzchen neut (PL die Schwätzchen)
□ to have a chat ein Schwätzchen halten
2 der Chat masc (PL die Chats) (online)

chat room NOUN
der Chatroom masc (PL die Chatrooms)

chat show NOUN
die Talkshow fem (PL die Talkshows)

chauvinist NOUN
■ **male chauvinist** der Chauvi

★ **cheap** ADJECTIVE
billig
□ a cheap T-shirt ein billiges T-Shirt □ It's
cheaper by bus. Mit dem Bus ist es billiger.

to **cheat** VERB
▷ see also **cheat** NOUN
betrügen (IMPERFECT betrog, PERFECT TENSE hat
betrogen)
□ He cheated me. Er hat mich betrogen.
■ **You're cheating!** (in games, at school) Du
schummelst!

cheat NOUN
▷ see also **cheat** VERB
der Betrüger masc (PL die Betrüger)
die Betrügerin fem

★ **check** NOUN
▷ see also **check** VERB
1 die Kontrolle fem
□ a security check eine Sicherheitskontrolle
2 die Rechnung fem (US: bill)
□ The waiter brought us the check. Der Kellner
brachte uns die Rechnung.
3 der Scheck masc (PL die Schecks) (US)
□ to write a check einen Scheck ausstellen

★ to **check** VERB
▷ see also **check** NOUN
nachsehen [64] (PRESENT TENSE sieht nach,
IMPERFECT sah nach, PERFECT TENSE hat
nachgesehen)
□ I'll check the time of the train. Ich sehe die
Abfahrtszeiten des Zuges nach. □ Could you
check the oil, please? Könnten Sie bitte das Öl
nachsehen?

to **check in** VERB
einchecken [4]
□ What time do I have to check in? Wann muss
ich einchecken?

★ = core vocabulary

to **check out** VERB
sich auschecken [4] (*from hotel*)

checked ADJECTIVE
kariert
□ a checked shirt ein kariertes Hemd

check-in NOUN
der Check-in *masc* (PL die Check-ins)

checking account NOUN (US)
das Girokonto *neut* (PL die Girokonten)

checkout NOUN
die Kasse *fem*

check-up NOUN
der Check-up *masc* (PL die Check-ups)

cheddar NOUN
der Cheddar *masc* (PL die Cheddars)

cheek NOUN
1 die Wange *fem*
□ He kissed her on the cheek. Er küsste sie auf die Wange.
2 die Frechheit *fem*
□ What a cheek! So eine Frechheit!

cheeky ADJECTIVE
frech
□ Don't be cheeky! Sei nicht so frech! □ a cheeky smile ein freches Lächeln

cheer NOUN
▷ *see also* **cheer** VERB
der Hurraruf *masc* (PL die Hurrarufe)
■ **to give a cheer** Hurra rufen [56]
■ **Cheers! 1** (*good health*) Prost! **2** (*thanks*) Danke schön!

to **cheer** VERB
▷ *see also* **cheer** NOUN
1 anfeuern [4] (PERFECT TENSE hat angefeuert) (*team*)
2 zujubeln [4] (PERFECT TENSE hat zugejubelt) (*speaker*)
□ The speaker was cheered. Dem Redner wurde zugejubelt.
■ **to cheer somebody up** jemanden aufheitern [88] □ I was trying to cheer him up. Ich habe versucht, ihn aufzuheitern.
■ **Cheer up!** Kopf hoch!

cheerful ADJECTIVE
fröhlich

cheerio EXCLAMATION
tschüs

cheese NOUN
der Käse *masc* (PL die Käse)

chef NOUN
der Küchenchef *masc* (PL die Küchenchefs)

chemical NOUN
die Chemikalie *fem*

chemist NOUN
1 der Apotheker *masc* (PL die Apotheker)
die Apothekerin *fem* (*pharmacist*)
2 die Apotheke *fem* (*pharmacy*)

□ You get it from the chemist. Du bekommst das in der Apotheke.
3 die Drogerie *fem* (*shop selling toiletries*)
4 der Chemiker *masc* (PL die Chemiker)
die Chemikerin *fem* (*scientist*)

chemistry NOUN
die Chemie *fem*
□ the chemistry lab das Chemielabor

cheque NOUN
der Scheck *masc* (PL die Schecks)
□ to write a cheque einen Scheck ausstellen
□ to pay by cheque mit Scheck bezahlen

chequebook NOUN
das Scheckheft *neut* (PL die Scheckhefte)

DID YOU KNOW...?
German banks provide customers with cheques in an envelope or wallet, usually ten at a time, rather than chequebooks.

cherry NOUN
die Kirsche *fem*

chess NOUN
das Schach *neut*
□ to play chess Schach spielen

chessboard NOUN
das Schachbrett *neut* (PL die Schachbretter)

chest NOUN
die Brust *fem* (PL die Brüste) (*of person*)
■ **his chest measurement** seine Oberweite
■ **a chest of drawers** eine Kommode

chestnut NOUN
die Kastanie *fem*

to **chew** VERB
kauen [38]

chewing gum NOUN
der Kaugummi *masc* (PL die Kaugummis)

chick NOUN
das Küken *neut* (PL die Küken)
□ a hen and her chicks eine Henne mit ihren Küken

chicken NOUN
1 das Hähnchen *neut* (PL die Hähnchen) (*food*)
□ I bought a chicken in the supermarket. Ich habe im Supermarkt ein Hähnchen gekauft.
2 das Huhn *neut* (PL die Hühner) (*live*)
□ They keep chickens. Sie halten Hühner.

chickenpox SING NOUN
die Windpocken *pl*
□ My sister has chickenpox. Meine Schwester hat Windpocken.

chickpeas PL NOUN
die Kichererbsen *fem pl*

chief NOUN
▷ *see also* **chief** ADJECTIVE
der Chef *masc* (PL die Chefs)
□ the chief of security der Sicherheitschef

Numbers in brackets refer to verb tables on pages 697 to 706.

401

chief – Christian name

★ **chief** ADJECTIVE
▷ *see also* **chief** NOUN
hauptsächlich
□ the chief reason der hauptsächliche Grund

★ **child** NOUN
das Kind *neut* (PL die Kinder)
□ all the children alle Kinder

childish ADJECTIVE
kindisch

child minder NOUN
die Tagesmutter *fem* (PL die Tagesmütter)

★ **children** PL NOUN ▷ *see* **child**

Chile NOUN
Chile *neut*
■ **from Chile** aus Chile
■ **to Chile** nach Chile

to **chill** VERB
kalt stellen [38]
□ Put the wine in the fridge to chill. Stell den Wein kalt.

chilli NOUN
der Chili *masc* (PL die Chilis)
■ **chilli peppers** die Peperoni *pl*

chilly ADJECTIVE
kühl

chimney NOUN
der Schornstein *masc* (PL die Schornsteine)

chin NOUN
das Kinn *neut* (PL die Kinne)

★ **China** NOUN
China *neut*
■ **from China** aus China
■ **to China** nach China

china NOUN
das Porzellan *neut*
□ a china plate ein Porzellanteller *masc*

Chinese ADJECTIVE
▷ *see also* **Chinese** NOUN
chinesisch
□ a Chinese restaurant ein chinesisches Restaurant
■ **a Chinese man** ein Chinese
■ **a Chinese woman** eine Chinesin

Chinese NOUN
▷ *see also* **Chinese** ADJECTIVE
das Chinesisch *neut* (GEN des Chinesischen) (*language*)
■ **the Chinese** (*people*) die Chinesen

★ **chip** NOUN
der Chip *masc* (PL die Chips) (*in computer*)

chips PL NOUN
1 die Pommes frites *fem pl* (*fried potatoes*)
□ We bought some chips. Wir haben Pommes frites gekauft.
2 die Kartoffelchips *masc pl* (US: *crisps*)

BE CAREFUL!
Do not translate **chips** by the German word **Chips**.

chiropodist NOUN
der Fußpfleger *masc* (PL die Fußpfleger)
die Fußpflegerin *fem*
□ He's a chiropodist. Er ist Fußpfleger.

chives PL NOUN
der Schnittlauch *masc*

★ **chocolate** NOUN
die Schokolade *fem*
□ a chocolate cake ein Schokoladenkuchen
□ hot chocolate heiße Schokolade

★ **choice** NOUN
die Wahl *fem*
□ I had no choice. Ich hatte keine andere Wahl.

choir NOUN
der Chor *masc* (PL die Chöre)
□ I sing in the school choir. Ich singe im Schulchor.

to **choke** VERB
ersticken [19] (PERFECT TENSE ist erstickt)
□ He's choking! Er erstickt!

★ to **choose** VERB
auswählen [4] (PERFECT TENSE hat ausgewählt)
□ She chose the red shirt. Sie hat das rote Hemd ausgewählt.

★ to **chop** VERB
▷ *see also* **chop** NOUN
klein hacken [48] (PERFECT TENSE hat klein gehackt)
□ She chopped the onions. Sie hackte die Zwiebeln klein.

★ **chop** NOUN
▷ *see also* **chop** VERB
das Kotelett *neut* (PL die Koteletts)
□ a pork chop ein Schweinekotelett

chopsticks PL NOUN
die Stäbchen *neut pl*

chose VERB ▷ *see* **choose**

chosen VERB ▷ *see* **choose**

Christ NOUN
Christus (GEN Christi)
□ the birth of Christ die Geburt Christi

christening NOUN
die Taufe *fem*

★ **Christian** NOUN
▷ *see also* **Christian** ADJECTIVE
der Christ *masc* (GEN des Christen, PL die Christen)
die Christin *fem*

★ **Christian** ADJECTIVE
▷ *see also* **Christian** NOUN
christlich

Christian name NOUN
der Vorname *masc* (GEN des Vornamens, PL die Vornamen)

★ **Christmas** NOUN
Weihnachten neut
□ Happy Christmas! Fröhliche Weihnachten!
■ **Christmas Day** der erste Weihnachtsfeiertag
■ **Christmas Eve** Heiligabend □ on Christmas Eve an Heiligabend

DID YOU KNOW...?
Traditionally, in Germany gifts are exchanged on Christmas Eve.

■ **a Christmas tree** ein Weihnachtsbaum masc
■ **a Christmas card** eine Weihnachtskarte

DID YOU KNOW...?
Most Germans send very few Christmas cards.

■ **Christmas dinner** das Weihnachtsessen

DID YOU KNOW...?
Germans traditionally eat goose at Christmas rather than turkey.

■ **Christmas pudding**

DID YOU KNOW...?
Germans don't have any traditional dessert at Christmas. Most know what Christmas pudding is, but almost always refer to it as **Plumpudding**.

to **chuck out** VERB
rauswerfen [92] (PRESENT TENSE wirft raus, IMPERFECT warf raus, PERFECT TENSE hat rausgeworfen)
□ Chuck out those old magazines. Wirf diese alten Zeitschriften raus.

chunk NOUN
das Stück neut (PL die Stücke)
□ Cut the meat into chunks. Schneiden Sie das Fleisch in Stücke.

★ **church** NOUN
die Kirche fem
□ I don't go to church. Ich gehe nicht in die Kirche.
■ **the Church of England** die anglikanische Kirche

cider NOUN
der Apfelwein masc

cigar NOUN
die Zigarre fem

★ **cigarette** NOUN
die Zigarette fem

cigarette lighter NOUN
der Zigarettenanzünder masc (PL die Zigarettenanzünder)

★ **cinema** NOUN
das Kino neut (PL die Kinos)
□ I'm going to the cinema this evening. Ich gehe heute Abend ins Kino.

cinnamon NOUN
der Zimt masc

★ **circle** NOUN
der Kreis masc (PL die Kreise)

circular ADJECTIVE
rund

circulation NOUN
1 der Kreislauf masc (of blood)
2 die Auflage fem (of newspaper)

circumstances PL NOUN
die Umstände masc pl

circus NOUN
der Zirkus masc (GEN des Zirkus, PL die Zirkusse)

★ **citizen** NOUN
der Bürger masc (PL die Bürger)
die Bürgerin fem
■ **a German citizen** ein deutscher Staatsbürger

★ **city** NOUN
die Stadt fem (PL die Städte)
■ **the city centre** die Innenstadt □ It's in the city centre. Es liegt in der Innenstadt.

city technology college NOUN
die technische Fachschule fem

civilization NOUN
die Zivilisation fem

civil partnership NOUN
die zivile Partnerschaft fem

civil servant NOUN
der Beamte masc (GEN des Beamten, PL die Beamten)
die Beamtin fem

DID YOU KNOW...?
In Germany the teaching profession is usually classed as part of the civil service and most teachers are therefore **Beamte**.

□ He's a civil servant. Er ist Beamter.

civil war NOUN
der Bürgerkrieg masc (PL die Bürgerkriege)

★ to **claim** VERB
1 behaupten [2] (PERFECT TENSE hat behauptet)
□ He claims to have found the money. Er behauptet, er habe das Geld gefunden.

Note the use of the subjunctive.

2 bekommen [40] (IMPERFECT bekam, PERFECT TENSE hat bekommen) (receive)
□ She's claiming unemployment benefit. Sie bekommt Arbeitslosenunterstützung.
■ **to claim on one's insurance** seine Versicherung in Anspruch nehmen [52] □ We claimed on our insurance. Wir haben unsere Versicherung in Anspruch genommen.

to **clap** VERB
klatschen [48] (applaud)
□ The audience clapped. Das Publikum klatschte.
■ **to clap one's hands** klatschen [48]

clarinet NOUN
die Klarinette fem
□ I play the clarinet. Ich spiele Klarinette.

clash – click on

to clash VERB

1 sich beißen [6] (IMPERFECT bissen sich, PERFECT TENSE haben sich gebissen) (colours)
□ These colours clash. Diese Farben beißen sich.

2 sich überschneiden [60] (IMPERFECT überschnitt sich, PERFECT TENSE hat sich überschnitten) (events)
□ The concert clashes with Ann's party. Das Konzert überschneidet sich mit Anns Party.

clasp NOUN
der Verschluss masc (GEN des Verschlusses, PL die Verschlüsse) (of necklace)

★ **class** NOUN

1 die Klasse fem (group)
□ We're in the same class. Wir sind in derselben Klasse.

2 die Stunde fem (lesson)
□ I go to dancing classes. Ich nehme Tanzstunden.

classic ADJECTIVE
▷ see also **classic** NOUN
klassisch
□ a classic example ein klassisches Beispiel

classic NOUN
▷ see also **classic** ADJECTIVE
der Klassiker masc (PL die Klassiker) (book, film)

classical ADJECTIVE
klassisch
□ I like classical music. Ich mag klassische Musik.

classmate NOUN
der Klassenkamerad masc (GEN des Klassenkameraden, PL die Klassenkameraden)
die Klassenkameradin fem

classroom NOUN
die Klassenzimmer fem (PL die Klassenzimmer)

classroom assistant NOUN
die Assistenzlehrkraft fem (PL die Assistenzlehrkräfte)

clause NOUN

1 die Klausel fem (in legal document)

2 der Satz masc (GEN des Satzes, PL die Sätze) (in grammar)

claw NOUN

1 die Kralle fem (of cat, dog)

2 die Klaue fem (of bird)

3 die Schere fem (of crab, lobster)

★ **clean** ADJECTIVE
▷ see also **clean** VERB
sauber
□ a clean shirt ein sauberes Hemd

★ **to clean** VERB
▷ see also **clean** ADJECTIVE
sauber machen [48] (PERFECT TENSE hat sauber gemacht)

cleaner NOUN
der Putzmann masc (PL die Putzmänner)
die Putzfrau fem
□ She's a cleaner. Sie ist Putzfrau.

cleaner's NOUN
die Reinigung fem

cleaning lady NOUN
die Putzfrau fem

cleansing lotion NOUN
die Reinigungslotion fem

★ **clear** ADJECTIVE
▷ see also **clear** VERB

1 klar
□ It's clear you don't believe me. Es ist klar, dass du mir nicht glaubst.

2 frei (road, way)
□ The road's clear now. Die Straße ist jetzt frei.

★ **to clear** VERB
▷ see also **clear** ADJECTIVE

1 räumen [38]
□ The police are clearing the road after the accident. Die Polizei räumt die Straße nach dem Unfall.

2 sich auflösen [4] (PERFECT TENSE hat sich aufgelöst) (fog, mist)
□ The mist soon cleared. Der Nebel löste sich bald auf.

■ **to be cleared of a crime** von einem Verbrechen freigesprochen werden [91] □ She was cleared of murder. Sie wurde von der Mordanklage freigesprochen.

■ **to clear the table** den Tisch abräumen [4]
□ I'll clear the table. Ich räume den Tisch ab.

to clear up VERB
aufräumen [4]
□ Who's going to clear all this up? Wer räumt das alles auf?

■ **I think it's going to clear up.** (weather) Ich glaube, es hellt sich auf.

clearly ADVERB
klar
□ She explained it very clearly. Sie hat es sehr klar erklärt. □ The English coast was clearly visible. Die englische Küste war klar zu sehen.

■ **to speak clearly** deutlich sprechen [70]

clementine NOUN
die Klementine fem

to clench VERB
■ **She clenched her fists.** Sie ballte die Fäuste.

★ **clever** ADJECTIVE

1 klug
□ She's very clever. Sie ist sehr klug.

2 genial (ingenious)
□ a clever system ein geniales System □ What a clever idea! Das ist eine geniale Idee!

to click on VERB
anklicken [4] (PERFECT TENSE hat angeklickt) (computer)

□ to click on an icon ein Icon anklicken
■ **to click on the mouse** mit der Maus klicken
[48]

★ **client** NOUN
der Klient masc (GEN des Klienten, PL die Klienten)
die Klientin fem

cliff NOUN
die Klippe fem

★ **climate** NOUN
das Klima neut (PL die Klimas)

climate change NOUN
der Klimawandel masc
□ We need to combat climate change. Wir müssen etwas gegen den Klimawandel tun.

★ to **climb** VERB
1 steigen [74] auf +acc (IMPERFECT stieg, PERFECT TENSE ist gestiegen)
□ We're going to climb Snowdon. Wir steigen auf den Snowdon.
2 hinaufgehen [29] (IMPERFECT ging hinauf, PERFECT TENSE ist hinaufgegangen) (stairs)
□ I watched him climb the stairs. Ich sah ihn die Treppe hinaufgehen.
■ **She finds it difficult to climb the stairs.** Das Treppensteigen fällt ihr schwer.

climber NOUN
der Kletterer masc (PL die Kletterer)
die Kletterin fem

climbing NOUN
das Klettern neut
■ **to go climbing** klettern gehen [29] □ We're going climbing in Scotland. Wir gehen in Schottland klettern.

clingfilm NOUN
die Frischhaltefolie fem

clinic NOUN
die Klinik fem

cloakroom NOUN
1 die Garderobe fem (for coats)
2 die Toilette fem (toilet)

★ **clock** NOUN
die Uhr fem
■ **a grandfather clock** eine Standuhr
■ **an alarm clock** ein Wecker masc
■ **a clock radio** ein Radiowecker masc

clockwork NOUN
das Uhrwerk neut
■ **to go like clockwork** wie am Schnürchen gehen [29] (informal)

clog NOUN
1 der Clog masc (PL die Clogs) (modern)
2 der Holzschuh masc (PL die Holzschuhe) (traditional, made of wood)

clone NOUN
▷ see also **clone** VERB
der Klon masc (PL die Klone)

to **clone** VERB
▷ see also **clone** NOUN
klonen [38]
□ a cloned sheep ein geklontes Schaf

★ **close** ADJECTIVE, ADVERB
▷ see also **close** VERB
1 nahe (near)
□ close relations nahe Verwandte □ I'm very close to my sister. Ich stehe meiner Schwester sehr nahe.
■ **The shops are very close.** Die Geschäfte sind ganz in der Nähe.
■ **She's a close friend of mine.** Sie ist eine gute Freundin von mir.
■ **Come closer!** Komm näher!
■ **close to** in der Nähe +gen □ The youth hostel is close to the station. Die Jugendherberge ist in der Nähe des Bahnhofs.
2 knapp (contest)
□ It's going to be very close. Das wird sehr knapp.
3 schwül (weather)
□ It's close today. Es ist schwül heute.

★ to **close** VERB
▷ see also **close** ADJECTIVE, ADVERB
schließen (IMPERFECT schloss, PERFECT TENSE hat geschlossen)
□ What time does the pool close? Wann schließt das Schwimmbad? □ The doors close automatically. Die Türen schließen automatisch.
■ **Please close the door.** Bitte mach die Tür zu.

★ **closed** ADJECTIVE
geschlossen
□ The bank's closed. Die Bank ist geschlossen.

closely ADVERB
genau (look, examine)

cloth NOUN
der Stoff masc (PL die Stoffe) (material)
■ **a cloth** ein Lappen masc □ Wipe it with a damp cloth. Wischen Sie es mit einem feuchten Lappen ab.

★ **clothes** PL NOUN
die Kleider neut pl
□ new clothes neue Kleider
■ **a clothes line** eine Wäscheleine
■ **a clothes peg** eine Wäscheklammer

★ **cloud** NOUN
1 die Wolke fem (in sky, of dust)
2 die Cloud fem (internet)
■ **cloud computing** das Cloud-Computing

cloudy ADJECTIVE
bewölkt

clove NOUN
■ **a clove of garlic** eine Knoblauchzehe

clown NOUN
der Clown masc (PL die Clowns)

Numbers in brackets refer to verb tables on pages 697 to 706.

405

club – Coke

★ **club** NOUN
der Klub masc (PL die Klubs)
□ a tennis club ein Tennisklub □ the youth club der Jugendklub
■ **clubs** (in cards) Kreuz neut □ the ace of clubs das Kreuzass

to **club together** VERB
zusammenlegen [15] (PERFECT TENSE hat zusammengelegt)
□ We clubbed together to buy her a present. Wir haben zusammengelegt, um ein Geschenk für sie zu kaufen.

clubbing NOUN
■ **to go clubbing** in Klubs gehen [29]

clue NOUN
der Hinweis masc (PL die Hinweise)
□ an important clue ein wichtiger Hinweis
■ **I haven't a clue.** Ich habe keine Ahnung.

clumsy ADJECTIVE
tollpatschig
□ Toby is even clumsier than his sister. Toby ist noch tollpatschiger als seine Schwester.

clutch NOUN
▷ see also **clutch** VERB
die Kupplung fem (of car)

to **clutch** VERB
▷ see also **clutch** NOUN
umklammern [34] (PERFECT TENSE hat umklammert)
□ She clutched my arm. Sie umklammerte meinen Arm.

clutter NOUN
der Kram masc
□ There's so much clutter in here. Hier liegt so viel Kram herum.

★ **coach** NOUN
1 der Reisebus masc (GEN des Reisebusses, PL die Reisebusse)
■ **by coach** mit dem Bus □ We went there by coach. Wir sind mit dem Bus dorthin gefahren.
■ **the coach station** der Busbahnhof
■ **a coach trip** eine Busreise
2 der Trainer masc (PL die Trainer)
die Trainerin fem (trainer)
□ the German coach der deutsche Trainer

★ **coal** NOUN
die Kohle fem
□ a coal mine eine Kohlezeche
■ **a coal miner** ein Bergarbeiter masc

coarse ADJECTIVE
1 grob
□ coarse black cloth grober schwarzer Stoff
2 grobkörnig
□ The sand is very coarse on that beach. Der Sand an diesem Strand ist sehr grobkörnig.

★ **coast** NOUN
die Küste fem
□ It's on the west coast of Scotland. Es liegt an der Westküste Schottlands.

coastguard NOUN
die Küstenwache fem

★ **coat** NOUN
der Mantel masc (PL die Mäntel)
□ a warm coat ein warmer Mantel
■ **a coat of paint** ein Anstrich masc

coat hanger NOUN
der Kleiderbügel masc (PL die Kleiderbügel)

cobweb NOUN
das Spinnennetz neut

cock NOUN
der Hahn masc (PL die Hähne) (bird)

cockerel NOUN
der Hahn masc (PL die Hähne)

cockney NOUN
der Cockney masc (PL die Cockneys)
□ I'm a cockney. Ich bin Cockney.

cocoa NOUN
der Kakao masc (PL die Kakaos or Kakao)
□ a cup of cocoa eine Tasse Kakao

When ordering more than one cup of cocoa use the plural form **Kakao**.

□ Two cocoas, please. Zwei Kakao bitte.

coconut NOUN
die Kokosnuss fem (PL die Kokosnüsse)

cod NOUN
der Kabeljau masc (PL die Kabeljaue)

★ **code** NOUN
▷ see also **code** VERB
der Code masc (PL die Codes)

★ **code** VERB
▷ see also **code** NOUN
codieren [76]

★ **coffee** NOUN
der Kaffee masc (PL die Kaffees or Kaffee)
□ A cup of coffee, please. Eine Tasse Kaffee, bitte.

When ordering more than one coffee use the plural form **Kaffee**.

□ Two coffees, please. Zwei Kaffee bitte.

coffeepot NOUN
die Kaffeekanne fem

coffee table NOUN
der Couchtisch masc (PL die Couchtische)

coffin NOUN
der Sarg masc (PL die Särge)

coin NOUN
die Münze fem
■ **a two-euro coin** ein Zweieurostück neut

coincidence NOUN
der Zufall masc (PL die Zufälle)

★ **Coke®** NOUN
die Cola fem (PL die Colas)
□ a can of Coke® eine Dose Cola

colander NOUN
der Seiher *masc* (PL die Seiher)

★ **cold** ADJECTIVE
▷ *see also* **cold** NOUN
kalt
□ The water's cold. Das Wasser ist kalt. □ It's cold today. Heute ist es kalt.

> When you talk about a person being 'cold', you use the impersonal construction.

□ I'm cold. Mir ist kalt. □ Are you cold? Ist dir kalt?

★ **cold** NOUN
▷ *see also* **cold** ADJECTIVE
1 die Kälte *fem*
□ I can't stand the cold. Ich kann Kälte nicht ausstehen.
2 der Schnupfen *masc* (PL die Schnupfen)
□ to catch a cold einen Schnupfen bekommen □ to have a cold einen Schnupfen haben □ I've got a bad cold. Ich habe einen üblen Schnupfen.
■ a cold sore ein Fieberbläschen *neut*

coleslaw NOUN
der Krautsalat *masc* (PL die Krautsalate)

★ to **collapse** VERB
zusammenbrechen [11] (PRESENT TENSE bricht zusammen, IMPERFECT brach zusammen, PERFECT TENSE ist zusammengebrochen)
□ He collapsed. Er brach zusammen.

collar NOUN
1 der Kragen *masc* (PL die Kragen) (*of coat, shirt*)
2 das Halsband *neut* (PL die Halsbänder) (*for animal*)

collarbone NOUN
das Schlüsselbein *neut* (PL die Schlüsselbeine)
□ I broke my collarbone. Ich habe mir das Schlüsselbein gebrochen.

★ **colleague** NOUN
der Kollege *masc* (GEN des Kollegen, PL die Kollegen)
die Kollegin *fem*

★ to **collect** VERB
1 einsammeln [4] (PERFECT TENSE hat eingesammelt)
□ The teacher collected the exercise books. Der Lehrer hat die Hefte eingesammelt.
2 sammeln [34]
□ I collect stamps. Ich sammle Briefmarken. □ They're collecting for charity. Sie sammeln für wohltätige Zwecke.
3 abholen [4] (PERFECT TENSE hat abgeholt) (*come to fetch*)
□ Their mother collects them from school. Ihre Mutter holt sie von der Schule ab. □ They collect the rubbish twice a week. Der Müll wird zweimal pro Woche abgeholt.

collect call NOUN (US)
das R-Gespräch *neut* (PL die R-Gespräche)

★ **collection** NOUN
die Sammlung *fem*
□ my CD collection meine CD-Sammlung □ a collection for charity eine Spendensammlung

collector NOUN
der Sammler *masc* (PL die Sammler)
die Sammlerin *fem*

★ **college** NOUN
die Fachhochschule *fem*

> **DID YOU KNOW...?**
> A **Fachhochschule** is an institute of higher education for pupils aged over 18, which combines academic studies with work experience. It is oriented towards the needs of industry and commerce.

to **collide** VERB
zusammenstoßen (PRESENT TENSE stößt zusammen, IMPERFECT stieß zusammen, PERFECT TENSE ist zusammengestoßen)

collie NOUN
der Collie *masc* (PL die Collies)

colliery NOUN
die Zeche *fem*

collision NOUN
der Zusammenstoß *masc* (GEN des Zusammenstoßes, PL die Zusammenstöße)

colon NOUN
der Doppelpunkt *masc* (*punctuation mark*)

colonel NOUN
der Oberst *masc* (GEN des Obersten, PL die Obersten)

★ **colour** (US **color**) NOUN
die Farbe *fem*
□ What colour is it? Welche Farbe hat es?

colourful (US **colorful**) ADJECTIVE
farbig

colouring (US **coloring**) NOUN
der Farbstoff *masc* (PL die Farbstoffe) (*for food*)

★ **comb** NOUN
▷ *see also* **comb** VERB
der Kamm *masc* (PL die Kämme)

★ to **comb** VERB
▷ *see also* **comb** NOUN
■ to comb one's hair sich kämmen [38] □ You haven't combed your hair. Du hast dich nicht gekämmt.

★ **combination** NOUN
die Kombination *fem*

★ to **combine** VERB
vereinen [84] (PERFECT TENSE hat vereint)
□ The film combines humour with suspense. Der Film vereint Humor und Spannung.

★ to **come** VERB
kommen [40] (IMPERFECT kam, PERFECT TENSE ist gekommen)
□ I'm coming! Ich komme! □ The letter came

Numbers in brackets refer to verb tables on pages 697 to 706.

407

C

this morning. Der Brief kam heute früh. □ Can I come too? Kann ich mitkommen? □ Some friends came to see us. Einige Freunde sind zu Besuch gekommen. □ I'll come with you. Ich komme mit dir.

to **come across** VERB
zufällig finden [24] (PERFECT TENSE hat sich beruhigt)

□ I came across some old photos. Ich fand zufällig einige alte Fotos.

■ **She comes across as a nice person.** Sie scheint ein netter Mensch zu sein.

to **come back** VERB
zurückkommen [40]

□ Come back! Komm zurück!.

to **come down** VERB
1 herunterkommen [40] (person, lift)
2 fallen [22] (prices)

to **come from** VERB
kommen [40] aus

□ I come from Germany. Ich komme aus Deutschland. □ Where do you come from? Woher kommen Sie?

to **come in** VERB
hereinkommen [40] aus

to **come out** VERB
herauskommen [40] aus

□ when we came out of the cinema als wir aus dem Kino kamen □ It's just come out on DVD. Es ist gerade als DVD herausgekommen.

to **come round** VERB
wieder zu sich finden [40] (after faint, operation)

to **come up** VERB
heraufkommen [40]

□ Come up here! Komm hier herauf!

■ **to come up to somebody** auf jemanden zukommen [40] □ She came up to me and kissed me. Sie kam auf mich zu und küsste mich.

comedian NOUN
der Komiker masc (PL die Komiker)
die Komikerin fem

★ **comedy** NOUN
die Komödie fem

★ **comfortable** ADJECTIVE
bequem

■ **I'm very comfortable, thanks.** Danke, ich fühle mich sehr wohl.

comic NOUN
das Comicheft neut (PL die Comichefte) (magazine)

comic strip NOUN
der Comicstrip masc (PL die Comicstrips)

coming ADJECTIVE
kommend

□ in the coming months in den kommenden Monaten

comma NOUN
das Komma neut (PL die Kommas)

★ **command** NOUN
der Befehl masc (PL die Befehle)

★ **comment** NOUN
▷ see also **comment** VERB
der Kommentar masc (PL die Kommentare)

□ He made no comment. Er gab keinen Kommentar ab. □ No comment! Kein Kommentar!

★ to **comment** VERB
▷ see also **comment** NOUN
■ **to comment on something** eine Bemerkung zu etwas machen [48]

commentary NOUN
der Kommentar masc (PL die Kommentare) (on TV, radio)

commentator NOUN
der Sportreporter masc (PL die Sportreporter)
die Sportreporterin fem (sports)

★ **commercial** NOUN
der Werbespot masc (PL die Werbespots)

★ to **commit** VERB
■ **to commit a crime** ein Verbrechen begehen [29]

■ **to commit oneself** sich festlegen [4] □ I don't want to commit myself. Ich will mich nicht festlegen.

■ **to commit suicide** Selbstmord begehen [29] □ He committed suicide. Er beging Selbstmord.

★ **committee** NOUN
der Ausschuss masc (GEN des Ausschusses, PL die Ausschüsse)

★ **common** ADJECTIVE
▷ see also **common** NOUN
gebräuchlich

□ 'Smith' is a very common surname. 'Smith' ist ein sehr gebräuchlicher Nachname.

■ **in common** gemein □ We've got a lot in common. Wir haben viel gemein.

★ **common** NOUN
▷ see also **common** ADJECTIVE
die Gemeindewiese fem

□ We went for a walk on the common. Wir sind auf der Gemeindewiese spazieren gegangen.

Commons PL NOUN
■ **the House of Commons** das britische Unterhaus

common sense NOUN
der gesunde Menschenverstand masc

□ Use your common sense! Benutze deinen gesunden Menschenverstand!

★ to **communicate** VERB
kommunizieren [76] (PERFECT TENSE hat kommuniziert)

★ **communication** NOUN
die Kommunikation *fem*

communion NOUN
die Kommunion *fem*
□ my First Communion meine Erstkommunion

communism NOUN
der Kommunismus *masc* (GEN des Kommunismus)

communist NOUN
▷ see also **communist** ADJECTIVE
der Kommunist *masc* (GEN des Kommunisten, PL die Kommunisten)
die Kommunistin *fem*

communist ADJECTIVE
▷ see also **communist** NOUN
kommunistisch
■ **the Communist Party** die Kommunistische Partei

★ **community** NOUN
die Gemeinschaft *fem*
■ **the local community** die Gemeinde

to **commute** VERB
pendeln [34] (PERFECT TENSE ist gependelt)
□ She commutes between Liss and London. Sie pendelt zwischen Liss und London.

compact disc NOUN
die Compact Disc *fem* (PL die Compact Discs)
■ **compact disc player** der CD-Spieler

companion NOUN
der Gefährte *masc* (GEN des Gefährten, PL die Gefährten)
die Gefährtin *fem*

★ **company** NOUN
1 das Unternehmen *neut* (PL die Unternehmen)
□ He works for a big company. Er arbeitet für ein großes Unternehmen.
2 die Gesellschaft *fem*
□ an insurance company eine Versicherungsgesellschaft
■ **a theatre company** ein Theaterensemble *neut*
■ **to keep somebody company** jemandem Gesellschaft leisten [2] □ I'll keep you company. Ich leiste dir Gesellschaft.

comparatively ADVERB
relativ

★ to **compare** VERB
vergleichen (IMPERFECT verglich, PERFECT TENSE hat verglichen)
□ People always compare him with his brother. Die Leute vergleichen ihn immer mit seinem Bruder.
■ **compared with** im Vergleich zu □ Oxford is small compared with London. Im Vergleich zu London ist Oxford klein.

★ **comparison** NOUN
der Vergleich *masc* (PL die Vergleiche)

compartment NOUN
das Abteil *neut* (PL die Abteile)

compass NOUN
der Kompass *masc* (GEN des Kompasses, PL die Kompasse)

compensation NOUN
der Schadenersatz *masc*
□ I got a thousand pounds compensation. Ich bekam tausend Pfund Schadenersatz.

compere NOUN
der Conférencier *masc* (PL die Conférenciers)

★ to **compete** VERB
teilnehmen [52] (PRESENT TENSE nimmt teil, IMPERFECT nahm teil, PERFECT TENSE hat teilgenommen)
□ I'm competing in the marathon. Ich nehme am Marathon teil.
■ **to compete for something** um etwas kämpfen [38] □ They are competing for a place in the UEFA cup. Sie kämpfen um einen Platz im UEFA-Pokal.
■ **There are fifty students competing for six places.** Fünfzig Studenten bewerben sich auf sechs Studienplätze.

competent ADJECTIVE
kompetent

★ **competition** NOUN
der Wettbewerb *masc* (PL die Wettbewerbe) (*organized event*)
□ a singing competition ein Gesangswettbewerb

★ **competitive** ADJECTIVE
■ **I'm a very competitive person.** Ich bin ein sehr ehrgeiziger Mensch.

★ **competitor** NOUN
der Teilnehmer *masc* (PL die Teilnehmer)
die Teilnehmerin *fem* (*participant*)

★ to **complain** VERB
sich beschweren [18] (PERFECT TENSE hat sich beschwert)
□ I'm going to complain to the manager. Ich werde mich beim Geschäftsführer beschweren.
□ We complained about the noise. Wir haben uns über den Lärm beschwert.

★ **complaint** NOUN
die Beschwerde *fem*
□ There were lots of complaints about the food. Es gab viele Beschwerden über das Essen.

★ **complete** ADJECTIVE
vollständig

★ **completely** ADVERB
völlig

complexion NOUN
der Teint *masc* (PL die Teints)

★ **complicated** ADJECTIVE
kompliziert

compliment NOUN
▷ see also **compliment** VERB
das Kompliment neut (PL die Komplimente)

to **compliment** VERB
▷ see also **compliment** NOUN
■ **They complimented me on my German.**
Sie haben mir Komplimente zu meinem
Deutsch gemacht.

complimentary ADJECTIVE
■ **complimentary ticket** der Freifahrschein

to **compose** VERB
komponieren [76] (PERFECT TENSE hat
komponiert) (music)
■ **to be composed of something** aus etwas
bestehen [72] □ The team is composed of two
boys and three girls. Die Mannschaft besteht
aus zwei Jungen und drei Mädchen.

composer NOUN
der Komponist masc (GEN des Komponisten, PL
die Komponisten)
die Komponistin fem

comprehension NOUN
das Verständnis neut (school exercise)

comprehensive ADJECTIVE
umfassend
□ a comprehensive guide ein umfassender
Reiseführer

comprehensive school NOUN
die Gesamtschule fem

> DID YOU KNOW...?
> **Gesamtschulen** are the exception rather
> than the rule in Germany.

★ **compromise** NOUN
▷ see also **compromise** VERB
der Kompromiss masc (GEN des Kompromisses,
PL die Kompromisse)
□ We reached a compromise. Wir haben einen
Kompromiss gefunden.

★ to **compromise** VERB
▷ see also **compromise** NOUN
einen Kompromiss schließen (IMPERFECT
schloss, PERFECT TENSE hat geschlossen)

compulsory ADJECTIVE
obligatorisch

★ **computer** NOUN
der Computer masc (PL die Computer)

★ **computer game** NOUN
das Computerspiel neut (PL die Computerspiele)

computer programmer NOUN
der Programmierer masc (PL die
Programmierer)
die Programmiererin fem
□ She's a computer programmer. Sie ist
Programmiererin.

computer science NOUN
die Informatik fem

computing NOUN
die Informatik fem

★ to **concentrate** VERB
sich konzentrieren [76] (PERFECT TENSE hat sich
konzentriert)
□ I couldn't concentrate. Ich konnte mich nicht
konzentrieren.

concentration NOUN
die Konzentration fem

concern NOUN
▷ see also **concern** VERB
die Sorge fem
□ to express concern about something Sorge
über etwas ausdrücken

to **concern** VERB
▷ see also **concern** NOUN
betreffen [78] (PRESENT TENSE betrifft, IMPERFECT
betraf, PERFECT TENSE hat betroffen)
□ It concerns all of us. Es betrifft uns alle.

concerned ADJECTIVE
■ **to be concerned** sich Sorgen machen [48]
□ I am concerned about him. Ich mache mir
Sorgen um ihn.
■ **as far as I'm concerned** was mich betrifft

concerning PREPOSITION
bezüglich
□ For further information concerning the job,
contact Mr Ross. Für weitere Informationen
bezüglich der Stelle wenden Sie sich an Herrn
Ross.

★ **concert** NOUN
das Konzert neut (PL die Konzerte)

concrete NOUN
der Beton masc (PL die Betons)

to **condemn** VERB
verurteilen [84] (PERFECT TENSE hat verurteilt)

★ **condition** NOUN
1 die Bedingung fem
□ I'll do it, on one condition ... Ich mache es
unter einer Bedingung ...
2 der Zustand masc (PL die Zustände)
□ in good condition in gutem Zustand

conditional NOUN
der Konditional masc

conditioner NOUN
die Spülung fem (for hair)

condom NOUN
das Kondom neut (PL die Kondome)

to **conduct** VERB
dirigieren [76] (PERFECT TENSE hat dirigiert)
(orchestra)

conductor NOUN
der Dirigent masc (GEN des Dirigenten, PL die
Dirigenten)
die Dirigentin fem

cone NOUN
1 die Eistüte fem
□ an ice-cream cone eine Eistüte

★ = core vocabulary

2 der Kegel *masc* (PL die Kegel) (*geometric shape*)
■ **a traffic cone** ein Pylon *masc*

conference NOUN
die Konferenz *fem*

to confess VERB
gestehen [72] (IMPERFECT gestand, PERFECT TENSE hat gestanden)
□ He finally confessed. Er hat schließlich gestanden. □ He confessed to the murder. Er hat den Mord gestanden.

confession NOUN
1 das Geständnis *neut* (GEN des Geständnisses, PL die Geständnisse)
□ He signed a confession. Er unterschrieb ein Geständnis.
2 die Beichte *fem* (*in church*)
□ to go to confession zur Beichte gehen

confetti NOUN
das Konfetti *neut*

★ **confidence** NOUN
1 das Vertrauen *neut*
□ I've got confidence in you. Ich habe Vertrauen in dich.
2 das Selbstvertrauen *neut*
□ She lacks confidence. Sie hat zu wenig Selbstvertrauen.

★ **confident** ADJECTIVE
1 zuversichtlich (*sure of something*)
□ I'm confident everything will be okay. Ich bin zuversichtlich, dass alles gut gehen wird.
2 selbstbewusst (*self-assured*)
□ She seems to be a confident person. Sie scheint eine selbstbewusste Frau zu sein.

confidential ADJECTIVE
vertraulich

★ **to confirm** VERB
bestätigen [18] (PERFECT TENSE hat bestätigt) (*booking*)

confirmation NOUN
die Bestätigung *fem*

conflict NOUN
der Konflikt *masc* (PL die Konflikte)

to confuse VERB
durcheinanderbringen [13] (IMPERFECT brachte durcheinander, PERFECT TENSE hat durcheinandergebracht)
□ Don't confuse me! Bring mich nicht durcheinander!

confused ADJECTIVE
durcheinander

confusing ADJECTIVE
verwirrend

confusion NOUN
das Durcheinander *neut*

to congratulate VERB
beglückwünschen [7] (PERFECT TENSE hat beglückwünscht)

□ All my friends congratulated me. Alle meine Freunde haben mich beglückwünscht.

★ **congratulations** PL NOUN
der Glückwunsch *masc* (PL die Glückwünsche)
□ Congratulations on your new job! Herzlichen Glückwunsch zum neuen Job!

conjunction NOUN
die Konjunktion *fem*

conjurer NOUN
der Zauberkünstler *masc* (PL die Zauberkünstler)
die Zauberkünstlerin *fem*

★ **connection** NOUN
1 der Zusammenhang *masc* (PL die Zusammenhänge)
□ There's no connection between the two events. Es besteht kein Zusammenhang zwischen den beiden Ereignissen.
2 der Kontakt *masc* (PL die Kontakte) (*electrical*)
□ There's a loose connection. Da ist ein Wackelkontakt.
3 der Anschluss *masc* (GEN des Anschlusses, PL die Anschlüsse) (*of trains, planes*)
□ We missed our connection. Wir haben unseren Anschluss verpasst.

to conquer VERB
erobern [88] (PERFECT TENSE hat erobert)

conscience NOUN
das Gewissen *neut*
□ I have a guilty conscience. Ich habe ein schlechtes Gewissen.

★ **conscious** ADJECTIVE
bewusst
□ politically conscious politisch bewusst □ a conscious effort eine bewusste Anstrengung
■ **to be conscious of something 1** (*know*) sich einer Sache bewusst sein [65] □ I was conscious of his disapproval. Ich war mir seiner Missbilligung bewusst. **2** (*notice*) etwas bemerken [7] □ She was conscious of Max looking at her. Sie hatte bemerkt, dass Max sie ansah.

consciousness NOUN
das Bewusstsein *neut*
■ **to lose consciousness** bewusstlos werden [91] □ I lost consciousness. Ich wurde bewusstlos.

★ **consequence** NOUN
die Folge *fem*

consequently ADVERB
folglich

conservation NOUN
der Schutz *masc*
□ nature conservation der Naturschutz

★ **Conservative** NOUN
▷ see also **conservative** ADJECTIVE
der Konservative *masc* (GEN des Konservativen, PL die Konservativen)
die Konservative *fem*

Numbers in brackets refer to verb tables on pages 697 to 706.

411

□ a Conservative (man) ein Konservativer
■ **to vote Conservative** konservativ wählen [38]
■ **the Conservatives** die Konservativen

★ **conservative** ADJECTIVE
▷ see also **Conservative**
konservativ
■ **the Conservative Party** die Konservative Partei

conservatory NOUN
der Wintergarten masc (PL die Wintergärten)

★ **to consider** VERB
in Erwägung ziehen [96] (IMPERFECT zog in Erwägung, PERFECT TENSE hat in Erwägung gezogen)
□ We considered cancelling our holiday. Wir zogen in Erwägung, den Urlaub abzusagen.
■ **I'm considering the idea.** Ich denke darüber nach.
■ **He considered it a waste of time.** Er hielt es für Zeitverschwendung.

considerate ADJECTIVE
1 rücksichtsvoll
□ She's a very considerate person. Sie ist ein rücksichtsvoller Mensch.
2 aufmerksam (kind)
□ That was very considerate of you. Das war sehr aufmerksam von dir.

considering PREPOSITION
1 dafür, dass
□ Considering we were there for a month ... Dafür, dass wir einen Monat da waren ...
2 unter den Umständen
□ I got a good mark, considering. Unter den Umständen bekam ich eine gute Note.

to consist VERB
■ **to consist of** bestehen [72] aus □ The band consists of three guitarists and a drummer. Die Band besteht aus drei Gitarristen und einem Schlagzeuger.

consistent ADJECTIVE
beständig
□ He's our most consistent player. Er ist unser beständigster Spieler.

consonant NOUN
der Konsonant masc (GEN des Konsonanten, PL die Konsonanten)

★ **constant** ADJECTIVE
beständig

constantly ADVERB
dauernd

constipated ADJECTIVE
verstopft

to construct VERB
bauen [38]

construction NOUN
der Bau masc (PL die Bauten)

★ **to consult** VERB
1 um Rat fragen [38] (solicitor, doctor)
2 nachsehen [64] in +dat (PRESENT TENSE sieht nach, IMPERFECT sah nach, PERFECT TENSE hat nachgesehen) (book)
□ Consult the dictionary! Sieh im Wörterbuch nach!

★ **consumer** NOUN
der Verbraucher masc (PL die Verbraucher)
die Verbraucherin fem

★ **contact** NOUN
▷ see also **contact** VERB
der Kontakt masc (PL die Kontakte)
□ I'm in contact with her. Ich bin in Kontakt mit ihr.
■ **your contact details** Ihre Kontaktinformationen
■ **a contact number** eine Kontaktnummer

★ **to contact** VERB
▷ see also **contact** NOUN
sich in Verbindung setzen [36] mit
□ Please contact us immediately. Bitte setzen Sie sich sofort mit uns in Verbindung.
■ **Where can we contact you?** Wo können wir Sie erreichen?

contact lenses PL NOUN
die Kontaktlinsen fem pl

contactless ADJECTIVE
kontaktlos (payment)

★ **to contain** VERB
enthalten [33] (PRESENT TENSE enthält, IMPERFECT enthielt, PERFECT TENSE hat enthalten)

container NOUN
der Behälter masc (PL die Behälter)

contempt NOUN
die Verachtung fem

contents PL NOUN
der Inhalt masc
■ **table of contents** das Inhaltsverzeichnis

★ **contest** NOUN
der Wettbewerb masc (PL die Wettbewerbe)

contestant NOUN
der Teilnehmer masc (PL die Teilnehmer)
die Teilnehmerin fem

★ **context** NOUN
der Zusammenhang masc (PL die Zusammenhänge)

★ **continent** NOUN
der Kontinent masc (PL die Kontinente)
□ How many continents are there? Wie viele Kontinente gibt es?

continental breakfast NOUN
das kleine Frühstück neut

continental quilt NOUN
die Steppdecke fem

★ **to continue** VERB
weitermachen [48] (PERFECT TENSE hat weitergemacht)

　　　　★ = core vocabulary

□ We'll continue tomorrow. Wir machen morgen weiter.
- **Please continue!** Bitte fahren Sie fort!
- **She continued talking to her friend.** Sie redete weiter mit ihrer Freundin.

continuous ADJECTIVE
laufend
- **continuous assessment** laufende Leistungskontrolle

contraceptive NOUN
das Verhütungsmittel *neut* (PL die Verhütungsmittel)

★ **contract** NOUN
der Vertrag *masc* (PL die Verträge)

to **contradict** VERB
widersprechen [70] (PRESENT TENSE widerspricht, IMPERFECT widersprach, PERFECT TENSE hat widersprochen)
□ Don't contradict me! Widersprich mir nicht!

contrary NOUN
das Gegenteil *neut*
- **on the contrary** im Gegenteil

★ **contrast** NOUN
der Kontrast *masc* (PL die Kontraste)

★ to **contribute** VERB
1 beitragen [77] (PRESENT TENSE trägt bei, IMPERFECT trug bei, PERFECT TENSE hat beigetragen)
□ The treaty will contribute to world peace. Der Vertrag wird zum Weltfrieden beitragen.
2 spenden [54] (*donate*)
□ She contributed ten pounds. Sie hat zehn Pfund gespendet.

★ **contribution** NOUN
der Beitrag *masc* (PL die Beiträge)

★ **control** NOUN
▷ *see also* **control** VERB
die Kontrolle *fem*
- **to lose control** (*of vehicle*) die Kontrolle verlieren [85] □ He lost control of the car. Er hat die Kontrolle über das Auto verloren.
- **the controls** (*of machine*) die Bedienelemente *neut pl*
- **to be in control** das Sagen haben [32]
- **to keep control** (*of people*) Disziplin halten [33] □ He can't keep control of the class. Er kann in der Klasse keine Disziplin halten.
- **out of control** (*child, class*) außer Rand und Band

★ to **control** VERB
▷ *see also* **control** NOUN
1 unter Kontrolle haben [32] (PRESENT TENSE hat unter Kontrolle, IMPERFECT hatte unter Kontrolle, PERFECT TENSE hat unter Kontrolle gehabt) (*country, organization*)
2 Disziplin halten [33] in +*dat* (PRESENT TENSE hält Disziplin in, IMPERFECT hielt Disziplin in, PERFECT TENSE hat Disziplin gehalten in)

□ He can't control the class. Er kann in der Klasse keine Disziplin halten.
3 unter Kontrolle halten [33]
□ I couldn't control the horse. Ich konnte das Pferd nicht mehr unter Kontrolle halten.
4 regeln [34] (*regulate*)
□ You can control the volume. Sie können die Lautstärke regeln.
- **to control oneself** sich beherrschen [7]

★ **controversial** ADJECTIVE
umstritten
□ a controversial book ein umstrittenes Buch

convenient ADJECTIVE
günstig (*place*)
□ The hotel's convenient for the airport. Das Hotel ist in günstiger Lage zum Flughafen.
- **It's not convenient for me right now.** Es ist gerade ungünstig.
- **Would Monday be convenient for you?** Würde dir Montag passen?

conventional ADJECTIVE
konventionell

convent school NOUN
die Klosterschule *fem*

★ **conversation** NOUN
die Unterhaltung *fem*
- **a German conversation class** deutsche Konversation

to **convert** VERB
umbauen [4] (PERFECT TENSE hat umgebaut)
□ We've converted the loft into a spare room. Wir haben den Speicher zu einem Gästezimmer umgebaut.

convict NOUN
▷ *see also* **convict** VERB
der Häftling *masc*
□ an escaped convict ein entflohener Häftling

to **convict** VERB
▷ *see also* **convict** NOUN
überführen [18] (PERFECT TENSE hat überführt)
□ He was convicted of the murder. Er wurde des Mordes überführt.

conviction NOUN
die Überzeugung *fem*
□ She spoke with great conviction. Sie sprach mit großer Überzeugung.
- **He has three previous convictions for robbery.** Er ist bereits dreimal wegen Raubes vorbestraft.

★ to **convince** VERB
überzeugen [18] (PERFECT TENSE hat überzeugt)
□ I'm not convinced. Ich bin nicht überzeugt.

★ to **cook** VERB
▷ *see also* **cook** NOUN
kochen [48]
□ I can't cook. Ich kann nicht kochen. □ She's cooking lunch. Sie kocht das Mittagessen.
- **to be cooked** fertig sein [65] □ When the

Numbers in brackets refer to verb tables on pages 697 to 706.

413

potatoes are cooked ...Wenn die Kartoffeln fertig sind ...

★ **cook** NOUN
▷ *see also* **cook** VERB
der Koch *masc* (PLdie Köche)
die Köchin *fem*
□ Werner's an excellent cook.Werner ist ein ausgezeichneter Koch.

cookbook NOUN
das Kochbuch *neut* (PLdie Kochbücher)

★ **cooker** NOUN
der Herd *masc* (PLdie Herde)
□ a gas cookerein Gasherd

cookery NOUN
das Kochen *neut*
■ **a cookery class**ein Kochkurs *masc*

cookie NOUN (US)
der Keks *masc* (GENdes Kekses , PLdie Kekse)

★ **cooking** NOUN
das Kochen *neut*
■ **I like cooking.**Ich koche gern.

★ **cool** ADJECTIVE
▷ *see also* **cool** VERB
1 kühl
□ a cooler placeein kühlerer Ort
2 cool (*great*)
□ That's really cool!Das ist echt cool!
■ **to stay cool** (*keep calm*)ruhig bleiben [10]
□ He stayed cool.Er blieb ruhig.

★ to **cool** VERB
▷ *see also* **cool** ADJECTIVE
kühlen [38]
■ **Just cool it!**Immer mit der Ruhe! (*informal*)

cooperation NOUN
die Zusammenarbeit *fem*

cop NOUN
der Polizist *masc* (GENdes Polizisten , PLdie Polizisten)
die Polizistin *fem*

co-parent VERB
eine gemeinsame Elternschaft eingehen [29]

to **cope** VERB
es schaffen [48]
□ It was hard, but we coped.Es war schwer, aber wir haben es geschafft.
■ **to cope with**bewältigen [84] □ She's got a lot of problems to cope with.Sie hat eine Menge Probleme zu bewältigen.

copper NOUN
1 das Kupfer *neut*
□ a copper braceletein Kupferarmband
2 der Polizist *masc* (GENdes Polizisten , PLdie Polizisten)
die Polizistin *fem* (*police officer*)

★ **copy** NOUN
▷ *see also* **copy** VERB
1 die Kopie *fem* (*of letter, document*)
2 das Exemplar *neut* (PLdie Exemplare) (*of book*)

★ to **copy** VERB
▷ *see also* **copy** NOUN
1 abschreiben [61] (IMPERFECTschrieb ab , PERFECT TENSEhat abgeschrieben) (*write down*)
□ She copied the sentence.Sie schrieb den Satz ab. □ The teacher accused him of copying.Der Lehrer warf ihm vor, abgeschrieben zu haben.
2 nachmachen [4] (PERFECT TENSEhat nachgemacht) (*person*)
□ She always copies her sister.Sie macht ihrer Schwester alles nach.
3 kopieren [76] (PERFECT TENSEhat kopiert) (*computer*)
□ to copy and pastekopieren und einfügen

core NOUN
der Stein *masc* (*of fruit*)

cork NOUN
1 der Korken *masc* (PLdie Korken) (*of bottle*)
2 der Kork *masc* (*material*)
□ a cork table matein Korkuntersetzer *masc*

corkscrew NOUN
der Korkenzieher *masc* (PLdie Korkenzieher)

corn NOUN
1 das Getreide *neut* (PLdie Getreide) (*wheat*)
2 der Mais *masc* (*sweetcorn*)
■ **corn on the cob**der Maiskolben

★ **corner** NOUN
1 die Ecke *fem*
□ in a corner of the roomin einer Ecke des Zimmers □ the shop on the cornerdas Geschäft an der Ecke □ He lives just round the corner.Er wohnt gleich um die Ecke.
2 der Eckball *masc* (PLdie Eckbälle) (*in football*)

cornet NOUN
1 das Kornett *neut* (PLdie Kornette)
□ He plays the cornet.Er spielt Kornett.
2 die Eistüte *fem* (*ice cream*)

cornflakes PL NOUN
die Cornflakes *pl*

cornstarch NOUN (US)
das Maismehl *neut*

Cornwall NOUN
Cornwall *neut*
■ **in Cornwall**in Cornwall

corporal NOUN
der Stabsunteroffizier *masc* (PLdie Stabsunteroffiziere)

corporal punishment NOUN
die Prügelstrafe *fem*

corpse NOUN
die Leiche *fem*

★ **correct** ADJECTIVE
▷ *see also* **correct** VERB
richtig
□ That's correct.Das ist richtig. □ the correct answerdie richtige Antwort

★ to **correct** VERB
▷ *see also* **correct** ADJECTIVE
korrigieren [76] (PERFECT TENSE hat korrigiert)

correction NOUN
die Verbesserung *fem*

correctly ADVERB
richtig

correspondent NOUN
der Korrespondent *masc* (GEN des
Korrespondenten , PL die Korrespondenten)
die Korrespondentin *fem*

corridor NOUN
der Korridor *masc* (PL die Korridore)

corruption NOUN
die Korruption *fem*

cosmetics PL NOUN
die Kosmetika *neut pl*

cosmetic surgery NOUN
die Schönheitschirurgie *fem*

★ to **cost** VERB
▷ *see also* **cost** NOUN
kosten [2]
□ The meal cost seventy euros. Das Essen hat
siebzig Euro gekostet. □ How much does it
cost? Wie viel kostet das? □ It costs too much.
Das kostet zu viel.

★ **cost** NOUN
▷ *see also* **cost** VERB
die Kosten *pl*
□ the cost of living die Lebenshaltungskosten
■ **at all costs** um jeden Preis

costume NOUN
das Kostüm *neut* (PL die Kostüme)

cosy ADJECTIVE
gemütlich

cot NOUN
1 das Kinderbett *neut* (PL die Kinderbetten) (for
children)
2 die Campingliege *fem* (camp bed)

★ **cottage** NOUN
das kleine Haus *neut* (GEN des kleinen Hauses ,
PL die kleinen Häuser)

cottage cheese NOUN
der Hüttenkäse *masc*

★ **cotton** NOUN
die Baumwolle *fem*
□ a cotton shirt ein Baumwollhemd *neut*
■ **cotton candy** die Zuckerwatte
■ **cotton wool** die Watte

couch NOUN
die Couch *fem* (PL die Couchs)

couchette NOUN
der Platz im Liegewagen *masc* (PL die Plätze im
Liegewagen)

to **cough** VERB
▷ *see also* **cough** NOUN
husten [2]

★ **cough** NOUN
▷ *see also* **cough** VERB
der Husten *masc*
□ a bad cough ein schlimmer Husten □ I've got
a cough. Ich habe Husten.

★ **could** VERB ▷ *see* can

★ **council** NOUN
der Gemeinderat *masc* (PL die Gemeinderäte)
□ He's on the council. Er ist im Gemeinderat.
■ **a council estate** eine Siedlung des sozialen
Wohnungsbaus
■ **a council house** eine Sozialwohnung

> **DID YOU KNOW...?**
> In Germany the council provides flats rather
> than houses.

councillor NOUN
der Gemeinderat *masc* (PL die Gemeinderäte)
die Gemeinderätin *fem*
□ She's a local councillor. Sie ist Gemeinderätin.

★ to **count** VERB
zählen [38]

to **count on** VERB
zählen [38] auf +acc
□ You can count on me. Du kannst auf mich
zählen.

★ **counter** NOUN
1 der Ladentisch *masc* (PL die Ladentische) (in
shop)
2 der Schalter *masc* (PL die Schalter) (in post office,
bank)
3 die Spielmarke *fem* (in game)

★ **country** NOUN
das Land *neut* (PL die Länder)
□ the border between the two countries die
Grenze zwischen den beiden Ländern
■ **in the country** auf dem Land □ I live in the
country. Ich wohne auf dem Land.
■ **country dancing** der Volkstanz

★ **countryside** NOUN
die Landschaft *fem*

★ **county** NOUN
die Grafschaft *fem*

> **DID YOU KNOW...?**
> The nearest German equivalent of a county
> would be a Bundesland .

■ **the county council** der Grafschaftsrat

> **DID YOU KNOW...?**
> The nearest German equivalent of a county
> council would be the Landtag .

★ **couple** NOUN
das Paar *neut* (PL die Paare)
□ the couple who live next door das Paar von
nebenan
■ **a couple** ein paar

> Note that in this sense paar is spelt with a
> small 'p'.

□ **a couple of hours** ein paar Stunden □ **Could you wait a couple of minutes?** Könntest du ein paar Minuten warten?

★**courage** NOUN
der Mut *masc*

courgette NOUN
die Zucchini *fem* (PL die Zucchini)

courier NOUN
1 der Kurier *masc* (PL die Kuriere) (*delivery service*) □ **They sent it by courier.** Sie haben es mit Kurier geschickt.
2 der Reiseleiter *masc* (PL die Reiseleiter) die Reiseleiterin *fem* (*for tourists*)

★**course** NOUN
1 der Kurs *masc* (PL die Kurse) □ **a German course** ein Deutschkurs □ **to go on a course** einen Kurs machen
2 der Gang *masc* (PL die Gänge) □ **the first course** der erste Gang ▪ **the main course** das Hauptgericht
3 der Platz *masc* (PL die Plätze) □ **a golf course** ein Golfplatz ▪ **of course** natürlich □ **Do you like chocolate? — Of course I do!** Magst du Schokolade? — Aber natürlich!

★**court** NOUN
1 das Gericht *neut* (PL die Gerichte) (*of law*) □ **He was in court last week.** Er war letzte Woche vor Gericht.
2 der Platz *masc* (PL die Plätze) (*tennis*) □ **There are tennis and squash courts.** Es gibt Tennis- und Squashplätze.

courtyard NOUN
der Hof *masc* (PL die Höfe)

★**cousin** NOUN
1 der Cousin *masc* (PL die Cousins) (*man*)
2 die Cousine *fem* (*woman*)

★**cover** NOUN
▷ *see also* **cover** VERB
1 der Umschlag *masc* (PL die Umschläge) (*of book*)
2 der Bezug *masc* (PL die Bezüge) (*of duvet*)

★**to cover** VERB
▷ *see also* **cover** NOUN
bedecken [18] (PERFECT TENSE hat bedeckt) □ **Cover the dough with a cloth.** Bedecke den Teig mit einem Tuch. ▪ **My face was covered with mosquito bites.** Mein Gesicht war voller Mückenstiche. ▪ **to cover up a scandal** einen Skandal vertuschen [7]

covering letter NOUN
die Geleitbrief *masc*

★**cow** NOUN
die Kuh *fem* (PL die Kühe)

coward NOUN
der Feigling *masc* (PL die Feiglinge)

der Feigling is also used for women.

□ **She's a coward.** Sie ist ein Feigling.

cowardly ADJECTIVE
feige

crab NOUN
die Krabbe *fem*

★**crack** NOUN
▷ *see also* **crack** VERB
1 der Riss *masc* (GEN des Risses, PL die Risse) (*in wall*)
2 der Sprung *masc* (PL die Sprünge) (*in cup, window*) ▪ **I'll have a crack at it.** Ich werd's mal versuchen.

★**to crack** VERB
▷ *see also* **crack** NOUN
1 knacken [48] (*nut*)
2 aufschlagen [59] (PRESENT TENSE schlägt auf, IMPERFECT schlug auf, PERFECT TENSE hat aufgeschlagen) (*egg*) ▪ **to crack a joke** einen Witz reißen

to crack down on VERB
hart durchgreifen gegen □ **The police are cracking down on cybercrime.** Die Polizei greift hart gegen Cyberkriminalität durch.

cracked ADJECTIVE
kaputt (*cup, window*)

cracker NOUN
1 der Cracker *masc* (PL die Cracker) (*biscuit*)
2 das Knallbonbon *neut* (PL die Knallbonbons) (*Christmas cracker*)

cradle NOUN
die Wiege *fem*

★**craft** NOUN
das Werken *neut* □ **We do craft at school.** Wir haben Werken in der Schule. ▪ **a craft centre** ein Kunstgewerbezentrum *neut*

craftsman NOUN
der Kunsthandwerker *masc* (PL die Kunsthandwerker)

to cram VERB
1 stopfen [38] □ **We crammed our stuff into the boot.** Wir haben unsere Sachen in den Kofferraum gestopft.
2 pauken [38] (*for exams*)

crane NOUN
der Kran *masc* (*machine*)

★**to crash** VERB
▷ *see also* **crash** NOUN
kaputt fahren [21] (PRESENT TENSE fährt kaputt, IMPERFECT fuhr kaputt, PERFECT TENSE hat kaputt gefahren) □ **He's crashed his car.** Er hat sein Auto kaputt gefahren. ▪ **The plane crashed.** Das Flugzeug stürzte ab. ▪ **to crash into something** auf etwas fahren

[21] □ My brother crashed into the back of a lorry. Mein Bruder ist hinten auf einen Lastwagen gefahren.

crash NOUN
▷ see also **crash** VERB
1 der Unfall *masc* (PL die Unfälle) (*of car*)
2 das Unglück *neut* (PL die Unglücke) (*of plane*)
   ■ **a crash helmet** ein Sturzhelm *masc*
   ■ **a crash course** ein Crashkurs *masc*

to **crawl** VERB
▷ see also **crawl** NOUN
krabbeln [88] (PERFECT TENSE ist gekrabbelt) (*baby*)

crawl NOUN
▷ see also **crawl** VERB
das Kraulen *neut*
   ■ **to do the crawl** kraulen [38]

crazy ADJECTIVE
verrückt

cream ADJECTIVE
▷ see also **cream** NOUN
cremefarben (*colour*)

cream NOUN
▷ see also **cream** ADJECTIVE
die Sahne *fem*
   □ strawberries and cream Erdbeeren mit Sahne
   □ a cream cake eine Sahnetorte
   ■ **cream cheese** der Frischkäse
   ■ **sun cream** die Sonnencreme

crease NOUN
die Falte *fem*

creased ADJECTIVE
zerknittert

to **create** VERB
schaffen (IMPERFECT schuf, PERFECT TENSE hat geschaffen)

creation NOUN
die Schöpfung *fem*

creative ADJECTIVE
kreativ

creature NOUN
das Lebewesen *neut* (PL die Lebewesen)

crèche NOUN
die Kinderkrippe *fem*

credit NOUN
der Kredit *masc* (PL die Kredite)
   □ on credit auf Kredit

credit card NOUN
die Kreditkarte *fem*

creep NOUN
▷ see also **creep** VERB
   ■ **It gives me the creeps.** Es ist mir nicht geheuer.

to **creep** VERB
▷ see also **creep** NOUN
kriechen (IMPERFECT kroch, PERFECT TENSE ist gekrochen)

cress NOUN
die Kresse *fem*

crew NOUN
die Mannschaft *fem*

crew cut NOUN
der Bürstenhaarschnitt *masc* (PL die Bürstenhaarschnitte)

★ **cricket** NOUN
1 das Cricket *neut*

> **DID YOU KNOW...?**
> Cricket is practically never played in Germany.

   □ I play cricket. Ich spiele Cricket.
   ■ **a cricket bat** ein Cricketschläger *masc*
2 die Grille *fem* (*insect*)

★ **crime** NOUN
1 das Verbrechen *neut* (PL die Verbrechen)
   □ Murder is a crime. Mord ist ein Verbrechen.
2 die Kriminalität *fem* (*lawlessness*)
   □ Crime is rising. Die Kriminalität nimmt zu.

★ **criminal** NOUN
▷ see also **criminal** ADJECTIVE
der Verbrecher *masc* (PL die Verbrecher)
die Verbrecherin *fem*

★ **criminal** ADJECTIVE
▷ see also **criminal** NOUN
kriminell
   □ It's criminal! Das ist kriminell!
   ■ **It's a criminal offence.** Das ist eine strafbare Handlung.
   ■ **to have a criminal record** vorbestraft sein [65]

★ **crisis** NOUN
die Krise *fem*

crisp ADJECTIVE
knusprig (*food*)

★ **crisps** PL NOUN
die Chips *masc pl*
   □ a bag of crisps eine Tüte Chips

criterion NOUN
das Kriterium *neut* (PL die Kriterien)

★ **critic** NOUN
der Kritiker *masc* (PL die Kritiker)
die Kritikerin *fem*

critical ADJECTIVE
kritisch

★ **criticism** NOUN
die Kritik *fem*

★ to **criticize** VERB
kritisieren [76] (PERFECT TENSE hat kritisiert)

Croatia NOUN
Kroatien *neut*
   ■ **from Croatia** aus Kroatien
   ■ **to Croatia** nach Kroatien

to **crochet** VERB
häkeln [34]

crocodile NOUN
das Krokodil neut (PL die Krokodile)

crook NOUN
der Verbrecher masc (PL die Verbrecher)
die Verbrecherin fem (criminal)

★ **crop** NOUN
die Ernte fem
□ a good crop of apples eine gute Apfelernte

★ **cross** NOUN
▷ see also cross ADJECTIVE, VERB
das Kreuz neut (PL die Kreuze)

★ **cross** ADJECTIVE
▷ see also cross NOUN, VERB
böse
□ to be cross about something wegen etwas
böse sein

★ to **cross** VERB
▷ see also cross ADJECTIVE, NOUN
überqueren [7] (PERFECT TENSE hat überquert)
(street, bridge)

to **cross out** VERB
durchstreichen

to **cross over** VERB
hinübergehen [29]

cross-country NOUN
der Crosslauf masc (race)
■ cross-country skiing der Langlauf

★ **crossing** NOUN
1 die Überfahrt fem (by boat)
□ the crossing from Dover to Calais die
Überfahrt von Dover nach Calais
2 der Fußgängerüberweg masc (PL die
Fußgängerüberwege) (for pedestrians)

★ **crossroads** SING NOUN
die Kreuzung fem

crossword NOUN
das Kreuzworträtsel neut (PL die
Kreuzworträtsel)
□ I like doing crosswords. Ich mache gern
Kreuzworträtsel.

to **crouch down** VERB
sich niederkauern [15] (PERFECT TENSE hat sich
niedergekauert)

crow NOUN
die Krähe fem

★ **crowd** NOUN
▷ see also crowd VERB
die Menge fem
■ the crowd (at sports match) die Zuschauer
masc pl

★ to **crowd** VERB
▷ see also crowd NOUN
sich drängen [38]
□ The children crowded round the model. Die
Kinder drängten sich um das Modell.

crowded ADJECTIVE
voll

crowdfunding NOUN
das Crowdfunding neut

★ **crown** NOUN
die Krone fem

crucifix NOUN
das Kruzifix neut (PL die Kruzifixe)

crude ADJECTIVE
ordinär (vulgar)

cruel ADJECTIVE
grausam

cruise NOUN
die Kreuzfahrt fem
□ to go on a cruise eine Kreuzfahrt machen

crumb NOUN
der Krümel masc (PL die Krümel)

to **crush** VERB
▷ see also crush NOUN
1 zerquetschen [95] (PERFECT TENSE hat
zerquetscht)
□ The tomatoes got crushed. Die Tomaten
wurden zerquetscht.
2 quetschen [48] (finger)
□ I crushed my finger in the car door. Ich habe
mir den Finger in der Autotür gequetscht.

crush NOUN
▷ see also crush VERB
■ to have a crush on somebody für jemanden
schwärmen [38]

crutch NOUN
die Krücke fem

★ **cry** NOUN
▷ see also cry VERB
der Schrei masc (PL die Schreie)
□ a cry of fear ein Angstschrei
■ to have a good cry sich ausweinen [4]

★ to **cry** VERB
▷ see also cry NOUN
weinen [38]
□ The baby's crying. Das Baby weint.

crystal NOUN
der Kristall masc (PL die Kristalle)

CTC NOUN (= city technology college)
die technische Fachschule fem

cub NOUN
1 das Junge neut (GEN des Jungen, PL die Jungen)
□ the lioness and her cub die Löwin und ihr
Junges (animal)
2 der Wölfling masc (PL die Wölflinge) (scout)

cube NOUN
der Würfel masc (PL die Würfel)

cubic ADJECTIVE
■ a cubic metre ein Kubikmeter masc

★ **cucumber** NOUN
die Gurke fem

cuddle NOUN
▷ see also cuddle VERB

■ **Come and give me a cuddle.** Komm und nimm mich in den Arm.

to **cuddle** VERB
▷ *see also* **cuddle** NOUN
■ **to cuddle somebody** jemanden in den Arm nehmen [52]

cue NOUN
das Queue *neut* (PL die Queues) (*for snooker, pool*)

> Queue is pronounced as if spelt 'Kö'.

culottes PL NOUN
der Hosenrock *masc* (PL die Hosenröcke)
□ a pair of culottes ein Hosenrock

★ **culture** NOUN
die Kultur *fem*

cunning ADJECTIVE
durchtrieben

★ **cup** NOUN
1 die Tasse *fem*
□ a china cup eine Porzellantasse □ a cup of coffee eine Tasse Kaffee
2 der Pokal *masc* (PL die Pokale) (*trophy*)

★ **cupboard** NOUN
der Schrank *masc* (PL die Schränke)

to **cure** VERB
▷ *see also* **cure** NOUN
heilen [38]

cure NOUN
▷ *see also* **cure** VERB
das Mittel *neut* (PL die Mittel)
□ a cure for a cold ein Mittel gegen Schnupfen

★ **curious** ADJECTIVE
neugierig

curl NOUN
▷ *see also* **curl** VERB
die Locke *fem*

to **curl** VERB
▷ *see also* **curl** NOUN
in Locken legen [38] (*hair*)

curly ADJECTIVE
lockig
□ When I was young my hair was curlier. Als ich jung war, waren meine Haare lockiger.

currant NOUN
die Korinthe *fem* (*dried fruit*)

★ **currency** NOUN
die Währung *fem*
□ foreign currency ausländische Währung

current NOUN
▷ *see also* **current** ADJECTIVE
die Strömung *fem*
□ The current is very strong. Die Strömung ist sehr stark.

current ADJECTIVE
▷ *see also* **current** NOUN
aktuell
□ the current situation die aktuelle Lage

current account NOUN
das Girokonto *neut* (PL die Girokonten)

current affairs PL NOUN
die Tagespolitik *fem sing*

curriculum NOUN
der Lehrplan *masc* (PL die Lehrpläne)

curriculum vitae NOUN
der Lebenslauf *masc* (PL die Lebensläufe)

curry NOUN
das Curry *neut* (PL die Currys)

curse NOUN
der Fluch *masc* (PL die Flüche) (*spell*)

★ **curtain** NOUN
der Vorhang *masc* (PL die Vorhänge)

cushion NOUN
das Kissen *neut* (PL die Kissen)

custard NOUN
die Vanillesoße *fem* (*for pouring*)

custody NOUN
das Sorgerecht *neut* (*of child*)
□ He got custody of his son. Er bekam das Sorgerecht für seinen Sohn.
■ **to be remanded in custody** inhaftiert werden [91]

custom NOUN
der Brauch *masc* (PL die Bräuche)
□ It's an old custom. Es ist ein alter Brauch.

★ **customer** NOUN
der Kunde *masc* (GEN des Kunden, PL die Kunden)
die Kundin *fem*

customs PL NOUN
der Zoll *masc* (PL die Zölle)

customs officer NOUN
der Zollbeamte *masc* (GEN des Zollbeamten, PL die Zollbeamten)
die Zollbeamtin *fem*
□ a customs officer ein Zollbeamter

★ **cut** NOUN
▷ *see also* **cut** VERB
1 die Schnittwunde *fem*
□ He's got a cut on his forehead. Er hat eine Schnittwunde an der Stirn.
2 die Senkung *fem* (*in price*)
3 die Kürzung *fem* (*in spending*)
■ **a cut and blow-dry** Schneiden und Föhnen

★ to **cut** VERB
▷ *see also* **cut** NOUN
1 schneiden [60] (IMPERFECT schnitt, PERFECT TENSE hat geschnitten)
□ I'll cut some bread. Ich schneide Brot.
■ **I cut my foot on a piece of glass.** Ich habe mir den Fuß an einer Glasscherbe verletzt.
■ **to cut oneself** sich schneiden [60] □ Watch you don't cut yourself! Pass auf, dass du dich nicht schneidest!
2 senken [38] (*price*)
3 kürzen [36] (*spending*)

cutback – Czech

to **cut down** VERB
1 fällen [38] (*tree*)
2 einschränken [4]
□ I'm cutting down on chocolate. Ich bin dabei, meinen Schokoladenkonsum einzuschränken.

to **cut off** VERB
abschneiden (*hair*)
■ **The electricity was cut off.** Der Strom wurde abgestellt.

to **cut up** VERB
■ **to cut up** (*vegetables, meat*) klein schneiden [60]

cutback NOUN
die Kürzung *fem*
□ cutbacks in public services Kürzungen bei den öffentlichen Ausgaben

cute ADJECTIVE
niedlich

cutlery NOUN
das Besteck *neut* (PL die Bestecke)

★ **CV** NOUN (= *curriculum vitae*)
der Lebenslauf *masc* (PL die Lebensläufe)

cyberbully NOUN
der Cybermobber *masc* (PL die Cybermobber)
die Cybermobberin *fem*

cyberbullying NOUN
das Cybermobbing *neut*

cybercafé NOUN
das Internet-Café *neut* (PL die Internet-Cafés)

cybercrime NOUN
die Cyberkriminalität *fem*

★ to **cycle** VERB
▷ *see also* **cycle** NOUN
Rad fahren [21] (PRESENT TENSE fährt Rad, IMPERFECT fuhr Rad, PERFECT TENSE ist Rad gefahren)
□ I like cycling. Ich fahre gern Rad.
■ **I cycle to school.** Ich fahre mit dem Rad zur Schule.

★ **cycle** NOUN
▷ *see also* **cycle** VERB
das Fahrrad *neut* (PL die Fahrräder)
□ a cycle ride eine Fahrradfahrt

cycling NOUN
das Radfahren *neut*
□ My hobby is cycling. Radfahren ist mein Hobby.

cyclist NOUN
der Radfahrer *masc* (PL die Radfahrer)
die Radfahrerin *fem*

cylinder NOUN
der Zylinder *masc* (PL die Zylinder)

Cyprus NOUN
Zypern *neut*
■ **from Cyprus** aus Zypern
■ **in Cyprus** auf Zypern
■ **to Cyprus** nach Zypern

Czech ADJECTIVE
▷ *see also* **Czech** NOUN
tschechisch
■ **the Czech Republic** die Tschechische Republik

Czech NOUN
▷ *see also* **Czech** ADJECTIVE
1 der Tscheche *masc* (GEN des Tschechen, PL die Tschechen)
die Tschechin *fem* (*person*)
2 das Tschechisch *neut* (GEN des Tschechischen) (*language*)

★ = core vocabulary

Dd

★ **dad** NOUN
   der Papa masc (PL die Papas)
   □ his dad sein Papa □ I'll ask Dad. Ich werde
   Papa fragen.

daddy NOUN
   der Papa masc (PL die Papas)
   □ my daddy mein Papa

daffodil NOUN
   die Osterglocke fem

daft ADJECTIVE
   verrückt

★ **daily** ADJECTIVE, ADVERB
   täglich
   □ It's part of my daily routine. Es gehört zu
   meiner täglichen Routine. □ The pool is open
   daily from nine a.m. to six p.m. Das
   Schwimmbad ist täglich von neun bis achtzehn
   Uhr geöffnet.

dairy NOUN
   die Molkerei fem (company)

dairy products PL NOUN
   die Milchprodukte neut pl

daisy NOUN
   das Gänseblümchen neut (PL die
   Gänseblümchen)

dam NOUN
   der Damm masc (PL die Dämme)

★ **damage** NOUN
   ▷ see also **damage** VERB
   der Schaden masc (PL die Schäden)
   □ The storm did a lot of damage. Der Sturm hat
   viel Schaden angerichtet.

★ to **damage** VERB
   ▷ see also **damage** NOUN
   beschädigen [7] (PERFECT TENSE hat beschädigt)

damp ADJECTIVE
   feucht

★ **dance** NOUN
   ▷ see also **dance** VERB
   der Tanz masc (PL die Tänze)
   □ Are you going to the dance tonight? Gehst du
   heute Abend zum Tanz?
   ■ I like to have a dance at parties. Ich tanze
   gern auf Partys.

★ to **dance** VERB
   ▷ see also **dance** NOUN
   tanzen [36]

dancer NOUN
   der Tänzer masc (PL die Tänzer)
   die Tänzerin fem

dancing NOUN
   das Tanzen neut
   ■ to go dancing tanzen gehen [29] □ Let's go
   dancing! Lass uns tanzen gehen!

dandruff NOUN
   die Schuppen fem pl

Dane NOUN
   der Däne masc (GEN des Dänen, PL die Dänen)
   die Dänin fem

★ **danger** NOUN
   die Gefahr fem
   ■ in danger in Gefahr □ His life is in danger.
   Sein Leben ist in Gefahr.
   ■ I'm in danger of failing maths. Es könnte
   durchaus sein, dass ich in Mathe durchfalle.

★ **dangerous** ADJECTIVE
   gefährlich

★ **Danish** ADJECTIVE
   ▷ see also **Danish** NOUN
   dänisch

★ **Danish** NOUN
   ▷ see also **Danish** ADJECTIVE
   das Dänisch neut (GEN des Dänischen)
   (language)

Danube NOUN
   die Donau fem

to **dare** VERB
   sich trauen [38]
   ■ to dare to do something sich trauen [38]
   etwas zu tun □ I didn't dare to tell my parents.
   Ich habe mich nicht getraut, es meinen Eltern
   zu sagen.
   ■ I dare say it'll be okay. Ich denke, dass das
   in Ordnung ist.

daring ADJECTIVE
   mutig

★ **dark** ADJECTIVE
   ▷ see also **dark** NOUN
   dunkel
   □ It's dark. Es ist dunkel. □ It's getting dark. Es
   wird dunkel. □ She's got dark hair. Sie hat
   dunkle Haare. □ a dark green sweater ein
   dunkelgrüner Pullover

★ **dark** NOUN
   ▷ see also **dark** ADJECTIVE
   die Dunkelheit fem

darkness – dear

□ **after dark** nach Einbruch der Dunkelheit
- **in the dark** im Dunkeln
- **I'm afraid of the dark.** Ich habe Angst im Dunkeln.

darkness NOUN
die Dunkelheit *fem*
- **The room was in darkness.** Das Zimmer war dunkel.

darling NOUN
der Liebling *masc* (PL die Lieblinge)

> **der Liebling** is also used for women.

□ **Thank you, darling!** Danke, Liebling!

dart NOUN
der Pfeil *masc* (PL die Pfeile)
- **to play darts** Darts spielen [38]

dash NOUN
▷ *see also* **dash** VERB
der Bindestrich *masc* (*punctuation mark*)

to **dash** VERB
▷ *see also* **dash** NOUN
1 rennen [55] (IMPERFECT rannte, PERFECT TENSE ist gerannt)
□ **Everyone dashed to the window.** Alle rannten zum Fenster.
2 sich beeilen [7] (PERFECT TENSE hat sich beeilt)
□ **I've got to dash!** Ich muss mich beeilen!

dashboard NOUN
das Armaturenbrett *neut* (PL die Armaturenbretter)

★ **data** PL NOUN
die Daten *pl*

database NOUN
die Datenbank *fem* (PL die Datenbanken) (*on computer*)

★ **date** NOUN
1 das Datum *neut* (PL die Daten)
□ **my date of birth** mein Geburtsdatum
- **What's the date today?** Der Wievielte ist heute?
- **to have a date with somebody** mit jemandem eine Verabredung haben [32]
□ **She's got a date with Sejal tonight.** Sie hat heute Abend eine Verabredung mit Sejal.
- **out of date** 1 (*passport*) abgelaufen
2 (*technology*) veraltet 3 (*clothes*) altmodisch
2 die Dattel *fem* (*fruit*)

★ **daughter** NOUN
die Tochter *fem* (PL die Töchter)

daughter-in-law NOUN
die Schwiegertochter *fem* (PL die Schwiegertöchter)

dawn NOUN
das Morgengrauen *neut*
□ **at dawn** im Morgengrauen

★ **day** NOUN
der Tag *masc* (PL die Tage)
□ **We stayed in Vienna for three days.** Wir sind drei Tage in Wien geblieben. □ **I stayed at home**

all day. Ich war den ganzen Tag zu Hause.
- **every day** jeden Tag
- **during the day** tagsüber
- **the day before** der Tag davor
- **the day before my birthday** der Tag vor meinem Geburtstag
- **the day after** der Tag danach
- **the day after my birthday** der Tag nach meinem Geburtstag
- **the day before yesterday** vorgestern □ **He arrived the day before yesterday.** Er ist vorgestern angekommen.
- **the day after tomorrow** übermorgen
□ **We're leaving the day after tomorrow.** Wir fahren übermorgen ab.

★ **dead** ADJECTIVE, ADVERB
1 tot
□ **He was already dead.** Er war schon tot.
- **He was shot dead.** Er wurde erschossen.
2 völlig (*totally*)
□ **You're dead right!** Du hast völlig recht!
- **dead on time** ganz pünktlich □ **The train arrived dead on time.** Der Zug kam ganz pünktlich an.

dead end NOUN
die Sackgasse *fem*

★ **deadline** NOUN
der Termin *masc* (PL die Termine)
□ **We'll never meet the deadline.** Den Termin schaffen wir nie.

dead spot NOUN
das Funkloch *neut* (PL die Funklöcher) (*mobile*)

★ **deaf** ADJECTIVE
taub
- **She's profoundly deaf.** Sie ist gehörlos.

deafening ADJECTIVE
ohrenbetäubend

★ **deal** NOUN
▷ *see also* **deal** VERB
das Geschäft *neut* (PL die Geschäfte)
- **It's a deal!** Abgemacht!
- **a great deal** viel □ **a great deal of money** viel Geld

★ to **deal** VERB
▷ *see also* **deal** NOUN
geben [28] (PRESENT TENSE gibt, IMPERFECT gab, PERFECT TENSE hat gegeben) (*cards*)
□ **It's your turn to deal.** Du gibst!
- **to deal with something** sich um etwas kümmern [38] □ **He promised to deal with it immediately.** Er versprach, sich sofort darum zu kümmern.

dealer NOUN
der Händler *masc* (PL die Händler)
die Händlerin *fem*
□ **a drug dealer** ein Drogenhändler □ **an antique dealer** ein Antiquitätenhändler

★ **dear** ADJECTIVE
1 lieb
- **Dear Mrs Sinclair** 1 Liebe Frau Sinclair

★ = core vocabulary

2 (more formal) Sehr geehrte Frau Sinclair
■ **Dear Sir/Madam** (in a letter) Sehr geehrte Damen und Herren
2 teuer (expensive)

★ **death** NOUN
der Tod masc (PL die Tode)
□ after her death nach ihrem Tod □ I was bored to death. Ich habe mich zu Tode gelangweilt.

debate NOUN
▷ see also **debate** VERB
die Debatte fem

to **debate** VERB
▷ see also **debate** NOUN
debattieren [76] (PERFECT TENSE hat debattiert)
□ We debated the issue. Wir haben die Frage debattiert.

debt NOUN
die Schulden fem pl
□ He's got a lot of debts. Er hat viele Schulden.
■ **to be in debt** verschuldet sein [65]

★ **decade** NOUN
das Jahrzehnt neut (PL die Jahrzehnte)

decaffeinated ADJECTIVE
entkoffeiniert

decay NOUN
■ **tooth decay** die Karies

to **deceive** VERB
täuschen [48]

★ **December** NOUN
der Dezember masc
□ in December im Dezember

decent ADJECTIVE
ordentlich
□ a decent education eine ordentliche Ausbildung
■ **The new teacher seems quite decent.** Der neue Lehrer scheint ganz anständig zu sein.

★ to **decide** VERB
1 beschließen (IMPERFECT beschloss, PERFECT TENSE hat beschlossen)
□ I decided to write to her. Ich habe beschlossen, ihr zu schreiben. □ I decided not to go. Ich habe beschlossen, nicht hinzugehen.
2 sich entscheiden (IMPERFECT entschied sich, PERFECT TENSE hat sich entschieden)
□ I can't decide. Ich kann mich nicht entscheiden. □ Haven't you decided yet? Hast du dich noch nicht entschieden?
■ **to decide on something** über etwas entscheiden □ We haven't decided on the name yet. Wir haben noch nicht über den Namen entschieden.

decimal ADJECTIVE
dezimal
□ the decimal system das Dezimalsystem

★ **decision** NOUN
die Entscheidung fem
□ to make a decision eine Entscheidung treffen

decisive ADJECTIVE
entschlossen (person)

★ **deck** NOUN
1 das Deck neut (PL die Decks) (of ship)
□ on deck an Deck
2 das Spiel neut (PL die Spiele) (of cards)

deckchair NOUN
der Liegestuhl masc (PL die Liegestühle)

to **declare** VERB
erklären [19] (PERFECT TENSE hat erklärt)

to **decline** VERB
1 ablehnen [4] (PERFECT TENSE hat abgelehnt)
□ He declined to comment. Er lehnte einen Kommentar ab.
2 zurückgehen [29] (IMPERFECT ging zurück, PERFECT TENSE ist zurückgegangen)
□ The exam pass rate is declining. Die Erfolgsquote bei Prüfungen geht zurück.

★ to **decorate** VERB
1 dekorieren [76] (PERFECT TENSE hat dekoriert)
□ I decorated the cake with green icing. Ich habe den Kuchen mit grünem Zuckerguss dekoriert.
2 streichen (IMPERFECT strich, PERFECT TENSE hat gestrichen) (paint)
3 tapezieren [76] (PERFECT TENSE hat tapeziert) (wallpaper)

decorations PL NOUN
der Schmuck masc
□ Christmas decorations der Weihnachtsschmuck

decrease NOUN
▷ see also **decrease** VERB
die Abnahme fem
□ a decrease in the number of unemployed people eine Abnahme der Arbeitslosenzahl

to **decrease** VERB
▷ see also **decrease** NOUN
abnehmen [52] (PRESENT TENSE nimmt ab, IMPERFECT nahm ab, PERFECT TENSE hat abgenommen)

dedicated ADJECTIVE
engagiert
□ a very dedicated teacher ein sehr engagierter Lehrer

to **deduct** VERB
abziehen [96] (IMPERFECT zog ab, PERFECT TENSE hat abgezogen)

★ **deep** ADJECTIVE
tief (water, hole, cut)
□ How deep is the lake? Wie tief ist der See? □ a hole four metres deep ein vier Meter tiefes Loch □ He's got a deep voice. Er hat eine tiefe Stimme.
■ **to take a deep breath** tief einatmen [3]
■ **The snow was really deep.** Es lag sehr viel Schnee.

deeply ADVERB
zutiefst (depressed)

deer – demand

deer NOUN
das Reh neut (PLdie Rehe)

★ **defeat** NOUN
▷ see also **defeat** VERB
die Niederlage fem

★ to **defeat** VERB
▷ see also **defeat** NOUN
besiegen [7] (PERFECT TENSEhat besiegt)

defect NOUN
der Defekt masc (PLdie Defekte)

★ **defence** (US **defense**) NOUN
die Verteidigung fem

★ to **defend** VERB
verteidigen [84] (PERFECT TENSEhat verteidigt)

defender NOUN
der Verteidiger masc (PLdie Verteidiger)
die Verteidigerin fem

defense NOUN (US)
die Verteidigung fem

to **define** VERB
definieren [76] (PERFECT TENSEhat definiert)

definite ADJECTIVE
1 genau
  □ I haven't got any definite plans.Ich habe noch keine genauen Pläne.
2 eindeutig
  □ It's a definite improvement.Es ist eine eindeutige Verbesserung.
3 sicher
  □ We might go to Spain, but it's not definite. Wir fahren vielleicht nach Spanien, aber es ist noch nicht sicher.
  ■ He was definite about it.Er war sich sehr sicher.

★ **definitely** ADVERB
eindeutig
  □ He's definitely the best.Er ist eindeutig der Beste.
  ■ He's the best player. — Definitely!Er ist der beste Spieler. — Absolut!
  ■ I definitely think he'll come.Ich bin sicher, dass er kommt.

definition NOUN
die Definition fem

to **defriend** VERB
entfreunden [54]
  □ Her sister has defriended her on Facebook. Ihre Schwester hat sie auf Facebook entfreundet.

★ **degree** NOUN
1 der Grad masc (PLdie Grade)
  □ a temperature of thirty degreeseine Temperatur von dreißig Grad
2 der Universitätsabschluss masc (GENdes Universitätsabschlusses, PLdie Universitätsabschlüsse)
  □ a degree in Englishein Universitätsabschluss in Englisch

★ to **delay** VERB
▷ see also **delay** NOUN
verschieben (IMPERFECTverschob, PERFECT TENSE hat verschoben)
  □ We delayed our departure.Wir haben unsere Abreise verschoben.
  ■ to be delayedVerspätung haben [32] □ Our flight was delayed.Unser Flug hatte Verspätung.

★ **delay** NOUN
▷ see also **delay** VERB
die Verzögerung fem
  ■ without delayunverzüglich

to **delete** VERB
löschen [48] (on computer)

deliberate ADJECTIVE
absichtlich

deliberately ADVERB
absichtlich
  □ She did it deliberately.Sie hat es absichtlich getan.

delicate ADJECTIVE
1 zierlich
  □ She has very delicate hands.Sie hat sehr zierliche Hände.
2 zerbrechlich (object)
  □ That vase is very delicate.Die Vase ist sehr zerbrechlich.
3 anfällig (often ill)
  □ a delicate childein anfälliges Kind
4 heikel (situation)
  □ The situation is rather delicate.Die Lage ist ziemlich heikel.

delicatessen SING NOUN
das Feinkostgeschäft neut (PLdie Feinkostgeschäfte)

delicious ADJECTIVE
köstlich

delight NOUN
die Freude fem

★ **delighted** ADJECTIVE
hocherfreut
  □ He'll be delighted.Er wird hocherfreut sein.

delightful ADJECTIVE
wunderbar (meal, evening)

★ to **deliver** VERB
1 austragen [77] (PRESENT TENSEträgt aus, IMPERFECTtrug aus, PERFECT TENSEhat ausgetragen)
  □ I deliver newspapers.Ich trage Zeitungen aus.
2 ausliefern [4] (PERFECT TENSEhat ausgeliefert) (mail)

delivery NOUN
die Lieferung fem

★ to **demand** VERB
▷ see also **demand** NOUN
fordern [88] (PERFECT TENSEhat gefordert)

★ **demand** NOUN
▷ see also **demand** VERB
die Nachfrage fem (for product)

★ = core vocabulary

demanding ADJECTIVE
anspruchsvoll
□ a demanding job eine anspruchsvolle Arbeit

demo NOUN
die Demo fem (PLdie Demos) (protest)

★ **democracy** NOUN
die Demokratie fem

★ **democratic** ADJECTIVE
demokratisch

to demolish VERB
abreißen (IMPERFECTriss ab , PERFECT TENSEhat abgerissen) (building)

★ **to demonstrate** VERB
1 vorführen [4] (PERFECT TENSEhat vorgeführt) (show)
□ She demonstrated the technique.Sie hat die Methode vorgeführt.
2 demonstrieren [76] (PERFECT TENSEhat demonstriert) (protest)
□ to demonstrate against somethinggegen etwas demonstrieren

★ **demonstration** NOUN
1 die Vorführung fem (of method, technique)
2 die Demonstration fem (protest)

demonstrator NOUN
der Demonstrant masc (GENdes Demonstranten , PLdie Demonstranten)
die Demonstrantin fem (protester)

denim NOUN
der Jeansstoff masc
■ a denim jacketeine Jeansjacke

denims PL NOUN
die Jeans fem pl (jeans)
□ a pair of denimseine Jeans

★ **Denmark** NOUN
Dänemark neut
■ from Denmarkaus Dänemark
■ to Denmarknach Dänemark

dense ADJECTIVE
1 dicht (crowd, fog)
2 dick (smoke)
■ He's so dense!Er ist furchtbar blöd! (informal)

dent NOUN
▷ see also dent VERB
die Delle fem

to dent VERB
▷ see also dent NOUN
eindellen [4] (PERFECT TENSEhat eingedellt)

dental ADJECTIVE
■ dental treatmentdie Zahnbehandlung
■ dental flossdie Zahnseide
■ dental surgeonder Zahnarzt

★ **dentist** NOUN
der Zahnarzt masc (PLdie Zahnärzte)
die Zahnärztin fem
□ Catherine is a dentist.Catherine ist Zahnärztin.

to deny VERB
leugnen [53]
□ She denied everything.Sie hat alles geleugnet.

deodorant NOUN
das Deo neut (PLdie Deos)

to depart VERB
1 abreisen [4] (PERFECT TENSEist abgereist) (person)
2 abfahren [21] (PRESENT TENSEfährt ab , IMPERFECT fuhr ab , PERFECT TENSEist abgefahren) (train)

★ **department** NOUN
1 die Abteilung fem (in shop)
□ the shoe departmentdie Schuhabteilung
2 der Fachbereich masc (PLdie Fachbereiche) (university, school)
□ the English departmentder Fachbereich Englisch

department store NOUN
das Kaufhaus neut (GENdes Kaufhauses , PLdie Kaufhäuser)

★ **departure** NOUN
die Abfahrt fem

departure lounge NOUN
die Abflughalle fem

★ **to depend** VERB
■ to depend onabhängen [35]von □ The price depends on which model it is.Der Preis hängt vom Modell ab.
■ depending on the weatherje nach Wetterlage
■ It depends.Es kommt drauf an.

to deport VERB
abschieben (IMPERFECTschob ab , PERFECT TENSE hat abgeschoben)

★ **deposit** NOUN
1 die Anzahlung fem (part payment)
□ You have to pay a deposit when you book.Sie müssen eine Anzahlung leisten, wenn Sie buchen.
2 die Kaution fem (when hiring something)
□ You get the deposit back when you return the bike.Sie bekommen die Kaution zurück, wenn Sie das Fahrrad zurückbringen.
3 das Pfand neut (PLdie Pfänder) (on bottle)

depressed ADJECTIVE
deprimiert
□ I'm feeling depressed.Ich bin deprimiert.

depressing ADJECTIVE
deprimierend

★ **depth** NOUN
die Tiefe fem

deputy head NOUN
der Konrektor masc (PLdie Konrektoren)
die Konrektorin fem

to descend VERB
hinuntersteigen [74] (IMPERFECTstieg hinunter , PERFECT TENSEist hinuntergestiegen)

d

Numbers in brackets refer to verb tables on pages 697 to 706.

425

d

★to **describe** VERB
beschreiben [61] (IMPERFECT beschrieb, PERFECT TENSE hat beschrieben)

★**description** NOUN
die Beschreibung fem

★**desert** NOUN
die Wüste fem

desert island NOUN
die einsame Insel fem

★to **deserve** VERB
verdienen [84] (PERFECT TENSE hat verdient)
□ He deserves a holiday. Er hat einen Urlaub verdient.
■ She deserves to be punished. Sie gehört bestraft.

★**design** NOUN
▷ see also **design** VERB
1 das Design neut (PL die Designs)
□ fashion design das Modedesign
2 der Entwurf masc (process)
3 das Muster neut (PL die Muster) (pattern)
□ a geometric design ein geometrisches Muster
4 die Konstruktion fem (car, machine)
□ It's a completely new design. Es ist eine völlig neue Konstruktion.

★to **design** VERB
▷ see also **design** NOUN
entwerfen [92] (PRESENT TENSE entwirft, IMPERFECT entwarf, PERFECT TENSE hat entworfen) (clothes, furniture)

designer NOUN
der Modeschöpfer masc (PL die Modeschöpfer)
die Modeschöpferin fem (of clothes)
■ designer clothes die Designerkleidung sing

★**design technology** NOUN
das Werken neut

desire NOUN
▷ see also **desire** VERB
das Verlangen neut (PL die Verlangen)

to **desire** VERB
▷ see also **desire** NOUN
wünschen [48] (PERFECT TENSE hat gewünscht)
□ if desired falls gewünscht

★**desk** NOUN
1 der Schreibtisch masc (PL die Schreibtische) (in office)
2 die Bank fem (PL die Bänke) (in school)
3 die Rezeption fem (in hotel)
4 der Schalter masc (PL die Schalter) (at airport)

desktop NOUN
der Desktop masc (PL die Desktops)
■ desktop PC der Desktop-PC masc

despair NOUN
die Verzweiflung fem
■ I was in despair. Ich war verzweifelt.

★**desperate** ADJECTIVE
verzweifelt
□ a desperate situation eine verzweifelte Lage
■ to get desperate fast verzweifeln [7] □ I was

getting desperate. Ich bin fast verzweifelt.
■ I'm desperate for a cold drink. Ich brauche dringend etwas Kaltes zu trinken.

desperately ADVERB
1 äußerst
□ We're desperately worried. Wir sind äußerst besorgt.
2 verzweifelt
□ He was desperately trying to persuade her. Er versuchte verzweifelt, sie zu überzeugen.

to **despise** VERB
verachten [18] (PERFECT TENSE hat verachtet)

despite PREPOSITION
trotz
□ despite the bad weather trotz des schlechten Wetters

dessert NOUN
der Nachtisch masc
□ for dessert zum Nachtisch

destination NOUN
das Ziel neut (PL die Ziele)

★to **destroy** VERB
zerstören [95] (PERFECT TENSE hat zerstört)

destruction NOUN
die Zerstörung fem

detached house NOUN
das Einfamilienhaus neut (GEN des Einfamilienhauses, PL die Einfamilienhäuser)

★**detail** NOUN
das Detail neut (PL die Details)
■ in detail ganz genau

★**detailed** ADJECTIVE
ausführlich

★**detective** NOUN
der Detektiv masc (PL die Detektive)
die Detektivin fem
■ a private detective ein Privatdetektiv
■ a detective story eine Detektivgeschichte

★**detention** NOUN
■ to get a detention nachsitzen müssen [51]
□ He got a detention. Er musste nachsitzen.

detergent NOUN
das Waschmittel neut (PL die Waschmittel)

determined ADJECTIVE
entschlossen
■ to be determined to do something entschlossen sein [65], etwas zu tun □ She's determined to become an engineer. Sie ist entschlossen, Ingenieurin zu werden.

detour NOUN
der Umweg masc (PL die Umwege)

devaluation NOUN
die Abwertung fem

devastated ADJECTIVE
am Boden zerstört
□ I was devastated. Ich war am Boden zerstört.

devastating ADJECTIVE
1 erschütternd (upsetting)
2 verheerend (flood, storm)

to **develop** VERB

1 entwickeln [34] (PERFECT TENSE hat entwickelt)
□ The teacher helped them develop their writing skills. Der Lehrer half ihnen, ihre Schreibfertigkeiten zu entwickeln.

2 sich entwickeln [34] (PERFECT TENSE hat sich entwickelt)
□ Girls develop faster. Mädchen entwickeln sich schneller. □ The argument developed into a fight. Der Streit entwickelte sich zu einer Schlägerei.
■ **a developing country** ein Entwicklungsland *neut*

development NOUN
die Entwicklung *fem*
□ the latest developments die neuesten Entwicklungen

device NOUN
das Gerät *neut* (PL die Geräte)

devil NOUN
der Teufel *masc* (PL die Teufel)
□ Poor devil! Armer Teufel!

to **devise** VERB
sich ausdenken [14] (IMPERFECT dachte sich aus, PERFECT TENSE hat sich ausgedacht)
□ We have devised a way to help him. Wir haben uns etwas ausgedacht, um ihm zu helfen.

devoted ADJECTIVE
■ **He's completely devoted to her.** Er liebt sie über alles.

diabetes NOUN
der Zucker *masc*
□ She's got diabetes. Sie hat Zucker.

diabetic NOUN
der Zuckerkranke *masc* (GEN des Zuckerkranken, PL die Zuckerkranken)
die Zuckerkranke *fem* (GEN der Zuckerkranken)
■ **I'm a diabetic.** Ich habe Zucker.

diagonal ADJECTIVE
diagonal

diagram NOUN
das Diagramm *neut* (PL die Diagramme)

to **dial** VERB
wählen [38] (PERFECT TENSE hat gewählt)
(*number*)
■ **He dialled the wrong number.** Er hat sich verwählt.

dialling tone NOUN
das Amtszeichen *neut* (PL die Amtszeichen)

dialogue NOUN
der Dialog *masc* (PL die Dialoge)

diamond NOUN
der Diamant *masc* (GEN des Diamanten, PL die Diamanten)
□ a diamond ring ein Diamantring *masc*
■ **diamonds** (*in cards*) das Karo □ the ace of diamonds das Karoass

diaper NOUN (US)
die Windel *fem*

diarrhoea NOUN
der Durchfall *masc* (PL die Durchfälle)
□ I've got diarrhoea. Ich habe Durchfall.

★ **diary** NOUN

1 der Kalender *masc* (PL die Kalender)
□ Put the date of the concert in your diary. Schreib das Datum für das Konzert in deinen Kalender.

2 das Tagebuch *neut* (PL die Tagebücher)
□ I keep a diary. Ich führe ein Tagebuch.

dice NOUN
der Würfel *masc* (PL die Würfel)

dictation NOUN
das Diktat *neut* (PL die Diktate)

dictator NOUN
der Diktator *masc* (PL die Diktatoren)

★ **dictionary** NOUN
das Wörterbuch *neut* (PL die Wörterbücher)

did VERB ▷ see **do**

★ to **die** VERB
sterben [75] (PRESENT TENSE stirbt, IMPERFECT starb, PERFECT TENSE ist gestorben)
□ She's dying. Sie stirbt. □ He died last year. Er ist letztes Jahr gestorben.
■ **to be dying to do something** es kaum erwarten können [41] etwas zu tun □ I'm dying to see you. Ich kann es kaum erwarten, dich zu sehen.

to **die down** VERB
nachlassen [42] (PRESENT TENSE lässt nach, IMPERFECT ließ nach, PERFECT TENSE hat nachgelassen)
□ The wind is dying down. Der Wind lässt nach.

diesel NOUN

1 der Diesel *masc* (*fuel*)
□ thirty litres of diesel Dreißig Liter Diesel

2 der Diesel *masc* (PL die Diesel) (*car*)
□ Our car's a diesel. Unser Auto ist ein Diesel.

★ **diet** NOUN
▷ see also **diet** VERB

1 die Nahrung *fem*
□ a healthy diet gesunde Nahrung

2 die Diät *fem* (*for slimming*)
■ **I'm on a diet.** Ich mache eine Diät.

★ to **diet** VERB
▷ see also **diet** NOUN
eine Diät machen [48]
□ I've been dieting for two months. Ich mache seit zwei Monaten eine Diät.

★ **difference** NOUN
der Unterschied *masc* (PL die Unterschiede)
□ There's not much difference in age between us. Es besteht kein großer Altersunterschied zwischen uns.
■ **It makes no difference.** Das ist egal.

d

different – director

★ **different** ADJECTIVE
verschieden
□ We are very different. Wir sind sehr verschieden.
■ **Berlin is different from London.** Berlin ist anders als London.

★ **difficult** ADJECTIVE
schwierig
□ It's difficult to choose. Es ist schwierig, sich zu entscheiden.

★ **difficulty** NOUN
die Schwierigkeit fem
□ to have difficulty doing something Schwierigkeiten haben, etwas zu tun
■ **without difficulty** problemlos

★ to **dig** VERB
1 graben (PRESENT TENSE gräbt, IMPERFECT grub, PERFECT TENSE hat gegraben) (hole)
2 umgraben (PERFECT TENSE hat umgegraben) (garden)
■ **to dig something up** etwas ausgraben

digestion NOUN
die Verdauung fem

digger NOUN
der Bagger masc (PL die Bagger)

digital ADJECTIVE
digital
□ the digital revolution die digitale Revolution
■ **a digital camera** eine Digitalkamera
■ **a digital radio** ein DAB-Radio neut
■ **a digital watch** eine Digitaluhr
■ **digital TV** das Digitalfernsehen

dim ADJECTIVE
1 schwach (light)
2 beschränkt (stupid)

dimension NOUN
das Maß neut (GEN des Maßes, PL die Maße) (measurement)

to **diminish** VERB
abnehmen [52] (PRESENT TENSE nimmt ab, IMPERFECT nahm ab, PERFECT TENSE hat abgenommen)

din NOUN
der Krach masc (PL die Kräche)

diner NOUN (US)
die Gaststätte fem

dinghy NOUN
■ **a rubber dinghy** ein Gummiboot neut
■ **a sailing dinghy** ein Segelboot neut

dining car NOUN
der Speisewagen masc (PL die Speisewagen)

dining room NOUN
das Esszimmer neut (PL die Esszimmer)

★ **dinner** NOUN
1 das Mittagessen neut (PL die Mittagessen) (at midday)
2 das Abendessen neut (PL die Abendessen) (in the evening)

dinner jacket NOUN
die Smokingjacke fem

dinner party NOUN
die Abendgesellschaft fem
■ **Emma's having a dinner party on Saturday.** Emma hat am Samstag Leute zum Essen eingeladen.

dinner time NOUN
die Essenszeit fem

dinosaur NOUN
der Dinosaurier masc (PL die Dinosaurier)

dip NOUN
▷ see also **dip** VERB
der Dip masc (PL die Dips)
□ a spicy dip ein pikanter Dip
■ **to go for a dip** kurz mal ins Wasser gehen [29]

to **dip** VERB
▷ see also **dip** NOUN
1 tauchen [48]
□ She dipped her hand in the water. Sie tauchte ihre Hand ins Wasser.
2 tunken [38]
□ He dipped a biscuit into his tea. Er tunkte einen Keks in seinen Tee.

diploma NOUN
das Diplom neut (PL die Diplome)
■ **She has a diploma in social work.** Sie hat Sozialarbeiterin gelernt.

diplomat NOUN
der Diplomat masc (GEN des Diplomaten, PL die Diplomaten)
die Diplomatin fem

★ **diplomatic** ADJECTIVE
diplomatisch

★ **direct** ADJECTIVE, ADVERB
▷ see also **direct** VERB
direkt
□ the most direct route der direkteste Weg
□ You can't fly to Stuttgart direct from Glasgow. Sie können von Glasgow nicht direkt nach Stuttgart fliegen.

★ to **direct** VERB
▷ see also **direct** ADJECTIVE, ADVERB
Regie führen [38] bei (film, play)
□ Who directed the film? Wer hat bei dem Film Regie geführt?

★ **direction** NOUN
die Richtung fem
□ We're going in the wrong direction. Wir fahren in die falsche Richtung.
■ **to ask somebody for directions** jemanden nach dem Weg fragen [38]

★ **director** NOUN
1 der Direktor masc (PL die Direktoren)
die Direktorin fem (of company)
2 der Regisseur masc (PL die Regisseure)
die Regisseurin fem (of play, film)
3 der Leiter masc (PL die Leiter)
die Leiterin fem (of programme)

★ = core vocabulary

directory NOUN
1 das Verzeichnis *neut* (GEN des Verzeichnisses, PL die Verzeichnisse) (*on computer*)
□ file directory das Dateiverzeichnis
2 das Telefonbuch *neut* (PL die Telefonbücher) (*telephone book*)

dirt NOUN
der Schmutz *masc*

★ **dirty** ADJECTIVE
schmutzig
□ to get dirty sich schmutzig machen □ to get something dirty etwas schmutzig machen □ a dirty joke ein schmutziger Witz

disabled ADJECTIVE
behindert

disadvantage NOUN
der Nachteil *masc* (PL die Nachteile)

to **disagree** VERB
■ We always disagree. Wir sind nie einer Meinung.
■ I disagree! Ich bin anderer Meinung.
■ He disagreed with me. Er war anderer Meinung als ich.

disagreement NOUN
die Meinungsverschiedenheit *fem*

★ to **disappear** VERB
verschwinden [86] (IMPERFECT verschwand, PERFECT TENSE ist verschwunden)

disappearance NOUN
das Verschwinden *neut*

disappointed ADJECTIVE
enttäuscht

disappointing ADJECTIVE
enttäuschend

disappointment NOUN
die Enttäuschung *fem*

★ **disaster** NOUN
die Katastrophe *fem*

disastrous ADJECTIVE
katastrophal

disc NOUN
die Platte *fem*

★ **discipline** NOUN
die Disziplin *fem*

disco NOUN
die Disco *fem* (PL die Discos)
□ There's a disco at the school tonight. Heute Abend gibt es in der Schule eine Disco.

to **disconnect** VERB
1 ausstecken [4] (PERFECT TENSE hat ausgesteckt) (*electrical equipment*)
2 abstellen [4] (PERFECT TENSE hat abgestellt) (*telephone, water supply*)

★ **discount** NOUN
der Rabatt *masc* (PL die Rabatte)
□ a discount of twenty per cent zwanzig Prozent Rabatt

■ a discount for students eine Studentenermäßigung

to **discourage** VERB
entmutigen [18] (PERFECT TENSE hat entmutigt)
■ to get discouraged sich entmutigen lassen [42] □ Don't get discouraged! Lass dich nicht entmutigen!

★ to **discover** VERB
entdecken [18] (PERFECT TENSE hat entdeckt)

discovery NOUN
die Entdeckung *fem*

discrimination NOUN
die Diskriminierung *fem*
□ racial discrimination die Rassendiskriminierung

★ to **discuss** VERB
1 besprechen [70] (PRESENT TENSE bespricht, IMPERFECT besprach, PERFECT TENSE hat besprochen)
□ I'll discuss it with my parents. Ich werde es mit meinen Eltern besprechen.
2 diskutieren [76] über +acc (PERFECT TENSE hat diskutiert) (*topic*)
□ We discussed the problem of pollution. Wir haben über das Problem der Umweltverschmutzung diskutiert.

★ **discussion** NOUN
die Diskussion *fem*

disease NOUN
die Krankheit *fem*

disgraceful ADJECTIVE
schändlich

to **disguise** VERB
verkleiden [54] (PERFECT TENSE hat verkleidet)
□ He was disguised as a police officer. Er war als Polizist verkleidet.

disgusted ADJECTIVE
angewidert
□ I was absolutely disgusted. Ich war total angewidert.

disgusting ADJECTIVE
1 widerlich (*food, smell*)
□ It looks disgusting. Es sieht widerlich aus.
2 abscheulich (*disgraceful*)
□ That's disgusting! Das ist abscheulich!

★ **dish** NOUN
1 die Schüssel *fem*
□ a china dish eine Porzellanschüssel
■ the dishes das Geschirr *sing*
■ to do the dishes abwaschen [89] □ He never does the dishes. Er wäscht nie ab.
2 das Gericht *neut* (PL die Gerichte) (*food*)
□ a vegetarian dish ein vegetarisches Gericht

dishonest ADJECTIVE
unehrlich

dish soap NOUN (US)
das Spülmittel *neut* (PL die Spülmittel)

dish towel NOUN (US)
das Geschirrtuch neut (PL die Geschirrtücher)

dishwasher NOUN
die Geschirrspülmaschine fem

disinfectant NOUN
das Desinfektionsmittel neut (PL die Desinfektionsmittel)

disk NOUN
die Platte fem
▪ **the hard disk** die Festplatte

to **dislike** VERB
▷ see also **dislike** NOUN
nicht mögen [50] (PRESENT TENSE mag nicht, IMPERFECT mochte nicht, PERFECT TENSE hat nicht gemocht)
□ I've always disliked cabbage. Kohl habe ich noch nie gemocht.

dislike NOUN
▷ see also **dislike** VERB
▪ **my likes and dislikes** was ich mag und nicht mag

dismal ADJECTIVE
kläglich
□ a dismal failure ein kläglicher Fehlschlag
▪ **The weather was dismal yesterday.** Gestern war das Wetter trostlos.

to **dismiss** VERB
entlassen [42] (PRESENT TENSE entlässt, IMPERFECT entließ, PERFECT TENSE hat entlassen) (employee)

disobedient ADJECTIVE
ungehorsam

display NOUN
▷ see also **display** VERB
die Auslage fem (of goods)
▪ **to be on display** ausgestellt sein [65] □ Her best paintings were on display. Ihre besten Bilder waren ausgestellt.
▪ **a firework display** ein Feuerwerk neut

to **display** VERB
▷ see also **display** NOUN
1 zeigen [38]
□ She proudly displayed her medal. Sie zeigte stolz ihre Medaille.
2 ausstellen [4] (PERFECT TENSE hat ausgestellt) (in shop window)
□ the fruit displayed in the shop window ... das Obst, das im Schaufenster ausgestellt war ...

disposable ADJECTIVE
zum Wegwerfen
▪ **disposable nappies** die Wegwerfwindeln fem pl

to **disqualify** VERB
disqualifizieren [76] (PERFECT TENSE hat disqualifiziert)
▪ **to be disqualified** disqualifiziert werden [91] □ He was disqualified. Er wurde disqualifiziert.

to **disrupt** VERB
1 stören [38]

□ Protesters disrupted the meeting. Protestierende haben die Versammlung gestört.
2 unterbrechen [11] (PRESENT TENSE unterbricht, IMPERFECT unterbrach, PERFECT TENSE hat unterbrochen) (service)
□ Train services were disrupted. Der Zugverkehr wurde unterbrochen.

dissatisfied ADJECTIVE
unzufrieden
□ We were dissatisfied with the service. Wir waren mit dem Service unzufrieden.

to **dissolve** VERB
1 auflösen [4] (PERFECT TENSE hat aufgelöst)
□ Dissolve the crystals in water. Löse die Kristalle in Wasser auf.
2 sich auflösen [4]
□ Sugar dissolves quickly in hot tea. Zucker löst sich in heißem Tee schnell auf.

★ **distance** NOUN
die Entfernung fem
□ a distance of forty kilometres eine Entfernung von vierzig Kilometern
▪ **It's within walking distance.** Man kann zu Fuß hingehen.
▪ **in the distance** in der Ferne

distant ADJECTIVE
weit
□ in the distant future in weiter Zukunft

distillery NOUN
die Brennerei fem
□ a whisky distillery eine Whiskybrennerei

distinction NOUN
1 die Unterscheidung fem
▪ **to make a distinction between ...** unterscheiden zwischen ...
2 die Auszeichnung fem
□ I got a distinction in my piano exam. Ich habe meine Klavierprüfung mit Auszeichnung bestanden.

distinctive ADJECTIVE
auffällig

to **distract** VERB
ablenken [4] (PERFECT TENSE hat abgelenkt)

to **distribute** VERB
verteilen [84] (PERFECT TENSE hat verteilt)

★ **district** NOUN
1 das Viertel neut (PL die Viertel) (of town)
2 die Gegend fem (of country)

to **disturb** VERB
stören [38]
▪ **I'm sorry to disturb you.** Verzeihen Sie die Störung.

ditch NOUN
▷ see also **ditch** VERB
der Graben masc (PL die Gräben)

to **ditch** VERB
▷ see also **ditch** NOUN
Schluss machen [48] mit (informal)

◻ **She's just ditched her boyfriend.** Sie hat gerade mit ihrem Freund Schluss gemacht.

dive NOUN
▷ see also **dive** VERB
der Kopfsprung *masc* (PL die Kopfsprünge)

to **dive** VERB
▷ see also **dive** NOUN
1 tauchen [48] (*under water*)
◻ **They are diving for pearls.** Sie tauchen nach Perlen.
2 einen Kopfsprung machen [48] (*into water*)
◻ **She dived into the water.** Sie machte einen Kopfsprung ins Wasser.

diver NOUN
der Taucher *masc* (PL die Taucher)
die Taucherin *fem* (*with breathing apparatus*)

diversion NOUN
die Umleitung *fem* (*for traffic*)

★ to **divide** VERB
1 teilen [38]
◻ **Divide the pastry in half.** Teilen Sie den Teig in zwei Teile. ◻ **Twelve divided by three is four.** Zwölf geteilt durch drei macht vier.
2 sich aufteilen [4] (PERFECT TENSE hat sich aufgeteilt)
◻ **We divided into two groups.** Wir haben uns in zwei Gruppen aufgeteilt.

diving NOUN
1 das Tauchen *neut* (*under water*)
2 das Springen *neut* (*into water*)
■ **diving board** das Sprungbrett

★ **division** NOUN
1 die Division *fem*
◻ **division and multiplication** Division und Multiplikation
2 die Liga *fem* (PL die Ligen) (*in football*)

divorce NOUN
die Scheidung *fem*

★ **divorced** ADJECTIVE
geschieden
◻ **My parents are divorced.** Meine Eltern sind geschieden.

Diwali NOUN
das Diwali *neut*

★ **DIY** NOUN (= *do-it-yourself*)
das Heimwerken *neut*
■ **to do DIY** Heimwerker sein [65]
■ **a DIY shop** ein Geschäft für Heimwerker
■ **DIY superstore** der Baumarkt

dizzy ADJECTIVE
■ **I feel dizzy.** Mir ist schwindlig.

DJ NOUN (= *disc jockey*)
der Diskjockey *masc* (PL die Diskjockeys)

★ to **do** VERB
1 machen [48]
◻ **What are you doing this evening?** Was macht ihr heute Abend? ◻ **I haven't done my homework.** Ich habe meine Hausaufgaben noch nicht gemacht. ◻ **She did it by herself.** Sie hat es allein gemacht.

2 tun [81] (IMPERFECT tat, PERFECT TENSE hat getan)
◻ **What shall I do?** Was soll ich tun? ◻ **I'll do my best.** Ich werde mein Bestes tun. ◻ **I'll tell you what to do.** Ich sage dir, was du tun sollst.

> In combination with certain nouns and verbs 'do' is not translated.

◻ **I do a lot of cycling.** Ich fahre viel Rad. ◻ **She was doing her knitting.** Sie strickte. ◻ **to do the ironing** bügeln
■ **to do well** erfolgreich sein [65] ◻ **The football team is doing well.** Die Fußballmannschaft ist sehr erfolgreich.
■ **She's doing well at school.** Sie ist gut in der Schule.

3 reichen [48] (*be enough*)
◻ **It's not very good, but it'll do.** Es ist nicht besonders gut, aber es wird reichen. ◻ **That'll do, thanks.** Danke, das reicht.

> In English 'do' is used to make questions. In German, questions are expressed by reversing the order of verb and subject.

◻ **Do you like German food?** Magst du deutsches Essen? ◻ **Where does he live?** Wo wohnt er? ◻ **Do you speak English?** Sprechen Sie Englisch? ◻ **What do you do in your spare time?** Was machen Sie in Ihrer Freizeit?
◻ **Where did you go for your holidays?** Wohin seid ihr in den Ferien gefahren?

> Use **nicht** in negative sentences for 'don't'.

◻ **I don't understand.** Ich verstehe nicht. ◻ **Why didn't you come?** Warum bist du nicht gekommen?

> 'do' is not translated when it is used in place of another verb.

◻ **I hate maths. — So do I.** Ich hasse Mathe. — Ich auch. ◻ **I didn't like the film. — Neither did I.** Ich mochte den Film nicht. — Ich auch nicht. ◻ **Do you like horses? — No, I don't.** Magst du Pferde? — Nein.

> Questions like 'doesn't it?' don't exist in German.

◻ **The bus stops at the youth hostel, doesn't it?** Der Bus hält an der Jugendherberge, nicht wahr? ◻ **You go swimming on Fridays, don't you?** Du gehst freitags schwimmen, nicht wahr?
■ **How do you do?** Guten Tag!
■ **I could do with a holiday.** Ich könnte einen Urlaub gebrauchen.

to **do up** VERB
1 zumachen [4] (*shirt, cardigan*)
◻ **Do up your jacket!** Mach deine Jacke zu!
2 renovieren [76] (*renovate*)
◻ **They're doing up my grandparents' house.** Sie renovieren das Haus meiner Großeltern.

to **do without** VERB
ohne etwas auskommen [40]
◻ **I couldn't do without my computer.** Ich käme nicht ohne meinen Computer aus.

d

dock NOUN
das Dock neut (PL die Docks) (for ships)

★ **doctor** NOUN
der Arzt masc (PL die Ärzte)
die Ärztin fem
□ She's a doctor. Sie ist Ärztin. □ She'd like to be a doctor. Sie möchte gerne Ärztin werden.

document NOUN
das Dokument neut (PL die Dokumente)

documentary NOUN
der Dokumentarfilm masc (PL die Dokumentarfilme)

to **dodge** VERB
ausweichen (IMPERFECT wich aus, PERFECT TENSE ist ausgewichen) (attacker)
□ to dodge something einer Sache ausweichen

Dodgems® PL NOUN
der Autoskooter masc sing (PL die Autoskooter)
□ to go on the Dodgems Autoskooter fahren

does VERB ▷ see do

★ **doesn't** = does not

★ **dog** NOUN
der Hund masc (PL die Hunde)
□ Have you got a dog? Hast du einen Hund?

do-it-yourself NOUN
das Heimwerken neut

dole NOUN
die Arbeitslosenunterstützung fem
■ to be on the dole stempeln gehen [29] □ A lot of people are on the dole. Viele Menschen gehen stempeln.
■ to go on the dole sich arbeitslos melden [54]

doll NOUN
die Puppe fem

★ **dollar** NOUN
der Dollar masc (PL die Dollars or Dollar)

When talking about amounts of money use the plural form **Dollar**.

□ That costs fifty dollars. Das kostet fünfzig Dollar.

dolphin NOUN
der Delfin masc (PL die Delfine)

★ **domestic** ADJECTIVE
■ a domestic flight ein Inlandsflug masc

dominoes SING NOUN
■ to have a game of dominoes Domino spielen [38]

to **donate** VERB
spenden [54]

★ **done** VERB ▷ see do

dongle NOUN
der Dongle masc (PL die Dongles)

donkey NOUN
der Esel masc (PL die Esel)

donor NOUN
der Spender masc (PL die Spender)
die Spenderin fem

★ **don't** = do not

★ **door** NOUN
die Tür fem

doorbell NOUN
die Klingel fem
■ to ring the doorbell klingeln [34]
■ Suddenly the doorbell rang. Es klingelte plötzlich.

doorman NOUN
der Portier masc (PL die Portiers)

doorstep NOUN
die Eingangsstufe fem

dormitory NOUN
der Schlafsaal masc (PL die Schlafsäle)

dose NOUN
die Dosis fem (PL die Dosen)

dosh NOUN
die Kohle fem (informal: money)

dot NOUN
der Punkt masc (PL die Punkte) (on letter 'i', in email address)
■ on the dot genau □ He arrived at nine o'clock on the dot. Er kam genau um neun Uhr.

★ to **double** VERB
▷ see also double ADJECTIVE, ADVERB
sich verdoppeln [34] (PERFECT TENSE hat sich verdoppelt)
□ The number of students has doubled. Die Zahl der Studenten hat sich verdoppelt.

★ **double** ADJECTIVE, ADVERB
▷ see also double VERB
doppelt
□ a double helping eine doppelte Portion
■ to cost double doppelt so viel kosten [2]
□ First-class tickets cost double. Fahrscheine erster Klasse kosten doppelt so viel.
■ a double bed ein Doppelbett neut
■ a double room ein Doppelzimmer neut
■ a double-decker bus ein Doppeldeckerbus masc

double bass NOUN
der Kontrabass masc (GEN des Kontrabasses, PL die Kontrabässe)
□ I play the double bass. Ich spiele Kontrabass.

to **double-click** VERB
doppelklicken [15] (PERFECT TENSE hat doppelgeklickt) (computer)

double glazing NOUN
das Doppelfenster neut (PL die Doppelfenster)

doubles PL NOUN
das Doppel neut (PL die Doppel) (in tennis)
□ to play mixed doubles gemischtes Doppel spielen

★ **doubt** NOUN
▷ see also doubt VERB

der Zweifel masc (PL die Zweifel)
□ I have my doubts. Ich habe meine Zweifel.

★ to **doubt** VERB
▷ see also **doubt** NOUN
bezweifeln [34] (PERFECT TENSE hat bezweifelt)
□ I doubt it. Das bezweifle ich.
■ **to doubt that** bezweifeln, dass □ I doubt he'll agree. Ich bezweifle, dass er zustimmt.

doubtful ADJECTIVE
■ **to be doubtful about doing something** nicht wissen [93], ob man etwas tun soll □ I'm doubtful about going by myself. Ich weiß nicht, ob ich allein gehen soll.
■ **It's doubtful.** Es ist fraglich.
■ **You sound doubtful.** Du scheinst nicht sicher zu sein.

dough NOUN
der Teig masc (PL die Teige)

doughnut NOUN
der Berliner masc (PL die Berliner)
□ a jam doughnut ein gefüllter Berliner

Dover NOUN
Dover neut
□ We went from Dover to Boulogne. Wir sind von Dover nach Boulogne gefahren.

★ **down** ADVERB, ADJECTIVE, PREPOSITION
1 unten (below)
□ down on the first floor unten im ersten Stock
□ It's down there. Es ist da unten.
2 auf den Boden (to the ground)
□ He threw down his racket. Er warf seinen Schläger auf den Boden.
■ **They live just down the road.** Sie wohnen etwas weiter unten.
■ **to come down** herunterkommen [40]
□ Come down here! Komm herunter!
■ **to go down** hinuntergehen [29] □ They went down into the cellar. Sie gingen in den Keller hinunter.
■ **to sit down** sich hinsetzen [15] □ Sit down! Setz dich hin!
■ **to feel down** niedergeschlagen sein [65]
□ I'm feeling a bit down. Ich bin etwas niedergeschlagen.
■ **The computer's down.** Der Computer ist abgestürzt.

★ to **download** VERB
▷ see also **download** NOUN
herunterladen (PRESENT TENSE lädt herunter, IMPERFECT lud herunter, PERFECT TENSE hat heruntergeladen) (computer)
□ to download a file eine Datei herunterladen

★ **download** NOUN
▷ see also **download** VERB
der Download masc (PL die Downloads)
□ a free download ein Gratis-Download

downpour NOUN
der Regenguss masc (GEN des Regengusses, PL die Regengüsse)
□ a sudden downpour ein plötzlicher Regenguss

★ **downstairs** ADVERB, ADJECTIVE
1 unten
□ The bathroom's downstairs. Das Badezimmer ist unten.
■ **the people downstairs** die Leute von unten
■ **to go downstairs** nach unten gehen [29]
2 untere
□ the downstairs bathroom das untere Badezimmer

downtown ADVERB (US)
im Stadtzentrum

to **doze** VERB
dösen [38]

to **doze off** VERB
einnicken [4]

★ **dozen** NOUN
das Dutzend neut (PL die Dutzende or Dutzend)

> When talking about more than one dozen use the plural form **Dutzend**.

□ two dozen zwei Dutzend □ a dozen eggs ein Dutzend Eier
■ **I've told you that dozens of times.** Ich habe dir das schon x-mal gesagt.

drab ADJECTIVE
trist (clothes)

★ **draft** NOUN (US)
der Luftzug masc (PL die Luftzüge)
■ **There's a draft!** Es zieht!

to **drag** VERB
▷ see also **drag** NOUN
schleppen [48] (thing, person)

drag NOUN
▷ see also **drag** VERB
■ **It's a real drag!** Das ist echt öde! (informal)
■ **in drag** in Frauenkleidern □ He was in drag. Er hatte Frauenkleider an.

dragon NOUN
der Drache masc (GEN des Drachen, PL die Drachen)

★ **drain** NOUN
▷ see also **drain** VERB
der Abfluss masc (GEN des Abflusses, PL die Abflüsse)
□ The drains are blocked. Der Abfluss ist verstopft.

★ to **drain** VERB
▷ see also **drain** NOUN
abtropfen lassen [42] (PRESENT TENSE lässt abtropfen, IMPERFECT ließ abtropfen, PERFECT TENSE hat abtropfen lassen) (vegetables, pasta)

draining board NOUN
das Ablaufbrett neut (PL die Ablaufbretter)

drainpipe NOUN
das Regenrohr neut (PL die Regenrohre)

★ **drama** NOUN
das Drama neut (PL die Dramen)
□ Drama is my favourite subject. Drama ist mein Lieblingsfach.

d

■ **drama school** die Schauspielschule □ I'd like to go to drama school. Ich würde gerne auf die Schauspielschule gehen.

★ **dramatic** ADJECTIVE
dramatisch
□ It was really dramatic! Es war wirklich dramatisch! □ a dramatic improvement eine dramatische Besserung

drank VERB ▷ see **drink**

drapes PL NOUN (US)
die Vorhänge masc pl

drastic ADJECTIVE
drastisch (change)
□ to take drastic action drastische Maßnahmen ergreifen

draught NOUN
der Luftzug masc (PL die Luftzüge)
■ **There's a draught!** Es zieht!

★ **draw** NOUN
▷ see also **draw** VERB
1 das Unentschieden neut (PL die Unentschieden) (sport)
□ The game ended in a draw. Das Spiel endete mit einem Unentschieden.
2 die Ziehung fem (in lottery)
□ The draw takes place on Saturday. Die Ziehung findet am Samstag statt.

★ to **draw** VERB
▷ see also **draw** NOUN
1 malen [38]
□ He's good at drawing. Er kann gut malen. □ to draw a picture ein Bild malen
■ **to draw a line** einen Strich machen [48]
2 unentschieden spielen [38] (sport)
□ We drew two all. Wir haben zwei zu zwei gespielt.
■ **to draw the curtains** die Vorhänge zuziehen [96]
■ **to draw lots** losen [38]

to **draw on** VERB
zurückgreifen auf (IMPERFECT griff zurück, PERFECT TENSE hat zurückgegriffen)
□ Draw on your own experience. Greife auf deine eigenen Erfahrungen zurück.

to **draw up** VERB
halten [33] (PRESENT TENSE hält, IMPERFECT hielt, PERFECT TENSE hat gehalten)
□ The car drew up in front of the house. Das Auto hielt vor dem Haus.

drawback NOUN
der Nachteil masc (PL die Nachteile)

drawer NOUN
die Schublade fem

★ **drawing** NOUN
die Zeichnung fem

drawing pin NOUN
die Reißzwecke fem

drawn VERB ▷ see **draw**

dreadful ADJECTIVE
1 furchtbar
□ a dreadful mistake ein furchtbarer Fehler □ You look dreadful. (ill) Du siehst furchtbar aus. □ I feel dreadful. Ich fühle mich furchtbar.
2 schrecklich
□ The weather was dreadful. Das Wetter war schrecklich.

★ to **dream** VERB
▷ see also **dream** NOUN
träumen [38]
□ I dreamt I was playing basketball. Ich habe geträumt, ich spiele Basketball.

Note the use of the subjunctive.

★ **dream** NOUN
▷ see also **dream** VERB
der Traum masc (PL die Träume)
□ It was just a dream. Es war nur ein Traum. □ a bad dream ein böser Traum

to **drench** VERB
■ **to get drenched** klatschnass werden [91]
□ We got drenched. Wir wurden klatschnass.

★ **dress** NOUN
▷ see also **dress** VERB
das Kleid neut (PL die Kleider)

★ to **dress** VERB
▷ see also **dress** NOUN
sich anziehen [96] (IMPERFECT zog sich an, PERFECT TENSE hat sich angezogen)
□ I got up, dressed, and went downstairs. Ich stand auf, zog mich an und ging hinunter.
■ **to dress somebody** jemanden anziehen [96] □ She dressed the children. Sie zog die Kinder an.
■ **to get dressed** sich anziehen [96] □ I got dressed quickly. Ich habe mich schnell angezogen.

to **dress up** VERB
sich verkleiden [54]
□ I dressed up as a ghost. Ich habe mich als Gespenst verkleidet.

★ **dressed** ADJECTIVE
angezogen
□ I'm not dressed yet. Ich bin noch nicht angezogen. □ How was she dressed? Wie war sie angezogen?
■ **She was dressed in a green jumper and jeans.** Sie hatte einen grünen Pullover und Jeans an.

dresser NOUN
die Kommode fem (furniture)

dressing NOUN
das Dressing neut (PL die Dressings) (for salad)

dressing gown NOUN
der Morgenmantel masc (PL die Morgenmäntel)

dressing table NOUN
der Frisiertisch masc (PL die Frisiertische)

drew VERB ▷ see **draw**

★ = core vocabulary

drier NOUN
1 der Wäschetrockner *masc* (PLdie Wäschetrockner) (*for washing*)
2 der Haartrockner *masc* (PLdie Haartrockner) (*for hair*)

drift NOUN
▷ *see also* **drift** VERB
■ **a snow drift**eine Schneeverwehung

to **drift** VERB
▷ *see also* **drift** NOUN
treiben (IMPERFECTtrieb , PERFECT TENSEist getrieben) (*boat, snow*)

drill NOUN
▷ *see also* **drill** VERB
der Bohrer *masc* (PLdie Bohrer)

to **drill** VERB
▷ *see also* **drill** NOUN
bohren [38]

to **drink** VERB
▷ *see also* **drink** NOUN
trinken [80] (IMPERFECTtrank , PERFECT TENSEhat getrunken)
□ What would you like to drink?Was möchtest du trinken? □ She drank three cups of tea.Sie trank drei Tassen Tee. □ He'd been drinking.Er hatte getrunken. □ I don't drink.Ich trinke nicht.

drink NOUN
▷ *see also* **drink** VERB
1 das Getränk *neut* (PLdie Getränke)
□ a cold drinkein kaltes Getränk □ a hot drink ein heißes Getränk
2 der Drink *masc* (PLdie Drinks) (*alcoholic*)
■ **They've gone out for a drink.**Sie sind etwas trinken gegangen.
■ **to have a drink**etwas trinken [80]

drinking water NOUN
das Trinkwasser *neut*

drive NOUN
▷ *see also* **drive** VERB
1 die Fahrt *fem*
□ It's a long drive.Es ist eine lange Fahrt.
■ **to go for a drive**fahren [21] □ We went for a drive in the country.Wir sind aufs Land gefahren.
2 die Auffahrt *fem* (*of house*)
□ He parked his car in the drive.Er parkte sein Auto in der Auffahrt.

to **drive** VERB
▷ *see also* **drive** NOUN
1 fahren [21] (PRESENT TENSEfährt , IMPERFECTfuhr , PERFECT TENSEist/hat gefahren)
□ My mum drives me to school.Meine Mama fährt mich in die Schule. □ We drove down to London.Wir sind nach London gefahren.

When **fahren** is used with an object it takes **haben** not **sein** .

□ He drove me home.Er hat mich nach Hause gefahren.

2 Auto fahren [21] (PRESENT TENSEfährt Auto , IMPERFECTfuhr Auto , PERFECT TENSEist Auto gefahren) (*operate a car*)
□ Can you drive?Kannst du Auto fahren?
■ **She's learning to drive.**Sie macht den Führerschein.
3 mit dem Auto fahren [21] (*go by car*)
□ Did you go by train? — No, we drove.Seid ihr mit dem Zug gefahren? — Nein, wir sind mit dem Auto gefahren.
■ **to drive somebody mad**jemanden wahnsinnig machen [48] □ He drives her mad. Er macht sie wahnsinnig.

★ **driver** NOUN
der Fahrer *masc* (PLdie Fahrer)
die Fahrerin *fem*
□ She's an excellent driver.Sie ist eine ausgezeichnete Fahrerin. □ He's a bus driver.Er ist Busfahrer.

driver's license NOUN (US)
der Führerschein *masc* (PLdie Führerscheine)

driving instructor NOUN
der Fahrlehrer *masc* (PLdie Fahrlehrer)
die Fahrlehrerin *fem*
□ She's a driving instructor.Sie ist Fahrlehrerin.

driving lesson NOUN
die Fahrstunde *fem*

driving licence NOUN
der Führerschein *masc* (PLdie Führerscheine)

driving test NOUN
die Fahrprüfung *fem*
■ **to take one's driving test**die Fahrprüfung machen [48] □ He's taking his driving test tomorrow.Er macht morgen die Fahrprüfung.
■ **She's just passed her driving test.**Sie hat gerade ihren Führerschein gemacht.

drizzle NOUN
▷ *see also* **drizzle** VERB
der Nieselregen *masc*

to **drizzle** VERB
▷ *see also* **drizzle** NOUN
nieseln [88]

drone NOUN
die Drohne *fem*

★ **drop** NOUN
▷ *see also* **drop** VERB
der Tropfen *masc* (PLdie Tropfen)
□ a drop of waterein Wassertropfen

★ to **drop** VERB
▷ *see also* **drop** NOUN
1 fallen lassen [42] (PRESENT TENSElässt fallen , IMPERFECTließ fallen , PERFECT TENSEhat fallen lassen)
□ I dropped the glass.Ich habe das Glas fallen lassen.
2 aufgeben [28] (PRESENT TENSEgibt auf , IMPERFECT gab auf , PERFECT TENSEhat aufgegeben) (*abandon*)
□ I'm going to drop chemistry.Ich gebe Chemie auf.

d

drought – dumb

3 absetzen [36] (PERFECT TENSE hat abgesetzt)
□ Could you drop me at the station? Könntest du mich am Bahnhof absetzen?

drought NOUN
die Dürre *fem*

drove VERB ▷ see **drive**

to **drown** VERB
ertrinken [80] (IMPERFECT ertrank, PERFECT TENSE ist ertrunken)
□ A boy drowned here yesterday. Hier ist gestern ein Junge ertrunken.

★**drug** NOUN
1 das Medikament *neut* (PL die Medikamente) (*medicine*)
□ They need food and drugs. Sie brauchen Nahrung und Medikamente.
2 die Droge *fem* (*illegal*)
□ hard drugs harte Drogen □ soft drugs weiche Drogen □ to take drugs Drogen nehmen
■ a drug addict (*man*) ein Drogensüchtiger
■ She's a drug addict. Sie ist drogensüchtig.
■ a drug dealer ein Dealer *masc*
■ a drugs smuggler ein Drogenschmuggler *masc*
■ the problem of drug abuse das Problem des Drogenmissbrauches

drugstore NOUN (US)
der Drugstore *masc* (PL die Drugstores)

★**drum** NOUN
die Trommel *fem*
□ an African drum eine afrikanische Trommel
■ a drum kit ein Schlagzeug *neut*
■ drums das Schlagzeug *sing* □ I play drums. Ich spiele Schlagzeug.

drummer NOUN
der Schlagzeuger *masc* (PL die Schlagzeuger)
die Schlagzeugerin *fem* (*in rock group*)

drunk VERB ▷ see **drink**

drunk ADJECTIVE
▷ see also **drunk** NOUN
betrunken
□ He was drunk. Er war betrunken.

drunk NOUN
▷ see also **drunk** ADJECTIVE
der Betrunkene *masc* (GEN des Betrunkenen, PL die Betrunkenen)
die Betrunkene *fem* (GEN der Betrunkenen)
□ a drunk (*man*) ein Betrunkener □ The streets were full of drunks. Die Straßen waren voll von Betrunkenen.

★**dry** ADJECTIVE
▷ see also **dry** VERB
trocken
□ The paint isn't dry yet. Die Farbe ist noch nicht trocken.
■ a long dry period eine lange Trockenzeit

★to **dry** VERB
▷ see also **dry** ADJECTIVE

1 trocknen [53]
□ The washing will dry quickly in the sun. Die Wäsche wird in der Sonne schnell trocknen.
□ some dried flowers getrocknete Blumen
■ to dry one's hair sich die Haare föhnen [38]
□ I haven't dried my hair yet. Ich habe mir noch nicht die Haare geföhnt.
2 trocknen lassen [42] (PRESENT TENSE lässt trocknen, IMPERFECT ließ trocknen, PERFECT TENSE hat trocknen lassen) (*clothes*)
□ There's nowhere to dry clothes here. Hier kann man nirgends Kleider trocknen lassen.
■ to dry the dishes das Geschirr abtrocknen [53]

dry-cleaner's NOUN
die Reinigung *fem*

dryer NOUN
der Wäschetrockner *masc* (PL die Wäschetrockner) (*for clothes*)
■ a tumble dryer ein Wäschetrockner
■ a hair dryer ein Föhn *masc*

DT NOUN (= *design technology*)
das Werken *neut*

DTP ABBREVIATION (= *Desktop Publishing*)
das DTP *neut*

dubbed ADJECTIVE
synchronisiert
□ The film was dubbed into German. Der Film war deutsch synchronisiert.

dubious ADJECTIVE
1 dubios (*situation, character*)
2 verdächtig (*package*)
■ My parents were a bit dubious about it. Meine Eltern hatten ihre Zweifel.

★**duck** NOUN
die Ente *fem*

★**due** ADJECTIVE, ADVERB
■ to be due to do something etwas tun sollen [69] □ He's due to arrive tomorrow. Er soll morgen ankommen.
■ The plane's due in half an hour. Das Flugzeug sollte in einer halben Stunde ankommen.
■ When's the baby due? Wann kommt das Baby?
■ due to wegen □ The trip was cancelled due to bad weather. Der Ausflug wurde wegen des schlechten Wetters abgesagt.

dug VERB ▷ see **dig**

dull ADJECTIVE
1 langweilig
□ He's nice, but a bit dull. Er ist nett, aber ein bisschen langweilig.
2 trüb (*weather, day*)

dumb ADJECTIVE (*rude*)
blöd
□ That was a really dumb thing I did! Da habe ich etwas echt Blödes gemacht!

★ = core vocabulary

dummy NOUN
der Schnuller *masc* (PL die Schnuller) *(for baby)*

★ **dump** NOUN
▷ *see also* **dump** VERB
■ **It's a real dump!** Das ist ein Dreckloch! *(informal)*
■ **a rubbish dump** eine Müllkippe

★ to **dump** VERB
▷ *see also* **dump** NOUN
1 abladen (PRESENT TENSE lädt ab, IMPERFECT lud ab, PERFECT TENSE hat abgeladen) *(waste)*
■ **'no dumping'** 'Schutt abladen verboten'
2 Schluss machen [48] mit *(informal: get rid of)*
□ He's just dumped his girlfriend. Er hat gerade mit seiner Freundin Schluss gemacht.

dungarees PL NOUN
die Latzhose *fem*
□ a pair of dungarees eine Latzhose

dungeon NOUN
das Verlies *neut* (PL die Verliese)

duration NOUN
die Dauer *fem*

★ **during** PREPOSITION
während
□ during the holidays während der Ferien
■ **during the day** tagsüber

dusk NOUN
die Dämmerung *fem*
□ at dusk bei Dämmerung

★ **dust** NOUN
▷ *see also* **dust** VERB
der Staub *masc*

★ to **dust** VERB
▷ *see also* **dust** NOUN
abstauben [4] (PERFECT TENSE hat abgestaubt)
□ I dusted the shelves. Ich habe das Regal abgestaubt.
■ **I hate dusting!** Ich hasse Staubwischen!

★ **dustbin** NOUN
der Mülleimer *masc* (PL die Mülleimer)

dustman NOUN
der Müllmann *masc* (PL die Müllmänner)
■ **He's a dustman.** Er arbeitet bei der Müllabfuhr.

dusty ADJECTIVE
staubig

★ **Dutch** ADJECTIVE
▷ *see also* **Dutch** NOUN
holländisch
■ **She's Dutch.** Sie ist Holländerin.

★ **Dutch** NOUN
▷ *see also* **Dutch** ADJECTIVE
das Holländisch *neut* (GEN des Holländischen) *(language)*
■ **the Dutch** die Holländer *masc pl*

★ **Dutchman** NOUN
der Holländer *masc* (PL die Holländer)

★ **Dutchwoman** NOUN
die Holländerin *fem*

★ **duty** NOUN
die Pflicht *fem*
□ It was his duty to tell the police. Es war seine Pflicht, die Polizei zu informieren.
■ **to be on duty** Dienst haben [32]

duty-free ADJECTIVE
zollfrei
■ **the duty-free shop** der Duty-free-Laden

★ **duvet** NOUN
das Deckbett *neut* (PL die Deckbetten)

★ **DVD** NOUN (= *digital video disc*)
die DVD *fem* (PL die DVDs)

DVD player NOUN
der DVD-Player *masc* (PL die DVD-Player)

dye NOUN
▷ *see also* **dye** VERB
der Farbstoff *masc*
■ **hair dye** das Haarfärbemittel

to **dye** VERB
▷ *see also* **dye** NOUN
färben [38]
□ to dye something red etwas rot färben □ She has dyed her hair blonde. Sie hat blond gefärbte Haare.

dynamic ADJECTIVE
dynamisch

dyslexia NOUN
die Legasthenie *fem*
■ **She has dyslexia.** Sie ist Legasthenikerin.

dyspraxia NOUN
Dyspraxie *fem*
■ **She has dyspraxia.** Sie leidet an Dyspraxie.

d

Ee

★ **each** ADJECTIVE, PRONOUN
jeder
  □ Each person has their own desk.Jeder hat seinen eigenen Schreibtisch. □ They have ten points each.Jeder hat zehn Punkte. □ He gave each of us ten pounds.Er gab jedem von uns zehn Pfund. □ each dayjeder Tag
jede
  □ Each woman gave an interesting talk.Jede Frau hielt einen interessanten Vortrag. □ There was a chair in each corner of the room.In jeder Ecke des Raums stand ein Stuhl.
jedes
  □ Each house has a garden.Jedes Haus hat einen Garten. □ The girls each have their own bedroom.Jedes der Mädchen hat sein eigenes Zimmer.
  ■ **each other**einander □ They hate each other. Sie hassen einander. □ We wrote to each other. Wir haben einander geschrieben.
  ■ **They don't know each other.**Sie kennen sich nicht.

eager ADJECTIVE
  ■ **He was eager to talk to us.**Er wollte unbedingt mit uns sprechen.

eagle NOUN
der Adler masc (pldie Adler)

★ **ear** NOUN
das Ohr neut (pldie Ohren)

earache NOUN
die Ohrenschmerzen masc pl
  □ to have earacheOhrenschmerzen haben

★ **earlier** ADVERB
1 vorhin
  □ I saw him earlier.Ich habe ihn vorhin gesehen.
2 früher (in the morning)
  □ I ought to get up earlier.Ich sollte früher aufstehen.

★ **early** ADVERB, ADJECTIVE
früh
  □ I have to get up early.Ich muss früh aufstehen. □ I came early to get a good seat.Ich bin früh gekommen, um einen guten Platz zu bekommen.
  ■ **to have an early night**früh ins Bett gehen
[29]

★ to **earn** VERB
verdienen [84] (PERFECT TENSEhat verdient)
  □ She earns twelve pounds an hour.Sie verdient zwölf Pfund pro Stunde.

★ **earnings** PL NOUN
der Verdienst masc (pldie Verdienste)

earphones PL NOUN
die Kopfhörer pl noun

earring NOUN
der Ohrring masc (pldie Ohrringe)

★ **earth** NOUN
die Erde fem

earthquake NOUN
das Erdbeben neut (pldie Erdbeben)

★ **easily** ADVERB
leicht

★ **east** ADJECTIVE, ADVERB
  ▷ see also **east** NOUN
nach Osten
  □ We were travelling east.Wir sind nach Osten gefahren.
  ■ **the east coast**die Ostküste
  ■ **an east wind**ein Ostwind masc
  ■ **east of**östlich von □ It's east of London.Es liegt östlich von London.

★ **east** NOUN
  ▷ see also **east** ADJECTIVE, ADVERB
der Osten masc
  □ in the eastim Osten

Easter NOUN
Ostern neut
  □ at Easteran Ostern □ We went to Spain for Easter.Wir waren über Ostern in Spanien.

Easter egg NOUN
das Osterei neut (pldie Ostereier)

★ **eastern** ADJECTIVE
östlich
  □ the eastern part of the islandder östliche Teil der Insel
  ■ **Eastern Europe**Osteuropa neut

★ **easy** ADJECTIVE
einfach

easy chair NOUN
der Sessel masc (pldie Sessel)

easy-going ADJECTIVE
locker
  □ She's very easy-going.Sie ist echt locker.

★ = core vocabulary

to **eat** VERB
essen [20] (PRESENT TENSE isst, IMPERFECT aß, PERFECT TENSE hat gegessen)
□ Would you like something to eat? Möchtest du etwas essen?

e-book NOUN
das E-Book neut (PL die E-Books)

e-card NOUN
die E-Card fem (PL die E-Cards)

eccentric ADJECTIVE
exzentrisch

echo NOUN
das Echo neut (PL die Echos)

ecology NOUN
die Ökologie fem

e-commerce NOUN
der E-Commerce masc (GEN des E-Commerce)

economic ADJECTIVE
rentabel (profitable)

economical ADJECTIVE
sparsam

economics SING NOUN
die Volkswirtschaft fem
□ He's studying economics. Er studiert Volkswirtschaft.

to **economize** VERB
sparen [38]
□ to economize on something mit etwas sparen

economy NOUN
die Wirtschaft fem
□ the German economy die deutsche Wirtschaft

ecotourism NOUN
der Ökotourismus masc

ecstasy NOUN
das Ecstasy neut (GEN des Ecstasy) (drug)
■ to be in ecstasy entzückt sein [65]

eczema NOUN
der Hautausschlag masc (PL die Hautausschläge)

edge NOUN
1 der Rand masc (PL die Ränder)
□ They live on the edge of the moors. Sie leben am Rand des Moors.
2 die Kante fem (of table)
3 das Ufer neut (PL die Ufer) (of lake)

edgy ADJECTIVE
nervös

Edinburgh NOUN
Edinburgh neut

editor NOUN
der Redakteur masc (PL die Redakteure)
die Redakteurin fem (of newspaper)

educated ADJECTIVE
gebildet

★ **education** NOUN
1 das Bildungswesen neut
□ There should be more investment in education. Es sollte mehr Geld ins Bildungswesen investiert werden.
2 das Lehramt neut (teaching)
□ She works in education. Sie ist im Lehramt tätig.

★ **educational** ADJECTIVE
lehrreich (experience)
□ It was very educational. Das war sehr lehrreich.

★ **effect** NOUN
der Effekt masc (PL die Effekte)
□ special effects Spezialeffekte

★ **effective** ADJECTIVE
effektiv

★ **efficient** ADJECTIVE
effizient

★ **effort** NOUN
die Bemühung fem
■ to make an effort to do something sich bemühen [7] etwas zu tun

e.g. ABBREVIATION
z. B. (=zum Beispiel)

★ **egg** NOUN
das Ei neut (PL die Eier)
□ a hard-boiled egg ein hart gekochtes Ei □ a soft-boiled egg ein weich gekochtes Ei
■ a fried egg ein Spiegelei
■ scrambled eggs die Rühreier neut pl

egg cup NOUN
der Eierbecher masc (PL die Eierbecher)

eggplant NOUN (US)
die Aubergine fem

Egypt NOUN
Ägypten neut
□ to Egypt nach Ägypten

★ **eight** NUMBER
acht
□ She's eight. Sie ist acht.

★ **eighteen** NUMBER
achtzehn
□ She's eighteen. Sie ist achtzehn.

★ **eighteenth** ADJECTIVE
achtzehnte
□ the eighteenth of August der achtzehnte August

★ **eighth** ADJECTIVE
achte
□ the eighth floor der achte Stock □ the eighth of August der achte August

★ **eighty** NUMBER
achtzig
□ She's eighty. Sie ist achtzig.

Numbers in brackets refer to verb tables on pages 697 to 706.

439

either – embarrassing

★ **either** ADVERB, CONJUNCTION, PRONOUN
  1 auch kein
    □ I don't like milk, and I don't like eggs either.
    Ich mag keine Milch und ich mag auch keine
    Eier.
  2 auch nicht
    □ I've never been to Spain. — I haven't either.
    Ich war noch nie in Spanien. — Ich auch nicht.
    ■ **either ... or ...** entweder ... oder ... □ You can
    have either ice cream or yoghurt. Du kannst
    entweder Eis oder Joghurt haben.
    ■ **either of them** einer von beiden □ Take
    either of them. Nimm einen von beiden.
    ■ **I don't like either of them.** Ich mag keinen
    von beiden.

elastic NOUN
  das Gummiband *neut* (PL die Gummibänder)

elastic band NOUN
  das Gummiband *neut* (PL die Gummibänder)

elbow NOUN
  der Ellbogen *masc* (PL die Ellbogen)

★ **elder** ADJECTIVE
  älter
    □ my elder sister meine ältere Schwester

★ **elderly** ADJECTIVE
  älter
    □ an elderly lady eine ältere Dame

★ **eldest** ADJECTIVE
  älteste
    □ my eldest brother mein ältester Bruder □ my
    eldest sister meine älteste Schwester □ He's
    the eldest. Er ist der Älteste.

to **elect** VERB
  wählen [38]

★ **election** NOUN
  die Wahl *fem*
    □ The general election takes place tomorrow.
    Morgen finden die allgemeinen Wahlen statt.

★ **electric** ADJECTIVE
  elektrisch
    □ an electric fire ein elektrischer Ofen □ an
    electric guitar eine elektrische Gitarre
    ■ **an electric blanket** eine Heizdecke

electrical ADJECTIVE
  elektrisch
    ■ **an electrical engineer** ein Elektrotechniker

electrician NOUN
  der Elektriker *masc* (PL die Elektriker)
  die Elektrikerin *fem*
    □ She's an electrician. Sie ist Elektrikerin.

★ **electricity** NOUN
  der Strom *masc*
    □ They cut off our electricity. Sie haben den
    Strom abgestellt.

★ **electronic** ADJECTIVE
  elektronisch

electronics SING NOUN
  die Elektronik *fem*
    □ My hobby is electronics. Elektronik ist mein
    Hobby.

★ **elegant** ADJECTIVE
  elegant

elementary school NOUN (US)
  die Grundschule *fem*

★ **elephant** NOUN
  der Elefant *masc* (GEN des Elefanten, PL die
  Elefanten)

elevator NOUN (US)
  der Aufzug *masc* (PL die Aufzüge)

★ **eleven** NUMBER
  elf
    □ She's eleven. Sie ist elf.

★ **eleventh** ADJECTIVE
  elfte
    □ the eleventh floor der elfte Stock □ the
    eleventh of August der elfte August

★ **else** ADVERB
  1 anders
    □ somebody else jemand anders □ nobody else
    niemand anders □ somewhere else irgendwo
    anders □ anywhere else irgendwo anders
  2 anderes
    □ nothing else nichts anderes □ something else
    etwas anderes □ anything else etwas anderes
    ■ **Would you like anything else?** Möchtest
    du noch etwas?
    ■ **I don't want anything else.** Ich will nichts
    anderes.
    ■ **Give me the money, or else!** Gib mir das
    Geld, sonst gibt's was!

★ **email** NOUN
    ▷ see also **email** VERB
  die E-Mail *fem* (PL die E-Mails)
    □ My email address is ... Meine E-Mail-Adresse
    ist ...

★ to **email** VERB
    ▷ see also **email** NOUN
  mailen [38] (PERFECT TENSE hat gemailt)
    □ Did you email it? Hast du es gemailt?
    ■ **to email somebody** jemandem eine E-Mail
    senden

embankment NOUN
  die Böschung *fem*

★ **embarrassed** ADJECTIVE
  verlegen
    □ He seemed pretty embarrassed. Er schien
    sehr verlegen.
    ■ **I was really embarrassed.** Es war mir
    wirklich peinlich.

embarrassing ADJECTIVE
  peinlich
    □ It was so embarrassing. Es war so peinlich.

★ = core vocabulary

embassy NOUN
die Botschaft *fem*

to embroider VERB
besticken [7] (PERFECT TENSE hat bestickt)

embroidery NOUN
die Stickerei *fem*
■ **I do embroidery.** Ich sticke.

emergency NOUN
der Notfall! *masc* (PL die Notfälle)
□ This is an emergency! Dies ist ein Notfall! □ in an emergency in einem Notfall
■ **an emergency exit** ein Notausgang *masc*
■ **an emergency landing** eine Notlandung *fem*
■ **the emergency services** die Rettungsdienste *masc pl*

to emigrate VERB
auswandern [88] (PERFECT TENSE ist ausgewandert)

emoji NOUN
das Emoji *neut* (PL die Emojis)

emotion NOUN
das Gefühl *neut* (PL die Gefühle)

emotional ADJECTIVE
emotional (*person*)

emperor NOUN
der Kaiser *masc* (PL die Kaiser)

to emphasize VERB
betonen [7] (PERFECT TENSE hat betont)

empire NOUN
das Reich *neut* (PL die Reiche)

to employ VERB
beschäftigen [18] (PERFECT TENSE hat beschäftigt)
□ The factory employs six hundred people. Die Fabrik beschäftigt sechshundert Leute.

employee NOUN
der Angestellte *masc* (GEN des Angestellten, PL die Angestellten)
die Angestellte *fem* (GEN der Angestellten)
□ He's an employee. Er ist Angestellter.

employer NOUN
der Arbeitgeber *masc* (PL die Arbeitgeber)
die Arbeitgeberin *fem*

employment NOUN
die Beschäftigung *fem*

empty ADJECTIVE
▷ *see also* **empty** VERB
leer

to empty VERB
▷ *see also* **empty** ADJECTIVE
leeren [38]
■ **to empty something out** etwas ausleeren [4]

to encourage VERB
ermutigen [7] (PERFECT TENSE hat ermutigt)
■ **to encourage somebody to do something** jemanden ermutigen [7], etwas zu tun

encouragement NOUN
die Ermutigung *fem*

encyclopedia NOUN
das Lexikon *neut* (PL die Lexika)

end NOUN
▷ *see also* **end** VERB
das Ende *neut* (PL die Enden)
□ the end of the holidays das Ende der Ferien
□ at the end of the street am Ende der Straße
□ at the other end of the table am anderen Ende des Tisches
■ **the end of the film** der Schluss des Films
■ **in the end** schließlich □ In the end I decided to stay at home. Schließlich habe ich beschlossen, zu Hause zu bleiben. □ It turned out all right in the end. Schließlich ging alles gut.
■ **for hours on end** stundenlang

to end VERB
▷ *see also* **end** NOUN
zu Ende sein [65] (PRESENT TENSE ist zu Ende, IMPERFECT TENSE war zu Ende, PERFECT TENSE ist zu Ende gewesen)
□ What time does the film end? Wann ist der Film zu Ende?
■ **to end up doing something** schließlich etwas tun [81] □ I ended up walking home. Ich bin schließlich zu Fuß nach Hause gegangen.

ending NOUN
der Schluss *masc* (GEN des Schlusses, PL die Schlüsse)
□ It was an exciting film, especially the ending. Es war ein spannender Film, besonders am Schluss.

endless ADJECTIVE
endlos
□ The journey seemed endless. Die Reise erschien endlos.

enemy NOUN
der Feind *masc* (PL die Feinde)
die Feindin *fem*

energetic ADJECTIVE
voller Energie (*person*)

energy NOUN
die Energie *fem*

engaged ADJECTIVE
1 besetzt (*busy, in use*)
□ I phoned, but it was engaged. Ich habe angerufen, aber es war besetzt.
2 verlobt (*to be married*)
□ She's engaged to Jacob. Sie ist mit Jacob verlobt.
■ **to get engaged** sich verloben [84]

engagement NOUN
die Verlobung *fem*
□ an engagement ring ein Verlobungsring *masc*

engine NOUN
der Motor *masc* (PL die Motoren)

Numbers in brackets refer to verb tables on pages 697 to 706.

441

engineer – envelope

★ **engineer** NOUN
1 der Ingenieur masc (PL die Ingenieure)
die Ingenieurin fem
□ He's an engineer. Er ist Ingenieur.
2 der Lokomotivführer masc (PL die Lokomotivführer)
die Lokomotivführerin fem (train driver)

★ **engineering** NOUN
die Technik fem
□ genetic engineering die Gentechnik
■ mechanical engineering der Maschinenbau

★ **England** NOUN
England neut
■ from England aus England
■ in England in England
■ to England nach England

DID YOU KNOW...?
Germans frequently use England to mean Great Britain or the United Kingdom.

★ **English** ADJECTIVE
▷ see also English NOUN
englisch
■ He's English. Er ist Engländer.
■ She's English. Sie ist Engländerin.
■ English people die Engländer masc pl

★ **English** NOUN
▷ see also English ADJECTIVE
das Englisch neut (GEN des Englischen) (language)
□ Do you speak English? Sprechen Sie Englisch?
■ the English (people) die Engländer masc pl

★ **Englishman** NOUN
der Engländer masc (PL die Engländer)

★ **Englishwoman** NOUN
die Engländerin fem

★ to **enjoy** VERB
genießen (IMPERFECT genoss, PERFECT TENSE hat genossen)
□ I enjoyed my holiday. Ich habe meinen Urlaub genossen.
■ Did you enjoy the film? Hat dir der Film gefallen?
■ Did you enjoy your meal? Hat es Ihnen geschmeckt?
■ to enjoy oneself sich amüsieren [76] □ I really enjoyed myself. Ich habe mich richtig amüsiert. □ Did you enjoy yourselves at the party? Habt ihr euch auf der Party amüsiert?

enjoyable ADJECTIVE
nett

enlargement NOUN
die Vergrößerung fem (of photo)

★ **enormous** ADJECTIVE
riesig

★ **enough** PRONOUN, ADJECTIVE
genug
□ enough time genug Zeit □ I didn't have enough money. Ich hatte nicht genug Geld.

□ big enough groß genug □ warm enough warm genug
■ Have you got enough? Reicht dir das?
■ I've had enough! Mir reicht's!
■ That's enough. Das reicht.

to **enquire** VERB
sich erkundigen [19] (PERFECT TENSE hat sich erkundigt)
■ to enquire about something sich nach etwas erkundigen [19] □ I'm going to enquire about train times. Ich werde mich nach den Abfahrtszeiten der Züge erkundigen.

enquiry NOUN
die Untersuchung fem (official investigation)
■ to make an enquiry sich erkundigen [19]
□ I'd like to make an enquiry about hotels. Ich möchte mich über Hotels erkundigen.

★ to **enter** VERB
betreten [79] (PRESENT TENSE betritt, IMPERFECT betrat, PERFECT TENSE hat betreten) (room)
■ to enter a competition an einem Wettbewerb teilnehmen [52]

★ to **entertain** VERB
unterhalten [33] (PRESENT TENSE unterhält, IMPERFECT unterhielt, PERFECT TENSE hat unterhalten) (guests)

entertainer NOUN
der Entertainer masc (PL die Entertainer)
die Entertainerin fem

entertaining ADJECTIVE
unterhaltsam

★ **enthusiasm** NOUN
die Begeisterung fem

enthusiast NOUN
■ a maths enthusiast ein Mathefan masc
■ She's a DIY enthusiast. Sie ist begeisterte Heimwerkerin.

enthusiastic ADJECTIVE
begeistert

entire ADJECTIVE
ganz
□ the entire world die ganze Welt

entirely ADVERB
ganz

★ **entrance** NOUN
der Eingang masc (PL die Eingänge)
■ an entrance exam eine Aufnahmeprüfung fem
■ entrance fee der Eintritt masc

★ **entry** NOUN
der Eingang masc (PL die Eingänge) (way in)
■ 'no entry' 1 (on door) 'kein Zutritt' 2 (on road sign) 'Einfahrt verboten'
■ an entry form ein Teilnahmeformular neut

entry phone NOUN
die Gegensprechanlage fem

envelope NOUN
der Umschlag masc (PL die Umschläge)

envious ADJECTIVE
neidisch

★ **environment** NOUN
die Umwelt *fem*

★ **environmental** ADJECTIVE
■ **environmental pollution** die Umweltverschmutzung
■ **environmental protection** der Umweltschutz

environment-friendly ADJECTIVE
umweltfreundlich

envy NOUN
▷ *see also* **envy** VERB
der Neid *masc*

to **envy** VERB
▷ *see also* **envy** NOUN
beneiden [54] (PERFECT TENSE hat beneidet)
□ I don't envy you! Ich beneide dich nicht!

epileptic ADJECTIVE
epileptisch

episode NOUN
die Folge *fem* (of TV programme, story)

★ **equal** ADJECTIVE
▷ *see also* **equal** VERB
gleich

★ to **equal** VERB
▷ *see also* **equal** ADJECTIVE
■ **Ten times two equals twenty.** Zehn mal zwei ist gleich zwanzig.

equality NOUN
die Gleichheit *fem*

to **equalize** VERB
ausgleichen (IMPERFECT glich aus, PERFECT TENSE hat ausgeglichen) (in sport)

equator NOUN
der Äquator *masc*

★ **equipment** NOUN
die Ausrüstung *fem*
□ fishing equipment die Anglerausrüstung
□ skiing equipment die Skiausrüstung

equipped ADJECTIVE
■ **equipped with** ausgerüstet mit
■ **to be well equipped** gut ausgestattet sein [65]

★ **equivalent** NOUN
das Äquivalent *neut* (PL die Äquivalente)
■ **to be equivalent to something** einer Sache entsprechen [70] □ Twenty-five per cent is equivalent to a quarter. Fünfundzwanzig Prozent entspricht einem Viertel.

e-reader NOUN
das E-Book-Lesegerät *neut* (PL die E-Book-Lesegeräte)

★ **error** NOUN
der Fehler *masc* (PL die Fehler)

escalator NOUN
die Rolltreppe *fem*

★ **escape** NOUN
▷ *see also* **escape** VERB
der Ausbruch *masc* (PL die Ausbrüche) (from prison)

★ to **escape** VERB
▷ *see also* **escape** NOUN
ausbrechen [11] (PRESENT TENSE bricht aus, IMPERFECT brach aus, PERFECT TENSE ist ausgebrochen)
□ A lion has escaped. Ein Löwe ist ausgebrochen. □ to escape from prison aus dem Gefängnis ausbrechen

escort NOUN
die Eskorte *fem*
□ a police escort eine Polizeieskorte

★ **especially** ADVERB
besonders
□ It's very hot there, especially in the summer. Dort ist es sehr heiß, besonders im Sommer.

essay NOUN
der Aufsatz *masc* (PL die Aufsätze)
□ a history essay ein Aufsatz in Geschichte

★ **essential** ADJECTIVE
wichtig
□ It's essential to bring warm clothes. Es ist ganz wichtig, warme Kleidung mitzubringen.

estate NOUN
die Siedlung *fem* (housing estate)
□ I live on an estate. Ich wohne in einer Siedlung.

estate agent NOUN
der Immobilienmakler *masc* (PL die Immobilienmakler)
die Immobilienmaklerin *fem*

estate car NOUN
der Kombiwagen *masc* (PL die Kombiwagen)

★ to **estimate** VERB
schätzen [36]
□ They estimated it would take three weeks. Sie schätzten, dass es drei Wochen dauern würde.

★ **etc** ABBREVIATION (= et cetera)
usw. (= und so weiter)

Ethiopia NOUN
Äthiopien *neut*
■ **in Ethiopia** in Äthiopien

★ **ethnic** ADJECTIVE
1 ethnisch (racial)
□ an ethnic minority eine ethnische Minderheit
2 folkloristisch (clothes, music)

e-ticket NOUN
das E-Ticket *neut* (PL die E-Tickets)

EU NOUN (= European Union)
die EU *fem* (= Europäische Union)

★ **euro** NOUN
der Euro *masc* (PL die Euros or Euro)

> When talking about amounts of money use the plural form **Euro**.

□ fifty euros fünfzig Euro

★ **Europe** NOUN
Europa *neut*
- **from Europe** aus Europa
- **in Europe** in Europa
- **to Europe** nach Europa

★ **European** ADJECTIVE
▷ see also **European** NOUN
europäisch
- **He's European.** Er ist Europäer.

★ **European** NOUN
▷ see also **European** ADJECTIVE
der Europäer *masc* (PL die Europäer)
die Europäerin *fem* (person)

to **evacuate** VERB
evakuieren [76] (PERFECT TENSE hat evakuiert)

eve NOUN
- **Christmas Eve** der Heiligabend
- **New Year's Eve** Silvester *neut*

★ **even** ADVERB
▷ see also **even** ADJECTIVE
sogar
□ I like all animals, even snakes. Ich mag alle Tiere, sogar Schlangen.
- **even if** selbst wenn □ I'd never do that, even if you asked me. Ich würde das nie tun, selbst wenn du mich darum bitten würdest.
- **not even** nicht einmal □ He never stops working, not even at the weekend. Er hört nie auf zu arbeiten, nicht einmal am Wochenende.
- **even though** obwohl □ He's never got any money, even though his parents are quite rich. Er hat nie Geld, obwohl seine Eltern ziemlich reich sind.
- **I liked Hamburg even more than Munich.** Hamburg hat mir noch besser gefallen als München.

★ **even** ADJECTIVE
▷ see also **even** ADVERB
gleichmäßig
□ an even layer of snow eine gleichmäßige Schneeschicht
- **an even number** eine gerade Zahl
- **to get even with somebody** es jemandem heimzahlen [4]

★ **evening** NOUN
der Abend *masc* (PL die Abende)
□ in the evening am Abend □ all evening den ganzen Abend □ yesterday evening gestern Abend □ tomorrow evening morgen Abend
- **Good evening!** Guten Abend!

evening class NOUN
der Abendkurs *masc* (PL die Abendkurse)

★ **event** NOUN
das Ereignis *neut* (GEN des Ereignisses, PL die Ereignisse)
- **a sporting event** eine Sportveranstaltung

eventful ADJECTIVE
ereignisreich

eventual ADJECTIVE
schließlich
- **the eventual outcome** das Endergebnis

> **BE CAREFUL!**
> Do not translate **eventual** by the German word **eventuell**.

★ **eventually** ADVERB
schließlich

★ **ever** ADVERB
1 schon einmal
□ Have you ever been to America? Warst du schon einmal in Amerika? □ Have you ever seen her? Hast du sie schon einmal gesehen?
2 je
□ the best I've ever seen das Beste, was ich je gesehen habe
- **for the first time ever** das allererste Mal
- **ever since** seit □ ever since I met him seit ich ihn kenne
- **ever since then** seither

★ **every** ADJECTIVE
jeder
□ every student jeder Student □ every day jeder Tag
jede
□ every mother jede Mutter □ every week jede Woche
jedes
□ every child jedes Kind □ every year jedes Jahr
- **every time** jedes Mal □ Every time I see him, he's depressed. Jedes Mal, wenn ich ihn sehe, ist er deprimiert.
- **every now and then** ab und zu

★ **everybody** PRONOUN
1 alle
□ Everybody had a good time. Alle hatten ihren Spaß.
2 jeder
□ Everybody makes mistakes. Jeder macht mal Fehler.

★ **everyone** PRONOUN
1 alle
□ Everyone opened their presents. Alle machten ihre Geschenke auf.
2 jeder
□ Everyone should have a hobby. Jeder sollte ein Hobby haben.

★ **everything** PRONOUN
alles
□ You've thought of everything! Du hast an alles gedacht! □ Money isn't everything. Geld ist nicht alles.

★ = core vocabulary

★ **everywhere** ADVERB
überall
□ I've looked everywhere. Ich habe überall gesucht. □ There were police officers everywhere. Überall waren Polizisten.

★ **evil** ADJECTIVE
böse

ex- PREFIX
Ex-
□ his ex-wife seine Ex-Frau

★ **exact** ADJECTIVE
genau

★ **exactly** ADVERB
genau
□ exactly the same genau das gleiche □ It's exactly ten o'clock. Es ist genau zehn Uhr.

to **exaggerate** VERB
übertreiben (IMPERFECT übertrieb, PERFECT TENSE hat übertrieben)

exaggeration NOUN
die Übertreibung fem

★ **exam** NOUN
die Prüfung fem
□ a German exam eine Deutschprüfung □ the exam results die Prüfungsergebnisse

examination NOUN
die Prüfung fem
■ a medical examination eine ärztliche Untersuchung

to **examine** VERB
untersuchen [18] (PERFECT TENSE hat untersucht)
□ The doctor examined him. Der Arzt untersuchte ihn.
■ He examined her passport. Er prüfte ihren Pass.

examiner NOUN
der Prüfer masc (PL die Prüfer)
die Prüferin fem

★ **example** NOUN
das Beispiel neut (PL die Beispiele)
■ for example zum Beispiel

★ **excellent** ADJECTIVE
ausgezeichnet
□ Her results were excellent. Ihre Noten waren ausgezeichnet.

★ **except** PREPOSITION
außer
□ everyone except me alle außer mir
■ except for abgesehen von □ It was super except for the weather. Abgesehen vom Wetter war es super.
■ except that außer, dass □ The weather was great, except that it was a bit cold. Das Wetter war toll, außer dass es etwas kalt war.

exception NOUN
die Ausnahme fem

□ to make an exception eine Ausnahme machen

exceptional ADJECTIVE
außergewöhnlich

excess baggage NOUN
das Übergewicht neut (PL die Übergewichte)

★ to **exchange** VERB
tauschen [48]
□ I exchanged the book for a video game. Ich habe das Buch gegen ein Videospiel getauscht.

★ **exchange rate** NOUN
der Wechselkurs masc (PL die Wechselkurse)

★ **excited** ADJECTIVE
aufgeregt

★ **exciting** ADJECTIVE
aufregend

exclamation mark NOUN
das Ausrufezeichen neut (PL die Ausrufezeichen)

★ **excuse** NOUN
▷ see also **excuse** VERB
die Entschuldigung fem

★ to **excuse** VERB
▷ see also **excuse** NOUN
■ Excuse me! Entschuldigung!

to **execute** VERB
1 hinrichten [2] (PERFECT TENSE hat hingerichtet) (kill)
2 ausführen [4] (PERFECT TENSE hat ausgeführt) (plan)

execution NOUN
die Hinrichtung fem (punishment)
□ His execution took place yesterday. Seine Hinrichtung fand gestern statt.

executive NOUN
der leitende Angestellte masc (GEN des leitenden Angestellten, PL die leitenden Angestellten)
die leitende Angestellte fem (GEN der leitenden Angestellten) (in business)
□ He's an executive. Er ist leitender Angestellter.

★ **exercise** NOUN
1 die Übung fem
□ an exercise book ein Übungsheft
2 die Bewegung fem
□ You need more exercise. Sie brauchen mehr Bewegung.
■ an exercise bike ein Heimtrainer masc
■ She does her exercises every morning. Sie macht jeden Morgen ihre Gymnastik.

exhaust NOUN
der Auspuff masc
■ exhaust fumes die Abgase neut pl

★ **exhausted** ADJECTIVE
erschöpft

Numbers in brackets refer to verb tables on pages 697 to 706.

445

exhaust pipe NOUN
das Auspuffrohr *neut* (PL die Auspuffrohre)

★ **exhibition** NOUN
die Ausstellung *fem*

to **exist** VERB
existieren [76] (PERFECT TENSE hat existiert)
■ **It doesn't exist.** Das gibt es nicht.

★ **exit** NOUN
der Ausgang *masc* (PL die Ausgänge) (*way out*)

exotic ADJECTIVE
exotisch

★ to **expect** VERB
1 erwarten [2] (PERFECT TENSE hat erwartet)
□ I'm expecting him for dinner. Ich erwarte ihn zum Abendessen. □ She's expecting a baby. Sie erwartet ein Kind. □ I didn't expect that from him. Das habe ich von ihm nicht erwartet.
2 annehmen [1] (PRESENT TENSE nimmt an, IMPERFECT nahm an, PERFECT TENSE hat angenommen)
□ I expect he'll be late. Ich nehme an, dass er sich verspäten wird. □ I expect so. Das nehme ich mal an.

expedition NOUN
die Expedition *fem*

to **expel** VERB
■ **to get expelled** (*from school*) von der Schule verwiesen werden [91]

expenses PL NOUN
die Kosten *pl*

★ **expensive** ADJECTIVE
teuer

★ **experience** NOUN
▷ *see also* **experience** VERB
die Erfahrung *fem*

★ to **experience** VERB
▷ *see also* **experience** NOUN
1 haben [32] (PRESENT TENSE hat, IMPERFECT hatte, PERFECT TENSE hat gehabt)
□ They're experiencing some problems. Sie haben einige Probleme.
2 empfinden [24] (IMPERFECT empfand, PERFECT TENSE hat empfunden) (*feel*)
□ It's normal to experience some pain after surgery. Es ist normal, nach einer Operation Schmerzen zu empfinden.
■ **He experienced a few nerves before the exam.** Er war vor der Prüfung ziemlich nervös.

experienced ADJECTIVE
erfahren

★ **experiment** NOUN
das Experiment *neut* (PL die Experimente)

★ **expert** NOUN
der Fachmann *masc* (PL die Fachleute)
die Fachfrau *fem*
□ She's a computer expert. Sie ist Computerfachfrau.

■ **He's an expert cook.** Er kocht ausgezeichnet.

to **expire** VERB
ablaufen [43] (PRESENT TENSE läuft ab, IMPERFECT lief ab, PERFECT TENSE ist abgelaufen) (*passport*)

★ to **explain** VERB
erklären [19] (PERFECT TENSE hat erklärt)

★ **explanation** NOUN
die Erklärung *fem*

★ to **explode** VERB
explodieren [76] (PERFECT TENSE ist explodiert)

to **exploit** VERB
ausbeuten [2] (PERFECT TENSE hat ausgebeutet)

exploitation NOUN
die Ausbeutung *fem*

to **explore** VERB
erkunden [18] (PERFECT TENSE hat erkundet) (*place*)

explorer NOUN
der Forscher *masc* (PL die Forscher)
die Forscherin *fem*

★ **explosion** NOUN
die Explosion *fem*

explosive ADJECTIVE
▷ *see also* **explosive** NOUN
explosiv

explosive NOUN
▷ *see also* **explosive** ADJECTIVE
der Sprengstoff *masc* (PL die Sprengstoffe)

to **export** VERB
exportieren [76] (PERFECT TENSE hat exportiert)

★ to **express** VERB
ausdrücken [4] (PERFECT TENSE hat ausgedrückt)
■ **to express oneself** sich ausdrücken [4] □ I can't express myself. Ich kann mich nicht ausdrücken.

★ **expression** NOUN
der Ausdruck *masc* (PL die Ausdrücke)
■ **It's an English expression.** Das ist eine englische Redewendung.

expressway NOUN (US)
die Schnellstraße *fem*

extension NOUN
1 der Anbau *masc* (PL die Anbauten) (*of building*)
2 der Apparat *masc* (PL die Apparate) (*telephone*)
□ Extension 3137, please. Apparat 3137, bitte.

extensive ADJECTIVE
1 ausgedehnt
□ The hotel is situated in extensive grounds. Das Hotel liegt auf einem ausgedehnten Gelände.
2 umfangreich
□ He has an extensive knowledge of the subject. Er hat ein umfangreiches Wissen auf diesem Gebiet.
■ **extensive damage** schwere Schäden *pl*

English-German

extensively ADVERB
viel
□ He has travelled extensively. Er ist viel gereist.

★ **extent** NOUN
■ **to some extent** in gewisser Weise

exterior ADJECTIVE
äußere
□ the exterior walls die äußeren Wände

extinct ADJECTIVE
■ **to become extinct** aussterben [75]
■ **to be extinct** ausgestorben sein [65] □ The species is almost extinct. Diese Art ist fast ausgestorben.

extinguisher NOUN
der Feuerlöscher masc (PL die Feuerlöscher) (fire extinguisher)

extortionate ADJECTIVE
überzogen

★ **extra** ADJECTIVE, ADVERB
zusätzlich
□ an extra blanket eine zusätzliche Decke
■ **to pay extra** extra bezahlen [7]
■ **Breakfast is extra.** Frühstück wird extra berechnet.
■ **It costs extra.** Das kostet extra.

★ **extraordinary** ADJECTIVE
außergewöhnlich

extravagant ADJECTIVE
verschwenderisch (person)

★ **extreme** ADJECTIVE
extrem

★ **extremely** ADVERB
äußerst

extremist NOUN
der Extremist masc (GEN des Extremisten, PL die Extremisten)
die Extremistin fem

★ **eye** NOUN
das Auge neut (PL die Augen)
□ I've got green eyes. Ich habe grüne Augen.
■ **to keep an eye on something** auf etwas aufpassen [31]

eyebrow NOUN
die Augenbraue fem

eyelash NOUN
die Wimper fem

eyelid NOUN
das Augenlid neut (PL die Augenlider)

eyeliner NOUN
der Eyeliner masc (PL die Eyeliner)

eye shadow NOUN
der Lidschatten masc (PL die Lidschatten)

eyesight NOUN
das Sehvermögen neut
□ Her eyesight is deteriorating. Ihr Sehvermögen lässt nach.
■ **to have good eyesight** gute Augen haben [32]

e

Ff

fabric NOUN
der Stoff *masc* (PLdie Stoffe)

fabulous ADJECTIVE
traumhaft
□ The show was fabulous.Die Show war
traumhaft.

★ **face** NOUN
▷ *see also* **face** VERB
1 das Gesicht *neut* (PLdie Gesichter) (*of person*)
2 das Zifferblatt *neut* (PLdie Zifferblätter) (*of clock*)
3 die Wand *fem* (PLdie Wände) (*of cliff*)
  ■ on the face of itauf den ersten Blick
  ■ in the face of these difficultiesangesichts
  dieser Schwierigkeiten
  ■ face to faceAuge in Auge
  ■ a face clothein Waschlappen *masc*

★ **to face** VERB
▷ *see also* **face** NOUN
konfrontiert sein [65]mit (PRESENT TENSEist
konfrontiert mit , IMPERFECTwar konfrontiert mit ,
PERFECT TENSEist konfrontiert gewesen mit)
(*place, problem*)
  ■ to face up to somethingsich einer Sache
  stellen [38] □ You must face up to your
  responsibilities.Sie müssen sich Ihrer
  Verantwortung stellen.

Facebook® NOUN
▷ *see also* **facebook** VERB
Facebook®
  ■ a Facebook pageeine Facebook-Seite

to facebook VERB
▷ *see also* **Facebook** NOUN
  ■ I facebooked her yesterday.Ich habe ihr
  gestern eine Nachricht auf Facebook gepostet.

facilities PL NOUN
die Einrichtungen *fem pl*
  ■ This school has excellent facilities.Diese
  Schule ist ausgezeichnet ausgestattet.
  ■ toilet facilitiesToiletten *fem pl*
  ■ cooking facilitiesdie Kochgelegenheit *sing*

★ **fact** NOUN
die Tatsache *fem*
  ■ in facttatsächlich

★ **factory** NOUN
die Fabrik *fem*

to fade VERB
1 verblassen [84] (PERFECT TENSEist verblasst)
(*colour*)
  □ The colour has faded.Die Farbe ist verblasst.

  ■ My jeans have faded.Meine Jeans sind
  verbleicht.
2 schwächer werden [91] (PRESENT TENSEwird
schwächer , IMPERFECTwurde schwächer , PERFECT
TENSEist schwächer geworden)
  □ The light was fading fast.Das Licht wurde
  schnell schwächer.
3 abnehmen [52] (PRESENT TENSEnimmt ab ,
IMPERFECTnahm ab , PERFECT TENSEhat
abgenommen)
  □ The noise gradually faded.Der Lärm nahm
  allmählich ab.

fag NOUN
die Kippe *fem* (*informal: cigarette*)

★ **to fail** VERB
▷ *see also* **fail** NOUN
1 durchfallen [22]in +dat (PRESENT TENSEfällt
durch , IMPERFECTfiel durch , PERFECT TENSEist
durchgefallen)
  □ I failed the history exam.Ich bin in der
  Geschichtsprüfung durchgefallen.
2 durchfallen [22]
  □ In our class, no one failed.In unserer Klasse
  ist niemand durchgefallen.
3 versagen [84] (PERFECT TENSEhat versagt)
  □ My brakes failed.Meine Bremsen haben
  versagt.
  ■ to fail to do somethingetwas nicht tun [81
  □ She failed to return her library books.Sie hat
  die Bücher aus der Bücherei nicht
  zurückgebracht.

★ **fail** NOUN
▷ *see also* **fail** VERB
  ■ without failganz bestimmt

★ **failure** NOUN
1 das Versagen *neut*
  □ a mechanical failureein mechanisches
  Versagen
  ■ feelings of failuredas Gefühl zu versagen
2 der Versager *masc* (PLdie Versager)
die Versagerin *fem*
  □ He's a failure.Er ist ein Versager.

faint ADJECTIVE
▷ *see also* **faint** VERB
schwach
  □ His voice was very faint.Seine Stimme war
  sehr schwach.
  ■ I feel faint.Mir ist schwindlig.

★ = core vocabulary

to **faint** VERB

▷ *see also* **faint** ADJECTIVE

ohnmächtig werden [91] (PRESENT TENSE wird ohnmächtig , IMPERFECT wurde ohnmächtig , PERFECT TENSE ist ohnmächtig geworden)

□ All of a sudden she fainted. Plötzlich wurde sie ohnmächtig.

fair ADJECTIVE

▷ *see also* **fair** NOUN

1 fair

□ That's not fair. Das ist nicht fair.

2 blond (*hair*)

□ He's got fair hair. Er hat blonde Haare.

3 hell (*skin*)

□ people with fair skin Menschen mit heller Haut

4 schön (*weather*)

□ The weather was fair. Das Wetter war schön.

5 gut (*good enough*)

□ I have a fair chance of winning. Ich habe gute Gewinnchancen.

6 ordentlich (*sizeable*)

□ That's a fair distance. Das ist eine ordentliche Entfernung.

fair NOUN

▷ *see also* **fair** ADJECTIVE

das Volksfest *neut* (PL die Volksfeste)

□ They went to the fair. Sie sind aufs Volksfest gegangen.

■ **a trade fair** eine Handelsmesse

fairground NOUN

der Rummelplatz *masc* (PL die Rummelplätze)

fair-haired ADJECTIVE

blond

fairly ADVERB

1 gerecht

□ The cake was divided fairly. Der Kuchen wurde gerecht verteilt.

2 ziemlich (*quite*)

□ That's fairly good. Das ist ziemlich gut.

fairness NOUN

die Fairness *fem*

fair trade NOUN

fairer Handel *masc*

fairy NOUN

die Fee *fem*

fairy tale NOUN

das Märchen *neut* (PL die Märchen)

faith NOUN

1 der Glaube *masc* (GEN des Glaubens)

□ the Catholic faith der katholische Glaube

2 das Vertrauen *neut*

□ People have lost faith in the government. Die Menschen haben das Vertrauen in die Regierung verloren.

faithful ADJECTIVE

treu

faithfully ADVERB

■ **Yours faithfully …** (*in letter*) Hochachtungsvoll …

fake NOUN

▷ *see also* **fake** ADJECTIVE

die Fälschung *fem*

□ The painting was a fake. Das Gemälde war eine Fälschung.

fake ADJECTIVE

▷ *see also* **fake** NOUN

gefälscht

□ a fake certificate eine gefälschte Urkunde

■ **She wore fake fur.** Sie trug eine Pelzimitation.

★ **fall** NOUN

▷ *see also* **fall** VERB

1 der Sturz *masc* (GEN des Sturzes , PL die Stürze)

■ **She had a nasty fall.** Sie ist übel gestürzt.

■ **a fall of snow** ein Schneefall *masc*

■ **Niagara Falls** die Niagarafälle

2 der Herbst *masc* (PL die Herbste) (US: *autumn*)

□ in fall im Herbst

★ to **fall** VERB

▷ *see also* **fall** NOUN

1 hinfallen [22] (PRESENT TENSE fällt hin , IMPERFECT fiel hin , PERFECT TENSE ist hingefallen)

□ He tripped and fell. Er ist gestolpert und hingefallen.

2 fallen [22]

□ Prices are falling. Die Preise fallen.

to **fall apart** VERB

auseinanderfallen [22]

□ The book fell apart when he opened it. Das Buch fiel auseinander, als er es öffnete.

to **fall down** VERB

1 hinfallen [22] (*person*)

□ She's fallen down. Sie ist hingefallen.

2 einfallen [22] (*building*)

□ The wall fell down. Die Mauer ist eingefallen.

to **fall for** VERB

1 hereinfallen [22] auf +acc

□ They fell for it. Sie sind darauf hereingefallen.

2 sich verlieben [84] in +acc

□ She's falling for him. Sie ist dabei, sich in ihn zu verlieben.

to **fall off** VERB

herunterfallen [22] von

□ The book fell off the shelf. Das Buch ist vom Regal heruntergefallen.

to **fall out** VERB

sich zerstreiten

□ Sarah's fallen out with her girlfriend. Sarah hat sich mit ihrer Freundin zerstritten.

to **fall through** VERB

ins Wasser fallen [22]

□ Our plans have fallen through. Unsere Pläne sind ins Wasser gefallen.

Numbers in brackets refer to verb tables on pages 697 to 706.

449

★ **false** ADJECTIVE
falsch
- **a false alarm** ein falscher Alarm *masc*
- **false teeth** das Gebiss *neut*

fame NOUN
der Ruhm *masc*

★ **familiar** ADJECTIVE
vertraut
□ a familiar face ein vertrautes Gesicht
- **to be familiar with something** mit etwas
vertraut sein [65] □ I'm familiar with his work.
Ich bin mit seiner Arbeit vertraut.

★ **family** NOUN
die Familie *fem*
□ the Airlie family die Familie Airlie

famine NOUN
die Hungersnot *fem* (PL die Hungersnöte)

★ **famous** ADJECTIVE
berühmt

★ **fan** NOUN
1 der Fächer *masc* (PL die Fächer) (*hand-held*)
2 der Ventilator *masc* (PL die Ventilatoren)
(*electric*)
3 der Fan *masc* (PL die Fans) (*of person, band,
sport*)

> **der Fan** is also used for women.

□ She's a fan of theirs. Sie ist ein Fan von ihnen.
□ football fans Fußballfans

fanatic NOUN
der Fanatiker *masc* (PL die Fanatiker)
die Fanatikerin *fem*

to **fancy** VERB
- **to fancy something** Lust auf etwas haben
[32] □ I fancy an ice cream. Ich habe Lust auf
ein Eis.
- **to fancy doing something** Lust haben [32],
etwas zu tun
- **He fancies her.** Er steht auf sie.

fancy dress NOUN
das Kostüm *neut* (PL die Kostüme)
- **He was wearing fancy dress.** Er war
kostümiert.
- **a fancy-dress ball** ein Kostümball *masc*

★ **fantastic** ADJECTIVE
fantastisch

★ **far** ADJECTIVE, ADVERB
weit
□ Is it far? Ist es weit? □ How far is it? Wie weit
ist es? □ How far is it to Geneva? Wie weit ist es
nach Genf?
- **far from 1** weit entfernt von □ It's not far
from Birmingham. Es ist nicht weit von
Birmingham entfernt. **2** überhaupt nicht □ It's
far from easy. Es ist überhaupt nicht einfach.
- **How far have you got?** (*with a task*) Wie weit
bist du gekommen?
- **at the far end** am anderen Ende □ at the far
end of the room am anderen Ende des Zimmers
- **far better** viel besser
- **as far as I know** soviel ich weiß
- **the Far East** der Ferne Osten

★ **fare** NOUN
der Fahrpreis *masc* (PL die Fahrpreise)
- **half fare** halber Preis
- **full fare** voller Preis

★ **farm** NOUN
der Bauernhof *masc* (PL die Bauernhöfe)

★ **farmer** NOUN
der Bauer *masc* (GEN des Bauern, PL die Bauern)
die Bäuerin *fem*
□ He's a farmer. Er ist Bauer.
- **a farmers' market** ein Bauernmarkt *masc*

farmhouse NOUN
das Bauernhaus *neut* (GEN des Bauernhauses,
PL die Bauernhäuser)

farming NOUN
die Landwirtschaft *fem*
- **dairy farming** die Milchwirtschaft

fascinating ADJECTIVE
faszinierend

★ **fashion** NOUN
die Mode *fem*
- **in fashion** in Mode

fashionable ADJECTIVE
modisch
□ Aisha wears very fashionable clothes. Aisha
trägt sehr modische Kleidung.
- **a fashionable restaurant** ein Restaurant,
das in Mode ist

★ **fast** ADJECTIVE, ADVERB
schnell
□ He can run fast. Er kann schnell laufen. □ a
fast car ein schnelles Auto
- **That clock's fast.** Die Uhr geht vor.
- **He's fast asleep.** Er schläft fest.

> **BE CAREFUL!**
> Do not translate **fast** by the German word
> fast.

★ **fat** ADJECTIVE
▷ *see also* **fat** NOUN
dick (*person*)

> **WORD POWER**
> You can use a number of other words instead
> of **fat**:
> **chubby** pummelig
> □ a chubby baby ein pummeliges Baby
> **overweight** übergewichtig
> □ an overweight man ein übergewichtiger
> Mann
> **plump** rundlich
> □ a plump woman eine rundliche Frau

★ **fat** NOUN
▷ *see also* **fat** ADJECTIVE
das Fett *neut* (PL die Fette)
- **It's very high in fat.** Es ist sehr fett.

atal ADJECTIVE
1 tödlich (*causing death*)
  □ a fatal accident ein tödlicher Unfall
2 fatal (*disastrous*)
  □ He made a fatal mistake. Er machte einen fatalen Fehler.

★ **father** NOUN
  der Vater *masc* (PL die Väter)
  □ my father mein Vater
  ■ **Father Christmas** der Weihnachtsmann

father-in-law NOUN
  der Schwiegervater *masc* (PL die Schwiegerväter)

faucet NOUN (US)
  der Wasserhahn *masc* (PL die Wasserhähne)

★ **fault** NOUN
1 die Schuld *fem* (*mistake*)
  □ It's my fault. Es ist meine Schuld.
2 der Fehler *masc* (PL die Fehler) (*defect*)
  □ a mechanical fault ein mechanischer Fehler

faulty ADJECTIVE
  defekt
  □ This machine is faulty. Die Maschine ist defekt.

★ **favour** (US **favor**) NOUN
  der Gefallen *masc* (PL die Gefallen)
  ■ **to do somebody a favour** jemandem einen Gefallen tun [81] □ Could you do me a favour? Könntest du mir einen Gefallen tun?
  ■ **to be in favour of something** für etwas sein [65] □ I'm in favour of recycling. Ich bin für das Recycling.

★ **favourite** (US **favorite**) ADJECTIVE
  ▷ *see also* **favourite** NOUN
  ■ **Blue's my favourite colour.** Blau ist meine Lieblingsfarbe.

★ **favourite** (US **favorite**) NOUN
  ▷ *see also* **favourite** ADJECTIVE
1 der Liebling *masc* (PL die Lieblinge)

  der Liebling is also used for women.

  □ She's his favourite. Sie ist sein Liebling.
2 der Favorit *masc* (PL die Favoriten)
  die Favoritin *fem*
  □ Liverpool are favourites to win the Cup. Der FC Liverpool ist Favorit für den Pokal.

★ **fear** NOUN
  ▷ *see also* **fear** VERB
  die Furcht *fem*

★ **to fear** VERB
  ▷ *see also* **fear** NOUN
  befürchten [2] (PERFECT TENSE hat befürchtet)
  □ You have nothing to fear. Sie haben nichts zu befürchten.

feather NOUN
  die Feder *fem*

★ **feature** NOUN
  die Eigenschaft *fem* (*of person, object*)

  □ an important feature eine wichtige Eigenschaft

★ **February** NOUN
  der Februar *masc*
  □ in February im Februar

fed VERB ▷ *see* **feed**

fed up ADJECTIVE
  ■ **to be fed up with something** etwas satthaben [32] □ I'm fed up with him. Ich habe ihn satt.

★ **to feed** VERB
  füttern [88]
  □ Have you fed the cat? Hast du die Katze gefüttert?
  ■ **She worked hard to feed her family.** Sie arbeitete hart, um ihre Familie zu ernähren.

★ **to feel** VERB
1 sich fühlen [38]
  □ I don't feel well. Ich fühle mich nicht wohl. □ I feel a bit lonely. Ich fühle mich etwas einsam.
2 spüren [38]
  □ I didn't feel much pain. Ich habe keine großen Schmerzen gespürt.
3 befühlen [7] (PERFECT TENSE hat befühlt)
  □ The doctor felt his forehead. Der Arzt hat ihm die Stirn befühlt.
  ■ **I was feeling hungry.** Ich hatte Hunger.
  ■ **I felt very cold.** Mir war sehr kalt.
  ■ **I feel like ...** (*want*) Ich habe Lust auf ... □ Do you feel like an ice cream? Hast du Lust auf ein Eis?

★ **feeling** NOUN
  das Gefühl *neut* (PL die Gefühle)
  □ a feeling of satisfaction ein Gefühl der Befriedigung
  ■ **an itchy feeling** ein Jucken *neut*

feet PL NOUN ▷ *see* **foot**

fell VERB ▷ *see* **fall**

felt VERB ▷ *see* **feel**

felt-tip pen NOUN
  der Filzschreiber *masc* (PL die Filzschreiber)

★ **female** ADJECTIVE
  ▷ *see also* **female** NOUN
  weiblich
  □ a female animal ein weibliches Tier □ the female sex das weibliche Geschlecht

  In many cases, the ending indicates clearly whether the noun refers to a man or a woman and there is therefore no need for the word 'female'.

  □ male and female students Studenten und Studentinnen

★ **female** NOUN
  ▷ *see also* **female** ADJECTIVE
  das Weibchen *neut* (PL die Weibchen) (*animal*)

feminine ADJECTIVE
  feminin

feminist – fight

feminist NOUN
der Feminist *masc* (GEN des Feministen , PL die Feministen)
die Feministin *fem*

★ **fence** NOUN
der Zaun *masc* (PL die Zäune)

fern NOUN
der Farn *masc* (PL die Farne)

ferocious ADJECTIVE
wild

ferry NOUN
die Fähre *fem*
■ **the ferry crossing** die Fährüberfahrt
■ **the ferry terminal** der Fährhafen

fertile ADJECTIVE
fruchtbar

fertilizer NOUN
das Düngemittel *neut* (PL die Düngemittel)

★ **festival** NOUN
das Festival *neut* (PL die Festivals)
□ a jazz festival ein Jazzfestival

to **fetch** VERB
1 holen [38]
□ Fetch the bucket. Hol den Eimer.
2 einbringen [13] (IMPERFECT brachte ein , PERFECT TENSE hat eingebracht) (*sell for*)
□ His painting fetched five thousand pounds. Sein Bild hat fünftausend Pfund eingebracht.

fever NOUN
das Fieber *neut* (*temperature*)

★ **few** ADJECTIVE, PRONOUN
wenige (*not many*)
□ few books wenige Bücher
■ **a few** ein paar □ a few hours ein paar Stunden □ How many apples do you want? — A few. Wie viele Äpfel willst du? — Ein paar.
■ **quite a few people** einige Leute

fewer ADJECTIVE
weniger
□ There are fewer people than there were yesterday. Es sind weniger Leute da als gestern.
□ There are fewer students in this class. In dieser Klasse sind weniger Schüler.

★ **fiancé** NOUN
der Verlobte *masc* (GEN des Verlobten , PL die Verlobten)
□ He's my fiancé. Er ist mein Verlobter.

★ **fiancée** NOUN
die Verlobte *fem* (GEN der Verlobten , PL die Verlobten)
□ She's my fiancée. Sie ist meine Verlobte.

fiction NOUN
die Romane *masc pl* (*novels*)

★ **field** NOUN
1 das Feld *neut* (PL die Felder) (*in countryside*)
□ a field of wheat ein Weizenfeld

2 der Platz *masc* (GEN des Platzes , PL die Plätze) (*for sport*)
□ a football field ein Fußballplatz
3 das Gebiet *neut* (PL die Gebiete) (*subject*)
□ He's an expert in his field. Er ist Fachmann auf seinem Gebiet.

★ **fierce** ADJECTIVE
1 gefährlich
□ The dog looked very fierce. Der Hund sah seh gefährlich aus.
2 heftig
□ a fierce attack ein heftiger Angriff
■ **The wind was very fierce.** Es wehte ein seh scharfer Wind.

★ **fifteen** NUMBER
fünfzehn
□ I'm fifteen. Ich bin fünfzehn.

★ **fifteenth** ADJECTIVE
fünfzehnte
□ the fifteenth of August der fünfzehnte August

★ **fifth** ADJECTIVE
fünfte
□ the fifth floor der fünfte Stock □ the fifth of August der fünfte August

★ **fifty** NUMBER
fünfzig
□ He's fifty. Er ist fünfzig.

fifty-fifty ADJECTIVE, ADVERB
halbe-halbe
□ They split the money fifty-fifty. Sie teilten das Geld halbe-halbe.
■ **a fifty-fifty chance** eine fünfzigprozentige Chance

★ **fight** NOUN
▷ *see also* **fight** VERB
1 die Prügelei *fem*
□ There was a fight in the school playground. Im Pausenhof gab es eine Prügelei.
2 der Kampf *masc* (PL die Kämpfe)
□ the fight against cancer der Kampf gegen Krebs

★ to **fight** VERB
▷ *see also* **fight** NOUN
1 sich prügeln [34] (*physically*)
□ They were fighting. Sie haben sich geprügelt.
2 streiten (IMPERFECT stritt , PERFECT TENSE hat gestritten) (*quarrel*)
□ He's always fighting with his wife. Er streitet dauernd mit seiner Frau.
3 bekämpfen [7] (PERFECT TENSE hat bekämpft) (*combat*)
□ This organization fights against racism. Diese Organisation bekämpft den Rassismus.
■ **Women are fighting for equal pay.** Frauen kämpfen für die Lohngleichheit.

to **fight back** VERB
sich wehren [38]

★ = core vocabulary

fighting NOUN
die Schlägerei *fem*
□ Fighting broke out on the football pitch. Auf dem Fußballplatz kam es zu einer Schlägerei.

★ **figure** NOUN
1 die Zahl *fem* (*number*)
□ Can you give me the exact figures? Können Sie mir genaue Zahlen nennen?
2 die Gestalt *fem* (*outline of person*)
□ Yasmin saw the figure of a man on the bridge. Yasmin sah die Gestalt eines Mannes auf der Brücke.
3 die Figur *fem* (*shape*)
□ She's got a good figure. Sie hat eine gute Figur. □ I have to watch my figure. Ich muss auf meine Figur achten.
4 die Persönlichkeit *fem* (*personality*)
□ She's an important political figure. Sie ist eine wichtige politische Persönlichkeit.

to **figure out** VERB
1 ausrechnen [4] (PERFECT TENSE hat ausgerechnet)
□ I'll figure out how much it'll cost. Ich werde ausrechnen, wie viel das kostet.
2 herausfinden [24] (IMPERFECT fand heraus, PERFECT TENSE hat herausgefunden)
□ I couldn't figure out what it meant. Ich konnte nicht herausfinden, was das bedeutet.
3 schlau werden [91] aus (PRESENT TENSE wird schlau, IMPERFECT wurde schlau, PERFECT TENSE ist schlau geworden)
□ I can't figure him out at all. Ich werde aus ihm überhaupt nicht schlau.

★ **file** NOUN
▷ *see also* **file** VERB
1 die Akte *fem* (*document*)
□ Have we got a file on the suspect? Haben wir über den Verdächtigen eine Akte?
2 die Aktenmappe *fem* (*folder*)
□ She keeps all her notes in a cardboard file. Sie bewahrt all ihre Notizen in einer Aktenmappe auf.
3 der Aktenordner *masc* (PL die Aktenordner) (*ring binder*)
4 die Datei *fem* (*on computer*)
5 die Feile *fem* (*for nails, metal*)

★ to **file** VERB
▷ *see also* **file** NOUN
1 abheften [2] (PERFECT TENSE hat abgeheftet) (*papers*)
2 feilen [38] (*nails, metal*)
□ I have to file my nails. Ich muss mir die Nägel feilen.

★ to **fill** VERB
füllen [38]
□ She filled the glass with water. Sie füllte das Glas mit Wasser.

to **fill in** VERB
1 ausfüllen [4]

□ Can you fill this form in, please? Können Sie bitte dieses Formular ausfüllen?
2 auffüllen [4]
□ He filled the hole in with soil. Er füllte das Loch mit Erde auf.

to **fill up** VERB
vollmachen [48]
□ He filled the cup up to the brim. Er machte die Tasse bis zum Rand voll.

★ **film** NOUN
der Film *masc* (PL die Filme)

film star NOUN
der Filmstar *masc* (PL die Filmstars)

der **Filmstar** is also used for women.

□ She's a film star. Sie ist ein Filmstar.

to **filter** VERB
filtern [88]

filthy ADJECTIVE
schmutzig

★ **final** ADJECTIVE
▷ *see also* **final** NOUN
1 letzte (*last*)
□ our final match of the season unser letztes Spiel der Saison
2 endgültig (*definite*)
□ a final decision eine endgültige Entscheidung
■ I'm not going and that's final. Ich gehe nicht, und damit basta.

★ **final** NOUN
▷ *see also* **final** ADJECTIVE
das Finale *neut* (PL die Finale)
□ Murray is in the final. Murray ist im Finale.

★ **finally** ADVERB
1 schließlich (*lastly*)
□ Finally, I would like to say ... Und schließlich möchte ich sagen ...
2 letztendlich (*eventually*)
□ They finally decided to leave on Saturday. Sie haben letztendlich beschlossen, am Samstag zu fahren.

financial ADJECTIVE
finanziell

★ to **find** VERB
finden [24] (IMPERFECT fand, PERFECT TENSE hat gefunden)
□ I can't find the exit. Ich kann den Ausgang nicht finden. □ Did you find your pen? Hast du deinen Schreiber gefunden?
■ to find something out etwas herausfinden [24] □ I'm determined to find out the truth. Ich bin entschlossen, die Wahrheit herauszufinden.
■ to find out about 1 (*make enquiries*) sich erkundigen [19] nach □ Try to find out about the exam. Versuche, dich nach der Prüfung zu erkundigen. 2 (*by chance*) erfahren [21] □ I found out about the party. Ich habe von der Party erfahren.

★ **fine** ADJECTIVE, ADVERB
 ▷ see also **fine** NOUN
 1 ausgezeichnet (very good)
  □ He's a fine musician. Er ist ein ausgezeichneter Musiker.
  ■ **How are you? — I'm fine.** Wie geht's? — Gut!
  ■ **I feel fine.** Mir geht's gut.
  ■ **The weather is fine today.** Das Wetter ist heute schön.
 2 fein (not coarse)
  □ She's got very fine hair. Sie hat sehr feine Haare.

★ **fine** NOUN
 ▷ see also **fine** ADJECTIVE, ADVERB
 1 die Geldbuße fem
  □ She got a fine. Sie hat eine Geldbuße bekommen.
 2 der Strafzettel masc (PL die Strafzettel) (for traffic offence)
  □ My dad got a fine for speeding. Mein Vater hat einen Strafzettel bekommen, weil er zu schnell gefahren ist.

★ **finger** NOUN
 der Finger masc (PL die Finger)
 □ my little finger mein kleiner Finger

fingernail NOUN
 der Fingernagel masc (PL die Fingernägel)

★ **finish** NOUN
 ▷ see also **finish** VERB
 das Finish neut (PL die Finishs) (of race)
 □ We saw the finish of the London Marathon. Wir sahen das Finish des Londoner Marathonlaufs.

★ to **finish** VERB
 ▷ see also **finish** NOUN
 1 fertig sein [65] (PRESENT TENSE ist fertig, IMPERFECT war fertig, PERFECT TENSE ist fertig gewesen)
  □ I've finished! Ich bin fertig!
 2 zu Ende sein [65] (PRESENT TENSE ist zu Ende, IMPERFECT war zu Ende, PERFECT TENSE ist zu Ende gewesen)
  □ The film has finished. Der Film ist zu Ende.
  ■ **I've finished the book.** Ich habe das Buch zu Ende gelesen.
  ■ **to finish doing something** etwas zu Ende machen [48] □ Let me finish writing this letter. Lass mich den Brief zu Ende schreiben.

★ **Finland** NOUN
 Finnland neut
 ■ **from Finland** aus Finnland
 ■ **to Finland** nach Finnland

Finn NOUN
 der Finne masc (GEN des Finnen, PL die Finnen)
 die Finnin fem

★ **Finnish** ADJECTIVE
 ▷ see also **Finnish** NOUN
 finnisch
 ■ **She's Finnish.** Sie ist Finnin.

★ **Finnish** NOUN
 ▷ see also **Finnish** ADJECTIVE
 das Finnisch neut (GEN des Finnischen) (language)

fir NOUN
 die Tanne fem
 ■ **fir cone** der Tannenzapfen
 ■ **fir tree** der Tannenbaum

★ **fire** NOUN
 ▷ see also **fire** VERB
 1 das Feuer neut (PL die Feuer)
  □ He made a fire to warm himself up. Er machte ein Feuer, um sich aufzuwärmen.
  ■ **to be on fire** brennen [12]
 2 der Brand masc (PL die Brände) (accidental)
  ■ **The house was destroyed by fire.** Das Haus ist abgebrannt.
 3 die Heizung fem (heater)
  □ Turn the fire on. Mach die Heizung an.
  ■ **the fire brigade** die Feuerwehr
  ■ **a fire alarm** ein Feueralarm masc
  ■ **a fire engine** ein Feuerwehrauto neut
  ■ **a fire escape** (stairs) eine Feuertreppe
  ■ **a fire extinguisher** ein Feuerlöscher masc
  ■ **a fire station** eine Feuerwehrstation

★ to **fire** VERB
 ▷ see also **fire** NOUN
 schießen (IMPERFECT schoss, PERFECT TENSE hat geschossen) (shoot)
 □ She fired twice. Sie hat zweimal geschossen.
 ■ **to fire at somebody** auf jemanden schießen
 □ He fired at me. Er hat auf mich geschossen.
 ■ **to fire a gun** einen Schuss abgeben [28]
 ■ **to fire somebody** jemanden feuern [34]
 □ He was fired from his job. Er wurde aus seinem Job gefeuert.

fire exit NOUN
 der Notausgang masc (PL die Notausgänge)

firefighter NOUN
 der Feuerwehrmann masc (PL die Feuerwehrleute)
 die Feuerwehrfrau fem
 □ She's a firefighter. Sie ist Feuerwehrfrau.

fireplace NOUN
 der offene Kamin masc (PL die offenen Kamine)

fireworks PL NOUN
 das Feuerwerk neut (PL die Feuerwerke)
 □ Are you going to see the fireworks? Seht ihr euch das Feuerwerk an?

★ **firm** ADJECTIVE
 ▷ see also **firm** NOUN
 streng
 □ to be firm with somebody streng mit jemandem sein

★ **firm** NOUN
 ▷ see also **firm** ADJECTIVE
 die Firma fem (PL die Firmen)
 □ He works for a large firm in Glasgow. Er arbeitet für eine große Firma in Glasgow.

★ = core vocabulary

★ **first** ADJECTIVE, ADVERB
▷ see also **first** NOUN

1 erste

□ my first boyfriend mein erster Freund □ the first time das erste Mal □ the first of August der erste August

■ **Rachel came first.** (in exam, race) Rachel war Erste.

■ **John came first.** (in exam, race) John war Erster.

2 zuerst

□ I want to get a job, but first I have to pass my exams. Ich will mir einen Job suchen, aber zuerst muss ich meine Prüfung bestehen.

■ **first of all** zuallererst

★ **first** NOUN
▷ see also **first** ADJECTIVE, ADVERB
der Erste masc (GEN des Ersten, PL die Ersten)
die Erste fem (GEN der Ersten)

□ She was the first to arrive. Sie ist als Erste angekommen.

■ **at first** zuerst

first aid NOUN
die Erste Hilfe fem

■ **a first aid kit** ein Verbandskasten masc

first-class ADJECTIVE, ADVERB

1 erster Klasse

□ a first-class ticket ein Ticket erster Klasse □ to travel first-class erster Klasse fahren

2 erstklassig

□ a first-class meal ein erstklassiges Essen

DID YOU KNOW...?
In Germany there is no first-class or second-class post. However, letters cost more to send than postcards, so you have to remember to say what you are sending when buying stamps. There is also an express service.

firstly ADVERB

1 zuerst

□ Firstly, let's see what the book is about. Zuerst wollen wir mal sehen, wovon das Buch handelt.

2 erstens

□ firstly ... secondly ... erstens ... zweitens ...

★ **fish** NOUN
▷ see also **fish** VERB
der Fisch masc (PL die Fische)

□ I caught three fish. Ich habe drei Fische gefangen. □ I don't like fish. Ich mag Fisch nicht.

★ to **fish** VERB
▷ see also **fish** NOUN

1 fischen [48]

2 angeln [34] (with a rod)

■ **to go fishing** fischen gehen [29] □ We went fishing in the River Dee. Wir haben im Dee gefischt.

fisherman NOUN
der Fischer masc (PL die Fischer)

□ He's a fisherman. Er ist Fischer.

fish finger NOUN
das Fischstäbchen neut (PL die Fischstäbchen)

★ **fishing** NOUN
das Angeln neut

□ My hobby is fishing. Angeln ist mein Hobby.

fishing boat NOUN
das Fischerboot neut (PL die Fischerboote)

fishing rod NOUN
die Angel fem

fishing tackle NOUN
das Angelzeug neut

fishmonger's NOUN
der Fischladen masc (PL die Fischläden)

fish sticks PL NOUN (US)
die Fischstäbchen fem

fist NOUN
die Faust fem (PL die Fäuste)

★ to **fit** VERB
▷ see also **fit** ADJECTIVE, NOUN

1 passen [31] (PERFECT TENSE hat gepasst) (be the right size)

□ Does it fit? Passt es? □ These trousers don't fit me. Diese Hose passt mir nicht.

2 einbauen [4] (PERFECT TENSE hat eingebaut) (install)

□ He fitted an alarm in his car. Er hat eine Alarmanlage in sein Auto eingebaut.

3 anbringen [13] (IMPERFECT brachte an, PERFECT TENSE hat angebracht) (attach)

□ She fitted a lock on her bedroom door. Sie brachte ein Schloss an der Schlafzimmertür an.

to **fit in** VERB

1 passen [31] (match up)

□ We won't all fit in. Wir passen nicht alle hinein. □ My clothes won't all fit in my backpack. Meine Kleider passen nicht alle in meinen Rucksack.

2 sich einpassen [4] (person)

□ She fitted in well at her new school. Sie hat sich in ihrer neuen Schule gut eingepasst.

■ **We fitted in a visit to Berlin.** Wir haben einen Besuch nach Berlin eingeschoben.

■ **Can you fit in lunch this week?** Kannst du diese Woche ein Mittagessen unterbringen?

★ **fit** ADJECTIVE
▷ see also **fit** VERB, NOUN
fit (healthy)

□ He felt relaxed and fit after his holiday. Nach seinem Urlaub fühlte er sich entspannt und fit.

★ **fit** NOUN
▷ see also **fit** ADJECTIVE, VERB

■ **to have a fit 1** (epileptic) einen Anfall haben [32] **2** (be angry) Zustände bekommen [40]

□ My mum will have a fit! Meine Mutter

bekommt Zustände!

fitness NOUN
die Fitness *fem*
■ **a fitness centre** ein Fitnesscenter *neut*

fitting room NOUN
die Umkleidekabine *fem*

★ **five** NUMBER
fünf
▢ He's five. Er ist fünf.

★ to **fix** VERB
1 reparieren [76] (PERFECT TENSE hat repariert)
(*mend*)
▢ Can you fix my bike? Kannst du mein Fahrrad reparieren?
2 festlegen [4] (PERFECT TENSE hat festgelegt)
(*decide*)
▢ Let's fix a date for the party. Lass uns einen Tag für die Party festlegen. ▢ They fixed a price for the laptop. Sie haben einen Preis für den Laptop festgelegt.
3 machen [48]
▢ Dylan's dad fixed some food for us. Dylan's Papa hat uns etwas zum Essen gemacht.

★ **fixed** ADJECTIVE
festgesetzt
▢ at a fixed price zu einem festgesetzten Preis
■ **at a fixed time** zu einer bestimmten Zeit
■ **My parents have very fixed ideas.** Meine Eltern haben ziemlich festgelegte Ansichten.

fizzy ADJECTIVE
mit Kohlensäure
▢ I don't like fizzy drinks. Ich mag keine Getränke mit Kohlensäure.

flabby ADJECTIVE
wabbelig

★ **flag** NOUN
die Fahne *fem*

flame NOUN
die Flamme *fem*

flamingo NOUN
der Flamingo *masc* (PL die Flamingos)

flan NOUN
1 die Quiche *fem* (PL die Quiches) (*savoury*)
▢ a cheese and onion flan eine Käse-Zwiebel-Quiche
2 der Kuchen *masc* (PL die Kuchen) (*sweet*)
▢ a raspberry flan ein Himbeerkuchen

flannel NOUN
der Waschlappen *masc* (PL die Waschlappen)
(*for face*)

to **flap** VERB
flattern [34] mit
▢ The bird flapped its wings. Der Vogel flatterte mit den Flügeln.

★ **flash** NOUN
▷ *see also* **flash** VERB
das Blitzlicht *neut* (PL die Blitzlichter)
■ **a flash of lightning** ein Blitz *masc*

■ **in a flash** blitzschnell

★ to **flash** VERB
▷ *see also* **flash** NOUN
1 blinken [38]
▢ The police car's blue light was flashing. Das Blaulicht des Polizeiautos blinkte.
2 leuchten [2] mit
▢ They flashed a torch in his face. Sie leuchteten ihm mit einer Taschenlampe ins Gesicht.
■ **She flashed her headlights.** Sie betätigte die Lichthupe.

flask NOUN
die Thermosflasche® *fem*

★ **flat** ADJECTIVE
▷ *see also* **flat** NOUN
1 flach
▢ flat shoes flache Schuhe
■ **a flat roof** ein Flachdach *neut*
2 platt (*tyre*)
▢ I've got a flat tyre. Ich habe einen platten Reifen.

★ **flat** NOUN
▷ *see also* **flat** ADJECTIVE
die Wohnung *fem*
▢ She lives in a flat. Sie wohnt in einer Wohnung.

flatscreen NOUN
■ **a flatscreen TV** ein Flachbildfernseher *masc*

to **flatter** VERB
schmeicheln [38]
▢ Are you trying to flatter me? Willst du mir schmeicheln? ▢ I feel flattered. Ich fühle mich geschmeichelt.

★ **flavour** (US **flavor**) NOUN
der Geschmack *masc* (PL die Geschmäcke)
▢ This cheese has a very strong flavour. Dieser Käse hat einen sehr pikanten Geschmack.
■ **Which flavour of ice cream would you like?** Was für ein Eis möchtest du?

flavouring NOUN
das Aroma *neut* (PL die Aromen)

flea NOUN
der Floh *masc* (PL die Flöhe)

flew VERB ▷ *see* **fly**

★ **flexible** ADJECTIVE
flexibel
■ **flexible working hours** gleitende Arbeitszeit

to **flick** VERB
schnipsen [48]
▢ She flicked the crumbs off her jumper. Sie schnipste die Krümel von ihrem Pullover.
■ **He flicked the switch and the light came on.** Er knipste den Schalter und das Licht ging an.
■ **to flick through a book** ein Buch durchblättern [15]

to **flicker** VERB
flackern [88]

★ = core vocabulary

□ The light flickered. Das Licht flackerte.

★ **flight** NOUN
der Flug *masc* (PL die Flüge)
□ What time is the flight to Munich? Um wie viel Uhr geht der Flug nach München?
■ **a flight of stairs** eine Treppe

flight attendant NOUN
der Flugbegleiter *masc* (PL die Flugbegleiter)
die Flugbegleiterin *fem*

to fling VERB
schmeißen (IMPERFECT schmiss, PERFECT TENSE hat geschmissen)
□ He flung the dictionary onto the floor. Er schmiss das Wörterbuch auf den Boden.

★ **to float** VERB
schwimmen [63] (IMPERFECT schwamm, PERFECT TENSE ist geschwommen)
□ A leaf was floating on the water. Auf dem Wasser schwamm ein Blatt.

flock NOUN
■ **a flock of sheep** eine Schafherde
■ **a flock of birds** ein Vogelschwarm *neut*

★ **flood** NOUN
▷ see also **flood** VERB
1 die Überschwemmung *fem*
□ The rain has caused many floods. Der Regen hat zu vielen Überschwemmungen geführt.
2 die Flut *fem*
□ He received a flood of emails. Er erhielt eine Flut von E-Mails.

★ **to flood** VERB
▷ see also **flood** NOUN
überschwemmen [18] (PERFECT TENSE hat überschwemmt)
□ The river has flooded the village. Der Fluss hat das Dorf überschwemmt.

flooding NOUN
die Überschwemmung *fem*

★ **floor** NOUN
1 der Fußboden *masc* (PL die Fußböden)
■ **a tiled floor** ein Fliesenboden
■ **on the floor** auf dem Boden
2 der Stock *masc* (PL die Stock) (storey)
■ **the first floor** der erste Stock □ on the first floor im ersten Stock
■ **the ground floor** das Erdgeschoss

BE CAREFUL!
Do not translate **floor** by **Flur**.

flop NOUN
der Flop *masc* (PL die Flops)
□ The film was a flop. Der Film war ein Flop.

florist NOUN
der Florist *masc* (GEN des Floristen, PL die Floristen)
die Floristin *fem*

flour NOUN
das Mehl *neut* (PL die Mehle)

★ **to flow** VERB
fließen [27] (IMPERFECT floss, PERFECT TENSE ist geflossen)
□ Water was flowing from the pipe. Aus dem Rohr floss Wasser.

★ **flower** NOUN
▷ see also **flower** VERB
die Blume *fem*

★ **to flower** VERB
▷ see also **flower** NOUN
blühen [38]

flown VERB ▷ see **fly**

flu NOUN
die Grippe *fem*
□ She's got flu. Sie hat Grippe.

fluent ADJECTIVE
■ **He speaks fluent German.** Er spricht fließend Deutsch.

flung VERB ▷ see **fling**

flush NOUN
▷ see also **flush** VERB
die Spülung *fem* (of toilet)

to flush VERB
▷ see also **flush** NOUN
■ **to flush the toilet** spülen [38]

flute NOUN
die Querflöte *fem*
□ I play the flute. Ich spiele Querflöte.

★ **fly** NOUN
▷ see also **fly** VERB
die Fliege *fem* (insect)

★ **to fly** VERB
▷ see also **fly** NOUN
fliegen [25] (IMPERFECT flog, PERFECT TENSE ist geflogen)
□ He flew from Berlin to New York. Er flog von Berlin nach New York.

to fly away VERB
wegfliegen [25]
□ The bird flew away. Der Vogel flog weg.

foal NOUN
das Fohlen *neut* (PL die Fohlen)

★ **focus** NOUN
▷ see also **focus** VERB
■ **to be out of focus** unscharf sein [65] □ The house is out of focus in this photo. Das Haus ist auf diesem Foto unscharf.

★ **to focus** VERB
▷ see also **focus** NOUN
scharf einstellen [4] (PERFECT TENSE hat scharf eingestellt)
□ Try to focus the binoculars. Versuch, das Fernglas scharf einzustellen.
■ **to focus on something 1** (with camera) die Kamera auf etwas einstellen [4] □ The cameraman focused on the bird. Der Kameramann stellte die Kamera auf den Vogel

ein. **2** (concentrate)sich auf etwas konzentrieren [76] □ Let's focus on the plot. Wir wollen uns auf die Handlung konzentrieren.

★ **fog** NOUN
der Nebel masc (PLdie Nebel)

★ **foggy** ADJECTIVE
neblig
□ a foggy dayein nebliger Tag

foil NOUN
die Alufolie fem (kitchen foil)
□ She wrapped the meat in foil.Sie wickelte das Fleisch in Alufolie.

★ **fold** NOUN
▷ see also **fold** VERB
die Falte fem

★ to **fold** VERB
▷ see also **fold** NOUN
falten [2]
□ He folded the newspaper in half.Er faltete die Zeitung in der Mitte zusammen.
■ **to fold up 1**zusammenfalten [2] (paper)
2zusammenklappen [4] (chair)
■ **to fold one's arms**die Arme verschränken [7] □ She folded her arms.Sie verschränkte die Arme.

folder NOUN
1 die Mappe fem
□ She kept all her letters in a folder.Sie bewahrte all ihre Briefe in einer Mappe auf.
2 der Ordner masc (PLdie Ordner) (ring binder, also on computer)

folding ADJECTIVE
■ **a folding chair**ein Klappstuhl masc
■ **a folding bed**ein Klappbett neut

★ to **follow** VERB
1 folgen [38] (PERFECT TENSEist gefolgt)
□ She followed him.Sie folgte ihm.
■ **You go first and I'll follow.**Geh du vor, ich komme nach.
2 followen [38]
□ Do you follow him on Twitter?Followst du ihm auf Twitter?

follower NOUN
der Follower masc (PLdie Follower)
die Followerin fem (on Twitter etc)

★ **following** ADJECTIVE
folgend
□ the following dayam folgenden Tag

fond ADJECTIVE
■ **to be fond of somebody**jemanden gernhaben [32] □ I'm very fond of her.Ich habe sie sehr gern.

★ **food** NOUN
die Nahrung fem
■ **We need to buy some food.**Wir müssen etwas zum Essen kaufen.
■ **cat food**das Katzenfutter
■ **dog food**das Hundefutter

★ **food bank** NOUN
die Tafel fem
□ Too many people now have to rely on food banks.Zu viele Menschen sind heutzutage von Tafeln abhängig.

food processor NOUN
die Küchenmaschine fem

★ **fool** NOUN
der Idiot masc (GENdes Idioten , PLdie Idioten)
die Idiotin fem

★ **foot** NOUN
1 der Fuß masc (GENdes Fußes , PLdie Füße) (of person)
□ My feet are aching.Mir tun die Füße weh.
■ **on foot**zu Fuß
2 der Fuß masc (PLdie Fuß) (12 inches)

DID YOU KNOW...?
In Germany measurements are in metres and centimetres rather than feet and inches. A foot is about 30 centimetres.

□ Susie is six foot tall.Susie ist ein Meter achtzig groß. □ That mountain is five thousand feet high.Dieser Berg ist eintausendsechshundert Meter hoch.

★ **football** NOUN
der Fußball masc (PLdie Fußbälle)
□ I like playing football.Ich spiele gern Fußball.
□ Paul threw the football over the fence.Paul warf den Fußball über den Zaun.

★ **footballer** NOUN
der Fußballer masc (PLdie Fußballer)
die Fußballerin fem

football player NOUN
der Fußballspieler masc (PLdie Fußballspieler)
die Fußballspielerin fem
□ She's a famous football player.Sie ist eine bekannte Fußballspielerin.

footpath NOUN
der Fußweg masc (PLdie Fußwege)
□ the footpath through the forestder Fußweg durch den Wald

footprint NOUN
der Fußabdruck masc (PLdie Fußabdrücke)
□ He saw footprints in the sand.Er sah Fußabdrücke im Sand.

footstep NOUN
der Schritt masc (PLdie Schritte)
□ I can hear footsteps on the stairs.Ich höre Schritte auf der Treppe.

★ **for** PREPOSITION

There are several ways of translating 'for'. Scan the examples to find one that is similar to what you want to say.

1 für
□ a present for meein Geschenk für mich □ He works for the government.Er arbeitet für die Regierung. □ I'll do it for you.Ich mache es für

★ = core vocabulary

dich. □ Are you for or against the idea?Bist du für oder gegen die Idee? □ Oxford is famous for its university.Oxford ist für seine Universität berühmt. □ I sold it for five pounds.Ich habe es für fünf Pfund verkauft.

■ **What for?**Wofür? □ Give me some money! — What for?Gib mir Geld! — Wofür? □ What's it for?Wofür ist das?

> When referring to periods of time, use**lang** for the future and completed action in the past, and**seit** (with the German verb in the present tense) for something that started in the past and is still going on.

2 lang

□ He worked in Germany for two years.Er hat zwei Jahre lang in Deutschland gearbeitet. □ She will be away for a month.Sie wird einen Monat lang weg sein.

3 seit

□ He's been learning German for two years.Er lernt seit zwei Jahren Deutsch. □ She's been away for a month.Sie ist seit einem Monat weg.
■ **What's the German for 'lion'?**Wie sagt man 'lion' auf Deutsch?
■ **It's time for lunch.**Es ist Zeit zum Mittagessen.
■ **There are roadworks for three kilometres.**Es gibt dort über drei Kilometer Bauarbeiten.
■ **the train for York**der Zug nach York
■ **for sale**zu verkaufen □ The factory's for sale. Die Fabrik ist zu verkaufen.

to **forbid** VERB
verbieten [8] (IMPERFECTverbot , PERFECT TENSE hat verboten)
■ **to forbid somebody to do something** jemandem verbieten, etwas zu tun [81] □ I forbid you to go out tonight!Ich verbiete dir, heute Abend auszugehen!

forbidden ADJECTIVE
verboten
□ Smoking is strictly forbidden.Rauchen ist streng verboten.

★ **force** NOUN
▷ see also **force** VERB
die Gewalt fem
□ the forces of naturedie Naturgewalten
■ **The force of the explosion blew out all the windows.**Die Explosion war so stark, dass alle Fenster kaputtgingen.
■ **in force**in Kraft □ The new law has been in force since May.Das neue Gesetz ist seit Mai in Kraft.

★ to **force** VERB
▷ see also **force** NOUN
zwingen [97] (IMPERFECTzwang , PERFECT TENSE hat gezwungen)
□ They forced him to open the safe.Sie zwangen ihn, den Safe aufzumachen.

★ **forecast** NOUN
■ **the weather forecast**die Wettervorhersage

foreground NOUN
der Vordergrund masc
□ in the foregroundim Vordergrund

forehead NOUN
die Stirn fem

★ **foreign** ADJECTIVE
ausländisch

★ **foreigner** NOUN
der Ausländer masc (PLdie Ausländer)
die Ausländerin fem

to **foresee** VERB
vorhersehen [64] (PRESENT TENSEsieht vorher , IMPERFECTsah vorher , PERFECT TENSEhat vorhergesehen)
□ He had foreseen the problem.Er hatte das Problem vorhergesehen.

★ **forest** NOUN
der Wald masc (PLdie Wälder)

forever ADVERB
1 für immer
□ He's gone forever.Er ist für immer weg.
2 dauernd (always)
□ She's forever complaining.Sie beklagt sich dauernd.

forgave VERB ▷ see **forgive**

to **forge** VERB
fälschen [38]
□ She tried to forge his signature.Sie versuchte, seine Unterschrift zu fälschen.

forged ADJECTIVE
gefälscht
□ forged banknotesgefälschte Banknoten

★ to **forget** VERB
vergessen [83] (PRESENT TENSEvergisst , IMPERFECT vergaß , PERFECT TENSEhat vergessen)
□ I've forgotten his name.Ich habe seinen Namen vergessen. □ I'm sorry, I completely forgot!Tut mir leid, das habe ich total vergessen!

forgetful ADJECTIVE
vergesslich

to **forgive** VERB
■ **to forgive somebody**jemandem verzeihen
□ I forgive you.Ich verzeihe dir.
■ **to forgive somebody for doing something** jemandem verzeihen, etwas getan zu haben
□ She forgave him for forgetting her birthday. Sie verzieh ihm, dass sie ihren Geburtstag vergessen hat.

forgot, forgotten VERB ▷ see **forget**

fork NOUN
1 die Gabel fem (for eating, gardening)
□ He ate his chips with a fork.Er aß seine Pommes frites mit einer Gabel.

2 die Gabelung *fem* (*in road*)
- **There was a fork in the road.** Die Straße gabelte sich.

★ **form** NOUN
1 das Formular *neut* (PL die Formulare) (*paper*)
□ to fill in a form ein Formular ausfüllen
2 die Form *fem* (*type*)
□ I'm against hunting in any form. Ich bin gegen die Jagd in jeglicher Form.
- **in top form** in Topform

★ **formal** ADJECTIVE
1 formell (*occasion*)
□ a formal dinner ein formelles Abendessen
2 förmlich (*person*)
3 gehoben (*language*)
□ a formal expression ein gehobener Ausdruck
- **formal clothes** die Gesellschaftskleidung *sing*
- **He's got no formal qualifications.** Er hat keinen offiziellen Abschluss.

★ **former** ADJECTIVE
ehemalig
□ a former pupil ein ehemaliger Schüler □ the former Prime Minister der ehemalige Premierminister

formerly ADVERB
früher

fort NOUN
das Fort *neut* (PL die Forts)

★ **forth** ADVERB
- **to go back and forth** hin- und hergehen [29]
- **and so forth** und so weiter

forthcoming ADJECTIVE
kommend
□ the forthcoming meeting die kommende Besprechung

fortnight NOUN
- **a fortnight** vierzehn Tage □ I'm going on holiday for a fortnight. Ich verreise für vierzehn Tage.

fortunate ADJECTIVE
- **to be fortunate** Glück haben [32] □ He was extremely fortunate to survive the accident. Er hatte Glück, den Unfall zu überleben.
- **It's fortunate that I remembered the map.** Zum Glück habe ich an die Landkarte gedacht.

fortunately ADVERB
zum Glück
□ Fortunately, it didn't rain. Zum Glück hat es nicht geregnet.

★ **fortune** NOUN
das Vermögen *neut* (PL die Vermögen)
□ Kate earns a fortune! Kate verdient ein Vermögen!
- **to tell somebody's fortune** jemandem wahrsagen [15]

★ **forty** NUMBER
vierzig
□ He's forty. Er ist vierzig.

★ **forward** ADVERB
▷ *see also* **forward** VERB
- **to move forward** sich vorwärtsbewegen [4]

★ **to forward** VERB
▷ *see also* **forward** ADVERB
nachsenden (IMPERFECT sandte nach, PERFECT TENSE hat nachgesandt)
□ He forwarded all the files. Er sandte alle Dateien nach.

to foster VERB
in Pflege nehmen [52] (PRESENT TENSE nimmt, IMPERFECT nahm, PERFECT TENSE hat genommen)
□ She has fostered more than fifteen children. Sie hat mehr als fünfzehn Kinder in Pflege genommen.

foster child NOUN
das Pflegekind *neut* (PL die Pflegekinder)
□ She's their foster child. Sie ist ihr Pflegekind.

fought VERB ▷ *see* **fight**

foul ADJECTIVE
▷ *see also* **foul** NOUN
furchtbar
□ The weather was foul. Das Wetter war furchtbar. □ What a foul smell! Was für ein furchtbarer Gestank!

foul NOUN
▷ *see also* **foul** ADJECTIVE
das Foul *neut* (PL die Fouls)
□ Ferguson committed a foul. Ferguson hat ein Foul begangen.

★ **found** VERB ▷ *see* **find**

★ **to found** VERB
gründen [54]
□ Baden-Powell founded the Scout Movement. Baden-Powell hat die Pfadfinderbewegung gegründet.

foundations PL NOUN
das Fundament *neut* (PL die Fundamente)

★ **fountain** NOUN
der Brunnen *masc* (PL die Brunnen)

fountain pen NOUN
der Füllfederhalter *masc* (PL die Füllfederhalter)

★ **four** NUMBER
vier
□ She's four. Sie ist vier.

★ **fourteen** NUMBER
vierzehn
□ I'm fourteen. Ich bin vierzehn.

★ **fourteenth** ADJECTIVE
vierzehnte
□ the fourteenth of August der vierzehnte August

fourth ADJECTIVE
vierte
□ the fourth floor der vierte Stock □ the fourth of August der vierte August

fox NOUN
der Fuchs masc (GEN des Fuchses, PL die Füchse)

fragile ADJECTIVE
zerbrechlich

frame NOUN
der Rahmen masc (PL die Rahmen) (for picture)

France NOUN
Frankreich neut
■ **from France** aus Frankreich
■ **in France** in Frankreich
■ **to France** nach Frankreich

frantic ADJECTIVE
■ **I was going frantic.** Ich bin fast durchgedreht.
■ **I was frantic with worry.** Ich habe mir furchtbare Sorgen gemacht.

fraud NOUN
1 der Betrug masc (crime)
□ He was jailed for fraud. Er kam wegen Betrugs ins Gefängnis.
2 der Betrüger masc (PL die Betrüger)
die Betrügerin fem (person)
□ He's not a real doctor, he's a fraud. Er ist kein echter Arzt, er ist ein Betrüger.

freckles PL NOUN
die Sommersprossen fem pl

free ADJECTIVE
▷ see also **free** VERB
1 kostenlos (free of charge)
□ a free brochure eine kostenlose Broschüre
2 frei (not busy, not taken)
□ Is this seat free? Ist dieser Platz frei?
■ **'admission free'** 'Eintritt frei'
■ **Are you free after school?** Hast du nach der Schule Zeit?

to free VERB
▷ see also **free** ADJECTIVE
befreien [7] (PERFECT TENSE hat befreit)

freedom NOUN
die Freiheit fem

freeway NOUN (US)
die Autobahn fem

to freeze VERB
1 gefrieren (IMPERFECT gefror, PERFECT TENSE ist gefroren)
□ The water had frozen. Das Wasser war gefroren.
2 einfrieren (food)
□ She froze the rest of the raspberries. Sie hat die restlichen Himbeeren eingefroren.

freezer NOUN
der Gefrierschrank masc (PL die Gefrierschränke)

freezing ADJECTIVE
■ **It's freezing!** Es ist eiskalt! (informal)
■ **I'm freezing!** Mir ist eiskalt! (informal)
■ **three degrees below freezing** drei Grad minus

freight NOUN
die Fracht fem (goods)
■ **a freight train** ein Güterzug masc

French ADJECTIVE
▷ see also **French** NOUN
französisch
■ **He's French.** Er ist Franzose.
■ **She's French.** Sie ist Französin.

French NOUN
▷ see also **French** ADJECTIVE
das Französisch neut (GEN des Französischen) (language)
□ Do you speak French? Sprechen Sie Französisch?
■ **the French** (people) die Franzosen masc pl

French beans PL NOUN
die grünen Bohnen fem pl
□ She really likes French beans. Sie mag grüne Bohnen besonders gern.

French fries PL NOUN
die Pommes frites fem pl

French horn NOUN
das Waldhorn neut (PL die Waldhörner)
□ I play the French horn. Ich spiele Waldhorn.

French kiss NOUN
der Zungenkuss masc (GEN des Zungenkusses, PL die Zungenküsse)

French loaf NOUN
das Stangenbrot neut (PL die Stangenbrote)

Frenchman NOUN
der Franzose masc (GEN des Franzosen, PL die Franzosen)

French windows PL NOUN
die Fenstertür fem

Frenchwoman NOUN
die Französin fem

frequent ADJECTIVE
häufig
□ frequent showers häufige Niederschläge
■ **There are frequent buses to the town centre.** Es gehen häufig Busse ins Stadtzentrum.

fresh ADJECTIVE
frisch
□ I need some fresh air. Ich brauche frische Luft.

to freshen up VERB
sich frisch machen [48]
□ I'd like to go and freshen up. Ich würde mich gerne frisch machen.

to fret VERB
sich verrückt machen [48]

f

Numbers in brackets refer to verb tables on pages 697 to 706.

461

□ Don't fret about your exams. Mach dich wegen der Prüfung nicht verrückt.

★ **Friday** NOUN

der Freitag *masc* (PL die Freitage)
□ on Friday am Freitag □ every Friday jeden Freitag □ last Friday letzten Freitag □ next Friday nächsten Freitag
■ on Fridays freitags

★ **fridge** NOUN

der Kühlschrank *masc* (PL die Kühlschränke)
■ a fridge magnet ein Kühlschrankmagnet

fried ADJECTIVE

gebraten
□ fried onions gebratene Zwiebeln
■ a fried egg ein Spiegelei *neut*

★ **friend** NOUN

▷ see also **friend** VERB
der Freund *masc* (PL die Freunde)
die Freundin *fem*

to **friend** VERB

▷ see also **friend** NOUN
sich befreunden [54] mit
□ I've friended her on Facebook. Ich habe mich mit ihr auf Facebook befreundet.

★ **friendly** ADJECTIVE

freundlich
□ She's really friendly. Sie ist wirklich freundlich. □ Liverpool is a very friendly city. Liverpool ist eine sehr freundliche Stadt.

★ **friendship** NOUN

die Freundschaft *fem*

fright NOUN

der Schrecken *masc* (PL die Schrecken)
□ I got a terrible fright! Ich habe einen furchtbaren Schrecken bekommen!

to **frighten** VERB

Angst machen [48]
□ Horror films frighten him. Horrorfilme machen ihm Angst.

★ **frightened** ADJECTIVE

■ to be frightened Angst haben [32] □ I'm frightened! Ich habe Angst!
■ to be frightened of something vor etwas Angst haben [32] □ Anna's frightened of spiders. Anna hat Angst vor Spinnen.

frightening ADJECTIVE

beängstigend

fringe NOUN

der Pony *masc* (PL die Ponys) (*of hair*)
□ She's got a fringe. Sie hat einen Pony.

Frisbee® NOUN

das Frisbee® *neut* (PL die Frisbees)
□ to play Frisbee Frisbee spielen

fro ADVERB

■ to and fro hin und her

★ **frog** NOUN

der Frosch *masc* (PL die Frösche)

★ **from** PREPOSITION

1 aus (*from country, town*)
□ I'm from Yorkshire. Ich bin aus Yorkshire. □ I come from Perth. Ich bin aus Perth.
■ Where do you come from? Woher sind Sie?

2 von (*from person*)
□ a text from my sister eine SMS von meiner Schwester
■ The hotel is one kilometre from the beach. Das Hotel ist einen Kilometer vom Strand entfernt.

3 ab (*number*)
□ from ten pounds ab zehn Pfund □ from the age of fourteen ab vierzehn
■ from ... to ... **1** (*distance*) von ... nach ... □ He flew from Manchester to Paris. Er flog von Manchester nach Paris. **2** (*time*) von ... bis ... □ from one o'clock to two von eins bis zwei
■ The price was reduced from ten pounds to five. Der Preis war von zehn auf fünf Pfund herabgesetzt.
■ from ... onwards ab ... □ We'll be at home from seven o'clock onwards. Wir werden ab sieben Uhr zu Hause sein.

★ **front** NOUN

▷ see also **front** ADJECTIVE
die Vorderseite *fem*
□ the front of the house die Vorderseite des Hauses
■ in front davor □ a house with a car in front ein Haus mit einem Auto davor
■ in front of vor

Use the accusative to express movement or a change of place. Use the dative when there is no change of place.

□ He stood in front of the house. Er stand vor dem Haus. □ He ran in front of a bus. Er lief vor einen Bus. □ the car in front of us das Auto vor uns
■ in the front (*of car*) vorn □ I was sitting in the front. Ich saß vorn.
■ at the front of the train vorn im Zug

★ **front** ADJECTIVE

▷ see also **front** NOUN
vordere
□ the front row die vordere Reihe □ the front seats of the car die vorderen Sitze des Autos
■ the front door die Haustür

frontier NOUN

die Grenze *fem*

★ **frost** NOUN

der Frost *masc* (PL die Fröste)

frosting NOUN (US)

der Zuckerguss *masc* (GEN des Zuckergusses, PL die Zuckergüsse)

★ **frosty** ADJECTIVE

frostig
□ It's frosty today. Heute ist es frostig.

to **frown** VERB
die Stirn runzeln [34]
□ He frowned. Er runzelte die Stirn.

froze, frozen VERB ▷ see **freeze**

frozen ADJECTIVE
tiefgefroren (food)
□ frozen chips tiefgefrorene Pommes frites

fruit NOUN
1 die Frucht fem (PL die Früchte)
□ an exotic fruit eine exotische Frucht
2 das Obst neut
□ Fruit is very healthy. Obst ist sehr gesund.
■ **fruit juice** der Fruchtsaft
■ **a fruit salad** ein Obstsalat masc

fruit machine NOUN
der Spielautomat masc (GEN des Spielautomaten, PL die Spielautomaten)

frustrated ADJECTIVE
frustriert

to **fry** VERB
braten (PRESENT TENSE brät, IMPERFECT briet, PERFECT TENSE hat gebraten)
□ Fry the onions for five minutes. Braten Sie die Zwiebeln fünf Minuten lang.

frying pan NOUN
die Bratpfanne fem

fuel NOUN
das Benzin neut (PL die Benzine) (for car)
□ to run out of fuel kein Benzin mehr haben

to **fulfil** VERB
erfüllen [7] (PERFECT TENSE hat erfüllt)
□ Cara fulfilled her dream of becoming a pilot. Cara hat ihren Traum erfüllt und ist Pilotin geworden.

full ADJECTIVE, ADVERB
1 voll
□ The tank's full. Der Tank ist voll.
2 ausführlich
□ He asked for full information about the job. Er bat um ausführliche Informationen über die Stelle.
■ **your full name** Name und Vornamen
■ **My full name is Connor John Marr.** Mein vollständiger Name ist Connor John Marr.
■ **I'm full.** (after meal) Ich bin satt.
■ **at full speed** mit Höchstgeschwindigkeit
□ He drove at full speed. Er fuhr Höchstgeschwindigkeit.
■ **There was a full moon.** Es war Vollmond.

full stop NOUN
der Punkt masc (PL die Punkte)

full-time ADJECTIVE, ADVERB
ganztags
□ She works full-time. Sie arbeitet ganztags.
■ **She's got a full-time job.** Sie hat einen Ganztagsjob.

fully ADVERB
ganz
□ He hasn't fully recovered yet. Er hat sich noch nicht ganz erholt.

fumes PL NOUN
die Abgase neut pl
□ dangerous fumes gefährliche Abgase
■ **exhaust fumes** Autoabgase

fun ADJECTIVE
▷ see also **fun** NOUN
lustig
□ She's a fun person. Sie ist ein lustiger Mensch.

fun NOUN
▷ see also **fun** ADJECTIVE
■ **to have fun** Spaß haben [32] □ We had great fun playing in the snow. Wir hatten beim Spielen im Schnee unseren Spaß.
■ **for fun** zum Spaß □ He entered the competition just for fun. Er hat am Wettbewerb nur zum Spaß mitgemacht.
■ **to make fun of somebody** sich über jemanden lustig machen [48] □ They made fun of him. Sie machten sich über ihn lustig.
■ **It's fun!** Das macht Spaß!
■ **Have fun!** Viel Spaß!

funds PL NOUN
■ **to raise funds** Spenden sammeln [34]

funeral NOUN
die Beerdigung fem

funfair NOUN
das Volksfest neut (PL die Volksfeste)

funny ADJECTIVE
1 lustig (amusing)
□ It was really funny. Es war wirklich lustig.
2 komisch (strange)
□ There's something funny about him. Er hat etwas Komisches an sich.

fur NOUN
1 der Pelz masc (GEN des Pelzes, PL die Pelze)
□ a fur coat ein Pelzmantel masc
2 das Fell neut (PL die Felle)
□ the dog's fur das Fell des Hundes

furious ADJECTIVE
wütend
□ Dad was furious with me. Papa war wütend auf mich.

furniture NOUN
die Möbel neut pl
□ a piece of furniture ein Möbelstück neut

further ADVERB, ADJECTIVE
weiter entfernt
□ London is further from Manchester than Leeds is. London ist weiter von Manchester entfernt als Leeds.
■ **How much further is it?** Wie weit ist es noch?

f

Numbers in brackets refer to verb tables on pages 697 to 706.

463

further education – future

further education NOUN

die Weiterbildung *fem*

fuse NOUN

die Sicherung *fem*

□ The fuse has blown. Die Sicherung ist durchgebrannt.

fuss NOUN

die Aufregung *fem*

□ What's all the fuss about? Was soll die ganze Aufregung?

■ **to make a fuss** Theater machen [48] □ He's always making a fuss about nothing. Er macht immer Theater wegen nichts.

fussy ADJECTIVE

pingelig

□ She is very fussy about her food. Sie ist mit dem Essen sehr pingelig.

★ **future** NOUN

1 die Zukunft *fem*

■ **in future** in Zukunft □ Be more careful in future. Sei in Zukunft vorsichtiger.

■ **What are your plans for the future?** Was für Zukunftspläne haben Sie?

2 das Futur *neut* (*in grammar*)

□ Put this sentence into the future. Setzt dieser Satz ins Futur.

★ = core vocabulary

Gg

to **gain** VERB
- **to gain weight** zunehmen [52]
- **to gain speed** schneller werden [91]

gallery NOUN
die Galerie *fem*
□ an art gallery eine Kunstgalerie

to **gamble** VERB
spielen [38]

gambler NOUN
der Spieler *masc* (PL die Spieler)
die Spielerin *fem*

gambling NOUN
das Glücksspiel *neut* (PL die Glücksspiele)
- **He likes gambling.** Er spielt gern.

★ **game** NOUN
das Spiel *neut* (PL die Spiele)
□ The children were playing a game. Die Kinder
spielten ein Spiel. □ a game of football ein
Fußballspiel □ a game of cards ein Kartenspiel

gamer NOUN
der Gamer *masc* (PL die Gamer)
die Gamerin *fem* (on computer)

games console NOUN
die Spielkonsole *fem*

gaming NOUN
das Gaming *neut* (on computer)

★ **gang** NOUN
die Gang *fem* (PL die Gangs)

gangster NOUN
der Gangster *masc* (PL die Gangster)

gap NOUN
1 die Lücke *fem*
□ There's a gap in the hedge. In der Hecke ist
eine Lücke.
2 die Pause *fem*
□ a gap of four years eine Pause von vier Jahren

gap year NOUN
das Gap-Year *neut*
□ My sister's in Australia on her gap year. Meine
Schwester macht ein Gap-Year in Australien.

garage NOUN
1 die Garage *fem* (for parking cars)
2 die Werkstatt *fem* (PL die Werkstätten) (for
repairs)

garbage NOUN
der Müll *masc*
□ the garbage can die Mülltonne
- **That's garbage!** Das ist Blödsinn!

★ **garden** NOUN
der Garten *masc* (PL die Gärten)

garden centre NOUN
das Gartencenter *neut* (PL die Gartencenter)

gardener NOUN
der Gärtner *masc* (PL die Gärtner)
die Gärtnerin *fem*
□ He's a gardener. Er ist Gärtner.

gardening NOUN
die Gartenarbeit *fem*
□ My gran loves gardening. Meine Oma liebt
Gartenarbeit.

gardens PL NOUN
der Park *masc sing* (PL die Parks)

garlic NOUN
der Knoblauch *masc*

garment NOUN
das Kleidungsstück *neut* (PL die
Kleidungsstücke)

★ **gas** NOUN
1 das Gas *neut* (PL die Gase)
- **a gas cooker** ein Gasherd *masc*
- **a gas cylinder** eine Gasflasche
- **a gas fire** ein Gasofen *masc*
- **a gas leak** eine undichte Stelle in der
Gasleitung
2 das Benzin *neut* (US)
- **a gas station** eine Tankstelle

gasoline NOUN (US)
das Benzin *neut*

★ **gate** NOUN
1 das Tor *neut* (PL die Tore) (of garden)
2 das Gatter *neut* (PL die Gatter) (of field)
3 der Flugsteig *masc* (PL die Flugsteige) (at airport)

gateau NOUN
die Torte *fem*

to **gather** VERB
sich versammeln [34] (PERFECT TENSE haben sich
versammelt) (assemble)
□ People gathered in front of the church.
Menschen versammelten sich vor der Kirche.
- **to gather speed** schneller werden [91]
□ The train gathered speed. Der Zug wurde
schneller.

gave VERB ▷ *see* give

gay ADJECTIVE
schwul (homosexual)

gaze – gesture

to **gaze** VERB
■ **to gaze at something** etwas anstarren [4]
□ He gazed at her. Er starrte sie an.

★ **GCSE** NOUN (= *General Certificate of Secondary Education*)
die mittlere Reife *fem*

gear NOUN
1 der Gang *masc* (PL die Gänge) (*in car*)
□ in first gear im ersten Gang
■ **to change gear** schalten [2]
2 die Ausrüstung *fem*
□ camping gear die Campingausrüstung
■ **your sports gear** (*clothes*) dein Sportzeug *neut*

gear lever NOUN
der Schalthebel *masc* (PL die Schalthebel)

gearshift NOUN (US)
der Schaltknüppel *masc* (PL die Schaltknüppel)

geese PL NOUN ▷ see **goose**

gel NOUN
das Gel *neut* (PL die Gele)

> Note that in German the 'g' in Gel is pronounced like the 'g' in girl.

□ hair gel das Haargel

gem NOUN
der Edelstein *masc* (PL die Edelsteine)

Gemini SING NOUN
die Zwillinge *masc pl*
□ I'm Gemini. Ich bin Zwilling.

gender NOUN
das Geschlecht *neut* (PL die Geschlechter)

★ **general** NOUN
▷ see also **general** ADJECTIVE
der General *masc* (PL die Generäle)

★ **general** ADJECTIVE
▷ see also **general** NOUN
allgemein
■ **in general** im Allgemeinen

general knowledge NOUN
die Allgemeinbildung *fem*

★ **generally** ADVERB
normalerweise
□ I generally go shopping on Saturday. Ich gehe normalerweise samstags einkaufen.

★ **generation** NOUN
die Generation *fem*
□ the younger generation die jüngere Generation

generator NOUN
der Generator *masc* (PL die Generatoren)

★ **generous** ADJECTIVE
großzügig
□ That's very generous of you. Das ist sehr großzügig von Ihnen.

genetic ADJECTIVE
genetisch

genetically ADVERB
genetisch
■ **genetically modified** genmanipuliert

Geneva NOUN
Genf *neut*
■ **to Geneva** nach Genf
■ **Lake Geneva** der Genfer See

genius NOUN
das Genie *neut* (PL die Genies)
□ She's a genius! Sie ist ein Genie!

★ **gentle** ADJECTIVE
sanft

★ **gentleman** NOUN
der Gentleman *masc* (PL die Gentlemen)
■ **Good morning, gentlemen.** Guten Morgen, meine Herren.

gently ADVERB
sanft

gents SING NOUN
die Herrentoilette *fem*
■ **'gents'** (*on sign*) 'Herren'

★ **genuine** ADJECTIVE
1 echt (*real*)
□ These are genuine diamonds. Das sind echte Diamanten.
2 aufrichtig (*sincere*)
□ She's a very genuine person. Sie ist ein sehr aufrichtiger Mensch.

geography NOUN
die Geografie *fem*

gerbil NOUN
die Wüstenrennmaus *fem* (PL die Wüstenrennmäuse)

germ NOUN
die Bazille *fem*

★ **German** ADJECTIVE
▷ see also **German** NOUN
deutsch
■ **He is German.** Er ist Deutscher.
■ **She is German.** Sie ist Deutsche.
■ **German shepherd** der Schäferhund

★ **German** NOUN
▷ see also **German** ADJECTIVE
1 der Deutsche *masc* (GEN des Deutschen, PL die Deutschen)
die Deutsche *fem* (GEN der Deutschen) (*person*)
□ a German ein Deutscher, eine Deutsche
■ **the Germans** die Deutschen
2 das Deutsch *neut* (GEN des Deutschen) (*language*)
□ Do you speak German? Sprechen sie Deutsch?

★ **Germany** NOUN
Deutschland *neut*
■ **from Germany** aus Deutschland
■ **in Germany** in Deutschland
■ **to Germany** nach Deutschland

gesture NOUN
die Geste *fem*

★ = core vocabulary

★ to **get** VERB
1 bekommen [40] (IMPERFECT bekam, PERFECT TENSE hat bekommen) (*receive*)
□ I got lots of presents. Ich habe viele Geschenke bekommen. □ He got first prize. Er hat den ersten Preis bekommen. □ Olivia got good exam results. Olivia hat gute Noten bekommen.
■ **have got** haben [32] □ How many have you got? Wie viele hast du?
2 holen [38] (*fetch*)
□ Get help! Hol Hilfe!
3 fassen [31] (*catch*)
□ They've got the thief. Sie haben den Dieb gefasst.
4 nehmen [52] (PRESENT TENSE nimmt, IMPERFECT nahm, PERFECT TENSE hat genommen) (*train, bus*)
□ I'm getting the bus into town. Ich nehme den Bus in die Stadt.
5 verstehen [72] (IMPERFECT verstand, PERFECT TENSE hat verstanden) (*understand*)
□ I don't get the joke. Ich verstehe den Witz nicht.
6 kommen [40] (IMPERFECT kam, PERFECT TENSE ist gekommen) (*go*)
□ How do you get to the castle? Wie kommt man zur Burg?
7 werden [91] (PRESENT TENSE wird, IMPERFECT wurde, PERFECT TENSE ist geworden) (*become*)
□ to get old alt werden
■ **to get something done** etwas machen lassen [42] □ to get something repaired etwas reparieren lassen □ to get one's hair cut sich die Haare schneiden lassen
■ **to get something for somebody** jemandem etwas holen [38] □ She got the book for me. Sie holte mir das Buch.
■ **to have got to do something** etwas tun müssen [51] □ I've got to tell him. Ich muss es ihm sagen.
■ **to get over something 1** sich von etwas erholen [19] □ It took her a long time to get over her illness. Sie brauchte lange Zeit, um sich von der Krankheit zu erholen. **2** etwas überwinden [86] □ He managed to get over the problem. Er konnte das Problem überwinden.
■ **to get round to something** zu etwas kommen [40] □ I'll get round to it eventually. Ich werde schon noch dazu kommen.

to **get away** VERB
entkommen [40]
□ One of the burglars got away. Einer der Einbrecher ist entkommen.
■ **You'll never get away with it.** Das wird man dir niemals durchgehen lassen.

to **get back** VERB
1 zurückkommen [40]
□ What time did you get back? Wann seid ihr zurückgekommen?
2 zurückbekommen [40]
□ He got his money back. Er hat sein Geld zurückbekommen.

to **get down** VERB
herunterkommen [40]
□ Get down from there! Komm da runter!

to **get in** VERB
nach Hause kommen [40]
□ What time did you get in last night? Wann bist du heute Nacht nach Hause gekommen?

to **get into** VERB
einsteigen [74] in +*acc*
□ Marek got into the car. Marek stieg ins Auto ein.

to **get off** VERB
1 aussteigen [74] aus
□ Ella got off the train. Ella stieg aus dem Zug aus.
2 absteigen [74] von
□ He got off his bike. Er stieg vom Fahrrad ab.

to **get on** VERB
1 einsteigen [74] in +*acc* (*vehicle*)
□ Mohammed got on the bus. Mohammed stieg in den Bus ein.
2 steigen [74] auf +*acc* (*bike*)
□ Jessica got on her bike. Jessica stieg auf ihr Fahrrad.
■ **to get on with somebody** sich mit jemandem verstehen [72] □ He doesn't get on with his parents. Er versteht sich nicht mit seinen Eltern. □ We got on really well. Wir haben uns wirklich gut verstanden.

to **get out** VERB
aussteigen [74] aus
□ Jake got out of the car. Jake stieg aus dem Auto aus.
■ **Get out!** Raus!
■ **to get something out** etwas herausholen [4] □ She got the map out. Sie holte die Karte heraus.

to **get together** VERB
sich treffen [78]
□ Could we get together this evening? Könnten wir uns heute Abend treffen?

to **get up** VERB
aufstehen [72]
□ What time do you get up? Wann stehst du auf?

ghost NOUN
das Gespenst *neut* (PL die Gespenster)

★ **giant** ADJECTIVE
▷ *see also* **giant** NOUN
riesig
□ They ate a giant meal. Sie haben ein riesiges Essen vertilgt.

★ **giant** NOUN
▷ *see also* **giant** ADJECTIVE
der Riese *masc* (GEN des Riesen, PL die Riesen)
die Riesin *fem*

★ **gift** NOUN
1 das Geschenk *neut* (PL die Geschenke) (*present*)
2 die Begabung *fem* (*talent*)

g

■ **to have a gift for something** für etwas begabt sein [65] □ Lucas has a gift for painting. Lucas ist künstlerisch begabt.

> **BE CAREFUL!**
> Do not translate **gift** by the German word **Gift**.

gifted ADJECTIVE
begabt
□ Maryam is a gifted pianist. Maryam ist eine begabte Pianistin.

gift shop NOUN
der Geschenkladen masc (PL die Geschenkläden)

gig NOUN
1 der Gig masc (PL die Gigs) (performance)
2 das Gigabyte neut (PL die Gigabytes) (gigabyte)

gigantic ADJECTIVE
riesengroß

to **giggle** VERB
kichern [88]

gin NOUN
der Gin masc (PL die Gins or Gin)

> When ordering more than one gin use the plural form **Gin**.

□ Three gins, please. Drei Gin bitte.
■ **a gin and tonic** ein Gin Tonic

ginger NOUN
▷ see also **ginger** ADJECTIVE
der Ingwer masc
□ Add a teaspoon of ginger. Fügen Sie einen Teelöffel Ingwer zu.

ginger ADJECTIVE
▷ see also **ginger** NOUN
rot
□ Robbie has ginger hair. Robbie hat rote Haare.

★ **giraffe** NOUN
die Giraffe fem

★ **girl** NOUN
das Mädchen neut (PL die Mädchen)
□ They've got a girl and two boys. Sie haben ein Mädchen und zwei Jungen. □ a five-year-old girl ein fünfjähriges Mädchen
■ **an English girl** eine junge Engländerin

★ **girlfriend** NOUN
die Freundin fem
□ Jake's girlfriend is called Erin. Jakes Freundin heißt Erin. □ She often went out with her girlfriends. Sie ging oft mit ihren Freundinnen aus.

★ to **give** VERB
geben [28] (PRESENT TENSE gibt, IMPERFECT gab, PERFECT TENSE hat gegeben)
■ **to give something to somebody** jemandem etwas geben [28] □ She gave me ten pounds. Sie gab mir zehn Pfund.
■ **to give something back to somebody** jemandem etwas zurückgeben [28] □ I gave the book back to her. Ich habe ihr das Buch zurückgegeben.

to **give in** VERB
nachgeben [28]
□ His mum gave in and let him watch TV. Seine Mama hat nachgegeben und ihn fernsehen lassen.

to **give out** VERB
austeilen [4]
□ The teacher gave out the books. Der Lehrer hat die Bücher ausgeteilt.

to **give up** VERB
aufgeben [28]
□ I couldn't do it, so I gave up. Ich habe es nicht gekonnt, also habe ich aufgegeben.
■ **to give up doing something** etwas aufgeben [28] □ He gave up smoking. Er hat das Rauchen aufgegeben.
■ **to give oneself up** sich ergeben [28] □ He gave himself up. Er hat sich ergeben.
■ **to give way** (in traffic) die Vorfahrt achten [2]

★ **glad** ADJECTIVE
froh
□ She's glad she's done it. Sie ist froh, dass sie es getan hat.

glamorous ADJECTIVE
glamourös (person)

to **glance** VERB
▷ see also **glance** NOUN
■ **to glance at something** einen Blick auf etwas werfen [92] □ He glanced at his watch. Er warf einen Blick auf seine Uhr.

glance NOUN
▷ see also **glance** VERB
der Blick masc (PL die Blicke)
□ at first glance auf den ersten Blick

to **glare** VERB
■ **to glare at somebody** jemanden wütend ansehen [64] □ He glared at me. Er sah mich wütend an.

glaring ADJECTIVE
■ **a glaring mistake** ein eklatanter Fehler

★ **glass** NOUN
das Glas neut (GEN des Glases, PL die Gläser)
□ a glass of milk ein Glas Milch

glasses PL NOUN
die Brille fem
□ Veronika wears glasses. Veronika trägt eine Brille.

to **gleam** VERB
funkeln [88]
□ Her eyes gleamed with excitement. Ihre Augen funkelten vor Aufregung.

glider NOUN
das Segelflugzeug neut (PL die Segelflugzeuge)

gliding NOUN
das Segelfliegen neut
□ My hobby is gliding. Segelfliegen ist mein Hobby.

glimpse NOUN
■ **to catch a glimpse of somebody** jemanden kurz zu sehen bekommen [40]

to **glitter** VERB
glitzern [88]

★ **global** ADJECTIVE
weltweit
■ **on a global scale** weltweit

global warming NOUN
die globale Erwärmung *fem*

globe NOUN
der Globus *masc* (GEN des Globus, PL die Globen)

gloomy ADJECTIVE
1 düster
□ a small gloomy flat eine kleine, düstere Wohnung
2 niedergeschlagen
□ She's been feeling very gloomy recently. Sie fühlt sich in letzter Zeit sehr niedergeschlagen.

glorious ADJECTIVE
herrlich

glove NOUN
der Handschuh *masc* (PL die Handschuhe)

glove compartment NOUN
das Handschuhfach *neut* (PL die Handschuhfächer)

to **glow** VERB
leuchten [2]
□ Her watch glows in the dark. Ihre Uhr leuchtet im Dunkeln.

glue NOUN
▷ see also **glue** VERB
der Klebstoff *masc* (PL die Klebstoffe)

to **glue** VERB
▷ see also **glue** NOUN
kleben [38]
□ to glue something together etwas zusammenkleben

GM ABBREVIATION (= *genetically modified*)
genmanipuliert
□ GM food genmanipulierte Lebensmittel *pl*

GMO NOUN (= *genetically modified organism*)
der genmanipulierte Organismus *masc* (GEN des genmanipulierten Organismus, PL die genmanipulierten Organismen)

★ **go** NOUN
▷ see also **go** VERB
■ **to have a go at doing something** etwas versuchen [84] □ He had a go at making a cake. Er hat versucht, einen Kuchen zu backen.
■ **Whose go is it?** Wer ist dran?

★ to **go** VERB
▷ see also **go** NOUN
1 gehen [29] (IMPERFECT ging, PERFECT TENSE ist gegangen)
□ I'm going to the cinema tonight. Ich gehe heute Abend ins Kino. □ I'm going now. Ich gehe jetzt.

2 weggehen [29] (IMPERFECT wegging, PERFECT TENSE ist weggegangen) (*leave*)
□ Where's Thomas? — He's gone. Wo ist Thomas? — Er ist weggegangen.

3 fahren [21] (PRESENT TENSE fährt, IMPERFECT fuhr, PERFECT TENSE ist gefahren) (*vehicle*)
□ My car won't go. Mein Auto fährt nicht.
■ **to go home** nach Hause gehen [29] □ I go home at about four o'clock. Ich gehe um etwa vier Uhr nach Hause.
■ **to go for a walk** einen Spaziergang machen [48] □ Shall we go for a walk? Sollen wir einen Spaziergang machen?
■ **How did it go?** Wie ist es gelaufen?
■ **I'm going to do it tomorrow.** Ich werde es morgen tun.
■ **It's going to be difficult.** Es wird schwierig werden.

to **go after** VERB
nachgehen [29] +*dat* (IMPERFECT ging nach, PERFECT TENSE ist nachgegangen) (*follow*)
□ I went after him. Ich ging ihm nach.
■ **Quick, go after them!** Schnell, ihnen nach!

to **go ahead** VERB
vorangehen [29] (IMPERFECT ging voran, PERFECT TENSE ist vorangegangen)
■ **to go ahead with something** etwas durchführen [4]

to **go around** VERB
herumgehen [29] (IMPERFECT ging herum, PERFECT TENSE ist herumgegangen)
□ There's a rumour going around that they're getting married. Es geht das Gerücht herum, sie würden heiraten.

to **go away** VERB
weggehen [29] (IMPERFECT ging weg, PERFECT TENSE ist weggegangen)
□ Go away! Geh weg!

to **go back** VERB
zurückgehen [29] (IMPERFECT ging zurück, PERFECT TENSE ist zurückgegangen)
□ We went back to the same place. Wir sind an denselben Ort zurückgegangen.
■ **Is he still here? — No, he's gone back home.** Ist er noch hier? — Nein, er ist nach Hause gegangen.

to **go by** VERB
vorbeigehen [29] (IMPERFECT ging vorbei, PERFECT TENSE ist vorbeigegangen)
□ A group of tourists went by. Eine Gruppe von Touristen ging vorbei.

to **go down** VERB
1 hinuntergehen [29] (IMPERFECT ging hinunter, PERFECT TENSE ist hinuntergegangen) (*person*)
□ to go down the stairs die Treppe hinuntergehen
2 sinken [67] (IMPERFECT sank, PERFECT TENSE ist gesunken) (*decrease*)
□ The price of computers has gone down. Die Preise für Computer sind gesunken.

3 Luft verlieren [85] (IMPERFECT verlor Luft, PERFECT TENSE hat Luft verloren) (*deflate*)
□ My airbed kept going down. Meine Luftmatratze verlor dauernd Luft.
■ **My brother's gone down with flu.** Mein Bruder hat die Grippe bekommen.

to **go for** VERB
angreifen (IMPERFECT griff an, PERFECT TENSE hat angegriffen) (*attack*)
□ The dog went for me. Der Hund griff mich an.
■ **Go for it!** (*go on!*) Na los!

to **go in** VERB
hineingehen [29] (IMPERFECT ging hinein, PERFECT TENSE ist hineingegangen)
□ He knocked and went in. Er klopfte und ging hinein.

to **go off** VERB
1 losgehen [29] (IMPERFECT ging los, PERFECT TENSE ist losgegangen)
□ The bomb went off. Die Bombe ging los.
□ The fire alarm went off. Der Feueralarm ging los.
2 klingeln [34]
□ My alarm clock goes off at seven every morning. Mein Wecker klingelt jeden Morgen um sieben Uhr.
3 schlecht werden [91] (PRESENT TENSE wird schlecht, IMPERFECT wurde schlecht, PERFECT TENSE ist schlecht geworden)
■ **The milk's gone off.** Die Milch ist sauer geworden.
4 weggehen [29] (*go away*)
□ He went off in a huff. Er ist beleidigt weggegangen.

to **go on** VERB
1 los sein [65] (PRESENT TENSE ist los, IMPERFECT war los, PERFECT TENSE ist los gewesen) (*happen*)
□ What's going on? Was ist los?
2 dauern [88] (*carry on*)
□ The concert went on until eleven o'clock at night. Das Konzert hat bis nach elf Uhr nachts gedauert.
■ **to go on doing something** etwas weiter tun [81] □ He went on reading. Er las weiter.
■ **to go on at somebody** an jemandem herumkritisieren [76] □ My parents always go on at me. Meine Eltern kritisieren dauernd an mir herum.
■ **Go on!** Na los! □ Go on, tell us! Na los, sag schon!

to **go out** VERB
ausgehen [29] (IMPERFECT ging aus, PERFECT TENSE ist ausgegangen)
□ Are you going out tonight? Gehst du heute Abend aus? □ Suddenly the lights went out. Plötzlich ging das Licht aus.
■ **to go out with somebody** mit jemandem ausgehen [29] □ Are you going out with him? Gehst du mit ihm aus?

to **go past** VERB
■ **to go past something** an etwas vorbeigehen

[29] □ He went past the shop. Er ging an dem Geschäft vorbei.

to **go round** VERB
■ **to go round a corner** um die Ecke biegen
■ **to go round to somebody's house** jemanden besuchen [7]
■ **to go round a museum** sich ein Museum ansehen [64]
■ **to go round the shops** einen Einkaufsbummel machen [48]

to **go through** VERB
fahren [21] durch (PRESENT TENSE fährt, IMPERFECT fuhr, PERFECT TENSE ist gefahren) (*by car*)
■ **We went through London to get to Birmingham.** Wir sind über London nach Birmingham gefahren.

to **go up** VERB
1 hinaufgehen [29] (IMPERFECT ging hinauf, PERFECT TENSE ist hinaufgegangen) (*person*)
□ to go up the stairs die Treppe hinaufgehen
2 steigen [74] (IMPERFECT stieg, PERFECT TENSE ist gestiegen) (*increase*)
□ The price has gone up. Der Preis ist gestiegen.
■ **to go up in flames** in Flammen aufgehen [29] □ The factory went up in flames. Die Fabrik ist in Flammen aufgegangen.

to **go with** VERB
passen [31] zu
□ Does this T-shirt go with these jeans? Passt dieses T-Shirt zu den Jeans?

★ **goal** NOUN
1 das Tor *neut* (PL die Tore) (*sport*)
□ to score a goal ein Tor schießen
2 das Ziel *neut* (PL die Ziele) (*aim*)
□ His goal is to become the world champion. Sein Ziel ist es, Weltmeister zu werden.

goalkeeper NOUN
der Torwart *masc* (PL die Torwarte)
die Torwartin *fem*

goat NOUN
die Ziege *fem*
■ **goat's cheese** der Ziegenkäse

god NOUN
der Gott *masc* (PL die Götter)
□ I believe in God. Ich glaube an Gott.

goddaughter NOUN
die Patentochter *fem* (PL die Patentöchter)

goddess NOUN
die Göttin *fem* (PL die Göttinnen)

godfather NOUN
der Patenonkel *masc* (PL die Patenonkel)
□ my godfather mein Patenonkel

godmother NOUN
die Patentante *fem*
□ my godmother meine Patentante

godson NOUN
der Patensohn *masc* (PL die Patensöhne)

goes VERB ▷ see go

★ = core vocabulary

goggles PL NOUN
die Schutzbrille *fem*

★ **gold** NOUN
das Gold *neut*
□ They found some gold. Sie haben Gold gefunden.
■ **a gold necklace** eine goldene Halskette

goldfish NOUN
der Goldfisch *masc* (PL die Goldfische)
□ I've got five goldfish. Ich habe fünf Goldfische.

gold-plated ADJECTIVE
vergoldet

★ **golf** NOUN
das Golf *neut*
□ My dad plays golf. Mein Papa spielt Golf.
■ **a golf club 1** (*stick*) ein Golfschläger *masc*
2 (*place*) ein Golfklub *masc*

golf course NOUN
der Golfplatz *masc* (GEN des Golfplatzes, PL die Golfplätze)

★ **gone** VERB ▷ *see* go

★ **good** ADJECTIVE
1 gut
□ It's a very good film. Das ist ein sehr guter Film.
■ **Vegetables are good for you.** Gemüse ist gesund.
■ **to be good at something** gut in etwas sein [65] □ Layla's very good at maths. Layla ist sehr gut in Mathe.

WORD POWER
You can use a number of other words instead of **good** to mean 'great':
excellent ausgezeichnet
□ an excellent book ein ausgezeichnetes Buch
fantastic fantastisch
□ fantastic weather fantastisches Wetter
great toll
□ a great film ein toller Film
fabulous traumhaft
□ a fabulous idea eine traumhafte Idee

2 freundlich (*kind*)
□ They were very good to me. Sie waren sehr freundlich zu mir. □ That's very good of you. Das ist sehr freundlich von Ihnen.
3 artig (*not naughty*)
□ Be good! Sei artig!
■ **for good** für immer □ One day he left for good. Eines Tages ist er für immer weggegangen.
■ **Good morning!** Guten Morgen!
■ **Good afternoon!** Guten Tag!
■ **Good evening!** Guten Abend!
■ **Good night!** Gute Nacht!
■ **It's no good complaining.** Es hat keinen Wert, sich zu beklagen.

goodbye EXCLAMATION
auf Wiedersehen

Good Friday NOUN
der Karfreitag *masc* (PL die Karfreitage)

good-looking ADJECTIVE
gut aussehend
■ **Alex is very good-looking.** Alex sieht sehr gut aus.

good-natured ADJECTIVE
gutmütig

★ **goods** PL NOUN
die Ware *fem* (*in shop*)
■ **a goods train** ein Güterzug *masc*

to **google** VERB
googeln [88]

goose NOUN
die Gans *fem* (PL die Gänse)

gooseberry NOUN
die Stachelbeere *fem*

gorgeous ADJECTIVE
1 hinreißend
□ She's gorgeous! Sie sieht hinreißend aus!
2 herrlich
□ The weather was gorgeous. Das Wetter war herrlich.

gorilla NOUN
der Gorilla *masc* (PL die Gorillas)

gospel NOUN
das Evangelium *neut* (PL die Evangelien)

gossip NOUN
▷ *see also* **gossip** VERB
1 der Tratsch *masc* (*rumours*)
□ Tell me the gossip! Erzähl mir den neuesten Tratsch!
2 die Klatschtante *fem* (*woman*)
□ She's such a gossip! Sie ist eine furchtbare Klatschtante!
3 das Klatschweib *neut* (PL die Klatschweiber) (*man*)
□ What a gossip! So ein Klatschweib!

to **gossip** VERB
▷ *see also* **gossip** NOUN
1 schwatzen [48] (*chat*)
□ They were always gossiping. Sie haben dauernd geschwatzt.
2 tratschen [48] (*about somebody*)
□ They gossiped about her. Sie haben über sie getratscht.

★ **got** VERB ▷ *see* get

gotten VERB ▷ *see* get

★ **government** NOUN
die Regierung *fem*

★ **GP** NOUN
der praktische Arzt *masc* (PL die praktischen Ärzte)
die praktische Ärztin *fem*
■ **My sister is a GP in Glasgow.** Meine Schwester ist praktische Ärztin in Glasgow.

GPS NOUN (= *global positioning system*)
das GPS *neut* (PL die GPS)

★ to **grab** VERB
packen [38]

□ She grabbed her umbrella and ran out the door. Sie packte ihren Schirm und lief zur Tür hinaus.

graceful ADJECTIVE
anmutig

★ **grade** NOUN
die Note *fem* (*mark*)
□ He got good grades. Er hat gute Noten bekommen.

grade school NOUN (US)
die Grundschule *fem*

gradual ADJECTIVE
allmählich

★ **gradually** ADVERB
allmählich
□ We gradually got used to it. Wir haben uns allmählich daran gewöhnt.

★ **graduate** NOUN
▷ see also **graduate** VERB
der Hochschulabsolvent *masc* (GEN des Hochschulabsolventen, PL die Hochschulabsolventen)
die Hochschulabsolventin *fem*

★ to **graduate** VERB
▷ see also **graduate** NOUN
den Abschluss machen [48]

graffiti PL NOUN
die Graffiti *pl*

grain NOUN
das Korn *neut* (PL die Körner)

gram NOUN
das Gramm *neut* (PL die Gramme or Gramm)

When specifying a quantity of something use the plural form **Gramm**.

□ five hundred grams of cheese fünfhundert Gramm Käse

grammar NOUN
die Grammatik *fem*

grammar school NOUN
das Gymnasium *neut* (PL die Gymnasien)

DID YOU KNOW...?
Gymnasium education begins after year 4 of the **Grundschule** and lasts until year 13. (However, pupils can leave after year 10.) It mainly prepares children for university education.

grammatical ADJECTIVE
grammatisch

gramme NOUN
das Gramm *neut* (PL die Gramme or Gramm)

When specifying a quantity of something use the plural form **Gramm**.

□ five hundred grammes of cheese fünfhundert Gramm Käse

grand ADJECTIVE
prachtvoll

□ She lives in a very grand house. Sie wohnt in einem prachtvollen Haus.

★ **grandchild** NOUN
der Enkel *masc* (PL die Enkel)

granddad NOUN
der Opa *masc* (PL die Opas)
□ my granddad mein Opa

★ **granddaughter** NOUN
die Enkelin *fem*

★ **grandfather** NOUN
der Großvater *masc* (PL die Großväter)
□ my grandfather mein Großvater

grandma NOUN
die Oma *fem* (PL die Omas)
□ my grandma meine Oma

★ **grandmother** NOUN
die Großmutter *fem* (PL die Großmütter)
□ my grandmother meine Großmutter

grandpa NOUN
der Opa *masc* (PL die Opas)
□ my grandpa mein Opa

★ **grandparents** PL NOUN
die Großeltern *pl*
□ my grandparents meine Großeltern

★ **grandson** NOUN
der Enkel *masc* (PL die Enkel)

granny NOUN
die Oma *fem* (PL die Omas)
□ my granny meine Oma

grant NOUN
1 das Stipendium *neut* (PL die Stipendien) (*for study*)
2 die Unterstützung *fem* (*for industry, organization*)

★ **grape** NOUN
die Traube *fem*

grapefruit NOUN
die Grapefruit *fem* (PL die Grapefruits)

graph NOUN
die grafische Darstellung *fem*

graphics PL NOUN
die Grafik *fem sing*

to **grasp** VERB
1 packen [38] (*with hand*)
2 verstehen [72] (IMPERFECT verstand, PERFECT TENSE hat verstanden)
□ I couldn't grasp the difference. Ich habe den Unterschied nicht verstanden.

★ **grass** NOUN
das Gras *neut* (GEN des Grases)
□ The grass is long. Das Gras ist hoch.
■ to cut the grass den Rasen mähen [48]

grasshopper NOUN
die Heuschrecke *fem*

to **grate** VERB
reiben [61] (IMPERFECT rieb, PERFECT TENSE hat gerieben)
□ to grate some cheese Käse reiben

★ = core vocabulary

grateful ADJECTIVE
dankbar

grave NOUN
das Grab neut (PL die Gräber)

gravel NOUN
der Kies masc

graveyard NOUN
der Friedhof masc (PL die Friedhöfe)

gravy NOUN
die Bratensoße fem

grease NOUN
das Fett neut (PL die Fette)

greasy ADJECTIVE
fettig
□ He has greasy hair. Er hat fettige Haare.
■ **The food was very greasy.** Das Essen war
sehr fett.

★ **great** ADJECTIVE
1 toll
□ That's great! Das ist toll!

WORD POWER
You can use a number of other words instead
of **great** to mean 'good':
amazing ausgezeichnet
□ an amazing cook ein ausgezeichneter Koch
marvellous wunderbar
□ a marvellous idea eine wunderbare Idee
superb großartig
□ a superb meal ein großartiges Essen
wonderful wunderbar
□ a wonderful opportunity eine wunderbare
Gelegenheit

2 groß (big)
□ a great mansion eine große Villa

★ **Great Britain** NOUN
Großbritannien neut
■ **from Great Britain** aus Großbritannien
■ **in Great Britain** in Großbritannien
■ **to Great Britain** nach Großbritannien

great-grandfather NOUN
der Urgroßvater masc (PL die Urgroßväter)

great-grandmother NOUN
die Urgroßmutter fem (PL die Urgroßmütter)

★ **Greece** NOUN
Griechenland neut
■ **from Greece** aus Griechenland
■ **to Greece** nach Griechenland

greedy ADJECTIVE
gierig
□ Don't be so greedy! Sei nicht so gierig!

Greek ADJECTIVE
▷ see also **Greek** NOUN
griechisch
□ I love Greek food. Ich mag griechisches Essen
sehr gern.
■ **Dionysis is Greek.** Dionysis ist Grieche.
■ **She's Greek.** Sie ist Griechin.

Greek NOUN
▷ see also **Greek** ADJECTIVE
1 der Grieche masc (GEN des Griechen, PL die
Griechen)
die Griechin fem (person)
2 das Griechisch neut (GEN des Griechischen)
(language)

★ **green** ADJECTIVE
▷ see also **green** NOUN
grün
□ a green car ein grünes Auto □ a green salad
ein grüner Salat
■ **the Green Party** die Grünen masc pl

★ **green** NOUN
▷ see also **green** ADJECTIVE
das Grün neut
□ a dark green ein dunkles Grün
■ **greens** (vegetables) das Grüngemüse sing
■ **the Greens** (party) die Grünen masc pl

★ **greengrocer** NOUN
der Gemüsehändler masc (PL die
Gemüsehändler)
die Gemüsehändlerin fem

greenhouse NOUN
das Treibhaus neut (GEN des Treibhauses, PL die
Treibhäuser)
■ **the greenhouse effect** der Treibhauseffekt
■ **greenhouse gas** das Treibhausgas

Greenland NOUN
Grönland neut

to **greet** VERB
begrüßen [31] (PERFECT TENSE hat begrüßt)
□ He greeted me with a kiss. Er begrüßte mich
mit einem Kuss.

greeting NOUN
■ **Greetings from Vienna!** Grüße aus Wien!
■ **'Season's Greetings'** 'fröhliche
Weihnachten und ein glückliches neues Jahr'

greetings card NOUN
die Grußkarte fem

grew VERB ▷ see **grow**

★ **grey** ADJECTIVE
grau
□ She's got grey hair. Sie hat graue Haare.
□ He's going grey. Er wird grau.

grey-haired ADJECTIVE
grauhaarig

grid NOUN
1 das Gitter neut (PL die Gitter) (on map)
2 das Netz neut (GEN des Netzes, PL die Netze) (of
electricity)

grief NOUN
der Kummer masc

grill NOUN
▷ see also **grill** VERB
der Grill masc (PL die Grills) (of cooker)

to **grill** VERB
▷ see also **grill** NOUN
grillen [48]

g

Numbers in brackets refer to verb tables on pages 697 to 706.

473

grim – guarantee

grim ADJECTIVE
schlimm
□ Things look grim. Es sieht schlimm aus.

to **grin** VERB
▷ see also **grin** NOUN
grinsen [38]
□ Aziz grinned at me. Aziz grinste mich an.

grin NOUN
▷ see also **grin** VERB
das Grinsen neut

to **grind** VERB
1 mahlen (PERFECT TENSE hat gemahlen) (coffee, pepper)
2 hacken [48] (meat)

to **grip** VERB
packen [38]
□ He gripped my arm tightly. Er packte mich fest am Arm.

gripping ADJECTIVE
spannend (exciting)

grit NOUN
der Splitt masc (PL die Splitte)

to **groan** VERB
▷ see also **groan** NOUN
stöhnen [38]
□ He groaned with pain. Er stöhnte vor Schmerzen.

groan NOUN
▷ see also **groan** VERB
das Stöhnen neut (of pain)

grocer NOUN
der Lebensmittelhändler masc (PL die Lebensmittelhändler)
die Lebensmittelhändlerin fem
□ He's a grocer. Er ist Lebensmittelhändler.

groceries PL NOUN
die Einkäufe masc pl

grocer's (shop) NOUN
das Lebensmittelgeschäft neut (PL die Lebensmittelgeschäfte)

grocery store NOUN (US)
das Lebensmittelgeschäft neut (PL die Lebensmittelgeschäfte)

groom NOUN
der Bräutigam masc (PL die Bräutigame) (bridegroom)
□ the groom and his best man der Bräutigam und sein Trauzeuge

to **grope** VERB
■ to grope for something nach etwas tasten [2] □ He groped for the light switch. Er tastete nach dem Lichtschalter.

★ **gross** ADJECTIVE
abscheulich (revolting)
□ It was really gross! Es war wirklich abscheulich!

grossly ADVERB
total

□ We're grossly underpaid. Wir sind total unterbezahlt.

★ **ground** NOUN
1 der Boden masc (PL die Böden) (earth)
□ The ground's wet. Der Boden ist nass.
2 der Platz masc (GEN des Platzes, PL die Plätze) (for sport)
□ a football ground ein Fußballplatz
3 der Grund masc (PL die Gründe) (reason)
□ We've got grounds for complaint. Wir haben Grund zur Klage.
■ **on the ground** auf dem Boden □ We sat on the ground. Wir saßen auf dem Boden.

★ **ground** VERB ▷ see grind
■ **ground coffee** gemahlener Kaffee

★ **group** NOUN
die Gruppe fem

★ to **grow** VERB
1 wachsen [87] (PRESENT TENSE wächst, IMPERFECT wuchs, PERFECT TENSE ist gewachsen) (plant, person, animal)
□ Grass grows quickly. Gras wächst schnell.
□ Haven't you grown! Bist du aber gewachsen!
■ **to grow a beard** sich einen Bart wachsen lassen [42] □ You should grow a beard. Du solltest dir einen Bart wachsen lassen.
■ **He's grown out of his jacket.** Er ist aus der Jacke herausgewachsen.
2 zunehmen [52] (PRESENT TENSE nimmt zu, IMPERFECT nahm zu, PERFECT TENSE hat zugenommen) (increase)
□ The number of pupils who go onto university has grown. Die Zahl der Schüler, die weiter studieren, hat zugenommen.
3 anbauen [4] (PERFECT TENSE hat angebaut) (cultivate)
□ My aunt grows potatoes. Meine Tante baut Kartoffeln an.

to **grow up** VERB
erwachsen werden [91]
□ Oh, grow up! Werd endlich erwachsen!

to **growl** VERB
knurren [38]

grown VERB ▷ see grow

growth NOUN
das Wachstum neut
□ economic growth das Wirtschaftswachstum

grub NOUN
die Fressalien fem pl (informal)

grudge NOUN
■ **to bear a grudge against somebody** einen Groll gegen jemanden haben [32] □ He's always borne a grudge against me. Er hat schon immer einen Groll gegen mich gehabt.

gruesome ADJECTIVE
furchtbar

guarantee NOUN
▷ see also **guarantee** VERB
die Garantie fem

★ = core vocabulary

□ a five-year guarantee eine Garantie von fünf Jahren

to guarantee VERB
▷ *see also* **guarantee** NOUN
garantieren [76] (PERFECT TENSE hat garantiert)
□ I can't guarantee he'll come. Ich kann nicht garantieren, dass er kommt.

to guard VERB
▷ *see also* **guard** NOUN
bewachen [7] (PERFECT TENSE hat bewacht)
□ They guarded the palace. Sie bewachten den Palast.
■ **to guard against something** gegen etwas Vorsichtsmaßnahmen ergreifen

guard NOUN
▷ *see also* **guard** VERB
der Zugbegleiter *masc* (PL die Zugbegleiter)
die Zugbegleiterin *fem* (*of train*)
■ **a security guard** ein Wachmann *masc*
■ **a guard dog** ein Wachhund *masc*

to guess VERB
▷ *see also* **guess** NOUN
raten (PRESENT TENSE rät, IMPERFECT riet, PERFECT TENSE hat geraten)
□ Can you guess what it is? Rate mal, was das ist. □ to guess wrong falsch raten

guess NOUN
▷ *see also* **guess** VERB
die Vermutung *fem*
□ It's just a guess. Es ist nur eine Vermutung.
■ **Have a guess!** Rate mal!

guest NOUN
der Gast *masc* (PL die Gäste)

der Gast is also used for women.

□ She is our guest. Sie ist unser Gast.
□ We have guests staying with us. Wir haben Gäste.

guesthouse NOUN
die Pension *fem*
□ We stayed in a guesthouse. Wir haben in einer Pension gewohnt.

guide NOUN
1 der Führer *masc* (PL die Führer) (*book*)
□ We bought a guide to Cologne. Wir haben einen Führer von Köln gekauft.
2 der Führer *masc* (PL die Führer)
die Führerin *fem* (*person*)
□ The guide showed us round the castle. Unser Führer hat uns die Burg gezeigt.
3 die Pfadfinderin *fem* (*Girl Guide*)

■ **the Guides** die Pfadfinderinnen

guidebook NOUN
der Führer *masc* (PL die Führer)

guide dog NOUN
der Blindenhund *masc* (PL die Blindenhunde)

★ **guilty** ADJECTIVE
schuldig
□ to feel guilty sich schuldig fühlen □ She was found guilty. Sie wurde schuldig gesprochen.

★ **guinea pig** NOUN
das Meerschweinchen *neut* (PL die Meerschweinchen)

★ **guitar** NOUN
die Gitarre *fem*
□ I play the guitar. Ich spiele Gitarre.

gum NOUN
der Kaugummi *masc* (PL die Kaugummis) (*chewing gum*)
■ **gums** (*in mouth*) das Zahnfleisch *sing*

★ **gun** NOUN
1 die Pistole *fem* (*small*)
2 das Gewehr *neut* (PL die Gewehre) (*rifle*)

gunpoint NOUN
■ **at gunpoint** mit Waffengewalt

gust NOUN
■ **a gust of wind** ein Windstoß *masc*

guts PL NOUN
der Mumm *masc* (*informal: courage*)
□ He's certainly got guts. Er hat wirklich Mumm.
■ **I hate his guts.** Ich kann ihn nicht ausstehen.

★ **guy** NOUN
der Typ *masc* (PL die Typen)
□ Who's that guy? Wer ist der Typ?
■ **He's a nice guy.** Er ist ein netter Kerl.

★ **gym** NOUN
1 die Turnhalle *fem* (*at school*)
■ **gym classes** die Turnstunden
2 das Fitnessstudio *neut* (*fitness centre*)
■ **to go to the gym** ins Fitnessstudio gehen

gymnast NOUN
der Turner *masc* (PL die Turner)
die Turnerin *fem*
□ She's a gymnast. Sie ist Turnerin.

gymnastics NOUN
das Turnen *neut*
■ **to do gymnastics** turnen [38]

gypsy NOUN
der Sinto *masc* (PL die Sinti)
die Sinteza *fem*

g

Numbers in brackets refer to verb tables on pages 697 to 706.

475

Hh

★habit NOUN
die Angewohnheit *fem*
□ a bad habit eine schlechte Angewohnheit

hacker NOUN
der Hacker *masc* (PL die Hacker)
die Hackerin *fem*

had VERB ▷ *see* **have**

haddock NOUN
der Schellfisch *masc*

hadn't = had not

hail NOUN
▷ *see also* **hail** VERB
der Hagel *masc*

to hail VERB
▷ *see also* **hail** NOUN
hageln [88]
□ It's hailing. Es hagelt.

★hair NOUN
die Haare *neut pl*
□ She's got long hair. Sie hat lange Haare.
□ He's got black hair. Er hat schwarze Haare.
□ He's losing his hair. Ihm gehen die Haare aus.
■ **to brush one's hair** sich die Haare bürsten
[2] □ I brush my hair every morning. Ich bürste
mir jeden Morgen die Haare.
■ **to wash one's hair** sich die Haare waschen
[89] □ I need to wash my hair. Ich muss mir die
Haare waschen.
■ **to have one's hair cut** sich die Haare
schneiden lassen [42] □ I've just had my hair
cut. Ich habe mir gerade die Haare schneiden
lassen.
■ **a hair** ein Haar *neut*

hairbrush NOUN
die Haarbürste *fem*

hair clip NOUN
die Haarspange *fem*

haircut NOUN
der Haarschnitt *masc* (PL die Haarschnitte)
■ **to have a haircut** sich die Haare schneiden
lassen [42] □ I've just had a haircut. Ich habe
mir gerade die Haare schneiden lassen.

★hairdresser NOUN
der Friseur *masc* (PL die Friseure)
die Friseurin *fem*
□ He's a hairdresser. Er ist Friseur.

★hairdresser's NOUN
der Friseur *masc* (PL die Friseure)
□ at the hairdresser's beim Friseur

hair dryer NOUN
der Haartrockner *masc* (PL die Haartrockner)

hair gel NOUN
das Haargel *neut* (PL die Haargele)

In German the 'g' in **Haargel** is pronounced
like the 'g' in girl.

hairgrip NOUN
die Haarklemme *fem*

hair spray NOUN
der Haarspray *masc* (PL die Haarsprays)

hair straighteners PL NOUN
der Haarglätter *masc sing* (PL die Haarglätter)

hairstyle NOUN
die Frisur *fem*

hairy ADJECTIVE
haarig
□ He's got hairy legs. Er hat haarige Beine.

★half NOUN
▷ *see also* **half** ADJECTIVE, ADVERB
1 die Hälfte *fem*
□ half of the cake die Hälfte des Kuchens
2 die Kinderfahrkarte *fem* (ticket)
□ A half to York, please. Eine Kinderfahrkarte
nach York bitte.
■ **two and a half** zweieinhalb
■ **half an hour** eine halbe Stunde
■ **half past ten** halb elf
■ **half a kilo** ein halbes Kilo
■ **to cut something in half** etwas in zwei Teile
schneiden [60]

★half ADJECTIVE, ADVERB
▷ *see also* **half** NOUN
1 halb
□ a half chicken ein halbes Hähnchen
2 fast
□ He was half asleep. Er schlief fast.

half-brother NOUN
der Halbbruder *masc*

half-hour NOUN
die halbe Stunde *fem*

half-price ADJECTIVE, ADVERB
zum halben Preis

half-sister NOUN
die Halbschwester *fem*

half-term NOUN
die kleinen Ferien *pl*

half-time NOUN
die Halbzeit *fem*

halfway ADVERB
1 auf halber Strecke
□ halfway between Oxford and Swindon auf halber Strecke zwischen Oxford und Swindon
2 in der Mitte
□ halfway through the chapter in der Mitte des Kapitels

★ **hall** NOUN
1 der Flur *masc* (PL die Flure) (*in house*)
2 der Saal *masc* (PL die Säle)
□ the village hall der Gemeindesaal
■ **hall of residence** das Wohnheim

Hallowe'en NOUN
der Abend vor Allerheiligen *masc*

hallway NOUN
der Flur *masc* (PL die Flure)

halt NOUN
■ **to come to a halt** zum Stehen kommen [40]

★ **ham** NOUN
der Schinken *masc* (PL die Schinken)
□ a ham sandwich ein Schinkensandwich *neut*

★ **hamburger** NOUN
der Hamburger *masc* (PL die Hamburger)

hammer NOUN
der Hammer *masc* (PL die Hämmer)

hamster NOUN
der Hamster *masc* (PL die Hamster)

★ **hand** NOUN
▷ *see also* **hand** VERB
1 die Hand *fem* (PL die Hände) (*of person*)
■ **to give somebody a hand** jemandem helfen [37] □ Can you give me a hand? Kannst du mir mal helfen?
■ **on the one hand ..., on the other hand ...** einerseits ..., anderseits ...
2 der Zeiger *masc* (PL die Zeiger) (*of clock*)

★ **to hand** VERB
▷ *see also* **hand** NOUN
reichen [48]
□ He handed me the book. Er reichte mir das Buch.
■ **to hand something in** etwas abgeben [28]
□ Ryan handed his exam paper in. Ryan gab seine Prüfungsarbeit ab.
■ **to hand something out** etwas austeilen [4]
□ The teacher handed out the books. Der Lehrer teilte die Bücher aus.
■ **to hand something over** etwas übergeben [28] □ She handed the keys over to me. Sie übergab mir die Schlüssel.

★ **handbag** NOUN
die Handtasche *fem*

handball NOUN
1 der Handball *masc* (*sport*)
2 das Handspiel *neut* (*foul*)

handbook NOUN
das Handbuch *neut* (PL die Handbücher)

handcuffs PL NOUN
die Handschellen *fem pl*

★ **handkerchief** NOUN
das Taschentuch *neut* (PL die Taschentücher)

★ **handle** NOUN
▷ *see also* **handle** VERB
1 die Klinke *fem* (*of door*)
2 der Henkel *masc* (PL die Henkel) (*of cup*)
3 der Griff *masc* (PL die Griffe) (*of knife*)
4 der Stiel *masc* (PL die Stiele) (*of saucepan*)

★ **to handle** VERB
▷ *see also* **handle** NOUN
■ He handled it well. Er hat das gut gemacht.
■ Helen's mum handled the travel arrangements. Die Mutter von Helen hat sich um die Reisevorbereitungen gekümmert.
■ She's good at handling children. Sie kann gut mit Kindern umgehen.

handlebars PL NOUN
die Lenkstange *fem sing*

handmade ADJECTIVE
handgemacht

★ **handsome** ADJECTIVE
gut aussehend
□ a handsome man ein gut aussehender Mann
■ He's very handsome. Er sieht sehr gut aus.

handwriting NOUN
die Handschrift *fem*

handy ADJECTIVE
1 praktisch
□ This knife's very handy. Dieses Messer ist sehr praktisch.
2 zur Hand
□ Have you got a pen handy? Hast du einen Schreiber zur Hand?

★ **to hang** VERB
1 aufhängen [35] (PERFECT TENSE hat aufgehängt)
□ Riley hung the painting on the wall. Riley hängte das Bild an der Wand auf.
2 hängen [35]
□ They hanged the criminal. Sie hängten den Verbrecher.

to hang around VERB
rumhängen [35] (IMPERFECT hing rum, PERFECT TENSE hat rumgehangen)
□ On Saturdays we hang around in the park. Samstags hängen wir im Park rum.

to hang on VERB
warten [2]
□ Hang on a minute, please. Bitte warte einen Moment.

h

hanger – haunted

to **hang up** VERB
aufhängen [35] (*clothes*)
□ Hang your jacket up on the hook. Häng deine Jacke am Haken auf. □ I tried to phone him but he hung up on me. Ich habe versucht, mit ihm zu telefonieren, aber er hat einfach aufgelegt.
auflegen [4] (*phone*)

hanger NOUN
der Bügel *masc* (PL die Bügel) (*for clothes*)

hang-gliding NOUN
das Drachenfliegen *neut*
■ **to go hang-gliding** Drachenfliegen gehen [29]

hangover NOUN
der Kater *masc* (PL die Kater)
□ to have a hangover einen Kater haben

Hanukkah NOUN
Hanukkah *neut*

to **happen** VERB
passieren [76] (PERFECT TENSE ist passiert)
□ What's happened? Was ist passiert?
■ **as it happens** zufälligerweise □ As it happens I saw him yesterday. Zufälligerweise habe ich ihn gestern gesehen.

happily ADVERB
1 fröhlich
□ 'Don't worry!' he said happily. 'Mach dir keine Sorgen!' sagte er fröhlich.
2 zum Glück (*fortunately*)
□ Happily, everything went well. Zum Glück ging alles gut.

happiness NOUN
das Glück *neut*

★ **happy** ADJECTIVE
glücklich
□ Jessica looks happy. Jessica sieht glücklich aus.
■ **I'm very happy with your work.** Ich bin sehr zufrieden mit Ihrer Arbeit.
■ **Happy birthday!** Herzlichen Glückwunsch zum Geburtstag!

> **WORD POWER**
> You can use a number of other words instead of **happy** to mean 'glad':
> **cheerful** fröhlich
> □ a cheerful little boy ein fröhlicher kleiner Junge
> **delighted** erfreut
> □ a delighted smile ein erfreutes Lächeln
> **glad** froh
> □ to be glad froh sein
> **satisfied** zufrieden
> □ a satisfied customer ein zufriedener Kunde

★ **harbour** (US **harbor**) NOUN
der Hafen *masc* (PL die Häfen)

★ **hard** ADJECTIVE, ADVERB
1 hart
□ This cheese is very hard. Dieser Käse ist sehr

hart. □ He's worked very hard. Er hat sehr hart gearbeitet.
2 schwierig
□ This question's too hard for me. Diese Frage ist für mich zu schwierig.

hard disk NOUN
die Festplatte *fem* (*of computer*)

★ **hardly** ADVERB
kaum
□ I've hardly got any money. Ich habe kaum Geld. □ I hardly know you. Ich kenne Sie kaum.
■ **hardly ever** fast nie

hard up ADJECTIVE
pleite

hardware NOUN
die Hardware *fem*

hare NOUN
der Feldhase *masc* (GEN des Feldhasen, PL die Feldhasen)

★ to **harm** VERB
■ **to harm somebody** jemandem wehtun [81]
□ I didn't mean to harm you. Ich wollte Ihnen nicht wehtun.
■ **to harm something** einer Sache schaden [54] □ Chemicals harm the environment. Chemikalien schaden der Umwelt.

harmful ADJECTIVE
schädlich
□ harmful chemicals schädliche Chemikalien

harmless ADJECTIVE
harmlos
□ Most spiders are harmless. Die meisten Spinnen sind harmlos.

harsh ADJECTIVE
1 hart
□ He deserves a harsh punishment. Er verdient es, hart bestraft zu werden.
2 rau
□ She's got a very harsh voice. Sie hat eine sehr raue Stimme.

harvest NOUN
die Ernte *fem*

has VERB ▷ *see* have

hashtag NOUN
der Hashtag *masc* (PL die Hashtags) (*on Twitter*)

hasn't = has not

★ **hat** NOUN
der Hut *masc* (PL die Hüte)

★ to **hate** VERB
hassen [31]
□ I hate maths. Ich hasse Mathe.

hatred NOUN
der Hass *masc* (GEN des Hasses)

haunted ADJECTIVE
■ **This house is haunted.** In diesem Haus spukt es.

★ **to have** VERB

1 haben [32] (PRESENT TENSE hat, IMPERFECT hatte, PERFECT TENSE hat gehabt)

□ Have you got a sister? Hast du eine Schwester? □ He has blue eyes. Er hat blaue Augen. □ I've got a cold. Ich habe eine Erkältung.

> The perfect tense of most verbs is formed with **haben**.

□ They have eaten. Sie haben gegessen. □ Have you done your homework? Hast du deine Hausaufgaben gemacht?

> Questions like 'hasn't he?' don't exist in German.

□ He's done it, hasn't he? Er hat es getan, nicht wahr?

> 'have' is not translated when it is used in place of another verb.

□ Have you got any money? — No, I haven't. Hast du Geld? — Nein. □ Does she have any pets? — Yes, she has. Hat sie Haustiere? — Ja. □ He hasn't done his homework. — Yes, he has. Er hat seine Hausaufgaben nicht gemacht. — Doch.

2 sein [65] (PRESENT TENSE ist, IMPERFECT war, PERFECT TENSE ist gewesen)

> The perfect tense of some verbs is formed with **sein**.

□ They have arrived. Sie sind angekommen. □ Has he gone? Ist er gegangen?

> 'have' plus noun is sometimes translated by a German verb.

□ He had his breakfast. Er hat gefrühstückt. □ to have a shower duschen □ to have a bath baden

■ **to have got to do something** etwas tun müssen [51] □ She's got to do it. Sie muss es tun.

■ **to have a party** eine Party machen [48]

■ **I had my hair cut yesterday.** Ich habe mir gestern die Haare schneiden lassen [42].

haven't = have not

hay NOUN
das Heu neut

hay fever NOUN
der Heuschnupfen masc

□ Do you get hay fever? Hast du manchmal Heuschnupfen?

hazelnut NOUN
die Haselnuss fem (PL die Haselnüsse)

★ **he** PRONOUN
er

□ He loves dogs. Er liebt Hunde.

★ **head** NOUN
▷ see also **head** VERB

1 der Kopf masc (PL die Köpfe) (of person)

□ I have a sore head. Ich habe Kopfschmerzen.

2 der Rektor masc (PL die Rektoren)
die Rektorin fem (of private or primary school)

3 der Direktor masc (PL die Direktoren)
die Direktorin fem (of state secondary school)

4 das Oberhaupt neut (PL die Oberhäupter) (leader)

□ a head of state ein Staatsoberhaupt

■ **Heads or tails? — Heads.** Kopf oder Zahl? — Kopf.

★ **to head** VERB
▷ see also **head** NOUN

■ **to head for something** auf etwas zugehen [29] □ He headed straight for the kitchen. Er ging direkt auf die Küche zu.

★ **headache** NOUN
die Kopfschmerzen masc pl

□ I've got a headache. Ich habe Kopfschmerzen.

headlight NOUN
der Scheinwerfer masc (PL die Scheinwerfer)

★ **headline** NOUN
die Schlagzeile fem

headmaster NOUN

1 der Rektor masc (PL die Rektoren) (of private or primary school)

2 der Direktor masc (PL die Direktoren) (of state secondary school)

headmistress NOUN

1 die Rektorin fem (of private or primary school)

2 die Direktorin fem (of state secondary school)

headphones PL NOUN
der Kopfhörer masc (PL die Kopfhörer)

□ a set of headphones ein Kopfhörer

★ **headquarters** PL NOUN
das Hauptquartier neut

□ The bank's headquarters are in London. Das Hauptquartier der Bank ist in London.

headteacher NOUN

1 der Rektor masc (PL die Rektoren)
die Rektorin fem (of private or primary school)

2 der Direktor masc (PL die Direktoren)
die Direktorin fem (of state secondary school)

★ **to heal** VERB

1 heilen [38] (PERFECT TENSE hat geheilt)
□ She healed her. Sie hat sie geheilt.

2 heilen [38] (PERFECT TENSE ist geheilt)
□ He healed very quickly. Er ist sehr schnell geheilt.

★ **health** NOUN
die Gesundheit fem

★ **healthy** ADJECTIVE
gesund

□ My grandparents are still very healthy. Meine Großeltern sind immer noch ganz gesund. □ a healthy diet eine gesunde Ernährung

h

heap - helpful

heap NOUN

der Haufen *masc* (PL die Haufen)
□ a rubbish heap ein Müllhaufen

★ **to hear** VERB

hören [38]
□ He heard the dog bark. Er hörte den Hund bellen. □ She can't hear very well. Sie hört nicht gut. □ I heard that she was ill. Ich habe gehört, dass sie krank war. □ Did you hear the good news? Hast du die gute Nachricht gehört?

■ **to hear about something** von etwas hören [38]

■ **to hear from somebody** von jemandem hören [38] □ I haven't heard from him recently. Ich habe in letzter Zeit nichts von ihm gehört.

★ **heart** NOUN

das Herz *neut* (GEN des Herzens, PL die Herzen)

■ **to learn something by heart** etwas auswendig lernen [38]

■ **the ace of hearts** das Herzass

heart attack NOUN

der Herzinfarkt *masc* (PL die Herzinfarkte)

heartbroken ADJECTIVE

zutiefst betrübt

★ **heat** NOUN

▷ see also **heat** VERB
die Hitze *fem*

★ **to heat** VERB

▷ see also **heat** NOUN
erhitzen [7] (PERFECT TENSE hat erhitzt)
□ Heat gently for five minutes. Erhitzen Sie es bei schwacher Hitze fünf Minuten lang.

to heat up VERB

1 aufwärmen [4] (cooked food)
□ He heated the soup up. Er hat die Suppe aufgewärmt.

2 heiß werden [91] (water, oven)
□ The water is heating up. Das Wasser wird heiß.

heater NOUN

der Heizofen *masc* (PL die Heizöfen)
□ an electric heater ein elektrischer Heizofen

heather NOUN

das Heidekraut *neut* (PL die Heidekräuter)

heating NOUN

die Heizung *fem*

heaven NOUN

der Himmel *masc* (PL die Himmel)

heavily ADVERB

schwer
□ The car was heavily loaded. Das Auto war schwer beladen.

■ **He drinks heavily.** Er trinkt viel.

■ **It was raining heavily.** Es regnete stark.

★ **heavy** ADJECTIVE

1 schwer
□ This bag's very heavy. Diese Tasche ist sehr schwer.

■ **heavy rain** starker Regen

2 anstrengend (busy)
□ I've got a very heavy week ahead. Ich habe eine anstrengende Woche vor mir.

■ **to be a heavy drinker** viel trinken [80]

he'd = he would, he had

hedge NOUN

die Hecke *fem*

hedgehog NOUN

der Igel *masc* (PL die Igel)

heel NOUN

der Absatz *masc* (GEN des Absatzes, PL die Absätze)

★ **height** NOUN

1 die Größe *fem* (of person)

2 die Höhe *fem* (of object, mountain)

heir NOUN

der Erbe *masc* (GEN des Erben, PL die Erben)

heiress NOUN

die Erbin *fem*

held VERB ▷ see **hold**

★ **helicopter** NOUN

der Hubschrauber *masc* (PL die Hubschrauber)

★ **hell** NOUN

die Hölle *fem*

■ **Hell!** Mist! (informal)

he'll = he will, he shall

★ **hello** EXCLAMATION

hallo

helmet NOUN

der Helm *masc* (PL die Helme)

★ **to help** VERB

▷ see also **help** NOUN
helfen [37] (PRESENT TENSE hilft, IMPERFECT half, PERFECT TENSE hat geholfen)

■ **to help somebody** jemandem helfen [37]
□ Can you help me? Kannst du mir helfen?

■ **Help!** Hilfe!

■ **Help yourself!** Bedienen Sie sich!

■ **He can't help it.** Er kann nichts dafür.

★ **help** NOUN

▷ see also **help** VERB
die Hilfe *fem*
□ Do you need any help? Brauchst du Hilfe?

help desk NOUN

der Helpdesk *masc* (PL die Helpdesks)

■ **an IT help desk** ein IT-Helpdesk

helpful ADJECTIVE

hilfreich
□ a helpful suggestion ein hilfreicher Vorschlag

■ **He was very helpful.** Er war eine große Hilfe.

helpline NOUN
> die Telefonberatung *fem*
■ **a customer helpline** ein Kundentelefon

help menu NOUN
> das Hilfemenü *neut* (PL die Hilfemenüs)

hen NOUN
> die Henne *fem*

★ **her** ADJECTIVE
> ▷ see also **her** PRONOUN
> ihr
> □ her father ihr Vater □ her mother ihre Mutter
> □ her child ihr Kind □ her parents ihre Eltern

> Do not use **ihr** with parts of the body.

> □ She's going to wash her hair. Sie wäscht sich
> die Haare. □ She's cleaning her teeth. Sie putzt
> sich die Zähne. □ She's hurt her foot. Sie hat
> sich am Fuß verletzt.

★ **her** PRONOUN
> ▷ see also **her** ADJECTIVE
> **1** sie
> □ I can see her. Ich kann sie sehen. □ Look at
> her! Sieh sie an! □ It's her again. Sie ist es schon
> wieder. □ I'm older than her. Ich bin älter als sie.

> Use **sie** after prepositions which take the
> accusative.

> □ I was thinking of her. Ich habe an sie gedacht.
> **2** ihr

> Use **ihr** after prepositions which take the
> dative.

> □ I'm going with her. Ich gehe mit ihr mit. □ He
> sat next to her. Er saß neben ihr.

> Use **ihr** when 'her' means 'to her'.

> □ I gave her a book. Ich gab ihr ein Buch. □ I told
> her the truth. Ich habe ihr die Wahrheit gesagt.

herb NOUN
> das Kraut *neut* (PL die Kräuter)

★ **here** ADVERB
> hier
> □ I live here. Ich wohne hier. □ Here's Helen.
> Hier ist Helen. □ Here are the books. Hier sind
> die Bücher. □ Here he is! Da ist er ja!

★ **hero** NOUN
> der Held *masc* (GEN des Helden, PL die Helden)
> □ He's a real hero! Er ist ein echter Held!

heroin NOUN
> das Heroin *neut*

★ **heroine** NOUN
> die Heldin *fem*
> □ the heroine of the novel die Heldin des
> Romans

hers PRONOUN
> **1** ihrer
> □ Is this her coat? — No, hers is black. Ist das
> ihr Mantel? — Nein, ihrer ist schwarz.
> ihre

□ Is this her cup? — No, hers is red. Ist das ihre
Tasse? — Nein, ihre ist rot.
ihres
□ Is this her car? — No, hers is white. Ist das ihr
Auto? — Nein, ihres ist weiß.
2 ihre
□ my parents and hers meine Eltern und ihre □ I
have my reasons and she has hers. Ich habe
meine Gründe und sie hat ihre.
■ **Is this hers?** Gehört das ihr? □ This book is
hers. Dieses Buch gehört ihr. □ Whose is this?
— It's hers. Wem gehört das? — Es gehört ihr.

★ **herself** PRONOUN
1 sich
□ She's hurt herself. Sie hat sich verletzt. □ She
talked mainly about herself. Sie redete
hauptsächlich über sich selbst.
2 selbst
□ She did it herself. Sie hat es selbst gemacht.
■ **by herself** allein □ She doesn't like travelling
by herself. Sie verreist nicht gern allein.

he's = he is, he has

to **hesitate** VERB
zögern [88]

heterosexual ADJECTIVE
heterosexuell

★ **hi** EXCLAMATION
hallo

hiccups PL NOUN
der Schluckauf *masc sing*
□ He had hiccups. Er hatte einen Schluckauf.

★ to **hide** VERB
sich verstecken [7] (PERFECT TENSE hat sich
versteckt)
□ He hid behind a bush. Er versteckte sich
hinter einem Busch.
■ **to hide something** etwas verstecken [7]
□ Sejal hid the present. Sejal hat das Geschenk
versteckt.

hide-and-seek NOUN
■ **to play hide-and-seek** Verstecken spielen
[38]

hideous ADJECTIVE
scheußlich

hi-fi NOUN
die Hi-Fi-Anlage *fem*

★ **high** ADJECTIVE, ADVERB
hoch
□ It's too high. Es ist zu hoch. □ How high is the
wall? Wie hoch ist die Mauer? □ The wall's two
metres high. Die Mauer ist zwei Meter hoch.

> Before a noun or after an article, use **hohe**.

□ She's got a very high voice. Sie hat eine sehr
hohe Stimme. □ a high price ein hoher Preis □ a
high temperature eine hohe Temperatur □ at
high speed mit hoher Geschwindigkeit
■ **It's very high in fat.** Es ist sehr fetthaltig.

h

★ **higher education** NOUN
die Hochschulbildung *fem*

high-heeled ADJECTIVE
- **high-heeled shoes** hochhackige Schuhe

high jump NOUN
der Hochsprung *masc* (PL die Hochsprünge) (*sport*)

★ **highlight** NOUN
▷ *see also* **highlight** VERB
der Höhepunkt *masc* (PL die Höhepunkte)
□ the highlight of the evening der Höhepunkt des Abends

★ to **highlight** VERB
▷ *see also* **highlight** NOUN
markieren [76] (PERFECT TENSE hat markiert)
□ She highlighted the word in yellow. Sie markierte das Wort in Gelb.

highlighter NOUN
der Textmarker *masc* (PL die Textmarker)

high-rise NOUN
das Hochhaus *neut* (GEN des Hochhauses, PL die Hochhäuser)
□ I live in a high-rise. Ich wohne in einem Hochhaus.

high school NOUN
das Gymnasium *neut* (PL die Gymnasien)

to **hijack** VERB
entführen [18] (PERFECT TENSE hat entführt)

hijacker NOUN
der Entführer *masc* (PL die Entführer)
die Entführerin *fem*

hike NOUN
die Wanderung *fem*

hiking NOUN
- **to go hiking** wandern gehen [29]

hilarious ADJECTIVE
urkomisch
□ It was hilarious! Es war urkomisch!

★ **hill** NOUN
der Hügel *masc* (PL die Hügel)
□ She walked up the hill. Sie ging den Hügel hinauf.

hill-walking NOUN
das Bergwandern *neut*
- **to go hill-walking** Bergwanderungen machen [48]

★ **him** PRONOUN
1 ihn
□ I can see him. Ich kann ihn sehen. □ Look at him! Sieh ihn an!

> Use **ihn** after prepositions which take the accusative.

□ I did it for him. Ich habe es für ihn getan.
2 ihm

> Use **ihm** after prepositions which take the dative.

□ I travelled with him. Ich bin mit ihm gereist.
□ I haven't heard from him. Ich habe nichts von ihm gehört.

> Use **ihm** when 'him' means 'to him'.

□ I gave him a book. Ich gab ihm ein Buch. □ I told him the truth. Ich habe ihm die Wahrheit gesagt.
3 er
□ It's him again. Er ist es schon wieder. □ I'm older than him. Ich bin älter als er.

★ **himself** PRONOUN
1 sich
□ He's hurt himself. Er hat sich verletzt. □ He talked mainly about himself. Er redete hauptsächlich über sich selbst.
2 selbst
□ He did it himself. Er hat es selbst gemacht.
- **by himself** allein □ He was travelling by himself. Er reiste allein.

Hindu ADJECTIVE
hinduistisch
- **a Hindu temple** ein Hindutempel *masc*

★ **hint** NOUN
▷ *see also* **hint** VERB
die Andeutung *fem*
□ to drop a hint eine Andeutung machen
- **I can take a hint.** Ich verstehe schon.

★ to **hint** VERB
▷ *see also* **hint** NOUN
andeuten [2] (PERFECT TENSE hat angedeutet)
□ He hinted that I'd passed the exam. Er deutete an, dass ich die Prüfung bestanden hätte.

★ **hip** NOUN
die Hüfte *fem*

hippo NOUN
das Nilpferd *neut* (PL die Nilpferde)

hipster NOUN
der Hipster *masc* (PL die Hipsters)

★ to **hire** VERB
▷ *see also* **hire** NOUN
1 mieten [2]
□ to hire a car ein Auto mieten
2 anstellen [4] (PERFECT TENSE hat angestellt) (*person*)
□ They hired a cleaner. Sie haben eine Putzfrau angestellt.

★ **hire** NOUN
▷ *see also* **hire** VERB
der Verleih *masc* (PL die Verleihe)
- **car hire** der Autoverleih
- **for hire** zu vermieten

hire car NOUN
der Mietwagen *masc* (PL die Mietwagen)

★ **his** ADJECTIVE
▷ *see also* **his** PRONOUN
sein

□ his father sein Vater □ his mother seine Mutter □ his child sein Kind □ his parents seine Eltern

> Do not use sein with parts of the body.

□ He's going to wash his hair. Er wäscht sich die Haare. □ He's cleaning his teeth. Er putzt sich die Zähne. □ He's hurt his foot. Er hat sich am Fuß verletzt.

★ his PRONOUN
▷ see also **his** ADJECTIVE
1 seiner
□ Is this his coat? — No, his is black. Ist das sein Mantel? — Nein, seiner ist schwarz.
seine
□ Is this his cup? — No, his is red. Ist das seine Tasse? — Nein, seine ist rot.
seines
□ Is this his car? — No, his is white. Ist das sein Auto? — Nein, seines ist weiß.
2 seine
□ my parents and his meine Eltern und seine □ I have my reasons and he has his. Ich habe meine Gründe und er hat seine.
■ **Is this his?** Gehört das ihm? □ This book is his. Dieses Buch gehört ihm. □ Whose is this? — It's his. Wem gehört das? — Das gehört ihm.

★ history NOUN
die Geschichte *fem*

★ to hit VERB
▷ see also **hit** NOUN
1 schlagen [59] (PRESENT TENSE schlägt, IMPERFECT schlug, PERFECT TENSE hat geschlagen)
□ Andrew hit him. Andrew hat ihn geschlagen.
2 anfahren [21] (PRESENT TENSE fährt an, IMPERFECT fuhr an, PERFECT TENSE hat angefahren)
□ He was hit by a car. Er wurde von einem Auto angefahren.
3 treffen [78] (PRESENT TENSE trifft, IMPERFECT traf, PERFECT TENSE hat getroffen)
□ The arrow hit the target. Der Pfeil traf sein Ziel.

★ hit NOUN
▷ see also **hit** VERB
1 der Hit *masc* (PL die Hits) (*song*)
□ their latest hit ihr neuester Hit
2 der Erfolg *masc* (PL die Erfolge) (*success*)
□ The film was a massive hit. Der Film war ein enormer Erfolg.

hitch NOUN
das Problem *neut* (PL die Probleme)
□ a slight hitch ein kleines Problem

to hitchhike VERB
per Anhalter fahren [21] (PRESENT TENSE fährt, IMPERFECT fuhr, PERFECT TENSE ist gefahren)

hitchhiker NOUN
der Anhalter *masc* (PL die Anhalter)
die Anhalterin *fem*

hitchhiking NOUN
das Trampen *neut*
□ Hitchhiking can be dangerous. Trampen kann gefährlich sein.

hit man NOUN
der Killer *masc* (PL die Killer)

HIV-negative ADJECTIVE
HIV-negativ

HIV-positive ADJECTIVE
HIV-positiv

hobby NOUN
das Hobby *neut* (PL die Hobbys)
□ What are your hobbies? Welche Hobbys haben Sie?

hockey NOUN
das Hockey *neut*
□ I play hockey. Ich spiele Hockey.

★ to hold VERB
1 halten [33] (PRESENT TENSE hält, IMPERFECT hielt, PERFECT TENSE hat gehalten) (*hold on to*)
□ Hold this end of the rope, please. Halt bitte dieses Ende des Seils.
■ **She held a bottle in her hand.** Sie hatte eine Flasche in der Hand.
2 fassen [31] (*contain*)
□ This bottle holds two litres. Diese Flasche fasst zwei Liter.
■ **to hold a meeting** eine Versammlung abhalten [33]
■ **Hold it!** (*wait*) Moment!
■ **to get hold of something** (*obtain*) etwas bekommen [40] □ I couldn't get hold of it. Ich habe es nicht bekommen.

to hold on VERB
1 sich festhalten [33] (PRESENT TENSE hält sich fest, IMPERFECT hielt sich fest, PERFECT TENSE hat sich festgehalten) (*keep hold*)
□ The cliff was slippery, but he managed to hold on. Die Klippe war rutschig, aber er konnte sich festhalten.
■ **to hold on to something** **1** sich an etwas klammern [34] □ He held on to the railing. Er klammerte sich an das Geländer. **2** etwas behalten [33] □ He held on to the book, just in case. Er hat das Buch vorsichtshalber behalten.
2 warten [2] (*wait*)
□ Hold on, I'm coming! Warte, ich komme!
■ **Hold on!** (*on telephone*) Bleiben Sie am Apparat!

to hold up VERB
■ **to hold up one's hand** die Hand heben □ I held up my hand. Ich hob die Hand.
■ **to hold somebody up** (*delay*) jemanden aufhalten [33] □ I was held up at the office. Ich wurde im Büro aufgehalten.
■ **to hold up a bank** (*rob*) eine Bank überfallen [22]

h

hold-up – hook

hold-up NOUN
1 der Überfall *masc* (PL die Überfälle) (*at bank*)
2 die Verzögerung *fem* (*delay*)
3 der Stau *masc* (PL die Staus) (*traffic jam*)

★ **hole** NOUN
das Loch *neut* (PL die Löcher)

★ **holiday** NOUN
1 die Ferien *pl* (*from school*)
 □ Did you have a good holiday? Hattet ihr
 schöne Ferien?
 ■ **on holiday** in den Ferien
 ■ **to go on holiday** in die Ferien fahren
 ■ **We are on holiday.** Wir haben Ferien.
 ■ **the school holidays** die Schulferien
2 der Urlaub *masc* (PL die Urlaube) (*from work*)
 □ Did you have a good holiday? Hattet ihr einen
 schönen Urlaub?
 ■ **on holiday** im Urlaub □ We are on holiday.
 Wir sind im Urlaub.
 ■ **to go on holiday** in Urlaub fahren
3 der Feiertag *masc* (PL die Feiertage) (*public
 holiday*)
 □ Next Wednesday is a holiday. Nächsten
 Mittwoch ist ein Feiertag.
4 der freie Tag *masc* (PL die freien Tage) (*day off*)
 ■ **He took a day's holiday.** Er nahm einen Tag
 frei.
 ■ **a holiday camp** ein Ferienlager *neut*
 ■ **a holiday home** eine Ferienwohnung *fem*

★ **Holland** NOUN
Holland *neut*
 ■ **from Holland** aus Holland
 ■ **in Holland** in Holland
 ■ **to Holland** nach Holland

hollow ADJECTIVE
hohl

holly NOUN
die Stechpalme *fem*

★ **holy** ADJECTIVE
heilig

★ **home** NOUN
▷ *see also* **home** ADVERB
das Zuhause *neut* (GEN des Zuhause)
 ■ **at home** zu Hause
 ■ **Make yourself at home.** Machen Sie es sich
 bequem.

★ **home** ADVERB
▷ *see also* **home** NOUN
1 zu Hause
 □ to be at home zu Hause sein
2 nach Hause
 □ to go home nach Hause gehen
 ■ **to get home** nach Hause kommen [40]
 □ What time did he get home? Wann ist er nach
 Hause gekommen?

home address NOUN
die Adresse *fem*
 □ What's your home address? Wie ist Ihre
 Adresse?

homeland NOUN
das Heimatland *neut* (PL die Heimatländer)

★ **homeless** ADJECTIVE
obdachlos
 ■ **homeless people** die Obdachlosen *masc pl*

home match NOUN
das Heimspiel *neut* (PL die Heimspiele)

homeopathy NOUN
die Homöopathie *fem*

★ **home page** NOUN
die Homepage *fem* (PL die Homepages)
(*internet*)

homesick ADJECTIVE
 ■ **to be homesick** Heimweh haben [32]

★ **homework** NOUN
die Hausaufgaben *fem pl*
 □ Have you done your homework? Hast du
 deine Hausaufgaben gemacht? □ my geography
 homework meine Erdkundeaufgaben

homosexual ADJECTIVE
▷ *see also* **homosexual** NOUN
homosexuell

homosexual NOUN
▷ *see also* **homosexual** ADJECTIVE
der Homosexuelle *masc* (GEN des
Homosexuellen, PL die Homosexuellen)
die Homosexuelle *fem*

★ **honest** ADJECTIVE
ehrlich
 □ She's an honest person. Sie ist ein ehrlicher
 Mensch. □ He was honest with her. Er war
 ehrlich zu ihr.

honestly ADVERB
ehrlich
 □ I honestly don't know. Ich weiß es ehrlich
 nicht.

honesty NOUN
die Ehrlichkeit *fem*

honey NOUN
der Honig *masc*

honeymoon NOUN
die Flitterwochen *fem pl*

★ **honour** (US **honor**) NOUN
die Ehre *fem*

hood NOUN
1 die Kapuze *fem*
 □ a coat with a hood ein Mantel mit Kapuze
2 die Motorhaube *fem* (US: *of car*)

★ **hook** NOUN
der Haken *masc* (PL die Haken)
 □ He hung the painting on the hook. Er hängte
 das Bild an den Haken.
 ■ **to take the phone off the hook** das Telefon
 aushängen [35]
 ■ **a fish hook** ein Angelhaken

★ = core vocabulary

hooligan NOUN
der Rowdy masc (PL die Rowdys)

hooray EXCLAMATION
hurra

Hoover® NOUN
der Staubsauger masc (PL die Staubsauger)

to hoover VERB
staubsaugen [38]
□ She hoovered the lounge. Sie hat im Wohnzimmer gestaubsaugt.

to hop VERB
hüpfen [38] (PERFECT TENSE ist gehüpft)

to hope VERB
▷ see also hope NOUN
hoffen [38]
□ I hope he comes. Ich hoffe, er kommt. □ I'm hoping for good exam results. Ich hoffe, dass ich gute Noten bekomme.
■ I hope so. Hoffentlich.
■ I hope not. Hoffentlich nicht.

hope NOUN
▷ see also hope VERB
die Hoffnung fem
■ to give up hope die Hoffnung aufgeben [28]
□ Don't give up hope! Gib die Hoffnung nicht auf!

hopeful ADJECTIVE
1 zuversichtlich
□ I'm hopeful. Ich bin zuversichtlich.
■ He's hopeful of winning. Er rechnet sich Gewinnchancen aus.
2 aussichtsreich (situation)
■ The future looks hopeful. Die Zukunft sieht gut aus.

hopefully ADVERB
hoffentlich
□ Hopefully he'll make it in time. Hoffentlich schafft er es noch.

hopeless ADJECTIVE
hoffnungslos
□ I'm hopeless at maths. In Mathe bin ich ein hoffnungsloser Fall.

horizon NOUN
der Horizont masc (PL die Horizonte)

horizontal ADJECTIVE
horizontal

horn NOUN
1 die Hupe fem (of car)
■ He sounded his horn. Er hat gehupt.
2 das Horn neut (PL die Hörner) (of instrument, animal)
□ I play the horn. Ich spiele Horn.

horoscope NOUN
das Horoskop neut (PL die Horoskope)

horrible ADJECTIVE
furchtbar
□ What a horrible dress! Was für ein furchtbares Kleid!

to horrify VERB
entsetzen [18]
□ I was horrified by the news. Ich war über die Neuigkeiten entsetzt.

horrifying ADJECTIVE
schrecklich
□ a horrifying accident ein schrecklicher Unfall

★ **horror** NOUN
der Horror masc

horror film NOUN
der Horrorfilm masc (PL die Horrorfilme)

★ **horse** NOUN
das Pferd neut (PL die Pferde)

horse-racing NOUN
das Pferderennen neut (PL die Pferderennen)

horseshoe NOUN
das Hufeisen neut (PL die Hufeisen)

hose NOUN
der Schlauch masc (PL die Schläuche)
□ a garden hose ein Gartenschlauch

> **BE CAREFUL!**
> Do not translate **hose** by the German word Hose.

hosepipe NOUN
der Schlauch masc (PL die Schläuche)

★ **hospital** NOUN
das Krankenhaus neut (GEN des Krankenhauses, PL die Krankenhäuser)
□ Take me to the hospital! Bringen Sie mich ins Krankenhaus! □ in hospital im Krankenhaus

hospitality NOUN
die Gastfreundschaft fem

host NOUN
1 der Gastgeber masc (PL die Gastgeber)
die Gastgeberin fem
2 der Moderator masc (PL die Moderatoren)
die Moderatorin fem (television)

★ **hostage** NOUN
die Geisel fem
□ to take somebody hostage jemanden als Geisel nehmen

hostel NOUN
die Herberge fem

hostile ADJECTIVE
feindlich

★ **hot** ADJECTIVE
1 heiß (warm)
□ a hot bath ein heißes Bad □ a hot country ein heißes Land □ It's hot. Es ist heiß. □ It's very hot today. Heute ist es sehr heiß.

> When you talk about a person being 'hot', you use the impersonal construction.

□ I'm hot. Mir ist heiß. □ I'm too hot. Mir ist es zu heiß.

h

hot dog – hunting

2 scharf (*spicy*)
□ a very hot curry ein sehr scharfes Curry

hot dog NOUN
der Hotdog *masc* (PL die Hotdogs)

★ **hotel** NOUN
das Hotel *neut* (PL die Hotels)
□ We stayed in a hotel. Wir haben in einem Hotel übernachtet.

★ **hour** NOUN
die Stunde *fem*
□ She always takes hours to get ready. Sie braucht immer Stunden, bis sie fertig ist.
■ **a quarter of an hour** eine Viertelstunde
■ **half an hour** eine halbe Stunde
■ **two and a half hours** zweieinhalb Stunden

hourly ADJECTIVE, ADVERB
stündlich
□ There are hourly buses. Der Bus verkehrt stündlich.
■ **to be paid hourly** stundenweise bezahlt werden [91]

★ **house** NOUN
das Haus *neut* (GEN des Hauses, PL die Häuser)
■ **at his house** bei ihm zu Hause
■ **We stayed at their house.** Wir haben bei ihnen übernachtet.

housewife NOUN
die Hausfrau *fem*
□ She's a housewife. Sie ist Hausfrau.

housework NOUN
die Hausarbeit *fem*
□ to do the housework die Hausarbeit machen

hovercraft NOUN
das Luftkissenfahrzeug *neut* (PL die Luftkissenfahrzeuge)

★ **how** ADVERB
wie
□ How old are you? Wie alt bist du? □ How far is it to Edinburgh? Wie weit ist es nach Edinburgh? □ How long have you been here? Wie lange sind Sie schon hier? □ How are you? Wie geht's?
■ **How much?** Wie viel? □ How much sugar do you want? Wie viel Zucker willst du?
■ **How many?** Wie viele? □ How many girls are there in the class? Wie viele Mädchen sind in der Klasse?

★ **however** CONJUNCTION
aber
□ This, however, isn't true. Das ist aber nicht wahr.

to howl VERB
heulen [38]

HTML ABBREVIATION (= *hypertext markup language*)
HTML

to hug VERB
▷ *see also* **hug** NOUN

umarmen [7] (PERFECT TENSE hat umarmt)
□ He hugged her. Er umarmte sie.

hug NOUN
▷ *see also* **hug** VERB
■ **to give somebody a hug** jemanden umarmen [7] □ She gave them a hug. Sie umarmte sie.

★ **huge** ADJECTIVE
riesig

to hum VERB
summen [38]
□ She hummed to herself. Sie summte vor sich hin.

★ **human** ADJECTIVE
menschlich
□ the human body der menschliche Körper

human being NOUN
der Mensch *masc* (GEN des Menschen, PL die Menschen)

humble ADJECTIVE
bescheiden

★ **humour** (US **humor**) NOUN
der Humor *masc*
■ **to have a good sense of humour** viel Humor haben [32]

★ **hundred** NUMBER
■ **a hundred** einhundert □ a hundred euros einhundert Euro
■ **five hundred** fünfhundert
■ **five hundred and one** fünfhundertundeins
■ **hundreds of people** Hunderte von Menschen

hung VERB ▷ *see* **hang**

Hungarian ADJECTIVE
ungarisch

Hungary NOUN
Ungarn *neut*
■ **from Hungary** aus Ungarn
■ **to Hungary** nach Ungarn

hunger NOUN
der Hunger *masc*

hungry ADJECTIVE
■ **to be hungry** Hunger haben [32] □ I'm hungry. Ich habe Hunger.

to hunt VERB
jagen [38]
□ It is illegal to hunt foxes. Es ist verboten, Füchse zu jagen.
■ **to go hunting** auf die Jagd gehen [29]
■ **The police are hunting the killer.** Die Polizei sucht den Mörder.
■ **to hunt for something** (*search*) nach etwas suchen [48] □ I hunted everywhere for that book. Ich habe überall nach diesem Buch gesucht.

hunting NOUN
das Jagen *neut*

★ = core vocabulary

□ I'm against hunting. Ich bin gegen Jagen.
■ **fox-hunting** die Fuchsjagd □ Fox-hunting is illegal. Die Fuchsjagd ist verboten.

hurdle NOUN
die Hürde _fem_
□ the 100 metres hurdles die 100 Meter Hürden

hurricane NOUN
der Orkan _masc_ (PL die Orkane)

to **hurry** VERB
▷ see also **hurry** NOUN
eilen [38] (PERFECT TENSE ist geeilt)
□ Amber hurried back home. Amber eilte nach Hause.
■ **Hurry up!** Beeil dich!

hurry NOUN
▷ see also **hurry** VERB
■ **to be in a hurry** in Eile sein [65]
■ **to do something in a hurry** etwas auf die Schnelle machen [48]
■ **There's no hurry.** Das eilt nicht.

★ to **hurt** VERB
▷ see also **hurt** ADJECTIVE
wehtun [81] (IMPERFECT tat weh, PERFECT TENSE hat wehgetan)
□ That hurts. Das tut weh. □ My leg hurts. Mein Bein tut weh. □ It hurts to have a tooth out. Es tut weh, wenn einem ein Zahn gezogen wird.
■ **to hurt somebody 1** jemandem wehtun [81] □ You're hurting me! Du tust mir weh!

2 (_offend_) jemanden verletzen [36] □ His remarks hurt me. Seine Bemerkungen haben mich verletzt.
■ **to hurt oneself** sich wehtun [81] □ I fell over and hurt myself. Ich bin hingefallen und habe mir wehgetan.

★ **hurt** ADJECTIVE
▷ see also **hurt** VERB
verletzt
□ Is he badly hurt? Ist er schlimm verletzt? □ He was hurt in the leg. Er hatte ein verletztes Bein. □ Luckily, nobody got hurt. Zum Glück wurde niemand verletzt. □ I was hurt by what he said. Was er sagte hat mich verletzt.

★ **husband** NOUN
der Ehemann _masc_ (PL die Ehemänner)

hut NOUN
die Hütte _fem_

hybrid ADJECTIVE
hybrid
■ **a hybrid car** ein Hybridauto

hymn NOUN
das Kirchenlied _neut_ (PL die Kirchenlieder)

hypermarket NOUN
der Verbrauchermarkt _masc_ (PL die Verbrauchermärkte)

hyphen NOUN
der Bindestrich _masc_ (PL die Bindestriche)

I i

★ **I** PRONOUN
ich
□ I speak German. Ich spreche Deutsch. □ Alex and I Alex und ich

★ **ice** NOUN
1 das Eis neut
■ There was ice on the lake. Der See war gefroren.
2 das Glatteis neut (on road)

iceberg NOUN
der Eisberg masc (PL die Eisberge)

icebox NOUN (US)
der Kühlschrank masc (PL die Kühlschränke)

★ **ice cream** NOUN
das Eis neut (PL die Eis)
□ vanilla ice cream das Vanilleeis

ice cube NOUN
der Eiswürfel masc (PL die Eiswürfel)

ice hockey NOUN
das Eishockey neut

Iceland NOUN
Island neut
■ from Iceland aus Island
■ to Iceland nach Island

ice lolly NOUN
das Eis am Stiel neut

ice rink NOUN
die Eisbahn fem

ice-skating NOUN
das Schlittschuhlaufen neut
■ I like ice-skating. Ich laufe gern Schlittschuh.
■ to go ice-skating Schlittschuh laufen gehen [29]

icing NOUN
der Zuckerguss masc (GEN des Zuckergusses, PL Zuckergüsse) (on cake)
■ icing sugar der Puderzucker

icon NOUN
das Icon neut (PL die Icons) (computer)
□ to click on an icon ein Icon anklicken

ICT NOUN (= Information and Communications Technology)
die IuK (= Informations- und Kommunikationstechnik)

icy ADJECTIVE
eiskalt

□ There was an icy wind. Es wehte ein eiskalter Wind.
■ The roads are icy. Die Straßen sind vereist.

I'd = I had, I would

★ **idea** NOUN
die Idee fem
□ Good idea! Gute Idee!

★ **ideal** ADJECTIVE
ideal

identical ADJECTIVE
identisch
□ identical to identisch mit

identification NOUN
die Identifikation fem
■ Have you got any identification? Können Sie sich ausweisen?

★ to **identify** VERB
identifizieren [76] (PERFECT TENSE hat identifiziert)

identity card NOUN
der Personalausweis masc (PL die Personalausweise)

idiom NOUN
die Redewendung fem

idiot NOUN
der Idiot masc (GEN des Idioten, PL die Idioten)
die Idiotin fem

idiotic ADJECTIVE
idiotisch

idle ADJECTIVE
faul (lazy)
□ to be idle faul sein
■ idle gossip sinnloses Geschwätz
■ I asked out of idle curiosity. Ich habe aus reiner Neugier gefragt.

i.e. ABBREVIATION
d. h. (= das heißt)

★ **if** CONJUNCTION
1 wenn
□ You can have it if you like. Wenn du willst, kannst du es haben.
2 ob (whether)
□ Do you know if he's there? Weißt du, ob er da ist?
■ if only wenn doch nur □ If only I had more money! Wenn ich doch nur mehr Geld hätte!

★ = core vocabulary

■ **if not** falls nicht □ Are you coming? If not, I'll go with Zhu. Kommst du? Falls nicht, gehe ich mit Zhu.

ignorant ADJECTIVE
unwissend

★ to **ignore** VERB
1 nicht beachten [2] (PERFECT TENSE hat nicht beachtet)
□ She ignored my advice. Sie hat meinen Rat nicht beachtet.
2 ignorieren [76] (PERFECT TENSE hat ignoriert)
□ She saw me, but she ignored me. Sie sah mich, hat mich aber ignoriert.
■ **Just ignore him!** Beachte ihn einfach nicht!

★ **ill** ADJECTIVE
krank (*sick*)
■ **to be taken ill** krank werden [91] □ She was taken ill while on holiday. Sie wurde im Urlaub krank.

I'll = I will

★ **illegal** ADJECTIVE
illegal

illegible ADJECTIVE
unleserlich

★ **illness** NOUN
die Krankheit *fem*

to **ill-treat** VERB
misshandeln [88] (PERFECT TENSE hat misshandelt)

illusion NOUN
die Illusion *fem*

★ **illustration** NOUN
die Illustration *fem*

I'm = I am

★ **image** NOUN
das Image *neut* (GEN des Image, PL die Images) (*public image*)
□ Erin wants to change her image. Erin will ihr Image ändern.

★ **imagination** NOUN
die Fantasie *fem*
□ You need a lot of imagination to be a writer. Als Schriftsteller braucht man viel Fantasie.
■ **It's just your imagination!** Das bildest du dir nur ein!

★ to **imagine** VERB
sich vorstellen [4] (PERFECT TENSE hat sich vorgestellt)
□ Imagine how I felt! Stell dir vor, wie mir zumute war!
■ **Is he angry? — I imagine so.** Ist er böse? — Ich denke schon.

to **imitate** VERB
nachmachen [4] (PERFECT TENSE hat nachgemacht)

imitation NOUN
die Imitation *fem*

★ **immediate** ADJECTIVE
sofortig
□ We need an immediate answer. Wir brauchen eine sofortige Antwort.
■ **in the immediate future** in unmittelbarer Zukunft

★ **immediately** ADVERB
sofort
□ I'll do it immediately. Ich mache es sofort.

★ **immigrant** NOUN
der Einwanderer *masc* (PL die Einwanderer)
die Einwanderin *fem*

immigration NOUN
die Einwanderung *fem*

immoral ADJECTIVE
unmoralisch

immune ADJECTIVE
■ **to be immune to something** gegen etwas immun sein [65] □ She is immune to measles. Sie ist gegen Masern immun.

impartial ADJECTIVE
unparteiisch

impatience NOUN
die Ungeduld *fem*

impatient ADJECTIVE
ungeduldig
□ People are getting impatient. Die Leute werden ungeduldig.

impersonal ADJECTIVE
unpersönlich

to **implement** VERB
ausführen [4] (PERFECT TENSE hat ausgeführt)
□ The headteacher will implement the plan. Die Direktorin wird den Plan ausführen.

to **imply** VERB
andeuten [2] (PERFECT TENSE hat angedeutet)
□ Are you implying I stole it? Wollen Sie andeuten, ich hätte es gestohlen?

to **import** VERB
importieren [76] (PERFECT TENSE hat importiert)

★ **importance** NOUN
die Wichtigkeit *fem*
□ the importance of a good knowledge of German die Wichtigkeit guter Deutschkenntnisse

★ **important** ADJECTIVE
wichtig

to **impose** VERB
auferlegen [4] (PERFECT TENSE hat auferlegt)
□ to impose a penalty eine Strafe auferlegen

★ **impossible** ADJECTIVE
unmöglich

to **impress** VERB
beeindrucken [7] (PERFECT TENSE hat beeindruckt)
□ She's trying to impress you. Sie will dich beeindrucken.

i

Numbers in brackets refer to verb tables on pages 697 to 706.

489

impressed ADJECTIVE
beeindruckt
□ I'm very impressed! Ich bin sehr beeindruckt!

impression NOUN
der Eindruck *masc* (PL die Eindrücke)
□ I was under the impression that ... Ich hatte den Eindruck, dass ...

impressive ADJECTIVE
beeindruckend

★ to **improve** VERB
1 verbessern [88] (PERFECT TENSE hat verbessert) (*make better*)
□ They have improved the sports facilities. Sie haben die Sporteinrichtungen verbessert.
2 besser werden [91] (PRESENT TENSE wird besser, IMPERFECT wurde besser, PERFECT TENSE ist besser geworden) (*get better*)
□ The weather is improving. Das Wetter wird besser. □ My German has improved. Mein Deutsch ist besser geworden.

★ **improvement** NOUN
1 die Verbesserung *fem* (*of condition*)
□ It's a great improvement. Das ist eine gewaltige Verbesserung.
2 der Fortschritt *masc* (PL die Fortschritte) (*of learner*)
□ There's been an improvement in her physics. Sie hat in Physik Fortschritte gemacht.

★ **in** PREPOSITION, ADVERB

Use the accusative to express movement or a change of place. Use the dative when there is no change of place.

1 in
□ It's in my bag. Es ist in meiner Tasche. □ Put it in my bag. Tu es in meine Tasche. □ I read it in this book. Ich habe es in diesem Buch gelesen. □ Write it in your exercise book. Schreib es in dein Übungsheft. □ in hospital im Krankenhaus □ in school in der Schule □ in Cardiff in Cardiff □ in Germany in Deutschland □ in Switzerland in der Schweiz □ in May im Mai □ in spring im Frühling □ in the rain im Regen □ I'll see you in three weeks. Ich sehe dich in drei Wochen.

Sometimes 'in' is not translated.

□ It happened in 2017. Es geschah 2017. □ in the morning morgens □ in the afternoon nachmittags □ at six in the evening um sechs Uhr abends
2 mit
□ the boy in the blue shirt der Junge mit dem blauen Hemd □ It was written in pencil. Es war mit Bleistift geschrieben. □ in a loud voice mit lauter Stimme □ She paid in dollars. Sie hat mit Dollar bezahlt.
3 auf
□ in German auf Deutsch □ in English auf Englisch

'in' is sometimes translated using the genitive.

□ the best pupil in the class der beste Schüler der Klasse □ the tallest person in the family der Größte der Familie
■ **in the beginning** am Anfang
■ **in the country** auf dem Land
■ **in time** rechtzeitig □ We arrived in time for dinner. Wir kamen rechtzeitig zum Abendessen.
■ **in here** hier drin □ It's hot in here. Hier drin ist es heiß.
■ **one person in ten** einer von zehn
■ **to be in** (*at home, work*) da sein [65] □ He wasn't in. Er war nicht da.
■ **to ask somebody in** jemanden hereinbitten [9]

inaccurate ADJECTIVE
1 ungenau (*not precise*)
□ an inaccurate translation eine ungenaue Übersetzung
2 unrichtig (*not correct*)
□ What he said was inaccurate. Was er sagte war unrichtig.

inadequate ADJECTIVE
unzulänglich

incentive NOUN
die Motivation *fem*
□ There is no incentive to work. Es gibt keine Motivation zu arbeiten.

★ **inch** NOUN
der Zoll *masc* (PL die Zoll)

DID YOU KNOW...?
In Germany measurements are given in metres and centimetres rather than feet and inches. An inch is about 2.5 centimetres.

■ **six inches** fünfzehn Zentimeter

★ **incident** NOUN
der Vorfall *masc* (PL die Vorfälle)

inclined ADJECTIVE
■ **to be inclined to do something** dazu tendieren [76], etwas zu tun □ He's inclined to be lazy. Er tendiert dazu, faul zu sein.

★ to **include** VERB
einschließen (IMPERFECT schloss ein, PERFECT TENSE hat eingeschlossen)
□ Service is not included. Bedienung ist nicht eingeschlossen.

★ **including** PREPOSITION
inklusive
□ That will be two hundred euros, including VAT. Das macht zweihundert Euro, inklusive Mehrwertsteuer.

inclusive ADJECTIVE
■ **from Monday to Thursday inclusive** von Montag bis einschließlich Donnerstag
■ **inclusive of VAT** inklusive Mehrwertsteuer

★ = core vocabulary

income NOUN
das Einkommen *neut* (PL die Einkommen)

income tax NOUN
die Einkommensteuer *fem*

incompetent ADJECTIVE
inkompetent

incomplete ADJECTIVE
unvollständig

inconsistent ADJECTIVE
1 widersprüchlich
  ■ **to be inconsistent with …** im Widerspruch
  stehen [72] zu …
2 unbeständig
  □ Your work is very inconsistent. Die Qualität
  deiner Arbeit ist sehr unbeständig.

inconvenience NOUN
  ■ **I don't want to cause any inconvenience.**
  Ich möchte keine Umstände machen.

inconvenient ADJECTIVE
  ■ **That's very inconvenient for me.** Das passt
  mir gar nicht.

incorrect ADJECTIVE
unrichtig

★ **increase** NOUN
  ▷ *see also* **increase** VERB
  die Zunahme *fem*
  □ an increase in road accidents eine Zunahme
  an Verkehrsunfällen

★ to **increase** VERB
  ▷ *see also* **increase** NOUN
1 zunehmen [52] (PRESENT TENSE nimmt zu,
  IMPERFECT nahm zu, PERFECT TENSE hat
  zugenommen) (*traffic, number*)
  □ Traffic on motorways has increased. Der
  Verkehr auf den Autobahnen hat zugenommen.
2 steigen [74] (IMPERFECT stieg, PERFECT TENSE ist
  gestiegen) (*price, demand*)
  □ with increasing demand bei steigender
  Nachfrage
3 stärker werden [91] (PRESENT TENSE wird stärker,
  IMPERFECT wurde stärker, PERFECT TENSE ist stärker
  geworden) (*pain, wind*)
  ■ **to increase in size** größer werden [91]
  ■ **to increase something** etwas erhöhen [19]
  □ They have increased the price. Sie haben den
  Preis erhöht.
  ■ **increased cost of living** höhere
  Lebenshaltungskosten

★ **incredible** ADJECTIVE
unglaublich

indecisive ADJECTIVE
unentschlossen (*person*)

★ **indeed** ADVERB
wirklich
  □ It's very hard indeed. Es ist wirklich schwer.
  ■ **Know what I mean? — Indeed I do.** Weißt
  du, was ich meine? — Ja, ganz genau.
  ■ **Thank you very much indeed!** Ganz
  herzlichen Dank!

★ **independence** NOUN
die Unabhängigkeit *fem*

★ **independent** ADJECTIVE
unabhängig
  ■ **an independent school** eine Privatschule

★ **index** NOUN
das Verzeichnis *neut* (GEN des Verzeichnisses, PL
die Verzeichnisse) (*in book*)

India NOUN
Indien *neut*
  ■ **from India** aus Indien
  ■ **to India** nach Indien

Indian ADJECTIVE
  ▷ *see also* **Indian** NOUN
1 indisch
2 indianisch (*American Indian*)

Indian NOUN
  ▷ *see also* **Indian** ADJECTIVE
der Inder *masc* (PL die Inder)
die Inderin *fem* (*person*)
  ■ **an American Indian** ein Indianer *masc*

to **indicate** VERB
1 zeigen [38]
  □ Her exam results indicate how hard she has
  worked all year. Ihre Prüfungsergebnisse
  zeigen, wie hart sie das ganze Jahr über
  gearbeitet hat.
2 andeuten [2] (PERFECT TENSE hat angedeutet)
  (*make known*)
  □ He indicated that he wasn't very pleased with
  her. Er hat angedeutet, dass er ziemlich
  unzufrieden mit ihr war.
3 anzeigen [4] (PERFECT TENSE hat angezeigt)
  (*technical device*)
  □ The thermometer indicated that he had a
  fever. Das Thermometer zeigte an, dass er
  Fieber hatte.
  ■ **to indicate left** links blinken [38]

indicator NOUN
der Blinker *masc* (PL die Blinker) (*in car*)

indigestion NOUN
die Magenverstimmung *fem*
  ■ **I've got indigestion.** Ich habe eine
  Magenverstimmung.

★ **individual** NOUN
  ▷ *see also* **individual** ADJECTIVE
das Individuum *neut* (PL die Individuen)

★ **individual** ADJECTIVE
  ▷ *see also* **individual** NOUN
individuell

indoor ADJECTIVE
  ■ **an indoor swimming pool** ein Hallenbad
  neut

indoors ADVERB
im Haus
  □ They're indoors. Sie sind im Haus.
  ■ **to go indoors** hineingehen [29] □ We'd
  better go indoors. Wir gehen besser hinein.

i

industrial – injure

industrial ADJECTIVE
industriell

industrial estate NOUN
das Industriegebiet *neut* (PL die Industriegebiete)

industry NOUN
die Industrie *fem*
□ the tourist industry die Tourismusindustrie
□ the oil industry die Erdölindustrie
■ **I'd like to work in industry.** Ich würde gern in der freien Wirtschaft arbeiten.

inefficient ADJECTIVE
ineffizient

inevitable ADJECTIVE
unvermeidlich

inexpensive ADJECTIVE
preiswert
□ an inexpensive hotel ein preiswertes Hotel
■ **inexpensive holidays** günstige Ferien

inexperienced ADJECTIVE
unerfahren

infant school NOUN
die Grundschule *fem*

DID YOU KNOW...?
The **Grundschule** is a primary school which children attend from the age of 6 to 10. This is the nearest equivalent to the infant school, which is attended by children from the age of 5 to 7. Many children attend **Kindergarten** before going to the **Grundschule**.

★ **infection** NOUN
die Entzündung *fem*
□ an ear infection eine Ohrenentzündung □ a throat infection eine Halsentzündung

infectious ADJECTIVE
ansteckend
□ It's not infectious. Es ist nicht ansteckend.

infinitive NOUN
der Infinitiv *masc* (PL die Infinitive)

infirmary NOUN
das Krankenhaus *neut* (GEN des Krankenhauses, PL die Krankenhäuser)

inflatable ADJECTIVE
■ **an inflatable mattress** eine Luftmatratze
■ **an inflatable dinghy** ein Gummiboot *neut*

★ **inflation** NOUN
die Inflation *fem*

★ **influence** NOUN
▷ see also **influence** VERB
der Einfluss *masc* (GEN des Einflusses, PL die Einflüsse)
□ He's a bad influence on her. Er hat einen schlechten Einfluss auf sie.

★ to **influence** VERB
▷ see also **influence** NOUN
beeinflussen [7] (PERFECT TENSE hat beeinflusst)

influenza NOUN
die Grippe *fem*

★ to **inform** VERB
informieren [76] (PERFECT TENSE hat informiert)
■ **to inform somebody of something** jemanden über etwas informieren [76]
□ Nobody informed me that the class was cancelled. Niemand hat mich darüber informiert, dass der Unterricht ausgefallen ist.

informal ADJECTIVE
1 locker (*person*)
2 zwanglos (*party*)
3 umgangssprachlich (*colloquial*)
■ **informal language** die Umgangssprache
■ **an informal visit** ein inoffizieller Besuch

★ **information** NOUN
die Information *fem*
□ important information wichtige Informationen
■ **a piece of information** eine Information
■ **Could you give me some information about Berlin?** Können Sie mir einige Informationen über Berlin geben?

information office NOUN
die Auskunft *fem* (PL die Auskünfte)

information technology NOUN
die Informationstechnik *fem*

infuriating ADJECTIVE
äußerst ärgerlich

ingenious ADJECTIVE
genial

★ **ingredient** NOUN
die Zutat *fem*

inhabitant NOUN
der Einwohner *masc* (PL die Einwohner)
die Einwohnerin *fem* (*of country, town*)

inhaler NOUN
der Inhalator *masc* (PL die Inhalatoren)

to **inherit** VERB
erben [38]
□ She inherited her father's house. Sie erbte das Haus ihres Vaters.

initials PL NOUN
die Initialen *fem pl*
□ Her initials are CDT. Ihre Initialen sind CDT.

initiative NOUN
die Initiative *fem*

to **inject** VERB
spritzen [36] (*drug*)
□ They injected me with antibiotics. Sie haben mir Antibiotika gespritzt.

injection NOUN
die Spritze *fem*

to **injure** VERB
verletzen [36] (PERFECT TENSE hat verletzt)

★ = core vocabulary

injured ADJECTIVE
verletzt

injury NOUN
die Verletzung fem

injustice NOUN
die Ungerechtigkeit fem

ink NOUN
die Tinte fem

in-laws PL NOUN
die Schwiegereltern pl

inn NOUN
das Gasthaus neut (GEN des Gasthauses, PL die Gasthäuser)

inner ADJECTIVE
■ **the inner city** die Innenstadt

inner tube NOUN
der Schlauch masc (PL die Schläuche)

innocent ADJECTIVE
unschuldig

inquest NOUN
die gerichtliche Untersuchung fem

to inquire VERB
■ **to inquire about something** sich nach etwas erkundigen [19]

inquiries office NOUN
die Auskunft fem (PL die Auskünfte)

inquiry NOUN
die Untersuchung fem (official investigation)

inquisitive ADJECTIVE
neugierig

insane ADJECTIVE
wahnsinnig

inscription NOUN
die Inschrift fem

insect NOUN
das Insekt neut (PL die Insekten)

insect repellent NOUN
das Insektenschutzmittel neut (PL die Insektenschutzmittel)

insensitive ADJECTIVE
gefühllos

to insert VERB
einwerfen [92] (PRESENT TENSE wirft ein, IMPERFECT warf ein, PERFECT TENSE hat eingeworfen)
□ I inserted a coin. Ich warf eine Münze ein.

inside NOUN
▷ see also **inside** ADVERB, PREPOSITION
das Innere neut (GEN des Inneren)

inside ADVERB, PREPOSITION
▷ see also **inside** NOUN
innen
□ inside and outside innen und außen
■ **They're inside.** Sie sind drinnen.
■ **to go inside** hineingehen [29]
■ **Come inside!** Kommt herein!

Use the accusative to express movement or a change of place. Use the dative when there is no change of place.

□ She was inside the house. Sie war im Haus.
□ She went inside the house. Sie ging ins Haus.

insincere ADJECTIVE
unaufrichtig

to insist VERB
darauf bestehen [72] (IMPERFECT bestand darauf, PERFECT TENSE hat darauf bestanden)
□ I didn't want to, but he insisted. Ich wollte nicht, aber er hat darauf bestanden.
■ **to insist on doing something** darauf bestehen [72], etwas zu tun □ She insisted on paying. Sie hat darauf bestanden zu bezahlen.
■ **He insisted he was innocent.** Er beteuerte seine Unschuld.

to inspect VERB
kontrollieren [76] (PERFECT TENSE hat kontrolliert)

inspector NOUN
der Kommissar masc (PL die Kommissare)
die Kommissarin fem (police)
□ Inspector Jill Brown Kommissarin Jill Brown

to install VERB
installieren [76] (PERFECT TENSE hat installiert)

instalment (US **installment**) NOUN
1 die Rate fem
□ to pay in instalments in Raten zahlen
2 die Folge fem (of TV, radio serial)
3 der Teil masc (of publication)

instance NOUN
■ **for instance** zum Beispiel

instant ADJECTIVE
sofortig
□ It was an instant success. Es war ein sofortiger Erfolg.
■ **instant coffee** der Pulverkaffee

instantly ADVERB
sofort

instead ADVERB
■ **instead of 1** (followed by noun) anstelle von
□ Use honey instead of sugar. Nehmen Sie Honig anstelle von Zucker. **2** (followed by verb) statt □ We played tennis instead of going swimming. Wir spielten Tennis statt schwimmen zu gehen.
■ **The pool was closed, so we played tennis instead.** Das Schwimmbad war zu, also spielten wir stattdessen Tennis.

instinct NOUN
der Instinkt masc (PL die Instinkte)

institute NOUN
das Institut neut (PL die Institute)

institution NOUN
die Institution fem

i

instruct – interview

to instruct VERB
anweisen (IMPERFECT wies an, PERFECT TENSE hat
angewiesen)
■ **to instruct somebody to do something**
jemanden anweisen, etwas zu tun □ She
instructed us to wait outside. Sie wies uns an,
draußen zu warten.

★ **instructions** PL NOUN
1 die Anweisungen _fem pl_
□ Follow the instructions carefully. Befolgen Sie
die Anweisungen genau.
2 die Gebrauchsanweisung _fem (manual)_
□ Where are the instructions? Wo ist die
Gebrauchsanweisung?

instructor NOUN
der Lehrer _masc_ (PL die Lehrer)
die Lehrerin _fem_
□ a skiing instructor ein Skilehrer □ a driving
instructor ein Fahrlehrer

★ **instrument** NOUN
das Instrument _neut_ (PL die Instrumente)
□ Do you play an instrument? Spielst du ein
Instrument?

insufficient ADJECTIVE
unzureichend

insulin NOUN
das Insulin _neut_

insult NOUN
▷ see also **insult** VERB
die Beleidigung _fem_

to insult VERB
▷ see also **insult** NOUN
beleidigen [7] (PERFECT TENSE hat beleidigt)

★ **insurance** NOUN
die Versicherung _fem_
□ his car insurance seine
Kraftfahrzeugversicherung
■ **an insurance policy** eine
Versicherungspolice

★ **intelligent** ADJECTIVE
intelligent

★ **to intend** VERB
■ **to intend to do something** beabsichtigen
[7], etwas zu tun □ I intend to do modern
languages at university. Ich beabsichtige,
Moderne Sprachen zu studieren.

★ **intense** ADJECTIVE
stark

intensive ADJECTIVE
intensiv

★ **intention** NOUN
die Absicht _fem_

intercom NOUN
die Sprechanlage _fem_

★ **interest** NOUN
▷ see also **interest** VERB
das Interesse _neut_ (PL die Interessen)

□ to show an interest in something Interesse an
etwas zeigen □ What interests do you have?
Welche Interessen hast du?
■ **My main interest is music.** Ich interessiere
mich hauptsächlich für Musik.

★ **to interest** VERB
▷ see also **interest** NOUN
interessieren [76] (PERFECT TENSE hat
interessiert)
□ It doesn't interest me. Das interessiert mich
nicht.
■ **to be interested in something** sich für
etwas interessieren [76] □ I'm not interested in
politics. Ich interessiere mich nicht für Politik.

★ **interesting** ADJECTIVE
interessant

★ **interior** NOUN
das Innere _neut_ (GEN des Inneren)

interior designer NOUN
der Innenarchitekt _masc_ (GEN des
Innenarchitekten, PL die Innenarchitekten)
die Innenarchitektin _fem_

intermediate ADJECTIVE
■ **an intermediate course** ein Kurs für
fortgeschrittene Anfänger

★ **internal** ADJECTIVE
innere
□ the internal organs die inneren Organe

★ **international** ADJECTIVE
international

★ **internet** NOUN
das Internet _neut_
□ on the internet im Internet

internet user NOUN
der Internetbenutzer _masc_ (PL die
Internetbenutzer)
die Internetbenutzerin _fem_

to interpret VERB
dolmetschen [48] (PERFECT TENSE hat
gedolmetscht)
□ Ossi couldn't speak German, so his friend
interpreted. Ossi konnte kein Deutsch, also
dolmetschte sein Freund.

interpreter NOUN
der Dolmetscher _masc_ (PL die Dolmetscher)
die Dolmetscherin _fem_

to interrupt VERB
unterbrechen [11] (PRESENT TENSE unterbricht,
IMPERFECT unterbrach, PERFECT TENSE hat
unterbrochen)

interruption NOUN
die Unterbrechung _fem_

interval NOUN
die Pause _fem (in play, concert)_

★ **interview** NOUN
▷ see also **interview** VERB
1 das Interview _neut_ (PL die Interviews) _(on TV, radio)_

2 das Vorstellungsgespräch *neut* (PLdie Vorstellungsgespräche) (*for job*)

to **interview** VERB

▷ *see also* **interview** NOUN

interviewen [84] (PERFECT TENSEhat interviewt) (*on TV, radio*)

□ I was interviewed on the radio.Ich wurde im Radio interviewt.

interviewer NOUN

der Moderator *masc* (PLdie Moderatoren)
die Moderatorin *fem* (*on TV, radio*)

intimate ADJECTIVE

eng

□ an intimate friendshipeine enge Freundschaft

■ **my intimate feelings**meine innersten Gefühle

into PREPOSITION

in

In this sense in is followed by the accusative.

□ He got into the car.Er stieg ins Auto. □ I'm going into town.Ich gehe in die Stadt.
□ Translate it into German.Übersetze das ins Deutsche. □ Divide into two groups.Teilt euch in zwei Gruppen.

intranet NOUN

das Intranet *neut* (PLdie Intranets)

to **introduce** VERB

vorstellen [4] (PERFECT TENSEhat vorgestellt)
□ He introduced me to his parents.Er stellte mich seinen Eltern vor.

introduction NOUN

die Einleitung *fem* (*in book*)

intruder NOUN

der Eindringling *masc* (PLdie Eindringlinge)

der Eindringling is also used for women.

intuition NOUN

die Intuition *fem*

to **invade** VERB

eindringen in +acc (IMPERFECTdrang ein, PERFECT TENSEist eingedrungen)

□ to invade a countryin ein Land eindringen

invalid NOUN

der Kranke *masc* (GENdes Kranken, PLdie Kranken)
die Kranke *fem* (GENder Kranken)
□ an invalid (*man*)ein Kranker

to **invent** VERB

erfinden [24] (IMPERFECTerfand, PERFECT TENSE hat erfunden)

invention NOUN

die Erfindung *fem*

inventor NOUN

der Erfinder *masc* (PLdie Erfinder)
die Erfinderin *fem*

to **invest** VERB

investieren [76] (PERFECT TENSEhat investiert)

investigation NOUN

die Untersuchung *fem* (*police*)

investment NOUN

die Investition *fem*

invigilator NOUN

die Aufsicht *fem*

die Aufsicht is also used for men.

□ You have to ask the invigilator.Du musst die Aufsicht fragen.

invisible ADJECTIVE

unsichtbar

★ **invitation** NOUN

die Einladung *fem*

★ to **invite** VERB

einladen (PRESENT TENSElädt ein, IMPERFECTlud ein, PERFECT TENSEhat eingeladen)

□ He's not invited.Er ist nicht eingeladen.

■ **to invite somebody to a party**jemanden zu einer Party einladen

★ to **involve** VERB

mit sich bringen [13] (IMPERFECTbrachte mit sich, PERFECT TENSEhat mit sich gebracht)

□ This will involve a lot of work.Das wird viel Arbeit mit sich bringen.

■ **His job involves a lot of travelling.**Er muss in seinem Job viel reisen.

■ **to be involved in something** (*crime, drugs*) in etwas verwickelt sein [65] □ He was involved in the murder.Er war in den Mord verwickelt.

■ **to be involved with somebody** (*in relationship*)mit jemandem eine Beziehung haben [32]

■ **I don't want to get involved.**Ich will damit nichts zu tun haben.

iPad® NOUN

das iPad® *neut* (PLdie iPads)

iPhone® NOUN

das iPhone® *neut* (PLdie iPhones)

iPod® NOUN

der iPod® *masc* (PLdie iPods)

IQ NOUN (= *intelligence quotient*)

der IQ *masc* (GENdes IQ, PLdie IQ)
(=*Intelligenzquotient*)

Iran NOUN

der Iran *masc*

Note that the definite article is used in German for countries which are masculine.

■ **from Iran**aus dem Iran
■ **in Iran**im Iran
■ **to Iran**in den Iran

Iraq NOUN

der Irak *masc*

Note that the definite article is used in German for countries which are masculine.

i

Numbers in brackets refer to verb tables on pages 697 to 706.

495

- **from Iraq** aus dem Irak
- **in Iraq** im Irak
- **to Iraq** in den Irak

Iraqi NOUN
▷ *see also* **Iraqi** ADJECTIVE
der Iraker *masc* (PL die Iraker)
die Irakerin *fem*

Iraqi ADJECTIVE
▷ *see also* **Iraqi** NOUN
irakisch

★ **Ireland** NOUN
Irland *neut*
- **from Ireland** aus Irland
- **in Ireland** in Irland
- **to Ireland** nach Irland

★ **Irish** ADJECTIVE
▷ *see also* **Irish** NOUN
irisch
☐ Irish music irische Musik
- **He's Irish.** Er ist Ire.
- **She's Irish.** Sie ist Irin.

★ **Irish** NOUN
▷ *see also* **Irish** ADJECTIVE
das Irisch *neut* (GEN des Irischen) (*language*)
- **the Irish** (*people*) die Iren *masc pl*

★ **Irishman** NOUN
der Ire *masc* (GEN des Iren, PL die Iren)

★ **Irishwoman** NOUN
die Irin *fem*

★ **iron** NOUN
▷ *see also* **iron** VERB
1 das Eisen *neut* (*metal*)
2 das Bügeleisen *neut* (PL die Bügeleisen) (*for clothes*)

★ to **iron** VERB
▷ *see also* **iron** NOUN
bügeln [34]

ironic ADJECTIVE
ironisch

ironing NOUN
das Bügeln *neut*
- **to do the ironing** bügeln [34]

ironing board NOUN
das Bügelbrett *neut* (PL die Bügelbretter)

ironmonger's (shop) NOUN
die Eisenwarenhandlung *fem*

irrelevant ADJECTIVE
irrelevant
☐ That's irrelevant. Das ist irrelevant.

irresponsible ADJECTIVE
verantwortungslos (*person*)
- **That was irresponsible of him.** Das war unverantwortlich von ihm.

irritating ADJECTIVE
nervend

is VERB ▷ *see* be

Islam NOUN
der Islam *masc*

> Note that the definite article is used in German.

Islamic ADJECTIVE
islamisch
☐ Islamic fundamentalists islamische Fundamentalisten
- **Islamic law** das Recht des Islams

★ **island** NOUN
die Insel *fem*

isle NOUN
- **the Isle of Man** die Insel Man
- **the Isle of Wight** die Insel Wight

isolated ADJECTIVE
abgelegen (*place*)
- **She feels very isolated.** Sie fühlt sich sehr isoliert.
- **an isolated case** ein Einzelfall *masc*

ISP ABBREVIATION (= *Internet Service Provider*)
der Internet-Anbieter *masc* (PL die Internet-Anbieter)

Israel NOUN
Israel *neut*
- **from Israel** aus Israel
- **to Israel** nach Israel

Israeli NOUN
▷ *see also* **Israeli** ADJECTIVE
der Israeli *masc* (GEN des Israeli, PL die Israeli)
die Israeli *fem* (GEN der Israeli)

Israeli ADJECTIVE
▷ *see also* **Israeli** NOUN
israelisch
- **He's Israeli.** Er ist Israeli.

issue NOUN
▷ *see also* **issue** VERB
1 die Frage *fem* (*matter*)
☐ a controversial issue eine umstrittene Frage
2 die Ausgabe *fem* (*of magazine*)

to **issue** VERB
▷ *see also* **issue** NOUN
ausgeben [28] (PRESENT TENSE gibt aus, IMPERFE gab aus, PERFECT TENSE hat ausgegeben) (*equipment, supplies*)

★ **it** PRONOUN

> Remember to check if 'it' stands for a masculine, feminine or neuter noun, and use the appropriate gender and case.

1 er
☐ Have you seen my hat? — It's on the table. Hast du meinen Hut gesehen? — Er ist auf der Tisch.
sie
☐ Where's your watch? — It's broken. Wo ist deine Uhr? — Sie ist kaputt.
es

★ = core vocabulary

□ She's wearing her new dress, it's very pretty. Sie trägt ihr neues Kleid, es ist sehr hübsch.

2 ihn

□ Where's my hat? — I haven't seen it. Wo ist mein Hut? — Ich habe ihn nicht gesehen.

sie

□ Where's your jacket? — I've lost it. Wo ist deine Jacke? — Ich habe sie verloren.

es

□ Take my ruler, I don't need it. Nimm mein Lineal, ich brauche es nicht.

■ **It's raining.** Es regnet.
■ **It's six o'clock.** Es ist sechs Uhr.
■ **It's Friday tomorrow.** Morgen ist Freitag.
■ **Who is it? — It's me.** Wer ist's? — Ich bin's.
■ **It's expensive.** Das ist teuer.

Italian ADJECTIVE
▷ see also **Italian** NOUN
italienisch
■ **She's Italian.** Sie ist Italienerin.

Italian NOUN
▷ see also **Italian** ADJECTIVE

1 der Italiener masc (PL die Italiener)
die Italienerin fem (person)

2 das Italienisch neut (GEN des Italienischen) (language)

italics PL NOUN
die Kursivschrift fem
■ **in italics** kursiv

★ **Italy** NOUN
Italien neut
■ **from Italy** aus Italien
■ **in Italy** in Italien
■ **to Italy** nach Italien

to **itch** VERB
jucken [38]
□ It itches. Es juckt. □ My head's itching. Mein Kopf juckt.

itchy ADJECTIVE
■ **My arm is itchy.** Mein Arm juckt.

it'd = it had, it would

★ **item** NOUN
der Artikel masc (PL die Artikel) (object)

itinerary NOUN
die Reiseroute fem

it'll = it will

★ **its** ADJECTIVE

Remember to check if 'its' refers back to a masculine, feminine or neuter noun, and use the appropriate gender and case.

sein
□ The dog is in its kennel. Der Hund ist in seiner Hütte.

ihr
□ The cup is in its usual place. Die Tasse ist an ihrem üblichen Platz.

sein
□ The baby is in its cot. Das Baby ist in seinem Bett.

it's = it is, it has

★ **itself** PRONOUN

1 sich
□ The dog scratched itself. Der Hund kratzte sich.

2 selbst
□ The heating switches itself off. Die Heizung schaltet von selbst aus.

I've = I have

Jj

jab NOUN
die Spritze *fem* (injection)

jack NOUN
1 der Wagenheber *masc* (PL die Wagenheber) (for car)
2 der Bube *masc* (GEN des Buben, PL die Buben) (playing card)

★ **jacket** NOUN
die Jacke *fem*
∎ **jacket potatoes** gebackene Kartoffeln

jackpot NOUN
der Jackpot *masc* (PL die Jackpots)
□ **to win the jackpot** den Jackpot gewinnen

★ **jail** NOUN
▷ see also **jail** VERB
das Gefängnis *neut* (GEN des Gefängnisses, PL die Gefängnisse)
∎ **She was sent to jail.** Sie musste ins Gefängnis.

★ to **jail** VERB
▷ see also **jail** NOUN
einsperren [4] (PERFECT TENSE hat eingesperrt)
∎ **He was jailed for ten years.** Er hat zehn Jahre Gefängnis bekommen.

jam NOUN
die Marmelade *fem*
□ **strawberry jam** Erdbeermarmelade
∎ **a traffic jam** ein Verkehrsstau *masc*

jam jar NOUN
das Marmeladenglas *neut* (GEN des Marmeladenglases, PL die Marmeladengläser)

jammed ADJECTIVE
∎ **The window's jammed.** Das Fenster klemmt.

jam-packed ADJECTIVE
gerammelt voll
□ **The café was jam-packed.** Das Café war gerammelt voll.

janitor NOUN
der Hausmeister *masc* (PL die Hausmeister)
die Hausmeisterin *fem*
□ **He's a janitor.** Er ist Hausmeister.

★ **January** NOUN
der Januar *masc*
□ **in January** im Januar

★ **Japan** NOUN
Japan *neut*
∎ **from Japan** aus Japan
∎ **to Japan** nach Japan

Japanese ADJECTIVE
▷ see also **Japanese** NOUN
japanisch

Japanese NOUN
▷ see also **Japanese** ADJECTIVE
1 der Japaner *masc* (PL die Japaner)
die Japanerin *fem* (person)
∎ **the Japanese** die Japaner *masc pl*
2 das Japanisch *neut* (GEN des Japanischen) (language)

jar NOUN
das Glas *neut* (GEN des Glases, PL die Gläser)
□ **an empty jar** ein leeres Glas □ **a jar of honey** ein Glas Honig

jaundice NOUN
die Gelbsucht *fem*
□ **She's suffering from jaundice.** Sie hat Gelbsucht.

javelin NOUN
der Speer *masc* (PL die Speere)

jaw NOUN
der Kiefer *masc* (PL die Kiefer)

★ **jazz** NOUN
der Jazz *masc* (GEN des Jazz)

★ **jealous** ADJECTIVE
eifersüchtig

★ **jeans** PL NOUN
die Jeans *fem pl*
□ **a pair of jeans** eine Jeans

Jello® NOUN (US)
der Wackelpudding *masc*

jelly NOUN
1 der Wackelpudding *masc* (dessert)
2 das Gelee *neut* (jam)

jellyfish NOUN
die Qualle *fem*

★ **jersey** NOUN
der Pullover *masc* (PL die Pullover)

Jesus NOUN
Jesus *masc* (GEN des Jesus)

jet NOUN
das Düsenflugzeug *neut* (PL die Düsenflugzeuge) (plane)

★ = core vocabulary

jetlag NOUN
- **to be suffering from jetlag** unter der Zeitverschiebung leiden [44]

jetty NOUN
die Mole *fem*

Jew NOUN
der Jude *masc* (GEN des Juden, PL die Juden)
die Jüdin *fem*

jewel NOUN
der Edelstein *masc* (PL die Edelsteine) (*stone*)

jeweller NOUN
der Juwelier *masc* (PL die Juweliere)
die Juwelierin *fem*
□ He's a jeweller. Er ist Juwelier.

jeweller's shop NOUN
das Juweliergeschäft *neut* (PL die Juweliergeschäfte)

jewellery NOUN
der Schmuck *masc*

Jewish ADJECTIVE
jüdisch

jigsaw NOUN
das Puzzle *neut* (PL die Puzzles)

★ **job** NOUN
1 der Job *masc* (PL die Jobs)
□ He's lost his job. Er hat seinen Job verloren.
□ I've got a Saturday job. Ich habe einen Samstagsjob.
2 die Arbeit *fem* (*chore, task*)
□ That was a difficult job. Das war eine schwierige Arbeit.

job centre NOUN
das Arbeitsamt *neut* (PL die Arbeitsämter)

jobless ADJECTIVE
arbeitslos

jockey NOUN
der Jockey *masc* (PL die Jockeys)

to jog VERB
joggen [48]

jogging NOUN
das Jogging *neut*
□ I like jogging. Ich mag Jogging.
- **to go jogging** joggen [48]

john NOUN (US)
das Klo *neut* (PL die Klos) (*informal*)

★ **to join** VERB
1 beitreten [79] (PRESENT TENSE tritt bei, IMPERFECT trat bei, PERFECT TENSE ist beigetreten) (*become member of*)
□ I'm going to join the tennis club. Ich trete dem Tennisklub bei.
2 sich anschließen (IMPERFECT schloss sich an, PERFECT TENSE hat sich angeschlossen) (*accompany*)
□ Do you mind if I join you? Macht es dir etwas aus, wenn ich mich dir anschließe?

to join in VERB
1 mitmachen [48] (PERFECT TENSE hat mitgemacht)
□ He doesn't join in with what we do. Er macht nicht mit bei den Dingen, die wir tun.
2 einstimmen [4] (PERFECT TENSE hat eingestimmt)
□ She started singing, and the audience joined in. Sie begann zu singen, und das Publikum stimmte mit ein.

joiner NOUN
der Schreiner *masc* (PL die Schreiner)
die Schreinerin *fem*
□ She's a joiner. Sie ist Schreinerin.

★ **joint** NOUN
1 das Gelenk *neut* (PL die Gelenke) (*in body*)
2 der Braten *masc* (PL die Braten) (*of meat*)
3 der Joint *masc* (PL die Joints) (*drugs*)

★ **joke** NOUN
▷ *see also* **joke** VERB
der Witz *masc* (GEN des Witzes, PL die Witze)
□ **to tell a joke** einen Witz erzählen

★ **to joke** VERB
▷ *see also* **joke** NOUN
Spaß machen [48]
□ I'm only joking. Ich mache nur Spaß.

jolly ADJECTIVE
fröhlich

Jordan NOUN
Jordanien *neut* (*country*)
- **from Jordan** aus Jordanien
- **to Jordan** nach Jordanien

to jot down VERB
notieren [76] (PERFECT TENSE hat notiert)

jotter NOUN
der Notizblock *masc* (PL die Notizblöcke) (*pad*)

journalism NOUN
der Journalismus *masc* (GEN des Journalismus)

★ **journalist** NOUN
der Journalist *masc* (GEN des Journalisten, PL die Journalisten)
die Journalistin *fem*
□ She's a journalist. Sie ist Journalistin.

★ **journey** NOUN
1 die Reise *fem*
□ I don't like long journeys. Ich mag lange Reisen nicht.
- **to go on a journey** eine Reise machen [48]
2 die Fahrt *fem* (*to school, work*)
□ the journey to school die Fahrt zur Schule
- **a bus journey** eine Busfahrt

★ **joy** NOUN
die Freude *fem*

joystick NOUN
der Joystick *masc* (PL die Joysticks) (*for computer game*)

★ **judge** NOUN
▷ *see also* **judge** VERB

Numbers in brackets refer to verb tables on pages 697 to 706.

499

judge – justify

der Richter *masc* (PL die Richter)
die Richterin *fem*
□ She's a judge. Sie ist Richterin.

★ to **judge** VERB
▷ *see also* **judge** NOUN
beurteilen [7] (PERFECT TENSE hat beurteilt)
(*assess*)
□ You can judge for yourself which is better. Du kannst das selbst beurteilen, welches besser ist.

judo NOUN
das Judo *neut* (GEN des Judo)
□ My hobby is judo. Judo ist mein Hobby.

jug NOUN
der Krug *masc* (PL die Krüge)

juggler NOUN
der Jongleur *masc* (PL die Jongleure)
die Jongleurin *fem*

★ **juice** NOUN
der Saft *masc* (PL die Säfte)
□ orange juice der Orangensaft

★ **July** NOUN
der Juli *masc*
□ in July im Juli

jumble sale NOUN
der Flohmarkt *masc* (PL die Flohmärkte)

★ to **jump** VERB
springen [71] (IMPERFECT sprang, PERFECT TENSE ist gesprungen)
□ to jump out of the window aus dem Fenster springen □ to jump off the roof vom Dach springen
■ **to jump over something** über etwas springen [71] □ He jumped over the fence. Er sprang über den Zaun.

★ **jumper** NOUN
1 der Pullover *masc* (PL die Pullover)
2 das Trägerkleid *neut* (PL die Trägerkleider)
(US: *dress*)

junction NOUN
1 die Kreuzung *fem* (*of roads*)
2 die Ausfahrt *fem* (*motorway exit*)

★ **June** NOUN
der Juni *masc*
□ in June im Juni

jungle NOUN
der Dschungel *masc* (PL die Dschungel)

junior NOUN
■ **the juniors** die Grundschüler *masc pl*

junior school NOUN
die Grundschule *fem*

> **DID YOU KNOW...?**
> The **Grundschule** is a primary school which children attend from the age of 6 to 10.

junk NOUN
der Krempel *masc* (*old things*)
□ The attic's full of junk. Der Speicher ist voller Krempel.
■ **junk food** Junkfood *neut*
■ **a junk shop** ein Trödelladen *masc*

★ **jury** NOUN
die Geschworenen *masc pl* (*in court*)

★ **just** ADVERB
1 gerade (*barely*)
□ We had just enough money. Wir hatten gerade genug Geld. □ just in time gerade noch rechtzeitig
2 kurz (*shortly*)
□ just after Christmas kurz nach Weihnachten
3 genau (*exactly*)
□ just here genau hier
4 eben (*this minute*)
□ I did it just now. Ich habe es eben gemacht.
□ He's just arrived. Er ist eben angekommen.
■ **I'm rather busy just now.** Ich bin gerade ziemlich beschäftigt.
■ **I'm just coming!** Ich komme schon!
5 nur (*only*)
□ It's just a suggestion. Es ist nur ein Vorschlag.

★ **justice** NOUN
die Gerechtigkeit *fem*

★ to **justify** VERB
rechtfertigen [38]

★ = core vocabulary

Kk

kangaroo NOUN
das Känguru neut (PL die Kängurus)

karate NOUN
das Karate neut (GEN des Karate)
□ I like karate. Ich mag Karate.

kebab NOUN
der Kebab masc (PL die Kebabs)

★ **keen** ADJECTIVE
1 begeistert (*enthusiastic*)
□ He doesn't seem very keen. Er scheint nicht gerade begeistert.
2 eifrig (*hardworking*)
□ She's a keen student. Sie ist eine eifrige Studentin.
■ **to be keen on something** etwas mögen [50] □ I'm keen on maths. Ich mag Mathe.
□ I'm not very keen on maths. Ich mag Mathe nicht besonders.
■ **to be keen on somebody** (*fancy them*) auf jemanden stehen [72] □ He's keen on her. Er steht auf sie.
■ **to be keen on doing something** Lust haben [32], etwas zu tun □ I'm not very keen on going. Ich habe keine große Lust zu gehen.

★ to **keep** VERB
1 behalten [33] (PRESENT TENSE behält, IMPERFECT behielt, PERFECT TENSE hat behalten) (*retain*)
□ You can keep it. Das kannst du behalten.
2 sein [65] (PRESENT TENSE ist, IMPERFECT war, PERFECT TENSE ist gewesen) (*remain*)
□ Keep quiet! Sei still!
■ **Keep still!** Halt still!
■ **I keep forgetting my keys.** Ich vergesse dauernd meine Schlüssel.
■ **to keep on doing something 1** (*continue*) etwas weiter tun [81] □ He kept on reading. Er las weiter. **2** (*repeatedly*) etwas dauernd tun [81] □ The car keeps on breaking down. Das Auto ist dauernd kaputt.
■ **'keep out'** 'Kein Zutritt'

to **keep up** VERB
mithalten [33]
□ Matthew walks so fast I can't keep up. Matthew geht so schnell, da kann ich nicht mithalten.

keep-fit NOUN
das Fitnesstraining neut

□ I like keep-fit. Ich mache gern Fitnesstraining.
■ **I go to keep-fit classes.** Ich gehe zum Fitnesstraining.

kennel NOUN
die Hundehütte *fem*

kept VERB ▷ *see* **keep**

kerosene NOUN (US)
das Petroleum neut

kettle NOUN
der Wasserkessel masc (PL die Wasserkessel)

★ **key** NOUN
der Schlüssel masc (PL die Schlüssel)

keyboard NOUN
1 die Tastatur *fem* (*of piano, computer*)
2 das Keyboard neut (PL die Keyboards) (*musical instrument*)
□ He sings and his sister is on keyboards. Er singt und seine Schwester spielt Keyboard.

keyring NOUN
der Schlüsselring masc (PL die Schlüsselringe)

★ **kick** NOUN
▷ *see also* **kick** VERB
der Tritt masc (PL die Tritte)
□ He gave me a kick. Er hat mir einen Tritt versetzt.

★ to **kick** VERB
▷ *see also* **kick** NOUN
treten [79] (PRESENT TENSE tritt, IMPERFECT trat, PERFECT TENSE hat getreten)
□ He kicked me. Er hat mich getreten.
■ **He kicked the ball hard.** Er hat den Ball kräftig gekickt.

to **kick off** VERB
anfangen [23] (*in football*)

kick-off NOUN
der Anstoß masc (GEN des Anstoßes, PL die Anstöße)
□ Kick-off is at ten o'clock. Um zehn Uhr ist Anstoß.

★ **kid** NOUN
▷ *see also* **kid** VERB
das Kind neut (PL die Kinder) (*child*)

★ to **kid** VERB
▷ *see also* **kid** NOUN
Spaß machen [48]
□ I'm just kidding. Ich mache nur Spaß.

k

Numbers in brackets refer to verb tables on pages 697 to 706.

kidnap – knife

to kidnap VERB
entführen [18] (PERFECT TENSE hat entführt)

kidney NOUN
die Niere *fem*
□ He's got kidney trouble. Er hat Nierenprobleme. □ I don't like kidney. Ich mag Nieren nicht.

★ **to kill** VERB
töten [2]
□ Hundreds of innocent people were killed in the bomb attack. Hunderte von unschuldigen Menschen wurden durch den Bombenangriff getötet.
■ **to be killed** umkommen [40] □ He was killed in a car accident. Er kam bei einem Unfall um. □ Luckily, nobody was killed. Zum Glück ist niemand dabei umgekommen.
■ **to kill oneself** sich umbringen [13] □ He killed himself. Er hat sich umgebracht.

★ **killer** NOUN
1 der Mörder *masc* (PL die Mörder)
die Mörderin *fem* (*murderer*)
□ The police are searching for the killer. Die Polizei sucht nach dem Mörder.
2 der Killer *masc* (PL die Killer) (*hitman*)
□ a hired killer ein Auftragskiller
■ **Meningitis can be a killer.** Hirnhautentzündung kann tödlich sein.

★ **kilo** NOUN
das Kilo *neut* (PL die Kilos *or* Kilo)
□ twenty euros a kilo zwanzig Euro das Kilo

> When specifying a quantity of something use the plural form **Kilo**.

□ three kilos of tomatoes drei Kilo Tomaten

★ **kilometre** NOUN
der Kilometer *masc* (PL die Kilometer)
□ a hundred kilometres hundert Kilometer

kilt NOUN
der Kilt *masc* (PL die Kilts)

★ **kind** ADJECTIVE
▷ *see also* **kind** NOUN
nett
□ Thank you for being so kind. Vielen Dank, dass Sie so nett waren.
■ **to be kind to somebody** zu jemandem nett sein [65]

★ **kind** NOUN
▷ *see also* **kind** ADJECTIVE
die Art *fem*
□ It's a kind of sausage. Es ist eine Art Wurst.
■ **a new kind of dictionary** ein neuartiges Wörterbuch

kindergarten NOUN
der Kindergarten *masc* (PL die Kindergärten)

> **DID YOU KNOW...?**
> Many German children go to **Kindergarten** from the age of 3 to 6.

kindly ADVERB
freundlicherweise

kindness NOUN
die Freundlichkeit *fem*

★ **king** NOUN
der König *masc* (PL die Könige)

kingdom NOUN
das Königreich *neut* (PL die Königreiche)

kiosk NOUN
1 die Telefonzelle *fem* (*phone box*)
2 der Kiosk *masc* (PL die Kioske)
□ a newspaper kiosk ein Zeitungskiosk

kipper NOUN
der Räucherhering *masc* (PL die Räucherheringe)

★ **kiss** NOUN
▷ *see also* **kiss** VERB
der Kuss *masc* (GEN des Kusses, PL die Küsse)

★ **to kiss** VERB
▷ *see also* **kiss** NOUN
1 küssen [48]
□ He kissed me. Er küsste mich.
2 sich küssen [48]
□ They kissed passionately. Sie küssten sich leidenschaftlich.

kit NOUN
1 das Zeug *neut* (*clothes for sport*)
□ I've forgotten my gym kit. Ich habe mein Sportzeug vergessen.
2 der Kasten *masc* (PL die Kästen)
□ a tool kit ein Werkzeugkasten □ a first-aid kit ein Erste-Hilfe-Kasten
■ **puncture repair kit** das Flickzeug
■ **sewing kit** das Nähzeug

★ **kitchen** NOUN
die Küche *fem*
□ a fitted kitchen eine Einbauküche
■ **the kitchen units** die Küchenschränke *masc pl*
■ **a kitchen knife** ein Küchenmesser *neut*

kite NOUN
der Drachen *masc* (PL die Drachen)

kitten NOUN
das Kätzchen *neut* (PL die Kätzchen)

★ **knee** NOUN
das Knie *neut* (PL die Knie)
□ He was on his knees. Er lag auf den Knien.

to kneel (down) VERB
sich hinknien [4] (PERFECT TENSE hat sich hingekniet)

knew VERB ▷ *see* **know**

★ **knickers** PL NOUN
die Unterhose *fem*
□ a pair of knickers eine Unterhose

★ **knife** NOUN
das Messer *neut* (PL die Messer)
■ **a penknife** ein Taschenmesser *neut*

k

to knit VERB

stricken [48]

knitting NOUN

das Stricken *neut*
- **I like knitting.** Ich stricke gern.

knives PL NOUN ▷ *see* **knife**

knob NOUN

1 der Griff *masc* (*on door*)
2 der Knopf *masc* (PL die Knöpfe) (*on radio, TV*)

★ **to knock** VERB

▷ *see also* **knock** NOUN

klopfen [38]

□ to knock on the door an die Tür klopfen
- **Someone's knocking at the door.** Es klopft.
- **She was knocked down by a car.** Ein Auto hat sie umgefahren.
- **He was knocked out.** (*made unconscious*) Er wurde bewusstlos geschlagen.
- **to knock somebody out** (*defeat*) jemanden schlagen [59] □ Liverpool knocked Aston Villa out of the cup. Der FC Liverpool hat Aston Villa im Pokalspiel geschlagen.
- **They were knocked out early in the tournament.** Sie schieden beim Turnier früh aus.
- **to knock something over** etwas umstoßen □ I accidentally knocked the milk over. Ich habe aus Versehen die Milch umgestoßen.

★ **knock** NOUN

▷ *see also* **knock** VERB

- **There was a knock on the door.** Es hat geklopft.

knot NOUN

der Knoten *masc* (PL die Knoten)

★ **to know** VERB

Use **wissen** for knowing facts, **kennen** for knowing people and places.

1 wissen [93] (PRESENT TENSE weiß, IMPERFECT wusste, PERFECT TENSE hat gewusst)
□ It's a long way. — Yes, I know. Es ist weit. — Ja, ich weiß. □ I don't know. Ich weiß nicht. □ I don't know what to do. Ich weiß nicht, was ich tun soll. □ I don't know how to do it. Ich weiß nicht, wie ich es machen soll.
2 kennen [39] (IMPERFECT kannte, PERFECT TENSE hat gekannt)
□ I know her. Ich kenne sie. □ I know Frankfurt well. Ich kenne Frankfurt gut.
- **I don't know any French.** Ich kann kein Französisch.

- **to know that …** wissen [93], dass … □ I know that you like chocolate. Ich weiß, dass du Schokolade magst. □ I didn't know that your dad was a police officer. Ich wusste nicht, dass dein Vater Polizist ist.
- **to know about something 1** (*be aware of*) von etwas wissen [93] □ Do you know about football training this afternoon? Weißt du von dem Fußballtraining heute Nachmittag? **2** (*be knowledgeable about*) sich mit etwas auskennen [39] □ He knows a lot about cars. Er kennt sich mit Autos aus. □ I don't know much about computers. Mit Computern kenne ich mich nicht besonders aus.
- **to get to know somebody** jemanden kennenlernen [4]
- **How should I know?** (*I don't know!*) Wie soll ich das wissen?
- **You never know!** Man kann nie wissen!

know-all NOUN

der Besserwisser *masc* (PL die Besserwisser)
die Besserwisserin *fem*
□ He's such a know-all! So ein Besserwisser!

know-how NOUN

das Know-how *neut* (GEN des Know-how)

★ **knowledge** NOUN

1 das Wissen *neut* (*general knowledge*)
□ Our knowledge of the universe is limited.
Unser Wissen über das Universum ist begrenzt.
2 die Kenntnisse *fem pl* (*things learnt*)
□ my knowledge of German meine Deutschkenntnisse

knowledgeable ADJECTIVE

- **to be knowledgeable about something** viel über etwas wissen [93] □ She is very knowledgeable about coding. Sie weiß viel über Programmierung.
- **She's very knowledgeable about martial arts.** Sie kennt sich mit Kampfsport gut aus.

known VERB ▷ *see* **know**

Koran NOUN

der Koran *masc*

Korea NOUN

Korea *neut*
- **from Korea** aus Korea
- **to Korea** nach Korea

kosher ADJECTIVE

koscher

k

Ll

lab NOUN (= *laboratory*)
das Labor *neut* (PL die Labors)
■ **a lab technician** ein Laborant *masc*

★ **label** NOUN
1 der Aufkleber *masc* (PL die Aufkleber) (*sticker*)
2 das Etikett *neut* (PL die Etiketts) (*on clothes*)
3 der Anhänger *masc* (PL die Anhänger) (*for luggage*)

★ **laboratory** NOUN
das Labor *neut* (PL die Labors)

labor union NOUN (US)
die Gewerkschaft *fem*

Labour NOUN
die Labour-Party *fem*
□ My parents vote Labour. Meine Eltern wählen die Labour-Party.
■ **the Labour Party** die Labour-Party

labourer NOUN
der Arbeiter *masc* (PL die Arbeiter)
die Arbeiterin *fem*
■ **a farm labourer** ein Landarbeiter

lace NOUN
1 der Schnürsenkel *masc* (PL die Schnürsenkel) (*of shoe*)
2 die Spitze *fem*
□ a lace collar ein Spitzenkragen

★ **lack** NOUN
der Mangel *masc* (PL die Mängel)
□ his lack of experience sein Mangel an Erfahrung

lacquer NOUN
der Lack *masc* (PL die Lacke)

lad NOUN
der Junge *masc* (GEN des Jungen, PL die Jungen)

ladder NOUN
1 die Leiter *fem*
2 die Laufmasche *fem* (*in tights*)

★ **lady** NOUN
die Dame *fem*
□ a young lady eine junge Dame
■ **Ladies and gentlemen ...** Meine Damen und Herren ...
■ **the ladies** die Damentoilette
■ **'ladies'** (*on sign*) 'Damen'

ladybird NOUN
der Marienkäfer *masc* (PL die Marienkäfer)

to lag behind VERB
hinterherhinken [15] (PERFECT TENSE ist hinterhergehinkt)

lager NOUN
das helle Bier *neut* (PL die hellen Biere)

> **DID YOU KNOW...?**
> German beers are completely different from British ones. There is no real equivalent to 'lager'.

laid VERB ▷ see **lay**

laid-back ADJECTIVE
locker

lain VERB ▷ see **lie**

★ **lake** NOUN
der See *masc* (PL die Seen)
■ **Lake Geneva** der Genfer See
■ **Lake Constance** der Bodensee

lamb NOUN
das Lamm *neut* (PL die Lämmer)
■ **a lamb chop** ein Lammkotelett *neut*

lame ADJECTIVE
lahm
■ **My pony is lame.** Mein Pony lahmt.

lamp NOUN
die Lampe *fem*

lamppost NOUN
der Laternenpfahl *masc* (PL die Laternenpfähle)

lampshade NOUN
der Lampenschirm *masc*

★ **land** NOUN
▷ see also **land** VERB
das Land *neut* (PL die Länder)
□ a piece of land ein Stück Land

★ **to land** VERB
▷ see also **land** NOUN
landen [54] (PERFECT TENSE ist gelandet) (*plane, passenger*)

landing NOUN
1 die Landung *fem* (*of plane*)
2 der Treppenabsatz *masc* (GEN des Treppenabsatzes, PL die Treppenabsätze) (*of staircase*)

landlady NOUN
die Vermieterin *fem*

★ = core vocabulary

landline NOUN
das Festnetz neut (PL die Festnetze)
□ Shall I call you on the landline?

landlord NOUN
der Vermieter masc (PL die Vermieter)

landmark NOUN
das Wahrzeichen neut (PL die Wahrzeichen)
□ Big Ben is a London landmark. Big Ben ist ein Londoner Wahrzeichen.

landowner NOUN
der Grundbesitzer masc (PL die Grundbesitzer)
die Grundbesitzerin fem

★ **landscape** NOUN
die Landschaft fem

★ **lane** NOUN
1 das Sträßchen neut (PL die Sträßchen) (in country)
2 die Spur fem (on motorway)

★ **language** NOUN
die Sprache fem
□ a difficult language eine schwierige Sprache
■ to use bad language Kraftausdrücke benutzen [36]

language laboratory NOUN
das Sprachlabor neut (PL die Sprachlabors)

★ **lap** NOUN
die Runde fem (sport)
□ I ran ten laps. Ich bin zehn Runden gelaufen.
■ on my lap auf meinem Schoß

★ **laptop** NOUN
der Laptop masc (PL die Laptops) (computer)

larder NOUN
die Speisekammer fem

★ **large** ADJECTIVE
groß
□ a large house ein großes Haus □ a large dog ein großer Hund

★ **largely** ADVERB
größtenteils

laser NOUN
der Laser masc (PL die Laser)

lass NOUN
das Mädchen neut (PL die Mädchen)

★ **last** ADJECTIVE, ADVERB
▷ see also last VERB
1 letzte
□ one last time ein letztes Mal □ the last question die letzte Frage □ last Friday letzten Freitag □ last week letzte Woche
2 als Letzte
□ He arrived last. Er kam als Letzter an.
3 zuletzt
□ I've lost my bag. — When did you see it last? Ich habe meine Tasche verloren. — Wann hast du sie zuletzt gesehen?
■ When I last saw him, he was okay. Als ich ihn das letzte Mal sah, war er in Ordnung.

■ the last time das letzte Mal □ the last time I saw her als ich sie das letzte Mal sah □ That's the last time I take your advice! Das ist das letzte Mal, dass ich auf deinen Rat höre!
■ last night 1 (evening) gestern Abend □ I got home at midnight last night. Ich bin gestern Abend um Mitternacht nach Hause gekommen.
2 (sleeping hours) heute Nacht □ I couldn't sleep last night. Ich konnte heute Nacht nicht schlafen.
■ at last endlich

★ to **last** VERB
▷ see also last ADJECTIVE, ADVERB
dauern [88]
□ The concert lasts two hours. Das Konzert dauert zwei Stunden.

lastly ADVERB
schließlich
□ Lastly I'd like to mention that ... Und schließlich möchte ich erwähnen, dass ...

★ **late** ADJECTIVE, ADVERB
1 zu spät
□ Hurry up or you'll be late! Beeil dich, du kommst sonst zu spät! □ I'm often late for school. Ich komme oft zu spät zur Schule.
■ to arrive late zu spät kommen [40] □ She arrived late. Sie kam zu spät.
2 spät
□ I went to bed late. Ich bin spät ins Bett gegangen. □ in the late afternoon am späten Nachmittag
■ in late May Ende Mai

lately ADVERB
in letzter Zeit
□ I haven't seen him lately. Ich habe ihn in letzter Zeit nicht gesehen.

★ **later** ADVERB
später
□ I'll do it later. Ich mache es später. □ See you later! Bis später!

★ **latest** ADJECTIVE
neueste
□ the latest news die neuesten Nachrichten
□ their latest album ihr neuestes Album
■ at the latest spätestens □ by ten o'clock at the latest bis spätestens zehn Uhr

★ **Latin** NOUN
das Latein neut
□ I do Latin. Ich lerne Latein.

Latin America NOUN
Lateinamerika neut
■ from Latin America aus Lateinamerika
■ to Latin America nach Lateinamerika

Latin American ADJECTIVE
lateinamerikanisch

★ **laugh** NOUN
▷ see also laugh VERB
das Lachen neut

Numbers in brackets refer to verb tables on pages 697 to 706.

505

English-German

laugh – leak

■ **It was a good laugh.** (*it was fun*) Es war lustig.

★ to **laugh** VERB
▷ *see also* **laugh** NOUN
lachen [48]
■ **to laugh at something** über etwas lachen [48] □ She didn't laugh at my joke. Sie hat über meinen Witz nicht gelacht.
■ **to laugh at somebody** jemanden auslachen [4] □ They laughed at her. Sie lachten sie aus.

to **launch** VERB
1 auf den Markt bringen [13] (IMPERFECT brachte, PERFECT TENSE hat gebracht) (*product*)
2 abschießen (IMPERFECT schoss ab, PERFECT TENSE hat abgeschossen) (*rocket*)

Launderette® NOUN
der Waschsalon *masc* (PL die Waschsalons)

Laundromat® NOUN (US)
der Waschsalon *masc* (PL die Waschsalons)

laundry NOUN
die Wäsche *fem* (*clothes*)

lavatory NOUN
die Toilette *fem*

lavender NOUN
der Lavendel *masc*

★ **law** NOUN
1 das Gesetz *neut* (GEN des Gesetzes, PL die Gesetze)
□ It's against the law. Das ist gegen das Gesetz.
2 Jura (*subject*)
□ She's studying law. Sie studiert Jura.

lawn NOUN
der Rasen *masc* (PL die Rasen)

lawnmower NOUN
der Rasenmäher *masc* (PL die Rasenmäher)

law school NOUN (US)
die juristische Fakultät *fem*

★ **lawyer** NOUN
der Rechtsanwalt *masc* (PL die Rechtsanwälte)
die Rechtsanwältin *fem*
□ My mother's a lawyer. Meine Mutter ist Rechtsanwältin.

★ to **lay** VERB
'lay' is also a form of 'lie (2)' verb
legen [38]
□ She laid the baby in her cot. Sie legte das Baby ins Bettchen.
■ **to lay the table** den Tisch decken [38]
■ **to lay something on** 1 (*provide*) etwas bereitstellen [15] □ They laid on extra buses. Sie stellten zusätzliche Busse bereit.
2 (*prepare*) etwas vorbereiten [2] □ They had laid on a special meal. Sie hatten ein besonderes Essen vorbereitet.

to **lay off** VERB
entlassen [42]
□ My mother's been laid off. Meine Mutter ist entlassen worden.

lay-by NOUN
der Rastplatz *masc* (GEN des Rastplatzes, PL die Rastplätze)

★ **layer** NOUN
die Schicht *fem*

layout NOUN
das Design *neut* (PL die Designs) (*of house, garden*)

★ **lazy** ADJECTIVE
faul

lb. ABBREVIATION (= *pound*)
Pfund

★ **lead (1)** NOUN
▷ *see also* **lead** VERB
1 das Kabel *neut* (PL die Kabel) (*cable*)
2 die Hundeleine *fem* (*for dog*)
■ **to be in the lead** in Führung sein [65] □ Our team is in the lead. Unsere Mannschaft ist in Führung.

★ **lead (2)** NOUN
das Blei *neut* (*metal*)

★ to **lead** VERB
▷ *see also* **lead** NOUN
führen [38]
□ the road that leads to the lake die Straße, die zum See führt
■ **to lead the way** vorangehen [29] □ She led the way. Sie ist vorangegangen.
■ **to lead somebody away** jemanden abführen [4] □ The police led the man away. Die Polizei führte den Mann ab.

★ **leader** NOUN
1 der Führer *masc* (PL die Führer)
die Führerin *fem* (*of political party, expedition*)
2 der Anführer *masc* (PL die Anführer)
die Anführerin *fem* (*of gang*)

lead singer NOUN
der Leadsinger *masc* (PL die Leadsinger)
die Leadsingerin *fem*

★ **leaf** NOUN
das Blatt *neut* (PL die Blätter)

leaflet NOUN
der Prospekt *masc* (PL die Prospekte) (*advertising*)
□ a leaflet about their products einen Prospekt über ihre Produkte

★ **league** NOUN
die Liga *fem* (GEN der Liga, PL die Ligen)
□ the Premier League die erste Liga

DID YOU KNOW...?
The 'Premier League' is similar to the German **Bundesliga**.

■ **They are at the top of the league.** Sie sind Tabellenführer.

★ **leak** NOUN
▷ *see also* **leak** VERB
die undichte Stelle *fem*

506   ★ = core vocabulary

□ a gas leak eine undichte Stelle in der Gasleitung

★ to leak VERB
  ▷ see also **leak** NOUN
  1 undicht sein [65] (PRESENT TENSE ist undicht, IMPERFECT war undicht, PERFECT TENSE ist undicht gewesen) (*pipe*)
  2 auslaufen [43] (PRESENT TENSE läuft aus, IMPERFECT lief aus, PERFECT TENSE ist ausgelaufen) (*water*)
  3 austreten [79] (PRESENT TENSE tritt aus, IMPERFECT trat aus, PERFECT TENSE ist ausgetreten) (*gas*)

★ to lean VERB
  sich lehnen [38]
  □ Don't lean over too far. Lehn dich nicht zu weit vor. □ She leant out of the window. Sie lehnte sich zum Fenster hinaus.
  ■ **to be leaning against something** gegen etwas gelehnt sein [65] □ The ladder was leaning against the wall. Die Leiter war gegen die Wand gelehnt.
  ■ **to lean something against a wall** etwas an einer Mauer anlehnen [4] □ He leant his bike against the wall. Er lehnte sein Fahrrad an der Mauer an.

to lean forward VERB
  sich nach vorn beugen [38]

to lean on VERB
  ■ **to lean on something** sich auf etwas stützen [48] □ He leant on the wall. Er stützte sich auf die Mauer.

★ to leap VERB
  springen [71] (IMPERFECT sprang, PERFECT TENSE ist gesprungen)
  □ He leapt out of his chair when his team scored. Er sprang vom Stuhl auf, als seine Mannschaft ein Tor schoss.

leap year NOUN
  das Schaltjahr *neut* (PL die Schaltjahre)

★ to learn VERB
  lernen [38]
  □ I'm learning to ski. Ich lerne Ski fahren.

learner NOUN
  ■ **She's a quick learner.** Sie lernt schnell.
  ■ **German learners** (*people learning German*) Deutschschüler *masc pl*

learner driver NOUN
  der Fahrschüler *masc* (PL die Fahrschüler)
  die Fahrschülerin *fem*

learnt VERB ▷ see **learn**

★ least ADVERB, ADJECTIVE, PRONOUN
  ■ **the least 1** (*followed by noun*) wenigste
  □ the least time die wenigste Zeit □ She has the least money. Sie hat das wenigste Geld. **2** (*followed by adjective*) am wenigsten ... □ the least intelligent pupil der am wenigsten intelligente Schüler □ the least difficult question die am wenigsten schwierige Frage

□ the least interesting book das am wenigsten interessante Buch **3** (*after a verb*) am wenigsten □ Maths is the subject I like the least. Mathe ist das Fach, das ich am wenigsten mag.
  ■ **It's the least I can do.** Das ist das wenigste, was ich tun kann.
  ■ **at least 1** mindestens □ It'll cost at least two hundred pounds. Das kostet mindestens zweihundert Pfund. **2** wenigstens □ ... but at least nobody was hurt. ... aber wenigstens wurde niemand verletzt.
  ■ **It's totally unfair – at least, that's my opinion.** Das ist total ungerecht – zumindest meiner Meinung nach.

★ leather NOUN
  das Leder *neut* (PL die Leder)
  □ a black leather jacket eine schwarze Lederjacke

★ to leave VERB
  ▷ see also **leave** NOUN
  1 lassen [42] (PRESENT TENSE lässt, IMPERFECT ließ, PERFECT TENSE hat gelassen) (*deliberately*)
  □ He always leaves his camera in the car. Er lässt immer seinen Fotoapparat im Auto.
  2 vergessen [83] (PRESENT TENSE vergisst, IMPERFECT vergaß, PERFECT TENSE hat vergessen) (*by mistake*)
  □ I've left my book at home. Ich habe mein Buch zu Hause vergessen.
  ■ **Don't leave anything behind.** Lassen Sie nichts liegen.
  3 abfahren [21] (PRESENT TENSE fährt ab, IMPERFECT fuhr ab, PERFECT TENSE ist abgefahren) (*bus, train*)
  □ The bus leaves at eight. Der Bus fährt um acht ab.
  4 abfliegen [25] (IMPERFECT flog ab, PERFECT TENSE ist abgeflogen) (*plane*)
  □ The plane leaves at six. Das Flugzeug fliegt um sechs ab.
  5 weggehen [29] (IMPERFECT ging weg, PERFECT TENSE ist weggegangen) (*person*)
  □ She's just left. Sie ist eben weggegangen.
  ■ **She left home last year.** Sie ist letztes Jahr von zu Hause weggezogen.
  6 verlassen [42] (PRESENT TENSE verlässt, IMPERFECT verließ, PERFECT TENSE hat verlassen) (*abandon*)
  □ She left her husband. Sie hat ihren Mann verlassen.
  ■ **to leave somebody alone** jemanden in Ruhe lassen [42] □ Leave me alone! Lass mich in Ruhe!

to leave out VERB
  auslassen [42]
  □ You've left out a comma. Du hast ein Komma ausgelassen.
  ■ **I felt really left out.** Ich fühlte mich richtig ausgeschlossen.

★ leave NOUN
  ▷ see also **leave** VERB
  der Urlaub *masc* (PL die Urlaube) (*from job, army*)
  □ a week's leave eine Woche Urlaub

I

Numbers in brackets refer to verb tables on pages 697 to 706.

507

leaves PL NOUN ▷ *see* **leaf**

Lebanon NOUN
der Libanon *masc*

> Note that the definite article is used in German for countries which are masculine.

- **from Lebanon** aus dem Libanon
- **in Lebanon** im Libanon
- **to Lebanon** in den Libanon

★ **lecture** NOUN
▷ *see also* **lecture** VERB
1 der Vortrag *masc* (PL die Vorträge) (*public*)
2 die Vorlesung *fem* (*at university*)

> **BE CAREFUL!**
> Do not translate **lecture** by Lektüre.

★ to **lecture** VERB
▷ *see also* **lecture** NOUN
1 unterrichten [2] (PERFECT TENSE hat unterrichtet)
□ She lectures at the university. Sie unterrichtet an der Universität.
2 belehren [7] (PERFECT TENSE hat belehrt) (*tell off*)
□ He's always lecturing us. Er belehrt uns andauernd.

lecturer NOUN
der Dozent *masc* (GEN des Dozenten, PL die Dozenten)
die Dozentin *fem*
□ She's a lecturer. Sie ist Dozentin.

led VERB ▷ *see* **lead** VERB

leek NOUN
der Lauch *masc* (PL die Lauche)

★ **left** VERB ▷ *see* **leave**

★ **left** ADJECTIVE, ADVERB
▷ *see also* **left** NOUN
1 linke
□ the left foot der linke Fuß □ my left arm mein linker Arm □ your left hand deine linke Hand □ her left eye ihr linkes Auge
2 links
□ Turn left at the traffic lights. Biegen Sie an der Ampel links ab.
- **Look left!** Sehen Sie nach links!
- **I haven't got any money left.** Ich habe kein Geld mehr.

★ **left** NOUN
▷ *see also* **left** ADJECTIVE, ADVERB
die linke Seite *fem*
- **on the left** links □ Remember to drive on the left. Vergiss nicht, links zu fahren.

left-hand ADJECTIVE
- **the left-hand side** die linke Seite
- **It's on the left-hand side.** Es liegt links.

left-handed ADJECTIVE
linkshändig

left-luggage office NOUN
die Gepäckaufbewahrung *fem*

★ **leg** NOUN
das Bein *neut* (PL die Beine)
□ I've broken my leg. Ich habe mir das Bein gebrochen.
- **a chicken leg** eine Hähnchenkeule
- **a leg of lamb** eine Lammkeule

★ **legal** ADJECTIVE
legal

leggings PL NOUN
die Leggings *pl*

leisure NOUN
die Freizeit *fem*
□ What do you do in your leisure time? Was machen Sie in Ihrer Freizeit?

leisure centre NOUN
das Freizeitzentrum *neut* (PL die Freizeitzentren)

lemon NOUN
die Zitrone *fem*

lemonade NOUN
die Limonade *fem*

★ to **lend** VERB
leihen (IMPERFECT lieh, PERFECT TENSE hat geliehen)
□ I can lend you some money. Ich kann dir Geld leihen.

★ **length** NOUN
die Länge *fem*
- **It's about a metre in length.** Es ist etwa einen Meter lang.

★ **lens** NOUN
1 die Kontaktlinse *fem* (*contact lens*)
2 das Glas *neut* (GEN des Glases, PL die Gläser) (*of spectacles*)
3 das Objektiv *neut* (PL die Objektive) (*of camera*)

Lent NOUN
die Fastenzeit *fem*
□ during Lent während der Fastenzeit

lent VERB ▷ *see* **lend**

lentil NOUN
die Linse *fem*

Leo NOUN
der Löwe *masc* (GEN des Löwen)
□ I'm Leo. Ich bin Löwe.

leotard NOUN
der Gymnastikanzug *masc* (PL die Gymnastikanzüge)

lesbian NOUN
die Lesbierin *fem*
- **She's a lesbian.** Sie ist lesbisch.

★ **less** PRONOUN, ADVERB, ADJECTIVE
weniger
□ A bit less, please. Etwas weniger, bitte. □ I've got less time for hobbies now. Ich habe jetzt weniger Zeit für Hobbys.
- **He's less intelligent than his brother.** Er ist nicht so intelligent wie sein Bruder.
- **less than** weniger als □ It costs less than a

hundred euros. Es kostet weniger als hundert Euro. □ **less than half** weniger als die Hälfte □ **He spent less than me.** Er hat weniger als ich ausgegeben. □ **I've got less than you.** Ich habe weniger als du.

★ **lesson** NOUN
1 die Lektion *fem*
□ **'Lesson Sixteen'** *(in textbook)* 'Lektion sechzehn'
2 die Stunde *fem (class)*
□ **A lesson lasts forty minutes.** Eine Stunde dauert vierzig Minuten.

★ **to let** VERB
1 lassen [42] (PRESENT TENSE lässt, IMPERFECT ließ, PERFECT TENSE hat gelassen) *(allow)*
■ **to let somebody do something** jemanden etwas tun lassen [42] □ **Let me have a look.** Lass mich mal sehen. □ **My parents won't let me go out tonight.** Meine Eltern lassen mich heute Abend nicht ausgehen.
■ **to let somebody down** jemanden enttäuschen [18] □ **I won't let you down.** Ich werde dich nicht enttäuschen.
■ **to let somebody know** jemandem Bescheid sagen [38] □ **I'll let you know as soon as possible.** Ich sage Ihnen sobald wie möglich Bescheid.
■ **Let's go to the cinema!** Lass uns ins Kino gehen!
■ **Let's go!** Gehen wir!
2 vermieten [2] (PERFECT TENSE hat vermietet) *(hire out)*
■ **'to let'** 'zu vermieten'

to let go VERB
loslassen [42] *(release)*
□ **Let me go!** Lass mich los!

to let in VERB
hineinlassen [42]
□ **They wouldn't let me in.** Sie wollten mich nicht hineinlassen.

★ **letter** NOUN
1 der Brief *masc* (PL die Briefe)
□ **She wrote me a long letter.** Sie hat mir einen langen Brief geschrieben.
2 der Buchstabe *masc* (GEN des Buchstaben, PL die Buchstaben) *(of alphabet)*
□ **the letters of the alphabet** die Buchstaben des Alphabets

letterbox NOUN
der Briefkasten *masc* (PL die Briefkästen)

lettuce NOUN
der Kopfsalat *masc* (PL die Kopfsalate)

leukaemia NOUN
die Leukämie *fem*
□ **He suffers from leukaemia.** Er leidet an Leukämie.

★ **level** ADJECTIVE
▷ *see also* **level** NOUN
eben

□ **A snooker table must be perfectly level.** Ein Snookertisch muss ganz eben sein.

★ **level** NOUN
▷ *see also* **level** ADJECTIVE
1 das Niveau *neut (social, intellectual)*
□ **She's on a level with the very best students.** Sie ist auf gleichem Niveau wie die allerbesten Studenten.
2 der Wasserstand *masc* (PL die Wasserstände) *(of river, lake)*
□ **The level of the river is rising.** Der Wasserstand des Flusses steigt.
3 die Höhe *fem (height)*
□ **at eye level** in Augenhöhe
■ **A levels** das Abitur

DID YOU KNOW...?
On average, Germans take their **Abitur** at the age of 19. The students sit examinations in a variety of subjects to attain an overall grade. If you pass, you have the right to a place at university.

level crossing NOUN
der Bahnübergang *masc* (PL die Bahnübergänge)

lever NOUN
der Hebel *masc* (PL die Hebel)

liable ADJECTIVE
■ **He's liable to lose his temper.** Er wird leicht wütend.

liar NOUN
der Lügner *masc* (PL die Lügner)
die Lügnerin *fem*

★ **liberal** ADJECTIVE
liberal *(opinions)*
■ **the Liberal Democrats** die Liberaldemokraten

liberation NOUN
die Befreiung *fem*

Libra NOUN
die Waage *fem*
□ **I'm Libra.** Ich bin Waage.

librarian NOUN
der Bibliothekar *masc* (PL die Bibliothekare)
die Bibliothekarin *fem*
□ **She's a librarian.** Sie ist Bibliothekarin.

★ **library** NOUN
1 die Bücherei *fem (public lending library)*
2 die Bibliothek *fem (of school, university)*

Libya NOUN
Libyen *neut*
■ **from Libya** aus Libyen
■ **to Libya** nach Libyen

★ **licence** NOUN
der Schein *masc* (PL die Scheine)
■ **a driving licence** ein Führerschein *masc*

to lick VERB
lecken [48]

lid – like

lid NOUN
der Deckel *masc* (PL die Deckel)

★ **lie** NOUN
▷ *see also* **lie** VERB
die Lüge *fem*
□ That's a lie! Das ist eine Lüge!
■ **to tell a lie** lügen [47]

★ **to lie (1)** VERB
▷ *see also* **lie** NOUN
lügen [47] (IMPERFECT log, PERFECT TENSE hat
gelogen) (*not tell the truth*)
□ I know she's lying. Ich weiß, dass sie lügt.

★ **to lie (2)** VERB
liegen [46] (IMPERFECT lag, PERFECT TENSE hat
gelegen)
□ He was lying on the sofa. Er lag auf dem Sofa.
□ When I'm on holiday I lie on the beach all day.
In den Ferien liege ich den ganzen Tag am
Strand.
■ **to lie down** sich hinlegen [4]
■ **to be lying down** liegen [46]

lie-in NOUN
■ **to have a lie-in** ausschlafen [58] □ She has a
lie-in on Sundays. Sonntags schläft sie aus.

lieutenant NOUN
der Leutnant *masc* (PL die Leutnants)
die Leutnantin *fem*

★ **life** NOUN
das Leben *neut* (PL die Leben)

lifebelt NOUN
der Rettungsring *masc* (PL die Rettungsringe)

lifeboat NOUN
das Rettungsboot *neut* (PL die Rettungsboote)

lifeguard NOUN
1 der Rettungsschwimmer *masc* (PL die
Rettungsschwimmer)
die Rettungsschwimmerin *fem* (*at beach*)
2 der Bademeister *masc* (PL die Bademeister)
die Bademeisterin *fem* (*at swimming pool*)

life jacket NOUN
die Schwimmweste *fem*

life-saving NOUN
das Rettungsschwimmen *neut*
□ I've done a course in life-saving. Ich habe
einen Kurs im Rettungsschwimmen gemacht.

lifestyle NOUN
der Lebensstil *masc* (PL die Lebensstile)

★ **to lift** VERB
▷ *see also* **lift** NOUN
hochheben (IMPERFECT hob hoch, PERFECT TENSE
hat hochgehoben)
□ I can't lift it. Ich kann es nicht hochheben.

★ **lift** NOUN
▷ *see also* **lift** VERB
der Aufzug *masc* (PL die Aufzüge)
□ The lift isn't working. Der Aufzug geht nicht.
■ **He gave me a lift to the cinema.** Er hat
mich zum Kino gefahren.

■ **Would you like a lift?** Kann ich Sie
mitnehmen?

★ **light** ADJECTIVE
▷ *see also* **light** NOUN, VERB
1 leicht (*not heavy*)
□ a light jacket eine leichte Jacke □ a light meal
ein leichtes Essen
2 hell (*colour*)
□ a light blue coat ein hellblauer Mantel

★ **light** NOUN
▷ *see also* **light** ADJECTIVE, VERB
1 das Licht *neut* (PL die Lichter)
□ to switch on the light das Licht anmachen
□ to switch off the light das Licht ausmachen
2 die Lampe *fem*
□ There's a light by my bed. Ich habe am Bett
eine Lampe.
■ **the traffic lights** die Ampel *sing*
■ **Have you got a light?** (*for cigarette*) Haben
Sie Feuer?

★ **to light** VERB
▷ *see also* **light** ADJECTIVE, NOUN
anzünden [54] (PERFECT TENSE hat angezündet)
(*candle, cigarette, fire*)

light bulb NOUN
die Glühbirne *fem*

lighter NOUN
das Feuerzeug *neut* (PL die Feuerzeuge)

lighthouse NOUN
der Leuchtturm *masc* (PL die Leuchttürme)

★ **lightning** NOUN
der Blitz *masc* (GEN des Blitzes, PL die Blitze)
■ **a flash of lightning** ein Blitz
■ **There was a flash of lightning.** Es hat
geblitzt.

★ **to like** VERB
▷ *see also* **like** PREPOSITION
mögen [50] (PRESENT TENSE mag, IMPERFECT
mochte, PERFECT TENSE hat gemocht)
□ I don't like mustard. Ich mag Senf nicht. □ I
like Kieran, but I don't want to go out with him.
Ich mag Kieran, aber ich will nicht mit ihm
ausgehen.
■ **I like riding.** Ich reite gern.
■ **Would you like ...?** Möchtest du ...? □ Would
you like some coffee? Möchtest du Kaffee?
□ Would you like to go for a walk? Möchtest du
einen Spaziergang machen?
■ **I'd like ...** Ich hätte gern ... □ I'd like an
orange juice, please. Ich hätte gern einen
Orangensaft, bitte.
■ **I'd like to ...** Ich würde gern ... □ I'd like to go
to Russia one day. Eines Tages würde ich gern
nach Russland fahren. □ I'd like to wash my
hands. Ich würde mir gern die Hände waschen.
■ **... if you like** ... wenn du möchtest

★ **like** PREPOSITION
▷ *see also* **like** VERB

★ = core vocabulary

1 so (*this way*)
□ It's fine like that. So ist es gut. □ Do it like this. Mach das so.
2 wie (*similar to*)
□ a city like Munich eine Stadt wie München □ It's a bit like salmon. Es ist ein bisschen wie Lachs.
■ **What's the weather like?** Wie ist das Wetter?
■ **to look like somebody** jemandem ähnlich sehen [64] □ You look like my brother. Du siehst meinem Bruder ähnlich.

★ **likely** ADJECTIVE
wahrscheinlich
□ That's not very likely. Das ist nicht sehr wahrscheinlich.
■ **She's likely to come.** Sie kommt wahrscheinlich.
■ **She's not likely to come.** Sie kommt wahrscheinlich nicht.

Lilo® NOUN
die Luftmatratze *fem*

lime NOUN
die Limone *fem* (*fruit*)

★ **limit** NOUN
die Grenze *fem*
■ **the speed limit** die Geschwindigkeitsbegrenzung

limousine NOUN
die Limousine *fem*

to **limp** VERB
hinken [38]

★ **line** NOUN
1 die Linie *fem*
□ a straight line eine gerade Linie
2 der Strich *masc* (PL die Striche) (*to divide, cancel*)
□ Draw a line under each answer. Machen Sie unter jede Antwort einen Strich.
3 das Gleis *neut* (GEN des Gleises, PL die Gleise) (*railway track*)
4 die Schlange *fem*
□ to stand in line Schlange stehen
■ **It's a very bad line.** (*on telephone*) Die Verbindung ist sehr schlecht.

linen NOUN
das Leinen *neut*
□ a linen jacket eine Leinenjacke

liner NOUN
der Überseedampfer *masc* (PL die Überseedampfer) (*ship*)

linguist NOUN
■ **to be a good linguist** sprachbegabt sein [65] □ She's a good linguist. Sie ist sehr sprachbegabt.

lining NOUN
das Futter *neut* (PL die Futter) (*of clothes*)

★ **link** NOUN
▷ see also **link** VERB

1 der Zusammenhang *masc* (PL die Zusammenhänge)
□ the link between smoking and cancer der Zusammenhang zwischen Rauchen und Krebs
2 der Link *masc* (PL die Links) (*computer*)

★ to **link** VERB
▷ see also **link** NOUN
verbinden (IMPERFECT verband, PERFECT TENSE hat verbunden)

lino NOUN
das Linoleum *neut*

★ **lion** NOUN
der Löwe *masc* (GEN des Löwen, PL die Löwen)

★ **lioness** NOUN
die Löwin *fem*

★ **lip** NOUN
die Lippe *fem*

to **lip-read** VERB
von den Lippen ablesen [4] (PRESENT TENSE liest von den Lippen ab, IMPERFECT las von den Lippen ab, PERFECT TENSE hat von den Lippen abgelesen)
■ **I'm learning to lip-read.** Ich lerne gerade Lippenlesen.

lip salve NOUN
der Lippenpflegestift *masc* (PL die Lippenpflegestifte)

lipstick NOUN
der Lippenstift *masc* (PL die Lippenstifte)

liqueur NOUN
der Likör *masc* (PL die Liköre)

liquid NOUN
die Flüssigkeit *fem*

liquidizer NOUN
der Mixer *masc* (PL die Mixer)

★ **list** NOUN
▷ see also **list** VERB
die Liste *fem*

★ to **list** VERB
▷ see also **list** NOUN
aufzählen [4] (PERFECT TENSE hat aufgezählt)
□ List your hobbies. Zählen Sie Ihre Hobbys auf.

★ to **listen** VERB
zuhören [4] (PERFECT TENSE hat zugehört)
□ Listen to me! Hör mir zu!
■ **Listen to this!** Hör dir das an!

listener NOUN
der Zuhörer *masc* (PL die Zuhörer)
die Zuhörerin *fem*

lit VERB ▷ see **light**

liter NOUN (US)
der Liter *masc* (PL die Liter)

literally ADVERB
buchstäblich (*completely*)
□ It was literally impossible to find a seat. Es war buchstäblich unmöglich, einen Platz zu finden.

literature – lock

■ **to translate literally** wörtlich übersetzen
[36]

★ **literature** NOUN
die Literatur fem
□ I'm studying English Literature. Ich studiere
englische Literatur.

litre NOUN
der Liter masc (PL die Liter)
□ three litres drei Liter

litter NOUN
der Abfall masc (PL die Abfälle)

litter bin NOUN
der Abfalleimer masc (PL die Abfalleimer)

★ **little** ADJECTIVE
klein
□ a little girl ein kleines Mädchen

> **WORD POWER**
> You can use a number of other words instead
> of **little** to mean 'small':
> **miniature** Miniatur-
> □ a miniature version eine Miniaturversion
> **minute** winzig
> □ a minute flat eine winzige Wohnung
> **tiny** winzig
> □ a tiny garden ein winziger Garten

■ **a little** ein bisschen □ How much would you
like? — Just a little. Wie viel möchtest du?
— Nur ein bisschen.
■ **very little** sehr wenig □ We've got very little
time. Wir haben sehr wenig Zeit.
■ **little by little** nach und nach

★ **live** ADJECTIVE
▷ see also **live** VERB
1 lebendig (animal)
2 live (broadcast)
■ **There's live music on Fridays.** Freitags gibt
es Livemusik.

★ **to live** VERB
▷ see also **live** ADJECTIVE
1 leben [38]
□ I live with my grandmother. Ich lebe bei
meiner Großmutter. □ They're living together.
Sie leben zusammen.
2 wohnen [38] (in house, town)
□ Where do you live? Wo wohnst du? □ I live in
Edinburgh. Ich wohne in Edinburgh.

to live on VERB
■ **to live on something** von etwas leben [38]
□ He lived on bread and water. Er lebte von Brot
und Wasser. □ He lives on benefits. Er lebt von
der Unterstützung.

lively ADJECTIVE
lebhaft
□ She's got a lively personality. Sie ist ein
lebhafter Typ.

liver NOUN
die Leber fem

lives PL NOUN ▷ see **life**

livestream NOUN
▷ see also **livestream** VERB
Livestream masc (PL die Livestreams)

to livestream VERB
▷ see also **livestream** NOUN
livestreamen [76]

living NOUN
■ **to make a living** sich seinen
Lebensunterhalt verdienen [84]
■ **What does she do for a living?** Was macht
sie beruflich?

living room NOUN
das Wohnzimmer neut (PL die Wohnzimmer)

lizard NOUN
die Echse fem

★ **load** NOUN
▷ see also **load** VERB
■ **loads of** eine Menge □ loads of people eine
Menge Leute □ loads of money eine Menge
Geld
■ **You're talking a load of rubbish!** Du redest
vielleicht einen Unsinn!

★ **to load** VERB
▷ see also **load** NOUN
beladen (PRESENT TENSE belädt, IMPERFECT belud,
PERFECT TENSE hat beladen)
□ He's loading the van right now. Er belädt
gerade den Lieferwagen.

loaf NOUN
der Laib masc (PL die Laibe)
■ **a loaf of bread** ein Brot neut

★ **loan** NOUN
▷ see also **loan** VERB
das Darlehen neut (PL die Darlehen) (money)

★ **to loan** VERB
▷ see also **loan** NOUN
ausleihen (IMPERFECT lieh aus, PERFECT TENSE hat
ausgeliehen)

to loathe VERB
verabscheuen [84] (PERFECT TENSE hat
verabscheut)
□ I loathe her. Ich verabscheue sie.

loaves PL NOUN ▷ see **loaf**

lobster NOUN
der Hummer masc (PL die Hummer)

★ **local** ADJECTIVE
örtlich
□ the local police die örtliche Polizei
■ **the local paper** das Lokalblatt

loch NOUN
der See masc (PL die Seen)

★ **lock** NOUN
▷ see also **lock** VERB
das Schloss neut (GEN des Schlosses, PL die
Schlösser)
□ The lock is broken. Das Schloss ist kaputt.

★ to **lock** VERB
  ▷ see also **lock** NOUN
  abschließen (IMPERFECT schloss ab, PERFECT
  TENSE hat abgeschlossen)
  □ Make sure you lock your door. Schließen Sie
  die Tür ab.
  ■ **to be locked out** ausgesperrt sein [65]
  □ The door slammed and I was locked out. Die
  Tür schlug zu und ich war ausgesperrt.

locker NOUN
  das Schließfach neut (PL die Schließfächer)
  ■ **the locker room** der Umkleideraum
  ■ **the left-luggage lockers** die
  Gepäckschließfächer

locket NOUN
  das Medaillon neut (PL die Medaillons)

lodger NOUN
  der Untermieter masc (PL die Untermieter)
  die Untermieterin fem

loft NOUN
  der Speicher masc (PL die Speicher)

★ **log** NOUN
  das Scheit neut (PL die Scheite) (of wood)

to **log in** VERB
  einloggen [4] (PERFECT TENSE hat eingeloggt)
  (computer)

to **log off** VERB
  ausloggen [4] (PERFECT TENSE hat ausgeloggt)
  (computer)

to **log on** VERB
  einloggen [4] (PERFECT TENSE hat eingeloggt)
  (computer)

to **log out** VERB
  ausloggen [4] (PERFECT TENSE hat ausgeloggt)
  (computer)

logical ADJECTIVE
  logisch

lollipop NOUN
  der Lutscher masc (PL die Lutscher)

lolly NOUN
  das Eis am Stiel neut (ice lolly)

★ **London** NOUN
  London neut
  ■ **from London** aus London
  ■ **to London** nach London

★ **Londoner** NOUN
  der Londoner masc (PL die Londoner)
  die Londonerin fem

loneliness NOUN
  die Einsamkeit fem

lonely ADJECTIVE
  einsam
  ■ **to feel lonely** sich einsam fühlen [38] □ She
  feels lonely. Sie fühlt sich einsam.

★ **long** ADJECTIVE, ADVERB
  ▷ see also **long** VERB
  lang

□ She's got long hair. Sie hat lange Haare. □ The
room is six metres long. Das Zimmer ist sechs
Meter lang.
  ■ **how long?** (time) wie lange? □ How long did
you stay there? Wie lange bist du
dortgeblieben? □ How long is the flight? Wie
lange dauert der Flug?

When you want to say how long you 'have
been' doing something, use the present
tense in German.

□ How long have you been here? Wie lange bist
du schon da? □ I've been waiting a long time.
Ich warte schon lange.
  ■ **It takes a long time.** Das dauert lange.
  ■ **as long as** solange □ I'll come as long as it's
not too expensive. Ich komme mit, solange es
nicht zu teuer ist.

★ to **long** VERB
  ▷ see also **long** ADJECTIVE, ADVERB
  ■ **to long to do something** es kaum erwarten
können [41], etwas zu tun □ I'm longing to see
my boyfriend again. Ich kann es kaum erwarten,
bis ich meinen Freund wiedersehe.

long-distance ADJECTIVE
  ■ **a long-distance call** ein Ferngespräch neut

longer ADVERB
  ■ **They're no longer going out together.** Sie
gehen nicht mehr miteinander.
  ■ **I can't stand it any longer.** Ich halte das
nicht länger aus.

long jump NOUN
  der Weitsprung masc (PL die Weitsprünge)

loo NOUN
  das Klo neut (PL die Klos) (informal)
  □ Where's the loo? Wo ist das Klo?
  ■ **I need the loo.** Ich muss mal. (informal)

★ **look** NOUN
  ▷ see also **look** VERB
  ■ **to have a look** ansehen [64] □ Have a look
at this! Sieh dir das mal an!
  ■ **I don't like the look of it.** Das gefällt mir
nicht.

★ to **look** VERB
  ▷ see also **look** NOUN
  1 sehen [64] (PRESENT TENSE sieht, IMPERFECT sah,
  PERFECT TENSE hat gesehen)
  ■ **Look!** Sieh mal!
  ■ **to look at something** etwas ansehen [64]
  □ Look at the picture. Sieh dir das Bild an.
  2 aussehen [64] (PERFECT TENSE hat ausgesehen)
  (seem)
  □ She looks surprised. Sie sieht überrascht aus.
  □ That cake looks nice. Der Kuchen sieht gut
aus. □ It looks fine. Es sieht gut aus.
  ■ **to look like somebody** jemandem ähnlich
sehen [64] □ He looks like his brother. Er sieht
seinem Bruder ähnlich.
  ■ **What does she look like?** Wie sieht sie aus?
  ■ **Look out!** Pass auf!

I

loose – lovely

■ **to look forward to something** sich auf etwas freuen [38] □ I'm looking forward to the holidays. Ich freue mich auf die Ferien.

■ **Looking forward to hearing from you ...** In der Hoffnung, bald etwas von dir zu hören, ... (*at the end of email, letter*)

to **look after** VERB
sich kümmern [34] um
□ I look after my little sister. Ich kümmere mich um meine kleine Schwester.

to **look for** VERB
suchen [48]
□ I'm looking for my passport. Ich suche meinen Pass.

to **look round** VERB
sich umsehen [64]
□ I shouted and he looked round. Ich habe gerufen, und er sah sich um. □ I'm just looking round. Ich sehe mich nur um. □ I like looking round the shops. Ich sehe mich gern in den Geschäften um.

■ **to look round a museum** ein Museum ansehen [64]

to **look up** VERB
nachschlagen [59] (*word, name*)
□ If you don't know a word, look it up in the dictionary. Wenn du ein Wort nicht weißt, schlage es im Wörterbuch nach.

★ **loose** ADJECTIVE
weit (*clothes*)
■ **loose change** das Kleingeld

lord NOUN
der Lord *masc* (PL die Lords) (*feudal*)
■ **the House of Lords** das Oberhaus

lorry NOUN
der Lastwagen *masc* (PL die Lastwagen)

lorry driver NOUN
der Lastwagenfahrer *masc* (PL die Lastwagenfahrer)
die Lastwagenfahrerin *fem*
□ He's a lorry driver. Er ist Lastwagenfahrer.

★ to **lose** VERB
verlieren [85] (IMPERFECT verlor, PERFECT TENSE hat verloren)
□ I've lost my purse. Ich habe meinen Geldbeutel verloren.
■ **to get lost** sich verlaufen [43] □ I was afraid I'd get lost. Ich hatte Angst, mich zu verlaufen.

★ **loss** NOUN
der Verlust *masc* (PL die Verluste)

★ **lost** VERB ▷ see lose

★ **lost** ADJECTIVE
verloren

lost-and-found NOUN (US)
das Fundbüro *neut* (PL die Fundbüros)

lost property office NOUN
das Fundbüro *neut* (PL die Fundbüros)

★ **lot** NOUN
■ **a lot** viel
■ **a lot of 1** viel □ He earns a lot of money. Er verdient viel Geld. **2** viele □ We saw a lot of interesting things. Wir sahen viele interessante Dinge gesehen.
■ **lots of** eine Menge □ lots of money eine Menge Geld □ lots of friends eine Menge Freunde
■ **What did you do at the weekend? — Not a lot.** Was hast du am Wochenende gemacht? — Nicht viel.
■ **Do you like football? — Not a lot.** Magst du Fußball? — Nicht besonders.
■ **That's the lot.** Das ist alles.

lottery NOUN
das Lotto *neut*
■ **to win the lottery** im Lotto gewinnen [30]

★ **loud** ADJECTIVE
laut
□ The television is too loud. Der Fernseher ist zu laut.

loudly ADVERB
laut

loudspeaker NOUN
der Lautsprecher *masc* (PL die Lautsprecher)

lounge NOUN
das Wohnzimmer *neut* (PL die Wohnzimmer)

lousy ADJECTIVE
lausig schlecht (*informal*)
□ The food in the canteen is lousy. Das Essen in der Kantine ist lausig schlecht.
■ **I feel lousy.** Mir geht's lausig schlecht.

★ **love** NOUN
▷ see also **love** VERB
die Liebe *fem*
■ **to be in love** verliebt sein [65] □ She's in love with Maya. Sie ist in Maya verliebt.
■ **Give your sister my love.** Grüß deine Schwester von mir.
■ **Love, Dad.** Alles Liebe, Papa.

★ to **love** VERB
▷ see also **love** NOUN
1 lieben [38] (*person, thing*)
□ I love you. Ich liebe dich. □ I love chocolate. Ich liebe Schokolade.
2 mögen [50] (PRESENT TENSE mag, IMPERFECT mochte, PERFECT TENSE hat gemocht) (*like a lot*)
□ Everybody loves her. Alle mögen sie.
■ **I'd love to come.** Ich würde liebend gern kommen.
■ **I love skiing.** Ich fahre unheimlich gern Ski.

★ **lovely** ADJECTIVE
1 wunderbar
□ What a lovely surprise! Was für eine wunderbare Überraschung!
2 schön (*pretty*)
□ They've got a lovely house. Sie haben ein schönes Haus.

★ = core vocabulary

■ **It's a lovely day.** Es ist ein herrlicher Tag.
■ **She's a lovely person.** Sie ist ein sehr netter Mensch.
■ **Is your meal OK? — Yes, it's lovely.** Schmeckt dein Essen? — Ja, prima.
■ **Have a lovely time!** Viel Spaß!

lover NOUN
der Liebhaber *masc* (PL die Liebhaber)
die Liebhaberin *fem*

★ **low** ADJECTIVE, ADVERB
niedrig
□ low prices niedrige Preise
■ **That plane is flying very low.** Das Flugzeug fliegt sehr tief.
■ **the low season** die Nebensaison □ **in the low season** in der Nebensaison

low-fat ADJECTIVE
mager
■ **a low-fat yoghurt** ein Magerjoghurt *masc*

loyalty NOUN
die Treue *fem*

loyalty card NOUN
die Kundenkarte *fem*

L-plates PL NOUN
das L-Schild *neut* (PL die L-Schilder)

★ **luck** NOUN
das Glück *neut*
□ She hasn't had much luck. Sie hat nicht viel Glück gehabt.
■ **Good luck!** Viel Glück!
■ **Bad luck!** So ein Pech!

luckily ADVERB
zum Glück

★ **lucky** ADJECTIVE
■ **to be lucky** **1** (*be fortunate*) Glück haben [32] □ He's lucky, he's got a job. Er hat Glück, er hat Arbeit. **2** (*bring luck*) Glück bringen [13] □ Black cats are lucky. Schwarze Katzen bringen Glück.
■ **He wasn't hurt. — That was lucky!** Er wurde nicht verletzt. — Das war Glück!

luggage NOUN
das Gepäck *neut*

lukewarm ADJECTIVE
lauwarm

lump NOUN
1 das Stück *neut* (PL die Stücke)
□ a lump of coal ein Stück Kohle
2 die Beule *fem* (*swelling*)
□ He's got a lump on his forehead. Er hat eine Beule an der Stirn.

★ **lunch** NOUN
das Mittagessen *neut* (PL die Mittagessen)
■ **to have lunch** zu Mittag essen [20] □ We have lunch at twelve o'clock. Wir essen um zwölf Uhr zu Mittag.

luncheon voucher NOUN
die Essensmarke *fem*

lung NOUN
die Lunge *fem*
□ lung cancer der Lungenkrebs

luscious ADJECTIVE
köstlich

lush ADJECTIVE
üppig

lust NOUN
das Verlangen *neut*

★ **Luxembourg** NOUN
Luxemburg *neut* (*country, city*)
■ **from Luxembourg** aus Luxemburg
■ **to Luxembourg** nach Luxemburg

luxurious ADJECTIVE
luxuriös

★ **luxury** NOUN
der Luxus *masc* (GEN des Luxus)
□ It was luxury! Das war wirklich ein Luxus!
■ **a luxury hotel** ein Luxushotel *neut*

lying VERB ▷ *see* lie

lyrics PL NOUN
der Text *masc sing* (PL die Texte) (*of song*)

Mm

mac NOUN
der Regenmantel *masc* (PL die Regenmäntel)

macaroni SING NOUN
die Makkaroni *pl*

★ **machine** NOUN
die Maschine *fem*

machine gun NOUN
das Maschinengewehr *neut*

machinery NOUN
die Maschinen *fem pl*

mackerel NOUN
die Makrele *fem*

★ **mad** ADJECTIVE
1 verrückt (*insane*)
□ You're mad! Du bist verrückt!
■ **to be mad about** verrückt sein [65] nach □ Aiden is mad about Ellie. Aiden ist verrückt nach Ellie. □ She's mad about football. Sie ist verrückt nach Fußball.
2 wütend (*angry*)
□ She'll be mad when she finds out. Wenn sie das erfährt, wird sie wütend sein.
■ **to be mad at somebody** wütend auf jemanden sein [65] □ He was mad at me. Er war wütend auf mich.

madam NOUN

> In German no form of address is normally used apart from **Sie**.

□ Would you like to order, Madam? Möchten Sie bestellen?

made VERB ▷ *see* **make**

madly ADVERB
■ **They're madly in love.** Sie sind wahnsinnig verliebt.

madman NOUN
der Verrückte *masc* (GEN des Verrückten, PL die Verrückten)
□ a madman ein Verrückter

madness NOUN
der Wahnsinn *masc*
□ It's absolute madness. Das ist totaler Wahnsinn.

★ **magazine** NOUN
die Zeitschrift *fem*

maggot NOUN
die Made *fem*

★ **magic** ADJECTIVE
▷ *see also* **magic** NOUN
1 magisch (*magical*)
□ magic powers magische Kräfte
■ **a magic trick** ein Zaubertrick *masc*
■ **a magic wand** ein Zauberstab *masc*
2 echt toll (*brilliant*)
□ It was magic! Es war echt toll!

★ **magic** NOUN
▷ *see also* **magic** ADJECTIVE
das Zaubern *neut*
□ My hobby is magic. Zaubern ist mein Hobby.

magician NOUN
der Zauberkünstler *masc* (PL die Zauberkünstler)
die Zauberkünstlerin *fem* (*conjurer*)

magnet NOUN
der Magnet *masc*

magnificent ADJECTIVE
1 wundervoll (*beautiful*)
□ a magnificent view eine wundervolle Aussicht
2 ausgezeichnet (*outstanding*)
□ It was a magnificent film. Es war ein ausgezeichneter Film.

magnifying glass NOUN
die Lupe *fem*

maid NOUN
die Hausangestellte *fem* (GEN der Hausangestellten) (*servant*)

maiden name NOUN
der Mädchenname *masc* (GEN des Mädchennamens, PL die Mädchennamen)

★ **mail** NOUN
▷ *see also* **mail** VERB
1 die Post *fem*
□ Here's your mail. Hier ist deine Post.
■ **by mail** per Post
2 die E-Mail *fem* (PL die E-Mails) (*email*)
□ Can I check my mail on your laptop? Kann ich meine E-Mails auf deinem Laptop checken?

★ to **mail** VERB
▷ *see also* **mail** NOUN
■ **to mail something to somebody** (*email*)
jemandem etwas mailen [38] □ I'll mail you my address. Ich maile dir meine Adresse.

mailbox NOUN (US)
der Briefkasten *masc* (PL die Briefkästen)

★ = core vocabulary

mailing list NOUN
die Mailingliste fem

mailman NOUN (US)
der Briefträger masc (PL die Briefträger)

mailwoman NOUN (US)
die Briefträgerin fem (PL die Briefträgerinnen)

★ **main** ADJECTIVE
■ **the main problem** das Hauptproblem
■ **the main thing** die Hauptsache

★ **mainly** ADVERB
hauptsächlich

main road NOUN
die Hauptstraße fem
□ I don't like cycling on main roads. Ich fahre
nicht gern auf Hauptstraßen Rad.

★ to **maintain** VERB
instand halten [33] (PRESENT TENSE hält instand,
IMPERFECT hielt instand, PERFECT TENSE hat
instand gehalten) (machine, building)

maintenance NOUN
die Instandhaltung fem (of machine, building)

maize NOUN
der Mais masc

majesty NOUN
die Majestät fem
■ **Your Majesty** Eure Majestät

★ **major** ADJECTIVE
groß
□ a major problem ein großes Problem
■ **a major operation** eine schwere Operation
■ **in C major** in C-Dur

Majorca NOUN
Mallorca neut
■ **to Majorca** nach Mallorca

★ **majority** NOUN
die Mehrheit fem

★ **make** NOUN
▷ see also **make** VERB
die Marke fem
□ What make is that car? Welche Marke ist das
Auto?

★ to **make** VERB
▷ see also **make** NOUN
1 machen [48]
□ He made it himself. Er hat es selbst gemacht.
□ I make my bed every morning. Ich mache
jeden Morgen mein Bett. □ Two and two make
four. Zwei und zwei macht vier.
■ **to make lunch** das Mittagessen machen
[48] □ She's making lunch. Sie macht das
Mittagessen.
■ **I'm going to make a cake.** Ich werde einen
Kuchen backen.
2 herstellen [4] (PERFECT TENSE hat hergestellt)
(manufacture)
□ made in Germany in Deutschland hergestellt
3 verdienen [84] (PERFECT TENSE hat verdient)
(earn)

□ He makes a lot of money. Er verdient viel
Geld.
■ **to make somebody do something**
jemanden zwingen [97], etwas zu tun □ My
mum makes me do my homework. Meine
Mama zwingt mich, meine Hausaufgaben zu
machen.
■ **to make a phone call** telefonieren [76] □ I'd
like to make a phone call. Ich würde gern
telefonieren.
■ **to make fun of somebody** sich über
jemanden lustig machen [48] □ They made fun
of him. Sie haben sich über ihn lustig gemacht.
■ **What time do you make it?** Wie viel Uhr
hast du?

to **make out** VERB
1 entziffern [34] (PERFECT TENSE hat entziffert)
□ I can't make out the address. Ich kann die
Adresse nicht entziffern.
2 verstehen [72] (IMPERFECT verstand, PERFECT
TENSE hat verstanden)
□ I can't make her out at all. Ich kann sie
überhaupt nicht verstehen.
3 behaupten [2] (PERFECT TENSE hat behauptet)
□ They're making out it was my fault. Sie
behaupten, es wäre meine Schuld gewesen.

to **make up** VERB
1 erfinden [24] (IMPERFECT erfand, PERFECT TENSE
hat erfunden) (invent)
□ He made up the whole story. Er hat die ganze
Geschichte erfunden.
2 sich versöhnen [84] (PERFECT TENSE haben sich
versöhnt) (after argument)
□ They soon made up. Sie haben sich bald
wieder versöhnt.

★ **maker** NOUN
1 der Hersteller masc (PL die Hersteller)
□ Germany's biggest car maker Deutschlands
größter Autohersteller
■ **She is a successful film maker.** Sie ist eine
erfolgreiche Filmemacherin.
2 die Maschine fem
□ a bread maker eine Brotmaschine □ a pasta
maker eine Nudelmaschine □ an ice-cream
maker eine Eismaschine

★ **make-up** NOUN
das Make-up neut (PL die Make-ups)

Malaysia NOUN
Malaysia neut
■ **to Malaysia** nach Malaysia

★ **male** ADJECTIVE
männlich
□ a male kitten ein männliches Katzenjunges
□ Sex: male Geschlecht: männlich

In many cases, the ending in German
indicates clearly whether the noun refers to
a man or a woman and there is therefore no
need for the word 'male'.

m

□ male and female students Studenten und Studentinnen

■ **a male nurse** ein Krankenpfleger *masc*

mall NOUN
das Einkaufszentrum *neut* (PL die Einkaufszentren)

Malta NOUN
Malta *neut*
■ **from Malta** aus Malta
■ **to Malta** nach Malta

mammoth ADJECTIVE
monumental
□ a mammoth task eine monumentale Aufgabe

★ **man** NOUN
der Mann *masc* (PL die Männer)
□ an old man ein alter Mann

★ to **manage** VERB
1 leiten [2] (*be in charge of*)
□ She manages a big store. Sie leitet ein großes Geschäft.
2 managen [48] (*band, football team*)
□ She manages the team. Sie managt die Mannschaft.
3 klarkommen [40] (IMPERFECT kam klar, PERFECT TENSE ist klargekommen) (*get by*)
□ We haven't got much money, but we manage. Wir haben nicht viel Geld, aber wir kommen klar. □ It's okay, I can manage. Das ist okay, ich komme klar.
4 schaffen [48]
□ Can you manage okay? Schaffst du es? □ I can't manage all that. (*food*) Das schaffe ich nicht alles.
■ **to manage to do something** es schaffen [48], etwas zu tun □ I managed to pass the exam. Ich habe die Prüfung geschafft.

manageable ADJECTIVE
machbar (*task*)

★ **management** NOUN
die Leitung *fem* (*organization*)
□ the management of the company die Leitung des Unternehmens □ 'under new management' 'unter neuer Leitung'

★ **manager** NOUN
1 der Geschäftsführer *masc* (PL die Geschäftsführer)
die Geschäftsführerin *fem* (*of company, shop, restaurant*)
2 der Manager *masc* (PL die Manager)
die Managerin *fem* (*of performer, football team*)

manageress NOUN
die Geschäftsführerin *fem*

mandarin NOUN
die Mandarine *fem* (*fruit*)

mango NOUN
die Mango *fem* (PL die Mangos)

mania NOUN
die Manie *fem*

maniac NOUN
der Verrückte *masc* (GEN des Verrückten, PL die Verrückten)
die Verrückte *fem* (GEN der Verrückten)
□ He drives like a maniac. Er fährt wie ein Verrückter.

to **manipulate** VERB
manipulieren [76] (PERFECT TENSE hat manipuliert)

mankind NOUN
die Menschheit *fem*

man-made ADJECTIVE
synthetisch (*fibre*)

★ **manner** NOUN
die Art und Weise *fem*
□ in this manner auf diese Art und Weise
■ **He was behaving in an odd manner.** Er benahm sich eigenartig.
■ **She has a confident manner.** Sie wirkt selbstsicher.

manners PL NOUN
das Benehmen *neut sing*
□ good manners gutes Benehmen
■ **Her manners are appalling.** Sie benimmt sich schrecklich.
■ **It's bad manners to speak with your mouth full.** Es gehört sich nicht, mit vollem Mund zu sprechen.

manpower NOUN
die Arbeitskräfte *fem pl*

mansion NOUN
die Villa *fem* (PL die Villen)

mantelpiece NOUN
der Kaminsims *masc* (GEN des Kaminsimses, PL die Kaminsimse)

manual NOUN
das Handbuch *neut* (PL die Handbücher)

★ to **manufacture** VERB
herstellen [4] (PERFECT TENSE hat hergestellt)

★ **manufacturer** NOUN
der Hersteller *masc* (PL die Hersteller)

manure NOUN
der Mist *masc*

manuscript NOUN
das Manuskript *neut* (PL die Manuskripte)

★ **many** ADJECTIVE, PRONOUN
viele
□ The country has many natural resources. Das Land hat viele Bodenschätze. □ He hasn't got many friends. Er hat nicht viele Freunde.
□ Were there many people at the concert? Waren viele Leute in dem Konzert?
■ **very many** sehr viele □ I haven't got very many books. Ich habe nicht sehr viele Bücher.
■ **Not many.** Nicht viele.
■ **How many?** Wie viele? □ How many do you want? Wie viele möchten Sie?

■ **How many euros do you get for a hundred pounds?** Wie viel Euro bekommt man für (ein)hundert Pfund?

■ **too many** zu viele □ That's too many. Das sind zu viele. □ She makes too many mistakes. Sie macht zu viele Fehler.

■ **so many** so viele □ I didn't know that so many would come. Ich wusste nicht, dass so viele kommen würden. □ I've never seen so many policewomen. Ich habe noch nie so viele Polizistinnen gesehen.

★ **map** NOUN
1 die Landkarte *fem* (*of country, area*)
2 der Stadtplan *masc* (PL die Stadtpläne) (*of town*)

> **BE CAREFUL!**
> Do not translate **map** by **Mappe**.

marathon NOUN
der Marathonlauf *masc* (PL die Marathonläufe)
□ the London marathon der Londoner Marathonlauf

marble NOUN
der Marmor *masc*
□ a marble statue eine Marmorstatue
■ **to play marbles** Murmeln spielen [38]

★ **March** NOUN
der März *masc*
□ in March im März

★ **march** NOUN
▷ *see also* **march** VERB
der Protestmarsch *masc* (GEN des Protestmarsches, PL die Protestmärsche) (*demonstration*)

★ to **march** VERB
▷ *see also* **march** NOUN
1 marschieren [76] (PERFECT TENSE ist marschiert) (*soldiers*)
2 aufmarschieren [76] (PERFECT TENSE ist aufmarschiert) (*protesters*)

mare NOUN
die Stute *fem*

margarine NOUN
die Margarine *fem*

★ **margin** NOUN
der Rand *masc* (PL die Ränder)
□ I wrote notes in the margin. Ich schrieb Notizen an den Rand.

marijuana NOUN
das Marihuana *neut*

marital status NOUN
der Familienstand *masc*

★ **mark** NOUN
▷ *see also* **mark** VERB
1 die Note *fem* (*in school*)
□ I get good marks for biology. Ich habe in Biologie gute Noten.
2 der Fleck *masc* (PL die Flecken) (*stain*)
□ You've got a mark on your shirt. Du hast einen Fleck auf dem Hemd.

★ to **mark** VERB
▷ *see also* **mark** NOUN
korrigieren [76] (PERFECT TENSE hat korrigiert)
□ The teacher hasn't marked my homework yet. Der Lehrer hat meine Hausarbeit noch nicht korrigiert.

★ **market** NOUN
der Markt *masc* (PL die Märkte)

★ **marketing** NOUN
das Marketing *neut* (GEN des Marketing)

marketplace NOUN
der Marktplatz *masc* (GEN des Marktplatzes, PL die Marktplätze)

marmalade NOUN
die Orangenmarmelade *fem*

maroon ADJECTIVE
kastanienbraun (*colour*)

★ **marriage** NOUN
die Ehe *fem*

★ **married** ADJECTIVE
verheiratet
□ They are not married. Sie sind nicht verheiratet. □ They have been married for fifteen years. Sie sind seit fünfzehn Jahren verheiratet.
■ **a married couple** ein Ehepaar *neut*

marrow NOUN
der Kürbis *masc* (GEN des Kürbisses, PL die Kürbisse) (*vegetable*)

★ to **marry** VERB
heiraten [2]
□ He wants to marry him. Er will ihn heiraten.
■ **to get married** heiraten [2] □ My sister's getting married in June. Meine Schwester heiratet im Juni.

marvellous ADJECTIVE
wunderbar
□ She's a marvellous cook. Sie ist eine wunderbare Köchin. □ The weather was marvellous. Das Wetter war wunderbar.

marzipan NOUN
der Marzipan *masc* (PL die Marzipane)

mascara NOUN
die Wimperntusche *fem*

masculine ADJECTIVE
männlich

mashed potatoes PL NOUN
der Kartoffelbrei *masc*
□ chicken with mashed potatoes Hähnchen mit Kartoffelbrei

★ **mask** NOUN
die Maske *fem*

★ **mass** NOUN
1 der Haufen *masc* (PL die Haufen)
□ a mass of books and papers ein Haufen Bücher und Papiere

m

Numbers in brackets refer to verb tables on pages 697 to 706.

519

2 die Messe *fem* (*in church*)
□ We go to mass on Sunday. Wir gehen am Sonntag zur Messe.
■ **the mass media** die Massenmedien

massage NOUN
die Massage *fem*

★ **massive** ADJECTIVE
enorm

★ to **master** VERB
beherrschen [7] (PERFECT TENSE hat beherrscht)
□ to master a language eine Sprache beherrschen

masterpiece NOUN
das Meisterstück *neut* (PL die Meisterstücke)

mat NOUN
der Vorleger *masc* (PL die Vorleger) (*doormat*)
■ **a table mat** ein Untersetzer *masc*
■ **a place mat** ein Set *neut*

★ **match** NOUN
▷ *see also* **match** VERB
1 das Streichholz *neut* (GEN des Streichholzes, PL die Streichhölzer)
□ a box of matches eine Schachtel Streichhölzer
2 das Spiel *neut* (PL die Spiele) (*sport*)
□ a football match ein Fußballspiel

★ to **match** VERB
▷ *see also* **match** NOUN
passen [31] zu
□ The jacket matches the trousers. Die Jacke passt zu der Hose. □ The carpet and the curtains don't match. Der Teppich und die Vorhänge passen nicht zueinander.

matching ADJECTIVE
farblich abgestimmt
□ matching wallpaper and curtains farblich abgestimmte Tapeten und Vorhänge

★ **mate** NOUN
der Kumpel *masc* (PL die Kumpel) (*informal*)

der Kumpel is also used for women.

□ On Friday night I go out with my mates. Freitag Abend gehe ich mit meinen Kumpels aus.

★ **material** NOUN
1 der Stoff *masc* (PL die Stoffe) (*cloth*)
2 das Material *neut* (PL die Materialien) (*information, data*)
□ I'm collecting material for my project. Ich sammle Material für mein Referat.
■ **raw materials** die Rohstoffe

mathematics SING NOUN
die Mathematik *fem*

maths SING NOUN
die Mathe *fem*

matron NOUN
die Oberschwester *fem* (*in hospital*)

★ **matter** NOUN
▷ *see also* **matter** VERB
die Angelegenheit *fem*
□ It's a serious matter. Das ist eine ernste Angelegenheit.
■ **It's a matter of life and death.** Es geht um Leben und Tod.
■ **What's the matter?** Was ist los?
■ **as a matter of fact** tatsächlich

★ to **matter** VERB
▷ *see also* **matter** NOUN
■ **it doesn't matter** **1** (*I don't mind*) das macht nichts □ I can't give you the money today. — It doesn't matter. Ich kann dir das Geld heute nicht geben. — Das macht nichts.
2 (*makes no difference*) das ist egal □ Shall I phone today or tomorrow? — Whenever, it doesn't matter. Soll ich heute oder morgen anrufen? — Wann du willst, das ist egal.
■ **It matters a lot to me.** Das ist mir sehr wichtig.

mattress NOUN
die Matratze *fem*

mature ADJECTIVE
reif
□ She's very mature for her age. Sie ist sehr reif für ihr Alter.

★ **maximum** NOUN
▷ *see also* **maximum** ADJECTIVE
das Maximum *neut* (PL die Maxima)

★ **maximum** ADJECTIVE
▷ *see also* **maximum** NOUN
■ **the maximum speed** die Höchstgeschwindigkeit
■ **the maximum amount** der Höchstbetrag

★ **May** NOUN
der Mai *masc*
□ in May im Mai
■ **May Day** der Erste Mai

★ **may** VERB
■ **He may come.** Er kommt vielleicht.
■ **It may rain.** Es regnet vielleicht.
■ **Are you going to the party? — I don't know, I may.** Gehst du zur Party? — Ich weiß nicht, vielleicht.
■ **May I sit down?** Darf ich mich hinsetzen?

★ **maybe** ADVERB
vielleicht
□ maybe not vielleicht nicht □ a bit boring, maybe vielleicht etwas langweilig □ Maybe she's at home. Vielleicht ist sie zu Hause.
□ Maybe he'll change his mind. Vielleicht überlegt er es sich anders.

mayonnaise NOUN
die Mayonnaise *fem*

★ **mayor** NOUN
der Bürgermeister *masc* (PL die Bürgermeister)
die Bürgermeisterin *fem*

maze NOUN
der Irrgarten masc (PL die Irrgärten)

★ **me** PRONOUN
1 mich
□ Can you hear me? Kannst du mich hören?
□ Look at me! Sieh mich an!

Use **mich** after prepositions which take the accusative.

□ Is this present for me? Ist das Geschenk für mich? □ Wait for me! Warte auf mich!

2 mir

Use **mir** after prepositions which take the dative.

□ Will you come with me? Kommst du mit mir mit? □ He sat next to me. Er saß neben mir.

Use **mir** when 'me' means 'to me'.

□ Give me the book, please! Gib mir bitte das Buch! □ She told me the truth. Sie hat mir die Wahrheit erzählt.

3 ich
□ It's me! Ich bin's! □ Me too! Ich auch! □ She's older than me. Sie ist älter als ich.

★ **meal** NOUN
das Essen neut (PL die Essen)

mealtime NOUN
■ **at mealtimes** zur Essenszeit

★ **to mean** VERB
▷ see also **mean** ADJECTIVE
1 bedeuten [2] (PERFECT TENSE hat bedeutet) (signify)
□ What does 'besetzt' mean? Was bedeutet 'besetzt'? □ I don't know what it means. Ich weiß nicht, was es bedeutet.

2 meinen [38] (mean to say)
□ What do you mean? Was meinst du damit? □ That's not what I meant. Das habe ich nicht gemeint. □ Which one do you mean? Welchen meinst du? □ Do you really mean it? Meinst du das wirklich?

■ **to mean to do something** etwas tun wollen [94] □ I didn't mean to offend you. Ich wollte dich nicht kränken.

★ **mean** ADJECTIVE
▷ see also **mean** VERB
1 geizig (with money)
□ He's too mean to buy Christmas presents. Er ist zu geizig, um Weihnachtsgeschenke zu kaufen.

2 gemein (unkind)
□ You're being mean to me. Du bist gemein zu mir. □ That's a really mean thing to say! Das ist gemein, so etwas zu sagen!

★ **meaning** NOUN
die Bedeutung fem

BE CAREFUL!
Do not translate **meaning** by Meinung.

★ **means** NOUN
die Möglichkeit fem
□ a means of storing power eine Möglichkeit, Energie zu speichern □ We have the means to do that. Wir haben die Möglichkeit, das zu tun.
■ **a means of transport** ein Transportmittel neut
■ **He'll do it by any possible means.** Er wird es tun, egal wie.
■ **by means of** mit □ He got in by means of a stolen key. Er kam mit einem gestohlenen Schlüssel hinein.
■ **by all means** selbstverständlich □ Can I come? — By all means! Kann ich kommen? — Selbstverständlich!
■ **by no means** keineswegs □ That was by no means the end of the matter. Damit war die Sache keineswegs erledigt.

meant VERB ▷ see **mean**

★ **meanwhile** ADVERB
inzwischen

measles SING NOUN
die Masern pl
□ She's got measles. Sie hat Masern.

★ **to measure** VERB
1 ausmessen (PRESENT TENSE misst aus, IMPERFECT maß aus, PERFECT TENSE hat ausgemessen)
□ I measured the page. Ich habe die Seite ausgemessen.

2 messen
□ The room measures three metres by four. Das Zimmer misst drei auf vier Meter.

measurement NOUN
das Maß neut (PL die Maße) (of object)
□ What are the measurements of the room? Wie sind die Maße des Zimmers? □ What are your measurements? Was sind Ihre Maße?
■ **my waist measurement** meine Taillenweite
■ **What's your neck measurement?** Welche Kragenweite haben Sie?

★ **meat** NOUN
das Fleisch neut
□ I don't eat meat. Ich esse kein Fleisch.

Mecca NOUN
Mekka neut

mechanic NOUN
der Mechaniker masc (PL die Mechaniker)
die Mechanikerin fem
□ He's a mechanic. Er ist Mechaniker.

mechanical ADJECTIVE
mechanisch

★ **medal** NOUN
die Medaille fem
■ **the gold medal** die Goldmedaille

★ **media** PL NOUN
die Medien neut pl

median strip NOUN (US)
der Mittelstreifen masc (PL die Mittelstreifen)

★ **media studies** PL NOUN
die Medienwissenschaft *fem sing*

★ **medical** ADJECTIVE
▷ *see also* **medical** NOUN
medizinisch
□ **medical treatment** die medizinische Behandlung
■ **medical insurance** die Krankenversicherung
■ **She's a medical student.** Sie ist Medizinstudentin.

★ **medical** NOUN
▷ *see also* **medical** ADJECTIVE
■ **to have a medical** sich ärztlich untersuchen lassen [42]

★ **medicine** NOUN
die Medizin *fem*
□ **I want to study medicine.** Ich möchte Medizin studieren. □ **I need some medicine.** Ich brauche Medizin.
■ **alternative medicine** die alternative Medizin

Mediterranean ADJECTIVE
▷ *see also* **Mediterranean** NOUN
südländisch (*person, character, scenery*)

Mediterranean NOUN
▷ *see also* **Mediterranean** ADJECTIVE
■ **the Mediterranean** das Mittelmeer

★ **medium** ADJECTIVE
mittlere
□ **a man of medium height** ein Mann von mittlerer Größe

medium-sized ADJECTIVE
mittelgroß
□ **a medium-sized town** eine mittelgroße Stadt

★ to **meet** VERB
1 treffen [78] (PRESENT TENSE trifft, IMPERFECT traf, PERFECT TENSE hat getroffen) (*by chance*)
□ **I met Ali when I was walking the dog.** Ich habe Ali getroffen, als ich mit dem Hund spazieren war.
2 sich treffen [78] (*by arrangement*)
□ **Let's meet in front of the tourist office.** Treffen wir uns doch vor dem Verkehrsbüro.
□ **I'm going to meet my friends.** Ich treffe mich mit meinen Freunden.
3 kennenlernen [4] (PERFECT TENSE hat kennengelernt) (*get to know*)
□ **I like meeting new people.** Ich lerne gerne neue Leute kennen.
■ **Have you met him before?** Kennen Sie ihn?
4 abholen [4] (PERFECT TENSE hat abgeholt) (*pick up*)
□ **I'll meet you at the station.** Ich hole dich am Bahnhof ab.

★ **meeting** NOUN
1 die Besprechung *fem* (*for work*)
□ **a business meeting** eine geschäftliche Besprechung

2 das Treffen *neut* (PL die Treffen) (*socially*)
□ **their first meeting** ihr erstes Treffen

meg NOUN (= *megabyte*)
das Megabyte *neut* (PL die Megabytes)

mega ADJECTIVE
■ **He's mega rich.** Er ist superreich. (*informal*)

melody NOUN
die Melodie *fem*

melon NOUN
die Melone *fem*

to **melt** VERB
schmelzen (PRESENT TENSE schmilzt, IMPERFECT schmolz, PERFECT TENSE ist geschmolzen)
□ **The snow is melting.** Der Schnee schmilzt.

★ **member** NOUN
das Mitglied *neut* (PL die Mitglieder)
■ **a Member of Parliament 1** (*man*) ein Abgeordneter **2** (*woman*) eine Abgeordnete

★ **membership** NOUN
die Mitgliedschaft *fem* (*of club*)
□ **I'm going to apply for membership.** Ich werde mich um Mitgliedschaft bewerben.

membership card NOUN
der Mitgliedsausweis *masc* (PL die Mitgliedsausweise)

meme NOUN
das Meme *neut* (PL die Memes) (*internet*)

memento NOUN
das Andenken *neut* (PL die Andenken)

memorial NOUN
das Denkmal *neut* (PL die Denkmäler)
■ **a war memorial** ein Kriegerdenkmal

to **memorize** VERB
auswendig lernen [38]

★ **memory** NOUN
1 das Gedächtnis *neut* (GEN des Gedächtnisses)
□ **I haven't got a good memory.** Ich habe kein gutes Gedächtnis.
2 die Erinnerung *fem* (*recollection*)
□ **to bring back memories** Erinnerungen wecken
3 der Speicher *masc* (GEN die Speicher) (*computer*)

memory card NOUN
die Speicherkarte *fem*

memory stick NOUN
der Memorystick® *masc* (PL die Memorysticks) (*for computer*)

men PL NOUN ▷ *see* **man**

to **mend** VERB
flicken [48]

meningitis NOUN
die Hirnhautentzündung *fem*

★ **mental** ADJECTIVE
geistig
■ **a mental illness** eine Geisteskrankheit

★ to **mention** VERB
erwähnen [19] (PERFECT TENSE hat erwähnt)
■ **Thank you! — Don't mention it!** Danke!
— Bitte!

mentor NOUN
Mentor masc (PL die Mentoren)

menu NOUN
1 die Speisekarte fem
□ Could I have the menu, please? Könnte ich
bitte die Speisekarte haben?
2 das Menü neut (PL die Menüs) (on computer)

★ **merchant** NOUN
der Händler masc (PL die Händler)
die Händlerin fem
□ a wine merchant ein Weinhändler

mercy NOUN
die Gnade fem

mere ADJECTIVE
bloß
□ It's a mere formality. Das ist eine bloße
Formalität.
■ **a mere five percent** ganze fünf Prozent

meringue NOUN
die Meringe fem

merry ADJECTIVE
■ **Merry Christmas!** Fröhliche Weihnachten!

merry-go-round NOUN
das Karussell neut (PL die Karussells)

★ **mess** NOUN
die Unordnung fem
□ His bedroom's always in a mess. In seinem
Schlafzimmer herrscht ständig Unordnung.

to **mess about** VERB
■ **to mess about with something** (interfere
with) an etwas herumfummeln [4] □ Stop
messing about with my computer! Hör auf, an
meinem Computer herumzufummeln!
■ **Don't mess about with my things!** Lass
meine Sachen in Ruhe!

to **mess up** VERB
■ **to mess something up** etwas
durcheinanderbringen [13] □ My little brother
has messed up my room. Mein kleiner Bruder
hat mein Zimmer durcheinandergebracht.

★ **message** NOUN
▷ see also **message** VERB
die Nachricht fem

to **message** VERB
▷ see also **message** NOUN
■ **She messaged me on Facebook.** Sie
schickte mir eine Nachricht auf Facebook.

messenger NOUN
der Bote masc (GEN des Boten, PL die Boten)
die Botin fem

messy ADJECTIVE
1 schmutzig (dirty)
□ a messy job eine schmutzige Arbeit

2 unordentlich (untidy)
□ Your room's really messy. Dein Zimmer ist
wirklich unordentlich. □ She's so messy! Sie ist
so unordentlich!
■ **My writing is terribly messy.** Ich habe eine
schreckliche Schrift.

met VERB ▷ see **meet**

★ **metal** NOUN
das Metall neut (PL die Metalle)

meter NOUN
1 der Zähler masc (PL die Zähler) (for gas,
electricity, taxi)
2 die Parkuhr fem (parking meter)

★ **method** NOUN
die Methode fem

★ **metre** NOUN
der Meter masc (PL die Meter)

metric ADJECTIVE
metrisch

Mexico NOUN
Mexiko neut
■ **from Mexico** aus Mexiko
■ **to Mexico** nach Mexiko

to **miaow** VERB
miauen [7] (PERFECT TENSE hat miaut)

mice PL NOUN ▷ see **mouse**

microblog NOUN
das Mikroblog neut (PL die Mikroblogs)

microblogging site NOUN
der Mikroblogging-Dienst masc

microchip NOUN
der Mikrochip masc (PL die Mikrochips)

microphone NOUN
das Mikrofon neut (PL die Mikrofone)

microscope NOUN
das Mikroskop neut (PL die Mikroskope)

microwave NOUN
die Mikrowelle fem

microwave oven NOUN
der Mikrowellenherd masc (PL die
Mikrowellenherde)

mid ADJECTIVE
■ **in mid May** Mitte Mai

midday NOUN
der Mittag masc (PL die Mittage)
■ **at midday** mittags

★ **middle** NOUN
die Mitte fem
■ **in the middle of the road** mitten auf der
Straße
■ **in the middle of the night** mitten in der
Nacht
■ **the middle seat** der mittlere Sitz
■ **the Middle East** der Nahe Osten

middle-aged ADJECTIVE
mittleren Alters

m

□ a middle-aged man ein Mann mittleren Alters
□ She's middle-aged. Sie ist mittleren Alters.

Middle Ages PL NOUN
■ the Middle Ages das Mittelalter

middle-class ADJECTIVE
■ a middle-class family eine Familie der Mittelschicht

middle name NOUN
der zweite Vorname *masc* (GEN des zweiten Vornamens, PL die zweiten Vornamen)

midge NOUN
die Mücke *fem*

★ **midnight** NOUN
die Mitternacht *fem*
■ at midnight um Mitternacht

midwife NOUN
die Hebamme *fem*
□ She's a midwife. Sie ist Hebamme.

★ **might** VERB

Use **vielleicht** to express possibility.

□ He might come later. Er kommt vielleicht später. □ We might go to Spain next year. Wir fahren nächstes Jahr vielleicht nach Spanien. □ She might not have understood. Sie hat es vielleicht nicht verstanden.

migraine NOUN
die Migräne *fem*
□ I've got a migraine. Ich habe Migräne.

mike NOUN
das Mikro *neut* (PL die Mikros)

★ **mild** ADJECTIVE
mild
□ The winters are quite mild. Die Winter sind ziemlich mild.

★ **mile** NOUN
die Meile *fem*

DID YOU KNOW...?
In Germany distances and speeds are expressed in kilometres. A mile is about 1.6 kilometres.

□ It's five miles from here. Es ist acht Kilometer von hier. □ at fifty miles per hour mit achtzig Kilometern pro Stunde
■ We walked miles! Wir sind meilenweit gegangen!

★ **military** ADJECTIVE
militärisch

★ **milk** NOUN
▷ see also **milk** VERB
die Milch *fem*
□ tea with milk der Tee mit Milch

★ to **milk** VERB
▷ see also **milk** NOUN
melken (PERFECT TENSE hat gemolken)

milk chocolate NOUN
die Milchschokolade *fem*

milk shake NOUN
der Milchshake *masc* (PL die Milchshakes)

mill NOUN
die Mühle *fem* (for grain)

millennium NOUN
das Jahrtausend *neut*

millimetre NOUN
der Millimeter *masc* (PL die Millimeter)

★ **million** NOUN
die Million *fem*

millionaire NOUN
der Millionär *masc* (PL die Millionäre)
die Millionärin *fem*

to **mimic** VERB
nachmachen [4] (PERFECT TENSE hat nachgemacht)

mince NOUN
das Hackfleisch *neut*

★ to **mind** VERB
▷ see also **mind** NOUN
aufpassen [31] auf +*acc* (PERFECT TENSE hat aufgepasst)
□ Could you mind the baby this afternoon? Kannst du heute Nachmittag auf das Baby aufpassen? □ Could you mind my bags? Könner Sie auf mein Gepäck aufpassen?
■ Do you mind if I open the window? Macht es Ihnen etwas aus, wenn ich das Fenster aufmache?
■ I don't mind. Es macht mir nichts aus. □ I don't mind the noise. Der Lärm macht mir nichts aus.
■ Never mind! Macht nichts!
■ Mind that bike! Pass auf das Fahrrad auf!
■ Mind the step! Vorsicht Stufe!

★ **mind** NOUN
▷ see also **mind** VERB
■ to make up one's mind sich entscheiden □ I haven't made up my mind yet. Ich habe mich noch nicht entschieden.
■ to change one's mind es sich anders überlegen [82] □ I've changed my mind. Ich habe es mir anders überlegt.
■ Are you out of your mind? Bist du wahnsinnig?

mindfulness NOUN
die Achtsamkeit *fem*

★ **mine** PRONOUN
▷ see also **mine** NOUN
1 meiner
□ Is this your coat? — No, mine's black. Ist das dein Mantel? — Nein, meiner ist schwarz.
meine
□ Is this your cup? — No, mine's red. Ist das deine Tasse? — Nein, meine ist rot.
meines
□ Is this your car? — No, mine's green. Ist das dein Auto? — Nein, meines ist grün.

2 meine

□ her parents and mine ihre Eltern und meine
□ Your hands are dirty, mine are clean. Deine Hände sind schmutzig, meine sind sauber.
■ **It's mine.** Das gehört mir. □ This book is mine. Dieses Buch gehört mir. □ Whose is this? — It's mine. Wem gehört das? — Es gehört mir.

★ **mine** NOUN
▷ see also **mine** PRONOUN
die Mine *fem*
■ **a land mine** eine Landmine
■ **a coal mine** ein Kohlebergwerk *neut*

miner NOUN
der Bergarbeiter *masc* (PL die Bergarbeiter)

mineral water NOUN
das Mineralwasser *neut* (PL die Mineralwasser)

miniature NOUN
die Miniatur *fem*

minibus NOUN
der Minibus *masc* (GEN des Minibusses, PL die Minibusse)

minicab NOUN
das Kleintaxi *neut* (PL die Kleintaxis)

★ **minimum** NOUN
▷ see also **minimum** ADJECTIVE
das Mininum *neut* (PL die Minima)

★ **minimum** ADJECTIVE
▷ see also **minimum** NOUN
■ **minimum age** das Mindestalter
■ **minimum amount** der Mindestbetrag
■ **minimum wage** der Mindestlohn

miniskirt NOUN
der Minirock *masc* (PL die Miniröcke)

★ **minister** NOUN
1 der Minister *masc* (PL die Minister)
die Ministerin *fem* (*in government*)
2 der Pfarrer *masc* (PL die Pfarrer)
die Pfarrerin *fem* (*of church*)

ministry NOUN
das Ministerium *neut* (PL die Ministerien) (*in politics*)

★ **minor** ADJECTIVE
kleiner
□ a minor problem ein kleineres Problem □ a minor operation eine kleinere Operation
■ **in D minor** in d-Moll

minority NOUN
die Minderheit *fem*

mint NOUN
1 die Pfefferminze *fem* (*plant*)
■ **mint sauce** die Pfefferminzsoße
2 das Pfefferminzbonbon *neut* (PL die Pfefferminzbonbons) (*sweet*)

minus PREPOSITION
minus
□ Sixteen minus three is thirteen. Sechzehn minus drei ist dreizehn. □ It's minus two degrees outside. Draußen hat es zwei Grad minus. □ I got a B minus. Ich habe eine Zwei minus bekommen.

DID YOU KNOW...?
In Germany grades are given from 1 to 6, with 1 being the best.

★ **minute** NOUN
▷ see also **minute** ADJECTIVE
die Minute *fem*
■ **Wait a minute!** Einen Augenblick!

★ **minute** ADJECTIVE
▷ see also **minute** NOUN
winzig
□ Her flat is minute. Ihre Wohnung ist winzig.

miracle NOUN
das Wunder *neut* (PL die Wunder)

★ **mirror** NOUN
der Spiegel *masc* (PL die Spiegel)

to **misbehave** VERB
sich schlecht benehmen [52] (PRESENT TENSE benimmt sich schlecht, IMPERFECT benahm sich schlecht, PERFECT TENSE hat sich schlecht benommen)

miscellaneous ADJECTIVE
verschieden
□ miscellaneous items verschiedene Artikel

mischief NOUN
die Dummheiten *fem pl*
□ She's always up to mischief. Sie macht dauernd Dummheiten.

mischievous ADJECTIVE
verschmitzt

miser NOUN
der Geizhals *masc* (GEN des Geizhalses, PL die Geizhälse)

miserable ADJECTIVE
1 unglücklich (*person*)
□ You're looking miserable. Du siehst richtig unglücklich aus.
2 schrecklich (*weather*)
□ The weather was miserable. Das Wetter war schrecklich.
■ **to feel miserable** sich miserabel fühlen [38]
□ I'm feeling miserable. Ich fühle mich miserabel.

misery NOUN
1 das Elend *neut*
□ All that money brought nothing but misery. All das Geld hat nichts als Elend gebracht.
2 der Miesepeter *masc* (*informal*) (PL die Miesepeter)
□ She's a real misery. Sie ist ein richtiger Miesepeter.

misfortune NOUN
das Unglück *neut* (PL die Unglücke)

mishap NOUN
das Missgeschick *neut* (PL die Missgeschicke)

Numbers in brackets refer to verb tables on pages 697 to 706.

525

m

misjudge – mix

to misjudge VERB
falsch einschätzen [4] (PERFECT TENSE hat falsch
eingeschätzt) (person)
□ I've misjudged her. Ich habe sie falsch
eingeschätzt.
■ He misjudged the bend. Er hat sich in der
Kurve verschätzt.

to mislay VERB
verlegen [7] (PERFECT TENSE hat verlegt)
□ I've mislaid my passport. Ich habe meinen
Pass verlegt.

to mislead VERB
irreführen [4] (PERFECT TENSE hat irregeführt)

misleading ADJECTIVE
irreführend

misprint NOUN
der Druckfehler masc (PL die Druckfehler)

★ **Miss** NOUN
das Fräulein neut

□ Miss Jones Frau Jones

★ **to miss** VERB
verpassen [7] (PERFECT TENSE hat verpasst)
□ Hurry or you'll miss the bus. Beeil dich, sonst
verpasst du den Bus! □ to miss an opportunity
eine Gelegenheit verpassen
■ I miss you. Du fehlst mir.
■ I'm missing my family. Meine Familie fehlt
mir.
■ He missed the target. Er hat nicht
getroffen.

★ **missing** ADJECTIVE
fehlend
□ the missing part das fehlende Teil
■ to be missing fehlen [38] □ My rucksack is
missing. Mein Rucksack fehlt. □ Two members
of the group are missing. Zwei Mitglieder der
Gruppe fehlen.

missionary NOUN
der Missionar masc (PL die Missionare)
die Missionarin fem

mist NOUN
der Nebel masc (PL die Nebel)

★ **mistake** NOUN
▷ see also **mistake** VERB
der Fehler masc (PL die Fehler)
□ It was a mistake to buy those yellow shoes. Es
war ein Fehler, diese gelben Schuhe zu kaufen.
■ a spelling mistake ein Rechtschreibfehler
■ to make a mistake **1** (in writing, speaking)
einen Fehler machen [48] **2** (get mixed up) sich

vertun [81] □ I'm sorry, I made a mistake. Tut
mir leid, ich habe mich vertan.
■ by mistake aus Versehen □ I took his bag by
mistake. Ich habe aus Versehen seine Tasche
genommen.

★ **to mistake** VERB
▷ see also **mistake** NOUN
■ He mistook me for my sister. Er hat mich
mit meiner Schwester verwechselt.

mistaken ADJECTIVE
■ to be mistaken sich irren [38] □ If you think
I'm going to get up at six o'clock, you're
mistaken. Wenn du meinst, ich würde um
sechs Uhr aufstehen, dann irrst du dich.

mistakenly ADVERB
irrtümlicherweise

mistletoe NOUN
die Mistel fem

mistook VERB ▷ see **mistake**

to mistrust VERB
misstrauen [49] (PERFECT TENSE hat misstraut)
□ I mistrust her. Ich misstraue ihr.

misty ADJECTIVE
neblig
□ a misty morning ein nebliger Morgen

to misunderstand VERB
missverstehen [72] (IMPERFECT missverstand,
PERFECT TENSE hat missverstanden)
□ Sorry, I misunderstood you. Entschuldigung,
ich habe Sie missverstanden.

misunderstanding NOUN
das Missverständnis neut (GEN des
Missverständnisses, PL die Missverständnisse)

misunderstood VERB ▷ see **misunderstand**

★ **mix** NOUN
▷ see also **mix** VERB
die Mischung fem
□ It's a mix of science fiction and comedy. Es ist
eine Mischung aus Science-Fiction und
Komödie.
■ a cake mix eine Backmischung

★ **to mix** VERB
▷ see also **mix** NOUN
1 vermischen [7] (PERFECT TENSE hat vermischt)
□ Mix the flour with the sugar. Vermischen Sie
das Mehl mit dem Zucker.
2 verbinden (IMPERFECT verband, PERFECT TENSE hat
verbunden)
□ He's mixing business with pleasure. Er
verbindet das Geschäftliche mit dem
Vergnügen.
■ to mix with somebody (associate) mit
jemandem verkehren [7]
■ He doesn't mix much. Er geht nicht viel
unter Menschen.

to mix up VERB
verwechseln [34]
□ He always mixes me up with my sister. Er
verwechselt mich immer mit meiner Schwester.

□ The travel agent mixed up the bookings. Das Reisebüro hat die Buchungen verwechselt.
■ **I'm getting mixed up.** Ich werde ganz konfus.

★ **mixed** ADJECTIVE
gemischt
□ a mixed salad ein gemischter Salat □ a mixed school eine gemischte Schule

mixer NOUN
der Mixer *masc* (PL die Mixer) (*for food*)

★ **mixture** NOUN
die Mischung *fem*
□ a mixture of spices eine Gewürzmischung
■ **cough mixture** der Hustensaft

mix-up NOUN
die Verwechslung *fem*

MMS NOUN (= *multimedia messaging service*)
der MMS® *masc*

to **moan** VERB
sich beklagen [7] (PERFECT TENSE hat sich beklagt)
□ She's always moaning. Sie beklagt sich dauernd.

★ **mobile** NOUN
das Handy *neut* (PL die Handys) (*phone*)

mobile home NOUN
das Wohnmobil *neut* (PL die Wohnmobile)

★ **mobile phone** NOUN
das Handy *neut* (PL die Handys)

to **mock** VERB
▷ *see also* **mock** ADJECTIVE
sich lustig machen [48] über +*acc*
□ Stop mocking him! Mach dich nicht über ihn lustig!

mock ADJECTIVE
▷ *see also* **mock** VERB
■ **a mock exam** eine Übungsprüfung

★ **model** NOUN
▷ *see also* **model** ADJECTIVE, VERB
1 das Modell *neut* (PL die Modelle)
□ the latest model das neueste Modell □ a model of the castle ein Modell der Burg
2 das Model *neut* (PL die Models) (*fashion*)
□ She's a famous model. Sie ist ein berühmtes Model.

★ **model** ADJECTIVE
▷ *see also* **model** NOUN, VERB
■ **a model plane** ein Modellflugzeug *neut*
■ **a model railway** eine Modelleisenbahn
■ **He's a model pupil.** Er ist ein vorbildlicher Schüler.

★ to **model** VERB
▷ *see also* **model** NOUN, ADJECTIVE
als Model arbeiten [2]
□ She was modelling in New York. Sie arbeitete in New York als Model.

■ **She was modelling a Victoria Beckham outfit.** Sie führte ein Outfit von Victoria Beckham vor.

modem NOUN
das Modem *neut* (PL die Modems)

★ **moderate** ADJECTIVE
gemäßigt
□ His views are quite moderate. Er hat sehr gemäßigte Ansichten.
■ **a moderate amount of alcohol** wenig Alkohol
■ **a moderate price** ein annehmbarer Preis

★ **modern** ADJECTIVE
modern

to **modernize** VERB
modernisieren [76] (PERFECT TENSE hat modernisiert)

★ **modest** ADJECTIVE
bescheiden

to **modify** VERB
ändern [88]

moist ADJECTIVE
feucht
□ This cake is very moist. Dieser Kuchen ist sehr feucht.

moisture NOUN
die Feuchtigkeit *fem*

moisturizer NOUN
1 die Feuchtigkeitscreme *fem* (PL die Feuchtigkeitscremes) (*cream*)
2 die Feuchtigkeitslotion *fem* (*lotion*)

moldy ADJECTIVE (US)
schimmlig

mole NOUN
1 der Maulwurf *masc* (PL die Maulwürfe) (*animal*)
2 der Leberfleck *masc* (PL die Leberflecke) (*on skin*)

★ **moment** NOUN
der Augenblick *masc* (PL die Augenblicke)
□ Could you wait a moment? Können Sie einen Augenblick warten? □ in a moment in einem Augenblick □ Just a moment! Einen Augenblick!
■ **at the moment** momentan
■ **any moment now** jeden Moment □ They'll be arriving any moment now. Sie können jeden Moment kommen.

momentous ADJECTIVE
bedeutsam

monarch NOUN
der Monarch *masc* (GEN des Monarchen, PL die Monarchen)
die Monarchin *fem*

monarchy NOUN
die Monarchie *fem*

monastery NOUN
das Kloster *neut* (PL die Klöster)

★ **Monday** NOUN

m

der Montag masc (PL die Montage)
□ **on Monday** am Montag □ **every Monday** jeden Montag □ **last Monday** letzten Montag □ **next Monday** nächsten Montag
■ **on Mondays** montags

to **monetize** VERB
monetarisieren [76]

★ **money** NOUN
das Geld neut (PL die Gelder)
□ I need to change some money. Ich muss Geld wechseln.
■ **to make money** Geld verdienen [84]

mongrel NOUN
die Promenadenmischung fem
□ My dog's a mongrel. Mein Hund ist eine Promenadenmischung.

★ **monitor** NOUN
der Monitor masc (PL die Monitore) (of computer)

monk NOUN
der Mönch masc (PL die Mönche)

★ **monkey** NOUN
der Affe masc (GEN des Affen, PL die Affen)

monopoly NOUN
das Monopol neut

monotonous ADJECTIVE
monoton

monster NOUN
das Monster neut (PL die Monster)

★ **month** NOUN
der Monat masc (PL die Monate)
□ **this month** diesen Monat □ **next month** nächsten Monat □ **last month** letzten Monat □ **every month** jeden Monat □ **at the end of the month** Ende des Monats

★ **monthly** ADJECTIVE
monatlich

monument NOUN
das Denkmal neut (PL die Denkmäler)

★ **mood** NOUN
die Laune fem
□ **to be in a bad mood** schlechte Laune haben □ **to be in a good mood** gute Laune haben

moody ADJECTIVE
1 launisch (temperamental)
2 schlecht gelaunt (in a bad mood)

★ **moon** NOUN
der Mond masc (PL die Monde)
■ **There's a full moon tonight.** Heute ist Vollmond.
■ **to be over the moon** (happy) überglücklich sein [65]

moor NOUN
▷ see also **moor** VERB
das Moor neut (PL die Moore)

to **moor** VERB
▷ see also **moor** NOUN
festmachen [48] (PERFECT TENSE hat festgemacht) (boat)

mop NOUN
der Mopp masc (PL die Mopps) (for floor)

moped NOUN
das Moped neut (PL die Mopeds)

★ **moral** ADJECTIVE
▷ see also **moral** NOUN
moralisch

★ **moral** NOUN
▷ see also **moral** ADJECTIVE
die Moral fem
□ **the moral of the story** die Moral der Geschichte
■ **morals** die Moral sing

morale NOUN
die Stimmung fem
□ Their morale is very low. Ihre Stimmung ist sehr schlecht.

★ **more** ADJECTIVE, PRONOUN, ADVERB
mehr
□ **a bit more** etwas mehr □ **There are more girls in the class.** In der Klasse sind mehr Mädchen.
■ **more than** mehr als □ She practises more than I do. Sie übt mehr als ich. □ I spent more than two hundred euros. Ich habe mehr als zweihundert Euro ausgegeben. □ **More girls than boys do German.** Mehr Mädchen als Jungen lernen Deutsch.

> In comparisons you usually add -er to the adjective.

□ Could you speak more slowly? Könnten Sie langsamer sprechen? □ He's more intelligent than me. Er ist intelligenter als ich. □ The cost of living is more expensive in Britain. Die Lebensunterhaltungskosten sind in Großbritannien höher.

> When referring to an additional amount, over and above what there already is, you usually use noch.

□ Is there any more? Gibt es noch mehr? □ Would you like some more? Möchten Sie noch etwas? □ It'll take a few more days. Es braucht noch ein paar Tage. □ Could I have some more chips? Kann ich noch Pommes frites haben? □ Do you want some more tea? Möchten sie noch Tee?
■ **There isn't any more.** Es ist nichts mehr da.
■ **more or less** mehr oder weniger
■ **more than ever** mehr denn je

moreover ADVERB
außerdem

★ **morning** NOUN
der Morgen masc (PL die Morgen)
□ **every morning** jeden Morgen
■ **this morning** heute Morgen
■ **tomorrow morning** morgen früh □ I have to get up at six tomorrow morning. Ich muss morgen früh um sechs aufstehen.

■ **in the morning** morgens □ **at seven o'clock in the morning** um sieben Uhr morgens

Morocco NOUN
Marokko *neut*
■ **from Morocco** auf Marokko
■ **to Morocco** nach Marokko

mortgage NOUN
die Hypothek *fem* (PL die Hypotheken)

Moscow NOUN
Moskau *neut*
■ **to Moscow** nach Moskau

mosque NOUN
die Moschee *fem*

mosquito NOUN
die Stechmücke *fem*
■ **a mosquito bite** ein Mückenstich *masc*

★ **most** ADVERB, ADJECTIVE, PRONOUN
1 die meisten
□ **most of my friends** die meisten meiner Freunde □ **most of them** die meisten von ihnen □ **most people** die meisten Menschen □ **Most cats are affectionate.** Die meisten Katzen sind anhänglich.
2 am meisten
□ **what I hate most** was ich am meisten hasse
■ **most of the time** meist
■ **most of the evening** fast den ganzen Abend
■ **most of the money** fast das ganze Geld
■ **the most** am meisten □ **He's the one who talks the most.** Er ist derjenige, der am meisten redet.
■ **to make the most of something** das Beste aus etwas machen [48]
■ **at the most** höchstens □ **Two hours at the most.** Höchstens zwei Stunden.

For the superlative you usually add -ste to the adjective.

□ **the most expensive seat** der teuerste Platz
□ **the most boring work** die langweiligste Arbeit
□ **the most expensive restaurant** das teuerste Restaurant

★ **mostly** ADVERB
■ **The teachers are mostly quite nice.** Die meisten unserer Lehrer sind ganz nett.

MOT NOUN
der TÜV *masc* (= *Technischer Überwachungsverein*)
□ **Mum's car failed its MOT.** Das Auto meiner Mutter ist nicht durch den TÜV gekommen.

motel NOUN
das Motel *neut* (PL die Motels)

moth NOUN
die Motte *fem*

★ **mother** NOUN
die Mutter *fem* (PL die Mütter)
□ **my mother** meine Mutter
■ **mother tongue** die Muttersprache

mother-in-law NOUN
die Schwiegermutter *fem* (PL die Schwiegermütter)

Mother's Day NOUN
der Muttertag *masc* (PL die Muttertage)

DID YOU KNOW...?
In Germany **Muttertag** is on the second Sunday in May.

motionless ADJECTIVE
bewegungslos

motivated ADJECTIVE
motiviert
□ **He is highly motivated.** Er ist höchst motiviert.

motivation NOUN
die Motivation *fem*

motive NOUN
das Motiv *neut* (PL die Motive)
□ **the motive for the killing** das Motiv für den Mord

★ **motor** NOUN
der Motor *masc* (PL die Motoren)
□ **The boat has a motor.** Das Boot hat einen Motor.

motorbike NOUN
das Motorrad *neut* (PL die Motorräder)

motorboat NOUN
das Motorboot *neut* (PL die Motorboote)

motorcycle NOUN
das Motorrad *neut* (PL die Motorräder)

motorcyclist NOUN
der Motorradfahrer *masc* (PL die Motorradfahrer)
die Motorradfahrerin *fem*

motorist NOUN
der Autofahrer *masc* (PL die Autofahrer)
die Autofahrerin *fem*

motor mechanic NOUN
der Automechaniker *masc* (PL die Automechaniker)
die Automechanikerin *fem*

motor racing NOUN
das Autorennen *neut* (PL die Autorennen)

motorway NOUN
die Autobahn *fem*
□ **on the motorway** auf der Autobahn

mouldy ADJECTIVE
schimmlig

★ **mountain** NOUN
der Berg *masc* (PL die Berge)
■ **a mountain bike** ein Mountainbike *neut*

mountaineer NOUN
der Bergsteiger *masc* (PL die Bergsteiger)
die Bergsteigerin *fem*

mountaineering NOUN
das Bergsteigen *neut*
■ **I go mountaineering.** Ich gehe bergsteigen.

mountainous ADJECTIVE
bergig

★ **mouse** NOUN
die Maus fem (PL die Mäuse) (also for computer)

mouse mat NOUN
das Mousepad neut (PL die Mousepads)
(computer)

mousse NOUN
1 die Creme fem (PL die Cremes) (food)
■ **chocolate mousse** die Schokoladencreme
2 der Schaumfestiger masc (PL die
Schaumfestiger) (for hair)

moustache NOUN
der Schnurrbart masc (PL die Schnurrbärte)
□ He's got a moustache. Er hat einen
Schnurrbart.

★ **mouth** NOUN
der Mund masc (PL die Münder)

mouthful NOUN
der Bissen masc (PL die Bissen)

mouthwash NOUN
das Mundwasser neut (PL die Mundwasser)

★ **move** NOUN
▷ see also **move** VERB
1 der Zug masc (PL die Züge)
□ That was a good move. Das war ein guter Zug.
■ **It's your move.** Du bist dran.
2 der Umzug masc (PL die Umzüge)
□ our move from Oxford to Luton unser Umzug
von Oxford nach Luton
■ **to get a move on** schneller machen [48]
■ **Get a move on!** Nun mach schon!

★ to **move** VERB
▷ see also **move** NOUN
1 bewegen [7] (PERFECT TENSE hat bewegt)
□ I can't move my arm. Ich kann den Arm nicht
bewegen. □ I was very moved by the film. Der
Film hat mich sehr bewegt.
■ **Could you move your stuff?** Könntest du
dein Zeug wegtun?
■ **Could you move your car?** Könnten Sie Ihr
Auto wegfahren?
2 sich bewegen [7]
□ Try not to move. Versuche, dich nicht zu
bewegen.
■ **Don't move!** Keine Bewegung!
3 fahren [21] (PRESENT TENSE fährt, IMPERFECT fuhr,
PERFECT TENSE ist gefahren) (vehicle)
□ The lorry was moving very slowly. Der
Lastwagen fuhr sehr langsam.
■ **to move house** umziehen [96] □ She's
moving house in July. Sie zieht im Juli um.

to **move forward** VERB
sich vorwärtsbewegen [15]

to **move in** VERB
einziehen [96]
□ They're moving in next week. Sie ziehen
nächste Woche ein.

to **move over** VERB
rücken [38]
□ Could you move over a bit? Könnten Sie ein
Stückchen rücken?

★ **movement** NOUN
die Bewegung fem

movie NOUN
der Film masc (PL die Filme)
■ **the movies** das Kino sing □ Let's go to the
movies! Lass uns ins Kino gehen!

moving ADJECTIVE
1 fahrend (not stationary)
□ a moving bus ein fahrender Bus
2 ergreifend (touching)
□ a moving story eine ergreifende Geschichte

to **mow** VERB
mähen [48]
□ to mow the lawn den Rasen mähen

mower NOUN
der Rasenmäher masc (PL die Rasenmäher)

mown VERB ▷ see **mow**

★ **MP** NOUN (= Member of Parliament)
der Abgeordnete masc (GEN des Abgeordneten,
PL die Abgeordneten)
die Abgeordnete fem (GEN der Abgeordneten)
□ an MP (man) ein Abgeordneter □ She's an MP.
Sie ist Abgeordnete.

MP3 player NOUN
der MP3-Spieler masc (PL die MP3-Spieler)

mph ABBREVIATION (= miles per hour)
Meilen pro Stunde

★ **Mr** NOUN (= Mister)
Herr

★ **Mrs** NOUN
Frau

MS NOUN (= multiple sclerosis)
MS
□ She's got MS. Sie hat MS.

★ **Ms** NOUN
Frau

DID YOU KNOW...?
Generally **Frau** is used to address all women
whether married or not.

□ Ms Jones Frau Jones

★ **much** ADJECTIVE, ADVERB, PRONOUN
1 viel
□ I haven't got much money. Ich habe nicht viel
Geld. □ I haven't got very much money. Ich
habe nicht sehr viel Geld. □ This is much better.
Das ist viel besser. □ I feel much better now. Ich
fühle mich jetzt viel besser.
2 sehr

Use **sehr** with most verbs.

□ I didn't like it much. Es hat mir nicht sehr
gefallen. □ I enjoyed the film very much. Der
Film hat mir sehr gefallen.

3 viel

> Use **viel** with verbs implying physical activity.

□ She doesn't travel much. Sie reist nicht viel.
□ We didn't laugh much. Wir haben nicht viel gelacht.
■ **Do you go out much?** Gehst du oft aus?
■ **Thank you very much.** Vielen Dank!
■ **not much** nicht viel □ What's on TV? — Not much. Was kommt im Fernsehen? — Nicht viel. □ What do you think of it? — Not much. Was hältst du davon? — Nicht viel.
■ **How much?** Wie viel? □ How much do you want? Wie viel möchtest du? □ How much time have you got? Wie viel Zeit hast du? □ How much is it? (*cost*) Wie viel kostet das?
■ **too much** zu viel □ That's too much! Das ist zu viel! □ It costs too much. Das kostet zu viel. □ They gave us too much homework. Sie haben uns zu viele Hausaufgaben aufgegeben.
■ **so much** so viel □ I didn't think it would cost so much. Ich hatte nicht gedacht, dass es so viel kosten würde. □ I've never seen so much traffic. Ich habe noch nie so viel Verkehr erlebt.

mud NOUN
der Schlamm *masc*

muddle NOUN
das Durcheinander *neut*
■ **to be in a muddle** durcheinander sein [65]

to **muddle up** VERB
verwechseln [34] (PERFECT TENSE hat verwechselt) (*people*)
□ He muddles me up with my sister. Er verwechselt mich mit meiner Schwester.
■ **to get muddled up** durcheinanderkommen [40] □ I'm getting muddled up. Ich komme durcheinander.

muddy ADJECTIVE
schlammig

muesli NOUN
das Müsli *neut* (PL die Müsli)

muffler NOUN (US)
der Schalldämpfer *masc* (PL die Schalldämpfer)

mug NOUN
▷ *see also* **mug** VERB
der Becher *masc* (PL die Becher)
□ Do you want a cup or a mug? Möchtest du eine Tasse oder einen Becher?

to **mug** VERB
▷ *see also* **mug** NOUN
überfallen [22] (PRESENT TENSE überfällt, IMPERFECT überfiel, PERFECT TENSE hat überfallen)
□ He was mugged in the city centre. Er wurde in der Innenstadt überfallen.

mugger NOUN
der Straßenräuber *masc* (PL die Straßenräuber)
die Straßenräuberin *fem*

mugging NOUN
der Überfall *masc* (PL die Überfälle)
□ Mugging has increased in recent years. Die Zahl der Überfälle hat in den letzten Jahren zugenommen.

muggy ADJECTIVE
schwül
□ It's muggy today. Es ist schwül heute.

multiple choice test NOUN
der Multiple-Choice-Test *masc* (PL die Multiple-Choice-Tests)

multiple sclerosis NOUN
die multiple Sklerose *fem*
□ She's got multiple sclerosis. Sie hat multiple Sklerose.

multiplication NOUN
die Multiplikation *fem*

to **multiply** VERB
multiplizieren [76] (PERFECT TENSE hat multipliziert)
□ to multiply six by three sechs mit drei multiplizieren

multi-storey car park NOUN
das Parkhaus *neut* (GEN des Parkhauses, PL die Parkhäuser)

★ **mum** NOUN
die Mama *fem* (PL die Mamas)
□ my mum meine Mama □ I'll ask Mum. Ich frage Mama.

mummy NOUN
1 die Mutti *fem* (PL die Muttis) (*mum*)
□ Mummy says I can go. Mutti sagt, ich kann gehen.
2 die Mumie *fem* (*Egyptian*)

mumps SING NOUN
der Mumps *masc*

Munich NOUN
München *neut*
■ **to Munich** nach München

★ **murder** NOUN
▷ *see also* **murder** VERB
der Mord *masc* (PL die Morde)

> **BE CAREFUL!**
> Do not translate **murder** by **Mörder**.

★ to **murder** VERB
▷ *see also* **murder** NOUN
ermorden [53] (PERFECT TENSE hat ermordet)
□ He was murdered. Er wurde ermordet.

murderer NOUN
der Mörder *masc* (PL die Mörder)
die Mörderin *fem*

★ **muscle** NOUN
der Muskel *masc* (PL die Muskeln)

muscular ADJECTIVE
muskulös

m

museum – mythology

★ **museum** NOUN
das Museum neut (PL die Museen)

★ **mushroom** NOUN
1 der Pilz masc (PL die Pilze)
2 der Champignon masc (PL die Champignons) (*button mushroom*)
□ mushroom omelette das Champignonomelett

★ **music** NOUN
die Musik fem

★ **musical** ADJECTIVE
▷ see also **musical** NOUN
musikalisch
□ I'm not musical. Ich bin nicht musikalisch.
■ **a musical instrument** ein Musikinstrument neut

★ **musical** NOUN
▷ see also **musical** ADJECTIVE
das Musical neut (PL die Musicals)

music centre NOUN
die Stereoanlage fem

★ **musician** NOUN
der Musiker masc (PL die Musiker)
die Musikerin fem

Muslim NOUN
der Moslem masc (PL die Moslems)
die Moslime fem
□ He's a Muslim. Er ist Moslem.

mussel NOUN
die Miesmuschel fem

★ **must** VERB
1 müssen [51] (PRESENT TENSE muss, IMPERFECT musste, PERFECT TENSE hat gemusst)
□ I must buy some presents. Ich muss Geschenke kaufen. □ I really must go now. Ich muss jetzt wirklich gehen. □ You must be tired. Du musst müde sein. □ They must have plenty of money. Sie müssen viel Geld haben. □ You must come and see us. Sie müssen uns besuchen.
2 dürfen [16] (PRESENT TENSE darf, IMPERFECT durfte, PERFECT TENSE hat gedurft)

Use **dürfen** in negative sentences.

□ You mustn't say things like that. So was darfst du nicht sagen.
■ **You mustn't forget to send her a card.** Vergiss nicht, ihr eine Karte zu schicken.

mustard NOUN
der Senf masc (PL die Senfe)

to **mutter** VERB
murmeln [34]

mutton NOUN
das Hammelfleisch neut

mutual ADJECTIVE
gegenseitig
■ **a mutual friend** ein gemeinsamer Freund

★ **my** ADJECTIVE
mein
□ my father mein Vater □ my aunt meine Tante □ my car mein Auto □ my parents meine Eltern
■ **my friend 1** (*male*) mein Freund **2** (*female*) meine Freundin

Do not use **mein** with parts of the body.

□ I want to wash my hair. Ich will mir die Haare waschen. □ I'm going to clean my teeth. Ich putze mir die Zähne. □ I've hurt my foot. Ich habe mich am Fuß verletzt.

★ **myself** PRONOUN
1 mich
□ I've hurt myself. Ich habe mich verletzt. □ When I look at myself in the mirror … Wenn ich mich im Spiegel ansehe … □ I don't like talking about myself. Ich rede nicht gern über mich selbst.
2 mir
□ I said to myself … Ich sagte mir … □ I am not very pleased with myself. Ich bin mit mir selbst nicht sehr zufrieden.
3 selbst
□ I made it myself. Ich habe es selbst gemacht.
■ **by myself** allein □ I don't like travelling by myself. Ich verreise nicht gern allein.

mysterious ADJECTIVE
rätselhaft

★ **mystery** NOUN
das Rätsel neut (PL die Rätsel)
■ **a murder mystery** (*novel*) ein Krimi masc

myth NOUN
1 der Mythos masc (GEN des Mythos, PL die Mythen) (*legend*)
□ a Greek myth ein griechischer Mythos
2 das Märchen neut (PL die Märchen) (*untrue idea*)
□ That's a myth. Das ist ein Märchen.

mythology NOUN
die Mythologie fem

Nn

to nag VERB

herumnörgeln [15] an (PERFECT TENSE hat
herumgenörgelt) (scold)
□ She's always nagging me. Sie nörgelt dauernd
an mir herum.

nail NOUN

der Nagel masc (PL die Nägel)
□ Don't bite your nails! Kau nicht an den
Nägeln!

nailbrush NOUN

die Nagelbürste fem

nailfile NOUN

die Nagelfeile fem

nail scissors PL NOUN

die Nagelschere fem
□ a pair of nail scissors eine Nagelschere

nail varnish NOUN

der Nagellack masc (PL die Nagellacke)
■ **nail varnish remover** der
Nagellackentferner

naked ADJECTIVE

nackt

★ **name** NOUN

der Name masc (GEN des Namens, PL die
Namen)
■ **What's your name?** Wie heißt du?

nanny NOUN

das Kindermädchen neut (PL die
Kindermädchen)
□ She's a nanny. Sie ist Kindermädchen.

nap NOUN

das Nickerchen neut (PL die Nickerchen)
■ **to have a nap** ein Nickerchen machen [48]

napkin NOUN

die Serviette fem

nappy NOUN

die Windel fem

★ **narrow** ADJECTIVE

eng

narrow-minded ADJECTIVE

engstirnig

nasty ADJECTIVE

1 übel (bad)
□ a nasty cold eine üble Erkältung □ a nasty
smell ein übler Geruch

2 böse (unfriendly)
□ He gave me a nasty look. Er warf mir einen
bösen Blick zu.

★ **nation** NOUN

die Nation fem

★ **national** ADJECTIVE

national
■ **a national newspaper** eine überregionale
Zeitung
■ **national elections** die Parlamentswahlen

> **DID YOU KNOW...?**
> In Germany the national elections are called
> **Bundestagswahlen.**

national anthem NOUN

die Nationalhymne fem

National Health Service NOUN

der staatliche Gesundheitsdienst masc

> **DID YOU KNOW...?**
> In Germany there are a large number of
> health schemes, not just a single service.

nationalism NOUN

der Nationalismus masc (GEN des
Nationalismus)
□ Scottish Nationalism der schottische
Nationalismus

nationalist NOUN

der Nationalist masc (GEN des Nationalisten, PL
die Nationalisten)
die Nationalistin fem

nationality NOUN

die Staatsangehörigkeit fem

National Lottery NOUN

das Lotto neut

national park NOUN

der Nationalpark masc (PL die Nationalparks)

★ **native** ADJECTIVE

■ **my native country** mein Heimatland neut
■ **native language** die Muttersprache
□ English is not their native language. Englisch
ist nicht ihre Muttersprache.
■ **a Native American** ein Indianer masc

★ **natural** ADJECTIVE

natürlich

naturalist NOUN

der Naturforscher masc (PL die Naturforscher)
die Naturforscherin fem

n

★ **naturally** ADVERB
natürlich
□ Naturally, we were very disappointed. Natürlich waren wir sehr enttäuscht.

★ **nature** NOUN
die Natur *fem*

naughty ADJECTIVE
böse
□ Naughty boy! Böser Junge!
■ **Don't be naughty!** Sei nicht ungezogen!

★ **navy** NOUN
die Marine *fem*
□ He's in the navy. Er ist bei der Marine.

navy-blue ADJECTIVE
marineblau
□ a navy-blue shirt ein marineblaues Hemd

Nazi NOUN
der Nazi *masc* (PL die Nazis)
□ the Nazis die Nazis

der Nazi is also used for women.

□ She was a Nazi. Sie war ein Nazi.

★ **near** ADJECTIVE
▷ *see also* **near** PREPOSITION, ADVERB
nah
□ It's fairly near. Es ist ziemlich nah. □ It's near enough to walk. Es ist nah genug, um zu Fuß zu gehen.
■ **nearest** nächste □ Where's the nearest service station? Wo ist die nächste Tankstelle?
□ the nearest shops die nächsten Geschäfte

★ **near** PREPOSITION, ADVERB
▷ *see also* **near** ADJECTIVE
in der Nähe von
□ I live near Liverpool. Ich wohne in der Nähe von Liverpool. □ near my house in der Nähe meines Hauses
■ **near here** hier in der Nähe □ Is there a bank near here? Ist hier in der Nähe eine Bank?
■ **near to** in der Nähe +gen □ It's very near to the school. Es ist ganz in der Nähe der Schule.

★ **nearby** ADVERB, ADJECTIVE
1 in der Nähe
□ There's a supermarket nearby. Es gibt einen Supermarkt in der Nähe.
2 nahe gelegen (*close*)
□ a nearby garage eine nahe gelegene Tankstelle

★ **nearly** ADVERB
fast
□ Dinner's nearly ready. Das Essen ist fast fertig. □ I'm nearly fifteen. Ich bin fast fünfzehn.
□ I nearly missed the train. Ich habe fast meinen Zug verpasst.

★ **neat** ADJECTIVE
ordentlich
□ She has very neat writing. Sie hat eine sehr ordentliche Schrift.

neatly ADVERB
ordentlich
□ neatly folded ordentlich gefaltet □ neatly dressed ordentlich gekleidet

★ **necessarily** ADVERB
■ **not necessarily** nicht unbedingt

★ **necessary** ADJECTIVE
nötig

necessity NOUN
die Notwendigkeit *fem*
□ A car is a necessity, not a luxury. Ein Auto ist eine Notwendigkeit und kein Luxus.

★ **neck** NOUN
1 der Hals *masc* (GEN des Halses, PL die Hälse) (*of body*)
2 der Ausschnitt *masc* (PL die Ausschnitte) (*of garment*)
□ a V-neck sweater ein Pullover mit V-Ausschnitt

necklace NOUN
die Halskette *fem*

★ to **need** VERB
▷ *see also* **need** NOUN
brauchen [48]
□ I need a bigger size. Ich brauche eine größere Größe.
■ **to need to do something** etwas tun müssen [51] □ I need to change some money. Ich muss Geld wechseln.

★ **need** NOUN
▷ *see also* **need** VERB
■ **There's no need to book.** Man braucht nicht zu buchen.

needle NOUN
die Nadel *fem*

negative NOUN
▷ *see also* **negative** ADJECTIVE
das Negativ *neut* (PL die Negative) (*photo*)

★ **negative** ADJECTIVE
▷ *see also* **negative** NOUN
negativ
□ He's got a very negative attitude. Er hat eine sehr negative Einstellung.

neglected ADJECTIVE
ungepflegt (*untidy*)
□ The garden is neglected. Der Garten ist ungepflegt.

negligee NOUN
das Negligé *neut* (PL die Negligés)

★ to **negotiate** VERB
verhandeln [34]

negotiations PL NOUN
die Verhandlungen *fem pl*

★ **neighbour** NOUN
der Nachbar *masc* (GEN des Nachbarn, PL die Nachbarn)
die Nachbarin *fem*

★ = core vocabulary

□ the neighbours' garden der Garten der Nachbarn

neighbourhood NOUN
die Nachbarschaft *fem*

★ **neither** PRONOUN, CONJUNCTION, ADVERB
weder noch

□ Carrots or peas? — Neither, thanks. Karotten oder Erbsen? — Weder noch, danke.
■ **Neither of them is coming.** Keiner von beiden kommt.
■ **neither ... nor ...** weder ... noch ... □ Neither Sarah nor Tamsin is coming to the party. Weder Sarah noch Tamsin kommen zur Party.
■ **Neither do I.** Ich auch nicht. □ I don't like him. — Neither do I! Ich mag ihn nicht. — Ich auch nicht!
■ **Neither have I.** Ich auch nicht. □ I've never been to Spain. — Neither have I. Ich war noch nie in Spanien. — Ich auch nicht.

neon NOUN
das Neon *neut*
■ **a neon light** eine Neonlampe

★ **nephew** NOUN
der Neffe *masc* (GEN des Neffen, PL die Neffen)
□ my nephew mein Neffe

★ **nerve** NOUN
der Nerv *masc* (PL die Nerven)
□ She gets on my nerves. Sie geht mir auf die Nerven.
■ **He's got a nerve!** Der hat vielleicht Nerven!

nerve-racking ADJECTIVE
nervenaufreibend

★ **nervous** ADJECTIVE
nervös *(tense)*
□ I bite my nails when I'm nervous. Wenn ich nervös bin, kaue ich an den Nägeln.
■ **to be nervous about something** vor etwas Angst haben [32] □ I'm a bit nervous about flying to New Zealand by myself. Ich habe etwas Angst, allein nach Neuseeland zu fliegen.

nest NOUN
das Nest *neut* (PL die Nester)

★ **Net** NOUN
■ **the Net** das Internet

★ **net** NOUN
das Netz *neut* (GEN des Netzes, PL die Netze)
□ a fishing net ein Fischnetz

netball NOUN
der Netball *masc*

★ **Netherlands** PL NOUN
die Niederlande *pl*

Note that the definite article is used in German for countries which are plural.

■ **from the Netherlands** aus den Niederlanden
■ **in the Netherlands** in den Niederlanden
■ **to the Netherlands** in die Niederlande

★ **network** NOUN
1 das Netz *neut* (GEN des Netzes, PL die Netze)
2 das Netzwerk *neut* (PL die Netzwerke) *(for computers)*

neurotic ADJECTIVE
neurotisch

★ **never** ADVERB
nie
□ Have you ever been to Germany? — No, never. Waren Sie schon mal in Deutschland? — Nein, nie. □ I never write letters. Ich schreibe nie Briefe. □ Never again! Nie wieder!
■ **Never mind.** Macht nichts!

★ **new** ADJECTIVE
neu
□ her new boyfriend ihr neuer Freund □ I need a new dress. Ich brauche ein neues Kleid.

newborn ADJECTIVE
■ **a newborn baby** ein neugeborenes Kind

newcomer NOUN
der Neuling *masc* (PL die Neulinge)

der Neuling is also used for women.

★ **news** SING NOUN

Nachricht is a piece of news; Nachrichten is the news, for example on TV.

1 die Nachrichten *fem pl*
□ good news gute Nachrichten □ I've had some bad news. Ich habe schlechte Nachrichten bekommen. □ I watch the news every evening. Ich sehe mir jeden Abend die Nachrichten an. □ I listen to the news every morning. Ich höre jeden Morgen die Nachrichten.
2 die Nachricht *fem*
□ That's wonderful news! Das ist eine wunderbare Nachricht!

★ **newsagent** NOUN
der Zeitungshändler *masc* (PL die Zeitungshändler)
die Zeitungshändlerin *fem*

★ **newspaper** NOUN
die Zeitung *fem*
□ I deliver newspapers. Ich trage Zeitungen aus.

newsreader NOUN
der Nachrichtensprecher *masc* (PL die Nachrichtensprecher)
die Nachrichtensprecherin *fem*

★ **New Year** NOUN
das Neujahr *neut*
□ to celebrate New Year Neujahr feiern
■ **Happy New Year!** Ein gutes neues Jahr!
■ **New Year's Day** das Neujahr
■ **New Year's Eve** das Silvester □ a New Year's Eve party eine Silvesterparty

New Zealand NOUN
Neuseeland *neut*
■ **from New Zealand** aus Neuseeland
■ **in New Zealand** in Neuseeland
■ **to New Zealand** nach Neuseeland

English-German

New Zealander NOUN

der Neuseeländer*masc* (PL die Neuseeländer)
die Neuseeländerin*fem*

★**next** ADJECTIVE, ADVERB, PREPOSITION

1 nächste
  □ **next Saturday** nächsten Samstag □ **next week** nächste Woche □ **next year** nächstes Jahr □ **the next train** der nächste Zug
  ■ **Next please!** der Nächste, bitte!

2 danach (*afterwards*)
  □ **What happened next?** Was ist danach passiert?
  ■ **What shall I do next?** Was soll ich als Nächstes machen?
  ■ **next to** neben

> Use the accusative to express movement or a change of place. Use the dative when there is no change of place.

  □ **I sat down next to my sister.** Ich setzte mich neben meine Schwester. □ **The post office is next to the bank.** Die Post ist neben der Bank.
  ■ **the next day** am nächsten Tag □ **The next day we visited Heidelberg.** Am nächsten Tag haben wir Heidelberg besucht.
  ■ **the next time** das nächste Mal □ **the next time you see her** wenn du sie das nächste Mal siehst
  ■ **next door** nebenan □ **They live next door.** Sie wohnen nebenan. □ **the people next door** die Leute von nebenan
  ■ **the next room** das Nebenzimmer

NHS NOUN

Staatlicher Gesundheitsdienst (*in Britain*)

> **DID YOU KNOW...?**
> In Germany there are a large number of health schemes, not just a single service.

★**nice** ADJECTIVE

1 nett (*kind*)
  □ **Your parents are nice.** Deine Eltern sind nett.
  □ **It was nice of you to remember my birthday.** Es war nett, dass du an meinen Geburtstag gedacht hast. □ **to be nice to somebody** nett zu jemandem sein

2 hübsch (*pretty*)
  □ **That's a nice jacket!** Das ist eine hübsche Jacke! □ **Ulm is a nice town.** Ulm ist eine hübsche Stadt.

> **WORD POWER**
> You can use a number of other words instead of **nice** to mean 'pretty':
> **attractive** attraktiv
> □ **an attractive woman** eine attraktive Frau
> **beautiful** schön
> □ **a beautiful painting** ein schönes Bild
> **lovely** wunderbar
> □ **a lovely surprise** eine wunderbare Überraschung
> **pretty** hübsch
> □ **a pretty village** ein hübsches Dorf

3 schön
  □ **nice weather** schönes Wetter □ **It's a nice day.** Es ist ein schöner Tag.

4 lecker (*food*)
  □ **This pizza's very nice.** Diese Pizza ist sehr lecker.
  ■ **Have a nice time!** Viel Spaß!

nickname NOUN

der Spitzname*masc* (GEN des Spitznamens, PL die Spitznamen)

★**niece** NOUN

die Nichte*fem*
  □ **my niece** meine Nichte

Nigeria NOUN

Nigeria*neut*
  ■ **in Nigeria** in Nigeria

★**night** NOUN

1 die Nacht*fem* (PL die Nächte)
  □ **I want a single room for two nights.** Ich möchte ein Einzelzimmer für zwei Nächte.
  ■ **at night** nachts
  ■ **Good night!** Gute Nacht!
  ■ **a nightclub** ein Nachtklub*masc*

2 der Abend*masc* (PL die Abende) (*evening*)
  □ **last night** gestern Abend

nightdress NOUN

das Nachthemd*neut* (PL die Nachthemden)

nightie NOUN

das Nachthemd*neut* (PL die Nachthemden)

nightlife NOUN

das Nachtleben*neut*
  □ **There's plenty of nightlife.** Dort gibt es ein reges Nachtleben.

★**nightmare** NOUN

der Albtraum*masc* (PL die Albträume)
  □ **I had a nightmare.** Ich hatte einen Albtraum.
  □ **It was a real nightmare!** Es war ein Albtraum!

nightshirt NOUN

das Nachthemd*neut* (PL die Nachthemden)

nil NOUN

null
  □ **We won one nil.** Wir haben eins zu null gewonnen.

★**nine** NUMBER

neun
  □ **She's nine.** Sie ist neun.

★**nineteen** NUMBER

neunzehn
  □ **She's nineteen.** Sie ist neunzehn.

★**nineteenth** ADJECTIVE

neunzehnte
  □ **the nineteenth of August** der neunzehnte August

★**ninety** NUMBER

neunzig
  □ **She's ninety.** Sie ist neunzig.

n

★ **ninth** ADJECTIVE
neunte
▫ the ninth floor der neunte Stock ▫ the ninth of August der neunte August

★ **no** ADVERB, ADJECTIVE
1 nein
▫ Are you coming? — No. Kommst du? — Nein.
▫ Would you like some more? — No thank you. Möchten Sie noch etwas? — Nein danke.
2 kein *(not any)*
▫ There's no hot water. Es gibt kein heißes Wasser. ▫ There are no trains on Sundays. Sonntags verkehren keine Züge. ▫ No problem. Kein Problem. ▫ I've got no idea. Ich habe keine Ahnung.
■ **No way!** Auf keinen Fall!
■ **'no smoking'** 'Rauchen verboten'

★ **nobody** PRONOUN
niemand
▫ Who's going with you? — Nobody. Wer geht mit dir mit? — Niemand. ▫ There was nobody in the office. Es war niemand im Büro.

★ to **nod** VERB
nicken [48]

★ **noise** NOUN
der Lärm *masc*
▫ Please make less noise. Macht bitte weniger Lärm.

noisy ADJECTIVE
laut
▫ It's too noisy here. Hier ist es zu laut.

to **nominate** VERB
nominieren [76] (PERFECT TENSE hat nominiert)
▫ She was nominated for an Oscar. Sie war für einen Oscar nominiert.

★ **none** PRONOUN
keiner
▫ None of my friends wanted to come. Keiner meiner Freunde wollte kommen. ▫ How many brothers have you got? — None. Wie viele Brüder hast du? — Keinen.
keine
▫ I can't find the milk — There's none left Ich finde die Milch nicht — Es ist keine mehr da.
keines
▫ Which of the books have you read? — None. Welches der Bücher hast du gelesen? — Keines.
■ **There are none left.** Es sind keine mehr da.

nonsense NOUN
der Unsinn *masc*
▫ She talks a lot of nonsense. Sie redet viel Unsinn. ▫ Nonsense! Unsinn!

non-smoker NOUN
der Nichtraucher *masc* (PL die Nichtraucher)
die Nichtraucherin *fem*
▫ She's a non-smoker. Sie ist Nichtraucherin.

nonstop ADJECTIVE, ADVERB
1 nonstop
▫ We flew nonstop. Wir sind nonstop geflogen.
■ **a nonstop flight** ein Nonstop-Flug *masc*
2 ununterbrochen
▫ His gran talks nonstop. Seine Oma redet ununterbrochen.

noodles PL NOUN
die Nudeln *fem pl*

noon NOUN
der Mittag *masc* (PL die Mittage)
■ **at noon** um zwölf Uhr mittags

★ **no one** PRONOUN
niemand
▫ Who's going with you? — No one. Wer geht mit dir mit? — Niemand. ▫ There was no one in the office. Es war niemand im Büro.

★ **nor** CONJUNCTION
■ **neither ... nor** weder ... noch ▫ neither the cinema nor the swimming pool weder das Kino noch das Schwimmbad
■ **Nor do I.** Ich auch nicht. ▫ I didn't like the film. — Nor did I. Der Film hat mir nicht gefallen. — Mir auch nicht.
■ **Nor have I.** Ich auch nicht. ▫ I haven't seen him. — Nor have I. Ich habe ihn nicht gesehen. — Ich auch nicht.

★ **normal** ADJECTIVE
normal
▫ at the normal time zur normalen Zeit ▫ a normal car ein normales Auto

★ **normally** ADVERB
1 normalerweise *(usually)*
▫ I normally arrive at nine o'clock. Normalerweise komme ich um neun Uhr.
2 normal *(as normal)*
▫ In spite of the strike, the airports are working normally. Trotz des Streiks arbeiten die Flughäfen normal.

★ **north** ADJECTIVE, ADVERB
▷ *see also* **north** NOUN
nach Norden
▫ We were travelling north. Wir sind nach Norden gefahren.
■ **the north coast** die Nordküste
■ **a north wind** ein Nordwind *masc*
■ **north of** nördlich von ▫ It's north of London. Es liegt nördlich von London.

★ **north** NOUN
▷ *see also* **north** ADJECTIVE, ADVERB
der Norden *masc*
▫ in the north im Norden

North America NOUN
Nordamerika *neut*
■ **from North America** aus Nordamerika
■ **to North America** nach Nordamerika

northbound ADJECTIVE
in Richtung Norden
▫ northbound traffic der Verkehr in Richtung Norden

n

northeast NOUN
der Nordosten *masc*
□ in the northeast im Nordosten

★ **northern** ADJECTIVE
nördlich
□ the northern part of the island der nördliche Teil der Insel
■ **Northern Europe** Nordeuropa *neut*

★ **Northern Ireland** NOUN
Nordirland *neut*
■ **from Northern Ireland** aus Nordirland
■ **in Northern Ireland** in Nordirland
■ **to Northern Ireland** nach Nordirland

North Pole NOUN
der Nordpol *masc*

North Sea NOUN
die Nordsee *fem*

northwest NOUN
der Nordwesten *masc*
□ in the northwest im Nordwesten

★ **Norway** NOUN
Norwegen *neut*
■ **from Norway** aus Norwegen
■ **to Norway** nach Norwegen

★ **Norwegian** ADJECTIVE
▷ *see also* **Norwegian** NOUN
norwegisch
■ **He's Norwegian.** Er ist Norweger.

★ **Norwegian** NOUN
▷ *see also* **Norwegian** ADJECTIVE
1 der Norweger *masc* (PL die Norweger)
die Norwegerin *fem* (*person*)
2 das Norwegisch *neut* (GEN des Norwegischen) (*language*)

★ **nose** NOUN
die Nase *fem*

nosebleed NOUN
das Nasenbluten *neut*
□ I often get nosebleeds. Ich habe oft Nasenbluten.

nosey ADJECTIVE
neugierig
□ She's very nosey. Sie ist sehr neugierig.

★ **not** ADVERB
1 nicht
□ Are you coming or not? Kommst du oder nicht? □ I'm not sure. Ich bin nicht sicher. □ It's not raining. Es regnet nicht.
■ **not really** eigentlich nicht
■ **not at all** überhaupt nicht
■ **not yet** noch nicht □ Have you finished? — Not yet. Bist du fertig? — Noch nicht. □ They haven't arrived yet. Sie sind noch nicht angekommen.
2 nein
□ Can you lend me ten pounds? — I'm afraid not. Können Sie mir zehn Pfund leihen? — Leider nein.

★ **note** NOUN
1 die Notiz *fem*
■ **to take notes** sich Notizen machen [48]
□ You should take notes. Du solltest dir Notizen machen.
2 der Brief *masc* (PL die Briefe) (*letter*)
■ **I'll write her a note.** Ich werde ihr schreiben.
3 der Schein *masc* (PL die Scheine) (*banknote*)
□ a five-pound note ein Fünfpfundschein

to **note down** VERB
aufschreiben [61] (IMPERFECT schrieb auf, PERFECT TENSE hat aufgeschrieben)

notebook NOUN
1 das Notizbuch *neut* (PL die Notizbücher)
2 der Notebookcomputer *masc* (PL die Notebookcomputer) (*computer*)

notepad NOUN
der Notizblock *masc* (PL die Notizblöcke)

notepaper NOUN
das Briefpapier *neut*

★ **nothing** NOUN
nichts
□ What's wrong? — Nothing. Was ist los? — Nichts. □ nothing special nichts Besonderes □ He does nothing. Er tut nichts. □ He ate nothing for breakfast. Er hat nichts zum Frühstück gegessen.

★ **notice** NOUN
▷ *see also* **notice** VERB
die Notiz *fem* (*sign*)
□ to put up a notice eine Notiz aushängen
□ Don't take any notice of him! Nimm keine Notiz von ihm!
■ **a warning notice** ein Warnschild *neut*

★ to **notice** VERB
▷ *see also* **notice** NOUN
bemerken [7] (PERFECT TENSE hat bemerkt)

notice board NOUN
das Anschlagbrett *neut* (PL die Anschlagbretter)

nought NOUN
die Null *fem*

noun NOUN
das Substantiv *neut* (PL die Substantive)

★ **novel** NOUN
der Roman *masc* (PL die Romane)

novelist NOUN
der Romanautor *masc* (PL die Romanautoren)
die Romanautorin *fem*

★ **November** NOUN
der November *masc*
□ in November im November

★ **now** ADVERB, CONJUNCTION
jetzt
□ What are you doing now? Was tust du jetzt?
■ **just now** gerade □ I'm rather busy just now. Ich bin gerade ziemlich beschäftigt. □ I did it just now. Ich habe es gerade getan.

★ = core vocabulary

■ **by now** inzwischen ❑ He should be there by now. Er müsste inzwischen dort sein. ❑ It should be ready by now. Es müsste inzwischen fertig sein.

■ **now and then** ab und zu

★ **nowhere** ADVERB

nirgends

❑ **nowhere else** sonst nirgends

★ **nuclear** ADJECTIVE

nuklear

■ **nuclear power** die Kernkraft

■ **a nuclear power station** ein Kernkraftwerk *neut*

nude ADJECTIVE

▷ *see also* **nude** NOUN

nackt

nude NOUN

▷ *see also* **nude** ADJECTIVE

■ **in the nude** nackt

nudist NOUN

der Nudist *masc* (GEN des Nudisten, PL die Nudisten)

die Nudistin *fem*

nuisance NOUN

■ **It's a nuisance.** Es ist sehr lästig.

■ **Sorry to be a nuisance.** Tut mir leid, dass ich schon wieder ankomme.

numb ADJECTIVE

taub

❑ **numb with cold** taub vor Kälte

★ **number** NOUN

1 die Anzahl *fem* (*total amount*)

❑ **a large number of people** eine große Anzahl von Menschen

2 die Nummer *fem* (*of house, telephone, bank account*)

❑ They live at number five. Sie wohnen in der Nummer fünf. ❑ What's your phone number? Wie ist Ihre Telefonnummer?

■ **You've got the wrong number.** Sie sind falsch verbunden.

3 die Zahl *fem* (*figure, digit*)

❑ I can't read the second number. Ich kann die zweite Zahl nicht lesen.

number plate NOUN

das Nummernschild *neut* (PL die Nummernschilder)

DID YOU KNOW...?
The first letters of a German number plate tell you where the car's owner lives. Thus L stands for Leipzig, LB for Ludwigsburg, LU for Ludwigshafen, etc.

nun NOUN

die Nonne *fem*

❑ She's a nun. Sie ist Nonne.

★ **nurse** NOUN

der Krankenpfleger *masc*

die Krankenschwester *fem*

❑ He's a nurse. Er ist Krankenpfleger. ❑ She's a nurse. Sie ist Krankenschwester.

nursery NOUN

1 die Kindergarten *fem* (PL die Kindergärten) (*for children*)

2 die Baumschule *fem* (*for plants*)

nursery school NOUN

der Kindergarten *masc* (PL die Kindergärten)

DID YOU KNOW...?
German children go to **Kindergarten** from the age of 3 to 6.

nursery slope NOUN

der Idiotenhügel *masc* (PL die Idiotenhügel)

nut NOUN

1 die Nuss *fem* (PL die Nüsse)

2 die Mutter *fem* (*made of metal*)

nutmeg NOUN

der Muskat *masc*

nutritious ADJECTIVE

nahrhaft

nuts ADJECTIVE

■ **He's nuts.** Er spinnt. (*informal*)

nylon NOUN

das Nylon *neut*

n

Numbers in brackets refer to verb tables on pages 697 to 706.

539

oak NOUN
die Eiche *fem*
□ an oak table ein Eichentisch *masc*

oar NOUN
das Ruder *neut* (PL die Ruder)

oats PL NOUN
der Hafer *masc*

obedient ADJECTIVE
gehorsam

to **obey** VERB
gehorchen [48] (PERFECT TENSE hat gehorcht)
□ She didn't obey her mother. Sie hat ihrer Mutter nicht gehorcht.
■ to obey the rules die Regeln befolgen [7]

★ **object** NOUN
der Gegenstand *masc* (PL die Gegenstände)
□ a familiar object ein vertrauter Gegenstand

objection NOUN
der Einspruch *masc* (PL die Einsprüche)

★ **objective** NOUN
das Ziel *neut* (PL die Ziele)

oblong ADJECTIVE
länglich

oboe NOUN
die Oboe *fem*
□ I play the oboe. Ich spiele Oboe.

obscene ADJECTIVE
obszön

observant ADJECTIVE
aufmerksam

to **observe** VERB
beobachten [2] (PERFECT TENSE hat beobachtet)

obsessed ADJECTIVE
besessen
□ He's completely obsessed with trains. Er ist von Zügen ganz besessen.

obsession NOUN
die Leidenschaft *fem*
□ Football's an obsession of mine. Fußball ist meine Leidenschaft.

obsolete ADJECTIVE
veraltet

obstacle NOUN
das Hindernis *neut* (GEN des Hindernisses, PL die Hindernisse)

obstinate ADJECTIVE
stur

to **obstruct** VERB
behindern [88] (PERFECT TENSE hat behindert)
□ A lorry was obstructing the traffic. Ein Lastwagen hat den Verkehr behindert.

to **obtain** VERB
erhalten [33] (IMPERFECT erhielt, PERFECT TENSE hat erhalten)

★ **obvious** ADJECTIVE
offensichtlich

★ **obviously** ADVERB
1 natürlich (*of course*)
□ Do you want to pass the exam? — Obviously! Willst du die Prüfung bestehen? — Natürlich!
□ Obviously not! Natürlich nicht!
2 offensichtlich (*visibly*)
□ She was obviously exhausted. Sie war offensichtlich erschöpft.

★ **occasion** NOUN
die Gelegenheit *fem*
□ a special occasion eine besondere Gelegenheit
■ on several occasions mehrmals

occasionally ADVERB
ab und zu

occupation NOUN
die Beschäftigung *fem*

to **occupy** VERB
besetzen [7] (PERFECT TENSE hat besetzt)
□ That seat is occupied. Der Platz ist besetzt.

to **occur** VERB
passieren [76] (PERFECT TENSE ist passiert) (*happen*)
□ The accident occurred yesterday. Der Unfall ist gestern passiert.
■ It suddenly occurred to me that ... Plötzlich ist mir eingefallen, dass ...

OCD NOUN (= obsessive compulsive disorder)
Zwangsstörung *fem*

★ **ocean** NOUN
der Ozean *masc* (PL die Ozeane)

★ **o'clock** ADVERB
■ at four o'clock um vier Uhr
■ It's five o'clock. Es ist fünf Uhr.

★ = core vocabulary

★ **October** NOUN
   der Oktober *masc*
   □ in October im Oktober

octopus NOUN
   der Tintenfisch *masc* (PL die Tintenfische)

★ **odd** ADJECTIVE
1 eigenartig
   □ That's odd! Das ist eigenartig!
2 ungerade
   □ an odd number eine ungerade Zahl

★ **of** PREPOSITION
   von
   □ some photos of my holiday Fotos von meinen Ferien □ three of us drei von uns □ a friend of mine ein Freund von mir □ That's very kind of you. Das ist sehr nett von Ihnen. □ Can I have half of that? Kann ich die Hälfte davon haben?

   'of' is not translated when specifying a quantity of something.

   □ a kilo of oranges ein Kilo Orangen

   'of' is often expressed by using the genitive.

   □ the end of the film das Ende des Films □ the top of the stairs das obere Ende der Treppe □ the front of the house die Vorderseite des Hauses
   ■ a boy of ten ein zehnjähriger Junge
   ■ the fourteenth of September der vierzehnte September
   ■ It's made of wood. Es ist aus Holz.

★ **off** ADVERB, PREPOSITION, ADJECTIVE

   For other expressions with 'off', see the verbs 'get', 'take', 'turn' etc.

1 aus (*heater, light, TV*)
   □ All the lights are off. Alle Lichter sind aus.
2 zu (*tap, gas*)
   □ Are you sure the tap is off? Bist du sicher, dass der Hahn zu ist?
3 abgesagt (*cancelled*)
   □ The match is off. Das Spiel wurde abgesagt.
   ■ to be off sick krank sein [65]
   ■ a day off ein freier Tag
   ■ to take a day off work sich einen Tag freinehmen [52] □ I'm taking a day off work tomorrow. Ich werde mir morgen einen Tag freinehmen.
   ■ She's off school today. Sie ist heute nicht in der Schule.
   ■ I must be off now. Ich muss jetzt gehen.
   ■ I'm off. Ich gehe jetzt.

offence NOUN
   das Vergehen *neut* (PL die Vergehen) (*crime*)

offensive ADJECTIVE
   anstößig

★ **offer** NOUN
   ▷ *see also* **offer** VERB
   das Angebot *neut* (PL die Angebote)
   □ a good offer ein günstiges Angebot
   ■ 'on special offer' 'im Sonderangebot'

★ to **offer** VERB
   ▷ *see also* **offer** NOUN
   anbieten [8] (IMPERFECT bot an, PERFECT TENSE hat angeboten)
   □ He offered to help me. Er bot mir seine Hilfe an. □ I offered to go with them. Ich habe ihnen angeboten mitzugehen.

★ **office** NOUN
   das Büro *neut* (PL die Büros)
   □ She works in an office. Sie arbeitet in einem Büro.

★ **officer** NOUN
   der Offizier *masc* (PL die Offiziere)
   die Offizierin *fem* (*in army*)
   ■ a police officer ein Polizist/eine Polizistin

★ **official** ADJECTIVE
   offiziell

off-licence NOUN
   die Wein- und Spirituosenhandlung *fem*

off-peak ADJECTIVE, ADVERB
   außerhalb der Hauptreisezeit
   □ It's cheaper to travel off-peak. Es ist billiger, außerhalb der Hauptreisezeit zu fahren.

offside ADJECTIVE
   im Abseits (*in football*)

★ **often** ADVERB
   oft
   □ It often rains. Es regnet oft. □ How often do you go to the gym? Wie oft gehst du ins Fitnessstudio? □ I'd like to go skiing more often. Ich würde gern öfter Ski fahren.

★ **oil** NOUN
   ▷ *see also* **oil** VERB
1 das Öl *neut* (PL die Öle) (*for lubrication, cooking*)
   ■ an oil painting ein Ölgemälde *neut*
2 das Erdöl *neut* (*petroleum*)
   □ North Sea oil Erdöl aus der Nordsee

★ to **oil** VERB
   ▷ *see also* **oil** NOUN
   ölen [38]

oil rig NOUN
   die Bohrinsel *fem*
   □ He works on an oil rig. Er arbeitet auf einer Bohrinsel.

oil slick NOUN
   der Ölteppich *masc* (PL die Ölteppiche)

oil well NOUN
   die Ölquelle *fem*

ointment NOUN
   die Salbe *fem*

★ **okay** EXCLAMATION, ADJECTIVE
   okay
   □ Could you call back later? — Okay! Kannst du später anrufen? — Okay! □ I'll meet you at six o'clock, okay? Ich treffe dich um sechs Uhr, okay? □ Is that okay? Ist das okay? □ How was your holiday? — It was okay. Wie waren die Ferien? — Okay.

o

Numbers in brackets refer to verb tables on pages 697 to 706.

541

■ **I'll do it tomorrow, if that's okay with you.** Ich mache das morgen, wenn du einverstanden bist.
■ **Are you okay?** Bist du in Ordnung?

★ **old** ADJECTIVE

alt
□ an old dog ein alter Hund □ old people alte Menschen □ my old English teacher mein alter Englischlehrer □ How old are you? Wie alt bist du? □ He's ten years old. Er ist zehn Jahre alt. □ my older brother mein älterer Bruder □ my older sister meine ältere Schwester □ She's two years older than me. Sie ist zwei Jahre älter als ich. □ He's the oldest in the family. Er ist der Älteste der Familie.

old age pensioner NOUN

der Rentner *masc* (PL die Rentner)
die Rentnerin *fem*
□ She's an old age pensioner. Sie ist Rentnerin.

old-fashioned ADJECTIVE

altmodisch
□ She wears old-fashioned clothes. Sie trägt altmodische Kleidung. □ My parents are rather old-fashioned. Meine Eltern sind ziemlich altmodisch.

olive NOUN

die Olive *fem*

olive oil NOUN

das Olivenöl *neut* (PL die Olivenöle)

Olympic® ADJECTIVE

olympisch
■ **the Olympics®** die Olympischen Spiele

omelette NOUN

das Omelett *neut* (PL die Omeletts)

★ **on** PREPOSITION, ADVERB
▷ *see also* **on** ADJECTIVE

There are several ways of translating 'on'. Scan the examples to find one that is similar to what you want to say. For other expressions with 'on' see the verbs 'go', 'put', 'turn' etc.

1 auf

Use the accusative to express movement or a change of place. Use the dative when there is no change of place.

□ It's on the table. Es ist auf dem Tisch. □ Put it on the table, please. Stell es bitte auf den Tisch. □ on an island auf einer Insel □ on the left auf der linken Seite

2 an

□ on Friday am Freitag □ on Christmas Day am ersten Weihnachtsfeiertag □ on the twentieth of June am zwanzigsten Juni □ on my birthday an meinem Geburtstag
■ **on Fridays** freitags

Use the accusative to express movement or a change of place. Use the dative when there is no change of place.

□ There was not a single picture on the wall. An der Wand hing kein einziges Bild. □ **She hung a picture on the wall.** Sie hängte ein Bild an die Wand.

3 in

□ on the second floor im zweiten Stock □ on TV im Fernsehen □ What's on TV? Was kommt im Fernsehen? □ I heard it on the radio. Ich habe es im Radio gehört.
■ **on the bus** **1** (*by bus*) mit dem Bus □ I go into town on the bus. Ich fahre mit dem Bus in die Stadt. **2** (*inside*) im Bus □ There were no empty seats on the bus. Es gab keinen freien Platz im Bus.
■ **I go to school on my bike.** Ich fahre mit dem Fahrrad zur Schule.
■ **on holiday** in den Ferien □ They're on holiday. Sie sind in den Ferien.
■ **They are on strike.** Sie streiken.

★ **on** ADJECTIVE
▷ *see also* **on** PREPOSITION, ADVERB

1 an (*heater, light, TV*)
□ I left the light on. Ich habe das Licht angelassen. □ Is the dishwasher on? Ist die Spülmaschine an?

2 auf (*tap, gas*)
□ Leave the tap on. Lass den Hahn auf.
■ **What's on at the cinema?** Was gibt's im Kino?

★ **once** ADVERB

einmal
□ once a week einmal pro Woche □ once more noch einmal □ I've been to Germany once before. Ich war schon einmal in Deutschland.
■ **Once upon a time ...** Es war einmal ...
■ **at once** sofort
■ **once in a while** ab und zu

★ **one** NUMBER, PRONOUN

Use ein for masculine and neuter nouns, eine for feminine nouns.

1 ein
□ one man ein Mann □ one child ein Kind □ We stayed there for one day. Wir sind einen Tag dortgeblieben.

2 eine
□ one minute eine Minute □ Do you need a stamp? — No thanks, I've got one. Brauchst du eine Briefmarke? — Nein danke, ich habe eine. □ I've got one brother and one sister. Ich habe einen Bruder und eine Schwester.

3 eins

Use eins when counting.

□ one, two, three eins, zwei, drei

4 man (*impersonal*)
□ One never knows. Man kann nie wissen.
■ **this one** **1** (*masculine*) dieser □ Which foot hurts? — This one. Welcher Fuß tut weh? — Dieser. **2** (*feminine*) diese □ Which is your cup? — This one. Welche ist deine Tasse? — Diese.

3 (*neuter*) dieses □ Which is the best photo? — This one. Welches ist das beste Foto? — Dieses.
■ **that one 1** (*masculine*) der da □ Which pen did you use? — That one. Welchen Schreiber hast du benützt? — Den da. **2** (*feminine*) die da □ Which bag is yours? — That one. Welche ist deine Tasche? — Die da. **3** (*neuter*) das da □ Which is your car? — That one. Welches ist Ihr Auto? — Das da.

oneself PRONOUN
1 sich
□ to hurt oneself sich wehtun
2 selbst
□ It's quicker to do it oneself. Es geht schneller, wenn man es selbst macht.

one-way ADJECTIVE
■ a one-way street eine Einbahnstraße

★ **onion** NOUN
die Zwiebel *fem*
□ onion soup die Zwiebelsuppe

online ADJECTIVE, ADVERB
online
■ online bullying das Internet-Mobben

★ **only** ADVERB, ADJECTIVE, CONJUNCTION
1 einzig
□ Monday is the only day I'm free. Montag ist mein einziger freier Tag. □ German is the only subject I like. Deutsch ist das einzige Fach, das ich mag.
2 nur
□ How much was it? — Only twenty euros. Wie viel hat es gekostet? — Nur zwanzig Euro. □ We only want to stay for one night. Wir wollen nur eine Nacht bleiben. □ the same jumper, only in black der gleiche Pullover, nur in Schwarz
■ an only child ein Einzelkind *neut*

onwards ADVERB
ab
□ from July onwards ab Juli

★ **open** ADJECTIVE
▷ *see also* **open** VERB
offen
□ The window was open. Das Fenster war offen.
■ The baker's is open on Sunday morning. Die Bäckerei hat am Sonntagmorgen auf.
■ in the open air im Freien

★ to **open** VERB
▷ *see also* **open** ADJECTIVE
1 aufmachen [4] (PERFECT TENSE hat aufgemacht)
□ Can I open the window? Kann ich das Fenster aufmachen? □ What time do the shops open? Um wie viel Uhr machen die Geschäfte auf?
2 aufgehen [29] (IMPERFECT ging auf, PERFECT TENSE ist aufgegangen)
□ The door opens automatically. Die Tür geht automatisch auf. □ The door opened and in came the teacher. Die Tür ging auf und die Lehrerin kam herein.

opening hours PL NOUN
die Öffnungszeiten *fem pl*

opera NOUN
die Oper *fem*

to **operate** VERB
bedienen [7] (PERFECT TENSE hat bedient) (*machine*)
■ to operate on someone jemanden operieren [76]
■ The light operates on a timer. Das Licht wird durch einen Timer betrieben.
■ How do you operate the remote control? Wie funktioniert die Fernbedienung?

operating system NOUN
das Betriebssystem *neut*

★ **operation** NOUN
die Operation *fem*
□ a major operation eine größere Operation
■ to have an operation operiert werden [91]
□ I have never had an operation. Ich bin noch nie operiert worden.

operator NOUN
der Telefonist *masc* (GEN des Telefonisten, PL die Telefonisten)
die Telefonistin *fem* (*on telephone*)

★ **opinion** NOUN
die Meinung *fem*
□ He asked me my opinion. Er fragte mich nach meiner Meinung. □ What's your opinion? Was ist deine Meinung?
■ in my opinion meiner Meinung nach

opinion poll NOUN
die Meinungsumfrage *fem*

★ **opponent** NOUN
der Gegner *masc* (PL die Gegner)
die Gegnerin *fem*

★ **opportunity** NOUN
die Gelegenheit *fem*
■ to have the opportunity to do something
die Gelegenheit haben [32], etwas zu tun □ I've never had the opportunity to go abroad. Ich hatte noch nie die Gelegenheit, ins Ausland zu fahren.

opposed ADJECTIVE
■ to be opposed to something gegen etwas sein [65] □ I'm opposed to eating meat. Ich bin gegen den Fleischkonsum.

opposing ADJECTIVE
gegnerisch (*team*)

★ **opposite** ADJECTIVE, ADVERB, PREPOSITION
1 entgegengesetzt
□ It's in the opposite direction. Es ist in der entgegengesetzten Richtung.
2 gegenüber
□ They live opposite. Sie wohnen gegenüber. □ the girl sitting opposite me das Mädchen, das mir gegenüber saß
■ the opposite sex das andere Geschlecht

Numbers in brackets refer to verb tables on pages 697 to 706.

543

O

opposition – ornament

★ **opposition** NOUN
die Opposition *fem*

optician NOUN
der Optiker *masc* (PL die Optiker)
die Optikerin *fem*
□ She's an optician. Sie ist Optikerin.

optimist NOUN
der Optimist *masc* (GEN des Optimisten, PL die Optimisten)
die Optimistin *fem*
□ She's an optimist. Sie ist Optimistin.

★ **optimistic** ADJECTIVE
optimistisch

★ **option** NOUN
1 die Wahl *fem* (*choice*)
□ I've got no option. Ich habe keine andere Wahl.
2 das Wahlfach *neut* (PL die Wahlfächer) (*optional subject*)
□ I'm doing geology as my option. Ich habe Geologie als Wahlfach.

optional ADJECTIVE
fakultativ

★ **or** CONJUNCTION
1 oder
□ Tea or coffee? Tee oder Kaffee?

Use **weder … noch** in negative sentences.

□ I don't eat meat or fish. Ich esse weder Fleisch noch Fisch.
2 sonst (*otherwise*)
□ Hurry up or you'll miss the bus. Beeil dich, sonst verpasst du den Bus.
■ **Give me the money, or else!** Gib mir das Geld, sonst gibt's was!

oral ADJECTIVE
▷ *see also* **oral** NOUN
mündlich
□ an oral exam eine mündliche Prüfung

oral NOUN
▷ *see also* **oral** ADJECTIVE
die mündliche Prüfung *fem*
□ I've got my German oral soon. Ich habe bald meine mündliche Prüfung in Deutsch.

★ **orange** NOUN
▷ *see also* **orange** ADJECTIVE
die Orange *fem*
■ **an orange juice** ein Orangensaft *masc*

★ **orange** ADJECTIVE
▷ *see also* **orange** NOUN
orange (*colour*)

orchard NOUN
der Obstgarten *masc* (PL die Obstgärten)

orchestra NOUN
das Orchester *neut* (PL die Orchester)
□ I play in the school orchestra. Ich spiele im Schulorchester.

★ **order** NOUN
▷ *see also* **order** VERB
1 die Reihenfolge *fem* (*sequence*)
□ in alphabetical order in alphabetischer Reihenfolge
2 die Bestellung *fem* (*at restaurant, in shop*)
□ The waiter took our order. Der Ober nahm unsere Bestellung auf.
3 der Befehl *masc* (PL die Befehle) (*instruction*)
□ That's an order. Das ist ein Befehl.
■ **in order to** um zu □ He does it in order to earn money. Er tut es, um Geld zu verdienen.
■ **'out of order'** 'außer Betrieb'

★ **to order** VERB
▷ *see also* **order** NOUN
bestellen [7] (PERFECT TENSE hat bestellt)
□ We ordered steak and chips. Wir haben Steak mit Pommes frites bestellt. □ Are you ready to order? Möchten Sie bestellen?

to order about VERB
herumkommandieren [15] (PERFECT TENSE hat herumkommandiert)
□ She was fed up with being ordered about. Sie hatte es satt, herumkommandiert zu werden.

★ **ordinary** ADJECTIVE
1 gewöhnlich
□ an ordinary day ein gewöhnlicher Tag
2 normal (*people*)
□ an ordinary family eine normale Familie
□ He's just an ordinary guy. Er ist ein ganz normaler Mensch.

organ NOUN
die Orgel *fem* (*instrument*)
□ I play the organ. Ich spiele Orgel.

organic ADJECTIVE
biologisch angebaut (*fruit*)
■ **organic vegetables** das Biogemüse *sing*
■ **organic milk** die Biomilch

★ **organization** NOUN
die Organisation *fem*

★ **to organize** VERB
organisieren [76] (PERFECT TENSE hat organisiert)

origin NOUN
der Ursprung *masc* (PL die Ursprünge)

★ **original** ADJECTIVE
originell
□ It's a very original idea. Das ist eine sehr originelle Idee.
■ **Our original plan was to go camping.** Ursprünglich wollten wir zelten.

★ **originally** ADVERB
ursprünglich

Orkney NOUN
die Orkneyinseln *fem pl*
■ **in Orkney** auf den Orkneyinseln

ornament NOUN
die Vezierung *fem*

★ = core vocabulary

orphan

orphan NOUN

das Waisenkind *neut* (PL die Waisenkinder)
□ She's an orphan. Sie ist ein Waisenkind.

ostrich NOUN

der Strauß *masc* (GEN des Straußes, PL die Sträuße)

★ **other** ADJECTIVE, PRONOUN

andere
□ Have you got these jeans in other colours? Haben Sie diese Jeans in anderen Farben? □ on the other side of the street auf der anderen Straßenseite
■ **the other day** neulich
■ **the other one 1** (*masculine*) der andere □ This hat? — No, the other one. Dieser Hut? — Nein, der andere. **2** (*feminine*) die andere □ This cup? — No, the other one. Diese Tasse? — Nein, die andere. **3** (*neuter*) das andere □ This photo? — No, the other one. Dieses Foto? — Nein, das andere.
■ **the others** die anderen □ The others are going but I'm not. Die anderen gehen, ich nicht.

★ **otherwise** ADVERB, CONJUNCTION

sonst
□ Note down the number, otherwise you'll forget it. Schreib dir die Nummer auf, sonst vergisst du sie. □ Put some sunscreen on, you'll get burned otherwise. Creme dich ein, sonst bekommst du einen Sonnenbrand. □ I'm tired, but otherwise I'm fine. Ich bin müde, aber sonst geht's mir gut.

★ **ought** VERB

If you want to say that you feel obliged to do something, use the conditional tense of **sollen**.

□ I ought to phone my parents. Ich sollte meine Eltern anrufen. □ You ought not to do that. Du solltest das nicht tun.

If you want to say that something is likely, use the conditional tense of **müssen**.

□ He ought to win. Er müsste gewinnen.

ounce NOUN

die Unze *fem*

★ **our** ADJECTIVE

unser
□ Our history teacher is quite nice. Unser Geschichtelehrer ist ganz nett. □ Our company is going to expand. Unsere Firma wird expandieren. □ Our house is quite big. Unser Haus ist ziemlich groß. □ Our neighbours are very nice. Unsere Nachbarn sind sehr nett.

Do not use **unser** with parts of the body.

□ We had to shut our eyes. Wir mussten die Augen zumachen.

ours PRONOUN

1 unserer
□ Your garden is very big, ours is much smaller.

orphan – outbreak

Euer Garten ist sehr groß, unserer ist viel kleiner.
unsere
□ Your school is very different from ours. Eure Schule ist ganz anderes als unsere.
unseres
□ Your house is bigger than ours. Euer Haus ist größer als unseres.
2 unsere
□ Our teachers are strict. — Ours are too. Unsere Lehrer sind streng. — Unsere auch.
■ **Is this ours?** Gehört das uns? □ This car is ours. Das Auto gehört uns. □ Whose is this? — It's ours. Wem gehört das? — Uns.

★ **ourselves** PRONOUN

1 uns
□ We really enjoyed ourselves. Wir haben uns wirklich amüsiert.
2 selbst
□ We baked the cake ourselves. Wir haben den Kuchen selbst gebacken

★ **out** ADVERB

There are several ways of translating 'out'. Scan the examples to find one that is similar to what you want to say. For other expressions with 'out', see the verbs 'go', 'put', 'turn' etc.

1 draußen (*outside*)
□ It's cold out. Es ist kalt draußen.
2 aus (*light, fire*)
□ All the lights are out. Alle Lichter sind aus.
■ **She's out.** Sie ist weg. □ She's out for the afternoon. Sie ist den ganzen Nachmittag weg.
■ **She's out shopping.** Sie ist zum Einkaufen.
■ **out there** da draußen □ It's cold out there. Es ist kalt da draußen.
■ **to go out** ausgehen [29] □ I'm going out tonight. Ich gehe heute Abend aus.
■ **to go out with somebody** mit jemandem gehen [29] □ I've been going out with him for two months. Ich gehe seit zwei Monaten mit ihm.
■ **out of 1** aus □ to drink out of a glass aus einem Glas trinken **2** von □ in nine cases out of ten in neun von zehn Fällen **3** außerhalb □ He lives out of town. Er wohnt außerhalb der Stadt. □ three kilometres out of town drei Kilometer außerhalb der Stadt
■ **out of curiosity** aus Neugier
■ **out of work** arbeitslos
■ **That is out of the question.** Das kommt nicht infrage.
■ **You're out!** (*in game*) Du bist draußen!
■ **'way out'** 'Ausgang'

outbreak NOUN

der Ausbruch *masc* (PL die Ausbrüche)
□ a flu outbreak ein Ausbruch der Grippe □ the outbreak of war der Kriegsausbruch

O

★**outcome** NOUN

das Ergebnis*neut* (PL die Ergebnisse)

outdoor ADJECTIVE

im Freien
□ outdoor activities Aktivitäten im Freien
■ **an outdoor swimming pool** ein Freibad*neut*

outdoors ADVERB

im Freien

outfit NOUN

das Outfit*neut* (PL die Outfits)
□ a cowboy outfit ein Cowboyoutfit

outgoing ADJECTIVE

aufgeschlossen
□ She's very outgoing. Sie ist sehr
aufgeschlossen.

outing NOUN

der Ausflug*masc* (PL die Ausflüge)
□ to go on an outing einen Ausflug machen

★**outline** NOUN

1 der Grundriss*masc* (GEN des Grundrisses PL die
Grundrisse) (summary)
□ This is an outline of the plan. Das ist der
Grundriss des Plans.
2 der Umriss*masc* (GEN des Umrisses PL die
Umrisse) (shape)
□ We could see the outline of the mountain.
Wir konnten den Umriss des Berges erkennen.

outlook NOUN

1 die Einstellung*fem* (attitude)
□ my outlook on life meine Einstellung zum
Leben
2 die Aussichten*fem pl* (prospects)
□ The outlook for the future is quite positive.
Die Zukunftsaussichten sind ziemlich positiv.

outrageous ADJECTIVE

1 unerhört (behaviour)
2 unverschämt (price)

outset NOUN

der Anfang*masc* (PL die Anfänge)
□ at the outset am Anfang

★**outside** NOUN

▷ see also **outside** ADJECTIVE, ADVERB, PREPOSITION
die Außenseite*fem*

★**outside** ADJECTIVE, ADVERB, PREPOSITION

▷ see also **outside** NOUN

1 äußere
□ the outside walls die äußeren Mauern
2 draußen
□ It's very cold outside. Draußen ist es sehr kalt.
3 außerhalb
□ outside the school außerhalb der Schule
□ outside school hours außerhalb der Schulzeit

outskirts PL NOUN

der Stadtrand*masc sing*
□ on the outskirts of the town am Stadtrand

★**outstanding** ADJECTIVE

bemerkenswert

oval ADJECTIVE

oval

oven NOUN

der Backofen*masc* (PL die Backöfen)

★**over** PREPOSITION, ADVERB, ADJECTIVE

1 über

> Use the accusative to express movement or a
> change of place. Use the dative when there is
> no change of place.

□ The ball went over the wall. Der Ball flog über
die Mauer. □ There's a mirror over the
washbasin. Über dem Becken ist ein Spiegel.
2 über+acc (more than)
□ It's over twenty kilos. Es ist über zwanzig Kilo
schwer. □ The temperature was over thirty
degrees. Die Temperatur lag über dreißig Grad.
3 vorbei (finished)
□ I'll be happy when the exams are over. Ich bin
froh, wenn die Prüfungen vorbei sind.
■ **over the holidays** die Ferien über
■ **over Christmas** über Weihnachten
■ **over here** hier
■ **over there** dort
■ **the house over the road** das Haus
gegenüber
■ **I spilled coffee all over my shirt.** Ich habe
Kaffee über mein Hemd geschüttet.
■ **all over Scotland** in ganz Schottland

★**overall** ADVERB

insgesamt (generally)
□ My results were quite good overall. Insgesamt
hatte ich ganz gute Noten.

overalls PL NOUN

der Overall*masc sing* (PL die Overalls)

overcast ADJECTIVE

bedeckt
□ The sky was overcast. Der Himmel war
bedeckt.

to **overcharge** VERB

zu viel berechnen [53] (PERFECT TENSE hat zu viel
berechnet)
□ He overcharged me. Er hat mir zu viel
berechnet. □ They overcharged us for the meal.
Sie haben uns für das Essen zu viel berechnet.

overcoat NOUN

der Mantel*masc* (PL die Mäntel)

overdone ADJECTIVE

verkocht (food)

overdraft NOUN

der Überziehungskredit*masc*

to **overestimate** VERB

überschätzen [36] (PERFECT TENSE hat
überschätzt)

to **overlook** VERB

1 einen Blick haben [32] auf+acc (PRESENT TENSE
hat einen Blick auf, IMPERFECT hatte einen Blick
auf, PERFECT TENSE hat einen Blick auf gehabt)
(have view of)

★ = core vocabulary

□ The hotel overlooked the beach. Vom Hotel hat man einen Blick auf den Strand.
2 übersehen [64] (PRESENT TENSE übersieht, IMPERFECT übersah, PERFECT TENSE hat übersehen) (*forget about*)
□ He had overlooked one important problem. Er hatte ein wichtiges Problem übersehen.

★ **overseas** ADVERB
1 im Ausland
□ I'd like to work overseas. Ich würde gern im Ausland arbeiten.
2 ins Ausland
□ Mia and her family are going overseas for a year. Mia zieht für ein Jahr mit ihrer Familie ins Ausland.

oversight NOUN
das Versehen *neut* (PL die Versehen)

to **oversleep** VERB
verschlafen [58] (PRESENT TENSE verschläft, IMPERFECT verschlief, PERFECT TENSE hat verschlafen)
□ I overslept this morning. Ich habe heute morgen verschlafen.

to **overtake** VERB
überholen [18] (PERFECT TENSE hat überholt)
□ He overtook me. Er hat mich überholt.

overtime NOUN
die Überstunden *fem pl*
□ to work overtime Überstunden machen

overtook VERB ▷ see **overtake**

overweight ADJECTIVE
■ to be overweight Übergewicht haben [32]

★ to **owe** VERB
schulden [54]
■ to owe somebody something jemandem etwas schulden [54] □ You owe me five pounds. Du schuldest mir fünf Pfund.

owing to PREPOSITION
wegen
□ owing to bad weather wegen des schlechten Wetters

owl NOUN
die Eule *fem*

★ **own** ADJECTIVE
▷ see also **own** VERB
eigen
□ I've got my own bathroom. Ich habe mein eigenes Badezimmer.
■ I'd like a room of my own. Ich hätte gern ein eigenes Zimmer.
■ on one's own allein □ on her own allein □ on our own allein

★ to **own** VERB
▷ see also **own** ADJECTIVE
besitzen [68] (IMPERFECT besaß, PERFECT TENSE hat besessen)
□ My father owns a small business. Mein Vater besitzt ein kleines Geschäft.

to **own up** VERB
zugeben [28] (PRESENT TENSE gibt zu, IMPERFECT gab zu, PERFECT TENSE hat zugegeben)
□ to own up to something etwas zugeben

★ **owner** NOUN
der Besitzer *masc* (PL die Besitzer)
die Besitzerin *fem*

oxygen NOUN
der Sauerstoff *masc*

oyster NOUN
die Auster *fem*

ozone layer NOUN
die Ozonschicht *fem*

o

Pp

PA NOUN (= *personal assistant*)
der Chefsekretär *masc* (PL die Chefsekretäre)
die Chefsekretärin *fem*
□ She's a PA. Sie ist Chefsekretärin.
■ **the PA system** (*public address*) die
Lautsprecheranlage

pace NOUN
das Tempo *neut* (*speed*)
□ Technology is developing at a rapid pace. Die
Technologie entwickelt sich in schnellem
Tempo.
■ **He was walking at a brisk pace.** Er ging mit
schnellen Schritten.

Pacific NOUN
der Pazifik *masc*

pacifier NOUN (US)
der Schnuller *masc* (PL die Schnuller)

★ **to pack** VERB
▷ *see also* **pack** NOUN
packen [38]
□ I'll help you pack. Ich helfe dir packen. □ I've
packed my case. Ich habe meinen Koffer
gepackt.
■ **Pack it in!** (*stop it*) Lass es!

★ **pack** NOUN
▷ *see also* **pack** VERB
1 die Packung *fem* (*packet*)
□ a pack of chewing gum eine Packung
Kaugummi
2 der Pack *masc* (PL die Packs) (*of yoghurts, cans*)
□ a six-pack ein Sechserpack
■ **a pack of cards** ein Spiel Karten *neut*

★ **package** NOUN
das Paket *neut* (PL die Pakete)
■ **a package holiday** eine Pauschalreise

packed ADJECTIVE
gerammelt voll
□ The cinema was packed. Das Kino war
gerammelt voll.

packed lunch NOUN
das Lunchpaket *neut* (PL die Lunchpakete)
■ **I take a packed lunch to school.** Ich nehme
für mittags etwas zum Essen in die Schule mit.

packet NOUN
die Packung *fem*
□ a packet of cigarettes eine Packung
Zigaretten

pad NOUN
der Notizblock *masc* (PL die Notizblöcke)
(*notepad*)

to paddle VERB
▷ *see also* **paddle** NOUN
1 paddeln [34] (*canoe*)
2 planschen [48] (*in water*)

paddle NOUN
▷ *see also* **paddle** VERB
das Paddel *neut* (PL die Paddel) (*for canoe*)
■ **to go for a paddle** planschen gehen [29]

padlock NOUN
das Vorhängeschloss *neut* (GEN des
Vorhängeschlosses, PL die Vorhängeschlösser)

★ **page** NOUN
die Seite *fem* (*of book*)

pager NOUN
der Pager *masc* (PL die Pager)

paid VERB ▷ *see* **pay**

paid ADJECTIVE
bezahlt
□ three weeks' paid holiday drei Wochen
bezahlter Urlaub

pail NOUN
der Eimer *masc* (PL die Eimer)

★ **pain** NOUN
der Schmerz *masc* (GEN des Schmerzes, PL die
Schmerzen)
□ a terrible pain ein furchtbarer Schmerz
■ **I've got pains in my stomach.** Ich habe
Bauchschmerzen.
■ **to be in pain** Schmerzen haben [32] □ She's
in a lot of pain. Sie hat starke Schmerzen.
■ **He's a real pain.** Er geht einem echt auf die
Nerven. (*informal*)

★ **painful** ADJECTIVE
schmerzhaft
■ **to suffer from painful periods** starke
Periodenschmerzen haben [32]
■ **to be painful** wehtun [81] □ Is it painful? Tut
es weh?

painkiller NOUN
das Schmerzmittel *neut* (PL die Schmerzmittel)

★ **paint** NOUN
▷ *see also* **paint** VERB
die Farbe *fem*

---

p

★ = core vocabulary

★ to **paint** VERB
▷ see also **paint** NOUN
1 streichen (IMPERFECT strich, PERFECT TENSE hat gestrichen)
□ to paint something green etwas grün streichen
2 malen [38] (pictures)
□ She painted a picture of the house. Sie hat von dem Haus ein Bild gemalt.

paintbrush NOUN
der Pinsel masc (PL die Pinsel)

painter NOUN
der Maler masc (PL die Maler)
die Malerin fem
■ a painter and decorator ein Anstreicher masc

★ **painting** NOUN
1 das Malen neut
□ My hobby is painting. Malen ist mein Hobby.
2 das Bild neut (PL die Bilder) (picture)
□ a painting by Picasso ein Bild von Picasso

★ **pair** NOUN
das Paar neut (PL die Paare)
□ a pair of shoes ein Paar Schuhe
■ a pair of scissors eine Schere
■ a pair of trousers eine Hose
■ a pair of jeans eine Jeans
■ in pairs paarweise □ We work in pairs. Wir arbeiten paarweise.

pajamas PL NOUN (US)
der Schlafanzug masc (PL die Schlafanzüge)
□ my pajamas mein Schlafanzug
■ a pair of pajamas ein Schlafanzug

Pakistan NOUN
Pakistan neut
■ from Pakistan aus Pakistan
■ to Pakistan nach Pakistan

Pakistani NOUN
▷ see also **Pakistani** ADJECTIVE
der Pakistani masc (PL die Pakistani)
die Pakistani fem

Pakistani ADJECTIVE
▷ see also **Pakistani** NOUN
pakistanisch
■ He's Pakistani. Er ist Pakistani.

pal NOUN
der Kumpel masc (PL die Kumpel) (informal)
der Kumpel is also used for women.

★ **palace** NOUN
der Palast masc (PL die Paläste)

★ **pale** ADJECTIVE
blass
□ You're very pale. Du bist sehr blass.
■ a pale blue shirt ein hellblaues Hemd

Palestine NOUN
Palästina neut
■ from Palestine aus Palästina
■ to Palestine nach Palästina

Palestinian ADJECTIVE
▷ see also **Palestinian** NOUN
palästinensisch
■ He's Palestinian. Er ist Palästinenser.

Palestinian NOUN
▷ see also **Palestinian** ADJECTIVE
der Palästinenser masc (PL die Palästinenser)
die Palästinenserin fem

palm NOUN
der Handteller masc (PL die Handteller) (of hand)
■ a palm tree eine Palme

pamphlet NOUN
die Broschüre fem

★ **pan** NOUN
1 der Topf masc (PL die Töpfe) (saucepan)
2 die Pfanne fem (frying pan)

pancake NOUN
der Pfannkuchen masc (PL die Pfannkuchen)

pandemic NOUN
die Pandemie fem
□ a flu pandemic eine Grippepandemie

★ **panic** NOUN
▷ see also **panic** VERB
die Panik fem

★ to **panic** VERB
▷ see also **panic** NOUN
in Panik geraten (PRESENT TENSE gerät in Panik, IMPERFECT geriet in Panik, PERFECT TENSE ist in Panik geraten)
□ She panicked. Sie geriet in Panik.
■ Don't panic! Nur keine Panik!

panther NOUN
der Panther masc (PL die Panther)

panties PL NOUN
der Slip masc (PL die Slips)
□ a pair of panties ein Slip

pantomime NOUN
das Weihnachtsmärchen neut (PL die Weihnachtsmärchen)

pants PL NOUN
1 die Unterhose fem (underwear)
□ a pair of pants eine Unterhose
2 die Hose fem (trousers)
□ a pair of pants eine Hose

pantyhose PL NOUN (US)
die Strumpfhose fem

★ **paper** NOUN
1 das Papier neut (PL die Papiere)
□ a piece of paper ein Stück Papier □ a paper towel ein Papierhandtuch
2 die Zeitung fem (newspaper)
□ an advert in the paper eine Anzeige in der Zeitung
■ an exam paper eine Klausur

paperback NOUN
das Taschenbuch neut (PL die Taschenbücher)

P

Numbers in brackets refer to verb tables on pages 697 to 706.

549

paper boy NOUN
der Zeitungsjunge masc (GEN des
Zeitungsjungen, PL die Zeitungsjungen)

paper clip NOUN
die Büroklammer fem

paper girl NOUN
das Zeitungsmädchen neut (PL die
Zeitungsmädchen)

paper round NOUN
■ to do a paper round Zeitungen austragen
[77]

paperweight NOUN
der Briefbeschwerer masc (PL die
Briefbeschwerer)

paperwork NOUN
die Schreibarbeit fem
□ I've got a lot of paperwork to do. Ich habe eine
Menge Schreibarbeit zu erledigen.

parachute NOUN
der Fallschirm masc (PL die Fallschirme)

parade NOUN
die Parade fem

paradise NOUN
das Paradies neut (GEN des Paradieses, PL die
Paradiese)

paragraph NOUN
der Paragraf masc (GEN des Paragrafen, PL die
Paragrafen)

parallel ADJECTIVE
parallel

paralyzed ADJECTIVE
gelähmt

paramedic NOUN
der Sanitäter masc (PL die Sanitäter)
die Sanitäterin fem

parcel NOUN
das Paket neut (PL die Pakete)

pardon NOUN
■ Pardon? Wie bitte?

★ **parent** NOUN
1 der Vater masc (father)
2 die Mutter fem (mother)
■ my parents meine Eltern

Paris NOUN
Paris neut

★ **park** NOUN
▷ see also park VERB
der Park masc (PL die Parks)
■ a national park ein Nationalpark
■ a theme park ein Themenpark
■ a car park ein Parkplatz masc

★ to **park** VERB
▷ see also park NOUN
parken [38]
□ Where can I park my car? Wo kann ich mein
Auto parken?
■ We couldn't find anywhere to park. Wir
haben nirgends einen Parkplatz gefunden.

parking NOUN
das Parken neut
□ 'no parking' 'Parken verboten'

parking lot NOUN (US)
der Parkplatz masc (GEN des Parkplatzes, PL die
Parkplätze)

parking meter NOUN
die Parkuhr fem

parking ticket NOUN
der Strafzettel masc (PL die Strafzettel)

★ **parliament** NOUN
das Parlament neut (PL die Parlamente)

parrot NOUN
der Papagei masc (PL die Papageien)

parsley NOUN
die Petersilie fem

★ **part** NOUN
1 der Teil masc (PL die Teile) (section)
□ The first part of the film was boring. Der erste
Teil des Films war langweilig.
2 das Teil neut (PL die Teile) (component)
□ spare parts Ersatzteile
3 die Rolle fem (in play, film)
■ to take part in something an etwas
teilnehmen [52] □ A lot of people took part in
the demonstration. An der Demonstration
haben viele Menschen teilgenommen.

particular ADJECTIVE
bestimmt
□ I am looking for a particular book. Ich suche
ein bestimmtes Buch. □ Are you looking for
anything particular? Suchen Sie nach etwas
Bestimmtem?
■ nothing in particular nichts Bestimmtes

particularly ADVERB
besonders

parting NOUN
der Scheitel masc (PL die Scheitel) (in hair)

★ **partly** ADVERB
zum Teil

★ **partner** NOUN
der Partner masc (PL die Partner)
die Partnerin fem

part-time ADJECTIVE, ADVERB
Teilzeit
□ a part-time job eine Teilzeitarbeit □ He works
part-time. Er arbeitet Teilzeit.

★ **party** NOUN
1 die Party fem (PL die Partys)
□ a birthday party eine Geburtstagsparty □ a
Christmas party eine Weihnachtsparty □ a New
Year party eine Silvesterparty
2 die Partei fem (political)
□ the Conservative Party die Konservative Partei
3 die Gruppe fem (group)
□ a party of tourists eine Gruppe Touristen

★ **pass** NOUN

▷ *see also* **pass** VERB

der Pass *masc* (GEN des Passes, PL die Pässe)
□ The pass was blocked with snow. Der Pass war zugeschneit. □ That was a good pass by Ferguson. Das war ein guter Pass von Ferguson.
■ **to get a pass** (*in exam*) bestehen [72] □ She got a pass in her piano exam. Sie hat ihre Klavierprüfung bestanden. □ I got six passes. Ich habe in sechs Fächern bestanden.
■ **a bus pass 1** (*monthly*) eine Monatskarte für den Bus **2** (*for old-age pensioners*) eine Seniorenkarte für den Bus

> **DID YOU KNOW...?**
> Almost all German cities operate an integrated public transport system; you can buy a weekly (**Wochenkarte**), monthly (**Monatskarte**) or yearly (**Jahreskarte**) pass which is valid for that period on all buses, trams and light railway vehicles in a particular zone.

★ to **pass** VERB

▷ *see also* **pass** NOUN

1 geben [28] (PRESENT TENSE gibt, IMPERFECT gab, PERFECT TENSE hat gegeben) (*give*)
□ Could you pass me the salt? Könntest du mir das Salz geben?

2 vergehen [29] (IMPERFECT verging, PERFECT TENSE ist vergangen) (*go by*)
□ The time has passed quickly. Die Zeit ist schnell vergangen.

3 vorbeigehen [29] an +*dat* (IMPERFECT ging vorbei, PERFECT TENSE ist vorbeigegangen) (*on foot*)
□ I pass his house on my way to school. Auf dem Weg zur Schule gehe ich an seinem Haus vorbei.

4 vorbeifahren [21] an +*dat* (PRESENT TENSE fährt vorbei, IMPERFECT fuhr vorbei, PERFECT TENSE ist vorbeigefahren) (*in vehicle*)
□ We passed the post office. Wir sind an der Post vorbeigefahren.

5 bestehen [72] (IMPERFECT bestand, PERFECT TENSE hat bestanden) (*exam*)
□ Did you pass? Hast du bestanden?
■ **to pass an exam** eine Prüfung bestehen [72] □ I hope I'll pass the exam. Ich hoffe, dass ich die Prüfung bestehe.

to **pass out** VERB

ohnmächtig werden [91] (PRESENT TENSE wird ohnmächtig, IMPERFECT wurde ohnmächtig, PERFECT TENSE ist ohnmächtig geworden) (*faint*)

passage NOUN

1 der Abschnitt *masc* (PL die Abschnitte) (*piece of writing*)
□ Read the passage carefully. Lest den Abschnitt sorgfältig durch.

2 der Gang *masc* (PL die Gänge) (*corridor*)

★ **passenger** NOUN

der Passagier *masc* (PL die Passagiere)
die Passagierin *fem*

passion NOUN

die Leidenschaft *fem*

passive ADJECTIVE

passiv
■ **passive smoking** das Passivrauchen

Passover NOUN

das Passahfest *neut*

passport NOUN

der Pass *masc* (GEN des Passes, PL die Pässe)
■ **passport control** die Passkontrolle

★ **password** NOUN

das Passwort *neut* (PL die Passwörter)

★ **past** ADVERB, PREPOSITION

▷ *see also* **past** NOUN

nach (*beyond*)
□ It's on the right, just past the hospital. Es ist auf der rechten Seite, gleich nach dem Krankenhaus. □ It's quarter past nine. Es ist Viertel nach neun. □ It's past midnight. Es ist nach Mitternacht.
■ **It's half past ten.** Es ist halb elf.
■ **to go past 1** (*vehicle*) vorbeifahren [21]
□ The bus went past without stopping. Der Bus ist vorbeigefahren, ohne anzuhalten. □ The bus goes past our house. Der Bus fährt an unserem Haus vorbei. **2** (*on foot*) vorbeigehen [29] □ He went past without saying hello. Er ging vorbei, ohne Hallo zu sagen. □ I went past your house yesterday. Ich bin gestern an eurem Haus vorbeigegangen.

★ **past** NOUN

▷ *see also* **past** ADVERB, PREPOSITION

die Vergangenheit *fem*
□ She lives in the past. Sie lebt in der Vergangenheit.
■ **in the past** (*previously*) früher □ That was common in the past. Das war früher üblich.

★ **pasta** NOUN

die Teigwaren *fem pl*
□ Pasta is easy to cook. Teigwaren sind leicht zu kochen.

paste NOUN

der Leim *masc* (PL die Leime) (*glue*)

pasteurized ADJECTIVE

pasteurisiert

pastime NOUN

der Zeitvertreib *masc* (PL die Zeitvertreibe)
□ a popular pastime ein beliebter Zeitvertreib
■ **Her favourite pastime is running.** Laufen ist ihre Lieblingsbeschäftigung.

pastry NOUN

der Teig *masc*
■ **pastries** (*cakes*) das Gebäck *sing*

to **pat** VERB

streicheln [88] (PERFECT TENSE hat gestreichelt) (*dog, cat*)

patch NOUN

1 das Stück *neut* (PL die Stücke)
□ a patch of material ein Stück Stoff

P

patched – peanut butter

2 der Flicken masc (PL die Flicken) *(for flat tyre)*
- **He's got a bald patch.** Er hat eine kahle Stelle.

patched ADJECTIVE
geflickt
□ a pair of patched jeans eine geflickte Jeans

★ **pâté** NOUN
die Fleischpastete fem
- **liver pâté** die Leberwurst

★ **path** NOUN
der Weg masc (PL die Wege)

pathetic ADJECTIVE
schrecklich schlecht
□ Our team was pathetic. Unsere Mannschaft war schrecklich schlecht.

patience NOUN
1 die Geduld fem
□ He hasn't got much patience. Er hat nicht viel Geduld.
2 die Patience fem *(card game)*
□ to play patience Patience spielen

★ **patient** NOUN
▷ see also **patient** ADJECTIVE
der Patient masc (GEN des Patienten, PL die Patienten)
die Patientin fem

★ **patient** ADJECTIVE
▷ see also **patient** NOUN
geduldig

patio NOUN
die Terrasse fem

patriotic ADJECTIVE
patriotisch

patrol NOUN
1 die Patrouille fem *(military)*
2 die Streife fem *(of police)*

patrol car NOUN
der Streifenwagen masc (PL die Streifenwagen)

★ **pattern** NOUN
das Muster neut (PL die Muster)
□ a geometric pattern ein geometrisches Muster □ a sewing pattern ein Nähmuster

★ **pause** NOUN
die Pause fem

pavement NOUN
der Bürgersteig masc (PL die Bürgersteige)

pavilion NOUN
der Pavillon masc (PL die Pavillons)

paw NOUN
die Pfote fem

★ **pay** NOUN
▷ see also **pay** VERB
die Bezahlung fem

★ to **pay** VERB
▷ see also **pay** NOUN
bezahlen [7] (PERFECT TENSE hat bezahlt)
□ They pay me more on Sundays. Sie bezahlen

mir sonntags mehr. □ to pay by credit card mit Kreditkarte bezahlen
- **to pay for something** für etwas bezahlen [7]
□ I paid fifty euros for it. Ich habe fünfzig Euro dafür bezahlt. □ I paid for my ticket. Ich habe meine Fahrkarte bezahlt.
- **to pay extra for something** für etwas extra bezahlen [7] □ You have to pay extra for parking. Fürs Parken müssen Sie extra bezahlen.
- **to pay attention** aufpassen [31] □ You should pay more attention. Du solltest besser aufpassen.
- **Don't pay any attention to him.** Beachte ihn einfach nicht.
- **to pay somebody a visit** jemanden besuchen [7] □ Johnnie paid us a visit last night. Johnnie hat uns gestern Abend besucht.
- **to pay somebody back** *(money)* es jemandem zurückzahlen [15] □ I'll pay you back tomorrow. Ich zahle es dir morgen zurück.

★ **payment** NOUN
die Bezahlung fem

payphone NOUN
der Münzfernsprecher masc (PL die Münzfernsprecher)

★ **PC** NOUN (= *personal computer*)
der PC masc (PL die PCs)
□ She typed the essay on her PC. Sie hat den Aufsatz am PC getippt.

PE NOUN (= *physical education*)
der Sportunterricht masc

★ **pea** NOUN
die Erbse fem

★ **peace** NOUN
1 der Frieden masc *(after war)*
2 die Stille fem *(quietness)*

★ **peaceful** ADJECTIVE
1 ruhig *(calm)*
□ a peaceful afternoon ein ruhiger Nachmittag
2 friedlich *(not violent)*
□ a peaceful protest ein friedlicher Protest

★ **peach** NOUN
der Pfirsich masc (PL die Pfirsiche)

peacock NOUN
der Pfau masc (PL die Pfauen)

peak NOUN
der Gipfel masc (PL die Gipfel) *(of mountain)*
- **in peak season** in der Hochsaison
- **It's more expensive during peak travel times.** Während der Hauptreisezeit ist es teurer.

★ **peanut** NOUN
die Erdnuss fem (PL die Erdnüsse)
□ a packet of peanuts eine Packung Erdnüsse

peanut butter NOUN
die Erdnussbutter fem
□ a peanut-butter sandwich ein Brot mit Erdnussbutter

★ = core vocabulary

pear NOUN
die Birne*fem*

pearl NOUN
die Perle*fem*

pebble NOUN
der Kieselstein *masc* (PL die Kieselsteine)
■ **a pebble beach** ein Kieselstrand *masc*

peckish ADJECTIVE
■ **to feel a bit peckish** ein bisschen Hunger haben [32]

peculiar ADJECTIVE
eigenartig
□ He's a peculiar person. Er ist ein eigenartiger Mensch. □ It tastes peculiar. Es schmeckt eigenartig.

pedal NOUN
das Pedal *neut* (PL die Pedale)

pedestrian NOUN
der Fußgänger *masc* (PL die Fußgänger)
die Fußgängerin*fem*

pedestrian crossing NOUN
der Fußgängerüberweg *masc* (PL die Fußgängerüberwege)

pedestrianized ADJECTIVE
■ **a pedestrianized street** eine Fußgängerzone

pedigree ADJECTIVE
reinrassig *(animal)*
□ a pedigree labrador ein reinrassiger Labrador

pee NOUN
■ **to have a pee** pinkeln [88] *(informal)*

peek NOUN
■ **to have a peek at something** einen kurzen Blick auf etwas werfen [92] □ I had a peek at the baby. Ich habe einen kurzen Blick auf das Baby geworfen.

peel NOUN
▷ *see also* **peel** VERB
die Schale*fem* *(of orange)*

to **peel** VERB
▷ *see also* **peel** NOUN
1 schälen [38]
□ Shall I peel the potatoes? Soll ich die Kartoffeln schälen?
2 sich schälen [38]
□ My nose is peeling. Meine Nase schält sich.

peg NOUN
1 der Haken *masc* (PL die Haken) *(for coats)*
2 die Wäscheklammer*fem* *(clothes peg)*
3 der Hering *masc* (PL die Heringe) *(tent peg)*

Pekinese NOUN
der Pekinese *masc* (GEN des Pekinesen, PL die Pekinesen)

pelican crossing NOUN
die Fußgängerampel*fem*

pellet NOUN
die Schrotkugel*fem* *(for gun)*

pelvis NOUN
das Becken *neut* (PL die Becken)

★ **pen** NOUN
der Schreiber *masc* (PL die Schreiber)

to **penalize** VERB
bestrafen [7] *(PERFECT TENSE* hat bestraft)

★ **penalty** NOUN
1 die Strafe*fem* *(punishment)*
□ the death penalty die Todesstrafe
2 der Elfmeter *masc* (PL die Elfmeter) *(in football)*
3 der Strafstoß *masc* (GEN des Strafstoßes, PL die Strafstöße) *(in rugby)*
■ **a penalty shoot-out** ein Elfmeterschießen *neut*

pence PL NOUN
die Pence *masc pl*

★ **pencil** NOUN
der Bleistift *masc* (PL die Bleistifte)
■ **in pencil** mit Bleistift

pencil case NOUN
das Federmäppchen *neut* (PL die Federmäppchen)

pencil sharpener NOUN
der Bleistiftspitzer *masc* (PL die Bleistiftspitzer)

pendant NOUN
der Anhänger *masc* (PL die Anhänger)

pen friend NOUN
der Brieffreund *masc* (PL die Brieffreunde)
die Brieffreundin*fem*

penguin NOUN
der Pinguin *masc* (PL die Pinguine)

penicillin NOUN
das Penizillin *neut*

penis NOUN
der Penis *masc* (GEN des Penis, PL die Penisse)

penitentiary NOUN *(US)*
das Gefängnis *neut* (GEN des Gefängnisses, PL die Gefängnisse)

penknife NOUN
das Taschenmesser *neut* (PL die Taschenmesser)

★ **penny** NOUN
der Penny *masc* (PL die Pennys *or* Pence)

★ **pension** NOUN
die Rente*fem*

pensioner NOUN
der Rentner *masc* (PL die Rentner)
die Rentnerin*fem*

pentathlon NOUN
der Fünfkampf *masc* (PL die Fünfkämpfe)

★ **people** PL NOUN
1 die Leute *pl*
□ The people were nice. Die Leute waren nett.
□ a lot of people viele Leute
2 die Menschen *masc pl* *(individuals)*
□ six people sechs Menschen □ several people mehrere Menschen

P

■ **German people** die Deutschen
■ **People say that ...** Man sagt, dass ...

★ **pepper** NOUN
1 der Pfeffer *masc* (*spice*)
    □ **Pass the pepper, please.** Gib mir mal bitte den Pfeffer.
2 die Paprikaschote *fem* (*vegetable*)
    □ **a green pepper** eine grüne Paprikaschote

peppermill NOUN
die Pfeffermühle *fem*

peppermint NOUN
das Pfefferminzbonbon *neut* (PL die Pfefferminzbonbons) (*sweet*)
    ■ **peppermint chewing gum** der Kaugummi mit Pfefferminzgeschmack

★ **per** PREPOSITION
pro
    □ **per day** pro Tag □ **per week** pro Woche
    ■ **thirty miles per hour** dreißig Meilen in der Stunde

★ **per cent** ADVERB
das Prozent *neut*
    □ **fifty per cent** fünfzig Prozent

★ **percentage** NOUN
der Prozentsatz *masc* (GEN des Prozentsatzes, PL die Prozentsätze)

percussion NOUN
das Schlagzeug *neut* (PL die Schlagzeuge)
    □ **I play percussion.** Ich spiele Schlagzeug.

★ **perfect** ADJECTIVE
perfekt
    □ **He speaks perfect English.** Er spricht perfekt Englisch.

★ **perfectly** ADVERB
1 ganz
    □ **You know perfectly well what happened.** Du weißt ganz genau, was passiert ist.
2 perfekt (*very well*)
    □ **The system worked perfectly.** Das System hat perfekt funktioniert.

★ to **perform** VERB
spielen [38] (*act, play*)

★ **performance** NOUN
1 die Vorstellung *fem* (*show*)
    □ **The performance lasts two hours.** Die Vorstellung dauert zwei Stunden.
2 die Darstellung *fem* (*acting*)
    □ **his performance as Hamlet** seine Darstellung des Hamlet
3 die Leistung *fem* (*results*)
    □ **the team's poor performance** die schwache Leistung der Mannschaft

perfume NOUN
das Parfüm *neut* (PL die Parfüme)

★ **perhaps** ADVERB
vielleicht
    □ **a bit boring, perhaps** etwas langweilig vielleicht □ **Perhaps he's ill.** Vielleicht ist er krank. □ **perhaps not** vielleicht nicht

★ **period** NOUN
1 die Zeit *fem*
    □ **for a limited period** für eine begrenzte Zeit
2 die Epoche *fem* (*in history*)
    □ **the Victorian period** die viktorianische Epoche
3 die Periode *fem* (*menstruation*)
    □ **I'm having my period.** Ich habe meine Periode.
4 die Stunde *fem* (*lesson time*)
    □ **Each period lasts forty minutes.** Jede Stunde dauert vierzig Minuten.

★ **permanent** ADJECTIVE
1 dauerhaft (*damage, solution, relationship*)
    □ **a permanent solution** eine dauerhafte Lösung
2 dauernd (*difficulties, tension*)
    □ **a permanent headache** dauernde Kopfschmerzen
3 fest (*job, address*)
    □ **a permanent job** eine feste Arbeit

★ **permission** NOUN
die Erlaubnis *fem* (PL die Erlaubnisse)
    □ **to ask somebody's permission** jemanden um Erlaubnis bitten
    ■ **Could I have permission to leave early?** Darf ich früher gehen?

★ **permit** NOUN
der Schein *masc* (PL die Scheine)
    □ **a fishing permit** ein Angelschein

to **persecute** VERB
verfolgen [84] (PERFECT TENSE hat verfolgt)

Persian ADJECTIVE
    ■ **a Persian cat** eine Perserkatze

persistent ADJECTIVE
hartnäckig (*person*)

★ **person** NOUN
1 der Mensch *masc* (GEN des Menschen, PL die Menschen)
    □ **She's a very nice person.** Sie ist ein netter Mensch.
2 die Person *fem* (*in grammar*)
    □ **first person singular** erste Person Singular
    ■ **in person** persönlich

★ **personal** ADJECTIVE
persönlich

★ **personality** NOUN
die Persönlichkeit *fem*

★ **personally** ADVERB
persönlich
    □ **I don't know him personally.** Ich kenne ihn nicht persönlich. □ **Personally I don't agree.** Ich persönlich bin nicht einverstanden.

personnel NOUN
das Personal *neut*

perspiration NOUN
der Schweiß *masc*

★ to **persuade** VERB
überreden [54] (PERFECT TENSE hat überredet)
    ■ **to persuade somebody to do something**

★ = core vocabulary

jemanden überreden [54] etwas zu tun □ She persuaded me to go with her. Sie hat mich überredet mitzukommen.

Peru NOUN
Peru neut

Peruvian ADJECTIVE
peruanisch

pessimist NOUN
der Pessimist masc (GEN des Pessimisten, PL die Pessimisten)
die Pessimistin fem
□ I'm a pessimist. Ich bin Pessimist.

pessimistic ADJECTIVE
pessimistisch

pest NOUN
die Nervensäge fem (person)
□ He's a real pest! Er ist eine echte Nervensäge!

to **pester** VERB
belästigen [7] (PERFECT TENSE hat belästigt)
□ Stop pestering me! Hör auf, mich zu belästigen!
■ **The children pestered her to take them to the zoo.** Die Kinder ließen ihr keine Ruhe, mit ihnen in den Zoo zu gehen.

pesticide NOUN
das Pestizid neut

★ **pet** NOUN
das Haustier neut (PL die Haustiere)
□ Have you got a pet? Hast du ein Haustier?
■ **She's the teacher's pet.** Sie ist das Schätzchen der Lehrerin.

petition NOUN
die Petition fem

petrified ADJECTIVE
■ **to be petrified of something** panische Angst vor etwas haben [32] □ She's petrified of spiders. Sie hat panische Angst vor Spinnen.

★ **petrol** NOUN
das Benzin neut (PL die Benzine)
■ **unleaded petrol** bleifreies Benzin

petrol station NOUN
die Tankstelle fem

petrol tank NOUN
der Benzintank masc (PL die Benzintanks)

phantom NOUN
der Geist masc (PL die Geister)

pharmacy NOUN
die Apotheke fem

pheasant NOUN
der Fasan masc (PL die Fasane)

★ **philosophy** NOUN
die Philosophie fem

phobia NOUN
die Phobie fem

★ **phone** NOUN
▷ see also **phone** VERB
1 das Telefon neut (PL die Telefone)

□ Where's the phone? Wo ist das Telefon? □ Is there a phone here? Gibt es hier ein Telefon?
■ **by phone** telefonisch
2 das Handy neut (PL die Handys) (mobile)
□ I've got a new phone. Ich habe ein neues Handy.
■ **to be on the phone** (speaking) telefonieren [76] □ She's on the phone at the moment. Sie telefoniert gerade.
■ **Can I use your phone, please?** Kann ich mal bitte telefonieren?

★ to **phone** VERB
▷ see also **phone** NOUN
anrufen [56] (IMPERFECT rief an, PERFECT TENSE hat angerufen)
□ I tried to phone you yesterday. Ich habe gestern versucht, dich anzurufen.

phone bill NOUN
die Telefonrechnung fem

phone book NOUN
das Telefonbuch neut (PL die Telefonbücher)

★ **phone box** NOUN
die Telefonzelle fem

★ **phone call** NOUN
der Anruf masc (PL die Anrufe)
□ There's a phone call for you. Da ist ein Anruf für Sie.
■ **to make a phone call** telefonieren [76]
□ Can I make a phone call? Kann ich telefonieren?

phonecard NOUN
die Telefonkarte fem

★ **phone number** NOUN
die Telefonnummer fem

★ **photo** NOUN
das Foto neut (PL die Fotos)
□ to take a photo ein Foto machen □ to take a photo of somebody ein Foto von jemandem machen

photocopier NOUN
der Fotokopierer masc (PL die Fotokopierer)

photocopy NOUN
▷ see also **photocopy** VERB
die Fotokopie fem

to **photocopy** VERB
▷ see also **photocopy** NOUN
fotokopieren [76] (PERFECT TENSE hat fotokopiert)

★ **photograph** NOUN
▷ see also **photograph** VERB
das Foto neut (PL die Fotos)
□ to take a photograph ein Foto machen □ to take a photograph of somebody ein Foto von jemandem machen

BE CAREFUL!
Do not translate **photograph** by **Fotograf**.

★ to **photograph** VERB
▷ see also **photograph** NOUN

Numbers in brackets refer to verb tables on pages 697 to 706.

555

fotografieren [76] (PERFECT TENSE hat fotografiert)

★ photographer NOUN

der Fotograf*masc* (GEN des Fotografen, PL die Fotografen)

die Fotografin*fem*

□ She's a photographer. Sie ist Fotografin.

photography NOUN

die Fotografie*fem*

□ My hobby is photography. Mein Hobby ist die Fotografie.

Photoshop® NOUN

▷ see also **Photoshop** VERB

Photoshop®

to Photoshop VERB

▷ see also **Photoshop** NOUN

■ **to Photoshop a picture** ein Bild mit Photoshop® bearbeiten [2]

★ phrase NOUN

die Wendung*fem*

phrase book NOUN

der Sprachführer*masc* (PL die Sprachführer)

★ physical ADJECTIVE

▷ see also **physical** NOUN

körperlich (of the body)

□ physical exercise körperliche Bewegung

■ **physical education** der Sportunterricht

■ **physical therapist 1** (man) der Krankengymnast **2** (woman) die Krankengymnastin

★ physical NOUN

▷ see also **physical** ADJECTIVE

die ärztliche Untersuchung*fem*

physicist NOUN

der Physiker*masc* (PL die Physiker)

die Physikerin*fem*

□ He's a physicist. Er ist Physiker.

★ physics NOUN

die Physik*fem*

□ She teaches physics. Sie unterrichtet Physik.

physiotherapist NOUN

der Krankengymnast*masc* (GEN des Krankengymnasten, PL die Krankengymnasten)

die Krankengymnastin*fem*

physiotherapy NOUN

die Krankengymnastik*fem*

pianist NOUN

der Pianist*masc* (GEN des Pianisten, PL die Pianisten)

die Pianistin*fem*

★ piano NOUN

das Klavier*neut* (PL die Klaviere)

□ I play the piano. Ich spiele Klavier. □ I have piano lessons. Ich nehme Klavierstunden.

★ pick NOUN

▷ see also **pick** VERB

■ **Take your pick!** Du hast die Wahl!

★ to pick VERB

▷ see also **pick** NOUN

1 auswählen [4] (PERFECT TENSE hat ausgewählt) (choose)

□ I picked the biggest piece. Ich habe das größte Stück ausgewählt.

2 pflücken [48] (fruit, flowers)

to pick on VERB

■ **to pick on somebody** auf jemandem herumhacken [15] □ She's always picking on me. Sie hackt dauernd auf mir herum.

to pick out VERB

auswählen [4]

□ I like them all – it's difficult to pick one out. Sie gefallen mir alle – es ist schwierig, eins auszuwählen.

to pick up VERB

1 abholen [4] (collect)

□ We'll come to the airport to pick you up. Wir holen dich am Flughafen ab.

2 aufheben (from floor)

□ Could you help me pick up the toys? Kannst du mir helfen, die Spielsachen aufzuheben?

3 aufschnappen [4] (informal: learn)

□ I picked up some Spanish during my holiday. Ich habe während der Ferien etwas Spanisch aufgeschnappt.

pickpocket NOUN

der Taschendieb*masc* (PL die Taschendiebe)

die Taschendiebin*fem*

★ picnic NOUN

das Picknick*neut* (PL die Picknicke)

■ **to have a picnic** picknicken [48] □ We had a picnic on the beach. Wir haben am Strand gepicknickt.

★ picture NOUN

1 das Bild*neut* (PL die Bilder)

□ The book has lots of pictures. Das Buch ist voller Bilder.

■ **to draw a picture of something** etwas zeichnen [53]

2 das Foto*neut* (PL die Fotos)

□ My picture was in the paper. Mein Foto war in der Zeitung.

3 das Gemälde*neut* (PL die Gemälde) (painting)

□ a famous picture ein berühmtes Gemälde

■ **to paint a picture of something** etwas malen [38]

picture messaging NOUN

das Picture Messaging*neut*

picturesque ADJECTIVE

malerisch

★ pie NOUN

1 die Pastete*fem* (savoury)

2 der Obstkuchen*masc* (PL die Obstkuchen) (sweet)

■ **an apple pie** ein gedeckter Apfelkuchen

★ piece NOUN

das Stück*neut* (PL die Stücke)

□ A small piece, please. Ein kleines Stück, bitte.
- **a piece of furniture** ein Möbelstück *neut*
- **a piece of advice** ein Ratschlag *masc*

pier NOUN
der Pier *masc* (PL die Piere)

pierced ADJECTIVE
1 durchstochen
□ I've got pierced ears. Ich habe durchstochene Ohrläppchen.
2 gepierct
□ She's got a pierced nose. Sie hat eine gepiercte Nase.

piercing ADJECTIVE
durchdringend *(cry)*

pig NOUN
das Schwein *neut* (PL die Schweine)

pigeon NOUN
die Taube *fem*

piggyback NOUN
- **to give somebody a piggyback** jemanden huckepack nehmen [52]

piggy bank NOUN
das Sparschwein *neut* (PL die Sparschweine)

pigtail NOUN
der Zopf *masc* (PL die Zöpfe)

pile NOUN
1 der Stapel *masc* (PL die Stapel) *(tidy)*
2 der Haufen *masc* (PL die Haufen) *(untidy)*

pile-up NOUN
der Auffahrunfall *masc* (PL die Auffahrunfälle)

pill NOUN
die Pille *fem*
- **to be on the pill** die Pille nehmen [52]

pillar NOUN
die Säule *fem*

pillar box NOUN
der Briefkasten *masc* (PL die Briefkästen)

pillow NOUN
das Kopfkissen *neut* (PL die Kopfkissen)

pilot NOUN
der Pilot *masc* (GEN des Piloten, PL die Piloten)
die Pilotin *fem*
□ He's a pilot. Er ist Pilot.

pimple NOUN
der Pickel *masc* (PL die Pickel)

PIN NOUN (= personal identification number)
die PIN-Nummer *fem*

pin NOUN
die Stecknadel *fem*
- **I've got pins and needles in my foot.** Mein Fuß ist eingeschlafen.

pinafore NOUN
die Schürze *fem*

pinball NOUN
der Flipper *masc* (PL die Flipper)
- **to play pinball** flippern [34]
- **a pinball machine** ein Flipper

to **pinch** VERB
1 kneifen (IMPERFECT kniff, PERFECT TENSE hat gekniffen)
□ He pinched me! Er hat mich gekniffen!
2 klauen [38] *(informal: steal)*
□ Who's pinched my pen? Wer hat meinen Schreiber geklaut?

pine NOUN
die Kiefer *fem*
□ a pine table ein Kieferntisch *masc*

★ **pineapple** NOUN
die Ananas *fem* (PL die Ananas)

★ **pink** ADJECTIVE
rosa

rosa is invariable.

□ a pink shirt ein rosa Hemd

pint NOUN
das Pint *neut* (PL die Pints)

DID YOU KNOW...?
In Germany measurements are in litres and centilitres. A pint is about 0.6 litres. German people don't drink pints of beer, they are more likely to order **ein großes Bier**.

- **to have a pint** ein Bier trinken [80] □ He's gone out for a pint. Er ist ein Bier trinken gegangen.

★ **pipe** NOUN
1 das Rohr *neut* (PL die Rohre) *(for water, gas)*
□ The pipes froze. Die Rohre sind eingefroren.
2 die Pfeife *fem* *(for smoking)*
□ He smokes a pipe. Er raucht Pfeife.
- **the pipes** *(bagpipes)* der Dudelsack *sing* □ He plays the pipes. Er spielt Dudelsack.

pirate NOUN
der Pirat *masc* (GEN des Piraten, PL die Piraten)
die Piratin *fem*

Pisces SING NOUN
die Fische *masc pl*
□ I'm Pisces. Ich bin Fisch.

pistol NOUN
die Pistole *fem*

★ **pitch** NOUN
▷ see also **pitch** VERB
der Platz *masc* (GEN des Platzes, PL die Plätze)
□ a football pitch ein Fußballplatz

★ to **pitch** VERB
▷ see also **pitch** NOUN
aufschlagen [59] (PRESENT TENSE schlägt auf, IMPERFECT schlug auf, PERFECT TENSE hat aufgeschlagen) *(tent)*
□ We pitched our tent near the beach. Wir haben unser Zelt in der Nähe des Strandes aufgeschlagen.

pity NOUN
▷ see also **pity** VERB
das Mitleid *neut*
- **What a pity!** Wie schade!

Numbers in brackets refer to verb tables on pages 697 to 706.

557

P

pity – platform

to pity VERB
▷ see also **pity** NOUN
bemitleiden [7] (PERFECT TENSE hat bemitleidet)

★ **pizza** NOUN
die Pizza fem (PL die Pizzas)

★ **place** NOUN
▷ see also **place** VERB
1 der Ort masc (PL die Orte) (location)
   □ It's a quiet place. Es ist ein ruhiger Ort.
   □ interesting places interessante Orte
2 der Platz masc (GEN des Platzes, PL die Plätze) (space)
   □ a parking place ein Parkplatz □ a university place ein Studienplatz
   ■ **to change places** die Plätze tauschen [48]
   □ Emma, change places with Sejal! Emma, tausch die Plätze mit Sejal!
   ■ **to take place** stattfinden [24]
   ■ **at your place** bei dir □ Shall we meet at your place? Sollen wir uns bei dir treffen?
   ■ **to my place** zu mir □ Do you want to come round to my place? Willst du noch zu mir mitkommen?

★ **to place** VERB
▷ see also **place** NOUN
legen [38]
   □ He placed his hand on hers. Er legte seine Hand auf ihre.
   ■ **He was placed third.** Er wurde Dritter.

plaid ADJECTIVE
kariert
   □ a plaid shirt ein kariertes Hemd

★ **plain** NOUN
▷ see also **plain** ADJECTIVE, ADVERB
die Ebene fem

★ **plain** ADJECTIVE, ADVERB
▷ see also **plain** NOUN
1 einfarbig (self-coloured)
   □ a plain carpet ein einfarbiger Teppich
2 einfach (not fancy)
   □ a plain white blouse eine einfache weiße Bluse

plain chocolate NOUN
die bittere Schokolade fem

plait NOUN
der Zopf masc (PL die Zöpfe)
   □ She wears her hair in a plait. Sie trägt einen Zopf.

★ **plan** NOUN
▷ see also **plan** VERB
der Plan masc (PL die Pläne)
   □ What are your plans for the holidays? Welche Ferienpläne habt ihr? □ to make plans Pläne machen □ a plan of the campsite ein Plan des Zeltplatzes
   ■ **Everything went according to plan.** Alles lief nach Plan.
   ■ **my essay plan** das Konzept für meinen Aufsatz

★ **to plan** VERB
▷ see also **plan** NOUN
planen [38]
   □ We're planning a trip to Canada. Wir planen eine Reise nach Kanada. □ Plan your revision carefully. Plant eure Stoffwiederholung sorgfältig.
   ■ **to plan to do something** vorhaben [32] etwas zu tun □ I'm planning to get a job in the holidays. Ich habe vor, mir einen Ferienjob zu suchen.

★ **plane** NOUN
das Flugzeug neut (PL die Flugzeuge)
   □ by plane mit dem Flugzeug

★ **planet** NOUN
der Planet masc (GEN des Planeten, PL die Planeten)

★ **planning** NOUN
die Planung fem
   ■ **family planning** die Familienplanung
   ■ **The trip needs careful planning.** Die Reis muss sorgfältig geplant werden.

★ **plant** NOUN
▷ see also **plant** VERB
1 die Pflanze fem
   □ to water the plants die Pflanzen gießen
2 die Fabrik fem (factory)

★ **to plant** VERB
▷ see also **plant** NOUN
pflanzen [36]

plant pot NOUN
der Blumentopf masc (PL die Blumentöpfe)

plaque NOUN
1 die Gedenktafel fem (to famous person, event)
2 der Zahnbelag masc (on teeth)

plaster NOUN
1 das Pflaster neut (PL die Pflaster) (sticking plaster)
   □ Have you got a plaster? Hast du ein Pflaster?
2 der Gips masc (GEN des Gipses, PL die Gipse) (fo fracture)
   □ Her leg's in plaster. Sie hat das Bein in Gips.

★ **plastic** NOUN
▷ see also **plastic** ADJECTIVE
das Plastik neut
   □ It's made of plastic. Es ist aus Plastik.

plastic ADJECTIVE
▷ see also **plastic** NOUN
aus Plastik
   □ They still sell plastic toys. Sie verkaufen immer noch Spielzeug aus Plastik.
   ■ **a plastic bag** eine Plastiktüte

★ **plate** NOUN
der Teller masc (PL die Teller) (for food)

★ **platform** NOUN
1 der Bahnsteig masc (PL die Bahnsteige) (at station)
   □ on platform seven auf Bahnsteig sieben
2 das Podium neut (PL die Podien) (for performers

★ **play** NOUN
▷ see also **play** VERB
das Stück neut (PL die Stücke)
□ a play by Shakespeare ein Stück von
Shakespeare □ to put on a play ein Stück
aufführen

★ to **play** VERB
▷ see also **play** NOUN
1 spielen [38]
□ He's playing with his friends. Er spielt mit
seinen Freunden. □ What sort of music do they
play? Welche Art von Musik spielen sie? □ I play
hockey. Ich spiele Hockey. □ I play the guitar.
Ich spiele Gitarre. □ She's always playing that
song. Sie spielt dauernd dieses Lied.
2 spielen [38] gegen (against person, team)
□ Germany are playing Scotland. Deutschland
spielt gegen Schottland.

to **play down** VERB
herunterspielen [15] (PERFECT TENSE hat
heruntergespielt)
□ He tried to play down his illness. Er versuchte,
die Schwere seiner Krankheit
herunterzuspielen.

to **play up** VERB
■ The engine's playing up. Der Motor macht
Schwierigkeiten.

★ **player** NOUN
der Spieler masc (PL die Spieler)
die Spielerin fem
□ a football player ein Fußballspieler

playful ADJECTIVE
verspielt

★ **playground** NOUN
1 der Schulhof masc (PL die Schulhöfe) (at school)
2 der Spielplatz masc (GEN des Spielplatzes, PL die
Spielplätze) (in park)

playgroup NOUN
die Spielgruppe fem

playing card NOUN
die Spielkarte fem

playing field NOUN
der Sportplatz masc (GEN des Sportplatzes, PL
die Sportplätze)

★ **playtime** NOUN
die Pause fem

playwright NOUN
der Dramatiker masc (PL die Dramatiker)
die Dramatikerin fem

★ **pleasant** ADJECTIVE
angenehm

★ **please** EXCLAMATION
bitte
□ Two coffees, please. Zwei Kaffee bitte.

★ **pleased** ADJECTIVE
1 erfreut (happy)
□ My mum's not going to be very pleased.
Meine Mama wird nicht sehr erfreut sein.
2 zufrieden (satisfied)
□ It's beautiful, she'll be pleased with it. Es ist
wunderschön, sie wird damit sehr zufrieden
sein.
■ to be pleased about something sich über
etwas freuen [38] □ Are you pleased about the
exam results? Freust du dich über die
Prüfungsergebnisse?
■ Pleased to meet you! Angenehm!

★ **pleasure** NOUN
das Vergnügen neut (PL die Vergnügen)
□ I read for pleasure. Ich lese zum Vergnügen.

★ **plenty** NOUN
mehr als genug
□ I've got plenty. Ich habe mehr als genug.
□ That's plenty, thanks. Danke, das ist mehr als
genug.
■ I've got plenty to do. Ich habe viel zu tun.
■ plenty of 1 viele □ plenty of opportunities
viele Möglichkeiten 2 (more than enough)
genügend □ I've got plenty of money. Ich habe
genügend Geld. □ We've got plenty of time. Wir
haben genügend Zeit.

pliers PL NOUN
die Zange fem sing
■ a pair of pliers eine Zange

★ **plot** NOUN
▷ see also **plot** VERB
1 die Handlung fem (of story, play)
2 die Verschwörung fem (against somebody)
□ a plot against the president eine
Verschwörung gegen den Präsidenten
■ a plot of land ein Stück Land neut
■ a vegetable plot ein Gemüsebeet neut

★ to **plot** VERB
▷ see also **plot** NOUN
planen [38]
□ They were plotting to kill him. Sie planten, ihn
zu töten.

plough NOUN
▷ see also **plough** VERB
der Pflug masc (PL die Pflüge)

to **plough** VERB
▷ see also **plough** NOUN
pflügen [38]

plug NOUN
1 der Stecker masc (PL die Stecker) (electrical)
□ The plug is faulty. Der Stecker ist kaputt.
2 der Stöpsel masc (PL die Stöpsel) (for sink)

to **plug in** VERB
einstecken [4] (PERFECT TENSE hat eingesteckt)
□ Is it plugged in? Ist es eingesteckt?

plum NOUN
die Pflaume fem
□ plum jam die Pflaumenmarmelade

plumber NOUN
der Klempner masc (PL die Klempner)
die Klempnerin fem
□ He's a plumber. Er ist Klempner.

plump – pole

plump ADJECTIVE
rundlich

to **plunge** VERB
tauchen [48]

plural NOUN
der Plural masc (PL die Plurale)

★ **plus** PREPOSITION, ADJECTIVE
plus
□ four plus three equals seven. Vier plus drei
macht sieben.
■ **three children plus a dog** drei Kinder und
ein Hund

p.m. ABBREVIATION
■ **at eight p.m.** um acht Uhr abends

> **DID YOU KNOW...?**
> In Germany times are often given using the
> 24-hour clock.

□ at two p.m. um vierzehn Uhr

pneumonia NOUN
die Lungenentzündung fem

poached ADJECTIVE
■ **a poached egg** ein verlorenes Ei neut

★ **pocket** NOUN
die Tasche fem
■ **pocket money** das Taschengeld □ eight
pounds a week pocket money acht Pfund
Taschengeld pro Woche

pocket calculator NOUN
der Taschenrechner masc (PL die
Taschenrechner)

podcast NOUN
der Podcast masc (PL die Podcasts)
□ to download a podcast einen Podcast
herunterladen

★ **poem** NOUN
das Gedicht neut (PL die Gedichte)

★ **poet** NOUN
der Dichter masc (PL die Dichter)
die Dichterin fem

★ **poetry** NOUN
die Gedichte neut pl
□ to write poetry Gedichte schreiben

★ **point** NOUN
▷ see also **point** VERB
1 der Punkt masc (PL die Punkte) (spot, score)
□ a point on the horizon ein Punkt am Horizont
□ They scored five points. Sie machten fünf
Punkte.
2 die Bemerkung fem (comment)
□ He made some interesting points. Er machte
ein paar interessante Bemerkungen.
3 die Spitze fem (tip)
□ a pencil with a sharp point ein Bleistift mit
einer scharfen Spitze
4 der Zeitpunkt masc (in time)
□ At that point, we were three one up. Zu dem
Zeitpunkt lagen wir mit drei zu eins in Führung.

■ **a point of view** ein Gesichtspunkt masc
■ **to get the point** begreifen □ I don't get the
point. Ich begreife das nicht.
■ **That's a good point!** Da hast du recht.
■ **There's no point.** Das hat keinen Wert.
□ There's no point in waiting. Es hat keinen
Wert zu warten.
■ **What's the point?** Wozu? □ What's the
point of leaving so early? Wozu so früh gehen?
■ **Physics isn't my strong point.** Die Physik
ist nicht meine Stärke.
■ **two point five (2.5)** zwei Komma fünf (2,5)

★ to **point** VERB
▷ see also **point** NOUN
mit dem Finger zeigen [38]
□ Don't point! Man zeigt nicht mit dem Finger!
■ **to point at somebody** auf jemanden zeigen
[38] □ She pointed at Maryam. Sie zeigte auf
Maryam.
■ **to point a gun at somebody** auf jemanden
mit der Waffe zielen [38]

to **point out** VERB
■ **to point something out 1** (show) auf etwas
zeigen [38] □ The guide pointed out Big Ben.
Unser Führer zeigte auf Big Ben. **2** (mention)
auf etwas hinweisen □ I should point out that ...
Ich möchte darauf hinweisen, dass ...

pointless ADJECTIVE
nutzlos
□ It's pointless to argue. Es ist nutzlos zu
streiten.

poison NOUN
▷ see also **poison** VERB
das Gift neut (PL die Gifte)

to **poison** VERB
▷ see also **poison** NOUN
vergiften [2] (PERFECT TENSE hat vergiftet)

poisonous ADJECTIVE
giftig

to **poke** VERB
■ **He poked me in the eye.** Er stieß mir ins
Auge.

poker NOUN
das Poker neut
□ I play poker. Ich spiele Poker.

★ **Poland** NOUN
Polen neut
■ **from Poland** aus Polen
■ **to Poland** nach Polen

polar bear NOUN
der Eisbär masc (GEN des Eisbären, PL die
Eisbären)

Pole NOUN
der Pole masc (GEN des Polen, PL die Polen)
die Polin fem (Polish person)

★ **pole** NOUN
der Mast masc (PL die Masten)
□ a telegraph pole ein Telegrafenmast
■ **a tent pole** eine Zeltstange

★ = core vocabulary

- **a ski pole** ein Skistock *masc*
- **the North Pole** der Nordpol
- **the South Pole** der Südpol

pole vault NOUN

das Stabhochspringen *neut*

★ **police** PL NOUN

die Polizei *fem*
□ We called the police. Wir haben die Polizei gerufen.

> Note that 'police' is used with a plural verb and **Polizei** with a singular verb.

□ The police haven't arrived yet. Die Polizei ist noch nicht da.
- **a police car** ein Polizeiwagen *masc*
- **a police station** ein Polizeirevier *neut*

★ **policeman** NOUN

der Polizist *masc* (GEN des Polizisten, PL die Polizisten)
□ He's a policeman. Er ist Polizist.

★ **policewoman** NOUN

die Polizistin *fem*
□ She's a policewoman. Sie ist Polizistin.

polio NOUN

die Kinderlähmung *fem*

★ **Polish** ADJECTIVE

▷ see also **Polish** NOUN

polnisch
- **He's Polish.** Er ist Pole.
- **She's Polish.** Sie ist Polin.

★ **Polish** NOUN

▷ see also **Polish** ADJECTIVE

das Polnisch *neut* (GEN des Polnischen)
(language)

polish NOUN

▷ see also **polish** VERB

1 die Schuhcreme *fem* (PL die Schuhcremes) *(for shoes)*
2 die Politur *fem* *(for furniture)*

to **polish** VERB

▷ see also **polish** NOUN

1 eincremen [4] (PERFECT TENSE hat eingecremt) *(shoes)*
2 polieren [76] (PERFECT TENSE hat poliert) *(glass, furniture)*

★ **polite** ADJECTIVE

höflich

politely ADVERB

höflich

politeness NOUN

die Höflichkeit *fem*

★ **political** ADJECTIVE

politisch

★ **politician** NOUN

der Politiker *masc* (PL die Politiker)
die Politikerin *fem*

★ **politics** PL NOUN

die Politik *fem*

□ I'm not interested in politics. Ich interessiere mich nicht für Politik.

poll NOUN

die Umfrage *fem*
□ The poll revealed that ... Die Umfrage ergab, dass ...

pollen NOUN

der Pollen *masc* (PL die Pollen)

to **pollute** VERB

verschmutzen [7] (PERFECT TENSE hat verschmutzt)

polluted ADJECTIVE

verschmutzt

★ **pollution** NOUN

die Umweltverschmutzung *fem*
- **air pollution** die Luftverschmutzung

polo-necked sweater NOUN

der Rollkragenpullover *masc* (PL die Rollkragenpullover)

polo shirt NOUN

das Polohemd *neut* (PL die Polohemden)

polythene bag NOUN

die Plastiktüte *fem*

pond NOUN

der Teich *masc* (PL die Teiche)
□ We've got a pond in our garden. Wir haben einen Teich im Garten.

pony NOUN

das Pony *neut* (PL die Ponys)

ponytail NOUN

der Pferdeschwanz *masc* (GEN des Pferdeschwanzes, PL die Pferdeschwänze)
□ He's got a ponytail. Er hat einen Pferdeschwanz.

pony trekking NOUN

- **to go pony trekking** Pony reiten gehen [29]

poodle NOUN

der Pudel *masc* (PL die Pudel)

★ **pool** NOUN

1 die Pfütze *fem* *(puddle)*
2 der Teich *masc* (PL die Teiche) *(pond)*
3 das Schwimmbecken *neut* (PL die Schwimmbecken) *(for swimming)*
4 das Poolbillard *neut* *(game)*
□ Shall we have a game of pool? Sollen wir eine Partie Poolbillard spielen?

★ **poor** ADJECTIVE

1 arm
□ a poor family eine arme Familie □ They are poorer than we are. Sie sind ärmer als wir.
□ Poor David! Der arme David!
- **the poor** die Armen *masc pl*
2 schlecht *(bad)*
□ a poor mark eine schlechte Note

poorly ADJECTIVE

- **She's poorly.** Es geht ihr schlecht.

Numbers in brackets refer to verb tables on pages 697 to 706.

561

P

★ **pop** ADJECTIVE
- **pop music** die Popmusik
- **a pop star** ein Popstar masc
- **a pop group** eine Popgruppe
- **a pop song** ein Popsong masc

to **pop in** VERB
vorbeikommen [40] (IMPERFECT kam vorbei, PERFECT TENSE ist vorbeigekommen)

to **pop out** VERB
kurz weggehen [29] (IMPERFECT ging weg, PERFECT TENSE ist weggegangen)
□ I'm just popping out for an hour. Ich gehe nur mal kurz für eine Stunde weg.

to **pop round** VERB
- **I'm just popping round to my aunt's.** Ich gehe nur mal kurz zu meiner Tante.

popcorn NOUN
das Popcorn neut

poppy NOUN
der Mohn masc

Popsicle® NOUN (US)
das Eis am Stiel neut (GEN des Eises am Stiel, PL die Eis am Stiel)

★ **popular** ADJECTIVE
beliebt
□ She's a very popular girl. Sie ist sehr beliebt.

★ **population** NOUN
die Bevölkerung fem

porch NOUN
die Veranda fem (PL die Veranden)

pork NOUN
das Schweinefleisch neut
□ I don't eat pork. Ich esse kein Schweinefleisch.
- **a pork chop** ein Schweinekotelett neut

pornography NOUN
die Pornografie fem

porridge NOUN
der Haferbrei masc

★ **port** NOUN
1 der Hafen masc (PL die Häfen) (harbour)
2 der Portwein masc (wine)
□ a glass of port ein Glas Portwein

portable ADJECTIVE
tragbar

porter NOUN
1 der Portier masc (PL die Portiers) (in hotel)
2 der Gepäckträger masc (PL die Gepäckträger) (at station)

portion NOUN
die Portion fem
□ a large portion of chips eine große Portion Pommes frites

portrait NOUN
das Porträt neut (PL die Porträts)

★ **Portugal** NOUN
Portugal neut

- **from Portugal** aus Portugal
- **to Portugal** nach Portugal

★ **Portuguese** ADJECTIVE
▷ see also **Portuguese** NOUN
portugiesisch
- **She's Portuguese.** Sie ist Portugiesin.

★ **Portuguese** NOUN
▷ see also **Portuguese** ADJECTIVE
1 der Portugiese masc (GEN des Portugiesen, PL die Portugiesen)
die Portugiesin fem (person)
2 das Portugiesisch neut (GEN des Portugiesischen) (language)

posh ADJECTIVE
vornehm
□ a posh hotel ein vornehmes Hotel

★ **position** NOUN
die Stellung fem
□ an uncomfortable position eine unbequeme Stellung

★ **positive** ADJECTIVE
1 positiv (good)
□ a positive attitude eine positive Einstellung
2 ganz sicher (sure)
□ I'm positive. Ich bin ganz sicher.

to **possess** VERB
besitzen [68] (IMPERFECT besaß, PERFECT TENSE hat besessen)

possession NOUN
- **Have you got all your possessions?** Hast du all deine Sachen?

★ **possibility** NOUN
die Möglichkeit fem
□ It's a possibility. Das ist eine Möglichkeit.

★ **possible** ADJECTIVE
möglich
□ as soon as possible sobald wie möglich

★ **possibly** ADVERB
vielleicht (perhaps)
□ Are you coming to the party? — Possibly. Kommst du zur Party? — Vielleicht.
- **... if you possibly can.** ... wenn du irgend kannst.
- **I can't possibly come.** Ich kann unmöglich kommen.

★ **post** NOUN
▷ see also **post** VERB
1 die Post fem (letters)
□ Is there any post for me? Ist Post für mich da?
2 der Pfosten masc (PL die Pfosten) (pole)
□ The ball hit the post. Der Ball traf den Pfosten.
3 der Beitrag masc (PL die Beiträge) (on forum, blog)

★ to **post** VERB
▷ see also **post** NOUN
1 aufgeben [28] (PRESENT TENSE gibt auf, IMPERFECT gab auf, PERFECT TENSE hat aufgegeben)
□ I've got some cards to post. Ich muss ein paar

★ = core vocabulary

Karten aufgeben.

2 posten [2] (*on website*)

postage NOUN
das Porto *neut* (PL die Portos)

postbox NOUN
der Briefkasten *masc* (PL die Briefkästen)

★ **postcard** NOUN
die Postkarte *fem*

postcode NOUN
die Postleitzahl *fem*

> **DID YOU KNOW...?**
> German postcodes consist of a 5-figure
> number which precedes the name of the
> city.

★ **poster** NOUN
1 das Poster *neut* (PL die Poster)
  □ I've got posters on my bedroom walls. Ich
  habe in meinem Zimmer Poster an den
  Wänden.
2 das Plakat *neut* (PL die Plakate) (*advertising*)
  □ There are posters all over town. In der ganzen
  Stadt hängen Plakate.

★ **postman** NOUN
der Briefträger *masc* (PL die Briefträger)
  □ He's a postman. Er ist Briefträger.

postmark NOUN
der Stempel *masc* (PL die Stempel)

★ **post office** NOUN
das Postamt *neut* (PL die Postämter)
  □ Where's the post office, please? Wo ist das
  Postamt, bitte?
  ■ **She works for the post office.** Sie arbeitet
  bei der Post.

★ **to postpone** VERB
verschieben (IMPERFECT verschob, PERFECT TENSE
hat verschoben)
  □ The match has been postponed. Das Spiel
  wurde verschoben.

★ **postwoman** NOUN
die Briefträgerin *fem*
  □ She's a postwoman. Sie ist Briefträgerin.

★ **pot** NOUN
1 der Topf *masc* (PL die Töpfe)
  □ a pot of jam ein Marmeladentopf
2 die Kanne *fem* (*for hot drinks*)
  ■ **pots and pans** Töpfe und Pfannen

★ **potato** NOUN
die Kartoffel *fem*
  □ a baked potato eine gebackene Kartoffel
  □ potato salad der Kartoffelsalat
  ■ **mashed potatoes** der Kartoffelbrei

★ **potential** NOUN
  ▷ *see also* **potential** ADJECTIVE
  ■ **He has great potential.** Er ist sehr
  vielversprechend.

★ **potential** ADJECTIVE
  ▷ *see also* **potential** NOUN

möglich
  □ a potential problem ein mögliches Problem

pothole NOUN
das Schlagloch *neut* (PL die Schlaglöcher) (*in
road*)

pot plant NOUN
die Topfpflanze *fem*

pottery NOUN
die Keramik *fem*

★ **pound** NOUN
  ▷ *see also* **pound** VERB
das Pfund *neut* (PL die Pfunde or Pfund) (*weight,
money*)

> When talking about an amount of money or
> specifying a quantity of something use the
> plural form **Pfund**.

  □ two pounds of carrots zwei Pfund Karotten
  □ How many euros do you get to the pound?
  Wie viel Euro bekommt man für ein Pfund? □ a
  pound coin eine Pfundmünze

★ **to pound** VERB
  ▷ *see also* **pound** NOUN
pochen [48]
  □ My heart was pounding. Mein Herz hat
  gepocht.

★ **to pour** VERB
gießen [31] (IMPERFECT goss, PERFECT TENSE hat
gegossen) (*liquid*)
  □ She poured some water into the pan. Sie goss
  etwas Wasser in den Topf. □ It's pouring. Es
  gießt. □ She poured him a drink. Sie goss ihm
  einen Drink ein.
  ■ **Shall I pour you a cup of tea?** Soll ich Ihnen
  eine Tasse Tee einschenken?
  ■ **in the pouring rain** im strömenden Regen

★ **poverty** NOUN
die Armut *fem*

powder NOUN
1 das Pulver *neut*
2 der Puder *masc* (PL die Puder) (*face powder*)

★ **power** NOUN
1 der Strom *masc* (*electricity*)
  □ The power's off. Es gibt keinen Strom.
  ■ **a power cut** ein Stromausfall *masc*
  ■ **a power point** eine Steckdose
  ■ **a power station** ein Kraftwerk *neut*
2 die Energie *fem* (*energy*)
  □ nuclear power die Kernenergie □ solar power
  die Sonnenenergie
3 die Macht *fem* (PL die Mächte) (*authority*)
  □ to be in power an der Macht sein

★ **powerful** ADJECTIVE
1 mächtig
  □ a powerful man ein mächtiger Mann
2 kräftig (*physically*)
3 leistungsstark (*machine*)

★ **practical** ADJECTIVE
praktisch

P

□ a practical suggestion ein praktischer Vorschlag □ She's very practical. Sie ist sehr praktisch.

practically ADVERB

praktisch

□ It's practically impossible. Es ist praktisch unmöglich.

★ **practice** NOUN

1 das Training neut (for sport)

□ football practice das Fußballtraining

2 die Übung fem

□ You need more practice. Du brauchst mehr Übung.

■ I've got to do my piano practice. Ich muss Klavier üben.

■ It's normal practice in our school. Das ist in unserer Schule so üblich.

■ in practice in der Praxis

■ a medical practice eine Arztpraxis

★ to **practise** VERB

1 üben [38] (music, hobby, language)

□ I ought to practise more. Ich sollte mehr üben. □ I practise the flute every evening. Ich übe jeden Abend Flöte. □ I practised my German when we were on holiday. Ich habe in den Ferien mein Deutsch geübt.

2 trainieren [76] (PERFECT TENSE hat trainiert) (sport)

□ The team practises on Thursdays. Die Mannschaft trainiert donnerstags. □ I don't practise enough. Ich trainiere nicht genug.

practising ADJECTIVE

praktizierend

□ She's a practising Catholic. Sie ist praktizierende Katholikin.

★ to **praise** VERB

loben [38]

□ The teacher praised her work. Der Lehrer lobte ihre Arbeit.

pram NOUN

der Kinderwagen masc (PL die Kinderwagen)

prawn NOUN

die Garnele fem

prawn cocktail NOUN

der Krabbencocktail masc (PL die Krabbencocktails)

to **pray** VERB

beten [2]

□ to pray for something für etwas beten

prayer NOUN

das Gebet neut (PL die Gebete)

precaution NOUN

die Vorsichtsmaßnahme fem

□ to take precautions Vorsichtsmaßnahmen treffen

preceding ADJECTIVE

vorherig

precinct NOUN

■ a shopping precinct ein Einkaufsviertel neut

■ a pedestrian precinct eine Fußgängerzone

precious ADJECTIVE

kostbar

precise ADJECTIVE

genau

□ at that precise moment genau in diesem Augenblick

★ **precisely** ADVERB

genau

□ Precisely! Genau!

■ at ten o'clock precisely um Punkt zehn Uhr

to **predict** VERB

vorhersagen [15] (PERFECT TENSE hat vorhergesagt)

predictable ADJECTIVE

vorhersehbar

prefect NOUN

DID YOU KNOW...?

German schools do not have prefects.

■ My sister's a prefect. Meine Schwester ist im letzten Schuljahr und führt die Aufsicht bei den Jüngeren.

★ to **prefer** VERB

lieber mögen [50] (PRESENT TENSE mag lieber, IMPERFECT mochte lieber, PERFECT TENSE hat lieber gemocht)

□ Which would you prefer? Was magst du lieber? □ I prefer biology to chemistry. Ich mag Biologie lieber als Chemie.

■ I preferred the first version. Die erste Version hat mir besser gefallen.

preference NOUN

die Vorliebe fem

□ his preference for detective stories seine Vorliebe für Kriminalromane

★ **pregnant** ADJECTIVE

schwanger

□ She's six months pregnant. Sie ist im siebten Monat schwanger.

prehistoric ADJECTIVE

prähistorisch

prejudice NOUN

1 das Vorurteil neut (PL die Vorurteile)

□ That's just a prejudice. Das ist ein Vorurteil.

2 die Vorurteile neut pl

□ There's a lot of racial prejudice. Es gibt viele Rassenvorurteile.

prejudiced ADJECTIVE

voreingenommen

■ to be prejudiced against somebody gegen jemanden voreingenommen sein [65]

premature ADJECTIVE

verfrüht

■ a premature baby eine Frühgeburt

★ = core vocabulary

Premier League NOUN

die erste Liga *fem*

□ in the Premier League in der ersten Liga

> **DID YOU KNOW...?**
> The 'Premier League' is similar to the German **Bundesliga**.

premises PL NOUN

die Geschäftsräume *masc pl*

□ They're moving to new premises. Sie ziehen in neue Geschäftsräume um.

premonition NOUN

die Vorahnung *fem*

preoccupied ADJECTIVE

■ He's preoccupied with his exams. Er denkt nur an seine Prüfungen.

prep NOUN

die Hausaufgaben *fem pl* (*homework*)

□ history prep die Hausaufgaben in Geschichte

preparation NOUN

die Vorbereitung *fem*

★ to **prepare** VERB

vorbereiten [2] (PERFECT TENSE hat vorbereitet)

□ She prepares lessons in the evening. Abends bereitet sie Stunden vor.

■ to prepare for something Vorbereitungen für etwas treffen [78] □ We're preparing for our holiday. Wir treffen Vorbereitungen für unseren Urlaub.

★ **prepared** ADJECTIVE

■ to be prepared to do something bereit sein [65], etwas zu tun □ I'm prepared to help you. Ich bin bereit, dir zu helfen.

prep school NOUN

die private Grundschule *fem*

to **prescribe** VERB

verschreiben [61] (IMPERFECT verschrieb, PERFECT TENSE hat verschrieben) (*medicine*)

□ He prescribed me a course of antibiotics. Er hat mir eine Antibiotikakur verschrieben.

prescription NOUN

das Rezept *neut* (PL die Rezepte)

□ You can't get it without a prescription. Das bekommt man nicht ohne Rezept.

presence NOUN

die Anwesenheit *fem*

■ presence of mind die Geistesgegenwart

★ **present** ADJECTIVE

▷ *see also* **present** NOUN, VERB

1 anwesend (*in attendance*)

□ He wasn't present at the meeting. Er war bei der Besprechung nicht anwesend.

2 gegenwärtig (*current*)

□ the present situation die gegenwärtige Situation

■ the present tense die Gegenwart

★ **present** NOUN

▷ *see also* **present** ADJECTIVE, VERB

1 das Geschenk *neut* (PL die Geschenke) (*gift*)

□ I'm going to buy presents. Ich kaufe Geschenke.

■ to give somebody a present jemandem etwas schenken [38]

2 die Gegenwart *fem* (*time*)

□ She was living in the past, not the present. Sie lebte in der Vergangenheit, nicht in der Gegenwart.

■ up to the present bis heute

■ for the present momentan

■ at present im Augenblick

■ the present tense das Präsens

★ to **present** VERB

▷ *see also* **present** ADJECTIVE, NOUN

■ to present somebody with something (*prize, medal*) jemandem etwas verleihen

presenter NOUN

der Moderator *masc* (PL die Moderatoren)

die Moderatorin *fem* (*on TV*)

presently ADVERB

1 sofort (*soon*)

□ You'll feel better presently. Sie werden sich sofort besser fühlen.

2 im Moment (*at present*)

□ They're presently on tour. Sie sind im Moment auf Tournee.

★ **president** NOUN

der Präsident *masc* (GEN des Präsidenten, PL die Präsidenten)

die Präsidentin *fem*

★ **press** NOUN

▷ *see also* **press** VERB

die Presse *fem*

■ a press conference eine Pressekonferenz

★ to **press** VERB

▷ *see also* **press** NOUN

drücken [38]

□ Don't press too hard! Nicht zu fest drücken! □ He pressed the start button. Er drückte auf den Startknopf.

pressed ADJECTIVE

■ We are pressed for time. Wir haben wenig Zeit.

press-up NOUN

der Liegestütz *masc* (GEN des Liegestützes, PL die Liegestütze)

□ I do twenty press-ups every morning. Ich mache jeden Morgen zwanzig Liegestütze.

★ **pressure** NOUN

▷ *see also* **pressure** VERB

der Druck *masc*

□ He's under a lot of pressure. Er steht unter viel Druck.

■ a pressure group 1 (*small-scale, local*) eine Bürgerinitiative 2 (*large-scale, more political*) eine Pressure-Group

★ to **pressure** VERB

▷ *see also* **pressure** NOUN

p

Druck ausüben [4] auf +acc (PERFECT TENSE hat Druck ausgeübt)

□ They are pressuring me. Sie üben Druck auf mich aus.

prestige NOUN
das Ansehen neut

prestigious ADJECTIVE
angesehen

★ **presumably** ADVERB
vermutlich

to **presume** VERB
annehmen [1] (PRESENT TENSE nimmt an, IMPERFECT nahm an, PERFECT TENSE hat angenommen)

□ I presume so. Das nehme ich an.

★ to **pretend** VERB
■ **to pretend to do something** so tun [81], als ob man etwas täte

Note that **als ob** is followed by the subjunctive.

□ He pretended to be asleep. Er tat so, als ob er schliefe.

★ **pretty** ADJECTIVE, ADVERB
1 hübsch
□ She's very pretty. Sie ist sehr hübsch.
2 ziemlich (rather)
□ That film was pretty bad. Der Film war ziemlich schlecht.
■ **It's pretty much the same.** Das ist mehr oder weniger dasselbe.

★ to **prevent** VERB
verhindern [88] (PERFECT TENSE hat verhindert)
■ **to prevent somebody from doing something** jemanden davon abhalten [33], etwas zu tun □ They tried to prevent us from staying out late. Sie haben versucht, uns davon abzuhalten, zu lange auszubleiben.

★ **previous** ADJECTIVE
vorherig

previously ADVERB
früher

prey NOUN
die Beute fem
■ **a bird of prey** ein Raubvogel masc

★ **price** NOUN
der Preis masc (GEN des Preises, PL die Preise)

price list NOUN
die Preisliste fem

to **prick** VERB
stechen (PRESENT TENSE sticht, IMPERFECT stach, PERFECT TENSE hat gestochen)

□ I've pricked my finger. Ich habe mir in den Finger gestochen.

★ **pride** NOUN
der Stolz masc (GEN des Stolzes)

★ **priest** NOUN
der Priester masc (PL die Priester)

die Priesterin fem
□ He's a priest. Er ist Priester.

★ **primarily** ADVERB
vor allem

★ **primary** ADJECTIVE
hauptsächlich

primary school NOUN
die Grundschule fem

DID YOU KNOW...?
Children in Germany begin **Grundschule** at the age of 6. The **Grundschule** provides primary education in school years 1 to 4.

□ She's still at primary school. Sie ist noch in der Grundschule.

prime minister NOUN
der Premierminister masc (PL die Premierminister)
die Premierministerin fem

primitive ADJECTIVE
primitiv

★ **prince** NOUN
der Prinz masc (GEN des Prinzen, PL die Prinzen)
□ the Prince of Wales der Prinz von Wales

★ **princess** NOUN
die Prinzessin fem
□ Princess Anne Prinzessin Anne

★ **principal** ADJECTIVE
▷ see also **principal** NOUN
■ **the principal reason** der Hauptgrund
■ **my principal concern** mein Hauptanliegen neut

★ **principal** NOUN
▷ see also **principal** ADJECTIVE
der Direktor masc (PL die Direktoren)
die Direktorin fem (of college)

principle NOUN
das Prinzip neut (PL die Prinzipien)
■ **on principle** aus Prinzip

★ **print** NOUN
1 die Schrift fem (letters)
■ **in small print** klein gedruckt
2 der Fingerabdruck masc (PL die Fingerabdrücke) (fingerprint)
3 der Kunstdruck masc (PL die Kunstdrucke) (picture)
□ a framed print ein gerahmter Kunstdruck

printer NOUN
der Drucker masc (PL die Drucker) (machine)

printout NOUN
der Ausdruck masc (PL die Ausdrucke)

★ **priority** NOUN
die Priorität fem

★ **prison** NOUN
das Gefängnis neut (GEN des Gefängnisses, PL die Gefängnisse)
■ **in prison** im Gefängnis

★ = core vocabulary

prisoner NOUN

der Gefangene *masc* (GEN des Gefangenen, PL die Gefangenen)

die Gefangene *fem* (GEN der Gefangenen)

□ a prisoner (*man*) ein Gefangener

prison officer NOUN

der Gefängniswärter *masc* (PL die Gefängniswärter)

die Gefängniswärterin *fem*

privacy NOUN

das Privatleben *neut*

□ an invasion of my privacy ein Eingriff in mein Privatleben

private ADJECTIVE

privat

■ **a private school** eine Privatschule

■ **private property** das Privateigentum

■ **'private'** (*on envelope*) 'persönlich'

■ **a private bathroom** ein eigenes Badezimmer

■ **I have private lessons.** Ich bekomme Nachhilfestunden.

to **privatize** VERB

privatisieren [76] (PERFECT TENSE hat privatisiert)

privilege NOUN

das Privileg *neut* (PL die Privilegien)

prize NOUN

der Preis *masc* (GEN des Preises, PL die Preise)

□ to win a prize einen Preis gewinnen

prize-giving NOUN

die Preisverleihung *fem*

prizewinner NOUN

der Preisträger *masc* (PL die Preisträger)

die Preisträgerin *fem*

pro NOUN

der Profi *masc* (PL die Profis)

> der Profi is also used for women.

□ This was her first year as a pro. Dies war ihr erstes Jahr als Profi.

■ **the pros and cons** das Für und Wider □ We weighed up the pros and cons. Wir haben das Für und Wider abgewogen.

probability NOUN

die Wahrscheinlichkeit *fem*

probable ADJECTIVE

wahrscheinlich

probably ADVERB

wahrscheinlich

□ probably not wahrscheinlich nicht

problem NOUN

das Problem *neut* (PL die Probleme)

□ No problem! Kein Problem!

proceeds PL NOUN

der Erlös *masc sing* (GEN des Erlöses, PL die Erlöse)

process NOUN

der Prozess *masc* (GEN des Prozesses, PL die Prozesse)

□ the peace process der Friedensprozess

■ **to be in the process of doing something** gerade dabei sein [65], etwas zu tun □ We're in the process of painting the kitchen. Wir sind gerade dabei, die Küche zu streichen.

procession NOUN

die Prozession *fem* (*religious*)

★ to **produce** VERB

1 herstellen [4] (PERFECT TENSE hat hergestellt) (*manufacture*)

2 inszenieren [76] (PERFECT TENSE hat inszeniert) (*play, show*)

3 produzieren [76] (PERFECT TENSE hat produziert) (*film*)

★ **producer** NOUN

1 der Regisseur *masc* (PL die Regisseure)

die Regisseurin *fem* (*of play, show*)

2 der Produzent *masc* (GEN des Produzenten, PL die Produzenten)

die Produzentin *fem* (*of film*)

★ **product** NOUN

das Produkt *neut* (PL die Produkte)

★ **production** NOUN

1 die Produktion *fem*

□ The latest smartphone has just gone into production. Das neueste Smartphone ist gerade in Produktion gegangen.

2 die Inszenierung *fem* (*play, show*)

□ a production of 'Hamlet' eine Hamletinszenierung

★ **profession** NOUN

der Beruf *masc* (PL die Berufe)

★ **professional** NOUN

▷ see also **professional** ADJECTIVE

der Profi *masc* (PL die Profis)

> der Profi is also used for women.

□ She now plays as a professional. Sie spielt jetzt als Profi.

★ **professional** ADJECTIVE

▷ see also **professional** NOUN

professionell (*player*)

□ a very professional piece of work eine sehr professionelle Arbeit

■ **a professional musician** ein Berufsmusiker *masc*

professionally ADVERB

■ **She sings professionally.** Sie ist Sängerin von Beruf.

★ **professor** NOUN

der Professor *masc* (PL die Professoren)

die Professorin *fem*

■ **She's the German professor.** Sie hat den Lehrstuhl für Deutsch inne.

★ **profit** NOUN

der Gewinn *masc* (PL die Gewinne)

profitable ADJECTIVE

gewinnbringend

P

Numbers in brackets refer to verb tables on pages 697 to 706.

567

program NOUN

▷ see also **program** VERB

das Programm neut (PL die Programme)

□ a computer program ein Computerprogramm

to program VERB

▷ see also **program** NOUN

programmieren [76] (PERFECT TENSE hat programmiert)

□ to program a computer einen Computer programmieren

programme NOUN

das Programm neut (PL die Programme)

programmer NOUN

der Programmierer masc (PL die Programmierer)

die Programmiererin fem

□ She's a programmer. Sie ist Programmiererin.

programming NOUN

das Programmieren neut

progress NOUN

der Fortschritt masc (PL die Fortschritte)

□ You're making progress! Du machst Fortschritte!

to prohibit VERB

verbieten [8] (IMPERFECT verbat, PERFECT TENSE hat verboten)

□ Smoking is prohibited. Das Rauchen ist verboten.

project NOUN

1 das Projekt neut (PL die Projekte) (plan)

2 das Referat neut (PL die Referate) (at school)

□ I'm doing a project on Berlin. Ich schreibe ein Referat über Berlin.

projector NOUN

der Projektor masc (PL die Projektoren)

promenade NOUN

die Strandpromenade fem

promise NOUN

▷ see also **promise** VERB

das Versprechen neut (PL die Versprechen)

□ You didn't keep your promise. Du hast dein Versprechen nicht gehalten.

■ **That's a promise!** Versprochen!

to promise VERB

▷ see also **promise** NOUN

versprechen [70] (PRESENT TENSE verspricht, IMPERFECT versprach, PERFECT TENSE hat versprochen)

□ She promised to write. Sie hat versprochen zu schreiben. □ I'll text you, I promise! Versprochen, ich schicke dir eine SMS!

promising ADJECTIVE

vielversprechend

to promote VERB

■ **to be promoted** befördert werden [91]

□ She was promoted after six months. Sie wurde nach sechs Monaten befördert.

promotion NOUN

1 die Beförderung fem (in job)

2 die Werbung fem (advertising)

prompt ADJECTIVE, ADVERB

schnell

□ a prompt reply eine schnelle Antwort

■ **at eight o'clock prompt** genau um acht Uh

promptly ADVERB

pünktlich

□ We left promptly at seven. Wir sind pünktlich um sieben gegangen.

pronoun NOUN

das Pronomen neut (PL die Pronomen)

to pronounce VERB

aussprechen [70] (PRESENT TENSE spricht aus, IMPERFECT sprach aus, PERFECT TENSE hat ausgesprochen)

□ How do you pronounce that word? Wie spricht man das Wort aus?

pronunciation NOUN

die Aussprache fem

proof NOUN

der Beweis masc (GEN des Beweises, PL die Beweise)

proper ADJECTIVE

1 echt (genuine)

□ proper German bread echtes deutsches Brot

2 ordentlich (decent)

□ We didn't have a proper lunch. Wir hatten kein ordentliches Mittagessen. □ It's difficult to get a proper job. Es ist schwierig, einen ordentlichen Job zu bekommen. □ We need proper training. Wir brauchen eine ordentliche Ausbildung.

3 richtig (appropriate)

□ You have to have the proper equipment. Sie brauchen die richtige Ausrüstung.

■ **If you had come at the proper time ...** Wenn du zur rechten Zeit gekommen wärst ...

properly ADVERB

1 richtig (correctly)

□ You're not doing it properly. Du machst das nicht richtig.

2 anständig (appropriately)

□ Dress properly for your interview. Zieh dich zum Vorstellungsgespräch anständig an.

property NOUN

das Eigentum neut

■ **'private property'** 'Privateigentum'

■ **stolen property** das Diebesgut

proportional ADJECTIVE

■ **proportional representation** das Verhältniswahlrecht

proposal NOUN

der Vorschlag masc (PL die Vorschläge) (suggestion)

to propose VERB

vorschlagen [59] (PRESENT TENSE schlägt vor,

★ = core vocabulary

IMPERFECT schlug vor, PERFECT TENSE hat vorgeschlagen)

□ I propose a new plan. Ich schlage einen neuen Plan vor.

■ **to propose to do something** vorhaben [32], etwas zu tun □ What do you propose to do? Was haben Sie zu tun vor?

■ **to propose to somebody** (*for marriage*) jemandem einen Heiratsantrag machen [48] □ He's proposed to her. Er hat ihr einen Heiratsantrag gemacht.

to **prosecute** VERB
strafrechtlich verfolgen [84] (PERFECT TENSE hat verfolgt)

□ They were prosecuted for murder. Sie wurden wegen Mordes strafrechtlich verfolgt.

■ **'Shoplifters will be prosecuted'** 'Jeder Diebstahl wird zur Anzeige gebracht'

prospect NOUN
die Aussicht *fem*
□ It'll improve my career prospects. Das wird meine Berufsaussichten verbessern.

BE CAREFUL!
Do not translate **prospect** by Prospekt.

prospectus NOUN
das Lehrprogramm *neut* (PL die Lehrprogramme) (*for school, university*)

to **protect** VERB
schützen [36]

protection NOUN
der Schutz *masc* (GEN des Schutzes)

protein NOUN
das Protein *neut* (PL die Proteine)

★ **protest** NOUN
▷ see also **protest** VERB
der Protest *masc* (PL die Proteste)
□ He ignored their protests. Er hat ihre Proteste ignoriert.

■ **a protest march** ein Protestmarsch *masc*

★ to **protest** VERB
▷ see also **protest** NOUN
protestieren [76] (PERFECT TENSE hat protestiert)

Protestant NOUN
▷ see also **Protestant** ADJECTIVE
der Protestant *masc* (GEN des Protestanten, PL die Protestanten)
die Protestantin *fem*
□ She's a Protestant. Sie ist Protestantin.

Protestant ADJECTIVE
▷ see also **Protestant** NOUN
protestantisch
□ a Protestant church eine protestantische Kirche

protester NOUN
der Demonstrant *masc* (GEN des Demonstranten, PL die Demonstranten)
die Demonstrantin *fem*

★ **proud** ADJECTIVE
stolz
□ Her parents are proud of her. Ihre Eltern sind stolz auf sie.

★ to **prove** VERB
beweisen (IMPERFECT bewies, PERFECT TENSE hat bewiesen)
□ The police couldn't prove it. Die Polizei konnte es nicht beweisen.

proverb NOUN
das Sprichwort *neut* (PL die Sprichwörter)

★ to **provide** VERB
stellen [38]
□ We'll provide the food. Wir stellen das Essen.
■ **to provide somebody with something** jemandem etwas zur Verfügung stellen [38]
□ They provided us with maps. Sie haben uns Karten zur Verfügung gestellt.

to **provide for** VERB
versorgen [7] (PERFECT TENSE hat versorgt)
□ He can't provide for his family any more. Er kann seine Familie nicht mehr versorgen.

provided CONJUNCTION
vorausgesetzt, dass
□ He'll play provided he's fit. Er spielt, vorausgesetzt, dass er fit ist.

provisional ADJECTIVE
vorläufig

prowler NOUN
der Herumtreiber *masc* (PL die Herumtreiber)
die Herumtreiberin *fem*

prune NOUN
die Backpflaume *fem*

pseudonym NOUN
das Pseudonym *neut* (PL die Pseudonyme)

psychiatrist NOUN
der Psychiater *masc* (PL die Psychiater)
die Psychiaterin *fem*
□ She's a psychiatrist. Sie ist Psychiaterin.

psychoanalyst NOUN
der Psychoanalytiker *masc* (PL die Psychoanalytiker)
die Psychoanalytikerin *fem*

★ **psychological** ADJECTIVE
psychologisch

psychologist NOUN
der Psychologe *masc* (GEN des Psychologen, PL die Psychologen)
die Psychologin *fem*
□ She's a psychologist. Sie ist Psychologin.

psychology NOUN
die Psychologie *fem*

PTO ABBREVIATION (= *please turn over*)
b. w. (= *bitte wenden*)

★ **pub** NOUN
die Kneipe *fem*

P

public – puncture

★ **public** NOUN
> ▷ see also **public** ADJECTIVE
> die Öffentlichkeit*fem*
> □ open to the public der Öffentlichkeit zugänglich
> ■ in public in der Öffentlichkeit

★ **public** ADJECTIVE
> ▷ see also **public** NOUN
> öffentlich
> □ public opinion die öffentliche Meinung
> □ public transport öffentliche Verkehrsmittel *neut pl*
> ■ a public holiday ein gesetzlicher Feiertag
> ■ the public address system die Lautsprecheranlage

publican NOUN
> der Gastwirt *masc*
> die Gastwirtin *fem*
> □ He's a publican. Er ist Gastwirt.

★ **publicity** NOUN
> die Publicity *fem*

public school NOUN
> die Privatschule *fem*

★ to **publish** VERB
> veröffentlichen [84] (PERFECT TENSE hat veröffentlicht)

★ **publisher** NOUN
> der Verlag *masc* (PL die Verlage) (company)

pudding NOUN
> der Nachtisch *masc*
> □ What's for pudding? Was gibt's zum Nachtisch?
> ■ rice pudding der Milchreis
> ■ black pudding die Blutwurst

puddle NOUN
> die Pfütze *fem*

puff pastry NOUN
> der Blätterteig *masc*

★ to **pull** VERB
> ziehen [96] (IMPERFECT zog, PERFECT TENSE hat gezogen)
> □ Pull! Zieh!
> ■ He pulled the trigger. Er drückte ab.
> ■ to pull a muscle sich einen Muskel zerren [38] □ I've pulled a muscle. Ich habe mir einen Muskel gezerrt.
> ■ You're pulling my leg! Du willst mich wohl auf den Arm nehmen! (informal)

to **pull down** VERB
> abreißen

to **pull out** VERB
> 1 herausziehen [96] (tooth, weed)
> 2 ausscheren [4] (car)
> □ The car pulled out to overtake. Das Auto scherte aus, um zu überholen.
> 3 aussteigen [74] (withdraw)
> □ She pulled out of the tournament. Sie ist aus dem Turnier ausgestiegen.

to **pull through** VERB
> durchkommen [40] (survive)
> □ They think he'll pull through. Sie meinen, er kommt durch.

to **pull up** VERB
> anhalten [33] (car)
> □ A car pulled up beside me. Ein Auto hielt neben mir an.

pullover NOUN
> der Pullover *masc* (PL die Pullover)

pulse NOUN
> der Puls *masc* (GEN des Pulses, PL die Pulse)
> □ The nurse felt his pulse. Die Schwester fühlte ihm den Puls.

pulses PL NOUN
> die Hülsenfrüchte *fem pl*

★ **pump** NOUN
> ▷ see also **pump** VERB
> 1 die Pumpe *fem*
> □ a bicycle pump eine Fahrradpumpe
> ■ a petrol pump eine Zapfsäule
> 2 der Sportschuh *masc* (PL die Sportschuhe) (shoe)

★ to **pump** VERB
> ▷ see also **pump** NOUN
> pumpen [38]

to **pump up** VERB
> aufpumpen [4] (tyre)

pumpkin NOUN
> der Kürbis *masc* (GEN des Kürbisses, PL die Kürbisse)

★ **punch** NOUN
> ▷ see also **punch** VERB
> 1 der Schlag *masc* (PL die Schläge) (blow)
> □ a violent punch ein heftiger Schlag
> 2 der Punsch *masc* (drink)

★ to **punch** VERB
> ▷ see also **punch** NOUN
> 1 schlagen [59] (PRESENT TENSE schlägt, IMPERFECT schlug, PERFECT TENSE hat geschlagen) (hit)
> □ He punched me! Er hat mich geschlagen!
> 2 entwerten [18] (PERFECT TENSE hat entwertet) (in ticket machine)
> □ Punch your ticket before you get on the train. Entwerten Sie Ihre Fahrkarte, bevor Sie in den Zug steigen.
> 3 knipsen [48] (by ticket inspector)
> □ He forgot to punch my ticket. Er hat vergessen, meine Fahrkarte zu knipsen.

punch-up NOUN
> die Schlägerei *fem* (informal)

punctual ADJECTIVE
> pünktlich

punctuation NOUN
> die Zeichensetzung *fem*

puncture NOUN
> die Reifenpanne *fem*
> □ to have a puncture eine Reifenpanne haben

to punish VERB
bestrafen [7] (PERFECT TENSE hat bestraft)
□ The teacher punished him. Der Lehrer bestrafte ihn.

punishment NOUN
die Strafe fem

★ **pupil** NOUN
der Schüler masc (PL die Schüler)
die Schülerin fem

puppet NOUN
die Marionette fem

puppy NOUN
der junge Hund masc (PL die jungen Hunde)

★ **to purchase** VERB
erwerben [90] (PRESENT TENSE erwirbt, IMPERFECT erwarb, PERFECT TENSE hat erworben)

★ **pure** ADJECTIVE
rein
□ pure orange juice reiner Orangensaft
■ He's doing pure maths. Er macht rein theoretische Mathematik.

★ **purple** ADJECTIVE
lila

★ **purpose** NOUN
der Zweck masc (PL die Zwecke)
□ What is the purpose of these changes? Welchen Zweck haben diese Veränderungen?
■ his purpose in life sein Lebensinhalt
■ on purpose absichtlich □ He did it on purpose. Er hat es absichtlich getan.

to purr VERB
schnurren [48]

purse NOUN
1 der Geldbeutel masc (PL die Geldbeutel) (for money)
2 die Handtasche fem (US: handbag)

to pursue VERB
verfolgen [84] (PERFECT TENSE hat verfolgt)

pursuit NOUN
die Aktivität fem
□ outdoor pursuits Aktivitäten im Freien

★ **push** NOUN
▷ see also **push** VERB
■ to give somebody a push jemanden stoßen
□ He gave me a push. Er hat mich gestoßen.

★ **to push** VERB
▷ see also **push** NOUN
1 drücken [38] (button)
2 drängeln [34]
□ Don't push! Nicht drängeln!
■ to push somebody to do something jemanden drängen [38], etwas zu tun □ They're pushing me to go to university. Sie drängen mich zu studieren.
■ to push drugs mit Drogen handeln [34]
■ Push off! Hau ab! (informal)

to push around VERB
herumkommandieren [76]

□ He likes pushing people around. Er kommandiert die Leute gern herum.

to push through VERB
■ I pushed my way through. Ich drängelte mich durch.

pushchair NOUN
der Sportwagen masc (PL die Sportwagen)

push-up NOUN
der Liegestütz masc (GEN des Liegestützes, PL die Liegestütze)
□ I do twenty push-ups every morning. Ich mache jeden Morgen zwanzig Liegestütze.

★ **to put** VERB

Use **legen** when you're putting something down flat, use **stellen** when you're standing something upright.

1 legen [38]
□ Where shall I put my things? Wohin soll ich meine Sachen legen? □ She's putting the baby to bed. Sie legt das Baby ins Bett.
2 stellen [38]
□ Put the vase on the table. Stell die Vase auf den Tisch.
■ Don't forget to put your name on the paper. Vergiss nicht, deinen Namen auf das Papier zu schreiben.

to put aside VERB
zurücklegen [15] (PERFECT TENSE hat zurückgelegt)
□ Can you put this aside for me till tomorrow? Können Sie mir das bis morgen zurücklegen?

to put away VERB
wegräumen [4] (PERFECT TENSE hat weggeräumt)
□ Can you put away the dishes, please? Kannst du bitte das Geschirr wegräumen?

to put back VERB
1 zurücklegen [15] (PERFECT TENSE hat zurückgelegt)
□ Put it back when you've finished with it. Leg es zurück, wenn du es nicht mehr brauchst.
2 zurückstellen [15] (PERFECT TENSE hat zurückgestellt)
□ to put the clock back die Uhr zurückstellen
□ Put the milk back in the fridge. Stell die Milch in den Kühlschrank zurück.

to put down VERB
1 abstellen [4] (PERFECT TENSE hat abgestellt)
□ I'll put these bags down for a minute. Ich stelle diese Taschen für eine Minute ab.
2 aufschreiben [61] (IMPERFECT schrieb auf, PERFECT TENSE hat aufgeschrieben) (in writing)
□ I've put down a few ideas. Ich habe ein paar Ideen aufgeschrieben.
■ to have an animal put down ein Tier einschläfern lassen [42] □ We had to have our old dog put down. Wir mussten unseren alten Hund einschläfern lassen.

P

Numbers in brackets refer to verb tables on pages 697 to 706.

571

puzzle – Pyrenees

to **put forward** VERB
<u>vorstellen</u> [4] (PERFECT TENSE hat vorgestellt)
□ to put the clock forward die Uhr vorstellen

to **put in** VERB
<u>einbauen</u> [4] (PERFECT TENSE hat eingebaut)
(*install*)
□ We've put in central heating. Wir haben eine
Zentralheizung einbauen lassen.
■ **He has put in a lot of work on this project.**
Er hat viel Arbeit in dieses Projekt gesteckt.

to **put off** VERB
1 <u>ausmachen</u> [48] (PERFECT TENSE hat
ausgemacht) (*switch off*)
□ Shall I put the light off? Soll ich das Licht
ausmachen?
2 <u>verschieben</u> (IMPERFECT verschob, PERFECT TENSE
hat verschoben) (*postpone*)
□ I keep putting it off. Ich verschiebe es
dauernd.
3 <u>stören</u> [38] (*distract*)
□ Stop putting me off! Hör auf, mich zu stören!
4 <u>entmutigen</u> [18] (PERFECT TENSE hat entmutigt)
(*discourage*)
□ He's not easily put off. Er lässt sich nicht so
schnell entmutigen.

to **put on** VERB
1 <u>anziehen</u> [96] (IMPERFECT zog an, PERFECT TENSE
hat angezogen) (*clothes*)
□ I'll put my coat on. Ich ziehe mir den Mantel
an.
2 <u>anmachen</u> [4] (PERFECT TENSE hat angemacht)
(*light, heater, TV*)
□ Shall I put the heater on? Soll ich den
Heizofen anmachen?
3 <u>aufführen</u> [4] (PERFECT TENSE hat aufgeführt)
(*play, show*)
□ We're putting on 'Bugsy Malone'. Wir führen
'Bugsy Malone' auf.
4 <u>aufstellen</u> [4] (PERFECT TENSE hat aufgestellt)
□ I'll put the potatoes on. Ich stelle die
Kartoffeln auf.
5 <u>auftragen</u> [77] (PRESENT TENSE trägt auf,
IMPERFECT trug auf, PERFECT TENSE hat
aufgetragen) (*lipstick*)
■ **to put on weight** zunehmen [52] □ He's put
on a lot of weight. Er hat viel zugenommen.

to **put out** VERB
1 <u>ausmachen</u> [48] (PERFECT TENSE hat
ausgemacht) (*light, cigarette*)
□ Put the light out. Mach das Licht aus.
2 <u>löschen</u> [48] (*fire*)

□ It took them five hours to put out the fire. Sie
haben fünf Stunden gebraucht, um das Feuer
zu löschen.

to **put through** VERB
<u>verbinden</u> (IMPERFECT verband, PERFECT TENSE hat
verbunden)
□ Can you put me through to him? Können Sie
mich mit ihm verbinden?
■ **I'm putting you through.** Ich verbinde.

to **put up** VERB
1 <u>aufhängen</u> [35] (PERFECT TENSE hat aufgehängt)
(*pin up*)
□ I'll put the poster up in my room. Ich hänge
das Poster in meinem Zimmer auf.
2 <u>aufschlagen</u> [59] (PRESENT TENSE schlägt auf,
IMPERFECT schlug auf, PERFECT TENSE hat
aufgeschlagen) (*tent*)
□ We put up our tent in a field. Wir haben unser
Zelt auf einem Feld aufgeschlagen.
3 <u>erhöhen</u> [19] (PERFECT TENSE hat erhöht) (*price*)
□ They've put up the price. Sie haben den Preis
erhöht.
4 <u>übernachten lassen</u> [42] (PRESENT TENSE lässt
übernachten, IMPERFECT ließ übernachten,
PERFECT TENSE hat übernachten lassen)
(*accommodate*)
□ My friend will put me up for the night. Mein
Freund lässt mich bei sich übernachten.
■ **to put one's hand up** sich melden [54] □ If
you have any questions, put up your hand.
Wenn ihr Fragen habt, dann meldet euch.
■ **to put up with something** sich etwas
gefallen lassen [42] □ I'm not going to put up
with it. Ich lasse mir das nicht gefallen.

puzzle NOUN
das Puzzle *neut* (PL die Puzzles) (*jigsaw*)

puzzled ADJECTIVE
verdutzt
□ You look puzzled! Du siehst verdutzt aus!

puzzling ADJECTIVE
rätselhaft

pyjamas PL NOUN
der Schlafanzug *masc* (PL die Schlafanzüge)
□ my pyjamas mein Schlafanzug
■ **a pair of pyjamas** ein Schlafanzug
■ **a pyjama top** ein Schlafanzugoberteil *neut*

pyramid NOUN
die Pyramide *fem*

Pyrenees PL NOUN
■ **the Pyrenees** die Pyrenäen *pl*

Qq

quad bike NOUN
das Quad *neut* (PL die Quads)

quaint ADJECTIVE
malerisch (*house, village*)

qualification NOUN
die Qualifikation *fem*
□ vocational qualifications die beruflichen Qualifikationen
■ **to leave school without any qualifications** die Schule ohne einen Abschluss verlassen [42]

★ **qualified** ADJECTIVE
ausgebildet
□ a qualified driving instructor eine ausgebildete Fahrlehrerin □ a qualified nurse ein ausgebildeter Krankenpfleger

★ **to qualify** VERB
1 seinen Abschluss machen [48] (*for job*)
□ She qualified as a teacher last year. Sie hat letztes Jahr ihren Abschluss als Lehrerin gemacht.
2 sich qualifizieren [76] (PERFECT TENSE hat sich qualifiziert) (*in competition*)
□ Our team didn't qualify. Unsere Mannschaft konnte sich nicht qualifizieren.

★ **quality** NOUN
1 die Qualität *fem*
□ a good quality of life eine gute Lebensqualität
■ **good-quality ingredients** qualitativ hochwertige Zutaten
2 die Eigenschaft *fem* (*of person*)
□ good qualities gute Eigenschaften

★ **quantity** NOUN
die Menge *fem*

quarrel NOUN
▷ see also **quarrel** VERB
der Streit *masc* (PL die Streite)

to quarrel VERB
▷ see also **quarrel** NOUN
sich streiten (IMPERFECT stritt sich, PERFECT TENSE hat sich gestritten)

quarry NOUN
der Steinbruch *masc* (PL die Steinbrüche) (*for stone*)

★ **quarter** NOUN
das Viertel *neut* (PL die Viertel)
□ three quarters drei Viertel □ a quarter of an hour eine viertel Stunde

■ **three quarters of an hour** eine Dreiviertelstunde
■ **a quarter past ten** Viertel nach zehn
■ **a quarter to eleven** Viertel vor elf

quarter final NOUN
das Viertelfinale *neut* (PL die Viertelfinale)

quartet NOUN
das Quartett *neut* (PL die Quartette)
□ a string quartet ein Streichquartett

quay NOUN
der Kai *masc* (PL die Kais)

queasy ADJECTIVE
■ **I'm feeling queasy.** Mir ist schlecht.

★ **queen** NOUN
1 die Königin *fem*
□ Queen Elizabeth Königin Elisabeth
2 die Dame *fem* (*playing card*)
□ the queen of hearts die Herzdame

query NOUN
▷ see also **query** VERB
die Frage *fem*

to query VERB
▷ see also **query** NOUN
infrage stellen [38]
□ No one queried my decision. Niemand hat meine Entscheidung infrage gestellt.
■ **They queried the bill.** Sie reklamierten die Rechnung.

★ **question** NOUN
▷ see also **question** VERB
die Frage *fem*
□ That's a difficult question. Das ist eine schwierige Frage.
■ **Can I ask a question?** Kann ich etwas fragen?
■ **It's out of the question.** Das kommt nicht infrage.

★ **to question** VERB
▷ see also **question** NOUN
befragen [7] (PERFECT TENSE hat befragt)
■ **He was questioned by the police.** Die Polizei hat ihn vernommen.

question mark NOUN
das Fragezeichen *neut* (PL die Fragezeichen)

questionnaire NOUN
der Fragebogen *masc* (PL die Fragebögen)

q

Numbers in brackets refer to verb tables on pages 697 to 706.

queue - quote

queue NOUN
▷ see also **queue** VERB
die Schlange *fem*

to queue VERB
▷ see also **queue** NOUN
Schlange stehen [72] (IMPERFECT stand
Schlange, PERFECT TENSE hat Schlange
gestanden)
□ We queued for an hour. Wir haben eine
Stunde lang Schlange gestanden.
■ **to queue for something** für etwas anstehen
[72] □ We had to queue for tickets. Wir mussten
für Karten anstehen.

★ **quick** ADJECTIVE, ADVERB
schnell
□ a quick lunch ein schnelles Mittagessen
□ Quick, phone the police! Schnell, rufen Sie die
Polizei! □ It's quicker by train. Mit dem Zug geht
es schneller.
■ **Be quick!** Beeil dich!
■ **She's a quick learner.** Sie lernt schnell.

★ **quickly** ADVERB
schnell
□ It was all over very quickly. Es war alles sehr
schnell vorbei.

★ **quiet** ADJECTIVE
1 ruhig (*not talkative, peaceful*)
□ You're very quiet today. Du bist heute sehr
ruhig. □ a quiet little town eine ruhige, kleine
Stadt
2 leise (*not noisy*)
□ The engine's very quiet. Der Motor ist sehr
leise.
■ **Be quiet!** Sei still!
■ **Quiet!** Ruhe!

★ **quietly** ADVERB
leise
□ He quietly opened the door. Er öffnete leise
die Tür.

quilt NOUN
die Steppdecke *fem* (*duvet*)

★ **to quit** VERB
1 aufgeben [28] (PRESENT TENSE gibt auf, IMPERFECT

gab auf, PERFECT TENSE hat aufgegeben)
□ I quit my job last week. Ich habe meine Stelle
letzte Woche aufgegeben.
2 aufhören [4]
□ I quit smoking. Ich habe mit dem Rauchen
aufgehört.

★ **quite** ADVERB
1 ziemlich (*rather*)
□ It's quite warm today. Heute ist es ziemlich
warm. □ I've been there quite a lot. Ich war
schon ziemlich oft da. □ quite a lot of money
ziemlich viel Geld □ quite a few people ziemlich
viele Leute □ It costs quite a lot. Es ist ziemlich
teuer. □ It's quite a long way. Es ist ziemlich
weit. □ It was quite a shock. Es war ein
ziemlicher Schock.
■ **I quite liked the film, but ...** Der Film hat
mir ganz gut gefallen, aber ...
2 ganz (*entirely*)
□ I'm not quite sure. Ich bin mir nicht ganz
sicher. □ It's not quite the same. Das ist nicht
ganz das Gleiche.
■ **quite good** ganz gut

quiz NOUN
das Quiz *neut* (GEN des Quiz, PL die Quiz)

quota NOUN
die Quote *fem*

quotation NOUN
das Zitat *neut* (PL die Zitate)
□ a quotation from Shakespeare ein
Shakespearezitat

quotation marks PL NOUN
die Anführungszeichen *neut pl*

★ **quote** NOUN
▷ see also **quote** VERB
das Zitat *neut* (PL die Zitate)
□ a Shakespeare quote ein Shakespearezitat
■ **quotes** (*quotation marks*) die
Anführungszeichen □ in quotes in
Anführungszeichen

★ **to quote** VERB
▷ see also **quote** NOUN
zitieren [76] (PERFECT TENSE hat zitiert)

Rr

rabbi NOUN
der Rabbiner *masc* (PL die Rabbiner)
die Rabbinerin *fem*

★ **rabbit** NOUN
das Kaninchen *neut* (PL die Kaninchen)
■ **a rabbit hutch** ein Kaninchenstall *masc*

rabies SING NOUN
die Tollwut *fem*
■ **a dog with rabies** ein tollwütiger Hund

★ **race** NOUN
▷ *see also* **race** VERB
1 das Rennen *neut* (PL die Rennen) (*sport*)
□ **a cycle race** ein Radrennen
2 die Rasse *fem* (*species*)
□ **the human race** die Menschheit
■ **race relations** Rassenbeziehungen *fem pl*

★ to **race** VERB
▷ *see also* **race** NOUN
1 rennen [55] (IMPERFECT rannte, PERFECT TENSE ist gerannt)
□ **We raced to catch the bus.** Wir sind gerannt, um den Bus zu erreichen.
2 um die Wette laufen [43] mit (PRESENT TENSE läuft um die Wette, IMPERFECT lief um die Wette, PERFECT TENSE ist um die Wette gelaufen) (*have a race*)
□ **I'll race you!** Ich laufe mit dir um die Wette!

racecourse NOUN
die Pferderennbahn *fem*

racehorse NOUN
das Rennpferd *neut* (PL die Rennpferde)

racer NOUN
das Rennrad *neut* (PL die Rennräder) (*bike*)

racetrack NOUN
die Rennbahn *fem*

racial ADJECTIVE
■ **racial discrimination** die Rassendiskriminierung

racing car NOUN
der Rennwagen *masc* (PL die Rennwagen)

racing driver NOUN
der Rennfahrer *masc* (PL die Rennfahrer)
die Rennfahrerin *fem*

racism NOUN
der Rassismus *masc* (GEN des Rassismus)

racist ADJECTIVE
▷ *see also* **racist** NOUN
rassistisch
■ **He's racist.** Er ist ein Rassist.

racist NOUN
▷ *see also* **racist** ADJECTIVE
der Rassist *masc* (GEN des Rassisten, PL die Rassisten)
die Rassistin *fem*

rack NOUN
der Gepäckträger *masc* (PL die Gepäckträger) (*for luggage*)

racket NOUN
1 der Schläger *masc* (PL die Schläger) (*for sport*)
□ **my tennis racket** mein Tennisschläger
2 der Krach *masc* (*noise*)
□ **a terrible racket** ein furchtbarer Krach

racquet NOUN
der Schläger *masc* (PL die Schläger)

radar NOUN
das Radar *neut*

radiation NOUN
die Strahlung *fem*

radiator NOUN
der Heizkörper *masc* (PL die Heizkörper)

★ **radio** NOUN
das Radio *neut* (PL die Radios)
■ **on the radio** im Radio
■ **a radio station** ein Rundfunksender *masc*

radioactive ADJECTIVE
radioaktiv

radio-controlled ADJECTIVE
ferngesteuert (*model plane, car*)

radish NOUN
1 das Radieschen *neut* (PL die Radieschen) (*small red*)
2 der Rettich *masc* (PL die Rettiche) (*long white*)

RAF NOUN (= Royal Air Force)
die britische Luftwaffe *fem*
□ **He's in the RAF.** Er ist bei der britischen Luftwaffe.

raffle NOUN
die Tombola *fem* (PL die Tombolas)
□ **a raffle ticket** ein Los *neut* (*für die Tombola*)

raft NOUN
das Floß *neut* (GEN des Floßes, PL die Flöße)

rag – rank

rag NOUN
der Lumpen *masc* (PL die Lumpen)
□ dressed in rags in Lumpen gekleidet
■ **a piece of rag** ein Lappen *masc*

★ **rage** NOUN
die Wut *fem*
□ mad with rage wild vor Wut
■ **to be in a rage** wütend sein [65] □ She was in a rage. Sie war wütend.

raid NOUN
▷ *see also* **raid** VERB
1 der Überfall *masc* (PL die Überfälle) (*burglary*)
□ There was a bank raid near my house. Es gab einen Banküberfall in der Nähe meines Hauses.
2 die Razzia *fem* (PL die Razzien)
□ a police raid eine Polizeirazzia

to **raid** VERB
▷ *see also* **raid** NOUN
eine Razzia machen [48] in +*dat* (*police*)
□ The police raided the club. Die Polizei machte eine Razzia in dem Klub.

★ **rail** NOUN
1 das Geländer *neut* (PL die Geländer) (*on stairs, bridge, balcony*)
2 die Schiene *fem* (*on railway line*)
■ **by rail** mit dem Zug

railcard NOUN
die Bahncard® *fem* (PL die Bahncards)

railroad NOUN (US)
die Eisenbahn *fem*
■ **a railroad station** ein Bahnhof *masc*

★ **railway** NOUN
die Eisenbahn *fem*
■ **a railway line** eine Eisenbahnlinie
■ **a railway station** ein Bahnhof *masc*

★ **rain** NOUN
▷ *see also* **rain** VERB
der Regen *masc*
□ in the rain im Regen

★ to **rain** VERB
▷ *see also* **rain** NOUN
regnen [53]
□ It rains a lot here. Hier regnet es viel.
■ **It's raining.** Es regnet.

rainbow NOUN
der Regenbogen *masc* (PL die Regenbogen)

raincoat NOUN
der Regenmantel *masc* (PL die Regenmäntel)

rainfall NOUN
der Niederschlag *masc* (PL die Niederschläge)

rainforest NOUN
der Regenwald *masc* (PL die Regenwälder)

★ **rainy** ADJECTIVE
regnerisch

★ to **raise** VERB
1 hochheben (IMPERFECT hob hoch, PERFECT TENSE hat hochgehoben) (*lift*)
□ He raised his hand. Er hob die Hand hoch.

2 heben (IMPERFECT hob, PERFECT TENSE hat gehoben) (*improve*)
□ They want to raise standards in schools. Sie wollen das Niveau in den Schulen heben.
■ **to raise money** Spenden sammeln [34]
□ We're raising money for a new gym. Wir sammeln Spenden für eine neue Turnhalle.

raisin NOUN
die Rosine *fem*

rake NOUN
der Rechen *masc* (PL die Rechen)

rally NOUN
1 die Kundgebung *fem* (*of people*)
2 die Rallye *fem* (PL die Rallyes) (*sport*)
□ a rally driver ein Rallyefahrer *masc*
3 der Ballwechsel *masc* (PL die Ballwechsel) (*in tennis*)

Ramadan NOUN
der Ramadan *masc*

ramble NOUN
die Wanderung *fem*
□ to go for a ramble eine Wanderung machen

rambler NOUN
der Wanderer *masc* (PL die Wanderer)
die Wanderin *fem*

ramp NOUN
die Rampe *fem* (*for wheelchairs*)

ran VERB ▷ *see* **run**

ranch NOUN
die Ranch *fem* (PL die Ranches)

random ADJECTIVE
■ **a random selection** eine Zufallsauswahl
■ **at random** aufs Geratewohl □ We picked the number at random. Wir haben die Nummer aufs Geratewohl ausgewählt.

rang VERB ▷ *see* **ring**

★ **range** NOUN
▷ *see also* **range** VERB
die Auswahl *fem*
□ a wide range of colours eine große Auswahl an Farben
■ **a range of subjects** verschiedene Themen
□ We study a range of subjects. Wir studieren verschiedene Themen.
■ **a mountain range** eine Bergkette

★ to **range** VERB
▷ *see also* **range** NOUN
■ **to range from ... to** gehen [29] von ... bis
□ Temperatures in summer range from twenty to thirty-five degrees. Die Temperaturen im Sommer gehen von zwanzig bis fünfunddreißig Grad.
■ **Tickets range from two to twenty pounds.** Karten kosten von zwei bis zwanzig Pfund.

rank NOUN
▷ *see also* **rank** VERB
■ **a taxi rank** ein Taxistand *masc*

★ = core vocabulary

to rank VERB
▷ see also **rank** NOUN
rangieren [76] (PERFECT TENSE hat rangiert)
□ He's ranked third in the United States. Er
rangiert in den Vereinigten Staaten an dritter
Stelle.

ransom NOUN
das Lösegeld neut (PL die Lösegelder)

rap NOUN
der Rap masc (music)

rape NOUN
▷ see also **rape** VERB
die Vergewaltigung fem

to rape VERB
▷ see also **rape** NOUN
vergewaltigen [7] (PERFECT TENSE hat
vergewaltigt)

rapids PL NOUN
die Stromschnellen fem pl

rare ADJECTIVE
1 selten (unusual)
□ a rare plant eine seltene Pflanze
2 blutig (steak)

rash NOUN
der Ausschlag masc (PL die Ausschläge)
□ I've got a rash. Ich habe einen Ausschlag.

rasher NOUN
■ an egg and two rashers of bacon ein Ei
und zwei Streifen Speck

raspberry NOUN
die Himbeere fem
□ raspberry jam die Himbeermarmelade

rat NOUN
die Ratte fem

rate NOUN
▷ see also **rate** VERB
1 der Preis masc (GEN des Preises, PL die Preise)
(price)
□ There are reduced rates for students.
Studenten bekommen ermäßigte Preise.
2 die Rate fem (level)
□ the divorce rate die Scheidungsrate
■ a high rate of interest ein hoher Zinssatz

to rate VERB
▷ see also **rate** NOUN
einschätzen [4] (PERFECT TENSE hat eingeschätzt)
□ He was rated the best. Man schätzte ihn als
den Besten ein.

rather ADVERB
ziemlich
□ I was rather disappointed. Ich war ziemlich
enttäuscht. □ Twenty pounds! That's rather a
lot! Zwanzig Pfund! Das ist aber ziemlich viel!
■ rather a lot of ziemlich viel □ rather a lot of
work ziemlich viel Arbeit
■ rather than statt □ We decided to camp,
rather than stay at a hotel. Wir haben

beschlossen zu zelten statt im Hotel zu
übernachten.
■ I'd rather ... Ich würde lieber ... □ I'd rather
stay in tonight. Ich würde heute Abend lieber zu
Hause bleiben. □ Would you like a sweet? — I'd
rather have an apple. Möchtest du ein Bonbon?
— Ich hätte lieber einen Apfel.

rattle NOUN
die Rassel fem (for baby)

rattlesnake NOUN
die Klapperschlange fem

to rave VERB
schwärmen [38]
□ They raved about the film. Sie schwärmten
von dem Film.

raven NOUN
der Rabe masc (GEN des Raben, PL die Raben)

ravenous ADJECTIVE
■ to be ravenous einen Riesenhunger haben
[32] □ I'm ravenous! Ich habe einen
Riesenhunger!

raving ADVERB
■ raving mad total verrückt (informal)

★ **raw** ADJECTIVE
roh (food)
■ raw materials die Rohstoffe masc pl

razor NOUN
der Rasierapparat masc (PL die Rasierapparate)
■ a razor blade eine Rasierklinge

RE NOUN (= religious education)
der Religionsunterricht masc

★ **reach** NOUN
▷ see also **reach** VERB
■ out of reach außer Reichweite □ The light
switch was out of reach. Der Lichtschalter war
außer Reichweite.
■ within easy reach of leicht zu erreichen
□ The campsite is within easy reach of the town
centre. Der Zeltplatz ist vom Stadtzentrum
leicht zu erreichen.

★ **to reach** VERB
▷ see also **reach** NOUN
1 ankommen [40] in +dat (IMPERFECT kam an,
PERFECT TENSE ist angekommen)
□ We reached the hotel at ten o'clock. Wir sind
um zehn Uhr im Hotel angekommen.
■ We hope to reach the final. Wir wollen ins
Endspiel kommen.
2 treffen [78] (PRESENT TENSE trifft, IMPERFECT traf,
PERFECT TENSE hat getroffen) (decision)
□ Eventually they reached a decision. Sie haben
schließlich eine Entscheidung getroffen.
■ He reached for his phone. Er griff nach
seinem Handy.

★ **to react** VERB
reagieren [76] (PERFECT TENSE hat reagiert)

★ **reaction** NOUN
die Reaktion fem

r

Numbers in brackets refer to verb tables on pages 697 to 706.

577

reactor NOUN
der Reaktor *masc* (PL die Reaktoren)
□ a nuclear reactor ein Kernreaktor

★ to **read** VERB
lesen [45] (PRESENT TENSE liest, IMPERFECT las, PERFECT TENSE hat gelesen)
□ I don't read much. Ich lese nicht viel. □ Have you read it? Hast du es gelesen? □ Read the text out loud. Lies den Text laut.

★ **reader** NOUN
der Leser *masc* (PL die Leser)
die Leserin *fem* (person)

readily ADVERB
bereitwillig
□ She readily agreed. Sie stimmte bereitwillig zu.

★ **reading** NOUN
das Lesen *neut*
□ Reading is one of my hobbies. Lesen ist eines meiner Hobbies.

★ **ready** ADJECTIVE
fertig
□ She's nearly ready. Sie ist fast fertig.
■ **He's always ready to help.** Er ist immer bereit zu helfen.
■ **a ready meal** ein Fertiggericht *neut*
■ **to get ready** sich fertig machen [48] □ She's getting ready to go out. Sie macht sich zum Ausgehen fertig.
■ **to get something ready** etwas machen [48]

★ **real** ADJECTIVE
1 echt (not fake)
□ He wasn't a real police officer. Er war kein echter Polizist. □ It's real leather. Es ist echtes Leder.
2 wirklich
□ Her real name is Cordelia. Ihr wirklicher Name ist Cordelia. □ in real life im wirklichen Leben
■ **It was a real nightmare.** Es war wirklich ein Albtraum.

realistic ADJECTIVE
realistisch

★ **reality** NOUN
die Wirklichkeit *fem*

reality TV NOUN
das Reality-TV *neut*

★ to **realize** VERB
■ **to realize that ...** bemerken [7], dass ...
□ We realized that something was wrong. Wir bemerkten, dass irgendetwas nicht stimmte.

★ **really** ADVERB
wirklich
□ She's really nice. Sie ist wirklich nett. □ I'm learning Italian. — Really? Ich lerne Italienisch. — Wirklich? □ Do you really think so? Meinst du wirklich?
■ **Do you want to go? — Not really.** Willst du gehen? — Eigentlich nicht.

realtor NOUN (US)
der Immobilienhändler *masc* (PL die Immobilienhändler)
die Immobilienhändlerin *fem*

rear ADJECTIVE
▷ see also **rear** NOUN
hintere
□ the rear windows die hinteren Fenster
■ **the rear wheel** das Hinterrad

rear NOUN
▷ see also **rear** ADJECTIVE
das hintere Ende *neut* (PL die hinteren Enden)
□ at the rear of the train am hinteren Ende des Zuges

★ **reason** NOUN
der Grund *masc* (PL die Gründe)
□ There's no reason to think that ... Es gibt keinen Grund zu meinen, dass ...
■ **for security reasons** aus Sicherheitsgründe
■ **That was the main reason I went.** Das wa der Hauptgrund, warum ich gegangen bin.

★ **reasonable** ADJECTIVE
1 vernünftig (sensible)
□ Felix is a very sensible boy. Felix ist ein sehr vernünftiger Junge. □ That wasn't a sensible idea. Das war keine vernünftige Idee.
2 ganz ordentlich (not bad)
□ She wrote a reasonable essay. Sie hat einen ganz ordentlichen Aufsatz geschrieben.

reasonably ADVERB
ziemlich
□ reasonably well ziemlich gut
■ **reasonably priced trainers** preiswerte Turnschuhe

to **reassure** VERB
beruhigen [18] (PERFECT TENSE hat beruhigt)

reassuring ADJECTIVE
beruhigend

rebel NOUN
▷ see also **rebel** VERB
der Rebell *masc* (PL die Rebellen)
die Rebellin *fem*

to **rebel** VERB
▷ see also **rebel** NOUN
rebellieren [76] (PERFECT TENSE hat rebelliert)

rebellious ADJECTIVE
aufmüpfig

★ **receipt** NOUN
die Quittung *fem*

★ to **receive** VERB
erhalten [33] (PRESENT TENSE erhält, IMPERFECT erhielt, PERFECT TENSE hat erhalten)

receiver NOUN
der Hörer *masc* (PL die Hörer) (of phone)
□ to pick up the receiver den Hörer abnehmen

★ **recent** ADJECTIVE
neueste

□ the recent developments in ... die neuesten Entwicklungen in ...
■ **in recent years** in den letzten Jahren

★ **recently** ADVERB
in letzter Zeit
□ I've been doing a lot of training recently. Ich habe in letzter Zeit viel trainiert.

reception NOUN
1 die Rezeption fem (in hotel)
□ Please leave your key at reception. Bitte geben Sie Ihren Schlüssel an der Rezeption ab.
2 der Empfang masc (PL die Empfänge) (party)
□ The reception will be at a hotel. Der Empfang findet in einem Hotel statt.

receptionist NOUN
der Empfangschef masc (PL die Empfangschefs)
die Empfangsdame fem

★ **recession** NOUN
die Rezession fem

★ **recipe** NOUN
das Rezept neut (PL die Rezepte)

★ to **reckon** VERB
meinen [38]
□ What do you reckon? Was meinst du?

reclining ADJECTIVE
■ **a reclining seat** ein Liegesitz masc

recognizable ADJECTIVE
wiederzuerkennen
□ He was scarcely recognizable after the accident. Er war nach dem Unfall kaum wiederzuerkennen.

★ to **recognize** VERB
erkennen [39] (IMPERFECT erkannte, PERFECT TENSE hat erkannt)
□ You'll recognize me by my red hair. Du wirst mich an meinen roten Haaren erkennen.

★ to **recommend** VERB
empfehlen [17] (PRESENT TENSE empfiehlt, IMPERFECT empfahl, PERFECT TENSE hat empfohlen)
□ What do you recommend? Was können Sie empfehlen?

to **reconsider** VERB
■ **to reconsider something** sich etwas noch einmal überlegen [82] □ I think you should reconsider your decision. Ich denke, du solltest dir die Entscheidung noch einmal überlegen.

★ **record** NOUN
▷ see also **record** VERB
1 der Rekord masc (PL die Rekorde) (sport)
□ the world record der Weltrekord
2 die Schallplatte fem (recording)
□ my favourite record meine Lieblingsschallplatte
■ **in record time** in Rekordzeit □ She finished the job in record time. Sie war in Rekordzeit mit der Arbeit fertig.
■ **He's got a criminal record.** Er ist vorbestraft.

■ **records** (of police, hospital) die Akten □ I'll check in the records. Ich sehe in den Akten nach.
■ **There is no record of your booking.** Ihre Buchung ist nirgends belegt.

★ to **record** VERB
▷ see also **record** NOUN
aufnehmen [52] (PRESENT TENSE nimmt auf, IMPERFECT nahm auf, PERFECT TENSE hat aufgenommen) (on film, tape)
□ They've just recorded their new album. Sie haben eben ihr neues Album aufgenommen.

recorded delivery NOUN
■ **to send something recorded delivery** etwas per Einschreiben senden

recorder NOUN
die Blockflöte fem (instrument)
□ She plays the recorder. Sie spielt Blockflöte.

★ **recording** NOUN
die Aufnahme fem

record player NOUN
der Plattenspieler masc (PL die Plattenspieler)

★ to **recover** VERB
sich erholen [19] (PERFECT TENSE hat sich erholt)
□ He's recovering from a knee injury. Er erholt sich von einer Knieverletzung.

★ **recovery** NOUN
die Erholung fem
■ **Best wishes for a speedy recovery!** Gute Besserung!

rectangle NOUN
das Rechteck neut (PL die Rechtecke)

rectangular ADJECTIVE
rechteckig

to **recycle** VERB
wiederverwerten [7] (PERFECT TENSE hat wiederverwertet)

recycling NOUN
das Recycling neut

★ **red** ADJECTIVE
rot
□ a red rose eine rote Rose □ red meat rotes Fleisch □ Robbie's got red hair. Robbie hat rote Haare.
■ **to go through a red light** bei Rot über die Ampel fahren [21]

Red Cross NOUN
das Rote Kreuz neut

redcurrant NOUN
die Rote Johannisbeere fem

to **redecorate** VERB
renovieren [76] (PERFECT TENSE hat renoviert)

red-haired ADJECTIVE
rothaarig

red-handed ADJECTIVE
■ **to catch somebody red-handed** jemanden auf frischer Tat ertappen [19] □ He was caught red-handed. Er wurde auf frischer Tat ertappt.

r

redhead NOUN

der Rothaarige *masc* (GEN des Rothaarigen, PL die Rothaarigen)

die Rothaarige *fem* (GEN der Rothaarigen)

□ a redhead (man) ein Rothaariger

to **redo** VERB

noch einmal machen [48]

★ to **reduce** VERB

ermäßigen [7] (PERFECT TENSE hat ermäßigt)

□ at a reduced price zu ermäßigtem Preis

★ **reduction** NOUN

der Nachlass *masc* (GEN des Nachlasses, PL die Nachlässe)

□ a five per cent reduction ein Nachlass von fünf Prozent

redundancy NOUN

die Entlassung *fem*

□ There were fifty redundancies. Es gab fünfzig Entlassungen.

■ his redundancy payment seine Abfindung

redundant ADJECTIVE

■ to be made redundant entlassen werden [91] □ He was made redundant yesterday. Er wurde gestern entlassen.

reed NOUN

das Schilf *neut* (plant)

reel NOUN

die Spule *fem* (of thread)

★ to **refer** VERB

■ to refer to anspielen [4] auf +acc □ What are you referring to? Auf was spielst du an?

referee NOUN

der Schiedsrichter *masc* (PL die Schiedsrichter)

die Schiedsrichterin *fem*

★ **reference** NOUN

das Arbeitszeugnis *neut* (GEN des Arbeitszeugnisses, PL die Arbeitszeugnisse) (for job application)

□ Would you please give me a reference? Können Sie mir bitte ein Arbeitszeugnis geben?

■ a reference book ein Nachschlagewerk *neut*

to **refill** VERB

nachfüllen [4] (PERFECT TENSE hat nachgefüllt)

□ He refilled my glass. Er füllte mein Glas nach.

refinery NOUN

die Raffinerie *fem*

to **reflect** VERB

reflektieren [76] (PERFECT TENSE hat reflektiert) (light, image)

reflection NOUN

das Spiegelbild *neut* (PL die Spiegelbilder) (in mirror)

reflex NOUN

der Reflex *masc* (GEN des Reflexes, PL die Reflexe)

reflexive ADJECTIVE

reflexiv

□ a reflexive verb ein reflexives Verb

refresher course NOUN

der Wiederholungskurs *masc* (GEN des Wiederholungskurses, PL die Wiederholungskurse)

refreshing ADJECTIVE

erfrischend

refreshments PL NOUN

die Erfrischungen *fem pl*

refrigerator NOUN

der Kühlschrank *masc* (PL die Kühlschränke)

to **refuel** VERB

auftanken [4] (PERFECT TENSE hat aufgetankt)

□ Our plane refuelled in Boston. Unser Flugzeug hat in Boston aufgetankt.

refuge NOUN

die Zuflucht *fem*

★ **refugee** NOUN

der Flüchtling *masc* (PL die Flüchtlinge)

der Flüchtling is also used for women.

refund NOUN

▷ see also **refund** VERB

die Rückvergütung *fem*

to **refund** VERB

▷ see also **refund** NOUN

zurückerstatten [2] (PERFECT TENSE hat zurückerstattet)

refusal NOUN

die Weigerung *fem*

★ to **refuse** VERB

▷ see also **refuse** NOUN

sich weigern [88]

★ **refuse** NOUN

▷ see also **refuse** VERB

der Müll *masc*

■ refuse collection die Müllabfuhr

to **regain** VERB

■ to regain consciousness wieder zu Bewusstsein kommen [40]

regard NOUN

▷ see also **regard** VERB

■ Give my regards to Alice. Grüße an Alice.

■ Martin sends his regards. Martin lässt grüßen.

■ 'Kind regards' 'mit freundlichen Grüßen'

to **regard** VERB

▷ see also **regard** NOUN

■ to regard something as etwas betrachten [7] als

■ as regards ... was ... betrifft □ As regards your behaviour ... Was dein Benehmen betrifft, ...

regarding PREPOSITION

betreffend

□ the laws regarding the export of animals die Gesetze den Export von Tieren betreffend

■ Regarding your sister, ... Was deine Schwester betrifft, ...

★ = core vocabulary

regardless ADVERB
trotzdem
□ to carry on regardless trotzdem
weitermachen

regiment NOUN
das Regiment neut (PL die Regimenter)

★ **region** NOUN
die Gegend fem

regional ADJECTIVE
regional

★ **register** NOUN
▷ see also **register** VERB
das Klassenbuch neut (PL die Klassenbücher) (in school)

★ to **register** VERB
▷ see also **register** NOUN
sich einschreiben [61] (IMPERFECT schrieb sich ein, PERFECT TENSE hat sich eingeschrieben) (at school, college)

registered ADJECTIVE
■ a registered letter ein eingeschriebener Brief

registration NOUN
1 der Namensaufruf masc (PL die Namensaufrufe) (in school)
2 das polizeiliche Kennzeichen neut (PL die polizeilichen Kennzeichen) (of car)

★ **regret** NOUN
▷ see also **regret** VERB
das Bedauern neut
□ I've got no regrets. Ich bedaure nichts.

★ to **regret** VERB
▷ see also **regret** NOUN
bedauern [88] (PERFECT TENSE hat bedauert)
□ You'll regret it! Du wirst es bedauern!
■ to regret doing something es bedauern [88], etwas getan zu haben □ I regretted saying that. Ich habe bedauert, dass ich das gesagt habe.

★ **regular** ADJECTIVE
1 regelmäßig
□ at regular intervals in regelmäßigen Abständen □ a regular verb ein regelmäßiges Verb
■ to take regular exercise regelmäßig Sport machen [48]
2 normal (average)
□ a regular portion of fries eine normale Portion Pommes frites

regularly ADVERB
regelmäßig

regulation NOUN
die Bestimmung fem

rehearsal NOUN
die Probe fem

to **rehearse** VERB
proben [38]

rein NOUN
der Zügel masc (PL die Zügel)
□ the reins die Zügel

★ **reindeer** NOUN
das Rentier neut (PL die Rentiere)

to **reject** VERB
verwerfen [92] (PRESENT TENSE verwirft, IMPERFECT verwarf, PERFECT TENSE hat verworfen) (idea, suggestion)
□ We rejected the idea. Wir haben die Idee verworfen.
■ I applied but they rejected me. Ich habe mich beworben, wurde aber abgelehnt.

relapse NOUN
der Rückfall masc (PL die Rückfälle)
□ to have a relapse einen Rückfall haben

★ **related** ADJECTIVE
verwandt (people)
□ Are you related to her? Bist du mit ihr verwandt? □ We're related. Wir sind miteinander verwandt.
■ The two events were not related. Es bestand kein Zusammenhang zwischen den beiden Ereignissen.

★ **relation** NOUN
1 der Verwandte masc (GEN des Verwandten, PL die Verwandten)
die Verwandte fem (GEN der Verwandten) (person)
□ He's a distant relation. Er ist ein entfernter Verwandter. □ I've got relations in Spain. Ich habe Verwandte in Spanien. □ my close relations meine engsten Verwandten
2 der Bezug masc (PL die Bezüge) (connection)
□ It has no relation to reality. Es hat keinen Bezug zur Wirklichkeit.
■ in relation to verglichen mit

★ **relationship** NOUN
die Beziehung fem
□ We have a good relationship. Wir haben eine gute Beziehung. □ I'm not in a relationship at the moment. Ich habe im Moment keine Beziehung.

★ **relative** NOUN
der Verwandte masc (GEN des Verwandten, PL die Verwandten)
die Verwandte fem (GEN der Verwandten)
□ a relative (man) ein Verwandter □ my close relatives meine engsten Verwandten
■ all her relatives ihre ganze Verwandtschaft

★ **relatively** ADVERB
relativ

★ to **relax** VERB
sich entspannen [18] (PERFECT TENSE hat sich entspannt)
□ I relax by listening to music. Ich entspanne mich mit Musikhören.

r

Numbers in brackets refer to verb tables on pages 697 to 706.

581

relaxation - remember

■ **Relax! Everything's fine.** Immer mit der Ruhe! Alles ist in Ordnung.

relaxation NOUN

die Entspannung *fem*

□ I don't have much time for relaxation. Ich habe nicht viel Zeit für Entspannung.

relaxed ADJECTIVE

entspannt

relaxing ADJECTIVE

entspannend

□ I find cooking relaxing. Ich finde Kochen entspannend.

relay NOUN

■ **a relay race** ein Staffellauf *masc*

★ to **release** VERB

▷ *see also* **release** NOUN

1 freilassen [42] (PRESENT TENSE lässt frei, IMPERFECT ließ frei, PERFECT TENSE hat freigelassen) (*prisoner*)

2 veröffentlichen [84] (PERFECT TENSE hat veröffentlicht) (*report, news*)

3 herausbringen [13] (IMPERFECT brachte heraus, PERFECT TENSE hat herausgebracht) (*film, album*)

★ **release** NOUN

▷ *see also* **release** VERB

die Freilassung *fem* (*from prison*)

□ the release of the hostages die Freilassung der Geisel

■ **the band's latest release** die neueste Platte der Band

relegated ADJECTIVE

abgestiegen (*sport*)

□ the relegated team die abgestiegene Mannschaft

relevant ADJECTIVE

entsprechend (*documents*)

■ **That's not relevant.** Das ist nicht relevant.

■ **to be relevant to something** einen Bezug zu etwas haben [32] □ Education should be relevant to real life. Die Ausbildung sollte einen Bezug zum wirklichen Leben haben.

★ **reliable** ADJECTIVE

zuverlässig

□ a reliable car ein zuverlässiges Auto □ He's not very reliable. Er ist nicht sehr zuverlässig.

★ **relief** NOUN

die Erleichterung *fem*

□ That's a relief! Das ist eine Erleichterung!

to **relieve** VERB

lindern [34]

□ This injection will relieve the pain. Diese Spritze wird den Schmerz lindern.

relieved ADJECTIVE

erleichtert

□ I was relieved to hear ... Ich war erleichtert zu hören ...

★ **religion** NOUN

die Religion *fem*

□ What religion are you? Welche Religion hast du?

★ **religious** ADJECTIVE

religiös

□ I'm not religious. Ich bin nicht religiös.

■ **my religious beliefs** mein Glaube *masc*

★ **reluctant** ADJECTIVE

■ **to be reluctant to do something** etwas nur ungern tun [81] □ They were reluctant to help us. Sie haben uns nur ungern geholfen.

reluctantly ADVERB

ungern

□ She reluctantly accepted. Sie hat ungern angenommen.

to **rely on** VERB

sich verlassen [42] auf +*acc* (PRESENT TENSE verlässt sich, IMPERFECT verließ sich, PERFECT TENSE hat sich verlassen)

□ I'm relying on you. Ich verlasse mich auf dich.

★ to **remain** VERB

bleiben [10] (IMPERFECT blieb, PERFECT TENSE ist geblieben)

■ **to remain silent** schweigen

★ **remaining** ADJECTIVE

restlich

□ the remaining ingredients die restlichen Zutaten

remains PL NOUN

die Reste *masc pl*

□ the remains of the picnic die Reste des Picknicks

■ **human remains** die menschlichen Überreste

■ **Roman remains** römische Ruinen

remake NOUN

das Remake *neut* (PL die Remakes) (*of film*)

★ **remark** NOUN

die Bemerkung *fem*

★ **remarkable** ADJECTIVE

bemerkenswert

remarkably ADVERB

bemerkenswert

to **remarry** VERB

wieder heiraten [2]

□ She remarried three years ago. Sie hat vor drei Jahren wieder geheiratet.

remedy NOUN

das Mittel *neut* (PL die Mittel)

□ a good remedy for a sore throat ein gutes Mittel gegen Halsschmerzen

★ to **remember** VERB

sich erinnern [88] (PERFECT TENSE hat sich erinnert)

□ I can't remember his name. Ich kann mich nicht an seinen Namen erinnern. □ I don't remember. Ich erinnere mich nicht.

★ = core vocabulary

In German you often say 'don't forget' rather than 'remember' when reminding somebody about something.

□ Remember your passport! Vergiss deinen Pass nicht! □ Remember to write your name on the form. Vergiss nicht, deinen Namen auf das Formular zu schreiben.

Remembrance Day NOUN
der Volkstrauertag *masc*
□ on Remembrance Day am Volkstrauertag

★ to **remind** VERB
erinnern [88] (PERFECT TENSE hat erinnert)
□ It reminds me of Scotland. Es erinnert mich an Schottland. □ I'll remind you tomorrow. Ich werde dich morgen daran erinnern. □ Remind me to speak to Zain. Erinnere mich, dass ich mit Zain sprechen will.

remorse NOUN
die Reue *fem*
□ He showed no remorse. Er zeigte keine Reue.

★ **remote** ADJECTIVE
abgelegen
□ a remote village ein abgelegenes Dorf

remote control NOUN
die Fernbedienung *fem*

remotely ADVERB
entfernt
□ There was nobody remotely resembling this description. Niemand sah dieser Beschreibung auch nur entfernt ähnlich.
■ **It's remotely possible that ...** Es ist gerade eben noch möglich, dass ...

removable ADJECTIVE
abnehmbar

removal NOUN
der Umzug *masc* (PL die Umzüge) *(from house)*
■ **a removal van** ein Möbelwagen *masc*

★ to **remove** VERB
entfernen [18] (PERFECT TENSE hat entfernt)
□ Did you remove the stain? Hast du den Fleck entfernt?

rendezvous NOUN
das Treffen *neut* (PL die Treffen)

★ to **renew** VERB
verlängern lassen [42] (PRESENT TENSE lässt verlängern, IMPERFECT ließ verlängern, PERFECT TENSE hat verlängern lassen) *(passport, licence)*
□ You'll need to renew your passport. Du musst deinen Pass verlängern lassen.
■ **to renew a contract** einen Vertrag verlängern [88]

renewable ADJECTIVE
erneuerbar *(energy, resource, passport)*

to **renovate** VERB
renovieren [76] (PERFECT TENSE hat renoviert)
□ The leisure centre has been renovated. Das Freizeitzentrum ist renoviert worden.

Remembrance Day - repetitive

renowned ADJECTIVE
berühmt

★ **rent** NOUN
▷ see also **rent** VERB
die Miete *fem*

BE CAREFUL!
Do not translate **rent** by **Rente**.

★ to **rent** VERB
▷ see also **rent** NOUN
mieten [2]
□ We rented a car. Wir haben ein Auto gemietet.

rental NOUN
die Miete *fem*
□ Car rental is included in the price. Die Automiete ist im Preis inbegriffen.

rental car NOUN (US)
der Mietwagen *masc* (PL die Mietwagen)

to **reoffend** VERB
erneut straffällig werden [91]

to **reorganize** VERB
umorganisieren [4] (PERFECT TENSE hat umorganisiert)

rep NOUN (= representative)
der Vertreter *masc* (PL die Vertreter)
die Vertreterin *fem*

repaid VERB ▷ see **repay**

★ to **repair** VERB
▷ see also **repair** NOUN
reparieren [76] (PERFECT TENSE hat repariert)
■ **to get something repaired** etwas reparieren lassen [42] □ I got the washing machine repaired. Ich habe die Waschmaschine reparieren lassen.

★ **repair** NOUN
▷ see also **repair** VERB
die Reparatur *fem*

to **repay** VERB
zurückzahlen [15] (PERFECT TENSE hat zurückgezahlt) *(money)*

repayment NOUN
die Rückzahlung *fem*

★ to **repeat** VERB
▷ see also **repeat** NOUN
wiederholen [4] (PERFECT TENSE hat wiederholt)

★ **repeat** NOUN
▷ see also **repeat** VERB
die Wiederholung *fem*
□ There are too many repeats on TV. Es gibt zu viele Wiederholungen im Fernsehen.

repeatedly ADVERB
wiederholt

repellent NOUN
■ **insect repellent** das Insektenschutzmittel

repetitive ADJECTIVE
monoton *(movement, work)*

r

★ to **replace** VERB
ersetzen [36] (PERFECT TENSE hat ersetzt)

replay NOUN
▷ see also **replay** VERB
■ **There will be a replay on Friday.** Das Spiel wird am Freitag wiederholt.

to **replay** VERB
▷ see also **replay** NOUN
wiederholen [4] (PERFECT TENSE hat wiederholt) (match)

replica NOUN
die Kopie fem

★ **reply** NOUN
▷ see also **reply** VERB
die Antwort fem

★ to **reply** VERB
▷ see also **reply** NOUN
antworten [2]

★ **report** NOUN
▷ see also **report** VERB
1 der Bericht masc (PL die Berichte) (of event)
□ a report in the paper ein Zeitungsbericht
2 das Zeugnis neut (GEN des Zeugnisses, PL die Zeugnisse) (at school)
□ I got a good report. Ich habe ein gutes Zeugnis bekommen.
■ **report card** das Zeugnis

★ to **report** VERB
▷ see also **report** NOUN
1 melden [54]
□ I've reported the theft. Ich habe den Diebstahl gemeldet.
2 sich melden [54]
□ Report to the caretaker when you arrive. Melden Sie sich bei Ihrer Ankunft beim Hausmeister.

★ **reporter** NOUN
der Reporter masc (PL die Reporter)
die Reporterin fem
□ She'd like to be a reporter. Sie möchte gern Reporterin werden.

★ to **represent** VERB
vertreten [79] (PRESENT TENSE vertritt, IMPERFECT vertrat, PERFECT TENSE hat vertreten) (person)
□ My lawyer represented me in court. Mein Anwalt hat mich vor Gericht vertreten.

★ **representative** ADJECTIVE
repräsentativ

reproduction NOUN
die Reproduktion fem

reptile NOUN
das Reptil neut (PL die Reptilien)

★ **republic** NOUN
die Republik fem

repulsive ADJECTIVE
abstoßend

reputable ADJECTIVE
angesehen

★ **reputation** NOUN
der Ruf masc

★ **request** NOUN
▷ see also **request** VERB
die Bitte fem

★ to **request** VERB
▷ see also **request** NOUN
bitten [9] um (IMPERFECT bat, PERFECT TENSE hat gebeten)
□ He requested information. Er bat um Informationen.

★ to **require** VERB
erfordern [19] (PERFECT TENSE hat erfordert)
□ Her job requires a lot of patience. Ihre Arbeit erfordert viel Geduld.

★ **requirement** NOUN
die Voraussetzung fem
□ What are the requirements for the job? Was sind die Voraussetzungen für diese Arbeit?
■ **entry requirements** (for university) die Aufnahmebedingungen

resat VERB ▷ see **resit**

★ to **rescue** VERB
▷ see also **rescue** NOUN
retten [2]

★ **rescue** NOUN
▷ see also **rescue** VERB
die Rettung fem
□ a rescue operation eine Rettungsaktion
■ **a mountain rescue team** ein Team der Bergwacht
■ **the rescue services** der Rettungsdienst sing
■ **to come to somebody's rescue** jemandem zu Hilfe kommen [40] □ He came to my rescue Er kam mir zu Hilfe.

★ **research** NOUN
die Forschung fem (experimental)
□ He's doing research. Er ist in der Forschung tätig.
■ **Research has shown that ...** Forschungen haben ergeben, dass ...
■ **She's doing some research in the library.** Sie sammelt in der Bibliothek Material.

resemblance NOUN
die Ähnlichkeit fem

to **resent** VERB
übel nehmen [52] (PRESENT TENSE nimmt übel, IMPERFECT nahm übel, PERFECT TENSE hat übel genommen)
□ I really resent your criticism. Ich nehme Ihnen Ihre Kritik wirklich übel.
■ **I resent being dependent on her.** Ich ärgere mich darüber, von ihr abhängig zu sein.

resentful ADJECTIVE
verärgert
□ He was resentful about the way they were treated. Er war verärgert darüber, wie sie behandelt wurden.

★ = core vocabulary

reservation NOUN

1 die Reservierung *fem* (*at restaurant*)
■ **I'd like to make a reservation for this evening.** Ich möchte für heute Abend einen Tisch reservieren.

2 die Buchung *fem* (*for journey, at hotel*)
■ **I've got a reservation for two nights.** Ich habe für zwei Nächte gebucht.

★ **reserve** NOUN
▷ *see also* **reserve** VERB

1 das Schutzgebiet *neut* (PL die Schutzgebiete) (*place*)
□ a nature reserve ein Naturschutzgebiet

2 der Reservespieler *masc* (PL die Reservespieler)
die Reservespielerin *fem* (*person*)
□ She was reserve in the game last Saturday. Sie war beim Spiel letzten Samstag Reservespielerin.

★ to **reserve** VERB
▷ *see also* **reserve** NOUN

reservieren [76] (PERFECT TENSE hat reserviert)
□ I'd like to reserve a table for tomorrow evening. Ich möchte für morgen Abend einen Tisch reservieren.

reserved ADJECTIVE

reserviert
□ a reserved seat ein reservierter Platz □ He's quite reserved. Er ist ziemlich reserviert.

reservoir NOUN

das Reservoir *neut* (PL die Reservoire)

★ **resident** NOUN

der Bewohner *masc* (PL die Bewohner)
die Bewohnerin *fem*

residential ADJECTIVE
■ **a residential area** ein Wohngebiet *neut*

★ to **resign** VERB

1 zurücktreten [79] (PRESENT TENSE tritt zurück, IMPERFECT trat zurück, PERFECT TENSE ist zurückgetreten)
□ The politician resigned. Die Politikerin ist zurückgetreten.

2 kündigen [38] (*employee*)
□ She resigned to take up a post abroad. Sie kündigte, um einen Posten im Ausland zu übernehmen.

resistance NOUN

der Widerstand *masc* (PL die Widerstände)

to **resit** VERB

wiederholen [4] (PERFECT TENSE hat wiederholt)
□ I'm resitting the exam in May. Ich wiederhole die Prüfung im Mai.

★ **resolution** NOUN

der Beschluss *masc* (GEN des Beschlusses, PL die Beschlüsse) (*decision*)
■ **Have you made any New Year's resolutions?** Hast du zum neuen Jahr gute Vorsätze gefasst?

★ **resort** NOUN

der Badeort *masc* (PL die Badeorte) (*at seaside*)
□ It's a resort on the Costa del Sol. Es ist ein Badeort an der Costa del Sol.
■ **a ski resort** ein Skiort
■ **as a last resort** als letzter Ausweg

★ **resources** PL NOUN

die Mittel *neut pl* (*financial*)
□ We haven't the resources to build a swimming pool. Wir haben nicht die Mittel, um ein Schwimmbad zu bauen.
■ **natural resources** Bodenschätze *masc pl*

★ **respect** NOUN
▷ *see also* **respect** VERB
der Respekt *masc*

★ to **respect** VERB
▷ *see also* **respect** NOUN
respektieren [76] (PERFECT TENSE hat respektiert)

respectable ADJECTIVE

1 anständig
□ respectable people anständige Leute *pl*

2 ordentlich (*standard, marks*)

respectively ADVERB

beziehungsweise
□ Britain and Germany were third and fourth respectively. Großbritannien und Deutschland belegten den dritten beziehungsweise vierten Platz.

★ **responsibility** NOUN

die Verantwortung *fem*

★ **responsible** ADJECTIVE

1 verantwortlich
□ to be responsible for something für etwas verantwortlich sein
■ **It's a responsible job.** Es ist ein verantwortungsvoller Posten.

2 verantwortungsbewusst (*mature*)
□ You should be more responsible. Du solltest verantwortungsbewusster sein.

★ **rest** NOUN
▷ *see also* **rest** VERB

1 die Pause *fem* (*relaxation*)
□ five minutes' rest eine fünfminütige Pause
■ **to have a rest** sich ausruhen [4] □ We stopped to have a rest. Wir haben Halt gemacht, um uns auszuruhen.

2 der Rest *masc* (PL die Reste) (*remainder*)
□ I'll do the rest. Ich mache den Rest. □ the rest of the money der Rest des Geldes
■ **the rest of them** die anderen □ The rest of them went swimming. Die anderen sind schwimmen gegangen.

★ to **rest** VERB
▷ *see also* **rest** NOUN

1 sich ausruhen [4] (PERFECT TENSE hat sich ausgeruht) (*relax*)
□ She's resting in her room. Sie ruht sich in ihrem Zimmer aus.

2 schonen [38] (*not overstrain*)

r

Numbers in brackets refer to verb tables on pages 697 to 706.

585

□ He has to rest his knee. Er muss sein Knie schonen.

3 lehnen [38] (*lean*)

□ I rested my bike against the window. Ich habe mein Fahrrad ans Fenster gelehnt.

★ **restaurant** NOUN
das Restaurant *neut* (PL die Restaurants)
□ We don't often go to restaurants. Wir gehen nicht oft ins Restaurant.

restful ADJECTIVE
ruhig

restless ADJECTIVE
unruhig

restoration NOUN
die Restauration *fem*

to **restore** VERB
restaurieren [76] (PERFECT TENSE hat restauriert) (*building, picture*)

to **restrict** VERB
beschränken [18] (PERFECT TENSE hat beschränkt)

rest room NOUN (US)
die Toilette *fem*

★ **result** NOUN
das Ergebnis *neut* (GEN des Ergebnisses, PL die Ergebnisse)
□ my exam results meine Prüfungsergebnisse
■ **What was the result? — One nil.** Wie ist das Spiel ausgegangen? — Eins zu null.

résumé NOUN
1 die Zusammenfassung *fem*
□ a résumé of her speech eine Zusammenfassung ihrer Rede
2 der Lebenslauf *masc* (PL die Lebensläufe) (US: *CV*)

★ to **retire** VERB
in Rente gehen [29] (IMPERFECT ging in Rente, PERFECT TENSE ist in Rente gegangen)
□ He retired last year. Er ist letztes Jahr in Rente gegangen.

retired ADJECTIVE
im Ruhestand
□ She's retired. Sie ist im Ruhestand. □ a retired teacher ein Lehrer im Ruhestand

★ **retirement** NOUN
der Ruhestand *masc*

to **retrace** VERB
■ **to retrace one's steps** zurückgehen [29] □ I retraced my steps. Ich bin zurückgegangen.

★ **return** NOUN
▷ *see also* **return** VERB
1 die Rückkehr *fem*
□ after our return nach unserer Rückkehr
■ **the return journey** die Rückfahrt
■ **a return match** ein Rückspiel *neut*
2 die Rückfahrkarte *fem* (*ticket*)
□ A return to Freiburg, please. Eine Rückfahrkarte nach Freiburg, bitte.

■ **in return** dafür □ ... and I help her in return ... und dafür helfe ich ihr
■ **in return for** für
■ **Many happy returns!** Herzlichen Glückwunsch zum Geburtstag!

★ to **return** VERB
▷ *see also* **return** NOUN
1 zurückkommen [40] (IMPERFECT kam zurück, PERFECT TENSE ist zurückgekommen) (*come back*)
□ I've just returned from holiday. Ich bin gerade aus den Ferien zurückgekommen.
■ **to return home** wieder nach Hause kommen [40]
2 zurückkehren [15] (PERFECT TENSE ist zurückgekehrt) (*go back*)
□ He returned to China the following year. Er ist im Jahr danach nach China zurückgekehrt.
3 zurückgeben [28] (PRESENT TENSE gibt zurück, IMPERFECT gab zurück, PERFECT TENSE hat zurückgegeben) (*give back*)
□ She borrows my things and doesn't return them. Sie leiht sich meine Sachen aus und gibt sie dann nicht zurück.

retweet NOUN
▷ *see also* **retweet** VERB
der Retweet *masc* (PL die Retweets)

to **retweet** VERB
▷ *see also* **retweet** NOUN
retweeten [2]

reunion NOUN
das Treffen *neut* (PL die Treffen)

to **reuse** VERB
wiederverwenden (PERFECT TENSE hat wiederverwendet)

to **reveal** VERB
ans Licht bringen [13] (IMPERFECT brachte ans Licht, PERFECT TENSE hat ans Licht gebracht) (*truth, facts*)
□ The survey reveals that many people are overweight. Die Untersuchung bringt ans Licht, dass viele Menschen Übergewicht haben.
■ **She refused to reveal the whereabouts of her daughter.** Sie weigerte sich, den Aufenthaltsort ihrer Tochter preiszugeben.
■ **It was revealed that ...** Es wurde bekannt gegeben, dass ...

revenge NOUN
die Rache *fem*
□ in revenge aus Rache
■ **to take revenge** sich rächen [48] □ They planned to take revenge on him. Sie haben geplant, sich an ihm zu rächen.

★ to **reverse** VERB
▷ *see also* **reverse** ADJECTIVE
rückwärtsfahren [21] (PRESENT TENSE fährt rückwärts, IMPERFECT fuhr rückwärts, PERFECT TENSE ist rückwärtsgefahren) (*car*)
□ He reversed without looking. Er fuhr rückwärts ohne zu sehen.

r

★ = core vocabulary

★ **reverse** ADJECTIVE
▷ see also **reverse** VERB
umgekehrt
□ in reverse order in umgekehrter Reihenfolge
■ **in reverse gear** im Rückwärtsgang

★ **review** NOUN
1 die Überprüfung *fem* (*of policy, salary*)
2 die Kritik *fem* (*of book, film*)
■ **to be under review** überprüft werden [91]

to **revise** VERB
den Stoff wiederholen [38]
□ I haven't started revising yet. Ich habe noch
nicht angefangen, den Stoff zu wiederholen.
■ **I've revised my opinion.** Ich habe meine
Meinung geändert.

revision NOUN
die Wiederholung des Stoffes *fem*
■ **Have you done a lot of revision?** Hast du
schon viel Stoff wiederholt?

to **revive** VERB
wiederbeleben [4] (PERFECT TENSE hat
wiederbelebt)
□ They tried to revive him. Sie versuchten, ihn
wiederzubeleben.

revolting ADJECTIVE
ekelhaft

★ **revolution** NOUN
die Revolution *fem*

★ **revolutionary** ADJECTIVE
revolutionär

revolver NOUN
der Revolver *masc* (PL die Revolver)

★ **reward** NOUN
die Belohnung *fem*

rewarding ADJECTIVE
dankbar
□ a rewarding job eine dankbare Arbeit

rheumatism NOUN
das Rheuma *neut*

Rhine NOUN
der Rhein *masc*

rhinoceros NOUN
das Nashorn *neut* (PL die Nashörner)

rhubarb NOUN
der Rhabarber *masc*
□ a rhubarb tart ein Rhabarberkuchen

★ **rhythm** NOUN
der Rhythmus *masc* (GEN des Rhythmus, PL die
Rhythmen)

rib NOUN
die Rippe *fem*

ribbon NOUN
das Band *neut* (PL die Bänder)

★ **rice** NOUN
der Reis *masc*
■ **rice pudding** der Milchreis

★ **rich** ADJECTIVE
reich
■ **the rich** die Reichen *masc pl*

★ to **rid** VERB
■ **to get rid of** loswerden [91] □ I want to get
rid of some old clothes. Ich will ein paar alte
Kleider loswerden.

★ **ride** NOUN
▷ see also **ride** VERB
■ **to go for a ride** 1 (*on horse*) reiten gehen
[29] 2 (*on bike*) mit dem Fahrrad fahren [21]
■ **We went for a bike ride.** Wir haben eine
Fahrt mit dem Fahrrad gemacht.
■ **It's a short bus ride to the town centre.**
Die Stadtmitte ist nur eine kurze Busfahrt
entfernt.

★ to **ride** VERB
▷ see also **ride** NOUN
reiten (IMPERFECT ritt, PERFECT TENSE ist geritten)
(*on horse*)
□ I'm learning to ride. Ich lerne reiten.
■ **to ride a bike** Fahrrad fahren [21] □ Can you
ride a bike? Kannst du Fahrrad fahren?

★ **rider** NOUN
1 der Reiter *masc* (PL die Reiter)
die Reiterin *fem* (*on horse*)
□ She's a good rider. Sie ist eine gute Reiterin.
2 der Fahrradfahrer *masc* (PL die Fahrradfahrer)
die Fahrradfahrerin *fem* (*on bike*)

ridiculous ADJECTIVE
lächerlich
□ Don't be ridiculous! Mach dich nicht
lächerlich!

riding NOUN
das Reiten *neut*
■ **to go riding** reiten gehen [29]
■ **a riding school** eine Reitschule

rifle NOUN
das Gewehr *neut* (PL die Gewehre)

rig NOUN
■ **an oil rig** eine Bohrinsel

★ **right** ADJECTIVE, ADVERB
▷ see also **right** NOUN

There are several ways of translating 'right'.
Scan the examples to find one that is similar
to what you want to say.

1 richtig (*correct, suitable*)
□ the right answer die richtige Antwort □ Am I
pronouncing it right? Spreche ich das richtig
aus? □ It isn't the right size. Es ist nicht die
richtige Größe. □ We're on the right train. Wir
sind im richtigen Zug. □ It's not right to behave
like that. Es ist nicht richtig, sich so zu
benehmen.
■ **Is this the right road for Hamburg?** Sind
wir hier richtig nach Hamburg?
■ **I think you did the right thing.** Ich glaube,
du hast das Richtige getan.

r

Numbers in brackets refer to verb tables on pages 697 to 706.

587

right – rip-off

■ **to be right 1** (*person*) recht haben [32]
□ You were right! Du hattest recht!
2 (*statement, opinion*) richtig sein [65] □ That's right! Das ist richtig!

2 genau (*accurate*)
□ Do you have the right time? Haben Sie die genaue Zeit?

3 rechte (*not left*)
□ **the right foot** der rechte Fuß □ **my right arm** mein rechter Arm □ **your right hand** deine rechte Hand □ **her right eye** ihr rechtes Auge

4 rechts (*turn*)
□ Turn right at the lights. Biegen Sie an der Ampel rechts ab.
■ **Look right!** Sehen Sie nach rechts!
■ **Right! Let's get started.** Okay! Fangen wir an.
■ **right away** sofort □ I'll do it right away. Ich mache es sofort.

★ **right** NOUN
▷ *see also* **right** ADJECTIVE, ADVERB
1 das Recht *neut* (PL die Rechte)
□ You've got no right to do that. Du hast kein Recht, das zu tun.
2 die rechte Seite *fem* (*not left*)
■ **on the right** rechts □ Remember to drive on the right. Vergiss nicht, rechts zu fahren.
■ **right of way** die Vorfahrt □ We had right of way. Wir hatten Vorfahrt.

right-hand ADJECTIVE
■ **the right-hand side** die rechte Seite
■ **It's on the right-hand side.** Es liegt rechts.

right-handed ADJECTIVE
rechtshändig

rightly ADVERB
richtig
□ If I remember rightly … Wenn ich mich richtig erinnere, … □ She rightly decided not to go to the party. Sie kam zu dem richtigen Schluss, dass sie nicht an die Party gehen soll.

rim NOUN
der Rand *masc* (PL die Ränder)
□ glasses with wire rims eine Brille mit Metallrand

★ **ring** NOUN
▷ *see also* **ring** VERB
1 der Ring *masc* (PL die Ringe)
□ a gold ring ein goldener Ring □ a diamond ring ein Diamantring
■ **a wedding ring** ein Ehering
2 der Kreis *masc* (GEN des Kreises, PL die Kreise) (*circle*)
□ to stand in a ring im Kreis stehen
3 das Klingeln *neut* (*of bell*)
■ **There was a ring at the door.** Es klingelte.
■ **to give somebody a ring** jemanden anrufen [56] □ I'll give you a ring this evening. Ich rufe dich heute Abend an.

★ **to ring** VERB
▷ *see also* **ring** NOUN
1 anrufen [56] (IMPERFECT rief an, PERFECT TENSE hat angerufen)
□ Your mother rang. Deine Mutter hat heute früh angerufen.
■ **to ring somebody** jemanden anrufen [56]
□ I'll ring you tomorrow morning. Ich rufe dich morgen früh an.
2 klingeln [34]
□ The phone's ringing. Das Telefon klingelt.
■ **to ring the bell** (*doorbell*) klingeln [34] □ I rang the bell three times. Ich habe dreimal geklingelt.

to ring up VERB
■ **to ring somebody up** jemanden anrufen [56]

to ring back VERB
zurückrufen [56]
□ I'll ring back later. Ich rufe später zurück.

ring binder NOUN
das Ringheft *neut* (PL die Ringhefte)

ring road NOUN
die Ringstraße *fem*

★ **ringtone** NOUN
der Klingelton *masc* (PL die Klingeltöne)

rink NOUN
1 die Eisbahn *fem* (for ice-skating)
2 die Rollschuhbahn *fem* (for roller-skating)

to rinse VERB
spülen [38]

★ **riot** NOUN
▷ *see also* **riot** VERB
die Krawalle *masc pl*

★ **to riot** VERB
▷ *see also* **riot** NOUN
randalieren [76] (PERFECT TENSE hat randaliert)

to rip VERB
zerreißen (IMPERFECT zerriss, PERFECT TENSE hat zerrissen)
□ I've ripped my jeans. Ich habe meine Jeans zerrissen. □ My skirt's ripped. Mein Rock ist zerrissen.

to rip off VERB
ausnehmen [52] (PRESENT TENSE nimmt aus, IMPERFECT nahm aus, PERFECT TENSE hat ausgenommen) (*informal*)
□ The hotel ripped us off. Das Hotel hat uns ausgenommen.

to rip up VERB
zerreißen (IMPERFECT zerriss, PERFECT TENSE hat zerrissen)

ripe ADJECTIVE
reif

rip-off NOUN
■ **It's a rip-off!** Das ist Nepp! (*informal*)

★ = core vocabulary

★ **rise** NOUN
  ▷ *see also* **rise** VERB
  1 der Anstieg *masc* (PL die Anstiege) (*in prices, temperature*)
    □ **a sudden rise in temperature** ein plötzlicher Temperaturanstieg
  2 die Gehaltserhöhung *fem* (*pay rise*)

★ **to rise** VERB
  ▷ *see also* **rise** NOUN
  1 steigen [74] (IMPERFECT stieg, PERFECT TENSE ist gestiegen) (*increase*)
    □ **Prices are rising.** Die Preise steigen.
  2 aufgehen [29] (IMPERFECT ging auf, PERFECT TENSE ist aufgegangen)
    □ **The sun rises early in June.** Die Sonne geht im Juni früh auf.

riser NOUN
  ■ **to be an early riser** ein Frühaufsteher sein [65]

★ **risk** NOUN
  ▷ *see also* **risk** VERB
  das Risiko *neut* (PL die Risiken)
  ■ **to take risks** Risiken eingehen [29] □ I don't want to take risks. Ich möchte kein Risiko eingehen.
  ■ **It's at your own risk.** Auf eigene Gefahr.

★ **to risk** VERB
  ▷ *see also* **risk** NOUN
  riskieren [76] (PERFECT TENSE hat riskiert)
  □ **You risk getting a fine.** Du riskierst einen Strafzettel. □ I wouldn't risk it. Das würde ich an deiner Stelle nicht riskieren.

risky ADJECTIVE
  gefährlich

★ **rival** NOUN
  ▷ *see also* **rival** ADJECTIVE
  der Rivale *masc* (GEN des Rivalen, PL die Rivalen)
  die Rivalin *fem*

★ **rival** ADJECTIVE
  ▷ *see also* **rival** NOUN
  rivalisierend
  □ **a rival gang** eine rivalisierende Bande
  ■ **a rival company** ein Konkurrenzunternehmen *neut*

rivalry NOUN
  die Rivalität *fem* (*between towns, schools*)

★ **river** NOUN
  der Fluss *masc* (GEN des Flusses, PL die Flüsse)
  ■ **the river Rhine** der Rhein

Riviera NOUN
  die Riviera *fem*
  ■ **the Italian Riviera** die italienische Riviera
  ■ **the French Riviera** die Côte d'Azur

★ **road** NOUN
  die Straße *fem*
  □ **There's a lot of traffic on the roads.** Es herrscht viel Verkehr auf den Straßen.
  ■ **They live across the road.** Sie wohnen gegenüber.

road map NOUN
  die Straßenkarte *fem*

road rage NOUN
  die Aggressivität im Straßenverkehr *fem*

road sign NOUN
  das Verkehrsschild *neut* (PL die Verkehrsschilder)

roadworks PL NOUN
  die Bauarbeiten *fem pl*

roast ADJECTIVE
  ■ **roast chicken** das Brathähnchen
  ■ **roast potatoes** die Bratkartoffeln
  ■ **roast pork** der Schweinebraten
  ■ **roast beef** der Rindsbraten

to rob VERB
  ■ **to rob somebody** jemanden berauben [7]
  □ **I've been robbed.** Ich bin beraubt worden.
  ■ **to rob a bank** eine Bank ausrauben [4]
  ■ **to rob somebody of something** jemandem etwas rauben [38] □ He was robbed of his wallet. Man hat ihm seine Brieftasche geraubt.

robber NOUN
  der Räuber *masc* (PL die Räuber)
  die Räuberin *fem*
  ■ **a bank robber** ein Bankräuber

robbery NOUN
  der Raub *masc* (PL die Raube)
  ■ **a bank robbery** ein Bankraub
  ■ **armed robbery** der bewaffnete Raubüberfall

robin NOUN
  das Rotkehlchen *neut* (PL die Rotkehlchen)

robot NOUN
  der Roboter *masc* (PL die Roboter)

★ **rock** NOUN
  ▷ *see also* **rock** VERB
  1 der Fels *masc* (GEN des Fels) (*substance*)
    □ **They tunnelled through the rock.** Sie gruben einen Tunnel durch den Fels.
  2 der Felsbrocken *masc* (PL die Felsbrocken) (*boulder*)
    □ **I sat on a rock.** Ich saß auf einem Felsbrocken.
  3 der Stein *masc* (PL die Steine) (*stone*)
    □ **The crowd threw rocks.** Die Menge fing an, Steine zu werfen.
  4 der Rock *masc* (*music*)
    □ **a rock concert** ein Rockkonzert □ She's a rock star. Sie ist ein Rockstar.
    ■ **rock and roll** der Rock 'n' Roll

★ **to rock** VERB
  ▷ *see also* **rock** NOUN
  erschüttern [19] (PERFECT TENSE hat erschüttert)
  □ **The explosion rocked the building.** Die Explosion erschütterte das Gebäude.

rockery NOUN
  der Steingarten *masc* (PL die Steingärten)

★ **rocket** NOUN
  die Rakete *fem* (*firework, spacecraft*)

rocking chair NOUN
der Schaukelstuhl *masc* (PL die Schaukelstühle)

rocking horse NOUN
das Schaukelpferd *neut* (PL die Schaukelpferde)

rod NOUN
die Angel *fem* (*for fishing*)

rode VERB ▷ *see* ride

★ **role** NOUN
die Rolle *fem*

role play NOUN
das Rollenspiel *neut* (PL die Rollenspiele)
□ to do a role play ein Rollenspiel machen

★ **roll** NOUN
▷ *see also* roll VERB
1 die Rolle *fem*
□ a roll of tape eine Rolle Klebstreifen □ a toilet roll eine Rolle Toilettenpapier
2 das Brötchen *neut* (PL die Brötchen) (*bread*)

★ to **roll** VERB
▷ *see also* roll NOUN
rollen [38]
■ **to roll out the pastry** den Teig ausrollen [4]

roll call NOUN
der Namensaufruf *masc* (PL die Namensaufrufe)

roller NOUN
die Walze *fem*

Rollerblade® NOUN
der Rollerblade® *masc* (PL die Rollerblades)

roller coaster NOUN
die Achterbahn *fem*

roller skates PL NOUN
die Rollschuhe *masc pl*

roller-skating NOUN
das Rollschuhlaufen *neut*
■ **to go roller-skating** Rollschuh laufen [43]

rolling pin NOUN
das Nudelholz *neut* (PL die Nudelhölzer)

Roman ADJECTIVE, NOUN
römisch (*ancient*)
□ a Roman villa eine römische Villa □ the Roman empire das Römische Reich
■ **the Romans** die Römer *masc pl*

Roman Catholic NOUN
der Katholik *masc* (GEN des Katholiken, PL die Katholiken)
die Katholikin *fem*
□ He's a Roman Catholic. Er ist Katholik.

romance NOUN
1 die Romantik *fem* (*love*)
□ There is no romance between them. Es besteht keine Romantik zwischen ihnen.
2 der romantische Zauber *masc* (*glamour*)
□ the romance of Venice der romantische Zauber von Venedig
■ **a holiday romance** ein Ferienflirt *masc*

Romania NOUN
Rumänien *neut*
■ **from Romania** aus Rumänien
■ **to Romania** nach Rumänien

Romanian ADJECTIVE
rumänisch

★ **romantic** ADJECTIVE
romantisch

★ **roof** NOUN
das Dach *neut* (PL die Dächer)

roof rack NOUN
der Dachträger *masc* (PL die Dachträger)

★ **room** NOUN
1 das Zimmer *neut* (PL die Zimmer)
□ the biggest room in the house das größte Zimmer des Hauses □ She's in her room. Sie ist in ihrem Zimmer. □ the music room das Musikzimmer
■ **a single room** ein Einzelzimmer
■ **a double room** ein Doppelzimmer
2 der Platz *masc* (GEN des Platzes) (*space*)
□ There's no room for that box. Es ist kein Platz für diese Schachtel.

roommate NOUN
der Zimmergenosse *masc* (GEN des Zimmergenossen, PL die Zimmergenossen)
die Zimmergenossin *fem*

★ **root** NOUN
die Wurzel *fem*

rope NOUN
das Seil *neut* (PL die Seile)

★ **rose** VERB ▷ *see* rise

★ **rose** NOUN
die Rose *fem* (*flower*)

to **rot** VERB
verfaulen [7] (PERFECT TENSE ist verfault)

rotten ADJECTIVE
faulig (*decayed*)
□ a rotten apple ein fauliger Apfel
■ **rotten weather** das Mistwetter (*informal*)
■ **That's a rotten thing to do.** Das ist gemein.
■ **to feel rotten** sich mies fühlen [38] (*informal*)

★ **rough** ADJECTIVE
1 rau
□ My hands are rough. Meine Hände sind rau.
□ It's a rough area. Das ist eine raue Gegend.
2 hart (*game*)
□ Rugby's a rough sport. Rugby ist ein harter Sport.
3 stürmisch (*water*)
□ The sea was rough. Das Meer war stürmisch.
4 ungefähr
□ I've got a rough idea. Ich habe eine ungefähre Vorstellung.
■ **to feel rough** sich nicht wohlfühlen [4] □ I feel rough. Ich fühle mich nicht wohl.

★ = core vocabulary

roughly ADVERB
ungefähr
□ It weighs roughly twenty kilos. Es wiegt ungefähr zwanzig Kilo.

★ **round** ADJECTIVE, ADVERB, PREPOSITION
▷ see also **round** NOUN
1 rund
□ a round table ein runder Tisch
2 um (around)
□ We were sitting round the table. Wir saßen um den Tisch herum. □ She wore a scarf round her neck. Sie trug einen Schal um den Hals.
■ **It's just round the corner.** (very near) Es ist gleich um die Ecke.
■ **to go round to somebody's house** bei jemandem vorbeigehen [29] □ I went round to my friend's house. Ich bin bei meiner Freundin vorbeigegangen.
■ **to have a look round** sich umsehen [64]
□ We're going to have a look round. Wir möchten uns umsehen.
■ **to go round a museum** sich ein Museum ansehen [64] □ I went round the local museum. Ich habe mir das örtliche Museum angesehen.
■ **round here** hier in der Gegend □ Is there a chemist's round here? Gibt es hier in der Gegend eine Apotheke? □ He lives round here. Er wohnt hier in der Gegend.
■ **all year round** das ganze Jahr über
■ **round about** (roughly) etwa □ It costs round about a hundred pounds. Es kostet etwa hundert Pfund. □ round about eight o'clock etwa um acht Uhr

★ **round** NOUN
▷ see also **round** ADJECTIVE, ADVERB, PREPOSITION
die Runde fem (of tournament, boxing match)
□ a round of golf eine Runde Golf
■ **a round of drinks** eine Runde □ He bought a round of drinks. Er hat eine Runde ausgegeben.

roundabout NOUN
1 der Kreisverkehr masc (PL die Kreisverkehre) (at junction)
2 das Karussell neut (PL die Karussells) (at funfair)

rounders SING NOUN
der Schlagball masc

round trip NOUN (US)
die Hin- und Rückfahrt fem
■ **a round-trip ticket** eine Rückfahrkarte

★ **route** NOUN
die Route fem
□ We're planning our route. Wir planen unsere Route.

route planner NOUN
der Routenplaner masc (PL die Routenplaner)

★ **routine** NOUN
die Routine fem

★ **row (1)** NOUN
die Reihe fem

□ a row of houses eine Reihe Häuser □ Our seats are in the front row. Unsere Plätze sind in der ersten Reihe.
■ **five times in a row** fünfmal hintereinander

★ **row (2)** NOUN
1 der Krach masc (noise)
□ What's that terrible row? Was ist das für ein furchtbarer Krach?
2 der Streit masc (PL die Streite) (quarrel)
■ **to have a row** Streit haben [32] □ They've had a row. Sie haben Streit gehabt.

★ **to row** VERB
rudern [88]
□ We took turns to row. Wir haben abwechselnd gerudert.

rowboat NOUN (US)
das Ruderboot neut (PL die Ruderboote)

rowing NOUN
das Rudern neut (sport)
□ My hobby is rowing. Rudern ist mein Hobby.
■ **a rowing boat** ein Ruderboot neut

★ **royal** ADJECTIVE
königlich
□ the royal family die königliche Familie

to rub VERB
1 reiben (IMPERFECT rieb, PERFECT TENSE hat gerieben) (stain)
2 sich reiben (part of body)
□ Don't rub your eyes! Reib dir nicht die Augen!
■ **I rubbed myself dry with a towel.** Ich rieb mich mit einem Handtuch trocken.
■ **to rub something out** etwas ausradieren [4]

rubber NOUN
1 der Gummi masc (PL die Gummis)
□ rubber soles die Gummisohlen
2 der Radiergummi masc (PL die Radiergummis) (eraser)
□ Can I borrow your rubber? Kann ich deinen Radiergummi ausleihen?
■ **a rubber band** ein Gummiband neut

★ **rubbish** NOUN
▷ see also **rubbish** ADJECTIVE
1 der Müll masc (refuse)
□ When do they collect the rubbish? Wann wird der Müll abgeholt?
2 der Krempel masc (junk)
□ They sell a lot of rubbish at the market. Sie verkaufen eine Menge Krempel auf dem Markt.
3 der Unsinn masc (nonsense)
□ Don't talk rubbish! Red keinen Unsinn!
■ **That's a load of rubbish!** Das ist doch Unsinn! (informal)
■ **a rubbish bin** ein Mülleimer masc
■ **a rubbish dump** eine Müllkippe

★ **rubbish** ADJECTIVE
▷ see also **rubbish** NOUN
miserabel (informal)
□ They're a rubbish team! Sie sind eine miserable Mannschaft!

■ **This magazine is rubbish!** Die Zeitschrift ist Schrott! (*informal*)

★ **rucksack** NOUN
der Rucksack *masc* (PL die Rucksäcke)

rude ADJECTIVE
1 unhöflich (*impolite*)
□ It's rude to interrupt. Es ist unhöflich dazwischenzureden. □ He was very rude to me. Er war sehr unhöflich zu mir.
2 unanständig (*offensive*)
□ a rude joke ein unanständiger Witz
■ **a rude word** ein Schimpfwort *neut*

rug NOUN
1 der Teppich *masc* (PL die Teppiche)
□ a Persian rug ein Perserteppich
2 die Decke *fem* (*blanket*)
□ a tartan rug eine karierte Decke

★ **rugby** NOUN
das Rugby *neut*
□ I play rugby. Ich spiele Rugby.

★ **ruin** NOUN
▷ *see also* **ruin** VERB
die Ruine *fem*
□ the ruins of the castle die Ruine der Burg
■ **My life is in ruins.** Mein Leben ist ruiniert.

★ to **ruin** VERB
▷ *see also* **ruin** NOUN
ruinieren [76] (PERFECT TENSE hat ruiniert)
□ You'll ruin your shoes. Du ruinierst dir deine Schuhe.
■ **One single mistake had ruined the company.** Ein einziger Fehler hatte die Firma zerstört.
■ **It ruined our holiday.** Es hat uns den Urlaub verdorben.

★ **rule** NOUN
▷ *see also* **rule** VERB
1 die Regel *fem*
□ the rules of grammar die Grammatikregeln
■ **as a rule** in der Regel
2 die Vorschrift *fem* (*regulation*)
□ It's against the rules. Das ist gegen die Vorschriften.

★ to **rule** VERB
▷ *see also* **rule** NOUN
regieren [76] (PERFECT TENSE hat regiert)

to **rule out** VERB
ausschließen (IMPERFECT schloss aus, PERFECT TENSE hat ausgeschlossen) (*possibility*)

ruler NOUN
das Lineal *neut* (PL die Lineale)
□ Can I borrow your ruler? Kann ich dein Lineal ausleihen?

rum NOUN
der Rum *masc*

★ **rumour** NOUN
das Gerücht *neut* (PL die Gerüchte)
□ It's just a rumour. Es ist nur ein Gerücht.

rump steak NOUN
das Rumpsteak *neut* (PL die Rumpsteaks)

★ **run** NOUN
▷ *see also* **run** VERB
der Lauf *masc* (PL die Läufe) (*in cricket*)
□ to score a run einen Lauf machen
■ **to go for a run** einen Dauerlauf machen [48]
□ I go for a run every morning. Ich mache jeden Morgen einen Dauerlauf.
■ **I did a ten-kilometre run.** Ich bin zehn Kilometer gelaufen.
■ **on the run** auf der Flucht □ The criminals are still on the run. Die Verbrecher sind noch auf der Flucht.
■ **in the long run** auf Dauer

★ to **run** VERB
▷ *see also* **run** NOUN
1 laufen [43] (PRESENT TENSE läuft, IMPERFECT lief, PERFECT TENSE ist gelaufen)
□ I ran five kilometres. Ich bin fünf Kilometer gelaufen.
■ **to run a marathon** an einem Marathonlauf teilnehmen [52]
2 leiten [2] (*manage*)
□ He runs a large company. Er leitet ein großes Unternehmen.
3 veranstalten [2] (PERFECT TENSE hat veranstaltet) (*organize*)
□ They run music courses in the holidays. Sie veranstalten Musikkurse während der Ferien.
4 laufen [43] (*water*)
□ Don't leave the tap running. Lass das Wasser nicht laufen.
■ **to run a bath** ein Bad einlaufen lassen [42]
5 fahren [21] (PRESENT TENSE fährt, IMPERFECT fuhr, PERFECT TENSE hat gefahren) (*by car*)
□ I can run you to the station. Ich kann dich zum Bahnhof fahren.

to **run away** VERB
weglaufen [43]
□ They ran away before the police came. Sie sind weggelaufen, bevor die Polizei kam.

to **run out** VERB
■ **Time is running out.** Die Zeit wird knapp.
■ **We ran out of money.** Uns ist das Geld ausgegangen.

to **run over** VERB
■ **to run somebody over** jemanden überfahren [21]
■ **to get run over** überfahren werden [91]
□ Be careful, or you'll get run over! Pass auf, sonst wirst du überfahren!

rung VERB ▷ *see* **ring**

★ **runner** NOUN
der Läufer *masc* (PL die Läufer)
die Läuferin *fem*

★ = core vocabulary

runner beans PL NOUN
die Stangenbohnen *fem pl*

runner-up NOUN
der Zweite *masc* (GEN des Zweiten, PL die Zweiten)
die Zweite *fem* (GEN der Zweiten)

★ **running** NOUN
das Laufen *neut*
□ Running is my favourite sport. Laufen ist mein Lieblingssport.

run-up NOUN
▪ in the run-up to Christmas in der Zeit vor Weihnachten

runway NOUN
die Startbahn *fem*

★ **rural** ADJECTIVE
ländlich

★ **rush** NOUN
▷ *see also* **rush** VERB
die Eile *fem*
▪ in a rush in Eile

★ to **rush** VERB
▷ *see also* **rush** NOUN
1 rennen [55] (IMPERFECT rannte, PERFECT TENSE ist gerannt) (*run*)
□ Everyone rushed outside. Alle rannten hinaus.
2 sich beeilen [7] (PERFECT TENSE hat sich beeilt) (*hurry*)
□ There's no need to rush. Wir brauchen uns nicht zu beeilen.

rush hour NOUN
die Hauptverkehrszeit *fem*
□ in the rush hour in der Hauptverkehrszeit

rusk NOUN
der Zwieback *masc* (PL die Zwiebacke)

★ **Russia** NOUN
Russland *neut*
▪ from Russia aus Russland
▪ to Russia nach Russland

Russian ADJECTIVE
▷ *see also* **Russian** NOUN
russisch
▪ He's Russian. Er ist Russe.
▪ She's Russian. Sie ist Russin.

Russian NOUN
▷ *see also* **Russian** ADJECTIVE
1 der Russe *masc* (GEN des Russen, PL die Russen)
die Russin *fem* (*person*)
2 das Russisch *neut* (GEN des Russischen)
(*language*)

rust NOUN
der Rost *masc*

rusty ADJECTIVE
rostig
□ a rusty bike ein rostiges Fahrrad
▪ My German is very rusty. Mein Deutsch ist ziemlich eingerostet.

ruthless ADJECTIVE
rücksichtslos

rye NOUN
der Roggen *masc*
▪ rye bread das Roggenbrot

r

Ss

Sabbath NOUN
1 der Sonntag *masc* (PL die Sonntage) *(Christian)*
2 der Sabbat *masc* (PL die Sabbate) *(Jewish)*

★ **sack** NOUN
▷ *see also* **sack** VERB
der Sack *masc* (PL die Säcke)
■ **to get the sack** gefeuert werden [91]

to **sack** VERB
▷ *see also* **sack** NOUN
■ **to sack somebody** jemanden feuern [34]
□ He was sacked. Er wurde gefeuert.

sacred ADJECTIVE
heilig

★ **sacrifice** NOUN
das Opfer *neut* (PL die Opfer)

★ **sad** ADJECTIVE
traurig

saddle NOUN
der Sattel *masc* (PL die Sättel)

saddlebag NOUN
die Satteltasche *fem*

sadly ADVERB
1 traurig
□ 'She's gone,' he said sadly. 'Sie ist weg,' sagte er traurig.
2 leider *(unfortunately)*
□ Sadly, it was too late. Leider war es zu spät.

★ **safe** NOUN
▷ *see also* **safe** ADJECTIVE
der Safe *masc* (PL die Safes)
□ She put the money in the safe. Sie tat das Geld in den Safe.

★ **safe** ADJECTIVE
▷ *see also* **safe** NOUN
1 sicher
□ It's perfectly safe. Es ist völlig sicher. □ This car isn't safe. Das Auto ist nicht sicher.
2 in Sicherheit *(out of danger)*
□ You're safe now. Sie sind jetzt in Sicherheit.
■ **to feel safe** sich sicher fühlen [38]
■ **safe sex** Safer Sex

★ **safety** NOUN
die Sicherheit *fem*
■ **a safety belt** ein Sicherheitsgurt *masc*
■ **a safety pin** eine Sicherheitsnadel

Sagittarius NOUN
der Schütze *masc* (GEN des Schützen)
□ I'm Sagittarius. Ich bin Schütze.

Sahara NOUN
■ **the Sahara Desert** die Wüste Sahara

said VERB ▷ *see* **say**

★ **sail** NOUN
▷ *see also* **sail** VERB
das Segel *neut* (PL die Segel)

★ to **sail** VERB
▷ *see also* **sail** NOUN
1 segeln [34] (PERFECT TENSE ist gesegelt) *(travel)*
2 abfahren [21] (PRESENT TENSE fährt ab, IMPERFECT fuhr ab, PERFECT TENSE ist abgefahren) *(set off)*
□ The boat sails at eight o'clock. Das Schiff fährt um acht Uhr ab.

sailing NOUN
das Segeln *neut*
□ His hobby is sailing. Segeln ist sein Hobby.
■ **to go sailing** segeln gehen [29]
■ **a sailing boat** ein Segelboot *neut*
■ **a sailing ship** ein Segelschiff *neut*

sailor NOUN
der Matrose *masc* (GEN des Matrosen, PL die Matrosen)
die Matrosin *fem*
□ He's a sailor. Er ist Matrose.

★ **saint** NOUN
der Heilige *masc* (GEN des Heiligen, PL die Heiligen)
die Heilige *fem* (GEN der Heiligen)
□ a saint *(man)* ein Heiliger

★ **sake** NOUN
■ **for the sake of** um ... willen □ for the sake of your parents um deiner Eltern willen

salad NOUN
der Salat *masc* (PL die Salate)
■ **salad cream** die Salatmayonnaise
■ **salad dressing** die Salatsoße

salami NOUN
die Salami *fem* (GEN der Salami, PL die Salamis)

★ **salary** NOUN
das Gehalt *neut* (PL die Gehälter)

★ **sale** NOUN
der Schlussverkauf *masc* (PL die Schlussverkäufe) *(reductions)*

★ = core vocabulary

□ There's a sale on at the Nike Store. Beim Nike Store ist Schlussverkauf.
- **on sale** erhältlich
- **'for sale'** 'zu verkaufen'

sales assistant NOUN
der Verkäufer *masc* (PL die Verkäufer)
die Verkäuferin *fem*
□ He's a sales assistant. Er ist Verkäufer.

salesman NOUN
1 der Vertreter *masc* (PL die Vertreter) (*sales rep*)
□ He's a salesman. Er ist Vertreter.
- **a double-glazing salesman** ein Vertreter für Doppelfenster
2 der Verkäufer *masc* (PL die Verkäufer) (*sales assistant*)

sales rep NOUN
der Vertreter *masc* (PL die Vertreter)
die Vertreterin *fem*

saleswoman NOUN
1 die Vertreterin *fem* (*sales rep*)
□ She's a saleswoman. Sie ist Vertreterin.
2 die Verkäuferin *fem* (*sales assistant*)

salmon NOUN
der Lachs *masc* (GEN des Lachses, PL die Lachse)

salon NOUN
der Salon *masc* (PL die Salons)
□ a hair salon ein Friseursalon □ a beauty salon ein Kosmetiksalon

saloon car NOUN
die Limousine *fem*

★ **salt** NOUN
das Salz *neut* (GEN des Salzes, PL die Salze)

salty ADJECTIVE
salzig

to **salute** VERB
grüßen [31]

Salvation Army NOUN
die Heilsarmee *fem*

★ **same** ADJECTIVE
gleiche
□ The same coat is cheaper elsewhere. Der gleiche Mantel ist anderswo billiger. □ He asked me the same question. Er hat mir die gleiche Frage gestellt. □ I have the same tablet. Ich habe das gleiche Tablet. □ We obviously have the same problems. Wir haben offensichtlich die gleichen Probleme.
- **at the same time** zur gleichen Zeit
- **It's not the same.** Das ist nicht das Gleiche.
- **They're exactly the same.** Sie sind genau gleich.

same-sex ADJECTIVE
gleichgeschlechtlich
- **a same-sex marriage** eine gleichgeschlechtliche Ehe

★ **sample** NOUN
die Probe *fem*

□ a free sample of perfume eine kostenlose Parfümprobe

★ **sand** NOUN
der Sand *masc*

sandal NOUN
die Sandale *fem*
□ a pair of sandals ein Paar Sandalen

sand castle NOUN
die Sandburg *fem*

★ **sandwich** NOUN
- **I normally have a sandwich for lunch.** Zu Mittag esse ich meistens ein belegtes Brot.
- **a cheese sandwich** ein Käsebrot

sang VERB ▷ *see* **sing**

sanitary napkin NOUN (US)
die Damenbinde *fem*

sanitary towel NOUN
die Damenbinde *fem*

sank VERB ▷ *see* **sink**

Santa Claus NOUN
der Weihnachtsmann *masc* (PL die Weihnachtsmänner)

sarcastic ADJECTIVE
sarkastisch

sardine NOUN
die Sardine *fem*

sat VERB ▷ *see* **sit**

satchel NOUN
der Schulranzen *masc* (PL die Schulranzen)

★ **satellite** NOUN
der Satellit *masc* (GEN des Satelliten, PL die Satelliten)
- **a satellite dish** eine Satellitenschüssel
- **satellite television** das Satellitenfernsehen

satisfactory ADJECTIVE
befriedigend

satisfied ADJECTIVE
zufrieden

sat nav NOUN
das GPS *neut* (PL die GPS)

★ **Saturday** NOUN
der Samstag *masc* (PL die Samstage)
□ on Saturday am Samstag □ every Saturday jeden Samstag □ last Saturday letzten Samstag □ next Saturday nächsten Samstag
- **on Saturdays** samstags
- **a Saturday job** ein Samstagsjob

★ **sauce** NOUN
die Soße *fem*

saucepan NOUN
der Kochtopf *masc* (PL die Kochtöpfe)

saucer NOUN
die Untertasse *fem*

Saudi Arabia NOUN
Saudi-Arabien *neut*
- **to Saudi Arabia** nach Saudi-Arabien

sauna – scene

sauna NOUN
die Sauna*fem* (PL die Saunas)

★**sausage** NOUN
die Wurst*fem* (PL die Würste)
■ **a sausage roll** eine Wurst im Blätterteig

★to **save** VERB
1 sparen [38] (*money, time*)
□ I've saved fifty pounds. Ich habe fünfzig Pfund gespart. □ I saved money by waiting for the sales. Ich habe Geld gespart, weil ich bis zum Schlussverkauf gewartet habe. □ We took a taxi to save time. Wir haben ein Taxi genommen, um Zeit zu sparen.
2 retten [2] (*rescue*)
□ Luckily, all the passengers were saved. Zum Glück wurden alle Passagiere gerettet.
3 speichern [88] (*on computer*)
□ Don't forget to save your work regularly. Vergiss nicht, deine Arbeit regelmäßig zu speichern.

to **save up** VERB
sparen [38]
□ I'm saving up for a bike. Ich spare für ein Fahrrad.

savings PL NOUN
die Ersparnisse*fem pl*
□ She spent all her savings on a computer. Sie gab all ihre Ersparnisse für einen Computer aus.

savoury ADJECTIVE
pikant (*spicy*)

saw VERB ▷ *see* **see**

saw NOUN
die Säge*fem*

sax NOUN
das Saxofon*neut* (PL die Saxofone)
□ I play the sax. Ich spiele Saxofon.

saxophone NOUN
das Saxofon*neut* (PL die Saxofone)
□ I play the saxophone. Ich spiele Saxofon.

★to **say** VERB
sagen [38]
□ What did he say? Was hat er gesagt? □ Did you hear what she said? Hast du gehört, was sie gesagt hat? □ Could you say that again? Können Sie das noch einmal sagen?
■ **That goes without saying.** Das ist selbstverständlich.

saying NOUN
die Redensart*fem*
□ It's just a saying. Das ist so eine Redensart.

★**scale** NOUN
1 der Maßstab*masc* (PL die Maßstäbe) (*of map*)
□ a large-scale map eine Karte großen Maßstabs
2 das Ausmaß*neut* (GEN des Ausmaßes, PL die Ausmaße) (*size, extent*)
□ a disaster on a massive scale eine Katastrophe von riesigem Ausmaß
3 die Tonleiter*fem* (*in music*)

scales PL NOUN
die Waage*fem sing* (*in kitchen, shop*)
■ **bathroom scales** die Personenwaage

scampi PL NOUN
die Scampi*pl*

★**scandal** NOUN
1 der Skandal*masc* (PL die Skandale) (*outrage*)
□ It caused a scandal. Es hat einen Skandal verursacht.
2 der Tratsch*masc* (*gossip*)
□ It's just scandal. Das ist nur Tratsch.

Scandinavia NOUN
Skandinavien*neut*
■ **from Scandinavia** aus Skandinavien
■ **to Scandinavia** nach Skandinavien

Scandinavian ADJECTIVE
skandinavisch
■ **He's Scandinavian.** Er ist Skandinavier.

scar NOUN
die Narbe*fem*

scarce ADJECTIVE
1 knapp
□ scarce resources knappe Geldmittel
2 rar
□ Jobs are scarce. Jobs sind rar.

scarcely ADVERB
kaum
□ I scarcely knew him. Ich kannte ihn kaum.

scare NOUN
▷ *see also* **scare** VERB
der Schrecken*masc* (PL die Schrecken)
■ **a bomb scare** ein Bombenalarm*masc*

to **scare** VERB
▷ *see also* **scare** NOUN
■ **to scare somebody** jemandem Angst machen [48] □ He scares me. Er macht mir Angst.

scarecrow NOUN
die Vogelscheuche*fem*

scared ADJECTIVE
■ **to be scared** Angst haben [32] □ I was scared stiff. Ich hatte furchtbar Angst.
■ **to be scared of** Angst haben [32] vor □ Are you scared of him? Hast du vor ihm Angst?

scarf NOUN
1 der Schal*masc* (PL die Schals) (*long*)
2 das Halstuch*neut* (PL die Halstücher) (*square*)

scary ADJECTIVE
furchterregend
□ It was really scary. Es war wirklich furchterregend.

★**scene** NOUN
1 der Ort*masc* (PL die Orte) (*place*)
□ The police were soon on the scene. Die Polizei war schnell vor Ort. □ the scene of the crime der Ort des Verbrechens

2 das Spektakel *neut* (PL die Spektakel) (*event, sight*)

□ It was an amazing scene. Es war ein erstaunliches Spektakel.

■ **to make a scene** eine Szene machen [48]

scenery NOUN

die Landschaft *fem* (*landscape*)

scent NOUN

der Duft *masc* (PL die Düfte) (*perfume*)

★ **schedule** NOUN

das Programm *neut* (PL die Programme)

□ a busy schedule ein volles Programm

■ **on schedule** planmäßig

■ **to be behind schedule** Verspätung haben [32]

scheduled flight NOUN

der Linienflug *masc* (PL die Linienflüge)

★ **scheme** NOUN

1 der Plan *masc* (PL die Pläne) (*idea*)

□ a crazy scheme ein verrückter Plan

2 das Projekt *neut* (PL die Projekte) (*project*)

□ a scheme to make extra pocket money ein Projekt, um mehr Taschengeld zu verdienen

scholarship NOUN

das Stipendium *neut* (PL die Stipendien)

★ **school** NOUN

die Schule *fem*

■ **to go to school** in die Schule gehen [29]

schoolbook NOUN

das Schulbuch *neut* (PL die Schulbücher)

★ **schoolboy** NOUN

der Schuljunge *masc* (GEN des Schuljungen, PL die Schuljungen)

★ **schoolchildren** PL NOUN

die Schulkinder *neut pl*

★ **schoolgirl** NOUN

das Schulmädchen *neut* (PL die Schulmädchen)

★ **science** NOUN

die Wissenschaft *fem*

science fiction NOUN

die Science-Fiction *fem*

scientific ADJECTIVE

wissenschaftlich

★ **scientist** NOUN

der Wissenschaftler *masc* (PL die Wissenschaftler)

die Wissenschaftlerin *fem* (*doing research*)

□ She's a scientist. Sie ist Wissenschaftlerin.

■ **He trained as a scientist.** Er hat eine wissenschaftliche Ausbildung.

★ **scissors** PL NOUN

die Schere *fem*

□ a pair of scissors eine Schere

to scoff VERB

futtern [34] (*informal: eat*)

□ Mark scoffed all the sandwiches. Mark hat alle Brote gefuttert.

scooter NOUN

1 der Motorroller *masc* (PL die Motorroller)

2 der Roller *masc* (PL die Roller) (*child's toy*)

★ **score** NOUN

▷ *see also* **score** VERB

der Spielstand *masc* (PL die Spielstände)

■ **What's the score?** Wie steht das Spiel?

■ **The score was three nil.** Es stand drei zu null.

★ **to score** VERB

▷ *see also* **score** NOUN

1 schießen (IMPERFECT schoss, PERFECT TENSE hat geschossen) (*goal*)

□ to score a goal ein Tor schießen

2 machen [48] (*point*)

□ to score six out of ten sechs von zehn Punkten machen

3 zählen [38] (*keep score*)

□ Who's going to score? Wer zählt?

■ **Our team didn't score.** Unsere Mannschaft hat nicht gepunktet.

Scorpio NOUN

der Skorpion *masc*

□ I'm Scorpio. Ich bin Skorpion.

Scot NOUN

der Schotte *masc* (GEN des Schotten, PL die Schotten)

die Schottin *fem*

Scotch tape® NOUN (US)

der Tesafilm® *masc*

★ **Scotland** NOUN

Schottland *neut*

■ **from Scotland** aus Schottland

■ **in Scotland** in Schottland

■ **to Scotland** nach Schottland

Scots ADJECTIVE

schottisch

□ a Scots accent ein schottischer Akzent

★ **Scotsman** NOUN

der Schotte *masc* (GEN des Schotten, PL die Schotten)

★ **Scotswoman** NOUN

die Schottin *fem*

★ **Scottish** ADJECTIVE

schottisch

□ a Scottish accent ein schottischer Akzent

■ **He's Scottish.** Er ist Schotte.

■ **She's Scottish.** Sie ist Schottin.

scout NOUN

der Pfadfinder *masc* (PL die Pfadfinder)

die Pfadfinderin *fem*

□ I'm in the Scouts. Ich bin bei den Pfadfindern.

scrambled eggs PL NOUN

die Rühreier *neut pl*

scrap NOUN

▷ *see also* **scrap** VERB

S

scrap – seat belt

1 das Stück neut (PL die Stücke)
□ a scrap of paper ein Stück Papier

2 die Schlägerei fem (fight)
■ scrap iron das Alteisen

to **scrap** VERB
▷ see also **scrap** NOUN
verwerfen [92] (PRESENT TENSE verwirft, IMPERFECT verwarf, PERFECT TENSE hat verworfen) (plan, idea)
□ The plan was scrapped. Der Plan wurde verworfen.

scrapbook NOUN
das Album neut (PL die Alben)

to **scratch** VERB
▷ see also **scratch** NOUN
kratzen [36]
□ Stop scratching! Hör auf zu kratzen!

scratch NOUN
▷ see also **scratch** VERB
der Kratzer masc (PL die Kratzer) (on skin)
■ to start from scratch von vorn anfangen [23]

★ **scream** NOUN
▷ see also **scream** VERB
der Schrei masc (PL die Schreie)

★ to **scream** VERB
▷ see also **scream** NOUN
schreien [62] (IMPERFECT schrie, PERFECT TENSE hat geschrien)

★ **screen** NOUN
1 die Leinwand fem (PL die Leinwände) (cinema)
2 der Bildschirm masc (PL die Bildschirme) (television, computer)
□ An error message appeared on the screen. Auf dem Bildschirm erschien eine Fehlermeldung.

screen saver NOUN
der Bildschirmschoner masc (PL die Bildschirmschoner) (computer)

screw NOUN
die Schraube fem

screwdriver NOUN
der Schraubenzieher masc (PL die Schraubenzieher)

to **scribble** VERB
kritzeln [34]

to **scrub** VERB
schrubben [48]
□ He scrubbed the floor. Er schrubbte den Boden.

sculpture NOUN
die Skulptur fem

★ **sea** NOUN
das Meer neut (PL die Meere)

★ **seafood** NOUN
die Meeresfrüchte fem pl
□ I don't like seafood. Ich mag Meeresfrüchte nicht.

seagull NOUN
die Möwe fem

seal NOUN
▷ see also **seal** VERB
1 der Seehund masc (PL die Seehunde) (animal)
2 das Siegel neut (PL die Siegel) (on container)

to **seal** VERB
▷ see also **seal** NOUN
1 versiegeln [84] (PERFECT TENSE hat versiegelt) (container)
2 zukleben [4] (PERFECT TENSE hat zugeklebt) (letter)

seaman NOUN
der Seemann masc (PL die Seeleute)

★ to **search** VERB
▷ see also **search** NOUN
durchsuchen [18] (PERFECT TENSE hat durchsucht)
□ They searched the woods for her. Sie haben den Wald nach ihr durchsucht.
■ to search for something nach etwas suchen [48] □ He was searching for gold. Er suchte nach Gold.

★ **search** NOUN
▷ see also **search** VERB
die Suche fem

search engine NOUN
die Suchmaschine fem (Internet)

search party NOUN
der Suchtrupp masc (PL die Suchtrupps)

seashore NOUN
der Strand masc (PL die Strände)
□ on the seashore am Strand

seasick ADJECTIVE
seekrank
□ to be seasick seekrank sein

★ **seaside** NOUN
■ at the seaside am Meer
■ We're going to the seaside. Wir fahren ans Meer.

★ **season** NOUN
die Jahreszeit fem
□ What's your favourite season? Welche Jahreszeit hast du am liebsten?
■ out of season außerhalb der Saison □ We went there out of season. Wir sind außerhalb der Saison dorthin gefahren.
■ during the holiday season während der Ferienzeit
■ a season ticket eine Dauerkarte

★ **seat** NOUN
der Platz masc (GEN des Platzes, PL die Plätze)

seat belt NOUN
der Sicherheitsgurt masc (PL die Sicherheitsgurte)
■ Fasten your seat belt! Schnalle dich an!

sea water NOUN
das Meerwasser *neut*

seaweed NOUN
die Alge *fem*

★ **second** ADJECTIVE
▷ *see also* **second** NOUN
zweite
□ **the second man from the right** der zweite Mann von rechts □ **her second husband** ihr zweiter Mann □ **on the second page** auf der zweiten Seite □ **my second child** mein zweites Kind
■ **to come second** (*in race*) Zweiter werden [91] □ She came second. Sie wurde Zweite.
■ **the second of August** der zweite August

second NOUN
▷ *see also* **second** ADJECTIVE
die Sekunde *fem*
□ It'll only take a second. Es dauert nur eine Sekunde.

★ **secondary school** NOUN
1 das Gymnasium *neut* (PL die Gymnasien)
2 die Realschule *fem*

DID YOU KNOW...?
Germans always specify the type of secondary school. **Gymnasium** takes nine years and leads to **Abitur**, **Realschule** takes six years and leads to **mittlere Reife**.

second-class ADJECTIVE, ADVERB
1 zweiter Klasse (*ticket, compartment*)
□ to travel second-class zweiter Klasse fahren
2 normal (*stamp, letter*)

DID YOU KNOW...?
In Germany there is no first-class or second-class post. However, letters cost more to send than postcards, so you have to remember to say what you are sending when buying stamps. There is also an express service.

□ **to send something second-class** etwas mit normaler Post schicken

second-hand ADJECTIVE
gebraucht
■ **a second-hand car** ein Gebrauchtwagen *masc*

secondly ADVERB
zweitens
□ **firstly ... secondly ...** erstens ... zweitens ...

★ **secret** ADJECTIVE
▷ *see also* **secret** NOUN
geheim
□ **a secret mission** eine geheime Mission

★ **secret** NOUN
▷ *see also* **secret** ADJECTIVE
das Geheimnis *neut* (GEN des Geheimnisses, PL die Geheimnisse)

□ It's a secret. Es ist ein Geheimnis. □ **Can you keep a secret?** Kannst du ein Geheimnis für dich behalten?
■ **in secret** heimlich

secretary NOUN
der Sekretär *masc* (PL die Sekretäre)
die Sekretärin *fem*
□ He's a secretary. Er ist Sekretär.

secretly ADVERB
heimlich

★ **section** NOUN
1 der Teil *masc* (PL die Teile)
□ I passed the written section of the exam. Ich habe den schriftlichen Teil der Prüfung bestanden.
2 die Abteilung *fem* (*in shop*)
□ the food section die Lebensmittelabteilung

★ **security** NOUN
die Sicherheit *fem*
□ airport security die Sicherheit auf den Flughäfen
■ **to have no job security** keinen sicheren Job haben [32]
■ **a security guard** ein Sicherheitsbeamter

security guard NOUN
der Wächter *masc* (PL die Wächter)
die Wächterin *fem*
■ She's a security guard. Sie ist beim Sicherheitsdienst.

sedan NOUN (US)
die Limousine *fem*

★ to **see** VERB
sehen [64] (PRESENT TENSE sieht, IMPERFECT sah, PERFECT TENSE hat gesehen)
□ I can't see. Ich kann nichts sehen. □ I saw him yesterday. Ich habe ihn gestern gesehen.
□ Have you seen him? Hast du ihn gesehen?
■ **See you!** Tschüs! (*informal*)
■ **See you soon!** Bis bald!
■ **to see to something** sich um etwas kümmern [38] □ Can you see to lunch, please? Kümmerst du dich bitte um das Mittagessen?

★ **seed** NOUN
der Samen *masc* (PL die Samen)
■ **sunflower seeds** die Sonnenblumenkerne *masc pl*

★ to **seem** VERB
scheinen [57] (IMPERFECT schien, PERFECT TENSE hat geschienen)
□ The shop seemed to be closed. Das Geschäft schien geschlossen zu haben. □ That seems like a good idea. Das scheint eine gute Idee zu sein.
■ **She seems tired.** Sie wirkt müde.
■ **It seems that ...** Es sieht so aus, dass ... □ It seems she's getting married. Es sieht so aus, dass sie heiratet.
■ **There seems to be a problem.** Anscheinend gibt's ein Problem.

seen – send

seen VERB ▷ *see* **see**

seesaw NOUN
die Wippe *fem*

see-through ADJECTIVE
durchsichtig

seldom ADVERB
selten

★ to **select** VERB
auswählen [4] (PERFECT TENSE hat ausgewählt)

★ **selection** NOUN
die Auswahl *fem*

self-assured ADJECTIVE
selbstsicher
□ He's very self-assured. Er ist sehr selbstsicher.

self-catering ADJECTIVE
▪ a self-catering apartment eine Wohnung
für Selbstversorger

self-centred ADJECTIVE
egozentrisch

self-confidence NOUN
das Selbstvertrauen *neut*
□ He hasn't got much self-confidence. Er hat
nicht viel Selbstvertrauen.

self-conscious ADJECTIVE
gehemmt

self-contained ADJECTIVE
▪ a self-contained flat eine separate
Wohnung

self-control NOUN
die Selbstbeherrschung *fem*

self-defence NOUN
die Selbstverteidigung *fem*
□ self-defence classes der Selbstverteidigungskurs
▪ She killed him in self-defence. Sie hat ihn
in Notwehr getötet.

self-discipline NOUN
die Selbstdisziplin *fem*

self-employed ADJECTIVE
▪ to be self-employed selbstständig sein [65]
□ He's self-employed. Er ist selbstständig.
▪ the self-employed die Selbstständigen *masc
pl*

selfie NOUN
das Selfie *neut*

selfie stick NOUN
der Selfie-Stick *masc* (PL die Selfie-Sticks)

selfish ADJECTIVE
egoistisch
□ Don't be so selfish. Sei nicht so egoistisch.

self-respect NOUN
die Selbstachtung *fem*

self-service ADJECTIVE
▪ It's self-service. (*café, shop*) Da ist
Selbstbedienung.

▪ a self-service restaurant ein
Selbstbedienungsrestaurant *neut*

★ to **sell** VERB
verkaufen [84] (PERFECT TENSE hat verkauft)
□ He sold it to me. Er hat es mir verkauft.

to **sell off** VERB
verkaufen [84]

to **sell out** VERB
▪ The tickets are all sold out. Alle Karten sind
ausverkauft.
▪ The tickets sold out in three hours. Die
Karten waren in drei Stunden ausverkauft.

sell-by date NOUN
das Verfallsdatum *neut* (PL die Verfallsdaten)

selling price NOUN
der Verkaufspreis *masc* (GEN des
Verkaufspreises, PL die Verkaufspreise)

Sellotape® NOUN
der Tesafilm® *masc*

semi NOUN
die Doppelhaushälfte *fem*
□ We live in a semi. Wir wohnen in einer
Doppelhaushälfte.

semicircle NOUN
der Halbkreis *masc* (GEN des Halbkreises, PL die
Halbkreise)

semicolon NOUN
der Strichpunkt *masc* (PL die Strichpunkte)

semi-detached house NOUN
die Doppelhaushälfte *fem*
□ We live in a semi-detached house. Wir
wohnen in einer Doppelhaushälfte.

semi-final NOUN
das Halbfinale *neut* (PL die Halbfinale)

semi-skimmed milk NOUN
die fettarme Milch *fem*

★ to **send** VERB
schicken [48]
□ She sent me money. Sie hat mir Geld
geschickt.

to **send back** VERB
zurückschicken [4]

to **send off** VERB
1 abschicken [4] (*goods, letter*)
2 vom Platz schicken [48] (*in sports match*)
□ She was sent off. Sie wurde vom Platz
geschickt.
▪ to send off for something 1 (*free*) etwas
kommen lassen [42] □ I've sent off for a
catalogue. Ich habe mir einen Katalog kommen
lassen. 2 (*paid for*) etwas bestellen [7]
▪ She sent off for a new passport. Sie hat
einen neuen Pass beantragt

to **send out** VERB
verschicken [7]
▪ to send out for something etwas
telefonisch bestellen [7] □ Shall we send out for
pizza? Wollen wir Pizza bestellen?

S

★ = core vocabulary

sender NOUN
der Absender *masc* (PL die Absender)
die Absenderin *fem*

★ **senior** ADJECTIVE
leitend
▫ senior management die leitenden Angestellten
■ **senior school** die weiterführende Schule
■ **senior pupils** die Oberstufenschüler

senior citizen NOUN
der Senior *masc* (PL die Senioren)
die Seniorin *fem*

sensational ADJECTIVE
sensationell

★ **sense** NOUN
1 der Sinn *masc* (PL die Sinne) (*faculty*)
▫ the five senses die fünf Sinne ▫ the sixth sense der sechste Sinn
■ **the sense of touch** der Tastsinn
■ **the sense of smell** der Geschmackssinn
■ **sense of humour** der Sinn für Humor ▫ He's got no sense of humour. Er hat keinen Sinn für Humor.
2 der Verstand *masc* (*wisdom*)
■ **Use your common sense!** Benutze deinen gesunden Menschenverstand!
■ **It makes sense.** Das macht Sinn.
■ **It doesn't make sense.** Das macht keinen Sinn.

senseless ADJECTIVE
sinnlos

★ **sensible** ADJECTIVE
1 vernünftig
▫ Be sensible! Sei vernünftig! ▫ It would be sensible to check first. Es wäre vernünftig, zuerst nachzusehen. ▫ Felix is a very sensible boy. Felix ist ein sehr vernünftiger Junge.

BE CAREFUL!
Do not translate **sensible** by the German word **sensibel**.

2 sinnvoll
▫ That wasn't a sensible idea. Das war nicht sinnvoll.

★ **sensitive** ADJECTIVE
sensibel
▫ She's very sensitive. Sie ist sehr sensibel.

sensuous ADJECTIVE
sinnlich

sent VERB ▷ *see* **send**

★ **sentence** NOUN
▷ *see also* **sentence** VERB
1 der Satz *masc* (GEN des Satzes, PL die Sätze)
▫ What does this sentence mean? Was bedeutet dieser Satz?
2 das Urteil *neut* (PL die Urteile) (*judgment*)
▫ The court will pass sentence tomorrow. Das Gericht wird morgen das Urteil verkünden.

3 die Strafe *fem* (*punishment*)
▫ the death sentence die Todesstrafe
■ **He got a life sentence.** Er hat lebenslänglich bekommen.

★ **to sentence** VERB
▷ *see also* **sentence** NOUN
verurteilen [84] (PERFECT TENSE hat verurteilt)
▫ to sentence somebody to life imprisonment jemanden zu einer lebenslangen Gefängnisstrafe verurteilen ▫ to sentence somebody to death jemanden zum Tode verurteilen

sentimental ADJECTIVE
sentimental

★ **separate** ADJECTIVE
▷ *see also* **separate** VERB
getrennt
▫ separate rooms getrennte Zimmer
■ **I wrote it on a separate sheet.** Ich habe es auf ein extra Blatt geschrieben.
■ **on separate occasions** bei verschiedenen Gelegenheiten
■ **on two separate occasions** zweimal

to separate VERB
▷ *see also* **separate** ADJECTIVE
1 trennen [38]
2 sich trennen [38] (*married couple*)

separately ADVERB
extra

separation NOUN
die Trennung *fem*

★ **September** NOUN
der September *masc*
▫ in September im September

sequel NOUN
die Fortsetzung *fem* (*book, film*)

sequence NOUN
1 die Reihenfolge *fem*
▫ in the correct sequence in der richtigen Reihenfolge
■ **in sequence** der Reihenfolge nach
■ **a sequence of events** eine Folge von Ereignissen
2 die Sequenz *fem* (*in film*)

sergeant NOUN
1 der Feldwebel *masc* (PL die Feldwebel)
die Feldwebelin *fem* (*army*)
2 der Polizeimeister *masc* (PL die Polizeimeister)
die Polizeimeisterin *fem* (*police*)

serial NOUN
die Fernsehserie *fem*

★ **series** SING NOUN
1 die Sendereihe *fem*
▫ a TV series eine Sendereihe im Fernsehen
2 die Reihe *fem* (*of numbers*)

★ **serious** ADJECTIVE
1 ernst

Numbers in brackets refer to verb tables on pages 697 to 706.

601

S

seriously – settle

□ You look very serious. Du siehst sehr ernst
aus.
■ **Are you serious?** Ist das dein Ernst?
2 schwer (*illness, mistake*)

> **BE CAREFUL!**
> Do not translate **serious** by seriös.

★ **seriously** ADVERB
im Ernst
□ No, but seriously ... Nein, aber im Ernst ...
■ **to take somebody seriously** jemanden
ernst nehmen [52]
■ **seriously injured** schwer verletzt
■ **Seriously?** Im Ernst?

sermon NOUN
die Predigt *fem*

servant NOUN
der Diener *masc* (PL die Diener)
die Dienerin *fem*

★ to **serve** VERB
▷ *see also* **serve** NOUN
1 servieren [76] (PERFECT TENSE hat serviert)
□ Dinner is served. Das Essen ist serviert.
2 aufschlagen [59] (PRESENT TENSE schlägt auf,
IMPERFECT schlug auf, PERFECT TENSE hat
aufgeschlagen)
□ It's Murray's turn to serve. Murray schlägt auf.
3 absitzen [68] (IMPERFECT saß ab, PERFECT TENSE
hat abgesessen) (*prison sentence*)
■ **to serve time** im Gefängnis sein [65]
■ **It serves you right.** Das geschieht dir recht.

★ **serve** NOUN
▷ *see also* **serve** VERB
der Aufschlag *masc* (PL die Aufschläge) (*tennis*)
■ **It's your serve.** Du hast Aufschlag.

server NOUN
der Server *masc* (PL die Server) (*computer*)

★ to **service** VERB
▷ *see also* **service** NOUN
überholen [18] (PERFECT TENSE hat überholt) (*car,
washing machine*)

★ **service** NOUN
▷ *see also* **service** VERB
1 die Bedienung *fem*
□ Service is included. Die Bedienung ist
inklusive.
2 die Inspektion *fem* (*of car*)
3 der Gottesdienst *masc* (PL die Gottesdienste)
(*church service*)
■ **the Fire Service** die Feuerwehr
■ **the armed services** die Streitkräfte

service area NOUN
die Raststätte *fem*

service charge NOUN
die Bedienung *fem*
□ There's no service charge. Die Bedienung
wird nicht extra berechnet.

serviceman NOUN
der Militärangehörige *masc* (GEN des
Militärangehörigen, PL die Militärangehörigen)
□ a serviceman ein Militärangehöriger
■ **He's a serviceman.** Er ist beim Militär.

service station NOUN
die Tankstelle *fem*

servicewoman NOUN
die Militärangehörige *fem* (GEN der
Militärangehörigen, PL die Militärangehörigen)
□ a servicewoman eine Militärangehörige
■ **She's a servicewoman.** Sie ist beim Militär.

serviette NOUN
die Serviette *fem*

session NOUN
die Sitzung *fem*

★ **set** NOUN
▷ *see also* **set** VERB
der Satz *masc* (GEN des Satzes, PL die Sätze)
□ a set of keys ein Satz Schlüssel □ **Williams
won the set.** (*tennis*) Williams hat den Satz
gewonnen.
■ **a chess set** ein Schachspiel *neut*
■ **a train set** eine Spielzeugeisenbahn

★ to **set** VERB
▷ *see also* **set** NOUN
1 stellen [38] (*alarm clock*)
□ I set the alarm for seven o'clock. Ich habe den
Wecker auf sieben Uhr gestellt.
2 aufstellen [4] (PERFECT TENSE hat aufgestellt)
(*record*)
□ The world record was set last year. Der
Weltrekord wurde letztes Jahr aufgestellt.
3 untergehen [29] (IMPERFECT ging unter, PERFECT
TENSE ist untergegangen) (*sun*)
□ The sun was setting. Die Sonne ging unter.
■ **The film is set in Morocco.** Der Film spielt in
Marokko.
■ **to set the table** den Tisch decken [38]

to **set off** VERB
aufbrechen [11]
□ We set off for Newcastle at nine o'clock. Wir
sind um neun Uhr nach Newcastle
aufgebrochen.

to **set out** VERB
aufbrechen [11]
□ We set out for Newcastle at nine o'clock. Wir
sind um neun Uhr nach Newcastle
aufgebrochen.

settee NOUN
das Sofa *neut* (PL die Sofas)

★ to **settle** VERB
1 lösen [38] (*problem*)
2 beilegen [4] (PERFECT TENSE hat beigelegt)
(*argument*)
■ **to settle an account** eine Rechnung
begleichen

to **settle down** VERB
ruhiger werden [91] (*calm down*)
■ **Settle down!** Beruhige dich!

to **settle in** VERB
sich einleben [4]

to **settle on** VERB
■ **to settle on something** sich für etwas
entscheiden □ **I finally settled on Crete for my
holidays.** Ich habe mich endlich dafür
entschieden, nach Kreta in Urlaub zu fahren.

★ **seven** NUMBER
sieben
□ **She's seven.** Sie ist sieben.

★ **seventeen** NUMBER
siebzehn
□ **He's seventeen.** Er ist siebzehn.

★ **seventeenth** ADJECTIVE
siebzehnte
□ **the seventeenth of August** der siebzehnte
August

★ **seventh** ADJECTIVE
siebte
□ **the seventh floor** der siebte Stock □ **the
seventh of August** der siebte August

★ **seventy** NUMBER
siebzig
□ **She's seventy.** Sie ist siebzig.

★ **several** ADJECTIVE, PRONOUN
einige
□ **several schools** einige Schulen □ **several of
them** einige von ihnen

to **sew** VERB
nähen [38]

to **sew up** VERB
flicken [48] (*tear*)

sewing NOUN
das Nähen *neut*
■ **I like sewing.** Ich nähe gern.
■ **a sewing machine** eine Nähmaschine

sewn VERB ▷ *see* **sew**

sex NOUN
das Geschlecht *neut* (PL die Geschlechter)
■ **to have sex with somebody** mit jemandem
Verkehr haben [32]
■ **sex education** der Aufklärungsunterricht

sexism NOUN
der Sexismus *masc* (GEN des Sexismus)

sexist ADJECTIVE
sexistisch

sexual ADJECTIVE
sexuell
□ **sexual harassment** die sexuelle Belästigung
■ **sexual discrimination** die Diskriminierung
aufgrund des Geschlechts

sexuality NOUN
die Sexualität *fem*

sexy ADJECTIVE
sexy

shabby ADJECTIVE
schäbig

★ **shade** NOUN
1 der Schatten *masc* (PL die Schatten)
□ **in the shade** im Schatten
2 der Ton *masc* (PL die Töne) (*colour*)
□ **a shade of blue** ein Blauton

★ **shadow** NOUN
der Schatten *masc* (PL die Schatten)

★ to **shake** VERB
1 ausschütteln [4] (PERFECT TENSE hat
ausgeschüttelt)
□ **She shook the rug.** Sie hat den Teppich
ausgeschüttelt.
2 schütteln [34]
□ **She shook the bottle.** Sie hat die Flasche
geschüttelt.
3 zittern [88] (*tremble*)
□ **He was shaking with fear.** Er zitterte vor
Angst.
■ **to shake one's head** (*in refusal*) den Kopf
schütteln [34]
■ **to shake hands with somebody** jemandem
die Hand geben [28] □ **They shook hands.** Sie
gaben sich die Hand.

shaken ADJECTIVE
mitgenommen
□ **I was feeling a bit shaken.** Ich war etwas
mitgenommen.

shaky ADJECTIVE
zittrig (*hand, voice*)

★ **shall** VERB
■ **Shall I shut the window?** Soll ich das
Fenster zumachen?
■ **Shall we ask him to come with us?** Sollen
wir ihn fragen, ob er mitkommt?

shallow ADJECTIVE
flach (*water, pool*)

shambles SING NOUN
das Chaos *neut* (GEN des Chaos)
□ **It's a complete shambles.** Es ist ein völliges
Chaos.

★ **shame** NOUN
die Schande *fem*
□ **The shame of it!** Diese Schande!
■ **What a shame!** Wie schade!
■ **It's a shame that ...** Es ist schade, dass ...
□ **It's a shame he isn't here.** Es ist schade, dass
er nicht da ist.

★ **shampoo** NOUN
das Shampoo *neut* (PL die Shampoos)
□ **a bottle of shampoo** eine Flasche Shampoo

shandy NOUN
das Bier mit Limonade *neut*

S

DID YOU KNOW...?
Shandy is also called **das Alsterwasser** in North Germany and **der Radler** in South Germany.

shan't = shall not

★ **shape** NOUN
die Form fem

★ **share** NOUN
▷ see also **share** VERB
1 die Aktie fem (in company)
□ They've got shares in the tech company. Sie haben Aktien von dem Hightech-Unternehmen.
2 der Anteil masc (PL die Anteile) (portion)
□ I want my share. Ich will meinen Anteil.

★ to **share** VERB
▷ see also **share** NOUN
teilen [38]
□ to share a room with somebody ein Zimmer mit jemandem teilen

to **share out** VERB
verteilen [84]
□ They shared out the sweets. Sie haben die Bonbons verteilt.

shark NOUN
der Hai masc (PL die Haie)

★ **sharp** ADJECTIVE
1 scharf (razor, knife)
□ I need a sharper knife. Ich brauche ein schärferes Messer.
2 spitz (spike, point)
3 gescheit (clever)
□ She's very sharp. Sie ist sehr gescheit.
■ **at two o'clock sharp** Punkt zwei Uhr

to **shave** VERB
sich rasieren [76] (PERFECT TENSE hat sich rasiert) (have a shave)
■ **to shave one's legs** sich die Beine rasieren [76] □ I don't shave my legs. Ich rasiere mir die Beine nicht.

shaver NOUN
■ **an electric shaver** ein Elektrorasierer masc

shaving cream NOUN
die Rasiercreme fem (PL die Rasiercremes)

shaving foam NOUN
der Rasierschaum masc

★ **she** PRONOUN
sie
□ She's very nice. Sie ist sehr nett.

★ **shed** NOUN
der Schuppen masc (PL die Schuppen)

she'd = she had, she would

★ **sheep** NOUN
das Schaf neut (PL die Schafe)
□ dozens of sheep Dutzende von Schafen

sheepdog NOUN
der Schäferhund masc (PL die Schäferhunde)

sheer ADJECTIVE
rein
□ It's sheer greed. Das ist die reine Gier.

★ **sheet** NOUN
das Leintuch neut (PL die Leintücher) (on bed)
■ **a sheet of paper** ein Blatt Papier neut

shelf NOUN
das Regal neut (PL die Regale)

★ **shell** NOUN
1 die Muschel fem (on beach)
2 die Schale fem (of egg, nut)
3 die Granate fem (explosive)

she'll = she will

shellfish NOUN
das Schalentier neut (PL die Schalentiere)

shell suit NOUN
der Jogginganzug masc (PL die Jogginganzüge)

★ **shelter** NOUN
■ **to take shelter** sich unterstellen [4] □ They took shelter beneath a bridge. Sie stellten sich unter eine Brücke unter.
■ **a bus shelter** eine überdachte Bushaltestelle

shelves PL NOUN ▷ see **shelf**

shepherd NOUN
der Schäfer masc (PL die Schäfer)
die Schäferin fem

sheriff NOUN
der Sheriff masc (PL die Sheriffs)

sherry NOUN
der Sherry masc (PL die Sherrys)

she's = she is, she has

Shetland Islands PL NOUN
die Shetlandinseln fem pl

shield NOUN
der Schild masc (PL die Schilde)

shift NOUN
▷ see also **shift** VERB
die Schicht fem
□ His shift starts at eight o'clock. Seine Schicht fängt um acht Uhr an. □ the night shift die Nachtschicht
■ **to do shift work** Schicht arbeiten [2]

to **shift** VERB
▷ see also **shift** NOUN
verschieben (IMPERFECT verschob, PERFECT TENSE hat verschoben) (move)
□ I couldn't shift the wardrobe. Ich konnte den Schrank nicht verschieben.
■ **Shift yourself!** Jetzt aber los! (informal)

shifty ADJECTIVE
1 zwielichtig (person)
□ He looked shifty. Er sah zwielichtig aus.
2 unstet (eyes)

★ = core vocabulary

shin NOUN
das Schienbein neut (PLdie Schienbeine)

to **shine** VERB
scheinen [57] (IMPERFECT schien , PERFECT TENSE hat geschienen)
□ The sun was shining. Die Sonne schien.

shiny ADJECTIVE
glänzend

★ **ship** NOUN
das Schiff neut (PLdie Schiffe)

shipbuilding NOUN
der Schiffbau masc

shipwreck NOUN
der Schiffbruch masc (PLdie Schiffbrüche)
(accident)

shipwrecked ADJECTIVE
■ to be shipwrecked Schiffbruch erleiden [44]

shipyard NOUN
die Werft fem

★ **shirt** NOUN
1 das Hemd neut (PLdie Hemden) (man's)
2 die Bluse fem (woman's)

to **shiver** VERB
zittern [88]

★ **shock** NOUN
▷ see also **shock** VERB
der Schock masc (PLdie Schocks)
■ to get a shock 1 (surprise)einen Schock bekommen [40] 2 (electric)einen Schlag bekommen [40]
■ an electric shock ein elektrischer Schlag

★ to **shock** VERB
▷ see also **shock** NOUN
schockieren [76] (PERFECT TENSE hat schockiert)
(upset)
□ I was shocked by the tragedy. Ich war über die Tragödie schockiert. □ Nothing shocks me any more. Mich schockiert nichts mehr.

shocked ADJECTIVE
schockiert
□ He'll be shocked if you say that. Wenn du das sagst, wird er schockiert sein.

shocking ADJECTIVE
schockierend
□ It's shocking! Es ist schockierend! □ a shocking waste eine schockierende Verschwendung

★ **shoe** NOUN
der Schuh masc (PLdie Schuhe)

shoelace NOUN
der Schnürsenkel masc (PLdie Schnürsenkel)

shoe polish NOUN
die Schuhcreme fem (PLdie Schuhcremes)

shoe shop NOUN
das Schuhgeschäft neut (PLdie Schuhgeschäfte)

shone VERB ▷ see **shine**

shook VERB ▷ see **shake**

★ to **shoot** VERB
1 schießen (IMPERFECT schoss , PERFECT TENSE hat geschossen) (gun, in football)
□ Don't shoot! Nicht schießen!
■ to shoot at somebody auf jemanden schießen
■ He was shot in the leg. (wounded)Er wurde ins Bein getroffen.
■ to shoot an arrow einen Pfeil abschießen
2 erschießen (IMPERFECT erschoss , PERFECT TENSE hat erschossen) (kill)
□ She was shot by a police officer. Sie wurde von einer Polizistin erschossen.
■ to shoot oneself (dead)sich erschießen □ He shot himself with a revolver. Er erschoss sich mit einem Revolver.
3 drehen [38] (film)
□ The film was shot in Prague. Der Film wurde in Prag gedreht.

shooting NOUN
1 die Schüsse masc pl
□ They heard shooting. Sie hörten Schüsse.
■ a shooting eine Schießerei
2 die Jagd fem (hunting)
□ to go shooting auf die Jagd gehen

★ **shop** NOUN
das Geschäft neut (PLdie Geschäfte)
□ a sports shop ein Sportgeschäft

★ **shop assistant** NOUN
der Verkäufer masc (PLdie Verkäufer)
die Verkäuferin fem
□ She's a shop assistant. Sie ist Verkäuferin.

★ **shopkeeper** NOUN
der Ladenbesitzer masc (PLdie Ladenbesitzer)
die Ladenbesitzerin fem
□ He's a shopkeeper. Er ist Ladenbesitzer.

shoplifting NOUN
der Ladendiebstahl masc (PLdie Ladendiebstähle)

★ **shopping** NOUN
die Einkäufe masc pl (purchases)
□ Can you get the shopping from the car? Kannst du die Einkäufe aus dem Auto holen?
■ I love shopping. Ich gehe gern einkaufen.
■ to go shopping einkaufen gehen [29]
■ a shopping bag eine Einkaufstasche
■ a shopping centre ein Einkaufszentrum neut

shop window NOUN
das Schaufenster neut (PLdie Schaufenster)

shore NOUN
die Küste fem
■ on shore an Land

★ **short** ADJECTIVE
1 kurz
□ a short skirt ein kurzer Rock □ short hair kurze Haare □ a short break eine kurze Pause □ a short walk ein kurzer Spaziergang

S

Numbers in brackets refer to verb tables on pages 697 to 706.

605

shortage – shrink

■ **too short** zu kurz □ Our holiday was too short. Unser Urlaub war zu kurz.
2 klein (*person*)
□ She's quite short. Sie ist ziemlich klein.
■ **to be short of something** knapp an etwas sein [65] □ I'm short of money. Ich bin knapp an Geld.
■ **In short, the answer's no.** Kurz, die Antwort ist nein.
■ **at short notice** kurzfristig

shortage NOUN
der Mangel *masc*
□ a water shortage ein Wassermangel

short cut NOUN
die Abkürzung *fem*
□ I took a short cut. Ich habe eine Abkürzung genommen.

shorthand NOUN
das Steno *neut*

★ **shortly** ADVERB
1 bald
□ He'll be arriving shortly. Er kommt bald.
2 kurz
□ shortly after the accident kurz nach dem Unfall

shorts PL NOUN
die Shorts *pl*
□ a pair of shorts ein Paar Shorts

short-sighted ADJECTIVE
kurzsichtig

short story NOUN
die Kurzgeschichte *fem*

★ **shot** VERB ▷ *see* **shoot**

★ **shot** NOUN
1 der Schuss *masc* (GEN des Schusses, PL die Schüsse) (*gunshot*)
2 das Foto *neut* (PL die Fotos) (*photo*)
□ a shot of the church ein Foto der Kirche
3 die Spritze *fem* (*injection*)

shotgun NOUN
die Flinte *fem*

★ **should** VERB
sollen [69]
□ You should take more exercise. Du solltest mehr Sport machen.
■ **He should be there by now.** Er müsste jetzt da sein.
■ **That shouldn't be too hard.** Das dürfte nicht zu schwer sein.
■ **I should have told you before.** Ich hätte es dir vorher sagen sollen.

When 'should' means 'would' use **würde**

□ I should go if I were you. Ich würde gehen, wenn ich du wäre.
■ **I should be so lucky!** Das wäre zu schön!

★ **shoulder** NOUN
die Schulter *fem*
■ **a shoulder bag** eine Umhängetasche

shouldn't = should not

★ **to shout** VERB
▷ *see also* **shout** NOUN
schreien [62] (IMPERFECT schrie, PERFECT TENSE hat geschrien)
□ Don't shout! Schrei doch nicht so! □ 'Go away!' he shouted. 'Geh weg!' schrie er.

★ **shout** NOUN
▷ *see also* **shout** VERB
der Schrei *masc* (PL die Schreie)

shovel NOUN
die Schaufel *fem*

★ **show** NOUN
▷ *see also* **show** VERB
1 die Show *fem* (PL die Shows) (*performance*)
2 die Sendung *fem* (*programme*)
3 die Ausstellung *fem* (*exhibition*)

★ **to show** VERB
▷ *see also* **show** NOUN
1 zeigen [38]
■ **to show somebody something** jemandem etwas zeigen [38] □ Have I shown you my new trainers? Habe ich dir meine neuen Turnschuhe schon gezeigt?
2 beweisen (IMPERFECT bewies, PERFECT TENSE hat bewiesen)
□ She showed great courage. Sie hat großen Mut bewiesen.
■ **It shows.** Das sieht man. □ I've never been riding before. — It shows. Ich bin noch nie geritten. — Das sieht man.

to show off VERB
angeben [28] (*informal*)

to show up VERB
aufkreuzen [4] (*turn up*)
□ He showed up late. Er kreuzte zu spät auf.

★ **shower** NOUN
1 die Dusche *fem*
■ **to have a shower** duschen [48]
2 der Schauer *masc* (PL die Schauer) (*of rain*)

showerproof ADJECTIVE
regendicht

showing NOUN
die Vorführung *fem* (*of film*)

shown VERB ▷ *see* **show**

show-off NOUN
der Angeber *masc* (PL die Angeber)
die Angeberin *fem*

shrank VERB ▷ *see* **shrink**

to shriek VERB
kreischen [38]

shrimps PL NOUN
die Krabben *fem pl*

to shrink VERB
einlaufen [43] (PRESENT TENSE läuft ein, IMPERFECT lief ein, PERFECT TENSE ist eingelaufen) (*clothes, fabric*)

★ = core vocabulary

Shrove Tuesday NOUN
der Fastnachtsdienstag *masc*

to shrug VERB
■ **He shrugged his shoulders.** Er zuckte mit den Schultern.

shrunk VERB ▷ *see* **shrink**

to shudder VERB
sich schütteln [34]

to shuffle VERB
■ **to shuffle the cards** die Karten mischen [48]

★ **to shut** VERB
zumachen [4] (PERFECT TENSE hat zugemacht)
□ What time do you shut? Wann machen Sie zu? □ What time does the left-luggage office shut? Wann macht die Gepäckaufbewahrung zu?

to shut down VERB
schließen
□ The cinema shut down last year. Das Kino hat letztes Jahr geschlossen.

to shut up VERB
1 verschließen (*close*)
2 den Mund halten [33] (*be quiet*)
□ Shut up! Halt den Mund!

shutters PL NOUN
die Fensterläden *masc pl*

shuttle NOUN
1 das Pendelflugzeug *neut* (PL die Pendelflugzeuge) (*plane*)
2 der Pendelzug *masc* (PL die Pendelzüge) (*train*)
3 der Pendelbus *masc* (GEN des Pendelbusses, PL die Pendelbusse) (*bus*)

shuttlecock NOUN
der Federball *masc* (PL die Federbälle) (*badminton*)

shy ADJECTIVE
schüchtern

Sicily NOUN
Sizilien *neut*
■ **from Sicily** aus Sizilien
■ **to Sicily** nach Sizilien

★ **sick** ADJECTIVE
1 krank (*ill*)
□ He was sick for four days. Er war vier Tage krank.
2 übel (*joke, humour*)
□ That's really sick! Das war wirklich übel!
■ **to be sick** (*vomit*) sich übergeben [28]
■ **I feel sick.** Mir ist schlecht.
■ **to be sick of something** etwas leid sein [65]
□ I'm sick of your jokes. Ich bin deine Witze leid.

sickening ADJECTIVE
ekelhaft

sick leave NOUN
■ **to be on sick leave** krankgeschrieben sein [65] □ Rudi's on sick leave. Rudi ist krankgeschrieben.

sickness NOUN
die Krankheit *fem*

sick note NOUN
1 die Entschuldigung *fem* (*from parents*)
2 das ärztliche Attest *neut* (PL die ärztlichen Atteste) (*from doctor*)

sick pay NOUN
die Bezahlung im Krankheitsfall *fem*

★ **side** NOUN
1 die Seite *fem*
□ He was driving on the wrong side of the road. Er fuhr auf der falschen Straßenseite. □ He's on my side. Er ist auf meiner Seite.
■ **side by side** nebeneinander
■ **the side entrance** der Seiteneingang
■ **to take sides** Partei ergreifen □ She always takes your side. Sie ergreift immer für dich Partei.
2 der Rand *masc* (PL die Ränder) (*edge*)
□ by the side of the road am Straßenrand
3 das Ufer *neut* (PL die Ufer) (*of pool, river*)
□ by the side of the lake am Ufer des Sees

sideboard NOUN
die Anrichte *fem*

side effect NOUN
der Nebeneffekt *masc* (PL die Nebeneffekte)

side street NOUN
die Seitenstraße *fem*

sidewalk NOUN (US)
der Bürgersteig *masc* (PL die Bürgersteige)

sideways ADVERB
1 von der Seite (*look*)
2 zur Seite (*move, be facing*)
■ **sideways on** von der Seite

sieve NOUN
das Sieb *neut* (PL die Siebe)

sigh NOUN
▷ *see also* **sigh** VERB
der Seufzer *masc* (PL die Seufzer)

to sigh VERB
▷ *see also* **sigh** NOUN
seufzen [36]

sight NOUN
der Anblick *masc*
□ an amazing sight ein irrer Anblick
■ **in sight** in Sicht
■ **out of sight** nicht zu sehen
■ **to have poor sight** schlechte Augen haben [32]
■ **to know somebody by sight** jemanden vom Sehen kennen [39]
■ **the sights** (*tourist spots*) die Sehenswürdigkeiten □ to see the sights sich die Sehenswürdigkeiten ansehen

★ **sightseeing** NOUN
das Sightseeing *neut*
■ **to go sightseeing** Sightseeing machen [48]

S

sign – single

★ **sign** NOUN
> ▷ see also **sign** VERB
1 das Schild neut (PL die Schilder) (notice)
□ There was a big sign saying 'private'. Da war ein großes Schild, auf dem 'privat' stand.
■ **a road sign** ein Verkehrsschild
2 das Zeichen neut (PL die Zeichen) (gesture, indication)
□ There's no sign of improvement. Es gibt kein Zeichen einer Besserung.
■ **What sign are you?** (star sign) Was für ein Sternzeichen sind Sie?

★ **to sign** VERB
> ▷ see also **sign** NOUN
unterschreiben [61] (IMPERFECT unterschrieb, PERFECT TENSE hat unterschrieben)

to sign in VERB
anmelden [54] (to website)

to sign on VERB
sich arbeitslos melden [54] (as unemployed)

to sign up VERB
sich einschreiben [61] (for course)

★ **signal** NOUN
> ▷ see also **signal** VERB
das Signal neut (PL die Signale)

★ **to signal** VERB
> ▷ see also **signal** NOUN
■ **to signal to somebody** jemandem ein Zeichen geben [28]

signature NOUN
die Unterschrift fem

significance NOUN
die Bedeutung fem

★ **significant** ADJECTIVE
bedeutend

sign language NOUN
die Zeichensprache fem

signpost NOUN
der Wegweiser masc (PL die Wegweiser)

★ **silence** NOUN
die Stille fem
□ There was absolute silence. Es herrschte absolute Stille.

★ **silent** ADJECTIVE
still

silicon chip NOUN
der Siliciumchip masc (PL die Siliciumchips)

silk NOUN
> ▷ see also **silk** ADJECTIVE
die Seide fem

silk ADJECTIVE
> ▷ see also **silk** NOUN
seiden
□ a silk scarf ein seidener Schal

silky ADJECTIVE
seidig

★ **silly** ADJECTIVE
dumm
□ That's the silliest excuse I've ever heard. Das ist die dümmste Ausrede, die ich je gehört habe.

★ **silver** NOUN
das Silber neut
□ a silver medal eine Silbermedaille

★ **similar** ADJECTIVE
ähnlich
□ My sister is very similar to me. Meine Schwester ist mir sehr ähnlich.

★ **simple** ADJECTIVE
einfach
□ It's very simple. Das ist sehr einfach.

★ **simply** ADVERB
einfach
□ It's simply not possible. Es ist einfach nicht möglich.

simultaneous ADJECTIVE
gleichzeitig

sin NOUN
> ▷ see also **sin** VERB
die Sünde fem

to sin VERB
> ▷ see also **sin** NOUN
sündigen [84]

★ **since** PREPOSITION, ADVERB, CONJUNCTION
1 seit
□ since Christmas seit Weihnachten □ I haven't seen her since she left. Ich habe sie nicht gesehen, seit sie weggezogen ist.
■ **since then** seither □ I haven't seen him since then. Ich habe ihn seither nicht gesehen.
■ **ever since** seitdem
2 da (because)
□ Since you're tired, let's stay at home. Da du müde bist, bleiben wir doch zu Hause.

sincere ADJECTIVE
aufrichtig

sincerely ADVERB
■ **Yours sincerely ...** Mit freundlichen Grüßen ...

★ **to sing** VERB
singen [66] (IMPERFECT sang, PERFECT TENSE hat gesungen)
□ He sang out of tune. Er hat falsch gesungen.
□ Have you ever sung this tune before? Hast du die Melodie schon mal gesungen?

★ **singer** NOUN
der Sänger masc (PL die Sänger)
die Sängerin fem

singing NOUN
das Singen neut

★ **single** ADJECTIVE
> ▷ see also **single** NOUN
alleinstehend (without a partner)

★ = core vocabulary

single – skateboard

- **a single room** ein Einzelzimmer neut
- **not a single thing** absolut nichts

★ **single** NOUN
▷ see also **single** ADJECTIVE
die einfache Fahrkarte fem (ticket)
□ **A single to Kiel, please.** Eine einfache Fahrkarte nach Kiel, bitte.

single parent NOUN
der Alleinerziehende masc (GEN des Alleinerziehenden, PL die Alleinerziehenden)
die Alleinerziehende fem (GEN der Alleinerziehenden)
- **a single-parent family** eine Einelternteilfamilie

singles PL NOUN
das Einzel neut sing (PL die Einzel) (in tennis)
□ **the women's singles** das Dameneinzel

singular NOUN
der Singular masc (PL die Singulare)
□ **in the singular** im Singular

sinister ADJECTIVE
unheimlich

★ **sink** NOUN
▷ see also **sink** VERB
die Spüle fem

★ **to sink** VERB
▷ see also **sink** NOUN
sinken [67] (IMPERFECT sank, PERFECT TENSE ist gesunken)

★ **sir** NOUN

In German no form of address is normally used apart from Sie.

□ **Would you like to order, sir?** Möchten Sie bestellen?
- **Yes sir.** Ja.
- **Could I have your email address please, sir?** Darf ich Sie um Ihre E-Mail-Adresse bitten?

siren NOUN
die Sirene fem

★ **sister** NOUN
die Schwester fem
□ **my little sister** meine kleine Schwester □ **I wanted to speak to the sister on the ward.** Ich wollte die Stationsschwester sprechen.

sister-in-law NOUN
die Schwägerin fem

★ **to sit** VERB
1 sitzen [68] (IMPERFECT saß, PERFECT TENSE hat gesessen) (be sitting)
□ **She was sitting on the floor.** Sie saß auf dem Boden.
2 sich setzen [36] (sit down)
□ **Sit on that chair.** Setz dich auf den Stuhl.
- **to be sitting** sitzen [68]
- **to sit an exam** eine Prüfung machen [48]

to sit down VERB
sich setzen [36]

sitcom NOUN
die Situationskomödie fem

site NOUN
1 die Stätte fem
□ **an archaeological site** eine archäologische Stätte
- **the site of the accident** der Unfallort
2 der Campingplatz masc (GEN des Campingplatzes, PL die Campingplätze) (campsite)
- **a building site** eine Baustelle

sitting room NOUN
das Wohnzimmer neut (PL die Wohnzimmer)

situated ADJECTIVE
- **to be situated** liegen [46] □ **The village is situated on the side of the hill.** Das Dorf liegt am Berghang.

★ **situation** NOUN
die Situation fem

★ **six** NUMBER
sechs
□ **He's six.** Er ist sechs.

★ **sixteen** NUMBER
sechzehn
□ **He's sixteen.** Er ist sechzehn.

★ **sixteenth** ADJECTIVE
sechzehnte
□ **the sixteenth of August** der sechzehnte August

★ **sixth** ADJECTIVE
sechste
□ **the sixth floor** der sechste Stock □ **the sixth of August** der sechste August

★ **sixty** NUMBER
sechzig
□ **She's sixty.** Sie ist sechzig.

★ **size** NOUN

DID YOU KNOW...?
Germany uses the European system for clothing and shoe sizes.

1 die Größe fem (of object, clothing)
□ **What size do you take?** Welche Größe haben Sie?
- **I'm a size ten.** Ich habe Größe achtunddreißig.
2 die Schuhgröße fem (of shoes)
□ **I take size six.** Ich habe Schuhgröße neununddreißig.

to skate VERB
1 Schlittschuh laufen [43] (PRESENT TENSE läuft Schlittschuh, IMPERFECT lief Schlittschuh, PERFECT TENSE ist Schlittschuh gelaufen) (ice-skate)
2 Rollschuh laufen [43] (PRESENT TENSE läuft Rollschuh, IMPERFECT lief Rollschuh, PERFECT TENSE ist Rollschuh gelaufen) (roller-skate)

skateboard NOUN
das Skateboard neut (PL die Skateboards)

skateboarding NOUN
das Skateboardfahren *neut*
■ **to go skateboarding** Skateboard fahren
[21]

skates PL NOUN
1 die Schlittschuhe *masc pl*
2 die Rollschuhe *masc pl* (*roller skates*)

skating NOUN
1 das Schlittschuhlaufen *neut*
■ **to go skating** Schlittschuh laufen [43]
■ **a skating rink** eine Eisbahn
2 das Rollschuhlaufen *neut* (*roller-skating*)
■ **to go skating** Rollschuh laufen [43]
■ **a skating rink** eine Rollschuhbahn

skeleton NOUN
das Skelett *neut* (PL die Skelette)

sketch NOUN
▷ *see also* **sketch** VERB
die Skizze *fem* (*drawing*)

to **sketch** VERB
▷ *see also* **sketch** NOUN
skizzieren [76] (PERFECT TENSE hat skizziert)

★ to **ski** VERB
▷ *see also* **ski** NOUN
Ski fahren [21] (PRESENT TENSE fährt Ski,
IMPERFECT fuhr Ski, PERFECT TENSE ist Ski gefahren)
□ Can you ski? Kannst du Ski fahren?

★ **ski** NOUN
▷ *see also* **ski** VERB
der Ski *masc* (PL die Skier)
■ **ski boots** die Skistiefel
■ **a ski lift** ein Skilift *masc*
■ **ski pants** die Skihose *sing*
■ **a ski pole** ein Skistock *masc*
■ **a ski slope** eine Skipiste
■ **a ski suit** ein Skianzug *masc*

to **skid** VERB
schleudern [88] (PERFECT TENSE ist geschleudert)

skier NOUN
der Skifahrer *masc* (PL die Skifahrer)
die Skifahrerin *fem*

★ **skiing** NOUN
das Skifahren *neut*
■ **to go skiing** Ski fahren [21]
■ **to go on a skiing holiday** in den Skiurlaub
fahren [21]

skilful ADJECTIVE
geschickt

★ **skill** NOUN
das Können *neut*
□ a lot of skill viel Können

skilled ADJECTIVE
■ **a skilled worker** ein Facharbeiter *masc*

skimmed milk NOUN
die Magermilch *fem*

skimpy ADJECTIVE
knapp (*clothes*)

★ **skin** NOUN
die Haut *fem* (PL die Häute)
■ **skin cancer** der Hautkrebs

skinhead NOUN
der Skinhead *masc* (PL die Skinheads)

der Skinhead is also used for women.

skinny ADJECTIVE
mager

skin-tight ADJECTIVE
hauteng

skip NOUN
▷ *see also* **skip** VERB
der Container *masc* (PL die Container) (*container*)

to **skip** VERB
▷ *see also* **skip** NOUN
1 seilspringen [71] (PERFECT TENSE ist
seilgesprungen) (*with rope*)
2 auslassen [42] (PRESENT TENSE lässt aus,
IMPERFECT ließ aus, PERFECT TENSE hat
ausgelassen)
□ to skip a meal eine Mahlzeit auslassen
■ **I skipped the maths lesson.** Ich habe die
Mathestunde geschwänzt.

★ **skirt** NOUN
der Rock *masc* (PL die Röcke)

skittles SING NOUN
das Kegeln *neut*
■ **to play skittles** kegeln [88]

to **skive** VERB
faulenzen [36] (*be lazy*)

to **skive off** VERB
schwänzen [36] (*informal*)
□ to skive off school die Schule schwänzen

skull NOUN
der Schädel *masc* (PL die Schädel)

★ **sky** NOUN
der Himmel *masc* (PL die Himmel)

Skype® NOUN
▷ *see also* **Skype** VERB
Skype®

to **Skype** VERB
▷ *see also* **Skype** NOUN
skypen [38]

skyscraper NOUN
der Wolkenkratzer *masc* (PL die Wolkenkratzer)

slack ADJECTIVE
1 locker (*rope*)
2 nachlässig (*person*)

to **slag off** VERB
■ **to slag somebody off** über jemanden
herziehen [96] (*informal*) □ She's always
slagging me off. Sie zieht dauernd über mich
her.

to **slam** VERB
zuknallen [4] (PERFECT TENSE hat/ist zugeknallt)

For the perfect tense use **haben** when the verb has an object and **sein** when there is no object.

□ The door slammed. Die Tür ist zugeknallt.
□ She slammed the door. Sie hat die Tür zugeknallt.

slang NOUN
der Slang *masc* (PL die Slangs)

slap NOUN
▷ *see also* **slap** VERB
die Ohrfeige *fem*

to **slap** VERB
▷ *see also* **slap** NOUN
■ **to slap somebody** jemandem einen Klaps geben [28] □ She slapped him. Sie gab ihm einen Klaps.

slate NOUN
1 der Schiefer *masc* (PL die Schiefer)
2 der Schieferziegel *masc* (PL die Schieferziegel) (*for roof*)

sledge NOUN
der Schlitten *masc* (PL die Schlitten)

sledging NOUN
■ **to go sledging** Schlitten fahren [21]

★ **sleep** NOUN
▷ *see also* **sleep** VERB
der Schlaf *masc*
□ I need some sleep. Ich brauche Schlaf.
■ **to go to sleep** einschlafen [58]

★ to **sleep** VERB
▷ *see also* **sleep** NOUN
schlafen [58] (PRESENT TENSE schläft, IMPERFECT schlief, PERFECT TENSE hat geschlafen)
□ I couldn't sleep. Ich konnte nicht schlafen.
■ **to sleep with somebody** mit jemandem schlafen [58]

to **sleep in** VERB
verschlafen [58]

to **sleep together** VERB
miteinander schlafen [58]

★ **sleeping bag** NOUN
der Schlafsack *masc* (PL die Schlafsäcke)

sleeping car NOUN
der Schlafwagen *masc* (PL die Schlafwagen)

sleeping pill NOUN
die Schlaftablette *fem*

sleepover NOUN
die Übernachtung *fem*
■ **to have a sleepover** bei Freunden übernachten [2]

sleepy ADJECTIVE
schläfrig
■ **to feel sleepy** schläfrig sein [65] □ I was feeling sleepy. Ich war schläfrig.
■ **a sleepy little village** ein verschlafenes kleines Dorf

sleet NOUN
▷ *see also* **sleet** VERB
der Schneeregen *masc*

to **sleet** VERB
▷ *see also* **sleet** NOUN
■ **It's sleeting.** Es fällt Schneeregen.

sleeve NOUN
1 der Ärmel *masc* (PL die Ärmel)
□ long sleeves lange Ärmel □ short sleeves kurze Ärmel
2 die Hülle *fem* (*record sleeve*)

sleigh NOUN
der Pferdeschlitten *masc* (PL die Pferdeschlitten)

slept VERB ▷ *see* **sleep**

★ **slice** NOUN
▷ *see also* **slice** VERB
die Scheibe *fem*

★ to **slice** VERB
▷ *see also* **slice** NOUN
aufschneiden [60] (IMPERFECT schnitt auf, PERFECT TENSE hat aufgeschnitten)

slick NOUN
■ **an oil slick** ein Ölteppich *masc*

★ **slide** NOUN
▷ *see also* **slide** VERB
1 die Rutschbahn *fem* (*in playground*)
2 das Dia *neut* (PL die Dias) (*photo*)
3 die Klemme *fem* (*hair slide*)

★ to **slide** VERB
▷ *see also* **slide** NOUN
rutschen [48] (PERFECT TENSE ist gerutscht)

★ **slight** ADJECTIVE
klein
□ a slight problem ein kleines Problem □ a slight improvement eine kleine Verbesserung

★ **slightly** ADVERB
etwas

★ **slim** ADJECTIVE
▷ *see also* **slim** VERB
schlank

★ to **slim** VERB
▷ *see also* **slim** ADJECTIVE
abnehmen [52] (PRESENT TENSE nimmt ab, IMPERFECT nahm ab, PERFECT TENSE hat abgenommen) (*be on a diet*)
□ I'm slimming. Ich nehme gerade ab.

sling NOUN
die Schlinge *fem*
□ She had her arm in a sling. Sie hatte den Arm in der Schlinge.

★ **slip** NOUN
▷ *see also* **slip** VERB
1 der Schnitzer *masc* (PL die Schnitzer) (*mistake*)
2 der Unterrock *masc* (PL die Unterröcke) (*underskirt*)
■ **a slip of paper** ein Zettel *masc*
■ **a slip of the tongue** ein Versprecher *masc*

S

Numbers in brackets refer to verb tables on pages 697 to 706.

611

slip – smelly

★ **to slip** VERB
▷ *see also* **slip** NOUN
ausrutschen [4] (PERFECT TENSE ist ausgerutscht)
□ He slipped on the ice. Er ist auf dem Eis ausgerutscht.

to slip up VERB
einen Fehler machen [48] (*make a mistake*)

slipper NOUN
der Hausschuh *masc* (PL die Hausschuhe)
□ a pair of slippers ein Paar Hausschuhe

slippery ADJECTIVE
glatt

slip-up NOUN
der Schnitzer *masc* (PL die Schnitzer)
■ There's been a slip-up. Da ist etwas schiefgelaufen.

slope NOUN
der Abhang *masc* (PL die Abhänge)

sloppy ADJECTIVE
schlampig

slot NOUN
der Schlitz *masc* (GEN des Schlitzes, PL die Schlitze)

slot machine NOUN
1 der Geldspielautomat *masc* (GEN des Geldspielautomaten, PL die Geldspielautomaten) (*for gambling*)
2 der Automat *masc* (GEN des Automaten, PL die Automaten) (*vending machine*)

★ **slow** ADJECTIVE
langsam
□ My computer's a bit slow. Mein Computer ist etwas langsam.
■ My watch is slow. Meine Uhr geht nach.

to slow down VERB
verlangsamen [84] (PERFECT TENSE hat verlangsamt)

★ **slowly** ADVERB
langsam
■ to go slowly 1 (*person*) langsam gehen [29]
2 (*car*) langsam fahren [21]

slug NOUN
die Nacktschnecke *fem* (*animal*)

slum NOUN
der Slum *masc* (PL die Slums)

slush NOUN
der Matsch *masc*

sly ADJECTIVE
gerissen (*person*)
■ a sly smile ein verschmitztes Lächeln

smack NOUN
▷ *see also* **smack** VERB
der Klaps *masc* (GEN des Klapses, PL die Klapse) (*slap*)

to smack VERB
▷ *see also* **smack** NOUN
■ to smack somebody jemandem einen Klaps

geben [28] □ She smacked him. Sie gab ihm einen Klaps.

★ **small** ADJECTIVE
klein
■ small change das Kleingeld

BE CAREFUL!
Do not translate **small** by schmal.

WORD POWER
You can use a number of other words instead of small to mean 'little':
miniature Miniatur-
□ a miniature version eine Miniaturversion
minute winzig
□ a minute cat eine winzige Katze
tiny winzig
□ a tiny garden ein winziger Garten

★ **smart** ADJECTIVE
1 schick (*elegant*)
2 intelligent (*clever*)
□ a smart idea eine intelligente Idee

smart card NOUN
die Smartcard *fem* (PL die Smartcards)

smartphone NOUN
das Smartphone *neut* (PL die Smartphones)

★ **smash** NOUN
▷ *see also* **smash** VERB
der Zusammenstoß *masc* (GEN des Zusammenstoßes, PL die Zusammenstöße)

★ **to smash** VERB
▷ *see also* **smash** NOUN
1 kaputt machen [48] (PERFECT TENSE hat kaputt gemacht) (*break*)
□ I've smashed my watch. Ich habe meine Uhr kaputt gemacht.
2 zerbrechen [11] (PRESENT TENSE zerbricht, IMPERFECT zerbrach, PERFECT TENSE ist zerbrochen) (*get broken*)
□ The glass smashed into tiny pieces. Das Glas zerbrach in winzige Scherben.

★ **smell** NOUN
▷ *see also* **smell** VERB
der Geruch *masc* (PL die Gerüche)
■ the sense of smell der Geruchsinn

★ **to smell** VERB
▷ *see also* **smell** NOUN
1 stinken (IMPERFECT stank, PERFECT TENSE hat gestunken)
□ That old dog really smells! Der alte Hund stinkt!
■ to smell of something nach etwas riechen
□ It smells of petrol. Es riecht nach Benzin.
2 riechen (IMPERFECT roch, PERFECT TENSE hat gerochen) (*detect*)
□ I can't smell anything. Ich kann nichts riechen.

smelly ADJECTIVE
stinkend
■ He's got smelly feet. Seine Füße stinken.

★ = core vocabulary

smelt VERB ▷ see **smell**

★ **smile** NOUN
▷ see also **smile** VERB
das Lächeln neut

★ to **smile** VERB
▷ see also **smile** NOUN
lächeln [34]

smiley NOUN
das Smiley neut (PL die Smileys)

★ **smoke** NOUN
▷ see also **smoke** VERB
der Rauch masc

★ to **smoke** VERB
▷ see also **smoke** NOUN
rauchen [48]
□ I don't smoke. Ich rauche nicht. □ He smokes cigars. Er raucht Zigarren.

smoker NOUN
der Raucher masc (PL die Raucher)
die Raucherin fem

★ **smoking** NOUN
das Rauchen neut
□ to give up smoking mit dem Rauchen aufhören □ Smoking is bad for you. Rauchen schadet der Gesundheit.
■ 'no smoking' 'Rauchen verboten'

★ **smooth** ADJECTIVE
1 glatt (surface)
2 aalglatt (person)

smoothie NOUN
der Smoothie masc (PL die Smoothies)

SMS NOUN (= short message service)
die SMS fem

smudge NOUN
der Dreck masc

smug ADJECTIVE
selbstgefällig
□ He's looking smug. Er wirkt selbstgefällig.

to **smuggle** VERB
schmuggeln [34]

smuggler NOUN
der Schmuggler masc (PL die Schmuggler)
die Schmugglerin fem

smuggling NOUN
das Schmuggeln neut

snack NOUN
der Snack masc (PL die Snacks)
□ to have a snack einen Snack zu sich nehmen

snack bar NOUN
die Imbissstube fem

snail NOUN
die Schnecke fem

snake NOUN
die Schlange fem

★ to **snap** VERB
brechen [11] (PRESENT TENSE bricht, IMPERFECT brach, PERFECT TENSE ist gebrochen) (break)

□ The branch snapped. Der Zweig brach.
■ to snap one's fingers mit dem Finger schnipsen [48]

snapshot NOUN
das Foto neut (PL die Fotos)

to **snarl** VERB
knurren [38] (animal)

to **snatch** VERB
■ to snatch something from somebody jemandem etwas entreißen □ He snatched the keys from me. Er entriss mir die Schlüssel.
■ My bag was snatched. Man hat mir meine Handtasche entrissen.

to **sneak** VERB
■ to sneak in sich hineinschleichen
■ to sneak out sich hinausschleichen
■ to sneak up on somebody an jemanden heranschleichen

to **sneeze** VERB
niesen [38]

to **sniff** VERB
1 schniefen [38]
□ Stop sniffing! Hör auf zu schniefen!
2 schnüffeln [88] an +dat
□ The dog sniffed my hand. Der Hund schnüffelte an meiner Hand.

snob NOUN
der Snob masc (PL die Snobs)

der Snob is also used for women.

□ She is such a snob. Sie ist ein furchtbarer Snob.

snooker NOUN
das Snooker neut
□ to play snooker Snooker spielen

snooze NOUN
das Nickerchen neut (PL die Nickerchen)
□ to have a snooze ein Nickerchen machen

to **snore** VERB
schnarchen [48]

★ **snow** NOUN
▷ see also **snow** VERB
der Schnee masc

★ to **snow** VERB
▷ see also **snow** NOUN
schneien [38]
□ It's snowing. Es schneit.

snowball NOUN
der Schneeball masc (PL die Schneebälle)

snowboard NOUN
das Snowboard neut

snowboarding NOUN
das Snowboarding neut

snowflake NOUN
die Schneeflocke fem

snowman NOUN
der Schneemann masc (PL die Schneemänner)

S

□ **to build a snowman** einen Schneemann machen

★ **so** CONJUNCTION, ADVERB

1 also

□ The shop was closed, so I went home. Das Geschäft war zu, also ging ich nach Hause. □ It rained, so I got wet. Es hat geregnet, also bin ich nass geworden. □ So, have you always lived in Leeds? Also, hast du schon immer in Leeds gewohnt?

■ **So what?** Na und?

2 so

□ It was so heavy! Es war so schwer! □ It's not so heavy! Es ist nicht so schwer! □ He was talking so fast I couldn't understand. Er hat so schnell geredet, dass ich nichts verstanden habe. □ How's your father? — Not so good. Wie geht's deinem Vater? — Nicht so gut. □ He's like his sister but not so clever. Er ist wie seine Schwester, aber nicht so klug.

■ **so much** (a lot) so sehr □ I love you so much. Ich liebe dich so sehr!

■ **so much ...** so viel ... □ I've got so much work. Ich habe so viel Arbeit.

■ **so many ...** so viele ... □ I've got so many things to do today. Ich muss heute so viele Dinge erledigen.

■ **so do I** ich auch □ I love horses. — So do I. Ich mag Pferde. — Ich auch.

■ **so have we** wir auch □ I've been to Hamburg. — So have we. Ich war schon einmal in Hamburg. — Wir auch.

■ **I think so.** Ich glaube schon.

■ **I hope so.** Hoffentlich.

■ **That's not so.** Das ist nicht so.

■ **so far** bis jetzt □ It's been easy so far. Bis jetzt war es einfach.

■ **so far so good** so weit, so gut

■ **ten or so people** so etwa zehn Leute

■ **at five o'clock or so** so gegen fünf Uhr

to **soak** VERB

einweichen [4] (PERFECT TENSE hat eingeweicht)

soaked ADJECTIVE

völlig durchnässt

□ We were soaked. Wir waren völlig durchnässt.

soaking ADJECTIVE

völlig durchnässt

□ We were soaking. Wir waren völlig durchnässt.

■ **soaking wet** patschnass □ Your shoes are soaking wet. Deine Schuhe sind patschnass.

★ **soap** NOUN

die Seife fem

soap opera NOUN

die Seifenoper fem

soap powder NOUN

das Waschpulver neut (PL die Waschpulver)

to **sob** VERB

schluchzen [36]

□ She was sobbing. Sie schluchzte.

sober ADJECTIVE

nüchtern

to **sober up** VERB

nüchtern werden [91] (PRESENT TENSE wird nüchtern, IMPERFECT wurde nüchtern, PERFECT TENSE ist nüchtern geworden)

★ **soccer** NOUN

der Fußball masc

□ to play soccer Fußball spielen

■ **a soccer player** ein Fußballspieler masc

★ **social** ADJECTIVE

sozial

□ social problems soziale Probleme

■ **a social class** eine gesellschaftliche Schicht

■ **I have a good social life.** Ich komme viel unter Leute.

■ **social media** Social Media pl noun

socialism NOUN

der Sozialismus masc (GEN des Sozialismus)

socialist ADJECTIVE

▷ see also **socialist** NOUN

sozialistisch

socialist NOUN

▷ see also **socialist** ADJECTIVE

der Sozialist masc (GEN des Sozialisten, PL die Sozialisten)

die Sozialistin fem

□ She's a Socialist. Sie ist Sozialistin.

social networking site NOUN

das soziale Netzwerk neut

social security NOUN

1 die Sozialhilfe fem (money)

■ **to be on social security** Sozialhilfe bekommen [40]

2 die Sozialversicherung fem (organization)

social worker NOUN

der Sozialarbeiter masc (PL die Sozialarbeiter)

die Sozialarbeiterin fem

□ She's a social worker. Sie ist Sozialarbeiterin.

society NOUN

1 die Gesellschaft fem

□ We live in a multicultural society. Wir leben in einer multikulturellen Gesellschaft.

2 der Verein masc (PL die Vereine) (club)

■ **a drama society** eine Theatergruppe

sociology NOUN

die Soziologie fem

sock NOUN

die Socke fem

socket NOUN

die Steckdose fem

soda NOUN

das Sodawasser neut (PL die Sodawasser) (soda water)

soda pop NOUN (US)

die Limo fem (PL die Limos)

sofa NOUN

das Sofa neut (PL die Sofas)

★ **soft** ADJECTIVE
weich
■ **soft cheese** der Weichkäse
■ **to be soft on somebody** (*be kind to*) nachsichtig mit jemandem sein [65]
■ **a soft drink** ein alkoholfreies Getränk
■ **soft drugs** weiche Drogen
■ **a soft option** eine bequeme Lösung

★ **software** NOUN
die Software *fem*

soggy ADJECTIVE
1 nass (*soaked*)
□ a soggy tissue ein nasses Taschentuch
2 weich (*not crisp*)
□ soggy chips weiche Pommes frites

★ **soil** NOUN
der Boden *masc* (PL die Böden)

solar ADJECTIVE
■ **solar eclipse** die Sonnenfinsternis
■ **solar panel** der Sonnenkollektor

solar power NOUN
die Sonnenenergie *fem*

sold VERB ▷ see **sell**

★ **soldier** NOUN
der Soldat *masc* (GEN des Soldaten, PL die Soldaten)
die Soldatin *fem*
□ He's a soldier. Er ist Soldat.

★ **solicitor** NOUN
1 der Rechtsanwalt *masc* (PL die Rechtsanwälte)
die Rechtsanwältin *fem* (*for lawsuits*)
□ He's a solicitor. Er ist Rechtsanwalt.
2 der Notar *masc* (PL die Notare)
die Notarin *fem* (*for property, wills*)
□ She's a solicitor. Sie ist Notarin.

★ **solid** ADJECTIVE
1 stabil
□ a solid wall eine stabile Wand
2 massiv
□ solid gold massives Gold
■ **for three hours solid** drei geschlagene Stunden lang

solo NOUN
das Solo *neut* (PL die Soli)
□ a guitar solo ein Gitarrensolo

★ **solution** NOUN
die Lösung *fem*

★ **to solve** VERB
lösen [38]

★ **some** ADJECTIVE, PRONOUN
1 ein paar
> Use **ein paar** with plural nouns.
□ some nice pictures ein paar nette Bilder □ I only sold some of them. Ich habe nur ein paar verkauft.
■ **Some people say that …** Manche Leute sagen, dass …

■ **some day** eines Tages
■ **some day next week** irgendwann nächste Woche
2 einige (*some but not all*)
□ Are these mushrooms poisonous? — Only some. Sind diese Pilze giftig? — Nur einige.
■ **I only took some of it.** Ich habe nur etwas davon genommen.
■ **I'm going to buy some sweets. Do you want some too?** Ich kaufe Bonbons. Willst du auch welche?
■ **Would you like some coffee? — No thanks, I've got some.** Möchten Sie Kaffee? — Nein danke, ich habe schon welchen.

> 'some' is frequently not translated.

□ Would you like some bread? Möchtest du Brot? □ Have you got some mineral water? Haben Sie Mineralwasser?

★ **somebody** PRONOUN
jemand
□ Somebody stole my bag. Jemand hat meine Tasche gestohlen.

★ **somehow** ADVERB
irgendwie
□ I'll do it somehow. Ich mache es irgendwie.
□ Somehow I don't think he believed me. Irgendwie hat er mir anscheinend nicht geglaubt.

★ **someone** PRONOUN
jemand
□ Someone stole my bag. Jemand hat meine Tasche gestohlen.

★ **something** PRONOUN
etwas
□ something special etwas Besonderes □ Wear something warm. Zieh etwas Warmes an.
■ **That's really something!** Das ist echt toll!
■ **It cost a hundred pounds, or something like that.** Es kostet hundert Pfund, oder so in der Gegend.
■ **His name is Phil or something.** Er heißt Phil oder so ähnlich.

sometime ADVERB
mal
□ You must come and see us sometime. Du musst uns mal besuchen.
■ **sometime last month** irgendwann letzten Monat

★ **sometimes** ADVERB
manchmal
□ Sometimes I think she hates me. Manchmal denke ich, sie hasst mich.

★ **somewhere** ADVERB
irgendwo
□ I've left my keys somewhere. Ich habe irgendwo meine Schlüssel liegen lassen. □ I'd like to live somewhere sunny. Ich würde gern irgendwo leben, wo es sonnig ist.

★ **son** NOUN
der Sohn *masc* (PL die Söhne)

★ **song** NOUN
das Lied *neut* (PL die Lieder)

son-in-law NOUN
der Schwiegersohn *masc* (PL die Schwiegersöhne)

★ **soon** ADVERB
bald
□ very soon sehr bald
■ **soon afterwards** kurz danach
■ **as soon as possible** sobald wie möglich

sooner ADVERB
früher
□ a bit sooner etwas früher □ sooner or later früher oder später

soot NOUN
der Ruß *masc*

soppy ADJECTIVE
sentimental

soprano NOUN
der Sopran *masc* (PL die Soprane)

sorcerer NOUN
der böse Zauberer *masc* (PL die bösen Zauberer)

sore ADJECTIVE
▷ see also **sore** NOUN
■ It's sore. Es tut weh.
■ **My feet are sore** Meine Füße tun weh.
■ **That's a sore point.** Das ist ein wunder Punkt.

sore NOUN
▷ see also **sore** ADJECTIVE
die Wunde *fem*

★ **sorry** ADJECTIVE
■ I'm really sorry. Es tut mir wirklich leid.
□ I'm sorry, I haven't got any change. Es tut mir leid, aber ich habe kein Kleingeld. □ I'm sorry I'm late. Es tut mir leid, dass ich zu spät komme.
□ I'm sorry about the noise. Es tut mir leid wegen des Lärms. □ You'll be sorry! Das wird dir leidtun!
■ **Sorry!** Entschuldigung!
■ **Sorry?** Wie bitte?
■ **I feel sorry for her.** Sie tut mir leid.

★ **sort** NOUN
die Art *fem*
□ There are different sorts of mushrooms. Es gibt verschiedene Arten von Pilzen.
■ **what sort of ...** 1 was für ein ... □ What sort of cake is that? Was für ein Kuchen ist das?
□ What sort of bike have you got? Was für ein Fahrrad hast du? 2 was für eine ... □ What sort of school do you go to? In was für eine Schule gehst du?

to sort out VERB
1 sortieren [76] (PERFECT TENSE hat sortiert) (*objects*)
2 lösen [38] (*problems*)

so-so ADVERB
so lala (*informal*)
□ How are you feeling? — So-so. Wie geht's dir? — So lala.

soul NOUN
1 die Seele *fem* (*spirit*)
2 der Soul *masc* (*music*)

★ **sound** NOUN
▷ see also **sound** VERB, ADJECTIVE, ADVERB
1 das Geräusch *neut* (PL die Geräusche) (*noise*)
■ **Don't make a sound!** Still!
■ **I heard the sound of footsteps.** Ich hörte Schritte.
2 die Lautstärke *fem*
□ Can I turn the sound down? Kann ich die Lautstärke runterdrehen?

★ **to sound** VERB
▷ see also **sound** NOUN, ADJECTIVE, ADVERB
klingen (IMPERFECT klang, PERFECT TENSE hat geklungen)
□ That sounds interesting. Das klingt interessant.
■ **It sounds as if she's doing well at school.** Allem Anschein nach ist sie gut in der Schule.
■ **That sounds like a good idea.** Das scheint eine gute Idee zu sein.

★ **sound** ADJECTIVE, ADVERB
▷ see also **sound** NOUN, VERB
gut
□ That's sound advice. Das ist ein guter Rat.
■ **to be sound asleep** fest schlafen [58]

soundtrack NOUN
der Soundtrack *masc* (PL die Soundtracks)

★ **soup** NOUN
die Suppe *fem*
□ vegetable soup die Gemüsesuppe

sour ADJECTIVE
sauer

★ **south** ADJECTIVE, ADVERB
▷ see also **south** NOUN
nach Süden
□ We were travelling south. Wir sind nach Süden gefahren.
■ **the south coast** die Südküste
■ **a south wind** ein Südwind *masc*
■ **south of** südlich von □ It's south of London. Es liegt südlich von London.

★ **south** NOUN
▷ see also **south** ADJECTIVE, ADVERB
der Süden *masc*
□ in the south im Süden
■ **in the south of Germany** in Süddeutschland

South Africa NOUN
Südafrika *neut*
■ **from South Africa** aus Südafrika
■ **to South Africa** nach Südafrika

South America NOUN
Südamerika *neut*

★ = core vocabulary

■ **from South America** aus Südamerika
■ **to South America** nach Südamerika

South American NOUN
▷ *see also* **South American** ADJECTIVE
der Südamerikaner *masc* (PL die Südamerikaner)
die Südamerikanerin *fem*

South American ADJECTIVE
▷ *see also* **South American** NOUN
südamerikanisch

southbound ADJECTIVE
in Richtung Süden
□ southbound traffic der Verkehr in Richtung Süden

southeast NOUN
der Südosten *masc*
■ **Southeast Asia** Südostasien *neut*

★ **southern** ADJECTIVE
südlich
□ the southern part of the island der südliche Teil der Insel
■ **southern England** Südengland *neut*

South Pole NOUN
der Südpol *masc*

South Wales NOUN
Südwales *neut*
■ **to South Wales** nach Südwales

southwest NOUN
der Südwesten *masc*
■ **southwest Germany** Südwestdeutschland *neut*

souvenir NOUN
das Souvenir *neut* (PL die Souvenirs)
□ a souvenir shop ein Souvenirgeschäft

soya NOUN
die Soja *fem*

soy sauce NOUN
die Sojasoße *fem*

★ **space** NOUN
1 der Platz *masc* (GEN des Platzes)
□ There's enough space. Es ist genug Platz da.
■ **a parking space** ein Parkplatz
2 der Raum *masc* (*outer space*)

spacecraft NOUN
das Raumschiff *neut* (PL die Raumschiffe)

spade NOUN
der Spaten *masc* (PL die Spaten)
■ **spades** (*in cards*) das Pik □ the ace of spades das Pikass

★ **Spain** NOUN
Spanien *neut*
■ **from Spain** aus Spanien
■ **in Spain** in Spanien
■ **to Spain** nach Spanien

★ **Spaniard** NOUN
der Spanier *masc* (PL die Spanier)
die Spanierin *fem*

spaniel NOUN
der Spaniel *masc* (PL die Spaniel)

★ **Spanish** ADJECTIVE
▷ *see also* **Spanish** NOUN
spanisch
■ **He's Spanish.** Er ist Spanier.
■ **She's Spanish.** Sie ist Spanierin.

★ **Spanish** NOUN
▷ *see also* **Spanish** ADJECTIVE
das Spanisch *neut* (GEN des Spanischen) (*language*)
■ **the Spanish** die Spanier *masc pl*

to spank VERB
■ **to spank somebody** jemandem den Hintern versohlen [84]

spanner NOUN
der Schraubenschlüssel *masc* (PL die Schraubenschlüssel)

★ **to spare** VERB
▷ *see also* **spare** ADJECTIVE, NOUN
■ **Can you spare a moment?** Hast du mal einen Moment Zeit?
■ **I can't spare the time.** Ich habe die Zeit nicht.
■ **There's no room to spare.** Es ist kein Platz übrig.
■ **We arrived with time to spare.** Wir waren zu früh da.

BE CAREFUL!
Do not translate **to spare** by **sparen**.

★ **spare** NOUN
▷ *see also* **spare** ADJECTIVE, VERB
das Ersatzteil *neut* (PL die Ersatzteile)
■ **I've lost my key. — Have you got a spare?** Ich habe meinen Schlüssel verloren. — Hast du einen Ersatzschlüssel?

★ **spare** ADJECTIVE
▷ *see also* **spare** VERB, NOUN
■ **spare batteries** die Ersatzbatterien *fem pl*
■ **a spare part** ein Ersatzteil *neut*
■ **a spare room** ein Gästezimmer *neut*
■ **spare time** die Freizeit □ What do you do in your spare time? Was machen Sie in Ihrer Freizeit?
■ **spare wheel** das Reserverad

sparkling ADJECTIVE
mit Kohlensäure (*water*)
■ **sparkling wine** der Sekt

sparrow NOUN
der Spatz *masc* (GEN des Spatzen, PL die Spatzen)

spat VERB ▷ *see* **spit**

★ **to speak** VERB
sprechen [70] (PRESENT TENSE spricht, IMPERFECT sprach, PERFECT TENSE hat gesprochen)
□ Do you speak English? Sprechen Sie Englisch?
■ **to speak to somebody** mit jemandem reden [54] □ Have you spoken to him? Hast du mit ihm geredet? □ She spoke to him about it. Sie hat mit ihm darüber geredet.
■ **spoken German** gesprochenes Deutsch

speaker – spelt

to speak up VERB
lauter sprechen [70] (PRESENT TENSE spricht, IMPERFECT sprach, PERFECT TENSE hat gesprochen)
□ Speak up, we can't hear you. Sprechen Sie lauter, wir können Sie nicht hören.

★ **speaker** NOUN
1 der Lautsprecher *masc* (PL die Lautsprecher) (*loudspeaker*)
2 der Redner *masc* (PL die Redner) die Rednerin *fem* (*in debate*)

★ **special** ADJECTIVE
besondere
□ a special occasion ein besonderer Anlass

★ **specialist** NOUN
der Fachmann *masc* (PL die Fachleute) die Fachfrau *fem*

speciality NOUN
die Spezialität *fem*

★ **to specialize** VERB
sich spezialisieren [76] (PERFECT TENSE hat sich spezialisiert)
□ We specialize in skiing equipment. Wir haben uns auf Skiausrüstung spezialisiert.

specially ADVERB
1 besonders
□ It can be very cold here, specially in winter. Es kann hier sehr kalt werden, besonders im Winter.
2 speziell
□ It's specially designed for teenagers. Das ist speziell für Teenager gedacht.
■ **not specially** nicht besonders □ Do you like tennis? — Not specially. Magst du Tennis? — Nicht besonders.

★ **species** SING NOUN
die Art *fem*

★ **specific** ADJECTIVE
1 speziell (*particular*)
□ certain specific issues gewisse spezielle Fragen
2 genau (*precise*)
□ Could you be more specific? Könnten Sie sich etwas genauer ausdrücken?

★ **specifically** ADVERB
1 extra
□ It's specifically designed for teenagers. Es ist extra für Teenager gedacht.
2 genau
□ in Britain, or more specifically in England in Großbritannien, oder genauer gesagt in England □ I specifically said that ... Ich habe ganz genau gesagt, dass ...

specs PL NOUN
die Brille *fem sing*
□ a pair of specs eine Brille

spectacles PL NOUN
die Brille *fem sing*
□ a pair of spectacles eine Brille

★ **spectacular** ADJECTIVE
spektakulär

spectator NOUN
der Zuschauer *masc* (PL die Zuschauer) die Zuschauerin *fem*

★ **speech** NOUN
die Rede *fem*
□ to make a speech eine Rede halten

speechless ADJECTIVE
sprachlos
□ speechless with admiration sprachlos vor Bewunderung □ I was speechless. Ich war sprachlos.

★ **speed** NOUN
1 der Gang *masc* (PL die Gänge)
■ a ten-speed bike ein Zehngangrad *neut*
2 die Geschwindigkeit *fem*
□ at top speed mit Höchstgeschwindigkeit

to speed up VERB
schneller werden [91]

speedboat NOUN
das Schnellboot *neut* (PL die Schnellboote)

speeding NOUN
das zu schnelle Fahren *neut*
□ He was fined for speeding. Er hat wegen zu schnellen Fahrens einen Strafzettel bekommen.

speed limit NOUN
die Geschwindigkeitsbegrenzung *fem*
□ to break the speed limit die Geschwindigkeitsbegrenzung überschreiten

speedometer NOUN
der Tachometer *masc* (PL die Tachometer)

★ **to spell** VERB
▷ *see also* **spell** NOUN
1 schreiben [61] (IMPERFECT schrieb, PERFECT TENSE hat geschrieben) (*in writing*)
□ How do you spell that? Wie schreibt man das?
2 buchstabieren [76] (PERFECT TENSE hat buchstabiert) (*out loud*)
□ Can you spell that please? Können Sie das bitte buchstabieren?
■ **I can't spell.** Ich kann keine Rechtschreibung.

★ **spell** NOUN
▷ *see also* **spell** VERB
■ **to cast a spell on somebody** jemanden verhexen [7]
■ **to be under somebody's spell** von jemandem wie verzaubert sein [65]

spelling NOUN
die Rechtschreibung *fem*
□ My spelling is terrible. Meine Rechtschreibung ist furchtbar.
■ **a spelling mistake** ein Rechtschreibfehler *masc*

spelt VERB ▷ *see* **spell**

★ = core vocabulary

to spend VERB
1 ausgeben [28] (PRESENT TENSE gibt aus, IMPERFECT gab aus, PERFECT TENSE hat ausgegeben) (money)
2 verbringen [13] (IMPERFECT verbrachte, PERFECT TENSE hat verbracht) (time)
□ He spent a month in Italy. Er verbrachte einen Monat in Italien.

BE CAREFUL!
Do not translate **to spend** by spenden.

spice NOUN
das Gewürz neut (GEN des Gewürzes, PL die Gewürze)

spicy ADJECTIVE
scharf
□ Indian food's much spicier than German food. Indisches Essen ist viel schärfer als deutsches.

spider NOUN
die Spinne fem

to spill VERB
verschütten [7] (PERFECT TENSE hat verschüttet) (tip over)
□ He spilled his coffee. Er hat seinen Kaffee verschüttet.
■ **to get spilt** verschüttet werden [91]

spinach NOUN
der Spinat masc

spin drier NOUN
die Schleuder fem

spine NOUN
das Rückgrat neut (PL die Rückgrate)

spire NOUN
der Kirchturm masc (PL die Kirchtürme)

spirit NOUN
1 der Mut masc (courage)
2 die Energie fem (energy)
■ **to be in good spirits** gut gelaunt sein [65]

spirits PL NOUN
die Spirituosen pl

spiritual ADJECTIVE
geistlich
□ the spiritual leader of Tibet der geistliche Führer Tibets

to spit VERB
spucken [38]
■ **to spit something out** etwas ausspucken [4]
■ **It's spitting.** Es tröpfelt.

spite NOUN
▷ see also **spite** VERB
■ **in spite of** trotz □ in spite of the bad weather trotz des schlechten Wetters
■ **out of spite** aus Gehässigkeit

to spite VERB
▷ see also **spite** NOUN
ärgern [88]
□ He just did it to spite me. Er tat es nur, um mich zu ärgern.

spiteful ADJECTIVE
1 gemein (action)
2 gehässig (person)

to splash VERB
▷ see also **splash** NOUN
bespritzen [7] (PERFECT TENSE hat bespritzt)
□ Don't splash me! Bespritz mich nicht!

splash NOUN
▷ see also **splash** VERB
der Platsch masc
□ I heard a splash. Ich hörte einen Platsch.
■ **a splash of colour** ein Farbfleck masc

splendid ADJECTIVE
wunderbar

splint NOUN
die Schiene fem

splinter NOUN
der Splitter masc (PL die Splitter)

to split VERB
1 zerteilen [95] (PERFECT TENSE hat zerteilt)
□ He split the wood with an axe. Er zerteilte das Holz mit einer Axt.
2 zerbrechen [11] (PRESENT TENSE zerbricht, IMPERFECT zerbrach, PERFECT TENSE ist zerbrochen)
□ The ship hit a rock and split in two. Das Schiff lief auf einen Fels auf und zerbrach in zwei Teile.
3 teilen [38] (divide up)
□ They split the profits. Sie teilten den Gewinn.

to split up VERB
1 sich trennen [38] (couple)
2 sich auflösen [4] (group)

to spoil VERB
1 verderben (PRESENT TENSE verdirbt, IMPERFECT verdarb, PERFECT TENSE hat verdorben)
□ It spoiled our evening. Es hat uns den Abend verdorben.
2 verwöhnen [84] (PERFECT TENSE hat verwöhnt) (child)

spoiled ADJECTIVE
verwöhnt
□ a spoiled child ein verwöhntes Kind

spoilsport NOUN
der Spielverderber masc (PL die Spielverderber)
die Spielverderberin fem

spoilt VERB ▷ see **spoil**

spoilt ADJECTIVE
verwöhnt
□ a spoilt child ein verwöhntes Kind

spoke VERB ▷ see **speak**

spoke NOUN
die Speiche fem (of wheel)

spoken VERB ▷ see **speak**

spokesman NOUN
der Sprecher masc (PL die Sprecher)

spokeswoman NOUN
die Sprecherin fem

Numbers in brackets refer to verb tables on pages 697 to 706.

619

sponge NOUN
der Schwamm *masc* (PL die Schwämme)
■ **a sponge cake** ein Rührkuchen *masc*

★ **sponsor** NOUN
▷ *see also* **sponsor** VERB
der Sponsor *masc* (PL die Sponsoren)
die Sponsorin *fem*

★ to **sponsor** VERB
▷ *see also* **sponsor** NOUN
sponsern [88]
□ The festival was sponsored by ... Das Festival wurde gesponsert von ...

spontaneous ADJECTIVE
spontan

spooky ADJECTIVE
1 gruselig (*eerie*)
□ a spooky story eine gruselige Geschichte
2 komisch (*strange*)
□ a spooky coincidence ein komischer Zufall

★ **spoon** NOUN
der Löffel *masc* (PL die Löffel)
□ a spoon of sugar ein Löffel Zucker

spoonful NOUN
■ **a spoonful of soup** ein Löffel Suppe

★ **sport** NOUN
der Sport *masc*
□ What's your favourite sport? Was ist dein Lieblingssport?
■ **a sports bag** eine Sporttasche
■ **a sports car** ein Sportwagen *masc*

sportsman NOUN
der Sportler *masc* (PL die Sportler)

sportswear NOUN
die Sportkleidung *fem*

sportswoman NOUN
die Sportlerin *fem*

sporty ADJECTIVE
sportlich
□ I'm not very sporty. Ich bin nicht besonders sportlich.

★ **spot** NOUN
▷ *see also* **spot** VERB
1 der Fleck *masc* (PL die Flecke) (*mark*)
□ There's a spot of blood on your shirt. Du hast einen Blutfleck auf dem Hemd.
2 der Punkt *masc* (PL die Punkte) (*in pattern*)
□ a red dress with white spots ein rotes Kleid mit weißen Punkten
3 der Pickel *masc* (PL die Pickel) (*pimple*)
□ I've got a big spot on my chin. Ich habe einen großen Pickel am Kinn.
4 der Platz *masc* (GEN des Platzes, PL die Plätze) (*place*)
□ It's a lovely spot for a picnic. Es ist ein herrlicher Platz für ein Picknick.
■ **on the spot 1** (*immediately*) sofort □ They gave her the job on the spot. Sie haben ihr den

Job sofort gegeben. **2** (*at the same place*) an Ort und Stelle □ They were able to repair the car on the spot. Sie konnten das Auto an Ort und Stelle reparieren.

★ to **spot** VERB
▷ *see also* **spot** NOUN
entdecken [18] (PERFECT TENSE hat entdeckt)
□ I spotted Ossi. Ich habe Ossi entdeckt.

spotless ADJECTIVE
makellos

spotlight NOUN
das Scheinwerferlicht *neut*

spotty ADJECTIVE
pickelig (*pimply*)

spouse NOUN
der Ehemann *masc* (PL die Ehemänner)
die Ehefrau *fem*

to **sprain** VERB
▷ *see also* **sprain** NOUN
■ **I've sprained my ankle.** Ich habe mir den Fuß verstaucht.

sprain NOUN
▷ *see also* **sprain** VERB
die Verstauchung *fem*
□ It's just a sprain. Es ist nur eine Verstauchung.

★ **spray** NOUN
▷ *see also* **spray** VERB
das Spray *neut* (PL die Sprays)
■ **hair spray** das Haarspray

★ to **spray** VERB
▷ *see also* **spray** NOUN
sprühen [38]
□ to spray perfume on one's wrist sich Parfüm auf das Handgelenk sprühen □ Somebody had sprayed graffiti on the wall. Irgendjemand hatte Graffiti auf die Wand gesprüht.

★ **spread** NOUN
▷ *see also* **spread** VERB
■ **cheese spread** der Streichkäse
■ **chocolate spread** der Schokoladenaufstrich

★ to **spread** VERB
▷ *see also* **spread** NOUN
1 streichen (IMPERFECT strich, PERFECT TENSE hat gestrichen)
□ to spread butter on a cracker Butter auf einen Cracker streichen
2 sich verbreiten [2] (PERFECT TENSE hat sich verbreitet) (*disease, news*)
□ The news spread rapidly. Die Nachricht verbreitete sich schnell.

to **spread out** VERB
sich verteilen [84] (*people*)
□ They spread out across the field. Sie verteilten sich über das Feld.

spreadsheet NOUN
die Tabellenkalkulation *fem* (*computer program*)

★ = core vocabulary

spring NOUN
1 der Frühling *masc* (PL die Frühlinge) (*season*)
□ in spring im Frühling
2 die Feder *fem* (*metal coil*)
3 die Quelle *fem* (*water hole*)

spring-cleaning NOUN
der Frühjahrsputz *masc* (GEN des Frühjahrsputzes)

springtime NOUN
das Frühjahr *neut* (PL die Frühjahre)
□ in springtime im Frühjahr

sprinkler NOUN
der Rasensprenger *masc* (PL die Rasensprenger) (*for lawn*)

sprint NOUN
▷ *see also* **sprint** VERB
der Sprint *masc* (PL die Sprints)
■ a hundred-metre sprint ein Einhundertmeterlauf *masc*

to sprint VERB
▷ *see also* **sprint** NOUN
rennen [55] (IMPERFECT rannte, PERFECT TENSE ist gerannt)
□ She sprinted for the bus. Sie rannte, um den Bus zu erreichen.

sprinter NOUN
der Sprinter *masc* (PL die Sprinter)
die Sprinterin *fem*

sprouts PL NOUN
■ Brussels sprouts der Rosenkohl *sing*

spy NOUN
▷ *see also* **spy** VERB
der Spion *masc* (PL die Spione)
die Spionin *fem*

to spy VERB
▷ *see also* **spy** NOUN
■ to spy on somebody jemandem nachspionieren [4] □ She's spying on me. Sie spioniert mir nach.

spying NOUN
die Spionage *fem*

to squabble VERB
sich kabbeln [34]
□ Stop squabbling! Hört auf, euch zu kabbeln!

★ **square** NOUN
▷ *see also* **square** ADJECTIVE
1 das Quadrat *neut* (PL die Quadrate)
□ a square and a triangle ein Quadrat und ein Dreieck
2 der Platz *masc* (GEN des Platzes, PL die Plätze)
□ the town square der Rathausplatz

★ **square** ADJECTIVE
▷ *see also* **square** NOUN
■ two square metres zwei Quadratmeter
■ It's two metres square. Es misst zwei mal zwei Meter.

squash NOUN
▷ *see also* **squash** VERB
das Squash *neut* (*sport*)
□ I play squash. Ich spiele Squash.
■ a squash court ein Squashcourt *masc*
■ a squash racket ein Squashschläger *masc*
■ orange squash das Orangen-Fruchtsaftgetränk

to squash VERB
▷ *see also* **squash** NOUN
zerdrücken [95] (PERFECT TENSE hat zerdrückt)
□ You're squashing me. Du zerdrückst mich.

to squeak VERB
1 quieksen [48] (*mouse, child*)
2 quietschen [48] (*creak*)

★ **to squeeze** VERB
1 pressen [31] (*fruit, toothpaste*)
2 drücken [38] (*hand, arm*)
□ to squeeze somebody's arm jemandem den Arm drücken
■ It was a tiny room but we all managed to squeeze in. Der Raum war winzig, aber wir haben uns alle hineingezwängt.
■ I can squeeze you in at 2 o'clock. Ich kann Sie um 2 Uhr einschieben.

to squint VERB
▷ *see also* **squint** NOUN
schielen [38]

squint NOUN
▷ *see also* **squint** VERB
■ He has a squint. Er schielt.

★ **squirrel** NOUN
das Eichhörnchen *neut* (PL die Eichhörnchen)

to stab VERB
■ to stab somebody 1 (*wound*) jemanden mit dem Messer verletzen [36] 2 (*kill*) jemanden erstechen

★ **stable** NOUN
▷ *see also* **stable** ADJECTIVE
der Stall *masc* (PL die Ställe)

★ **stable** ADJECTIVE
▷ *see also* **stable** NOUN
stabil
□ a stable relationship eine stabile Beziehung

stack NOUN
der Stapel *masc* (PL die Stapel)
□ a stack of books ein Stapel Bücher

★ **stadium** NOUN
das Stadion *neut* (PL die Stadien)

★ **staff** NOUN
1 die Belegschaft *fem* (*in company*)
2 die Lehrerschaft *fem* (*in school*)

★ **stage** NOUN
1 die Bühne *fem* (*in plays*)
2 das Podium *neut* (PL die Podien) (*for speeches, lectures*)

■ **at this stage 1** an diesem Punkt □ at this stage in the negotiations an diesem Punkt der Verhandlungen **2** im Augenblick □ At this stage, we can't be sure. Im Augenblick können wir noch nicht sicher sein.
■ **to do something in stages** etwas in Etappen machen [48]

to **stagger** VERB
taumeln [88] (PERFECT TENSE ist getaumelt)

stain NOUN
▷ *see also* **stain** VERB
der Fleck *masc* (PL die Flecke)

to **stain** VERB
▷ *see also* **stain** NOUN
beflecken [7] (PERFECT TENSE hat befleckt)

stainless steel NOUN
der Edelstahl *masc*

stain remover NOUN
der Fleckenentferner *masc* (PL die Fleckenentferner)

stair NOUN
die Stufe *fem* (step)

staircase NOUN
die Treppe *fem*

★ **stairs** PL NOUN
die Treppe *fem sing*

stale ADJECTIVE
altbacken (bread)

stalemate NOUN
das Patt *neut* (PL die Patts) (in chess)

stall NOUN
der Stand *masc* (PL die Stände)
□ He's got a market stall. Er hat einen Marktstand.
■ **the stalls** (in theatre) das Parkett *sing*

stamina NOUN
das Durchhaltevermögen *neut*

stammer NOUN
das Stottern *neut*
■ **He's got a stammer.** Er stottert.

★ to **stamp** VERB
▷ *see also* **stamp** NOUN
abstempeln [4] (PERFECT TENSE hat abgestempelt) (passport)
■ **to stamp one's foot** mit dem Fuß aufstampfen [4]

★ **stamp** NOUN
▷ *see also* **stamp** VERB
1 die Briefmarke *fem*
□ I need a stamp. Ich brauche eine Briefmarke.
□ a stamp album ein Briefmarkenalbum □ a stamp collection eine Briefmarkensammlung
2 der Stempel *masc* (PL die Stempel) (rubber stamp)

stamped ADJECTIVE
■ **a stamped addressed envelope** ein frankierter und adressierter Rückumschlag

★ to **stand** VERB
1 stehen [72] (IMPERFECT stand, PERFECT TENSE hat gestanden) (be standing)
□ He was standing by the door. Er stand an der Tür.
2 aufstehen [72] (PERFECT TENSE ist aufgestanden) (stand up)
3 aushalten [33] (PRESENT TENSE hält aus, IMPERFECT hielt aus, PERFECT TENSE hat ausgehalten) (tolerate, withstand)
□ I can't stand all this noise. Ich halte diesen Lärm nicht aus.

to **stand for** VERB
1 stehen [72] für (be short for)
□ 'DM' stands for 'Direct Message'. 'DM' steht für 'direct message'.
2 dulden [54] (tolerate)
□ I won't stand for it! Ich dulde das nicht!
■ **to stand in for somebody** jemanden vertreten [79]

to **stand out** VERB
herausragen [15]

to **stand up** VERB
aufstehen [72] (get up)
■ **to stand up for** eintreten [79] für □ Stand up for your rights! Tretet für eure Rechte ein!

★ **standard** ADJECTIVE
▷ *see also* **standard** NOUN
normal
□ the standard procedure die normale Vorgehensweise
■ **standard German** das Hochdeutsch
■ **standard equipment** die Standardausrüstung

★ **standard** NOUN
▷ *see also* **standard** ADJECTIVE
das Niveau *neut* (PL die Niveaus)
□ The standard is very high. Das Niveau ist sehr hoch.
■ **the standard of living** der Lebensstandard
■ **She's got high standards.** Sie hat hohe Ansprüche.

stand-by ticket NOUN
das Stand-by-Ticket *neut* (PL die Stand-by-Tickets)

standpoint NOUN
der Standpunkt *masc* (PL die Standpunkte)

stands PL NOUN
die Tribüne *fem sing* (at sports ground)

stank VERB ▷ *see* **stink**

staple NOUN
▷ *see also* **staple** VERB
die Heftklammer *fem*

to **staple** VERB
▷ *see also* **staple** NOUN
zusammenheften [4] (PERFECT TENSE hat zusammengeheftet)

★ = core vocabulary

stapler NOUN
die Heftmaschine *fem*

★ **star** NOUN
▷ *see also* **star** VERB
1 der Stern *masc* (PL die Sterne) (*in sky*)
2 der Star *masc* (PL die Stars) (*celebrity*)

der Star is also used for women.

□ She's a TV star. Sie ist ein Fernsehstar.
■ **the stars** (*horoscope*) die Sterne

★ to **star** VERB
▷ *see also* **star** NOUN
die Hauptrolle spielen [38]
□ The film stars Kristen Stewart. Kristen Stewart spielt in dem Film die Hauptrolle.
■ **... starring Viola Davis** ... mit Viola Davis in der Hauptrolle

★ to **stare** VERB
■ **to stare at something** etwas anstarren [4]

stark ADVERB
■ **stark naked** splitternackt

★ **start** NOUN
▷ *see also* **start** VERB
1 der Anfang *masc* (PL die Anfänge)
□ It's not much, but it's a start. Es ist nicht viel, aber es ist immerhin ein Anfang.
■ **Shall we make a start on the washing-up?** Sollen wir den Abwasch in Angriff nehmen?
2 der Start *masc* (PL die Starts) (*of race*)

★ to **start** VERB
▷ *see also* **start** NOUN
1 anfangen [23] (PRESENT TENSE fängt an, IMPERFECT fing an, PERFECT TENSE hat angefangen)
□ What time does it start? Wann fängt es an?
■ **to start doing something** anfangen [23], etwas zu tun □ I started learning German three years ago. Ich habe vor drei Jahren angefangen, Deutsch zu lernen.
2 gründen [54] (*organization*)
□ He wants to start his own business. Er möchte ein eigenes Geschäft gründen.
3 ins Leben rufen [56] (IMPERFECT rief ins Leben, PERFECT TENSE hat ins Leben gerufen) (*campaign*)
□ She started the campaign. Sie hat die Kampagne ins Leben gerufen.
4 anlassen [42] (PRESENT TENSE lässt an, IMPERFECT ließ an, PERFECT TENSE hat angelassen) (*car*)
□ He couldn't start the car. Er konnte das Auto nicht anlassen.
■ **The car wouldn't start.** Das Auto ist nicht angesprungen.

to **start off** VERB
beginnen [5]
□ Things started off badly. Die ganze Sache begann schlecht. □ Let's start off with a reminder of what we did last week. Beginnen wir mit der Erinnerung, was wir letzte Woche gemacht haben.

starter NOUN
die Vorspeise *fem* (*first course*)

to **starve** VERB
verhungern [88] (PERFECT TENSE ist verhungert) (*die*)
□ People were literally starving. Die Menschen sind förmlich verhungert.
■ **I'm starving!** Ich bin am Verhungern!
■ **They starved us in prison.** Sie ließen uns im Gefängnis hungern.

★ **state** NOUN
▷ *see also* **state** VERB
1 der Zustand *masc* (PL die Zustände)
■ **He was in a real state.** (*upset*) Er ist fast durchgedreht.
2 der Staat *masc* (*government*)
■ **the States** (*USA*) die Staaten □ in the States in den Staaten

★ to **state** VERB
▷ *see also* **state** NOUN
1 erklären [19] (PERFECT TENSE hat erklärt) (*say*)
■ **She stated her opinion.** Sie sagte ihre Meinung.
2 angeben [28] (PRESENT TENSE gibt an, IMPERFECT gab an, PERFECT TENSE hat angegeben) (*give*)
□ Please state your name and address. Geben Sie bitte Ihren Namen und Ihre Adresse an.

stately home NOUN
das Schloss *neut* (GEN des Schlosses, PL die Schlösser)

★ **statement** NOUN
die Erklärung *fem*

★ **station** NOUN
der Bahnhof *masc* (PL die Bahnhöfe) (*railway*)
■ **the bus station** der Busbahnhof
■ **a police station** eine Polizeiwache
■ **a radio station** ein Rundfunksender *masc*

stationer's NOUN
das Schreibwarengeschäft *neut* (PL die Schreibwarengeschäfte)

station wagon NOUN (US)
der Kombiwagen *masc* (PL die Kombiwagen)

statue NOUN
die Statue *fem*

status NOUN
der Status *masc* (PL die Status)

★ to **stay** VERB
▷ *see also* **stay** NOUN
1 bleiben [10] (IMPERFECT blieb, PERFECT TENSE ist geblieben) (*remain*)
□ Stay here! Bleiben Sie hier!
2 übernachten [2] (PERFECT TENSE hat übernachtet) (*spend the night*)
□ to stay with friends bei Freunden übernachten
■ **Where are you staying?** Wo wohnen Sie?
■ **to stay the night** über Nacht bleiben [10]
■ **We stayed in Belgium for a few days.** Wir waren ein paar Tage in Belgien.

stay – stiff

to stay in VERB
zu Hause bleiben [10] (*not go out*)

to stay up VERB
aufbleiben [10]
□ We stayed up till midnight. Wir sind bis um Mitternacht aufgeblieben.

★ **stay** NOUN
▷ *see also* **stay** VERB
der Aufenthalt *masc* (PL die Aufenthalte)
□ my stay in Vienna mein Aufenthalt in Wien

★ **steady** ADJECTIVE
1 stetig
□ steady progress stetiger Fortschritt
2 fest
□ a steady job eine feste Arbeit
3 ruhig (*voice, hand*)
4 solide (*person*)
■ a steady boyfriend ein fester Freund
■ a steady girlfriend eine feste Freundin
■ Steady on! Immer mit der Ruhe!

steak NOUN
das Steak *neut* (PL die Steaks) (*beef*)
□ steak and chips Steak mit Pommes frites

★ **to steal** VERB
stehlen [73] (PRESENT TENSE stiehlt, IMPERFECT stahl, PERFECT TENSE hat gestohlen)

★ **steam** NOUN
der Dampf *masc* (PL die Dämpfe)
□ a steam engine eine Dampflokomotive

★ **steel** NOUN
der Stahl *masc*
□ a steel door eine Stahltür

steep ADJECTIVE
steil (*slope*)

steeple NOUN
der Kirchturm *masc* (PL die Kirchtürme)

steering wheel NOUN
das Lenkrad *neut* (PL die Lenkräder)

★ **step** NOUN
▷ *see also* **step** VERB
1 der Schritt *masc* (PL die Schritte) (*pace*)
□ He took a step forward. Er machte einen Schritt nach vorn.
2 die Stufe *fem* (*stair*)
□ She tripped over the step. Sie stolperte über die Stufe.

★ **to step** VERB
▷ *see also* **step** NOUN
■ to step aside zur Seite treten [79] □ She stepped aside to let him pass. Sie trat zur Seite, um ihn vorbeizulassen.
■ to step back zurücktreten [79]

★ **stepbrother** NOUN
der Stiefbruder *masc* (PL die Stiefbrüder)

★ **stepdaughter** NOUN
die Stieftochter *fem* (PL die Stieftöchter)

★ **stepfather** NOUN
der Stiefvater *masc* (PL die Stiefväter)

stepladder NOUN
die Trittleiter *fem*

★ **stepmother** NOUN
die Stiefmutter *fem* (PL die Stiefmütter)

★ **stepsister** NOUN
die Stiefschwester *fem*

★ **stepson** NOUN
der Stiefsohn *masc* (PL die Stiefsöhne)

stereo NOUN
die Stereoanlage *fem*

★ **sterling** ADJECTIVE
■ five hundred pounds sterling fünfhundert britische Pfund

stew NOUN
der Eintopf *masc* (PL die Eintöpfe)

★ **steward** NOUN
der Steward *masc* (PL die Stewards)

★ **stewardess** NOUN
die Stewardess *fem* (PL die Stewardessen)

★ **stick** NOUN
▷ *see also* **stick** VERB
der Stock *masc* (PL die Stöcke)

★ **to stick** VERB
▷ *see also* **stick** NOUN
kleben [38] (*with adhesive*)
■ I can't stick it any longer. Ich halte das nicht mehr aus.

to stick out VERB
herausstrecken [15] (PERFECT TENSE hat herausgestreckt)
□ Lucy stuck out her tongue. Lucy streckte ihre Zunge heraus.

sticker NOUN
der Aufkleber *masc* (PL die Aufkleber)

stick insect NOUN
die Gespenstheuschrecke *fem* (PL die Gespenstheuschrecken)

sticky ADJECTIVE
klebrig
□ to have sticky hands klebrige Hände haben
■ a sticky label ein Aufkleber *masc*

stiff ADJECTIVE, ADVERB
steif (*rigid*)
■ to have a stiff neck einen steifen Hals haben [32]
■ to feel stiff 1 steif sein [65] □ I feel stiff after the long journey. Ich bin nach der langen Reise ganz steif. 2 Muskelkater haben [32] □ I feel stiff after playing football yesterday. Ich habe gestern Fußball gespielt und habe jetzt Muskelkater.
■ to be bored stiff sich zu Tode langweilen [38]
■ to be frozen stiff total durchgefroren sein [65]

★ = core vocabulary

■ **to be scared stiff** furchtbare Angst haben [32]

★ **still** ADVERB
▷ see also **still** ADJECTIVE
1 immer noch
□ I still haven't finished. Ich bin immer noch nicht fertig. □ Are you still in bed? Bist du immer noch im Bett?
■ **better still** noch besser
2 trotzdem (even so)
□ We lost but it was still a good match. Wir haben verloren, es war aber trotzdem ein gutes Spiel.
3 immerhin (after all)
□ Still, it's the thought that counts. Es war immerhin gut gemeint.

★ **still** ADJECTIVE
▷ see also **still** ADVERB
still
□ Keep still! Halt still! □ Sit still! Sitz still!

sting NOUN
▷ see also **sting** VERB
der Stich masc (PL die Stiche)
□ a wasp sting ein Wespenstich

to **sting** VERB
▷ see also **sting** NOUN
stechen (PRESENT TENSE sticht, IMPERFECT stach, PERFECT TENSE hat gestochen)
□ I've been stung. Ich bin gestochen worden.

stingy ADJECTIVE
geizig

to **stink** VERB
▷ see also **stink** NOUN
stinken (IMPERFECT stank, PERFECT TENSE hat gestunken)
□ It stinks! Es stinkt!

stink NOUN
▷ see also **stink** VERB
der Gestank masc

★ to **stir** VERB
umrühren [4] (PERFECT TENSE hat umgerührt)

to **stitch** VERB
▷ see also **stitch** NOUN
nähen [38] (cloth)

stitch NOUN
▷ see also **stitch** VERB
der Stich masc (PL die Stiche)
□ I had five stitches. Ich wurde mit fünf Stichen genäht.

stock NOUN
▷ see also **stock** VERB
1 der Vorrat masc (PL die Vorräte) (supply)
2 das Lager neut (PL die Lager) (in shop)
□ in stock auf Lager
■ **out of stock** ausverkauft
3 die Brühe fem
□ chicken stock die Hühnerbrühe

to **stock** VERB
▷ see also **stock** NOUN
führen [38] (have in stock)
□ Do you stock earphones? Führen Sie Kopfhörer?

to **stock up** VERB
sich eindecken [4]
□ We stocked up with food. Wir deckten uns mit Lebensmitteln ein.

stock cube NOUN
der Brühwürfel masc (PL die Brühwürfel)

stocking NOUN
der Strumpf masc (PL die Strümpfe)

stole, stolen VERB ▷ see **steal**

★ **stomach** NOUN
1 der Magen masc (PL die Mägen)
□ on a full stomach mit vollem Magen
2 der Bauch masc (PL die Bäuche)
□ to lie on one's stomach auf dem Bauch liegen

stomachache NOUN
■ **to have a stomachache** Bauchschmerzen haben [32]

★ **stone** NOUN
der Stein masc (PL die Steine) (rock)
□ a stone wall eine Steinmauer □ a peach stone ein Pfirsichstein

DID YOU KNOW...?
In Germany weight is expressed in kilos. A stone is about 6.3 kg.

□ I weigh eight stone. Ich wiege fünfzig Kilo.

stood VERB ▷ see **stand**

stool NOUN
der Hocker masc (PL die Hocker)

★ to **stop** VERB
▷ see also **stop** NOUN
1 aufhören [4] (PERFECT TENSE hat aufgehört)
□ He stopped crying. Er hörte auf zu weinen. □ I think the rain's going to stop. Ich glaube, es hört auf zu regnen. □ You should stop smoking. Du solltest aufhören zu rauchen.
■ **to stop somebody doing something** jemanden daran hindern [88], etwas zu tun
■ **Stop it!** Hör auf!
2 halten [33] (PRESENT TENSE hält, IMPERFECT hielt, PERFECT TENSE hat gehalten) (bus, train, car)
□ The bus doesn't stop here. Der Bus hält hier nicht.
3 stoppen [48]
□ a campaign to stop hunting eine Kampagne, um das Jagen zu stoppen
■ **Stop!** Halt!

★ **stop** NOUN
▷ see also **stop** VERB
die Haltestelle fem
□ a bus stop eine Bushaltestelle
■ **This is my stop.** Ich muss jetzt aussteigen.

S

Numbers in brackets refer to verb tables on pages 697 to 706.

625

stopwatch – stretch

stopwatch NOUN
die Stoppuhr *fem*

store NOUN
▷ *see also* **store** VERB
1 das Geschäft *neut* (PL die Geschäfte) (*shop*)
□ a furniture store ein Möbelgeschäft
2 das Lager *neut* (PL die Lager) (*stock, storeroom*)

to store VERB
▷ *see also* **store** NOUN
1 lagern [88]
□ They store potatoes in the cellar. Sie lagern Kartoffeln im Keller.
2 speichern [88] (*information*)

storey NOUN
der Stock *masc* (PL die Stock)
□ the first storey der erste Stock
■ a three-storey building ein dreistöckiges Gebäude

★ **storm** NOUN
1 der Sturm *masc* (PL die Stürme) (*gale*)
2 das Gewitter *neut* (PL die Gewitter) (*thunderstorm*)

stormy ADJECTIVE
stürmisch

★ **story** NOUN
die Geschichte *fem*

stove NOUN
1 der Herd *masc* (PL die Herde) (*in kitchen*)
2 der Kocher *masc* (PL die Kocher) (*camping stove*)

★ **straight** ADJECTIVE
1 gerade
□ a straight line eine gerade Linie
2 glatt
□ straight hair glatte Haare
3 hetero (*heterosexual*)
■ straight away sofort
■ straight on geradeaus

straightforward ADJECTIVE
einfach

strain NOUN
▷ *see also* **strain** VERB
die Anstrengung *fem* (*stress*)
■ It was a strain. Es war anstrengend.

to strain VERB
▷ *see also* **strain** NOUN
sich verrenken [7] (PERFECT TENSE hat sich verrenkt)
□ I strained my back. Ich habe mir den Rücken verrenkt.
■ I strained a muscle. Ich habe mir einen Muskel gezerrt.

strained ADJECTIVE
■ a strained muscle eine Muskelzerrung

stranded ADJECTIVE
■ We were stranded. Wir saßen fest.

★ **strange** ADJECTIVE
sonderbar
□ That's strange! Das ist sonderbar!

stranger NOUN
der Fremde *masc* (GEN des Fremden, PL die Fremden)
die Fremde *fem* (GEN der Fremden)
□ a stranger (man) ein Fremder
■ Don't talk to strangers. Sprich nicht mit fremden Menschen.
■ I'm a stranger here. Ich bin hier fremd.

to strangle VERB
erwürgen [19] (PERFECT TENSE hat erwürgt)

strap NOUN
1 der Riemen *masc* (PL die Riemen) (*of bag, camera, shoe, suitcase*)
2 der Träger *masc* (PL die Träger) (*of bra, dress*)
3 das Armband *neut* (PL die Armbänder) (*of watch*)

straw NOUN
das Stroh *neut*
■ That's the last straw! Jetzt reicht's aber!

★ **strawberry** NOUN
die Erdbeere *fem*
□ strawberry jam die Erdbeermarmelade □ a strawberry ice cream ein Erdbeereis

stray NOUN
■ a stray cat eine streunende Katze

★ **stream** NOUN
▷ *see also* **stream** VERB
der Bach *masc* (PL die Bäche)

★ **stream** VERB
▷ *see also* **stream** NOUN
streamen (*recording, video*)
□ The concert will be streamed live. Das Konzert wird live gestreamt.

★ **street** NOUN
die Straße *fem*
□ in the street auf der Straße

streetcar NOUN (US)
die Straßenbahn *fem*

streetlamp NOUN
die Straßenlampe *fem*

street plan NOUN
der Stadtplan *masc* (PL die Stadtpläne)

streetwise ADJECTIVE
gewieft (*informal*)

★ **strength** NOUN
die Kraft *fem* (PL die Kräfte)

★ **to stress** VERB
▷ *see also* **stress** NOUN
betonen [7] (PERFECT TENSE hat betont)
□ I would like to stress that ... Ich möchte betonen, dass ...

★ **stress** NOUN
▷ *see also* **stress** VERB
der Stress *masc* (GEN des Stresses)

★ **to stretch** VERB
1 sich strecken [48] (*person, animal*)
□ The dog woke up and stretched. Der Hund wachte auf und streckte sich.

★ = core vocabulary

2 ausleiern [4] (PERFECT TENSE ist ausgeleiert) (*get bigger*)
□ My sweater stretched when I washed it. Mein Pullover ist in der Wäsche ausgeleiert.
3 spannen [38] (*stretch out*)
□ They stretched a rope between the trees. Sie spannten ein Seil zwischen den Bäumen.
■ **to stretch out one's arms** die Arme ausbreiten [4]

stretcher NOUN
die Trage *fem*

stretchy ADJECTIVE
elastisch

★ **strict** ADJECTIVE
streng

★ **strike** NOUN
▷ *see also* **strike** VERB
der Streik *masc* (PL die Streiks)
■ **to be on strike** streiken [38]
■ **to go on strike** in den Streik treten [79]

★ to **strike** VERB
▷ *see also* **strike** NOUN
1 schlagen [59] (PRESENT TENSE schlägt, IMPERFECT schlug, PERFECT TENSE hat geschlagen)
□ The clock struck three. Die Uhr schlug drei.
□ She struck him across the mouth. Sie schlug ihm auf den Mund.
2 streiken [38] (*go on strike*)
■ **to strike a match** ein Streichholz anzünden [54]

striker NOUN
1 der Streikende *masc* (GEN des Streikenden, PL die Streikenden)
die Streikende *fem* (GEN der Streikenden) (*person on strike*)
□ a striker ein Streikender (*man*)
2 der Torschütze *masc* (GEN des Torschützen, PL die Torschützen)
die Torschützin *fem* (*footballer*)

striking ADJECTIVE
1 streikend (*on strike*)
□ striking bus drivers die streikenden Busfahrer
2 auffällig (*noticeable*)
□ a striking difference ein auffälliger Unterschied

★ **string** NOUN
1 die Schnur *fem* (PL die Schnüre)
□ a piece of string eine Schnur
2 die Saite *fem* (*of violin, guitar*)

to **strip** VERB
▷ *see also* **strip** NOUN
sich ausziehen [96] (IMPERFECT zog sich aus, PERFECT TENSE hat sich ausgezogen) (*get undressed*)

strip NOUN
▷ *see also* **strip** VERB
der Streifen *masc* (PL die Streifen)
■ **a strip cartoon** ein Comicstrip *masc*

stripe NOUN
der Streifen *masc* (PL die Streifen)

striped ADJECTIVE
gestreift
□ a striped skirt ein gestreifter Rock

stripper NOUN
der Stripper *masc* (PL die Stripper)
die Stripperin *fem*

stripy ADJECTIVE
gestreift
□ a stripy shirt ein gestreiftes Hemd

to **stroke** VERB
▷ *see also* **stroke** NOUN
streicheln [88]

stroke NOUN
▷ *see also* **stroke** VERB
der Schlag *masc* (PL die Schläge)
□ to have a stroke einen Schlag bekommen

stroll NOUN
■ **to go for a stroll** einen Spaziergang machen [48]

stroller NOUN (US)
der Sportwagen *masc* (PL die Sportwagen) (*for child*)

★ **strong** ADJECTIVE
stark
□ She's very strong. Sie ist sehr stark. □ Mark is stronger than David. Mark ist stärker als David.

strongly ADVERB
dringend
□ We strongly recommend that ... Wir empfehlen dringend, dass ...
■ **He smelt strongly of garlic.** Er roch stark nach Knoblauch.
■ **strongly built** solide gebaut
■ **I don't feel strongly about it.** Das ist mir ziemlich egal.

struck VERB ▷ *see* **strike**

to **struggle** VERB
▷ *see also* **struggle** NOUN
sich wehren [38] (*physically*)
□ He struggled, but he couldn't escape. Er wehrte sich, aber er konnte sich nicht befreien.
■ **to struggle to do something 1** (*fight*) kämpfen [38], um etwas zu tun □ He struggled to get custody of his daughter. Er kämpfte, um das Sorgerecht für seine Tochter zu bekommen.
2 (*have difficulty*) Mühe haben [32], etwas zu tun □ She struggled to get the door open. Sie hatte Mühe, die Tür aufzubekommen.

struggle NOUN
▷ *see also* **struggle** VERB
der Kampf *masc* (PL die Kämpfe) (*for independence, equality*)
□ It was a struggle. Es war ein Kampf.

stub NOUN
die Kippe *fem* (*of cigarette*)

S

stubborn – subtitles

to **stub out** VERB
ausdrücken [4] (PERFECT TENSE hat ausgedrückt)

stubborn ADJECTIVE
stur

stuck VERB ▷ see **stick**

stuck ADJECTIVE
■ **It's stuck.** Es klemmt.
■ **to get stuck** stecken bleiben [10] ▢ We got stuck in a traffic jam. Wir sind im Stau stecken geblieben.

stuck-up ADJECTIVE
hochnäsig (*informal*)

stud NOUN
1 der Ohrstecker *masc* (PL die Ohrstecker) (*earring*)
2 der Stollen *masc* (PL die Stollen) (*on football boots*)

★ **student** NOUN
der Student *masc* (GEN des Studenten, PL die Studenten)
die Studentin *fem*

studio NOUN
das Studio *neut* (PL die Studios)
▢ a TV studio ein Fernsehstudio
■ **a studio flat** eine Einzimmerwohnung

★ to **study** VERB
1 studieren [76] (PERFECT TENSE hat studiert) (*at university*)
▢ I plan to study biology. Ich habe vor, Biologie zu studieren.
2 lernen [38] (*do homework*)
▢ I've got to study tonight. Ich muss heute Abend lernen.

★ **stuff** NOUN
1 die Sachen *fem pl* (*things*)
▢ There's some stuff on the table for you. Auf dem Tisch stehen Sachen für dich.
2 das Zeug *neut* (*possessions*)
▢ Have you got all your stuff? Hast du all dein Zeug?

stuffy ADJECTIVE
stickig (*room*)
▢ It's really stuffy in here. Hier drin ist es wirklich stickig.

to **stumble** VERB
stolpern [88] (PERFECT TENSE ist gestolpert)

stung VERB ▷ see **sting**

stunk VERB ▷ see **stink**

stunned ADJECTIVE
sprachlos (*amazed*)
▢ I was stunned. Ich war sprachlos.

stunning ADJECTIVE
umwerfend

stunt NOUN
der Stunt *masc* (PL die Stunts) (*in film*)

★ **stupid** ADJECTIVE
blöd
▢ a stupid joke ein blöder Witz
■ **Me, go jogging? Don't be stupid!** Ich und joggen? Du spinnst wohl!

to **stutter** VERB
▷ *see also* **stutter** NOUN
stottern [88]

stutter NOUN
▷ *see also* **stutter** VERB
■ **He's got a stutter.** Er stottert.

★ **style** NOUN
der Stil *masc* (PL die Stile)
▢ That's not his style. Das ist nicht sein Stil.

★ **subject** NOUN
1 das Thema *neut* (PL die Themen)
▢ The subject of my presentation was social media. Das Thema meines Vortrags war Social Media.
2 das Fach *neut* (PL die Fächer) (*at school*)
▢ What's your favourite subject? Was ist dein Lieblingsfach?

subjunctive NOUN
der Konjunktiv *masc*

submarine NOUN
das U-Boot *neut* (PL die U-Boote)

subscription NOUN
das Abonnement *neut* (PL die Abonnements) (*to paper, magazine*)
■ **to take out a subscription to something** etwas abonnieren [76]

subsequently ADVERB
später

to **subsidize** VERB
subventionieren [76] (PERFECT TENSE hat subventioniert)

★ **subsidy** NOUN
die Subvention *fem*

★ **substance** NOUN
die Substanz *fem*

★ **substitute** NOUN
▷ *see also* **substitute** VERB
1 der Ersatz *masc* (*replacement*)
▢ Tofu is often used as a meat substitute. Tofu wird oft als Fleischersatz benutzt.
2 der Ersatzspieler *masc* (PL die Ersatzspieler)
die Ersatzspielerin *fem* (*in sport*)

★ to **substitute** VERB
▷ *see also* **substitute** NOUN
ersetzen [36] (PERFECT TENSE hat ersetzt)
▢ to substitute water for lemonade Limonade durch Wasser ersetzen

subtitled ADJECTIVE
mit Untertiteln

subtitles PL NOUN
die Untertitel *masc pl*
▢ an English film with German subtitles ein englischer Film mit deutschen Untertiteln

★ = core vocabulary

S

subtle ADJECTIVE
  fein
  □ a subtle difference ein feiner Unterschied

to subtract VERB
  abziehen [96] (IMPERFECT zog ab, PERFECT TENSE hat abgezogen)
  □ to subtract three from five drei von fünf abziehen

suburb NOUN
  die Vorstadt fem (PL die Vorstädte)
  □ a suburb of Berlin eine Vorstadt von Berlin
  □ They live in the suburbs. Sie wohnen in der Vorstadt.

suburban ADJECTIVE
  ■ a suburban train eine S-Bahn

subway NOUN
  1 die Unterführung fem (underpass)
  2 die U-Bahn fem (underground)

★ **to succeed** VERB
  Erfolg haben [32] (PRESENT TENSE hat Erfolg, IMPERFECT hatte Erfolg, PERFECT TENSE hat Erfolg gehabt)
  □ He succeeded in his plan. Er hatte mit seinem Plan Erfolg.
  ■ I succeeded in convincing him. Es ist mir gelungen, ihn zu überzeugen.

★ **success** NOUN
  der Erfolg masc (PL die Erfolge)
  □ The play was a great success. Das Stück war ein großer Erfolg.

★ **successful** ADJECTIVE
  erfolgreich
  □ a successful attempt ein erfolgreicher Versuch □ She's a successful architect. Sie ist eine erfolgreiche Architektin.
  ■ to be successful in doing something etwas mit Erfolg tun [81]

successfully ADVERB
  mit Erfolg

successive ADJECTIVE
  ■ on four successive occasions viermal hintereinander

★ **such** ADJECTIVE, ADVERB
  so
  □ such nice people so nette Leute □ such a long journey eine so lange Reise
  ■ such a lot of 1 (so much) so viel □ such a lot of work so viel Arbeit 2 (so many) so viele
  □ such a lot of mistakes so viele Fehler
  ■ such as (like) wie zum Beispiel □ hot countries, such as India heiße Länder, wie zum Beispiel Indien
  ■ not as such nicht eigentlich □ He's not an expert as such, but ... Er ist nicht eigentlich ein Experte, aber ...
  ■ There's no such thing. So was gibt es nicht.
  □ There's no such thing as the yeti. So was wie den Yeti gibt es nicht.

such-and-such ADJECTIVE
  der und der
  □ such-and-such a place der und der Ort
  die und die
  □ such-and-such a time die und die Zeit
  das und das
  □ such-and-such a problem das und das Problem

to suck VERB
  lutschen [48] (sweets)
  □ to suck one's thumb am Daumen lutschen

★ **sudden** ADJECTIVE
  plötzlich
  □ a sudden change eine plötzliche Änderung
  ■ all of a sudden plötzlich

★ **suddenly** ADVERB
  plötzlich
  □ Suddenly, the door opened. Plötzlich ging die Tür auf.

suede NOUN
  das Wildleder neut
  □ a suede jacket eine Wildlederjacke

★ **to suffer** VERB
  leiden [44] (IMPERFECT litt, PERFECT TENSE hat gelitten)
  □ She was really suffering. Sie hat wirklich gelitten.
  ■ to suffer from a disease an einer Krankheit leiden [44]

to suffocate VERB
  ersticken [19] (PERFECT TENSE ist erstickt)

★ **sugar** NOUN
  der Zucker masc (PL die Zucker)

★ **to suggest** VERB
  vorschlagen [59] (PRESENT TENSE schlägt vor, IMPERFECT schlug vor, PERFECT TENSE hat vorgeschlagen)
  □ I suggested they set off early. Ich habe vorgeschlagen, dass sie früh aufbrechen sollen.

★ **suggestion** NOUN
  der Vorschlag masc (PL die Vorschläge)

★ **suicide** NOUN
  der Selbstmord masc (PL die Selbstmorde)
  □ to commit suicide Selbstmord begehen

suicide bomber NOUN
  der Selbstmordattentäter masc (PL die Selbstmordattentäter)
  die Selbstmordattentäterin fem

suicide bombing NOUN
  das Selbstmordattentat neut (PL die Selbstmordattentate)

★ **suit** NOUN
  ▷ see also **suit** VERB
  1 der Anzug masc (PL die Anzüge) (man's)
  2 das Kostüm neut (PL die Kostüme) (woman's)

★ **to suit** VERB
  ▷ see also **suit** NOUN

S

Numbers in brackets refer to verb tables on pages 697 to 706.

629

suitable – supernatural

1 passen [31] (*be convenient for*)
□ What time would suit you? Welche Zeit würde Ihnen passen? □ That suits me fine. Das passt mir gut.
■ **Suit yourself!** Wie du willst!

2 stehen [72] (IMPERFECT stand, PERFECT TENSE hat gestanden) (*look good on*)
□ That dress really suits you. Das Kleid steht dir wirklich.

★ **suitable** ADJECTIVE
1 passend
□ a suitable time eine passende Zeit
2 angemessen (*clothes*)
□ suitable clothing angemessene Kleidung

suitcase NOUN
der Koffer *masc* (PL die Koffer)

suite NOUN
1 die Suite *fem* (*in hotel*)
2 die Garnitur *fem* (*furniture*)
■ **a bathroom suite** eine Badezimmergarnitur

to **sulk** VERB
schmollen [48]

sulky ADJECTIVE
beleidigt

sultana NOUN
die Sultanine *fem*

★ **sum** NOUN
1 das Rechnen *neut* (*calculation*)
■ **She's good at sums.** Sie kann gut rechnen.
2 die Summe *fem* (*amount*)
□ a sum of money eine Geldsumme

to **sum up** VERB
zusammenfassen [15] (PERFECT TENSE hat zusammengefasst)

to **summarize** VERB
zusammenfassen [15] (PERFECT TENSE hat zusammengefasst)

summary NOUN
die Zusammenfassung *fem*

★ **summer** NOUN
der Sommer *masc* (PL die Sommer)
□ in summer im Sommer
■ **summer clothes** die Sommerkleidung *sing*
■ **the summer holidays** die Sommerferien

summertime NOUN
der Sommer *masc* (PL die Sommer)
□ in summertime im Sommer

★ **summit** NOUN
der Gipfel *masc* (PL die Gipfel)

★ **sun** NOUN
die Sonne *fem*
□ in the sun in der Sonne

to **sunbathe** VERB
sonnenbaden [54] (PERFECT TENSE hat sonnengebadet)

sunblock NOUN
das Sonnenschutzmittel *neut* (PL die Sonnenschutzmittel)

sunburn NOUN
der Sonnenbrand *masc* (PL die Sonnenbrände)

sunburnt ADJECTIVE
■ **I got sunburnt.** Ich habe einen Sonnenbrand bekommen.

★ **Sunday** NOUN
der Sonntag *masc* (PL die Sonntage)
□ every Sunday jeden Sonntag □ last Sunday letzten Sonntag □ next Sunday nächsten Sonntag □ on Sunday am Sonntag
■ **on Sundays** sonntags

Sunday school NOUN
die Sonntagsschule *fem*

sunflower NOUN
die Sonnenblume *fem*

sung VERB ▷ *see* sing

sunglasses PL NOUN
die Sonnenbrille *fem sing*
□ a pair of sunglasses eine Sonnenbrille

sunk VERB ▷ *see* sink

sunlight NOUN
das Sonnenlicht *neut*

sunny ADJECTIVE
sonnig
□ a sunny morning ein sonniger Morgen
■ **It's sunny.** Die Sonne scheint.

sunrise NOUN
der Sonnenaufgang *masc* (PL die Sonnenaufgänge)

sunroof NOUN
das Schiebedach *neut* (PL die Schiebedächer)

sunscreen NOUN
die Sonnenschutzcreme *fem* (PL die Sonnenschutzcremes)

sunset NOUN
der Sonnenuntergang *masc* (PL die Sonnenuntergänge)

sunshine NOUN
der Sonnenschein *masc*

sunstroke NOUN
der Hitzschlag *masc* (PL die Hitzschläge)
□ to get sunstroke einen Hitzschlag bekommen

suntan NOUN
■ **to have a suntan** braun sein [65]
■ **suntan lotion** die Sonnenmilch

★ **super** ADJECTIVE
klasse

klasse is invariable.

□ a super film ein klasse Film

★ **superb** ADJECTIVE
großartig

★ **supermarket** NOUN
der Supermarkt *masc* (PL die Supermärkte)

supernatural ADJECTIVE
übernatürlich

★ = core vocabulary

superstitious ADJECTIVE
abergläubisch

to supervise VERB
beaufsichtigen [84] (PERFECT TENSE hat
beaufsichtigt)

supervisor NOUN
1 der Vorarbeiter *masc* (PL die Vorarbeiter)
die Vorarbeiterin *fem* (*in factory*)
2 der Abteilungsleiter *masc* (PL die
Abteilungsleiter)
die Abteilungsleiterin *fem* (*in department store*)

supper NOUN
das Abendessen *neut* (PL die Abendessen)

supplement NOUN
1 die Beilage *fem* (*of newspaper, magazine*)
2 der Zuschlag *masc* (PL die Zuschläge) (*money*)

supplies PL NOUN
die Vorräte *masc pl* (*food*)

★ **to supply** VERB
▷ *see also* **supply** NOUN
1 liefern [88] (*goods, material*)
□ The farm supplied us with food. Der
Bauernhof lieferte uns die Lebensmittel.
2 stellen [38] (*put at somebody's disposal*)
□ The centre supplied all the necessary
equipment. Das Zentrum hat die ganze
notwendige Ausrüstung gestellt.

★ **supply** NOUN
▷ *see also* **supply** VERB
der Vorrat *masc* (PL die Vorräte)
□ a supply of paper ein Papiervorrat
■ **the water supply** (*to town*) die
Wasserversorgung

supply teacher NOUN
der Aushilfslehrer *masc* (PL die Aushilfslehrer)
die Aushilfslehrerin *fem*

★ **to support** VERB
▷ *see also* **support** NOUN
1 unterstützen [36] (PERFECT TENSE hat
unterstützt)
□ My mum has always supported me. Meine
Mutti hat mich immer unterstützt.
■ **What team do you support?** Für welche
Mannschaft bist du?
2 sorgen [38] für (*financially*)
□ She had to support five children on her own.
Sie musste allein für ihre fünf Kinder sorgen.

★ **support** NOUN
▷ *see also* **support** VERB
die Unterstützung *fem* (*backing*)

★ **supporter** NOUN
1 der Fan *masc* (PL die Fans)

> **der Fan** is also used for women.

□ a Liverpool supporter ein Liverpool-Fan
2 der Anhänger *masc* (PL die Anhänger)
die Anhängerin *fem*
□ She's a supporter of the Labour Party. Sie ist
Anhängerin der Labour-Party.

★ **to suppose** VERB
annehmen [1] (PRESENT TENSE nimmt an,
IMPERFECT nahm an, PERFECT TENSE hat
angenommen)
□ I suppose he's late. Ich nehme an, er kommt
zu spät. □ Suppose you won the lottery. Nimm
mal an, du gewinnst im Lotto. □ I suppose so.
Das nehme ich an.
■ **to be supposed to do something** etwas tun
sollen [69] □ You're supposed to go straight
home. Du solltest sofort nach Hause gehen.
■ **You're supposed to show your passport.**
Sie müssen Ihren Pass zeigen.

supposing CONJUNCTION
angenommen
□ Supposing you won the lottery ...
Angenommen, du gewinnst im Lotto ...

surcharge NOUN
der Zuschlag *masc* (PL die Zuschläge)

★ **sure** ADJECTIVE
sicher
□ Are you sure? Bist du sicher?
■ **Sure!** Klar!
■ **to make sure that ...** sich vergewissern [88],
dass ... □ I'm going to make sure the door's
locked. Ich werde mich vergewissern, dass die
Tür abgeschlossen ist.

★ **surely** ADVERB
sicherlich
□ She'll get into university, surely? Sie bekommt
doch sicherlich einen Platz an der Uni?
■ **Surely you haven't forgotten?** Du hast es
bestimmt nicht vergessen, oder?

surf NOUN
▷ *see also* **surf** VERB
die Brandung *fem*

to surf VERB
▷ *see also* **surf** NOUN
surfen [38] (PERFECT TENSE hat gesurft)
■ **to surf the Net** im Internet surfen [38]

★ **surface** NOUN
die Oberfläche *fem*

surfboard NOUN
das Surfbrett *neut* (PL die Surfbretter)

surfing NOUN
das Surfen *neut*
■ **to go surfing** surfen gehen [29]

surgeon NOUN
der Chirurg *masc* (GEN des Chirurgen, PL die
Chirurgen)
die Chirurgin *fem*
□ She's a surgeon. Sie ist Chirurgin.

★ **surgery** NOUN
die Arztpraxis *fem* (PL die Arztpraxen) (*doctor's
surgery*)
■ **surgery hours** die Sprechstunden

surname NOUN
der Nachname *masc* (GEN des Nachnamens, PL
die Nachnamen)

S

surprise – sweaty

★ **surprise** NOUN
die Überraschung *fem*

★ **surprised** ADJECTIVE
überrascht
□ I was surprised to see him. Ich war überrascht, ihn zu sehen.

★ **surprising** ADJECTIVE
überraschend

★ to **surrender** VERB
sich ergeben [28] (PRESENT TENSE ergibt sich, IMPERFECT ergab sich, PERFECT TENSE hat sich ergeben)

surrogate mother NOUN
die Leihmutter *fem* (PL die Leihmütter)

★ to **surround** VERB
umstellen [4] (PERFECT TENSE hat umstellt)
□ The police surrounded the house. Die Polizei hat das Haus umstellt.
■ **surrounded by** umgeben von □ The house is surrounded by trees. Das Haus ist von Bäumen umgeben.

surroundings PL NOUN
die Umgebung *fem sing*
□ a hotel in beautiful surroundings ein Hotel in wunderschöner Umgebung

★ **survey** NOUN
die Umfrage *fem* (*research*)

surveyor NOUN
1 der Gebäudesachverständige *masc* (GEN des Gebäudesachverständigen, PL die Gebäudesachverständigen)
die Gebäudesachverständige *fem* (GEN der Gebäudesachverständigen) (*of buildings*)
□ a surveyor (*man*) ein Gebäudesachverständiger
2 der Landvermesser *masc* (PL die Landvermesser)
die Landvermesserin *fem* (*of land*)

to **survive** VERB
überleben [18] (PERFECT TENSE hat überlebt)

survivor NOUN
der Überlebende *masc* (GEN des Überlebenden, PL die Überlebenden)
die Überlebende *fem* (GEN der Überlebenden)
□ There were no survivors. Es gab keine Überlebenden.

★ to **suspect** VERB
▷ see also **suspect** NOUN
verdächtigen [84] (PERFECT TENSE hat verdächtigt)

★ **suspect** NOUN
▷ see also **suspect** VERB
der Verdächtige *masc* (GEN des Verdächtigen, PL die Verdächtigen)
die Verdächtige *fem* (GEN der Verdächtigen)
□ a suspect (*man*) ein Verdächtiger

★ to **suspend** VERB
1 verweisen (IMPERFECT verwies, PERFECT TENSE hat verwiesen) (*from school*)

□ He was suspended. Er wurde von der Schule verwiesen.
2 sperren [38] (*from team*)
3 suspendieren [76] (PERFECT TENSE hat suspendiert) (*from job*)

suspense NOUN
1 die Ungewissheit *fem* (*waiting*)
□ The suspense was terrible. Die Ungewissheit war furchtbar.
2 die Spannung *fem* (*in story*)
■ **a film with lots of suspense** ein sehr spannender Film

suspension NOUN
1 der Ausschluss *masc* (GEN des Ausschlusses, PL die Ausschlüsse) (*from school*)
2 die Sperre *fem* (*from team*)
3 die Suspendierung *fem* (*from job*)

suspicious ADJECTIVE
1 argwöhnisch
□ He was suspicious at first. Zuerst war er argwöhnisch.
2 verdächtig (*suspicious-looking*)
□ a suspicious person eine verdächtige Person

to **swallow** VERB
schlucken [48]

swam VERB ▷ see swim

swan NOUN
der Schwan *masc* (PL die Schwäne)

to **swap** VERB
tauschen [48]
□ Do you want to swap? Willst du tauschen?
■ **to swap an apple for a sweet** einen Apfel für ein Bonbon eintauschen [4]

to **swat** VERB
totschlagen [59] (PRESENT TENSE schlägt tot, IMPERFECT schlug tot, PERFECT TENSE hat totgeschlagen)

to **sway** VERB
schwanken [38]

to **swear** VERB
1 schwören (IMPERFECT schwor, PERFECT TENSE hat geschworen) (*make an oath*)
2 fluchen [38] (*curse*)

swearword NOUN
der Kraftausdruck *masc* (PL die Kraftausdrücke)

sweat NOUN
▷ see also **sweat** VERB
der Schweiß *masc* (GEN des Schweißes)

to **sweat** VERB
▷ see also **sweat** NOUN
schwitzen [36]

sweater NOUN
der Pullover *masc* (PL die Pullover)

sweaty ADJECTIVE
1 verschwitzt (*person, face*)
□ I'm all sweaty. Ich bin ganz verschwitzt.
2 feucht (*hands*)

★ = core vocabulary

Swede NOUN

der Schwede masc (GEN des Schweden, PL die Schweden)

die Schwedin fem (person)

swede NOUN

die Steckrübe fem (vegetable)

Sweden NOUN

Schweden neut

■ **from Sweden** aus Schweden

■ **to Sweden** nach Schweden

Swedish ADJECTIVE

▷ see also **Swedish** NOUN

schwedisch

■ **He's Swedish.** Er ist Schwede.

■ **She's Swedish.** Sie ist Schwedin.

Swedish NOUN

▷ see also **Swedish** ADJECTIVE

das Schwedisch neut (GEN des Schwedischen) (language)

to sweep VERB

fegen [38]

□ **to sweep the floor** den Boden fegen

sweet NOUN

▷ see also **sweet** ADJECTIVE

1 das Bonbon neut (PL die Bonbons) (candy)

□ **a bag of sweets** eine Tüte Bonbons

2 der Nachtisch masc (pudding)

□ **What sweet did you have?** Was für einen Nachtisch hattest du?

sweet ADJECTIVE

▷ see also **sweet** NOUN

1 süß

□ **Isn't he sweet?** Ist er nicht süß?

2 nett (kind)

□ **That was really sweet of you.** Das war wirklich nett von dir.

■ **sweet and sour chicken** Hähnchen süß-sauer

sweetcorn NOUN

der Mais masc

sweltering ADJECTIVE

■ **It was sweltering.** Es war eine Bruthitze.

swept VERB ▷ see **sweep**

to swerve VERB

ausscheren [4] (PERFECT TENSE ist ausgeschert)

□ **He swerved to avoid the cyclist.** Er scherte aus, um dem Fahrradfahrer auszuweichen.

swim NOUN

▷ see also **swim** VERB

■ **to go for a swim** schwimmen gehen [29]

to swim VERB

▷ see also **swim** NOUN

schwimmen [63] (IMPERFECT schwamm, PERFECT TENSE ist geschwommen)

□ **Can you swim?** Kannst du schwimmen?

□ **She swam across the river.** Sie schwamm über den Fluss.

swimmer NOUN

der Schwimmer masc (PL die Schwimmer)

die Schwimmerin fem

□ **She's a good swimmer.** Sie ist eine gute Schwimmerin.

★ **swimming** NOUN

das Schwimmen neut

■ **to go swimming** schwimmen gehen [29]

■ **Do you like swimming?** Schwimmst du gern?

■ **a swimming cap** eine Bademütze

■ **a swimming costume** ein Badeanzug masc

■ **a swimming pool** ein Schwimmbad neut

■ **swimming trunks** die Badehose sing □ **a pair of swimming trunks** eine Badehose

swimsuit NOUN

der Badeanzug masc (PL die Badeanzüge)

★ **swing** NOUN

▷ see also **swing** VERB

die Schaukel fem (in playground, garden)

★ **to swing** VERB

▷ see also **swing** NOUN

schaukeln [34]

★ **Swiss** ADJECTIVE

▷ see also **Swiss** NOUN

Schweizer

□ **I like Swiss cheese.** Ich mag Schweizer Käse.

■ **Andreas is Swiss.** Andreas ist Schweizer.

■ **Claudie is Swiss.** Claudie ist Schweizerin.

★ **Swiss** NOUN

▷ see also **Swiss** ADJECTIVE

der Schweizer masc (PL die Schweizer)

die Schweizerin fem (person)

■ **the Swiss** die Schweizer

★ **switch** NOUN

▷ see also **switch** VERB

der Schalter masc (PL die Schalter) (for light, radio etc)

★ **to switch** VERB

▷ see also **switch** NOUN

tauschen [48]

□ **to switch A for B** A gegen B tauschen

to switch off VERB

ausschalten [2] (PERFECT TENSE hat ausgeschaltet)

to switch on VERB

anschalten [2] (PERFECT TENSE hat angeschaltet)

★ **Switzerland** NOUN

die Schweiz fem (GEN der Schweiz)

> Note that the definite article is used in German for countries which are feminine.

■ **from Switzerland** aus der Schweiz

■ **in Switzerland** in der Schweiz

■ **to Switzerland** in die Schweiz

Numbers in brackets refer to verb tables on pages 697 to 706.

633

S

swollen - system

swollen ADJECTIVE
geschwollen (*arm, leg*)

to **swop** VERB
tauschen [48]
□ Do you want to swop? Willst du tauschen?
■ **to swop an apple for a sweet** einen Apfel für ein Bonbon eintauschen [4]

sword NOUN
das Schwert *neut* (PL die Schwerter)

swore VERB ▷ *see* **swear**

sworn VERB ▷ *see* **swear**

to **swot** VERB
▷ *see also* **swot** NOUN
pauken [38] (*informal*)
□ I'll have to swot for the maths exam. Ich muss für die Matheprüfung pauken.

swot NOUN
▷ *see also* **swot** VERB
der Streber *masc* (PL die Streber)
die Streberin *fem* (*informal*)

swum VERB ▷ *see* **swim**

swung VERB ▷ *see* **swing**

syllabus NOUN
der Lehrplan *masc* (PL die Lehrpläne)
□ on the syllabus auf dem Lehrplan

★ **symbol** NOUN
das Symbol *neut* (PL die Symbole)

sympathetic ADJECTIVE
verständnisvoll

BE CAREFUL!
Do not translate **sympathetic** by the German word **sympathisch**.

to **sympathize** VERB
■ **to sympathize with somebody** (*pity*)
Mitgefühl mit jemandem haben [32]

★ **sympathy** NOUN
das Mitleid *neut*

★ **symptom** NOUN
das Symptom *neut*

syringe NOUN
die Spritze *fem*

★ **system** NOUN
das System *neut* (PL die Systeme)

★ = core vocabulary

Tt

★ table NOUN
der Tisch *masc* (PL die Tische)
□ to lay the table den Tisch decken

tablecloth NOUN
die Tischdecke *fem*

tablespoon NOUN
der Esslöffel *masc* (PL die Esslöffel)
□ a tablespoon of sugar ein Esslöffel Zucker

tablespoonful NOUN
■ a tablespoonful of sugar ein Esslöffel Zucker

tablet NOUN
1 die Tablette *fem* (*medicine*)
2 das Tablet *neut* (PL die Tablets) (*computer*)

table tennis NOUN
das Tischtennis *neut* (GEN des Tischtennis)
□ to play table tennis Tischtennis spielen

tabloid NOUN
das Boulevardblatt *neut* (PL die Boulevardblätter)

★ tackle NOUN
▷ see also **tackle** VERB
der Angriff *masc* (PL die Angriffe) (*in sport*)
■ fishing tackle das Angelzeug

★ to tackle VERB
▷ see also **tackle** NOUN
angreifen (IMPERFECT griff an, PERFECT TENSE hat angegriffen) (*in sport*)
■ to tackle a problem ein Problem angehen [29]

tact NOUN
der Takt *masc*

tactful ADJECTIVE
taktvoll

tactics PL NOUN
die Taktik *fem sing*

tactless ADJECTIVE
taktlos

tadpole NOUN
die Kaulquappe *fem*

tag NOUN
das Etikett *neut* (PL die Etiketts) (*label*)

★ tail NOUN
der Schwanz *masc* (GEN des Schwanzes, PL die Schwänze)
■ Heads or tails? Kopf oder Zahl?

tailor NOUN
der Schneider *masc* (PL die Schneider)
die Schneiderin *fem*
□ He's a tailor. Er ist Schneider.

★ to take VERB
1 nehmen [52] (PRESENT TENSE nimmt, IMPERFECT nahm, PERFECT TENSE hat genommen)
□ He took a plate from the cupboard. Er nahm einen Teller aus dem Schrank. □ We took a taxi. Wir haben ein Taxi genommen.
2 mitnehmen [52] (PRESENT TENSE nimmt mit, IMPERFECT nahm mit, PERFECT TENSE hat mitgenommen) (*take along*)
□ Are you taking your camera? Nimmst du deine Kamera mit? □ Don't take anything valuable with you. Nehmen Sie nichts Wertvolles mit. □ When will you take me to Venice? Wann nimmst du mich nach Venedig mit? □ Do you take your exercise books home? Nehmt ihr eure Hefte mit nach Hause?
3 bringen [13] (IMPERFECT brachte, PERFECT TENSE hat gebracht) (*to a certain place*)
□ She always takes him to school. Sie bringt ihn immer zur Schule. □ I'm taking my coat to the cleaner's. Ich bringe meinen Mantel in die Reinigung.
4 brauchen [48] (*require*)
□ She always takes hours to get ready. Sie braucht immer Stunden, bis sie fertig ist. □ It takes five people to do this job. Für diese Arbeit braucht man fünf Leute. □ That takes a lot of courage. Dazu braucht man viel Mut.
■ It takes a lot of money to do that. Das kostet viel Geld.
5 dauern [88] (*last*)
□ The journey took three hours. Die Fahrt dauerte drei Stunden. □ It won't take long. Das dauert nicht lange.
6 ertragen [77] (PRESENT TENSE erträgt, IMPERFECT ertrug, PERFECT TENSE hat ertragen) (*tolerate*)
□ He can't take being criticized. Er kann es nicht ertragen, kritisiert zu werden.
7 machen [48] (*exam, test, subject*)
□ Have you taken your driving test yet? Hast du deine Fahrprüfung schon gemacht? □ I'm taking German instead of French. Ich mache Deutsch statt Französisch.

to take after VERB
nachschlagen [59] (PRESENT TENSE schlägt nach, IMPERFECT schlug nach, PERFECT TENSE hat nachgeschlagen)

◻ She takes after her mother. Sie schlägt ihrer Mutter nach.

to **take apart** VERB
▪ to take something apart etwas auseinandernehmen [52]

to **take away** VERB
1 wegnehmen [52] (PRESENT TENSE nimmt weg, IMPERFECT nahm weg, PERFECT TENSE hat weggenommen) (object)
2 wegbringen [13] (IMPERFECT brachte weg, PERFECT TENSE hat weggebracht) (person)
▪ hot meals to take away warme Mahlzeiten zum Mitnehmen

to **take back** VERB
zurückbringen [13] (IMPERFECT brachte zurück, PERFECT TENSE hat zurückgebracht)
◻ I took it back to the shop. Ich habe es in den Laden zurückgebracht.
▪ I take it all back! Ich nehme alles zurück!

to **take down** VERB
1 herunternehmen [52] (PRESENT TENSE nimmt herunter, IMPERFECT nahm herunter, PERFECT TENSE hat heruntergenommen)
◻ She took down the painting. Sie nahm das Gemälde herunter.
2 abbauen [38] (PRESENT TENSE baut ab, IMPERFECT baute ab, PERFECT TENSE hat abgebaut) (tent)
3 sich notieren [66] (PRESENT TENSE schreibt auf, IMPERFECT schrieb auf, PERFECT TENSE hat aufgeschrieben) (note down)
◻ I took it down in my notebook. Ich habe es mir in meinem Notizbuch notiert.

to **take in** VERB
verstehen [72] (IMPERFECT verstand, PERFECT TENSE hat verstanden) (understand)
◻ I didn't really take it in. Ich habe das nicht richtig verstanden.

to **take off** VERB
1 abfliegen [25] (IMPERFECT flog ab, PERFECT TENSE ist abgeflogen) (plane)
◻ The plane took off twenty minutes late. Das Flugzeug ist mit zwanzig Minuten Verspätung abgeflogen.
2 ausziehen [96] (IMPERFECT zog aus, PERFECT TENSE hat ausgezogen) (clothes)
◻ Take your coat off. Zieh den Mantel aus.

to **take out** VERB
herausnehmen [52] (PRESENT TENSE nimmt heraus, IMPERFECT nahm heraus, PERFECT TENSE hat herausgenommen) (from container, pocket)
▪ He took her out to the theatre. Er führte sie ins Theater aus.

to **take over** VERB
übernehmen [52] (PRESENT TENSE übernimmt, IMPERFECT übernahm, PERFECT TENSE hat übernommen)
◻ I'll take over now. Ich übernehme jetzt.
▪ to take over from somebody jemanden ablösen [4] ◻ Sarah has taken over from Emma. Sarah hat Emma abgelöst.

takeaway NOUN
1 das Essen zum Mitnehmen neut (PL die Essen zum Mitnehmen) (meal)
2 die Imbissstube fem (shop)
◻ a Chinese takeaway eine chinesische Imbissstube

takeoff NOUN
der Abflug masc (PL die Abflüge) (of plane)

talcum powder NOUN
der Puder masc (PL die Puder)

★ **tale** NOUN
die Geschichte fem (story)

★ **talent** NOUN
das Talent neut (PL die Talente)
◻ She's got lots of talent. Sie hat sehr viel Talent.
▪ to have a talent for something eine Begabung für etwas haben [32]
▪ He's got a real talent for languages. Er ist wirklich sprachbegabt.

talented ADJECTIVE
begabt

★ **talk** NOUN
▷ see also talk VERB
1 der Vortrag masc (PL die Vorträge) (speech)
◻ She gave a talk on rock climbing. Sie hielt einen Vortrag über das Klettern.
2 das Gespräch neut (PL die Gespräche) (conversation)
◻ We had a talk about her problems. Wir hatten ein Gespräch über ihre Probleme.
▪ I had a talk with my mum about it. Ich habe mit meiner Mama darüber gesprochen.
3 das Gerede neut (gossip)
◻ It's just talk. Das ist nur Gerede.

★ to **talk** VERB
▷ see also talk NOUN
reden [54]
◻ We talked about the weather. Wir haben über das Wetter geredet.
▪ to talk something over with somebody etwas mit jemandem besprechen [70]

talkative ADJECTIVE
redselig

★ **tall** ADJECTIVE
1 groß (person, tree)
◻ They've cut down the tallest tree in the park. Sie haben den größten Baum im Park gefällt.
◻ He's two metres tall. Er ist zwei Meter groß.
2 hoch (building)

Before a noun or after an article, use hohe.

◻ a tall building ein hohes Gebäude

tame ADJECTIVE
zahm (animal)

tampon NOUN
der Tampon masc (PL die Tampons)

tan NOUN
▪ She's got a lovely tan. Sie ist schön braun.

★ = core vocabulary

tangerine NOUN
die Mandarine *fem*

tank NOUN
1 der Tank *masc* (PL die Tanks) (*for water, petrol*)
2 der Panzer *masc* (PL die Panzer) (*military*)
■ **a fish tank** ein Aquarium *neut*

tanker NOUN
1 der Tanker *masc* (PL die Tanker) (*ship*)
□ an oil tanker ein Öltanker
2 der Tankwagen *masc* (PL die Tankwagen) (*truck*)
□ a petrol tanker ein Benzintankwagen

★ **tap** NOUN
1 der Wasserhahn *masc* (PL die Wasserhähne) (*water tap*)
2 der Klaps *masc* (PL die Klapse) (*gentle blow*)

tap-dancing NOUN
das Stepptanzen *neut*
■ **I do tap-dancing.** Ich mache Stepptanz.

★ **tape** NOUN
der Klebstreifen *masc* (PL die Klebstreifen) (*sticky tape*)

tape deck NOUN
das Kassettendeck *neut* (PL die Kassettendecks)

tape measure NOUN
das Maßband *neut* (PL die Maßbänder)

tape recorder NOUN
der Kassettenrekorder *masc* (PL die Kassettenrekorder)

★ **target** NOUN
das Ziel *neut* (PL die Ziele)

tarmac NOUN
der Asphalt *masc* (*on road*)

tart NOUN
der Kuchen *masc* (PL die Kuchen)
□ an apple tart ein Apfelkuchen

tartan ADJECTIVE
im Schottenkaro
□ a tartan scarf ein Schal im Schottenkaro

★ **task** NOUN
die Aufgabe *fem*

★ **taste** NOUN
▷ *see also* **taste** VERB
der Geschmack *masc* (PL die Geschmäcke)
□ It's got a really strange taste. Es hat einen sehr eigenartigen Geschmack. □ She has good taste. Sie hat einen guten Geschmack.
■ **a joke in bad taste** ein geschmackloser Witz
■ **Would you like a taste?** Möchtest du mal probieren?

★ **to taste** VERB
▷ *see also* **taste** NOUN
1 probieren [76] (PERFECT TENSE hat probiert)
□ Would you like to taste it? Möchtest du mal probieren?
2 schmecken [48]
□ You can taste the garlic in it. Man kann den Knoblauch schmecken.

■ **to taste of something** nach etwas schmecken [48] □ It tastes of fish. Es schmeckt nach Fisch.

tasteful ADJECTIVE
geschmackvoll

tasteless ADJECTIVE
1 fade (*food*)
2 geschmacklos (*in bad taste*)
□ a tasteless remark eine geschmacklose Bemerkung

tasty ADJECTIVE
schmackhaft

tattoo NOUN
die Tätowierung *fem*

taught VERB ▷ *see* **teach**

Taurus NOUN
der Stier *masc*
□ I'm Taurus. Ich bin Stier.

★ **tax** NOUN
die Steuer *fem* (*on goods, income*)

taxi NOUN
das Taxi *neut* (PL die Taxis)
□ a taxi driver ein Taxifahrer

taxi rank NOUN
der Taxistand *masc* (PL die Taxistände)

TB NOUN (= *tuberculosis*)
die TB *fem* (= *Tuberkulose*)

★ **tea** NOUN
1 der Tee *masc* (PL die Tees)
□ a cup of tea eine Tasse Tee

> **DID YOU KNOW...?**
> Usually, tea is not drunk with milk and sugar in Germany, but is served with lemon, and is referred to as **Schwarztee**. Fruit teas and herbal teas are also very widespread.

■ **a tea bag** ein Teebeutel *masc*
2 das Abendessen *neut* (PL die Abendessen) (*evening meal*)
□ We were having tea. Wir saßen beim Abendessen.

★ **to teach** VERB
1 beibringen [13] (IMPERFECT brachte bei, PERFECT TENSE hat beigebracht)
□ My sister taught me to swim. Meine Schwester hat mir das Schwimmen beigebracht.
■ **That'll teach you!** Das wird dir eine Lehre sein!
2 unterrichten [2] (PERFECT TENSE hat unterrichtet) (*in school*)
□ She teaches physics. Sie unterrichtet Physik.

★ **teacher** NOUN
der Lehrer *masc* (PL die Lehrer)
die Lehrerin *fem*
□ a maths teacher ein Mathelehrer □ She's a teacher. Sie ist Lehrerin. □ He's a primary school teacher. Er ist Grundschullehrer.

t

Numbers in brackets refer to verb tables on pages 697 to 706.

637

teacher's pet – television

teacher's pet NOUN
Lehrers Schätzchen *neut*
□ She's the teacher's pet. Sie ist Lehrers Schätzchen.

teaching assistant NOUN
der Lehrassistent *masc* (GEN des Lehrassistenten, PL die Lehrassistenten)
die Lehrassistentin *fem*

tea cloth NOUN
das Geschirrtuch *neut* (PL die Geschirrtücher)

★ **team** NOUN
die Mannschaft *fem*
□ a football team eine Fußballmannschaft
□ She was in my team. Sie war in meiner Mannschaft.

teapot NOUN
die Teekanne *fem*

★ **tear** NOUN
▷ see also **tear** VERB
die Träne *fem*
□ She was in tears. Sie war in Tränen aufgelöst.

★ to **tear** VERB
▷ see also **tear** NOUN
zerreißen (IMPERFECT zerriss, PERFECT TENSE hat/ist zerrissen)
□ Mind you don't tear the page. Pass auf, dass du die Seite nicht zerreißt.

> For the perfect tense use **haben** when the verb has an object and **sein** when there is no object.

□ You've torn your shirt. Du hast dein Hemd zerrissen. □ Your shirt is torn. Dein Hemd ist zerrissen. □ It won't tear, it's very strong. Es zerreißt nicht, es ist sehr stark.

to **tear up** VERB
zerreißen
□ He tore up the letter. Er zerriss den Brief.

tear gas NOUN
das Tränengas *neut* (GEN des Tränengases)

to **tease** VERB
1 quälen [38] (*unkindly*)
□ Stop teasing that poor animal! Hör auf, das arme Tier zu quälen!
2 necken [48] (*jokingly*)
□ He's teasing you. Er neckt dich nur.
■ I was only teasing. Ich habe nur einen Scherz gemacht.

teaspoon NOUN
der Teelöffel *masc* (PL die Teelöffel)
□ a teaspoon of sugar ein Teelöffel Zucker

teaspoonful NOUN
■ a teaspoonful of sugar ein Teelöffel Zucker

teatime NOUN
die Abendessenszeit *fem* (*in evening*)
□ It was nearly teatime. Es war fast Abendessenszeit.

tea towel NOUN
das Geschirrtuch *neut* (PL die Geschirrtücher)

★ **technical** ADJECTIVE
technisch

technician NOUN
der Techniker *masc* (PL die Techniker)
die Technikerin *fem*

★ **technique** NOUN
die Technik *fem*

techno NOUN
der Techno *masc* (*music*)

technological ADJECTIVE
technologisch

★ **technology** NOUN
die Technologie *fem*

teddy bear NOUN
der Teddybär *masc* (GEN des Teddybären, PL die Teddybären)

teenage ADJECTIVE
1 für Teenager
□ a teenage magazine eine Zeitschrift für Teenager
2 heranwachsend (*boys*, *girls*)
□ She has two teenage daughters. Sie hat zwei heranwachsende Töchter.

★ **teenager** NOUN
der Teenager *masc* (PL die Teenager)

> **der Teenager** is also used for girls.

teens PL NOUN
■ She's in her teens. Sie ist ein Teenager.

tee-shirt NOUN
das T-Shirt *neut* (PL die T-Shirts)

teeth PL NOUN ▷ see **tooth**

to **teethe** VERB
zahnen [38]

teetotal ADJECTIVE
■ I'm teetotal. Ich trinke keinen Alkohol.

telecommunications PL NOUN
die Nachrichtentechnik *fem sing*

teleconferencing NOUN
die Telekonferenzen *fem pl*

★ **telephone** NOUN
das Telefon *neut* (PL die Telefone)
□ on the telephone am Telefon
■ a telephone box eine Telefonzelle
■ a telephone call ein Anruf *masc*
■ a telephone number eine Telefonnummer

telesales SING NOUN
der Telefonverkauf *masc* (PL die Telefonverkäufe)

telescope NOUN
das Teleskop *neut* (PL die Teleskope)

★ **television** NOUN
das Fernsehen *neut*
■ on television im Fernsehen
■ a television programme eine Fernsehsendung

t

★ to **tell** VERB
sagen [38]
■ **to tell somebody something** jemandem
etwas sagen [38] □ Did you tell your dad? Hast
du es deinem Papa gesagt? □ I told him that I
was going on holiday. Ich habe ihm gesagt, dass
ich in Urlaub fahre.
■ **to tell somebody to do something**
jemandem sagen [38], er solle etwas tun □ He
told me to wait a moment. Er sagte mir, ich
solle einen Moment warten.
■ **to tell lies** lügen [47]
■ **to tell a story** eine Geschichte erzählen [19]
■ **I can't tell the difference between them.**
Ich kann sie nicht unterscheiden.

to **tell off** VERB
schimpfen [38]

telly NOUN
der Fernseher masc (PL die Fernseher)
■ **to watch telly** fernsehen [64]
■ **on telly** im Fernsehen

temper NOUN
■ **to be in a temper** wütend sein [65]
■ **to lose one's temper** wütend werden [91]
□ I lost my temper. Ich bin wütend geworden.
■ **He's got a terrible temper.** Er ist furchtbar
jähzornig.

★ **temperature** NOUN
die Temperatur fem (of oven, water, person)
■ **The temperature was thirty degrees.** Es
waren dreißig Grad.
■ **to have a temperature** Fieber haben [32]

★ **temple** NOUN
der Tempel masc (PL die Tempel)

★ **temporary** ADJECTIVE
vorläufig

to **tempt** VERB
in Versuchung führen [38]
□ to tempt somebody to do something
jemanden in Versuchung führen, etwas zu tun
■ **I'm very tempted!** Das reizt mich sehr!

temptation NOUN
die Versuchung fem

tempting ADJECTIVE
verlockend

★ **ten** NUMBER
zehn
□ She's ten. Sie ist zehn.

tenant NOUN
der Mieter masc (PL die Mieter)
die Mieterin fem

tender ADJECTIVE
1 zärtlich (loving)
2 empfindlich
□ My neck is still tender. Mein Hals ist noch
immer empfindlich.

to **tend to** VERB
■ **to tend to do something** dazu neigen [38],
etwas zu tun □ He tends to arrive late. Er neigt
dazu, zu spät zu kommen.

★ **tennis** NOUN
das Tennis neut (GEN des Tennis)
□ Do you play tennis? Spielst du Tennis?
■ **a tennis ball** ein Tennisball masc
■ **a tennis court** ein Tennisplatz masc

tennis player NOUN
der Tennisspieler masc (PL die Tennisspieler)
die Tennisspielerin fem
□ She's a tennis player. Sie ist Tennisspielerin.

tenor NOUN
der Tenor masc (PL die Tenöre)

tenpin bowling NOUN
das Bowling neut
■ **to go tenpin bowling** Bowling spielen [38]

tense ADJECTIVE
▷ see also **tense** NOUN
angespannt
□ a tense situation eine angespannte Situation

tense NOUN
▷ see also **tense** ADJECTIVE
■ **the present tense** das Präsens
■ **the future tense** das Futur

tension NOUN
die Spannung fem

tent NOUN
das Zelt neut (PL die Zelte)

★ **tenth** ADJECTIVE
zehnte
□ the tenth floor der zehnte Stock □ the tenth
of August der zehnte August

★ **term** NOUN
das Trimester neut (PL die Trimester) (at school)

DID YOU KNOW...?
In Germany the school and university year
is divided into two semesters rather than
three terms.

■ **to come to terms with something** sich mit
etwas abfinden [24]

terminal ADJECTIVE
▷ see also **terminal** NOUN
unheilbar (illness, patient)

terminal NOUN
▷ see also **terminal** ADJECTIVE
das Terminal neut (PL die Terminals) (of
computer)
■ **an oil terminal** ein Ölterminal masc
■ **an air terminal** ein Terminal masc

terminally ADVERB
■ **to be terminally ill** unheilbar krank sein [65]

terrace NOUN
1 die Terrasse fem (patio)
2 die Häuserreihe fem (row of houses)
■ **the terraces** (at stadium) die Ränge

terraced ADJECTIVE
■ **a terraced house** ein Reihenhaus neut

★ **terrible** ADJECTIVE
furchtbar

Numbers in brackets refer to verb tables on pages 697 to 706.

639

t

□ My German is terrible. Mein Deutsch ist furchtbar.

terribly ADVERB

furchtbar

□ He suffered terribly. Er litt furchtbar. □ I'm terribly sorry. Es tut mir furchtbar leid.

terrier NOUN

der Terrier masc (PL die Terrier)

terrific ADJECTIVE

super (wonderful)

> super is invariable.

□ That's terrific! Das ist super! □ You look terrific! Du siehst super aus!

terrified ADJECTIVE

■ **I was terrified!** Ich hatte furchtbare Angst!

terrorism NOUN

der Terrorismus masc (GEN des Terrorismus)

★ **terrorist** NOUN

der Terrorist masc (GEN des Terroristen, PL die Terroristen)

die Terroristin fem

■ **a terrorist attack** ein Terrorangriff masc

★ **test** NOUN

▷ see also **test** VERB

1 die Arbeit fem (at school)

□ I've got a test tomorrow. Ich schreibe morgen eine Arbeit.

2 der Test masc (PL die Tests) (trial, check)

□ nuclear tests Atomtests

3 die Untersuchung fem (medical)

□ a blood test eine Blutuntersuchung □ They're going to do some more tests tomorrow. Sie machen morgen noch weitere Untersuchungen.

■ **driving test** die Fahrprüfung □ He's got his driving test tomorrow. Er hat morgen seine Fahrprüfung.

★ to **test** VERB

▷ see also **test** NOUN

1 probieren [76] (PERFECT TENSE hat probiert)

■ **to test something out** etwas ausprobieren [4]

2 abfragen [4] (PERFECT TENSE hat abgefragt) (class)

□ He tested us on the new vocabulary. Er hat uns die neuen Wörter abgefragt.

■ **She was tested for drugs.** Man hat bei ihr ein Drogentest gemacht.

test match NOUN

das Länderspiel neut (PL die Länderspiele)

test tube NOUN

das Reagenzglas neut (GEN des Reagenzglases, PL die Reagenzgläser)

tetanus NOUN

der Tetanus masc (GEN des Tetanus)

□ a tetanus injection eine Tetanusspritze

★ **text** NOUN

▷ see also **text** VERB

die SMS fem (PL die SMS) (text message)

★ **text** VERB

▷ see also **text** NOUN

eine SMS schicken [48]

□ I'll text you. Ich schicke dir eine SMS.

textbook NOUN

das Lehrbuch neut (PL die Lehrbücher)

■ **a German textbook** ein Deutschbuch

textiles PL NOUN

die Textilien fem pl

■ **a textiles factory** eine Textilfabrik

★ **text message** NOUN

die SMS fem (PL die SMS)

text messaging NOUN

das Versenden von SMS neut

Thames NOUN

die Themse fem

★ **than** CONJUNCTION

als

□ She's taller than me. Sie ist größer als ich. □ I've got more books than him. Ich habe mehr Bücher als er. □ more than ten years mehr als zehn Jahre □ more than once mehr als einmal

★ to **thank** VERB

sich bedanken [7] bei (PERFECT TENSE hat sich bedankt)

□ Don't forget to thank them. Vergiss nicht, dich bei ihnen zu bedanken.

■ **thank you** danke

■ **thank you very much** vielen Dank

thanks EXCLAMATION

danke

■ **thanks to** dank □ Thanks to him, everything went OK. Dank ihm ging alles gut.

★ **that** ADJECTIVE, PRONOUN, CONJUNCTION

1 dieser

□ that man dieser Mann

diese

□ that woman diese Frau

dieses

□ that book dieses Buch

■ **that one 1** (masculine) der da □ This man? — No, that one. Dieser Mann? — Nein, der da. **2** (feminine) die da □ This woman? — No, that one. Diese Frau? — Nein, die da. **3** (neuter) das da □ Do you like this photo? — No, I prefer that one. Gefällt dir dieses Foto? — Nein, das da gefällt mir besser.

2 das

□ Did you see that? Hast du das gesehen? □ What's that? Was ist das? □ Who's that? Wer ist das? □ Is that you? Bist du das?

■ **That's ...** Das ist ... □ That's my German teacher. Das ist meine Deutschlehrerin.

■ **That's what he said.** Das hat er gesagt.

> In relative clauses use **der**, **die** or **das**, depending on the gender of the noun 'that' refers to.

3 der

□ the man that saw us der Mann, der uns sah

★ = core vocabulary

die
□ **the woman that saw us** die Frau, die uns sah

das
□ **the child that saw us** das Kind, das uns sah

die
□ **the people that helped us** die Leute, die uns geholfen haben

4 dass
□ **He thought that Henry was ill.** Er dachte, dass Henry krank war. □ **I know that she likes chocolate.** Ich weiß, dass sie Schokolade mag.

5 so
□ **It was that big.** Es war so groß. □ **It's about that high.** Es ist etwa so hoch. □ **It's not that difficult.** Es ist nicht so schwierig.

★ **the** ARTICLE

Use **der** with a masculine noun, **die** with a feminine noun, and **das** with a neuter noun. For plural nouns always use **die**.

1 der
□ **the boy** der Junge
die
□ **the orange** die Orange
das
□ **the girl** das Mädchen

2 die
□ **the children** die Kinder

★ **theatre** NOUN
das Theater neut (PL die Theater)

theft NOUN
der Diebstahl masc (PL die Diebstähle)

★ **their** ADJECTIVE
ihr
□ **their father** ihr Vater □ **their mother** ihre Mutter □ **their child** ihr Kind □ **their parents** ihre Eltern

Do not use **ihr** with parts of the body.

□ **They can't bend their arms.** Sie können die Arme nicht bewegen.

theirs PRONOUN

1 ihrer
□ **This is our computer, not theirs.** Das ist unser Computer, nicht ihrer.
ihre
□ **It's not our garage, it's theirs.** Das ist nicht unsere Garage, sondern ihre.
ihres
□ **It's not our car, it's theirs.** Das ist nicht unser Auto, sondern ihres.

2 ihre
□ **Our teachers are stricter than theirs.** Unsere Lehrer sind strenger als ihre.
■ **Is this theirs?** Gehört das ihnen? □ **This car is theirs.** Das Auto gehört ihnen. □ **Whose is this?** — **It's theirs.** Wem gehört das? — Ihnen.

★ **them** PRONOUN

1 sie
□ **I didn't see them.** Ich habe sie nicht gesehen.

Use **sie** after prepositions which take the accusative.

□ **It's for them.** Es ist für sie.

2 ihnen

Use **ihnen** when 'them' means 'to them'.

□ **I gave them some brochures.** Ich habe ihnen ein paar Broschüren gegeben. □ **I told them the truth.** Ich habe ihnen die Wahrheit gesagt.

Use **ihnen** after prepositions which take the dative.

□ **Layla and Sophie came. Louis was with them.** Layla und Sophie sind gekommen. Louis war bei ihnen.

★ **theme** NOUN
das Thema neut (PL die Themen)

★ **themselves** PRONOUN

1 sich
□ **Did they hurt themselves?** Haben sie sich verletzt?

2 selbst
□ **They did it themselves.** Sie haben es selbst gemacht.

★ **then** ADVERB, CONJUNCTION

1 dann
□ **I get dressed. Then I have breakfast.** Ich ziehe mich an. Dann frühstücke ich. □ **My pen's run out. — Use a pencil then!** Mein Kugelschreiber ist leer. — Dann nimm einen Bleistift!

2 damals (at that time)
□ **There was no electricity then.** Damals gab es keinen Strom.
■ **now and then** ab und zu □ **Do you play chess? — Now and then.** Spielst du Schach? — Ab und zu.
■ **By then it was too late.** Da war es schon zu spät.

★ **therapy** NOUN
die Therapie fem

★ **there** ADVERB

Use **dort** when something is in a fixed position, **dorthin** when there is movement involved.

1 dort
□ **Can you see that house there?** Siehst du das Haus dort? □ **Brussels? I've never been there.** Brüssel? Ich war noch nie dort.
■ **over there** dort drüben
■ **in there** dort drin
■ **on there** darauf
■ **up there** dort oben
■ **down there** dort unten

2 dorthin
□ **Put it there.** Stell es dorthin. □ **He went there on Friday.** Er ging am Freitag dorthin.
■ **There he is!** Da ist er ja!
■ **There is ...** 1 Es ist ... □ **There's a factory near my house.** In der Nähe von meinem Haus ist eine Fabrik. 2 Es gibt ... □ **There is a lot of**

poverty in the world. Es gibt viel Armut auf der Welt.
- **There are ...** **1** Es sind ... □ There are five people in my family. In meiner Familie sind fünf Leute. **2** Es gibt ... □ There are many schools in this city. In dieser Stadt gibt es viele Schulen.
- **There has been an accident.** Es hat einen Unfall gegeben.

★ **therefore** ADVERB
deshalb

there's = there is, there has

thermometer NOUN
das Thermometer neut (PL die Thermometer)

Thermos® NOUN
die Thermosflasche® fem

★ **these** ADJECTIVE, PRONOUN
1 die
□ these shoes die Schuhe
- **THESE shoes** diese Schuhe hier
2 die hier
□ I want these! Ich möchte die hier! □ I'm looking for some sandals. Can I try these? Ich suche Sandalen. Kann ich die hier anprobieren?

★ **they** PRONOUN
sie
□ Are there any tickets left? — No, they're all sold out. Gibt es noch Karten? — Nein, sie sind schon alle ausverkauft. □ Do you like those shoes? — No, they're horrible. Gefallen dir die Schuhe? — Nein, sie sind furchtbar.
- **They say that ...** Man sagt, dass ...

they'd = they had, they would

they'll = they will

they're = they are

they've = they have

★ **thick** ADJECTIVE
1 dick (not thin)
□ one metre thick einen Meter dick
2 dumm (stupid)

★ **thief** NOUN
der Dieb masc (PL die Diebe)
die Diebin fem

thigh NOUN
der Schenkel masc

★ **thin** ADJECTIVE
dünn

> **WORD POWER**
> You can use a number of other words instead of **thin** to mean 'skinny':
> **lanky** schlaksig
> □ a lanky boy ein schlaksiger Junge
> **skinny** mager
> □ a skinny dog ein magerer Hund
> **slim** schlank
> □ a slim girl ein schlankes Mädchen

★ **thing** NOUN
das Ding neut (PL die Dinge)
□ beautiful things schöne Dinge □ What's that

thing called? Wie heißt das Ding da?
- **my things** (belongings) meine Sachen
- **You poor thing!** **1** (man) Du Armer! **2** (woman) Du Arme!

★ **to think** VERB
1 denken [14] (IMPERFECT dachte, PERFECT TENSE hat gedacht)
□ I think you're wrong. Ich denke, du hast unrecht. □ What are you thinking about? Woran denkst du?
- **What do you think about the suggestion?** Was halten Sie von dem Vorschlag?
2 glauben [38]
□ I don't think I can come. Ich glaube nicht, dass ich kommen kann.
- **I think so.** Ich glaube schon.
- **I don't think so.** Ich glaube nicht.
3 nachdenken [14] (PERFECT TENSE hat nachgedacht) (spend time thinking)
□ Think carefully before you reply. Denk gut nach, bevor du antwortest. □ I'll think about it. Ich denke darüber nach.
4 sich vorstellen [4] (PERFECT TENSE hat sich vorgestellt) (imagine)
□ Just think, this time next week we'll be on holiday! Stell dir vor, heute in einer Woche haben wir Ferien!
- **I'll think it over.** Ich werde es mir überlegen.

★ **third** ADJECTIVE
▷ see also **third** NOUN
dritte
□ the third day der dritte Tag □ the third time das dritte Mal □ the third of August der dritte August
- **He came third.** Er wurde Dritter.

★ **third** NOUN
▷ see also **third** ADJECTIVE
das Drittel neut (PL die Drittel)
□ a third of the population ein Drittel der Bevölkerung

thirdly ADVERB
drittens

★ **Third World** NOUN
die Dritte Welt fem

thirst NOUN
der Durst masc

★ **thirsty** ADJECTIVE
- **to be thirsty** Durst haben [32] □ Are you thirsty? Hast du Durst?

★ **thirteen** NUMBER
dreizehn
□ I'm thirteen. Ich bin dreizehn.

★ **thirteenth** ADJECTIVE
dreizehnte
□ the thirteenth of August der dreizehnte August

★ **thirty** NUMBER
dreißig
□ She's thirty. Sie ist dreißig.

★ = core vocabulary

this ADJECTIVE, PRONOUN

1 dieser

□ this man dieser Mann

diese

□ this woman diese Frau

dieses

□ this child dieses Kind

■ **this one 1** (*masculine*) der hier □ That man over there? — No, this one. Der Mann dort? — Nein, der hier. **2** (*feminine*) die hier □ That woman over there? — No, this one. Die Frau dort? — Nein, die hier. **3** (*neuter*) das hier □ I don't like that picture over there, I prefer this one. Das Bild dort gefällt mir nicht, das hier gefällt mir besser.

2 das

□ You see this? Siehst du das? □ What's this? Was ist das? □ This is my mother. (*introduction*) Das ist meine Mutter.

■ **This is Dylan speaking.** (*on the phone*) Hier spricht Dylan.

thistle NOUN

die Distel *fem*

thorough ADJECTIVE

gründlich

□ She's very thorough. Sie ist sehr gründlich.

thoroughly ADVERB

gründlich (*examine*)

those ADJECTIVE, PRONOUN

1 diese

□ those shoes diese Schuhe

■ **THOSE shoes** diese Schuhe dort

2 die da

□ I want those! Ich möchte die da! □ I'm looking for some sandals. Can I try those? Ich suche Sandalen. Kann ich die da anprobieren?

though CONJUNCTION, ADVERB

obwohl

□ It's warm, though it's raining. Es ist warm, obwohl es regnet.

■ **He's nice, though not very clever.** Er ist nett, aber nicht besonders klug.

thought VERB ▷ *see* **think**

thought NOUN

der Gedanke *masc* (GEN des Gedankens, PL die Gedanken) (*idea*)

□ I've just had a thought. Mir ist eben ein Gedanke gekommen.

■ **It was a nice thought, thank you.** Das war nett, vielen Dank.

■ **It's the thought that counts.** Es war gut gemeint.

thoughtful ADJECTIVE

1 nachdenklich (*deep in thought*)

□ You look thoughtful. Du siehst nachdenklich aus.

2 aufmerksam (*considerate*)

□ She's very thoughtful. Sie ist sehr aufmerksam.

thoughtless ADJECTIVE

gedankenlos

★ **thousand** NUMBER

■ **a thousand** eintausend □ a thousand euros eintausend Euro

■ **two thousand pounds** zweitausend Pfund

■ **thousands of people** Tausende von Menschen

thousandth ADJECTIVE

tausendste

thread NOUN

der Faden *masc* (PL die Fäden)

★ **threat** NOUN

die Drohung *fem*

★ to **threaten** VERB

drohen [38]

□ He threatened me. Er hat mir gedroht. □ to threaten to do something drohen, etwas zu tun

★ **three** NUMBER

drei

□ She's three. Sie ist drei.

three-dimensional ADJECTIVE

dreidimensional

three-piece suite NOUN

die dreiteilige Polstergarnitur *fem*

threw VERB ▷ *see* **throw**

thrifty ADJECTIVE

sparsam

thrill NOUN

der Reiz *masc* (GEN des Reizes, PL die Reize) (*excitement*)

■ **It was a great thrill.** Es war sehr aufregend.

thrilled ADJECTIVE

■ **I was thrilled.** (*pleased*) Ich habe mich unheimlich gefreut.

thriller NOUN

der Thriller *masc* (PL die Thriller)

thrilling ADJECTIVE

spannend

★ **throat** NOUN

der Hals *masc* (GEN des Halses, PL die Hälse)

■ **to have a sore throat** Halsweh haben [32]

to **throb** VERB

■ **a throbbing pain** ein pochender Schmerz

■ **My arm's throbbing.** Mir pocht es im Arm.

throne NOUN

der Thron *masc* (PL die Throne)

★ **through** PREPOSITION, ADJECTIVE, ADVERB

durch

□ through the window durch das Fenster □ to go through Leeds durch Leeds fahren □ to go through a tunnel durch einen Tunnel fahren

■ **I know her through my sister.** Ich kenne sie über meine Schwester.

■ **He doesn't live here – he's just passing through.** Er wohnt nicht hier - er ist nur auf der Durchreise.

t

- **a through train** ein durchgehender Zug
- **'no through road'** 'keine Durchfahrt'

★ **throughout** PREPOSITION
  - **throughout Britain** in ganz Großbritannien
  - **throughout the year** das ganze Jahr über

★ to **throw** VERB
  werfen [92] (PRESENT TENSE wirft, IMPERFECT warf, PERFECT TENSE hat geworfen)
  □ He threw the ball to me. Er warf mir den Ball zu.
  - **to throw a party** eine Party machen [48]
  - **That really threw him.** Das hat ihn aus der Fassung gebracht.

to **throw away** VERB
  1 wegwerfen [92] (object)
  2 vergeben [28] (chance)

to **throw out** VERB
  1 wegwerfen [92] (object)
  2 rauswerfen [92] (person)
  □ I threw him out. Ich habe ihn rausgeworfen.

to **throw up** VERB
  sich übergeben [28]

thug NOUN
  der Schlägertyp masc (PL die Schlägertypen)

thumb NOUN
  der Daumen masc (PL die Daumen)

thumb tack NOUN (US)
  die Reißzwecke fem

to **thump** VERB
  - **to thump somebody** jemandem eine verpassen [7] (informal) □ I thumped him. Ich habe ihm eine verpasst.

thunder NOUN
  der Donner masc (PL die Donner)

thunderstorm NOUN
  das Gewitter neut (PL die Gewitter)

thundery ADJECTIVE
  gewitterig

★ **Thursday** NOUN
  der Donnerstag masc (PL die Donnerstage)
  □ on Thursday am Donnerstag □ every Thursday jeden Donnerstag □ last Thursday letzten Donnerstag □ next Thursday nächsten Donnerstag
  - **on Thursdays** donnerstags

thyme NOUN
  der Thymian masc (PL die Thymiane)

tick NOUN
  ▷ see also **tick** VERB
  1 das Häkchen neut (PL die Häkchen) (mark)
  2 das Ticken neut (of clock)
  - **in a tick** in einer Sekunde

to **tick** VERB
  ▷ see also **tick** NOUN
  1 ankreuzen [36] (PERFECT TENSE hat angekreuzt)
  □ Tick the correct answer. Kreuzen Sie die richtige Antwort an.
  2 ticken [48] (clock)

to **tick off** VERB
  1 abhaken [4] (on list)
  2 ausschimpfen [4] (scold)

★ **ticket** NOUN
  1 die Fahrkarte fem (for bus, tube, train)
  □ an underground ticket eine Fahrkarte für die U-Bahn
  2 das Ticket neut (PL die Tickets) (for plane)
  3 die Eintrittskarte fem (for theatre, concert, cinema, museum)
  - **a parking ticket** ein Strafzettel masc

ticket inspector NOUN
  der Fahrscheinkontrolleur masc (PL die Fahrscheinkontrolleure)
  die Fahrscheinkontrolleurin fem

ticket office NOUN
  1 der Fahrkartenschalter masc (PL die Fahrkartenschalter) (for travel)
  2 die Kasse fem (for theatre, cinema)

to **tickle** VERB
  kitzeln [34]

ticklish ADJECTIVE
  kitzlig
  □ Are you ticklish? Bist du kitzlig?

★ **tide** NOUN
  - **high tide** die Flut
  - **low tide** die Ebbe

★ **tidy** ADJECTIVE
  ▷ see also **tidy** VERB
  ordentlich
  □ Your room is very tidy. Dein Zimmer ist sehr ordentlich. □ She's very tidy. Sie ist sehr ordentlich.

★ to **tidy** VERB
  ▷ see also **tidy** ADJECTIVE
  aufräumen [4] (PERFECT TENSE hat aufgeräumt)
  □ Go and tidy your room. Geh und räum dein Zimmer auf.

to **tidy up** VERB
  aufräumen [4]
  □ Don't forget to tidy up afterwards. Vergesst nicht, nachher aufzuräumen.

★ **tie** NOUN
  ▷ see also **tie** VERB
  die Krawatte fem (necktie)
  - **It was a tie.** (in sport) Es gab ein Unentschieden.

★ to **tie** VERB
  ▷ see also **tie** NOUN
  1 zubinden (IMPERFECT band zu, PERFECT TENSE hat zugebunden) (ribbon, shoelaces)
  - **I tied a knot in the rope.** Ich machte einen Knoten in das Seil.
  2 unentschieden spielen [38] (in sport)
  - **They tied three all.** Sie haben drei zu drei gespielt.

to **tie up** VERB
  1 zuschnüren [4] (parcel)
  2 anbinden (dog, boat)

3 fesseln [34] (*prisoner*)

tiger NOUN
der Tiger *masc* (PL die Tiger)

★ **tight** ADJECTIVE
1 eng (*tight-fitting*)
  □ tight jeans enge Jeans
2 zu eng (*too tight*)
  □ This dress is a bit tight. Das Kleid ist etwas zu eng.

to **tighten** VERB
1 spannen [38] (*rope*)
2 anziehen [96] (IMPERFECT zog an, PERFECT TENSE hat angezogen) (*screw*)

tightly ADVERB
fest (*hold*)

tights PL NOUN
die Strumpfhose *fem sing*
  □ a pair of tights eine Strumpfhose

tile NOUN
1 der Dachziegel *masc* (PL die Dachziegel) (*on roof*)
2 die Fliese *fem* (*on wall, floor*)

tiled ADJECTIVE
1 gekachelt (*wall*)
2 mit Fliesen ausgelegt (*floor, room*)
  ■ a tiled roof ein Ziegeldach *neut*

★ **till** NOUN
  ▷ *see also* **till** PREPOSITION, CONJUNCTION
  die Kasse *fem*

★ **till** PREPOSITION, CONJUNCTION
  ▷ *see also* **till** NOUN
1 bis
  □ I waited till ten o'clock. Ich habe bis zehn Uhr gewartet.
  ■ till now bis jetzt
  ■ till then bis dann
2 vor

> Use **vor** if the sentence you want to translate contains a negative such as 'not' or 'never'.

  □ It won't be ready till next week. Vor nächster Woche wird es nicht fertig. □ Till last year I'd never been to Germany. Vor letztem Jahr war ich nie in Deutschland.

★ **time** NOUN
1 die Zeit *fem*
  □ It's time to get up. Es ist Zeit zum Aufstehen.
  □ It was two o'clock, German time. Es war zwei Uhr, deutsche Zeit. □ I'm sorry, I haven't got time. Ich habe leider keine Zeit.
  ■ What time is it? Wie viel Uhr ist es?
  ■ What time do you get up? Um wie viel Uhr stehst du auf?
  ■ on time pünktlich □ He never arrives on time. Er kommt nie pünktlich.
  ■ from time to time von Zeit zu Zeit
  ■ in time rechtzeitig □ We arrived in time for lunch. Wir kamen rechtzeitig zum Mittagessen.
  ■ just in time gerade noch rechtzeitig
  ■ in no time im Nu □ It was ready in no time. Es war im Nu fertig.

2 der Moment *masc* (PL die Momente) (*moment*)
  □ This isn't a good time to ask him. Das ist kein guter Moment, um ihn zu fragen.
  ■ for the time being momentan

3 das Mal *neut* (PL die Male) (*occasion*)
  □ next time nächstes Mal
  ■ this time diesmal
  ■ two at a time jeweils zwei
  ■ How many times? Wie oft?
  ■ at times manchmal
  ■ a long time lange □ Have you lived here a long time? Wohnst du schon lange hier?
  ■ in a week's time in einer Woche □ I'll come back in a month's time. Ich komme in einem Monat wieder.
  ■ Come and see us any time. Besuchen sie uns, wann Sie wollen.
  ■ to have a good time sich amüsieren [76]
  □ Did you have a good time? Habt ihr euch amüsiert?
  ■ two times two zwei mal zwei

time bomb NOUN
die Zeitbombe *fem*

time off NOUN
die Freizeit *fem*

timer NOUN
1 die Schaltuhr *fem* (*time switch*)
2 der Kurzzeitmesser *masc* (PL die Kurzzeitmesser) (*for cooking*)
  ■ an egg timer eine Eieruhr

time-share NOUN
das Timesharing-Appartement *neut* (PL die Timesharing-Appartements)

★ **timetable** NOUN
1 der Fahrplan *masc* (PL die Fahrpläne) (*for train, bus*)
2 der Stundenplan *masc* (PL die Stundenpläne) (*at school*)

time zone NOUN
die Zeitzone *fem*

★ **tin** NOUN
1 die Dose *fem*
  □ a tin of beans eine Dose Bohnen □ a biscuit tin eine Keksdose
2 das Zinn *neut* (*type of metal*)

tinned ADJECTIVE
in Dosen (*food*)
  □ tinned peaches Pfirsiche in Dosen

tin opener NOUN
der Dosenöffner *masc* (PL die Dosenöffner)

tinsel NOUN
die Rauschgoldgirlande *fem*

tinted ADJECTIVE
getönt (*spectacles, glass*)

★ **tiny** ADJECTIVE
winzig

★ **tip** NOUN
  ▷ *see also* **tip** VERB
1 das Trinkgeld *neut* (PL die Trinkgelder) (*money*)

Numbers in brackets refer to verb tables on pages 697 to 706.

645

t

□ **Shall I give him a tip?** Soll ich ihm ein Trinkgeld geben?

2 der Tipp *masc* (PL die Tipps) (*advice*)
□ **a useful tip** ein guter Tipp

3 die Spitze *fem* (*end*)
■ **It's on the tip of my tongue.** Es liegt mir auf der Zunge.
■ **a rubbish tip** eine Müllkippe
■ **This place is a complete tip!** Was für ein Saustall! (*informal*)

★ **to tip** VERB
▷ *see also* **tip** NOUN
■ **to tip somebody** jemandem ein Trinkgeld geben [28] □ He tipped the taxi driver generously. Er gab dem Taxifahrer ein großzügiges Trinkgeld.

tipsy ADJECTIVE
beschwipst
□ **I'm feeling a bit tipsy.** Ich bin etwas beschwipst.

tiptoe NOUN
■ **on tiptoe** auf Zehenspitzen

★ **tired** ADJECTIVE
müde
□ **I'm tired.** Ich bin müde.
■ **to be tired of something** etwas leid sein [65]

tiring ADJECTIVE
ermüdend

★ **tissue** NOUN
das Papiertaschentuch *neut* (PL die Papiertaschentücher)
□ **Have you got a tissue?** Hast du ein Papiertaschentuch?

★ **title** NOUN
der Titel *masc* (PL die Titel)

title role NOUN
die Titelrolle *fem*

★ **to** PREPOSITION
1 nach
□ **to go to Munich** nach München fahren □ We went to Italy. Wir sind nach Italien gefahren. □ the train to London der Zug nach London □ the road to Edinburgh die Straße nach Edinburgh □ **to the left** nach links
■ **I've never been to Munich.** Ich war noch nie in München.
2 in
□ **to go to school** in die Schule gehen □ to go to the theatre ins Theater gehen
3 zu

> Use **zu** when you talk about going to a particular place or person.

□ **We drove to the station.** Wir fuhren zum Bahnhof. □ to go to the doctor's zum Arzt gehen □ to go to the baker's zum Bäcker gehen □ Let's go to Ossi's house. Lass uns zu Ossi nach Hause gehen.
■ **a letter to his mother** ein Brief an seine Mutter

■ **It's hard to say.** Es ist schwer zu sagen.
■ **It's easy to criticize.** Es ist leicht zu kritisieren.
■ **something to drink** etwas zu trinken
4 bis (*as far as, until*)
□ **to count to ten** bis zehn zählen □ It's ninety kilometres to the border. Es sind neunzig Kilometer bis zur Grenze.
■ **from ... to** von ... bis □ from nine o'clock to half past three von neun bis halb vier
■ **ten to nine** zehn vor neun

> Use the dative when you say or give something to somebody.

□ **Give it to me!** Gib es mir! □ That's what he said to me. Das ist, was er zu mir gesagt hat. □ We said goodbye to the neighbours. Wir sagten den Nachbarn Auf Wiedersehen. □ I sold it to a friend. Ich habe es einem Freund verkauft.
■ **to talk to somebody** mit jemandem reden [54]

> When 'to' is used with the infinitive, it is often not translated.

□ **I'd like to go.** Ich würde gern gehen. □ I don't want to see him. Ich möchte ihn nicht sehen.
5 um ... zu (*in order to*)

> **um ... zu** is used with the infinitive.

□ **I did it to help you.** Ich tat es, um dir zu helfen. □ She's too young to go to school. Sie ist noch zu jung, um in die Schule zu gehen.
■ **the key to the front door** der Schlüssel für die Haustür
■ **the answer to the question** die Antwort auf die Frage

toad NOUN
die Kröte *fem*

toadstool NOUN
der Giftpilz *masc* (GEN des Giftpilzes, PL die Giftpilze)

★ **toast** NOUN
1 der Toast *masc* (PL die Toasts)
□ **a piece of toast** eine Scheibe Toast
2 der Trinkspruch *masc* (PL die Trinksprüche) (*speech*)
□ **to drink a toast to somebody** einen Trinkspruch auf jemanden ausbringen

toaster NOUN
der Toaster *masc* (PL die Toaster)

toastie NOUN
der Toast *masc* (PL die Toasts)
□ **a cheese toastie** ein Käsetoast

tobacco NOUN
der Tabak *masc*

tobacconist's NOUN
der Tabakladen *masc* (PL die Tabakläden)

toboggan NOUN
der Schlitten *masc* (PL die Schlitten)

tobogganing NOUN
- **to go tobogganing** Schlitten fahren [21]

★ **today** ADVERB
heute
□ What did you do today? Was hast du heute gemacht?

toddler NOUN
das Kleinkind neut (PL die Kleinkinder)

★ **toe** NOUN
der Zeh masc (PL die Zehen)
□ my big toe mein großer Zeh

toffee NOUN
der Karamell masc

★ **together** ADVERB
1 zusammen
□ Are they still together? Sind sie noch zusammen?
2 gleichzeitig (at the same time)
□ Don't all speak together! Redet nicht alle gleichzeitig!
- **together with** (with person) zusammen mit

★ **toilet** NOUN
die Toilette fem

toilet paper NOUN
das Toilettenpapier neut

toiletries PL NOUN
die Toilettenartikel masc pl

toilet roll NOUN
die Rolle Toilettenpapier fem

token NOUN
- **a gift token** ein Geschenkgutschein masc

told VERB ▷ see tell

tolerant ADJECTIVE
tolerant

toll NOUN
die Benutzungsgebühr fem (on bridge, motorway)

★ **tomato** NOUN
die Tomate fem
□ tomato soup die Tomatensuppe

tomboy NOUN
der Wildfang masc
□ She's a real tomboy. Sie ist ein echter Wildfang.

★ **tomorrow** ADVERB
morgen
□ tomorrow morning morgen früh □ tomorrow night morgen Abend
- **the day after tomorrow** übermorgen

★ **ton** NOUN
die Tonne fem
□ That old bike weighs a ton. Das alte Fahrrad wiegt ja eine Tonne.

★ **tongue** NOUN
die Zunge fem
- **to say something tongue in cheek** etwas nicht so ernst meinen [38]

tonic NOUN
das Tonic neut (PL die Tonics) (tonic water)
- **a gin and tonic** ein Gin Tonic masc

★ **tonight** ADVERB
1 heute Abend (this evening)
□ Are you going out tonight? Gehst du heute Abend aus?
2 heute Nacht (during the night)
□ I'll sleep well tonight. Ich werde heute Nacht gut schlafen.

tonsillitis NOUN
die Mandelentzündung fem
□ She's got tonsillitis. Sie hat eine Mandelentzündung.

tonsils PL NOUN
die Mandeln fem pl

★ **too** ADVERB, ADJECTIVE
1 auch (as well)
□ My sister came too. Meine Schwester ist auch mitgekommen.
2 zu (excessively)
□ The water's too hot. Das Wasser ist zu heiß.
□ We arrived too late. Wir sind zu spät gekommen.
- **too much** zu viel □ too much noise zu viel Lärm □ At Christmas we always eat too much. Zu Weihnachten essen wir immer zu viel.
□ Seventy euros? That's too much. Siebzig Euro? Das ist zu viel.
- **too many** zu viele □ too many burgers zu viele Burger
- **Too bad!** Da kann man nichts machen!

took VERB ▷ see take

★ **tool** NOUN
das Werkzeug neut (PL die Werkzeuge)
- **a tool box** ein Werkzeugkasten masc

★ **tooth** NOUN
der Zahn masc (PL die Zähne)

★ **toothache** NOUN
die Zahnschmerzen masc pl
□ to have toothache Zahnschmerzen haben

★ **toothbrush** NOUN
die Zahnbürste fem

★ **toothpaste** NOUN
die Zahnpasta fem (PL die Zahnpasten)

★ **top** NOUN
▷ see also top ADJECTIVE
1 die Spitze fem (of tree)
2 der Gipfel masc (PL die Gipfel) (of mountain)
3 das Oberteil neut (PL die Oberteile) (of garment)
□ a bikini top ein Bikinioberteil
4 das Kopfende neut (PL die Kopfenden) (of table)
5 der Deckel masc (PL die Deckel) (of box, jar)
6 der Verschluss masc (GEN des Verschlusses, PL die Verschlüsse) (of bottle)
- **at the top of the page** oben auf der Seite
- **to reach the top of the ladder** oben auf der Leiter ankommen [40]
- **on top of** (on) oben auf □ on top of the

Numbers in brackets refer to verb tables on pages 697 to 706.

t

647

cupboard oben auf dem Schrank
■ **There's a surcharge on top of that.** Es
kommt noch ein Zuschlag dazu.
■ **from top to bottom** von oben bis unten □ I
searched the house from top to bottom. Ich
habe das Haus von oben bis unten durchsucht.

★ **top** ADJECTIVE
▷ see also **top** NOUN
erstklassig (first-class)
□ a top hotel ein erstklassiges Hotel
■ **a top surgeon** ein Spitzenchirurg masc
■ **a top model** (fashion) ein Topmodel neut
■ **He always gets top marks.** Er bekommt
immer Spitzennoten.
■ **the top floor** der oberste Stock □ on the top
floor im obersten Stock

topic NOUN
das Thema neut (PL die Themen)
□ The essay can be on any topic. Der Aufsatz
kann über ein beliebiges Thema sein.

topical ADJECTIVE
aktuell
□ a topical issue ein aktuelles Problem

torch NOUN
die Taschenlampe fem

tore, torn VERB ▷ see **tear**

tortoise NOUN
die Schildkröte fem

★ **torture** NOUN
▷ see also **torture** VERB
die Folter fem
■ **It was pure torture.** Es war die Hölle.
(informal)

★ to **torture** VERB
▷ see also **torture** NOUN
quälen [38]
□ Stop torturing that poor animal! Hör auf, das
arme Tier zu quälen!

Tory ADJECTIVE
▷ see also **Tory** NOUN
konservativ
□ the Tory government die konservative
Regierung

Tory NOUN
▷ see also **Tory** ADJECTIVE
der Konservative masc (GEN des Konservativen,
PL die Konservativen)
die Konservative fem (GEN der Konservativen)
□ a Tory (man) ein Konservativer
■ **the Tories** die Konservativen

to **toss** VERB
■ **to toss pancakes** Pfannkuchen in der Luft
wenden
■ **Shall we toss for it?** Sollen wir eine Münze
werfen?

★ **total** ADJECTIVE
▷ see also **total** NOUN
gesamt
□ the total amount der gesamte Betrag

★ **total** NOUN
▷ see also **total** ADJECTIVE
1 die Gesamtmenge fem (amount)
2 die Endsumme fem (money, figures)
■ **the grand total** die Gesamtsumme

totally ADVERB
völlig
□ He's totally useless. Er ist völlig unfähig.

★ **touch** NOUN
▷ see also **touch** VERB
■ **to get in touch with somebody** sich mit
jemandem in Verbindung setzen [36]
■ **to keep in touch with somebody** mit
jemandem in Verbindung bleiben [10]
■ **Keep in touch!** Lass von dir hören!
■ **to lose touch** sich aus den Augen verlieren
[85]
■ **to lose touch with somebody** jemanden
aus den Augen verlieren [85]

★ to **touch** VERB
▷ see also **touch** NOUN
berühren [18] (PERFECT TENSE hat berührt)
■ **'Do not touch'** 'Nicht berühren'
■ **Don't touch that!** Fass das nicht an!

touchdown NOUN
die Landung fem

touched ADJECTIVE
gerührt
□ I was really touched. Ich war wirklich gerührt.

touching ADJECTIVE
rührend

touchline NOUN
die Seitenlinie fem

touchscreen NOUN
das Touchscreen neut

touchy ADJECTIVE
empfindlich
□ She's a bit touchy. Sie ist etwas empfindlich.

★ **tough** ADJECTIVE
1 hart
□ It was tough, but I managed OK. Es war hart,
aber ich habe es geschafft. □ It's a tough job.
Das ist eine harte Arbeit. □ He thinks he's a
tough guy. Er meint, er sei ein harter Bursche.
2 zäh (meat)
□ The meat's tough. Das Fleisch ist zäh.
3 fest (strong)
□ tough leather gloves feste Lederhandschuhe
■ **Tough luck!** Das ist Pech!

toupee NOUN
das Toupet neut (PL die Toupets)

★ **tour** NOUN
▷ see also **tour** VERB
1 die Besichtigung fem (of town, museum)
■ **We went on a tour of the city.** Wir haben
die Stadt besichtigt.
■ **a guided tour** eine Führung
■ **a package tour** eine Pauschalreise

★ = core vocabulary

2 die Tournee *fem* (*by singer, group*)
□ **on tour** auf Tournee □ **to go on tour** auf Tournee gehen

★ to **tour** VERB
▷ *see also* **tour** NOUN
■ **Rihanna's touring Europe.** Rihanna ist auf Europatournee.

tour guide NOUN
der Reiseleiter *masc* (PL die Reiseleiter)
die Reiseleiterin *fem*

tourism NOUN
der Tourismus *masc* (GEN des Tourismus)

★ **tourist** NOUN
der Tourist *masc* (GEN des Touristen, PL die Touristen)
die Touristin *fem*
■ **tourist information office** das Verkehrsbüro

★ **tournament** NOUN
das Turnier *neut* (PL die Turniere)

tour operator NOUN
der Reiseveranstalter *masc* (PL die Reiseveranstalter)

★ **towards** PREPOSITION
1 auf ... zu (*in the direction of*)
□ **He came towards me.** Er kam auf mich zu.
2 gegenüber (*of attitude*)
□ **my feelings towards him** meine Empfindungen ihm gegenüber

★ **towel** NOUN
das Handtuch *neut* (PL die Handtücher)

★ **tower** NOUN
der Turm *masc* (PL die Türme)
■ **a tower block** ein Hochhaus *neut*

★ **town** NOUN
die Stadt *fem* (PL die Städte)
■ **a town plan** ein Stadtplan *masc*
■ **the town centre** die Stadtmitte
■ **the town hall** das Rathaus

tow truck NOUN (US)
der Abschleppwagen *masc* (PL die Abschleppwagen)

★ **toy** NOUN
das Spielzeug *neut* (PL die Spielzeuge)
■ **a toy shop** ein Spielwarengeschäft *neut*
■ **a toy car** ein Spielzeugauto *neut*

trace NOUN
▷ *see also* **trace** VERB
die Spur *fem*
□ **There was no trace of him.** Von ihm fehlte jede Spur.

to **trace** VERB
▷ *see also* **trace** NOUN
nachziehen [96] (IMPERFECT zog nach, PERFECT TENSE hat nachgezogen) (*draw*)

tracing paper NOUN
das Pauspapier *neut*

track NOUN
1 der Pfad *masc* (PL die Pfade) (*dirt road*)
2 das Gleis *neut* (GEN des Gleises, PL die Gleise) (*railway line*)
3 die Rennbahn *fem* (*in sport*)
□ **two laps of the track** zwei Runden der Rennbahn
4 das Stück *neut* (PL die Stücke) (*song*)
□ **This is my favourite track.** Das ist mein Lieblingsstück.
5 die Spur *fem* (*trail*)
□ **They followed the tracks for miles.** Sie folgten der Spur meilenweit.

to **track down** VERB
■ **to track somebody down** jemanden finden [24] □ **The police never tracked down the thief.** Die Polizei hat den Dieb nie gefunden.

★ **tracksuit** NOUN
der Jogginganzug *masc* (PL die Jogginganzüge)

tractor NOUN
der Traktor *masc* (PL die Traktoren)

trade NOUN
das Handwerk *neut* (*skill, job*)
□ **to learn a trade** ein Handwerk erlernen

trade union NOUN
die Gewerkschaft *fem*

> **DID YOU KNOW...?**
> Unions in Germany are organized within the **Deutscher Gewerkschaftsbund (DGB)**.

trade unionist NOUN
der Gewerkschafter *masc* (PL die Gewerkschafter)
die Gewerkschafterin *fem*

★ **tradition** NOUN
die Tradition *fem*

★ **traditional** ADJECTIVE
traditionell

traffic NOUN
der Verkehr *masc*
□ **The traffic was terrible.** Es war furchtbar viel Verkehr.

traffic circle NOUN (US)
der Kreisverkehr *masc* (PL die Kreisverkehre)

traffic jam NOUN
der Stau *masc* (PL die Staus)

★ **traffic lights** PL NOUN
die Ampel *fem sing*

traffic warden NOUN
1 der Hilfspolizist *masc* (GEN des Hilfspolizisten, PL die Hilfspolizisten) (*man*)
2 die Politesse *fem* (*woman*)

★ **tragedy** NOUN
die Tragödie *fem*

tragic ADJECTIVE
tragisch

trailer NOUN
1 der Anhänger *masc* (PL die Anhänger) (*vehicle*)

train – travel agent

2 der Wohnwagen *masc* (PL die Wohnwagen) (*caravan*)

3 die Vorschau *fem* (*advert for film*)

★ **train** NOUN
▷ *see also* **train** VERB
der Zug *masc* (PL die Züge)

★ to **train** VERB
▷ *see also* **train** NOUN
trainieren [76] (PERFECT TENSE hat trainiert) (*sport*)
□ to train for a race für ein Rennen trainieren
■ **to train as a teacher** eine Lehrerausbildung machen [48]
■ **to train an animal to do something** ein Tier dressieren [76], etwas zu tun

trained ADJECTIVE
gelernt
□ She's a trained nurse. Sie ist gelernte Krankenschwester.

trainee NOUN
1 der Praktikant *masc* (GEN des Praktikanten, PL die Praktikanten)
die Praktikantin *fem* (*in profession*)
□ She's a trainee. Sie ist Praktikantin.
2 der Lehrling *masc* (PL die Lehrlinge) (*apprentice*)

der Lehrling is also used for women.

□ She's a trainee plumber. Sie ist Klempnerlehrling.

trainer NOUN
1 der Trainer *masc* (PL die Trainer)
die Trainerin *fem* (*sports coach*)
2 der Dresseur *masc* (PL die Dresseure)
die Dresseuse *fem* (*of animals*)

★ **trainers** PL NOUN
die Turnschuhe *masc pl*
□ a pair of trainers ein Paar Turnschuhe

★ **training** NOUN
1 die Ausbildung *fem*
□ a training course ein Ausbildungskurs *masc*
2 das Training *neut* (PL die Trainings) (*sport*)

tram NOUN
die Straßenbahn *fem*

tramp NOUN
der Landstreicher *masc* (PL die Landstreicher)
die Landstreicherin *fem*

trampoline NOUN
das Trampolin *neut* (PL die Trampoline)

transfer NOUN
das Abziehbild *neut* (PL die Abziehbilder) (*sticker*)

transfusion NOUN
die Transfusion *fem*

transistor NOUN
der Transistor *masc* (PL die Transistoren)

transit lounge NOUN
die Transithalle *fem*

to **translate** VERB
übersetzen [36] (PERFECT TENSE hat übersetzt)

□ to translate something into English etwas ins Englische übersetzen

translation NOUN
die Übersetzung *fem*

translator NOUN
der Übersetzer *masc* (PL die Übersetzer)
die Übersetzerin *fem*
□ Anita's a translator. Anita ist Übersetzerin.

transparent ADJECTIVE
durchsichtig

transplant NOUN
die Transplantation *fem*
□ a heart transplant eine Herztransplantation

★ **transport** NOUN
▷ *see also* **transport** VERB
der Transport *masc* (PL die Transporte)
□ the transport of goods der Warentransport

★ to **transport** VERB
▷ *see also* **transport** NOUN
transportieren [76] (PERFECT TENSE hat transportiert)

trap NOUN
die Falle *fem*

trash NOUN (US)
der Müll *masc*

trash can NOUN (US)
der Mülleimer *masc* (PL die Mülleimer)

trashy ADJECTIVE
trashig (*informal*)
□ a really trashy film ein echt trashiger Film

traumatic ADJECTIVE
traumatisch
□ a traumatic experience ein traumatisches Erlebnis

★ **travel** NOUN
▷ *see also* **travel** VERB
das Reisen *neut*

★ to **travel** VERB
▷ *see also* **travel** NOUN
reisen [36] (PERFECT TENSE ist gereist)
□ I prefer to travel by train. Ich reise lieber mit dem Zug.
■ **I'd like to travel round the world.** Ich würde gern eine Weltreise machen.
■ **We travelled over eight hundred kilometres.** Wir haben über achthundert Kilometer zurückgelegt.
■ **News travels fast!** Neuigkeiten sprechen sich schnell herum!

travel agency NOUN
das Reisebüro *neut* (PL die Reisebüros)

travel agent NOUN
der Reisebürokaufmann *masc* (PL die Reisebürokaufleute)
die Reisebürokauffrau *fem*
□ She's a travel agent. Sie ist Reisebürokauffrau.
■ **at the travel agent's** im Reisebüro

★ = core vocabulary

traveller NOUN
1 der Fahrgast _masc_ (PL die Fahrgäste) (_on bus, train_)

   der Fahrgast is also used for women.

2 der Passagier _masc_ (PL die Passagiere)
   die Passagierin _fem_ (_on plane_)

travelling NOUN
■ I love travelling. Ich reise sehr gern.

travel sickness NOUN
die Reisekrankheit _fem_

tray NOUN
das Tablett _neut_ (PL die Tabletts)

to tread VERB
treten [79] (PRESENT TENSE tritt, IMPERFECT trat, PERFECT TENSE ist getreten)
□ to tread on something auf etwas treten □ He trod on her foot. Er ist ihr auf den Fuß getreten.

treasure NOUN
der Schatz _masc_ (GEN des Schatzes, PL die Schätze)

★ **treat** NOUN
▷ _see also_ **treat** VERB
1 das Geschenk _neut_ (PL die Geschenke) (_present_)
2 der Leckerbissen _masc_ (PL die Leckerbissen) (_food_)
■ to give somebody a treat jemandem eine besondere Freude machen [48]

★ **to treat** VERB
▷ _see also_ **treat** NOUN
behandeln [34] (PERFECT TENSE hat behandelt) (_well, badly_)
■ to treat somebody to something jemandem etwas spendieren [76] □ He treated us to an ice cream. Er hat uns ein Eis spendiert.

★ **treatment** NOUN
die Behandlung _fem_

to treble VERB
sich verdreifachen [7] (PERFECT TENSE hat sich verdreifacht)
□ The price has trebled. Der Preis hat sich verdreifacht.

★ **tree** NOUN
der Baum _masc_ (PL die Bäume)

to tremble VERB
zittern [88]

tremendous ADJECTIVE
1 fantastisch
   □ Messi is a tremendous player. Messi ist ein fantastischer Spieler.
2 gewaltig
   □ a tremendous success ein gewaltiger Erfolg

★ **trend** NOUN
1 der Tendenz _fem_ (_tendency_)
2 der Trend _masc_ (PL die Trends) (_fashion_)

trendy ADJECTIVE
modisch

★ **trial** NOUN
der Prozess _masc_ (GEN des Prozesses, PL die Prozesse) (_in court_)

triangle NOUN
das Dreieck _neut_ (PL die Dreiecke)

tribe NOUN
der Stamm _masc_ (PL die Stämme)

★ **trick** NOUN
▷ _see also_ **trick** VERB
1 der Streich _masc_ (PL die Streiche)
   □ to play a trick on somebody jemandem einen Streich spielen
2 der Trick _masc_ (PL die Tricks) (_knack_)
   □ It's not easy: there's a trick to it. Das ist nicht leicht: Da ist ein Trick dabei.

★ **to trick** VERB
▷ _see also_ **trick** NOUN
■ to trick somebody jemanden reinlegen [4]

tricky ADJECTIVE
knifflig

tricycle NOUN
das Dreirad _neut_ (PL die Dreiräder)

trifle NOUN
das Trifle _neut_ (PL die Trifles) (_dessert_)

to trim VERB
▷ _see also_ **trim** NOUN
1 schneiden [60] (IMPERFECT schnitt, PERFECT TENSE hat geschnitten) (_hair_)
2 stutzen [36]
   □ He trimmed his moustache. Er stutzte seinen Schnurrbart.
3 mähen [48] (_grass_)

trim NOUN
▷ _see also_ **trim** VERB
■ to have a trim sich die Haare schneiden lassen [42] □ You need a trim. Du solltest dir die Haare schneiden lassen.

★ **trip** NOUN
▷ _see also_ **trip** VERB
die Reise _fem_
□ to go on a trip eine Reise machen □ Have a good trip! Gute Reise!
■ a day trip ein Tagesausflug _masc_

★ **to trip** VERB
▷ _see also_ **trip** NOUN
stolpern [88] (PERFECT TENSE ist gestolpert) (_stumble_)

triple ADJECTIVE
dreifach

triplets PL NOUN
die Drillinge _masc pl_

trivial ADJECTIVE
trivial

trod, trodden VERB ▷ _see_ tread

troll NOUN
die Troll _masc_ (PL die Trolle) (_internet_)

trolley NOUN
1 der Einkaufswagen _masc_ (PL die Einkaufswagen) (_for shopping_)
2 der Kofferkuli _masc_ (PL die Kofferkulis) (_for luggage_)

trolling NOUN
die Trolling neut (internet)

trombone NOUN
die Posaune fem
□ I play the trombone. Ich spiele Posaune.

troops PL NOUN
die Truppen fem pl
□ British troops die britischen Truppen

trophy NOUN
die Trophäe fem
□ to win a trophy eine Trophäe gewinnen

tropical ADJECTIVE
tropisch
□ tropical plants tropische Pflanzen
■ The weather was tropical. Es war tropisch heiß.

to **trot** VERB
traben [38] (PERFECT TENSE ist getrabt)

★ **trouble** NOUN
das Problem neut (PL die Probleme)
□ The trouble is ... Das Problem ist ...
■ What's the trouble? Was ist das Problem?
■ to be in trouble in Schwierigkeiten sein [65]
■ stomach trouble die Magenbeschwerden fem pl
■ to take a lot of trouble over something sich mit etwas viel Mühe geben [28] □ I took a lot of trouble over that project. Ich habe mir mit dem Referat viel Mühe gegeben.
■ Don't worry, it's no trouble. Keine Sorge, das macht keine Mühe.

troublemaker NOUN
der Unruhestifter masc (PL die Unruhestifter)
die Unruhestifterin fem

★ **trousers** PL NOUN
die Hose fem sing
□ a pair of trousers eine Hose

trout NOUN
die Forelle fem

truant NOUN
■ to play truant die Schule schwänzen [36]

★ **truck** NOUN
der Lastwagen masc (PL die Lastwagen)
■ She's a truck driver. Sie ist Lastwagenfahrerin.

★ **true** ADJECTIVE
wahr
□ true love wahre Liebe □ That's true. Das ist wahr.
■ to come true wahr werden [91] □ I hope my dream will come true. Ich hoffe, mein Traum wird wahr.

trumpet NOUN
die Trompete fem
□ She plays the trumpet. Sie spielt Trompete.

trunk NOUN
1 der Stamm masc (PL die Stämme) (of tree)
2 der Rüssel masc (PL die Rüssel) (of elephant)

3 der Schrankkoffer masc (PL die Schrankkoffer) (luggage)
4 der Kofferraum masc (PL die Kofferräume) (US: of car)

trunks PL NOUN
■ swimming trunks die Badehose sing □ a pair of trunks eine Badehose

★ **trust** NOUN
▷ see also **trust** VERB
das Vertrauen neut
□ to have trust in somebody Vertrauen zu jemandem haben

★ to **trust** VERB
▷ see also **trust** NOUN
■ to trust somebody jemandem vertrauen [84] □ Don't you trust me? Vertraust du mir nicht?
■ Trust me! Glaub mir!

trusting ADJECTIVE
vertrauensvoll

★ **truth** NOUN
die Wahrheit fem

truthful ADJECTIVE
ehrlich

★ **try** NOUN
▷ see also **try** VERB
der Versuch masc (PL die Versuche)
□ his third try sein dritter Versuch
■ to have a try es versuchen [84] □ I'll have a try. Ich werd's versuchen.
■ It's worth a try. Der Versuch lohnt sich.
■ to give something a try etwas versuchen [84]

★ to **try** VERB
▷ see also **try** NOUN
1 versuchen [84] (PERFECT TENSE hat versucht) (attempt)
□ to try to do something versuchen, etwas zu tun
■ to try again es noch einmal versuchen [84]
2 probieren [76] (PERFECT TENSE hat probiert) (taste)
□ Would you like to try some? Möchtest du etwas probieren?

to **try on** VERB
anprobieren [76] (clothes)

to **try out** VERB
■ to try something out etwas ausprobieren [4]

T-shirt NOUN
das T-Shirt neut (PL die T-Shirts)

★ **tube** NOUN
die Tube fem
■ the Tube (underground) die U-Bahn

tuberculosis NOUN
die Tuberkulose fem

★ **Tuesday** NOUN
der Dienstag masc (PL die Dienstage)
□ on Tuesday am Dienstag □ every Tuesday

★ = core vocabulary

jeden Dienstag □ **last Tuesday** letzten Dienstag
□ **next Tuesday** nächsten Dienstag
■ **on Tuesdays** dienstags

tug of war NOUN
das Tauziehen *neut*

tuition NOUN
1 der Unterricht *masc*
■ **extra tuition** die Nachhilfestunden *fem pl*
□ She receives extra tuition. Sie bekommt
Nachhilfestunden.
2 die Studiengebühren *fem pl* (*tuition fees*)

tulip NOUN
die Tulpe *fem*

tumble dryer NOUN
der Wäschetrockner *masc* (PL die
Wäschetrockner)

tummy NOUN
der Bauch *masc* (PL die Bäuche)
□ I've got a sore tummy. Ich habe
Bauchschmerzen.

tuna NOUN
der Thunfisch *masc* (PL die Thunfische)

★ **tune** NOUN
die Melodie *fem* (*melody*)
■ **to play in tune** richtig spielen [38]
■ **to sing out of tune** falsch singen [66]

Tunisia NOUN
Tunesien *neut*
■ **in Tunisia** in Tunesien

★ **tunnel** NOUN
der Tunnel *masc* (PL die Tunnel)
■ **the Channel Tunnel** der Kanaltunnel

Turk NOUN
der Türke *masc* (GEN des Türken, PL die Türken)
die Türkin *fem*

★ **Turkey** NOUN
die Türkei *fem*

> Note that the definite article is used in
> German for countries which are feminine.

■ **from Turkey** aus der Türkei
■ **in Turkey** in der Türkei
■ **to Turkey** in die Türkei

turkey NOUN
der Truthahn *masc* (PL die Truthähne)

★ **Turkish** ADJECTIVE
▷ *see also* **Turkish** NOUN
türkisch

★ **Turkish** NOUN
▷ *see also* **Turkish** ADJECTIVE
das Türkische *neut* (GEN des Türkischen)
(*language*)

★ **turn** NOUN
▷ *see also* **turn** VERB
die Abbiegung *fem* (*in road*)
■ **'no left turn'** 'links abbiegen verboten'
■ **Whose turn is it?** Wer ist an der Reihe?
■ **It's my turn!** Ich bin an der Reihe!

★ to **turn** VERB
▷ *see also* **turn** NOUN

1 abbiegen (IMPERFECT bog ab, PERFECT TENSE ist
abgebogen)
□ Turn right at the lights. Biegen Sie an der
Ampel rechts ab.
2 werden [91] (PRESENT TENSE wird, IMPERFECT
wurde, PERFECT TENSE ist geworden) (*become*)
□ to turn red rot werden
■ **to turn into something** sich in etwas
verwandeln [34] □ The frog turned into a
prince. Der Frosch verwandelte sich in einen
Prinzen.

to **turn back** VERB
umkehren [4] (PERFECT TENSE ist umgekehrt)
□ We turned back. Wir sind umgekehrt.

to **turn down** VERB
1 ablehnen [4] (PERFECT TENSE hat abgelehnt)
(*offer*)
2 leiser stellen [38] (*radio, TV*)
3 herunterdrehen [15] (PERFECT TENSE hat
heruntergedreht) (*heating*)

to **turn off** VERB
1 ausmachen [48] (PERFECT TENSE hat
ausgemacht) (*light, radio*)
2 zudrehen [15] (PERFECT TENSE hat zugedreht)
(*tap*)
3 ausschalten [2] (PERFECT TENSE hat
ausgeschaltet) (*engine*)

to **turn on** VERB
1 anmachen [4] (PERFECT TENSE hat angemacht)
(*light, radio*)
2 aufdrehen [15] (PERFECT TENSE hat aufgedreht)
(*tap*)
3 anlassen [42] (PRESENT TENSE lässt an, IMPERFECT
ließ an, PERFECT TENSE hat angelassen) (*engine*)

to **turn out** VERB
■ **It turned out to be a mistake.** Es stellte
sich heraus, dass das ein Fehler war.
■ **It turned out that she was right.** Es stellte
sich heraus, dass sie recht hatte.

to **turn round** VERB
1 umkehren [4] (PERFECT TENSE ist umgekehrt)
(*car*)
□ At the end of the street we turned round. Am
Ende der Straße kehrten wir um.
2 sich umdrehen [4] (PERFECT TENSE hat sich
umgedreht) (*person*)
□ I turned round. Ich drehte mich um.

to **turn up** VERB
1 aufkreuzen [4] (PERFECT TENSE ist aufgekreuzt)
(*arrive*)
2 höherstellen [15] (*heater*)
3 lauter machen [48] (*radio, TV*)

turning NOUN
■ **It's the third turning on the left.** Es ist die
dritte Straße links.
■ **We took the wrong turning.** Wir sind falsch
abgebogen.

turnip NOUN
die Steckrübe *fem*

t

turquoise ADJECTIVE
türkis (colour)

turtle NOUN
die Meeresschildkröte fem

tutor NOUN
der Lehrer masc (PL die Lehrer)
die Lehrerin fem (private teacher)

tuxedo NOUN (US)
der Smoking masc (PL die Smokings)

★ **TV** NOUN
das Fernsehen neut

tweet NOUN
▷ see also **tweet** VERB
der Tweet masc (PL die Tweets) (on Twitter)

to **tweet** VERB
▷ see also **tweet** NOUN
twittern [34] (on Twitter)

tweezers PL NOUN
die Pinzette fem sing
□ a pair of tweezers eine Pinzette

★ **twelfth** ADJECTIVE
zwölfte
□ the twelfth floor der zwölfte Stock □ the twelfth of August der zwölfte August

★ **twelve** NUMBER
zwölf
□ She's twelve. Sie ist zwölf. □ at twelve o'clock um zwölf Uhr

★ **twentieth** ADJECTIVE
zwanzigste
□ the twentieth of August der zwanzigste August

★ **twenty** NUMBER
zwanzig
□ He's twenty. Er ist zwanzig.
■ in twenty nineteen im Jahr zweitausendneunzehn

★ **twice** ADVERB
zweimal
■ twice as much doppelt so viel □ He gets twice as much pocket money as me. Er bekommt doppelt so viel Taschengeld wie ich.

★ **twin** NOUN
der Zwilling masc (PL die Zwillinge)

> der Zwilling is also used for women.

■ my twin brother mein Zwillingsbruder masc
■ her twin sister ihre Zwillingsschwester
■ identical twins eineiige Zwillinge
■ a twin room ein Doppelzimmer mit zwei Betten

twinned ADJECTIVE
■ Oxford is twinned with Bonn. Oxford und Bonn sind Partnerstädte.

★ to **twist** VERB
1 biegen (IMPERFECT bog, PERFECT TENSE hat gebogen) (bend)
■ I've twisted my ankle. Ich habe mir den Fuß vertreten.
2 verdrehen [84] (PERFECT TENSE hat verdreht) (distort)
□ You're twisting my words. Sie verdrehen meine Worte.

twit NOUN
der Trottel masc (PL die Trottel) (informal)

> der Trottel is also used for women.

Twitter® NOUN
Twitter® neut

★ **two** NUMBER
zwei
□ She's two. Sie ist zwei.

★ **type** NOUN
▷ see also **type** VERB
die Art fem
□ What type of smartphone have you got? Welche Art von Smartphone hast du?

★ to **type** VERB
▷ see also **type** NOUN
Schreibmaschine schreiben [61] (IMPERFECT schrieb Schreibmaschine, PERFECT TENSE hat Schreibmaschine geschrieben)

typewriter NOUN
die Schreibmaschine fem

★ **typical** ADJECTIVE
typisch
□ That's just typical! Das ist typisch!

tyre NOUN
der Reifen masc (PL die Reifen)

Uu

UFO NOUN (= *unidentified flying object*)
das UFO *neut* (PL die UFOs) (=*unbekanntes Flugobjekt*)

ugh EXCLAMATION
igitt

★ **ugly** ADJECTIVE
hässlich

★ **UK** NOUN (= *United Kingdom*)
das Vereinigte Königreich *neut*
■ **from the UK** aus dem Vereinigten Königreich
■ **in the UK** im Vereinigten Königreich
■ **to the UK** in das Vereinigte Königreich

ulcer NOUN
das Geschwür *neut* (PL die Geschwüre)

Ulster NOUN
Ulster *neut*
■ **from Ulster** aus Ulster
■ **in Ulster** in Ulster
■ **to Ulster** nach Ulster

ultimate ADJECTIVE
äußerste
□ **the ultimate challenge** die äußerste Herausforderung
■ **It was the ultimate adventure.** Das war das große Abenteuer.

ultimately ADVERB
schließlich
□ **Ultimately, it's your decision.** Schließlich ist es deine Entscheidung.

★ **umbrella** NOUN
1 der Regenschirm *masc* (PL die Regenschirme)
2 der Sonnenschirm *masc* (PL die Sonnenschirme) (*for sun*)

umlaut NOUN
der Umlaut *masc*
□ **The plural of 'Haus' is written with an umlaut.**
Der Plural von 'Haus' wird mit Umlaut gebildet.
■ **a umlaut** ä
■ **o umlaut** ö
■ **u umlaut** ü

umpire NOUN
der Schiedsrichter *masc* (PL die Schiedsrichter)
die Schiedsrichterin *fem*

UN NOUN (= *United Nations*)
die UN *pl*

★ **unable** ADJECTIVE
■ **to be unable to do something** etwas nicht tun können [41] □ **I was unable to come.** Ich konnte nicht kommen.

unacceptable ADJECTIVE
unannehmbar

unanimous ADJECTIVE
einstimmig
□ **a unanimous decision** ein einstimmiger Beschluss

unavoidable ADJECTIVE
unvermeidlich

unaware ADJECTIVE
■ **to be unaware** 1 (*not know about*) nichts wissen [93] □ **I was unaware of the regulations.**
Ich wusste nichts von den Bestimmungen.
2 (*not notice*) nicht merken [38] □ **She was unaware that she was being filmed.** Sie merkte nicht, dass sie gefilmt wurde.

unbearable ADJECTIVE
unerträglich

unbeatable ADJECTIVE
unschlagbar

unbelievable ADJECTIVE
unglaublich

unborn ADJECTIVE
ungeboren
□ **the unborn child** das ungeborene Kind

unbreakable ADJECTIVE
unzerbrechlich

uncanny ADJECTIVE
unheimlich
□ **That's uncanny!** Das ist unheimlich!
■ **an uncanny resemblance to** eine verblüffende Ähnlichkeit mit

uncertain ADJECTIVE
ungewiss
□ **The future is uncertain.** Die Zukunft ist ungewiss.
■ **to be uncertain about something** sich über etwas nicht im Klaren sein [65] □ **I'm uncertain about her plans.** Ich bin mir über ihre Pläne nicht im Klaren.

uncivilized ADJECTIVE
unzivilisiert

★ **uncle** NOUN
der Onkel *masc* (PL die Onkel)
□ **my uncle** mein Onkel

uncomfortable – undo

★ **uncomfortable** ADJECTIVE
  unbequem
  □ The seats are rather uncomfortable. Die Sitze sind ziemlich unbequem.

unconscious ADJECTIVE
  bewusstlos

uncontrollable ADJECTIVE
  unkontrollierbar

unconventional ADJECTIVE
  unkonventionell

★ **under** PREPOSITION
  unter

  Use the accusative to express movement or a change of place. Use the dative when there is no change of place.

  □ The ball rolled under the table. Der Ball rollte unter den Tisch. □ The cat's under the table. Die Katze ist unter dem Tisch. □ children under ten Kinder unter zehn
  ■ **under there** da drunter □ What's under there? Was ist da drunter?
  ■ **under twenty people** weniger als zwanzig Leute

underage ADJECTIVE
  minderjährig

undercover ADJECTIVE, ADVERB
  ■ **an undercover agent** (secret agent) ein Geheimagent masc
  ■ **She was working undercover.** Sie führte verdeckte Ermittlungen durch.

underdog NOUN
  der Underdog masc (PL die Underdogs)
  □ We were the underdogs in this match. Wir waren in diesem Spiel die Underdogs.

to underestimate VERB
  unterschätzen [36] (PERFECT TENSE hat unterschätzt)
  □ I underestimated her. Ich habe sie unterschätzt.

to undergo VERB
  sich unterziehen [96] (IMPERFECT unterzog sich, PERFECT TENSE hat sich unterzogen) (operation)

★ **underground** ADJECTIVE, ADVERB
  ▷ see also **underground** NOUN
  1 unterirdisch
  □ underground water pipes unterirdische Wasserrohre
  ■ **an underground car park** eine Tiefgarage
  2 unter der Erde
  □ Moles live underground. Maulwürfe leben unter der Erde.

★ **underground** NOUN
  ▷ see also **underground** ADJECTIVE, ADVERB
  die U-Bahn fem
  □ Is there an underground in Frankfurt? Gibt es in Frankfurt eine U-Bahn?

to underline VERB
  unterstreichen (IMPERFECT unterstrich, PERFECT TENSE hat unterstrichen)

underneath PREPOSITION, ADVERB
  1 unter

  Use the accusative to express movement or a change of place. Use the dative when there is no change of place.

  □ I put it underneath that pile. Ich habe es unter diesen Stapel gelegt. □ It was hidden underneath the carpet. Es war unter dem Teppich versteckt.
  2 darunter
  □ I got out of the car and looked underneath. Ich stieg aus dem Auto aus und sah darunter.

underpaid ADJECTIVE
  unterbezahlt
  □ I'm underpaid. Ich bin unterbezahlt.

underpants PL NOUN
  die Unterhose fem sing
  □ a pair of underpants eine Unterhose

underpass NOUN
  die Unterführung fem

underscore NOUN
  der Unterstrich masc (PL die Unterstriche)

undershirt NOUN (US)
  das Unterhemd neut (PL die Unterhemden)

underskirt NOUN
  der Unterrock masc (PL die Unterröcke)

★ **to understand** VERB
  verstehen [72] (IMPERFECT verstand, PERFECT TENSE hat verstanden)
  □ Do you understand? Verstehst du? □ I don't understand this word. Ich verstehe dieses Wort nicht. □ Is that understood? Ist das verstanden?

★ **understanding** ADJECTIVE
  verständnisvoll
  □ She's very understanding. Sie ist sehr verständnisvoll.

understood VERB ▷ see **understand**

undertaker NOUN
  der Beerdigungsunternehmer masc (PL die Beerdigungsunternehmer)
  die Beerdigungsunternehmerin fem

underwater ADJECTIVE, ADVERB
  unter Wasser
  □ It was filmed underwater. Es wurde unter Wasser gefilmt.
  ■ **an underwater camera** eine Unterwasserkamera

★ **underwear** NOUN
  die Unterwäsche fem

underwent VERB ▷ see **undergo**

to undo VERB
  aufmachen [4] (PERFECT TENSE hat aufgemacht)

★ = core vocabulary

to **undress** VERB
sich ausziehen [96] (IMPERFECT zog sich aus, PERFECT TENSE hat sich ausgezogen) (*get undressed*)
□ The doctor told me to get undressed. Der Arzt bat mich, mich auszuziehen.

uneconomic ADJECTIVE
unrentabel

★ **unemployed** ADJECTIVE
arbeitslos
□ He's unemployed. Er ist arbeitslos. □ He's been unemployed for a year. Er ist seit einem Jahr arbeitslos.
■ **the unemployed** die Arbeitslosen *masc pl*

★ **unemployment** NOUN
die Arbeitslosigkeit *fem*

★ **unexpected** ADJECTIVE
unerwartet
□ an unexpected visitor ein unerwarteter Gast

unexpectedly ADVERB
überraschend
□ They arrived unexpectedly. Sie sind überraschend gekommen.

★ **unfair** ADJECTIVE
unfair
□ It's unfair to girls. Es ist Mädchen gegenüber unfair.

unfamiliar ADJECTIVE
unbekannt
□ I heard an unfamiliar voice. Ich hörte eine unbekannte Stimme.

unfashionable ADJECTIVE
unmodern

unfit ADJECTIVE
nicht fit
□ I'm rather unfit at the moment. Ich bin im Moment nicht sehr fit.

to **unfold** VERB
auseinanderfalten [15] (PERFECT TENSE hat auseinandergefaltet)
□ She unfolded the map. Sie faltete die Karte auseinander.

unforgettable ADJECTIVE
unvergesslich

★ **unfortunately** ADVERB
leider
□ Unfortunately, I arrived late. Ich bin leider zu spät gekommen.

to **unfriend** VERB
entfreunden [54]
□ Her sister has unfriended her on Facebook. Ihre Schwester hat sie auf Facebook entfreundet.

unfriendly ADJECTIVE
unfreundlich
□ They're a bit unfriendly. Sie sind etwas unfreundlich.

ungrateful ADJECTIVE
undankbar

★ **unhappy** ADJECTIVE
unglücklich
□ He was very unhappy as a child. Er war als Kind sehr unglücklich. □ to look unhappy unglücklich aussehen

unhealthy ADJECTIVE
ungesund

uni NOUN
die Uni *fem* (PL die Unis)
□ to go to uni zur Uni gehen

★ **uniform** NOUN
die Uniform *fem*
□ the school uniform die Schuluniform

> **DID YOU KNOW...?**
> School uniforms are virtually nonexistent in Germany.

uninhabited ADJECTIVE
unbewohnt

union NOUN
die Gewerkschaft *fem* (*trade union*)

Union Jack NOUN
die britische Flagge *fem*

unique ADJECTIVE
einzigartig

unit NOUN
die Einheit *fem*
□ a unit of measurement eine Maßeinheit
■ **a kitchen unit** ein Kücheneinbauschrank *masc*

★ **United Kingdom** NOUN
das Vereinigte Königreich *neut*
■ **from the United Kingdom** aus dem Vereinigten Königreich
■ **in the United Kingdom** im Vereinigten Königreich
■ **to the United Kingdom** in das Vereinigte Königreich

United Nations PL NOUN
■ **The United Nations is extremely important.** Die Vereinten Nationen *fem pl* sind äußerst wichtig.

★ **United States** NOUN
■ **The United States play a big role.** Die Vereinigten Staaten *masc pl* spielen eine große Rolle.
■ **from the United States** aus den Vereinigten Staaten
■ **in the United States** in den Vereinigten Staaten
■ **to the United States** in die Vereinigten Staaten

★ **universe** NOUN
das Universum *neut*

★ **university** NOUN
die Universität *fem*

□ Do you want to go to university? Möchtest du auf die Universität gehen? □ **Lancaster University** die Universität von Lancaster
■ **She's at university.** Sie studiert.

★ **unless** CONJUNCTION
es sei denn
□ **unless he leaves** es sei denn, er geht □ **I won't come unless you phone me.** Ich komme nicht, es sei denn, du rufst an.

unlike PREPOSITION
im Gegensatz zu
□ **Unlike him, I really enjoy flying.** Im Gegensatz zu ihm fliege ich wirklich gern.

★ **unlikely** ADJECTIVE
unwahrscheinlich
□ **It's possible, but unlikely.** Es ist möglich, aber unwahrscheinlich.

to **unload** VERB
ausladen (PRESENT TENSE lädt aus, IMPERFECT lud aus, PERFECT TENSE hat ausgeladen)
□ **We unloaded the car.** Wir haben das Auto ausgeladen.
■ **The lorries go there to unload.** Die Lastwagen fahren dorthin um abzuladen.

to **unlock** VERB
aufschließen (IMPERFECT schloss auf, PERFECT TENSE hat aufgeschlossen)
□ **He unlocked the door.** Er schloss die Tür auf.

unlucky ADJECTIVE
■ **to be unlucky 1** (number, object) Unglück bringen [13] □ **They say thirteen is an unlucky number.** Es heißt, dass die Zahl dreizehn Unglück bringt. **2** (person) kein Glück haben [32] □ **Did you win? — No, I was unlucky.** Hast du gewonnen? — Nein, ich habe kein Glück gehabt.

unmarried ADJECTIVE
unverheiratet
□ **an unmarried couple** ein unverheiratetes Paar

unnatural ADJECTIVE
unnatürlich

unnecessary ADJECTIVE
unnötig

unofficial ADJECTIVE
1 inoffiziell (meeting, leader)
2 wild (strike)

to **unpack** VERB
auspacken [4] (PERFECT TENSE hat ausgepackt) (clothes, case)
□ **I went to my room to unpack.** Ich ging auf mein Zimmer, um auszupacken.

unpleasant ADJECTIVE
unangenehm

to **unplug** VERB
ausstecken [4] (PERFECT TENSE hat ausgesteckt)
□ **She unplugged the TV.** Sie hat den Fernseher ausgesteckt.

unpopular ADJECTIVE
unbeliebt

unpredictable ADJECTIVE
unvorhersehbar (event)

unreal ADJECTIVE
unglaublich (incredible)
□ **It was unreal!** Es war unglaublich!

unrealistic ADJECTIVE
unrealistisch

unreasonable ADJECTIVE
unmöglich
□ **Her attitude was completely unreasonable.** Ihre Haltung war völlig unmöglich.

unreliable ADJECTIVE
unzuverlässig
□ **He's completely unreliable.** Er ist total unzuverlässig.

to **unroll** VERB
aufrollen [4] (PERFECT TENSE hat aufgerollt)

unsatisfactory ADJECTIVE
unbefriedigend

to **unscrew** VERB
aufschrauben [4] (PERFECT TENSE hat aufgeschraubt)
□ **She unscrewed the top of the bottle.** Sie schraubte den Flaschenverschluss auf.

unshaven ADJECTIVE
unrasiert

unskilled ADJECTIVE
ungelernt
□ **an unskilled worker** ein ungelernter Arbeiter

unstable ADJECTIVE
1 nicht stabil (object)
2 labil (person)

unsteady ADJECTIVE
unsicher (walk, voice)
■ **He was unsteady on his feet.** Er war wackelig auf den Beinen.

unsuccessful ADJECTIVE
erfolglos (attempt)
□ **an unsuccessful artist** ein erfolgloser Künstler
■ **to be unsuccessful in doing something** keinen Erfolg bei etwas haben [32] □ **He was unsuccessful in getting a job.** Er hatte bei der Arbeitssuche keinen Erfolg.

unsuitable ADJECTIVE
ungeeignet (clothes, equipment)

untidy ADJECTIVE
unordentlich

to **untie** VERB
1 aufmachen [4] (PERFECT TENSE hat aufgemacht) (knot, parcel)
2 losbinden (IMPERFECT band los, PERFECT TENSE hat losgebunden) (animal)

★ **until** PREPOSITION, CONJUNCTION
1 bis
□ I waited until ten o'clock. Ich habe bis zehn Uhr gewartet.
■ **until now** bis jetzt □ It's never been a problem until now. Es war bis jetzt nie ein Problem.
■ **until then** bis dahin □ Until then I'd never been to Germany. Bis dahin war ich noch nie in Deutschland gewesen.

2 vor

> Use **vor** if the sentence you want to translate contains a negative, such as 'not' or 'never'.

□ It won't be ready until next week. Es wird nicht vor nächster Woche fertig sein. □ Until last year I'd never been to Germany. Vor letztem Jahr war ich noch nie in Deutschland.

★ **unusual** ADJECTIVE
ungewöhnlich
□ an unusual shape eine ungewöhnliche Form □ It's unusual to get snow at this time of year. Es ist ungewöhnlich, dass es um diese Jahreszeit schneit.

unwilling ADJECTIVE
■ **to be unwilling to do something** nicht gewillt sein [65], etwas zu tun □ He was unwilling to help me. Er war nicht gewillt, mir zu helfen.

to **unwind** VERB
sich entspannen [18] (PERFECT TENSE hat sich entspannt) (relax)

unwise ADJECTIVE
unklug (person)
□ That was unwise of you. Das war unklug von dir.

unwound VERB ▷ see unwind

to **unwrap** VERB
auspacken [4] (PERFECT TENSE hat ausgepackt)
□ Let's unwrap the presents. Packen wir die Geschenke aus.

★ **up** PREPOSITION, ADVERB
auf

> Use the accusative to express movement or a change of place. Use the dative when there is no change of place.

□ He drove me up the hill. Er hat mich den Berg hinaufgefahren. □ the chapel up on the hill die Kapelle auf dem Berg
■ **up here** hier oben
■ **up there** dort oben
■ **up north** oben im Norden
■ **to be up** (out of bed) auf sein [65] □ We were up at six. Wir waren um sechs Uhr auf. □ He's not up yet. Er ist noch nicht auf.
■ **What's up?** Was gibt's?
■ **What's up with her?** Was ist los mit ihr?
■ **to get up** (in the morning) aufstehen [72]
□ What time do you get up? Um wie viel Uhr stehst du auf?

■ **to go up 1** hinauffahren [4] □ The bus went up the hill. Der Bus ist den Berg hinaufgefahren.
2 (on foot) hinaufgehen [29] □ We went up the hill. Wir sind den Berg hinaufgegangen.
■ **to go up to somebody** auf jemanden zugehen [29]
■ **She came up to me.** Sie kam auf mich zu.
■ **up to** (as far as) bis □ to count up to fifty bis fünfzig zählen □ up to three hours bis zu drei Stunden □ up to now bis jetzt
■ **It's up to you.** Das ist dir überlassen.

> For other expressions with 'up', see the verbs 'go', 'come', 'put', 'turn' etc.

upbringing NOUN
die Erziehung fem

uphill ADVERB
bergauf

to **upload** VERB
hochladen

upright ADJECTIVE
■ **to stand upright** aufrecht stehen [72]

★ **upset** NOUN
▷ see also **upset** ADJECTIVE, VERB
■ **a stomach upset** eine Magenverstimmung

★ **upset** ADJECTIVE
▷ see also **upset** NOUN, VERB
1 gekränkt (hurt)
□ She was upset when he said that. Sie fühlte sich gekränkt, als er das sagte.
2 betrübt (sad)
□ I was very upset when my father died. Ich war sehr betrübt, als mein Vater starb.
■ **an upset stomach** eine Magenverstimmung

★ to **upset** VERB
▷ see also **upset** NOUN, ADJECTIVE
aufregen [4] (PERFECT TENSE hat aufgeregt)
□ Don't say anything to upset her! Sag nichts, was sie aufregen könnte.

upside down ADVERB
verkehrt herum
□ It's upside down. Es ist verkehrt herum.

upstairs ADVERB
oben
□ Where's your coat? — It's upstairs. Wo ist dein Mantel? — Er ist oben.
■ **the people upstairs** die Leute von oben
■ **to go upstairs** hinaufgehen [29]

uptight ADJECTIVE
nervös (nervous)
□ She's really uptight. Sie ist echt nervös.

★ **up-to-date** ADJECTIVE
1 modern (car, phone, tv)
2 aktuell (information)
□ an up-to-date timetable ein aktueller Fahrplan
■ **to bring something up to date** etwas auf den neuesten Stand bringen [13]

u

■ **to keep somebody up to date** jemanden auf dem Laufenden halten [33]

upwards ADVERB
hinauf
□ **to look upwards** hinaufsehen

★ **urgent** ADJECTIVE
dringend
□ **Is it urgent?** Ist es dringend?

urine NOUN
der Urin *masc*

★ **US** SING NOUN
die USA *pl*
■ **from the US** aus den USA
■ **in the US** in den USA
■ **to the US** in die USA

★ **us** PRONOUN
uns
□ **They saw us.** Sie haben uns gesehen. □ **They gave us a map.** Sie gaben uns eine Karte.
■ **Who is it? — It's us!** Wer ist da? — Wir sind's!

★ **USA** NOUN
die USA *pl*
■ **from the USA** aus den USA
■ **in the USA** in den USA
■ **to the USA** in die USA

USB stick NOUN
der USB-Stick *masc* (PL die USB-Sticks)

★ **use** NOUN
▷ *see also* **use** VERB
■ **It's no use.** Es hat keinen Zweck. □ **It's no use shouting, she's deaf.** Es hat keinen Zweck zu brüllen, sie ist taub. □ **It's no use, I can't do it.** Es hat keinen Zweck, ich kann's nicht.
■ **to make use of something** etwas benützen [7]

★ **to use** VERB
▷ *see also* **use** NOUN
benützen [7] (PERFECT TENSE hat benützt)
□ **Can we use a dictionary in the exam?** Können wir in der Prüfung ein Wörterbuch benützen?
■ **Can I use your phone?** Kann ich mal telefonieren?
■ **to use the toilet** auf die Toilette gehen [29]
■ **I used to live in London.** Ich habe früher mal in London gelebt.

■ **I used to not like maths, but now I do.** Früher habe ich Mathe nicht gemocht, aber jetzt doch.

■ **to be used to something** an etwas gewöhnt sein [65] □ **He wasn't used to driving on the right.** Er war nicht daran gewöhnt, rechts zu fahren. □ **Don't worry, I'm used to it.** Keine Sorge, ich bin daran gewöhnt.
■ **a used car** ein Gebrauchtwagen *masc*

to use up VERB
aufbrauchen [4]
□ **We've used up all the paint.** Ich habe die ganze Farbe aufgebraucht.

★ **useful** ADJECTIVE
nützlich

★ **useless** ADJECTIVE
nutzlos
□ **This app is just useless.** Diese App ist echt nutzlos.
■ **You're useless!** Du bist zu nichts zu gebrauchen!
■ **It's useless asking her!** Es ist zwecklos, sie zu fragen!

★ **user** NOUN
der Benutzer *masc* (PL die Benutzer)
die Benutzerin *fem*

user-friendly ADJECTIVE
benutzerfreundlich

username NOUN
der Benutzername *masc* (GEN des Benutzernamens, PL die Benutzernamen)
□ **What's your username?** Was ist dein Benutzername?

★ **usual** ADJECTIVE
üblich
□ **as usual** wie üblich

★ **usually** ADVERB
normalerweise
□ **I usually get to school at half past eight.** Ich bin normalerweise um halb neun in der Schule.

utility room NOUN
der Abstellraum *masc* (PL die Abstellräume)

U-turn NOUN
die Wende *fem*
■ **to do a U-turn** wenden

u

Vv

vacancy NOUN
1 die freie Stelle *fem* (*job*)
2 das freie Zimmer *neut* (PL die freien Zimmer)
(*room in hotel*)

vacant ADJECTIVE
1 frei (*seat, job*)
2 leer stehend (*building*)
3 leer (*look*)
□ a vacant look ein leerer Blick

vacation NOUN (US)
1 die Ferien *pl* (*from school*)
□ They went on vacation to Mexico. Sie haben in Mexiko Ferien gemacht.
2 der Urlaub *masc* (PL die Urlaube) (*from work*)
□ I have thirty days' vacation a year. Ich habe dreißig Tage Urlaub im Jahr.

to **vaccinate** VERB
impfen [38]

to **vacuum** VERB
staubsaugen [38] (IMPERFECT staubsaugte, PERFECT TENSE hat gestaubsaugt)
□ to vacuum the hall den Flur staubsaugen

vacuum cleaner NOUN
der Staubsauger *masc* (PL die Staubsauger)

vagina NOUN
die Vagina *fem* (PL die Vaginen)

vague ADJECTIVE
vage

vain ADJECTIVE
eitel
□ He's so vain! Er ist so eitel!
■ in vain umsonst

Valentine card NOUN
die Valentinskarte *fem*

> **DID YOU KNOW...?**
> Germans celebrate Valentine's Day by giving flowers rather than sending cards.

Valentine's Day NOUN
der Valentinstag *masc* (PL die Valentinstage)

valid ADJECTIVE
gültig
□ This ticket is valid for three months. Dieser Fahrschein ist drei Monate lang gültig.

★ **valley** NOUN
das Tal *neut* (PL die Täler)

★ **valuable** ADJECTIVE
wertvoll
□ a valuable picture ein wertvolles Bild
□ valuable help wertvolle Hilfe

valuables PL NOUN
die Wertsachen *fem pl*
□ Don't take any valuables with you. Nehmen Sie keine Wertsachen mit.

★ **value** NOUN
der Wert *masc* (PL die Werte)

★ **van** NOUN
der Lieferwagen *masc* (PL die Lieferwagen)

vandal NOUN
der Vandale *masc* (GEN des Vandalen, PL die Vandalen)
die Vandalin *fem*

vandalism NOUN
der Vandalismus *masc* (GEN des Vandalismus)

to **vandalize** VERB
mutwillig zerstören [95] (PERFECT TENSE hat mutwillig zerstört)

vanilla NOUN
die Vanille *fem*
■ vanilla ice cream das Vanilleeis

to **vanish** VERB
verschwinden [86] (IMPERFECT verschwand, PERFECT TENSE ist verschwunden)

to **vape** VERB
dampfen [48]

vaping NOUN
das Dampfen *neut*

variable ADJECTIVE
wechselhaft (*mood, weather*)

varied ADJECTIVE
abwechslungsreich
□ a varied diet eine abwechslungsreiche Kost
□ a varied life ein abwechslungsreiches Leben
■ a varied selection eine reichhaltige Auswahl

★ **variety** NOUN
1 die Abwechslung *fem*
□ She likes variety in her life. Sie hat gern Abwechslung im Leben.
2 die Sorte *fem* (*kind*)
□ a new variety of coffee eine neue Kaffeesorte

★ **various** ADJECTIVE
verschieden

V

□ We visited various villages. Wir haben verschiedene Dörfer besucht.

to **vary** VERB
schwanken [38]
□ It varies between two and four per cent. Es schwankt zwischen zwei und vier Prozent.
■ It varies. Das ist unterschiedlich.

vase NOUN
die Vase *fem*

VAT NOUN (= *value added tax*)
die Mehrwertsteuer *fem*

veal NOUN
das Kalbfleisch *neut*

vegan NOUN
▷ *see also* **vegan** ADJECTIVE
der Veganer *masc* (PL die Veganer)
die Veganerin *fem*
□ I'm a vegan. Ich bin Veganerin.

vegan ADJECTIVE
▷ *see also* **vegan** NOUN
veganisch

★ **vegetable** NOUN
die Gemüsesorte *fem*
■ **vegetables** das Gemüse *sing*
■ **vegetable soup** die Gemüsesuppe

★ **vegetarian** ADJECTIVE
▷ *see also* **vegetarian** NOUN
vegetarisch
□ vegetarian lasagne die vegetarische Lasagne
■ He's vegetarian. Er ist Vegetarier.

★ **vegetarian** NOUN
▷ *see also* **vegetarian** ADJECTIVE
der Vegetarier *masc* (PL die Vegetarier)
die Vegetarierin *fem*
□ She's a vegetarian. Sie ist Vegetarierin.

★ **vehicle** NOUN
das Fahrzeug *neut* (PL die Fahrzeuge)

vein NOUN
die Vene *fem*

velvet NOUN
der Samt *masc*

vending machine NOUN
der Automat *masc* (GEN des Automaten, PL die Automaten)

Venetian blind NOUN
die Jalousie *fem*

verb NOUN
das Verb *neut* (PL die Verben)

★ **verdict** NOUN
das Urteil *neut* (PL die Urteile)

vertical ADJECTIVE
senkrecht

vertigo NOUN
das Schwindelgefühl *neut*
■ He had an attack of vertigo. Ihm wurde schwindlig.

★ **very** ADVERB
sehr
□ very tall sehr groß □ not very interesting nicht sehr interessant
■ **very much 1** sehr viel □ He didn't eat very much. Er hat nicht sehr viel gegessen. **2** (*like, love, respect*) sehr □ I love her very much. Ich liebe sie sehr.
■ **Thank you very much.** Vielen Dank.

vest NOUN
1 das Unterhemd *neut* (PL die Unterhemden)
2 die Weste *fem* (*waistcoat*)

vet NOUN
der Tierarzt *masc* (GEN des Tierarztes, PL die Tierärzte)
die Tierärztin *fem*
□ She's a vet. Sie ist Tierärztin.

★ **via** PREPOSITION
über
□ We went to Munich via Ulm. Wir sind über Ulm nach München gefahren.

vicar NOUN
der Pastor *masc* (PL die Pastoren)
die Pastorin *fem*
□ He's a vicar. Er ist Pastor.

★ **vice** NOUN
der Schraubstock *masc* (PL die Schraubstöcke) (*for holding things*)

vice versa ADVERB
umgekehrt

vicious ADJECTIVE
1 brutal
□ a vicious attack ein brutaler Überfall
2 bissig (*dog*)
3 bösartig (*person*)
■ **a vicious circle** ein Teufelskreis *masc*

★ **victim** NOUN
das Opfer *neut* (PL die Opfer)
□ He was the victim of a mugging. Er wurde das Opfer eines Straßenüberfalls.

★ **victory** NOUN
der Sieg *masc* (PL die Siege)

★ to **video** VERB
▷ *see also* **video** NOUN
auf Video aufnehmen [52] (PRESENT TENSE nimmt auf Video auf, IMPERFECT nahm auf Video auf, PERFECT TENSE hat auf Video aufgenommen)

★ **video** NOUN
▷ *see also* **video** VERB
das Video *neut* (PL die Videos) (*film*)
□ to watch a video ein Video ansehen □ a video of my family on holiday ein Video von meiner Familie in den Ferien
■ **a video camera** eine Videokamera
■ **a video game** ein Videospiel *neut* □ She likes playing video games. Sie spielt gern Videospiele.

Vienna NOUN
Wien *neut*
■ **to Vienna** nach Wien

★ = core vocabulary

Vietnamese NOUN
▷ *see also* **Vietnamese** ADJECTIVE
der Vietnamese *masc* (PL die Vietnamesen)
die Vietnamesin *fem*

Vietnamese ADJECTIVE
▷ *see also* **Vietnamese** NOUN
vietnamesisch

★ **view** NOUN
1 die Aussicht *fem*
□ There's an amazing view. Man hat dort eine tolle Aussicht.
2 die Meinung *fem* (*opinion*)
□ in my view meiner Meinung nach

★ **viewer** NOUN
der Fernsehzuschauer *masc* (PL die Fernsehzuschauer)
die Fernsehzuschauerin *fem*

viewpoint NOUN
der Standpunkt *masc* (PL die Standpunkte)

vile ADJECTIVE
ekelhaft (*smell, food*)

villa NOUN
die Villa *fem* (PL die Villen)

★ **village** NOUN
das Dorf *neut* (PL die Dörfer)

villain NOUN
1 der Verbrecher *masc* (PL die Verbrecher)
die Verbrecherin *fem* (*criminal*)
2 der Bösewicht *masc* (PL die Bösewichte) (*in film*)

vine NOUN
die Weinrebe *fem*

★ **vinegar** NOUN
der Essig *masc*

vineyard NOUN
der Weinberg *masc* (PL die Weinberge)

viola NOUN
die Bratsche *fem*
□ I play the viola. Ich spiele Bratsche.

★ **violence** NOUN
die Gewalt *fem*

★ **violent** ADJECTIVE
1 gewalttätig (*person, film*)
■ **a violent crime** ein Gewaltverbrechen *neut*
2 gewaltig (*explosion*)

★ **violin** NOUN
die Geige *fem*
□ I play the violin. Ich spiele Geige.

violinist NOUN
der Geigenspieler *masc* (PL die Geigenspieler)
die Geigenspielerin *fem*

viral ADJECTIVE
viral
■ **a viral video** ein virales Video

virgin NOUN
die Jungfrau *fem*
□ to be a virgin Jungfrau sein

Virgo NOUN
die Jungfrau *fem*
□ I'm Virgo. Ich bin Jungfrau.

virtual reality NOUN
die virtuelle Realität *fem*

★ **virus** NOUN
das Virus *neut* (GEN des Virus, PL die Viren)

visa NOUN
das Visum *neut* (PL die Visa)

visible ADJECTIVE
sichtbar

★ **visit** NOUN
▷ *see also* **visit** VERB
1 der Besuch *masc* (PL die Besuche)
□ my last visit to her mein letzter Besuch bei ihr
2 der Aufenthalt *masc* (PL die Aufenthalte) (*to country*)
□ Did you enjoy your visit to Germany? Hat euer Deutschlandaufenthalt Spaß gemacht?

★ **to visit** VERB
▷ *see also* **visit** NOUN
1 besuchen [7] (PERFECT TENSE hat besucht) (*person*)
2 besichtigen [18] (PERFECT TENSE hat besichtigt) (*place*)
□ We'd like to visit the castle. Wir würden gern die Burg besichtigen.

★ **visitor** NOUN
der Besucher *masc* (PL die Besucher)
die Besucherin *fem*
■ **to have a visitor** Besuch haben [32]

visual ADJECTIVE
visuell

★ **vital** ADJECTIVE
äußerst wichtig
□ It's vital that you do plenty of revision. Es ist äußerst wichtig, dass du so viel wie möglich wiederholst.
■ **of vital importance** äußerst wichtig

★ **vitamin** NOUN
das Vitamin *neut* (PL die Vitamine)

vivid ADJECTIVE
lebhaft
□ to have a vivid imagination eine lebhafte Fantasie haben

vocabulary NOUN
der Wortschatz *masc* (GEN des Wortschatzes, PL die Wortschätze)

vocational ADJECTIVE
beruflich
□ vocational training die berufliche Ausbildung

vodka NOUN
der Wodka *masc* (PL die Wodkas)

★ **voice** NOUN
die Stimme *fem*

voice mail NOUN
die Voicemail *fem*

v

volcano – vulgar

volcano NOUN
der Vulkan *masc* (PL die Vulkane)

volleyball NOUN
der Volleyball *masc*
□ to play volleyball Volleyball spielen

volt NOUN
das Volt *neut* (GEN des Volt, PL die Volt)

voltage NOUN
die Spannung *fem*

★ **voluntary** ADJECTIVE
freiwillig (*contribution, statement*)
■ **to do voluntary work** ehrenamtlich tätig
sein [65]

★ **volunteer** NOUN
▷ *see also* **volunteer** VERB
der Freiwillige *masc* (GEN des Freiwilligen, PL die
Freiwilligen)
die Freiwillige *fem* (GEN der Freiwilligen)
□ a volunteer ein Freiwilliger (*man*)

★ to **volunteer** VERB
▷ *see also* **volunteer** NOUN

■ **to volunteer to do something** sich freiwillig
melden [54], etwas zu tun

to **vomit** VERB
sich übergeben [28] (PRESENT TENSE übergibt
sich, IMPERFECT übergab sich, PERFECT TENSE hat
sich übergeben)

★ **vote** NOUN
▷ *see also* **vote** VERB
die Stimme *fem*

★ to **vote** VERB
▷ *see also* **vote** NOUN
wählen [38]
□ to vote Labour Labour wählen
■ **to vote for somebody** für jemanden
stimmen [38] □ I voted for him. Ich habe für
ihn gestimmt.

voucher NOUN
der Gutschein *masc* (PL die Gutscheine)
□ a gift voucher ein Geschenkgutschein

vowel NOUN
der Vokal *masc* (PL die Vokale)

vulgar ADJECTIVE
vulgär

v

Ww

wafer NOUN
die Waffel *fem*

★ **wage** NOUN
der Lohn *masc* (PL die Löhne)
□ He collected his wages. Er hat seinen Lohn abgeholt.

waist NOUN
die Taille *fem*

waistcoat NOUN
die Weste *fem*

★ to **wait** VERB
warten [2]
■ **to wait for something** auf etwas warten [2]
□ We were waiting for the bus. Wir haben auf den Bus gewartet.
■ **to wait for somebody** auf jemanden warten [2] □ I'll wait for you. Ich warte auf dich. □ Wait for me! Warte auf mich!
■ **Wait a minute!** Einen Augenblick!
■ **to keep somebody waiting** jemanden warten lassen [42] □ They kept us waiting for hours. Sie haben uns stundenlang warten lassen.
■ **I can't wait for the holidays.** Ich kann die Ferien kaum erwarten.
■ **I can't wait to see him again.** Ich kann's kaum erwarten, bis ich ihn wiedersehe.

to **wait up** VERB
aufbleiben [10] (IMPERFECT blieb auf, PERFECT TENSE ist aufgeblieben)
□ My mum always waits up till I get in. Meine Mutti bleibt immer auf, bis ich nach Hause komme.

★ **waiter** NOUN
der Kellner *masc* (PL die Kellner)

waiting list NOUN
die Warteliste *fem*

waiting room NOUN
das Wartezimmer *neut* (PL die Wartezimmer)

★ **waitress** NOUN
die Kellnerin *fem*

to **wake up** VERB
aufwachen [4] (PERFECT TENSE ist aufgewacht)
□ I woke up at six o'clock. Ich bin um sechs Uhr aufgewacht.
■ **to wake somebody up** jemanden wecken [38] □ Would you wake me up at seven o'clock? Könntest du mich um sieben Uhr wecken?

★ **Wales** NOUN
Wales *neut*
□ the Prince of Wales der Prinz von Wales
■ **from Wales** aus Wales
■ **in Wales** in Wales
■ **to Wales** nach Wales

★ to **walk** VERB
▷ *see also* **walk** NOUN
1 gehen [29] (IMPERFECT ging, PERFECT TENSE ist gegangen)
□ He walks fast. Er geht schnell.
2 zu Fuß gehen (*go on foot*)
□ Are you walking or going by bus? Geht ihr zu Fuß oder nehmt ihr den Bus? □ We walked ten kilometres. Wir sind zehn Kilometer zu Fuß gegangen.
■ **to walk the dog** mit dem Hund spazieren gehen [29]

★ **walk** NOUN
▷ *see also* **walk** VERB
der Spaziergang *masc* (PL die Spaziergänge)
□ to go for a walk einen Spaziergang machen
■ **It's ten minutes' walk from here.** Von hier ist es zehn Minuten zu Fuß.

walking NOUN
das Wandern *neut*
■ **I did some walking in the Alps last summer.** Ich bin letzten Sommer in den Alpen gewandert.

walking stick NOUN
der Spazierstock *masc* (PL die Spazierstöcke)

★ **wall** NOUN
1 die Mauer *fem*
□ There's a wall round the garden. Um den Garten ist eine Mauer.
2 die Wand *fem* (PL die Wände)
□ They have lots of pictures on the wall. Sie haben viele Bilder an der Wand.

wallet NOUN
die Brieftasche *fem*

wallpaper NOUN
die Tapete *fem*

walnut NOUN
die Walnuss *fem* (PL die Walnüsse)

to **wander** VERB
■ **to wander around** herumlaufen □ I just wandered around for a while. Ich bin einfach eine Zeit lang herumgelaufen.

want - waste

★ to **want** VERB

möchten (PRESENT TENSE mag, IMPERFECT mochte, PERFECT TENSE hat gemocht)
□ Do you want some cake? Möchtest du Kuchen?
■ **to want to do something** etwas tun wollen [94] □ I want to go to the cinema. Ich will ins Kino gehen. □ What do you want to do? Was willst du machen?

★ **war** NOUN

der Krieg masc (PL die Kriege)

ward NOUN

der Krankensaal masc (PL die Krankensäle) (room in hospital)

warden NOUN

der Herbergsvater masc (PL die Herbergsväter) die Herbergsmutter fem (PL die Herbergsmütter) (of youth hostel)

wardrobe NOUN

der Kleiderschrank masc (PL die Kleiderschränke) (piece of furniture)

warehouse NOUN

das Lagerhaus neut (GEN des Lagerhauses, PL die Lagerhäuser)

★ **warm** ADJECTIVE

1 warm
□ warm water warmes Wasser □ It's warm in here. Hier drin ist es warm. □ It's warmer in the kitchen. In der Küche ist es wärmer.

> When you talk about a person being 'warm', you use the impersonal construction.

□ I'm warm. Mir ist warm. □ I'm too warm. Mir ist zu warm.
2 herzlich
□ a warm welcome ein herzlicher Empfang

to **warm over** VERB

aufwärmen

to **warm up** VERB

1 sich aufwärmen (for sport)
2 aufwärmen (food)
□ I'll warm up some pasta for you. Ich wärme dir ein paar Nudeln auf.

★ to **warn** VERB

warnen [38]
□ Well, I warned you! Ich habe dich ja gewarnt.
■ **to warn somebody not to do something** jemanden davor warnen, etwas zu tun [81]
□ He warned me not to go there. Er warnte mich davor, dort hinzugehen.

★ **warning** NOUN

die Warnung fem

Warsaw NOUN

Warschau neut
■ **to Warsaw** nach Warschau

wart NOUN

die Warze fem

was VERB ▷ see be

★ **wash** NOUN

▷ see also **wash** VERB
■ **to have a wash** sich waschen [89] □ I had a wash. Ich habe mich gewaschen.
■ **to give something a wash** etwas waschen [89] □ He gave the car a wash. Er hat das Auto gewaschen.

★ to **wash** VERB

▷ see also **wash** NOUN
1 waschen [89] (PRESENT TENSE wäscht, IMPERFECT wusch, PERFECT TENSE hat gewaschen)
□ to wash something etwas waschen
2 sich waschen [89] (have a wash)
□ Every morning I get up, wash and get dressed. Jeden Morgen stehe ich auf, wasche mich und ziehe mich an.
■ **to wash one's hands** sich die Hände waschen [89] □ Where can I wash my hands? Wo kann ich mir die Hände waschen?
■ **to wash one's hair** sich die Haare waschen [89] □ You should wash your hair. Du solltest dir die Haare waschen.

to **wash up** VERB

abwaschen [89]

washbasin NOUN

das Waschbecken neut (PL die Waschbecken)

washcloth NOUN (US)

der Waschlappen masc (PL die Waschlappen)

washing NOUN

die Wäsche fem (clothes)
■ **Have you got any washing?** Hast du etwas zu waschen?
■ **to do the washing** Wäsche waschen [89]

washing machine NOUN

die Waschmaschine fem

washing powder NOUN

das Waschpulver neut (PL die Waschpulver)

★ **washing-up** NOUN

der Abwasch masc
□ to do the washing-up den Abwasch machen

washing-up liquid NOUN

das Spülmittel neut (PL die Spülmittel)

wasn't = was not

wasp NOUN

die Wespe fem

★ **waste** NOUN

▷ see also **waste** VERB
1 die Verschwendung fem
□ It's such a waste! Es ist so eine Verschwendung! □ It's a waste of time. Es ist Zeitverschwendung!
2 der Müll masc (rubbish)
□ nuclear waste der Atommüll

★ to **waste** VERB

▷ see also **waste** NOUN
verschwenden [7] (PERFECT TENSE hat verschwendet)

★ = core vocabulary

□ I don't like wasting money. Ich verschwende nicht gerne Geld. □ There's no time to waste. Wir haben keine Zeit zu verschwenden.

wastepaper basket NOUN
der Papierkorb *masc* (PL die Papierkörbe)

★ **watch** NOUN
▷ *see also* **watch** VERB
die Uhr *fem*

★ to **watch** VERB
▷ *see also* **watch** NOUN
1 ansehen [64] (PRESENT TENSE sieht an, IMPERFECT sah an, PERFECT TENSE hat angesehen) (*film, video*)
□ Did you watch that film last night? Hast du dir gestern Abend den Film angesehen?
■ **to watch television** fernsehen [64]
2 zusehen [64] (PRESENT TENSE sieht zu, IMPERFECT sah zu, PERFECT TENSE hat zugesehen)
□ Watch me! Sieh mir zu!
3 beobachten [2] (PERFECT TENSE hat beobachtet) (*keep a watch on*)
□ The police were watching the house. Die Polizei beobachtete das Haus.

to **watch out** VERB
aufpassen [31]
■ **Watch out!** Pass auf!

★ **water** NOUN
▷ *see also* **water** VERB
das Wasser *neut* (PL die Wasser)

★ to **water** VERB
▷ *see also* **water** NOUN
1 gießen (IMPERFECT goss, PERFECT TENSE hat gegossen) (*plant*)
□ He was watering his tulips. Er goss seine Tulpen.
2 sprengen (*garden*)
□ We should water the lawn. Wir sollten den Rasen sprengen.

waterfall NOUN
der Wasserfall *masc* (PL die Wasserfälle)

watering can NOUN
die Gießkanne *fem*

watermelon NOUN
die Wassermelone *fem*

waterproof ADJECTIVE
wasserdicht
□ Is this jacket waterproof? Ist die Jacke wasserdicht?

water-skiing NOUN
das Wasserskifahren *neut*
■ **to go water-skiing** Wasserski fahren [21]

★ **wave** NOUN
▷ *see also* **wave** VERB
die Welle *fem* (*in water*)
■ **We gave him a wave.** Wir haben ihm zugewinkt.

★ to **wave** VERB
▷ *see also* **wave** NOUN
winken [38]
■ **to wave at somebody** jemandem zuwinken
□ I waved at my friend. Ich winkte meinem Freund zu.
■ **to wave goodbye** zum Abschied winken [38] □ I waved her goodbye. Ich habe ihr zum Abschied gewinkt.

wavy ADJECTIVE
wellig
□ wavy hair welliges Haar

wax NOUN
das Wachs *neut* (GEN des Wachses)

★ **way** NOUN
1 die Art und Weise *fem* (*manner*)
□ That's no way to talk to your mother! Das ist keine Art und Weise, mit deiner Mutter zu reden!
■ **She looked at me in a strange way.** Sie sah mich sonderbar an.
■ **This book tells you the right way to do it.** Dieses Buch erklärt, wie man es machen muss.
■ **You're doing it the wrong way.** Du machst das falsch.
■ **In a way you're right.** In gewisser Weise hast du recht.
■ **a way of life** eine Art zu leben
2 der Weg *masc* (*route*)
□ I don't know the way. Ich kenne den Weg nicht.
■ **on the way** unterwegs □ We stopped for lunch on the way. Wir haben unterwegs angehalten und zu Mittag gegessen. □ He's on his way. Er ist unterwegs.
■ **It's a long way.** Es ist weit. □ Sydney is a long way from London. Sydney ist weit von London entfernt.
■ **Which way is it?** In welcher Richtung ist es?
■ **The supermarket is this way.** Zum Supermarkt geht es in diese Richtung.
■ **Do you know the way to the hotel?** Wissen Sie, wie man zum Hotel kommt?
■ **'way in'** 'Eingang'
■ **'way out'** 'Ausgang'
■ **by the way ...** übrigens ...

★ **we** PRONOUN
wir
□ We're staying here for a week. Wir sind eine Woche lang hier.

★ **weak** ADJECTIVE
schwach
□ Maths is my weakest subject. In Mathe bin ich am schwächsten.

wealthy ADJECTIVE
reich

★ **weapon** NOUN
die Waffe *fem*

w

wear – well-dressed

★ to **wear** VERB
tragen [77] (PRESENT TENSE trägt, IMPERFECT trug, PERFECT TENSE hat getragen) (clothes)
□ She was wearing a sweatshirt and leggings. Sie trug ein Sweatshirt und Leggings. □ She was wearing black. Sie trug Schwarz.

★ **weather** NOUN
das Wetter neut
□ What was the weather like? Wie war das Wetter? □ The weather was lovely. Das Wetter war herrlich.

★ **weather forecast** NOUN
die Wettervorhersage fem

Web NOUN
■ the Web das Web

web address NOUN
die Internetadresse fem

★ **webcam** NOUN
die Webcam fem (PL die Webcams)

★ **webmail** NOUN
die Webmail fem

web page NOUN
die Webseite fem

★ **website** NOUN
die Website fem (PL die Websites)

webzine NOUN
das Web-Magazin neut (PL die Web-Magazine)

we'd = we had, we would

★ **wedding** NOUN
die Hochzeit fem
■ wedding anniversary der Hochzeitstag
■ wedding dress das Brautkleid
■ wedding ring der Ehering

★ **Wednesday** NOUN
der Mittwoch masc (PL die Mittwoche)
□ on Wednesday am Mittwoch □ every Wednesday jeden Mittwoch □ last Wednesday letzten Mittwoch □ next Wednesday nächsten Mittwoch
■ on Wednesdays mittwochs

weed NOUN
das Unkraut neut
□ The garden's full of weeds. Der Garten ist voller Unkraut.

★ **week** NOUN
die Woche fem
□ last week letzte Woche □ every week jede Woche □ next week nächste Woche □ in a week's time in einer Woche
■ a week on Friday Freitag in einer Woche

weekday NOUN
■ on weekdays werktags

★ **weekend** NOUN
das Wochenende neut (PL die Wochenenden)
□ at the weekend am Wochenende □ at weekends am Wochenende □ last weekend letztes Wochenende □ next weekend nächstes Wochenende

★ to **weigh** VERB
wiegen (IMPERFECT wog, PERFECT TENSE hat gewogen)
□ How much do you weigh? Wie viel wiegst du? □ First, weigh the flour. Wiegen Sie zuerst das Mehl.
■ to weigh oneself sich wiegen

★ **weight** NOUN
das Gewicht neut (PL die Gewichte)
■ to lose weight abnehmen [52]
■ to put on weight zunehmen [52]

weightlifter NOUN
der Gewichtheber masc (PL die Gewichtheber)

weightlifting NOUN
das Gewichtheben neut

weight training NOUN
das Krafttraining neut

weird ADJECTIVE
sonderbar

★ **welcome** NOUN
▷ see also welcome VERB
■ They gave her a warm welcome. Sie haben sie herzlich empfangen.
■ Welcome! Herzlich willkommen! □ Welcome to Germany! Herzlich willkommen in Deutschland!

★ to **welcome** VERB
▷ see also welcome NOUN
■ to welcome somebody jemanden begrüßen [31]
■ Thank you! — You're welcome! Danke! — Bitte!

★ **well** ADJECTIVE, ADVERB
▷ see also well NOUN
1 gut
□ You did that really well. Das hast du wirklich gut gemacht.
■ to do well gut sein [65] □ She's doing well at school. Sie ist gut in der Schule.
■ to be well (in good health) gesund sein [65] □ I'm not very well at the moment. Ich bin im Moment nicht gesund.
■ Get well soon! Gute Besserung!
■ Well done! Gut gemacht!
2 na ja
□ It's enormous! Well, quite big anyway. Es ist riesig! Na ja, jedenfalls ziemlich groß.
■ as well auch □ We worked hard, but we had some fun as well. Wir haben hart gearbeitet, aber auch Spaß gehabt.

★ **well** NOUN
▷ see also well ADJECTIVE, ADVERB
der Brunnen masc (PL die Brunnen)

we'll = we will

well-behaved ADJECTIVE
artig

well-dressed ADJECTIVE
gut angezogen

★ = core vocabulary

wellingtons PL NOUN
die Gummistiefel *masc pl*

★ **well-known** ADJECTIVE
bekannt
□ **a well-known film star** ein bekannter Filmstar

well-off ADJECTIVE
gut situiert

★ **Welsh** ADJECTIVE
▷ *see also* **Welsh** NOUN
walisisch
■ **He's Welsh.** Er ist Waliser.
■ **She's Welsh.** Sie ist Waliserin.
■ **Welsh people** die Waliser *masc pl*

★ **Welsh** NOUN
▷ *see also* **Welsh** ADJECTIVE
das Walisisch *neut* (GEN des Walisischen) *(language)*

★ **Welshman** NOUN
der Waliser *masc* (PL die Waliser)

★ **Welshwoman** NOUN
die Waliserin *fem*

went VERB ▷ *see* **go**

were VERB ▷ *see* **be**

we're = we are

weren't = were not

★ **west** NOUN
▷ *see also* **west** ADJECTIVE, ADVERB
der Westen *masc*
□ **in the west** im Westen

★ **west** ADJECTIVE, ADVERB
▷ *see also* **west** NOUN
nach Westen
□ **We were travelling west.** Wir fuhren nach Westen.
■ **the west coast** die Westküste
■ **a west wind** ein Westwind *masc*
■ **west of** westlich von □ **Stroud is west of Oxford.** Stroud liegt westlich von Oxford.
■ **the West Country** der Südwesten Englands

★ **western** NOUN
▷ *see also* **western** ADJECTIVE
der Western *masc* (GEN des Western, PL die Western) *(film)*

★ **western** ADJECTIVE
▷ *see also* **western** NOUN
westlich
■ **the western part of the island** der westliche Teil der Insel
■ **Western Europe** Westeuropa *neut*

West Indian ADJECTIVE
▷ *see also* **West Indian** NOUN
westindisch
■ **He's West Indian.** Er ist aus Westindien.

West Indian NOUN
▷ *see also* **West Indian** ADJECTIVE
der Westinder *masc* (PL die Westinder)
die Westinderin *fem* *(person)*

West Indies PL NOUN
die Westindischen Inseln *fem pl*
■ **in the West Indies** auf den Westindischen Inseln

★ **wet** ADJECTIVE
nass
□ **wet clothes** nasse Kleider □ **to get wet** nass werden
■ **wet weather** regnerisches Wetter
■ **dripping wet** klatschnass
■ **It was wet all week.** Es hat die ganze Woche geregnet.

wet suit NOUN
der Neoprenanzug *masc* (PL die Neoprenanzüge)

we've = we have

whale NOUN
der Wal *masc* (PL die Wale)

★ **what** ADJECTIVE, PRONOUN
1 was
□ **What are you doing?** Was tust du? □ **What did you say?** Was hast du gesagt? □ **What is it?** Was ist das? □ **What's the matter?** Was ist los? □ **What happened?** Was ist passiert? □ **I saw what happened.** Ich habe gesehen, was passiert ist. □ **I heard what he said.** Ich habe gehört, was er gesagt hat.
■ **What?** Was?
2 welcher
□ **What name?** Welcher Name?
welche
□ **What colour is it?** Welche Farbe hat es?
welches
□ **What book do you want?** Welches Buch möchten Sie?
welche
□ **What subjects are you studying?** Welche Fächer studierst du?
■ **What's the capital of Finland?** Wie heißt die Hauptstadt von Finnland?
■ **What a mess!** So ein Chaos!

wheat NOUN
der Weizen *masc*

★ **wheel** NOUN
das Rad *neut* (PL die Räder)
■ **the steering wheel** das Lenkrad

wheelchair NOUN
der Rollstuhl *masc* (PL die Rollstühle)

★ **when** ADVERB, CONJUNCTION
1 wann
□ **When did he go?** Wann ist er gegangen?
2 als
□ **She was reading when I came in.** Sie las, als ich hereinkam.

★ **where** ADVERB, CONJUNCTION
wo
□ **Where's Emma today?** Wo ist Emma heute? □ **Where do you live?** Wo wohnst du? □ **a shop**

w

where you can buy jewellery ein Geschäft, wo man Schmuck kaufen kann
- **Where are you from?** Woher sind Sie?
- **Where are you going?** Wohin gehst du?

> **BE CAREFUL!**
> Do not translate **where** by the German word **wer**.

★ **whether** CONJUNCTION
ob
□ I don't know whether to go or not. Ich weiß nicht, ob ich gehen soll oder nicht.

★ **which** ADJECTIVE, PRONOUN
1 welcher
□ Which coat is yours? Welcher Mantel ist deiner?
welche
□ Which jacket did you buy? Welche Jacke hast du gekauft?
welches
□ Which book do you want? Welches Buch willst du?
welche
□ Which shoes should I wear? Welche Schuhe soll ich anziehen?

> When asking 'which one' use **welcher** or **welche** or **welches**, depending on whether the noun is masculine, feminine or neuter.

- **I know his brother. — Which one?** Ich kenne seinen Bruder. — Welchen?
- **I know his sister. — Which one?** Ich kenne seine Schwester. — Welche?
- **I took one of your books. — Which one?** Ich habe eines deiner Bücher genommen. — Welches?
- **Which would you like?** Welches möchtest du?
- **Which of these are yours?** Welche davon gehören dir?

> In relative clauses use **der**, **die** or **das**, depending on the gender of the noun 'which' refers to.

2 der
□ the film which is on now der Film, der gerade läuft
die
□ the jacket which Ella bought die Jacke, die Ella gekauft hat
das
□ the book which I am reading das Buch, das ich lese
die
□ the sweets which I ate die Süßigkeiten, die ich gegessen habe

★ **while** CONJUNCTION
> ▷ see also **while** NOUN
während
□ You hold the torch while I look inside. Halt du die Taschenlampe, während ich hineinsehe.

□ She's dynamic, while he's more laid-back. Sie ist dynamisch, während er eher lässig ist.

★ **while** NOUN
> ▷ see also **while** CONJUNCTION
die Weile fem
□ after a while nach einer Weile
- **a while ago** vor einer Weile □ **He was here a while ago.** Er war vor einer Weile hier.
- **for a while** eine Zeit lang □ I lived in London for a while. Ich habe eine Zeit lang in London gelebt.
- **quite a while** ziemlich lange □ That happened quite a while ago. Das ist schon ziemlich lange her. □ I haven't seen him for quite a while. Ich habe ihn schon ziemlich lange nicht mehr gesehen.

★ **whip** NOUN
> ▷ see also **whip** VERB
die Peitsche fem

★ to **whip** VERB
> ▷ see also **whip** NOUN
1 peitschen
□ She whipped her horse. Sie peitschte ihr Pferd.
2 schlagen [59] (PRESENT TENSE schlägt, IMPERFECT schlug, PERFECT TENSE hat geschlagen) (cream)

whipped cream NOUN
die Schlagsahne fem

whisk NOUN
der Schneebesen masc (PL die Schneebesen)

whiskers PL NOUN
die Schnurrhaare neut pl

whisky NOUN
der Whisky masc (PL die Whiskys)

★ to **whisper** VERB
flüstern [88]

whistle NOUN
> ▷ see also **whistle** VERB
die Pfeife fem
- **The referee blew his whistle.** Der Schiedsrichter hat gepfiffen.

to **whistle** VERB
> ▷ see also **whistle** NOUN
pfeifen (IMPERFECT pfiff, PERFECT TENSE hat gepfiffen)

★ **white** ADJECTIVE
weiß
□ He's got white hair. Er hat weiße Haare.
- **white wine** der Weißwein
- **white bread** das Weißbrot
- **white coffee** der Kaffee mit Milch
- **a white man** ein Weißer
- **a white woman** eine Weiße
- **white people** die Weißen masc pl

whiteboard NOUN
die Weißwandtafel fem
□ an interactive whiteboard eine interaktive Weißwandtafel

★ = core vocabulary

Whitsun NOUN
das Pfingsten *neut* (GEN des Pfingsten, PL die Pfingsten)

★ **who** PRONOUN

1 wer
□ Who said that? Wer hat das gesagt? □ Who's he? Wer ist er?

> In relative clauses use **der**, **die** or **das**, depending on the gender of the noun 'who' refers to.

2 der
□ the man who saw us der Mann, der uns gesehen hat □ the man who we saw der Mann, den wir gesehen haben
die
□ the woman who saw us die Frau, die uns gesehen hat □ the woman who we saw die Frau, die wir gesehen haben
das
□ the child who saw us das Kind, das uns gesehen hat □ the child who we saw das Kind, das wir gesehen haben
die
□ the people who saw us die Leute, die uns gesehen haben

> **BE CAREFUL!**
> Do not translate **who** by **wo**.

★ **whole** ADJECTIVE
▷ *see also* **whole** NOUN
ganz
□ the whole class die ganze Klasse □ the whole day den ganzen Tag □ the whole world die ganze Welt

★ **whole** NOUN
▷ *see also* **whole** ADJECTIVE
■ **The whole of Wales was affected.** Ganz Wales war davon betroffen.
■ **on the whole** im Großen und Ganzen

wholemeal ADJECTIVE
■ **wholemeal bread** das Vollkornbrot
■ **wholemeal flour** das Vollkornmehl

wholewheat ADJECTIVE (US)
■ **wholewheat bread** das Vollkornbrot

★ **whom** PRONOUN
wen
□ Whom did you see? Wen hast du gesehen?
■ **the man to whom I spoke** der Mann, mit dem ich gesprochen habe
■ **the woman to whom I spoke** die Frau, mit der ich gesprochen habe

★ **whose** PRONOUN, ADJECTIVE
wessen
□ Whose book is this? Wessen Buch ist das?
■ **Whose is this?** Wem gehört das?
■ **I know whose it is.** Ich weiß, wem das gehört.
■ **the man whose picture was in the paper** der Mann, dessen Bild in der Zeitung war

■ **the woman whose picture was in the paper** die Frau, deren Bild in der Zeitung war
■ **the girl whose picture was in the paper** das Mädchen, dessen Bild in der Zeitung war

★ **why** ADVERB
warum
□ Why did you do that? Warum hast du das getan? □ Tell me why. Sag mir warum. □ Why not? Warum nicht? □ All right, why not? Also gut, warum auch nicht?
■ **That's why he did it.** Deshalb hat er es getan.

★ **wicked** ADJECTIVE
1 böse (*evil*)
2 geil (*informal: really great*)

wicket NOUN
das Mal *neut* (PL die Male) (*stumps*)

★ **wide** ADJECTIVE, ADVERB
breit
□ a wide road eine breite Straße
■ **wide open** weit offen □ The door was wide open. Die Tür stand weit offen. □ The windows were wide open. Die Fenster waren weit offen.
■ **wide awake** hellwach

widow NOUN
die Witwe *fem*
□ She's a widow. Sie ist Witwe.

widower NOUN
der Witwer *masc* (PL die Witwer)
□ He's a widower. Er ist Witwer.

width NOUN
die Breite *fem*

★ **wife** NOUN
die Frau *fem*
□ his wife seine Frau

Wi-Fi NOUN
das Wi-Fi *neut*

wig NOUN
die Perücke *fem*

★ **wild** ADJECTIVE
1 wild
□ a wild animal ein wildes Tier
2 verrückt (*crazy*)
□ She's a bit wild. Sie ist ein bisschen verrückt.

wild card NOUN
die Wildcard *fem* (PL die Wildcards)

wildlife NOUN
die Tierwelt *fem*
□ I'm interested in wildlife. Ich interessiere mich für die Tierwelt.

★ **will** NOUN
▷ *see also* **will** VERB
das Testament *neut* (PL die Testamente)
□ He left me some money in his will. Er hat mir in seinem Testament Geld vermacht.
■ **He came of his own free will.** Er ist freiwillig gekommen.

★ **will** VERB
▷ *see also* **will** NOUN

In German the present tense is often used to express somebody's intention to do something.

□ **I'll show you your room.** Ich zeige Ihnen Ihr Zimmer. □ **I'll give you a hand.** Ich helfe dir.
■ **Will you help me?** Hilfst du mir?
■ **Will you wash up? — No, I won't.** Wäschst du ab? — Nein.

Use the German future tense when referring to the more distant future.

□ **I will come back one day.** Ich werde eines Tages zurückkommen. □ **It won't take long.** Es wird nicht lange dauern.
■ **That'll be Oscar.** Das wird Oscar sein.
■ **Will you be quiet!** Werdet ihr wohl still sein!

★ **willing** ADJECTIVE
■ **to be willing to do something** bereit sein, etwas zu tun [81]

★ to **win** VERB
▷ *see also* **win** NOUN
gewinnen [30] (IMPERFECT gewann, PERFECT TENSE hat gewonnen)
□ **Did you win?** Hast du gewonnen?
■ **to win a prize** einen Preis bekommen [40]

★ **win** NOUN
▷ *see also* **win** VERB
der Sieg *masc* (PL die Siege)

★ to **wind** VERB
▷ *see also* **wind** NOUN
1 wickeln (*rope, wool, wire*)
□ **He wound the rope round the tree.** Er wickelte das Seil um den Baum.
2 sich schlängeln (*river, path*)
□ **The road winds through the valley.** Die Straße schlängelt sich durch das Tal.

★ **wind** NOUN
▷ *see also* **wind** VERB
der Wind *masc* (PL die Winde)
□ **a strong wind** ein starker Wind
■ **a wind farm** eine Windfarm
■ **a wind instrument** ein Blasinstrument *neut*
■ **wind power** die Windkraft
■ **a wind turbine** eine Windturbine

windmill NOUN
die Windmühle *fem*

★ **window** NOUN
das Fenster *neut* (PL die Fenster)
□ **to break a window** ein Fenster kaputt machen
□ **a broken window** ein kaputtes Fenster
■ **a shop window** ein Schaufenster

windscreen NOUN
die Windschutzscheibe *fem*

windscreen wiper NOUN
der Scheibenwischer *masc* (PL die Scheibenwischer)

windshield NOUN (US)
die Windschutzscheibe *fem*

windshield wiper NOUN (US)
der Scheibenwischer *masc* (PL die Scheibenwischer)

windy ADJECTIVE
windig (*place*)
□ **It's windy.** Es ist windig.

★ **wine** NOUN
der Wein *masc* (PL die Weine)
□ **a bottle of wine** eine Flasche Wein □ **a glass of wine** ein Glas Wein
■ **white wine** der Weißwein
■ **red wine** der Rotwein
■ **a wine glass** ein Weinglas *neut*
■ **the wine list** die Getränkekarte

★ **wing** NOUN
der Flügel *masc* (PL die Flügel)

to **wink** VERB
■ **to wink at somebody** jemandem zublinzeln
□ **He winked at me.** Er hat mir zugeblinzelt.

★ **winner** NOUN
der Sieger *masc* (PL die Sieger)
die Siegerin *fem*

★ **winning** ADJECTIVE
■ **the winning team** die Siegermannschaft
■ **the winning goal** das entscheidende Tor

★ **winter** NOUN
der Winter *masc* (PL die Winter)
□ **in winter** im Winter

winter sports PL NOUN
der Wintersport *masc sing*

★ to **wipe** VERB
abwischen [4] (PERFECT TENSE hat abgewischt)
■ **to wipe one's feet** sich die Füße abstreifen
□ **Wipe your feet!** Streif dir die Füße ab!

to **wipe up** VERB
aufwischen

★ **wire** NOUN
der Draht *masc* (PL die Drähte)

wireless ADJECTIVE
drahtlos
□ **wireless technology** drahtlose Technologie

wisdom tooth NOUN
der Weisheitszahn *masc* (PL die Weisheitszähne)

★ **wise** ADJECTIVE
weise

★ to **wish** VERB
▷ *see also* **wish** NOUN
■ **to wish for something** sich etwas wünschen [48] □ **What more could I wish for?** Was mehr könnte ich mir wünschen?
■ **to wish to do something** etwas tun mögen
□ **I wish to make a complaint.** Ich möchte mich beschweren.

★ = core vocabulary

■ **I wish you were here!** Ich wünschte, du wärst da!

■ **I wish you'd told me!** Wenn du mir das doch nur gesagt hättest!

★ **wish** NOUN

▷ *see also* **wish** VERB

der Wunsch *masc* (PL die Wünsche)

■ **to make a wish** sich etwas wünschen [48]

□ You can make a wish. Du darfst dir etwas wünschen.

■ **'best wishes'** **1** (*on greetings card*) 'Alles Gute' **2** (*at end of email, letter*) 'alles Liebe' □ 'with best wishes, Jo' (*friends, family*) 'alles Liebe, Jo' □ 'with best wishes' (*more formal*) 'mit freundlichen Grüßen'

wit NOUN

der geistreiche Humor *masc* (*humour*)

★ **with** PREPOSITION

1 mit

□ Come with me. Komm mit mir. □ a woman with blue eyes eine Frau mit blauen Augen

■ **Fill the jug with water.** Tu Wasser in den Krug.

■ **He walks with a stick.** Er geht am Stock.

2 bei (*at the home of*)

□ We stayed with friends. Wir haben bei Freunden übernachtet.

3 vor

□ green with envy grün vor Neid □ to shake with fear vor Angst zittern

★ **within** PREPOSITION

■ **The shops are within easy reach.** Die Geschäfte sind schnell zu erreichen.

■ **within the week** innerhalb dieser Woche

★ **without** PREPOSITION

ohne

□ without a coat ohne einen Mantel □ without speaking ohne etwas zu sagen

★ **witness** NOUN

der Zeuge *masc* (GEN des Zeugen, PL die Zeugen) die Zeugin *fem*

□ There were no witnesses. Es gab keine Zeugen.

■ **witness box** der Zeugenstand

■ **witness stand** der Zeugenstand

witty ADJECTIVE

geistreich

wives PL NOUN ▷ *see* **wife**

woken up VERB ▷ *see* **wake up**

woke up VERB ▷ *see* **wake up**

wolf NOUN

der Wolf *masc* (PL die Wölfe)

★ **woman** NOUN

die Frau *fem*

won VERB ▷ *see* **win**

★ **to wonder** VERB

sich fragen [38]

□ I wonder why she said that. Ich frage mich, warum sie das gesagt hat. □ I wonder what that means. Ich frage mich, was das bedeutet.

■ **I wonder where Caroline is.** Wo Caroline wohl ist?

★ **wonderful** ADJECTIVE

wunderbar

won't = **will not**

★ **wood** NOUN

1 das Holz *neut* (PL die Hölzer) (*timber*)

□ It's made of wood. Es ist aus Holz.

2 der Wald *masc* (PL die Wälder) (*forest*)

□ We went for a walk in the wood. Wir sind im Wald spazieren gegangen.

★ **wooden** ADJECTIVE

hölzern

■ **a wooden chair** ein Holzstuhl *masc*

woodwork NOUN

das Schreinern *neut*

□ Dieter's hobby is woodwork. Schreinern ist Dieters Hobby.

wool NOUN

die Wolle *fem*

□ It's made of wool. Es ist aus Wolle.

★ **word** NOUN

das Wort *neut* (PL die Wörter)

□ a difficult word ein schwieriges Wort

■ **What's the word for 'shop' in German?** Wie heißt 'shop' auf Deutsch?

■ **in other words** in anderen Worten

■ **to have a word with somebody** mit jemandem reden [54]

■ **the words** (*lyrics*) der Text *sing* □ I really like the words of this song. Der Text dieses Liedes gefällt mir wirklich gut.

word processing NOUN

die Textverarbeitung *fem*

word processor NOUN

das Textverarbeitungssystem *neut* (PL die Textverarbeitungssysteme)

wore VERB ▷ *see* **wear**

★ **work** NOUN

▷ *see also* **work** VERB

die Arbeit *fem*

□ She's looking for work. Sie sucht Arbeit. □ He's at work at the moment. Er ist zurzeit bei der Arbeit. □ It's hard work. Das ist harte Arbeit.

■ **to be off work** (*sick*) krank sein [65]

■ **He's out of work.** Er ist arbeitslos.

★ **to work** VERB

▷ *see also* **work** NOUN

1 arbeiten [2] (*person*)

□ She works in a shop. Sie arbeitet in einem Laden. □ to work hard hart arbeiten

2 funktionieren [76] (PERFECT TENSE hat funktioniert) (*machine, plan*)

□ The heating isn't working. Die Heizung funktioniert nicht. □ My plan worked perfectly. Mein Plan hat prima funktioniert.

w

worker – would

to **work out** VERB

1 trainieren [76] (*exercise*)
□ I work out twice a week. Ich trainiere zweimal pro Woche.

2 klappen [48] (*turn out*)
□ In the end it worked out really well. Am Ende hat es richtig gut geklappt.

■ **to work something out** (*figure out*) auf etwas kommen [40] □ I just couldn't work it out. Ich bin einfach nicht darauf gekommen.

■ **It works out at ten pounds each.** Das macht für jeden zehn Pfund.

★ **worker** NOUN

der Arbeiter *masc* (PL die Arbeiter)
die Arbeiterin *fem*
□ He's a factory worker. Er ist Fabrikarbeiter.
■ **She's a good worker.** Sie macht gute Arbeit.

work experience NOUN

das Praktikum *neut* (PL die Praktika)
□ work experience in a factory ein Praktikum in einer Fabrik

working-class ADJECTIVE

der Arbeiterklasse *masc*
□ a working-class family eine Familie der Arbeiterklasse

workman NOUN

der Arbeiter *masc* (PL die Arbeiter)

works NOUN

das Werk *neut* (PL die Werke) (*factory*)

worksheet NOUN

das Arbeitsblatt *neut* (PL die Arbeitsblätter)

workshop NOUN

die Werkstatt *fem* (PL die Werkstätten)
■ **a drama workshop** ein Theaterworkshop *masc*

workspace NOUN

der Arbeitsplatz *masc* (GEN des Arbeitsplatzes, PL die Arbeitsplätze)

workstation NOUN

der Arbeitsplatzcomputer *masc* (PL die Arbeitsplatzcomputer)

★ **world** NOUN

die Welt *fem*
■ **She's the world champion.** Sie ist die Weltmeisterin.

World Wide Web NOUN

■ **the World Wide Web** das World Wide Web

worm NOUN

der Wurm *masc* (PL die Würmer)

worn VERB ▷ *see* wear

worn ADJECTIVE

abgenutzt
□ The carpet is a bit worn. Der Teppich ist etwas abgenutzt.
■ **worn out** (*tired*) erschöpft

★ **worried** ADJECTIVE

besorgt
□ She's very worried. Sie ist sehr besorgt.

■ **to be worried about something** sich wegen etwas Sorgen machen [48] □ I'm worried about the exam. Ich mache mir wegen der Prüfung Sorgen.

■ **to look worried** besorgt aussehen [64]
□ She looks worried. Sie sieht besorgt aus.

★ to **worry** VERB

sich Sorgen machen
□ You worry too much. Du machst dir zu viele Sorgen.
■ **Don't worry!** Keine Sorge!

★ **worse** ADJECTIVE, ADVERB

schlechter
□ My results were bad, but his were even worse. Meine Noten waren schlecht, aber seine waren noch schlechter. □ I'm feeling worse. Mir geht es schlechter.
■ **It was even worse than that.** Es war sogar noch schlimmer.

to **worship** VERB

anbeten (PERFECT TENSE hat angebetet)
□ He worships Lucy. Er betet Lucy an.

★ **worst** ADJECTIVE

▷ *see also* **worst** NOUN

■ **the worst 1** der schlechteste □ the worst student in the class der schlechteste Schüler der Klasse **2** die schlechteste □ He got the worst mark in the whole class. Er hat von der ganzen Klasse die schlechteste Note bekommen. **3** das schlechteste □ the worst report I've ever had das schlechteste Zeugnis, das ich je hatte

■ **my worst enemy** mein schlimmster Feind
■ **Maths is my worst subject.** In Mathe bin ich am schlechtesten.

★ **worst** NOUN

▷ *see also* **worst** ADJECTIVE

das Schlimmste *neut* (GEN des Schlimmsten)
□ The worst of it is that ... Das Schlimmste daran ist, dass ...
■ **at worst** schlimmstenfalls
■ **if the worst comes to the worst** schlimmstenfalls

★ **worth** ADJECTIVE

■ **to be worth** wert sein [65] □ It's worth a lot of money. Es ist sehr viel Geld wert. □ How much is it worth? Wie viel ist das wert?
■ **It's worth it.** Das lohnt sich. □ Is it worth it? Lohnt es sich? □ It's not worth it. Das lohnt sich nicht.

★ **would** VERB

■ **Would you like ...?** Möchtest du ...? □ Would you like a biscuit? Möchtest du einen Keks? □ Would you like to go and see a film? Möchtest du ins Kino gehen?
■ **Would you close the door please?** Würden Sie bitte die Tür zumachen?
■ **I'd like ...** Ich würde gern ... □ I'd like to go to America. Ich würde gern nach Amerika fahren.

■ **Shall we go to the concert? — Yes, I'd like that.** Sollen wir ins Konzert gehen? — Au ja!
■ **I said I'd do it.** Ich sagte, ich würde es tun.
■ **If you asked him he'd do it.** Wenn du ihn fragen würdest, würde er es tun.
■ **If you had asked him he would have done it.** Wenn du ihn gefragt hättest, hätte er es getan.

wouldn't = would not

★ **wound** VERB ▷ see **wind**

★ **to wound** VERB
▷ see also **wound** NOUN
verwunden [7] (PERFECT TENSE hat verwundet)
□ He was wounded. Er wurde verwundet.

★ **wound** NOUN
▷ see also **wound** VERB
die Wunde fem

★ **to wrap** VERB
einpacken [4] (PERFECT TENSE hat eingepackt)
□ She's wrapping the present. Sie packt das Geschenk ein.
■ **Can you wrap it for me please?** (in shop)
Können Sie es mir bitte in Geschenkpapier einpacken?

to wrap up VERB
einpacken [4]

wrapping paper NOUN
das Geschenkpapier neut

wreck NOUN
▷ see also **wreck** VERB
das Wrack neut (PL die Wracks)
□ That car is a wreck! Das Auto ist ein Wrack.
□ After the exam I was a complete wreck. Nach der Prüfung war ich ein totales Wrack.

to wreck VERB
▷ see also **wreck** NOUN
1 zerstören [95] (PERFECT TENSE hat zerstört) (building)
□ The explosion wrecked the whole house. Die Explosion hat das ganze Haus zerstört.
2 kaputt fahren [21] (PRESENT TENSE fährt kaputt, IMPERFECT fuhr kaputt, PERFECT TENSE hat kaputt gefahren) (car)
□ He's wrecked his car. Er hat sein Auto kaputt gefahren.
3 verderben (PRESENT TENSE verdirbt, IMPERFECT verdarb, PERFECT TENSE hat verdorben) (plan, holiday)
□ Our trip was wrecked by bad weather. Das schlechte Wetter hat uns den Ausflug verdorben.

wreckage NOUN
1 das Wrack neut (PL die Wracks) (of vehicle)
2 die Trümmer pl (of building)

wrestler NOUN
der Ringer masc (PL die Ringer)
die Ringerin fem

wrestling NOUN
das Ringen neut
□ His hobby is wrestling. Ringen ist sein Hobby.

wrinkled ADJECTIVE
faltig

wrist NOUN
das Handgelenk neut (PL die Handgelenke)

★ **to write** VERB
schreiben [61] (IMPERFECT schrieb, PERFECT TENSE hat geschrieben)
□ to write a letter einen Brief schreiben
■ **to write to somebody** jemandem schreiben
[61] □ I'm going to write her an email. Ich werde ihr eine E-Mail schreiben.

to write down VERB
aufschreiben [61]
□ I wrote down the address. Ich habe die Adresse aufgeschrieben. □ Can you write it down for me, please? Können Sie es mir bitte aufschreiben?

★ **writer** NOUN
der Schriftsteller masc (PL die Schriftsteller)
die Schriftstellerin fem
□ She's a writer. Sie ist Schriftstellerin.

★ **writing** NOUN
die Schrift fem
□ I can't read your writing. Ich kann deine Schrift nicht lesen.
■ **in writing** schriftlich

★ **written** VERB ▷ see **write**

★ **wrong** ADJECTIVE, ADVERB
1 falsch (incorrect)
□ The information was wrong. Die Information war falsch. □ the wrong answer die falsche Antwort
■ **You've got the wrong number.** Sie haben sich verwählt.
2 unrecht (morally bad)
□ I think fox hunting is wrong. Ich meine, dass Fuchsjagden unrecht sind.
■ **to be wrong** (mistaken) unrecht haben [32]
□ You're wrong about that. Sie haben da unrecht.
■ **to do something wrong** etwas falsch machen [48] □ You've done it wrong. Du hast das falsch gemacht. □ Have I done something wrong? Habe ich etwas falsch gemacht?
■ **to go wrong** (plan) schiefgehen [29] □ The robbery went wrong. Der Überfall ist schiefgegangen.
■ **What's wrong?** Was ist los?
■ **What's wrong with her?** Was ist mit ihr los?

wrote VERB ▷ see **write**

WWW ABBREVIATION
= World Wide Web
■ **the WWW** das WWW

w

Xx

Xmas NOUN (= *Christmas*)
Weihnachten *neut*

to **X-ray** VERB
▷ *see also* **X-ray** NOUN
röntgen [54]
□ They X-rayed my arm. Sie haben meinen Arm geröntgt.

X-ray NOUN
▷ *see also* **X-ray** VERB
die Röntgenaufnahme *fem*
■ to have an X-ray geröntgt werden [91]

★ = core vocabulary

Yy

★ **yacht** NOUN
1 das Segelboot *neut* (PL die Segelboote) (*sailing boat*)
2 die Jacht *fem* (*luxury motorboat*)

★ **yard** NOUN
der Hof *masc* (PL die Höfe) (*of building*)
□ **in the yard** auf dem Hof

to **yawn** VERB
gähnen [38]

★ **year** NOUN
das Jahr *neut* (PL die Jahre)
□ **last year** letztes Jahr □ **next year** nächstes Jahr □ **to be fifteen years old** fünfzehn Jahre alt sein
■ **an eight-year-old child** ein achtjähriges Kind

DID YOU KNOW...?
In Germany secondary schools, years are counted from the **fünfte Klasse** (youngest) to the **dreizehnte Klasse** (oldest).

□ **year seven** die fünfte Klasse □ **She's in year eleven.** Sie ist in der neunten Klasse. □ **year eight** die sechste Klasse
■ **She's a first-year at university.** Sie ist Studienanfängerin.

to **yell** VERB
schreien [62] (IMPERFECT schrie, PERFECT TENSE hat geschrien)

★ **yellow** ADJECTIVE
gelb

★ **yes** ADVERB
1 ja
□ **Do you like it? — Yes.** Gefällt es dir? — Ja. □ **Yes please.** Ja bitte.
2 doch

Use **doch** to contradict a negative statement or question.

□ **Don't you like it? — Yes!** Gefällt es dir nicht? — Doch! □ **You're not Swiss, are you? — Yes I am!** Sie sind nicht Schweizer, oder? — Doch, ich bin Schweizer. □ **That's not true. — Yes it is!** Das ist nicht wahr. — Doch!

★ **yesterday** ADVERB
gestern
□ **yesterday morning** gestern früh □ **yesterday afternoon** gestern Nachmittag □ **yesterday evening** gestern Abend □ **all day yesterday** gestern den ganzen Tag
■ **the day before yesterday** vorgestern

★ **yet** ADVERB
1 noch
□ **It has yet to be proved that ...** Es muss noch bewiesen werden, dass ...
2 schon (*in questions*)
□ **Has the murderer been caught yet?** Ist der Mörder schon gefasst worden?
■ **not yet** noch nicht □ **It's not finished yet.** Es ist noch nicht fertig.
■ **not as yet** noch nicht □ **There's no news as yet.** Es gibt noch keine Nachricht.
■ **Have you finished yet?** Bist du fertig?

yob NOUN
der Rowdy *masc* (PL die Rowdys)

yoga NOUN
das Yoga *neut*

★ **yoghurt** NOUN
der Joghurt *masc* (PL die Joghurts)

yolk NOUN
das Eigelb *neut* (PL die Eigelbe)

★ **you** PRONOUN

Only use **du** when speaking to one person, and when the person is your own age or younger. Use **ihr** for several people of your own age or younger. If in doubt use the polite form **Sie**.

1 Sie (*polite form, singular and plural*)
□ **Do you like athletics?** Mögen Sie Leichtathletik? □ **Can I help you?** Kann ich Ihnen behilflich sein? □ **I saw you yesterday.** Ich habe Sie gestern gesehen. □ **It's for you.** Das ist für Sie.
2 du (*familiar singular*)
□ **Do you like sport?** Magst du Sport? □ **She's younger than you.** Sie ist jünger als du. □ **I know you.** Ich kenne dich. □ **I gave it to you.** Ich habe es dir gegeben. □ **It's for you.** Es ist für dich. □ **I'll come with you.** Ich komme mit dir mit.
3 ihr (*familiar plural*)
□ **Do you two like football?** Mögt ihr beiden Fußball? □ **I told you to be quiet.** Ich habe euch gesagt, ihr sollt still sein. □ **This is for you two.** Es ist für euch beide. □ **Can I come with you?** Kann ich mit euch mitkommen?

★ young ADJECTIVE
jung
□ young people junge Leute

younger ADJECTIVE
jünger
□ He's younger than me. Er ist jünger als ich.
□ my younger brother mein jüngerer Bruder
□ my younger sister meine jüngere Schwester

youngest ADJECTIVE
jüngste
□ his youngest brother sein jüngster Bruder
□ She's the youngest. Sie ist die Jüngste.

★ your ADJECTIVE

> Only use **dein** when speaking to one person, and when the person is your own age or younger. For several people of your own age or younger use **euer**. If in doubt use the polite form **Ihr**.

1 Ihr (*polite form, singular and plural*)
□ your father Ihr Vater □ your mother Ihre Mutter □ your house Ihr Haus □ your seats Ihre Plätze

2 dein (*familiar singular*)
□ your brother dein Bruder □ your sister deine Schwester □ your book dein Buch □ your parents deine Eltern

3 euer (*familiar plural*)
□ your father euer Vater □ your mother eure Mutter □ your car euer Auto □ your teachers eure Lehrer

> Do not use **Ihr**, **dein** or **euer** with parts of the body.

□ Would you like to wash your hands? Möchten Sie sich die Hände waschen? □ Do you want to wash your hair? Möchtest du dir die Haare waschen? □ You two, go upstairs and brush your teeth. Ihr beide geht nach oben und putzt euch die Zähne.

★ yours PRONOUN

> Only use **deiner/deine/deines** when speaking to one person of your own age or younger. Use **euer/eure/eures** when speaking to several people of your own age or younger. If in doubt use the polite form **Ihrer/Ihre/Ihres**.

1 Ihrer (*polite form, singular and plural*)
□ That's a nice coat. Is it yours? Das ist ein hübscher Mantel. Ist es Ihrer?
Ihre
□ What a pretty jacket. Is it yours? Was für eine hübsche Jacke. Ist das Ihre?
Ihres
□ I like that car. Is it yours? Das Auto gefällt mir. Ist es Ihres?

Ihre
□ my parents and yours meine Eltern und Ihre
■ **Is this yours?** Gehört das Ihnen? □ This book is yours. Das Buch gehört Ihnen.
■ **Yours sincerely, ...** Mit freundlichen Grüßen ...

2 deiner (*familiar singular*)
□ I've lost my pen. Can I use yours? Ich habe meinen Schreiber verlegt. Kann ich deinen benützen?
deine
□ Nice jacket. Is it yours? Hübsche Jacke. Ist das deine?
deines
□ I like that car. Is it yours? Das Auto gefällt mir. Ist das deines?
deine
□ my parents and yours meine Eltern und deine
□ My hands are dirty, yours are clean. Meine Hände sind schmutzig, deine sind sauber.
■ **Is this yours?** Gehört das dir? □ This book is yours. Das Buch gehört dir. □ Whose is this? — It's yours. Wem gehört das? — Es gehört dir.

3 euer (*familiar plural*)
□ My computer is broken. Can I use yours? Mein Computer ist kaputt. Kann ich euren benutzen?
eure
□ I haven't got a torch. Can I use yours? Ich habe keine Taschenlampe. Kann ich eure benutzen?
eures
□ Our house is bigger than yours. Unser Haus ist größer als eures.
eure
□ our parents and yours unsere Eltern und eure
■ **Is this yours?** Gehört das euch? □ These books are yours. Diese Bücher gehören euch.
□ Whose is it? — It's yours. Wem gehört das? — Es gehört euch.

★ yourself PRONOUN

> Only use **dich/dir** when speaking to one person of your own age or younger. If in doubt use the polite form **sich**.

1 sich (*polite form*)
□ Have you hurt yourself? Haben Sie sich verletzt? □ Tell me about yourself! Erzählen Sie etwas von sich!

2 dich (*familiar form*)
□ Have you hurt yourself? Hast du dich verletzt?

3 dir (*familiar form*)
□ Tell me about yourself! Erzähl mir etwas von dir! □ If you are not happy with yourself ... Wenn du mit dir selbst nicht zufrieden bist ...

4 selbst
■ **Do it yourself!** 1 Machen Sie es selbst!
2 Mach's selbst!

yourselves PRONOUN

> Only use **euch** when speaking to people of your own age or younger. If in doubt use the polite form **sich**.

1 sich (*polite form*)
  □ Did you enjoy yourselves? Haben Sie sich amüsiert?
2 euch (*familiar form*)
  □ Did you enjoy yourselves? Habt ihr euch amüsiert?

3 selbst
  ■ **Did you make it yourselves? 1** Haben Sie es selbst gemacht? **2** Habt ihr es selbst gemacht?

youth club NOUN
  das Jugendzentrum *neut* (PL die Jugendzentren)

youth hostel NOUN
  die Jugendherberge *fem*

y

Zz

zany ADJECTIVE
irre komisch
□ a zany film ein irre komischer Film

zebra NOUN
das Zebra neut (PL die Zebras)

zebra crossing NOUN
der Zebrastreifen masc (PL die Zebrastreifen)

★ **zero** NOUN
die Null fem

Zimbabwe NOUN
Simbabwe neut
□ in Zimbabwe in Simbabwe

Zimmer frame® NOUN
der Gehapparat masc (PL die Gehapparate)

zip NOUN
der Reißverschluss masc (GEN des
Reißverschlusses, PL die Reißverschlüsse)

zip code NOUN (US)
die Postleitzahl fem

zip drive NOUN
das Zip-Laufwerk neut (PL die Zip-Laufwerke)

zipper NOUN (US)
der Reißverschluss masc (GEN des
Reißverschlusses, PL die Reißverschlüsse)

zit NOUN
der Pickel masc (PL die Pickel)

zodiac NOUN
der Tierkreis masc (GEN des Tierkreises)
■ the signs of the zodiac die Sternzeichen

★ **zone** NOUN
die Zone fem

★ **zoo** NOUN
der Zoo masc (PL die Zoos)

zoom lens NOUN
das Zoomobjektiv neut (PL die Zoomobjektive)

zucchini PL NOUN (US)
die Zucchini pl

★ = core vocabulary

Contents

German verb tables

This section is designed to help you find all the verb forms you need in German. From pages 686–696 you will find 11 very common regular and irregular verbs shown in full, with example phrases.

From pages 697–706 you will see a list of 97 regular and irregular verbs with a summary of their main forms.

How to find the verb you need

Many German verbs on both sides of the dictionary, when they appear in the infinitive form (-en), are followed by a number in square brackets. Each of these numbers corresponds to a verb in this section. For example:

> ★ **lachen** VERB [48]
>   to laugh

Here, the number [48] after the verb **lachen** means that **lachen** follows the same pattern as verb number 48 in the list at the end of this section, which is **machen**:

> **diskutieren** (PERFECT TENSE **hat diskutiert**)
>   VERB [76]
>   to discuss

Here, **diskutieren** follows the same pattern as verb number [76] in the list at the end of this section, which is **studieren**. On page 704 of this section, you can see that the main forms of **studieren** are given to show you how this verb (and others like it) works.

In the full verb tables, you will find examples of **weak**, **strong** and **mixed** verb forms. **Weak** verbs follow regular patterns, **strong** verbs follow irregular patterns and **mixed** verbs follow a mixture of regular and irregular patterns. In these tables, **machen** is an example of a **weak** verb, **wissen** is an example of a **mixed** verb and the rest are **strong** verbs.

Verb tenses

The present tense

The present tense is used to talk about what is true at the moment, what happens regularly and what is happening now, for example, 'I'm a student'; 'She works as a consultant'; 'I'm studying German'.

There is more than one way to express the present tense in English. For example, you can either say 'I give', 'I am giving' or occasionally 'I do give'. In German, you use the same form **ich gebe** for all these.

In English you can also use the present tense to talk about something that is going to happen in the near future. You can do the same in German.

Morgen **spiele ich** Tennis.	**I'm going** to play tennis tomorrow.
Wir nehmen den Zug um zehn Uhr.	**We're getting** the 10 o'clock train.

The future tense

The future tense is used to talk about something that will happen or will be true. There are several ways to express the future tense in English: you can use the future tense ('I'll ask him on Tuesday'), the present tense ('I'm not working tomorrow'), or 'going to' followed by an infinitive ('She's going to study in Switzerland for a year'). In German you can also use the future tense (if you want to emphasize the future, express doubt or suppose something about the future) or the present tense. You cannot use the verb **gehen** (to go) followed by an infinitive.

Das **werde ich** erst nächstes Jahr **machen können**.	**I won't be able to do** that until next year.
Ich nehme den letzten Zug.	**I'm taking** the last train.
Das **wirst du** bereuen.	**You're going to** regret that.

The imperfect tense

The imperfect tense is one of the tenses used to talk about the past, especially in descriptions, and to say what used to happen, for example 'I used to work in Manchester'; 'It was sunny yesterday'.

Ich war ganz traurig, als sie wegging.	**I was** very sad when she left.
Es gab ein großes Problem mit Drogen.	**There was** a big problem with drugs.
Samstags **spielte ich** Tennis.	**I used to play** tennis on Saturdays.

The perfect tense

The perfect tense is made up of two parts: the present tense of **haben** or **sein**, and the German past participle (like 'given', 'finished' and 'done' in English).

Most verbs form the perfect tense with **haben**. There are two main groups of verbs which form their perfect tense with **sein** instead of **haben**: two verbs which mean 'to happen' (**geschehen** and **passieren**) and a group of verbs that are mainly used to talk about movement or a change of some kind, including:

gehen	to go
kommen	to come
ankommen	to arrive
abfahren	to leave
aussteigen	to get off
einsteigen	to get on
sterben	to die
sein	to be
werden	to become
bleiben	to remain
begegnen	to meet
gelingen	to succeed
aufstehen	to get up
fallen	to fall

Gestern **bin ich** ins Kino **gegangen**.   **I went** to the cinema yesterday.
Sie ist ganz früh **abgefahren**.   **She left** really early.

The imperative

The imperative is a form of the verb used when giving orders and instructions, for example, 'Be quiet!', 'Shut the door!', 'Don't go!'

In German, there are several forms of the imperative that are used to give instructions or orders to someone. These correspond to **du**, **ihr** and **Sie**. For the **du** form most verbs simply use the verb stem (an -e can be added to help pronunciation). The **ihr** form adds a -t to the stem and the **Sie** form adds -en.

Hol(e)!	**Fetch!**
Holt!	**Fetch!**
Holen Sie!	**Fetch!**

The subjunctive

The subjunctive is a verb form that is used in certain circumstances to express some sort of feeling, or to show there is doubt about whether something will happen or something is true. It is used much more frequently in German than in English, for example in indirect speech.

Direct Speech

Sie sagte: „Er **kennt** deine Schwester." She said, "He **knows** your sister."

Indirect Speech

Sie sagte, er **kenne** meine Schwester. She said he **knew** my sister.

The conditional

The conditional is a verb form used to talk about things that would happen or that would be true under certain conditions, for instance, 'I would help you if I could'. It is also used to say what you would like or need, for example, 'Could you give me the bill?'. The conditional tense in German is made up of two parts: the **würde** form – the imperfect subjunctive of the verb **werden** (*to become*) – and the infinitive of the main verb, which normally goes at the end of the sentence.

Was **würden** Sie an meiner Stelle **tun**? What **would** you do in my position?

Das **würde** ich nie von dir **verlangen**. I **would** never ask that of you.

essen (to eat)

PRESENT		PRESENT SUBJUNCTIVE	
ich	esse	ich	esse
du	isst	du	essest
er/sie/es	isst	er/sie/es	esse
wir	essen	wir	essen
ihr	esst	ihr	esset
sie/Sie	essen	sie/Sie	essen

PERFECT		IMPERFECT	
ich	habe gegessen	ich	aß
du	hast gegessen	du	aßest
er/sie/es	hat gegessen	er/sie/es	aß
wir	haben gegessen	wir	aßen
ihr	habt gegessen	ihr	aßt
sie/Sie	haben gegessen	sie/Sie	aßen

FUTURE		CONDITIONAL	
ich	werde essen	ich	würde essen
du	wirst essen	du	würdest essen
er/sie/es	wird essen	er/sie/es	würde essen
wir	werden essen	wir	würden essen
ihr	werdet essen	ihr	würdet essen
sie/Sie	werden essen	sie/Sie	würden essen

PAST PARTICIPLE	PRESENT PARTICIPLE
gegessen	essend

IMPERATIVE

iss!/essen wir!/esst!/essen Sie!

EXAMPLE PHRASES

Ich **esse** kein Fleisch. I don't eat meat.
Wir **haben** nichts **gegessen**. We haven't had anything to eat.
Ich möchte etwas **essen**. I'd like something to eat.

ich = I du = you er = he/it sie = she/it es = it/he/she wir = we ihr = you sie = they Sie = you

fahren (to drive; to go)

	PRESENT		**PRESENT SUBJUNCTIVE**
ich	fahre	ich	fahre
du	fährst	du	fahrest
er/sie/es	fährt	er/sie/es	fahre
wir	fahren	wir	fahren
ihr	fahrt	ihr	fahret
sie/Sie	fahren	sie/Sie	fahren

	PERFECT		**IMPERFECT**
ich	bin gefahren	ich	fuhr
du	bist gefahren	du	fuhrst
er/sie/es	ist gefahren	er/sie/es	fuhr
wir	sind gefahren	wir	fuhren
ihr	seid gefahren	ihr	fuhrt
sie/Sie	sind gefahren	sie/Sie	fuhren

	FUTURE		**CONDITIONAL**
ich	werde fahren	ich	würde fahren
du	wirst fahren	du	würdest fahren
er/sie/es	wird fahren	er/sie/es	würde fahren
wir	werden fahren	wir	würden fahren
ihr	werdet fahren	ihr	würdet fahren
sie/Sie	werden fahren	sie/Sie	würden fahren

PAST PARTICIPLE

gefahren

PRESENT PARTICIPLE

fahrend

IMPERATIVE

fahr(e)!/fahren wir!/fahrt!/fahren Sie!

EXAMPLE PHRASES

Sie **fahren** mit dem Bus in die Schule. They go to school by bus.
Rechts **fahren**! Drive on the right!
Ich **bin** mit der Familie nach Spanien **gefahren**. I went to Spain with my family.
Sie **hat** das Auto **gefahren**. She drove the car.

ich = I **du** = you **er** = he/it **sie** = she/it **es** = it/he/she **wir** = we **ihr** = you **sie** = they **Sie** = you

gehen (to go)

	PRESENT		**PRESENT SUBJUNCTIVE**
ich	gehe	ich	gehe
du	gehst	du	gehest
er/sie/es	geht	er/sie/es	gehe
wir	gehen	wir	gehen
ihr	geht	ihr	gehet
sie/Sie	gehen	sie/Sie	gehen

	PERFECT		**IMPERFECT**
ich	bin gegangen	ich	ging
du	bist gegangen	du	gingst
er/sie/es	ist gegangen	er/sie/es	ging
wir	sind gegangen	wir	gingen
ihr	seid gegangen	ihr	gingt
sie/Sie	sind gegangen	sie/Sie	gingen

	FUTURE		**CONDITIONAL**
ich	werde gehen	ich	würde gehen
du	wirst gehen	du	würdest gehen
er/sie/es	wird gehen	er/sie/es	würde gehen
wir	werden gehen	wir	würden gehen
ihr	werdet gehen	ihr	würdet gehen
sie/Sie	werden gehen	sie/Sie	würden gehen

PAST PARTICIPLE

gegangen

PRESENT PARTICIPLE

gehend

IMPERATIVE

geh(e)!/gehen wir!/geht!/gehen Sie!

EXAMPLE PHRASES

Die Kinder **gingen** ins Haus. The children went into the house.
Wie **geht** es dir? How are you?
Wir **sind** gestern schwimmen **gegangen**. We went swimming yesterday.

ich = I du = you er = he/it sie = she/it es = it/he/she wir = we ihr = you sie = they Sie = you

haben (to have)

	PRESENT		**PRESENT SUBJUNCTIVE**
ich	habe	ich	habe
du	hast	du	habest
er/sie/es	hat	er/sie/es	habe
wir	haben	wir	haben
ihr	habt	ihr	habet
sie/Sie	haben	sie/Sie	haben

	PERFECT		**IMPERFECT**
ich	habe gehabt	ich	hatte
du	hast gehabt	du	hattest
er/sie/es	hat gehabt	er/sie/es	hatte
wir	haben gehabt	wir	hatten
ihr	habt gehabt	ihr	hattet
sie/Sie	haben gehabt	sie/Sie	hatten

	FUTURE		**CONDITIONAL**
ich	werde haben	ich	würde haben
du	wirst haben	du	würdest haben
er/sie/es	wird haben	er/sie/es	würde haben
wir	werden haben	wir	würden haben
ihr	werdet haben	ihr	würdet haben
sie/Sie	werden haben	sie/Sie	würden haben

PAST PARTICIPLE

gehabt

PRESENT PARTICIPLE

habend

IMPERATIVE

hab(e)!/haben wir!/habt!/haben Sie!

EXAMPLE PHRASES

Hast du eine Schwester? Have you got a sister?
Er **hatte** Hunger. He was hungry.
Sie **hat** heute Geburtstag. It's her birthday today.

ich = I **du** = you **er** = he/it **sie** = she/it **es** = it/he/she **wir** = we **ihr** = you **sie** = they **Sie** = you

kommen (to come)

	PRESENT		**PRESENT SUBJUNCTIVE**
ich	komme	ich	komme
du	kommst	du	kommest
er/sie/es	kommt	er/sie/es	komme
wir	kommen	wir	kommen
ihr	kommt	ihr	kommet
sie/Sie	kommen	sie/Sie	kommen

	PERFECT		**IMPERFECT**
ich	bin gekommen	ich	kam
du	bist gekommen	du	kamst
er/sie/es	ist gekommen	er/sie/es	kam
wir	sind gekommen	wir	kamen
ihr	seid gekommen	ihr	kamt
sie/Sie	sind gekommen	sie/Sie	kamen

	FUTURE		**CONDITIONAL**
ich	werde kommen	ich	würde kommen
du	wirst kommen	du	würdest kommen
er/sie/es	wird kommen	er/sie/es	würde kommen
wir	werden kommen	wir	würden kommen
ihr	werdet kommen	ihr	würdet kommen
sie/Sie	werden kommen	sie/Sie	würden kommen

PAST PARTICIPLE

gekommen

PRESENT PARTICIPLE

kommend

IMPERATIVE

komm(e)!/kommen wir!/kommt!/kommen Sie!

EXAMPLE PHRASES

Er **kam** die Straße entlang. He was coming along the street.
Ich **komme** zu deiner Party. I'm coming to your party.
Woher **kommst** du? Where do you come from?

ich = I **du** = you **er** = he/it **sie** = she/it **es** = it/he/she **wir** = we **ihr** = you **sie** = they **Sie** = you

können (to be able to; can)

PRESENT

ich	**kann**
du	**kannst**
er/sie/es	**kann**
wir	**können**
ihr	**könnt**
sie/Sie	**können**

PRESENT SUBJUNCTIVE

ich	**könne**
du	**könnest**
er/sie/es	**könne**
wir	**können**
ihr	**könnet**
sie/Sie	**können**

PERFECT

ich	**habe gekonnt/können**
du	**hast gekonnt/können**
er/sie/es	**hat gekonnt/können**
wir	**haben gekonnt/können**
ihr	**habt gekonnt/können**
sie/Sie	**haben gekonnt/können**

IMPERFECT

ich	**konnte**
du	**konntest**
er/sie/es	**konnte**
wir	**konnten**
ihr	**konntet**
sie/Sie	**konnten**

FUTURE

ich	**werde können**
du	**wirst können**
er/sie/es	**wird können**
wir	**werden können**
ihr	**werdet können**
sie/Sie	**werden können**

CONDITIONAL

ich	**würde können**
du	**würdest können**
er/sie/es	**würde können**
wir	**würden können**
ihr	**würdet können**
sie/Sie	**würden können**

PAST PARTICIPLE

gekonnt/können*

PRESENT PARTICIPLE

könnend

*This form is used when combined with another infinitive.

....

EXAMPLE PHRASES

Er **kann** gut schwimmen. He can swim well.
Sie **konnte** kein Wort Deutsch. She couldn't speak a word of German.
Kann ich gehen? Can I go?

ich = I **du** = you **er** = he/it **sie** = she/it **es** = it/he/she **wir** = we **ihr** = you **sie** = they **Sie** = you

machen (to do; to make)

	PRESENT		**PRESENT SUBJUNCTIVE**
ich	mache	ich	mache
du	machst	du	machest
er/sie/es	macht	er/sie/es	mache
wir	machen	wir	machen
ihr	macht	ihr	machet
sie/Sie	machen	sie/Sie	machen

	PERFECT		**IMPERFECT**
ich	habe gemacht	ich	machte
du	hast gemacht	du	machtest
er/sie/es	hat gemacht	er/sie/es	machte
wir	haben gemacht	wir	machten
ihr	habt gemacht	ihr	machtet
sie/Sie	haben gemacht	sie/Sie	machten

	FUTURE		**CONDITIONAL**
ich	werde machen	ich	würde machen
du	wirst machen	du	würdest machen
er/sie/es	wird machen	er/sie/es	würde machen
wir	werden machen	wir	würden machen
ihr	werdet machen	ihr	würdet machen
sie/Sie	werden machen	sie/Sie	würden machen

PAST PARTICIPLE

gemacht

PRESENT PARTICIPLE

machend

IMPERATIVE

mach!/macht!/machen Sie!

EXAMPLE PHRASES

Was **machst** du? What are you doing?
Ich **habe** die Betten **gemacht**. I made the beds.
Ich **werde** es morgen **machen**. I'll do it tomorrow.

ich = I **du** = you **er** = he/it **sie** = she/it **es** = it/he/she **wir** = we **ihr** = you **sie** = they **Sie** = you

692

müssen (to have to)

	PRESENT			**PRESENT SUBJUNCTIVE**
ich	muss		ich	müsse
du	musst		du	müssest
er/sie/es	muss		er/sie/es	müsse
wir	müssen		wir	müssen
ihr	müsst		ihr	müsset
sie/Sie	müssen		sie/Sie	müssen

	PERFECT			**IMPERFECT**
ich	habe gemusst/müssen		ich	musste
du	hast gemusst/müssen		du	musstest
er/sie/es	hat gemusst/müssen		er/sie/es	musste
wir	haben gemusst/müssen		wir	mussten
ihr	habt gemusst/müssen		ihr	musstet
sie/Sie	haben gemusst/müssen		sie/Sie	mussten

	FUTURE			**CONDITIONAL**
ich	werde müssen		ich	würde müssen
du	wirst müssen		du	würdest müssen
er/sie/es	wird müssen		er/sie/es	würde müssen
wir	werden müssen		wir	würden müssen
ihr	werdet müssen		ihr	würdet müssen
sie/Sie	werden müssen		sie/Sie	würden müssen

PAST PARTICIPLE	**PRESENT PARTICIPLE**
gemusst/müssen*	müssend

*This form is used when combined with another infinitive.

....

EXAMPLE PHRASES

Ich **muss** auf die Toilette. I must go to the loo.
Wir **müssen** jeden Abend unsere Hausaufgaben machen. We have to do our homework every night.
Sie **hat** abwaschen **müssen**. She had to wash up.

ich = I **du** = you **er** = he/it **sie** = she/it **es** = it/he/she **wir** = we **ihr** = you **sie** = they **Sie** = you

sein (to be)

	PRESENT		**PRESENT SUBJUNCTIVE**
ich	bin	ich	sei
du	bist	du	sei(e)st
er/sie/es	ist	er/sie/es	sei
wir	sind	wir	seien
ihr	seid	ihr	seiet
sie/Sie	sind	sie/Sie	seien

	PERFECT		**IMPERFECT**
ich	bin gewesen	ich	war
du	bist gewesen	du	warst
er/sie/es	ist gewesen	er/sie/es	war
wir	sind gewesen	wir	waren
ihr	seid gewesen	ihr	wart
sie/Sie	sind gewesen	sie/Sie	waren

	FUTURE		**CONDITIONAL**
ich	werde sein	ich	würde sein
du	wirst sein	du	würdest sein
er/sie/es	wird sein	er/sie/es	würde sein
wir	werden sein	wir	würden sein
ihr	werdet sein	ihr	würdet sein
sie/Sie	werden sein	sie/Sie	würden sein

PAST PARTICIPLE

gewesen

PRESENT PARTICIPLE

seiend

IMPERATIVE

sei!/seien wir!/seid!/seien Sie!

EXAMPLE PHRASES

Er **ist** zehn Jahre alt. He is ten years old.
Wir **waren** gestern im Theater. We were at the theatre yesterday.
Mir **war** kalt. I was cold.

ich = I **du** = you **er** = he/it **sie** = she/it **es** = it/he/she **wir** = we **ihr** = you **sie** = they **Sie** = you

werden (to become)

	PRESENT		**PRESENT SUBJUNCTIVE**
ich	werde	ich	werde
du	wirst	du	werdest
er/sie/es	wird	er/sie/es	werde
wir	werden	wir	werden
ihr	werdet	ihr	werdet
sie/Sie	werden	sie/Sie	werden

	PERFECT		**IMPERFECT**
ich	bin geworden	ich	wurde
du	bist geworden	du	wurdest
er/sie/es	ist geworden	er/sie/es	wurde
wir	sind geworden	wir	wurden
ihr	seid geworden	ihr	wurdet
sie/Sie	sind geworden	sie/Sie	wurden

	FUTURE		**CONDITIONAL**
ich	werde werden	ich	würde werden
du	wirst werden	du	würdest werden
er/sie/es	wird werden	er/sie/es	würde werden
wir	werden werden	wir	würden werden
ihr	werdet werden	ihr	würdet werden
sie/Sie	werden werden	sie/Sie	würden werden

PAST PARTICIPLE

geworden

PRESENT PARTICIPLE

werdend

IMPERATIVE

werde!/werden wir!/werdet!/werden Sie!

EXAMPLE PHRASES

Mir **wird** schlecht. I feel ill.
Ich will berühmt **werden**. I want to become famous.
Der Kuchen **ist** gut **geworden**. The cake turned out well.

ich = I **du** = you **er** = he/it **sie** = she/it **es** = it/he/she **wir** = we **ihr** = you **sie** = they **Sie** = you

695

wissen (to know)

	PRESENT		**PRESENT SUBJUNCTIVE**
ich	weiß	ich	wisse
du	weißt	du	wissest
er/sie/es	weiß	er/sie/es	wisse
wir	wissen	wir	wissen
ihr	wisst	ihr	wisset
sie/Sie	wissen	sie/Sie	wissen

	PERFECT		**IMPERFECT**
ich	habe gewusst	ich	wusste
du	hast gewusst	du	wusstest
er/sie/es	hat gewusst	er/sie/es	wusste
wir	haben gewusst	wir	wussten
ihr	habt gewusst	ihr	wusstet
sie/Sie	haben gewusst	sie/Sie	wussten

	FUTURE		**CONDITIONAL**
ich	werde wissen	ich	würde wissen
du	wirst wissen	du	würdest wissen
er/sie/es	wird wissen	er/sie/es	würde wissen
wir	werden wissen	wir	würden wissen
ihr	werdet wissen	ihr	würdet wissen
sie/Sie	werden wissen	sie/Sie	würden wissen

PAST PARTICIPLE

gewusst

PRESENT PARTICIPLE

wissend

IMPERATIVE

wisse!/wissen wir!/wisset!/wissen Sie!

....

EXAMPLE PHRASES

Ich **weiß** nicht. I don't know.
Er **hat** nichts davon **gewusst**. He didn't know anything about it.
Sie **wussten**, wo das Kino war. They knew where the cinema was.

ich = I **du** = you **er** = he/it **sie** = she/it **es** = it/he/she **wir** = we **ihr** = you **sie** = they **Sie** = you

German verb forms

		PRESENT	PERFECT	IMPERFECT	FUTURE	PRESENT SUBJUNCTIVE	PAST PARTICIPLE
1	**annehmen** to accept *verb with a spelling change*	ich nehme an	habe **angenommen**	**nahm** an	werde annehmen	nehme an	**angenommen**
		du nimmst an	hast angenommen	**nahmst** an	wirst annehmen	nehmest an	
		er/sie/es nimmt an	hat angenommen	**nahm** an	wird annehmen	nehme an	
		wir nehmen an	haben angenommen	**nahmen** an	werden annehmen	nehmen an	
		ihr nehmt an	habt angenommen	**nahmt** an	werdet annehmen	nehmet an	
		sie/Sie nehmen an	haben angenommen	**nahmen** an	werden annehmen	nehmen an	
2	**arbeiten** to work	ich arbeite	habe gearbeitet	arbeitete	werde arbeiten	arbeite	gearbeitet
		du arbeitest	hast gearbeitet	arbeitetest	wirst arbeiten	arbeitest	
		er/sie/es arbeitet	hat gearbeitet	arbeitete	wird arbeiten	arbeite	
		wir arbeiten	haben gearbeitet	arbeiteten	werden arbeiten	arbeiten	
		ihr arbeitet	habt gearbeitet	arbeitetet	werdet arbeiten	arbeitet	
		sie/Sie arbeiten	haben gearbeitet	arbeiteten	werden arbeiten	arbeiten	
3	**atmen** to breathe	ich atme	habe geatmet	atmete	werde atmen	atme	geatmet
		du atmest	hast geatmet	atmetest	wirst atmen	atmest	
		er/sie/es atmet	hat geatmet	atmete	wird atmen	atme	
		wir atmen	haben geatmet	atmeten	werden atmen	atmen	
		ihr atmet	habt geatmet	atmetet	werdet atmen	atmet	
		sie/Sie atmen	haben geatmet	atmeten	werden atmen	atmen	
4	**ausreichen** to suffice	ich reiche aus	habe ausgereicht	reichte aus	werde ausreichen	reiche aus	ausgereicht
		du reichst aus	hast ausgereicht	reichtest aus	wirst ausreichen	reichest aus	
		er/sie/es reicht aus	hat ausgereicht	reichte aus	wird ausreichen	reiche aus	
		wir reichen aus	haben ausgereicht	reichten aus	werden ausreichen	reichen aus	
		ihr reicht aus	habt ausgereicht	reichtet aus	werdet ausreichen	reichet aus	
		sie/Sie reichen aus	haben ausgereicht	reichten aus	werden ausreichen	reichen aus	
5	**beginnen** to begin *verb with a spelling change*	ich beginne	habe **begonnen**	**begann**	werde beginnen	beginne	**begonnen**
		du beginnst	hast begonnen	**begannst**	wirst beginnen	beginnest	
		er/sie/es beginnt	hat begonnen	**begann**	wird beginnen	beginne	
		wir beginnen	haben begonnen	**begannen**	werden beginnen	beginnen	
		ihr beginnt	habt begonnen	**begannt**	werdet beginnen	beginnet	
		sie/Sie beginnen	haben begonnen	**begannen**	werden beginnen	beginnen	
6	**beißen** to bite *verb with a spelling change*	ich beiße	habe **gebissen**	**biss**	werde beißen	beiße	**gebissen**
		du beißt	hast gebissen	**bissest**	wirst beißen	beißest	
		er/sie/es beißt	hat gebissen	**biss**	wird beißen	beiße	
		wir beißen	haben gebissen	**bissen**	werden beißen	beißen	
		ihr beißt	habt gebissen	**bisst**	werdet beißen	beißet	
		sie/Sie beißen	haben gebissen	**bissen**	werden beißen	beißen	
7	**bestellen** to order	ich bestelle	habe **bestellt**	bestellte	werde bestellen	bestelle	**bestellt**
		du bestellst	hast bestellt	bestelltest	wirst bestellen	bestellest	
		er/sie/es bestellt	hat bestellt	bestellte	wird bestellen	bestelle	
		wir bestellen	haben bestellt	bestellten	werden bestellen	bestellen	
		ihr bestellt	habt bestellt	bestelltet	werdet bestellen	bestellet	
		sie/Sie bestellen	haben bestellt	bestellten	werden bestellen	bestellen	
8	**bieten** to offer *verb with a spelling change*	ich biete	habe **geboten**	**bot**	werde bieten	biete	**geboten**
		du bietest	hast geboten	**bot(e)st**	wirst bieten	bietest	
		er/sie/es bietet	hat geboten	**bot**	wird bieten	biete	
		wir bieten	haben geboten	**boten**	werden bieten	bieten	
		ihr bietet	habt geboten	**botet**	werdet bieten	bietet	
		sie/Sie bieten	haben geboten	**boten**	werden bieten	bieten	

	PRESENT	PERFECT	IMPERFECT	FUTURE	PRESENT SUBJUNCTIVE	PAST PARTICIPLE
9 bitten to ask for verb with a spelling change	ich bitte du bittest er/sie/es bittet wir bitten ihr bittet sie/Sie bitten	habe **gebeten** hast gebeten hat gebeten haben gebeten habt gebeten haben gebeten	**bat** **bat(e)st** **bat** **baten** **batet** **baten**	werde bitten wirst bitten wird bitten werden bitten werdet bitten werden bitten	bitte bittest bitte bitten bittet bitten	**gebeten**
10 bleiben to stay verb with a spelling change	ich bleibe du bleibst er/sie/es bleibt wir bleiben ihr bleibt sie/Sie bleiben	bin **geblieben** bist geblieben ist geblieben sind geblieben seid geblieben sind geblieben	**blieb** **bliebst** **blieb** **blieben** **bliebt** **blieben**	werde bleiben wirst bleiben wird bleiben werden bleiben werdet bleiben werden bleiben	bleibe bleibest bleibe bleiben bleibet bleiben	**geblieben**
11 brechen to break verb with a spelling change	ich breche du brichst er/sie/es bricht wir brechen ihr brecht sie/Sie brechen	habe **gebrochen** hast gebrochen hat gebrochen haben gebrochen habt gebrochen haben gebrochen	**brach** **brachst** **brach** **brachen** **bracht** **brachen**	werde brechen wirst brechen wird brechen werden brechen werdet brechen werden brechen	breche brechest breche brechen brechet brechen	**gebrochen**
12 brennen to burn verb with a spelling change	ich brenne du brennst er/sie/es brennt wir brennen ihr brennt sie/Sie brennen	habe **gebrannt** hast gebrannt hat gebrannt haben gebrannt habt gebrannt haben gebrannt	**brannte** **branntest** **brannte** **brannten** **branntet** **brannten**	werde brennen wirst brennen wird brennen werden brennen werdet brennen werden brennen	brenne brennest brenne brennen brennet brennen	**gebrannt**
13 bringen to bring verb with a spelling change	ich bringe du bringst er/sie/es bringt wir bringen ihr bringt sie/Sie bringen	habe **gebracht** hast gebracht hat gebracht haben gebracht habt gebracht haben gebracht	**brachte** **brachtest** **brachte** **brachten** **brachtet** **brachten**	werde bringen wirst bringen wird bringen werden bringen werdet bringen werden bringen	bringe bringest bringe bringen bringet bringen	**gebracht**
14 denken to think verb with a spelling change	ich denke du denkst er/sie/es denkt wir denken ihr denkt sie/Sie denken	habe **gedacht** hast gedacht hat gedacht haben gedacht habt gedacht haben gedacht	**dachte** **dachtest** **dachte** **dachten** **dachtet** **dachten**	werde denken wirst denken wird denken werden denken werdet denken werden denken	denke denkest denke denken denket denken	**gedacht**
15 durchsetzen to enforce	ich setze durch du setzt durch er/sie/es setzt durch wir setzen durch ihr setzt durch sie/Sie setzen durch	habe durchgesetzt hast durchgesetzt hat durchgesetzt haben durchgesetzt habt durchgesetzt haben durchgesetzt	setzte durch setztest durch setzte durch setzten durch setztet durch setzten durch	werde durchsetzen wirst durchsetzen wird durchsetzen werden durchsetzen werdet durchsetzen werden durchsetzen	setze durch setzest durch setze durch setzen durch setzet durch setzen durch	durchgesetzt
16 dürfen to be allowed to verb with a spelling change	ich **darf** du **darfst** er/sie/es **darf** wir dürfen ihr dürft sie/Sie dürfen	habe **gedurft/ dürfen** hast **gedurft/ dürfen** hat **gedurft/ dürfen** haben **gedurft/ dürfen** habt **gedurft/ dürfen** haben **gedurft/ dürfen**	durfte durftest durfte durften durftet durften	werde dürfen wirst dürfen wird dürfen werden dürfen werdet dürfen werden dürfen	dürfe dürfest dürfe dürfen dürfet dürfen	**gedurft/ dürfen*** This form is used when combined with another infinitive
17 empfehlen to recommend verb with a spelling change	ich empfehle du empfiehlst er/sie/es empfiehlt wir empfehlen ihr empfehlt sie/Sie empfehlen	habe **empfohlen** hast empfohlen hat empfohlen haben empfohlen habt empfohlen haben empfohlen	**empfahl** **empfahlst** **empfahl** **empfahlen** **empfahlt** **empfahlen**	werde empfehlen wirst empfehlen wird empfehlen werden empfehlen werdet empfehlen werden empfehlen	empfehle empfehlest empfehle empfehlen empfehlet empfehlen	**empfohlen**

		PRESENT	PERFECT	IMPERFECT	FUTURE	PRESENT SUBJUNCTIVE	PAST PARTICIPLE
18 entdecken to discover	ich	entdecke	habe **entdeckt**	entdeckte	werde entdecken	entdecke	**entdeckt**
	du	entdeckst	hast entdeckt	entdecktest	wirst entdecken	entdeckest	
	er/sie/es	entdeckt	hat entdeckt	entdeckte	wird entdecken	entdecke	
	wir	entdecken	haben entdeckt	entdeckten	werden entdecken	entdecken	
	ihr	entdeckt	habt entdeckt	entdecktet	werdet entdecken	entdecket	
	sie/Sie	entdecken	haben entdeckt	entdeckten	werden entdecken	entdecken	
19 erzählen to tell	ich	erzähle	habe **erzählt**	erzählte	werde erzählen	erzähle	**erzählt**
	du	erzählst	hast erzählt	erzähltest	wirst erzählen	erzählest	
	er/sie/es	erzählt	hat erzählt	erzählte	wird erzählen	erzähle	
	wir	erzählen	haben erzählt	erzählten	werden erzählen	erzählen	
	ihr	erzählt	habt erzählt	erzähltet	werdet erzählen	erzählet	
	sie/Sie	erzählen	haben erzählt	erzählten	werden erzählen	erzählen	
20 essen to eat			see full verb table page 686				
21 fahren to drive; to go			see full verb table page 687				
22 fallen to fall verb with a spelling change	ich	falle	bin **gefallen**	fiel	werde fallen	falle	**gefallen**
	du	fällst	bist gefallen	**fielst**	wirst fallen	fallest	
	er/sie/es	fällt	ist gefallen	**fiel**	wird fallen	falle	
	wir	fallen	sind gefallen	**fielen**	werden fallen	fallen	
	ihr	fallt	seid gefallen	**fielt**	werdet fallen	fallet	
	sie/Sie	fallen	sind gefallen	**fielen**	werden fallen	fallen	
23 fangen to catch verb with a spelling change	ich	fange	habe gefangen	fing	werde fangen	fange	gefangen
	du	fängst	hast gefangen	fingst	wirst fangen	fangest	
	er/sie/es	fängt	hat gefangen	fing	wird fangen	fange	
	wir	fangen	haben gefangen	fingen	werden fangen	fangen	
	ihr	fangt	habt gefangen	fingt	werdet fangen	fanget	
	sie/Sie	fangen	haben gefangen	fingen	werden fangen	fangen	
24 finden to find verb with a spelling change	ich	finde	habe **gefunden**	**fand**	werde finden	finde	**gefunden**
	du	findest	hast gefunden	**fand(e)st**	wirst finden	findest	
	er/sie/es	findet	hat gefunden	**fand**	wird finden	finde	
	wir	finden	haben gefunden	**fanden**	werden finden	finden	
	ihr	findet	habt gefunden	**fandet**	werdet finden	findet	
	sie/Sie	finden	haben gefunden	**fanden**	werden finden	finden	
25 fliegen to fly verb with a spelling change	ich	fliege	bin **geflogen**	**flog**	werde fliegen	fliege	**geflogen**
	du	fliegst	bist geflogen	**flogst**	wirst fliegen	fliegest	
	er/sie/es	fliegt	ist geflogen	**flog**	wird fliegen	fliege	
	wir	fliegen .	sind geflogen	**flogen**	werden fliegen	fliegen	
	ihr	fliegt	seid geflogen	**flogt**	werdet fliegen	flieget	
	sie/Sie	fliegen	sind geflogen	**flogen**	werden fliegen	fliegen	
26 fliehen to flee verb with a spelling change	ich	fliehe	bin **geflohen**	**floh**	werde fliehen	fliehe	**geflohen**
	du	fliehst	bist geflohen	**flohst**	wirst fliehen	fliehest	
	er/sie/es	flieht	ist geflohen	**floh**	wird fliehen	fliehe	
	wir	fliehen	sind geflohen	**flohen**	werden fliehen	fliehen	
	ihr	flieht	seid geflohen	**floht**	werdet fliehen	fliehet	
	sie/Sie	fliehen	sind geflohen	**flohen**	werden fliehen	fliehen	
27 fließen to flow verb with a spelling change	ich	fließe	bin **geflossen**	**floss**	werde fließen	fließe	**geflossen**
	du	fließt	bist geflossen	**flossest**	wirst fließen	fließest	
	er/sie/es	fließt	ist geflossen	**floss**	wird fließen	fließe	
	wir	fließen	sind geflossen	**flossen**	werden fließen	fließen	
	ihr	fließt	seid geflossen	**flosst**	werdet fließen	fließet	
	sie/Sie	fließen	sind geflossen	**flossen**	werden fließen	fließen	
28 geben to give verb with a spelling change	ich	gebe	habe **gegeben**	**gab**	werde geben	gebe	**gegeben**
	du	gibst	hast gegeben	**gabst**	wirst geben	gebest	
	er/sie/es	gibt	hat gegeben	**gab**	wird geben	gebe	
	wir	geben	haben gegeben	**gaben**	werden geben	geben	
	ihr	gebt	habt gegeben	**gabt**	werdet geben	gebet	
	sie/Sie	geben	haben gegeben	**gaben**	werden geben	geben	
29 gehen to go			see full verb table page 688				

		PRESENT	PERFECT	IMPERFECT	FUTURE	PRESENT SUBJUNCTIVE	PAST PARTICIPLE
30 gewinnen to win verb with a spelling change	ich du er/sie/es wir ihr sie/Sie	gewinne gewinnst gewinnt gewinnen gewinnt gewinnen	habe **gewonnen** hast gewonnen hat gewonnen haben gewonnen habt gewonnen haben gewonnen	**gewann** **gewannst** **gewann** **gewannen** **gewannt** **gewannen**	werde gewinnen wirst gewinnen wird gewinnen werden gewinnen werdet gewinnen werden gewinnen	gewinne gewinnest gewinne gewinnen gewinnet gewinnen	gewonnen
31 grüßen to greet	ich du er/sie/es wir ihr sie/Sie	grüße grüßt grüßt grüßen grüßt grüßen	habe **gegrüßt** hast gegrüßt hat gegrüßt haben gegrüßt habt gegrüßt haben gegrüßt	grüßte grüßtest grüßte grüßten grüßtet grüßten	werde grüßen wirst grüßen wird grüßen werden grüßen werdet grüßen werden grüßen	grüße grüßest grüße grüßen grüßet grüßen	gegrüßt
32 haben to have			see full verb table page 689					
33 halten to hold verb with a spelling change	ich du er/sie/es wir ihr sie/Sie	halte hältst hält halten haltet halten	habe **gehalten** hast gehalten hat gehalten haben gehalten habt gehalten haben gehalten	**hielt** **hielt(e)st** **hielt** **hielten** **hieltet** **hielten**	werde halten wirst halten wird halten werden halten werdet halten werden halten	halte haltest halte halten haltet halten	gehalten
34 handeln to trade; to act	ich du er/sie/es wir ihr sie/Sie	handle handelst handelt handeln handelt handeln	habe **gehandelt** hast gehandelt hat gehandelt haben gehandelt habt gehandelt haben gehandelt	handelte handeltest handelte handelten handeltet handelten	werde handeln wirst handeln wird handeln werden handeln werdet handeln werden handeln	handle handelst hand(e)le handeln handelt handeln	gehandelt
35 hängen to hang verb with a spelling change	ich du er/sie/es wir ihr sie/Sie	hänge hängst hängt hängen hängt hängen	habe **gehangen** hast gehangen hat gehangen haben gehangen habt gehangen haben gehangen	**hing** **hingst** **hing** **hingen** **hingt** **hingen**	werde hängen wirst hängen wird hängen werden hängen werdet hängen werden hängen	hänge hängest hänge hängen hänget hängen	gehangen
36 heizen to heat	ich du er/sie/es wir ihr sie/Sie	heize heizt heizt heizen heizt heizen	habe **geheizt** hast geheizt hat geheizt haben geheizt habt geheizt haben geheizt	heizte heiztest heizte heizten heiztet heizten	werde heizen wirst heizen wird heizen werden heizen werdet heizen werden heizen	heize heizest heize heizen heizet heizen	geheizt
37 helfen to help verb with a spelling change	ich du er/sie/es wir ihr sie/Sie	helfe hilfst hilft helfen helft helfen	habe **geholfen** hast geholfen hat geholfen haben geholfen habt geholfen haben geholfen	**half** **halfst** **half** **halfen** **halft** **halfen**	werde helfen wirst helfen wird helfen werden helfen werdet helfen werden helfen	helfe helfest helfe helfen helfet helfen	geholfen
38 holen to fetch	ich du er/sie/es wir ihr sie/Sie	hole holst holt holen holt holen	habe **geholt** hast geholt hat geholt haben geholt habt geholt haben geholt	holte holtest holte holten holtet holten	werde holen wirst holen wird holen werden holen werdet holen werden holen	hole holest hole holen holet holen	geholt
39 kennen to know verb with a spelling change	ich du er/sie/es wir ihr sie/Sie	kenne kennst kennt kennen kennt kennen	habe **gekannt** hast gekannt hat gekannt haben gekannt habt gekannt haben gekannt	**kannte** **kanntest** **kannte** **kannten** **kanntet** **kannten**	werde kennen wirst kennen wird kennen werden kennen werdet kennen werden kennen	kenne kennest kenne kennen kennet kennen	gekannt
40 kommen to come			see full verb table page 690					
41 können to be able to			see full verb table page 691					

		PRESENT	PERFECT	IMPERFECT	FUTURE	PRESENT SUBJUNCTIVE	PAST PARTICIPLE
42	**lassen** to leave; to allow *verb with a spelling change*	ich lasse du lässt er/sie/es lässt wir lassen ihr lasst sie/Sie lassen	habe **gelassen** hast gelassen hat gelassen haben gelassen habt gelassen haben gelassen	ließ ließest ließ ließen ließt ließen	werde lassen wirst lassen wird lassen werden lassen werdet lassen werden lassen	lasse lassest lasse lassen lasset lassen	**gelassen**
43	**laufen** to run *verb with a spelling change*	ich laufe du läufst er/sie/es läuft wir laufen ihr lauft sie/Sie laufen	bin **gelaufen** bist gelaufen ist gelaufen sind gelaufen seid gelaufen sind gelaufen	lief liefst lief liefen lieft liefen	werde laufen wirst laufen wird laufen werden laufen werdet laufen werden laufen	laufe laufest laufe laufen laufet laufen	**gelaufen**
44	**leiden** to suffer *verb with a spelling change*	ich leide du leidest er/sie/es leidet wir leiden ihr leidet sie/Sie leiden	habe **gelitten** hast gelitten hat gelitten haben gelitten habt gelitten haben gelitten	litt litt(e)st litt litten littet litten	werde leiden wirst leiden wird leiden werden leiden werdet leiden werden leiden	leide leidest leide leiden leidet leiden	**gelitten**
45	**lesen** to read *verb with a spelling change*	ich lese du liest er/sie/es liest wir lesen ihr lest sie/Sie lesen	habe **gelesen** hast gelesen hat gelesen haben gelesen habt gelesen haben gelesen	las lasest las lasen last lasen	werde lesen wirst lesen wird lesen werden lesen werdet lesen werden lesen	lese lesest lese lesen leset lesen	**gelesen**
46	**liegen** to lie *verb with a spelling change*	ich liege du liegst er/sie/es liegt wir liegen ihr liegt sie/Sie liegen	habe **gelegen** hast gelegen hat gelegen haben gelegen habt gelegen haben gelegen	lag lagst lag lagen lagt lagen	werde liegen wirst liegen wird liegen werden liegen werdet liegen werden liegen	liege liegest liege liegen lieget liegen	**gelegen**
47	**lügen** to (tell a) lie *verb with a spelling change*	ich lüge du lügst er/sie/es lügt wir lügen ihr lügt sie/Sie lügen	habe **gelogen** hast gelogen hat gelogen haben gelogen habt gelogen haben gelogen	log logst log logen logt logen	werde lügen wirst lügen wird lügen werden lügen werdet lügen werden lügen	lüge lügest lüge lügen lüget lügen	**gelogen**

48 machen to do; to make   see full verb table page 692

		PRESENT	PERFECT	IMPERFECT	FUTURE	PRESENT SUBJUNCTIVE	PAST PARTICIPLE
49	**misstrauen** to mistrust	ich misstraue du misstraust er/sie/es misstraut wir misstrauen ihr misstraut sie/Sie misstrauen	habe **misstraut** hast misstraut hat misstraut haben misstraut habt misstraut haben misstraut	misstraute misstrautest misstraute misstrauten misstrautet misstrauten	werde misstrauen wirst misstrauen wird misstrauen werden misstrauen werdet misstrauen werden misstrauen	misstraue misstrauest misstraue misstrauen misstrauet misstrauen	**misstraut**
50	**mögen** to like *verb with a spelling change*	ich **mag** du **magst** er/sie/es **mag** wir mögen ihr mögt sie/Sie mögen	habe **gemocht/ mögen** hast **gemocht/ mögen** hat **gemocht/ mögen** haben **gemocht/ mögen** habt **gemocht/ mögen** haben **gemocht/ mögen**	mochte mochtest mochte mochten mochtet mochten	werde mögen wirst mögen wird mögen werden mögen werdet mögen werden mögen	möge mögest möge mögen möget mögen	**gemocht/ mögen*** This form is used when combined with another infinitive

51 müssen to have to   see full verb table page 693

		PRESENT	PERFECT	IMPERFECT	FUTURE	PRESENT SUBJUNCTIVE	PAST PARTICIPLE
52 nehmen to take *verb with a spelling change*	ich	nehme	habe **genommen**	nahm	werde nehmen	nehme	genommen
	du	**nimmst**	hast genommen	**nahmst**	wirst nehmen	nehmest	
	er/sie/es	**nimmt**	hat genommen	**nahm**	wird nehmen	nehme	
	wir	nehmen	haben genommen	**nahmen**	werden nehmen	nehmen	
	ihr	nehmt	habt genommen	**nahmt**	werdet nehmen	nehmet	
	sie/Sie	nehmen	haben genommen	**nahmen**	werden nehmen	nehmen	
53 rechnen to calculate	ich	rechne	habe **gerechnet**	rechnete	werde rechnen	rechne	gerechnet
	du	rechnest	hast gerechnet	rechnetest	wirst rechnen	rechnest	
	er/sie/es	rechnet	hat gerechnet	rechnete	wird rechnen	rechne	
	wir	rechnen	haben gerechnet	rechneten	werden rechnen	rechnen	
	ihr	rechnet	habt gerechnet	rechnetet	werdet rechnen	rechnet	
	sie/Sie	rechnen	haben gerechnet	rechneten	werden rechnen	rechnen	
54 reden to talk	ich	rede	habe **geredet**	redete	werde reden	rede	geredet
	du	redest	hast geredet	redetest	wirst reden	redest	
	er/sie/es	redet	hat geredet	redete	wird reden	rede	
	wir	reden	haben geredet	redeten	werden reden	reden	
	ihr	redet	habt geredet	redetet	werdet reden	redet	
	sie/Sie	reden	haben geredet	redeten	werden reden	reden	
55 rennen to run *verb with a spelling change*	ich	renne	bin **gerannt**	**rannte**	werde rennen	renne	gerannt
	du	rennst	bist gerannt	**ranntest**	wirst rennen	rennest	
	er/sie/es	rennt	ist gerannt	**rannte**	wird rennen	renne	
	wir	rennen	sind gerannt	**rannten**	werden rennen	rennen	
	ihr	rennt	seid gerannt	**ranntet**	werdet rennen	rennet	
	sie/Sie	rennen	sind gerannt	**rannten**	werden rennen	rennen	
56 rufen to shout; to call *verb with a spelling change*	ich	rufe	habe **gerufen**	rief	werde rufen	rufe	gerufen
	du	rufst	hast gerufen	riefst	wirst rufen	rufest	
	er/sie/es	ruft	hat gerufen	rief	wird rufen	rufe	
	wir	rufen	haben gerufen	riefen	werden rufen	rufen	
	ihr	ruft	habt gerufen	rieft	werdet rufen	rufet	
	sie/Sie	rufen	haben gerufen	riefen	werden rufen	rufen	
57 scheinen to shine; to seem *verb with a spelling change*	ich	scheine	habe **geschienen**	schien	werde scheinen	scheine	geschienen
	du	scheinst	hast geschienen	schienst	wirst scheinen	scheinest	
	er/sie/es	scheint	hat geschienen	schien	wird scheinen	scheine	
	wir	scheinen	haben geschienen	schienen	werden scheinen	scheinen	
	ihr	scheint	habt geschienen	schient	werdet scheinen	scheinet	
	sie/Sie	scheinen	haben geschienen	schienen	werden scheinen	scheinen	
58 schlafen to sleep *verb with a spelling change*	ich	schlafe	habe **geschlafen**	schlief	werde schlafen	schlafe	geschlafen
	du	schläfst	hast geschlafen	schliefst	wirst schlafen	schlafest	
	er/sie/es	schläft	hat geschlafen	schlief	wird schlafen	schlafe	
	wir	schlafen	haben geschlafen	schliefen	werden schlafen	schlafen	
	ihr	schlaft	habt geschlafen	schlieft	werdet schlafen	schlafet	
	sie/Sie	schlafen	haben geschlafen	schliefen	werden schlafen	schlafen	
59 schlagen to hit *verb with a spelling change*	ich	schlage	habe **geschlagen**	schlug	werde schlagen	schlage	geschlagen
	du	schlägst	hast geschlagen	schlugst	wirst schlagen	schlagest	
	er/sie/es	schlägt	hat geschlagen	schlug	wird schlagen	schlage	
	wir	schlagen	haben geschlagen	schlugen	werden schlagen	schlagen	
	ihr	schlagt	habt geschlagen	schlugt	werdet schlagen	schlaget	
	sie/Sie	schlagen	haben geschlagen	schlugen	werden schlagen	schlagen	
60 schneiden to cut *verb with a spelling change*	ich	schneide	habe **geschnitten**	schnitt	werde schneiden	schneide	geschnitten
	du	schneidest	hast geschnitten	schnittest	wirst schneiden	schneidest	
	er/sie/es	schneidet	hat geschnitten	schnittst	wird schneiden	schneide	
	wir	schneiden	haben geschnitten	schnitt	werden schneiden	schneiden	
	ihr	schneidet	habt geschnitten	schnitten	werdet schneiden	schneidet	
	sie/Sie	schneiden	haben geschnitten	schnittet	werden schneiden	schneiden	
61 schreiben to write *verb with a spelling change*	ich	schreibe	habe **geschrieben**	schrieb	werde schreiben	schreibe	geschrieben
	du	schreibst	hast geschrieben	schriebst	wirst schreiben	schreibest	
	er/sie/es	schreibt	hat geschrieben	schrieb	wird schreiben	schreibe	
	wir	schreiben	haben geschrieben	schrieben	werden schreiben	schreiben	
	ihr	schreibt	habt geschrieben	schriebt	werdet schreiben	schreibet	
	sie/Sie	schreiben	haben geschrieben	schrieben	werden schreiben	schreiben	

		PRESENT	PERFECT	IMPERFECT	FUTURE	PRESENT SUBJUNCTIVE	PAST PARTICIPLE
62 schreien to scream verb with a spelling change	ich	schreie	habe geschrie(e)n	**schrie**	werde schreien	schreie	**geschrien**
	du	schreist	hast geschrie(e)n	**schriest**	wirst schreien	schreiest	
	er/sie/es	schreit	hat geschrie(e)n	**schrie**	wird schreien	schreie	
	wir	schreien	haben geschrie(e)n	**schrien**	werden schreien	schreien	
	ihr	schreit	habt geschrie(e)n	**schriet**	werdet schreien	schreiet	
	sie/Sie	schreien	haben geschrie(e)n	**schrien**	werden schreien	schreien	
63 schwimmen to swim verb with a spelling change	ich	schwimme	bin **geschwommen**	schwamm	werde schwimmen	schwimme	**geschwommen**
	du	schwimmst	bist geschwommen	**schwammst**	wirst schwimmen	schwimmest	
	er/sie/es	schwimmt	ist geschwommen	**schwamm**	wird schwimmen	schwimme	
	wir	schwimmen	sind geschwommen	**schwammen**	werden schwimmen	schwimmen	
	ihr	schwimmt	seid geschwommen	**schwammt**	werdet schwimmen	schwimmet	
	sie/Sie	schwimmen	sind geschwommen	schwammen	werden schwimmen	schwimmen	
64 sehen to see verb with a spelling change	ich	sehe	habe **gesehen**	**sah**	werde sehen	sehe	**gesehen**
	du	siehst	hast gesehen	**sahst**	wirst sehen	sehest	
	er/sie/es	sieht	hat gesehen	**sah**	wird sehen	sehe	
	wir	sehen	haben gesehen	**sahen**	werden sehen	sehen	
	ihr	seht	habt gesehen	**saht**	werdet sehen	sehet	
	sie/Sie	sehen	haben gesehen	**sahen**	werden sehen	sehen	
65 sein to be			see full verb table page 694				
66 singen to sing verb with a spelling change	ich	singe	habe **gesungen**	sang	werde singen	singe	**gesungen**
	du	singst	hast gesungen	**sangst**	wirst singen	singest	
	er/sie/es	singt	hat gesungen	**sang**	wird singen	singe	
	wir	singen	haben gesungen	**sangen**	werden singen	singen	
	ihr	singt	habt gesungen	**sangt**	werdet singen	singet	
	sie/Sie	singen	haben gesungen	**sangen**	werden singen	singen	
67 sinken to sink verb with a spelling change	ich	sinke	bin gesunken	**sank**	werde sinken	sinke	**gesunken**
	du	sinkst	bist gesunken	**sankst**	wirst sinken	sinkest	
	er/sie/es	sinkt	ist gesunken	**sank**	wird sinken	sinke	
	wir	sinken	sind gesunken	**sanken**	werden sinken	sinken	
	ihr	sinkt	seid gesunken	**sankt**	werdet sinken	sinket	
	sie/Sie	sinken	sind gesunken	**sanken**	werden sinken	sinken	
68 sitzen to sit verb with a spelling change	ich	sitze	habe **gesessen**	**saß**	werde sitzen	sitze	**gesessen**
	du	sitzt	hast gesessen	**saßest**	wirst sitzen	sitzest	
	er/sie/es	sitzt	hat gesessen	**saß**	wird sitzen	sitze	
	wir	sitzen	haben gesessen	**saßen**	werden sitzen	sitzen	
	ihr	sitzt	habt gesessen	**saßt**	werdet sitzen	sitzet	
	sie/Sie	sitzen	haben gesessen	**saßen**	werden sitzen	sitzen	
69 sollen to be to	ich	soll	habe **gesollt/ sollen**	**sollte**	werde sollen	solle	**gesollt/ sollen***
	du	sollst	hast **gesollt/ sollen**	**solltest**	wirst sollen	sollest	This form is used when
	er/sie/es	soll	hat **gesollt/sollen**	**sollte**	wird sollen	solle	combined with another
	wir	sollen	haben **gesollt/ sollen**	**sollten**	werden sollen	sollen	infinitive
	ihr	sollt	habt **gesollt/ sollen**	**solltet**	werdet sollen	sollet	
	sie/Sie	sollen	haben **gesollt/ sollen**	**sollten**	werden sollen	sollen	
70 sprechen to speak verb with a spelling change	ich	spreche	habe **gesprochen**	sprach	werde sprechen	spreche	**gesprochen**
	du	sprichst	hast gesprochen	**sprachst**	wirst sprechen	sprechest	
	er/sie/es	spricht	hat gesprochen	**sprach**	wird sprechen	spreche	
	wir	sprechen	haben gesprochen	**sprachen**	werden sprechen	sprechen	
	ihr	sprecht	habt gesprochen	**spracht**	werdet sprechen	sprechet	
	sie/Sie	sprechen	haben gesprochen	**sprachen**	werden sprechen	sprechen	
71 springen to jump verb with a spelling change	ich	springe	habe **gesprungen**	sprang	werde springen	springe	**gesprungen**
	du	springst	hast gesprungen	**sprangst**	wirst springen	springest	
	er/sie/es	springt	hat gesprungen	**sprang**	wird springen	springe	
	wir	springen	haben gesprungen	**sprangen**	werden springen	springen	
	ihr	springt	habt gesprungen	**sprangt**	werdet springen	springet	
	sie/Sie	springen	haben gesprungen	**sprangen**	werden springen	springen	

		PRESENT	PERFECT	IMPERFECT	FUTURE	PRESENT SUBJUNCTIVE	PAST PARTICIPLE
72	**stehen**	ich stehe	habe **gestanden**	**stand**	werde stehen	stehe	**gestanden**
	to stand	du stehst	hast **gestanden**	**standest**	wirst stehen	stehest	
	verb with a spelling change	er/sie/es steht	hat gestanden	**standst**	wird stehen	stehe	
		wir stehen	haben gestanden	**stand**	werden stehen	stehen	
		ihr steht	habt gestanden	**standen**	werdet stehen	stehet	
		sie/Sie stehen	haben gestanden	**standet**	werden stehen	stehen	
73	**stehlen**	ich stehle	habe **gestohlen**	**stahl**	werde stehlen	stehle	**gestohlen**
	to steal	du stiehlst	hast **gestohlen**	**stahlst**	wirst stehlen	stehlest	
	verb with a spelling change	er/sie/es stiehlt	hat gestohlen	**stahl**	wird stehlen	stehle	
		wir stehlen	haben gestohlen	**stahlen**	werden stehlen	stehlen	
		ihr stehlt	habt gestohlen	**stahlt**	werdet stehlen	stehlet	
		sie/Sie stehlen	haben gestohlen	**stahlen**	werden stehlen	stehlen	
74	**steigen**	ich steige	bin **gestiegen**	**stieg**	werde steigen	steige	**gestiegen**
	to climb	du steigst	bist **gestiegen**	**stiegst**	wirst steigen	steigest	
	verb with a spelling change	er/sie/es steigt	ist gestiegen	**stieg**	wird steigen	steige	
		wir steigen	sind gestiegen	**stiegen**	werden steigen	steigen	
		ihr steigt	seid gestiegen	**stiegt**	werdet steigen	steiget	
		sie/Sie steigen	sind gestiegen	**stiegen**	werden steigen	steigen	
75	**sterben**	ich sterbe	bin **gestorben**	**starb**	werde sterben	sterbe	**gestorben**
	to die	du stirbst	bist **gestorben**	**starbst**	wirst sterben	sterbest	
	verb with a spelling change	er/sie/es stirbt	ist gestorben	**starb**	wird sterben	sterbe	
		wir sterben	sind gestorben	**starben**	werden sterben	sterben	
		ihr sterbt	seid gestorben	**starbt**	werdet sterben	sterbet	
		sie/Sie sterben	sind gestorben	**starben**	werden sterben	sterben	
76	**studieren**	ich studiere	habe **studiert**	studierte	werde studieren	studiere	**studiert**
	to study	du studierst	hast studiert	studiertest	wirst studieren	studierest	
		er/sie/es studiert	hat studiert	studierte	wird studieren	studiere	
		wir studieren	haben studiert	studierten	werden studieren	studieren	
		ihr studiert	habt studiert	studiertet	werdet studieren	studieret	
		sie/Sie studieren	haben studiert	studierten	werden studieren	studieren	
77	**tragen**	ich trage	habe **getragen**	**trug**	werde tragen	trage	**getragen**
	to wear; to carry	du trägst	hast getragen	**trugst**	wirst tragen	tragest	
	verb with a spelling change	er/sie/es trägt	hat getragen	**trug**	wird tragen	trage	
		wir tragen	haben getragen	**trugen**	werden tragen	tragen	
		ihr tragt	habt getragen	**trugt**	werdet tragen	traget	
		sie/Sie tragen	haben getragen	**trugen**	werden tragen	tragen	
78	**treffen**	ich treffe	habe **getroffen**	**traf**	werde treffen	treffe	**getroffen**
	to meet	du triffst	hast getroffen	**trafst**	wirst treffen	treffest	
	verb with a spelling change	er/sie/es trifft	hat getroffen	**traf**	wird treffen	treffe	
		wir treffen	haben getroffen	**trafen**	werden treffen	treffen	
		ihr trefft	habt getroffen	**traft**	werdet treffen	treffet	
		sie/Sie treffen	haben getroffen	**trafen**	werden treffen	treffen	
79	**treten**	ich trete	bin **getreten**	**trat**	werde treten	trete	**getreten**
	to kick; to step	du trittst	bist getreten	**tratest**	wirst treten	tretest	
	verb with a spelling change	er/sie/es tritt	ist getreten	**tratst**	wird treten	trete	
		wir treten	sind getreten	**trat**	werden treten	treten	
		ihr tretet	seid getreten	**traten**	werdet treten	tretet	
		sie/Sie treten	sind getreten	**tratet**	werden treten	treten	
80	**trinken**	ich trinke	habe **getrunken**	**trank**	werde trinken	trinke	**getrunken**
	to drink	du trinkst	hast getrunken	**trankst**	wirst trinken	trinkest	
	verb with a spelling change	er/sie/es trinkt	hat getrunken	**trank**	wird trinken	trinke	
		wir trinken	haben getrunken	**tranken**	werden trinken	trinken	
		ihr trinkt	habt getrunken	**trankt**	werdet trinken	trinket	
		sie/Sie trinken	haben getrunken	**tranken**	werden trinken	trinken	
81	**tun**	ich tue	habe **getan**	**tat**	werde tun	tue	**getan**
	to do	du tust	hast getan	**tatest**	wirst tun	tuest	
	verb with a spelling change	er/sie/es tut	hat getan	**tatst**	wird tun	tue	
		wir tun	haben getan	**tat**	werden tun	tuen	
		ihr tut	habt getan	**taten**	werdet tun	tuet	
		sie/Sie tun	haben getan	**tatet**	werden tun	tuen	

		PRESENT	PERFECT	IMPERFECT	FUTURE	PRESENT SUBJUNCTIVE	PAST PARTICIPLE
82	**sich überlegen** to consider	ich überlege mir	habe mir **überlegt**	überlegte mir	werde mir überlegen	überlege mir	**überlegt**
		du überlegst dir	hast dir überlegt	überlegtest dir	wirst dir überlegen	überlegst dir	
	verb with a spelling change	er/sie/es überlegt sich	hat sich überlegt	überlegte sich	wird sich überlegen	überlege sich	
		wir überlegen uns	haben uns überlegt	überlegten uns	werden uns überlegen	überlegen uns	
		ihr überlegt euch	habt euch überlegt	überlegtet euch	werdet euch überlegen	überleget euch	
		sie/Sie überlegen sich	haben sich überlegt	überlegten sich	werden sich überlegen	überlegen sich	
83	**vergessen** to forget	ich vergesse	habe **vergessen**	**vergaß**	werde vergessen	vergesse	**vergessen**
		du vergisst	hast vergessen	**vergaßest**	wirst vergessen	vergessest	
	verb with a spelling change	er/sie/es vergisst	hat vergessen	**vergaß**	wird vergessen	vergesse	
		wir vergessen	haben vergessen	**vergaßen**	werden vergessen	vergessen	
		ihr vergesst	habt vergessen	**vergaßt**	werdet vergessen	vergesset	
		sie/Sie vergessen	haben vergessen	**vergaßen**	werden vergessen	vergessen	
84	**verlangen** to demand	ich verlange	habe **verlangt**	verlangte	werde verlangen	verlange	**verlangt**
		du verlangst	hast verlangt	verlangtest	wirst verlangen	verlangest	
		er/sie/es verlangt	hat verlangt	verlangte	wird verlangen	verlange	
		wir verlangen	haben verlangt	verlangten	werden verlangen	verlangen	
		ihr verlangt	habt verlangt	verlangtet	werdet verlangen	verlanget	
		sie/Sie verlangen	haben verlangt	verlangten	werden verlangen	verlangen	
85	**verlieren** to lose	ich verliere	habe **verloren**	**verlor**	werde verlieren	verliere	**verloren**
		du verlierst	hast verloren	**verlorst**	wirst verlieren	verlierest	
	verb with a spelling change	er/sie/es verliert	hat verloren	**verlor**	wird verlieren	verliere	
		wir verlieren	haben verloren	**verloren**	werden verlieren	verlieren	
		ihr verliert	habt verloren	**verlort**	werdet verlieren	verlieret	
		sie/Sie verlieren	haben verloren	**verloren**	werden verlieren	verlieren	
86	**verschwinden** to disappear	ich verschwinde	bin **verschwunden**	**verschwand**	werde verschwinden	verschwinde	**verschwunden**
		du verschwindest	bist verschwunden	**verschwandest**	wirst verschwinden	verschwindest	
	verb with a spelling change	er/sie/es verschwindet	ist verschwunden	**verschwandst**	wird verschwinden	verschwinde	
		wir verschwinden	sind verschwunden	**verschwand**	werden verschwinden	verschwinden	
		ihr verschwindet	seid verschwunden	**verschwanden**	werdet verschwinden	verschwindet	
		sie/Sie verschwinden	sind verschwunden	**verschwandet**	werden verschwinden	verschwinden	
87	**wachsen** to grow	ich wachse	bin **gewachsen**	**wuchs**	werde wachsen	wachse	**gewachsen**
		du wächst	bist gewachsen	**wuchsest**	wirst wachsen	wachsest	
	verb with a spelling change	er/sie/es wächst	ist gewachsen	**wuchs**	wird wachsen	wachse	
		wir wachsen	sind gewachsen	**wuchsen**	werden wachsen	wachsen	
		ihr wachst	seid gewachsen	**wuchst**	werdet wachsen	wachset	
		sie/Sie wachsen	sind gewachsen	**wuchsen**	werden wachsen	wachsen	
88	**wandern** to hike	ich wandere	bin **gewandert**	wanderte	werde wandern	wandere	**gewandert**
		du wanderst	bist gewandert	wandertest	wirst wandern	wanderest	
	verb with a spelling change	er/sie/es wandert	ist gewandert	wanderte	wird wandern	wandrest	
		wir wandern	sind gewandert	wanderten	werden wandern	wandere	
		ihr wandert	seid gewandert	wandertet	werdet wandern	wanderen	
		sie/Sie wandern	sind gewandert	wanderten	werden wandern	wandren	
89	**waschen** to wash	ich wasche	habe **gewaschen**	**wusch**	werde waschen	wasche	**gewaschen**
		du wäschst	hast gewaschen	**wuschest**	wirst waschen	waschest	
	verb with a spelling change	er/sie/es wäscht	hat gewaschen	**wusch**	wird waschen	wasche	
		wir waschen	haben gewaschen	**wuschen**	werden waschen	waschen	
		ihr wascht	habt gewaschen	**wuscht**	werdet waschen	waschet	
		sie/Sie waschen	haben gewaschen	**wuschen**	werden waschen	waschen	
90	**werben** to recruit; to advertise	ich werbe	habe **geworben**	**warb**	werde werben	werbe	**geworben**
		du wirbst	hast geworben	**warbst**	wirst werben	werbest	
	verb with a spelling change	er/sie/es wirbt	hat geworben	**warb**	wird werben	werbe	
		wir werben	haben geworben	**warben**	werden werben	werben	
		ihr werbt	habt geworben	**warbt**	werdet werben	werbet	
		sie/Sie werben	haben geworben	**warben**	werden werben	werben	

		PRESENT	PERFECT	IMPERFECT	FUTURE	PRESENT SUBJUNCTIVE	PAST PARTICIPLE
91	**werden** to become		see full verb table page 695				
92	**werfen**	ich werfe	habe **geworfen**	**warf**	werde werfen	werfe	**geworfen**
	to throw	du wirfst	hast geworfen	**warfst**	wirst werfen	werfest	
	verb with a	er/sie/es wirft	hat geworfen	**warf**	wird werfen	werfe	
	spelling change	wir werfen	haben geworfen	**warfen**	werden werfen	werfen	
		ihr werft	habt geworfen	**warft**	werdet werfen	werfet	
		sie/Sie werfen	haben geworfen	**warfen**	werden werfen	werfen	
93	**wissen** to know		see full verb table page 696				
94	**wollen**	ich **will**	habe **gewollt/ wollen**	wollte	werde wollen	wolle	**gewollt/ wollen***
	to want	du **willst**	hast gewollt/ wollen	wolltest	wirst wollen	wollest	This form is
	verb with a spelling change	er/sie/es **will**	hat gewollt/wollen	wollte	wird wollen	wolle	used when combined
		wir wollen	haben gewollt/ wollen	wollten	werden wollen	wollen	with another infinitive
		ihr wollt	habt gewollt/ wollen	wolltet	werdet wollen	wollet	
		sie/Sie wollen	haben gewollt/ wollen	wollten	werden wollen	wollen	
95	**zerstören**	ich zerstöre	habe zerstört	zerstörte	werde zerstören	zerstöre	**zerstört**
	to destroy	du zerstörst	hast zerstört	zerstörtest	wirst zerstören	zerstörest	
		er/sie/es zerstört	hat zerstört	zerstörte	wird zerstören	zerstöre	
		wir zerstören	haben zerstört	zerstörten	werden zerstören	zerstören	
		ihr zerstört	habt zerstört	zerstörtet	werdet zerstören	zerstöret	
		sie/Sie zerstören	haben zerstört	zerstörten	werden zerstören	zerstören	
96	**ziehen**	ich ziehe	habe **gezogen**	**zog**	werde ziehen	ziehe	**gezogen**
	to go;	du ziehst	hast gezogen	**zogst**	wirst ziehen	ziehest	
	to pull	er/sie/es zieht	hat gezogen	**zog**	wird ziehen	ziehe	
	verb with a	wir ziehen	haben gezogen	**zogen**	werden ziehen	ziehen	
	spelling change	ihr zieht	habt gezogen	**zogt**	werdet ziehen	ziehet	
		sie/Sie ziehen	haben gezogen	**zogen**	werden ziehen	ziehen	
97	**zwingen**	ich zwinge	habe **gezwungen**	**zwang**	werde zwingen	zwinge	**gezwungen**
	to force	du zwingst	hast gezwungen	**zwangst**	wirst zwingen	zwingest	
	verb with	er/sie/es zwingt	hat gezwungen	**zwang**	wird zwingen	zwinge	
	a spelling	wir zwingen	haben gezwungen	**zwangen**	werden zwingen	zwingen	
	change	ihr zwingt	habt gezwungen	**zwangt**	werdet zwingen	zwinget	
		sie/Sie zwingen	haben gezwungen	**zwangen**	werden zwingen	zwingen	